4/96

THE GREAT
CONTEMPORARY
ISSUES

WOMEN: THEIR CHANGING ROLES

HE GREAT
ONTEMPORARY
SSUES

WOMEN: THEIR CHANGING ROLES

The New York Times

ARNO PRESS

NEW YORK/1973

ELIZABETH JANEWAY

Advisory Editor

Copyright © 1973 by The New York Times Company.
Library of Congress Cataloging in Publication Data
Main entry under title:
Women: their changing roles.
    (The Great contemporary issues)
    Contemporary accounts from the New York times.
    "A Hudson group book."
    Bibliography: p.
1. Woman–History and condition of women—Addresses, essays, lectures. 2. Women in the United States—Addresses, essays, lectures. 3. United States—Social conditions—Addresses, essays, lectures. I. Janeway, Elizabeth, ed. II. New York times. III. Series.
HQ1426.W65   301.41′2′0973   72-5020
ISBN 0-405-04164-0
Manufactured in the United States of America by Arno Press, Inc.

The editors express special thanks to The Associated Press, United Press International, and Reuters for permission to include in this series of books a number of dispatches originally distributed by those news services.

A HUDSON GROUP BOOK
Produced by Morningside Associates. Edited by Joanne Soderman.

Contents

A Publisher's Note About the Series

It would take even an accomplished speed-reader, moving at full throttle, some three and a half solid hours a day to work his way through all the news THE NEW YORK TIMES prints. The sad irony, of course, is that even such indefatigable devotion to life's carnival would scarcely assure a decent understanding of what it was really all about. For even the most dutiful reader might easily overlook an occasional long-range trend of importance, or perhaps some of the fragile, elusive relationships between events that sometimes turn out to be more significant than the events themselves.

This is why "The Great Contemporary Issues" was created—to help make sense out of some of the major forces and counterforces at large in today's world. The philosophical conviction behind the series is a simple one: that the past not only can illuminate the present but must. ("Continuity with the past," declared Oliver Wendell Holmes, "is a necessity, not a duty.") Each book in the series, therefore, has as its subject some central issue of our time that needs to be viewed in the context of its antecedents if it is to be fully understood. By showing, through a substantial selection of contemporary accounts from THE NEW YORK TIMES, the evolution of a subject and its significance, each book in the series offers a perspective that is available in no other way. For while most books on contemporary affairs specialize, for excellent reasons, in predigested facts and neatly drawn conclusions, the books in this series allow the reader to draw his own conclusions on the basis of the facts as they appeared at virtually the moment of their occurrence. This is not to argue that there is no place for events recollected in tranquility; it is simply to say that when fresh, raw truths are allowed to speak for themselves, some quite distinct values often emerge.

For this reason, most of the articles in "The Great Contemporary Issues" are reprinted in their entirety, even in those cases where portions are not central to a given book's theme. Editing has been done only rarely, and in all such cases it is clearly indicated. (Such an excision occasionally occurs, for example, in the case of a Presidential State of the Union Message, where only brief portions are germane to a particular volume, and in the case of some names, where for legal reasons or reasons of taste it is preferable not to republish specific identifications.) Similarly, typographical errors, where they occur, have been allowed to stand as originally printed.

"The Great Contemporary Issues" inevitably encompasses a substantial amount of history. In order to explore their subjects fully, some of the books go back a century or more. Yet their fundamental theme is not the past but the present. In this series the past is of significance insofar as it suggests how we got where we are today. These books, therefore, do not always treat a subject in a purely chronological way. Rather, their material is arranged to point up trends and interrelationships that the editors believe are more illuminating than a chronological listing would be.

Each volume in this series contains an index; cumulative indexes to the entire series will be issued from time to time. Each volume also contains a selective bibliography.

"The Great Contemporary Issues" series will ultimately constitute an encyclopedic library of today's major issues. Long before editorial work on the first volume had even begun, some fifty specific titles had already been either scheduled for definite publication or listed as candidates. Since then, events have prompted the inclusion of a number of additional titles, and the editors are, moreover, alert not only for new issues as they emerge but also for issues whose development may call for the publication of sequel volumes. We will, of course, also welcome readers' suggestions for future topics.

Reflections on the History of Women

American women are not the only people in the world who manage to lose track of themselves, but we do seem to mislay the past in a singularly absent-minded fashion. A century ago, observers as different as Mark Twain and Henry James noticed that our identities appeared to fit loosely and be readily subject to change. In part, this is because we are Americans, geographically and socially mobile, fellow-countrymen of the Henry Ford who said, "History is bunk." In part, it is because we are women, people whose lives are recurrently jolted away from continuity. Look at our personal histories, and you will find old scars of passage from one state of being to another: tomboy to junior miss; drum majorette to sociology student; art historian to computer programmer; candidate for an M.A. to harried wife-and-mother; priestess of the Feminine Mystique to divorcée; housewife to financial analyst; and older woman who has suffered the feared and fracturing shift from busy middle life to lonely, widowed age.

Acquaintance with change has some positive advantages. These transitions should, and often do, keep alive our capacity to adjust to new circumstances and to learn new rules and roles. Women are less surprised than men when they find that they do not control their lives. They have less pride invested in setting up and maintaining a consistent image of themselves to front the outside world. They are, in fact, less apt to be engaged directly with the outside world. The dooms pronounced on them by Sigmund Freud and Erik Erikson still exert force: "Anatomy is destiny." "Women are concerned with inner space, with family and child-rearing." Challenged as these dicta have been, they remain at least partially true as current, demonstrable fact. It will take more time than we have yet lived to reduce them to the level of superstition toward which they are tending. Women can't help but know that they live in a changing world. The very fashions of dress, which even nuns are now allowed to follow, tell them so.

In the abstract, then, this ability to accept change can be seen as healthy, as a responsive adjust-ment which contributes to survival. But when we say this, we are at once raising the question of *who is it that survives;* of what core within us remains the same in a world of change. Certainly some of the energy of the current liberation movement derives from the urge among women to find more secure identities, the need to know who and what they have been in the past, in order to see themselves as participants with a stake in the present and a valid reach into the future. Every emerging social group wants a history, rather as every aspirant nineteenth-century merchant wanted ancestors, roots and a coat of arms. Snobs can laugh but, in fact, a sense of one's own connection to the past, of one's continuity of being, is as much needed for healthy survival as one's ability to accept change. Particularly is this true for the sex which has been told for centuries by parents, prelates and philosophers that the traditional role of its members is to live for others and find their identities in personal relationships. To live in response to others is to live a life which is necessarily fragmented and ephemeral.

These reflections are called forth by the opportunity to take a long look at the social image of women in the last several generations, that period which hovers somewhere between hearsay and history. The first thing one discovers is that the scholarly historians who deride the idea of a special history of women are quite correct. Women have not been trend-setters, activists or protagonists in the drama of great events. If they turn up in the middle of some climactic scene, they are likely to have got there by the accident of marriage or, occasionally, of birth. Women monarchs have inherited power under laws made by men, not laid hands on it themselves, and rare indeed has been any influence their rule has had on the lives of other women *as* women. The history of women has not been made within their own ranks but has followed from external, male-initiated, processes. Like their personal lives, women's history is fragmented, interrupted; a shadow history of human beings whose existence has been shaped by the efforts and the demands of others.

Even as subordinates, women have not formed a distinct group or class whose development can be treated coherently as, for example, black history can. Though women's activities have been circumscribed, the background of their lives has always been enormously diverse. They have been queens and slaves and prostitutes, ladies and laborers, poets and procurers. True, none has been president, few if any have been pornographers. They have rarely headed major industrial firms, conducted symphonies, functioned as trial lawyers or orthopedic surgeons. In top level politics they are scarce on the ground. Once again, these limits are determined by external enforced conventions. Women's history must therefore deal less with what they have done than with what they have been allowed to do. Within the limits permitted, women have done everything, lived lives of variety and activity. They have simply behaved like human beings; and have, therefore, *no* special women's history. What is special is not their own plans and deeds but, rather, the roles, expectations and interpretations that have been projected onto them.

The paradoxical result is that any useful history of women has to be a history of what has been thought about them. It is the *image* of woman, originating in men's eyes, that alone gives her a special group identity. Which is not to say that women don't often accept such an identity—accept it whether they approve of it, resent it or (as today) see it as a unifying force, a challenge against which an attack can be mounted. The woman's movement, indeed, is seizing on the old, demeaning image of women, the old submissive identity, in order to escape from it by overthrowing it. It is a kind of outsize palace revolution which is taking place; and those who are startled or put off by the anger the movement activists voice might reflect on the frustration implicit in the situation of a group whose very identities have been forged by others, so that a woman's ego can hardly be trusted until it is reclaimed and made over. That will have happened on the day when women see themselves, and are seen, as human beings who happen to have been born with female sex; but it has not happened yet. The present and the recent past still bear out Simone de Beauvoir's admirable description: women are regarded as "object," misunderstood as "other" and dealt with as "the second sex."

Just the same, if we look at a compendium of popular attitudes toward women over the past century, we find much reason to hope that more realistic estimates of women's abilities are replacing the superstitions of the past. Collected here from *The New York Times* is a pertinent and revealing selection of news items, essays, reports and advertising appeals having to do with women, the earliest dating from the 1860's

when (not surprisingly) the drafting of men to fight had opened new opportunities for women.) True, a Victorian smog of condescension and contempt soon descended again; but from the 1890's on, we can trace a sort of social case-history of woman-as-she-is-seen which does document a growing, if uneven, advance toward personal dignity, autonomy and freedom of choice. These are annals of change, source material for the historian of ideas—or, perhaps better, of myth.

For one can't really sort out the articles and items here compiled in terms of factual news stories on the one hand and opinion pieces on the other. Opinion and news are thoroughly mixed up together, and what turns out to be most illuminating is often the taken-for-granted background, or even the tone of voice. A news item reporting the successful elopement of young Miss Double and her fiance, Mr. Wirth (pursued across Central Park by angry Mr. Double père), is a cheerful enough anecdote of young love. But it is also bread-and-butter evidence, worthy of Lévi-Strauss, that marriageable young girls were considered by their parents to be objects of barter just 70 years ago. Indeed, the patriarchal approach of men in general to women in general is a clear indication that women were habitually thought of then as being never quite grown-up. The authority of the father descended to the husband so that a kind of paternal sway was continued inside marriage; and the mode of address to women of such figures of authority as the writers of editorials apes the affectionate, rather waggish tone of the stage father. What we are witnessing in the background of what seem to be simple news developments (Carrie Nation arrested. Growing interest in athletics for women.) is the assumption and tacit assertion that women engaged in any activities outside the home are not to be taken seriously. We are being shown not only the limits of woman's place but also the means by which the limits were then enforced. That was seldom done by argument. Instead, it was continually suggested that *women weren't worth arguing with.* The effect was to devalue women's experience, weakening her sense of identity and her ability to hold to her convictions.

In short, the fight for women's rights has always involved more than a struggle for tangible goals like equal pay, equal opportunity, the vote itself. It has been a fight for the very right to fight, to assert one's demands, to declare that one's ambitions and needs are as important as those of men. I emphasize this point because it illuminates the purpose of those consciousness-raising groups which puzzle many people, both men and women. Why, it is asked, do women need to come together and tell each other their troubles? Aren't they just indulging in self-pity and airing emotions which should really be private? But sharing experience is really a declaration of the right to judge events and emotions by one's own lights instead of by received opinion. How distorting to women the received opinions of the recent past were is well documented here. A good example is the discussion among several men of women's literary interests. Do they read books at all? Don't they simply parrot the judgments put forward in reviews? No, is the reply, they do read; for they think that they may pick up ideas and information which will make them more attractive to men. And, of course, some of them are lonely. One is reminded of the caricatures of Jews which *Der Sturmer* printed in the 1930's and, chillingly, that both attitudes were eminently respectable.

To be fair, such views were in contention even at the time and not only by women. An editorial writer speculates that women may well turn away from the cultivation of higher values like literature, music and art because a concern for culture will "only unfit them for living with the dullards they marry." A few years later novelist Ellen Glasgow declares that "real women," human and articulate, are beginning to appear in fiction and drive out the stereotypes of the last century. But as late as 1913 we find that any serious discussion of women's work is apt to deal with— household management! Which turns out to mean the proper instructions to, and supervision of, a staff of servants, whose numbers may be 25 to 40 in a "large establishment" or the "typical" six.

Part of the interest of this work, then, is that it introduces us to a vanished world and does so in contemporary terms. It is very hard not to look at the past through our own hang-ups and psychic scars. To many, the early years of the century seem a haven of comfort and certainty. To others they are surrounded by an aura of nostalgic glamour. To a few they are remembered as years of deprivation and strife. But they are seldom seen without some bias of emotion. Well, here they are as they were. We can see what we have lost, and that much of it is well lost; not only the rigidly defined sex roles but also the hierarchy of class. So important was "position" that many progressive causes are reported on simply as the activities of "leading clubwomen" who interested themselves in do-gooding.

At the same time, the stark facts of life appear. Here is the report of an energetic young woman who has spent a year moving from city to city to discover what jobs are open to inexperienced girls and what wages are offered. In Chicago a department store will pay beginners $5 a week, and mother's helpers are offered as little as $10 a month. In New York addressing envelopes brings a dollar a thousand and a worker can soon manage to make $1.25 a day. Skill pays. Experienced stenographers ask for $15 to $18 a week

in the ads placed at about this period. But what can we say to "Wanted: A little girl handy with the needle to learn fancy work. $2.50 to begin."? Or to the study of tuberculosis rates among textile workers, two and a quarter to five times those of women in other occupations? Such details underline the fact that pre-World War I America, like Disraeli's England, was made up of two nations, the "Haves" and the "Have-nots."

Intellectually, however, change was already underway in the prewar years. Questions that have continued to engage the attention of women in their drive toward equality show up astonishingly early. In the two years 1905 and 1906 we find the brilliant theoretician of women's rights Charlotte Gilman noting (40 years before de Beauvoir) how women, seen as objects, take their standards and self-images from men; how social change has isolated them from the world of work until their contribution to the mainstream of life has dwindled to a point where the world could practically run without them, except for their services as domestic and industrial drudges. Susan B. Anthony discusses what women's unpaid work within marriage entitles them to after divorce. An Iowa couple (both, be it noted, veterans of earlier marriages) agrees on a detailed marriage contract, defining their roles, limiting the number of children they will have, providing for a division of money and setting a term at which they will review their life together and decide whether to renew their agreement or not. Elsie Clews Parson seriously sets forth the advantages of trial marriage. Here is the philosophic background of the suffrage movement.

Again, with the advent of World War I, we see how the need for women as workers paralleled their advance toward getting the vote. Unenthusiastic at first, President Wilson ended by presenting woman suffrage to Congress as a vital war measure. In 1918 women were being urged to go into war industry in order to free men to fight; or, more accurately, to be drafted. Jobs were being opened to women in order to force men out, for one aspect of the War between the Sexes not often noted is its manipulative use by the State and the Establishment.

With the twenties we are in the era of the "emancipated" woman. She had the vote, of course, She also had short hair and lipstick—sermons were preached on this topic. But though we tend to think of her as a Fitzgerald flapper, or as Zelda herself, the meaning of emancipation was wider than simple citizenship in the Jazz Generation. Thus, young women with jobs didn't have to marry the first man who asked them. Most of them were still in "women's jobs," but there were not only women doctors and lawyers listed in the 1920 census, but also women architects, engineers, dentists, opticians and taxi drivers. There were also protests over inequities of jobs and wages. And there was a hard-fought battle, paralleling the current struggle for abortion reform, over birth control. In a very real way the twenties forecast the seventies in the range of issues which questioned old ways and pointed up social change.

The depression years of the thirties produced contradictory tugs on women's status. Frances Perkins sat as Secretary of Labor in Franklin Roosevelt's cabinet, but massive male unemployment brought forth demands that married women be dismissed from jobs in order to spread work, and the National Recovery Administration put an official stamp on lower minimum wages for women workers. Another war changed this, drew women back into industry in the forties and for the first time in American history into the armed forces on a par with men. With the fifties another swing of opinion persuaded many women that home was where they belonged. Young girls married earlier than ever and the baby boom began the population explosion. But, as we all remember, the "Togetherness" of the fifties began to come apart in the sixties. This was not simply the effect of another change of mind. In spite of low wages and the restriction of women to subordinate, non-executive jobs, their participation in the labor force was steadily rising. Much of the affluence of the prosperous sixties was due to the rising number of working wives and mothers. When the new women's movement got under way, millions of women knew from their own experience that "equal rights for women" was a phrase but not a fact.

In his memoir *Speak Memory*, Vladimir Nabokov recalls how reading Hegel on historical development via thesis, antithesis and synthesis brought home to him "the essential spirality of all things in time." History is not a linear process, in which syllogisms are posited, proven and left behind. It is a matter of human emotions, beliefs and behavior challenged by new demands, rising reluctantly (and only sometimes successfully) to meet them, falling back and then, if need be, returning to cope again with unappeased pressures. The women's movement began as an unfocused and almost inarticulate search for a more honorable and worthy life. It was shaped by external restrictions, some of them economic, some of them social, some psychological. It fell from time to time into absurdity, but seldom into absurdity approaching the majestic, pompous nonsense with which the status quo condemned it; read, for example, the 1909 interview with *Ladies Home Journal* editor Edward W. Bok on the question of woman's suffrage. Most women, he

assured the *Times* interviewer, were *opposed* to receiving the vote, would not use it, were busy at home. Just so, psychology professor Joseph Adelson of the University of Michigan writes in March 1972 that the Women's Liberation Movement receives support from only 3 per cent of women interviewed and provokes in most "an attitude somewhere between irritation and indifference." So, though things have changed some, they have not changed all that much. The image of women, whose history is annotated here, still includes the belief that women are not capable of knowing what's good for them!

If every nation gets the government it deserves, every generation writes the history which corresponds with its view of the world. No one conceived that a record of the doings of women might be interesting or important until the old sex roles came into question. If, one day, sex roles blur so that women are fully integrated into mainstream activities, a history of women will cease to be significant. Historiography, that is, is nearly as transitory as historical events. Even so, the record of how women were thought of, what behavior was deemed proper to them, what doors were shut, and how sanctions were applied against the violation of assigned roles—these data will always be important. They explain the attitudes of the past, and the present is built on these attitudes. The value of this collection, therefore, is permanent, just because it is a chronicle of what was thought and not an interpretation of it. Historians return to source material long after they have ceased to read earlier historians.

For all of us, historians and laymen, men and women, the reproduction of past certainties which have lost their plausibility and persuasiveness is always useful. "I beseech you, in the bowels of Christ," wrote Oliver Cromwell to the Elders of the Church of Scotland, "think it possible that you may be mistaken." Every cocksure ideologue needs to hear such an injunction once in a while. The men and women who lived out the changes of role and relationship recorded here discovered for themselves how they were mistaken and sometimes, thank heaven, how they were right; right in their convictions and right also in their questioning. The most valuable thing we learn from the past (and I think sometimes the only thing) is that we may be mistaken. No certainty should be immune from questioning; and when the questioning springs from and is supported by experience, certainties will shift. There can be no better illustration of *this* certainty—that change occurs—than the documented annals of woman's changing role.

ELIZABETH JANEWAY

THE GREAT
CONTEMPORARY
ISSUES

WOMEN: THEIR CHANGING ROLES

CHAPTER 1

Social Feminism

Susan B. Anthony,
American feminist and reformer.

LONGEST REIGN IN ENGLISH HISTORY

She Was at One Time Much Criticised for Living in Seclusion.

In England eighteen is the age at which a royal Princess reaches her majority. Victoria passed this period on May 24, 1837, on the morning of which day she was awakened by a serenade. Among her many presents was a piano sent by the King, who lay then on a bed from which he did not rise. Less than a month afterward, on June 20, at 2:20 A. M., the King breathed his last, at Windsor. Immediately after this a carriage drawn by four horses and containing the Archbishop of Canterbury and the Lord Chamberlain departed for Kensington Palace, and at 5 o'clock dashed up the central avenue that led to the door. What followed has been described in the "Diary" of Miss Wynn:

"They knocked, they rang, they thumped for a considerable time before they could arouse a porter at the gate; they were again kept waiting in the courtyard; then turned into one of the lower rooms, where they seemed to be forgotten by everybody. They rang the bell and desired that the attendant of the Princess Victoria might be sent to inform her royal Highness that they requested an audience on business of importance. After another delay and another ringing to inquire the cause, the attendant was summoned, who stated that the Princess was in such a sweet sleep that she could not venture to disturb her. They then said: 'We are come on business of State to the Queen, and even her sleep must give way to that.' It did, and to prove that she did not keep them waiting, in a few moments she came into the room in a loose white nightgown and shawl, her nightcap thrown off and her hair falling upon her shoulders, her feet in slippers, tears in her eyes, but perfectly collected and dignified."

About the first words the young Queen spoke when she was told the news were to request the Archbishop to pray for the widowed Queen Adelaide. When they had departed she went to her mother and informed her of the mighty change in her fortunes. Then she addressed a letter of condolence to her aunt Adelaide, asking her to remain at Windsor as long as she pleased. The letter was addressed "To her Majesty the Queen." She was reminded that she ought to write instead, "To her Majesty the Queen Dowager," but her answer was: "I am aware of that, but I will not be the first to remind her of her altered position." It was arranged that a Council should be held that day at Kensington. The hour fixed was 11 A. M. In Greville's "Diary" the following account of this Council, which a familiar picture by Sir David Wilkie has made well known, is given, and Greville was not a man given to emotion:

"Never was anything like the first impression she produced, or the chorus of praise and admiration which it raised about her manner and behavior, and certainly not without justice. It was very extraordinary, and something far beyond what was looked for. Her extreme youth and inexperience, and the ignorance of the world concerning her, naturally excited intense curiosity to see how she would act on this trying occasion, and there was a considerable assemblage at the palace, notwithstanding the short notice that had been given. She was plainly dressed and in mourning. After she had read her speech and taken and signed the oath for the security of the Church of Scotland, administered by the Archbishop of Canterbury, the Privy Councilors were sworn; the two royal Dukes first by themselves, and, as these old men, her uncles, knelt before her swearing allegiance and kissing her hand, I saw her blush up to the eyes, as if she felt the contrast between their civil and their natural relations, and this was the only sign of emotion that she evinced. Her manner to them was very graceful and engaging; she kissed them both, and rose from her chair and moved toward the Duke of Sussex, who was furthest from her and too infirm to reach her. She seemed rather bewildered at the multitude of men who were sworn and who came one after the other to kiss her hand; but she did not speak to anybody, nor did she make the slightest difference in her manner, or show any in her countenance to any individual of any rank, station or party. I particularly watched her when Melbourne and the Ministers, and the Duke of Wellington, and Peel approached her. She went through the whole ceremony, occasionally looking at Melbourne for instruction when she had any doubt what to do, which hardly ever occurred, with perfect calmness and self-possession, but at the same time with a graceful modesty and propriety particularly interesting and ingratiating."

The New York Times

Queen Victoria (1837-1901)

On the following day occurred the ceremony of the proclamation, when, according to custom, the Queen made her appearance at the open window in St. James's Palace, surrounded by the great nobles of the realm in their robes of state. At Kensington a range of apartments separate from her mother's were at once set apart for her use, and there she lived until July 13, when she left the home of her childhood for Buckingham Palace. She did not go to Windsor until the September of that year, and she then reviewed her troops from on horseback. She opened the first Parliament of her reign in November, and in the following June she was formally crowned in Westminster Abbey. Harriet Martineau, an eye-witness, has described that scene with much felicity. "The throne," says she, "covered, as was its footstool, with cloth of gold, stood on an elevation of four steps in the centre of the area. The first peeress took her seat in the north transept opposite at 6:45, and three of the Bishops came next. From that time the peers and their ladies arrived faster and faster. Each peeress was conducted by Goldsticks, one of whom handed her to her seat and the other bore and arranged her train on her lap and saw that her coronet, footstool, and book were comfortably placed. About 9 the first gleams of the sun started into the Abbey, and presently traveled down to the peeresses. I had never before seen the full effect of diamonds. As the light traveled, each lady shone out as a rainbow. The brightness, vastness, and dreamy magnificence of the scene produced a strange effect of exhaustion and sleepiness."

WIFE AND MOTHER.

Albert, Prince Consort of England, was the second son of Ernest, Duke of Saxe-Coburg-Gotha, and was born Aug. 26, 1819, so that he was three months younger than Victoria. Five years after his birth his father and mother had separated, two years later the mother was divorced, and in 1831 she died, having never seen her son since the separation. Prince Albert first saw the Princess Victoria in the Spring of 1836, when he made a visit to England with his father and his elder brother. The visit lasted a month, and the cousins are believed to have parted very reluctantly. Victoria, in a letter to her uncle, begged him to "take care of the health of one now so dear to me, and to take him under your special protection." From a much earlier time the idea of a union between these two had been entertained at Saxe-Coburg, and as Victoria's accession became more and more a certainty it took firm hold. Meanwhile, great care was taken with the education of the Prince. For one thing, it was necessary that he should know English. The position he was likely to fill was kept clearly in view.

When Victoria had become Queen, Albert wrote that he had heard with great satisfaction of the "astonishing self-possession" she had shown. "You are Queen," said he, "of the mightiest land of Europe. In your hand lies the happiness of millions." Albert was not Victoria's only suitor. She was indeed a great catch; there was none like her in Europe. There had scarcely been one like her in England since Elizabeth. She was sought by Prince Alexander of the Netherlands, by Prince Adalbert of Prussia, by Duke Ernest of Würtemberg, and even, it is said, by Prince George of Cambridge, her cousin, afterward the Duke of Cambridge, and whose morganatic wife, Mrs. Fitz-George, died early in 1890, the only wife he ever chose to have. Albert well understood how the strict etiquette of the Court obliged the Queen to take the initiative, and hence, on his second visit, in October, 1839, when the purpose of his visit was clearly understood, he waited anxiously for some sign of the Queen's decision in his favor. This he had the happiness to obtain on the second evening of his visit, at a ball, when she gave him her bouquet, and he received a message from her that she desired to speak with him on the following day.

Victoria up to this time had been somewhat reluctant to consider an immediate marriage, as she thought both herself and Albert too young, but State reasons and the wise influence of Prince Leopold, who was uncle to both, prevailed to change her inclinations. In the following year occurred the wedding. Albert landed at Dover and went thence to Canterbury and London, being received at Buckingham Palace at the hall door by the Queen and her mother, attended by the whole household. In order that the people might be better pleased the Queen decided upon noon as the hour for the wedding, instead of the evening hour common with royal persons. The wedding took place in the Chapel of St. James's Palace, and thence Queen and Prince were driven to Windsor, the roads being lined with rejoicing crowds. Three days were passed at Windsor and then they returned to London to receive the congratulations of the people.

One of the most charming and wholesome domestic pictures that royal lives have afforded is furnished in the married life of Albert and Victoria. Its influence on English domestic life in general must have been far-reaching. Prince Albert was a man of honest purposes and devoted affections; he was endowed with noble ambitions guided by intelligence. Painting, etching, and music were accomplishments that afforded amusement to both, and the Prince was a man of taste and skill in landscape gardening. He loved a country life and early hours. To these tastes the Queen learned to conform, though she had formerly preferred town life; in fact, she became eventually as fond of the country as was he. Many glimpses of their domestic occupations and manners are afforded in the biography of the Prince and the journals kept by the Queen, which were made public several years ago. Elsewhere interesting glimpses have also been given. One of the most interesting is contained in a letter from Mendelssohn to his mother. He had been asked by the Prince to play on the organ at Buckingham Palace and called by appointment. "I found him alone," says Mendelssohn, "and as we were talking the Queen came in also, alone, in a simple morning dress. She said she was obliged to leave for Claremont in an hour, and then, suddenly interrupting herself, exclaimed: 'But, goodness, what a confusion!' for the wind had littered the whole room and even the pedals of the organ (which, by the way, made a very pretty figure in the room) with leaves of music from a large portfolio which lay open. As she spoke she knelt down and began picking up the music. Prince Albert helped, and I, too, was not idle."

The difficulties encountered at the outset of this union were incident to the peculiar relations of the Queen and Prince. Head of the family though the Prince was in his position as husband, his place in public affairs was necessarily subordinate. Great tact and a large amount of genuine sense and right feeling were necessary on his part to make the path a smooth one. Undoubtedly the common judgment now is that he bore himself with conspicuous good sense and dignity in this trying situation. His character was naturally strong. His disposition was essentially resolute, and a proper degree of independence was essential to his happiness. In the royal household many were reluctant to surrender the powers they had formerly exercised, and others were disappointed that the husband of the Queen was a foreigner. To a friend the Prince wrote, in the May following his marriage, that his difficulty was to fill his place "with proper dignity," because he "was only the husband and not the master of the house." The Queen, however, soon showed her determination that in all matters not affairs of State the Prince was to exercise paramount authority. Sir Theodore Martin, the biographer of the Prince, says the example of the Queen was itself "enough to quell resistance," while the Prince's own "tact, forbearance, and superior grasp of mind were not long in removing every obstacle to his legitimate authority.

"In finding his right position in regard to public affairs, the Prince had to feel his way cautiously and to inspire confidence in his ability and tact no less than in his freedom from personal ambition." A large degree of credit for his success belongs to Baron Stockmar, who, along with Prince Leopold, had been and still continued to be an efficient and successful guide and adviser to the Prince. No act of the Prince's life at this time showed his sense of his position with better effect on the English people than his letter to the Duke of Wellington declining to become Field Marshal Commander in Chief of the English Army. In this letter he said he had resolved "to sink his own individual existence in that of his wife; to aim at no power by himself or for himself; to shun all ostentations; to assume no separate responsibility before the public; to make his position entirely a part of hers."

The Queen became the mother of nine children. The first was born in November, 1840. This was the Princess Royal, (Victoria by name,) who afterward (1858) was married to the Crown Prince of Prussia, and has since become known as the Empress Frederick of Germany. On Nov. 9, 1841, was born Albert Edward, the Prince of Wales, who married the Princess Alexandra of Denmark in 1863. The third child was Princess Alice, born in 1843, married to Prince Louis of Hesse-Darmstadt in 1862, and who died in 1878. The fourth was Alfred, Duke of Edinburgh, born in 1844, married to the Grand Duchess Marie Alexandrovna of Russia in 1874, assumed the title of Duke of Saxe-Coburg Gotha, and died July 30, 1900; the fifth was Princess Helena, born in 1846, and married in 1866 to Prince Christian of Schleswig-Holstein; the sixth, Princess Louise, born in 1848, and married to the Marquis of Lorne in 1871; the seventh, Arthur, Duke of Connaught, born in 1850, and married to the Princess Louise of Hohenzollern in 1879; the eighth, Leopold, Duke of Albany, born in 1853, married to the Princess Hélène of Waldeck-Pyrmont in 1882, and died in 1884, and the ninth and last, Beatrice, born in 1857, married to Prince Henry of Battenberg in 1885, and widowed, Jan. 20, 1896.

These children of the Queen, with one exception, have each had children of their own. A few years ago the record stood: The Princess Royal, six, of whom the present Emperor of Germany is the oldest; the Prince of Wales, six, of whom one died in infancy, and the eldest of whom, Albert Victor, born in 1864, died in July, 1892, leaving his brother, the Duke of York, heir to the throne after his father; Princess Alice, one; the Duke of Edinburgh, five; Princess Helena, (sometimes called Princess Christian,) four; Princess Louise, none; the Duke of Connaught, three; the Duke of Albany, one, and Princess Beatrice, two. Several of the Queen's grandchildren are already married, and she has been for some years a great-grandmother. First among them is the present Emperor of Germany, whose first child was born in 1882; another is his sister Sophia, married to the Crown Prince of Greece, and another, the daughter of the Prince of Wales, married in 1889 to the Duke of Fife, a marriage which gave satisfaction in England for the negative reason that it was not contracted with a Prince of German blood. Antipathy to German Princes is now an instinctive feeling to a large class of the English people. It dates back to the beginning of the Hanoverian line, early in the eighteenth century. A saying of Lord Chesterfield's illustrates how deep this feeling was in his time. There had been discussion of the Stuart Pretender. Chesterfield said England ought to contrive to make him Elector of Hanover, for this would make it certain he could never mount the throne of England.

At the time of her first jubilee, which was celebrated with extraordinary splendor on a perfect June day in 1887, the Queen had thirty-one grandchildren living and six great-grandchildren. The second or diamond jubilee, ten years later, celebrating the sixtieth anniversary of her succession, was equally impressive in its pageantry.

UNTIL HER WIDOWHOOD.

The domestic life of the Queen for the twenty years her husband lived was singularly happy. Fate seemed to shower upon her every blessing to which a woman could aspire. It was not an eventful twenty years; eventful years are seldom years of happiness. The record of this period, besides the birth of children, embraces travel to various parts of her dominions and the Continent, return visits from European sovereigns, the purchase and enlargement of country homes, and the education of her children. Following the christening of the Prince of Wales with much state and splendor in 1842 came the visit of the King of Prussia, against which various Courts had intrigued in vain; then the first visit to Scotland, which she was subsequently to love so well, and then her visit to King Louis Philippe of France. The year 1844 was marked by several royal visits to London. First came the King of Saxony, then the Emperor of Russia, and then the King of the French. In 1845 the Queen went to Germany with the Prince, and was entertained by the King of Prussia.

A few years of married life had inspired a wish for homes remote from London. In September, 1846, possession was taken of the house at Osborne, on the Isle of Wight. It was private property, and the Prince enlarged and beautified it, bestowing upon it the best products of his taste in landscape gardening. The pride of the Prince in this place was that he made his farming pay. The place was really created by him. Even the trees in most cases owed their existence to him. By his will the Prince made Osborne the personal property of the Queen. In 1846 the royal family sailed around the west coast of Scotland, visited the Duke of Argyll, and explored Fingal's Cave. "It was the first time," wrote the Queen, "that the British standard with the Queen of Great Britain and her children had ever entered Fingal's Cave, and the men gave three cheers, which sounded very impressive there."

This visit renewed the Queen's liking for the Scotch Highland countries, and desire for a home there took definite form when her physician recommended the air and climate. The Balmoral property was then acquired. It was only a small castle, with a picturesque tower and a garden in front. Improvements on a vast scale were necessary ere it should take on its present fine proportions. It is built of red granite, in baronial style, with gables and turrets and a square clock tower. Like Osborne, Balmoral is private property. In the Autumn of 1855, when the Queen first occupied Balmoral, news reached her by telegraph of the fall of Sebastopol. Bonfires were lighted on the hills to commemorate the event. Here came in that Autumn the Crown Prince of Prussia to woo and win the eldest daughter of the Queen, who is now the Empress Frederick.

One of the royal visits that belongs to those happy twenty years was a visit to Ireland, one of three or four made by the Queen. It occurred in 1849, and was the first royal visit to Ireland since 1821. She landed in the Cove of Cork, on a spot to which was given the name of Queenstown. She went on to Dublin, and expressed much delight at the enthusiasm with which she was received. Waving her handkerchief from the paddlebox as the royal yacht was about to sail away, an old woman in the crowd below called out to her: "Och, Queen darlint, make one of the childer Prince Patrick and ould Oireland will die for ye!" Ten months later the Queen's fourth son was born. She named him Arthur, after Ireland's greatest soldier, the Duke of Wellington, and Patrick, after Ireland's patron saint.

Early in the sixties, sorrows thick and first came upon the Queen. Her mother, after a surgical operation upon her arm, was taken with a chill, and when the Queen arrived was unconscious. She died without recognition. Relatives of Queen and Prince by marriage, the King of Portugal and his brother, Prince Ferdinand, died of typhoid fever. Then came the unlooked-for illness of the Prince Consort. "Am full of rheumatic pains," wrote the Prince in his diary, "and thoroughly unwell. Have scarcely closed my eyes at night for the past fortnight." He had grown gradually worse, when news came of the seizure of Mason and Slidell from the British steamer Trent.

Lord John Russell advised the Queen to demand reparation and forwarded a dispatch for her approval. The terms of this dispatch seemed to the Prince too harsh. He wrote out his objections, telling the Queen he could scarcely hold his pen while doing so. These suggestions were adopted.

Late in December the Prince Consort breathed his last. The body was deposited in the royal vault in St. George's Chapel, and subsequently removed to the splendid mausoleum erected to hold it.

Victoria's life after her husband died continued for many years to be one of quiet seclusion. Her people saw little or nothing of her, and the projects with which she was occupied for doing honors in public to his memory were, for the most part, the only ones in which she manifested particular interest. So prolonged was this devotion of hers that many criticisms were at length made on the seclusion of the Queen. Radical leaders were not slow to make use of those circumstances and to point out her obligations to the country as things to which private sorrows should give way. One would search long to find a record of such absorbed devotion on the part of a reigning monarch. The memorials erected in Albert's honor suggest in their way the most notable that history records. On the Appian Way, beyond the walls of Rome, the wealthiest Roman of his time reared "a stern round tower" to the memory of his wife, which survives to our time as one of the most interesting monuments that the traveler in that land beholds. On the banks of a river in a land over which Victoria ruled, another eminent man set up a memorial to his wife, in what we know as the Taj Mahal, which has come to be accepted as the most beautiful architectural tribute that exists in memory of a lost wife. Victoria's tributes were to a lost husband.

The Prince Consort had been dead not three months when the Queen laid at Frogmore the first stone of the mausoleum that now holds his dust. A few years later she began at Balmoral the immense cairn bearing the inscription, "To the Beloved Memory of Albert, the Great and Good Prince Consort, Erected by His Broken-hearted Widow, Victoria, 21 August, 1862." Six of her children ("my poor six orphans" she called them) placed each a stone upon this pile. Granite without mortar was used in its construction, the shape being that of a pyramid. In various cities, among them Edinburgh and Aberdeen, statues of the Prince Consort were set up, and in London the colossal Albert Memorial, which was for a long time a spot of extensive pilgrimage to all visitors to London. In 1867 she laid the foundation stone of the Albert Hall of Arts and Sciences, in which was carried out a project the Prince had in hand when he died.

These years in the sixties were of further note in a domestic way for marriages, deaths, and births. In 1863 the Prince of Wales completed his twenty-first year, and was married. One of the grandest sights London had seen was the reception it gave to the bride of the Prince, the beautiful daughter of the King of Denmark. On hilltops throughout England, Scotland, and Wales, were set beacon lights. The marriage took place in St. George's Chapel, at Windsor, and was witnessed by the Queen from a recess or closet. She was still in deep mourning, and did not join the wedding party. Another marriage of special interest occurred in 1870, being that of Princess Louise and the Marquis of Lorne. This was a union between a Princess and a subject, as was the Fife marriage of 1889. Old George III. would never have sanctioned such a union. His Marriage act forbade it, except with the approval of the reigning sovereign.

Private grief came to the Queen in 1864, when her uncle Leopold, then King of the Belgians, passed away; he had been a friend of great value to the Princess Victoria in her childhood, and she felt the loss keenly. The five years now past had taken from her not only this uncle, who was like a father to her childhood, but her husband and her mother. Six years later came the illness of the Prince of Wales, when his life was for some days in great danger from typhoid fever. On his recovery the Queen went in state to St. Paul's Cathedral to give thanks, and the day was made a national festival. It was a day in February, and she sat in an open carriage with the Prince at her side. The route going lay along the Strand and Fleet Street, and returning along Oxford Street. In August of the same year a visit was paid to Edinburgh, when the Queen occupied rooms in the historic Palace of Holyrood. In September her half-sister, the Princess Hohenlohe-Langenburg, to whom she was much attached, died.

After the Franco-Prussian war England received the royal French exiles. Chislehurst, in Kent, became the home of the fallen Emperor, his wife, and son, and much kindness was shown to them by the Queen, who retained for many years afterward a special fondness for the afflicted ex-Empress Eugénie. When Napoleon died, in 1873, 40,000 persons were said to attend his funeral, 2,000 of them being French. The Queen in that year received a visit from the Shah of Persia and the Czar of Russia, whose daughter had just become the wife of the Queen's second son.

With Lord Beaconsfield as Prime Minister in 1877 a new eminence was acquired by the Queen. She was made Empress of India, and proclamation of the fact was formally made in the old Mogul capital of Delhi, as well as at Calcutta, Bombay, and Madras. She opened Parliament in person that year and did Lord Beaconsfield the great honor of a visit to his home, Hughenden Manor, where she took luncheon and planted a tree. In December of the next year, on the seventeenth anniversary of her father's death, died Princess Alice, and in March, 1884, another child of the Queen, the Duke of Albany, died. Readers will not fail to recall the message sent to Mrs. Garfield on the death of the President: "Words cannot express the deep sympathy I feel with you at this terrible moment. May God support you as He alone can!" Another event, the marriage of Princess Beatrice, in 1885, should be added to this domestic record. She was the youngest of the Queen's children and had long been her mother's inseparable companion. Mr. Frith, the artist who painted a picture of the Prince of Wales's marriage, related that he once asked the Princess at Windsor if she would not have liked to be one of the bridesmaids at her brother's wedding.

"No, I don't like weddings," she said. "I shall never be married; I shall stay with Mamma." This undoubtedly was the fate already fixed up as in store for her. Her marriage, however, was at the time understood to have taken place with the understanding that she was not to leave her mother. Her husband died in 1896.

Queen Victoria's life was several times in danger from violence. Serious illness she never knew until the last. When a Princess, some shot from a gun accidentally passed very near her. After she was a Queen repeated attempts were made to shoot her. Four months after her marriage, a young bartender out of employment fired at her twice while she was riding with the Prince at Windsor, both shots missing them. In the next year a man snapped a pistol at her carriage window as she was returning from church in London, but the charge failed to go off. On the day after this man's sentence of death was commuted to transportation for life another pistol was snapped at her carriage, but it, too, missed fire. Other attempts were made in later years, but the Queen was never hit. She appears to have been as safe from harm as Washington appeared to be to the Indians, who thought he bore a charmed life.

REFORM BILLS AND IRELAND.

From the foregoing review of what may be called the personal side of the Queen' life the course of this article naturally verts at this point to the public m and events of this remarkable re' Victoria assumed the statesmen had been fo' pied with measur' The new Ministr' that came ' William

WOMEN AND BOOKS.

Readers from All Parts Continue Their Replies to "Tiglath."

Our aggressive correspondent "Tiglath" continues to meet with protests against his onslaught on women as having no real interest in literature. THE SATURDAY REVIEW has already printed many of the letters inspired by him, but the more recent arrivals have become so numerous that we find it necessary to resort to rather drastic condensation in order to give them a representation. Our correspondence is rapidly growing, and, while we are always glad to hear from our readers, we must ask them to write with brevity and to deal with important topics that have general interest to readers of THE SATURDAY REVIEW.

May Harris of Robinson's Springs, Ala., writes: "I fancy 'Tiglath' is right when he suggests that the brilliant example of feminine intellect he instances furnished the waning glories of her 'thirty-five years' with 'a literary cosmetic.' Poor woman of thirty-five. She wished to make herself attractive, and we are not left in any reasonable doubt as to whom she wished to please with her 'cosmetic.' The ego, if not the heart, of 'Tiglath' should have been touched by her effort to 'quote intelligently from the rarer poets,' with whom he was on terms of unquestioned intimacy. 'Upon one occasion,' he adds, 'she spoke of Plautus in a way that made me look at her twice'! Women haven't any sense of humor—perhaps; but at least they can perceive the humorous lack of it in men. Perhaps 'Tiglath' will tell me who said—

" 'To thine own self be true,
And it must follow, as the night the day,
Thou canst not then be false to any man.' "

Byron wrote in his journal anent Mme. de Stael: "I don't talk, I can't flatter, and I won't listen, except to a pretty or a foolish woman." He adds, however, regretfully: "She ought to have been a man." Had "Tiglath's" unfortunate friend been a man, "Tiglath's" letter would have been lost to the readers of THE REVIEW, for men are sensible and selfish enough to prefer the passive to the active form of the verb amuse.

As to whether women care for literature, I am not considering the question. It is one to be individually answered, and perhaps not disappointingly. If men cared more, it would be better, for it may be they sometimes read too much and are inspired to show on how "many thousand lines" they can show "talent and power." It is hard to learn that "what we know we feel, and what we feel we know" is, if expressed, counted by "Tiglath," a literary cosmetic, but women are too prone to exhibit what they consider their best points for admiration, especially masculine.

"Then the craftsman thinks to grace the rose,
Plucks a mold flower,
For his gold flower.
Uses fine things that efface the rose."

And the rose, most sapient "Tiglath," is, after all, the thing. Had I the mantle of Macaulay, I would scathe "Tiglath," even as Robert Montgomery suffered, and I can fancy the contempt of Carlyle's growl—the sage of Chelsea would have wasted no words. "Tiglath" is an original study of contemporary egotism. He is a text and a sermon in himself.

Charles Wills, Jr., writes from Morristown, N. J.: "Although I think 'Tiglath' has gone a little beyond the truth in saying that no woman cares for literature beyond the 'ceaseless flight of trumpery novels,' I think he is right in saying that women—on the average, I mean—have not an inborn and self-sustaining love for good literature. The highest taste for reading that most of the women I have met possess is for the novels that are not heavy enough to make them do any thinking outside of their regular routine. A woman would far rather read the society page of a daily newspaper than any literature that would inspire her to new thoughts and new feelings. Many women profess to have a love for good literature, but their views on

books are almost always to be found in the book reviews."

Elma Stuart writes from Phoenix, Ariz.: "'Tiglath's' sweeping condemnation of my sex rather stirs me. His accusation may be true of some—unfortunately is—but surely not of all. I am a very average Englishwoman, and yet I think the keenest pleasure of my whole life has been to buy books. When I have found a good, noble, and beautiful book I could not rest till it was my very own.

The years roll back as I write, and I see myself, forty-three of them ago, young and just married. We had foolishly married against the consent of our parents, and they —God bless them, they are here no more— thought to unmarry us, I suppose, by a process of starvation. Many a time, my husband dining at an eating house, did I eat only dry bread for dinner, all the while treasuring up in secret a sovereign ($5) given me by a cousin, and which I destined to the purchase of "Boswell's Life of Johnson." I had to wait five months ere opportunity favored me, and not till I was at the Cape of Good Hope did I triumphantly carry home my volumes. But when at last I held them in my eager hands, what were exile and poverty and vexation in comparison?

Sir, every book on my shelves is dear to me, for every book means a sacrifice. But for what an end! In my many sorrows they (my books) have been unfailing in kindness and comfort; in foolishness they have given wisdom and guidance; they have been strength to my weakness, have helped me to help others, and in their possession has been deep joy, and, what is more, they have removed far from my home and from my heart that sore sorrow and trial of woman's life—loneliness. It is to me a small matter that I have mostly fed poorly and dressed plainly, since by so doing I have been enabled to gather under my roof the great and noble of the earth, who look down on me from my walls with the faces of friends. Had I—would to God I could have! —the boon of life once more, I should, so far as the blessed acquisition of books goes, live it all over again. I thank you most gratefully for the treat your paper is to me.

Ella Town Hamlin, writing from Orlando, Fla., asks: Is it possible that a being of such fossiliferous tendencies and origin as "Tiglath" can hail from enlightened New York? Where has the man been hibernating? His priggish communication with reference to women is so hopelessly nonsensical as hardly to merit a passing thought; but nevertheless he would arouse the ire of almost any self-respecting woman, advanced or otherwise. The man certainly evinces a conceit and vanity absolutely colossal. Hasn't he learned that this is the age of conscientious, earnest striving among our sex for higher education, for a better understanding of politics, for a knowledge of sociology, and all subjects worthy the thought and study of either sex? May I intimate that there are things to know quite as essential as a faithful study of the authors he names, most of whom were friends of our school days and worthy ones, too.

Christine V. W. Clarke of New York says: "The letter by 'Tiglath,' with the discussion which it has aroused seems to me very beneficial for any reader. I think honest criticism, even if it is founded on inaccurate impressions, which assumes that woman should be the peer of man is more acceptable than such chivalrous expressions as assume that she is by nature mentally an inferior being. I believe that in reading this discussion many an earnest woman is asking herself, What is true literature? and, with the thought that the homes make the nation, With what literature should homemaking women familiarize themselves? I hope not many of us assume to judge the world by our little environment. I can say that the only two authors I have known personally whose works were widely read were women. When I married and went to one of the Rocky Mountain States, I spent many congenial hours of the first year in a literary course which my husband was pursuing to secure a higher degree from his Alma Mater. The next year I was admitted to membership in a woman's literary club—the Aglaia, which was discussing American literature. This year the Aglaia is pursuing a Chicago University course in literature. In that Western town I found three literary clubs of women and a historical club. If there were any such organizations of men, I never heard of them. Personally, I have never observed such heartfelt appreciation of and enthusiasm for true literature in men as in women, but I should consider it folly to say it does not exist."

Mrs. Charles F. Hotchkiss of Glen Ridge, N. J., writes: I do not agree with you that the novel-reading men are not those who read serious literature. On the contrary, I believe that the men who are constantly using their brains in a serious study of science, history, or philosophy are the very ones who read most, and who certainly best appreciate the novel. Perhaps my opinion may carry more weight when I tell you that a close personal knowledge of the experiences of one who for forty years was librarian of a circulating book club in a university town leads me to this conclusion.

This librarian knew the tastes and demands of nearly every individual member of the club; and, while the women did full justice to the heavier reading matter, the men relaxed themselves with the novels. Yet they were all without exception men of weight in the world of letters.

Charles Augustus Davis sends this from Philadelphia: "I have not yet arrived at that period in life when I can claim an understanding of that charming combination of inconsistency and contrariety—woman. However, my experience in the world is of sufficient value to warrant the statement that woman, from the breadth of her sympathies and the nicety of her mental adjustment, is well qualified not only to enjoy, but to pass judgment on literary matters ranging from a Vedic hymn in the original Sanskrit to the Hibernianism of Mr. Dooley. It would be useless to deny the existence of many shallow women; fortunately, this class is in the minority. cently it was my privilege to make a symposium that included a member of the University of presence of a psychologi tensions—gave addition cussions. During ment I found reme C

THE DEVELOPMENT OF FEMININE SELF-RELIANCE.

The release of Mrs. Nation on bail from the Topeka Bastile was effected just in time to save the male portion of the human race from annihilation. A Michigan woman had formally notified Judge Hazen, who seems to have been the committing magistrate, that if the illustrious prisoner was longer detained "we propose to raise the greatest army of women the world has ever known and wipe man out of existence." Considering the facility with which armies of women, at least large enough to do great damage to property, can be raised in the West, it would be in the highest degree fatuous to dismiss this threat as idle vaporing. It might not be made good to the extent of wiping man out of existence, but even decimation would be undesirable from the male point of view. That a beginning would have been made in that direction is extremely probable. To the new woman all things appear to be possible. An army of them much less numerous than St. Ursula's following of eleven thousand virgins would be likely to give a good deal better account of themselves than those unhappy young women did at Cologne. Times have changed since that sad event "cast a gloom over Europe." At the head of eleven thousand new women armed with hatchets Mrs. Nation would have routed the Huns without difficulty.

The principal characteristic of the new woman which has hitherto escaped the recognition to which its importance entitles it is her exaggerated self-reliance. Up to a certain point this is admirable, but it can perhaps be carried too far for the good of society and the peace of mankind. Time was—and it was not very long ago—when the favorite attitude of the typical woman was that of complete theoretical dependence upon the strong arm and masterful intelligence of her male protector. We speak of this dependence as theoretical, advisedly. It accomplished its chief purpose in flattering the masculine vanity. A favorite figure of speech in describing the proper and normal relation of the sexes was to compare man to the sturdy oak which buffeted the storms and wrestled the strong winds, and woman to the clinging vine which embraced the oak and was upheld by it. This was very pretty and poetical, no doubt, and it did service for a good many centuries, until women began to take an interest in botany. Then they made the discovery that the figure was at least an unfortunate one, since

the clinging vine, however decorative to the rough and scraggy oak, was at best a parasite, and that the oak would best promote its own well-being and insure a green old age if it had as little as possible to do with vegetables of the clinging vine variety. Naturalists had pointed out that when the clinging vine got its growth its principal business in life was to embrace its victim so tightly as to squeeze the sap out of it, not in exuberance of affection, but because it was by nature a constrictor. No woman of good judgment cared to be put in that classification; so the clinging vine metaphor was dropped, and the woman who should now venture to suggest that view of the relation of the sexes in a paper before her club would be promptly invited to resign, as irredeemably ineligible for association with any one but hopeless old maids—whose views on that subject "don't count." Accepted conventions permit, and indeed demand, the amelioration of unpleasant truths to suit the fictions of social amenities. The favorite modern figure is safer. It pictures man as the sun, the source of life and light and power, perpetually eliminative of energizing forces; and woman as the earth, perpetually absorptive of the benefits radiated from the generous luminary which is the accredited source of all terrestrial phenomena. This is free from objection. The new woman is content with the earth and the fullness thereof, and makes no objection to any amount of solar radiation up to the limit of her absorptive powers. Moreover, the sun, while conferring inestimable benefits, remains some ninety-two millions of miles out of her way, and demands nothing in return for what he confers. This is as it should be.

Those who think that the development of self-reliance stops at intellectual independence, or even at political equality, have read history to small purpose. Circumstances partly of her own making and partly the result of influences which have always tended to promote a certain degree of artificiality in social relations, have operated to restrain woman from participation in much of the world's work which has profoundly interested them. It looks now as if this restraint was becoming steadily weaker. The swing of the arrested pendulum and the relaxation of the coiled spring are familiar phenomena, invariably illustrating the law of equality between action and reaction. This is a disquieting thought. We believe it is a statistical fact that there are more women than men in the world.

BRIDE MERRILY TELLS OF HER ELOPEMENT

Also of Her Papa's Futile Chase in Central Park.

Miss Edna Double's Parents Objected to Adolph Lee Wirth of Milwaukee as Their Son-in-Law.

With all the accessories known to romance Adolph Lee Wirth, a wealthy young business man of Milwaukee, and his bride, who was Miss Edna Double of New York and Boston, are at the Savoy Hotel spending their honeymoon, and waiting anxiously for a possible reconciliation with the father and mother of the bride. George E. Double, the father, and his wife are at their home at 235 West Seventy-fifth Street, and are making no move toward forgiveness.

"I did all I could to get the consent of my people to this marriage before the ceremony was performed," declared young Mrs. Wirth last evening, "but when they would not consent I went ahead. I knew Mr. Wirth was the only man in the world for me, and I was going to have him. That is all there was to it except for the chase papa gave us through Central Park in a cab. But we lost him." And with that the bride of three days let her merriment have full sway and laughed heartily as she told of the experience.

"As far as I was concerned there was but one thought," said Mr. Wirth. "I wanted the girl and she wanted me and I got her. Nothing else to it."

Mr. Double is the head of the cotton goods manufacturing firm, with main offices in Boston and with New York offices at 62 Walker Street, doing business under the firm name of George E. Double & Co. Mr. Wirth, who is thirty-two years of age, is a son of Lee Wirth of Milwaukee and has been brought up in the business of brewing and distilling. He at present is a Director of the National Distilling Company and is manager of its vinegar department, and also is a Director of the Bakers and Consumers' Yeast Company and of the Milwaukee Vinegar Company. All of these corporations are located in Milwaukee. His bride is twenty-four years of age and has had a thorough musical education in this country and Europe, and is an accomplished linguist as well. She does not conceal the fact that she considers the elopement, especially the encounter with her father, as a huge joke.

"It all is a very simple affair," she said as she told the details in the reception room of the Savoy, last evening. "Four years ago I was traveling in Europe and studying music. At Salzberg I met Mr. Wirth, who had gone to Europe for the purpose of studying chemistry in Berlin as an aid in his business. A mutual attachment immediately was formed, and in a short time there was an understanding between us, although no formal engagement was announced. My mother was with me at the time and there were other friends. Mr. Wirth and I were much in the company of each other all that year, and in the following Spring I returned to New York, while he remained in Berlin for another year.

"During all this time we were in constant correspondence, and when he came back to America two years ago he made a formal demand for my hand. My parents objected. Their only reason was that I was an only child; they called me 'the apple of their eye,' and they did not want me to marry at all, I guess. Finally they persuaded me for the time to give up all thought of marrying Mr. Wirth, and he went back to Milwaukee. We kept up our correspondence, however, and as a matter of fact we all the time had our eyes on the one goal we both sought.

"Last Wednesday Mr. Wirth came to New York for the purpose of marrying me. We had planned it before when he had been here and also in our letters. I told my mother on Wednesday morning that Mr. Wirth and I were to marry and asked her consent and aid, but it was refused. I did not, however, tell her that we were to marry that same day. When I left the house I told my grandmother I intended to bring Mr. Wirth to the house that evening, but I did not tell her we were to be married in the meantime. Later in the day I met Mr. Wirth downtown and with mutual friends, a married couple known to me well and to Mr. Wirth slightly, we went to The Little Church Around the Corner and were married by Dr. Houghton.

"After the ceremony we four went to the Waldorf for a dinner. While there my father came in. He and Mr. Wirth had words, although Mr. Wirth urged father to say nothing at that time to create a scene. Father, however, said my husband had stolen me, and he was very disagreeable, although we both begged him not to be. Then I told father we were going to go home and see my mother. He said there was no need to, as she was not home and would not see me anyway.

"Mr. Wirth became afraid something would happen to separate us. He was not a resident of New York and feared he might be arrested for taking me. So we at once left the hotel and jumped in a cab which was driven up Fifth Avenue. Father jumped into another cab and followed us, keeping right back of us all the time. Up Fifth Avenue we went to Fifty-ninth Street then over to Eighth Avenue, where we entered the Park. We were driving at a furious pace and it was a great chase. Our driver kept urging the horse on and I shouted to him.

"'Go on, do your best, there is money in it for you!'

"He kept right on, only he raised his hand and made some sort of a fraternity sign to the other cabman. From that time on father's cab kept dropping further and further back, and I afterward found our cabman had signaled to the other to get lost, and that he would divide with him when they got back to the Waldorf, with the result that there was no more father to be seen."

Still fearful that there might be an arrest, Wirth and his bride decided not to stay in the city, so they went over to Paterson, N. J., and stopped at the home of a Mr. Fletcher, who is the Eastern manager of the corporations with which Mr. Wirth is connected. The next day, Thursday, they came to New York again and put up at the Savoy. Mrs. Wirth says she did not send any more word to her home and has made no attempt to get her belongings and will make no attempt until she gets to Milwaukee, where she will make her home.

"But I do want to say that at getting a trousseau in two days I am a crackerjack," she remarked, laughingly. "On Thursday Mr. Wirth and I went shopping, and I got everything that was needed in the way of clothes and things to last me several weeks. We are going to take a trip through the South before we go to Milwaukee."

At the home of the Doubles last evening there was a sort of family conference between the father, mother, grandmother, and some other relatives from out of town who had been summoned to talk the affair over.

"I did not want my daughter to marry Mr. Wirth," said Mrs. Double, "because she was a girl much younger than her years, sensitive, of a musical disposition, and not at all suited to a man of Mr. Wirth's calibre. I never cared for him and hoped for an entirely different sort of marriage for her when it came time for a marriage. I never expected or desired her to go through life without marrying. No, there was no marriage we had in view for her, nothing of the sort.

"We never would give our consent to this marriage and since the marriage there has been no attempt at a reconciliation between my daughter and myself. There has been a communication received by us, but that is all. What I shall do if my daughter comes to me I cannot say. I love her very dearly and am heartbroken over her action."

"Do you mean, Mrs. Double, that your daughter would have to leave her husband and come to you alone before she would be received?" was asked.

"I do not say that or prescribe any other conditions," she answered.

"Would you receive Mr. Wirth?"

"That is a very hard question to answer, and one I do not care to answer at this time.

"I have no recollection of saying my daughter need not come home to see her mother on the night of her wedding," said Mr. Double, "but there were a good many lovely things said by both Mr. Wirth and myself at the Waldorf. We were both pretty angry, and did not mince matters at all."

March 22, 1903

March 11, 1905

SWEET GIRL UNDERGRADUATES.

That is a very dark saying which Mr. ANDREW CARNEGIE has promulgated to the female students of Dundee University College, in advising them to "cut their hair short for hygienic reasons, but to retain their long-haired ways."

We wonder what he really meant by it. The second branch of the proposition is of course perfectly clear. The "long-haired ways" of women have been familiar and delightful to mankind from the dynasty of RAMESES to that of ROOSEVELT, and have, during all these generations, secured the race from the danger of "suicide." Beauty has continued to draw us "by a single hair," and more powerfully by the multiple thereof involved in "a head." The tangles of Neaera's have enmeshed mankind, and will continue to do so so long as mankind is mankind. Sweet girl undergraduates with their golden hair will, in the form of "coeds," make matches before they come to be graduates, to the relief of the apprehension of the President of the United States—"for he lacks soldiers."

What troubles us is, what are the "hygienic reasons"? None such, that we know of, have been admitted by the consensus of mankind, or the doctors thereof. If they exist in Scotland, they must be peculiar to it. At the time when Scotchmen were as odious in London as Germans now are, and for much the same reasons, there was, to be sure, a South British imputation of a North British malady, of which the period was supposed to be a septenniad. MACAULAY treats the supposition as a fact. But, for this malady, cutting the hair was neither remedial nor prophylactic. The only palliatives were abundant sulphur and frequent posts, such as those which have handed down to posterity the name of the good Duke of ARGYLE. If the occasion still existed which his Grace so nobly met, we have no doubt that Mr. CARNEGIE would prove equal to it, and that ornamental scratching posts would appear at all needed crossroads, with neat inscriptions testifying to the munificence of the donor, and that around each would revolve a psoric chorus, "GOD bless the guid ANDREW CARNEGIE." But, even if the occasion still existed, it is hard to see how shingling the human hair would serve to meet it. It is for a larger and visibler and superficial instead of sub-cutaneous parasite that that remedy would alone prove efficacious. And of course Mr. CARNEGIE does not mean that.

Moreover, it would be interesting to know the foundations of his belief that short hair in women is compatible with "long-haired ways." The experience of mankind is to the contrary effect. A girl of collegiate age with her hair cut is, to the casual eye, only an inferior kind of boy. Since, and before, St. PAUL remarked that the glory of a woman is her hair, it has been considered that her shingling her head was, on the part of lovely woman, a token of masculinity. At the time of the Beecher trial, a generation ago, a clever woman remarked that all she could make out about the case was that all the women concerned wore their hair short and all the men wore theirs long, thus indicating a reversal of the normal position of the sexes. Let us hope that the lassies to whom the philanthropist addressed himself will not take him too seriously, but will retain their long hair in retaining their long-haired ways. We have no real apprehension that they will take him too seriously, or that they will cut off their hair on easier terms than a satisfactory endowment apiece.

WOMEN AT LAWN TENNIS

Tournaments Arranged Exclusively for the Fair Players.

Likelihood of Mrs. G. W. Hillyard, England's Foremost Feminine Expert, Competing in This Country.

Interest in developing the sport of lawn tennis among women has received more than the usual amount of attention during the past two seasons. It is evident that there is no abatement in the interest this year and that the game will be materially furthered. There was a meeting yesterday afternoon of the Board of Governors of the New York Lawn Tennis Club, at the courts, One Hundred and Twenty-third Street and St. Nicholas Avenue, at which it was decided to take the initiative in the Metropolitan district in holding tournaments for women players. This is one of the most important movements that has been started among the players of this city, and it appears probable that it may have a bearing on future international competitions.

The officers of the New York Lawn Tennis Club, with two additional members, compose the Board of Governors of the organization. They were elected at a recent meeting, and are as follows: Lindley H. Hill, President; Louis J. Grant, Vice President; Robert M. Beckley, Secretary; David S. Sands, Treasurer; A. T. Friedman, Captain; C. L. Cobb, First Lieutenant; Robert Le Roy, Second Lieutenant; additional Governors, G. Lorraine Wyeth and Harry McCallum. Ever since last season there has been considerable talk among the club members as to the advisability of holding a distinctive woman's tournament. This was because Mrs. George W. Hillyard, the ex-champion of England of the women, said to one of the club's members who was abroad last year that she would like to come to America to play through the season. Mrs. Hillyard has won at different times all of the woman's titles in England and on the Continent of Europe, such as those at Nice, Monte Carlo, Paris, Berlin, and elsewhere. She deplored the conditions which ruled in this country and the fact that there were so few tournaments in which women were allowed to compete. Furthermore, Mrs. Hillyard signified her intention of visiting this country in the event of her husband accompanying the challenging team of Britons for the tournaments of 1903.

It was partly with the view of stimulating the sport and preparing the women experts for such competitions as might arise and for the National woman's championship meeting that the Governors of the New York Lawn Tennis Club met yesterday. The club is perhaps better fitted than any other to make the proposed movement successful. It has a numerous membership among women players, the present holder of the National title, Miss Elizabeth H. Moore, heading the list. The most prominent among the others are Miss A. M. Risch, who last year won the mixed doubles at the Kings County Lawn Tennis Club paired with Robert Le Roy, the Columbia University player; Miss Edith H. White, Miss M. Hartley, Miss Gertrude Mahoney, Miss Mabel Compton, Miss Jeannette Allen, Miss Emma W. Hodkinson, Miss Virginia Mercer, Miss Cecil Mosby, Mrs. Harry McCallum, Mrs. C. H. Emerson, Mrs. W. E. Jones, and Mrs. Stephen H. Keating. These women are all desirous of bringing to a successful issue the plans that were briefly outlined by the Governors of the club and an auxiliary committee of women will later be appointed.

The plans which were made contemplate the holding of a tournament distinctly for women players sometime in the early part of June, the date to be decided upon later. It will be during some week that does not conflict with any other tournament within the Metropolitan district. If possible it will be arranged as an annual fixture under the direction of the United States National Lawn Tennis Association and will be given some designation as a woman's championship. The events will include singles, doubles, and mixed doubles.

Such a tournament has never before been held in New York, and it is believed by the members of the club promoting the meeting that it will attract a representative entry list. It will also induce many of the feminine players in this vicinity, notably those of the Staten Island Ladies' Club, of Livingston, S. I., the Kings County Lawn Tennis Club, and the clubs affiliated with the Hudson River Association of Country Clubs to enter an open tournament. Many of the woman players of this country fail to get the experience that match play in a big tournament affords. Because of this they are deterred from entering the meeting for the National championship that is held annually at Philadelphia. This is a feature which the proposed tournament hopes to overcome. It will be just in advance of the woman's championship and will give the competitors an opportunity to become used to playing through a series of matches against players of varying degrees of skill.

While the plans of the meeting are still in somewhat of an embryonic state, they include plans for other tournaments to be held throughout the season by other clubs. The New York Lawn Tennis Club's meeting will be the beginning of the series. The Kings County Lawn Tennis Club, the Orange Lawn Tennis Club, the West End Lawn Tennis Club, the Sleepy Hollow Lawn Tennis Club, and the Staten Island Ladies' Club will be asked to enter into the plans and further the sport among the women, who desire to get the same opportunities for tournament play as are now afforded to the men. This country is far behind England in respect to women playing on the courts, and it is doubtful if an American girl would be able to make a worthy opponent for several of the women who have won and held honors abroad. It may lead to international matches, which will be in every way as interesting as those in which the teams of Englishmen and American experts engage, and this is the end that it is believed will ultimately be attained.

The regular club tournament of the New York Lawn Tennis Club will be held on Decoration Day, May 30, and the following days. This is earlier than usual, but the members believe that the matches will give the best men of the club the sort of practice that is desirable before the regular metings of the season get in full swing. The Kings County Lawn Tennis Club also expects to begin its club tournament at the beginning of the season. It carried out the idea last year and with excellent results.

A special challenge match has been arranged to be played to-morrow at the Seventh Regiment Armory, the expert pair of the Regimental Tennis Association, Calhoun Cragin and Arthur Cragin, having challenged Wylie C. Grant and Robert Le Roy, the recent winners of the National Indoor Championship in the doubles. Grant has been playing on the Seventh Regiment courts a great deal and has held to the fine form which he displayed during the indoor meeting, which he won. His opponent has been William Cragin of the West Side organization, and Grant has defeated him in three special matches.

At the Crescent Athletic Club a new committee will have charge of the tennis affairs this year. F. Otto Affeld, Jr., has been elected Chairman of the committee, and he has begun to arrange the details of an active season on the fine turf courts at Bay Ridge. The Crescent clubmen and tennis followers have not yet given up hope that the international competitions for the Dwight F. Davis Challenge Cup may yet be played on their courts instead of those of the Longwood Cricket Club, Boston. Whatever may be the final decision relative to the English and American matches, there will be an abundance of play of a high order of excellence at Bay Ridge. The invitation tournament will bring together many of the old-time college champions of Yale, Harvard, and Princeton who are now members of the club. There will also be a numerous gathering of the present leaders and holders of National titles. In addition to this tournament the regular series of class, handicap, and scratch matches will fill out the season from June to October.

March 22, 1903

MISS MARY BROWNE

December 21, 1913

PERILS THAT WOMEN FIND IN ATHLETICS

Dr. Sargent Warns Them Against Emulating Men in Sports.

DANGERS OF COMPETITION

Let Women Stick to Lighter and Graceful Forms of Exercise, Says Harvard's Physical Director.

According to opinions expressed by authorities who addressed the Public School Physical Training Society at a mass meeting held last evening at the hall of the Board of Education in Fifty-ninth Street, woman for her own good should not strive to emulate man in the more strenuous forms of athletics, particularly competitive games, and should pursue physical training merely for recreation and pleasure.

These views were expressed at the first mass meeting on athletics for women that has ever been held in this country, and they are likely to affect the action of the educational authorities of this city, who intend to devote considerable attention to the question of athletics for women.

City Supt. Maxwell, who acted as Chairman of the meeting, got back briefly at some of his fads and frills critics.

"Some time ago," he said, "authorities of the financial department attacked the so-called fads and frills. I know not if physical training is a fad or a frill. But I do know that when the matter was referred to the people of this city they declared that progress should not be delayed, and there was no greater outburst in favor of any movement than that in favor of physical training. The people favor physical training because they see we are trying to give the child, hemmed in as he is in this city, an opportunity to develop physically."

Dr. Dudley Sargent, Physical Director at Harvard University, was the principal speaker. He struck the keynote of the evening in a discussion of "What athletic games, if any, are injurious for women in the form in which they are played by men?" Dr. Sargent said:

"In physical education women should not be expected to excel in physical exercises which are adapted to men, nor should they be required to teach athletics to men and boys, as is the case in some of the schools in the West. Such a requirement is not only injurious to the women, but equally injurious to the men. Let woman rather confine herself to the lighter and more graceful forms of gymnastics and athletics, and make herself supreme along these lines as she has already done in aesthetic dancing. Let her know enough about the rougher sports to be the sympathetic admirer of men and boys in their efforts to be strong, vigorous, and heroic.

"While admiring and applauding all there is in athletics which tends to make boys courageous and manly, let her not hesitate to condemn all that tends to make them mean, vicious, and cowardly. Let woman use her influence in trying to raise football and some of the rougher athletic games from their barbaric stage to a standard more in keeping with our present civilization, and she will do more for the moral and physical welfare of herself and the community than she could possibly do by entering the arena as a competitor in these contests."

The forms of gymnastics to which woman should confine herself Dr. Sargent classified thus: All forms of dancing, calisthenics, and light gymnastics, archery, lawn tennis, swimming, field hockey, lacrosse, sprint running, bicycling, rowing, canoeing, golf, skating, fencing, and all gymnastic plays and games. These were the athletic exercises and games, he thought, to which women were best adapted and in which they were most likely to excel.

Among the athletic sports and games that would be likely to prove injurious to most women, if played in the form in which they are played by men, Dr. Sargent particularly mentioned football, ice hockey, basket ball, boxing, pole vaulting, heavy gymnastics. These games prove injurious to women, he said, because of the limitations imposed upon her by her physical configuration, the tendency to become masculine in form and character if she tries to excel in masculine pursuits, and her inability to bear a prolonged mental and physical strain.

Nevertheless, he declared these sports and games could be so modified as to meet the peculiar requirements of woman, with the result that all of them could be played by her with reasonable hope of physical, mental, and moral development.

In his discussion of "Athletics from a Biological Viewpoint," Dr. Luther H. Gulick, President of the society, struck substantially the same note as Dr. Sargent by saying:

"I believe that athletics for women should for the present be restricted to sport within the school; that it should be used for recreation and pleasure; that the strenuous training of teams tends to be damaging to both body and mind, and that public general competition emphasizes qualities that are, on the whole, unnecessary and undesirable in women. Let us, then, have athletics for recreation, but not for serious public competition."

In the course of the day demonstrations of elementary and high school gymnastics, games, and athletics were given for the benefit of the members of the society. In the morning, at Public School No. 6, Madison Avenue and Eighty-fifth Street, of which Miss Katherine D. Blake and M. J. Thompson are Principals, a demonstration of regular physical training in the elementary schools was given, under the direction of Miss Jessie H. Bancroft, Asistant Director of Physical Training.

In the afternoon, at the Wadleigh High School, 114th Street, west of Seventh Avenue, an exhibition of athletics for girls, including indoor baseball, indoor hockey, and putting the shot, was given by the members of the Wadleigh Athletic Association.

March 31, 1906

AN ANARCHIST HONEYMOON.

Emma Goldman and Berkman Hold Hands on a Park Bench.

Special to The New York Times.

CHICAGO, May 25.—While the Chicago police were searching high and low for that terrible pair of "Reds," Alexander Berkman and Emma Goldman, the two Anarchists were on a bench in Lincoln Park to-day, holding hands and talking.

A reporter found them there, and they made no attempt to evade him.

"What shall I call you—Miss Goldman, Mrs. Goldman, or Mrs. Berkman?" the reporter asked.

"I am Emma Goldman, and I will live and die with that name," said the woman

"But are you two married?"

"We are Anarchists and don't believe in marriage, because marriage means the tyranny of government, and government means force," they replied almost in unison.

"But you are living together."

"Yes," said Emma Goldman, "and the basis of living together is a true spiritual love that still leaves free scope for individuality. That means companionship. But whenever one Anarchist ceases to love another more than any one else in the world, then he is free to go his way."

Berkman smiled fondly upon her.

May 26, 1906

EMMA GOLDMAN, ANARCHIST

Internationally Known Figure, Deported From the U. S., Is Stricken in Toronto

DISILLUSIONED BY SOVIETS

Deported for Opposing Draft

Emma Goldman, apostle of philosophic anarchism and of "voluntary communism," was born in Russia, spent thirty-three years of her life in the United States fighting for her ideals, for which she suffered imprisonment, and was an incorrigible revolutionist to the end.

She was deported from the United States in 1919 for obstructing conscription, fled in 1921 from Soviet Russia, where she had hoped to find the realization of her social dreams but found only disillusionment, and saw her ideals defeated again in the civil war in Spain, in which she took an active part. In the social history of the United States she wrote a chapter all her own, and in the history of the world-wide revolutionary movement of her time she made a place for herself beside that of her teacher, Peter Kropotkin.

Miss Goldman was a writer of distinction and an able critic of the drama. Her autobiography, "Living My Life," published in 1931, is regarded as one of the important books of its kind.

Thought Ideal Betrayed

After fighting for a generation against what she considered the ills of the social system in the United States she opposed Lenin and Trotsky because she believed them guilty of betraying the Socialist ideal by establishing what she denounced as a new despotism. Her experience in Russia confirmed her in the belief that all government was wrong and that the new society for which she stood could be established only on the basis of anarchism through the free cooperation of the masses. She never ceased to search for that new society even after the defeat in 1939 of the social experiment in Catalonia, where she thought she had finally found it.

Miss Goldman always had a warm feeling in her heart for America despite the long years of conflict with the authorities and public opinion in this country. In 1934 she was permitted to visit the United States for ninety days, and she lectured on political and literary topics.

It was not only because she had found an America that had undergone a profound transformation from the days when she had first come to know this country but also because of the striking contrast presented by the United States in comparison with nations in the grip of totalitarian regimes that Miss Goldman hailed America as a land of hope. She said she had never ceased to regard this country as her real home.

Found U. S. Still Free

"You are still free in America," she said. "You are free to come here and listen to me, with no army of police descending upon you. No spies enter your homes for incriminating documents. No legalized assassins shoot you down in the streets."

EMMA GOLDMAN

Emma Goldman was born in Kovno, June 27, 1869. She spent her childhood in the Russo-German province of Kurland, where her father had charge of the government-subsidized theatre and where she received her early education. Later she was sent to her grandmother in Koenigsberg, the city of Immanuel Kant, in East Prussia, where she continued her education in schools and through private instruction.

In 1882, when she was 13 years old, her parents moved to St. Petersburg. It was a stormy period in the life of the Russian people. Alexander II had been assassinated the year before and Russian society was in violent fermentation, marked by the execution of the assassins and the imprisonment of their ac complices. It was the period of the celebrated revolutionary party of the Narodnaya Volia, of activist "nihilism." Young Emma was deeply impressed by figures like Sophia Perovskaya, who was among those executed for the assassination of the Emperor, and Vera Figner. She determined to seek independence and an active career of her own. At the age of 17, with her sister Helene, she emigrated to America. They settled in Rochester, where she obtained employment in a clothing factory at $2.50 a week. There she gained her first knowledge and impressions of the labor problem.

Entered Anarchist Movement

In 1887 she was married to Jacob Kersner but the marriage soon broke up because of differences of opinion and ideas. Miss Goldman moved to New Haven, Conn., where she obtained employment in a corset factory. In New Haven she came into contact for the first time with anarchist circles. She read the Freiheit, the paper published by Johann Most.

These contacts, together with the impression made upon her by the execution of the Chicago anarchists in the Haymarket bombing tragedy of 1886, brought her actively into the anarchist movement. Made ill by her factory work, she returned to Rochester, where she remained until August, 1889, when she came to New York. Here she met Alexander Berkman. They became close friends and collaborators in anarchist work and propaganda.

This association was interrupted for fourteen years during which Berkman served a term of imprisonment in Atlanta for his attempt to assassinate Henry C. Frick during the Homestead steel strike in 1892. After his release from prison Berkman rejoined his companion in her work of going up and down the country preaching the abolition of government through education of the people to the point where they could govern themselves.

Miss Goldman's first imprisonment was in 1893, when she was arrested for inciting to riot at a Union Square demonstration in New York held in support of the Debs railway strike. She served seven months on Blackwell's Island. While in prison she acted as nurse in the hospital and devoted her leisure time to intensive study of American literature, with special attention to Bret Harte, Mark Twain, Walt Whitman, Thoreau and Emerson. She also studied particularly Fourier, the French Socialist. These and other studies fortified her for the literary aspect of her career.

Miss Goldman was 25 years old when she left Blackwell's Island in 1894. In addition to her work as a propagandist of anarchism she published for many years The Blast and later, until her deportation, Mother Earth, a literary and philosophic journal which came to be recognized as the authoritative spokesman of philosophic anarchism in this country.

On Sept. 6, 1901, Leon Czolgosz shot President McKinley at Buffalo. In his confession the assassin said he had been influenced by the writings of Emma Goldman and by some speeches which he had heard her make in Cleveland. She was arrested in Chicago and questioned for two weeks, the authorities being compelled to release her because of lack of evidence linking her in any way with the assassination. Eighteen years later, however, when the deportation proceedings were brought against her and Berkmen, A. Mitchell Palmer, Attorney General, revived the subject, contending that there was some evidence that she knew Czolgosz, at least by sight.

While she was often in trouble with the authorities because of her work on the lecture platform and in labor struggles, it was not until the war that Miss Goldman came into serious conflict with the government.

Served Two Years in Jail

Because of their agitation against the war draft and their opposition to the war Berkman was sent to Atlanta and Miss Goldman fined $10,000 and sentenced to two years in jail in Jefferson City, Mo. The deportation proceedings were brought by the government upon their release. The case was fought through the Supreme Court and, finally, on Dec. 1, 1919, together with 247 other aliens, they were deported on the transport Buford.

"We expect to be called back to Soviet America," she said as the Buford drew away from the pier.

Because of the absence of diplomatic relations with Russia at that time, the deportees were landed in Finland, whence they traveled by rail to Petrograd. They received a gala reception from the Bolsheviki, but it was not long before Miss Goldman and Berkman discovered that the regime set up by Lenin and Trotsky did not correspond to their conception of the new society. Within six months she wrote to a niece in Rochester that the Soviet regime was a new despotism under which the Russian people were deprived of all liberty.

The suppression of the Kronstadt rebellion of the Spring of 1921 moved them to open opposition against the Bolsheviki. They fled to the Ukraine and in December of the same year arrived in Riga, enemies of the Bolshevik system. Early in 1922 Miss Goldman was in Stockholm, going in April to Prague and thence to Berlin. Berkman wrote a book called "The Bolshevik Myth," while Miss Goldman traveled about Germany lecturing against bolshevism.

Wrote Two Books on Russia

In 1924 she published her book "My Disillusionment in Russia," followed next year with "My Further Disillusionment in Russia." This disillusionment was again emphasized in her autobiography. Incensed by her criticism, Communists in Germany tried to break up her meetings, just as the American police had frequently done in the earlier part of her career.

In 1924 Miss Goldman arrived in England, and two years later she turned up in Montreal as Mrs. E. G. Colton, wife of James Colton, a Welsh miner whom she had married in order to obtain British citizenship, having in the meanwhile lost her status as a Soviet citizen and become a woman without a country. From Canada she returned to the South of France, where she lived quietly and wrote "Living My Life."

Three years later came her American visit. She did not conceal her happiness at having been permitted to return to this country, if only for a brief span. She was warmly received here by old friends and left with deep regret and some hope that she might yet be permitted to return to the United States permanently.

Her antipathy to bolshevism was based upon a conclusion that the system had given "unhappy Russia a far worse tyranny than under the Czar."

Her impression of Russia was confirmed through the years in the establishment, finally, of the dictatorship of Stalin after the execution or exile of most of the old Bolshevik leaders. Lenin died in January, 1924. Ultimately, as Miss Goldman believed, Leninism, too, was dead, while nearly all the leading Leninists had been exterminated.

In July, 1936, while living at Nice, France, Miss Goldman suffered a shock in the death of her friend Berkman, who had committed suicide in a place near by.

SAYS DRINK MENACES WOMEN.

Dr. Peters Thinks Fashionable Tippling Threatens the Republic.

The Rev. Madison C. Peters has discovered that there is inebriety among "society women," and he talked about it yesterday at the People's Meeting in the Epiphany Baptist Church.

"The fashion that encourages women inebriates among the society women of New York," said Dr. Peters, "presents a deplorable outlook for the future of the Republic. The fashionables of this city are establishing a custom which is being followed by millions of American women, to the detriment of the race.

"Closely observe the goings on in the fashionable drinking places of our city, and nine out of ten women drink habitually, their tipples identical with those of men and the calls as frequent, drinking with men and women and alone, at luncheon, at dinner, at supper, and between times, young women and old, to say nothing of the drinking in their own homes, where nobody except their maids see them.

"Fashionable physicians know that I tell the truth. Alcoholism among women is alarmingly on the increase. I appeal to every woman who loves her kind to discourage the custom of social drinking and help to save the womanhood of the Nation from the curse of drunkenness."

'TOBACCO-SMOKING FEMALES'

Aldermen Moved to Invoke the Corporation Counsel Against Them.

The Aldermen intend to find out all about the rumors that women smoke in public places in the city, and they are going to stop it if they have to appeal to the Legislature. At yesterday's meeting Alderman Dowling, majority leader, offered this resolution:

Resolved, That the Corporation Counsel be and he is hereby requested to advise this board, at his earliest convenience, as to its power to prohibit tobacco smoking by females in public places, by legislative enactment.

It was adopted unanimously.

WRITERS BAFFLED BY 'GIRL OF TO-DAY'

Booth Tarkington Says She Might Be Anywhere from 17 to 30 Years Old.

TWO TYPES, STREET THINKS

One He Finds In Maine In Summer and the Other Is a New York Product.

Among authors who have written about American girls as they are, considerable interest is being taken in the search THE NEW YORK TIMES is making for the typical American girl of to-day. Booth Tarkington, whose portrayal of the American flirt and of the American boy have added fresh laurels to those he won by his earlier romances, and Julian Street, who has written much that is interesting about phases of the American girl that are seen in New York, said yesterday that a selection such as THE TIMES was undertaking to arrive at was beyond them.

"Typical American girl," said Mr. Tarkington, "is an epithet that makes me feel in a fog—as if I were trying to breathe with my nose in a plush cushion. Passing these symptoms, I think of sketches by Gibson and Flagg, tennis rackets, turkey-trotting, flat-soled shoes, college pins and the 'biological view of life.'

"A Frenchman could give you some color on this subject. I am too confused. I cannot be sure that I am able to think about a real type; it is probable that I am thinking only about what I have read of it and about the pictures I have seen of it.

"How old would I make this girl? Well, girls are 30, nowadays, as well as 17. Is there a new type? I incline to think so, but only from hearsay. I have heard, for instance, Julian Street speak of specimens unknown to me. Jesse Lynch Williams has gone so far as to assert that there is a new kind of girl—due to a new confrontation with old problems, if I understand him correctly. He told me they conversed most interestingly. As for myself, the fact is I can't answer questions about the American girl as well as I could ask them, though I would, of course, champion her against all other girls whatsoever. If I were questioner, I would ask:

"Is she less sentimental than her ancestresses were? Is she better educated than they? Does she think more? Is she less of a coquette? Does she know more about 'taking care of herself?'

Would she be better equipped to earn her own living? Has she humor?

"If the answers are all 'es' some people would claim that 'the world do move,' and, perhaps, 'it do.'

"So you see," added Mr. Tarkington, "I don't know anything about the subject, and, as I said before, it confuses me. All I know about it is what I can see, and all I can see is that she dresses enchantingly."

Mr. Street said he knew of at least two types of American girl of to-day thoughe he wouldn't want to say that either was THE type.

"If I lived in one of the hotels near Times Square," continued Mr. Street. "and were accustomed to spend my wakeful hours in the restaurants thereabout, I should be inclined to think the typical American girl is what I call a hectic.' I have no doubt that a great many foreigners who come over here and who see a great deal of the night life of New York picture the typical American girl as a sort of beauty of loose, red lips, feverish eyes, shining from the shadows of low-piled hair, like those of some wild creature gazing from a cave at night. This is distinctly a New York type, though it could not be called THE New York type.

"On the other hand, in Maine, in the Summer time, I see a lot of brown, strong girls, who can play golf or tennis, or send a canoe along with a powerful stroke. These are certainly of a more wholesome type than the other. Yet the other class is no less a type. Neither is the great American type.

"I cannot say what is the real American type of the girl of to-day. The type I should like to believe she is, if there is such a thing as the typical American girl, is a strong, healthy, thoroughly wholesome young person, sweetly sympathetic, who looks you squarely in the eyes. She is almost the antithesis of the extravagant, tight or slashed skirted little turkey-trotter who constitutes such a large portion of the afternoon population of Fifth Avenue and Broadway.

"I don't know that the creature I picture is typical, but I do know we have evolved in this country a girl with a remarkable amount of intelligence, a girl who, though she may be 'fashionable,' isn't altogether given up to fashion, but who reads good books, and thinks for herself and tries to understand what life is all about. I do not say this is THE American type, but it is an American type. One of the most striking things about her is her frankness, her charming friendliness. But again, when you try to describe such a girl, you find yourself describing an ideal of your own. A man who tries to describe a typical woman almost invariably pictures what he hopes she is—what he himself would like her to be."

THE NEW YORK TIMES is seeking the girl of to-day in order to present her to its readers by the most artistic method of photographic reproduction known. Everybody is invited to send in, before Nov. 1, photographs which have been taken within a year. With each photograph submitted must be sent the name and address of the subject, together with the date when the picture was taken.

From the pictures sent in, twenty-nine will be selected, which will be reproduced by the new rotogravure method in a special section of the Christmas number of THE TIMES. The judges will be seven artists, each of whom is famous as a creator of a type which represents a phase of the American girl. They will select from the twenty-nine photographs that which represents the typical American girl of to-day, and her picture will cover the entire front page of a rotogravure section of the Christmas number.

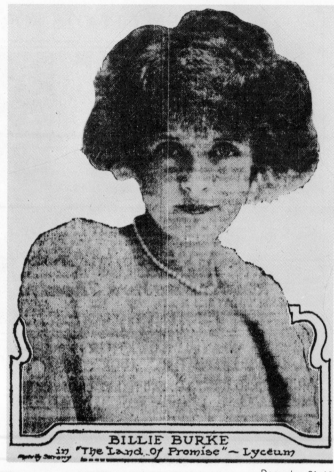

BILLIE BURKE in "The Land of Promise" — Lyceum

'THE GIRL OF TO-DAY' SEEKS TO BE USEFUL

One great trait that distinguishes The Girl of To-day, in the opinion of Mrs. May Wilson Preston, who, in her paintings and illustrations, has portrayed a great many phases of that delightful feminine person THE NEW YORK TIMES is seeking, is that she wants to do something useful in the world. She doesn't necessarily have to work for a living to be The Girl of To-day, according to Mrs. Preston, but just the same she works, and an idle person is not The Girl of To-day.

"There is no doubt that a new type of girl has come into being," said Mrs. Preston yesterday at her home in West Ninth Street. "In her development education has done a great deal, and it is a fact that the more a woman really knows the more she is apt to try to do something. Of course, a great many more girls go to college now than formerly. Then the spread of the woman's suffrage idea has had a great influence. In my opinion, the real Girl of To-day is one who wants to do something to be a self-supporting woman. She always does something, too. It may take one form with one and another with another. It may be that she goes in for philanthropic work, or suffrage, or the arts; at any rate, I believe the majority of women that are intelligent work in some way. If nowadays a girl is idle it is an indication that she has not much brain.

"I wouldn't say that athletics have had a great deal to do in the development of The Girl of To-day," said Mrs. Preston, in answer to a question, "although anything that has tended to strengthen the body has also had an effect upon making the mind stronger. At the same time, The Girl of To-day is not necessarily an athletic creature. I know a lot of women who are very brainy, but who have not the physique to go in for athletics.

"As I have always lived in New York I could not say whether The Girl of To-day is more closely approached by a Western girl or a Southern girl than by a New York girl, but from what I have read I should say that the typical American girl is not produced by any one locality to the exclusion of the rest. Certainly, New York produces her."

Do you think The Girl of To-day makes a better wife than her mother or her aunt?" Mrs. Preston was asked.

"It seems to me the more intelligent a girl is the better wife she will make," was the reply. "There is no question that The Girl of To-day is better groomed and better dressed than the girl of any other period. She devotes care to her appearance, and makes the most of the attractions that nature gave her. It is impossible to limit The Girl of To-day to any particular coloring or size. One of the most intelligent women I know is extremely small, while others are very tall. Of course the American girl of to-day has the ability to take care of herself. What distinguishes her mainly from the girls of any other nation is her independence.

"Taking it all in all, it seems to me the real high type of American woman—and that includes The Girl of To-day—is the sort who has brains, and wants to use them. She wants to do something that is worth while. She does not necessarily take up art or music or literature, but she may have her own way of doing good work. She may find in her own household enough to do to occupy all her time. Such a woman I consider may be doing equally important service in the world with the woman who is doing professional work."

FAIR PILOTS FOR GLIDDEN AUTO TOUR

These twin girls, clad in buckskins, drive a Metz in the A. A. A. reliability tour which started last week from the Twin Cities for the Glacier National Park.

July 31, 1913

Feminism . . . . By ELLEN GLASGOW

WHEN the most popular of men's heroines, after being blighted by love, went to the undertaker's to select her coffin, ordered that a broken lily should be engraved on the lid, and had it sent home to use as a writing table during her decline, an admiring eighteenth century public exclaimed that this touching episode had immortalized the womanly woman. No other heroine in fiction has been so passionately eulogized or so widely mourned, and even to-day she remains the most convincing of the feminine prigs with which the imagination of man has enriched the pages of literature. For Clarissa belongs not only to the evolving novel, but to the evolving masculine ideal of woman.

And since the hardest traditions to shake are those relating to women, since even a realist is apt to romance about women in English fiction, and so great a writer as Thackeray went to life for his heroes and to the Victorian pattern of femininity for his heroines, it is, perhaps, asking too much to expect an avowed sentimentalist to create a natural Clarissa. When woman herself has shown such eagerness to conform to man's ideal of her that she has cheerfully defied nature and reshaped both her soul and body after the model he put before her, one can hardly demand of a man novelist that he should write of her as she is and not as he desires that she should be. Ages of false thinking about her on the part of others have bred in woman the dangerous habit of false thinking about herself, and she has denied her own humanity so long and so earnestly that she has come at last almost to believe in the truth of her denial.

So it is not surprising that, until the day of George Meredith, English novelists, though they often wrote of men and things as they were, invariably treated woman as if she were the solitary exception to natural law, and particularly to the law of development. Fielding, Thackeray. Dickens, and a host of others prepared their womanly woman after the same recipe—modesty, goodness, self-sacrifice, an inordinate capacity for forgiveness, "about as much religion as my William likes," and, now and then, a little vivacity—all sufficiently diluted to make the mixture palatable to the opposite sex. And in time, after the manner of mankind, this formula received the sanction of custom.

From Richardson to George Meredith there was little change in man's ideal of the womanly woman. In fiction man might wear his cloak of many colors, but woman appeared changelessly white except on the occasions when, for purposes of plot, she was depicted as changelessly black. Never by design or accident could the colors run together—never could Amelia become Becky for an hour or Becky become Amelia. The womanly woman of the earlier novelists was wholly contented with her immemorial position as the spectator of man; and when she wasn't womanly, and wasn't contented, she was inevitably, as in the case of poor Beatrix, hunted to her destruction. Because it has pleased man to imagine that woman is passive and hates change, no English writer of fiction before George Meredith—or, I may say, instead, before Mr. Hardy—ever dared to recognize that she is, and has always been, in her heart at least, the adventurous sex. Even Fielding, who feared nothing else on earth, lived in terror of offending against the popular legend of the womanly woman, and was oppressed by the curious delusion that woman is made of different clay from man—that, while he progresses, she, corresponding to some fixed ideal of her, remains static. To be sure, the period in which he lived was one in which, to quote from his Mrs. James, "no woman could be genteel who was not entirely flat before," and for this reason, perhaps, his vision of the eternal feminine is as sentimental as Thackeray's. And yet, in spite of the fact that the world, or a part of it at least, has outgrown the belief that the worship of a dissolute husband is an exalted occupation for an immortal soul, it is impossible to resist the charm of Fielding's Amelia. Never before or since has man's womanly woman been made so lovable; and if she no longer commands our unquestioning esteem, she still continues to enchant and delight us. For, passive as she is in every quality except that of sex, she is drawn by the hand of a lover, and there is good red blood, not printer's ink, in her veins.

As for the two greatest novelists of the nineteenth century, they never forgot for a minute, like the kind-hearted gentlemen they were, that the souls of their heroines were encased in crinoline. The Victorian ideals of femininity lay as an incubus upon the **earlier fiction of the period—for it is, after all, an imperfect transcript of life that paints man as a human being and woman as a piece of faintly colored waxwork. It was a cherished tradition of the century, and in the beginning was probably construed into a delicate compliment to the young Queen, that the womanly woman had been created by the hand of God wholly passive and perfect, without the faults or even the ordinary impulses of human nature. It is true that when she became old and ugly she was permitted to be funny; and it is entirely to the saving fiction of the womanly woman's imperishable outward loveliness that we owe some of the most entrancing characters in Dickens's novels. His heroines belong in a gallery of waxwork figures; but his old women, his ugly women, and his wicked women are wholly delightful. For the old, the ugly, and the wicked, growing cramped in their positions or dissatisfied with their entertainment as the audience of man, become miraculously alive. When they cease to be valued as witnesses of the achievements of others, they display an amazing activity.**

But with Meredith and Hardy, **woman, for the first time in men's novels, drops her cloak of sentimentality and appears not less human and vital than does the source of her being.** And yet even here the ancient tradition is not completely discarded, and these great writers, unlike in so much else, are alike at least in this— that they both appear, in many of their books, if not in all, to regard caprice as the ruling principle of woman's nature. That a real Diana would have sold her lover's secret is exceedingly doubtful; that a real Sue would have deserted the suffering Jude is almost unbelievable—but caprice is probably the last quality that the masculine imagination will relinquish in its conception of woman; and certainly to make the womanly woman capricious is a pleasant change from the earlier fashion of making her insipid.

For before Meredith's splendid heroines appeared, when English novelists portrayed woman in heroic dimensions, it was invariably in di-

Ellen Glasgow
Author of "Virginia"   photo by Bradley

mensions of sex. She lived for man and failing this, she died for man and at long intervals she even disguised her sex and wore man's clothes for man—but the beginning, middle, and end of her existence was simply man. Without the prop of man she was as helplessly ineffectual as the "tender parasite" to which Thackeray compared her. And with the sacred inconsistency possible only to tradition, she was represented as passive even in the single activity to which her energies were directed— for in love, as in all else, she was supposed to sit with smiling patience and wait on the convenience of man. When she grew restless it proved merely that she was not the womanly woman—since to grow restless in the opinion of most novelists is the exclusive prerogative of man. And so deeply rooted in the masculine mind is this inherited belief in the right of the male to want to rove, if not actually to pack up and go, that we find so essentially modern a writer as Mr. Galsworthy speaking of "the aching for the wild the passionate, the new, that never quite dies in a man's heart."—implying, one gathers from the context, that this aching has either never been born

in the heart of a woman or has died there in its infancy. Yet Mr. Galsworthy possesses an understanding of woman's nature—of her strength, her weakness, her blindness to the virtue of expediency, her tragic wastefulness in love—that is not equaled—that is not even approached by any other of our younger novelists. In his perfect novel "The Dark Flower"— for it is impossible for one who is by temperament a novelist, not a reviewer, to speak in measured terms of praise of work so rare, so delicately wrought as this—he has painted the portraits of four women that stand out as softly glowing, as mysteriously lovely, as the figures in Titian's Sacred and Profane Love. About them one and all, ardently as they are imagined, there is a certain wistfulness—a pathos that seems inherent in sex—as if Mr. Galsworthy were oppressed by the feeling that woman could never really be happy—that Nature had, from the beginning, ordained her for suffering. These four women are but exquisite variations from the indestructible type of man's womanly woman—the woman who lives by love alone—the woman for whom Goldsmith wrote his famous advice on the simplest and most satisfactory way of wringing her lover's bosom. These women exist only in their relation to man; and, despite a feverish energy that love gives them, one feels that they could never become free women, that they are doomed to remain the slaves of passion or of memory. Only in self-sacrifice have they power, and it is not often that the beauty of self-sacrifice in woman is denied by one of the opposite sex. But it is Mr. Galsworthy's peculiar distinction that in his masculine insistence upon the beauty of self-sacrifice in women, he should understand the full cost of it to women themselves, the tragic waste of useless renunciation, the bitter loss to the world of that joy which is the crown and heritage of fulfillment, never of crucifixion.

Now, it is only by perfectly realizing this tradition of the womanly woman, it is only by completely understanding how deeply it has colored almost all that man has written about woman from the wisdom of Solomon to the folly of Sir Almroth Wright, that we shall begin to grasp the profound significance of the woman's movement. For what we call the woman's movement is a revolt from a pretense of being—it is at its best and worst a struggle for the liberation of personality. After centuries of silence or of idle chatter on the part of woman about their own natures, there has come, within the present decade, a rather startling burst of world confidences. Women novelists are still content, with some honorable exceptions, to copy the models as well as the methods of men; but in the brilliant and fearless books of Ellen Kay, of Rosa Mayreder, of Olive Schreiner, of C. Gasquoine Hartley (Mrs. Walter Gallichan), woman has become at last not only human, but articulate. Mrs. Gallichan's "The Truth About Woman" is an honest and courageous attempt to view woman, not through man's colored spectacles of tradition and sentiment, but by the clear, searching light of reality. It is not a book for babes, nor, for the matter of that, is it a book for octogenarians, unless they have abandoned most of the opinions held by the octogenarians of my acquaintance. She destroys much that the world has long valued, and particularly does she destroy the image worship of the womanly woman of fiction. One may not always agree with her conclusions; but she has admirably succeeded in freeing herself from sex prejudices and superstitions, and she brings to the familiar facts of biology and history an entirely fresh point of view and a remarkable keenness of insight. In preaching the gospel of freedom to women, however, it is well to remember—and it is not fair to imply that Mrs. Gallichan wholly forgets this—that the best use man has made of his liberty in the past has been to place restrictions upon it. For love, which would be so easy a solution of life's problems if it existed as a pure essence, may become sometimes, through

its strange interminglings, as morally destructive as hatred.

But Mrs. Gallichan writes with conviction, fairness, and sincerity, and she appears splendidly above that feminine priggishness, the irritating assumption of woman's moral superiority to man, which to the present writer at least sounds out of place, though not without humor, on a woman's lips. For virtue, after all, is not biological, but spiritual, and is of an infinite complexity—yet there are modern crusaders who seem to have forgotten that the Wisdom that forgave the thief and the Magdalen had only scorn for the Pharisee and drove the money changers out of the temple. So it is a pleasant change to find that Mrs. Gallichan rejects the popular doctrine of man's natural grossness as fearlessly as she denies the other sanctified fallacy of "woman's consecration to suffering." Of the one, she says wisely: "We women are so easily deceived by the outside appearances of things. The man who calls 'a spade a spade' is not really inferior to him who terms it 'an agricultural implement for the tilling of the soil,'" and of the other: "The female half of life has not been pre-ordained to suffer any more than the male half; this belief has done more to destroy the conscience of woman than any other single error. You have only to repeat any lie long enough to convince even yourself of its truth. But assuredly free woman will have to yield up her martyr's crown."

And it is just here, in this yielding up of the crown of the martyr and the manner of the Pharisee, that Mrs. Gallichan seems to make her greatest contribution to her subject. There is a song of joy in her pages—a song so different from the many mournful hymns with which men have celebrated the fact of sex, that one is tempted to ask if, after all, the sorrows of woman have existed chiefly in the imagination of men. She rejoices in womanhood, but it is a womanhood so free, so active, so conquering, that the word takes a new meaning from her interpretation, and she strikes her deepest note when she adds: "that from which woman must be freed is herself—the unsocial self that has been created by a restricted environment. * * * Woman is what she is because she has lived as she has. And no estimate of her character, no effort to fix the limit of her activities, can carry weight that ignores the totally different relations toward society that have artificially grown up, dividing so sharply the life of woman from that of man."

In the three main divisions of her book—the Biological Section, the Historical Section, and the Modern Section —Mrs. Gallichan discusses at length, and with a personal enthusiasm that makes it very interesting reading, the evolution of the woman's part in nature as the guardian of the life force, and therefore as "the predominant and responsible partner in the relations of the sexes." The ancient social

dominance of woman in the mother-age, the transition from this to the inferiority and dependence of the mother during the father-age, and the present unstable efforts of the sexes toward a balance of power—all these periods of bondage or of liberty she regards merely as nature's provisions for the better care of the race. In contrast with much that man has written about woman—in contrast with the intolerant bitterness of Weininger, of Nietzsche, of Schopenhauer—there is a large, calm justice in her criticism of this man's world in which we are living. To her clear vision man appears, not as a conscious tyrant, but, equally with woman, as a victim to the conditions of social evolution. Beneath the historic fact of man's dominance, she discerns the invincible purpose of nature without which man's efforts to dominate would have been as useless as a child's cries for the moon. If the balance of power passed from the matriarch to the patriarch, this was possible only because the growing race needed to cradle itself in the father-age before it could gather its strength. Not male tyranny, but the selective agency of life decided the issue. While the race needed woman's subjection, she was condemned to remain subject; when it needs her freedom, she is inevitably ordained to become free. It is as useless for men to fight progress as it is for women to fight men—"For to go on with man, not to get from man, this is the goal of woman's freedom. Just in measure as the sexes fall away from love and understanding of each other do they fall away from life into the futility of personal ends." In the harmonious adjustment of the future she sees:

"Neither mother-right alone, nor father-right alone, can satisfy the new ideals of the true relationship of the sexes. The spiritual force, slowly unfolding, that has uplifted, and is still uplifting, womanhood, is the foundation of woman's claim that the further progress of humanity is bound up with her restoration to a position of freedom and human equality. But this position she must not take from man—that, indeed, would be a step backward. No, she is to share it with him, and this for her own sake and for his, and, more than all, for the sake of their children and all the children of the race. This replacement of the mother side by side with the father in the home and in the larger home of the State is the true work of the Woman's Movement."

But where this very modern interpretation diverges most widely from the traditional ideal of the sexes is in the writer's rejection of the belief in woman's natural passivity, and by this single point, small as it may appear to some thinkers, will probably be decided the future success or failure of the movement we know as Feminism. If, as man has so confidently asserted in the past, woman exists, not as an active agent of life, but merely as the passive guardian of the life force, then, indeed, is her revolt doomed to fail and her struggle to bear fruit in her sorrow. If her fight is a fight against law, if it is nature's purpose that woman shall sit and watch, then, as surely as night follows day, she will continue to sit and watch until the end of time. To Mrs. Gallichan, of course, as to all feminists, this apparent passivity is not inherent, but acquired, and is obliged, therefore, to disappear in the higher development of the race. By an appeal to history, indeed, she shows how often it has vanished in the past when it ceased to be one of the necessary conditions of woman's relation to man. "Woman," she repeats, "is what she is because she has lived as she has." It is foolish to talk of a revolt against nature as if, by taking thought, one could change the principle of one's being; and it is not without deep significance that woman's long endeavor to exist artificially, instead of naturally, should result in the violent reaction of the present. For this hunger for freedom that is driving women to-day into strange countries, as it drove the pioneers of old across oceans to the wilderness of new continents, is bound up with the imperative striving of life.

Ellen Glasgow

WOMAN'S WEAKNESS DUE TO EDUCATION

Girls Do Not Belong to the Weaker Sex Necessarily, Mrs. Gilman Asserts.

MEN DICTATE FASHIONS

A Desire to Meet Their Approval Governs Feminine Customs, Even Among the Hottentots.

Discussing the normal woman and the coming world in the last of her lectures on the "Larger Feminism" at the Hotel Astor yesterday, Mrs. Charlotte Perkins Gilman announced at the outset that her subject treated of "two things about which we know nothing—since the normal woman doesn't exist and the coming world is beyond our ken." About 200 women listened to Mrs. Gilman.

First of all, she demolished the theory that woman is necessarily the "weaker vessel." Girl children at birth, she said, were stronger than boy babies. In Martinique, where the development of women wasn't checked as it is here, there were women porters who carried trays of merchandise so heavy that it took two men to put them on the woman's head. Little Japanese women loaded coal and carried it aboard ships, she pointed out. In her address she said:

"Here the conventional belief is that only indoor work at home, not work in the fresh air and sunlight, is good for women. As a matter of fact, we now find that only that small class of parasitic women are really weaker vessels—women beautiful with small, soft white hands and dimpled knuckles. They are beautiful for the same reason as are the six-inch fingernails of the upper class Chinamen—they do no work. Smallness, weakness, delicacy, and the visible evidence that she can't do much—that is the ideal we have evolved of feminine beauty. And it is a purely masculine ideal from which we women have slavishly formed our own. Man, being stronger—in some respects, in the shoulders—has preferred to have in his mate opposite qualities, just as women are naturally attracted to a big, strong, pugnacious, dominant man."

But this "true woman" ideal of the man's creation, Mrs. Gilman said, was not in accord with the facts.

"Nevertheless, it has begotten our modern form of so-called chivalry," she asserted, "this open-the-door and pick-up-the-handkerchief idea of chivalry. And the woman likes it; she likes the compliment of being lifted up by the elbow and put aboard a car. Why, it wouldn't be a compliment to a one-legged hunchback! Man, the artist, has invented this conventional ideal of woman and impressed it laboriously on all his art and literature; and we have accepted it.

I know a woman who would not go to a gymnasium, because, forsooth, exercise would widen her hands and make them stronger."

Mrs. Gilman decried the adoption by woman of such arbitrary standards of beauty. Hottentot women, she said, wore a sort of natural bustle, and thought that was essentially beautiful and feminine, when it was merely Hottentot; and another tribe of women bound up their legs "until the calf stood out like a Dutch cheese"—thinking that the ideal of womanly beauty. Still others were stuffed by their masters like Strassburg geese to make them ideally beautiful—fat. And then, coming down to the womenfolk of civilized men:

"Owing to standards of this age, women have been modified both physically and psychically," she said, "and to such an enormous extent that it's very hard to tell what qualities are normal. They used to picture the ideal man's shape as wedgelike, with broad shoulders and a straight back, tapering toward the waist; and woman's shape as oval, narrow at the top and bottom, until Gibson created a new ideal of woman and women came up and achieved it. Now we have a kind of curled up, slinking, drooping, slouching ideal. Did you ever notice any such changes in the shapes of men?"

Mrs. Gilman said she was glad to notice so much difference of opinion in her class. Any way, she continued, women had grown so helpless under these arbitrary changes, both as to what their shapes and what the fashion-makers put upon them, simply because they had no positive ideal of their own as to what was beautiful for women.

"Take for example the matter of size," she said. "It isn't good to have a small body, either for the mother or her sons and daughters. This ideal of small women came from the fact that the small and weak woman was much easier to manage. In primitive times the swiftest men caught the most women, and the swiftest women escaped the most men. That bred a race from slow women."

One man, a big broad-shouldered red-faced male in the midst of the larger feminists, let out a hearty laugh as Mrs. Gilman described the fleet she-race away from matrimony. But Mrs. Gilman continued:

"It is not convenient to be too small. Things are built men's size in the world; if you are small, your feet don't touch the floor when you sit down in cars; the hooks in your closet hang too high, and if you happen to be in a crowd you can't see out. The normal woman physically should meet the race type with only such modifications to sex as are essential to a healthy, happy, vigorous, normal motherhood."

Mrs. Gilman said the time would come when, instead of wearing what they considered beautiful one year and hideous the next, women would adopt standards of beauty that would make the world a joy to live in—for all except the fashion-pirates. In that day, too, the fine points in women would be definitely known, whereas now, she said, people knew the fine points in beauty of dogs at dog shows, but not of women at horse shows. The normal woman would be "grandly, healthfully beautiful in body, vigorous and competent for motherhood, and for getting on and off street cars without male help."

Yet motherhood, she said, wasn't the sum and substance of woman's life. The normal woman was going to be pre-eminently human. Even the little girl children were going to reap advantage from that day of glory.

In her five-minute whirlwind tour of "The Coming World," Mrs. Gilman described its essentials as, first, a sufficient income for all to live a comfortable life, and, secondly, a beauty replacing present ugliness—clean, healthy cities and fertile lands instead of present-day smoke-pits and miasma. In that day, she concluded, the world would be made finer and better by men and women, standing shoulder to shoulder, and co-operating without effort or strain to make the world the kind of place all wanted it to be. It could be such a place to-day, she added, if the two houses got together.

The Nestlé Permanent Hair Wave

Before Waving

The inroads of this science into existing habits are increasingly noticeable. Were it not for the fact that so much harm has been done by unscrupulous operators we believe that not a woman who is willing to spend a dollar a week on her hair

Nestlé Waved

would be without a good permanent hair wave in preference to straight hair or the daily, nightly, or weekly use of hot instruments. Many women spend ten or more dollars a week on their clothes and nothing on their hair. This is out of proportion. These women should save a dollar a week on their clothes and apply it to their hair. Have a Nestlé Wave every five or six months and your friends will consider you well groomed. Winter has started with all its social functions. Thousands of women are bent on looking their best. Money is no object to them. They can afford a hairdresser twice a day if they like. Yet if you could ask a large majority of them they would say that in former times they indulged in such extravagance, but now their hair is "Nestlé Waved"--!

It takes about two hours to wave your hair. The wave is guaranteed to be exactly as if it was naturally waved. No frizz. No injury. No dry and brittle appearance, in fact no evidence at all that such hair had been artificially waved.

An illustrated booklet giving more particulars is supplied free of charge.

C. NESTLÉ CO.
657-9 Fifth Avenue, Corner 52d Street, New York
Telephone 6541 Plaza
London, 48 South Molton St, and 43 Dover St.

Pupils of either sex and with a good education are now accepted by Mr. Nestlé for instructions in Permanent Hair Waving

DESCRIBES MAN AS THE 'WHOLE THING'

Mrs. Charlotte Perkins Gilman, in the first of six discussion-lectures, "The Large Feminism," given at the Civic Club, 14 West Twelfth Street, yesterday, took for her subject the "Biological Base." It is woman and the female of other species who form the "biological base," Mrs. Gilman told the members of her class, but while woman is the race superior, man has put it all over her in the conduct of human life.

"When it comes to human life," said Mrs. Gilman, "man is the whole thing."

She told the women—there were no men in the class—that woman had been the producer for the family in the early days of the world. She not only reared the children, but she grew and prepared the food, and made the clothes while the men devoted themselves to hunting and fighting. But somewhere along the ages, and this is something that history does not tell, man got the whole running of the world into his own hands and he has been running it ever since.

"In the human world the men are the best of everything," said Mrs. Gilman. "They are the best cooks, the best milliners; they build the ships and the big bridges, and do all the important work. If there should come a big pestilence and all the women of the world should die, the men could get along very well indeed without them. They would miss their wives, sisters, and daughters very much at first, but they would still have everything necessary. They would have their big manufactories, their ships and their bridges, their big clubs and the cooks to prepare meals in them. They would have the big games; for the big games of the world are all for men, aren't they? And they never want the women around in those, anyway. Even the boy doesn't want the girls around when he is playing. The men could be perfectly happy and satisfied as long as the race existed, but as to the women it would be different.

"The women, if all the men should be killed off, would miss all the big things in the world which the men have been doing. They could not make the ships or the bridges, the street cars or the subways, and they do not even run the big stores. I don't mean to say they couldn't do it, but they haven't been doing it and are not yet prepared to."

The real purpose of life, Mrs. Gilman said, is the development of the race, and it is the women there who are making good there.

"They call the bringing of children into the world and nursing them the handicaps of women. They are really her glory. If she had not developed these powers we would still be reptiles. In the development of human power man has gone so far ahead that he has subjugated woman. Women are the only animals that are subjugated, and anything else is so foreign to us now that it is difficult for us to accept it.

"Woman does the great work of the world in producing the children. What happens to the male in other species? See the great spider in the web. It is always a female, and as her little would-be suitors, much smaller than she, come along she eats them up. Even the one she accepts as a spouse she finally devours. It is the young roosters and the male calves in the barnyard that are always killed

"There are certain characteristics of the male which are their predominant forces—there is the all-powerful desire for the female, and it must be said that man has been very true to type. Then there is his desire to fight—combativeness. One little boy will go up to another and say: 'I can lick you.' Girls may fight sometimes, but they do it for some cause—not because they like it and to get acquainted. Sheep are the meekest and stupidest of animals, but you can't go into a pasture with a ram or he will attack you; the bull is the same, and on the plains you are at liberty to shoot a loose stallion, for he will jump on you with his front feet and kill you. You hear a yowling out in your yard at night, and it is the everlasting tomcat, who is fighting his rivals."

CALLS ON NATION TO HONOR MOTHERS

Pray for Them on This, Their Day, Says President, and for Their Fighting Sons.

BAKER'S WORD FROM FRONT

"Our Boys Are Cheerful, Earnest, and Full of Fight," Secretary of War Declares.

DANIELS TO BRAVE MOTHERS

Their Courage Reflected In Their Sons—Messages from Prominent Women.

WASHINGTON, May 11.—A nation's unity tomorrow in reverence and in homage to motherhood was asked tonight by President Wilson in a Mothers' Day message to the American people. The President's message, issued in response to a House resolution, read:

I take the liberty of calling special attention to the fact that this is Mothers' Day, and I take advantage of the occasion to suggest that during this day our attention be directed particularly to the patriotic sacrifices which are being so freely and generously made by the mothers of our land in unselfishly offering their sons to bear arms, and, if need be, to die in defense of liberty and justice, and that we especially remember these mothers in our prayers, praying God for His divine blessing upon them and upon their sons whose whole-hearted service is now given to the country which we love.

Messages to American mothers also were issued by Secretary of War Baker, Secretary of the Navy Daniels, and Dr. Anna Howard Shaw, Chairman of the Woman's Committee of the Council of National Defense. Mr. Baker's message read:

To the Mothers of America:

I bring you a message from your boys in France. They are cheerful and earnest and full of fight—as proud of their country as their country is proud of them.

From you they yet draw inspiration, and to you they send a message filled with determination and with hope. They hope to make this war the last war that America will ever have to fight against a military despotism, and they want to fight till that hope has been achieved.

They ask you to be of good cheer, to be with them fondly in your thoughts, and to sustain your hearts in the day of battle as they will sustain theirs. NEWTON D. BAKER.

Following is the message from Secretary Daniels:

To the Mothers of Defenders of Democracy:

The courage of the mothers in the homes is reflected by the bravery of the men at the front. It is always true that the morale of a nation's soldiers and the ideals for which they fight are born in the spiritual heroism of a nation's mothers. Let the nation join in international prayer to all mothers of defenders of democracy to cheer and strengthen them, their sons, and the nation itself to fight to win the fight that must be won.

Our country stands before the world as a nation fighting for the ideals of nations, and the world knows that the mothers of America are sending men of ideals to the front. In that lies our strength. Faith and prayer are the two basic supports of national idealism. International prayer, for all mothers of democracy—there are thirteen millions of them—cannot but aid every soldier in camp or trench as well as strengthen every mother at home. JOSEPHUS DANIELS.

Here is the message from Dr. Shaw:

To the Mothers of the World:

The mothers of the world are one in sacrifice, hope, and pride in their sons and daughters who are serving their country while their sons are on the battleline. The mothers rejoice that they, too, may serve in the same great struggle for justice, and that with every rising and setting sun their prayers of gratitude ascend and their hearts rejoice that they are the mothers of men who hold that honor is more precious than life and that the crowning glories of a nation are justice and mercy. ANNA HOWARD SHAW.

The National Association of Mothers of Defenders of Democracy announced tonight that it had set aside tomorrow as a day of prayer.

"The result desired," said the announcement, "is to cheer, console, and strengthen the hearts of the mothers who have sons in the camp or trench, and to secure through mothers' letters to sons a higher spiritual soldier morale."

May 12, 1918

THE THIRD SEX

By WILLIAM W. GREGG.

SOME years ago an imaginative writer narrated the inhabitants of another planet, either Mars or the Moon, according to my recollection. In describing their activities the author's fancy had free rein, but I now recall only a single distinguishing feature, a scientific, all-pervading system of specialization for each individual, far beyond anything that even German Kultur has yet produced on our planet. For by that system an individual's position in life was not only fixed and predetermined for him by social sanctions with an exactness surpassing that of the caste systems of the East, but these sanctions were reinforced by and bound up with such an education, training, and especially breeding of the individual that he must at maturity perforce fall into the notch assigned to him and into that notch only. For instance, the wise men, the brainworkers, were depicted as being almost all brain, with enormous heads, but with limbs and muscles so atrophied as to be all but nonexistent. The individuals who did the muscular work of the community were correspondingly of extreme muscular development, but possessed of only rudimentary brains.

Such a division of society into brain and muscle workers has obvious advantages. If the workers were sufficiently tractable, as they probably always would be if they produced no thinkers of their own, the supremacy of the thinkers would be assured and we would thus have a system where the workers acquiesced, with a degree of cheerfulness unknown even in the Reichstag, in having their thinking done for them by a permanent governing caste. In all society of which we have any knowledge, however, there have always, since the dawn of history, been mutterings more or less loud and more or less frequent on the part of the working castes, thus proving that in some individuals of such castes the brain was to some degree active and that even in the masses it was more than a rudimentary organ. Thus, not only the troubles of autocracies but also the emergence of democratic forms of government are due to the fact that no hard and fast line has ever been maintained in human society between the thinkers and the workers, between brainworkers and muscleworkers.

This impassable division line so portrayed as a prominent feature of Martian society was accompanied by other descriptions suggesting that the author's concept of the individual Martian was of something resembling a superinsect rather than a human being; for it is a peculiar fact that neither in human society, nor in subhuman life on the earth, except among insects, is there a well-defined instance of what may be called absolute caste, that is, caste so based on structural, biological differences as absolutely to preclude a member of it from ever escaping into another caste.

INSECT SOCIAL LIFE.

About the time of the publication of the Martian romance referred to came Maeterlinck's "Life of the Bee," which opened to most of us a new vision of life. This small insect, seemingly an insignificant byproduct of the great evolutionary process, is now recognized as having developed among certain of its species a communal form of life which, if there be any validity in the old argument from design, necessarily indicates a high order of intelligence. Moreover, certain species of ants are equally remarkable in that they possess what apparently correspond in human society to cows and slaves—to herds and servants. In brief, ants are known to make a practice of caring for and keeping in their nests certain insects, of a totally different species, which exude a liquid used by the ants as food.

17

The slaves are obtained by raids on other ant nests, and the captured ants then work in the nests of their captors, the ants of one species being so dependent upon this slave labor as to be incapable of caring for their own eggs without the assistance of their captives. As is well known, colonies of the "warrior ants" make long marches drawn up in battle columns, attacking and destroying every living thing in their path and as difficult to divert from their course, except by absolute destruction, as any human army of shock troops under the most rigorous military discipline.

But in addition to the practices mentioned, the most prominent feature of the communal life of the so-called social insects, such as the bees and the ants, is the existence of a neuter or third sex, if the expression be allowable, made up of imperfect females, that is, an absolute caste of workers; for if any group in a society can be said to constitute an absolute caste it is these insect workers, sexless at birth by the will of the society into which they are born. Although the eggs laid by the queen will produce either males or females, the polity of the social insects is such that only a few perfect females are produced out of the thousands of female eggs laid, the remainder producing only imperfect females or workers. After the eggs are laid by the queen the workers so manage them as to produce at will either perfect or imperfect females, thus exhibiting a degree of sex knowledge and control unknown even in human society. The bee and ant workers from birth accordingly are designedly precluded from parenthood and thus form a class unique in the entire animal world.

All life as we know it is based upon sex, and really upon a two-sex system when once we get beyond the rudimentary forms. The duality of sex emerges in the beginnings of life, and from then on every individual of every species may be classed at birth, barring accidental malformation, as belonging to one of the two sexes. Of course man has succeeded in producing many sterile hybrids both of plants and animals, but the entire animal world, except where man has interfered, contains no examples of the absence at birth of potential parenthood, except the so-called workers of the social insects mentioned. Here only among all the myriad forms of life upon this planet is found what may be called a true third sex.

A prominent woman lecturer of the day, with strong feminist leanings, frequently refers to the extraordinary size and strength of the female spider as compared with her mate, presumably by way of arguing that in an up-to-date human society women would be equally superior in physical powers to men, whom they then would tolerate solely as biological necessities. Such arguments from nature as applied to human affairs obviously are exceedingly tenuous. To take the single matter of sex relations in the nonhuman world: almost every conceivable human sex arrangement can be found exemplified and apparently working with success in some part of nature's laboratory. Thus, to use the female spider, addicted to the habit of eating her mate, as an example of probable or possible human female supremacy in the future, is as illogical as it would be to argue male supremacy from the harem system of the bull seals of the Aleutian Islands. It may be noted, however, that only in the insect world is the female ever physically superior to the male. Among all other forms of life, especially among the higher forms, including mankind, physical superiority usually is found in the males.

So much for the validity of so-called arguments from nature as applied to human society. Nevertheless, while conceding their invalidity as arguments proper, it must be admitted that comparisons between human and subhuman life are often suggestive.

THE TWO-SEX VIEW.

Coming now to human society, we of course find no true third sex, biologically speaking, such as is found among the social insects. But is there any class in human society which, although not based on unalterable anatomical differences, is yet sufficiently removed as a class from normal parenthood to correspond even roughly to a true third sex? For as the entire human race is divisible into two true sexes only, and can be perpetuated only by individuals in sex relations, if any considerable class of adults remains out of the sex relation such persons in effect and from a social viewpoint constitute a third or neuter sex, even if their status is apparently determined merely by their own choice and so is subject to possible change during considerable periods in the life of each individual.

Savage and primitive life shows practically all mature individuals mated, often on a polygamous basis, because of the greater mortality of the males through hunting and fighting. In the next higher stage of society the unmarried are still almost negligible numerically, consisting almost entirely of religious devotees, sterilized slaves, and women of the most ancient profession; and similar conditions, except as to the second group mentioned, have in general persisted down to modern times.

But what of the present situation? As we look over our civilization we see, especially in our older long-settled communities, in spite of the influence of a powerful church, a few unmarried men, but considerable numbers of unmarried women, and also many married couples producing either no children or else fewer than the average of almost three children per couple necessary merely to maintain the race at its present numbers. As the principal aim of marriage, viewed sociologically, is to continue the race, any marriage which does not meet its proportionate share of this total race obligation must be considered subnormal, and the parties to it necessarily to some extent aligned, broadly speaking, with this so-called third sex, which thus for practical purposes may fairly be used to cover all, but on account of their numbers, more especially women, whether married or single, who do not measure up to the race standard mentioned. The facts of the present situation are beyond dispute, its causes may be open to question. The whole subject is too large for full discussion here, but attention may be called to one or two aspects of the situation.

In all discussions of the so-called woman question, whether by suffragists, feminists, or conservatives, it will be found that the arguments almost invariably assume or predicate women as composing a single class. They are idealized or praised or condemned as a single sex, that is, all arguments about them naturally fall into a two-sex point of view. The tacit assumption is that any woman, qui a woman, can speak for and represent any other woman better than she can be represented by any man who, of course, belongs to the "opposite sex," and so has, it is assumed, different interests. Is this a logical assumption? If all adult men and women were living in the normal sex relationship outlined, if there were practically as well as biologically only two sexes, then the assumption would be just, but is it even reasonably accurate under present conditions or under conditions as they are rapidly coming to be?

WAR AND WOMEN'S WORK.

The woman wage worker is peculiarly a modern product. Women have usually done their share, and often more than their share, of the world's work. They have long worked in the home and on the farm and outside of the home as voluntary nurses and helpers to neighbors and relatives; but as workers for wages outside of the home, whether in factories or in business or in the professions, they present a comparatively new problem. To some women this emergence from the home has been a godsend, by which they have enjoyed a field of activity for talents that otherwise never would have been used. But because some women have found a new sphere of usefulness outside of the home many have jumped to the conclusion that all women should likewise seek for new worlds to conquer outside the home. Some even go a step further and advocate the immediate demolishment of the home so as to force out into the open any timorous or reluctant souls now ignobly sheltered within its portals. Perhaps the home is an anachronism; certainly it seems to be undergoing changes at the present day. But before discarding it entirely as an institution it might be well to consider who they are who are clamoring most loudly for its destruction. Are they men or women who themselves have lived, or are living, or probably ever will live, up to the normal sex standard mentioned, or are they very largely, if not almost exclusively, of the so-called third sex referred to; and, if the latter, is their judgment likely to be as sound on this very human question as that of others equally intelligent who also have the valuable social experience of normal married life?

The political importance of any class agitation seems to increase almost geometrically with its numbers. Until very recently the women living apart from the normal sex relations mentioned have been but few, albeit numbering some of high intelligence and social value. As the male birth rate is slightly higher than the female, heretofore there have been, theoretically, enough men to provide husbands for all women. As women wage-earning opportunities multiply, women tend to become more exacting in their choice of a mate and more inclined to delay marriage, the practical result being not that some women least attractive to men do not marry, but also that many attractive and capable women do not marry, or else marry so late as to be disinclined or unable to have the normal quota of children.

Such was in general the situation at the beginning of the world war, but the war, and especially our entrance into it, have radically altered the situation. What was before merely a side question of compartively little importance socially has now become a social problem of the first magnitude. Before the war the wage-earning woman as a relatively permanent class outside of marriage was comparatively few in numbers and relatively almost negligible in the body politic. Even ultraconservatives recognized that the few women who did not marry should in justice have every chance in the business and professional world to show their worth as individuals, and, as a matter of fact, in most modern communities women for many years have had practically equal opportunities with men in every possible field of endeavor sought by them, excepting only that of politics. But the war has changed all this by creating such an excessive labor demand that hosts of our unmarried, and even of our married, women have been recruited into the ranks as wage earners, and the end is not yet in sight. If the war ends soon, and without heavy American losses, most of these women will ultimately drift back into their former homes, or will marry and set up homes of their own; but if the war continues for one or two or five years longer, with attendant losses of hundreds of thousands, or even millions of our best young men, the result will be more and more women wage earners, and ultimately a large and permanent (for another generation at least) class of women wage earners after the war, for the reason that the normal quota of potential husbands for this generation has been enormously diminished by the ravages of war. And then we may expect to see the full force of the feminist movement, strongly backed, as it will be, principally by the influence and the votes of the third sex, although of course supported more or less by other social elements.

THE ECONOMIC FACTOR.

The use of the term "queen bee" suggests that she is the ruler and authority of the hive, but such is not the case. The rulers of the hive are the workers, the third sex. They, not the queen, determine how many young queens shall be produced and when the drones shall be "balled" and stung to death or driven out of the hive. Is there any evidence so far that the human third sex, once it gains power in the business and political world, will act other than primarily for its own interests, or that it will be any more altruistic than either of the other two sexes? Moreover, if the third sex principle is bound to be more in evidence in the near future in human society than formerly, the question naturally arises as to whether or not the interests of the third sex naturally coincide with or are opposed to those of either of the other sexes.

As mentioned, at present the assumption of the leaders of the third sex is that they and they alone are entitled to speak for all women, that is, that the interests of both classes of women, the sexed and the nonsexed, are the same, but is this so? Are not the economic interests of the normal married woman really identical with those of her husband, and thereby essentially antagonistic to his actual or possible competitors? When the third sex, for instance, claim "equal pay for equal work," and get it, do they not thereby in effect, under normal conditions, depress the wages of the married woman's husband, that is, reduce the total fund out of which both she and her husband with their children are supported? For however much feminists, themselves almost invariably without practical experience of the job of rearing two or three children, may scorn the married woman who is not also an "economic factor," it is very likely that the great majority of married women who do rear the normal number of children see nothing unreasonable in sharing a husband's wage for some years at least. A friend of mine, a professor in a woman's college, often hears this equal-pay argument from his unmarried feminine colleagues on the Faculty. He has a wife and three children, and his colleagues for the most part no dependents at all. A strict application of the equal-pay rule would reduce his salary rather than raise the salaries of his female associates to his present salary, the institution being none too well off financially. His wife, although a college graduate and a successful teacher before marriage, is not now a wage earner, although in addition to her household duties with young children she finds time to be an efficient member, and the only woman member, of an unsalaried city board of education. Evidently her interests financially are those of her husband and therefore necessarily opposed to the competing financial interests of the unattached teachers mentioned, and the same, is true of most normal couples where the woman meets her social obligations as child bearer and rearer and as home maker.

When thus employed woman's activities in the home seem of sufficient importance to society to merit more serious consideration than feminists usually deign to give them. Possibly society in the future may perfect a system of State-reared offspring. (The insect queen does not see her own eggs, much less care for them. And it must be admitted that she is not strictly an economic factor of the hive or nest, as she never leaves it to gather food and does no work in the hive except to lay eggs.) But even if all children were from birth State-reared the mothers would still be unable to be economic factors for considerable periods. For although in receipt of State pensions or bounties or compensation during such periods, they would still be handicapped in competition with men in a business world which demands long and continuous service from those who would achieve success. In short, the theory that the normal married woman could be in any true sense an economic factor in the same degree as her husband seems physiologically impossible except in those few and exceptional occupations or professions where one may be absolute master of his or her time for considerable periods and yet win success.

In the vast majority, however, of gainful occupations, even mediocre success requires continuous and painstaking application for many years, and this is impossible to the woman who bears children. Of course even the normal married woman may at times be able to enter or re-enter the wage-earning class, especially as her children grow up, and this is often most desirable, but such activities must normally be in the nature of avocations rather than vocations.

The equal-pay-for-equal-work principle is also in effect opposed to the law's view of marriage, that is, to the formulated opinion of majorities in society up to the present day. When the law exacts support of wife and children by the husband, but makes no corresponding exaction of the wife, no matter how rich she may be or how needy her husband and children, it necessarily thereby presupposes that the wife and mother, by virtue of her being such, has legitimate financial claims upon her husband; in other words, that she has not the same economic opportunities in the world that he has. Is there anything either untrue or humiliating in this assumption? Is not the woman's special mission of renewing the race really too high to be measured by mere economic standards, by the standards of commercialism? It would be interesting to know just how many of the so-called advanced women, who so resent the law's attitude toward the married woman as a protected and a privileged class, are themselves married, and, if married, are rearing the normal number of children. How many of all the women who now affect economic independence from their husbands, the pursuit of "careers," the retaining of their former names after marriage, &c., do in fact both support themselves and also produce the normal number of children, for, if economic independence of married women strongly tends to sterility, of what value is such independence as an ideal for the average married woman?

PARTISAN DIVISIONS.

It accordingly seems evident that the normal woman's interests, although different, are far more closely allied with those of men in general than with those of the third sex, and yet the so-called leaders of the various woman's movements almost always belong to this third sex. If the average woman who is meeting her obligations to society as home maker and child rearer once understood how few interests in common she really has with the leaders of suffrage and feminism she would be far less likely to follow blindly in their lead. One cannot blame such third-sex leaders from pushing their cause by every fair means, but always it should be remembered that primarily it is their cause and not that of women as a class that they are pushing, however much, either ignorantly or intentionally, they may seek to becloud this fact.

Probably most men instinctively sense the distinction here sought to be made and consequently distrust these feminine leaders of "causes." This distrust is sometimes set down as mere sex antagonism. There is, however, but little antagonism between the two sexes in their normal relations, although there undoubtedly is antagonism between the average man and the aggressive leaders of the third sex, especially as its numbers increase and as it gains added political as well as economic power. In all Central and Eastern suffrage States at least women's votes will soon have considerable majorities, and there are already indications that if the third-sex leaders could control the rest of the woman votes their power would be used directly against the male minority. Even now many of the suffrage leaders are trying upon various pretexts to keep the women voters outside of the men's parties, that is, to induce women to vote as a separate class, thus giving to their leaders the power that goes with the ability to "deliver the goods." With woman's political power increased by every casualty list that comes from abroad the third sex could soon win in any sex contest if only it could control the votes of the normal women. As it probably never can do this or do much more than control the vote of the woman contingent of the third sex, the danger of a solid woman's vote is small. Normal married women will ultimately gravitate largely into men's parties, as will some of the third sex, although with reluctance, but probably enough of the third sex will hold together and apart from men's political organizations to be a troublesome factor in politics in the future.

For even a small minority of women voters, outside of the large parties and under strong leadership, can and undoubtedly will in the future exert an influence upon legislation out of all proportion to its numbers, as is proved by the recent accomplishments of the suffragists. By skillfully playing off each party against the other, by alternately coaxing and threatening each party in turn, they finally succeeded in forcing the Federal suffrage amendment through the House of Representatives. Under pressure of threats of a solid woman's vote to be exerted against any reluctant member, we have seen Congressmen voting for the amendment not merely in the absence of any mandate from their constituents so to do, but also in some instances in spite of the wishes of their constituents, as where their States or districts had previously voted against suffrage. We have, moreover, the express declarations of suffrage leaders that it is easier to convert (or coerce) legislators than voters, and that the efforts of the suffragists in the future are to be aimed solely at Legislatures and Congress. If a movement is based upon majorities legally expressed it must, whether for good or ill, win in a democracy, but if it succeeds largely by an adroit playing upon the hopes and fears of legislators, every principle of democratic government is violated. Many of the very able third-sex leaders of the suffrage movement by their acts past and present appear to proclaim their belief in the principle that the end justifies the means, and with their recent advent into the political arena we may expect to see further use made of this same principle in politics.

MAINTAINING THE SPECIES.

It seems almost futile now to discuss the desirability or undesirability of a third sex, as no other possibility exists for the present even under our imperfect monogamous system, for probably the alternative of polygamy will never be acceptable, to our country at least, however much it may be considered elsewhere as a possible solution of the difficulty. But although the present surplus of women will probably increase until the end of the war, and then will continue for at least a generation after that time, so far as the relative numbers of the sexes are concerned, there would be no reason why a return to ante-bellum conditions might not be possible.

It is thus pertinent to consider whether the existence of a large number of women out of normal married life is desirable in the body politic. First of all it must be admitted that this is largely a matter of degree. When few in numbers a third sex may be a most desirable element in society. When much more numerous it may constitute a most undesirable element. In the extreme lies the danger, no matter how much we may disagree as to just when the situation is extreme.

Assuming, then, that our portion at least of the race should be kept up to its present numbers merely, which most would admit, this means that if some couples fail of the necessary average of more than two children the deficit must be made up by other couples, and this is the way our civilization does maintain its numbers, and even grows slowly. As to the argument of the "bachelor girl" who perchance marries late in life, if at all: "Why should I undertake the distasteful burden of bearing and rearing children when more than enough will be born anyway?" This seems to be the viewpoint, especially of the college woman, for the statistics of a leading woman's college show that its graduates have hardly reproduced themselves, to say nothing of meeting the minimum average of two and a fraction children per adult. And the figures for Harvard are not very much better. When we consider the birth rate in certain slum areas it seems as if society were continually dying off at the top and being kept up to its present numbers only by the fecundity of its least promising portions. Surely if this has been the rule it is not necessary that it should always continue to be the rule; but even with the passing of the slum, which we may reasonably hope in large measure to accomplish in time, and with the prevention of offspring to the notoriously unfit, society will still be the loser in the long run unless the most advanced or educated or worthy portion of society at least reproduces itself. If it tends to become sterile and the reproduction of society at large is mostly done by the less efficient, even if not by the least efficient, the result will be like trying to improve or "grade up" a dairy herd by saving the poorer members for breeding. No cattle breeder would think of attempting merely by better environment to improve a herd, or even much to improve the individuals of a herd, unless he took care at the same time both to breed his best individuals and either not breed his mediocre and poorest at all or else not retain their offspring in the herd. It is therefore inevitable that, in spite of examples of some prominent men of unknown antecedents, although usually of good stock, that is, human "sports," biologically speaking, environment of itself can never take the place of first-class foundation stock. Consequently the duty of parenthood by the best and fittest must be recognized as bearing the sanction of nature's categorical imperative.

THIRD SEX AS TEACHERS.

If the foregoing views are valid is there not much in our present educational system that must be recognized as far from the ideal even though we may differ as to the remedy? Our youth in the grade schools, for instance, meet almost exclusively teachers of the third sex only, in public high schools largely the same sex, and only in men's colleges and private schools for boys are mature male teachers found exclusively. So far as boys are concerned, however, the situation is not difficult. Few men living in civilized communities do not marry, although they may not live up to the racial standards mentioned. With girls, on the other hand, the problem is seen in its acute form, for many girls do not marry, and in women's colleges unmarried women professors predominate. Undoubtedly the viewpoint of many college girls upon graduation is largely that of their women instructors rather than of the normal women upon whom society is based, but upon whom the graduate frequently looks with mingled pity and contempt as mere barnacles upon the ship of State to be removed at once by the "new womanhood," whatever that term may mean. How, then, to give these graduates, who represent so much that is highest and best in our social organism, a broader and a more normal view of life in general than that now possessed by many of their instructors and the leaders of the various women's movements—this is a problem that deserves the best attention of our educators and even of our statesmen.

And what is true of our educational systems seems also true of certain other activities in which third-sex women predominate. It may be doubted, for instance, whether professional women settlement and charity workers as a class are not open to criticism for frequently using their great influence to further extreme and unsound views upon social and national questions. Does not their enthusiasm in their work frequently lead them to exalt unduly alluring schemes of social betterment based upon environment, and thereby to overlook certain fundamental principles of eugenics based upon heredity? In short, rightly or wrongly, they are supposed to be especially sympathetic with Socialist and pacifist theories. Certainly they were well represented in the "peace-ship" fiasco, and although the financial backer of that famous expedition has long since announced his support of our Government, no such declarations have been made public by the most prominent women members of his party. We accordingly have the spectacle of almost no men of national reputation now standing opposed to the Government's war policy, while a number of women of wide repute, some of whom have admittedly done great service in their particular lines, are now in the nation's crisis justly suspected of supporting their country, if at all, in a very lukewarm fashion, and of really being more sympathetic with certain portions of our un-American population with which they have come in contact. And thus the paradox that woman, long considered primarily the conserving and conservative element of society, is now found in the front ranks of every new movement, no matter how radical or seemingly ill-advised. Has then the average woman recently undergone such a remarkable transformation of her former self as some would have us believe? Does not the true explanation lie rather in the increasing numbers of a third sex restlessly alert to every novelty, although the great body of women living under more normal conditions take but little interest therein?

The matter of loyalty to our country in its present great need raises the woman's vote. Suffice it to say that ever since the last election in New York State suffrage leaders have been protesting that their victory was not due to the help received from the Socialists. The facts remain, however, that every Socialist is and long has been an ardent suffragist, that the Socialist leaders have all along asserted that the suffrage victory was due to their efforts and that the Socialists in this country as a party stand convicted of disloyalty to our Government, at least in its war aims. A further significant fact is that suffrage was defeated in New York State outside of the City of New York, but was carried in the city—that huge cosmopolitan centre of socialism where the total number of those native born with both parents native is only about 7 per cent. of the entire 5,500,000 population. Furthermore, and entirely apart from their connection with socialism, many of the third sex suffrage leaders throughout the country, judging by their expressed utterances, have long known but an amorphous form of patriotism. The only "cause" that has interested them for years is that of suffrage. Such international and worldwide problems as those leading up to our entry into the great war have seemed to them quite insignificant as compared with the cause upon which they have lavished time and money, and which has exhibited such forms of feminine political hysteria as hunger strikes and the picketing of the White House.

This concentration, not to say narrowness, of view, while admittedly a strong

factor in sustaining their enthusiasm, argues but ill for either the intelligence or the sincerity of such leaders. For any considerable class of voters to be represented by such leaders either in or out of Congress or State Legislatures, especially during the present life and death struggle of democracies with autocracy, must be recognized as a very definite danger to our nation. The women politicians may in the future prove their worth, but thus far their methods have been no less objectionable than those of the men politicians, while their sense of the impending national crisis has been in general far less acute. Since war—and war against men-ruled autocracies of high military efficiency—is now recognized as essential to the preservation of our democracy, for the present at least the talents of the third sex leaders, no matter how intellectual such leaders may be, will apparently be best exercised in other fields than international politics or military programs.

Until human society shall become as mechanical as the life of the social insects, with their apparent total disregard of the individual and thought only for the colony, a system now exalted in certain quarters, however, and which admittedly makes for military efficiency in humans as well as in the marching hosts of warrior ants; until insect polity shall have supplanted human polity as now generally understood and recognized (outside of the Central Powers), so long, it seems, will the best racial results be achieved through the great majority of citizens living in normal sex relationships, while the departure of any considerable body either of men or of women from this norm will invariably result in a very definite, although ofttimes insidious, weakening of the social structure.

August 4, 1918

WOMEN MUST REMOVE HATS.

That's What Equal Suffrage Means, Says Chicago Justice.

CHICAGO, Nov. 19.—Equal suffrage for women means that they must not wear their hats when in his courtroom, Justice of the Peace E. P. Aring declared when he fined two women $5 each for contempt of court when they refused to remove their hats. The women paid.

When the Justice called the court to order he said:

"Everybody will please remove their hats."

Mrs. Oscar McCann and Mrs. Frederick Ritter failed to do so. The court hesitated a moment, but the two continued to wear their hats.

"Five dollars and costs for contempt of court," said the Justice. "If women can have equal suffrage with men they can also remove their hats in my courtroom."

November 20, 1920

MRS. O. H. P. BELMONT

Mrs. Oliver H. P. Belmont, social leader, suffragist and former head of the National Woman's party, had long been one of the most colorful feminine figures in American life. With great wealth at her command and possessed of a forceful personality, she made both social and political history over a period of nearly sixty years.

Mrs. Belmont, who before her first marriage to William Kissam Vanderbilt in 1874 was Miss Alva Smith, was born in Mobile, Ala., on Jan. 17, 1853. She was the daughter of a cotton planter, Murray Forbes Smith, and Phoebe Ann Smith and a granddaughter of General Robert Desha of Tennessee. Her education was received in private schools in France. Even in her girlhood, her likes and dislikes were pronounced.

Although her marriage to Mr. Vanderbilt brought her a notable place in New York society, she captured its leadership five years later. "Every one of importance" acknowledged her sway, save only the Astors. Mrs. Vanderbilt issued invitations to a function at her home at 477 Madison Avenue — now occupied by the Catholic Charities as headquarters—and the names of the Astors were not included on the list. Emissaries inquired why the admitted leaders of the "Four Hundred" had been left out, and it was explained by Mrs. Vanderbilt that she could not ask persons who had never called on her. The Astors called on the forceful young matron, and the belated invitations were hurriedly dispatched.

Three children were born of her first marriage—Consuelo, the former Duchess of Marlborough, now Mme. Jacques Balsan of Paris; William Kissam Vanderbilt Jr. and Harold Stirling Vanderbilt. Her life was one of great social splendor. During the '90s Mr. Vanderbilt made her a birthday gift of her celebrated Newport villa, Marble House, on Bellevue Avenue. Its magnificence was her challenge to Newport society after she had successfully stormed the innermost social citadels of New York.

Newport House a Sensation.

Her Newport house was the sensation of the day. It cost $2,000,000 to build and $7,000,000 more was spent on the furniture and decorations. It was constructed of white Italian marble and resembled the Trianon with pilasters and Corinthian capitals as large as those of the Temple of the Sun at Baalbek. She ordered a marble driveway and surrounded the house with high marble walls. Various kinds of marble were used lavishly for the interior.

The house was designed by Richard M. Hunt, then a well-known architect, and was completed in 1892. Great secrecy was maintained and detectives guarded the entrance. In due course it was opened with a ball of the utmost splendor. For the first three years it was the centre of a social clique as impregnable as the stone of which it was built. Extravagance and ostentation marked every social gathering. The jewels worn at balls were valued at millions of dollars.

Then, in 1895, when rumors of marital differences and divorce had already been heard, the 24-year-old Duke of Marlborough arrived and his engagement to Mrs. Vanderbilt's daughter, Consuelo, then 17 years old, resulted. There was a ball that

MRS. OLIVER H. P. BELMONT.

outshone all previous functions. A brilliant wedding ceremony followed a $2,000,000 settlement on Consuelo, who became the Duchess of Marlborough.

Later the same year Mrs. Vanderbilt's marriage was terminated by a divorce, and in 1896 she became the wife of Oliver H. P. Belmont. Mr. Belmont never cared to have his wife entertain at Marble House. After his death in 1908, however, it had a renaissance which coincided with the suffrage movement, in which Mrs. Belmont was keenly interested. It was last used by Mrs. Belmont in 1914.

Organizer of Equality Association.

The most notable function of which it was the scene, the Marlborough betrothal, turned out unhappily, for the subsequent marriage was followed with years of separation, civil divorce and final annulment by the Papal Tribunal of the Rota. It was alleged in the evidence brought out before the Rota that Mrs. Belmont had forced her daughter to marry the Duke, despite the fact that she was in love with a young New York man, and that the mother had threatened suicide if Consuelo did not comply with her wishes. After the Marlborough divorce, the former Duchess became the wife of Jacques Balsan and had since lived in Paris.

A reverberation of Mrs. Belmont's divorce and subsequent remarriage was heard in society as late as 1926 when Bishop Manning of the Episcopal Diocese of New York asked her to resign from the directorate of the Seaside Home for Children, which she had given the church. Mrs. Belmont complied, but berated the Bishop and continued her philanthropic work and her advocacy of woman's suffrage.

Mrs. Belmont showed active interest in architecture, hospitals, children's homes, the abolition of child labor and better sanitary conditions for working women, as well as for suffrage. She gave $100,000 to the Nassau Hospital at Mineola, L. I. She was founder and president of the Political Equality Association and organized the National Woman's party convention in 1915 and presented to the organization a $100,000 home in Washington.

After the suffrage fight was won and the constitutional amendment adopted, Mrs. Belmont turned her attention to obtaining legal and industrial equality for women.

In addition to her Paris home at 9 Rue Monsieur—she sold her country place at Sands Point to Mrs. William Randolph Hearst in 1928—Mrs. Belmont, in 1926, purchased the estate known as Domaine d'Augerville la Rivière, Loiret, France, not far from the magnificent property owned by her daughter, Mme. Balsan, near Dreux.

The château was given by Charles VII to Jacques Coeur, some time in the first half of the fifteenth century. Among the art gems it contains are fifteenth-century tapestries, several portraits by Clouet and a series of of Italian primitives. Mrs. Belmont was interested in the development of the village at the château gates and, in 1928, erected a statue of Jeanne d'Arc in the Catholic church there.

An Authority on Architecture.

The art for which Mrs. Belmont cared most during her lifetime was architecture. She was not only an authority on the subject, but she supervised the building of some of the most beautiful homes in America and she was the only woman ever to become a member of the American Institute of Architecture. Besides the famed Marble House at Newport she built Beacon Towers at Sands Point, L. I., a reproduction in her favorite French Gothic.

The first place Mrs. Belmont purchased in France was a villa at Eze-sur-Mer overlooking the Mediterranean at one of the most picturesque spots along the coast of the Alpes Maritimes. High on the hills behind rises the Winter residence of her daughter. Mrs. Belmont's residence, known as Villa Isoletta, hangs high above the sea and is celebrated for its gardens.

The pièce de résistance of all her many dwellings, however, is the Château d'Augerville-la-Rivière, in the Department of Loiret, about forty miles south of Paris. It was built in 1495 for the granddaughter of the great French financier, Jacques Coeur, who furnished funds for the wars fought by Jeanne d'Arc. The estate of 375 acres was a grant from Charles VII, who gave the land to Coeur early in the fifteenth century. The home was built as a part of the granddaughter's dowry.

The structure is of the best French Gothic period, and, in the opinion of experts, the simple exterior as it now stands is approximately as it was built. The white stone walls of the château are surrounded by a moat, formed by the little river Essonne, which flows around the four sides. It stands in the centre of a vast tract of lovely woodlands, meadow and hills, cut by winding paths and tiny tributaries of the Essonne.

It was here that Mrs. Belmont spent the last years of a life of aggressive energy. She occupied herself first with the restoration of the château's interior to the simple dignity of the original period, removing the embellishments and decorations which more ornate centuries had gathered. Heavy-beamed ceilings dominate the interior, richly decorated in designs of bright colors. There are paneled walls of wood in the drawing rooms and massive walls of stone in the spacious foyer and dining hall.

Many of the furnishings of the house include genuine museum pieces. Among these are old carved chests, tables and cabinets, wrought-iron chandeliers which once held candles, and, most notable of all, many rare specimens of fifteenth and sixteenth century Flemish tapestries. There are also several portraits by Clouet and a series of Italian primitives. In collecting these rare objects, and in making various changes in the park and surrounding buildings, Mrs. Belmont was always the active directing force.

The arrival of the American chatelaine at Augerville meant immediate employment for the small group of villagers who, as in many of the small hamlets in France, depend almost wholly upon the owner of the nearest château for work and commissions. Mrs. Belmont became a force in the life of the countryside for miles around her home, improving the social conditions of the peasantry, providing them with recreation, entertainment, and instruction. She was particularly solicitous for the welfare of the peasant children of Augerville and Boulancourt.

Her Interest in Suffrage.

Mrs. Belmont's interest in the woman's suffrage movement throughout the world continued all her life. She alone had moved the suffrage association from obscure headquarters in a small town in Ohio into an -imposing home in New York, and the ultimate success of the movement in the United States was in no small part her own.

Her first interest in the movement came early in the twentieth century, after a meeting at the home of the then Mrs. Clarence H. Mackay, at which Dr. Anna Howard Shaw spoke. In 1913 she was the only leader of the older and more conservative suffrage societies to join the younger and more radical group formed in Washington to work solely for the adoption of the Federal suffrage amendment. When the Conference on the Codification of International Law was held at The Hague in 1930, she joined the feminist leaders from many countries in urging that laws affecting nationality be made identical for each sex, and that women should not be compelled to forfeit their nationalities upon marriage to a foreigner.

January 26, 1933

Crusading Forerunner of Women's Lib

By NADINE BROZAN

It was 1916 and young Jeannette Rankin of Missoula, Mont., had no Betty Friedans to tell her that she was enslaved, no consciousness-raising groups to liberate her ego. She just knew there was something wrong with the way society was treating its women, so she did the boldest thing she could think of: She ran for the House of Representatives —and won in a victory that ended the male monopoly in Congress.

Today, at age 91, the former suffragette, lifelong pacifist and activist— has the satisfaction of seeing the rest of the world—at least the female portion of it—inch up to her and her ideas.

Women's liberation and its aura of innovation notwithstanding, she was there first, and there's almost nothing being demanded by the youth movement that she didn't suggest in the early 1900's.

Item: She voted in the House of Representatives against American entry into World War I.

Item: She cast the sole dissenting vote against entry into World War II.

Item: She introduced the first bill to grant women citizenship independent of their husbands.

Instruction for Mothers

Item: She authored the first bill for Government-sponsored instruction of hygiene in maternity and infancy ("The Government had always offered instruction in hygiene of pigs," she said during a visit here to appear on two television shows.)

And so it went during her two terms in Congress, 1916-18 and 1940-42, and in all the decades between and since.

Although "It's sometimes a terrible bore to hear the same things," she has confidence in her spiritual descendants.

"The women's movement is going to take forward steps beyond anything we can envision today. I'm quite thrilled with what they're doing," she said, sitting ramrod straight in her Algonquin Hotel room. But she does part company with the movement on one issue: money.

"I wish they wouldn't waste their energy talking about money. Money shouldn't be a factor in our lives," she said, using herself to illustrate it superfluousness.

"I live without money. My house [in Watkinsville, Ga.; she also has a "smallish" ranch in Montana and an apartment in Carmel Valley, Calif.] was built in 1890, and I bought it and 33 acres for $500 in 1935. I have one cold water tap in the bathroom and kitchen, a dirt floor in the living room, a two-burner

21

hot plate, an electric fry pan, a fireplace, an oil stove, two gas heaters, an electric heater and an electric blanket."

Asked if she had ever considered modernizing her home, which she runs with the help of one person, she replied with astonishment, "What for? I give all my money to the peace movement."

Peace is one of her two most consuming interests; the other is the vote, and it was lack of the vote that inspired her activism in 1910 when she became a suffragette.

In fact, her decision to run for Congress in 1916 was a show of gratitude to the suffragette movement. "I ran to repay the women of Montana who had worked for suffrage." (Her state had given women the right to vote in 1914, six years before that right became a Constitutional Amendment.)

Miss Rankin, who has never been married, was gerrymandered out of her district in 1918. In 1940 she ran for the House again; this time the motive was peace. "The women elected me because they remembered that I'd been against our entering World War I."

She made headlines when she cast the only vote of opposition to American combat in World War II. When her term was up, she retired. "I always said that if we did go to war, I wouldn't run again because my friends and family would have to bear the brunt of criticism against me," she explained.

But she has never stopped agitating for peace by herself and as a member of such organizations as the Women's International League for Peace and Freedom, Another Mother for Peace and the War Resisters League. And in 1968, she led the Jeannette Rankin Brigade of 5,000 women to Washington to protest the Vietnam war.

Vietnam troubles her as much today as World War I did in its time. "We've

The New York Times/Jack Manning
Jeannette Rankin

done all the damage we can possibly do in Vietnam," she said. "You can't settle disputes by shooting nice young men."

How would she get the boys out of Vietnam? "By planes and boats—the same way we got them there."

And how would she achieve permanent peace?

Her response was unorthodox, but then Miss Rankin was never known for conformity. "We must have absolutely unilateral disarmament," she declared. "If we disarmed, we would be the safest country in the world. After all, you have to have a worthy adversary to fight. Would Cassius Clay fight a Boy Scout?"

Her hopes lie with women. "We could have peace in one year if women were organized," she said. (Miss Rankin once went to New Zealand to organize women and when her efforts floundered, she became a dressmaker and appealed to customers while pinning up their hems.)

The key to peace rests, she believes, in electoral reform, to allow a greater diversity of candidates. "Now we have a choice between a white male Republican and a white male Democrat."

She has devised a complex system of direct preferential election. Anyone who wished to ("as long as they're under 90") could raise a small bond and run and voters would specify not only a first choice, but a second through fifth.

She is also actively campaigning in Georgia and Montana for abolition of the single-member Congressional District in favor of larger multimember districts, again allowing a broader spectrum of representation.

In a way, the sprightly crusader, whose only concession to age is a cane, has come full circle. She first proposed such changes in 1917, "but they weren't practical then because we had no computers."

If she had her life to relive, she'd do it all again, she mused. "But this time I'd be nastier."

Marriage and the Home

NEW PUBLICATIONS.

—*The American Woman's Home*. By CATHARINE E. BEECHER and HARRIET BEECHER STOWE. 12mo. (New-York: (J. B. Ford & Co.) Here we have another installment of popular instruction from that family of "brains" which old Dr. LYMAN BEECHER was father of. How it happens that the instincts of the BEECHERS lead them to irradiate the common things of every-day life with their peculiar genius, instead of busying themselves to find new topics and strange fields of intellectual labor, we do not know. Fortunately, that is the fact, and to this gifted family the world owes much, in the fact that they know how to discover new meanings in old and hackneyed themes; to make the homely things of life show their bright sides; to simplify many of the complicated problems of humanity by the rule of a strong common sense which ignores traditions and studies nature, direct; to sympathize with both the joys and woes of the world and to apply to both the living principles of Christian philosophy; and finally, to pour the light of a poetic and happy temperament over all. This is the work they delight in: and in the solid and handsome volume above mentioned, we find a peculiarly apt illustration of their style of doing things.

The book might be called a housekeeper's manual of first principles. The table of contents discloses a remarkable variety of topics, from the planning and building of a house, its proper ventilation, furnishing and decoration, (in modes which cleverly combine the charms of beauty with the conveniences of economy,) to the best ways of living, so as to secure comfort and true happiness. The care of health, in all its moods and tenses, even from infancy to old age; healthful food and drinks, with significant hints for good cooking; personal cleanliness and clothing; the regulation of the household as to rising, good manners, good temper, habits of order, giving in charity, the management of young children, home amusements and social duties; sewing, fires and lights; the care of rooms, yards, gardens, plants, flowers, fruit and domestic animals; earth and water closets; ventilation and warming, with popularly scientific discussions of the whys and wherefores of all the advice given, based on physiology and the laws of matter, good sense, good taste and the laws of mind. These are some of the large round of themes discussed, and, we must say, made admirably clear and intelligible.

Young married women, and for the matter of that, old married women, and men too, if they will but read, may find many helps to pleasant and comfortable living in this volume. It is handsomely printed, profusely illustrated, and compactly and handsomely bound.

August 2, 1869

RIGHTS OF INDIAN WOMEN

Cannot Practice Medicine or Law, but May Rule Households.

MANY HENPECKED "BRAVES"

The Woman Holds All Property and Has Exclusive Control of the Children—Husband's Standing.

"The rights and privileges of an Indian woman," said a man who has lived much in Arizona and New Mexico, "compare very favorably with those of her more civilized sisters, notwithstanding the general impression to the contrary. She cannot practice medicine, nor does she dabble in the law; but she is absolute mistress of her household, her property rights are broader and better defined than those of a white woman, she owns her good man, body and soul; her children are under her own exclusive control, and she dominates in all those activities which are commonly termed woman's sphere. I refer particularly to the women of the Pueblo tribes, of the Southwest, but the same statements, slightly modified, could be made of the other tribes."

Continuing, the same man pointed out some of the advantages the Indian woman enjoyed.

Practically all property, both real and personal, belongs to the women, and they alone can dispose of it. The crops in the fields are the special charge of the man of the house, but only so long as they are in the ground. When the harvest is gathered and brought in it becomes the woman's property, and the man cannot dispose of it, even in the way of a social entertainment or feast, without first securing the wife's consent. No case has ever been known where a man has attempted to override these arrangements and assume control, for the result would be expulsion from the family, and probably also from the tribe. When a man marries he goes to the house of his wife's people, and his standing there is so peculiar and so insecure, as it were, that he dares not attempt to break through the rules which have governed him and his ancestors for many generations.

A HUSBAND IS ONLY A GUEST.

In fact, the standing of a man in his wife's household is but little better than that of an honored guest. The Pueblos, like all the other Indian tribes, are organized on the clan system; that is, the descendants, real or supposed, of a common ancestor constitute a family group, named after some animal or natural object, like the Rattlesnake gens, the Corn people, and so on. But descent is reckoned only in the female line, and the children, therefore, always belong to the mother's gens. By an ancient rule, still observed, marriage within the gens is not permitted. Thus it comes about that the man is, as it were, "in the house of his enemies," for in any difference of opinion the whole family is against him.

Each gens, or huge artificial family, lives by itself in the village, all its houses being connected with each other, but not with those of any other gens. The houses of the Pueblos are arranged in long rows, or in beehive-like clusters, the rooms being placed one above the other, so as to form terraces like a great stairway. When a family increases new rooms are built, but they always adjoin and are connected with those already standing. There is no way, therefore, in which a man can escape the dominating influences of his wife's people. The gens sometimes numbers 500 members or more, all animated by the same motives and bound to stand by each other. No matter how aggressive the man may be, he is necessarily of a different family, and the immense majority against him makes his case hopeless. Under these conditions family jars are extremely rare, for only in the most important cases will a man's gens take up his defense.

MAY BE SENT HOME TO HIS FATHER.

The woman has still another expedient, seldom used, but always held in reserve. If her husband does not behave himself he can be sent home to his father; in other words, he may be expelled from his wife's gens, into which he is adopted when he marries, and consequently has to leave the home of the gens. In that case he loses not only his wife, but all right to his children, since the latter are reckoned the children of the gens, and becomes practically, if not actually, an outcast. The Indian is very loath to give up the teachings and beliefs of a lifetime to adopt those of other men, and the average "brave" recognizes that his wife is the "boss" and conforms himself to the conditions which confront him, leaving his theories for discussion in the quiet of a "stag" gathering.

As a matter of fact, the average Indian "brave" is a very much henpecked man, and when at home hardly dares call his soul his own. Any one who watches the proceedings in any of the numerous trading posts scattered over the Indian reservations will quickly reach the conclusion that the men who are buying have explicit orders as to what they are to get. Not infrequently there is a small margin, which the man is allowed to spend for himself, if he has been good, and he may purchase some small ornament, like a looking glass, or some brass tacks to decorate his saddle. Often, however, the woman herself comes to the store to take part in the barter, and there is never the slightest doubt as to the part she takes.

WHAT WOMEN MUST NOT DO.

Old, gray-haired warriors, who have killed not one man, but five or six, and who are universally looked up to and respected in the tribe, whose word in council is accepted as the unwritten law, are as much under this domination as the youngest married man in the tribe. That domination, however, is confined to what may be termed its legitimate sphere. In matters of State, in the preservation and handing down of the myths and traditions of the tribe, which, to the Indian's mind, are its history; in the dances and other religious ceremonies, the women have no part, save in those especially set apart for them.

That this, "the way of our fathers," should always continue is provided for in a peculiar way. The chief medicine men, priests, and other high functionaries of the tribe educate their successors, for without a written language the ritual and the traditions must be taught by word of mouth. The successor of a priest, however, is never his son, but always his sister's son. The sacerdotal line of descent is from uncle to nephew. In this way the influence of the wife is eliminated.

In many of the religious ceremonies the women are allowed to participate, but only as spectators. In others they are not allowed to be present; the penalty for breaking the rule is death, swift and sudden. The women have their own dances and ceremonies, however, with their own priesthood and other functionaries. These priestesses have also much influence in the social life of the tribe. No girl, for example, would marry without the approval of the chief priestess of the gens.

ONE WIFE ENOUGH FOR THE PUEBLO.

Some of the tribes practice polygamy, with marriage by purchase; others have more or less distinct survivals of the very old form of marriage by capture, in which the man must abduct his wife, but among the Pueblos the form is strictly monogamous, and the Pueblo maiden must be wooed and won in much the regulation way. When a young man has reached the point where he believes that life without some particular girl would be but a dreary waste, he makes a formal proposition. But the way is made so smooth that even the most timid man has no difficulty in making his intentions known. All that it is necessary for him to do is to prepare a little "bundle of gifts," consisting, perhaps, of a piece of buckskin and an ornament or two. This he sends to the home of the girl. If she will have none of him it is returned, but if it is retained he becomes by that act an accepted suitor.

Thereafter the young couple can be seen almost every afternoon out on the terraces in the bright sunshine, the young man squatting on his haunches and the girl brushing his hair with a native brush formed of a bundle of straw, an act perhaps symbolical of their future relations. At the appointed time the man takes up his abode in the home of the girl, and devotes himself to the cultivation of amicable relations with his mother-in-law, if he be wise. When the children come other rooms are built for the new family, but only the women do the building, for the houses belong to them. One or two men are usually kept on hand, however, to hew the timbers, haul water to mix the mud mortar, lift heavy beams in place, and generally do what they are told to do.

THE MEN DO THE FIELD WORK.

By the addition of more rooms those first built become in time dark, inaccessible, and little better than cellars, but they are hardly less useful, for in them is stored the supply of food for the Winter. The Pueblos are a thrifty people, and not infrequently have stored away the harvest not of one year only, but of two or three. For many years prior to the American conquest of the country, in 1846, they were the natural prey of the wild, improvident tribes which surrounded them, and these conditions perhaps had something to do with bringing about the present practice that men only work in the fields. At the proper time in the Spring, which is determined by the priests from observations of the sun and stars, announcement is made that the time for planting has arrived, and on an appointed day the men go to the fields, sometimes a long distance from the village, and plant their corn. Thereafter they work the fields at regular intervals, returning, if possible, each evening to their families, where the good wife has prepared food during the day, besides attending to her other household duties and the care of the children.

When the corn begins to ripen the whole family adjourns to the fields, usually for a stay of several weeks, and assists in the care of the crops, which at this stage require much attention, for as there are usually no fences, or only crude ones, many robbers of all kinds must be guarded against. The birds are among the worst foes of the Indian farmer, and the children are delegated to keep down their depredations. Until quite recently, however, some of the wilder tribes, like the Navajos, made a practice of raiding through the fields at night, gathering what they wanted for their own use and destroying much more, and not always stopping at the murder of a lone Pueblo worker to round out the night's pleasure. Frequently several families combine for protection and mutual aid, and the harvest field becomes, as it were, an annex of the village.

THE WINTER SEASON OF REST.

With the harvest gathered and safely stored in the house, the season of hard work for the man ends, and the woman's duties, as the head of the household, become more arduous. She must grind the corn and make it into thin paper-like sheets of bread, cook all the food necessary, weave certain kinds of blankets, keep the house smoothly plastered and in good repair, renew the whitewash when necessary, and attend to the innumerable details inseparable from the care of a home. In addition, she must bring all the water used in the family from one of the near-by wells, and she is responsible for the proper care of the flocks of sheep and herds of goats, which form the family's principal wealth. This work, however, is usually delegated to the children.

The principle of the female ownership of property is so rigidly adhered to that the traveler in that country is sometimes embarrassed by it, although he seldom knows the cause of his trouble. The only fresh meat to be had in that region, away from the settlements, is mutton. The flocks of sheep range from a few dozen up to hundreds, and in a few cases to thousands, but to the hungry traveler, who sees more sheep than he can count, it may be a case of mutton, mutton everywhere, and not a bite to eat, for unless he can find a flock in charge of the woman of the house, who owns it, he can no more buy a sheep than he can purchase a slice of the moon.

July 23, 1900

MODERN VIEW OF MARRIAGE

Dr. Adler Discusses It Before the Ethical Culture Society.

Says the Tendency to the Fashion of Women Asserting Their Equality with Men Cannot Last.

"The New Attitude Toward Marriage" was the subject of a lecture by Dr. Felix Adler before the Society for Ethical Culture in Carnegie Music Hall yesterday morning.

He began by characterizing as nonsense the idea that woman is a slave, and the corresponding assumption that it is necessary to emancipate her.

"Some of those who talk of 'woman's rights,'" said he, "assume that in early times women were simply the slaves of men, and that they have gradually and steadily been rising to a higher position, with the growth of civilization. In a particular age, indeed, woman is an object of reverence, in another she is the plaything of man, in another the burden-bearer, and in still another, as in the days of chivalry, the object of an almost mystical devotion.

"And yet, whatever theory of marriage was dominant in particular ages, there have been noble marriages right along. In Euripides, and even in the far-off times depicted in Homer, and in the Hebrew records, we find examples. In all these will be found the upward look toward the wife, an appreciation of the delicacy of her imagination, of her ability to console while seeming to seek counsel. Yet a bad theory does work harm and tends to discourage our better impulses. I shall now consider three theories of marriage.

"The first of these theories is the one that was dominant in the age preceding our own, which emphasized the difference between the sexes as fundamental. According to that theory, sex is not a mere physical accident, but it is carried out through the whole being. Hence comes the idea of the mental inferiority of women. No one has ever questioned her moral quality—her ability to bear pain, her stanch conservatism as regards morality, her more delicate religious perceptions. But it was supposed that the power of sustained thinking was denied her. Man was the head of woman. It was he who in case of conflicting opinions was to have the casting vote.

"Opposed to that theory is the one which is based on the contention for the essential equality of the sexes. Its advocates regard sex as accidental and incidental, and refuse to recognize any ground of fundamental difference. They even try to do away with it as far as possible, and insist upon equality and similarity. Women try to do the same things, in the same way, as men. Women have entered into almost every profession. In some they have made good their claims to a place; in others they have not got that far. They have founded clubs, they do as men do, they go about alone at hours when formerly only men were supposed to be out.

"Now, in all this there is much of good, and whether we like it or not, it was inevitable that it should come about. But there are serious drawbacks as well. Is it well, for instance, to have all the work of the world simply duplicated? Would it not be better that in art, in literature, in all the activities of life, woman should import a new note, and that difference, not similarity, should be emphasized?

"This idea of freedom and equality is fraught with danger. Already it has been proclaimed in one quarter that a married woman should not depend upon her husband, but should have her own separate means of livelihood, so as to preserve her independence. And in a way that is logical—but what sort of a home would it produce when taken logically? Marriage means accepting restrictions from which we cannot withdraw.

"The third general theory which I shall consider returns to the emphasis on the fundamental difference between the sexes, but without the assertion of the inferiority of woman. Indeed, what sense is there in making such an assertion, since it can never be demonstrated? The tendency to the present fashion of women asserting their equality was perfectly natural as a reaction, but it cannot last. The great change that is coming about is to inspire and inform woman's life with more mentality, to take away the merely impulsive and empirical character of her acting.

"I imagine that women will live in the future very much as in the past. The most gifted will go into the professions, and a considerable number will have to be money-getters. But, unless the race is to perish, the great majority will be homekeepers. But they will be on a higher grade than heretofore. There is such a thing as domestic science, and she is not a modern woman who does not put science into her vocation. And what can be more intensely interesting than the study of child nature? The ignorant mother caresses her child, but sees nothing. The modern mother sees things, and will be more and more able to guide and shape her child's development.

"The home-keeper, however, must take part in the life of the world, not with any idea of merely getting away from home, from her tasks—that makes the gadabout woman of whom we have enough examples to-day. But she will get out into society, into the life of the world, in order that she may improve and ventilate her home. The wise woman is still the inspiration, the object of reverence, and the counselor of her children when they are grown men and women. To this end all sources of knowledge are needed by her to-day."

January 13, 1902

PORTIAS FROWN UPON WIFE'S-LIABILITY BILL

Store Judgments Against Married Women Wrong, They Decide.

ETHICS A LARGE FACTOR

Measure Might Stop the Cry-Baby Act When Husband Sees Big Bills, Club President Suggests.

The feminine legal element of New York, as represented by the Portia Club, is to protest against the bill to hold married women responsible for the necessities of life purchased by them for themselves and their families. The subject of that bill as presented by Mr. Wood to the State Legislature on Tuesday was the first business taken up by the Portias at their regular meeting at the Murray Hill Hotel yesterday afternoon.

"As long as woman is not allowed the full benefits of the law," said Mrs. R. F. Bent, Chairman of the Legislative Committee, "she should not be liable for any judgments against her husband, and we should work against this bill."

"In this State, as in others, where the present law is based upon the old common law," said Miss Emily Bullowa, the President, "women are a privileged class. That was right when the old law was in effect, for the husband owned everything. Now a married woman can hold her own property, and conditions are changed. The result can be seen in that famous case of the tradesman who sued a husband for his rich wife's large bills for clothes, and then found he had no money and sued the wife, but could not make her pay."

"I move that we protest against this bill," said Mrs. Bent. The motion was seconded.

"We want to be as sensible as men," said Mrs. Josephine Reuter," and we must bear our own responsibilities. Women often buy more than their husbands can afford and many business troubles are caused by them. If a woman can't afford a thing she shouldn't buy it, and as long as she controls her own property, she should pay her bills."

"A husband is entitled to the services of his wife and all her time, so that she is not able to earn her own living," said Mrs. W. H. Wood, "and I don't see why he shouldn't pay her bills. If a bill like this is passed some husbands would take advantage of it."

"If the trades people could collect from the married woman as from the single woman," said the President, "it would keep many of the former from doing the 'baby act,' the married woman act, in escaping from their bills. If the law allows a woman to control her property why shouldn't she be responsible if she buys things her husband can't afford?

"I think women should appreciate what has been done for them. In many ways they have more control of their property than men."

"Women act as purveyors of the home and agents of the husbands," said Mrs. Bent. "They do not buy everything that is eaten in the house or the clothes for the children for their own pleasure, and why should they be obliged to pay for them?"

"We ought to think of the poor tradespeople," interjected Mrs. Reuter.

"Of course, I am for the rights of women first, last, and all the time," said Mrs. Lillie Devereux Blake, "and the bill would be just if other things were different. See what the wealthy women in New York do now. Their word is as good as their bond and their names as good as their husbands. They open large accounts, pay their own bills, and are to be relied upon."

"Oh, no, they are not," cried a woman at one end of the room.

"As a matter of fact," said Mrs. Bent. "I don't believe a woman with a penniless husband could open a large account in any of the shops. The first step is to look a man up in Bradstreet's."

It was necessary to take a rising vote to decide the question. The Portias decided to protest against the Married Woman's Responsibility bill.

February 10, 1905

MISS ANTHONY FOR DIVORCE

WASHINGTON, April 14.—Over the bitter protest of Miss Susan B. Anthony, the National Council of Women to-day adopted a resolution pledging the organization to co-operate with Church and State to ascertain what are the chief causes which induce or lead up to divorce. Divorce, the resolution recites, is known to cause most disastrous results in the family and State.

"I do not consider divorce an evil by any means," asserted Miss Anthony, who was on her feet before the reading of the resolution had been concluded. "It is just as much a refuge for women married to brutal men as Canada was once a refuge from brutal masters. I will never vote for a resolution that will cut women off from refuge from designing and brutal men."

April 15, 1905

SOLVING MARITAL PROBLEMS

AT the further end of the long table in the Magistrates Council Chamber in the West Side Court the other day sat a group of some twenty or more well-dressed women, a few of them armed with important-looking documents, others with the ordinary packages and reticules that usually adorn the sex when on an outing, and all of them conversing in subdued whispers and casting expectant glances toward the head of the table, where sat Judge Wahle, President of the Board of City Magistrates and at that time presiding Judge in the West Side Court. As Judge Wahle had lately expressed his amazement at the number of women who came to him seeking summonses for non-supporting husbands, the gathering in his council chamber seemed possibly significant of matrimonial woes awaiting his consideration.

✦ ✦ ✦

"An average of ten to fifteen abandonment cases a day in this court has been the record," said Judge Wahle, looking up from his writing toward the feminine contingent occupying the opposite end of the room. "but I don't believe these ladies are here to see me on that kind of mission."

Then the Judge got up to investigate for himself, and was presently the centre of a group of fair petitioners, whose demands, whatever they were, seemed to meet ample satisfaction in the judicial smiles and bows that greeted them.

"No, their husbands are all right," laughed the Judge as he resumed his seat at the head of the table. "Abandoned wives rarely come in a body like that. These ladies are a delegation from the Prison Relief Association, and they are here to address the Magistrates' meeting in regard to the care of female prisoners. One way or another, women are very much in evidence always in our police courts."

"But ladies of such evident culture and refinement as these are seldom here to prosecute cases of abandonment, Judge?"

"Ah, that depends—that depends," answered the Judge slowly. "To a student of sociology there can be nothing more full of surprises than the ever-changing dramatis personae of a New York police court. No class or type is exclusively represented here; neither is there any crime that does not find its exponent sooner or later among those at the top as well as among those at the bottom of the social scale. This is especially true in cases of wife abandonment. From a study of these cases as they present themselves in the police courts this fact stands out with remarkable prominence: the class of people characterized by the lowest order of intelligence, without education or refinement, and the class where intelligence, education, refinement, are carried up to their highest development, are the two classes that give to the police courts the bulk of the cases of wife abandonment. What we might call the great middle class, the large average, standing between the highest and the lowest in the social scale, contributes a remarkably small proportion of such cases.

✦ ✦ ✦

"It was only last week that a lady of about forty-five came before me as complainant in an abandonment case that was characterized by some notable features. This lady was the daughter of a well-known college President. About twenty-five years ago she married the son of a prominent physician in this city. For fifteen years the pair lived happily together. Two sons were born to them, the elder of whom was sent to college to finish his education. In every way the little family gave evidence of a happy prosperity and the best kind of culture. But ten years ago another woman appeared on the scene—and everything was changed. The man was fascinated by the new-comer, fancied any number of shortcomings in the wife with whom he had lived for so many years, and finally left her altogether, choosing to live instead with the woman whose charms had caused the estrangement between them.

✦ ✦ ✦

"Ordinarily in a case of this kind divorce is resorted to. But in this instance the wife, poor little woman, either belonged to a religious denomination discountenancing divorce or else she was too proud to complain of the perfidy of the man who had abandoned her. At any rate, she said nothing, devoting herself instead to earning a livelihood for herself and her two sons. This she did by going out as a companion, then a governess—her age and her upbringing leaving few avenues for self-support open to her. Then her health broke down completely. Her son, a lad of nineteen, left college to do what he could to keep the family above water, but without success. It was at this crisis that the poor woman was forced to appeal to the courts for help.

"What did I do in the case? The law would have sanctioned sending the man to the Island for six months—and doubtless such a course would have been beneficial to him. But the wife would have fared ill with such a verdict. In cases of this kind more than in any other everything is left to the discretion of the Judge. So I put the man under bonds to pay his wife $15 a week for her support. He has a good income and will pay it—and probably he will get over his infatuation for the other woman.

"That is a typical case of abandonment among the educated classes. In the less intelligent classes these cases often assume a more brutal aspect—outwardly, at least. Only yesterday an aggravated instance of this character was brought before me. The wife was a thoroughly reputable woman, and a hard worker too. But her husband was utterly worthless and dissolute. I doubt if he had ever done much to contribute to her or his own support. At any rate, for some time past he had left it to his wife to earn their joint livelihood. The woman was devoted to him—is now, for that matter—and slaved away that he might have the wherewithal to enjoy himself. He was generally away from home, putting in an appearance only when the need for money forced him. Finally he became infatuated with another woman. The latter had no means of support, so the brute brought her to his wife, and the three lived together for a while on the wife's earnings.

✦ ✦ ✦

"Then came the climax that brought them all to the police court. The second woman became jealous. There was an ugly quarrel, culminating in an assault on the wife by the man and the woman. Obviously there was nothing to be done in a case like this except to set in motion the full rigor of the law. So I sent the man and the woman he had forced upon his home to the island. Such a solution, at least, meets the ends of justice and frees the wife for a time from the monster who has tormented and imposed on her. But the strange part of it is that she still cares for him, and when he has served out his sentence will undoubtedly drudge for him again. If in the meantime his confinement has had a reforming influence upon him, there may be some hope that a future catastrophe may be averted. But that is not probable.

"Sometimes the improbable does happen, though, in these cases. A short time ago a woman came to me and complained that her husband had abandoned her and her two children. She was unable to earn a livelihood, while he had a sufficient income for all of them. The man declared that it was impossible to live with the woman. True or not, I placed him under bonds to pay his wife $5 a week. A short time after she appeared before me again, declaring this time that their marital differences were made up; they were living amicably together, and asking for a removal of the restraint put upon her husband. It is a pleasure to grant requests like that.

"The law, of course, cannot cure marital woes, cannot patch up a broken home. But often it can step in and help to bring about a condition of things that does not bear quite so hard on the abandoned wife. Every Judge, probably, has his own set of rules to guide him in disposing of these cases. It never pays to be too severe always. Thus where a man is accused of abandonment for the first time, I generally give him a reprimand, advise him as much as possible, insist on his paying a fair part of his in-

come toward his wife's support, and let him go. If the case is one of willful neglect and the man is guilty besides of annoying his wife, or if he abandons her to go on prolonged sprees, a lenient decision will obviously do no good. So I give such cases the full benefit of a stay on the Island. That seldom solves the problem, as I have frequently had wives tell me that their hubands have been sent to the Island three or four times without any result in their favor. But it does work sometimes and it is the law.

✦ ✦ ✦

"The vast majority of wife abandonment cases are apparently due to the simple fact that the husbands have never accustomed themselves to handing over a stipulated portion of their wages to their wives. They commence by keeping it all themselves, doling it out in an irregular way as the wife asks for it. Then they get into the habit of spending more and more on themselves, until they finally absent themselves from their homes altogether, refusing to give anything for the support of their families. Sometimes, however, the woman is to blame. On investigation, a wife who has complained of abandonment by her husband is occasionally found to be the culprit herself, absenting herself from home, leading a life of dissipation, in which she insists that her husband should support her. But that is rare. What is far more common is to

find that the long-suffering wife has been supporting her worthless husband, only complaining of him when driven to it by absolute want or willful abuse on his part. This is found to be true in 80 per cent. of all the abandonment cases. Where a man is honestly out of work and thus unable to support his family, a wife has never been known to complain.

"I have stated that from ten to fifteen cases of abandonment daily came before me while I was presiding in the West Side Court. This court sits seventeen days in the month. Hence, according to my figures, there is an average of from 170 to 250 cases of this kind on trial here every month. So far as I can learn the same average is maintained in the other police courts of the city. There are fourteen police courts altogether, so that putting it roughly on the basis of this calculation, there are from 2,500 to 3,500 cases of wife abandonment on trial in the City of New York every month—a decided increase over the showing in this respect of former years, and giving a rather discouraging picture of marriage in the metropolis to the sociologist in search of facts."

✦ ✦ ✦

Judge Wahle recently moved to the Essex Market Court, where he will have a new set of experiences with the ups and downs of married life to compare with what he found on the west side.

August 20, 1905

Close-Range Studies
of
Darkest New York
What a Year and a Half's Investigation of the Family Life of a Score of Typical Middle West Side Tenement Dwellers
Revealed to Miss Elsa G. Herzfeld.

THAT darkest New York is still pretty dark is the opinion of Miss Elsa G. Herzfeld, who has spent a year and a half in investigating the family life of a selected number of tenement dwellers in one of the submerged districts of the city. Miss Herzfeld is a young woman, a graduate of Barnard College in the Class of 1903, who became interested in sociological studies during her undergraduate days and followed up the work after her graduation. The care and faithfulness to detail with which she has prosecuted the work which leads her to such pessimistic conclusions appear in every page of the unpretentious, paper-covered volume called "Family Monographs," in which she has recorded the results of her work.

What increases the sinister aspect of the truth learned by Miss Herzfeld is the fact that the subjects of her study are not by any means the most unenlightened of their class. Miss Herzfeld herself

regards them as quite typical of the tenement house average. These people are not reached by the activities of our schools and churches in any vital way, and, in this investigator's opinion, these institutions are losing ground all the time, rather than gaining it.

One turns from the pages of Miss Herzfeld's little volume with a feeling of discouraged amazement at the knowledge that there exist to-day within half a mile of Times Square, in the metropolis of this country, thousands of human beings still in a mental darkness and narrowness that was scarcely exceeded in the Middle Ages. It is a humiliating conviction that is forced upon us, namely, that the agencies upon which we have depended to reach these people and which we fondly hoped were shedding a light that would in time come to raise the whole body politic to the level of good citizenship are not only failing to do what we hoped, but, as a matter of fact, are less efficient to-day than they were ten years ago.

Through the narrow streets of the middle west side, in which Miss Herzfeld prosecuted her investigations, there stalk day and night the grim and threatening figures of Superstition, Ignorance, Suspicion, and Disease. The chains of these Potentates of Darkness are still heavy upon the limbs of the dwellers in these districts, nor have all the efforts of our best benevolence been able to loosen them or to lessen their weight.

All the twenty-four families studied so closely by Miss Herzfeld live in the district that lies between Fifty-third Street on the north and Fortieth Street on the south and between Ninth Avenue and the North River. It is almost exclusively a tenement house neighborhood, averaging nearly seven families to a house, though in the houses of the double-decker type, nineteen or twenty families usually find shelter. There are eighty-eight saloons in the district—all of them prosperous. "The streets," says Miss Herzfeld, "are always dirty. In Winter the unmelted snow is heaped up in the gutters. The pavement is chiefly of cobblestones, the sidewalks are narrow and badly paved. The garbage can and ash barrel standing before the doors are always running over." The families are for the most part German and Irish, though occasionally the Russian Jews or English are met. Between the members of these diverse races there is the greatest antipathy and distrust, while all unite in their contempt for the negro. They live entirely in the moment; providence is entirely unknown, except in the form of insurance. Their reading is almost exclusively confined to newspapers. "One man kept his papers for months and read them over and over. He persisted in saying that the 'old ones is better than the new.'"

In art the taste runs principally to crayons of grandparents and other members of the family. "These are copied from photographs or are original productions of an artist who 'comes round' and is pain on the installment plan. The crayon is also paid for in coupons given by the family grocer. One woman whose husband's family did not figure in her portrait gallery, said she 'felt awfully ashamed because you might think my husband had no folks.'"

Nothing is more indicative of the intellectual darkness which still enshrouds these people, despite all the efforts of settlement workers to put it to flight, than the superstitions which persist among them. All the folk-lore of the old country, the belief in witches, fairies, and so on, took ship with them on the other side and found their way hither in the steerage.

"Amulets," says Miss Herzfeld, "are worn for good luck; a scapular wards off disease. A heart worn as a 'charm' will bring a sweetheart. Dreams are prophetic, they foretell sorrow, joy, and the arrival of letters. It is unsafe to go out by another door than the one by which you enter a house. If a dog howls, bad luck is sure to come before sundown.' It is unlucky to comb your hair after dark. Never attempt anything new on Friday."

When a child is to be christened, it is carried through the house first, to protect it from disease. A child must be taken to church on a 'straight line' or it will lose its way in later life. A child on its way to church must not meet a funeral. It will die if it does."

It appears that sunshine on a wedding day is lucky, while bad luck will overtake you if you sell or pawn a wedding gift, particularly your wedding ring. Moreover, if you work on your wedding day you will have to work all the rest of your life.

As might be expected, the circumstance of death is surrounded with even more superstitions. Touching the crepe on the door of a house of mourning is particularly ominous. Miss Herzfeld once came across a small boy dissolved in tears. He was sure he was going to die. He had touched some crepe and his playfellows had told him, "God will damn you." The belief in the Banshee is widespread among the Irish residents, but it is unanimously agreed that this prophetess of ill does not cross the ocean, being afraid of the voyage. Even in the shadow of death these people are anxious to do the "proper thing." The strength of their own peculiar social laws is quite as compelling as in higher walks of society. "You attend the funeral of your kinsfold; they 'expect it.' You have to get new mourning clothes, and 'they cost.' 'A coach to Calvary Cemetery costs me \$9,' one woman said. The funeral display is an indication of one's social status. His funeral must be as 'fine' as his neighbor's. All things are sacrificed in order to avoid pauper burial."

"There exists among these people," said Miss Herzfeld, in discussing the matter with the writer, "the most invincible aversion to hospital treatment. To avoid it they are willing to go to almost any trouble or expense within the limits of possibility. This is particularly true of the women, and I am bound to say that their aversion rests upon quite comprehensible grounds. The thing that has gone far to make these people hate the hospitals is that when they resort to them they are almost invariably treated as if they had no feelings of delicacy whatever. If their cases possess any scientific interest the examining physician will often call in all the young medical students he can assemble in order that they may get the benefit of this opportunity for observation. What humiliates the victims all the more is their knowledge of the fact that these same physicians would never dare to act in this manner with well-to-do patients. If the hospital is to be of any use as a weapon in the hands of those who are trying to lift these people from the depths of physical and mental darkness in which they live, there will have to be a reform along these lines. At present the hospital is of practically no help at all, and the quack and charlatan are getting their innings instead."

Curious ideas survive among these narrow streets regarding medical, and, indeed, every other science. The Irish frequently speak of a doctor as a "charmer." Once, it was told, a man with a severe cold went to a "charmer" to be cured. The latter "pulled out his hair as much as a cap could cover, roasted two eggs and put them on the bald spot, then he muttered to himself, and when he got through the man could swaller and holler as loud as any one."

Political ideals prevailing among the men of this district go far to shed much light on the difficulty of achieving ideal government in this city. They rarely attend primaries, since it "makes no difference whether you go or not." The primaries are too complicated for the poor man. They are meant for the politician.

"The residents," says Miss Herzfeld, "speak about the great amount of election bribery that goes on. One man told me that he had had the strength to refuse a bribe of \$5. He spoke of it as though it were rather an unusual act. 'The boys had their laugh on me, but I'm an honest man.'

"The district boss is more successful in getting out men to vote than any educational influence or institution could be, for he knows how to minister to the social and individual needs of his ward. He pays the rent of the dispossessed man; he finds work for him. He gives bail when the poor man is fined. He invites whole families to annual picnics. He buys tickets for the benefit entertainments. He attends the funerals. He pays funeral expenses. He invites the neighbors 'to a drink' or a supper, and he gets a pass for a man going on a journey.

Upon these and other kindnesses 'not worth talking about' depends a man's vote.

"There are, it is true, shafts of sunlight that fall over this dark picture. One of them is the kindly way the neighbors have of standing by each other when trouble overtakes a family. They mind each other's children and watch over each other's sick, and in the house of death friendly and helpful feet are many. The young girl on the same floor is given a place in the family to 'keep her from fallin' into low company.' If your husband gets drunk a neighbor 'opens her door to you.' If you get separated or dispossessed, she has always room for one more. The neighbors lend everything they have, from the kettle or coffee pot to the best black skirt for a funeral. One woman lent her christening robe nineteen times."

+ + +

As for family economy, there is none. As for economics, about a half of each family's income, Miss Herzfeld found, went for food, a quarter for rent, and out of the remaining quarter has to come clothing and all the rest. The poorer the family the more wasteful the mother. About half of each family's food is wasted because of ignorance of its value. All buy in small quantities, and there is practically no saving, except for a specific purpose or where some settlement worker succeeds in cultivating habits of thrift. Most families consume what they earn almost at once, living literally from hand to mouth. There is one exception to this rule which takes the form of life, or, rather, burial insurance. Says Miss Herzfeld: "The fear of a plain pine box and cheap shroud and rest on Hart's Island makes life insurance a necessity. Every one in the family over a year old is insured. Sometimes the children are actually starved to pay the premium."

It will surprise a good many people to learn that these tenement house dwellers hate the model tenement, which was devised for their especial benefit. The reasons for this curious antipathy are many and such as could only be understood by one who knows the instincts upon which the life of these people is founded. "You are not likely," says Miss Herzfeld, "to move into 'one of them new-fangled' model tenements because you cannot pay your rent weekly. The housekeeper is too 'cranky,' and you do not like the 'crowd.' The Forty-second Street 'crowd' is the worst of all. You would not be seen living there. There is more to clean in the new kind of house. You must not use the fire-escape to put things on, and besides you want a place for your plants if you have any. 'New tenements? Not much, for me.'"

The housewives of this dark quarter take anything but a rosy view of the institution of marriage.

"Mothers warn their daughters not to marry, telling them that there are plenty of chances yet to come and that 'you can always get married.' They speak of marriage as a necessary evil. They advise all young women to remain single if they wish to be happy. Most of them are married at eighteen. 'Few is the husbands that don't abuse you or get drunk. I never knew any.' 'Saints and men who don't drink don't live on earth.'

"These people," declared Miss Herzfeld, "have as a rule not the smallest notion of the most elementary facts of hygiene. The food they give their children is of such a character that it is a wonder that any of them grow up, and makes it almost certain that a foundation of ill-health will be laid in childhood on which a structure of mature misery will be reared. The food, even when of fair quality, is ill cooked and no care is taken to keep it clean. Milk is left standing uncovered where it is likely to be contaminated. Cleanliness, when it is attained in person, is the result of instinct rather than of any knowledge that it is needful for health. Tea is drunk in enormous quantities by everybody, and whisky is not infrequently given to children to 'make them feel good.'

"The failure of our school system to reach these people," declared Miss Herzfeld to the writer, "is at the bottom of their failure to raise themselves. You may think that all these failings, all this darkness and unenlightenment is true only of the older generation who were not born in this country. This, unfortunately, is not the case. Our schools do not reach the younger generation. In the first place, startling as it may seem, New York, the largest city on the continent, has no school census. It is therefore impossible always to know who is evading school attendance. Our truant officers are ridiculously few. They cannot begin to follow up the cases of failure to attend school. Instead of realizing the importance of sending their offspring to school most of these people are constantly devising ways to avoid it. They are so poor that the moment their children become of age sufficient to make them of any use in the bitter struggle to maintain a bare existence the parents send them to work or keep them at home to help about the house. Often, when complaint is made to the truant officers, the family has moved, for these families are nomadic, and it is impossible to get trace of them again.

"There is no use in blinking these hard facts. Our schools, so far as reaching these people who constitute so large a percentage of our population and who need the elevation of schooling so much worse than any other class, are failures. Nobody, I think, who knows the facts from personal observation, will attempt to deny it."

November 5, 1905

ON CHOOSING WIVES.

Under the title of "The Choice of a Wife" The St. James's Gazette has opened a discussion which is always timely, and as apposite on one side of the Atlantic as on the other. Sometimes a single instance of it is of equally acute interest on both sides, as Lord CURZON has just reminded the Pilgrims' Club in London in saying that the best pilgrimage he ever made in his life was the one he made across the Atlantic to persuade an American pilgrim to continue her life pilgrimage in his company.

Our British contemporary admits that its title may be regarded as a misnomer, since in so many cases wives are not chosen, but "happen." In a great many more cases, one may pretty safely say, they choose, and the discussion might more properly proceed under the title of "The Choice of a Husband." Of course the male in this case is deeply unaware of its facts. He fancies himself the pursuer, when he is in fact the pursued, as GALATEA in the eclogue did not flee until she was aware that her lover was looking after. But it is none the less true that

she is, quite perhaps as often as not, the Valkyr, "the chooser of the slain," and the object of her choice the unresisting and willing victim. Not that this is at all necessarily to her discredit. There are, of course, women who take the warpath without serious intentions. Like the defiant Seminole, they battle for the joy they have to see the white man fall. But a young woman whose intentions are both serious and honorable has nothing at all to be ashamed of in endeavoring by all womanly means to acquire the man whom she believes she can make happy and knows that she means to try to.

Perhaps it is "Anglo-Saxon" or "English speaking," perhaps it is more general and "Teutonic." But in spite of the philosophers there is in this country, and we believe in England also, a general objection to the conduct of a man, at least of a young man, who marries for any other, or even any better, reason than that he is in love. How he came to be there he would by the nature of the case find it difficult or impossible to explain. If he could give satisfactory reasons all to whom those reasons appealed would be in love with the object of his affections, a result which would evidently lead to marriages of inconvenience or to no marriages at all. The marriage of reason is what is called on the Continent a mariage de convenance, of which the British writer rather atrociously says that it is an object of envy to those whose own marriages have combined romance with inconvenience.

If one is really bent on making a marriage of reason instead of waiting for a "call," excellent recipes may be given to him. A wise man once advised his son, who had shown some disposition to choose instead of waiting to be chosen, to "look for a good woman's daughter." It would be hard to find any better basis for a happy union. In general, of course, mixed marriages, whether the mixture be of religion or of country, would be viewed by a wise adviser with apprehension, although Lord CURZON's experience is only one of very many as to the possible happiness of marriages between persons of different nationalities, much more alike as are the nationalities of Lord and Lady CURZON than any other two nationalities. Dr. JOHNSON's famous saying that marriages would be happier if they were arranged by the Lord Chancellor, due regard being paid to the ages and conditions of the parties, has never been accepted as a working rule in his own country. There is the wholly "reasonable" and extremely circumspect Count BONI CASTELLANE, whose marriage of reason has so lately been shown to be so far

from a success. There are quite enough more failures of the same kind to offset the unhappy marriages of romance. It is of these, of course, that BURTON declares that matches are made in heaven, though matches of the sulphurous kind, of which all of us know some instances, suggest a very different place of manufacture.

SWIFT's saying that the reason why so few marriages are happy is that "young ladies spend their time in making nets, not in making cages," is doubly outrageous. In the first place it is an outrageous begging of the question. The testimony of less cynical observers in our day and country is that most marriages are entitled to be called happy. In the second place it outrageously puts the whole blame for unhappy marriages on the female partner, contrary alike to probability and to fact. But at least as many of the marriages are failures in which men "choose" their wives, or think they do, as in cases in which men become the prey of their own imaginations. And there is this to be said from the point of view of reason in favor of marriages with which reason has nothing to do. In the first months of married life there are necessarily very many differences to be adjusted and small incompatibilities of ways of thinking and feeling to be reconciled. That, as all experienced spouses know, is the trying period. Marriage is like life in that it is a school wherein whoso does not 'earn must suffer. Now, to diminish the friction of this trying time no better lubricant could possibly be provided than the romantic love, which cannot be expected to last forever, but which may very probably outlast this greatest necessity for it of the early connubial period. When the glamour of the romance "fades into the light of common day," and a real man and a real woman take the places of the creatures of each other's fancy, and passion cools into at best the tenderest of friendships, both parties are better off, and will acknowledge themselves to be better off because the romance has been. "In erring reason's spite" all mankind will continue to love a lover, and justly so.

Remarkable Wedding Contract

ISAIAH F. HARDING and Mrs. Isabella Engelbrecht of Dallas County, Iowa, have just entered into marriage on a fifteen-year plan, according to a special from Des Moines.

Neither had found smooth sailing upon the sea of matrimony, although both are, comparatively speaking, rich. Twice each had been married, and twice divorced.

When, therefore, seeking a consolation prize, Harding asked Mrs. Engelbrecht to be his, extreme caution attended her affirmative response. "We'd better lay down some rules to go by," she said, and Harding agreed.

The result was the most remarkable nuptial contract ever drawn in Iowa, and perhaps in the world. Veteran lawyers say they have never seen anything quite like it.

It arranges for almost every possible contingency that may arise in the wedded life of two people.

The contract plainly sets forth who shall build the fires, when the husband may bring home guests to meals, when the relatives of each shall visit them, how the money is to be divided, how often the wife may attend social functions without being scowled at—and even fixes a limit to the number of possible future Hardings.

By observing in minutest detail the terms of this remarkable document Harding and his third wife have already enjoyed two months of life together without a cloud appearing in the matrimonial sky. The contract provides:

"That we, by the terms of this agreement, made this third day of May, A. D. 1906, between Isaiah F. Harding of the County of Dallas and State of Iowa, party of the first part, and Isabella Engelbrecht, of the County of Polk and State of Iowa, of the second part, do hereby bind ourselves by this covenant to carry out entire and in detail the terms of this solemn obligation so that we, as man and wife, may dwell together in peace and harmony so long as this said covenant shall be in force, to wit: From this said 3d day of May, A. D. 1906, until the 3d day of May, A. D. 1921, a period of fifteen years.

"It is hereby agreed and stipulated between said Isaiah F. Harding, party of the first part, and said Isabella Engelbrecht, party of the second part, that if at the end of the fifteen years aforesaid cause to believe that such union is not for the best interest of either of us the said union shall be terminated by either without further formality, providing that, if at any time during the period above set forth, either should wish to relinquish the bonds of matrimony, such action shall not be taken except with due process of law.

"We hereby agree that we shall jointly and severally settle upon the children of each by former marriage one-half of the estate of the party of the first part to be settled upon his children, and the said one-half of the estate of the party of the second part upon her children. Deeds and papers to this effect shall be duly signed, transferred, and recorded upon the completion of this covenant. And this shall be regarded as applying to personal property as well as real.

"And we hereby bind ourselves to the faithful performance of the following stipulations, so far as within us lies:

"Isaiah F. Harding, party of the first part, agrees that Isabella Engelbrecht, party of the second part, shall, upon her wedding to him, the party of the first part, receive each week the sum of $15 with which to defray the household expenses, but it is understood that he, the party of the first part, shall furnish fuel and water.

"It is expressly understood that from this union shall come not more than three children. Upon the birth of each or any child the above amount of $15 per week shall be increased $3 per week.

"The party of the second part shall furnish domestic help and to assist her in this she shall be allowed the financial output of poultry and one cow from the farm herd. But if for any other reason it shall be found necessary to dispense with domestic help, then it shall be the duty of the husband to build the fires and prepare the morning meals for six months throughout the Winter, and for the wife to build the fires and prepare the morning meals for the remaining six months of the year.

❊ ❊ ❊

"Neither party shall invite guests to the house, except with the express permission of the other, and then not oftener than twice per week; relatives shall not be allowed to visit the family, except that relatives of the party of the first part shall be permitted to visit the home at any time within the first two weeks of the month of May; relatives of the party of the second part within the last two weeks of the month of October. This shall not relate in any way to the children of either of the parties of this covenant.

"If the parties of this covenant shall remove to the city to live it is agreed that in addition to the costs mentioned above party of the first part shall pay ice and gas expenses. Furthermore, it shall be the privilege of the party of the second part to attend two social functions each week, one of which, if the parties reside in the city, shall be the theatre, and this expense shall be borne by the party of the first part.

"Each Sunday the party of the first part shall escort and accompany the party of the second part to church in the morning and again in the evening, should she desire it.

"Party of the first part shall keep up the house insurance, keep the premises in good condition, furnish at all times respectable conveyance to and from town, see that both himself and wife are properly clothed, take an active part in any civic or rural improvement, and assist in any political movement for the general good. It is expressly declared that he shall vote according to the dictates of his conscience."

August 12, 1906

SUGGESTS TRIAL MARRIAGES.

Mrs. Clews Parsons in "The Family," Recommends a Radical Change.

Mrs. Elsie Clews Parsons's book, "The Family," will probably be on sale to-day or to-morrow. The book suggests some startling reforms, of which this one is perhaps the most radical:

"It would seem well to encourage early trial marriages, the relation to be entered into with a view to permanency, but with the privilege of breaking it, if it proves unsuccessful, without suffering any great degree of public condemnation."

The book, as explained by the publishers, G. P. Putnam's Sons, is principally intended as a textbook, useful to those who lecture to elementary students in sociology, and it is of interest to all in general who are interested in sociological questions.

Mrs. Parsons, the author of "The Family," is the daughter of Henry Clews, the banker, and the wife of Congressman Herbert Parsons, Chairman of the Republican County Committee. She is a Doctor of Philosophy and she was for six years lecturer in sociology in Barnard College.

November 17, 1906

WHERE THEY MAKE HOUSEKEEPING A LEARNED PROFESSION

THERE'S no denying the fact that throughout a goodly part of the civilized world a strike of vast proportions is in progress—the strike of a sex. For that is what the whole feminist movement, with its allied phenomena of dwindling birth rates, servant problems, housekeeping difficulties, and disappearing home life, amounts to.

The care of the home and the bearing and rearing of children are the employments which the divine right of sex makes woman's distinctive work, and they are the only work with which, by and large, until recent years, she has concerned herself. But she has found out that she can do other things that will bring her larger rewards and greater honor.

And, therefore, she has struck, not, indeed, consciously and with concerted intention to bring about stated results, but with a definite individual purpose to win, each for herself—and in some cases, for others as well—either higher pecuniary rewards or more social significance, or both. That is, the sex wants higher wages of one sort or another.

But the well-known method of endeavoring to get higher wages by declining to work for less is having in this strike an interesting and most promising variation. For the movement to make of the mother's and homekeeper's work a learned profession, to be prepared for, like the profession of law or medicine, by years of earnest study, is growing rapidly, and is bound to have results of the greatest importance.

If we look back along the course of civilization we see one vocation after another coming up out of the gutter of social disdain and gradually gaining for itself honor and emolument. The surgeon, whose profession is now honorable and lucrative, and to whom it is possible to attain heights of distinction, was once merely the barber, of no more importance in the social and economic scale than the barber is now.

So, also, the lawyer and the literary man were hardly more than hangers-on of some rich and distinguished person. Since the youth of the race, when the only employments in which there was profit or honor or glory were those of killing or of ruling others, every occupation which is of real service to mankind has had to pull itself up out of a mire of social contempt, prove its worth, and by the value of its social service win its way to social honor and pecuniary reward. And it is that course upon which woman's housekeeping vocation has started.

While it is only within recent years that the endeavor to base housekeeping firmly upon scientific principles has assumed definite form, the first glimmerings of the idea that it ought to be so date back almost to the beginning of education for women. We of the twentieth century, with its ample opportunities for women's education, find it difficult to realize what a little time ago it was when those beginnings made their appearance and how small they were.

It was only a little more than 100 years ago that a daring New England school board, which was almost the first to take a step in that direction, decided that two of the eight hours of daily instruction in the town school should be devoted to girls, "as they are a tender and interesting branch of the community, but have been much neglected in the public schools of this town." And it was as late as 1825 that the first High School for girls, in

Practice Dining Room at Columbia University.

Boston, swamped itself by its very success.

Before the end of its second year there was such a rush of applicants for admission and such a clamor among parents for larger and better accommodations that the School Committee decided to save itself a lot of trouble by abolishing the school and declaring it a failure. But the beginnings had been made, and, considering the youth of the country and all the pioneering that had to be done, they grew rapidly.

And before the middle of the century the idea began to spring up here and there that a part of the instruction of girls should be devoted to their particular needs. The two Beecher sisters, Catherine and Harriet, were among the very first to set forth this doctrine and Miss Catherine Beecher published in 1840 a "Treatise on Domestic Economy" which showed a remarkable appreciation, considering the limited nature of all scientific knowledge at that time, of the scope and importance of the matter.

In the decade after the civil war came other books, by several authors, which began to stir interest among educators, the organization of the first cooking schools and the establishing of domestic science departments in several Western State universities, and agricultural colleges. But at that time and for a good many years afterward it was little more than a sort of "trade school" movement. Its most ardent disciples, and they were not many, scarcely saw in it yet one of the important divisions of applied science, and they were content to teach the young women how cooking and sewing and washing ought to be done without leading them to the sciences in which are rooted all right methods of discharging household duties.

All this early development of the idea of training for household work, it is noteworthy, was nearly coincident with the beginnings of woman's revolt against household work. Trade school methods were not what she wanted. There was nothing in them to satisfy her newly awakened intellectual cravings, they opened no new path to financial independence, they offered no increase of social significance.

Industrial life was opening many doors before her, and she found that within them not only could she win economic independence, but that there her work was of consequence and her individuality to be reckoned with. If she entered commercial or professional life she knew that she would hold an important place in the social organization. Numbers of men and women would be ready to recognize and pay for her ability, her skill, her experience.

But even the help of the Domestic Science School in those days could not make of the housekeeper's vocation in the general estimate much more than a "pottering around the house," in which there was neither financial emolument nor social significance. It was not until the home economics movement advanced itself from the position of a trade school to that of an applied science whose principles are based on the pure sciences of almost every department of human knowledge that the modern young woman began to think it was really worth while.

For the last ten or fifteen years the growth of the movement has been remarkably rapid and significant. Domestic science departments have been organized, or those already existing have been revivified and enlarged in a great number of colleges and universities. In the higher institutions of learning in this country that are State aided or supported there are now more than thirty departments for the teaching of household arts and sciences.

Several of the Western State universities which established such courses in the last decade of the nineteenth century, only to drop them in a few years, have found in the last five or six years that they must re-establish the department or lag behind both the times and the demand of the State's young people. Kansas, which was the second State in the Union—Iowa was the first—to give household training in the State Agricultural College, where it has been carried on steadily for more than thirty years, has just organized, in addition, a School of Domestic Science in her State University.

A year ago Columbia University opened a School of Household Arts which had an attendance during its first year of about 400 students. Simmons College, in Boston, which was opened about eight years ago and from the beginning has paid much attention to this branch, finds its School of Household Economics well nigh swamped by the demands upon it.

The Agricultural Department of the United States Government has kept in close touch with this movement to bring about scientific housekeeping and finds many opportunities of giving it aid and comfort. A dozen years ago the Secretary of the Department dwelt in one of his reports upon the necessity of giving to this movement a thoroughly scientific basis.

"In this, as in other branches of instruction which have a vital relation to the arts and industries," he said, "the student should learn not only the best methods of doing the things required by the daily needs of home life, but also the reasons why certain things are to be done and others avoided. In other words, this teaching needs a scientific basis if it is to be thoroughly useful. In this respect domestic science is in the same category with medicine, engineering and agriculture.

"It is not so very long ago that medicine and engineering were very largely empirical arts, and the schools of medicine and engineering were principally engaged in teaching men the things they were to do when they became doctors or engineers. To-day no doctor or engineer is considered fitted to pursue his profession until he has drunk deep at the fountains of science and knows well the principles on which successful practice must be based. * * * Now, what has been done for the boy * * * needs to be done for the girl in domestic art and science. And already the beginnings 'of a far-reaching effort in this direction have been made."

Among the recent fruitions of the movement was the organization two years ago of the American Home Economics Association, which has already a membership of about fifteen hundred men and women, scattered all over this country, with a few in Canada. Its President is Mrs. Ellen H. Richards of the Faculty of the Massachusetts Institute of Technology, and the author of a number of books treating of various phases of the application of science and scientific methods to the problems of the home.

From the beginning of the domestic science movement Mrs. Richards has been one of its foremost leaders, and nearly the whole of her long and busy life has been devoted to the study of how to improve the conditions of human living by applying scientific truths and principles to the methods and environment of daily life. Dr. C. F. Langworthy of the United States Department of Agriculture, who is one of the Vice Presidents, presents at the annual meetings an extensive survey of the year's studies and results in the science of nutrition.

At last Winter's meeting in Boston among those who took a prominent part in the proceedings were members of the Faculties of Yale, Harvard, and Columbia Universities, of the Universities of Toronto and Wisconsin, and many men and women well known in educational and philanthropic work from all parts of the country. The association publishes a journal of home economics, an illustrated bi-monthly review of the whole field of domestic science, of which Mrs. Mary H. Abell is the editor.

It maintains also a graduate school of home economics which holds Summer sessions of a peripatetic sort, one or another institution, east or west, acting each year as its host. Wesleyan University housed it one Summer by invitation of Prof. Atwater, and with the offer of the use of his laboratories, while Cornell, Illinois, and Missouri Universities have each extended hospitality for a Summer term.

The courses offered to students of home economics vary somewhat according to the use which the young woman intends to make of her training. At the Columbia University School of Household and Industrial Arts last year about half of the 400 students were there solely for the purpose of becoming scientific homekeepers, better qualified when they become wives and mothers to administer their homes and rear their children. Others were studying to become teachers of domestic science in schools and colleges—a vocation in which the demand has been rapidly increasing during the last few years.

Institutional management was the career for which still others were preparing themselves. This, too, is one of the new pursuits which recent years have opened to women.

The need of trained women as managers of public and private institutions, as administering housekeepers in large hotels, as supervisors of women's dormitories in colleges has multiplied the call for them so fast that capable women prepared for such work find no difficulty in getting situations. Others were doing research work of one sort or another connected with housekeeping problems.

At all of the institutions of high grade which include departments of domestic science more or less of this research work is carried on. At the University of Chicago one young woman made an exhaustive study of the comparative cost of coal, coke, gas, and electricity for cooking.

At Columbia last Winter one student, who was engaged in post-graduate research work in nutrition, devoted much time to the work of finding out the most economical way of cooking green vegetables. Her test tubes, scales, and figures finally proved that there is a saving of about one-third their nutritive value if they are steamed instead of boiled. In other colleges the losses in the cooking of beef and the relation of yeast to flavor in bread were among the subjects of research.

In the School of Household Arts of Columbia University there was held last Spring an exhibit illustrative of the work of its departments. In household chemistry the students had made tests of textiles. Samples of alleged woolen goods, bought in New York stores, had been tested for admixtures of cotton, and the exhibit showed portions of the original samples as they appeared before and after taking the test, with the accompanying data of price, alleged quality, and the percentage of cotton admixture which had been proved.

Samples of silk had been tested, the results showing that in some cases the silks had owed their body and sheen to 60, 70, or even 80 per cent. of metallic dressing. Other work had been the analysis of milk, of coal, of water, of crackers, and of washing powders.

In the dietetics laboratory a series of tables daintily spread showed the results of the work of students who had evolved daily menus for children of varying ages, so as to adapt the food given to the child each year to the needs of that stage of its growth. In another room, amid odors that ascended to heaven of ether and sulphuric acid, an obliging young woman showed to visitors all the processes of analyzing a child's school luncheon to find out whether or not it contained all the necessary ingredients in proper proportion for the child's nourishment.

In the foods and cookery laboratory there was an exhibit of fireless cookers of many and varied kinds and of foods cooked in them. Students in this department had been making special investigation of the cost, the methods, and the possibilities of these cookers.

A full course of study in home economics is comprehensive of many things that once were thought entirely outside of "woman's sphere." It is of such nature and purpose as to show the responsibility of the homekeeper toward her family, the community, and the state to be of vastly more importance than she or any one else, until recent years, had ever dreamed it to be.

The basic principle of the new science of housekeeping, the fundamental idea upon which it rests, is that the wife and mother, the keeper of the home, has in her charge the well-being of the family and is responsible to it and to the state of which it is an integral part for its sanitary surroundings, its due care, its proper nourishment. Therefore her course of training must include instruction in how a house should be situated and built and what should be its sanitary arrangements in order to secure to its occupants the best advantages possible of drainage, ventilation, sunshine, heat, coolness, sanitation.

She must comprehend the principles of grace and beauty of form and of harmony in color so that she may furnish and decorate her home with good taste, simply, harmoniously, and in a way fitted to the family's needs. For its proper management she must have an understanding of household economy, how to keep her accounts, how to apportion the income to the various expenses in order to produce the best results, how to systematize work and how to supervise assistants.

For the proper nutrition of her family and the proper conservation of its income she must know the principles of nutrition, which necessitates a knowledge of physiology, chemistry, and bacteriology. She must be conversant with costs of foods and their comparative nutritive values.

And since she is the custodian of the family's investment in all the paraphernalia of living—which in every family represents a goodly portion of its income—it is her duty to be thoroughly familiar with the proper use and care of all these numerous and varied belongings—"household technique" they call this branch of the practical application of knowledge in the schools of domestic science.

In order to appreciate the necessity of hygienic conditions, if they would conscientiously discharge their obligations as wives, mothers, and homekeepers, those who are training young women to be scientific housewives think that they should be familiar with the sciences upon which hygiene is based, should know how to secure and maintain hygienic conditions, and should realize the tremendous cost the family and the community must pay in illness, in lessened strength and efficiency for unclean surroundings.

The theoretical and the practical are kept well balanced in this training for up-to-date housekeeping. The student must base her practical knowledge deeply and broadly upon the sciences whose principles enter into the routine of daily life.

Chemistry—physiological, organic and household—physiology, bacteriology, she must know as well as how to prepare and serve a meal. If she spends hours on one day among her test tubes, acids, and salts, on another she will go marketing with a teacher who will make the expedition a sort of walking lecture upon the points to observe in buying meats and vegetables, poultry and fish.

In the practice dining room, which is always arranged and furnished to show the beauty of simplicity and harmony, she will take turns with her fellow students at being hostess, guest, or serving maid at the breakfasts, luncheons, teas, and dinners which they have first cooked in the big, well-equipped kitchen, which is so spotlessly clean that it might be called chemically pure. After she has listened to lectures upon the historical evolution of the household she will make a practical study of plumbing and ventilation. Lessons in the principles of design are followed by the working out of schemes for the decoration and furnishing of a house or an apartment which combine economy with artistic effects.

Nowhere does this training lose sight of the importance to society of the woman's work in her home—which heretofore has been considered of no consequence whatever outside of her own four walls. Every one of her studies is a sort of index finger pointing toward the social responsibilities of the administrator of the home, of the woman who holds power over the physical and moral welfare and to a large extent the happiness of her own small kingdom, whose duty it is to protect and advance the well-being of the neighborhood by her close watch upon her own gates, whose thrift and wisdom in the spending of the income of her own family is not only an example for others but a factor in the prosperity of the whole community.

But according to this new view of the science of housekeeping the home warder's obligations to the social scheme of which she is a part do not stop with the discharge of her duties to her own family. For it holds that her expert training in scientific methods of housekeeping not only fits her to do her share in the larger housekeeping of the community but lays upon her shoulders the duty of helping to keep the neighborhood, the municipality, the State a wholesome place to live in. And so among her studies are such subjects as sanitary legislation, methods of street cleaning, and disposal of sewage, the sanitation of public places, the public health movement and its significance, the social aspects of crime, the influence of the home upon social life, the history and present tendencies of social legislation.

It is quite evident that all this training is bound to produce a housekeeper as different from the housekeeper of fifty years ago as the trained and experienced surgeon of to-day is different from the old-time barber-surgeon with his leeches and cupping glasses. And it looks, too, as if she will be as much more useful to society and in all her human relations as the services of the modern physician have advanced in value and consequence beyond those of his professional forebear.

And so it appears that a new profession is being born into the arena of human effort—a new one, although it deserves the title of the oldest profession in the world. For the wife and mother watched and cared for the home and the children inside the walls of the cave or upon a platform above a lake according to her best lights before man had evolved any more than the instinctive beginnings of his two primal professions, war and government. And however certain cynical authors may attempt to honor the sisterhood of shame with the same title, the fact remains that the homekeeper had swept and garnished her hearth and begun the loving discharge of her duties there long before the shadow of the harlot fell across it.

But ancient, honorable, and of highest importance though it is, the housekeeper's profession has been a long time coming into its own. For so many centuries social opinion—which was mainly of masculine gender—honored only that which was destructive that woman's distinctive work, essentially productive and conserving, shared in that social contempt which was the fate of all really useful effort. But after science began to go slumming and to rescue one after another of these outcasts of human endeavor, mankind realized how important they were for its welfare and its happiness, and now honors them accordingly.

There is no telling, as yet, what changes these new duties, new importance, and new honors which the domestic science movement is in a fair way to win for the housekeeper will make in woman's attitude toward the world and the world's attitude toward her. That it will in time put an end to the strike of the sex by according to woman's distinctive work the social emoluments and the pecuniary rewards which she feels she is capable of winning elsewhere can hardly be doubted.

Neither can it be doubted that it will effect a change in woman's position in society as profound as that which the feminist movement has already brought about. And those who believe in it and are helping it forward are quite sure that its influence will be for the betterment and the happiness of men, women, and children individually and the whole social body in general.

September 4, 1910

HOW ONE WOMAN MANAGES A LARGE HOUSEHOLD

By Katharine Lord.

(Miss Lord has had a wide experience in many lines of work. She was six years at Greenwich House, the well-known settlement where she organized and managed the handicraft school.)

THERE has been much discussion in the public prints of late of the ever-recurrent servant problem. There are mistresses bemoaning the scarcity of efficient servants and servants complaining of overwork, lack of consideration, curtailing of freedom, and menial position. Meanwhile nothing is heard from the satisfied and well served mistresses nor of the contented servants. They are too busily engaged in their respective jobs to have time or inclination to discuss the subject.

I speak advisedly of the mistress as well as the servant who is "on her job"; for the entirely efficient servant is seldom found except in the employ of the efficient mistress. The business of running a household demands system as much as the business of running a commercial enterprise. No man would employ from five to forty individuals and leave them to work out among themselves their divisions of duties and general responsibility. Yet many of the women who complain of inefficient servants are doing just this thing.

Such a woman has been taught for generations perhaps that she must "create a home," and many times she succeeds by sheer force of lovableness and charm, but at great cost to herself.

Unnecessary Martyrdom.

So far, so good. She is a noble, perhaps self-sacrificing, woman, but she is undergoing unnecessary martyrdom, simply because she is not using her mind and doing her part—the planning of the work.

We are hearing much just now of the budget system of administering the family income, however small it may be; the system by which the income is portioned out in advance, rather than being left to chance division.

What of the budget system of housework? Could it not be made more general with excellent effect? Would it not obviate many of the difficulties if duties were systematized, grouped more carefully, standardized as are the parts of any business enterprise?

That there is very general interest in this subject is shown by the crop of communications on the servant question which comes into a newspaper office. One which came recently to THE TIMES office spoke of the smooth running of English households, and the amount of work expected there of servants, quoting as evidence lists of work posted in an English household with which he or she was familiar. This fact that there were lists of work posted conspicuously where servants and mistress could refer to them really means much more than the writer realized. In how many of the households where "trouble with help" is the constant experience is there any such system in use? The

chances are that in most of them it is quite unknown. There are, of course, other causes of an unsatisfactory condition, both on the part of employer and employed. But this at least is one important cause—the failure of the mistress to do her part in putting the household on a systematic basis.

It is illogical in the extreme to demand of domestic servants what is not asked of any other kind of employe, namely, the initial planning of each one's sphere of labor.

A Standardized Household.

One devotee of the budget system is Mrs. William Jay Schieffelin, who is known among her large circle of friends for her well-ordered household, as she is known to the world at large for her constructive philanthropies and her intelligent interest in public affairs.

"The most important thing about planning the care of a large household," said Mrs. Schieffelin, "is to have every inch of the house covered. And it is only by sitting down and giving real time and thought to the matter that such lists can be made satisfactory.

"My lists are a logical growth," she continued. "Beginning in my young matron days with a much smaller household, I have revised and added to them each year as occasion demanded."

Each Autumn, on the return to town, Mrs. Schieffelin goes over her lists, making any necessary changes of detail. She makes sure that each servant understands his work thoroughly. Then dismisses the subject from her mind. A spirit of co-operation and of cheerful devotion to duty is cultivated.

Each individual servant is responsible for his assigned work and for every detail of it. Besides that the butler is generally responsible for the first and second floors, basement, and cellar and for the five servants that are under him. The cook is responsible for the kitchen, servants' dining room, storeroom, and men's rooms, and for the kitchen and pantry maids under her.

The lists of work consist of two parts. First, the work to be done every day, with approximate hours for doing each thing. And, second, a schedule of special work to be done on every day of the week. At the head of each list is a statement of the territory, as it were, for which that particular servant is responsible.

Three copies are made of each list. One is kept by Mrs. Schieffelin herself, one is given to the butler or cook, and one to the individual servant.

When a new servant is engaged Mrs. Schieffelin personally goes over the list of work with him until she is sure that it is thoroughly understood. Sometimes a second review of some details is necessary. After that she expects — and usually gets — satisfactory results. If after a trial it is found that the servant cannot do his work satisfactorily, that shows that he is not suited to the place and a change is made. But such cases are rare. Mrs. Schieffelin keeps her servants for long periods of time and when changes are made they are usually for reasons quite outside of the work itself.

The value of such a system in the household employing fifteen or twenty servants is apparent. But it is equally applicable to the smaller menage. The organization of a force of six or seven servants is exactly the same as that

33

of three or four times the number; it is simply a matter in the larger house of a greater number in each department.

Tho care of any household naturally falls into three departments—that of the kitchen and basement, that of the dining room and general living rooms, and that of the bedrooms. If there be children, there will be also a nursery department.

In a Six Servant House.

Take a typical six servant house for example. There will probably be a butler, footman or useful man, cook, laundress, and two maids. The butler and second man between them will have charge of the entire first floor, basement, heating plant, sidewalk and yard, and will serve the meals, wait on the door, take charge of telephone and other messages, family or guests' luggage and all packages. The cook will be supreme in her own domain, the kitchen, storerooms, servants' dining room, etc., and will probably have some specified assistance from the maids and possibly from the laundress. The housemaids will care for all bedrooms, upstairs sitting rooms, and have such other duties as are assigned to them. The exact division of duties will, of course, depend on the number and character of the family.

When the number of servants is increased, the departments, as they may be called, remain practically the same. The butler, if he is efficient, is very likely to become a sort of general factotum. In many households he even engages and dismisses servants and has general oversight of the entire force. Of course if there be children there will be a nursery with a governess, nurses, and perhaps a footman and maids especially attached to this department.

In Smaller Households.

Suppose the servant force be not larger, but smaller than the typical one just referred to. Is the budget system still applicable?

Assuredly it is. In the household of one or two servants it is just as necessary to have the duties understood, the time planned to the best advantage, the work distributed evenly throughout the week. And this is for the mistress to do, whether she has one servant or thirty; whether she be a housekeeper hired for the purpose or a woman who through preference or necessity keeps the reins of management in her own hands.

"There are only two of us, and we have four servants. You would think we might have the evening paper brought up when it comes!"

Who has not heard a peevish woman make some such plaint as this? It is just possible that this little detail is not the particular duty of any one of the four. Hence it is frequently forgotten.

In a portfolio of working lists collected from several different housekeepers I find the following:

HALL AND DOOR SERVICE.
(Butler's Copy.)

Bell and telephone to be answered promptly always.

Write all messages when family are out or resting and deliver at soonest possible moment.

Deliver telegrams and notes by hand at once.

All packages are to be taken at once to the third or fourth floor.

Heavy packages or packages to the fourth floor may be carried in elevator.

Announce callers to ladies at their rooms. Take cards on tray.

Use of Elevator—Always put out elevator light and close door immediately on arriving at any floor. Always walk down stairs.

Have tea and chocolate tray always ready.

Morning newspapers to be placed in the dining room.

Evening newspaper to be carried at once to the library.

There follows a schedule by days showing when each servant is on duty in the hall, and each one assigned to such duty has a copy, as does the butler, who has general supervision of this work.

Here are a few lists secured from other housekeepers which show how carefully every possible detail of work is provided for:

WAITRESS.

Up at 6:30.
Family prayers.
Open dining room.
Sweep and dust front stairs.
Set breakfast table.
Assist butler with breakfast.
Make coffee.
Warm milk.
Arrange trays and take them up when necessary.
Clear breakfast table and help dry dishes.
Leather silver after meals.
Clean and dust dining room.
Trim lamps and candles.
Prepare lunch table and be dressed by 11 o'clock.
Wait on door until lunch.
Clean coffee percolator.
When on duty empty and clean garbage pail.
When on duty draw down shades and curtains and light lamps.
Off duty every other afternoon until 5:45. (Same afternoons as butler.)
Every third evening off until 11 o'clock.
Every third evening answer front door bell, and answer basement bell after 9 o'clock.
Every other Sunday afternoon and evening off. (Same as butler.)
Two out of three Sunday mornings off; third Sunday morning on duty.
Serve children's supper when on duty.
Write down telephone messages and deliver as soon as possible.
Wednesday—Look over and put away linen.
Thursday—Turn out dining room.
Friday—Front stairs.

PARLOR-PANTRY MAID.

Down at 6:30—Open and dust library and print room. Draw up salon shades and empty scrap baskets.
Breakfast, 7:20; Saturday, 7:30; Sunday, 7:45. Dust salon and second floor hall. Use broom bag for dusting floors. Wash up breakfast things and empty grease trap. Every other day clean and dust pantry and tidy up after each meal. Clean and dust lavatory in front hall. Towels, &c. Window sill.

Monday—Turn out library. Wash window sills.
Tuesday—Wash stone border on second floor hall; dust walls, clean and tidy two closets.
Wednesday—Turn out print room. Wash window sills.
Thursday—Clean plumbing in lavatory. Clean pantry cupboards.
Friday—Turn out salon. Clean closet in front hall, first floor, under stairs.
Saturday—Clean both pantries, icebox, plate warmer, &c. Clean top pantry stairs, (between servants' dinner hour and dining room luncheon.) Window sills in all rooms to be kept clean.
Evenings out when convenient until 11 o'clock. Sunday morning out. Every other Sunday evening and afternoon out. One other afternoon and evening out.
Tuesday and Thursday afternoon for own laundry. Keep aprons, gloves, and children's bibs in good order. Wash dusters, brushes, &c.

(Copyright, 1913, by Sturgis, Walton & Co.)

April 6, 1913

TRAINING GIRLS IN THE CRAFT OF MOTHERHOOD

BY MARY L. READ,
Director of the New York School of Mothercraft.

LITTLE more than a year ago there was opened in New York City a School of Mothercraft. The name was new to America, and so was the idea, in practice but not in theory. This school was to give the special practical training for young women which educators, sociologists, physicians, biologists, have long been urging.

Steadily, slowly, persistently, this school has developed. It has attracted inquiries from young women and mothers not only in the immediate locality but from all parts of the United States. Commissioner Claxton of the United States Bureau of Education is one of its advisors. So also is Prof. Ross, the sociologist of the University of Wisconsin, as well as nearly a score of prominent university men and women, physicians, biologists, and educators of New York City.

Club women and society leaders are participating in its upbuilding. Young women, social workers, young mothers, not only in Manhattan, but from the suburbs, have been among its students. College women especially have attended its classes. As one applicant said, "I have been given every advantage of college and special education that money could buy except the special preparation for homemaking. Now I have my own home and all these problems, and I feel it is a very great responsibility and one to which I want to give special study."

"My little boy of four can do nothing with. He is very naughty and will not mind. What can I do to make him mind?"

"My little girl is always teasing for stories. Where can I find stories suited to her age, and how can I learn how to tell these stories?"

"My little girl is an only child. What can she do on rainy days when she must be in the house?"

"Is there any place where a mother can learn some of the things the children do in the kindergarten?"

These are some of the questions the mothers of little children come to ask. In the special classes in story-telling, nursery games and songs, children's handwork, child study, they find some answers to their questions.

Said the Superintendent of one of the hospitals where infants' nurses are trained: "I don't know the first thing about a baby or how to take care of it, but don't let the nurse know." And one father who came to us for an infant's nurse begged us to send her immediately, as the baby had had nothing to eat all day and would not have until the nurse came, because the mother knew nothing about how to prepare its bottle."

"The first time I had to bathe my baby, when it was a few weeks old, I was so afraid I would dislocate its arms or legs or injure it for life in some way, that I trembled and cried all the time. And I was sending for the doctor every few days because I thought something was the matter with it. Nothing ever was, but of course I didn't know, and I lived in constant fear."

These are typical experiences given by mothers of good general education, with means to provide not only the necessities and comforts but even the luxuries of life, for their homes and their children. Their fathers and mothers would have thought it a disgrace not to have provided training in all the social accomplishments.

"If I, with my love for my baby, and my college training, could only have had such an opportunity for training in the care of babies as the little immigrant girl of meagre schooling who came to me from one of the hospitals, how much better care I could have given my baby myself. As it was, I didn't even know whether this nursery maid was doing things right," was the comment of one of these young mothers.

Appeals From Brides.

"What kind of clothes must I get ready for the baby, and how many shall I need, and what kind of a crib—do tell me everything I need to get," earnestly begged a young Southern woman, as she took her notebook and pencil from her bag, preparatory to her first lesson. "And making them—I want to make them myself, and I never made a garment in my life. Will you not teach me?"

She was hundreds of miles from her own mother, in a strange city, and she never had so much as held a baby. There were so many problems and questions in getting things ready for the baby.

"Next year I am to be married, and I don't know the first thing about housekeeping, or babies, or how to cook, or sew, or market. I have just gone to school, and had a good time all my life. I need to begin at the beginning and learn everything. I think this school is just what I need, and have been looking for." This is a frequent form of letter. Then there are young women who write: "I am graduating in June. I should like such a training in homemaking and the care of children. Please tell me all about the course."

"Expected" to Marry.

"You know," said a young society mother to a group of her club friends, "all the girls in our set are expected to marry and have a family, but none of us have been expected to be trained for our work, and the babies come and we feel so helpless and ignorant. That is why I feel that such a school is so important and we all ought to take part in getting it established."

"I want my daughter and some of her friends to come for some of these classes," said another society mother, "for it seems to me so important that girls should have all this training while they are young."

But the craft of the mother is not limited to the care and training of one's own children. In these days of social service many young women are devoting their time to the mothering of children from less fortunate homes, and to do this efficiently requires a knowledge of child nature, the principles of his development, and acquaintance with his physical nature and needs.

"There are many young women of leisure in our parish who would like to do some social service work, especially with children or in clubs, but who have neither experience nor training, and who are likely to do as much harm as good," said the Secretary of a large and wealthy parish.

These young women could do an immense amount of lasting good for hundreds of children and have a great satisfaction and joy in it, and, incidentally, be acquiring training and experience with children that would be of great value to them in their own homes, by such a course of study and practical training as is given at the School of Mothercraft. If a young woman who is untrained and inexperienced has four or five hours a week that she wishes to devote to social service, she might profitably, for herself and those she would help, devote at least half of this time to training and preparation, and work at first under guidance, as young women do who are training as teachers or nurses. In this way she knows what progress she is making and how valuable her social service really is.

"What shall I do when I finish college or high school?" is the question thousands of young women are asking every year. In that interim between graduation and marriage, these young women feel that they should be doing something worth while.

"Do you know of a young woman who can assist me with my little children, who is fond of children, cultured, gracious, who is worthy to be a companion at this most impressionable age, and who is trained in their physical care and also in kindergarten or Montessori—a young woman who in personality, character and intelligence would be a congenial member of our family group—perhaps a college girl or a kindergartner? It is so important what kind of a person is with the children."

A New Vocation.

This is a request that comes repeatedly to the school. Here is a vocation for young women of education and personality that, instead of being overcrowded, is calling for workers; where the environment is that of a beautiful home, with often opportunities for travel, and an income above the average for teaching and superior to the usual commercial position. Such a young woman must be, of course, adaptable, resourceful, agreeable. She will be gaining lasting friends and acquiring experiences that will fit her the better for her own home-making, instead of being useless or a handicap. There may be some problems of adjustment to work out between her and the mother, but the mother who appreciates the importance of such an assistant will also appreciate the importance of such a young woman's own social and personal life.

The school has been making a study of this special vocational field from the standpoint of the mother and of her assistant, and a conference is being arranged to meet at the school in the early Fall, to which both mothers and assistants will be invited for a discussion of the problems of their relationship, and how this relationship can be made of the greatest mutual satisfaction and benefit.

Learn to Do by Doing.

The School of Mothercraft has applied to the vocation of mothering and home-making the principles of the new pedagogy. Students "learn to do by doing." For this reason the school has had its own kindergarten and residential nursery. Here, in the daily life with little children, these young women learn by experience as well as by class discussions how to take care of little children, as well as the baby—how to "manage" children. They learn to sympathize with childhood ways and interests, and to understand a little child, by being with the child through many hours of the day, as well as by reading the comments of psychologists.

They learn the close relation between the child's physical condition and his disposition, between the routine of his daily physical needs and the development of his character. While they are learning how to cook the cereal for three-year-old André's breakfast or buy a chop for his dinner they are also learning responsibility; in serving his supper they are learning not only how to feed children but how to live with them and how to make these daily functions a time of pleasure, beauty, and comradeship; in utilizing his help in clearing away the table and doing the dishes they are also learning patience and how to develop self-reliance in the child.

Work of the School Unique.

So far as the work of the school is unique, it is in these three points: the comprehensiveness of the training, which takes the child as the basis of its curriculum and so includes every phase of problem which the mother or mother-substitute will need, including biology, eugenics, child hygiene, child psychology, kindergarten, and the beginnings of home making and home economics. Again, in its methods: its practical work with the children, providing for these students guidance under trained instructors instead of leaving the young mother to experiment alone on her own firstborn.

And lastly: While schools of domestic science have trained women to meet the problems of food, shelter, and clothing, kindergarten schools have specialized in psychology and character training after the age of babyhood; hospital training has prepared at length for the care of the sick, this school has assembled and synthesized and simplified all these, and more. It provides an introduction to these problems of the home, the mother, the child, and the start for intelligent progress. Its students must have had at least a high school training, and some of them are college graduates.

The word "mothercraft" is far from new in England. The idea of such a course of training is still older, having first been organized there about twenty years ago. At present there are no less than a dozen such special schools there, and some of the girls' high schools have a nursery or mothercraft course, with their own resident children and kindergarten. Years before England began, such a school had been developed in Germany.

WANTS TO BE EUGENIC BRIDE

New York City Girl Offers to Accept Colorado Health Offer.

Special to The New York Times.

DENVER, Col., Nov. 2.—Miss Mary Brown of 142 Ninetieth Street, New York City, a nurse, is one of more than fifty young women from all parts of the United States who have appealed by letter to Dr. Paul S. Hunter, Secretary of the State Board of Health, to be the feminine half of a eugenic marriage, which the board is arranging. M. D. Bowen of Denver is the only man who has volunteered and Miss Brown said in her letter that if Mr. Bowen could meet a few requirements that she would impose she is willing to become a eugenic bride and live as the Health Board directed.

Miss Brown says Bowen may consider himself a martyr, but as she is interested in eugenics she will not regard it as martyrdom. A teacher of Onondaga County, New York, wishes to remain incognito, describes herself as a "progressive Western woman living in the East; good looking, of good figure and perfectly capable of doing all things wanted of her by a eugenic marriage." She is a teacher of physical training in a New York State High School.

TAKES UP PRENATAL CARE.

New Angle to the Battle to Reduce Infant Mortality.

Coincidental with the proposal to establish a chain of restaurants and rest stations throughout this city for the proper care and instruction of expectant mothers, the Children's Bureau of the Department of Labor at Washington has issued a monograph on "Prenatal Care," giving interesting vital statistics in relation to preventable infant mortality. The monograph is the first of a series of bulletins to be issued by the bureau on the care of children. The reasons for its publication are set forth by Miss Julia C. Lathrop, Chief of the bureau, in her letter transmitting the monograph to Secretary Wilson.

"A preliminary survey of the field prescribed by law for the bureau's investigations," she says, "showed at once the urgency of the question of infant mortality. The United States Census Bureau estimates that 300,000 babies less than 1 year old died last year in this country, and it is authoritatively stated that at least half of these deaths were needless. Accordingly the bureau's first field inquiry is upon the subject of infant mortality. The studies preliminary thereto have induced us to begin our study with this monograph on prenatal care, for consideration of which the following statement is significant:

"The latest reports of the Bureau of the Census on Mortality Statistics show that slightly more than 42 per cent. of the infants dying under one year of age in the registration area in 1911 did not live to complete the first month of life, and that of this 42 per cent. almost seven-tenths died as a result of conditions existing before they were born, or of injury and accident at birth. Of those that lived less than one week, about 83 per cent. died of such causes, and of the number that lived less than one day, 94 per cent. died of these causes.

"Thus the Children's Bureau was drawn inevitably to begin its contemplated series of monographs on the care of children by a statement regarding prenatal care of the mother and child. The preparation of such a statement has been requested by the National Congress of Mothers and by members of her representative bodies of women. It has been written by Mrs. Max West of the staff of the bureau, from the standpoint of a woman who has university training, experience in Government research, and who is herself the mother of a family of young children. It has been prepared after careful study of the literature on the subject. It has been read and criticised by a large number of well-known physicians and nurses and by many mothers. To mention by name all those to whom the bureau is indebted for valuable aid in its preparation would be impossible, but special appreciation may be expressed of the generous assistance of Dr. J. Morris Slemons, Professor of Obstetrics and Gynecology in the University of California.

"This monograph is addressed to the average mother of this country. There is no purpose to invade the field of the medical or nursing professions, but rather to furnish such statements regarding hygiene and normal living as every mother has a right to possess in the interest of herself and her children. A standard of life for the family high enough to permit a woman to conserve her strength for her family, if she knows the facts essential to her guidance, is necessarily taken for granted. The attempt is made here to present some of the most important of these facts."

WOMEN IN THE HOME.

Only 19.5 Per Cent. Are Single and 20 Per Cent. Self-Supporting.

To the Editor of The New York Times:

Relative to Miss Elizabeth Newport Hepburn's criticism of Mrs. John Martin's "Back to the Home" movement, it is interesting to consult the last United States Census to find out just how many women are out of the home. It tells us that we old maids are a vastly overrated group, constantly exploited by the suffragists.

The census informs us that of the women of 21 years of age and over in this country only 19.5 per cent. are single; of the women of 30 years of age, only 10 per cent. are unwed; and (evidently while there's life there's hope!) of the women of 60 years and over, only 6 per cent. are unappropriated blessings.

"But," cry our suffrage friends, "how about the many married women who support themselves?"

Well, as to this, let's consult the last report on statistics of women at work, issued by the Department of Commerce and Labor. It informs us that while 90 per cent. of the males in the United States of 16 years and over are wage earners, only 20 per cent. of the females of 16 years and over are engaged in any kind of gainful occupation.

The great majority of women are already "back to the home." Those of us who are single and self-supporting are in a hopeless minority, so far as any control of the ballot box is concerned. This is a married woman's country. MARJORIE DORMAN.

New York, April 6, 1914.

April 7, 1914

WIFE'S SAVINGS NOT HERS.

Court Rules Money She Accumulated by Economy Belongs to Husband.

That the savings of a wife accumulated from money given to her by her husband for household expenses do not belong to her was decided yesterday by Justice Blackmar in the Supreme Court, Brooklyn, in a suit brought by Charles S. Montgomery, Jr., against his wife, Mrs. Emma Lee Montgomery, and the Williamsburg Savings Bank. By the decision of the court Montgomery recovers $618.12, which his wife saved from his earnings and deposited to their joint account.

Mr. and Mrs. Montgomery had a disagreement last November, and when he went to the bank to draw out the money deposited by his wife he found that she had placed a stop order on the account. Then he brought suit. In his opinion, the court said:

"Our laws have not yet reached the point of holding that property which is the result of the husband's earnings and the wife's savings become their joint property. No matter how careful and prudent has been the wife, if the money originally belonged to the husband it is still his property, unless the evidence show that it was a gift to the wife. In this most important of all partnerships there is no partnership property."

December 16, 1914

SHE BUYS HARDWARE NOW.

The Dealer Has to Accommodate Himself to Women's Ways.

One of the things that is troubling the retail hardware dealer today is the fact that women are becoming the principal buyers in his line, just as they already are in all other lines, for a hardware store today carries every kind of utensil and tool that is used around the house, and women nowadays are the principal buyers of such things. Formerly hardware stores were all for men, carpenters, mechanics, machinists, farmers, lumbermen, and the like of husky humanity. So the average hardware dealer changes somewhat slowly, and only as he realizes that unless he adapts himself to new conditions women will go to the drug store for scissors and shears, to the five-and-ten cent stores for tackhammers and icepicks, to the jeweler for silver-plated ware, and to the department store for household and kitchen utensils.

Women as purchasers are a different proposition from men, inasmuch as they demand the very pink of courtesy and attention, and will not put up with those easy-going ways which characterized the old-fashioned dealer. They expect clean, bright stores, the very latest novelties, and are "sharks" on bargains, though, contrary to the usual belief, they buy, in the long run, on quality, namely, on goods that give satisfaction. They are rather argumentative, though they object to being answered back, and have to be handled with gloves, since, being sensitive creatures, they are apt "to fly the coop." Most of all, however, with them shopping is a matter of personality, and those dealers who get their liking because of courteous, fair treatment are the most sure of retaining their trade.

July 16, 1916

NEW DIVORCE CANON FAILS OF ADOPTION

Episcopalian Deputies Refuse to Condemn Remarriage of "Innocent Party."

DEFEATED BY LAY MEMBERS

Majority of the Clergy Favored the Change, Including Those from Chicago and Reno.

Special to The New York Times.

ST. LOUIS, Oct. 14.—The House of Deputies of the Protestant Episcopal Church today rejected a proposed canon forbidding the remarriage of persons who had been divorced. The law of the Church permitting its clergy to solemnize the marriage of the innocent party still stands. The defeat of the measure followed a heated debate carried over from Thursday. It was due to non-concurrence of the two orders, clerical and lay, of the lower house. The House of Bishops merely discussed the matter this afternoon in its secret conclave, for in the circumstances any action on their part at this time would be without force. The Church stands committed to the existing status for another three years.

The vote in the House was taken by dioceses and missionary districts, each of the sixty-eight dioceses being entitled to a ballot for each order, and the districts, of which there are twenty-four, to half a vote in each division. Each diocese is represented by four clergymen and four laymen, and the districts by one in each order. The results of the roll call were as follows:

Clerical—Yeas, 37 dioceses and 3½ districts; total, 40½ votes. Nays, 23 dioceses and 1¾ missionary districts; total, 24¾; majority for the measure, 15¾ votes.

In the lay order there were recorded in favor of the canon 28 votes from the dioceses and 1 from the districts, making 29 and against it were 32 dioceses and three-fourths of a missionary district, giving 32¾ votes in the clerical order. Thus, the defeat of the canon was compassed by only 3¾ votes in a single order. A few of the dioceses and districts were not represented.

The clergy, who are obliged to decide every few days whether or not they will give "the sanction of the Church" to the weddings of those who have been freed of their matrimonial partners by law, showed deep feeling throughout the discussion. The Southern dioceses were solid for the existing regulation, and the East was divided. The North and the West, where there has been much agitation in recent years for divorce reform were almost unanimously for the new canon. Chicago once denounced as the divorce mart, voted for the proposed restriction, as did all the dioceses of Illinois. The missionary district of Nevada, which includes Reno, voted yea.

The deputation from the Diocese of New York was divided. Of the four clerical deputies on the affirmative were Dean William M. Grosvenor of the Cathedral of St. John the Divine, the Rev. Dr. Ernest M. Stires, the rector of St. Thomas's, and the Rev. Dr. Leighton Parks of St. Bartholomew's. Voting "no" was the Rev. Dr. Henry Lubeck of Zion and St. Timothy. Of the lay deputies from New York, Francis Lynde Stetson and Justice Vernon M. Davis were for the canon and Edmund L. Baylies and Stephen Baker against it.

October 15, 1916

FOREIGNERS' WIVES LOSE.

Ruling Excludes American Women from Citizenship.

"An American woman married to a foreigner cannot regain her citizenship so long as the marital relation legally exists," was the statement made at the Board of Elections yesterday by S. Howard Cohen, Chief Clerk of the Board, who wrote Attorney General Merton E. Lewis for a ruling in the matter.

Mr. Cohen asked: "Can an American woman, married to an unnaturalized foreigner residing in the State of New York, obtain her own naturalization, although her husband does not choose to be naturalized?" Second, "Can the said woman cast her vote on the strength of her American birth without being naturalized, although married to the said unnaturalized foreigner?"

Attorney General Lewis, in reply, referred to Chapter 2,534, Section 3, of the United States statutes, enacted March 2, 1907, which provides that an American woman who marries a foreigner shall take the nationality of her husband. He further stated: "Expatriation may be a heavy penalty imposed for the privilege of contracting marriage with a foreigner, but when viewed from the standpoint of our national welfare it becomes the dictate of necessity. Inasmuch as citizenship is a requisite qualification for the exercise of suffrage, a woman married to a foreigner cannot vote until her husband has been naturalized, or she is restored to citizenship upon the legal termination of the marital relations, as provided in Chapter 2,534, Section 3, of the United States statutes."

January 31, 1918

Working Women's Protective Union.

MEETING AT COOPER INSTITUTE—SPEECHES BY JUDGE DALY, REV. WM. H. MILBURN, AND OTHERS.

Last evening, a mass meeting on behalf of the working women was held at the Cooper Institute. The hall was well filled with a very respectable and intelligent audience, among whom were numbers of the working women. Hon. CHARLES P. DALY presided. He said the members of the committee had submitted to him a constitution, which should attract the attention and admiration of all who were interested in the welfare and success of the 30,000 working women now employed in all branches of business in this great commercial City. They had more to struggle with than those of the so-called stronger sex, and the object of this society was to protect them from the frauds of designing men who would take from them a portion of their small earnings, or treat them in any way that was not right. He was astonished to hear that married women of comfortable means took employment to supply them with additional spending-money, and thought it necessary that they should leave the field for those who actually need it. And when they knew the great harm they were doing, he was satisfied they would do so. During the afternoon, MYNDERT VAN SCHAICK, Esq., had called on him and presented him with a check for $50 for the society. He hoped others would follow the good example. His speech was received with much enthusiasm. At its close Miss TERESA ESMONDE read "The Song of the Workingwomen," written by Mrs. ANN S. STEPHENS. At its close a practical workingwoman exhibited a number of articles made for various large mercantile houses, explained the amount of work they required and the prices paid. The following are a few of them:

A pair of drawers made of white cotton drilling, 1,800 stitches, sewed on the machine, and well made. Completely finished with buckles, buttonholes, straps and strings.

The woman who made these drawers was a smart operator, and could finish four pair per day, working from 7 A. M. until 9 P. M., receiving 4 1-6 cents per pair, or 16⅔ cents for her day's labor; resting, she says, long enough to make herself a cup of tea and eat a piece of bread.

Another very large pair of canton flannel drawers, 2,000 stitches, done by hand. Double seams, felled; with eyelets, buttonholes, buttons, stays and strings. The workingwoman to furnish her own thread—a rule adopted by employers since the price of a spool of cotton has risen from four to eight and ten cents.

This woman, the mother of three children, was very poor, and came to the rooms of the Working Women's Protective Union, No. 4, New-Chambers-street, where she threw down the work, saying she had been working on these drawers for seven months, and could not work any longer for the price paid. Said she—"I may as well starve without work as to work and starve at the same time." An inquiry revealed the fact, that the wealthy firm who employed her paid five and a half cents per pair for these drawers, of which she could make two pairs per day, remarking, "If I get to bed about daylight, and sleep two or three hours, I feel satisfied."

A coarse flannel army shirt, large size, made by hand-sewing. Collar, wristbands and gussets put on with double rows of stitching all round. The seams are felled, three buttonholes, buttons and stays, requiring upward of 2,000 stitches.

The woman who made this garment was sixty years of age, and too deaf to go to the stores for orders. She has worked on these shirts since the war broke out, receiving 7 cents each—one of them being a good day's work for her. Younger women might make two or perhaps three in twelve hours, furnishing their own thread. This old lady occupied, with another woman, a damp, dark basement, where she strained her eyes in the daytime, and sewed by the light of her neighbor's lamp during the evening. At the end of the week her net earnings, after paying for needles and thread, amounted to thirty-nine cents in "currency."

A fine white cotton shirt, with a fine linen plaited bosom, nicely stitched and well made throughout, containing 11,500 sewing machine stitches, six buttonholes, felled seams, &c., &c.

Two of these shirts are finished each day by the operator, who employs nearly every moment of her time, finds her own thread, and receives for the garment sixteen cents each, or thirty-two cents for more than twelve hours' labor. These shirts sell for $3 to $3 50 in the retail stores. Their total cost to the employer may be summed up as follows:

Three yards fine muslin, at 33 cents	99 cents.
Half-yard fine linen	38 cents.
Labor and thread	16 cents.
Buttons	6 cents.
Total cost	$1 59

Thus giving the merchant who so crushes the poor workingwomen a profit of $1 91 on each shirt. Numerous other articles of gentlemen's and ladies' apparel were exhibited and explained, and were in some instances even worse, if possible, than those given above.

Rev. WM. H. MILBURN being introduced, paid a glowing compliment to PETER COOPER, Esq., for his generosity, and thanked God that we had among us some few at least who would help to alleviate the sufferings of the poor. He had often pitied the workingwomen of London and other cities of the Old World, and had prided himself that here in New-York things were different; that in this chivalric country woman received the wages and treatment she was entitled to, but that fond idea had been suddenly destroyed, and he found that we, of the eighteenth century, had in this matter grown worse instead of better. Nearly three-quarters of the New-York merchants had done these women justice, but there were some few who would wring from them their miserable pittance of 16, 20 or 24 cents, "and then go, God knows where, to spend it." He drew a vivid picture of a poor, sick woman, lying in rags on the bare floor in a barren room, the mother crouching over the few remaining embers of fire, and a beautiful sister working steadily, desperately, for the trifling sum she could earn. On their support, can you, said he, with this picture before you, wonder that sometimes a star drops from Heaven and is lost, lost forever, here and hereafter. He asked the ladies who wanted sewing done to send to the rooms of the Association, No. 4 New Chambers-street, that a good and competent woman would be sent them, and he urged them to pay the woman when the work was done, and not make her call two or three times for her money, for it might be she needed that money to buy bread. His speech was listened to with eager attention, and frequently interrupted by applause.

Miss ESMONDE then read HOOD's song of the shirt, after which Mr. BEACH gave an interesting statement of the proceedings of the society since its commencement, and the great good it had done; he urged the citizens generally to help them. At its close he was presented with a beautiful basket of flowers—a present from the ladies.

JAMES T. BRADY, who was to have spoken, was delayed in Washington, and consequently could not attend. Letters were received from Judges ROOSEVELT and KIRTLAND, and numerous other distinguished gentlemen, expressing their interest in the movement, and wishes for its success.

A vote of thanks was then tendered to Judge DALY, and the meeting adjourned.

March 22, 1864

OUR WORKING CLASSES.

How the Female Portion of Our Population Earns a Living—Occupations Open to Women—Rates of Remuneration, &c.

Woman's field of labor in this part of the country has been very greatly enlarged during the past eight or ten years; and it is annually extending to embrace occupations, trades and professions heretofore considered as closed to the sex.

This extension has been and is less the result of the long-continued agitation of the woman's rights question than the inevitable consequence of the increasing excess in numbers of the females over the males in the more populous States. In all of the New-England, two of the Middle, and one of the Southern States, the females of all ages are in excess of the males to the aggregate of 100,000; and this excess is annually increasing, and doubtless will continue to increase.

Census reports reveal the fact that in all cases this excess is confined to persons aged between 15 and 30 years. There are more male than female children from 1 to 10 years of age, and more men than women from 40 years upward. But the excess of females from 15 to 30 over males of the same ages is several times greater than the aggregate excess of all ages. In other words, there are, in the New-England and Middle States, for instance, a quarter of a million young women who must support themselves, and who cannot reasonably look forward to any matrimonial alliance which will relieve them of this inevitable necessity. In the State of New-York alone there are 132,837 of this class of females who have this, to them, dreary prospect in view. And further, two-thirds of this number are located in the several large cities, which go to make up this Metropolis. The census statistics show that the excess of females is invariably confined wholly to the large cities and manufacturing, rather than to the rural and agricultural districts. Basing our inquiries on these well-established figures and facts, we have lately made inquiry into the number and condition of the working-women of this City, and find that there are hardly less than 75,000 women in this Metropolis—including Brooklyn, Jersey City and Hoboken—who are wholly dependent on their own labor for support, and engaged in various trades at wages averaging but little more than half that paid to men.

The industrial and social reform which is throwing all occupations open to the industry of woman is of very modern origin. It is only a few years since that custom and society prohibited respectable young women from standing in stores, acting as clerks, or working at trades; and happily the reform is not yet completed, but is daily enlarging the sphere and liberty of woman. All the lighter trades and manufactures are generally open at this time to women, as are some of the professions also. We find on examination that women are regularly and largely employed in this City in the following occupations and at about the following average rate of wages:

TABLE OF OCCUPATIONS FOR WOMEN AND WAGES PAID THEM.

	Per week.
Actresses	$15 00
Artificial-flower workers	8 00
Artists	—
Ballet-dancers	6 00
Book-folders	8 00
Book-sewers	8 00
Book-binders	10 00
Compositors	10 00
Copyists	6 00
Designers	12 00
Editors	18 00
Envelope-makers	7 00
Florists	7 00
Fur-trimmers	8 00
Hair-dressers	8 00
Hatters	8 00
Hoop-skirt makers	7 00
Jewelers	9 00
Lecturers	—
Mantua-makers	7 00
Milliners	7 00
Paper-box makers	5 00
Paper-collar makers	5 00
Photograph mounters	6 00
Physicians	—
Saleswomen	8 00
School-teachers	10 00
Sculptors	—
Seamtresses	4 50
Servants, household, (with board)	2 50
Shoefitters	9 00
Silver-burnishers	8 00
Singers	—
Telegraph operators	10 00
Toy-painters	8 00
Umbrella-makers	7 00
Wood-engravers	10 00

It is impossible, of course, to fix the weekly income of those engaged in purely professional work, as artists, physicians, lecturers, sculptors and singers; but it is well known that there are a large number of ladies who make large incomes in the pursuit of these professions. Ladies in charge of literary and fashion papers receive handsome salaries of from $40 to $50 per week. One fashion paper published here pays its literary conductors, who are all ladies, about $100 per week, and more than that amount for literary matter sent by lady contributors. There are about ten practicing physicians of the gentler sex in New-York, all of whom make handsome livings, and there are one or two schools for the education of others. Cooper Institute maintains for the benefit of young ladies an admirable school of design, and artists and sculptors of ability have graduated there, and are now doing well in pursuance of their professions in this City, while numerous designers educated there have found places in silverware, furniture and jeweler establishments in various parts of the City and country.

The churches and theatres and opera-houses give employment to a large number of choir and chorus singers at remunerative rates.

Although we would encourage no more young women to seek support and independence in the great cities, it is not to be denied that there is a demand for their labor in all these branches of manufacture and other occupations, particularly in the higher grades requiring skill, experience and general knowledge. This is true in spite of the fact that the rates are low and apparently unremunerative. The women are wanted—in fact are preferred to the men—at the wages they receive. The women cannot understand why the man's labor should be worth more than their's, and complain of this inequality, but they should remember that they are now engaged in driving young men from many of the occupations which they fill, and until they can prove their fitness for the positions, they can only succeed in gaining their places by underbidding the men. When men thus underbidden by the women seek, as they will, other fields, the wages for female labor must of necessity advance with the increased demand.

The wages now received will not support a young lady in very elegant style, but, as is the case with the great majority of them, they have only themselves to take care of; they may live comfortably and independently on their wages. Good board and comfortable lodging in respectable localities can be obtained from $4 to $5 per week; and the majority of young ladies with their peculiar tact at economical arrangement can dress neatly, not gaudily, on the balance.

Most of the occupations named, excepting those of the seamstress and household servants, are really desirable for young women. They are light, pleasant, not too confining, easily learned, and do not by any means, as many suppose, throw them too much before an impertinent public gaze. Very few of the immense throng which continually crowds A. T. STEWART's Tenth-street store suspect the existence and labor within it of nearly eight hundred young women engaged in a dozen different kinds of manufacture. The workshops of the principal manufacturers of this City are usually separated from the show and salesrooms, and admission to the former is obtained only by special permission of the employers. The privacy of the employes is thus obtained. Employers are careful also to guard their female employes from insult or rudeness on the part of their workmen, knowing that the reputation of their establishment depends in a great measure on that of their employes; and thus a protection is thrown around the industrious young woman by the industry itself. The female hands in a manufacturing establishment are no more exposed to publicity than they would be if at school; and not more liable to insult or annoyance on their way to and from school.

There are from 3,000 to 3,500 women engaged in the several book-publishing houses of this City in the various branches of "book-folding," "book-sewing" and "book-binding." "Book-folding" is a business which, when done by machinery, is not unlike sewing by machinery, but it is far less laborious, whether done by hand or machine, than plain sewing. It requires a great deal less skill, time and strength to fold a book than to make a shirt or jacket or a pair of pants, and the price which is received for the folding of the book is greater than for making the articles of wearing apparel. The sewing or stitching of these folded leaves, done by hand, is even lighter labor than the folding. It is accomplished with a large needle two or three inches long with an eye capable of holding the largest twine thread, and hence the eye's sight is untaxed and the fingers uncramped. Book-binding is more arduous, requiring greater skill and a longer apprenticeship to learn the trade, but it is better paid than the other two branches of the business.

Type-setting and telegraphy are at this time favorite occupations with young women, and numbers are learning these branches of industry. Among the results of the late strikes among the working classes was the establishment of a school of telegraphy, and the opening of one or two printing offices to female compositors. The first is connected with the Cooper Institute, and now numbers a large force of pupils, who promise in time to become good operatives. One of the training-schools for female compositors is at the establishment of JOHN A. GRAY & GREEN. It has been in operation six weeks, and during that time fifteen young women have graduated, and are now employed in the composing-room. Thirty-eight pupils are still in training. Large numbers have been dismissed in consequence of a lack of knowledge of the English language, punctuation, &c.

Of late—indeed, within the past four or five years—the number of shop girls or saleswomen in the stores on Broadway have greatly, almost visibly, increased. It is already evident that young men must eventually give up their places in this line to young women, as completely as they have done in Germany and France; and the father who places his son behind the counter of a dry goods, lace, or boot and shoe store, commits a great mistake, and does his son a grievous wrong. Parents are beginning to see that it is the daughters who ought properly to be apprenticed to such positions. The occupation of saleswoman is one to which young ladies have no other objection than its publicity; but those who have occupied these positions for years say that this publicity is really a protection, and that, contrary to their expectations when first entering upon it, it increases the outward show of respect on the part of customers.

The saleswomen of New-York are no longer exclusively foreigners, of Hebrew, German or French descent. One no longer sees on Broadway only numberless German Jewesses and an occasional French or Italian face behind the shop counters. American ladies of refinement and culture are found in almost every respectable store, and every year adds to their number.

The not very complimentary notion which once generally prevailed, that they were employed for their attractiveness rather than their usefulness, has been exploded; and they are coming to be recognized as the most valuable and desirable of saleswomen. More than a year ago Messrs. A. T. STEWART & Co. began to introduce saleswomen in various branches of their trade, and eventually propose to have only females in the whole of their magnificent structure on Broadway and Tenth street.

There are also employed in the various restaurants in this city a great many young women, but it is not the most popular nor the most respectable employment. Nor is it remunerative. From $5 to $6 is the maximum of wages. In fact it may be said with truth that the least respectable of employments—including ballet dancing, &c.—are the worst paid; and young women entering these occupations run great risks of losing reputation as well as being half-paid.

The worst paid, hardest worked, and most oppressed classes of workingwomen in New-York are those engaged in the branches of trade usually considered most appropriate for them—such as seamstresses, mantua-makers and milliners. There are a few needlewomen—skilled workers in embroidery and braiding—who gain a comfortable livelihood; but for every one of these there are ten plain sewers who live a life of want and misery in the vain effort to eke out a living at inadequate wages. The mantua-makers and milliners—employed in the larger establishments and selected because possessing a certain skill and taste—are underpaid, and, in fact, the needle is the worst instrument with which women can dig their way in the world. The reason that this labor, for which they are seemingly best fitted, is of all others the worst paid, is an obvious one. The supply of this kind of labor has always been greater than the demand. Every woman suddenly thrown on her own resources naturally thinks she can make the most money by the application of the needle, the only implement in the use of which her previous education has made her skillful, and she at once offers herself in that branch of manufacture with which she is best acquainted. Five women apply at clothing establishments for plain sewing where one applies to make umbrellas, shoes, or hats, or fold or sew books, or to trim furs or make artificial flowers. The consequence is that this branch of labor is over-supplied, and wages are kept down. The seamstresses underbid each other for work at which they can only postpone starvation. The hard-hearted employers are blamed by sympathetic persons, but it is really the poor impractical unfortunates—doubly unfortunate in being impractical as well as poor—who are at fault. They should turn to less crowded and more remunerative employments. "But these have to be learned by long apprenticeship," is suggested in reply. Very true; the new occupation must be learned, and in order to make a certain and ample income from it, it must be learned thoroughly. But any woman of average intelligence can earn in learning book-folding and sewing, envelope, paper-box and collar making, or as a saleswoman, more money than she can possibly earn as a seamstress unless of the most excellent and accomplished kind. Almost one-half of the working women of this City are now employed in this unremunerative occupation, instead of seeking those which are better paid.

March 17, 1869

WOMEN'S WAGES.

It is a complaint so common as to be monotonous, with those who are seeking to reform social evils, that women receive much less payment for their labor than men. We think there is less foundation for this reproach than appears on the surface. In certain fields of employment, women crowd the market with half-trained labor, and in consequence their wages fall to a very low point. They compete with one another. Employers pay less for their labor than for men's, because there are so many of their sex seeking that particular employment, and, of course, underbidding one another. Moreover, in many occupations, owing to

the chance of their marrying, to their physical weakness, and to their want of training, women are worth less than men.

No one who has not studied the habits of women of ordinary advantages can realize how inaccurate and careless their training is. This is often owing to the want of ambition, or the neglect of their parents. There is in this City, for instance, a very respectable and useful calling for women—teaching in the public schools—by means of which salaries of from six hundred dollars to two thousand dollars can be earned. The City offers gratuitously a three years' course of careful and thorough training for this employment in the Normal

College. When a graduate has finished this course, she is immediately of more value in the market. Her salary will be probably double what it would be if she undertook to teach without the preliminary training. But we venture to say that seventy-five out of the hundred of those girls who graduate at the City schools, and who mean to be teachers, never enter the Normal College. The usual alleged reason is poverty. But when one remembers the numbers of poor families in New-England who deny themselves every luxury to give a boy a good education, one can easily understand that the cause of this neglect in this City is rather want of principle than want of means. The result is that this class of girls soon settle down into the ranks of poor teachers, or become shop-girls and seamstresses.

But even in these places, their want of any thoroughness and accuracy of training must at once depress their scale of payment. For a certain period, female assistants were employed in a well-known library and reading-room of this City. A gentleman had occasion to ask for a certain kind of encyclopedia. The young lady in charge had not the remotest idea what particular encyclopedias were in the reading-room, nor even of the character or subject of the journals and magazines. An intelligent office-boy in that position would have naturally made it his business to know thoroughly every book and paper in the room. Such a lad at once enters into successful competition with the young lady, and brings down her wages.

A few years ago, some of our job printers in New-York undertook to employ female compositors. To their dismay, they soon discovered that the New-York working girls did not know the English language well enough, or could not spell accurately enough, to make good compositors, and they were forced to send for Massachusetts female workers, or to have the work done in New-England.

We may appeal to the common experience of our lady readers if the female clerks in our dry-goods shops are not more inattentive and uncivil than the male. Such a fact alone (if it be general) would depress their wages as compared with men's. But such defects are merely the result of want of training. The French petty female shopkeepers and clerks are unsurpassed. And in this country, take the branches where women are carefully educated, and they compete successfully with the other sex. The teachers, for instance, prepared by our best female normal schools, and drilled in the "object system," are more in request for primary and other schools than male teachers. A young lady has been known to receive as high as $1,500 and $2,000 salary soon after graduating. A good Latin teacher in this City can earn her $2 50 per hour.

Again, in a lower kind of service, the pay is excellent. A fair female cook will earn $25 per month and her board, and a skillful one $50, which is better pay than men of the same class receive. We have known clever operators on shoe-sewing machines earn $50 a week; and many just trained on the ordinary sewing-machines will make from $1 to $2 per day. A raw Irish peasant girl will often earn in our families $15 per month, which, with board, is equivalent to nearly $400 per annum. In higher branches, there are many female "editors" earning their $4,000 or $5,000 per annum. The most successful women novelists enjoy a much larger income than this, and the female lecturers receive, in many instances, from $5,000 to $10,000 per annum. Women have no ground whatever for complaining of being "kept down" in the present day.

"HIGHER EDUCATION."

The sterner sex is not commonly supposed to take much interest in the "higher education" of the softer. The reason of course is that the male of our species values the female as he finds her companionable and agreeable to himself, and it is very doubtful whether in most cases her attractiveness in this respect is increased with an increase of intellectual culture beyond a certain point. Dr. Johnson observed, with his usual soundness and sententiousness: "A man is in general better pleased when there is a good dinner on the table than when his wife knows Greek." This is undoubtedly true, and most women try to adapt themselves to men. The minority of women who feel that they are not mere "helpmeets," actual or potential, but that they exist for their own sake and owe duties to themselves, reprehend this view as the outcome of sexual selfishness. It is to this minority that the efforts for higher education that are so marked a feature of contemporary culture are very largely due.

We may admit the selfishness of the common masculine view without thereby admitting that women are at present under-educated for their own usefulness or their own happiness. A distinguished German who visited this country a few years ago shrewdly remarked as the result of his observations that there was more culture among American women than among American men. Reflection will confirm the justice of this remark. If we count out men whose business it is to keep abreast of the modern movement in all that constitutes culture, the preponderance is in favor of women is very marked. Matthew Arnold's definition of culture as a knowledge of the best that has been said and thought in the world is rather narrow, because it is quite evident that the critic was thinking of literature alone. If we broaden it so as to include an appreciation of the best that has been done in the world in all arts there can be no dispute that this appreciation is far more diffused among American women than among American men. For one man in ordinary business, or even professional, life who takes a real interest in the things of the mind, and has any conscientiousness in his desire to "admire rightly;" there are at least ten women. In literature and in music the proportion is probably much greater. American men who are themselves distinctly interested in culture do not appreciate this if they live in cities like New-York and Boston, for the reason that they are tolerably sure to come to know a considerable number of other men like-minded. But any publisher who has tried to educate the public taste, and any musician who has made

a similar endeavor in his own art, would tell the male dilettanti that if he relied upon their support he would go into bankruptcy. It is to the women even of the cities that the best in literature and in art makes its most hopeful appeal. Of course, this remark does not apply to "society" in the esoteric sense in which society means the small collection of people who make a business of pleasure, having no other business. In this country at least, society in this sense is entirely frivolous and uncultivated, as it is also in England, according to English observers. But the wives, and much more the daughters, of Americans who work for their living are almost sure to be the superiors of the men in general culture. The difference is more obvious in small towns than in large cities. It is quite possible to find American villages in which there is not a man who knows the difference between good and bad in any art, and in which there are a dozen or a score of women capable of this discrimination.

The reason for this difference is not far to seek. It is an old saying that this country is alone both in having no "leisure class" and in having a "leisure sex." To many young American women such culture as they have attained is not merely a superficial accomplishment, to be paraded in talk, but it is the very substance of their being. Sympathy, however, is even more necessary to women in the pursuit of any branch of knowledge than it is to men. A scholarly man, dropped into a remote community in which nobody shares his tastes or takes any interest in his pursuits, must be an exceptional man if he does not allow his scholarship to rust. Much more forlorn is the fate of a cultivated woman who marries an uncultivated man, as the great majority of cultivated American women are forced to do for lack of cultivated American men to marry. The husband, if he be an average American, is a well-disposed person, but he cherishes a tacit contempt for those things that his wife knows and he does not know, upon the ground that there is "no money in them;" so that she gets no sympathy in the quarter to which she must look for sympathy. If she be not naturally her husband's intellectual superior, her studies have made her a better equipped and more highly civilized human being. She is shut up to the alternatives of developing her intellectual life by herself, or of permitting it to die out. This is a dismal and to many women a tragical choice. Many thousands of American women have had to make it. So long as this is the common experience, it can hardly be said that there is any urgent demand for the higher education of American women.

MISS WILLARD

Well-Known Temperance Worker

A SKETCH OF HER BUSY LIFE

Frances E. Willard, social reformer and leader among the advocates of temperance, was born Sept. 29, 1839, in the village of Churchville, near Rochester, N. Y., of Puritan parentage. Her girlhood was passed on the banks of the Rock River, Wisconsin, in a wild environment of wood and prairie. Forest Home was the name of her father's cottage there.

Early in 1858 the family removed to Evanston, Ill., the seat of the Northwestern University, where Mr. Willard became a partner in the Chicago banking firm of Preston, Willard & Kean. Previous to this time Miss Willard attended the Milwaukee Female College, founded by Catharine Beecher, and in 1859 was graduated from the Northwestern University, at Evanston. Three years later she was made Professor of Natural Science in that institution, and subsequently she was called to the Pittsburg Female College. In 1866 she became Principal of Genesee Wesleyan Seminary, at Lima, N. Y., remaining there two years.

Studied in Foreign Cities.

In 1868-70, Miss Willard traveled through Europe and the East. She studied in Paris, Berlin, and Rome, and visited nearly every European capital. She also traveled in Palestine and Egypt. In Paris she studied in the College of France and the Petit Sorbonne, attending lectures by Guizot and other noted men. While abroad she wrote for The New York Independent, Harper's Monthly, The Christian Union, and various Chicago journals. From 1871 to 1874 she was Professor of Aesthetics in Northwestern University and Dean of the Woman's College, where she developed her system of self-government.

It was in 1874 that Miss Willard gave up her profession to identify herself with the Woman's Christian Temperance Union, serving as Corresponding Secretary of the National organization till 1879, and since that date as its President. Of her work a writer recently said in The Ram's Horn: "Her marvelous faculty for organizing developed, and made itself manifest. She purposed to herself to visit and speak in every town in the United States which numbered 10,000 inhabitants, afterward including many of 5,000, organizing and energizing the Woman's Christian Temperance Union in nearly every town which she visited. For ten years she averaged one public meeting a day, writing letters and articles, planning work while in transit between towns at which she spoke. In 1879 she was made President of the National Woman's Christian Temperance Union, and her skillful management and unprecedented travels throughout America have given it

the unique position it holds in the world to-day. The remarkable feature of her work is that she manifests equal capacity with pen, voice, and in administration."

On the death of her brother, Oliver A. Willard, in 1879, she succeeded him as the editor of The Chicago Evening Post. Since 1882 she has been a member of the Executive Committee of the Prohibition Party. In 1886 she accepted the leadership of the White Cross movement in her unions, which have obtained chiefly through her exertions enactments in twelve States for the protection of women. In 1888 she was made President of the American Branch of the International Council of Women and of the World's Christian Temperance Union.

After the foundation of the World's Christian Temperance Union, which was a child of Miss Willard's brain, her next great idea was to issue an immense polyglot petition, having signatures from people of the chief countries of the world, and to present it to the heads of the different Governments. This great scheme was undertaken with enthusiasm by the branches of the Woman's Christian Temperance Union in their respective towns, cities, and countries, and 7,000,000 names and indorsements were secured. At the last meeting of the World's Union in Toronto, October, 1897, the petition, its various parts pasted together in ribbon form, covered the walls of the Massey Music Hall, the meeting place of the convention, on all sides, leaving many yards to spare.

Remains as a Moral Example.

The weak point in the petition, which the temperance worker learned after it was well under way, was that no nation could accept officially petitions from any but its own subjects. But it still remains, the workers in its behalf aver, one of the greatest moral examples of the world.

In 1892, on the death of her mother, Lady Henry Somerset invited Miss Willard to England, where, in Exeter Hall, she was welcomed by the united philanthropic societies of Great Britain. In June, 1894, she returned home and was welcomed at a great meeting in New York, at which a telegram was read announcing that the Ohio Wesleyan University had conferred upon her the title of LL. D.

Miss Willard found time, amid all her work, to publish several volumes, among them "Nineteen Beautiful Years," a tribute to a dead sister; "Woman and Temperance," "Glimpses of Fifty Years," "How to Win," "Woman in the Pulpit," and "A Great Mother," the latter a memorial of her mother.

Personally, Miss Willard was a woman of attractive presence. She possessed that unknown quantity often called magnetism, which was felt in her private conversation as well as in her public addresses. She had an equable temper, a ready wit, and a great fund of humor. Her travels and acquaintance with many people of many climes had given her a fund of information and an insight into human nature which made her always an entertaining companion. Her gift of language was great. The strong point in her character, which was brought into play in her temperance work, was her power of organization. The loss of her mother, Mme. Willard, a woman of strong character and unusual common sense, after a close companionship of over fifty years, was a great blow to Miss Willard, and her friends often thought that she never entirely recovered from the shock.

HITS AT WOMEN'S CLUBS

Robert E. Erskine Says They Serve No Good Purpose.

A large gathering of New York clubwomen were treated to a discussion of their favorite topic, the woman's club, yesterday morning at a meeting of the League for Political Education. The question for debate, as regularly put, was: "That club life offers to woman a desirable opportunity for social and intellectual development."

On the affirmative were Mrs. J. Woolsey Shepard, President of the Society of New England Women; Mrs. St. John Gaffney, President of the International Council of Women, and J. C. Pumpelly. On the negative were Mrs. Henry M. Sanders, President of the League for Political Education, an organization to which men belong, and which devotes itself to the political education of the people; Mrs. Almon Hensley, President of the Society for the Study of Life, and Robert Erskine Ely of Cambridge. Mr. Ely struck straight out from the shoulder, to use a technical term not to be found in women's club papers, and the fall of a pin could have been heard while he was speaking.

"Club life for women has come to have a technical meaning," said Mr. Ely. "Organizations like the Red Cross Society, the patriotic societies, and the League for Political Education do not mean to come under the head of women's clubs. These organizations have a specific work, men may belong to them, and they would not be admitted to the federations of women's clubs. The woman's club is composed exclusively of women, and generally of one class of women. They are women who have no particular occupation, women who have a certain amount of leisure, and they are not the women who have distinguished themselves in art, literature, or philanthropy. Women of this latter class would not have the time or strength, if they had the inclination, to join such organizations.

"One reason why the club is not good for women is that it is not socially enlarging. They meet in it women with the same interests as themselves, and for the best kind of enlargement there should be a meeting of people of different stations in life and different points of view. From an intellectual standpoint the club is not beneficial. Its members are naturally not experts, and subjects for discussion are given out without regard to the writer. Naturally in the preparation of papers there must be a resort to elementary histories and the encyclopedia, and members of the club spend time in listening to matter of this kind when they might be reading the valuable essays in which our reviews of to-day abound.

"Another bad effect is that the club gives women a false standard. The women poets, artists, and philanthropists, the women we delight to honor, have not come from the women's clubs. Such women feel that they can spend their time better in other ways, or treat the club with silent contempt. There is a call for women to do a larger public service. There is work for them in the educational system, in domestic science, where drudgery may be reduced to a minimum, and much of the work should be done by machine, and there is the municipal housekeeping, which is only the domestic housekeeping on a larger scale. This is work for women, but they cannot do it if their time and strength are given to other things."

"Did he really mean what he said?" gasped Mrs. Henry A. Stimson, a prominent Sorosian, as Mr. Ely closed his remarks. "Why, it wasn't true."

"Shall we vote on clubs as they are or as they might be?" asked Mrs. Frederick Nathan, President of the Consumers' League, and she did not vote at all when told to vote on clubs as they are.

The vote stood 25 in the affirmative and 18 in the negative.

STRIKE AGITATORS JAILED.

"Mother" Jones and Associates Arrested for Exhorting Miners, Locked Up in Parkersburg, West Va.

CLARKSBURG, West Va., June 21.— "Mother" Jones, Thomas Haggerty, William Morgan, Bernard Rice, George Baron, Andrew Lascavash, and William Blakely of the United Mine Workers from different parts of the country, who were arrested here last night, were taken to Parkersburg by four Deputy Marshals and lodged in jail. The miners have leased a plot of ground at Clarksburg for the purpose of holding meetings, and will make the arrest their chief defense. The arrest was made under an injunction issued a few days ago by Judge J. Jackson of the United States Circuit Court.

The amount of their bail has not been fixed, but the men were provided with sufficient funds to secure their own releases.

This is the first time that "Mother" Jones has been arrested, although she has been served with innumerable injunctions.

SETTLEMENT WORKERS HOLD ANNUAL SESSION

Miss Addams of Hull House, Chicago, Praises Immigrants.

Commissioner De Forest Says Danger to Tenement House Reform Is Past Because of Public Sentiment and Not the City Administration.

There was an enthusiastic gathering yesterday afternoon at Sherry's, Fifth Avenue and Forty-fourth Street, on the occasion of the annual meeting of the University Settlement. The announcement that Miss Jane Addams of Hull House, Chicago, was to deliver the principal address brought together a large audience, largely of women, so that a glance over the hall revealed a bewildering scene of millinery and the art of the dressmaker. There were so many attractive bonnets and gowns that it would seem as if the wearers could have no other thought in life than to obtain suitable raiment, but the eagerness of the listeners to catch every word said and the spontaneity with which they caught and applauded the more telling points in the addresses showed that the women were in earnest and had apparently devoted more time to the problems of sociology than to the latest creations of the Parisian modistes.

President Nicholas Murray Butler of Columbia presided, making a brief opening address. In referring to a recent description of Oxford as the home of lost causes, abandoned beliefs, and discredited heroes, he said that there could be no such criticism of the modern university, which to-day looks forward and strives to be of real usefulness in the building up of the social structure and the advancement of mankind in the way of education and the higher civilization.

"The University Settlement work," he said, "is a natural outgrowth of the methods of thought and action inculcated at the modern university. The University Settlement affords the means of developing reciprocal regard among the various classes of society and is of especial importance in a country where there are no artificial lines among the various classes of society, especially important in a country where within a single lifetime one may see many instances of progress from one extreme of society to the other."

"NOT ALMS, BUT A FRIEND."

Robert W. De Forest, Tenement House Commissioner and President of the Charity Organization Society, was the first speaker. He told a number of instances of what had been accomplished by the society and the department, and then said, in part:

"There is a profound desire among both men and women to aid in social service. 'Service' is, in fact, the keynote of twentieth century uplifting, and that it is the right keynote we may know from the emphasis which Christ laid upon it. Social service affords the right means of relief, rather than charity. 'Not alms, but a friend' is a good motto.

"The Settlement, as I understand it, gives the friend. The Charity Organization Society and the University Settlement should co-operate in their labors. I hope that this policy will be continued and that in every case either society will limit its work to what the other is not doing effectively. There is no limit to the good that may be accomplished. I wish to express my appreciation of the good work that the University Settlements in this city have done in the matter of tenement house reform.

"Last January we were face to face with the most dangerous crisis that tenement house reform has encountered since the present law was enacted. Now I believe that I may say that all danger is over, and the fact that the danger is past is due not to the city administration, but to the voice of public sentiment. And in arousing this effective public sentiment, all of the Settlements, both in Manhattan and in Brooklyn, have taken an active and useful part."

Mrs. R. Y. Fitzgerald, manager of the west side branch of the Settlement, 38 King Street, told of the work under her direction.

"When the west side house was opened," she said, "some members of the society doubted whether the location had been well chosen. The streets were wide, the houses old-fashioned and roomy, and there were large back yards, but although the neighborhood was different from the large houses in Rivington Street, plenty of work was found to be done. On one side there was an Irish and Irish-American population, none too thrifty, and with a good capacity to get into troble.

"On the other were Italians, with abundance of thrift, but imposed upon on all sides and needing a friendly hand and very frequently words of advice. The house maintains a kindergarten and a school of carpentry, and will soon introduce some forms of art work such as wood carving, lace making, and rug making. There are a number of families among the Italians near by who are skilled in these industries, but do not know where to find a market, and are, therefore, engaged in work that pays very much less than they could earn, if properly started and aided."

Mrs. James Speyer, President of the Woman's Auxiliary of the University Settlement, was unable to be present on account of the serious illness of a relative. Miss Ella Clark read the report of the Woman's Auxiliary. It dwelt especially on the work in kindergartens and the library. Dickens had proved the favorite author in the neighborhood. It was distinctly stated that a trip through the neighborhood would do away with any notions of race suicide.

Robert Hunter, in charge of the house at Eldridge and Rivington Streets, and head worker of the Settlement, made a short address in which he found warrant for the Settlement in proof of its accomplishment. As an example he suggested the case of a young physician who, having completed his medical course, had opened his office in the crowded section of the east side. Mr. Hunter told of several young men whose education had been started in the Settlement, who, because of this education, were abundantly able to live in other parts of the city, but who held that they were under such obligations that to move elsewhere would be like desertion. They realized what had been done for them and were willing to undergo the discomforts of the crowded district that they might be near by to aid in the work that had done so much for them.

MISS JANE ADDAMS.

Miss Jane Addams was given the heartiest sort of a greeting. Speaking of the work at Hull House, Chicago, she said in part:

"Any list of the achievements of settlements must be pitifully meagre when compared with the needs to be met. Merely to build a great institution is not the main object, for there is a natural distrust of institutionalism. The real object is to get into personal relations with those who need our help, and in spite of their needs we shall find that there is in their lives a pathos, dignity, and worth which is like that of those who are more pleasantly situated.

"It is not so difficult to cultivate relations of friendship with persons who at first are prone to distrust you, because you are better dressed, speak a more refined tongue, and have great advantages. It is not necessary to go to the home of some unfortunate person, seat yourself down, and announce firmly that you have come to make friends. That is not the way to go about it. Friendships are never founded in this way.

"Friendship is a far more subtle thing, something like a growing flower that ripens into beauty, the feeling first a suspicion that you mean well, and have no thought of intrusion, a kindliness in the eyes and in the voice, and an illustration by the hands that you are willing and ready, even eager, to be of assistance. Before long the woman cleaning the ash can and the man tending the furnace, the laborer, his wife and his children come to trust you, and to appreciate you as a friend, the sort of friend, indeed, they can come to when in need.

"A cultured person is the first to avoid giving offense by seeming to see the difference in speech and manner, the last person to force acquaintance on those who are not friends, and it is our effort first to make friends of those we would aid. There is as much in making the friends as there is in afterward trying to help them.

"In our work in Hull House we have steadily grown in tolerance, until we have sometimes had to ask ourselves if we are not in danger of going too far and of reaching that optimism which will accept everything as good, and that is a very useless and dangerous optimism. Yet we are convinced that there is a latent force, a creative power in the people themselves with whom we deal, which will come out if it only has the chance.

"There are few who know how much good these immigrants bring with them, the love of art and useful accomplishments for which they find no market. I know a man in Chicago who was put out of his rooms in a tenement because he had carved his door in the evenings when he came home weary from work, and sought to tell what there was better in him. It was exquisite work, the same he had done in a church in Italy, he said proudly, which is double starred in Baedeker.

"Another had trouble with his landlord because he decorated his ceiling with stucco. This man said that he had been paid for such work at home, but he supposed he ought not to have attempted it here, where the 'American people like everything smooth and such a queer white.' These men were artists, but they were not appreciated in their new surroundings.

"The children are eager to learn, and in many families they have adequate instructors in their parents, from whom they have inherited artistic tastes; but they grow ashamed of it, as they see that it has no reward, and they lose their heritage in our materialistic surroundings. Of course, I meant Chicago when I said that—I don't know about the atmosphere of New York.

"We once had a Greek play in Hull House played by the fruit peddlers, who are laborers in the Summer time. We found that these Greeks knew and had read the stories of Homer, and they were delighted to play before the Americans that they might illustrate and emphasize the fact that they were not barbarians.

"One man always prayed before rehearsing his part, and I asked him the reason for his prayer. He told me that he prayed for power to properly present the honor and glory of ancient Greece to the ignorant people of America, and he was absolutely sincere. We very freely express our opinion of the immigrants in this country, but we don't always stop to think or to question what they may think of us. The answers would be informative and useful. The social gulf that we used to hear so much about is imaginary, but it is deepest in the imaginations that are the most shallow. There is good and great work to be done, and the settlements are trying to do it."

In conclusion Miss Addams said that she could not entirely accept the motto, "Not alms, but friends," as it was often necessary to give alms. She said that it was work and association that were the great thing, and protested against a tendency frequently shown to turn a particular branch of work over to the city as soon as it gave the greatest promise.

W. K. Brice, Franklin H. Giddings, F. J. Goodnow, R. A. Seligman, and Samuel Thorne, Jr., were elected members of the Council of the society, class of 1906.

March 22, 1903

TRADE SCHOOL FOR GIRLS.

New York Federation of Women's Clubs Votes to Establish Institution.

Special to The New York Times.

UTICA, N. Y., Nov. 13.—The New York Federation of Women's clubs to-day, after a four days' convention, decided to establish a trade school for girls, and coupled with this action was the assuming of the management of the industrial school at Amsterdam, N. Y., started there about twelve years ago.

This trade school idea originated in the Federation five years ago, and the State association now has sufficient funds to conduct the school for three years. By that time the Federation hopes to have liberal endowments or executive action whereby the State will provide financial support.

Mrs. Dore Lyon of New York is the Chairman of the committee on trade school, and she engineered the Federation approval of the project. The vote to establish the school was 95 to 51.

The President appointed the following delegates to the biennial convention of the General Federation of Women's Clubs at St. Louis next May: Mrs. Tod Helmuth, New York; Mrs. Cornelius Zabriskie, Brooklyn; Mrs. William Eastwood, Rochester; Mrs. Philip Carpenter, Mrs. Dore Lyon, New York; Mrs. George R. Baird, Oneonta; Mrs. Alfred Campbell, Binghamton; Mrs. Adelbert Moot, Buffalo; Mrs. Wolcott J. Humphrey, Warsaw; Miss Lucy C. Watson, Utica; Miss Flora Broadhead, Jamestown; Mrs. Charles M. Dow, Jamestown.

November 14, 1903

The Plight of the Homeless Woman Wage Earner

THE author of "The Long Day," which is "The True Story of a New York Working Girl as Told by Herself," says that the greatest of all the urgent needs of the young women who toil is a series of cheap hotels after the order of the Mills Hotels for men.

Long before the appearance of "The Long Day," Miss Alice Smith, through her work among young girls as a probation officer of the West Side Court and a resident of the West Side Neighborhood House, became so thoroughly convinced that this was the case that she left her work to open up a cheap boarding house for working girls with as extensive accommodations as the limited means then at her disposal would allow. Last Winter, John Arbuckle, the Brooklyn philanthropist and "coffee king," in recognition of the life-and-death need of working girls for cheap living quarters, turned his private sailing vessel, the Jacob A. Stamler, into a woman's hotel, where board and lodging could be procured at 40 cents a day. At the present moment Mrs. Robert E. Ely, wife of Dr. Ely, the sociologist, is trying to interest capital in an attempt to build a large working girls' hotel. In all New York there is not a settlement worker, a probation officer, a practical philanthropist, or a Police Magistrate who will deny that the lack of cheap, clean, and respectable lodgings is one of the chief causes of the disaster which so often overtakes young girls who come to New York to work.

The needs of the workman with a wife and family are the solicitous concern of a company which boasts that it makes business and philanthropy meet in the construction of cheap model tenements. The requirements of the single workingman are met, at least in part, by the Mills Hotels and various other cheap lodging houses of varying degrees of cleanliness and respectability. The case of the professional woman is considered and provided for in a fashionable and popular woman's hotel. There is hardly a need of any one class that is not cheerfully filled by the obliging real estate agents, except the imperative, desperate need of the young girl on starvation wages.

╋ ╋ ╋

For her there is absolutely no provision. She may seek herself out a furnished room for $1, $2, or $3 a week, if she can find one—but as a rule the landladies prefer "gentlemen lodgers." There are, it is true, a few "Christian homes," but in these it is universally acknowledged that the girls pay high for wretched returns, are placed under humiliating restrictions, and are considered objects of charity to boot.

It is readily admitted that, as a rule, the girl on low wages is prompt with her rent and not given to jumping her board bills. She keeps her room neat and clean, seldom damages the walls or furniture, and makes almost no demands upon her landlady in the way of service. Why, then, with the need freely acknowledged and the investment pronounced a safe one, are there no working women's hotels?

Dr. E. R. L. Gould, President of the City and Suburban Homes Company, and builder of the Phipps Model Tenements, has answered the question in two words:

"Conventional morality."

It is not, he says, that the girls are less moral as a class than the men who live in the Mills Hotels. In fact, Dr. Gould concedes that they are altogether more moral. The crux of the matter is simply that a man's neighbors are not concerned with his method of life so long as his conduct in the house is above reproach; while, in the case of a woman, be her deportment never so blameless in her home, it goes for naught if she is suspected of the slightest deflection abroad.

"I have an instance in mind right now," said Dr. Gould. "It comes from a certain one of our houses which I have reserved exclusively for business women who want to do light housekeeping. It seemed to me that I had succeeded in securing a highly desirable class of tenants, when a friend came to me and informed me that the reputation of the house was being injured by rumors that one of the inmates was an altogether undesirable person. I quietly went to work and looked up the record of every woman on my list of tenants. There was not one against whom there had ever been a breath of scandal. Still my friend insisted that the gossip continued, and I went up to the house to investigate.

"As we neared the entrance my friend pointed to one of my tenants who had just ridden up to the door on a bicycle.

"'There,' he said, 'that's the woman all the talk has been about.'

"I stared at him aghast.

"'Do you know what you are saying?' I asked. 'That woman is a missionary and a church worker. There isn't a more strait-laced person in all New York.'

"When I ran the story down I found that the whole thing had originated in the fact that she rode a bicycle in a short skirt and had a high color that could be mistaken for rouge.

"This matter of a cheap working woman's hotel is not a new one to me. I have been consulted time after time by various philanthropists and sociologists in regard to it, but, for the one reason I have mentioned, I have been actually afraid to embark on the enterprise. The moment you consider such an undertaking you are confronted with the question of restrictions. A. T. Stewart's experiment in what is now the Park Avenue Hotel went to pieces because of too many restrictions. In the hotel that Mrs. Ely is trying to get built she would have no restrictions at all. It is hard to say what would be right. Too many restrictions are, of course, humiliating to the girls, and none at all cause people to talk.

"I am perfectly willing to admit with the author of 'The Long Day' that working girls should be allowed to see their young men friends in the parlors and reception rooms, and I can see that it would be a lowering of any girl's pride and self-respect to require her to give an account of herself and her conduct during her absences from the hotel, but from the standpoint of the practical business man I can also see that the success of the enterprise might be seriously jeopardized without pretty strict regulations.

"Even with them the experiment would be dangerous. You see the reputation or appearance of a man has no effect upon the reputation or standing of his hotel. Just let a woman whose manner of dressing does not meet with all the exactions of conventionality be seen entering a hotel, and the place has received an indelible stamp. No matter how exemplary her conduct in the hotel, one woman whose appearance excites suspicion may wreck the whole enterprise.

"These things may be wrong, but they are facts, and a business man in considering a business enterprise must deal with facts. The enterprise, to attain a truly philanthropic purpose, must not be a philanthropy, but a good, paying business proposition. I know that the reason I have mentioned is what has kept us from yielding to numerous solicitations to build a woman's hotel, and I imagine that is what has kept others from doing it."

What Dr. Gould says means that, while the moral scruples of society stand in the way of the improvement of living conditions for girls on low wages, these girls are forced into conditions that absolutely imply loss of self-respect and loss of the sense of decency and propriety. They are rendered reckless of the consequences of any act that will bring them relief by the despair of ever obtaining anything better by means approved by society.

"The young girls who go wrong in a great city like this for want of the various necessities of a parlor must make the angels in Heaven weep!" exclaims the author of "The Long Day." Every young girl who has lived in a furnished room in New York can echo this sentiment with all the fervor of her soul. She knows that unless she is to deny herself the right that every girl, rich or poor, feels in the inmost depths of her heart to be hers, by every law of Heaven and earth—the right to select a man for her mate—she must entertain her young men friends in her tiny hall room, in the public parks, or in the back room of a saloon."

As a rule, the strictest girls elect to receive their callers in their own rooms—particularly as they are not thought the worse of for it, and are even expected to do it. Unless a landlady be unusually strait-laced the inquiries of all a girl's young men callers are answered with a gesture toward the stairs, and the words "Fourth floor rear"—or "front"—as the case may be.

"The young man goes up and knocks at the girl's door. If she is not dressed to receive callers she will call to him to sit down on the stairs and wait for her. If she is very particular she may suggest that they go for a walk.

Oh, the endless walks of homeless working girls trying to get a little joy and beauty and poetry out of their dull, hard, colorless lives without compromising with evil! In the Summer, when she and the young man who has brought a gleam of poetry into the deadly prose of her existence have walked the streets until they are tired they can go and sit on a park bench; but in the Winter, where are they to go?

Here is where the back room of the saloon, warm and bright and comfortable, looms up, an irresistible temptation. The alternatives are the street and the dark, stuffy, cold little room. Here there is privacy for talk, the requirements of physical comfort, an atmosphere of gayety and fun. Is it any wonder that a girl, though she has looked upon the saloon all her life with horror and repulsion, and would as soon think of entering one as of cutting off her right hand, comes to consider the back room "a different matter"? Is it any wonder that, to buy the right to sit there, she sips a glass of beer? Generally her friends at the factory or the shop look upon the back room as the naturally appointed place of assembly for all their hours of recreation. She begins to believe her prejudice against the saloon old-fashioned and provincial, and learns to make use of it as a factor in her daily life.

But leaving the matter of the necessity for a parlor entirely out of the question, the difficulties of finding any sort of a roof to cover her head, any sort of refuge into which she can crawl at night to sleep away the leaden weariness of the day's work, are almost insurmountable.

The author of "The Long Day" found a room with light housekeeping facilities for $1 a week. The present author has never been able to find the cheapest accommodation for less than $2. This room was somewhere in the vicinity of East Seventeenth Street and Second Avenue. The occupant, a young girl earning $6 a week, asked me if I didn't think she had stumbled across a "snap." The apartment was a hall bedroom containing a washstand, furnished with a bowl, pitcher and mirror; a cot bed, and a long shelf from which hung a cheap calico curtain. The shelf and the space behind it were designed to serve as a closet. The lucky possessor of these luxuries exhibited with pride a small round appliance which, she said, heated the room "grand" when attached to the gas jet, the only difficulty then being that it extinguished the light. Another attachable appliance, partaking of the nature of a bracket, enabled her to make coffee and boil eggs over the same gas jet

This is the way, in varying degrees of squalor, according to the amount of their wages, that the greater number of the working girls in New York live. The working girl's "clubs" and "Christian homes" are entirely too high-priced for most of those whose needs they are designed to meet. Besides, many young women of spirit prefer starving and freezing in independence to living in comparative comfort on a charitable basis.

Although it is universally conceded that the girls living in the various "homes" and "clubs" pay high prices for bad food and the poorest accommodations, they are invariably treated as inmates of an institution. The mere fact that a girl lives in one brands her as an object of charity. She is, moreover, surrounded by an atmosphere of suspicion and restraint and is usually spied upon, talked about, and constantly reproved and lectured.

A young girl who had tried in succession all the various "homes" and "clubs" in the city told the writer that she was done with them once for all, and that in future she would starve rather than subject herself to their system of surveillance and supervision.

"If they represent 'Christian charity,'" she said, "I want a little pagan cruelty. If I stay where I am now I shall soon begin to believe myself all they seem to think me."

The writer of "The Long Day" says of these institutions:

"We do not want any so-called 'working girls' homes'—God forbid the euphemism—which, while overcharging us for their miserable accommodations, at the same time would put us in the position of charity dependents. First and most important, there must be no semblance of charity. Let the working girls' hotel and the working girls' lodging house be not only self-supporting, but so built and conducted that they will pay a fair rate of interest upon the money invested. Otherwise they would fail of any truly philanthropic object.

"As to their conduct as institutions, there should be no rules, no regulations which are not in full operation in the Waldorf-Astoria or the Hotel St. Regis. The curse of all such attempts in the past has been the insistence upon coercive morality. Make them not only non-sectarian, but non-religious. There is no more need of conducting a working girls' hotel or lodging house in the name of God or under the auspices of a religious sentiment than there is a necessity of advertising the fashionable woman's hotel or bachelor apartment house as being under Divine guidance."

Dr. Gould suggests that, as the working girls' hotel appears to be an impossibility while society continues to cherish its present prejudices, the girls should take to light housekeeping in model tenement flats with two or three rooms. This is because Dr. Gould is a man. No man has yet realized that when a woman goes into the market place to engage in productive labor she has simply no more to do with housekeeping than a man. Even if other conditions were favorable, no girl could do the exhausting work demanded of her and discharge the various labors of housekeeping besides.

But other conditions are not favorable. Although highly desirable living quarters may be obtained in Dr. Gould's model tenements on the basis of $1.20 a room, they are placed as high as heaven beyond the reach of the working girl by the fact that they are unfurnished. The working girl's wages never leave the smallest surplus, and the necessity for the smallest outlay places the most alluring living arrangement as far beyond her means as the St. Regis.

FRANCES MAULE.

December 17, 1905

LABOR LAW HELD TO BE CLASS LEGISLATION

Court of Special Sessions Declares It Unconstitutional.

INDIVIDUAL RIGHTS VIOLATED

Protects Women in Factories, Justice Olmsted Says, but Doesn't Govern Their Work in the Home.

In an opinion written by Justice Olmsted, Justices McKean and Deuel concurring, the Court of Special Sessions yesterday declared Section 77 of the general labor law unconstitutional on the ground that it is class legislation. This section prohibits the employment of women or minors in factories before 6 o'clock in the morning or after 9 in the evening, or for more than ten hours a day or sixty hours a week.

This decision was handed down in the case of David L. Williams, the proprietor of a turning establishment at 437 Eleventh Avenue, who was arrested last January to test the constitutionality of the law. Williams admitted that his shop could be legally called a factory, and that he had at times employed women after hours.

Attorney General Mayer appeared for the State. As a matter of public policy he said that the law should be upheld. Frederick B. House, who represented Williams, asserted that the statute was a violation of the rights of the individual, and as such should not be enforced.

Justice Olmsted in a long opinion said that the welfare of future citizens was the only excuse for the law. He regarded the law as class legislation, he said, in that it only protected women in factories and made no provision for those who worked overtime in their own homes.

Therefore he considered the law an "unwarranted violation or invasion of constitutional rights." He granted an arrest of judgment in the case and discharged the defendant Williams.

August 4, 1906

A Young Woman's Chances of Getting Work in Five American Cities

NEW YORK has so often been called the grave-yard of village ambitions that it is rather interesting to note a contrary assertion by a young woman who made a series of labor experiments in the interests of her father's sociological researches. Her theory, after visiting the five representative cities of the Union, is that the great metropolis is a veritable treasure house of opportunity in every line of honest endeavor, from high art down to the lowliest form of manual labor. Chicago, San Francisco, Pittsburg, and Atlanta are the unfavorable contrasts cited, especially in the case of women wage earners.

Miss Brown, as we will call her, is young and resourceful, but not skilled in any particular line of work, as her education has been general. She left her home a year ago with exactly $5 in her pocket above the price of her railroad fare to San Francisco, assuming that even the poorest aspirant for work starts upon her quest with that meagre sum in reserve. Upon reaching San Francisco she immediately inserted the following advertisement in the three leading newspapers:

"A young Eastern woman, not afraid of work, desires position where energy and industry will be appreciated."

While waiting for replies Miss Brown engaged lodgings at $2 a week in one of the "rooming houses" with which the city teemed from end to end, and meanwhile the amazingly familiar manners of her fellow-boarders put her on her guard against too much friendliness. It was "a way they had out there," she was told when she remonstrated with an offensively forward young man.

*** *** ***

Answers came promptly and in gratifying numbers, but of a character hardly agreeable. Nine of the fourteen answers offered a sheltered "pleasant" life in exchange for "companionship"; three young bachelors wanted agreeable housekeepers, and only one answer offered an honest, respectable occupation, which happened to be a manufacturing concern, where experience was absolutely necessary. Miss Brown then tried answering advertisements, with slightly better success. Within the week she obtained temporary employment in a fruit packing house, which required a certain deftness of touch that she soon acquired. The pay was barely sufficient to cover her current expenses, but she kept at the work until she obtained a slightly better paying position in a dental office. All subsequent advertisements produced more or less objectional answers, and many of the wants which she answered were simply cleverly disguised "personals." Still she kept right on looking for work for the sake of the desired experience. Next she obtained a position in a shoe store, where the male customers treated her with jocund familiarity. Three weeks later the opportunity came to fill a vacancy in a telephone operating office, but Miss Brown soon discovered that the "hello girl" in California expects no consideration either from her employers or any of the men that frequent the offices. Miss Brown worked at the switchboard for ten days, however, determined to assure herself that her first impressions were correct; then she left in search of other employment.

All the while Miss Brown had managed by careful planning to make both ends meet, which was comparatively easy at that season of the year, when fruit was abundant and cheap and fuel unnecessary. At the end of three months, after having tried every form of employment that the city offered except the professional branches, she left for Chicago, with a very unfavorable report of San Francisco as a field for working women.

After a five days' hunt for profitable employment in Chicago Miss Brown obtained a nominal position in a big department store, at a salary of $5 a week. Her place of operation was in a basement, among tinware, artificially lighted and poorly ventilated; in fact, the only means of ventilation consisted of a double stairway, which let down the used-up atmosphere from the main floor of the store. Of course the day's work was extremely enervating under the circumstances. Miss Brown found a fairly clean boarding place at $4 a week, which left her only $1 for incidental expenses and dress, which necessitated great economy. As she had no time to answer advertisements personally she was obliged to rely on correspondence, and finally had the good fortune to secure a position as general office worker for a soap manufacturing concern at $7 a week. She was informed by her employer that she would be expected to make a good appearance at his desk on account of his business, which meant that every penny that she could possibly spare above the price of her bare living would have to go for dress. Still, the position was a pleasant one, so far as her relations with the business was concerned, for she received respectful treatment from every man with whom she was brought into the remotest contact. She left the office after four weeks, and resumed her quest of experience. The third position required strictly personal references, which Miss Brown could not give, for it had been agreed that she was to make her way unrecommended, in order to give due value to her experiments. She told her would-be employer frankly that she was a stranger in the city and could not therefore obtain references, whereupon he stated that he could not make use of her services, as the position involved great personal responsibility.

For two weeks Miss Brown remained idle, and meanwhile she lived very precariously and walked many weary miles each day in search of employment, and was finally obliged to accept a semi-menial position as mother's help at $10 a month and board. During that month she spent every spare hour in looking for other employment, and finally secured an engagement at a food demonstrating counter in a department store. Taking it all in all, the Chicago experience was less unpleasant than that of San Francisco, though neither was calculated to encourage the average working girl.

The next seat of experiment was Pittsburg, where Miss Brown had the good fortune to obtain employment at once in a cigar factory at $6 a week. Her boarding place was very unsanitary, and the locality was literally choked with smoke from the surrounding factories and docks. The field did not look promising, for the only remunerative work in demand was shorthand, which seemed to be in constant demand. There was a sprinkling of incidentals in the way of nursery governesses, seamstresses, flowermakers, and waitresses wanted here and there about the city, but generally the outlook was dull for the non-professional worker. Miss Brown tried five different occupations during her stay, and managed, by rigid economy, to pay her frugal expenses and save up the $5 necessary for her start in Atlanta. Her railway fare was supplied by her father, who stood in readiness to help her at a pinch, of course, but Miss Brown made out somehow without reinforcements.

*** *** ***

Atlanta offered still fewer opportunities than Pittsburg, and under vastly different social circumstances. The newspapers carried very few want advertisements, and those were generally of a purely domestic character. In business circles the attitude of the employer toward his prospective women employes was slightly misleading, and generally ended in polite regrets; one very discouraging feature of Southern methods was the universal readiness to hold out promises of employment in the near future to women applicants—a mistaken courtesy, because strangers do not understand that it is merely the custom of the country. Miss Brown was encouraged to call the second time in a great many instances that led to disappointment and waste of carfares. The supply of workers was greatly in excess of the demand. Office positions were limited to expert stenographers and skilled bookkeepers, and most of these positions were filled by young men. Comparatively few women were employed in the larger offices.

Finally, in despair of obtaining other employment, Miss Brown took a temporary position in a cotton factory, which tided her over a hard week or two until she found an opportunity to renew her original quest, but she was unable to obtain anything better than a humble sewing task during the remainder of her stay in the city. The social conditions of working women differed vitally from those of either of the other cities visited, as the Southern working woman seemed to be strictly confined to a very narrow circle of fellow-wage earners, with fewer privileges to better her condition than is generally the case in Northern cities. Broadly speaking, the Southern field is a very narrow one for non-professional women.

Toward the end of May Miss Brown arrived in New York City, a total stranger, without references and with only $5 in her pocket. She engaged a hall room in the vicinity of Irving Place for $2, and immediately set about a quest for employment by answering advertisements, both in person and by letter. Many of the advertisers required previous experience in manufacturing lines, and others demanded references, but there were half a dozen opportunities where neither of those requirements were mentioned. Miss Brown obtained employment on the third day at addressing envelopes for $1 a thousand. On the first day she was able to turn out 500 legibly written envelopes; the second day 600, and before the week ended she was making $1.25 a day, which satisfied her regarding that particular branch of emergency work by which any moderately intelligent woman can make enough to save her from

want. Her second experiment began a day after she gave up the addressing, in the line of artificial flower painting, at which she succeeded so well that she was offered a permanent position at the end of the second week at $8 a week to begin with, but as her object was not money-making she relinquished the position after three profitable weeks, and took the next thing that offered—a place in a fashionable Turkish bath establishment at $25 a month, with lunches thrown in. She pleased her employer so well that she was given a better offer before the week was up, including a free course in massage.

In the meanwhile Miss Brown had been reading the daily papers diligently in quest of other opportunities, and had run across an advertisement in which a lady offered board and lodging in exchange for light household duties. Miss Brown called, made arrangements to undertake the work of a pleasant little flat before and after business hours, which were, fortunately, short.

Mother's helper was the next venture. Although the "mother" hesitated about taking an unrecommended young stranger into her home, she overcame her scruples in Miss Brown's favor, and engaged her at a salary of $18 a month and board. It was an unpleasant position on account of domestic friction, but it afforded food and shelter and sufficient money to tide a girl through a waiting period while looking for better employment.

Miss Brown obtained a cashier's position in a "hurry" restaurant without references by making a small deposit. She finally succeeded in placing herself in the way of making a fine salary as an amanuensis. She sums up the result of her year's experience as follows: "My series of experiments have proved, to me at least, that a healthy, industrious, fairly intelligent young woman of any creed or nationality can obtain honest employment in New York City without push or pull of any sort whatever. There is no need of destitution or idleness among the strong and capable, even though they may not be skilled in any special branch of art. And, lastly, a girl need not be strikingly handsome or remarkable stylish in order to succeed in earning a good living in any of the numerous branches of industry open to women in our great metropolis. An agreeable, willing working girl can succeed nine times out of ten in New York City, four times in ten in Chicago, three times in Pittsburg, one in Atlanta, and once in fifty in the Far West."

August 12, 1906

ROOSEVELT QUIZZES GIRL DRESS STRIKERS

East Side Workers Gather Around Him While He Asks Them About Their Lives.

FIGHT WAIST PROTOCOL

Manufacturers of Low-Priced Goods Say Makers of Costly Garments Plotted with Union Against Them.

Col. Roosevelt visited the east side yesterday to study, at first hand, the conditions surrounding the young women now on strike in the kimono and wrapper industry. He made the trip at the request of Miss Madeline C. Doty, Secretary of the Child Welfare Committee of the Progressive Service, who last Saturday went to Oyster Bay and told the Colonel that most of the girls employed as kimono and wrapper makers were not more than 15 years old, and were forced to work at starvation wages for overlong hours.

Miss Doty and Miss Gertrude Barnum, an organizer of the International Garment Workers' Union, accompanied Col. Roosevelt. The party departed from The Outlook office in a taxicab at 4 o'clock in the afternoon and went to a hall at 49 Henry Street where between 500 and 600 girl strikers had assembled to meet the man who Miss Doty told them was a "personage." She had not revealed the Colonel's name. When those in the hall saw the Colonel in the taxicab they ran to the street to greet him.

Shaking hands with them as he walked toward the entrance, and, with his hat pressed under his elbow, the Colonel hurried into the hall. Inside there was no attempt at formality. Col. Roosevelt marched to the front of the room, but instead of standing on the platform, he leaned against a desk and waved his hand for silence.

"Now, young ladies," he began, "I want to know all about your lives; how you work, and how you manage to be cheerful. Just gather around me and tell your stories."

When this had been translated into Spanish, Italian, Turkish, and Greek, the girls, ranging in age from 18 to 14 years, formed a close circle around their visitor. He sat on a desk swinging his feet, and Miss Doty took down his questions and the answers.

"Now, tell me about yourself," the Colonel said, pointing to a tall and attractive-looking Spanish girl, seemingly some 16 years old.

Through an interpreter the girl said she had come to this country when she was 14 years old. She started at once, she asserted, to earn her living as a wrapper maker, and had been employed at that work ever since. She went to work at 8 o'clock in the morning, quit at 9 o'clock at night, and earned between $6 and $7 a week. She made 36 komonos a day at 4 cents each, she said. For the machine on which she did her sewing in the factory and which was owned by the company she had to pay $32, she told the Colonel, the price being taken out of her weekly wages. Her father had been ill in the hospital for a year, and all her wages went to the support of the family.

The Colonel could hardly wait till the story closed to express anger at such conditions. The smile of greeting which he had worn on entering the hall had by this time completely disappeared, and in its stead was an expression of anger mixed with sympathy. He next heard the story of Esther Bella, 17 years old, of 104 Allen Street, who had been forced to pay $32 for a machine which her employers owned. Her wages were $6 a week, from which she had to pay all her living expenses. The stories poured in upon the Colonel, girls pressing forward to take the places of those who had finished their recitals. No hesitation was shown; only eagerness to gain the Colonel's attention.

Occasionally the interviewer hastened the proceedings by talking directly to the French girls in their language. Always the story was the same; of extreme privations, long working hours and small wages. When the Colonel quit the hall at 6 o'clock he turned to the leaders and those accompanying him and exclaimed:

"This is crushing the future motherhood of the country. It must be stopped. It is too horrible for words."

From the Henry Street hall, and with the girls crowding about and cheering his departure, the Colonel went to Odd Fellows' Hall at 67 St. Mark's Place, where another gathering awaited him. The girls here had not been informed that a noted man was to visit them and they were startled at first when the Colonel pushed his way into the gathering. At this place most of the girls could speak English and the time needed for translation was saved. Col. Roosevelt's method of gaining the confidence of the girls was the same as at the other place. He was quite informal, and soon had the young women at their ease. One Jewish girl, some 15 years old, told the Colonel that she could earn only $5.50 a week because she could not work on Saturday. If the strike was successful she wanted as a condition of settlement that Sunday should be made a work day.

A story that touched the Colonel deeply was told by a fifteen-year-old Italian girl. At the end of her narrative she said with a catch in her voice:

"If only they would let us sing while we work."

"The brutes," Mr. Roosevelt muttered under his breath, "to prevent them from singing if they can be cheerful under such conditions."

It was here that one girl, when asked how she used her wages, explained that $2.75 of her $4.50 a week was spent on food and the rest provided all other necessities of life.

"You see," she said, "the boys can go to the saloons and get free luncheon with a nickel beer, but we have to buy from a pushcart."

When the Colonel departed for his home he said that he would continue his investigation on Thursday, his regular day in town, and that then he would have more to say about the conditions under which the girls labored. He said that he would speak to State Senator Salant, the only Progressive in the Legislature, and ask him to promote legislation more favorable to the young girls who were forced to earn their living in the garment industry.

January 22, 1913

HOUSEWORK HAS MOST PITFALLS FOR WOMEN EARNERS

IS THE trend of modern industry dangerous to the character of woman? The most casual observer sees that the conditions under which she works have changed and are changing rapidly. The difference between her industrial environment now and fifty years ago is so great that it must almost inevitably affect her physically and mentally. Are her moral qualities also affected? And if so, in what manner? As an indistinguishable unit in the industrial host of to-day, is she more or less anti-social in thought and deed than as an isolated worker under the simpler conditions of the past?"

These are the questions which Mary Conyngton undertakes to answer in her recently published study of the "Relation between Occupation and Criminality of Women." Miss Conyngton's work was done under the direction of the United States Commissioner of Labor and appeared as volume 15 in the monumental report on Woman and Child Wage-Earners, issued by the Government.

If all Government reports were as interesting as this study of Miss Conyngton's, we should not need to import so many sociological novels and plays from England to tell us about the effect of modern industry on human life and character. But Miss Conyngton's study is none the less a work of science for all that she has written it in a spirited, readable style. She is a skilled investigator of social and economic conditions, and if she did not wear the ring of Gyges in her search for truth, she had at least its modern equivalent, science and professional training. All of us who are interested in the changing character of women's work, in the gradual shifting of the scene of their labors from the home to the shop, from the kitchen to the factory, from domestic service to the newer occupations, cannot consider too seriously the findings of Miss Conyngton's little volume. She says:

The tailoress of 1870 might be and often was the village garment maker, going her rounds from house to house, a recognized and important figure in the community, and independent and respected personality. The tailoress of to-day is far more apt to be employed within a garment making factory, an automaton during work hours, from an indistinguishable atom of the crowded city life outside of them. This tendency is at work in a multitude of trades. Millinery and dressmaking are still disorganized and uncentralized, but the large establishments are crowding the small, and the independent worker is giving way to the apprentice, who serves her term and works under factory or shop conditions. The home industries are disappearing or giving place to the sweated trades. Hannah is no longer at the window binding shoes, but in a factory with fifty others straining every nerve to keep pace with the machinery. Everywhere the movement is going on, and so the census figures, striking as they are, do not show fully the change which has taken place within the last three or four decades, and which seems likely to progress still more rapidly in the future.

What has been the effect of these changes on the moral nature of women? There was only one answer to that, everybody supposed. It had been harmful, of course. Not only was this the popular belief, but the same idea had found its way into the works of more than one sociological writer. One author, for instance, had declared that it was an undeniable fact that women were the worse morally for the recent widening of their sphere of industrial and political activity. There is nothing which challenges the scientific expert like an apriori statement of this kind. To go around talking about "undeniable facts" in this manner in the hearing of Miss Conyngton's calibre is to court disaster of the worst kind. One day, having had this "undeniable fact" flung at her once too often, perhaps, she started to see whether it would stand the test of an examination of prison records.

She wanted to know just what were the occupations best represented in the reformatories and prisons for women throughout the country.

To ascertain this she studied the lives of 3,229 offenders distributed through the penal institutions of six different States. She went sleuthing into the past lives of each of the unfortunates. They were all over 16 years old, old enough to have been at work a longer or shorter period after leaving school, or else to have entered upon a period of home-making in the interim. Just how they had spent the years of their independence after leaving school was a fact which Miss Conyngton recorded

carefully for each one. She writes:

If we know that out of 100 following one pursuit 20 are in jail or in prison, while out of 100 following another occupation only 5 are under sentence, there is certainly ground for considering that the first pursuit needs looking into. It will probably be found either that the conditions under which it is carried on tend to break down character or that there is something about it which attracts those of weak or undeveloped morality. To this extent the jail, the workhouse, and the reformatory may serve as an index to the effect on women of different occupations, so far as lawbreaking is concerned.

Of the 3,229 offenders studied, 81 per cent. had come from the traditional pursuits of women—housework—within their own homes or in the homes of others. The newer pursuits, including work in factories and shops, in offices and stores, furnished but 12 per cent.

These percentages make an excellent showing for the newer occupations. They become still more striking when compared with the relative size of the different occupational groups, as reported by the census.

While 24 per cent. of the women breadwinners of the country are engaged in domestic service, this occupation furnishes 70 per cent. of the offenders in women's prisons, nearly three times their proper share. While 25 per cent. of the women breadwinners are at work in mills and factories, as garment and flower makers, as workers in fur and feathers, in all the overworked and sweated trades, still they furnish only 17 per cent. of the offenders, as against 70 per cent. from the group of servants and waiters.

The women engaged in trade and transportation, that is in offices, stores, and telephone exchanges, made even a better showing than their sisters in the factories and mills. In 1900 they constituted 10 per cent. of all the women gainfully employed and yet they supply only 3 per cent. of the offenders.

The last group includes "the cash girls, bookkeepers, clerks, saleswomen, stenographers, and telephone operators." It is here that the most rapid increase is taking place in the number of women employed. Here, too, is found the largest proportion of young women between 16 and 24, the age when the character is forming and when a girl might be expected to yield most easily to adverse influences—the crime age, according to some authorities. In this group it is necessary for a girl to make a good appearance, no matter how small her wages. Here as cash girl, bundle girl, or saleswoman, she has always before her eyes and within temptingly easy reach of her fingers ribbons and beads and a hundred and one pretty trinkets dear to the heart of girlhood. Here as bookkeeper or cashier she has endless opportunities for embezzlement or petty peculations. As stenographer she is thrown into close relations with employers who may or may not be honorable men, as telephone girl or clerk or teleg-

rapher she must keep all hours and meet all persons and see on every hand opportunities to go wrong so easily, so gradually, that she might well stray from the path of conventional safety before she realized that she had even stepped aside. Yet these workers furnish to the whole group of offenders studied only one-third of their proportionate representation.

Proceeding with the patience of science, Miss Conyngton next examines particular towns and States where local industrial conditions might be reflected in the prison population. She takes the town of Paterson, N. J., for instance, famous far and wide for its silk mills, which attract young women in great numbers as mill workers. In Paterson only 18 per cent. of the women breadwinners are in domestic service, while 69 per cent work in the mills of the town. Yet when we look into the prison population we find that domestic and personal service furnishes 64 per cent. of the offenders, which is considerably more than three times their proportion.

In the State of Massachusetts, with its army of textile workers, its girl shoemakers, its women weavers and spinners, where do the wrongdoers in the reformatories come from? Here, as everywhere else, the prison population is drafted mainly from the ranks of domestic service.

While 60,000 women work in the textile mills of Massachusetts, they furnish but 16 per cent. of the offenders. The 70,000 employed as servants and waitresses contribute 60 per cent.

From whatever point of view Miss Conyngton arranged her statistics, however she shifted them, the answer was always the same. "The prison population is not recruited from the ranks of the saleswomen, the clerks, and stenographers, the packers and shippers, the telephone and telegraph operators, who have increased in numbers so rapidly within the last few decades."

Of 3,000 women offenders she found that 80 per cent. came from the traditional pursuits of women, that is directly from their own homes or from domestic service, and a trifle less than 12 per cent. from all other lawful occupations.

One of the questions which Miss Conyngton considers further on in the study is whether low wages play any part in the social evil. She believes that before this can be answered one must make a strong distinction between taking the initial step in wrongdoing and becoming a habitual wrongdoer after the first error has been made. On this subject she says:

It was generally agreed that while it is the rarest of things for a girl to enter upon an immoral life directly through want, yet when she has once gone wrong through thoughtlessness, or affection, or some other cause, then low wages or irregular or insufficient wages are strongly effective in deciding her to adopt a life of immorality or in impelling her to drift into such a life without any definite decision.

If Miss Conyngton had found that

girls go wrong to any great extent because of low wages this would have tallied ill with the principal occupation in which they go wrong. It is a well-known fact that domestic service is an especially high-paid calling. The high standard of wages usually paid to servants influences the pay of the least efficient and poorest among them. If wages were a protection, the servant would stand a better chance than her sister in the mill.

We are not to suppose, however, that Miss Conyngton found among the women in prison any who were really skilled in the domestic arts. On the contrary the women were conspicuously untrained in every way.

"You never saw anything like the amount they don't know," said one Warden. "Till I came here I supposed it was as natural for a woman to know how to sew as to know how to eat, or how to put up her hair; it was part of being a woman. But give these women a needle and thread and they've no more idea what to do with them than my cat here. And its just the same with cooking and washing and all the things a woman is supposed to know about. I've found that mostly the women who really know how to do anything don't come here; they're doing it, and that keeps them out of harm's way."

The Warden's interpretation of the facts revealed by the report is homely and to the point. Miss Conyngton's explanation, which agrees in substance with the Warden's, is the illuminating explanation of a woman who knows the whole gamut of women's occupations and the details of each.

Here it is: The girl does not go wrong because she is a domestic or an unskilled worker, but she is a domestic or an unskilled worker because she is the kind of girl most likely to be tempted and least likely to resist.

The good showing made by the newer occupations is due to the fact that they have a disciplinary and educative value in themselves, and the kind of woman who goes to prison is hardly qualified to enter them. Miss Conyngton writes:

The stenographer or bookkeeper or cashier or confidential clerk must have a certain amount of intelligence and general education to begin with, and must usually have taken some special training in addition. Some force of character, some sustained and purposeful effort is required before a girl can enter such a position. The place once secured, it cannot be held without a considerable amount of patient application, of attention to uninteresting detail, of doing a thing because it is to be done, and of sacrificing present inclination to a definitely conceived plan of action. A saleswoman or a packer and shipper may not require as much preliminary training, but the discipline of the position is no less exacting. The training in systematic and sustained

industry, in promptness, in obedience to a recognized authority, tends to build up a type of character which renders its possessor very unlikely to come in conflict with the laws. By their very nature, these positions carry with them a training and discipline of high value.

But in addition to the disciplinary value which they share with the better grades of factory work, the newer occupations have certain advantages of their own. In most, probably in all of them, the girl has reached a position in which a jail or prison sentence for a woman is looked upon as an ineffaceable stigma, and the public sentiment of her class becomes a tremendous force to restrain her from any open break with respectability.

The poorest of the newer trades has the interest of working in company; the better ones have much more. It is entirely possible for the girl to go to her work with pleasurable zest and to find in it the interest and excitement of the day. The loneliness of domestic service and the deadening monotony of the poorer grades of factory work, both of which lead a girl to seek relief in the dubious pleasures open to her, are alike wanting. Her work itself may supply interest and companionship, both of which are safeguards against the temptations most likely to assail her. Add the element of ambition, the possibility that if the worker desires it she may rise to one of the really well-paid and responsible positions, and it will be admitted that the saleswoman or stenographer or clerk or cashier has some cogent inducements to avoid forfeiting her standing.

When we turn to personal and domestic service and to housekeeping, we find the situation reversed. It may be said with much truth that keeping one's own house or doing the work of another person's requires to the full as much intelligence and self-control and capacity for planning a course of action and carrying it out to the end as an industrial career of any kind. The difference is that the manager of a shop or the employer of the better grade of female workers will not accept service below a certain standard, while no such standard is set for the girl who marries and keeps her own house, or who enters the lower grades of domestic work. Again and again a girl who, in a reformatory, is classed as not quite capable of self-direction, marries soon after her release. Innumerable others of the same grade of intelligence who have not reached the reformatory also marry. It is small wonder that, having married, they go wrong. Given a certain moderate amount of temptation or of exposure to bad influences and the result is a foregone conclusion. They go wrong from their own homes rather than from the newer occupations simply because they are not capable of entering the latter.

Domestic service, as known to most of the women found under sentence, has the same two drawbacks as housekeeping; it is easily entered by the class most likely to be found in prison and has little in itself to restrain their tendencies. Moreover, domestic service, again as known to these women, has some dangerous features of its own. The principal reason for the large number of of-

fenders from its ranks undoubtedly is that it affords an opening for the low-grade and unskilled worker who could not possibly secure or retain a place in any well organized industry. The servant who finds her way into jail or prison is not ordinarily a trained domestic worker. A few such are found among those committed for intemperance or theft, but generally she is an unskilled worker of the poorest grade. Nothing is more surprising than that such women are able to secure places at all, but they rarely seem to have any difficulty in doing so.

These workers have little or no social standing, and so the incentive of maintaining their position, so powerful among workers of a better class, is wanting.

While domestic service is thus open to the lowest grade, it has for them little educative or disciplinary value. A confusion of speech frequently arises because the persons discussing the advantages of domestic service have in mind a well-ordered household, and a just, intelligent, and considerate mistress, while those discussing its disadvantages have in mind the exact reverse.

The servants who appear in jail do not as a class come from houses of the first kind. They are apt to work for people whose standards are but little higher than their own. Their work is often carried on under unhygienic conditions, their hours are long and irregular, and their mistresses frequently "awful aggravating." They cannot do their work well enough to take any intelligent interest in it, and the day becomes a lonesome and monotonous round of drudgery. They have no prospect of rising to anything higher, so that the spur of ambition does not drive them forward in the right way and there is no social standard of their own class to hold them back from the wrong.

On the whole, then, Miss Conyngton found that a girl's occupation played little part in her criminal or immoral record. Unfortunate early influences and defective mentality—the two often combined in a single case—seem to be the principal reasons why girls go wrong, but they are strengthened by a number of subsidiary causes.

Prominent among these is the lack of innocent amusement under suitable conditions. "Their work hasn't half as much to do with their going wrong as their amusements have." A desire for amusement is as natural as a desire for food; in the young it is well-nigh as imperious. It may be that the girls would really prefer safe amusements. The success of working girls' clubs and classes seems to indicate that she does not insist upon frequenting undesirable places when desirable ones are open to her.

But if safe amusements are not at hand she will take what she finds. The saloon and the dance hall realize this and take pains to be at hand, but the forces of morality have failed to recognize and supply the need adequately.

TUBERCULOSIS' HARVEST AMONG WOMEN IN COTTON MILLS

THE United States Government has just issued one of the most important of its series of nineteen volumes dealing with the condition of woman and child wage-earners in this country. It is Senate Document No. 645 of the second session of the Sixty-first Congress, the fourteenth volume of the series, and relates to "Causes of Death Among Woman and Child Cotton Mill Operatives."

This remarkable report was prepared by Dr. Arthur R. Perry, formerly a physician of Boston, who gave up his private practice to undertake an exhaustive investigation for the Government among the cotton-mill operatives of New England. He carried on his work under the immediate direction of Commissioner of Labor Charles P. Neill; but his labors were free-handed and unhampered. The result has been that the methods of gathering and tabulating mortality statistics have been practically revolutionized.

Dr. Perry went at his task in an original manner, his method being equivalent in value to a new and highly important invention. His mortality tables are probably the most complete that have ever been collected, and the deductions he draws from them are unfailing in their logic and accuracy.

In the first place, the three great cotton-mill centres in the East were selected for the investigation. They are Fall River, Mass.; Manchester, N. H., and Pawtucket, R. I. Then he undertook to find out the cause of the deaths of all persons in these cities from 10 to 44 years of age in the years 1905, 1906, and 1907, and to divide the decedents into two groups —operatives and non-operatives.

Only Reliable Method.

Dr. Perry declared that the only reliable method upon which to base the prospects of the living mill operatives was to obtain accurate data relating to the life histories of deceased mill operatives. He gathered them all. The results, mostly in the form of painstaking tabulations, make up a compact volume of 430 pages.

"The age period, 15 to 44 years," Dr. Perry explains, "was selected for special intensive study, because it represents a period of full industrial activity during which the death rate would normally be low. It is customary to present vital statistics by age groups of ten years. If this period from 15 to 44 years, inclusive, be divided into these customary groups

A Mill Child

of years, the death rates are sufficiently similar to justify considering the three together as a single age group characterized throughout by a low mortality.

"A second reason for choosing this age period for special study lies in the fact that more than one-half the entire population is found within its limits, so that it presents a wider field for study than a more limited age group could do. Moreover, for a study of causes of death among cotton operatives this group presents unique advantages, since more than four-fifths (85 per cent.) of the entire operative population is included within it.

"Also within its limits are found three-fourths (76 per cent.) of the entire number of tuberculous deaths of individuals of 10 years and over, nearly three-fourths (73 per cent.) of the whole operative mortality from all causes and fully nine-tenths (91 per cent.) of the entire operative deaths from tuberculosis. For all these reasons this age period was considered to demand special intensive study.

"In regard to sex, as the investigation was primarily into causes of death among woman and child cotton-mill operatives, special attention, naturally, has been given to the study of female decedents as compared with the corresponding classes of male decedents.

"At a very early stage of the investigation it became evident that the Irish in each age, sex, and occupation group almost without exception presented a higher death rate than any other race or people. This difference was so marked that the inclusion of the Irish in any tabulations of the aggregate population proved likely to cause erroneous and exceedingly misleading results. In the following tabulations, therefore, data will be given for three groups—the Irish, the non-Irish, and the total population.

"Cotton-mill work was selected for special investigation because it employs a larger number of women and children than any other industry, because it exhibits a deplorably high female death rate, and because it, more frequently perhaps than any other large industry, subjects its workers to inhalation of irritant vegetable dust, which in the underfed and overworked is especially conducive to bronchitic, asthmatic, and tuberculously infectious pulmonary diseases.

"And, finally, tuberculosis was selected for special intensive study because it was found to be the most prevalent ultimate or immediate cause of death within the age period 15 to 44, which comprised one-half the total population and four-fifths of the operative population of the cities selected for study.

How Data Was Acquired.

"Moreover, to bring out the facts more clearly, a method of comparison has been adopted. The present report, therefore, presents the results of a special intensive study into the basic antilongevity causes existent in the years 1905, 1906, and 1907 among (1) persons resident in Fall River, Mass., as compared with those in Fall River, Manchester, and Pawtucket combined; (2) persons aged 15 to 44 years as compared with the aggregate aged 10 years and over; (3) females as compared with males; (4) the Irish race or people as compared with the aggregate non-Irish races or peoples; (5) cotton operatives as compared with those not employed in cotton manufacturing, and (6) persons who ultimately fell victims to tuberculosis, as compared with those whose debility or casualty culminated in nontuberculous forms of death.

"As a result of these comparisons the following points seems to be clearly established:

"I. The effect of cotton operative work upon health, as reflected in the death rate, differs widely between the sexes. For the thirty-year age period from 15 to 44, in which the great majority of the operatives are found,

PHOTO & I COURTESY OF THE NATIONAL CHILD LABOR COMMITTEE

Worker So Small She Has to Stand on a Box to Reach Machine.

Children Employed in a Big Cotton Mill.

the death rates of males and females in the general population are almost identical, the male rate being 6.19 and the female rate 6.18. A comparison of the death rates of male and female non-operatives shows the rate for males to be 22 per cent. in excess of that for females, (male rate, 6.48; female rate, 5.31.) When, however, the comparison is confined to the death rates of operatives the female rate shows an excess of 33 per cent. over the male (male rate, 5.74; female rate, 7.63,) despite the younger ages of the female operatives.

Female Death Rate.

"II. In the age groups within which operatives and non-operatives are fairly comparable, female operatives have a decidedly higher death rate than non-operatives. This is most marked in respect to tuberculosis, the death rate of female operatives from this cause being in general more than twice that of non-operatives, and in some of the race and age groups running up to many times as high. Thus, in the age groups 15 to 24 years, 25 to 34 years, and 35 to 44 years, the death rates from tuberculosis per 1,000 were, respectively, two and one-fourth times, two and one-half times, and five times those among women of the same age groups outside the cotton industry.

"III. An examination of different factors which might affect the death rate, especially from tuberculosis, such as native or foreign birth, tuberculous kindred or intimates, overcrowding, sanitary condition of homes, &c., fails to show any such massing of unfortunate conditions among the female operatives as would explain their unvaryingly higher death rate.

"Hence it seems impossible to escape the conclusion that operative work is prejudicial to the health of females, that the combination of operative work with matrimony is especially harmful, and that, while the general hazard of the female operative is greater than that of the non-operative, she is in most danger from tuberculosis. Whether the harmful effects of operative work are greater than those of other industrial employments, and whether they inhere in cotton textile work as a whole or are due to certain occupations carried on within the mills, are questions for further investigations to answer. This has established the fact of the high mortality among female cotton operatives and of their special susceptibility to tuberculosis.

"In considering the real significance of these conclusions, weight must be given to the character of the death records on which they are based. This study has clearly established that such records, as at present made out, cannot safely be used as the basis of mortality studies without investigation of their accuracy. Two conspicuous errors or defects were discovered, the first relating to the decedents' occupation and the second to the cause of death.

Deficient Records.

"1. The official records contained many and serious errors as to the occupation of the decedent. This was especially the case where females were concerned. In Fall River more than one-half of the female decedents for the period covered who were found to have been cotton-mill operatives were not so recorded. On the other hand, one-seventh of the group recorded as operatives were found on investigation not to have been cotton-mill operatives. Among the male decedents of Fall River for the three years studied 28 per cent. of those who were proved to have been cotton operatives were recorded on the death certificate as having followed some other occupation, while one-third of those recorded as operatives could not properly be included among cotton workers. The effect of such inaccuracies upon any study of occupational mortality is obvious.

"2. In regard to the cause of death the certificates were found to err in two ways; in some cases the cause was described by a misleading or absolutely false term, and in others one of two contributory factors was arbitrarily assigned as the cause, with no mention of the other, which might have been equally or even more important.

This is the method of estimating the significance of contributory causes of death described by Dr. Perry:

"There are certain circumstances or experiences, common but not inevitable accompaniments of living, which may be active factors in the causation of both disease and death. Such, for instance, are (1) ignorance; (2) bad air, whether germ laden, dusty, humid, or chemically impure; (3) bad food, that is, ill chosen, ill cooked, or ill chewed; (4) bad or alcoholic drink; (5) bad personal, sexual, or apartment hygiene; (6) long labor and short sleep; (7) occupational stress, (hurry and worry;) (8) scant income, whether through thriftlessness, misfortune, or low wages; (9) accompaniments of the conjugal condition, such as child-birth and dependents; (10) overwork of non-resiliency from fatigue.

Some Percentages.

"These or some of these conditions might be encountered in the life history of any decedent, but as there are no data by age groups of the actual prevalence of such conditions it was impossible to obtain, through age group death rates, any precise data of their effect in shortening life. Throughout this study, therefore, it has been assumed tentatively that the significance of any such condition as a causative factor of death is established by the frequency with which it was found to have occurred as an antecedent of the deaths studied.

"For example, the following study shows that in Fall River 29 per cent. of the decedent female cotton operatives had had tuberculous relatives, while only 21 per cent. of the decedent male operatives had had similarly afflicted relatives. In accordance with the above principle it has therefore been tentatively assumed that tuberculous kindred have more influence as a causative factor of deaths among female than among male operatives.

"Again, the economic importance of any factor or group of factors is measured fundamentally by its longevity effect; i. e., its effect on the duration of life. In this study it has been tentatively assumed that this effect is shown by the rare occurrence of a given factor in the life history of young decedents; or conversely by its frequent occurrence in the life history of those who attained a high average age before death.

"For instance, it was found that in Fall River, during the three years covered by this study, four-fifths (79 per cent.) of the total number of deaths from tuberculosis among the female population aged 10 years or over occurred in the age period 15 to 44, while of the deaths in the same age and sex group from pneumonia and cancer only 29 per cent. of the first and 24 per cent. of the second occurred in the age period 15 to 44.

"In other words, tuberculosis had a far more marked anti-longevity effect in this group than either of the other diseases. But this period is that of the greatest industrial importance. It is evident, then, that so far as this section of the population is concerned, tuberculosis, which finds its greatest number of victims in the period of chief industrial activity, is economically far more important than pneumonia and cancer, which find their victims principally among those whose industrial effectiveness is either waning or practically at an end.

"This method of reaching conclusions as to the physical condition of a specified class of individuals by a comparison of death rates has been so seldom used and differs so radically from the customary method that the main points of variance between the two modes of investigation seem to need some preliminary consideration.

"The two methods may be respectively defined as the inspection method and the death-rate method. Under the first method a careful inspection is made of as many as possible of those engaged in a given industry and from the prevalence of ill health or disease among them conclusions are drawn as to the healthfulness of that pursuit. By the second method, the death rate among those engaged in a given industry is accurately determined for a period sufficiently long to exclude the effect of temporary disturbances, and from a comparison of this death rate with that prevailing in similar age and sex groups outside of the industry conclusions are drawn as to the healthful or non-healthful character of the industry."

This table shows the relation between the death rate and the annual rental per capita:

Operatives—
Tuberculous $21.00
Non-tuberculous 22.00
Non-operatives—
Tuberculous 23.00
Non-tuberculous 25.00
Both classes—
Tuberculous 22.00
Non-tuberculous 25.00

The National Child Labor Committee, commenting on Dr. Perry's report, says:

"The boy who works in a cotton mill has only half as good a chance to live to be 20 years old as the boy outside the cotton mill, and there are more child operatives under 16 in cotton mills than the total population of San Diego or Fitchburg or Kalamazoo. There has long been an impression that a cotton mill was not the health resort that some mill owners claim it to be. Now the latest volume of the Government report on the condition of woman and child wage-earners shows that it might be called a death resort. It reveals a death rate so high that the report throws upon the defenders of cotton-mill conditions the burden of proving that the general effect of cotton-mill work is not positively injurious to health.

"Boys and girls offer a curious contrast in their powers of resistance to the health hazards of the cotton industry. Women of every age between 14 and 54 show a higher death rate among those who work in a cotton mill than among those who do not. This difference reaches its climax with women 35 to 44 years of age, of whom twice as many operatives as non-operatives die. Boys on the other hand succumb in largest numbers before they are 20. Boys 15 to 19 make up one-sixth of all the male workers in cotton mills, and these boy operatives have a death rate nearly twice as high as the non-operative population of the same age. On the other hand, relatively more girl operatives than boy operatives die under 20. Not only do a large pro-

Girl Workers in a Cotton Mill.

portion of deaths among women operatives occur between 15 and 19, but the actual death rate per 1,000 operatives of this age period is higher for girls than for boys.

Argument Against Child Labor.

"In these facts the National Child Labor Committee finds another reason for believing that all children under 16 should be excluded from factory work. It is significant, they say, that although in almost every State the passage of child labor laws has les-

sened the numbers of children under 14 in factories, and in many States has excluded them altogether, the numbers of children under 16 reported in factories by the census of 1900 and the census of 1910 are almost identical. The decrease is less than 200 on a total of over 160,000. This is not surprising to those who have noted that local investigations in various places have been showing a marked increase in recent years in the numbers who leave school at 14, or as soon as the law allows them, to go to work.

"A striking example of this is offered by a report on Worcester, Mass., received last month from the United States Bureau of Education. In that city from 1905 to 1910 the number of girls under 16 taking out employment certificates had increased 40 per cent., while the population of Worcester had increased only 10 per cent.

"The report lends a sinister distinction to the third largest industry of the country, in which one-twentieth of all the six and a half million factory workers are employed.

"The three earlier volumes of the Government report presented facts on wages, hours, ages of workers, &c., in typical cotton communities North and South, which showed the South in so unfavorable a light that many voices arose to insinuate that the findings of the Bureau of Labor had been deliberately colored under the influence of the Northern cotton manufacturers. Now this latest and most damaging testimony about the influence of cotton mills upon health comes entirely from New England.

"The National Child Labor Committee has throughout the controversy defended the Bureau of Labor and the committee points to this volume on the 'Causes of Death Among Cotton Mill Operatives' as a final vindication of the Bureau's sincerity."

This Little Girl, Aged 12 Years, Works in a Cotton Mill and Helps Support an Ablebodied Father.

HENRY ST. SETTLEMENT CELEBRATING ITS 20TH BIRTHDAY

THE Henry Street Settlement which, with its founder and head, Miss Lillian Wald, has acquired a world-wide fame, is celebrating its twentieth anniversary. A feature of this will be a grand pageant to take place in Henry Street on the evenings of Friday and Saturday next, June 6 and 7. It will be an illustrated history of Henry Street from the days of the Indians. Five hundred people, men, women, and children, will take part in it, and it will represent the loving co-operation of all the varied forces of the settlement, from the little kindergarten graduates to the oldest beneficiaries, together with the various workers, residents, and many friends of the institution.

March is the actual birthday month of the Settlement. It was in that month, twenty years ago, that Miss Wald with one associate, Miss Mary M. Brewster, started the work which has developed to wonderful proportions and has led many valuable lines of civic work.

The celebration has been going on for some time and will continue until the Fall, when the work of the Settlement will be shown in a big exhibition.

All the city has been taking part in the anniversary rejoicing. There have been dinners and many gifts have been received. The latter represent the beautiful co-operative spirit of the donors. A newsboy, who had been connected with the Settlement, sent 25 cents for the pageant. A colored woman's club sent $5, and there has been a gift of $50,000 which will be the nest egg of a permanent fund.

A committee has been appointed to raise a permanent fund to support the work of the nurses. Many people are being asked by the committee to co-operate and the $50,000 from two people, a man and woman whose names have not yet ben announced, is one of the first large gifts.

The Nursing Education League, whose members are superintendents of hospitals and training schools, gave the Henry Street nurses a dinner at the Park Avenue Hotel. The library at Seward Park is to have a special evening celebration of the anniversary, when, among other things, stories of old New York will be told. As for the city itself, it is co-operating to make things smooth for the pageant, which will be the real birthday party of the Settlement, and is making great haste to get the asphalt in the streets in condition for the celebration.

The Misses Alice and Irene

HENRY STREET SETTLEMENT HOUSE

Lewisohn, two wealthy young women who are among the many prominent non-resident workers for the Settlement, have the entire management of the pageant and are at the Settlement daily rehearsing and superintending the work.

The costumes alone for the 500 people who will take part represent a fabulous amount of work. They have been designed and cut by Miss Ethel Frankau, a volunteer worker who has been years in the Settlement and has made a scientific study of costumes. The dramatic work of the clubs, which is a strong feature of the Settlement activities, is said to compare with the Irish Players, and the players are always correctly costumed from Miss Frankau's designs. The Settlement has developed through the pageant what it laughingly calls a sweatshop, a costume manufactory established in one of the buildings, where women and older children, and the regular workers in the Settlement go when they can spare a minute to do what work they can in sewing. A number of old Quaker gowns have been loaned.

Henry Street is an interesting part of the city historically and the managers of the pageant have much to work upon. Nathan Hale was executed in the vicinity. In Henry Street there still remains a church with a slave gallery, the only one left in the city. The houses which the Settlement occupies, seven of which are on Henry Street, are historic relics. They date back to the days when the finest residences of the city were there.

Miss Wald feels that one of the good pieces of civic work that the Settlement has done, aside from its philanthropies, has been the restoration and preservation of these charming old houses.

There is a legend to the effect that they were finished by fine cabinet-makers who came to New York during the War of 1812. The woodwork inside is a delight. The doors are of solid mahogany and the rosettes on the frames are hand-carved.

If you go into the big gymnasium of the Settlement, at the back of three of the Henry Street houses, any evening nowadays, you will see a lot of small boys hopping around in an excited way making strange noises. It is a rehearsal and the small boys, though without costume, may easily be recognized as Indians. They will figure in the group of Manhattas of the Island in early days, who will open the pageant.

"The Settlement," says Miss Lewisohn, "has always encouraged and stimulated the gathering together of beautiful old traditions and has always been eager to revive customs that have significance and meaning. A committee to plan the festivity decided that no more appropriate subject could be chosen than picturesque social gatherings of the people who have lived at different times in Henry Street, in order to create an atmosphere of old New York. The current number of the Settlement Journal says:

First, we shall be the Manhattas, gravely welcoming the White Strangers, initiating them into the ceremony of the peace pipe and burying the hatchet with joyous songs and dances. Then we shall be the Dutch vrouws and burghers with their large families and enjoying a strawberry picnic in the days when the fields of Manhattan Island were covered with wild berries. In the midst of the fun, the postie will dash by on horseback on his way to Boston carrying the monthly mail and, of course, every one will follow, waving and singing to speed him on his dangerous journey.

Then there will be a real May party with king, queen, court, chimney sweeps, Moorish dancers, milkmaids, and sailors, all dancing and playing round the Maypole just as in the Colonial days. There will be a glimpse, too, of the children who a little more than a century ago were taken by their Quaker parents to the first two public schools in New York, which were started in Henry and Madison Streets.

And then we shall have to imagine a moonlight Spring evening in the sixties, and we shall see the girls in hoop skirts and the young men in stocks gather on the stoops of the houses, singing old ballads and dancing old-fashioned polkas.

The last episode will be a picture of all the nationalities in Henry Street in the last fifty years—the Irish, the Scotch, the Germans, the Italians, and the Russians—and we shall sing again the songs and dance the dances that have added so much poetry to the life of the city.

Old music and songs are being revived for the pageant and prominent artists are designing scenery and painting beautiful banners. Boy carpenters of the Settlement have made properties. The streets are to be brilliantly illuminated and decorated.

One of the regrets of every one concerned in the pageant is that a general invitation cannot be sent out to the public to witness it. It will be so large in itself that with the people of the vicinity and the friends of the Settlement, who will be invited, there will be no room for those from other parts of the city.

The chorus will be a special feature. Mass meetings are being held in which all the clubs are brought together. These rehearsals require so much space that Public School 147 has been loaned for the purpose.

The work of the Henry Street Settlement, originally called the Nurses' Settlement, founded by Miss Lillian D. Wald, who is to New York what Miss Jane Addams is to Chicago, has grown to unimagined proportions since its establishment in 1893. Miss Wald came into it immediately after her graduation. She was taking a special course at the Woman's Hospital and giving lessons in home nursing to east side mothers, women from different parts of the Old World, when the special event which threw her into Settlement work took place.

A little girl came one morning to say that her mother was too ill to attend the class and asked Miss Wald if she would call on her. The place to which she was directed was unimaginable in its squalor. She says now that never in all her work on the east side has she seen anything more pitiful than that first case.

The so-called home was in a rear tenement reached through a yard that was in an unspeakably filthy condition. The sick woman was in a dark, unlighted room, the only air reaching it coming from a window opening into another small room in which were her husband, children, and boarders.

The beginning of the Henry Street Settlement was in a little upper floor on Jefferson Street which Miss Wald and Miss Brewster occupied, realizing that the only way to help the people was to live among them.

The settlement as it now is has, in addition to the seven houses on Henry Street, a Settlement House on Seventy-ninth Street and one on Sixtieth Street for colored nurses. Three stores are rented downtown which are used for stock rooms, milk stations, and clinics, and the Children's Aid Society Rooms are hired for dancing classes.

There are 3,000 members of the Henry Street classes and clubs alone. The other Settlement buildings have their own special membership lists. Miss Wald says that, though at first she did only nursing work, she always had in mind the citizenship work which is now one of the Settlement features.

The entire Boroughs of Manhattan and Bronx are now districted for nursing, and there are 92 nurses subject to call. Poor mothers with large families who cannot under any circumstances leave home to go to a hospital now receive all the attention that they need at home.

The nurses' uniform of the settlement is a pretty one, plain dark blue cotton, with little white collar and cuffs—very becoming also. It is an attractive sight to see the nurses coming in with their black visiting bags twice a day to the nurses' room in the Settlement to write out their reports, which are carefully preserved. Last year these nurses made 200,000 visits.

From 9 A. M. to 4 P. M. surgical cases, where it is possible, visit the settlement and are looked after by nurses in charge. Miss Wald's is considered the best-organized nursing staff in the world.

Jacob H. Schiff, who has been interested in the work from the beginning, gave the first Settlement House at 265 Henry Street, which is the administration building now where Miss Wald and her assistant, Miss Alice Gannett, live. Miss Helen McDowell, who was one of the first lay workers, and who is still a resident, gave the second house and fitted it up. Mrs. Butler Duncan was an up-town house, and John Crosby Brown, father of one of the residents, gave another house. Then Mrs. Sylvan Bier gave a house in the country, which became the first out-of-town branch of the work. The Settlement now has seven delightful country homes.

There are camps for boys, homes for mothers and babies, homes for girls, a convalescent home, a model family of eight being brought up under the best conditions of family life, and classes in agriculture.

There is co-operative housekeeping in all the homes and the little and big girls not only learn the benefits of the family spirit, but practical home-making and housekeeping.

The Settlement is conspicuous through the boxes of flowers in its diamond panel windows and its pretty window curtains. Inside the houses are as charming as outside. Everything in good and simple taste, with pictures and fine old brasses that have been picked up in the neighborhood.

The Settlement residents are prominent men and women. They include Miss Florence Kelley, Dr. Henry Moskowitz, Miss Elizabeth Farrell and Howard Bradstreet. From the beginning the value of the work has interested people of prominence and wealth. Many people of wealth have been among both residents and outside workers, and one of the things upon which the Settlement prides itself is that it has never been obliged to make a public appeal for funds.

The Settlement has initiated many valuable features of city life. At its first building, 265 Henry Street, the first public playground was started in the back yard with sand piles and the "scups" or swings. It was Miss Wald who volunteered the services of one of the nurses of the Settlement for public school work. After a month the School Board took this work over and the system has now spread throughout the world. It was Miss Wald who interviewed President Roosevelt in regard to the Federal Child's Bureau. One of the things the Settlement is proudest of is the scholarships it gives. There are fifty-five of these now.

Great pride is felt in the first girl to whom a scholarship was given. Her father was a student of the work of the Rabbis, a cultivated man in an Old-World way, but the little daughter was not walking along similar lines. Education had no fascination for her. She was a dear little imp of a girl with a talent for art. Finally, through a Settlement scholarship, she took a course in designing at the Manhattan Trade School and got a good position with a neckwear firm for whom she designs and buys. She goes on trips to Paris for her employers and yet she is only nineteen years old.

Miss Wald is on the Joint Board of Sanitary Control and is President of the Lower East Side Social Halls Association, which operates Clinton Hall. Among the Settlement's activities is work on the docks, in the parks, and in the schools.

June 1, 1913

WOMEN WHO ARE INVENTORS

A WELL-KNOWN physician whose achievements and writings have placed him among the best American medical authorities has been devoting time to the study of women as inventors. In a recent interview he gave a few ideas upon the subject which raised a storm of protest from the women inventors of the day.

The interview grants that "women excel in the most beautiful and effective qualities of genius for building civilization. Women have achieved in literature. But the encyclopedia fails to record the names of women painters, composers or inventors except in significant numbers. The test of history has shown that women have failed to produce works of genius, or have made any important discoveries to place themselves at the head of professions practically their own, the famous Chefs, modistes and dressmakers being men." All this may be true, but it must be remembered that woman, "attuned to maternity," has been pretty busy in that line for all the ages she has been assisting in the civilization of a world, while time and opportunity have been denied her to demonstrate her abilities along the creative and inventive line. Men have had the field to themselves so far. The "germ cell" accredited to them which gives them the capacity to seize opportunity and to make the most of it, has steadily developed, while women have been forced by circumstances to bide their time.

The time has come now, however, when men must look to their laurels, for the modern field is full of women inventors. The oldest of them and the one having most to her credit, is Miss Margaret E. Knight, who at the age of seventy is working twenty hours a day on her eighty-ninth invention. Her first achievement—at the age of twelve—was a covered shuttle which is in general use to-day in cotton mills, where it is a great protection to the operators. Her invention of the square paper bag now in universal use brought her in 1871 from the Queen of England the decoration of the Royal Legion of Honor. Among labor saving devices in cotton and woolen mills, rubber and shoe factories, her latest is a motor for driving them.

Miss Jane Anderson has three inventions on the market, one being on exhibition at the Museum of Safety in the Engineers Building. Her metal sanitary toilet cleanser, with the paper to use in connection with it, and her fire extinguisher — an accessory of tea tables where the alcohol kettle is a cause of more or less danger — entitle her to the gratitude of thousands of women.

A minor device, invented by Miss Anderson, is a metal open-work slipper rack, to fasten on the side of the bed, for night slippers; quite a convenience, as these particular articles have a depraved habit of becoming separated and betaking themselves to far distant corners when most needed. She also promises "more to come" in the near future.

Mrs. Nina Piffard-Frances is of a mechanical turn of mind, and her inventions run along that line. Her first was a self-threading machine needle which, she declares, was bought up and shelved by a firm having one of its own, though not so good, on the market. Her next was a non-corrosive metal lock faucet for wine, liquor, or oil barrels. It is simple yet effective, the key being the central telescope bolt which releases or closes the escape for the liquid. A stamp-affixing machine for office use is the third invention, and Mrs. Frances says she is at work now on something still better.

Mrs. Julia C. Phillips has come to the aid of her flat-dwelling sisters, whose cry of "more closet room" is so persistent, and has invented the "invisible wardrobe." This device is "strictly sanitary, requires no floor or wall space, creates a closet where there is none, has a metal framework and a dust-proof cover, and is swung like a drawer under the metal bed by peculiar hinges of its own. It also comes for crib use, and holds all the baby's clothes in its compartment tills." Other space economizers are already absorbing the new inventor's attention.

Mrs. Norma Ford Schafuss has recently invented a buckle for garters, belts, or other purposes, which for its simplicity and remarkable fastening powers brought a chorus of praise from the manufacturers. They said they had been at work for twenty years trying to get something like the thing, which this clever woman had worked out by means of common hairpins, fussed over at odd moments! Encouraged by her success, she is now at work on some sanitary devices which she thinks will fill a long felt need.

Mme. Bessie Lazelle has the distinction of owning and operating a factory for the making of certain items of women's apparel, where all the help, even to the office force, are women. A number of sanitary garments have been invented by Mme. Lazelle, but her latest is a rubberized bathing corset, which has among its good points the quality of drying so quickly that it may be worn three or four times a day if desired.

June Haughton, besides being an expert rifle shot and traveler, has found time to invent several small sanitary devices and a motor veil which fastens by a button and loop over large or small hats, and forms a scarf or shoulder drapery in a number of becoming ways.

Mrs. Homer Lind, in addition to keeping house, looking after the welfare of two kiddies, and playing a long season in vaudeville with her husband, has invented an attachment for the window frame in places where a pulley is used to bring the clothesline indoors. With this attachment the things can be hung by a person who stands beside the window instead of leaning out. When not in use it folds away like an umbrella. She has about perfected a wind shield to go with the frame.

Another woman inventor is also interested in vaudeville work, and in her case necessity was certainly the mother of invention. Mrs. Anita Lawrence Linton had great need in the sketch done by her husband and herself of an affective rainfall. All manner of things were investigated without much success. One day, in despair, she sat down to study just what a rainstorm really did, and she noted its string-like appearance in falling. At once a new idea came to her. After experimenting with chiffon, tinsel strings, and blue lights she finally succeeded in producing a really wonderful effect, and her "rain curtain" may now be used on any sized stage.

A mechanical washer, a twin rolling pin and a body vibrator were all invented by a woman. A vacuum washing machine with electric attachment, which does the washing while the housewife attends to her other duties, was the invention of a clever woman. Modern cake pans, jelly frames, hat pin safety attachments, and a dozen and one household conveniences are being patented by women, though these facts do not get into the encyclopaedia. President Whigelt of the Inventors' League of the United States says that they have welcomed a number of women inventors as members of the league, and have applications for membership on file now, while Mrs. Nina Piffard-Frances is one of the charter members of the league. These are but a few of the bright women whose inventions are patented and on the market in this immediate vicinity, and a trip further afield would discover many more.

October 19, 1913

PROHIBITION GAINS, W. C. T. U. WOMEN SAY

World's Convention Opens with Reports of Changing Conditions in Many Countries.

The opening of the business session of the Ninth Triennial Convention of the World's Woman's Christian Temperance Union in the Academy fo Music, Brooklyn, brought out yesterday a large crowd of women who filled every seat and stood in groups in the back of the house, though from there it was difficult to hear the speakers on the platform. There were 3,500 present.

The Academy presented a brilliant appearance, the platform, balconies, and boxes being draped with flags of all nations and myriads of colors. There were representatives from many nations, but not all natives of the countries from which they came. There was nothing picturesque in the dress of the women, who were all in European costume. Mme. Barrakat of Syria was one of the native women present. There are six organizations of W. C. T. U. women on Mount Lebanon, in the Holy Land, and their leader told the convention that in that far off land the women were gathered together while the convention was in session praying for its success.

The morning session opened with addresses of welcome from Mayor Kline, Borough President Lewis R. Pounds, and William A. Marble, President of the Merchants' Association of New York. Mayor Kline's words did not appeal to the women. He told them that they would be more successful if they were milder in their methods and advocated temperance rather than total abstinence. One of the women speakers in the afternoon, telling of the need of entire prohibition of liquor, added:

"And tell that to your Mayor."

Lady Aurea Howard, daughter of Lady Carlisle, President of the World's Union, represented her mother at the morning session and presented Mrs. Lillian M. N. Stevens, National W. C. T. U. President, and Vice President of the World's Union. In the name of the British delegates, Lady Howard gave Mrs. Stevens a silver and crystal vase.

It was announced yesterday that the big polyglot temperance petition with its 7,000,000 signatures which has, for some years, been working its way around the world would be sent to the Panama Exposition where a request has been made for it.

In the W. C. T. U., news of the work of the world's union it was said yesterday that there was an increase of 45,932 members since the last convention. There is an organization in Milan with 32 members; Ireland has for the first time a white ribbon band and there are 20 new unions in China. Work must be done in India to disassociate the name of Christian with liquor, the Christians having introduced it into the country, the native religions all opposing its use. Prince Albert Island is the only prohibition point in Canada and Halifax is the only place in Nova Scotia where liquor can be sold.

Nine of the United States are under prohibition laws, these taking in one-half of the population and two-thirds of the territory. The women applauded when reference was made to a famous temperance dinner at Washington.

Total abstinence is increasing in Germany, there are more than 200,000 white ribboneds there and 50 organizations. The most scientific study and instruction of the evil effects of alcohol is to be found in Germany. Physicians are promoting temperance in Sweden, but physicians in France are taking no steps in that direction. There is much scientific study in Italy. Miss Agnes Slack, one of the two Honorary Secretaries who read the reports told of the bad conditions in Belgium and how, in a first-class boarding school for girls, she saw little girls of seven drinking beer. The French women would join unions if moderate drinking was allowed and a new W. C. T. U., headquarters is to be put up in Paris and money is needed for it. They are enrolling the babies in England and the mothers come in after them.

"We have done enormous work for suffrage in England," said Miss Slack, who is from Derbyshire, "but I do not believe the vote for the women will ever be won by violence. The temperance women have worked for every suffrage bill."

Mrs. Carry Chapman Catt, the International Suffrage President, was received with applause in the afternoon and told the women that it was their organization which had driven her into suffrage.

"Your pledge was the first one I ever made," she said, "and I have never broken it. Your badge was the first one that I ever wore. It was in a little town in Iowa. The local paper had allowed the temperance women a column in its pages, they had some trouble to find anything to say and I undertook to do the work.

"Our town was a prohibition town, but there were five saloons in it and I knew it. An investigation was undertaken and different men testified to going into these places and asking for something to drink and being given milk. My column had been largely made up of extracts from The Union Signal, but here was something real to write about and I did it. I said that if these men were such idiots that when they received beer to drink they thought it was milk we women knew by the smell as we passed the doors of the places that it was beer.

"The president of our union was the wife of a grocer who was superintendent of the Sunday School and frequently had temperance afternoons. He obliged his wife to resign from the union after that and she did. The editor of the paper disavowed any responsibility for my work and the women never had a column again. My father said I was always too strong-minded for my own good and my mother felt that her chicken had turned out a duckling.

"I was a young girl of 22 then, but I made up my mind if that was the way things went in temperance work the thing I wanted was a vote, and I have been hunting it ever since."

Col. Moss, Medical Superintendent of the East Division of the army, was present with Mrs. Moss. The Colonel told the women that they were doing more to put down disease than any other organization; that Francis Willard, the founder of the work, deserved a noble monument; that the great numbers of moral and mental defectives in all parts of the country owed the curse of their defects to alcoholic parents.

There was much disappointment among the delegates because Miss Ellen Stone, who was kidnapped in the Near East, was obliged to leave before the time for her presentation to the audience. She will be at the sessions early next week.

The convention accomplishes much work in a short time, as action is taken in executive meetings and approved in bulk by the delegates as a whole. Tea is served for the delegates every afternoon at the close of the sessions in the assembly room in the upper part of the academy.

Telling what the English women were doing, Mrs. Ormiston Chant, a writer and public speaker of England at the evening meeting said:

"We have a woman at Whitehall, alongside a man Government official, and she draws £1,000 for looking after the children's work in the labor bureaus. And we would never have believed it, but we have women who wear the golden chain, are called 'Your Worship,' and sit on the Mayor's bench. We have all been praying for the vote, but I would like you American women to knew that we English women working for the vote, and who have born the heat and burden of the day, are almost all of us against any form of violence. We believe in the power of love and a sound mind. In God's time and when God's hour strikes we shall have the ballot."

Mrs. Gordon Wright of Canada claimed the most northern union in the world—"200 miles from the Arctic circle, twenty-two members in Dawson." Miss Agnes Slack of England and the Baroness de Laveleys of Belgium were other speakers. There will be another all day session at the Academy to-day.

October 25, 1913

WOMEN TO ASK CITY TO FIND THEM WORK

Mass Meeting of Unemployed Held at Cooper Union—Conference with Mayor To-day.

UNION ORGANIZATION URGED

Inequality of Pay of Men and Women Assailed — Trades League Throws Open Its Doors to Jobless.

A mass meeting of unemployed women was held in Cooper Union yesterday at 1 P. M. and Miss Melinda Scott presided as Chairman. She announced that the assembly room of the Woman's Trades Union League, 42 East Twenty-second Street, had been thrown open to women without work that they might not have to sit in the parks when not looking for a job.

"I understand," she said, "that girls who live in hired rooms are turned out of them at 8:30 o'clock in the morning and not allowed to come back until 6:30 at night. Now every one knows that there is no use in going around to look for work after 10:30 in the morning, so we have opened the league room for the women."

She also said that arrangements were being made to give those out of work temporary employment.

A resolution was passed making a demand on the State authorities for work. This will be taken to the Mayor to-day and the women will ask for immediate employment.

It had been planned for the women at the meeting to march down to City Hall after adjournment, but this was abandoned when a letter was read from Mr. Mitchel saying that he had arranged for a conference to-day to which he had asked Miss Mary Dreier to send a representative of the unemployed women. He had discussed the situation with Commissioner Kingsbury, he said.

One woman in the audience got up to say that she did not see when there was such a demand for domestic servants why any of the women who had been telling of their trials need suffer.

"Why will they suffer all these hardships," she asked, "when they could have comfortable homes and $20 a month? There is no need of any one starving."

"There must be some very good reason why the girls all prefer to go to factories or shops under the worst condition rather than go into people's homes to work," answered Miss Scott.

The stories of the girls were very similar. Many complaints told of looking for work where there seemed to be no real demand for girls. One girl after another told of name, address and pedigree being taken at these places and then being sent off. There would be small armies of girls all treated in the same way. It took their time and carfare needlessly, they complained.

"I had to walk home from Thirty-second Street way downtown, where I live," said one girl, "because I had taken my last ten cents to go there."

"They keep the advertisements in the paper because they like to have girls standing around outside their shops," said Miss Scott, "and then they can say to those who are working for them: 'See all the people waiting to take your place.'"

Another complaint was that the employers were continually bringing in younger girls who would begin for lower wages. A girl of 18 or 20 would break down in her work, it was asserted, after having worked up in two or three years to $9 or $10 a week, and then going back after an illness she would find her place taken by the younger girl at $5.

An expert stenographer said that a man's position with very hard work was given her with half his pay, and in a less difficult position she was replaced by some one less expert, who would take less money.

The cry of a middle-aged woman carrying a muff and having the appearance of being very well dressed, was one of the most pathetic.

"Why ain't I let to live?" she asked. "I was born and brought up in this city, I'm a citizen, I'm capable. This is a suicidal existence. Nobody cares, and if you say anything about your troubles they take out their watches. I want work. Give me a chance. I'm as capable as any one. Give me a chance."

A laundry worker who had helped organize a strike had not had work since. She is blacklisted.

Many of the speakers asserted that the women must organize to find relief. The meeting lasted three hours.

January 29, 1914

WOMEN SELL AUTOS.

They Demonstrate Them and Get as Much Pay as Men at Maxwell's.

Automobile Row saw an innovation yesterday in the form of a reception at the salesrooms of the Maxwell Motor Company, at Broadway and Fifty-ninth Street, to inaugurate the new policy of the company of employing women for demonstrators and sales agents on the same terms as men. Many of the women active in the woman's movement were present, and speeches were made by Mrs. Crystal Eastman Benedict, manager of the new enterprise; Miss Alice Carpenter, field organizer of the saleswoman's bureau; Mrs. Charles Beard, Mrs. Alice Burrows Fernandez, Director of the Vocational Guidance Survey and one of the founders of the Intercollegiate Bureau of Occupations, and Miss Mary Garrett Hay of the Woman's Suffrage Party.

Concrete evidence of the company's belief in the ability of women to handle machinery as well as sell motor cars was shown by Miss Jean Earl Moehle, a Barnard graduate of this year's class, who, in leather apron and blue jeans coat, stood on the show window platform during the afternoon assembling and disassembling a motor. Another saleswoman recently employed by the company, Miss Mabel Wiley, sold a car during the reception to Mrs. Edwin Stanton Bayer.

The speakers, who were introduced by Mrs. Inez Milholland Boissevain, dwelt on the opportunity which this new occupation gave to women to prove the contention of the feminist movement that women were not only equal to the task of sharing the occupations of men, but, when engaged in them, were worthy of equal pay for equal service. This condition and the prospect of proper hours and fair treatment, led them, they said, to indorse the enterprise.

During the reception tea was poured by Miss Florence Guernsey, President of the City Federation of Women's Clubs, and Mrs. Henry Bruere, while Miss Ethel Peyser and Miss Rose Young were at the coffee table.

December 16, 1914

PROTESTING WOMEN MARCH IN MOURNING

Muffled Drums Beat as the Sombre Parade Moves Down Fifth Avenue.

HATS RAISED TO PEACE FLAG

Only 1,500 Are in Line, but Crowds Along Thoroughfare Show Sympathy by Silence.

With muffled drums, a small army of women robed in black marched down Fifth Avenue from Fifty-eighth Street to Union Square yesterday afternoon as a protest against the war. It was not a large parade, for there were no more than 1,500 marchers, but it was impressive, and the crowd that lined Fifth Avenue from the beginning to the end of the march received it almost in silence.

Here and there a woman would lean forward from the crowd of spectators and clap vigorously. In another place a man would do the same, and once two or three persons aplauded at the same time, but the general silence of the great gathering was considered the best evidence of understanding. At different places men stood with raised hats as the peace flag passed.

The crowd which saw the parade was immense. It began at Fifty-eighth Street, and from there down the avenue the people stood three deep on both sides, while children sat on the curbstones at their feet. The crowd massed on the steps of St. Patrick's Cathedral, with its drapery of mourning for the Pope, and was greatest at the Public Library.

The parade started at 4:40, and at 5:45 it was disbanding at Union Square. There had been a misunderstanding with the police, who had not expected it to move until 5 o'clock. Following the mounted police, Miss Alice Carpenter, with Miss Rose Young and Mrs. Florence Woolston as aids, bore the big peace flag, a large yellow-fringed white banner with a dove carrying an olive branch in the centre and beneath it the word "Peace" in large letters of gold.

The banner carriers were dressed in white, with black bands on their arms, and so was Mrs. Henry Villard, who walked alone in front of the officers of the Committee of Two Hundred, Mrs. John Winters Brannan, Miss Lillian Deaver, Miss Lillian Wald, and Miss Katherine Leckey directly following her. Behind them were Miss Mary Shaw, Mrs. James Lees Laidlaw, Mrs. Charlotte Perkins Gilman, and Mrs. Mary Ware Dennett. Some of the women wore dresses of deep mourning.

Many women who were members of the Committee of Two Hundred and who had been working in the interest of the parade were not able to be present. Among the marchers were Mrs. Robert Ingersoll, Mrs. Wolston Hill Brown, Mrs. Henry Butterworth, Mrs. Haryot Holt Dey, Miss Mary Wood, Mrs. Edward Lauterbach, Miss Annie Peck, Mrs. Elmer Black, and Miss Helen Varick Boswell. Mme. Yorska of the French Theatre led a band of refugees.

In one of the automobiles were an Indian woman, (Mrs. Isabel Hide,) and a Chinese woman, (Miss Ruth Kiminsbee.) Each was in native costume. There were women of all nations, but they all wore the mourning symbol to show that they marched not as nations, but as sorrowing women together.

Miss Portia Willis, the Head Marshal, carried a bouquet of purple and white asters tied with black, and a great bunch of gladiolas and asters with broad ribbon bands was carried by Mrs. Bertha Mailly. The batons of the drum majors of some of the Boy Scout drum corps were wound with crape. One band of young girls, who identified themselves only as being "citizens of the world," wore printed bands: "Let Us Have Peace." One of them carried a globe tied with purple and white ribbons.

There were a number of children in the parade. One baby was wheeled by his mother in a carriage, another was carried in his mother's arms. Sylvia Manhardt, 2 years old, showed her mourning only in her feet. She wore a little red dress, but black and white striped stockings and black shoes. The smallest Boy Scout was Alfred Greenwald, 4 years old, who marched with one of the drum corps and attracted much attention. Little Alfred unknowingly broke the most stringent rule of the parade by carrying a flag. The peace banner was to be the only one. He carried a United States flag, but it was furled.

Miss Eleanor Garrison, granddaughter of William Lloyd Garrison, who arrived here on the Adriatic yesterday, did not know of the Peace Parade until she landed, but she was one of the marchers. Mrs. Elizabeth Worth Müller, leading one of the delegations, a tall distinguished woman wearing a cap and gown, was one of those who had war stories to tell. Her husband going to Germany had remained with the army, although past the age for service.

Mrs. Ida Harris, originally from Odessa, was one of the marchers. She is a suffrage leader in the Second Assembly District. Even the men in her district were wearing black yesterday, she said, honoring the Peace Parade and sorrowing for suffering relatives in Germany and in Russia. There was a large band of young women Socialists, all wearing red badges over black or white gowns and some red bands on black sleeves. There were also twenty negro women. Miss Lavine Dock of the Henry Street Settlement was a Marshal, and with her was a division of the settlement nurses in their blue uniforms.

Three hundred policemen from the Third and Fourth Inspection Districts were on duty on the line of parade under Inspectors Dwyer and Morris. Chief Inspector Schmittberger, who supervised the arrangements, said:

"The demonstration is one of the most orderly and impressive that I have seen in New York in many years of service in the Police Department."

August 30, 1914

ONLY HEROIC WOMEN WERE DOCTORS THEN

Dr. Anna Manning Comfort Tells of Indignities She Suffered at Bellevue in 1865.

PUBLIC ALSO ANTAGONISTIC

Member of Women's Medical College's First Class Honored at Luncheon—Memorial for Her.

Changes in the position of women in the world in the last fifty years were emphasized by Dr. Anna Manning Comfort, graduate of the New York Medical College and Hospital for Women in its first class in 1865, at a luncheon in her honor, given by the Faculty and Trustees of the college at Delmonico's yesterday. Dr. Comfort was graduated at the age of 20, and she is only in the early seventies, alert and well preserved, though she has had a vigorous career, has been married, and is the mother of three children.

"Students of today have no idea of conditions as they were when I studied medicine," said Dr. Comfort. "It is difficult to realize the changes that have taken place. I attended the first meeting when this institution was proposed, and was graduated from the first class. We had to go to Bellevue Hospital for our practical work, and the indignities we were made to suffer are beyond belief. There were 500 young men students taking post-graduate courses, and we were jeered at and catcalled, and the 'old war horses,' the doctors, joined the younger men.

"We were considered aggressive. They said women did not have the same brains as men and were not trustworthy. All the work at the hospital was made as repulsively unpleasant for us as possible. There were originally six in the class, but all but two were unable to put up with the treatment to which we were subjected and dropped out. I trembled whenever I went to the hospital and I said once that I could not bear it. Finally the women went to the authorities, who said that if we were not respectfully treated they would take the charter from the hospital.

"As a physician there was nothing that I could do that satisfied people. If I wore square-toed shoes and swung my arms they said I was mannish, and if I carried a parasol and wore a ribbon in my hair they said I was too feminine. If I smiled they said I had too much levity, and if I sighed they said I had no sand.

"They tore down my sign when I began to practice, the drug stores did not like to fill my prescriptions, and the older doctors would not consult with me. But that little band of women made it possible for the other women who have come later into the field to do their work. When my first patients came and saw me they said I was too young, and they asked in horrified tones if I had studied dissecting just like the men. They were shocked at that, but they were more shocked when my bills were sent in to find that I charged as much as a man.

"I believe in women entering professions," said Dr. Comfort, "but I also believe in motherhood. For the normal woman it is no more of a tax to have a profession as well as family life than it is for a man to carry on the multitudinous duties he has outside the family. I had three sons of my own and two adopted ones, and I am as proud of my motherhood as of my medical career. I gave as much of my personality to my children in an hour as some mothers do in ten. My children honored me and have been worth while in the world."

There were many expressions of esteem for Dr. Comfort and she was overcome when it was announced that money had been raised for an Anna Manning Comfort scholarship in the hospital.

Letters of regret were read from John Burroughs and Colonel Theodore Roosevelt among others.

"I believe in women in the medical profession, and in politics, and in all worthy pursuits," said John Burroughs.

"I am amazed to learn that this is the only institution in this State, and one of two in the United States, exclusively for the woman medical student," said Colonel Roosevelt. "There should be others and women of refinement would be drawn into the profession who will not study medicine in a coeducational college, and more women doctors are needed."

Dr. Walter G. Crump, who spoke of the need for medical colleges exclusively for women, said:

"We learn from the Flexner report that there is an overproduction of doctors, but nine out of ten of the women doctors practice. There are demands continually for women physicians which cannot be filled. They are needed in many places where women and girls are to be under a physician's care."

Dr. Mary A. Brinkman, who was one of the early graduates of the college, spoke. Sh said she could corroborate many of the things told by Dr. Comfort.

Dr. W. H. Diffenbach presided, and other speakers were the Rev. William L. Sullivan, Jefferson M. Levy, Dr. Katharine B. Davis, Dean Cornelia C. Brant of the college, and Mrs. Augustus C. Dexter, Second Vice President, who has been connected with the institution for eighteen years.

April 9, 1916

NEVER HEARD OF FEMINISM.

A Man Who Doesn't Know That Women Want to Do These Things.

To the Editor of The New York Times:

Wherefore these countless girls and women, jammed together with the laborers and men of affairs, filling the subways, elevated trains, and street cars, morning and night? Is man less fit and capable of supporting the weaker and gentler sex than of yore, or is it just because of the restlessness that overshadows our nation? Are a few extra dollars to be exchanged for all the womanliness, gentleness, refinement, and tenderness of womanhood? Are these to vanish altogether in the maelstrom of commercialism? Is home no more a place of interest and attraction?

Can you see the picture? Mothers, daughters, sisters, wives, swaying with the troubled masses, drudging in the dimness of the factory, screaming at the election polls, cheap and scanty meals in crowded restaurants, lost in the everlasting grind of office routine and "efficiency." Should all this be? Must all this be?

It is true that thousands of women—wage-earners—are such by sheer necessity, because they have no one to care for and support them. These are to be respected and their efforts are admired. Alas! a vast number of positions withheld from our army of unemployed are in the hands of young girls who are willing to expose the standard qualities of their sex to the contamination of the imbroglio of the "business world" for a few dollars less than the salary their employers would be obliged to part with were these positions filled by men.

It is surprising, however, that in this highly developed stage of efficiency this fact should have been overlooked: that skirts and trousers side by side in an office accomplish little and work many blunders. Many a man has neglected the shaping of his career because of a pretty face near by, out for fun, and eagerly awaiting the day of remuneration, when she will be able to get a hat a little neater than her rivals. Had Solomon lived to see these days, surely there would have been another "evil" and "vanity" added to the book of the Ecclesiastes.

The foregoing is not written in the interest of the unemployed men, but as a little reminder for our sisters that the downtown office is not the proper place for them. Men have not the time nor the opportunity to treat them with due consideration and respect while the "rush hours" are on. Our sisters are consequently obliged to harden themselves to the surrounding conditions.

ALLEN PALMER.

Brooklyn, May 11, 1916.

May 16, 1916.

Wasn't It All a Joke?

Perhaps if those correspondents of ours who are so vehemently belaboring the ALLEN PALMER who wrote the letter about working women would give a little earnest thought to him and his letter they would begin to wonder if they were not a little lacking in an excellent and valuable quality which he possesses. To wit, the sense of humor!

Of course, all that they are writing about him and his letter is quite true. They might even go still further in denunciation of him and it without exceeding the limits of truth and justice. They might, that is, if it were certain that he wrote as seriously as they are writing.

But presumably he is not the village idiot, and, if he isn't, of course he wrote, not to express his own sentiments and opinions, but to bring out exactly such sentiments and opinions almost as his indignant critics are now expressing. In other words, he has trapped them and is laughing at their needless rages.

This is all theory, we admit, but it is such a plausible theory that it deserves consideration. If it isn't true, if PALMER meant what he wrote, he deserves no mercy. Off with his head!

May 25, 1916.

AS WOMEN FEEL IN MAN'S ENVIRONS

New York, May 16, 1916.

To the Editor of The New York Times:

I note with interest and amusement the letter written you by Allen Palmer of Brooklyn regarding the women he meets in the crowded subways, going to and from their daily toil, and the appeal he makes to chivalrous manhood to take them from their employment and seat them in a home of their own to wash dishes, clean, &c. Mr. Palmer seems to think it is a crime against young womanhood to allow them to mingle with men in toil, but I fear there are many of us who prefer this daily routine to perhaps the dishwashing one. The women of today are no less gentle, no less refined, and the men of today no less capable of taking care of them, but the ideas of the women are changing, and some of them really do prefer taking care of themselves.

There are few men who blunder because of the pretty face of the girl or woman working at their sides. These men who do blunder usually go outside of their offices, as well as their homes, for that part of their life, and the girl who is priding herself on having a better hat than another girl is usually the one in the home for whom the man in the office is working. I suppose there is a lot of sympathy wasted by girls on their employers because perhaps they know better than any one else what the men are up against in their homes. Stenographers and other office girls and women have been called "love pirates," but the true "love pirates" are the wives and daughters of the men, not the girls who work for them. I think this will be found true in the majority of cases. A girl in business who understands the big and little things which happen every day to try the patience and nerve of the business men is better able to understand them and better able to help them to better things. If every woman in the United States had a year or more in a downtown office, that woman would make some man a better wife because of her wider understanding.

The girl who sits at home and takes things easy does not understand why, when a man comes home from business tired and nervous, he should not entertain them, go to dances, dinners, theatres, and go to his office the next day equipped to fight and win.

Mr. Palmer does not look deep enough into the pit—he skims the surface. Things would be all very lovely if we did not have to work and each one of us had some one to take good care of us, but times are changing, and the old order will never return. The girls in the offices do not expose their qualities to contamination, but rather make an office better for their being there, for the majority of men in offices and on the public highways respect girls and women of the working classes and curb their vehement language when they are around rather than give vent to it. I'm one of them and I know.

MARY J. SMITH.

May 24, 1916.

HOUSE, AT 3:12 A.M., VOTES FOR WAR

Special to The New York Times.

WASHINGTON, Friday, April 6.—At 3:12 o'clock this morning the House of Representatives by the overwhelming vote of 373 to 50 adopted the resolution that meant war between the Government and the people of the United States and the Imperial German Government.

War will formally begin this afternoon when President Wilson will approve the resolution which was passed by the Senate Wednesday night and was approved by the House this morning without the crossing of a "t" or the dotting of an "i."

The House presented an impressive spectacle as the roll call proceeded on the adoption of the war resolution. Nearly every member was in his seat.

The galleries were crowded for the most part by men and women who had sat there all the evening, some of them since 10 o'clock yesterday morning when the House met. Some of the men and women were in evening dress. Men and women who were in the diplomatic box had come directly from dinner parties.

There were crowds also in the corridors outside the galleries, seeking a chance for a peep at the events inside.

Usually when the roll of the House is called there is much confusion, and it is often difficult to hear the responses of the Representatives as their names are droned by the reading clerk.

But there was a marked difference this morning. The House, which had been full of levity at times during the long debate, felt the solemnity of the moment. No sound disturbed the proceedings. Every member's answer came distinctly and was heard by the throng that listened almost breathlessly to the "Ayes" and "Noes" that followed the calling of the roll.

Miss Rankin Votes "No."

Miss Jeanette Rankin, the woman Representative from Montana, had been absent from the House most of the evening, but took her accustomed place while the roll call was in progress. When her name was called she sat silent. "Miss Rankin," repeated the clerk. Still no answer. The clerk went on with his droning, and floor and galleries buzzed.

On the second roll call Miss Rankin's name was again called. She sat silent as before. The eyes of the galleries were turned on her. For a moment there was breathless silence. Then Miss Rankin rose. In a voice that broke a bit but could be heard all over the still chamber she said:

"I want to stand by my country, but I cannot vote for war. I vote no." The "No" was scarcely audible.

And the maiden speech of the first woman Congressman ended in a sob. She was deeply moved and big tears were in her eyes.

It was a sympathetic House, however, and although most of the persons there were plainly in favor of the war resolution, a wave of applause swept through floor and gallery.

When the roll call had been completed and a slip containing the count handed to Speaker Clark the latter's gavel came down with a bang. The House became quiet instantly.

"On this motion," said the Speaker, "the Ayes are 373 and the Noes are 50."

The cheers that followed drowned the Speaker's announcement that the resolution had been adopted. Then the floors and galleries cleared, Representatives and spectators knowing that war had again come to the United States.

The Senate adjourned Wednesday night, to meet again at noon today. As the resolution must be returned to the Senate, while that body is in session President Wilson will not receive the historical document for signature until this afternoon. From the moment of his approval war will be on.

The Early Morning Scene

At 1:20 o'clock this m----- Representative Kelly began to expre--- list showed --- m-

April 6, 1917.

58

Women as "Permanent Peacemakers"

The writer of this article is one of the women who attended the International Conference for Permanent Peace held in Zurich, Switzerland, in May. It was a gathering of people whose ardor for peace, according to the general impression in this country, carried them very far toward sympathy with conquered Germany. They went on record as disapproving vehemently the "severity" of the Allies' terms set forth in the draft of the Peace Treaty and sent a telegram of appeal to President Wilson in the name of the Fourteen Points.

WHITE slavery, prohibition, laws for women and children, and caring for the sick should be the subjects taken up by the Women's Congress now meeting in Switzerland. The women guided by the English, American, and Swiss must be practical and let international political questions alone. Their work today is to heal the wounds of a war-torn world."

Thus ran an editorial article in the Swiss Journal de Genève, welcoming the 200 women of the International Conference for Permanent Peace in Zurich on May 12.

But the editor had forgotten these were not club women of a few years ago. During the war many of them had become voters plunged sometimes against their will into the turbulent political life of their countries. Since their first congress at The Hague in 1915 they had daily eaten and drunk of international politics. They had come firmly to believe that today not only diplomats but ordinary men and even women could have a say on world questions. With a total disregard for the well-meaning, kindly editor's warning, they traveled together for a whole week through the mazes of the peace terms just presented to the Germans, the covenant of the League of Nations and the international blockade plans.

Even though the Governments of the world looked worried and frowned, even though passport difficulties were many and the journey at best tedious and haphazard, these women came together from fifteen different countries. Japan alone of the five great allied powers was unrepresented, and the Oriental point of view was entirely lacking in the various discussions. Each of the twenty-six Englishwomen received their passports after promising " to indulge in no Socialist propaganda." France refused passports to her women, but three finally arrived after combining personal business in Switzerland with the conference. One

Italian delegate was allowed to come " to study the costumes of tout le monde." Belgium had no delegate, for her threat to expatriate any woman attending proved so effective that only Mlle. la Fontaine sat as a silent onlooker.

For weeks the Munich women, too, were refused passports, but for quite a different reason. " There is no such country as Switzerland," said the Communist Government which held the power after Kurt Eisner's assassination. " I will telegraph as proof," said Frau Hallgarten, one of the delegates. But the Communists' creed recognizing no national boundaries was not to be swayed by telegraphed evidence. So the women waited until the counter-revolution took place and passports were in vogue again. Twenty-seven women finally arrived from Germany, four from Austria, and two from Hungary.

The neutral countries of Holland, Norway, Sweden, and Denmark sent twenty-five women. Russia was missing, as the International Committee has never had an active organization there. " The Irish Republic " sent three women, who sat, not with Great Britain as did Australia, but safely on the other side of the room with the Americans.

Headed by Jane Addams, who presided over the conference and had previously conferred with Secretary Lansing and Colonel House in Paris, the women of the United States were there twenty-six strong. The State Department allowed twelve to go from this country; the remaining fourteen were already in Europe in various capacities.

Whatever any one may think about woman's having her finger in the international pie, a little thing like a four months' voyage on the sea will never prove a deterrent. It took the three Australian women just one-sixth of a year to reach Zurich by way of India, Egypt, and England. They started in March, spent one week conferring with their sisters from many lands, and in July, if they hurry, they will be able to report back to those who sent them.

It was necessary for the Scandinavian women to cross through Germany. It was an eight instead of the usual three day journey, and the delegates took their luncheons with them—also their dinners and breakfasts. Sometimes they cooked their meals over their little spirit lamps on station platforms while waiting for trains which ran without time tables. Dr. Aletta Jacobs, the Dutch suffragist who in 1912 traveled around the world with Mrs. Catt organizing women for

suffrage, headed the delegation from Holland.

These women who met at Zurich were not women of great wealth or social position; neither were they, with one or two exceptions, workingwomen. Jane Addams termed them " just an ordinary group of citizens." They were, however, a little out of the ordinary in that they were typically " doers." Most of them were professional women—doctors, lawyers, teachers, professors, social and civic workers, writers. Nationally and sometimes internationally their names might be found linked with the suffrage movement, with work of all kinds for both women and children. Many of them hold public office in their communities. Jane Addams and Lillian Wald are the heads of our two greatest American settlements, Hull House of Chicago and Henry Street of New York. Florence Kelley, as Secretary of the National Consumers' League, has been instrumental in much of the labor legislation for women passed in the United States. Dr. Alice Hamilton of Harvard University is the first woman to receive a professorship in a man's college. In addition were unofficial representatives from the Y. W. C. A., the Society of Friends, and the National Catholic War Council.

The list of England's delegates read like the roster of her various suffrage societies during the struggle for the vote. Among them were Mrs. Despard, General French's sister and veteran suffragist, still speaking in spite of her seventy-odd years; Mrs. Philip Snowden, opponent of the Militant Suffragists, who has lectured in America often, and Mrs. Pethick Lawrence, who more than once broke into jail with Mrs. Pankhurst. Margaret Ashton, member of the Manchester City Council, and Miss Rayds, Secretary to the Scottish Women's Hospital and active in relief work in Saloniki and Serbia, were two other prominent Englishwomen there.

Lida Heymann and Anita Augsberg of Munich have been for years leaders in the German suffrage movement. Dr. Helene Stöcher of Berlin, another delegate, is the founder of the German League for the Protection of Mothers, and has under her control 400 homes for illegitimate children and their mothers. Frau Kulka, from Austria, is a well known child welfare expert, and the two delegates from Hungary, former active suffragists and feminists, are officials in the Communist Hungarian Government—one, Vilma Gluchlich, at the head of a bureau established to look into mat-

AMERICAN DELEGATION AT THE WOMEN'S GATHERING IN SWITZERLAND.

Left to Right, Bottom Row: Miss Elisabeth Sweeney, Miss Grace Drake, Miss Alice Hunt, Miss Jeannette Rankin, Mrs. Louis F. Post, Miss Jane Addams, Mrs. Lucia Ames Mead, and Miss Emily Balch.

Top Row: Miss Rose Nichols, Mrs. Stokes-Miller, Miss Caroline Wood, Miss Constance Drexel, Mrs. John Rickman, Miss Marion Burritt, Mrs. Rose Morgan French, Mrs. Marcy Church Tenell, Miss Lillian Wald, Mrs. Lucy Biddle Lewis, Mrs. John Jay White, Dr. Alice Hamilton. Miss Clara Savage, and Miss Florence Holbrook.

ters concerning women; the other, Paula Pogani, the editor of Woman, the Government newspaper devoted to women's interests. Rosika Schwimmer of Hungary, prominent in the 1915 Congress at The Hague, instigator of the Ford Peace Party, and Hungarian Minister to Switzerland under the Karolyi régime, was among the missing. "Was she perchance in prison?" it was whispered. Oh! no—only not in favor with the Soviet Republic of Bela Kun, and therefore keeping very much in the background and asking for no passport, waiting perhaps for the return of Karolyi into power.

Back in 1915 the International Congress at The Hague had voted to meet whenever the official Peace Conference should be "summoned." Not even a long and bitter war had deterred them. It was the same group, yet it was quite different. Then, the Socialists among them could be counted on one hand; now, they were not quite a majority. Then, the Socialists represented the extreme radical point of view; now, at least in Central Europe, they were the counter-revolutionists crushing Bolshevism. Then, a communist was unheard of among their ranks; now, women who belonged to the communist party were there from both Hungary and Germany. Then, to look at their faces the effects of the war were hardly discernible; now, many of the Scandinavians and Central Europeans

showed in their pinched, unhealthy looking faces the lack of food.

It was a coincidence that the women's first session found the ink on the peace terms hardly dry. The German women had received their copies while on the way, and arrived in a hopeless frame of mind. They said that "even President Wilson," whom they looked to for "a peace that would temper justice with mercy," had "apparently failed them." They had expected to give up Alsace and Lorraine, to restore the devastated territory, to pay indemnities, but they said they "could not sign the peace that was handed them." To sign would be fatal, yet not to sign they realized would be equally fatal.

If the Germans were submerged in hopelessness, the rest of the congress also voiced dissent from "the severity of the Allies." It hurled by wire at the Paris Conference a set of resolutions denouncing the treaty as a provoker of future wars and urging amendments in harmony with President Wilson's Fourteen Points. The women particularly assailed the blockade proposal, recalling that England had been holding meetings of protest backed by many persons of rank, clergymen and people of prominence, whose influence had been absolutely for the war, and that America and Herbert Hoover seemed ready to send all possible aid. From every part of the Balkans and Central Europe, enemy or

allied, came stories of starvation and under-nourishment of women and children. Train loads of little boys and girls kept coming into Switzerland for a two weeks' "feed," then to be sent back perhaps to starve again. The women at the congress continuously criticised the Big Five at Paris for favoring a blockade as a last weapon against the enemy.

A second resolution signed by Jane Addams and wired to Paris asked "that the Governments take immediate action to lift the blockade and to organize the resources of the world for the relief of the people from famine and pestilence." In reply, President Wilson telegraphed Miss Addams: "Your message appeals both to my head and heart, and I hope most surely that means may be found, though the present outlook is exceedingly unpromising because of unfortunate practical difficulties."

Then the conference set for itself the task of working out a constructive piece of criticism of the League of Nations covenant. There was gradually developing a radical and a conservative wing whose views had to be compromised if the covenant was not to be denounced entirely. Most of the Dutch, the Scandinavians, the Swiss, and the Americans were conservatives. Many of the English and naturally the women from Central Europe occupied the extreme Socialist, if not Communist, left. The Americans, headed by Jane Addams, possibly influenced by President Wilson's position, saw defects in the League's constitution, but wished it preserved and amended as a basis for world democracy. As finally passed and taken to Paris by Miss Addams and Mme. Duchesne of France, the League resolution indorsed the principle underlying a society of nations, but asked for certain amendments, including the admission of all nations on equal terms, worldwide reduction of armaments, and easy amendment to the covenant. Finally, last but not least, the congress provided for a permanent women's bureau to be established at Geneva, the seat of the League of Nations, with Emily Balch of the United States as permanent Secretary.

Probably the resolutions passed will prove but "scraps of paper." Yet American women return home with the knowledge that women the world over are becoming politically minded both nationally and internationally.

June 22, 1919

WOMEN IN 8-HOUR DAY FIGHT

An organized effort to induce President Wilson to urge Congress to legislate an eight-hour day for women promises to crystallize out of the interstate conference on that subject now in progress in this city under the auspices of the Women's Trade Union League of New York and Philadelphia and the Baltimore Committee of the National Women's Trade Union League.

Mrs. Florence Kelley, General Secretary of the National Consumers' League, read resolutions to that effect at yesterday morning's session at the Russell Sage Foundation. They were so cordially received that it was predicted they would be incorporated in the formal resolutions to be adopted today when the conference reconvenes at the Art Building, 311 Fourth Avenue.

Mrs. Kelley further enlivened the proceedings when she charged that hour-limiting laws in New York were farcical from the standpoint of the present degree of enforcement.

"Graded by our enforcement, we stand close to the bottom of the list of States having such laws," she said. "The non-enforcement of the fifty-four hours a week law is notorious. The 5 o'clock closing hour for children below 16 years of age is in parts of this city almost a mockery. Few employers pay fines. No employer is in any jail or penitentiary for any offense against this law. Suits are either not begun or are so ill prepared that they are lost in spite of the disposition of the court in recent years to sustain these laws.

"For this there is at present one sole remedy—publicity. Laggard servants of a negligent public can be made to do their duty only when the public exchanges negligence for vigilance."

Dr. F. S. Lee, Professor of Physiology in Columbia, spoke for a non-rigid day with hours determined by physical tests of reaction to conditions. Commissioner of Immigration F. C. Howe pleaded for the shorter day from the official's viewpoint, and Dr. Lee K. Frankel of the Metropolitan Life Insurance Company advocated it on behalf of the employer.

Miss Elizabeth Lowe charged at the afternoon session that she had been assaulted by an officer of a candy factory because she distributed before the factory leaflets advertising the conference, and named two candy factories where she said women were overworked and underpaid.

The conference will end today.

December 3, 1916

WOMEN IN BUSINESS.

Striking Figures That Show How Their Numbers Increase.

An interesting and comprehensive article, entitled "The Increasing Employment of Women in Business," written by Harry Franklin Porter of the Industrial Service Department of the National City Bank of New York, gives some statistics which will surprise the average casual reader regarding the part which women are now taking in work formerly done only by men. Mr. Porter's figures are concisely summarized in this wise:

From only a few thousand in 1860, the number has multiplied at double the rate of population increase. In 1880, the first year for which detailed statistics are available, 2,647,157 women were listed as breadwinners. This was approximately 5.3 per cent of the population. A decade later the number had increased to 4,000,532, which was roughly 6.3 per cent of the population. In 1900 the total was 5,319,397, or about 7 per cent; while in 1910 the figure was 8,075,722, being nearly 9 per cent of the population. Between 1900 and 1910 the percentage of increase was 52 per cent, as against a gain in population of only 21 per cent. Assuming the same rate of increase since then, the number of women now partially or wholly self-supporting must easily exceed ten million.

It is noticeable that the first real entry of women in this country into positions which had been almost entirely monopolized by men was at the beginning of the civil war. Now, at the opening of a war which may be vastly more important than the struggle between the North and the South, the tendency of women to enter permanently into business and industrial life is again rapidly becoming marked. What the outcome will be when peace is again restored is considered at length by Mr. Porter, but from the nature of the case the ultimate economic effect must be a matter of conjecture.—Rochester Democrat and Chronicle.

November 11, 1917

WOMEN IN FACTORIES.

Learn as Readily as Men, but Majority Object to Overalls.

Owing to the fact that nearly 1,000 men have been called to the colors from one of the large automobile factories, a school has been established to train women in upholstering, trimming, and other work calling for skilled operatives.

Women are now making tops and curtains, doing all sorts of inspection work, and handling various small chassis parts. A large number are operating drill presses and automatic screw machines. Clerical work, such as keeping the time cards and doing the routine office work of the various factory departments, is largely done by women.

The Safety First Department in the factory has prescribed costumes for the women workers. These may be either loose overalls or jumpers, or bungalow aprons made of khaki or overall material. Women must wear caps to protect their hair. Most of the women prefer not to wear overalls. Experience thus far shows that the women learn as quickly as men, and in some departments are even more efficient.

December 2, 1917

Where Women Supplant Men Because of War

ACCORDING to many signs, we are fast taking the road that England has followed in solving the labor problem brought on by the war. Women today are taking the places of men in many lines of work in which they had heretofore been barred. With quiet seriousness of purpose, proved by the fact that the vast majority of people know little of these changes, man labor is being replaced by woman's. And this is but a beginning of what it is expected to be as the war progresses. In many cases, it is not the present urgent need which is causing the change, but the anticipation of the increased shortage which will undoubtedly be felt at the time of the second draft.

Up to the present time, the women street-car conductors and subway guards are perhaps the most familiar to the public. These have been engaged by both the Interborough and Brooklyn Rapid Transit Companies. The need arose out of a real shortage of men. In the Rapid Transit Company alone 500 men have been called to the colors. At the present time the Interborough has ninety-two women who are either actually working on the cars or who are being trained for the work at the company schools. The Brooklyn Rapid Transit Company has more than 160 women in the place of men. Of these, 150 are employed as guards on Brooklyn subways. The remainder are conductors on low-step cars. The women get the same training as the men, must pass a similar physical examination, are subject to the same age limits, that is, 21 to 45, and receive the same pay, 27 cents an hour. The type of women employed are of average intelligence, and with one exception they come from occupational fields that are unusual in no way. In many cases they are members of the families of the men previously employed who have been drafted. The exception is a woman on the Brooklyn Rapid Transit who worked as a car conductor in Norway. This same company has also employed a colored woman station porter. Both companies are well pleased with the results so far, and are making arrangements to increase the numbers of women workers.

Another new occupation which women have taken up with great success is that of elevator running. In many of the apartment houses on the upper west side women have in large measure displaced the men. Some of the department stores are also turning to women for this work. One of these is entirely depending upon women for elevator operators. The Greenhut Company now employs twenty-five women elevator runners. Some changes in schedule that were considered necessary to insure the best service have been made. Where the men worked on three-hour shifts with relief, the women work on two-hour shifts, with a half hour's rest between. Where one man used to relieve four runners, a woman relieves only three. That has made it necessary for the company to employ four additional runners, but the ultimate result, very satisfactory, has made the additional expense worth while. The women draw the same pay as the men, $10 a week.

Women have also been drafted as workers in the fire-extinguishing industry. The Pyrene Company now employs 275 women at work that has previously been done by men. Women are taking part in every process, from the beginning to the end of the manufacture of the product. Here, too, the management is planning to add to the present number of women workers, in view of the shortage of men expected as a result of the second draft. So enthusiastic are the heads of department in praise of the work now being done that they are considering a policy of making their plant more largely dependent upon woman labor.

In the factory of the Otis Elevator Company at Yonkers there are about 160 women in the machine shops, which had before entirely been run by men. Compared to the 2,000 workers employed

there, this is a small number, but it is a beginning. This number will be raised as the exigencies demand. The women are employed in making the small machine tools, in drilling, in electrical work, and in other departments. Opportunity is given to the women to advance from the simpler to the more complex operations, with corresponding advance in pay. The salaries paid them are the same that the men received previous to the pre-war period. No girl gets less than $9 a week. They are during their work unsegregated from the men, with perfect good-fellowship. During the morning and afternoon, the women are allowed fifteen-minute rest periods, which they spend in rooms especially outfitted for them. To prepare for any accident that might happen, the plant has opened a separate first-aid room, under the supervision of the same nurse and doctor who are in charge of the men machinists' room. Every effort is made to insure the health and safety of the women. The work they turn out is on a par with that of the men.

Many women are employed in the munition works. The assembling of the parts of the shell calls for a type of work for which women are peculiarly adaptable. The fitting of the fine screw and the insertion of the tiny springs make the sensitive touch perceptions and delicate handling of a woman's hands really needed. For the last fourteen years women have been employed in these departments. The work now is therefore an extension of what has gone before, arising out of the increased demand for munitions. Some factories are going so far as to put women to work on the drill presses. Women are also being employed in powder cutting.

An industry from which women had always heretofore been barred is the felt hat industry. The reason was, in the main, purely physical. The work is heavy and the conditions under which the people employed have to work are such as to test even the powers of some men. At the present time, however, employers have sent out a call for strong women, and several of that type have responded, showing themselves able to do the work. The pay is commensurate with the kind of labor required.

Another industry in which women have heretofore not been seen as workers is radium plating. Now, in many of these factories women are used to meet

the shortage made by the departure of men. Again the judgment passed on her work is "entirely satisfactory."

A sight that is so far peculiar to the streets of Brooklyn alone is that of women drivers on laundry wagons. They are proving themselves efficient, clear-headed, and quick. One company in New Jersey reports the employment of women as steamfitters. The work is of the lighter kind, but women are taking to it amazingly well.

Women have for some time now been engaged in various kinds of railroad work. In Delaware, women are employed in railroad machine shops, in the drillrooms, and at the stations where light freight is unloaded. One station in New York can boast of a track forewoman, the head of a woman's gang.

The Sperry Gyroscope Company of Brooklyn has also gone into the employment of women in its factories. At the present time the firm is engaged in Government work, supplying the military forces with army compasses, boat compasses, and altometers. The women are engaged in the assembling of parts, in the glass bending processes, in cutting of tubes, and in inspection of instruments. Their salary to start with is $10 per week with advancement according to ability. Attention is paid to the physical well-being of the workers, and rest periods and reliefs form part of the schedule of labor. One of the reasons given by this firm for the employment of woman labor is significant. As the company is engaged in Government work, men employes might be subject to exemption.

Mrs. Edgar Strakosch, Secretary of the Employment Committee of the Mayor's Committee of Women on National Defense, who has made a study of women in industry, is of the opinion that it was not so much a shortage of labor caused by the war that brought on this new phase of industrial conditions, but that the public mind had been led by the conditions of the war to that point where it could countenance the entrance of women into industries which before had been controlled by men. It was a case of women taking advantage of the psychological moment, which, in a leap, advanced their entrance into new fields. Another point to be taken into consideration, she said, was the one that although women were receiving the pay that men had previously got, they were not, in a large measure, receiving the wages at which a man might today be willing to work.

Girl Laborers on Small Farms at $2 a Day
Land Army of America Starts Its Spring Drive

THE Woman's Land Army of America is getting ready for its Spring drive. It is an organization formed a few weeks ago to supply unskilled female labor for farms during the Spring and Summer months. Its first units will be sent out in March.

Units are groups of farmhands. The organizers, in explaining their purpose, begin by saying that "this is no society girl business." Neither is it an attempt to supply trained help. The girls who enlist with the army and will work to help the food supply next Spring and Summer are not expert farmers, or students of agriculture. They are unskilled, and they work for $2 a day. It has been shown that the small farmer needs help. It has also been shown that he does not need a highly educated young agriculturist to teach him how to run his farm. He needs workers. That is what the new association will give him.

Mrs. Robert C. Hill, Vice Chairman of the Land Army's Advisory Council, also a member of the Executive Board of the Women's Farm and Garden Association and of the War Work Council of the Garden Club of America, had this to say of the undertaking:

"There is a place for the woman who is a trained agricultural worker, of course; it is a fine thing for women to own and work their farms. But the great need that we are trying to meet is not for that kind of work. The girls in the land army must fill humble positions. They must just be day laborers, doing as they are told. There is some farm work that girls cannot do, and they are naturally not to be employed for work beyond their strength. That goes without saying.

"Another point we want to make is that the girls have a good time at the work. We hear an outcry that it is cruel to make women work in the fields, that it is un-American and all wrong generally. Well, we shall not allow it to be any of those things. Light farm work is healthy work. Only girls who are physically qualified are accepted. They are comfortably housed. They have a housemother who has general oversight over their health. And they have a jolly time.

"The reason women's work on farms has not generally been successful is because of the housing problem. You cannot expect girls to live as day laborers can—in tin boxes or corrugated iron shacks. You make provision for them to live in a healthy fashion. That is the great need behind our unit plan. And of course we want to make the life just as happy and bright for the girls as we can. As a matter of fact, those who worked in

trial units organized last Summer had a wonderful time, and are enlisting their sisters and cousins and friends for next Summer. It works out into an enjoyable sort of camping.

"Our unit consists of from ten to a hundred girls. The ideal unit has a small farmhouse for the housekeeper-cook, with a kitchen and living room, preferably with running water, but if that is not possible, situated near a stream. The unit is surrounded by the girls' tents. In the unit of more than ten we plan for a housemother, a cook, an agricultural leader, and a third-hand motor car.

"The girls must volunteer for not less than two months. They may apply to the Woman's University Club, or the Woman's Farm and Garden Association, or the office of the Advisory Council of the Woman's Land Army at 600 Lexington Avenue. A physical examination must be passed before they are assigned to a place.

"At first they are not so good as men. But after a little practice they become first-class workers. One farmer, George T. Powell, an apple expert, who has orchards near Ghent, N. Y., wrote us after

trying the girl farmhands that they 'made up in intelligence, willingness, and team work what they lacked in strength.' The system is simply this: A farmer calls up the unit, asks for workers, and gets them in the morning for the whole day. They take their luncheon with them, their day is over at 5 o'clock. Our experience in testing a few units last year taught us that the girls liked it, and that it did not tire them out. We used often to hear of the girls starting off in the evening, after a day in the fields, to walk to the village and back. There isn't any 'entertainment' provided for them at the unit house, but they are just a crowd of jolly, healthy young people, happy in their camp life.

"We work with the small farmers, such as are numerous in New York State. The Government sends out men for agricultural work, but they are for the great farms in the West. The need we strive to meet is different. At first the farmer is prejudiced against the idea, and does not want the 'farmerettes.' One farmer after another says, 'I won't have city girls fussing around on my farm!'

Then there comes a day when something must be done at once, and there aren't enough men. He decides to try a pair of these despised 'city girls.' They work well. After that he is a steady customer.

"The Bedford County farmers declared with one voice after the last season that they could not get along without the 'farmerettes.'"

Women cannot work in the fields in ordinary women's clothes, and the experiments with overalls on top of a lingerie waist have proved unsuccessful.

"Nothing tires a worker so much as improper clothing," Mrs. Hill went on. "You must have perfect freedom of movement. You must have the right sort of shoes and the right sort of stockings. You must be cool and neat. Several costumes have been designed. One of the best is the one we have named the Molly Pitcher, designed by Miss Charlotte Foss. It consists of a smock, and knickerbockers of heavy blue or khaki-colored twill, with a little hat, good heavy shoes, and golf stockings made of cotton. The girls do not like to wear woolen stockings, but an ordinary stocking won't do. It won't stay up. So one of the stores has had a cotton golf stocking especially made for this outfit, and it solves the problem. The whole costume—shoes, hat, everything—can be bought for $14.

Many of our recruits have sweethearts in the army. It means much to these girls to be helping the country. And we must face the likelihood that some of these young men will come back crippled from the war, and that there must be an entirely new beginning for them. It may be that they will be helped in their new start by the hundreds and hundreds of girls now learning farm work. With the money which the disabled men get from the Government they and their wives can live their new life together on farms, with good homes and a healthy future."

Last Spring the Woman's Farm and Garden Association and the Garden Club of America, which were our only agricultural organizations of women when we entered the war, were notified from Washington that they should undertake definite practical work to aid the food supply. They began to co-operate with successful results. At the same time the Mayor's Committee of Women on National Defense was attacking the problem. Farm units were organized, farm camps established, courses in farm work arranged in various schools, private farms given over as training and "experiment" stations, different methods tried out, all with the same purpose—to supply the farmers with the women workers. All that was the experimental stage. The Land Army has set out to furnish the stage of full development.

February 3, 1918

WOMEN TAKE 1,413,000 JOBS

Have Replaced That Number of Men Since 1914—Many Were Servants.

WASHINGTON, March 29.—An increase of 1,426,000 in the number of women employed since 1914 is shown in figures announced today by the Bureau of Labor Statistics. The greatest increase was in industries which took in 530,000 more women, but the largest proportionate increase was 214,000 additional women taken into Government service. Women have replaced 1,413,000 men since 1914.

Industrial and Government work has taken 400,000 women formerly employed in domestic service or in dressmaking.

March 30, 1918

ENEMY ALIEN WOMEN MUST REGISTER NOW

President Signs Bill Making the Espionage Law Applicable to Them.

WASHINGTON, April 19.—President Wilson today signed the bill extending provisions of the Espionage act to women and requiring registration of enemy alien women.

Within a few days the President is expected to issue a proclamation declaring women subjects of enemy countries subject to arrest and internment, and ordering German women to leave Washington at some definite future time. Women enemy aliens also will be forbidden to approach docks, wharves, and warehouses under the same restrictions now imposed on enemy alien males.

As soon as it was learned yesterday that the President had signed the bill which puts enemy alien women in the same class as male enemies, the Department of Justice started several investigations which had been held in abeyance.

It is understood that a large number of women are on the "suspicious list" and their records were being looked up last night by a large force of special agents belonging to the staff of Charles W. De Woody, Chief of the Department of Justice Bureau of Investigation for the New York district.

William Wallace, Jr., head of the Enemy Alien Bureau, said last night he would have nothing to give out concerning the investigation of women suspects before today.

That the Germans have used women spies in New York is well known to the Federal agents. Some of these women are among the most trusted agents in the enemy spy system. The names of many of them are in the possession of the authorities.

When asked about the statement that there were 20,000 dangerous enemy aliens in the city, Mr. Wallace said:

"We are now checking the police registration with the United States Marshal's registration, the registration for the selective draft, and the State registration, and as far as we have gone there has been substantial conformity in the registrations. The checking is not completed, and I am speaking only from partial checks. If any one else has made checks with different results I have yet to hear of it.

"If any information is submitted to this bureau, whether as the result of checks or otherwise, indicating aliens who have not registered, they will be promptly dealt with. It is the duty of any citizen having such information to furnish it."

April 20, 1918

BUSINESS STATUS OF COLLEGE WOMEN
Census of Nine Colleges Shows Wide Variety of Occupations.

THE Association of Collegiate Alumnae, in co-operation with several women's colleges, has made an investigation into certain phases of the economic and personal status of the alumnae of these colleges which presents many interesting facts. As the statistics include the graduates of 1915, the census is of special value because it establishes the status of a large group of women graduates practically up to the time of the entrance of the United States into the war.

Conditions caused by the war are likely to make a difference in the economic status of women, so that the census will offer valuable material for comparison with conditions and results after the changes due to the war have produced their effects.

Eight colleges for women, Barnard, Bryn Mawr, Mount Holyoke, Radcliffe, Smith, Vassar, Wellesley, and Wells, and one co-educational university, Cornell, are included in the survey. In the Journal of the association for May, Mary Van Kleeck makes a digest of the statistics.

The chief purpose of the inquiry, she says, was to obtain information about the occupations of college women, and therefore the greater part of the information it gives is concerned with their economic status. Reports were obtained from 16,739 graduates, and of these 11,663 (69.7 per cent.) had been gainfully employed. More than half of these have been employed in teaching, or have united teaching with some other gainful employment.

Those who have taken up other occupations than teaching, of whom the percentage is 22.8 of all graduates, have entered upon a long and most varied array of vocations. The list of them shows how rapidly and widely the doors of employment have been opening to women prepared to enter them. It has long been the general impression that this is true, and these figures offer the proof.

The list of occupations other than teaching in which college women were employed in 1915 fills two pages of the Journal. Under agriculture are included Shetland pony breeders, dairy farmers, farm managers, orange growers, greenhouse managers, estate superintendents, and ten other classifications.

In Government service there are inspectors of many sorts, civil service examiners, scientific workers, clerical workers, agents, commissioners.

The theatre has proved attractive to a few college women, of whom eleven are listed as actors and ten others as managers, producers, entertainers, and coaches.

Under business appears a great variety of vocations, the number of women thus engaged being the third largest in the list. Those engaged in social service work have the largest number, 471, while library work comes second with 293 and business claims 260. Under this classification one finds women engaged in such diverse employments as engineering and contracting, banking, printing, hotel management, as visiting household accountant, owner and manager of a riding school, manager detective agency.

Art, both fine and applied, has a representation, including scientific, engineering, mechanical, and architectural draftsmen, designers, landscape architects, and—unique among them all —a "painter of fishes for a taxidermist."

Practically all the professions are represented and more than a dozen of the sciences, from archaeology to zoology. Among the unclassified occupations are cable code expert and maker of codes, professional shopper, conductor of European tours, hostess, and manager of State House at expositions, judge of domestic science exhibits at State and county fairs in five States yearly.

More than four thousand women reported their earnings for the year, of whom 3,634 were teachers and 1,040 were in other occupations. Those in other occupations were better paid, for the median earnings for teachers amounted to $995 and for the others $1,065. The highest median earnings in the various groups were those of women in theatrical pursuits and the lowest in agriculture.

Some of the maximum earnings reported were that of the head and owner of a large school, $35,000; a literary woman, author of a novel which had been successful both as book and play, $24,000, (she added on her card that some years she made very little;) a physician and surgeon in private practice for fifteen years reported $9,000; an orange grower with twenty-one years' experience, $8,000; one business woman earned $5,000; one woman had $15,000 as half the joint earnings of her husband and herself in the management of a group of Summer camps for girls.

The statistics of marriages and birth rates, Miss Van Kleeck suggests, should be studied with caution, because the early classes of women graduates were small and the younger alumnae far outnumber the older ones. Therefore, since many of them are still young and unmarried, they overweight the percentages and make them not wholly representative. She thinks that "three decades or five decades hence it will be possible to study the statistics of college women as facts of a history which is closed for a sufficiently large number to make final statements."

Of 16,739 graduates of all ages included in the census, 6,544, or 39.1 per cent., were married. The distribution of percentages among the nine colleges shows that the higher percentage of marriages is found among the alumnae of the older institutions. Out of the total of 6,544 marriages only 37 had been divorced, with more than half of that number, 20, belonging to the group graduated between 1900 and 1910. The percentage of all divorces to marriages was only 57-100 of 1 per cent.

It appears that employment affects marriage, for of the total number who have been gainfully employed only 30.5 per cent. were married, while of those who had never been thus employed 58.9 were married. The percentage of marriage is higher among teachers than among those engaged in other vocations, while the lowest of all the percentages is among those who had tried both teaching and other work.

"Apparently," concludes Miss Van Kleeck, "the more varied the vocational experience the less frequent the marriage ,of college graduates." Collegiate education appears to defer marriage, for the average age at marriage of those who had been gainfully employed was 28 years and 1 month, and of those who had followed no vocation was 26 years and 1 month. As the average age at graduation is 22 years, it would seem that the tendency is to defer marriage for five or six years.

Of the married graduates 60.9 per cent. had children, averaging 2.1 per family. One Wellesley graduate reported 11 children, and for none of the colleges was the maximum number of children less than 6. In the entire group of married graduates 29 per cent. had 3 children or more. That the percentage of children is affected by the large number of younger graduates whose families are not complete is indicated by the much higher percentages of the older groups. Of the graduates in classes previous to 1890, the proportion having children is 80.7, and the average number of children per family 2.9.

But it is to be noted that the mortality rate among the children of college women is low. Of all the children born to women included in the census only 6.7 in every 100 had died and, only 4.5 per cent. had died during their first year. In studies of infant mortality made by the Federal Children's Bureau the rate in Manchester, N. H., was found to be 16.5; in Johnstown, Penn., 13.4, and in Montclair, N. J., a residential suburb having exceptionally good living conditions, 8.5.

College women appear to prefer college men for husbands, for 78.8 per cent. of the married women in this census had married college graduates. Wellesley held the highest percentage of the collegiate alliances, 91.2, while Cornell came next with 83.4, and Wells was the lowest. Nearly half of these husbands follow professional vocations.

PRESENT ECONOMIC STATUS OF WOMEN

New Opportunities Thrown Open to Them by the War

WOMEN workers are to be marshaled to shame men who dodge essential duties. Lists of occupations in which men should be replaced by women are to be published in the daily papers, with the implication that men who persist in remaining in them will be confessed industrial slackers.

These are the most radical features of the new plan of the United States Employment Service, designed to bring into the war industries large numbers of men now engaged in non-essential industries and needed for carrying out the new war program of an army of 5,000,000 men. The drastic aim deemed necessary by the labor situation is that no man shall occupy a position that a woman can fill.

Certain employments, after investigation by community labor boards, will be officially noted as "woman's work." The lists will be progressive in character; new occupations will be added to the published lists as new facts and new emergencies develop. The motive force relied upon to impel men to relinquish non-essential employments for the war industries will be, as the plan of publicity indicates, the pressure of public opinion, believed by the promoters of the plan to be the strongest force that could be appealed to in the present national determination to see the war through to a finish.

With more and more directness, as the campaign unfolds, attention will be focused on men who are working at jobs that women might do.

"It should be understood that this plan will be put into effect in no haphazard fashion," said N. A. Smyth, Assistant Director of the United States Employment Service in Washington, the other day, "but only after careful investigations conducted in a friendly spirit and with special precautions not to inflict injustice on any one, but the fact is that there is an alarming shortage of man power in the war industries. This made necessary the carrying out of this program.

"The employer who retains men of physical ability in these prescribed occupations, and the employe who delays leaving such positions for essential work, will alike be unenviably marked in the community. When the lists have been prepared by the community labor boards and approved by the Federal Directors and Advisory Directors of the various States, it is believed that the force of public opinion and self-respect will prevent any able-bodied man from keeping a position officially designated as 'woman's work.' The decent fellows will get out without delay; the slackers will be forced out and especially, I think, by the sentiment of women who stand ready, in order to bring the war

to a victorious conclusion as soon as possible, to take their places."

The lists will probably include, according to the United States Employment Service, " sales clerks and floor walkers in every sort of mercantile establishment; clerical, cashier, and office staffs in mercantile, manufacturing, and financial houses,; and the offices of transportation companies and other public utilities, waiters, attendants, and many other occupations."

Community labor boards will begin at once to study the industries in their respective communities with a view to determining those in which women can be used in war work and in what nonwar industries women can replace men. Two general orders have been prepared by the United States Employment Service defining the methods to be followed. In the first order employers engaged in war work who want women for employments which have hitherto not been customarily undertaken by women are directed to make application for approval to the community labor board in their district. After the propriety of using women in a given industry has been passed upon by the board the United States Employment Service is to give every assistance in filling the demand. In the second order two women are added to the community labor boards, one to represent the woman who works, the other to represent the management. They are to have full voting power on all questions concerning the utilization of women in the industries. Regulations to protect women from being drawn into employments that would be injurious to them or for which they are otherwise unfitted have been drawn up as follows:

First—Whether the kind of work is one which it is proper for women to perform.

Second—Whether the conditions surrounding the particular job are such that it is proper for women to be employed at that particular place and under existing conditions.

Third—What, if any, modifications in the conditions must be made in order that the employment of women may be sanctioned.

Fourth—What, if any, limitations are necessary as to the ages of women to be employed or otherwise.

"These orders," said Mr. Smyth, "indicate that steps in putting the new program into effect have been taken with care and that proper safeguards will be thrown around the now necessary larger introduction of women into the industries. Proper use of the reserves of women must be one of the principal weapons of overcoming the present labor deficit. The process cannot begin too soon.

"On the other hand, to carry on such a shift too impetuously, without proper direction and control, would result in great harm. If men are released too quickly they will suffer from unemployment while they are finding their new positions. If women go into industry too rapidly they will suffer from undertaking jobs for which they are not fitted or from laboring under conditions which are not suited for women. All decisions with relation to the use of women in industry will, of course, be in accord ance with the resolutions of the War Labor Policies Board. It will be seen that authority is given to community labor boards to take into consideration special local conditions, and in this way the system is given adaptability and elasticity, while the requirement that lists of 'women's work' be submitted for approval to the Federal Director and Advisory Boards in the respective States assures a reasonable uniformity."

Up to this time much has been heard about women in war work, but, according to these plans and others being made, the great call is about to be made. This, as pointing to the place of women in this country in the future, brings into new importance the questions as to what women have accomplished in the war thus far, what new occupations have been opened to them, what new rights as workers by the side of men have been accorded them, what economic gains have been won by them.

As to economic gains, here is a table showing changes in woman's wages in an Eastern metal work plant engaged in the manufacture of war supplies:

	Wages Per Hour, Cents. 1915.	1918.
Foot press operators.....	17.1	28.70
Trimmers	18.1	28.8
Bench workers...........	14.05	20
Power press operators...	15.7	29.5
Inspectors	16	34.9

The average of wages paid to women by this company are: In 1915, 15.9 cents per hour; in 1918, 35.1 cents per hour, a gain of more than 100 per cent. Women wage changes in four other factories engaged in similar work are:

1915, 13.7 cents per hour: 1918, 35.1 cents.

1915, 16.1 cents per hour; 1918, 27.5 cents.

1915; 16.1 cents per hour; 1918, 30 cents.

1915, 17.4 cents an hour; 27.6 cents.

In a textile factory the comparison of wages to women, hourly average based on a guarantee, is: 1915, 13.7 cents; 1918, 33.5 cents.

These increases are considered fairly typical throughout war industries in which women are employed. Miss Marie L. Obenauer, Chief Woman Examiner of the National War Labor Board at Washington, considered an authority on the subject of women employment, estimates the increase in women's wages in manufacturing war industries since 1915 to range between 80 and 100 per cent. But this advance refers only to employments in which women were engaged as machine workers before the war and not to occupations in which women have taken the place of men.

Where women do the work of men they have made their most substantial gain. The National War Labor Board, composed of representatives of employers and employes—"to bring about a settlement by mediation and conciliation of every controversy arising between employers and workers in the field of production necessary for the conduct of the war"—has laid down the following as a fundamental policy:

"If it shall become necessary to employ women on work ordinarily performed by men they must be allowed equal pay for equal work." • • •

Already this principle has been applied in several controversies. Two of greater importance were those of the Schenectady works and the Pittsfield works of the General Electric Company. In the Pittsfield case, in addition to the ruling of equal pay, a minimum standard was fixed for women's wages there—"that in no case shall any female 21 years of age or over, of six months' experience in the plant, receive less than 30 cents an hour." In the Schenectady Works a standard for women workers was—"in all classes of employment there shall be an increase of 20 per cent. in the wages of all adult women and no women shall receive less than $15 per week."

OUTPUT OF WOMEN

as compared with output of men in similar work, by industries.
(Compiled by National Industrial Conference Board.)

Classification of Establishments	Total No. of Establishments..	Greater in All Operations ...	Greater in Some Opera's; Equal in Some.....	Equal in All Operations ...	Greater in Some Opera's; Less in Some.....	Equal in Some Opera's; Less in Some.....	Less in All Operations ...	Not Comparable or Not Stated.
Automobiles and Automobile accessories....	10	1	..	3	1	2	1	2
Typewriters and other light machines........	6	2	..	2	..	1	..	1
Electrical machinery, apparatus, supplies...	18	2	..	6	2	2	2	4
Foundry and machine shop products.........	37	12	1	11	1	2	5	5
Munitions	13	4	..	1	2	1	2	3
Railway equipment.....	7	1	1	1	..	3	1	..
Tools, cutlery, and hardware	16	5	2	4	..	..	..	5
Miscellaneous metal products	20	3	2	2	1	..	4	8
Total	127	30	6	30	7	11	15	28

What actual gain for women is this standard of not less than $15 a week, as applied to this great company? In 1915 the Massachusetts Wage Commission, after investigation, fixed the amount necessary to maintain an adult worker at $8.71 a week. In July of this year the Bridgeport Employers' Association, after an extensive study of the cost of living, decided that such cost had increased 64.1 per cent. since 1915.

WAGE RATES OF WOMEN

as compared with rates to men by industries.

(Compiled by National Industrial Conference Board.)

Classification of Establishments.	Total No. of Establishments.	Wage Rates of Women. Equal to Men's.	Piece Rate Equal to Men's; Time Rate, Less.	Less Than Men's.	Not Comparable, or Not Stated.
Automobiles & auto access'r's	10	4	1	3	2
Typewr's, other light mach's..	6	2	2	2	..
Elec. machin'ry, appar., & supp.	18	3	2	8	5
Foundry. mach. shop products.	37	18	8	7	4
Munitions	13	5	6	..	2
Railway equip..	7	6	..	..	1
Tools, cutlery, and hardware	16	9	3	1	3
Miscellaneous metal products	20	6	7	3	4
Total........	127	53	29	24	21

In this table the column headed women's rates "equal to men's" means that rates were the same for men and women, whether on piece or daywork respectively; in some cases women were engaged exclusively on piecework; in other cases on timework.

According to this, the cost of maintenance a week of the worker in the New England territory for July of this year would be $13.08, and with variations for local conditions, these figures, if well computed, would be true for a large section of the country. The surplus gain in women's wages, therefore, is not as large as it appears, especially when compared with the advances obtained by some of the more powerful unions of male workers; but from one viewpoint the gain is great, for it marks an official recognition of the principle of the economic independence of the woman worker, that she shall earn enough to support herself, instead of being, often the case heretofore, one of a family group of wage earners dependent in part for her support on the larger earning power of male members.

This independence, or progress toward it, has just now a pertinent international bearing. The recent conductorette strike in London for recognition of the principle of equal pay for equal work is seen by some as the beginning of a revolution in women's wages in Great Britain. In France as early as 1916 a Ministerial circular said: "Women on work recognized as man's: If the women performed all the work they should be paid the same rates as the men, but if they had the help of men in some part of the work, or if special machinery had been installed to bring the work within their power, deductions might be made for these things. Their total earnings, however, plus what was paid to the men, or plus a fair allowance for the cost of the extra appliances, should equal the total which would be paid to men engaged in such work."

Just recently in France various writers on economic and social subjects have been discussing the effects of the economic emancipation of women, due to higher wages, and a main concern, as expressed by some of the writers, was that the admission of women to the new and better paid occupations would deter them, in greater numbers, from marrying or consenting to bear children and thus have a tendency to lower the birth rate in France. The views of writers who hold this opinion seem far-fetched to some persons in this country.

What is the attitude of employers to the new principle? That has not yet received a general expression of opinion. The National Industrial Conference Board on "Wartime Employment of Women in the Metal Trades" in its most recent research report says: "The principle of equal wages for equal work has found fairly general acceptance among employers in the metal trades." As to the attitude of men workers, this report says: "A large number of employers reported quiet acquiescence or even friendly co-operation of their men. A munition plant employing 694 women found that 'the male workers in the establishment accepted the introduction of female workers in new processes as inevitable, and there was no friction.' • • • Again and again the reported attitude is 'remarkably satisfactory,' 'very favorable,' 'friendly,' or is described by a brief but expressive 'O. K.'"

Where the War Labor Board has made awards of equal pay for equal work the earnings of women who were doing this work have gone up, in some classes of work, from 45 to 65 cents an hour. The working hours per week range from 48 to 52 hours. In a 52-hour week at 50 cents an hour one of these women substitutes would earn, including a 10 per cent. bonus for full time, $28.60. The earnings of some of the women run to $3[illegible] a week and more. Women who have won their way in the shops to doing a man's job are being received into unions. Women have been admitted to the International Machinists' Trades, the wire-workers', the ironworkers', and woodworkers' unions.

The increase in the earning power of women since 1915 in work outside the shops, in clerical work and the like, has not been so large, and is estimated to average not much more than 50 per cent., but the whole result is that the American woman has won her way to a new economic footing, and that the basis now recognized is, as defined by the rulings of the War Labor Board, that her pay shall be sufficient to support her and that for equal work she shall receive equal pay.

What new occupations have been opened to women by the war? Far in the lead are the various machinist trades, hitherto thought alien to them. The progress of women has been from the lighter to the heavier machines. Lines are being drawn as to the amount of exertion which may be required. A New York law provides that a woman shall not lift weights in excess of twenty-five pounds. The United States Ordnance Department, the American Foundrymen's Association, and the National Founders' Association have adopted the same rule. Grinding of metal parts may not be done by women in the State of New York. Under these safeguards, increasing in number, a great body of women has been inducted into the metal trades since 1914. In 1914 the percentage of women workers in the metal trades in the United States, as compiled by the National Industrial Conference Board from an abstract of census of manufactures, was 4.6 per cent. Of the 2,140,789 employes in these trades, says the research report of the board, 98,112 were women over 16 years of age. Clerical workers are included in these figures. This year, out of a total labor force of 384,709 in 131 establishments, 49,831 were women, as against 334,878 men; the proportion of women was 12.9 per cent.

It is estimated that 100,000 women are employed in munition plants and airplane factories, as against 3,500 in the last census year. In the chemical plants, on steam cars and electric cars, in elevators, as motor drivers, women have taken the place of men. There is in addition the work of women on the farms and as section hands on railroads. The Federal Railroad Administration announced a short time ago that they would be tried there to a limited extent, though the advisability of their work is still questioned by some labor directors, and Wisconsin has already passed a law throwing limitations around the employment of women on railways.

In England, due no doubt to the necessities of the war, a broader latitude is given in assigning women of strong build to heavier work. It is contended by one class of observers there that the physique of the women of Great Britain is to be permanently benefited by the ability which women have shown to stand up under work heavier than it was thought they could bear, and that this is especially true of outdoor work. Women there throughout the day are engaged in lifting weights of from 50 to 60 pounds. In some cases women have been employed in lifting 100 pound bags of coke and loading them on carts, though this is not approved, nor is the unloading of heavy pieces of limestone from cars. Those who contend that the health and vigor of women are to be increased by the exercise of their bodies in heavier work seem to have no medical tests to support their views.

In a summary as to the efficiency of women in the metal trades, which bears on the greater number of new occupations entered by women during the war, the recent research report of the National Industrial Conference Board says:

"Experience of employers in the metal trades in the United States has clearly demonstrated the practicability of employing women in a large variety of manufacturing operations. * * * In reviewing the record of efficient performance by women it must be emphasized that most of the tasks in which they are engaged are semi-skilled work of a repetitive character in which rapidity, lightness of touch and natural dexterity are more important than skill acquired through long training and experience. It is too early to form conclusions as to the ability of women to perform work of higher skill. The necessity for immediate increase of output made it essential to give women specialized training for particular jobs rather than to develop them into general mechanics. Even in England, where in one place or another women are used in practically all operations in the engineering and munitions trades, they have not received the broad training which skilled workmen receive."

Of the results found as to output, in the survey of 127 establishments in the metal trades made by the National Industrial Conference Board, this statement is made: "Eliminating the twenty-eight establishments in which, for one reason or another, no comparison can be made, this summary indicates that the output of women compares favorably with that of men, since it appears that in thirty establishments of the remaining ninety-nine the output of women was greater than that of men in all operations on which both were engaged; in six it was greater in some, equal in others; in thirty it was equal to that of the men. In other words, in sixty-six establishments, or two-thirds of those furnishing definite information as to output, women's production was equal to or greater than that of men in the operations on which both were employed. In only fifteen establishments was it found that women produced less than men in all operations in which they were engaged. Their production in the remaining eighteen establishments, although less in some operations, was equal, or greater in others.

"It appears, moreover, that the efficiency of women did not depend on the nature of the industry as such, or to any marked extent that they had but recently been introduced into an industry. In none of the classifications do a majority of the establishments report women less efficient than men, and it is significant that in the manufacture of foundry and machine shop products, on which women were in the past seldom employed except as coremakers, twenty-four establishments report women's work equal or superior to that of men in all operations as against five finding them inferior.

"In a steel establishment where women are employed in the manufacture of fuses, women operators of drill presses and milling machines are found to be from 25 to 50 per cent. faster than men. Another manufacturer of small metal parts for munitions states that women drill press operators handle 196 parts per hour on day work, while on night work men turn out only 148. Although the output of a day shift cannot fairly be compared with that of a night shift, this would not explain so marked a difference in results. In a bolt and nut establishment women working on drill presses and milling machines have achieved an average increase in output amounting to 30 per cent.

"A frequent commendation of women is that they are 'more teachable' and that they are 'more conscientious and painstaking' than men, although in some establishments they are reported to learn more slowly. A common experience was that they 'follow instructions better.'"

With regard to the physical limitations of women this statement is made: "It was the consensus among employers furnishing information that women should not be employed on work which required much lifting or straining, such as heavy machine operators, trucking, or yard labor. These opinions agree in substance with the experience of employers in Great Britain. According to the British Factory Inspectors' Report of 1916: 'There is hardly a process of any kind on which women are not employed to some extent, the one absolute limit lying in these heavy occupations, where adaptations of plant appliances cannot be effected so as to bring them within the compass even of selected women of physical capacity above the normal.'"

How many women have been drawn into gainful employments by the war who had hitherto been so engaged? There are no comprehensive statistics on this, but the consensus among employment experts is that the public has an exaggerated idea of the number of new recruits up to this time. What has given the impression of a vast induction of women into gainful employment for the first time is the extensive shifting, in greater and greater degree, from one occupation to another. From an economic standpoint, the two main factors in this shifting have been better pay and the lessening demand for workers in nonessential industries. The appeal was strong to domestic servants, and there was a heavy shift from this employment, and also from lodging house keepers, a calling known as not very remunerative. The vacant clerical positions had to be filled, but, in a considerable degree, this was done by shifting. The pay of women in city clerical positions was a strong inducement to country school teachers, and, according to an authoritative statement, 100,000 school teachers have left their schools for new employment. Many nurses also shifted over to new work.

From the time of our entry into the war this transfer to better paid employments connected with the production of supplies for the war received a new impetus. Women began to make the change not only for economic but also for patriotic reasons, and the war industries daily took on a new attraction. At the same time economic forces began to work more powerfully. People began to save, and this cut heavily into the nonessential industries. Women employed in the novelty industries, in artificial flower making, in feathers, in millinery, in a score of others, found the demand for labor there slackening. Then came the War Industries Board with control over the supplies for industries, and the singling out of nonessential industries, with the effect of accelerating the shifting of women from one employment to another.

The normal increase of women in the manufacturing industries is 100,000 a year, and prior to the activity brought on by the war business had been slack, so that there was a large surplus of unemployed women wage earners to draw upon. This shifting, as pointed out above, is an important factor in the new economic situation of America's women, for it is that which has opened new occupations to them, so that the foundation is laid for the great increase in women workers which the enlarged army plans call for.

That the greatest change up to this time has been the shifting is borne out by the investigation of the National Industrial Conference Board, which says: "Frequently women who have entered the metal trades in the present war labor emergency came from a great range of occupations to their new employment. An automobile manufacturer employing 423 women in twenty-three different departments reported that they had seldom been previously engaged on machine work. In another automobile plant the force of women was recruited approximately as follows: Twenty-five per cent. assemblers from other plants, 20 per cent. machine hands from other plants, 20 per cent. clerical workers from other plants, 20 per cent from housework, 5 per cent. from laundries, 5 per cent. from restaurants, 5 per cent. had not worked before."

ATTENDANCE AT WORK

of married women as compared with attendance of unmarried women and men.

(Compiled by National Industrial Conference Board.)

	Number of establishments	Number of women	Number of married women	Per C. of married women to total numb'r of women.
Women's attendance better than men's	33	4,965	575	11.6
Women's attendance equal to men's	23	3,488	723	20.7
Women's attendance worse than men's	20	7,213	924	12.8
Total	76	15,666	2,222	14.2

Supplementing this the statement is made: "In the establishments represented in this investigation women thus far have been chiefly drawn from other industrial occupations rather than from the ranks of the previously unemployed. It is probable, however, that an increasing number will be procured from the latter source if the available supply of men continues to decrease as the result of the war."

In 1910 8,075,772 women were engaged in gainful occupations, compared with 30,091,564 men. In 1914 the number of women in manufacturing industries was 1,649,697. According to the normal increase of 100,000 a year this would now have reached 2,000,000. The question here is how many women since the beginning of 1915 have been drawn into these industries who had not hitherto been gainfully employed and who, therefore, have swelled the total of women workers? This number is variously estimated at from 400,000 to 1,000,000.

"The tendency has been to exaggerate the number," Miss Obenauer said in Washington the other day, "and I have seen the estimate placed as high as 2,000,000, which is certainly much beyond the fact. No general statistics are available and I base my estimate of 400,000 on certain known increases, in typical instances; for the last two months the rate of influx has been gaining rapidly, and with the greater demands for women workers this is certain to continue."

Miss Obenauer thinks the increase of women in clerical work since the beginning of 1915 is about 500,000, or about double what it was in 1910; this would make a total gain of new women workers in these two fields of about 1,000,000. The total number of women in gainful employments in this country at this time is between 10,000,000 and 12,000,000, according to the summary of various estimates.

How many more women will be required when an army of 5,000,000 is in the field or in training? Here again the experts on these matters differ. Some at the upper end say not less than 4,000,000. Miss Obenauer thinks that 2,500,000 will be all it is necessary to enlist.

"In my opinion," she said, "one new woman will be required for every new soldier who goes into the field. I base this on the estimate of the statistician of the United States Chamber of Commerce that four workers will be required behind every soldier in the industries providing the supplies for the war. The equivalent of the other three men will be obtained, in my opinion, by greater conservation of skill, the maximum use of men unfit for military service, the elimination of non-essential industries, and the adaptation of all industries possible to war service and the use of labor-saving machinery."

Where will the women, certainly not likely to be less than 2,000,000, come from? The largest reservoir that can be drawn upon with the least disturbance to domestic life are women not now gainfully employed who are unmarried and not at the head of a household. Of this class of women in 1910 there were in the United States 2,000,000 between the ages of 16 and 45. Some of these were still in school, but the number, as compared with the total, was not large. It is from this class chiefly that the new women workers have been drawn, but there is undoubtedly still a surplus left in that class. Many of them are women of leisure, economically independent. But among the leaders of women workers there is strong opinion that, with the drafting of the man power of the country to meet the war needs, a new responsibility falls on the women of the country, and that women of independent means have as little excuse for not working as women who are driven to do so by the necessity of supporting children. Two of these women leaders declared that the principle of the draft was just as applicable, as matter of justice, to women as to men. One of these was Miss Obenauer, who said:

"I would be in favor of drafting all women who are physically fit and able to leave their families for industrial war service. There would be a great advantage in this. The selective method could be employed, and women could be fitted to the tasks best suited to them. There is much lost effort, owing to the lack of a system or any authority to provide one. Some women are in industrial work who should be in their homes, and some women are in their homes who should be at work, as women of leisure who are free from domestic responsibilities. It is a mistake to try to induce women who are needed at home to enter industrial work, even at this time. Certainly single women able to work should respond first and do so whether they are dependent on employment for a living or not."

Of the 47,000,000 women in the country, according to the last census, 35,000,000 are between the ages of 16 and 45. Of the employment of married women workers, the report of the National Industrial Conference Board says: "In eighty-five establishments reporting for the present investigation, 17.3 per cent. of a total of 22,750 women employes were married. Many of the men who have entered the national service were the only wage earners in their families, and very frequently wives who were employed before their marriage found themselves obliged to return to work. Employment of an increasing proportion of married women in industry has, however, been one of the striking social changes of the last thirty years."

With regard to the general bearing of the investigation, the board says: "In addition to the information secured from employers in the metal trades, scattered replies were received from a few other industries. Since the information was not sufficient to permit of conclusions, it has not been included in this report. In many of these instances, moreover, there had been no increase in the list of occupations of women since the outbreak of the war. The experience reported by these manufacturers in other lines was, broadly speaking, similar to that here presented by the metal trades, and therefore indicates, as already pointed out, that the conclusions reached for the metal trades are applicable to many other industries."

Miss Mary Van Kleek, Director of the new Women in Industrial Service of the Department of Labor, who is the only woman member of the War Labor Policies Board, co-ordinates women in industrial war work with the national labor problem.

"Every woman who is able to work will be needed, and the call is just as direct to women who are economically independent as to others," she said. "In some cities women of the leisure class are proposing to do volunteer work. I think that is a mistake. Women of the leisure class who go into labor should do so on exactly the same basis as other women. That is, they should conform to the standards and receive the pay for the particular work they undertake to do. For this they should undergo whatever training is necessary, so that they will be on a footing of efficiency with the others. If this were not done, if they approached the work in a merely voluntary, amateur way, it is readily seen that standards would be lowered and an injury inflicted; this is especially apparent in the effect there would be on wages—with women who are economically independent working without pay.

"This is the practical way, and the whole problem should be approached in that way. We shall need all the women workers that can be obtained, but I am not in favor of trying, by campaign methods, to enlist, say, 1,000,000 women, for occupations for which they have had no preparation, women without any industrial experience. There is great danger in inducting women into jobs for which they have had no previous training. In the first place, it should be determined for what kind of work the woman is suited, and then the preliminary training should be given. The question should not be considered from the standpoint of the woman and the job, but that of the worker and job; that is, suitability on the basis of efficiency.

"The success of the whole labor program depends on the observance of these principles, and unless they are applied to women as well as to men women would be taken in to serve in the capacities of unskilled workers, without consideration of their fitness for special and more useful tasks, and the result would be a positive loss in the labor output of the nation. In certain machine processes, for example, it has been found, according to reports of manufacturers, that the results obtained by women workers are more satisfactory than those by men. There is no question as to the efficiency of women where they are introduced under the right conditions to a work for which they are naturally suited. It is for this reason that we are placing so much emphasis on a study of occupations, with regard to the employment of women, and preliminary training for the occupations selected."

WOMEN RETURNING TO PEACE WORK

THE movement of women war workers to peace time production has begun. When a large number of gas mask workers were released from a Government plant in Long Island City recently the employment manager of this plant telephoned the United States Employment Service before notifying the women.

"Good," was the response of the service official. "The world is going out of mourning. Lingerie, waist, necktie and collar manufacturers are calling for power-machine operators. Corset factories, released by the War Industries Board from their restricted output, need skilled operators. Send us others as you release them and we will place them."

A large motor manufacturer in Detroit who has been employing hundreds of women reports:

"Our plant has unfilled contracts that will keep us at 100 per cent. production for two years. The questions are whether we can get materials and labor. The War Industries Board has already released steel supplies. Even before the war our great problem was a sufficient labor supply. We are ready to add to our force."

The first group of women to be released from war service in Washington was made the subject of special conference attention by the employment service. Their names, qualifications, and home addresses were requested by the United States Employment Service. Telegraphic machinery of the Clearance Division of Service was started, and within a few hours it was evident that nearly every woman would be offered a position, many of them in or near her home town. This offer of a position will be coincident with her release from war service.

Similar service can be rendered by the United States Employment Service throughout the country. A letter is being sent to each Federal Director, urging him to make special effort to list such clerical work as Washington women who have been engaged in war work can do, in order to be ready to place these women in their home States as rapidly as they are released from Government service.

With the war labor supplying machinery of the war equipment of the employment service reversed to meet the reconstruction needs, there need be no serious problem of unemployment for women who have been engaged in war work or for returning soldiers whose places have been taken by women. The one necessity is that employers and employes, whether scrub woman or professor, utilize the nation-wide facilities the Government has provided.

There remains the new factor of the woman who has been urged to take a man's place. Widespread pressure to this end really began only with the recent draft, which had scarcely started to operate. The great number of women on war work have been transferred merely from less to more essential industry. Like the gas mask workers, these women will naturally go back to their old trades.

The number of women who have taken men's places is larger, measured by the number who previously had taken similar work in an equal length of time.

A few hundred uniformed women chauffeurs concentrated in cities where publicity is facile have made a country-wide appeal, when earnest census takers could find not one in this calling eight years ago. The woman shipyard worker has likewise received much attention, yet at the greatest shipyard in the country, out of a total of 30,000 workers in late October, only 1½ per cent. were women in men's jobs, and these unskilled jobs where transfer is easiest.

Women who are highly skilled workers in their trades or professions were already, before the war, largely released from sex discrimination. Employers more and more are calling for so many skilled operators, so many chemists, &c. War pressure has merely accelerated a natural development.

December 1, 1918

Women in Men's Work While Needed Elsewhere.

To the Editor of The New York Times:

The problem of finding employment for the returning troops is, without doubt, a very big one, and unless every possible effort is made to solve it the situation promises to become quite serious. Many steps have been taken already, but there seems to be one measure which has been largely neglected, and yet it is of the most vital importance. I refer to the numerous positions now held by women which were formerly filled by men. In not a few instances the women are retained because they work for something less.

I see hundreds of girls holding jobs on the street railways, in apartment houses, and stores, running elevators, in hotels and restaurants as waitresses, and in various mercantile establishments doing clerical work. A great many of these women are married and their husbands work also. On the other hand there is a tremendous shortage of female help for household services, and I venture to claim that a tremendously large percentage of these women are better qualified for domestic positions than for the situations they now hold. Therefore, as a matter of patriotism, employers should be urged to give men, particularly discharged soldiers, the preference.

LOUIS H. SCHWARTZ.
New York, March 27, 1919.

The Third Sex in Industry

American Observer's View of a Movement Well Defined in England, in Which Women Seek Special Conditions and Favors

NOW comes the third sex in industry, formed of women workers who, like the militant suffragists, regard their interests as distinct from those of men workers, and requiring an organization or union separate from the men's.

In England this movement is already well defined, and is represented by the Women's Industrial Union under the leadership of Lady Rhondda. The members are referred to as the third sex, though they, like the militant suffragists, repudiate any such designation. In England much bitterness and strife have been caused by the new organization, but its appearance there at this time is considered to have some extenuating circumstances.

The war drew many women into the industries. It was their hearty co-operation during this period that was the main factor, it is asserted, in winning for them the suffrage. This is a point made by those who contend that extreme militant methods have never advanced women toward the attainment of their aim. But the counsel of continued co-operation with men workers in the trying period of readjustment following the war was not followed by the body of women who are now making a fight in England through the Women's Industrial Union. Unusual conditions, it is fair to say, surrounded some of the women who joined this movement. By the loss of their husbands in the war they had become the heads of families, and the fight for continued employment at the highest possible wages was seen to be a first necessity, with what they considered to be a first call over men upon whom no one was dependent.

What in Great Britain is called the third sex in industry made its American appearance in the dispute over the rights of women street car conductors in Cleveland, Ohio. Several suffrage associations, notably in Ohio and Massachusetts, have been holding protest meetings in favor of the women conductors, and it is asserted that the same exclusive appeal of women for women which was made in England is now being presented in this country. Unless checked in the beginning, much bitterness among men and women workers is expected to ensue, with much loss to the general cause of labor.

Women had not been employed on Cleveland street cars prior to the war. The Cleveland street car company advertised for women conductors in August, 1918. Bad feeling resulted among the men employes, who feared the effect this move would have on trade union policies and standards. Later this feeling was aggravated by what were said to be discriminations in favor of the women conductors. The company stated that women were being sought because there were not enough men available to run the cars with efficiency. This the union asserted to be untrue.

The Federal Department of Labor sent two investigators of the Investigation Service to Cleveland to determine whether or not sufficient men were available for conductors. The result of the investigation was against the company; according to its own books, the investigators reported, the company's employment agency had hired 1,142 men and had lost 1,273 men, of which 908 quit, 191 were discharged, 13 died, 2 were promoted, and but 159 joined the United-States forces. Later the War Labor Board made a decision that women conductors were not necessary in Cleveland because men were returning from the front, but an extension of time was allowed the company to hold its women conductors on duty.

Later the War Labor Board granted a rehearing of the case. Soon after the controversy reached an acute stage women suffrage associations stepped in with protests over what they termed the great injustice threatened the women conductors. On the other hand, labor representatives assert that if the position taken by the women conductors and their supporters is sustained a great injustice will be done them, and a blow struck at the strength of their organization.

Miss Gertrude Barnum, Assistant Chief of the Investigation Service of the Department of Labor, which sent the two inspectors to Cleveland, said in Washington the other day:

" The course of the women's suffrage associations in making protests before they knew what they were protesting about—for no hearing had then been held on the women's case and facts were not known—is to be condemned, for the effect of the protests is to stir up strife between men and women workers.

" If the movement succeeded and a separate organization for women workers were formed in this country, it would mean another division in the ranks of labor, with men and women arrayed against each other for the benefit of the employers, who could play one off against the other. From that would come a lowering of standards and a weakening in other ways of the unions, which have required years and years to build up. The men conductors in Cleveland asserted that the real reason the company desired women conductors was that they were not well versed in trade unionism and would prove more tractable.

" In a word, the men conductors saw in the move an effort to weaken their union; before the women conductors were taken on the men employes wanted to thrash out the consequences with the company, but this was refused.

" If the women were successful as a separate body of workers, they would not only harm the unions as they exist today, but also, ultimately, their own cause. There is but one fair and constructive viewpoint, but one way for the worker to proceed—neither as a woman nor as a man, but as a worker. Women in entering new industries, where the workers are highly organized, should remember that the ' rights ' which are spoken of are not natural ones, but that they have been won by twenty-five years or more of protracted effort on the part of the members of the unions, and as a result of many sacrifices. They should be willing to assume the responsibilities that belong to a fellow-worker and be willing to share not only the advantages, but also the disadvantages.

" Take the Cleveland street car conductors. They have been a long time in raising their standards, in shortening hours, and in increasing wages. When a man desires a job as conductor he applies for membership in the union and then seeks employment with the company through the union. That is what is called the ' front door,' and women should know that if they try to enter an industry in any other way than by the ' front door ' they will be certain to arouse the antagonism of the organized workers.

"I think women workers generally realize the wisdom and fairness of this. That is why the untimely interference in the Cleveland case by woman suffrage associations is to be deplored.

© Bachrach.
Miss Gertrude Barnum.

"Some might blame the Cleveland men conductors. But there are many questions that need to be thrashed out first; first, as to whether this is a suitable employment for women; that touches the men conductors in a practical way which outsiders could not realize. The men out of their earnings, not large, have created a sick benefit fund and strike funds, in which any member of the union shares. But if such work as closing the heavy doors of the large cars in use today should turn out to be too heavy for women, or long hours on their feet in the crowded cars on night runs prove too

much of a strain, then they frequently would be incapacitated and would draw on the sick fund much oftener than the men. Even if the men desired to extend this privilege in greater degree to the women they cannot afford it at present wages. The men conductors have thought, too, that women serving as street car conductors was more or less a war fad, only temporary, and that if received in the unions they would only 'muss things up' and then get out.

"When I say that men and women workers should be on the same footing, without any distinction as to sex, I do not mean that where there are health risks peculiar to women they should not be taken into consideration. They should. Before a woman is taken into a new industry her permanent fitness should be thoroughly investigated and determined. After that co-education and co-operation should be the rule for men and women workers. We have many illustrations of that kind of co-operation, where men and women join hands for the advancement of the general cause of labor. One is the Amalgamated Association of Street and Electric Railway Employes, an international organization. This association made a fight for the right of the women employes of the companies, used as ticket choppers, to organize, and since then have made other fights for the improvement of the conditions of the women workers."

"What do you understand as the third sex in industry?" was asked.

"In general," answered Miss Barnum, "it is a group, divorced from the women of the home, who believe that women's sphere is the home, and from the co-educationalists in labor who believe that women should receive labor education with men and should co-operate with men in raising the working standards of both men and women. This third group, the so-called third sex in industry, has lost faith in a chance to improve the conditions of the members by working with men, and believes that it should work primarily for women and against men. Most of those active in this group, I understand, are unmarried women."

Songs and Speeches in Four Languages at Opening Session in Washington.

WASHINGTON, Oct. 28.—Speeches in four languages and songs in as many more marked the opening session today of the first International Congress of Working Women. Some fifty of the delegates came from foreign countries, eleven nations besides the United States being represented. With the service of a corps of women interpreters, all of the addresses made during the day were fully understood, as was indicated by the waves of applause which swept over the hall.

Mrs. Raymond Robins, as President of the National Women's Trade Union League, in opening the congress hailed it as the forerunner of many similar ones to come. As she ended a woman who had taken her remarks down in shorthand read them in French, while others who followed recited them in Polish and Bohemian. These four languages generally sufficed, the Italian, Japanese, and other nationals getting the meaning through one of the four languages.

Luther Stewart, President of the Federation of Federal Employes, and Miss Mary Anderson of the United States Labor Department also spoke in welcome.

Mlle. Jeanne Bouvier and Mlle. Victoire Cappe spoke, respectively, for France and Belgium.

Dr. Alice Moreau, who responded to the welcome in behalf of Argentina, used French. She was warmly applauded for her assertion that "women must organize to overcome the old prejudice that she is some sort of an inferior animal to man."

Mrs. Margaret Bondfield, an English delegate, spoke of the conference as "working to build a new civilization that will not have the evils of the old." This also drew a triple demonstration, as each of the interpreters rendered it.

At the afternoon session, Miss Mary Van Kleeck, formerly of the Labor Department, discussed the participation of women in labor organization and industry, predicting that a few decades would find them out of the class needing special protection by reason of their ability and organization. Miss Van Kleeck condemned radicals and conservatives of extreme views and advocated a middle course in meeting social and industrial problems.

Each of the countries has ten votes in the congress, regardless of the number of delegates present. Most of the nations, however, have sent only two delegates, except Poland, which has five. The executive committee, so that each country's point of view may be represented, consists of one member from each delegation chosen by her co-delegates. The following members of this committee have been assigned: For Poland, Mlle. Sophie Dobranske; for Czechoslovakia, Mme. Marie Majerova; for France, Mlle. Jeanne Bouvier; for Belgium, Mlle. Victoire Cappe; for Canada, Mrs. Katherine Berry; for Switzerland, Frau Huni; for Japan, Dr. Tomo Inouyi; for Sweden, Dr. Anna Sundquist; for Italy, Signorina Cabrini Casartilli; for Argentina, Dr. Alicia Moreau; for Great Britain, either Miss Margaret Bondfield or Miss Mary McArthur, and for the United States, Mrs. Raymond Robins.

The ten delegates representing this country in the congress are Mrs. Robins; Miss Mary Anderson, of Washington, representing boot and shoe workers; Mrs. Lois B. Rantoul, of Boston, of the Federal Employes' Union; Mrs. Maud Swartz, of the printers; Miss Leonora O'Reilly, of the New York Women's Trade Union League; Miss Agnes Nestor and Miss Elizabeth Christian, representing the glove makers; Miss Rose Schneidermann, of the cap makers; Miss Julia O'Connor, president of the Telephone Operators' Union, and Miss Fania Cohn, of the Ladies' Garment Workers' Union of New York.

TOPICS OF THE TIMES.

America's "Spirit" Criticised.

In the current number of Good Housekeeping, decorated and introduced in a way that shows editorial approval and sympathy, there appears an article by a young woman with a significantly exotic name. It is notably well written, evidently the product of deep and sincere emotion, and it is a successful literary achievement in that the writer, using but little space, has expressed fully what she had in mind. That she does not lack intelligence is obvious, and yet she and the article itself, taken together, constitute a complete refutation of practically every statement and implication the article contains.

For this so eloquent young woman has much fault to find with something she calls " the spirit of America."

It seems that when she arrived here she did not receive the welcome she had expected. Exactly what sort of a welcome she did expect she does not reveal—possibly because the welcome she did get exactly corresponded with any reasonable or sane expectation. For she was allowed to land, to enter American life on exact social, economic and political equality with all the women in it already, and there was opened to her full opportunity for the display of whatever abilities and talents she possessed.

She seems to hold it a grievance that, instead of being allowed, as she desired, at once to serve with head and heart the America of her dreams, she had to become for awhile a mere " hand " in a sweatshop. That wasn't living the "free life" to which the young woman had aspired! And she reminds us that it was to gain the right to lead such a life that the first English colonists came over here!

Evidently she has forgotten, or never knew, what sort of a life those colonists led for many a year—the innumerable hardships, the grinding toil, the many dangers, they had to endure and did endure without a whimper until by work and thrift they attained to easier conditions.

Grievances Wholly Imaginary.

That the young woman with the eloquent pen had to work for awhile in a sweatshop was unpleasant for her, of course, and unpleasant for her, too, was it that her wages didn't rise as fast as the price of food and clothing, but surely " the spirit of America " was not blamable for either of those unpleasantnesses. And why does not her article put a lot of emphasis, instead of none at all, on the fact that, though America could find at first use only for her hands, it permitted her to get the education to which she aspired; that as soon as she was able to write articles worth reading editors accepted and paid for them so well that now she is, seemingly, in just about the position which the America of her dreams had promised?

Instead of complaint and criticism of America, why is she not writing praises of the country that has been so kind to her and done so much for her? Her grievances are wholly imaginary, and all her eloquence, boiled down, turns out to be nothing better than ingratitude—than failure to appreciate the very great benefits bestowed on terms as generous as any human being in reason can ask.

She need not believe nor say that America is perfect; we all know that it isn't; but at least she might have admitted, or even proclaimed, that—well, that in not many other lands would she have been as kindly treated or have done as well. Then her article, which now causes irritation and justifies resentment in the mind of every sensible reader, would have been worthy in substance of its admirable phrasing.

June 21, 1920

THE CRAZE FOR EMBROIDERIES

One Aspect Is a Movement to Interest Foreign-Born Women in Putting Their Home Work on the Market

IF it is not embroidered well, then it isn't fit to be called smart. This applies to clothes, to curtains, to decorations miscellaneous, and to many another appendage to feminine life and apparel. In the last few years the fad has been growing and growing until now we are in the middle of an embroidery era.

At first there were stray spots on the Frenchiest and most expensive of the gowns. Now there is scarcely an article of apparel that does not show a bit of embroidery somewhere in its make-up, if it is not entirely covered with the fine hand stitchery. Somebody who knows the situation well has said: " Batik has had its day, and now embroidery is coming into its own and rightful place." That is a far-visioned prophecy, but there seems every likelihood that it may be so.

While we are facing the immediate demand of our individual needs for Spring clothes and Spring decorations, an interesting little bit of research discloses the fact that here in America, under our very noses as it were, we have an abundant and overflowing source of supply for decoration and trimmings of this character. One fancies that all the really fine and colorful and artistic embroideries are imported—sent to us from the other side. And the customs duty these days runs to over half the cost of material, making foreign embroideries almost prohibitive in price. Then a lot of the foreign things, so-called antiques, have been woven just a week before they left, the other side and their makers have conscientiously rubbed them in the all pervading grime to give them that authenticity which is calculated to send their prices, even minus the duty, soaring skyward. We can do the same trick here, and we can even refrain from the dirt application when we become honest enough to see that the art lies in the thing itself, not in its age and raggedness.

Of course, it is a well known fact that we have representatives of all the nationalities gathered in our great country —forty-five of them, or something like that, they are. And all of the women of these people carry in their systems the knowledge of embroidery, what it is, and how to do it. Even if they are of the second generation or of the third, they have lingering somewhere in their consciousness the sleeping ability to stitch and stitch until the material plus the threads they are weaving into it becomes a work of art. When they first began to come to this country they found that their old work had no place here, where shirt waists and tailored suits were the things. Gradually they forgot to do the stitchery which had been their pleasure. It is a fact that in America there is little use for their solid and brilliantly colored embroideries except as stray and strange pieces of decoration, but in our latest embroidery craze we are beginning to see that their art can be employed. How to bring out this sleeping talent, how to get the workers together, how to market the embroideries and let the public know where they can be had— that is another problem and a poser, for it is hard, from all angles, to start on its way an idea that is so entirely new to the minds of every one.

Those who conduct the Art Alliance of America and those who are interested in the People's Institute recently got together and formed a plan to open four settlements of hand workers in New York City, just as an experiment. The one for the Ukrainians was the first. At the Ukrainian Settlement a room was opened and the women in the neighborhood who could embroider were invited to come and take the work away to their homes. The designs are made by artists at the settlement who are there for that purpose, and the danger is avoided of the women turning out work which is too bizarre and too un-American to be salable. The artist carefully studies the needs of her public and designs accordingly, and then the hand workers, who after all are only interested in the work itself, get the pieces to carry out and finish. The pay for the work is 30 cents an hour, so that for an eight-hour day an embroiderer can get $2.40. She can work at home, attending the while to her household duties and putting in just as much time at embroidery as she pleases. It is a great boon to many women who could not go out to work but who need a little extra money over and above their husbands' wages.

In this Ukrainian community they are making all sorts of beautiful specimens of embroidery which are extraordinarily inexpensive, when the labor and all are considered. With the prices of raw materials at such exorbitant figures it would seem a wise investment to put one's money into something of this sort which will live artistically and is calculated also to give a maximum amount of wear. Besides the embroidered smocks and bands for dresses, which are now greatly in demand, these women do exquisite pieces of table linen with borders and motifs carried out in true Ukrainian character. They have curtains in all sorts of lovely tones and colors and stitches, and they make whole sets of bedroom and porch fixings to be used by decorators in creating new and unusual rooms. Cretonne is a bit tiring in some ways, and besides it has been done and done. This new work can be developed in various intricacies of design and pattern, until it becomes an entirely individual thing and something which, because of its character and the work that has gone into it, will not outlive its usefulness nor its decorative possibilities in many years.

One of the bedroom sets is of natural toned linen of a very heavy quality. The edges are hemstitched for a finish. Then across the spread are sun lines of a deep pink embroidery, while in the centre of the cover is worked out a design that still carries out the squares in a little more elaborate way. In this pattern are touches of black, distributed by the designing artist so that they tell in the most effective manner. To go with this are curtains—long slim strips of the same linen decorated with the same embroidery, also bureau covers and a table cover, to which can be added any other decorative bit that the room may need.

The Ukrainians, under the expert direction that has come to visit them, are doing lovely porch sets, too. One of the leading decorators in town is handling these with great success. The work is done in heavy threads on extra heavy materials for foundations. The sets can be washed and kept clean and made to last out several Summers in the outdoor living room.

The same people who are conducting the Ukrainian experiment have arranged to establish groups of workers among the Italians, Sicilians, and negroes. Many others will follow if plans reach maturity. The Italians are to be led—in fact the work is beginning now—to make their own native embroideries, those dainty, delicate things in cool blues and whites with the backgrounds worked in solidly and the designs left blank with teetering black stitches to suggest their outlines. There is no more beautiful embroidery than this. We have the people right here among us who not only can do it but love to do it, and they should be able to turn out in this country as beautiful hand embroideries as they have produced abroad for many ages past. It is being done now in small quantities.

One of the arguments for pushing the work is the benefit to the workers. Of course we need the embroideries—fashion and its demands attend to that. But the women need the "expression" if they are to be the efficient American citizens that we all are crying loudly for them to become. For generations they have worked at this sort of thing in their own countries, but until now they have found little encouragement

here for their native arts. Psychologists, after their delvings and probings, have told us that the tips of the fingers are the instruments which demand to discharge the surplus energies of the human body, and that if they are denied their natural expression developed through the ages they "take it out in picking and stealing"—worse than that, in extreme nervousness and twitchiness. It seems simple enough to give them work to do, to let them supply the demand already created, in short, to help them through a little expert guidance to become adapted to this land that is so new and strange and inexplicable to their foreign intelligences.

A pretty story is told of an Italian woman, who brought in her stunt of embroidery after an unbelievably short space of time. She had made the large sum of $25 on the job, and finally confessed that her husband had helped with the work in the evenings. Perhaps, after all, that is the solution of handling the time left over from an eight-hour day. If it pleases the master of the house to turn his hand to sewing and to the making of beautiful things why might that not be his avocation? If he has another sort of temperament, then he can possibly fill his extra time in some other direction; but there are many of those men who enjoy the art of embroidery just as a woman does.

Later the people in charge hope to extend the work from New York to the remotest quarters of the country for the benefit of people living in isolated districts with much spare time in the evenings. Many are the sewing women of the rural community who wish that they could turn their handiwork to account, and yet know of no way to apply their talents commercially. The correspondence of a woman's magazine brings numerous requests by each mail from women who are reaching out blindly for a possible market for the stitches which they know so well how to make. The Art Alliance says that there must be primarily, if the work is to have any permanent success, trained supervisors, trained teachers, and trained designers. The managers are sure they can make the production of artistic needlework a permanent American institution.

Besides the dresses which are showing all sorts of embroideries this Spring, there are hats and scarfs which are pleasantly ornamented with designs of wool and silk woven from hand and machine stitches. Everything is carrying the semblance of embroidery in one form or another. It is the trimming of the hour, without a doubt, and it must be used if one is to be in the running of fashion. The machine embroidery now being developed in the United States are most astonishing of all. Of course, artistically they cannot be put in the same class as the hand work, but they have their place, and it is interesting to see how deftly the machine needles can produce the effect of hand embroidery when they are piloted by an expert.

There is one place in town where lessons in machine embroidery are given free, and the tale goes that the workers get extravagant wages. The machine needle makes a sort of French net stitch which can be huddled together, or strung out in a straight line, or scattered in small groups over the surface of the material until the effect becomes quite unusual.

February 1, 1920

EARLIEST WOMAN PASTOR DIES AT 96

The Rev. Dr. Antoinette L. Brown Blackwell, the first woman in the United States to be ordained a minister, an associate of Susan B. Anthony and Julia Ward Howe in the early days of the agitation for woman suffrage, died yesterday of arterio-sclerosis at the age of 96 at the home of her daughter, Mrs. Samuel T. Jones, 331 Elmore Avenue, Elizabeth, N. J. Services will be held at 2:30 o'clock Tuesday afternoon in Elizabeth, in All Souls' Unitarian Church, of which she was pastor emeritus.

Born in a log cabin in Henrietta, N. Y., May 20, 1825, Antoinette Brown began to work for her living when scarcely more than a child, teaching school for $1 a week before she was 16 years old. In the early forties she entered Oberlin College and there formed a friendship with Lucy Stone. Both were denied admission to the debating exercises of the men, and thereupon organized the first debating society ever formed among college girls.

When, in 1847, Antoinette applied for admission to the theological school the professors told her frankly they would have excluded her if the charter of Oberlin had permitted. To help pay her expenses she essayed to teach in the preparatory department, but the Ladies' Board, composed largely of the wives of the professors, blocked her by passing a rule against teaching by graduates of the college. She had made friends, however, and a private drawing class organized by them enabled her to pay her way after all.

After graduation she was engaged by a woman's society in this city to do missionary and social work. Her efforts met with the approval of her employers, but when she spoke at the first National Woman's Rights Convention in Worcester, Mass., in 1850, they were so scandalized her connection with the society ended abruptly. After that she worked as a free lance, lecturing and preaching where she could. She attained great popularity as a speaker, and occasionally received as much as $100 for a lecture, a high price for a woman in those days. Horace Greeley and Charles A. Dana offered to provide her with a hall and a salary of $1,000 a year if she would preach regularly in New York City. She felt herself insufficiently trained, however, and accepted a call from the Congregational Church at South Butler, N. Y., at $300 a year.

Her regular ordination at South Butler as an orthodox Congregational minister in 1853 aroused severe condemnation. The New York Independent called her an infidel. Her church appointed her a delegate to the World's Temperance Convention in this city. When she rose to speak the convention, composed chiefly of ministers, howled and hooted during the two days to drown her voice. Despite the aid of Channing, Phillips, Garrison and others, she was not allowed to be heard.

Later she went through a period of religious doubt, resigned her pulpit and became a Unitarian. She accompanied Susan B. Anthony and Julia Ward Howe in their tours for suffrage, and when the Federal Amendment was passed she declared it the happiest moment of her life.

Dr. Blackwell's vitality and enduring energy were remarkable. When 78 years old she visited the Holy Land alone, and at 93 wrote the last of her many books.

Her writings deal with religious, philosophical and scientific subjects, except the novel "The Island Life" and a volume of poems. The titles of some of the others are: "Studies in General Science," "The Sexes Throughout Nature," "The Philosophy of Individuality" and "The Making of the Universe."

In 1856 she married Samuel C. Blackwell. They had five children.

November 6, 1921

Women Win the Vote

WOMAN SUFFRAGE IN WYOMING.

The third biennial Legislature of Wyoming convened in Cheyenne on the 4th inst. Both houses elected Republican presiding officers, for first time in the history of the Territory, the first Legislature, in fact, having been entirely Democratic. Governor Campbell in his message speaks of woman suffrage in the following terms: "The experiment of granting to woman a voice in the Government, which was inaugurated for the first time in the history of the world by the first Legislature of our Territory, has now been tried for four years. I have heretofore taken occasion to express my views in regard to the wisdom and justice of this measure, and my conviction that its adoption has been attended only by good results. Two years more have only served to deepen my conviction that what we have done has been well done, and that our system of impartial suffrage is an undoubted success."

November 16, 1873

Women May Vote in Colorado.

DENVER, Col., Dec. 3.—The State Canvassing Board completed its work yesterday. The count shows that woman's suffrage was carried by 6,347 majority. Gov. Waite has issued a proclamation giving women the right to vote at all elections in this State.

December 4, 1893

Woman Suffrage in Colorado

Written for THE NEW YORK TIMES

By John Cotton Dana,

City Librarian, Springfield, Mass.

Colorado wives don't quarrel with their husbands over politics. The grim spectre of political partisanship may be threatening the peace and harmony of family firesides, but he has not yet made his presence actually felt. In Colorado, at least, a woman can vote and be a woman still. She hasn't lost her charm since 1894, when she first made acquaintance with the real thing in ballot boxes.

Colorado has not yet outgrown its newness. In the new Western community woman, being somewhat rare, much needed in housekeeping, in demand for marrying, a prop to the social life men are too busy to keep up, a necessity as school ma'am, and indispensable to the preacher—woman in this case, gets attention and deference not generally granted her. And in the new Western community she has usually risen to her opportunity. You will find the eternal sameness, but you will find her also a trifle more assertive, a bit more self-reliant, and, one may venture the statement, not infrequently more helpful. The men in Colorado had come to think of women, not less as women, but a little more as co-workers. A chance touch of legislation gave the opportunity to grant them the suffrage, and it was granted; rather, one must admit, to the men's surprise. But the thing was done, and the women hastened to equip themselves for the new duty—which they then spelled with a large D. Not in the history of the world has there been anything quite like the first attack of Colorado women on the fruit of the tree of political knowledge. They wanted to vote; they thought it a duty to vote; it was the thing—the fad—to vote; Populism was to be downed, or sustained, as the case might be; their reputation for ability and vim was at stake; ignorance of political and sociological matters was a disgrace, and in a few short months they felt that ignorance in that particular form was theirs no longer, and all, with one accord, voted.

Then they reflected. They found human nature was superior to political institutions; that even the vote of the more moral half—as they regarded it—of the community did not work any immediate noteworthy change in political methods or add much to the effectiveness of city, county, or State Government. They learned also that the politician found them an uncertain quantity;

not entirely negligible, to be sure, but so impossible of forecast as to make for a time the ward canvass a useless waste of campaign funds. He found it—so he had the effrontery to claim—easier to gain women-voters by being pleasant-spoken in the last half hour before ballot-casting, than it was to persuade them by arguments and torchlight processions during the campaign. And they found also, much to their dismay, that the political worker of their sex, as she arose, proved often to be such among women as is the man worker among the men. With the rich, the society element, voting ceased to be a fad. It remained a proper thing for those who chose to exercise the right; it was no longer a duty. The rank and file kept on voting. Certain special factors being held in view, one cannot say that the figures show any very notable falling off in the woman vote in the six years it has existed. The woman votes as most men do; though not quite so much as a partisan and a little more as the special case and the special candidate may move her. The dyed-in-the-wool partisan is born, not made. The political bias of the father passes naturally enough to the son. It will take a generation of woman suffrage to raise the first crop of born female Democrats.

The politician does not like the woman vote. It confuses his reckoning. The game is not in his hands, as it formerly was. The grip of the gang rule is a little weakened. Under ordinary circumstances this would be counted a distinct gain for good government. Here the gain is somewhat doubtful. The game is played, as before. The winnings go more by chance and less by calculation; the result is not so much the coming of better men into office as the coming into office of an unexpected group of the same old eager office seekers. Add a larger element of chance to the game of politics dishonestly played, and the result is not politics honestly played. It is simply the old thing plus a little chaos.

And what has woman, voting, done with her little vote? Very little. Good government is a matter of skill; it does not come by nature, even from women. You don't get the perfect state out of indifferentism, ignorance, and greed, plus a modicum of zeal, wisdom, and honor, in any community, and you don't get it in Colorado even when to half these qualities you add the feminine element. A good many Colorado women see this, and would give up their franchise if they could, realizing that the best society is born of the best people, and not of the right to vote. But the question of withdrawal or surrender of the right—if it could ever come to a popular vote—would immediately become a party issue, and would be answered in the negative. The right to vote once granted or once seized is never given up—by voting. Woman suffrage in Colorado is now a settled fact. It works. That is, it is in active operation, and there is no attendant revolution, no social upheaval, no panic, no loss of stability in any institutions, domestic, civil, educational, or religious. To the passing observer Colorado is as though woman suffrage were not. If ever the woman vote does produce marked changes in human society—by the vote direct—it will be, save in certain peculiar and isolated cases, not this side of the first quarter century of the experiment, and not until women have added to a native opportunism a fairly penetrating political foresight. They have proved now and again that they can make almost any polling place clean and decent; that they can—not always—mitigate the horrors of caucus and convention; that they can sometimes compel the machine to pick its candidates with a keener eye to the respectable element in the community; that they can, temporarily at least, elevate the tone and add to the efficiency of a city government; that they can learn what results it is right to expect of a city department, of public streets, for example, and can materially help in securing those results; that they can fill creditably a good many positions in the State, especially those connected with educational, penal, and charitable institutions, and that they can speak with more force in favor of the effective administration of laws regulating drinking, gambling, and the social evil.

Since women voted men have added to the deference they always granted them—a deference usually such as the superior can afford to pay to the inferior—a little of the deference which one's equal compels. Therefore, women have not lost in indirect influence on political affairs as they have gained in direct; rather the reverse is true.

The positive or objective results are not much; they can as yet hardly rise to be counted. A certain subjective result can be much more surely insisted on—the right of suffrage has compelled women to look a little further abroad. Women in Colorado to-day very commonly think of human society as part of that world of which they wish to know something. This wider outlook is, of course, not common among men; no one would claim it is more common among women, even in Colorado. But many women in Colorado now have it where formerly few had it. This is not a revolution. Perhaps it is not even progress. Certainly it is change—and it is the one change of importance in Colorado society which can as yet be definitely laid to the door of woman suffrage.

JOHN COTTON DANA.

March 11, 1900

ELIZABETH CADY STANTON

Mrs. Stanton was born Nov. 12, 1815, in Johnstown, N. Y. She was the daughter of Supreme Court Judge Daniel Cady and wife of the late Henry Brewster Stanton, noted abolitionist and journalist. She began her education at the Johnstown Academy, and later became a pupil at Emma Willard's Seminary, in Troy, a school noted then throughout the country. She was graduated with the class of '32. Eight years later, while attending a world's anti-slavery convention in London, she made the acquaintance of Lucretia Mott, which resulted in the joint passage of a call for a woman's rights convention. Mrs. Stanton was on her wedding trip at this time. The convention was held at her home, Seneca Falls, July 19 and 20, 1848.

The first formal claim for suffrage for women was then made. In 1854 she appeared before the New York Legislature and addressed it on "The Rights of Married Women." Six years later she took the stand that drunkenness should constitute a cause for divorce. She was instrumental in having the question of woman suffrage submitted to Kansas in 1867 and Michigan in 1874. She was President of the National Committee of her party from 1855 to 1865. She was also identified with the Women's Loyal League and was President of the National Women's Suffrage Association until 1883. In 1868 she sought to become an actual political factor by entering the lists for Congress. For the past quarter of a century and over she had annually addressed a committee of Congress in favor of an amendment for women to the Constitution of the United States.

"At the time of her death she was honorary President of the National Women's Suffrage Association. Mrs. Stanton's mother was Margaret Livingston, a daughter of James Livingston, an officer in the American Army during the Revolution. Her father's ancestors came from Connecticut. Mrs. Stanton began to take a great interest in the laws as they applied to women by having access to her father's office, and in which she spent a great deal of time. She began to hold that the statutes were unfair toward women. Before she knew how great a project was confronting her, she had become the evangel of equal rights.

"After graduation from the Willard Seminary in Troy, Mrs. Stanton came to find herself in sympathy with the principles enunciated by her cousin, Gerritt Smith, the anti-slavery agitator. She became desirous of knowing just what the conditions were in the South, and it was at the house of an abolitionist that she met her future husband.

Through her efforts, practically unaided, she caused the passage of a "Woman's Property bill" by the New York Legislature, delivering a two-hour speech thereon. With her work as an anti-slavery advocate and claimant for women's rights, she also found time to devote to the cause of temperance.

She was wont to tell that as early as her sixteenth year she became a believer in woman's rights. Her vexation and mortification were great when her brothers went to college and she could not also go. About this time she was often in a tilt with the law students in her father's office over the rights of women. When they could not score any other way they would mention "The Taming of the Shrew," not at all to the liking of their opponent.

Mrs. Stanton met Daniel O'Connell in London. "He was," she said, "tall, well developed, and a magnificent-looking man, and probably one of the most effective speakers Ireland ever produced." She was in Paris in 1840 at the time the body of Napoleon Bonaparte was brought to France from St. Helena by the Prince de Joinville, and witnessed the wild excitement over the event.

While the Stanton family was living at Chelsea, Mass., Whittier became a regular visitor. During such time he unfolded to Mrs. Stanton one of the most deeply interesting pages of his life, a sad romance of love and disappointment. Mrs. Stanton first met Miss Susan B. Anthony when the latter was a demure young Quakeress. The two ever worked together in friendship and sympathy. Mrs. Stanton said of their joint labors:

"We never met without issuing a pronunciamento on some question. In thought and sympathy we are one, and in the division of labor we exactly complemented each other. In writing we did better work than either could alone. While she is slow and analytical in composition, I am rapid and synthetic. I am the better writer, she the better critic. She supplies the facts and statistics, I the philosophy and rhetoric, and, together, we have made arguments that have stood unshaken through the storms of long years—arguments that no one has answered. Our speeches may be considered the united product of our two brains."

The crowning work of Mrs. Stanton's life is held to be by many the "Woman's Bible." Lady Henry Somerset and Miss Frances E. Willard discussed the project of this Bible with Mrs. Stanton, but finally withdrew their names from the committee, fearing that the work would be too radical. Miss Anthony and Mrs. Stanton were the founders of the Loyal League, which had for its object the relief of the suffering families of Union soldiers, the heads of which were at the front. In 1880 Mrs. Stanton and Miss Anthony issued in collaboration three volumes entitled "History of Women's Suffrage."

It is a noteworthy fact that Miss Anthony finished the fourth volume only last week. In 1895 Mrs. Stanton published "Eighty Years and More," being a volume of reminiscences of her life. She was the author of scores of essays upon marriage, divorce, and allied subjects. From 1870 to 1880 she devoted the greater part of her time to lecturing. On Nov. 12, 1895, she was the central figure in a most memorable reception which took place in the Metropolitan Opera House, this city, and was attended by prominent suffragists from every part of the country. This reception marked the completion of her eightieth year.

October 27, 1902

Susan B. Anthony

Susan B. Anthony's self-imposed task, for almost half a century, has been to secure equal rights for women—social, civil, and political. When she began her crusade woman in social life was "cabin'd, cribb'd, confined" to an extent which scarcely can be conceived by the present independent and self-reliant generation. In law she was but little better than a slave; in politics a mere cipher. To-day in society she has practically unlimited freedom; in the business world most of the obstacles have been removed; the laws, although still unjust in many respects, have been revolutionized in her favor; in four States women have the full franchise, in one the municipal ballot, in twenty-five a vote on school questions, and in four others some form of suffrage, while in each campaign their recognition as a political factor grows more marked. * * * She is the only woman who has given her whole time and effort to this end, with no diversion of interest in behalf of husband and children, no diversion of other public questions. Is there an example in all history of either man or woman who devoted half a century of the hardest, most persistent labor for one reform?

"Life and Letters of Susan B. Anthony"—Ida Husted Harper.—Vol. II., Chap. L.

MY first glimpse of Susan B. Anthony has always been a pleasant memory. It was in 1898, the first of a brief residence in Rochester, N. Y., when a small and informal gathering one Saturday afternoon offered a good opportunity to see and hear the notable woman. There is no memory left now of the details of that meeting, only of the impression left by Susan B. and Mary Anthony, and the memory of the younger sister is the more vivid. Miss Anthony spoke, of course, on woman's suffrage, simply and well, as she always did. But it is of the expression on Mary Anthony's face that I always think in connection with Miss Anthony. That afternoon she sat on the platform with her sister, and during Susan B. Anthony's informal address and the demonstration that followed Mary watched her with an expression of absorbed and adoring love that can be compared only to a lover's. All who knew the sisters saw that look many times; and friends knew that Mary Anthony's life was one of daily and hourly devotion to her more famous sister, tender, absolute, beautiful beyond all words.

It is good to know that the elder sister realized and appreciated as they deserved this devotion and the unselfish thoughtfulness that attended her. "Without Mary," Susan said many times, "my work would have been impossible."

A little removed from the lower stretch of Rochester's main street, even its plain red brick exterior impressing the chance passer with a certain old-fashioned air of dignity, stands the Anthony homestead, built in 1845 by the father, Daniel Anthony, where Susan B. Anthony and her sister, Mary, passed happily together the tranquil twilight following lives of unusual devotion and toil. "Homey" best expresses the atmosphere that greeted friend or stranger entering the door. Perfect hospitality is the memory cherished by the man or woman fortunate enough to enter that home for an hour or for a day.

In the front of the two old-fashioned parlors stood the mahogany table upon which was written the call and resolutions for the first woman's rights convention ever held, the gift of Mrs. Stanton. The rear parlor was the library. Miss Mary Anthony's study opened from this, and the dining room adjoining was rich in handsome old furniture. Upstairs were the quaintly furnished guest chamber, the family sleeping rooms, and what was Miss Anthony's study, a big, sunshiny room, lined with books and pictures, and made cheery by a gas log. What stories those walls could tell of hours and hours of labor, of plans and prophecies, of happy, familiar chat, of campaigns fought out in advance, and of letters—thousands—dictated, typewritten, and signed.

When at home Miss Anthony's daily routine varied little. There was always the cold sponge bath, the simple breakfast soon after 7, and then to her study to work busily until the plain noonday dinner, oftener than not shared by one or more friends. After a little rest, more work, until the sunset hour brought a time when the two sisters might sit with hands and brains at rest, talking lovingly of the dear ones gone before, of life's compensations, or the reunion at most but a few years distant. Often the evening brought guests. Monday evening was the regular at home, when young and old of all beliefs were made welcome. If there were no guests Miss Anthony went back to her study again and wrote, wrote, until, at 10 o'clock, she gathered together the big package of mail, put on wraps, and went out for a brisk walk of several squares, for which the posting of the letters was only an excuse.

It was into a home of unusual comfort and liberality of thought for the times that Susan Brownell Anthony, named for an aunt, was born Feb. 15, 1820, at Adams, Mass., the second child of Daniel Anthony, a "Hicksite Friend," and Lucy Read, who turned from the gay life of a popular belle when she married, to the quiet customs of the Quakers, though she never became a member of that society. Susan was one of a family of eight children, of whom Mary is now the only survivor.

Susan early showed unusual vigor of intellect, phenomenal memory, and insatiable ambition. When she was 3 years old her grandmother taught her to spell and read, and at 12 she earned her first money, $3 for two weeks' work in her father's cotton factory, taking the place of a sick "spooler" by her own eager request. At the father's wish his children early in life were made members of the Quaker society. Daniel Anthony's means and ambitions enabled him to give his children the advantages of a private school in his big, handsome house at Battenville, Washington County, New York State, where the family had moved in 1826, and Susan was the star pupil. Though her father was one of the wealthy men of the county, the daughter began teaching at the age of 17, the first Winter for a dollar a week and board. The next year she was sent to Deborah Moulson's Seminary, near Philadelphia; but her father's business reverses called both Susan and Guelma home in the Spring of 1888.

A year at the home school followed, and then the family left the happy home at Battenville and moved to Hardscrabble, where Daniel Anthony started to build up his fortunes anew. Susan had no difficulty in securing a school at New Rochelle, and thus began the work which she carried on with gratifying suc-

SUSAN B. ANTHONY.

cess for fifteen years. Pay was small—she and Hannah taught from 1840 to 1845 for $2 and $2.50 a week and board—but the good daughters lived with rigid economy and gave their father every penny they could spare to help pay interest on the mortgage which rested on factory, mills, and home. In 1845 the family moved to Rochester, making the trip from Palatine Bridge by "line boat." Susan accompanied her parents, returning to Palatine Bridge in 1846 to teach in Canajoharie Academy, a position which she held three years. This was perhaps the gayest time of the Quaker lass's life, and her letters home show that she enjoyed pretty clothes, good times, and the attention of the beaus quite as much as any girl who has no mission.

※ ※ ※

It was in the Spring of 1853 that Miss Anthony, who for several years past had found the work growing irksome, gave up teaching. She was deeply interested in temperance and anti-slavery, and hers was a nature that could have no divided interests. At a State gathering of the Sons of Temperance in 1852 at Albany a decisive step was taken. Susan B. Anthony represented the Rochester Union, but when she rose to speak she was told by the presiding officer that the sisters were not invited there "to speak, but to listen and learn." With several other women she left the hall, and the rebels held a meeting of their own. The result, after weeks of hard work, was the first Woman's State Temperance Convention, at Corinthian Hall, Rochester, April 20, 1852. Five hundred women were in attendance.

In September of the same year Susan attended her first woman's rights convention at Syracuse and took an active part in its proceedings. The work begun then was carried on with single-hearted zeal and steadfast devotion almost unparalleled. Abuse from press and audience, rebuffs, and insults commenced with the withdrawal from the Albany temperance meeting.

The years from 1852 to 1856 were spent in addressing temperance and teachers' conventions, in attending and taking part in woman's rights conventions at Rochester, Albany, and Saratoga; in a canvass of New York State for funds, and in trips to Washington, Saratoga, Philadelphia, and Boston. What seemed a distinct advancement of woman's cause and a recognition of Miss Anthony's efforts and abilities came in 1856, an urgent request from the American Anti-Slavery Society that she become its agent and go on a lecture trip through Central and Western New York. The Winter and the next few years were full of great physical hardships, many discouragements, and much bitter trial. Anti-slavery meetings, attempted in 1861, were mobbed and broken up in every city from Buffalo to Albany. Then, Nov. 25, 1862, came the death of Daniel Anthony, his children's idol; Susan's support, strength, and sympathetic guide in all her work and ambitions.

※ ※ ※

Organization of the Woman's National Loyal League kept Miss Anthony busy in 1863 and 1864, and a strong endeavor to rouse public protest against the Fourteenth Amendment was the most important work of the women suffragists in 1865. The year 1867 brought a hard-fought campaign to secure a woman's suffrage amendment to the New York State Constitution, but the amendment was defeated. Generous financial aid enabled the starting of The Revolution, the first woman's suffrage paper, and gave the leaders of the movement fresh courage to face the future.

The year 1869 saw another encouraging advance in the organization, May 15, in New York City, of the National Woman Suffrage Association, with Elizabeth Cady Stanton as President. Its especial object was "a Sixteenth Amendment to the Constitution securing the ballot to the women of the Nation on equal terms with men." The second National Woman's Suffrage Convention, held in Lincoln Hall, Washington, January, 1870, just preceded Miss Anthony's fiftieth birthday.

The ten years preceding had given her some encouragement; there had always been hosts of loyal friends to stand by her; but the years had also been full of almost incredible hardship, work well-nigh superhuman in its untiring energy, and abuse hard to understand to-day. She had been insultingly attacked by almost every paper of almost every State, driven from convention halls, been the object of harsh, often abusive, words from notable public speakers, had her audiences broken up by mobs, seen trusted co-laborers fail her at the most important crises, lost loved ones, and through everything held with deathlike grip to one central and paramount idea, the securing of the ballot to women.

In 1871 Miss Anthony and Mrs. Stanton started on a lecturing trip to the Pacific Coast, stopping at Salt Lake City, visiting the Yosemite and encountering a strongly hostile spirit in Oregon and California. The National Republican Convention at Philadelphia, June 7, 1872, contained in its platform the following:

"The Republican Party is mindful of its obligations to the loyal women of America for their noble devotion to the cause of freedom; their admission to wider fields of usefulness is received with satisfaction, and the honest demand of any class of citizens for equal rights should be treated with respectful consideration."

It was not what the leaders of the National organization for woman's suffrage had hoped and asked for; but it was the first time any National platform had mentioned woman, and it kindled hopes of better things to come.

※ ※ ※

From the adoption of the Fourteenth Amendment, July 28, 1868, several leaders in the movement had claimed women's right to vote under its provisions. Spurred to action in 1872 by an especially stirring appeal to all voters to register and cast their ballot, in the editorial columns of a Rochester daily, Miss Anthony with her three sisters went to the registry office and registered, the Inspectors consenting after some objections. The example was followed by nearly fifty strong-minded Rochester women. Such criticism followed the announcement of this action that when Election Day came the Inspectors in several wards refused the votes of the women they had registered; but Miss Anthony and fourteen others were permitted to vote in her ward. Election Day was Nov. 5. Nov. 18 Miss Anthony was arrested and taken into court to answer the charge of illegal voting, together with the fourteen other offenders and the three Inspectors involved. She was indicted by the Grand Jury at its next sitting, and the trial was held in Canandaigua the following Summer.

The case was bitterly and skillfully fought on both sides, and at its conclusion Judge Hunt directed the jury to bring in a verdict of guilty. A fine of $100 and the costs of the prosecution was the sentence pronounced. Miss Anthony promptly declared that she would "never pay a dollar of your unjust penalty," and the Judge did not resort to an order of commitment to force the issue. The costs of the trial Miss Anthony paid, actuated by a sense of justice to those who stood by her in this time of trial.

The Spring of 1880 brought the peaceful passing away of the saintlike mother at the age of 87. Bravely putting aside her personal sorrow, Miss Anthony, with Mrs. Stanton's aid, plunged into the arduous work of writing the "History of Woman Suffrage," the first volume of which appeared in 1881. Feb. 23, 1883, saw Miss Anthony and Miss Rachel Foster sailing for England. The year of travel and comparative rest that followed was probably the easiest, most care-free year of this unselfish, hard-working woman's life. Her welcome home in November of 1883 was a royal one, and Miss Anthony immediately plunged again into the thick of the countless demands of her life work. The seven years following were crowded with lecture and campaign work from Washington to South Dakota, appeals to and strivings with Congress, high officials, and the political parties for recognition and support, and work on the second volume of the history. Her seventieth birthday was celebrated by a fine banquet at the Riggs House, Washington, and sweeter to her were the strong words of loving appreciation from friends and of honorable recognition of her efforts from many leading papers.

Seventy years old and over forty years of almost herculean labor for the cause so dear to her, the suffrage of woman, yet, with all the vigor of twenty-five she started out on a campaign in South Dakota, kept up her lecture and convention work, accepted the burdens of the Presidency of the National Convention in 1892, was an active figure at the World's Fair, and in 1894 conducted two vigorous campaigns—one to secure from the Constitutional Convention an amendment abolishing the word "male" from the new Constitution; the other, in Kansas, to secure a majority vote on an amendment giving women full suffrage.

※ ※ ※

Disappointed exceedingly by her defeat in these two hard-fought battles, but undaunted, Miss Anthony went on with her lecturing wherever there was a call, made a trip through the Southern States in 1895, and visited California again, where her reception was so cordial that she was called back again in 1896 to conduct another aggressive campaign.

This was almost the last of Miss Anthony's long journeys and long campaigns. Every spare moment of the year following was given to lending a helping hand on her biography, which appeared in 1898. The years since were filled with visits, short trips, and, in the intervals of two rather serious illnesses, with eager, enthusiastic work for the cause so near her heart; but most of the time was spent at the Anthony homestead in Rochester. Like the mellow, golden sunset of a day of storm and stress were the closing years of a life which in concentration, single-mindedness of purpose, and strenuous labor has rarely been equaled.

With the friends of Susan B. Anthony will linger longest now the memory of the tender, womanly loveliness of the great reformer rather than the work of her public life. The writer remembers seeing one day at the Anthony home a young woman—one of the thousands of strangers who touched Miss Anthony's life every year. The girl asked for and received a few moments' interview; then, as she rose to go, she found that she had lost her handkerchief. Quickly Miss Anthony pressed into her hands a fresh bit of linen.

"Take this, my dear," said this busy, burdened woman cordially, "I always keep one of these on hand for just such emergencies."

"That little act," said an old friend of Miss Anthony who had witnessed the incident, "is characteristic of her life; but how she can think of all the little things she does we all wonder."

Those who knew Miss Anthony best can tell you, with wet eyes and breaking voice, of thousands of similar incidents. And it is good to remember now of this woman who was a public character so many years that to her sister and life-long companion she was the dearest and noblest soul on earth—it is not granted to every human being to inspire such love and devotion as dwelt in Mary Anthony's heart and shone on Mary Anthony's face—tribute to Susan B. Anthony.   J. E. T.

March 18, 1906

MISS LAURA CLAY NOTED SUFFRAGIST

Received Vote for President at 1920 Democratic Convention, First Woman So Honored

LEXINGTON, Ky., June 29 (AP) —Miss Laura Clay, nationally known as a pioneer in the women's suffrage movement, died today at her home here. Her age was 92.

She was one of the first women to take up the equal suffrage movement, her speaking trips taking her into several States. The high point of her career, however, came in 1920, when, at the Democratic National Convention, she became the first woman to receive a vote for the Presidential nomination. She received the honor as a tribute to the many years of service she rendered in political and suffragette movements.

Daughter of General Clay

Born of the famous Clay family of Kentucky, she had something of the power of her famous kinsman, Henry Clay, in her ability to sway an audience, and in the determination with which, through long years, she fought for equal rights for women.

Miss Clay was born on a farm in Madison County, Kentucky, on Feb. 9, 1849, the daughter of General Cassius M. Clay and Mary Jane Warfield Clay. Her father was Minister to Russia when Alaska was purchased by the United States. He was a cousin of Kentucky's famed statesman and orator, Henry Clay.

Miss Clay completed her schooling at the University of Michigan and at Kentucky State College, now Transylvania College, graduating from the latter in 1870.

She soon started an active public career. After eighteen years of effort by her and other Kentucky women, the Kentucky Equal Rights Association was formed at Covington in 1888. She was its first president and held the office twenty-two years.

One of the chief aims of the association was to extend the property rights of married women. Wives had few property rights then and the struggle to convert the Kentucky Legislature was a long one, but finally it was successful. Laws were also passed making husbands and wives joint guardians of their children instead of vesting all the authority in the father.

Spoke in Many States

Miss Clay carried this fight into other States, making many addresses in the Nineties in Indiana, Ohio and Kansas, where her eloquence won many converts. Next she enlisted in the nation-wide fight for equal suffrage. She was one of the women who took the stump in this campaign and on one tour was away from Kentucky for nearly a year, speaking chiefly in Kansas and Ohio.

The ability displayed by Miss Clay in the campaign for equal rights for women and her staunch adherence to the principle of State rights as opposed to Federal authority, combined to bring her into several political campaigns.

Her ability as a speaker was utilized frequently by the Democratic party, of which she was an ardent member. In 1928, at the age of 79, she made a dozen addresses in behalf of the Presidential candidacy of Alfred E. Smith.

The high point in her political career came, however, in 1920. She was a delegate to the National Democratic Convention of that year at San Francisco and when the gathering got into its long deadlock over the aspirations of William G. McAdoo and James M. Cox for the first place on the ticket, she had the thrill of hearing her own name placed in nomination for the place. She received one vote on the thirty-sixth allot.

June 30, 1941

DR. ANNA H. SHAW, SUFFRAGIST

Leader Fought Poverty In Her Youth, Taught School at 15, and Became Pioneer Woman Minister.

PHILADELPHIA, July 2.—Dr. Anna Howard Shaw, honorary President of the National American Woman's Suffrage Association, died at her home in Moylan, Penn., near here, at 7 o'clock this evening. She was 72 years old.

Dr. Shaw also was Chairman of the Woman's Committee of the Council of National Defense and recently was awarded the Distinguished Service Medal for her work during the war.

She was taken ill in Springfield, Illinois, about a month ago while on a lecture tour with former President Taft and President Lowell of Harvard University, in the interest of the League of Nations. Pneumonia developed and for two weeks she was confined to her room in a Springfield hospital. She returned to her home about the middle of June and apparently had entirely recovered. Last Saturday she drove to Philadelphia in her automobile, and upon her return said she was feeling "fine." She was taken suddenly ill again yesterday with a recurrence of the disease and grew rapidly worse until the end.

Her secretary, Miss Lucy E. Anthony, a niece of Susan B. Anthony, who has been with Dr. Shaw for thirty years, and two nieces, the Misses Lulu and Grace Greene, were at her bedside when she died.

No arrangements for the funeral have yet been made. They probably will be announced tomorrow.

Dr. Shaw continued her active participation in public affairs to the last. Immediately preceding the great war, in the early Summer of 1914, Dr. Shaw went to Rome as Chairman of the Committee on Suffrage and Right of Citizenship at the quinquennial session of the International Council of Women.

Immediately after hostilities had been terminated in France by the armistice Dr. Shaw signed the resolution she helped draft for the National American Woman Suffrage Association, addressed to the Peace Conference, asking for punishment of the Germans for their crimes against women and girls.

For her endeavors in the interest of women at home as well as soldiers in France during the war, Dr. Shaw received letters from Queen Mary of England, Mme. Poincaré, wife of the President of France; President Wilson, General Pershing, and other celebrities.

Dr. Shaw's Long Life of Service.

In the death of the Rev. Dr. Anna Howard Shaw there was brought to a close a life crowded with activities from her earliest youth until her last illness, a career as remarkable as it was rare. The whole course of her life was bent upon human betterment, and she was for many years a leader, especially in the cause of woman suffrage.

Dr. Shaw was born at Newcastle-on-Tyne, Eng., Feb. 14, 1847, and came to America with her parents in 1853, being nearly shipwrecked on the way over. When she was 9 years old her parents went from Massachusetts to Michigan, settling in what was then a wilderness, 40 miles from a post office and 100 miles from a railroad. In "The Story of a Pioneer," which Dr. Shaw published in 1915, she told the interesting story of her life. The family endured many hardships in that sparsely populated region. The little log cabin which they occupied had the earth for a floor, and holes in the walls instead of windows and doors. Her father was without horses or other farm animals, and without farming implements. Dr. Shaw helped plant corn and potatoes by chopping a hole in the ground with an axe. She did most of the work in the digging of a well, chopped wood for the big fireplace, felled trees, and later helped in the laying of a floor in the house and putting in doors and windows and partitions. The father was compelled to leave his wife and children at the mercy of Indians and wild animals while he earned a living for them.

When she was 15 she began teaching school, receiving $4 a week and walking eight miles a day. Later she went to live with a married sister in a Northern town. She was determined to have a college education, and by preaching and lecturing, which was frowned upon by members of her family and friends, she managed to pay her way through Albion College, where she studied from 1872 to 1875. She had only $18 in her pocket when she arrived at Albion. She later went to the Theological School of Boston University, where she graduated in 1878. She suffered extreme poverty during this period, living in an attic in Boston. She often went cold and hungry and knew the exhaustion due to continued insufficient food and hard work.

On account of her sex, she was refused when applying for ordination by the New England Conference and by the General Conference of the Methodist Episcopal Church, but in the same year had the honor of being the first woman ordained by the Methodist Protestant Church. In her struggles to become a minister she fought against ridicule, dissension, and lack of the barest necessities.

Pioneer Among Women in the Ministry.

She received a local preacher's license from the District Conference and in 1878 was pastor of the Methodist Episcopal Church at Hingham, Mass., and from 1878 to 1885 she was pastor at East Dennis, Mass. She was ordained by the Methodist Protestant Church on Oct. 12, 1880. While serving as pastor of the Dennis congregation Dr. Shaw studied medicine also at Boston University, graduating with the M. D. degree in 1885. Kansas City University conferred on her the honorary degree of D. D. in 1902 and the LL. D. degree in 1917.

When the suffrage movement began to show increasing energy in 1885, Dr. Shaw resigned her pastorate to devote her life to a fight for temperance, suffrage, and social purity. She became the lecturer for the Massachusetts Woman's Suffrage Association, and from 1886 to 1892 she was national superintendent of franchise of the Women's Christian Temperance Union. Her association through her preaching with such prominent women as Mary A. Livermore and Julia Ward Howe enlarged her view of life and aroused her enthusiasm for the causes of suffrage and liberty.

On the resignation of Dr. Shaw's most intimate friend, Susan B. Anthony, in 1900, the Presidency of the National Woman's Suffrage Association rested between Dr. Shaw and Mrs. Carrie B. Chapman, whom Miss Anthony finally chose as being the more experienced, while Dr. Shaw was made Vice President-at-Large. She had been national lecturer for the organization since 1886 and continued in this work until 1904, when Mrs. Chapman Catt was compelled to resign the Presidency on account of ill health, and Dr. Shaw succeeded her as head of the National Association. She served in this capacity until 1915, when she declined re-election.

Her administration was marked by unprecedented progress. The number of suffrage workers increased from 17,000 to 200,000, and one campaign in ten years was replaced by ten in one year; the expenditures of the association increased from $15,000 to $50,000 annually, while the number of States with full suffrage grew from four to twelve, and the whole suffrage movement changed from an academic discussion to a vital political force arousing the attention of the entire nation.

The year of 1912 was the banner year for Dr. Shaw and the cause, when Arizona, Kansas, and Oregon received full suffrage. During that year Dr. Shaw spoke in the principal cities in each of these States, making four or five speeches a day and traveling in any sort of conveyance, from freight cars to automobiles.

Dr. Shaw had spoken in every State in the Union, before many State Legislatures, and before committees of both houses of Congress. She is said to have been the only woman who ever preached in Gustav Vasa Cathedral, the State Church of Sweden, and the first ordained woman to preach in Berlin, Copenhagen, Christiania, Amsterdam, and London. In London Dr. Shaw visited all the suffrage headquarters, studying the methods and organization that prevailed there. On her return she said that she learned much, but that as to methods, the American suffrage advocates would have to work out their own. Dr. Shaw figured in a number of lively meetings of the antis, who were heckled by the suffrage advocates.

Earned Service Cross in the War.

As Chairman of the Committee of Women's Defense Work, appointed by the Council of National Defense, in April, 1917, Dr. Shaw performed great services throughout the war. The Government recently awarded the Distinguished Service Medal to her for her work in this capacity, the presentation being made by Secretary of War Baker in his office at the War Department on May 12 last. During the war she wrote articles and delivered addresses in arousing the people of the country to a realization of the true meaning of the struggle with Germany.

She was greatly pleased when word came that the League of Nations offices would be open to women as well as men. She was attending the annual convention of the National Association at the time.

"It is splendid," she said. "People of the United States will understand what democracy means by the time the Peace Conference gets through and recognizes the services of women—not only recognizes their services, but their intellectual counsel and experience. The world moves. The United States must hurry."

On Dec. 15 last Dr. Shaw was sworn in as a special member of the Washington police force, having remarked at a reception the night before on the fact that she had had a forty years' desire to serve as a policewoman. The regulation oath was administered by Superintendent Pullman and Dr. Shaw received a badge.

As a minister, Dr. Shaw would not perform a marriage ceremony in which it was insisted that the word "obey" be used.

"The marriage service," she said, "is a poll-parrot affair. The method used in reciting the pledge is ridiculous, to say the least. There is no solemnity, dignity or character to that kind of marriage ceremony."

She had said that she believed in making the ceremony fit the occasion, having a different service for each marriage. As evidence of the fact that her position was right, she pointed out that she had never known of a divorce among persons married by her.

One of Dr. Shaw's last appearances in New York City was at the National Conference on Lynching, held at Carnegie Hall early in May. She was one of the leaders in arranging for the conference, and in her address she urged the passage of the Suffrage Amendment as a solution of the lynching problem. She said that women of intelligence had been brought to a realization of the fact that womanhood was not being protected by the lynching of negroes, a pretext which she described as "merely camouflage on the part of men for exhibitions of barbarism."

Though an ardent suffragist, Dr. Shaw did not approve of the methods of the militant suffrage workers. She condemned the picketing of the White House when the President was being annoyed in November, 1917, saying that the pickets had endangered the life of the President by their actions, and asserting that the pickets at the time of the visit of the Russian Mission to Washington had carried treasonable banners. Her remarks were made at the annual meeting of the Pennsylvania Woman Suffrage Association, and a resolution condemning "the mistaken methods of the pickets" was almost unanimously adopted.

In 1913 Dr. Shaw figured in a lively skirmish with the authorities in Delaware County, Penn., where she lived. Dr. Shaw refused to make out a statement of her "personal property, mortgages, stocks," and other property, returning the blank that had been left at her home to be filled out on the ground that taxation without representation was tyranny.

The Tax Assessor assessed her property at $30,000, which she declared was excessive, but the Tax Commissioner declined to do anything about the matter unless Dr. Shaw personally made out the declaration. The result was that her automobile, a pale yellow roadster, given to her by admiring suffrage workers, was levied upon and sold by the Sheriff for the taxes. The car was bought in by her friends and returned to her.

Alighting from a Lehigh Valley train in the Jersey City Station one morning in February, in 1914, Dr. Shaw slipped on the icy car step and fractured her right ankle, which laid her up for some time right in the midst of a busy speaking tour in behalf of equal suffrage. She afterward brought suit for $25,000 against the railroad company, but lost the case.

Dr. Shaw never married. She was a member of the International Woman Suffrage Alliance, the League to Enforce Peace, National Society for Broader Education, the Women's Civic Club of New York, and editor of the Woman's Committee War Department of The Ladies' Home Journal. Besides writing "The Story of a Pioneer," she had contributed many short stories and articles to various magazines.

July 3, 1919

"VOTES FOR WOMEN"
----As Seen By EDWARD W. BOK

Real Opponents to the Suffrage Movement, Says Mr. Bok, Are the Women Themselves, Whose Peculiar Field of Work Lies Outside of Politics

PROBABLY few men in the United States have had better opportunities to form an opinion on the question of woman suffrage than Mr. Edward W. Bok. As editor of The Ladies' Home Journal he has been studying woman for many years—studying her wants, her ambitions, her recipes for content. This general course of study alone would entitle Mr. Bok to be considered an authority on anything appertaining to the American woman of to-day. But, in addition to his general observations, he has made a particularly close study of the suffrage question.

He has investigated it all over the United States. He has received hundreds of letters from women who are deeply interested in it.

And it was, seemingly, at the psychological moment that a SUNDAY TIMES reporter asked Mr. Bok to tell what he thought about the question. Apparently Mr. Bok had been thinking a great deal about it, had much to say, and was quite willing to say it.

✦ ✦ ✦

"From your knowledge of American women, do you find that the majority are in favor of woman suffrage or opposed to it?" Mr. Bok was asked.

"Neither. The greater part of American women that my lines have put me in touch with are absolutely indifferent to it. They do not regard the subject as either an important question, or a question at all for that matter. And when they do write or speak of it an overwhelming percentage are opposed to it and express themselves in no uncertain terms."

"Why, would you say, are they opposed or indifferent to the ballot?"

"Because the average American woman is too busy. Take the average wife or mother who has, say, two or three children and a home of her own. She likes her books, she is fond of music, she may have a taste for pictures. That woman is busy; she has not an idle hour in the day. You cannot interest her in extraneous subjects because there are too many things of a vital nature that are distinctly woman's own questions that take up all her time. And when you talk to her, as I have scores of times, about the ballot she invariably replies: 'Oh, that is for my husband to attend to. That doesn't concern me. I have my own problems that I understand much better and consider myself better to try and solve.' That is the invariable attitude of the average home-loving American woman, and all the suffragists cannot budge her an inch from that position."

"The point is taken by the suffragists, however, that these women would take an interest in civics if they had the right to vote. Do you believe that?"

✦ ✦ ✦

"I do not. That is tantamount to saying that the American woman does not know what she wants. And," continued Mr. Bok smilingly, "I pity the lack of discernment that would say that of the American woman. I have dealt with her now, journalistically, for twenty-five years, and during that time I have come into pretty close touch with American women, their needs and wants, and if there is any person on the face of the earth that knows what she wants it is the American woman. And, more than that, she gets what she wants."

"She could get the ballot, then, you think, if she really wanted it?" the reporter asked.

"Assuredly.

"The opponents to woman suffrage are not men; they are the women themselves. Look back of the adverse legislation for instance, and how do the legislators arrive at a decision to vote as they do against the ballot? A few weeks ago a State bill to allow women to vote was reported unfavorably by a vote of 9 to 2. I wrote to each of those nine legislators and asked them what influenced their vote. In each case they replied that they themselves professed to know nothing of the question, but had referred it to their 'women folks' and 'woman friends,' only to find that there was no demand for the vote among these women and no interest in it. One of the legislators wrote me: 'I felt if the women wanted to vote it was up to us to let them, so I made quite a little canvass of the situation. I asked every woman friend I had and asked my friends to do the same to see how far this desire extended. The result was practically nil. Out of over 150 women I questioned I couldn't find more than ten who had the least desire to vote, and they were, for the most part, lukewarm. And my fellow-members on the committee, when we came to compare notes, found the same condition of affairs. The women, as a whole, do not seem interested.' And he was right," ended Mr. Bok.

✦ ✦ ✦

"This is exactly in line," continued Mr. Bok, "with what I have discovered myself. For instance, not so long ago a President of the United States received the customary 'petition' that is familiar to every President, asking him to incorporate in his next message to Congress a recommendation that the subject of woman suffrage be seriously taken up with the view of giving to woman the right to vote. The President was fair-minded—he was willing to see both sides—so he determined to test the truth of the phrase in the petition that 'this was practically the unanimous desire of American womanhood as a whole,' but that 'men had refused to recognize the fact.'

"That evening he handed the petition to his wife and asked her: 'What do you think of this?'

"'I really don't know,' she answered. 'I have never thought about it.'

"The President was interested. 'But,' he insisted, 'the petition says it is the unanimous desire of American womanhood as a whole!'

"'Perhaps it is,' said the President's wife. 'I am not prepared to say. Why don't you find out?'

"'In what way?'" asked the President.

"'Pick fifty women that you know and whose opinions you respect, write to them and ask,' was the reply.

"The President did. There were forty-six answers, four of the women addressed being ill or absent from the country. Thirty-four had no desire whatever to vote—they either were 'too busy' or left politics to their husbands. Eleven were absolutely indifferent. 'Really, Mr. President, I am not interested,' voiced the prevailing sentiment; while one lonely lady thought she 'might vote, but,' she added, 'probably when the time came I wouldn't bother about it!'

"Here, then, were forty-odd intelligent, representative women, and yet not a single one actually wanted the ballot!

"Only a few evenings ago a group of six typical, intelligent American women were talking about this agitation, when I asked them: Suppose the question was put to you to vote upon, how would you vote, in favor of your sex voting or not?'

"The women looked amused, when one voiced the sentiment of the others, as it appeared: 'Why, we wouldn't vote—wouldn't bother about it; it doesn't interest us.'

"'But,' says the suffrage agitator, 'that is your clinging woman, the ivy kind!'

"'Very well. Suppose we take a club of women interested in civics, with a membership of 116. A careful poll was recently taken of the members of this club by the President, who is in favor of woman suffrage, and has upon several occasions talked to the club on the subject, and of a complete vote of 91 14 were in favor of women voting, 57 decidedly against, and 20 'really didn't care.'

"'But,' again says your suffrage agitator, 'that is only one club. All the women's clubs would show up differently.' But would they? Suppose we see.

EDWARD W. BOK.

"Last Summer in Boston I was introduced into one of the functions of the biennial convention of the General Federation of Woman's Clubs, and I took particular pains to ask the leading officers and workers of the movement how they believed the Federation, as a whole, stood on the question of woman suffrage. Said one of the principal officers: 'So overwhelmingly against it that I wouldn't like to see the Federation place itself on record on the subject.'

"'You are in favor of a woman's voting, then?' I asked.

"'I am, decidedly,' she answered. 'But I know only too well how the Federation, as a body, would express itself.'

"I said to another officer standing by: 'What do you think?'

"'Just as Mrs. — does. I have tried it on three clubs in different parts of the country, and I desisted from any further effort.'

"'Would you mind telling me the ratio?' I asked.

"'Oh, it was terrible!' she answered: '80 per cent. against! It was anything but encouraging.'

"I asked another leading worker in the movement—one who has, perhaps, traveled as extensively over the country as any officer of the Federation, and spoken before nearly every principal woman's club in America. 'What would be the vote of the Federation on this question? Would you, from your experience, hazard an opinion?' I asked.

"'It isn't hazarding an opinion. I know only too well. It would be a Waterloo for me and mine,' she laughingly answered.

"'You are a suffragist, then?' I asked.

"'Well, yes,' she replied. 'I suppose I am. I have said so often enough in public. But, somehow or other, I am free to say that whenever I have spoken on the subject I have not been surprised that my arguments have failed to convince. They do not seem convincing to myself.'

"'I dislike to say it, my dear,' said another woman standing by, 'but I feel as you do. I think the average American woman is pretty nearly right on this question—we had better let voting alone. We don't understand it, and we really wouldn't intelligently understand the questions that we would be asked to vote upon.'

"'I know I wouldn't,' said a third. 'Besides, I'm too busy with my home and my club work. Why take on anything more? Then, what would we gain that we haven't or that we couldn't get if we wanted? We'd better let well enough alone.'

"That," said Mr. Bok, "fairly illustrates the indifference of the great body of American women to this cry for the ballot. Remember, there is not a man's opinion voiced in these expressions, and on four different occasions upon which they were expressed they represented different classes of women, of varying interests, of wide observation and experience among their sex. And yet not a sign appears there in all the horizon that the wish to vote represents 'practically the unanimous desire of American womanhood as a whole.' On the contrary, it would certainly appear as if the exact opposite is nearer the truth.

"The simple fact of the matter is that the vast majority of American women have not only no desire to vote, but, to use their own words, they are not 'bothering' about the question; they are 'not even interested.' This is the actual condition that the American woman suffragists confront—not the antagonism of men, for men, as a body, are not antagonistic; they are indifferent, perfectly content to let the women fight this question out among themselves and give them the consensus of opinion. And up to date that consensus is distinctly that the average woman's common sense, and, particularly her knowledge of her own sex, teaches her that she is unwilling to run the risks which she knows, far better than men, would accompany an extension of the franchise to her sex.

"It comes down to this," said Mr. Bok, "that the field of politics as a new excitement for a few restless American women is barred to them by their own sex."

"Is it true, from your own knowledge, that the working class of women want the ballot more than do the women who have homes? That is said, you know."

"If that is so," replied Mr. Bok, "why, then, did only 5 per cent. of the workingwomen of Massachusetts vote that they wanted the ballot when they were asked to express themselves? That wouldn't prove they were so keen to vote. I saw this point practically tested twice within the past month, once in a New York manufactory where they employ 2,000 women and girls. A careful vote was taken, and only 211 asked to vote. In another place, where there are 600 girls and women employed only 81 wanted to vote. In nearly every case the women asked: 'What do we want to vote for?' You see, when you get this noisy clamor of the suffragists down to a practical test or two, their statements do not seem to hold water.

"But meeting the suffragists on their own contention that the workingwomen want the ballot more than the women who are sheltered in homes, how about these workingwomen when they marry? They seem to overlook the fact that 50 per cent. of the women who work marry at 25 years of age or before; that over two-thirds marry before they reach 35."

"You do not think that the average American woman is attracted to the vote, then, from what has been done in those States where women can vote?"

"How could they be attracted when so little has been done? Now, what has actually been accomplished, say in Colorado? They have raised the age of consent limit. Well, so has Massachusetts, where women can't vote. The suffragists point with pride to Judge Lindsay's Juvenile Court in Denver as the direct result of woman's ballot. No one can say one word save of the highest praise for what Judge Lindsay has done in his splendid work. But would the Denver Juvenile Court have never come into existence save through woman's ballot? Who can say? The fact remains that Chicago has a juvenile court equally as able and effective as the Denver court. Judge Mack's wonderful work in Chicago every one knows. But women can't vote in Illinois, so surely woman's vote didn't bring about the Chicago Juvenile Court.

"And how about the juvenile courts in the fourteen other States where they exist to-day and where women cannot vote? I have looked pretty carefully into political and moral conditions in Colorado since women began to vote there. I have had careful inquiries made of women who vote in that State, and I cannot see from what is told me that conditions are a whit better than they were before women voted, and I say this not as my own personal opinion but from what has been written me by Colorado women themselves. Take the question of morals in Denver. Now, surely, that is a condition to which women would naturally first of all turn. Only the other day I received a letter from a woman voter in Colorado in which she said 'I believe as strongly as can any woman in the right to vote as a right, but when it comes to the actual net result of her vote I must confess that I see no difference in our condition out here. If immorality was worse than it is now, it certainly must have been pretty bad.'

"One of the most significant facts in my correspondence from women," said Mr. Bok, "since this agitation for woman's suffrage has started, is the number of letters that have come to me from women living in States where woman suffrage exists, and almost invariably these women counsel against its extension. They vote, they say, but how do we vote?' they generally say. 'Exactly as our menfolk do or tell us to vote.' Again and again they strike the warning note. 'Don't be fooled by what these agitators say of the great work done by women's votes in our State.

The great work doesn't exist, except in the minds of those agitators themselves. The code books do not show it; neither our civic nor our moral condition shows it. We wish it did. We believed woman's vote would alter a great many existing evils. But it hasn't, and don't be misled into believing that it has.'

"Now, this is not from one woman, but from scores who have written me from Colorado, Wyoming, and the other States. These women have wanted to believe in the efficiency of the woman's ballot; they asked for it, they exercised the privilege, and now they acknowledge it is without the result they hoped for.

"Look at a woman like Phoebe Couzins. I notice the suffragists never refer to her. But the fact remains that here was one of the leaders of the suffrage movement who fought shoulder to shoulder with Susan B. Anthony, Elizabeth Cady Stanton, Julia Ward Howe, and the rest of them. For twenty-five years she gave up her life to the cause. She spent a year in Colorado, and was one of the leaders in the movement there, and one of the chief spirits in the enactment of the suffrage law in that State. What does she say now of the cause for which she gave up a quarter of a century of her life and of her work in Colorado? She freely acknowledges that she has come to the conviction that the cause of woman suffrage is not only a mistake but now in the full light of her experience that it would be a positive menace not only to her sex but to the country. There is a keen, brainy woman for you, who certainly knows every nook and corner of the woman suffrage question. The ripe conclusion of a woman of that sort is not to be put lightly aside, you know.

"Then, too," continued the Philadelphia editor, "when it comes to what has actually been accomplished by the woman's vote in the States where it has been tried, I am willing to listen to men who have been and are in a position to judge. Surely President Roosevelt, in his seven years' occupancy of the Presidency, had opportunities for observing what had been done in those States. And he is a believer in woman suffrage. Yet he had to acknowledge that 'I am unable to see that there has been any special improvement in the position of women in those States in the West that have adopted woman suffrage as compared with those States adjoining that have not adopted it.' Certainly Mr. Roosevelt, with his astute political knowledge, his opportunities for observation, his own belief in the ballot for women, would be the first to acknowledge the good that had been done if such were true. And he is not alone. A man like Senator Elihu Root is certainly perceiving, and he stands exactly where Mr. Roosevelt stands.

"Then take such a man as James Bryce, the present English Ambassador. There is certainly a disinterested judge for you; a keen observer of American tendencies and institutions, thoroughly in sympathy with our every progress. 'No evidence,' he says, 'has come in my way tending to show that politics either in Wyoming or Washington is in any way purer than in the adjoining States and Territories.' There is no getting away from such testimony as those—they come from careful, sane, and authoritative sources, and must be listened to with respect."

"You do not believe, then, that the claim of the suffragists that women would, if allowed to vote, purify politics, is well founded?"

"No, and I say this from the facts and conditions as they exist to-day in the States where the experiment has been tried. You can only go by results. And one of the results in two of these States has been (as women have written to me from those States) to bring into being a species which they call 'hen politicians,' as fully alive to political intrigues and tricks as the most out-and-out type of men politicians, and, if anything, worse. Take my own experience. The President of the company that publishes our magazine has again and again received from Wyoming and Colorado petitions several yards long with hundreds of names attached demanding my removal from the editorial chair. Why? Simply because I did not believe as these suffragists did, and that I said so in the magazine.

"In Wyoming a number of women suffragists, with a knowledge of laws that needs no comment from me, tried their best to get the Post Office Department to keep our magazine from entering Wyoming through the mails because of our position on the suffrage question. A committee of three suffragists waited on me once and put before me a proposition that if I would line up our magazine on their side they would at their next convention declare the periodical to be the official organ of their movement, and see to it that every suffragist subscribed to it; that if I persisted in my opposition to their cause they would pass a resolution condemning the magazine, and call upon every believer in woman suffrage to withhold their support.

"What do you call that but politics of the most peanut order, unless you call it attempted blackmail?

"Take the statement of one of the leaders of the woman suffragist movement herself in New York only the other day, after the defeat of the Suffrage bill at Albany. She delivered a speech calling upon every woman interested in suffrage not to lose heart by the defeat sustained, and particularly emphasized how legislation and politics in general would, when the woman's ballot was an actuality, be more chaste, purer, and receive an uplift from the present degrading influences that existed at Albany. And then she closed with a fervent plea that every woman present or interested in woman suffrage should see to it that not a single member of the committee who voted against the measure should be returned to the next Legislature! There's purification of politics for you, and spoken by one of the women foremost in the movement. In other words, we would have pure politics just so long as we believed as these women did and voted as they did. I see no difference in that sort of politics from what we have now."

"You believe, then, we would gain nothing in the way of higher politics as a Nation if women voted?"

"On the contrary, we would lose," emphatically declared Mr. Bok. "For this fundamental reason, as has been shown and is being shown every day where women are employed in business: women cannot lose sight of the personal equation. A woman, first of all and above all, sees everything in the personal, in the concrete; it is her nature, it is constitutional. It is in no respect a charge against her; it is fundamental, inherent, but that very elemental factor in her temperament would lead to a personal element in politics that would be disastrous to parties or policies. Women have confessed to me again and again that were they asked to vote they would invariably, because instinctively, lose sight of measures, no matter what measures they might be, and vote for men.

✦ ✦ ✦

"The ballot in woman's hand would bring about a condition of political polemics that would be surprising, even to its present supporters. We would have a feeling not only of sex against sex, of women against men, but you would create a feeling of the sex against itself that would be anything but picturesque. There is no enemy of woman greater than woman herself. A woman is relentless when it comes to her own sex. There are few women who really like their own sex, who have any use whatever for women as a whole. They like woman in the concrete, but not in the mass, and woe be to any people or condition that makes it possible for a woman to take it out of her sex."

"But how about the ballot as woman's right?" Mr. Bok was asked.

"The ballot is not a right for any woman any more than it is for a man. It is a privilege fixed by age, by residence, by educational qualification, that is conferred by a community upon an individual. But it never becomes a natural right; it always remains a prerogative. The argument constantly is put forth that because a woman pays taxes she should have a right to vote. That is not so. If that were so, I have a right to vote in New York, New Jersey, and Pennsylvania, for I pay taxes in all three States. Suppose some shiftless incompetent is put up as Governor of New York, and I protest with all my being against his election, and I walk into New York City and cast a ballot because I feel I have a right as a property holder and a taxpayer to say who shall or shall not be Governor of the State wherein my property lies—what would happen to me? I have no actual, no natural, right to vote anywhere, because a vote is not a right. The power to vote is granted to me, and it is granted upon conditions. It is for the State, the community, to say who shall have the right to cast a ballot, and when a man or a woman insists upon it as a right he or she is just a shade beside the facts."

✦ ✦ ✦

"What about the charge that women cannot do their work in the world without the dignity that the ballot would give them?"

"Dignity, bosh!" was the impatient response. "This idea that woman cannot do her work in the world without the right of suffrage is all rubbish. Just take the statement of a woman who is now very prominent in this suffrage excitement in New York. She says, in print, that if women were given the ballot they would immediately seek to ameliorate the hardships of the women among the working classes and 'uplift the asylums and hospitals,' whatever that may mean. That, she says, would be enough to keep a generation of American women busy. It

would, indeed. But why doesn't she get busy? How can woman's vote help the wage-earning woman?

"It didn't require woman's vote to induce the Supreme Court of the United States to give its recent humane decision declaring that the limiting of woman's hours at work was constitutional, and giving her a special right because of her sex to a protection that did not apply to her fellow-male worker.

"It didn't require the power to vote to lead Mrs. Vanderbilt to decide to build her tuberculosis tenements for the poor. The hundreds of women who are every day working and have been working for the betterment of our asylums and prisons and hospitals didn't fold their hands, or get on the stage of a theatre and say, 'Give us a vote, and we will do our work.' They did not pose as martyrs, as creatures bereft of a right; they went to work and are at work every day and every night.

"The great trouble with the suffragists is that they regard the ballot as a cure-all for every evil that exists. They seem not to be able to grasp the salient fact that legislation will right the evils they talk about more effectively than will the ballot, and that what cannot be done through legislation it is mighty hard, if not impossible, to do by the ballot. A woman has a thousand times more influence before a legislative body of men when she appears before them in a cause that they know she knows and feels than through all the ballots that she can cast.

"Take one prominent statement constantly made by suffragists: that an equal ballot will bring about an equal wage for both sexes. To make a statement such as that shows how far woman is removed from that accurate knowledge of affairs that would make her a safe voter. For every man knows that the question of an equal wage is not a political question or a theme for the ballot box; it is a purely economic question, and has to be reached through economic sources.

✦ ✦ ✦

But if the ballot for woman can bring about an equal wage, why hasn't it done so in Colorado, or Idaho, or Wyoming? Do women there receive an equal wage with men?"

"How do you interpret this increased agitation that has arisen on this subject of late, particularly in New York City?"

"In one way as the natural outcome of the unfeminine rumpus in England, of course. That gave the suffragists here a chance, and they took advantage of it to bring the excitement over here. I am inclined to believe, however, with regard to this English excitement over woman suffrage that the desire for the ballot is not so general over there as we are led to suppose. I was over there last October and was surprised myself to meet the number of women who had no desire to vote. I had been led to believe myself that the excitement over there was really a widespread movement, but Mrs. Humphry Ward assured me it was not so at all, and Frederic Harrison, who is very closely in touch with English conditions, says the same. It is another case, apparently, of a lot of noise made by a few—in larger numbers, I believe, than here, yet at the same time not expressive of the majority of English women, a number of whom smiled when I asked them if they wanted to vote."

"Then you do not think that this movement here has any special significance?" asked the reporter.

"Yes, I do," answered Mr. Bok. "But I notice you call it a movement. It is not that. It is an excitement, an outbreak, an expression, and, to my mind, an unnatural expression of an unnatural condition that goes much deeper than mere woman suffrage."

"What would you say is that unnatural condition?"

✛✛✛

"There is an old Swedish saying that reflects this situation pretty well. It is 'what we are pursuing is really only a runaway horse attached to our wagon.' Now woman, by her very nature, is a personification of nervous energy; of emotion; of sentiment. That nervous energy and emotion were given her for expression in her natural channels—that of motherhood. And when she reaches that expression she finds ample outlet for all her nervous energy. But for a number of years there has grown up in America a dangerous type of woman, a woman who, misunderstanding the modern currents of thought, has believed that her work in the world lay outside of the home or who for some reason of other has developed a positive aversion to motherhood.

"The feeling of love in this type of woman seems to be stunted; in some cases they ask for love but not motherhood. They consider children as a hindrance to their own greatest development; they believe that by paying their natural tribute to their sex and doing the greatest work in the world that a woman can do they would lose a certain power of brilliancy for themselves. It is notable

in the sense that they want the freedom of the man to go about as he does and not be tied down; to take their part in the work of the world, which under a mistaken sense they think they were created to do. They are working out for a fancied equality; an equality that they cannot see is impossible because of the inequality which nature itself has created, and which, if it is made an equality, always brings about the injury of the weaker factor.

"This aversion to motherhood, this unwillingness to be a woman in the highest sense of the word, leaves the woman unsatisfied; it leaves her with her nervous energies unspent. So, for what she cannot find a natural outlet in her home, she goes outside, looks around for what is going on, and plunges into the first excitement that she meets. It may be bridge; it may be vivisection; it may be woman's clubs; it may be woman suffrage.

✛✛✛

"She must have an outlet—any outlet save the natural outlet. She hasn't enough to do; her hands are idle; her mind is not full—to be frank, her lap is not full. This whole movement was well expressed by a prominent supporter of woman's rights not long ago when she said that 'celibacy is the aristocracy of the future.' They changed it in Chicago to the cry, 'No ballot, no babies.' Another suffragist simply said that 'it was

far more important for a woman to be a woman than to be a mother.' No matter how they phrase it, there is always the same undercurrent; the same basic aversion to motherhood.

"You can always seek growth of one movement by a corresponding excitement on the other extreme. And this whole tendency toward an aversion to motherhood on the part of one element of restless American womanhood has brought about a corresponding keenness on the part of another and larger element of American womanhood toward a close study of the conditions of childhood in America. You can see the signs of this on every hand; more attention is being given to the physical, mental, and moral questions of childhood than ever before; my mail from women is full of it; it is safe to say that seven out of every ten letters we get, of a serious order, ask some question about children. It is in the air, and the whole movement is coming naturally out of the people, where all great movements come from, and where woman suffrage does not come from.

"That is an excitement of the restless few; the question of the child is a great operating movement, being born of the many. That is the great ethical question we are facing: the future of the child, and in comparison with it, so far as the real interest and deep anxiety of the American woman as a sex is concerned, the question of woman suffrage fades into absolute insignificance."

April, 18, 1909

Map Showing the Progress of Woman Suffrage

INDICATES FULL WOMANS SUFFRAGE

INDICATES SCHOOL AND OTHER FORMS OF PARTIAL WOMANS SUFFRAGE

INDICATES NO WOMANS SUFFRAGE

October 13, 1911

WOMEN AS A FACTOR IN THE POLITICAL CAMPAIGN

For the First Time in American History

Their Active Support

Is Openly Sought by All Parties.

IF any one had suggested during the Presidential campaign of 1908, or even less than a year ago, for that matter, that in this Presidential year of 1912 women would take almost as prominent a part in the management of the campaign as the men, that each of the big political parties would have thoroughly organized women's bureaus, and, more marvelous still, that one of the big parties would unequivocally declare for woman's suffrage, and even go to the extent of electing women delegates at large to its National and State Conventions as well as putting women on its National and State Committees, that person would have been scoffed at if not actually called insane.

Yet all this has happened in the short space between Presidential campaigns, and it has created less excitement than any window-smashing tournament by London suffragettes. It is all an indication of how rapidly they do things in America, and with what little fuss. It may also foreshadow the coming within a very short time of the granting of equal franchise rights to women in America. At least the suffragists look upon it in that way and cheerfully maintain that they will obtain without trouble or martyrdom all the rights their London sisters have been battling for so long.

But whatever the ultimate result is to be, the remarkable thing about it is the way in which the present Presidential campaign has suddenly become feminized. Of course, many sacred traditions and precedents have been thrown overboard this year by the bolting of Col. Roosevelt and his followers from the regular Republican organization and the formation of the Bull Moose Party. This alone is responsible in large measure for the sudden interest taken by the campaign managers of the other parties in the affairs of women and the recognition of their ability as vote gatherers.

The Bull Moosers set the pace when they declared for woman suffrage and welcomed women to their ranks, and as the race is merely a vote-getting one after all, the managers of the other

two parties couldn't very well afford to lag behind.

After the campaign is over and it is no longer necessary to struggle madly for votes, the sudden and suspicious interest taken by the wily campaign managers in the women may just as suddenly subside, and the suffragists may fall back to the condition they were in before the feverish interest began. On the other hand, the suffragists—and all the women workers connected with the political organizations are suffragists—say that no matter which party wins, the impetus given this year to their movement by the recognition of their ability to think and work along the same lines as men will do more to popularize the suffragist cause than anything that has happened in the history of the movement. The women workers, so far from feeling that interest in their cause will subside, predict that there will be a suffrage plank in the platform of every party four years hence.

Women Divided Politically.

To many people the proposition of votes for women sounds like the last word in progressivism, but how far behind the times they must feel when they realize that already the suffragist cause has advanced far enough to admit of a split in their own ranks into progressives and conservatives. There are a large body of suffragists who frown upon the idea of their sisters allying themselves with any political party whatever, on the ground that a non-partisan attitude will accomplish much more for the cause. These are the conservatives. The radicals or progressives are the women who have gone right into the Republican, Democratic, or Bull Moose organizations and are fighting hard to elect their respective candidates to the Presidency, believing that each candidate, in his own way, will bring to a realization the good they are fighting for.

As a matter of fact, very little is being said about votes for women by any of the women connected with the three parties. Laws to better the lot of women and children is what is being urged, and each organization is doing

everything possible to prove that this result will be brought about more rapidly by the election of Gov. Wilson, Mr. Taft, or Col. Roosevelt, as the case may be.

It was the managers of the Bull Moose Party, as has been said, that set the rapid pace for the women in this campaign. The Democratic campaign managers quickly saw the drift of things and followed suit by organizing a woman's bureau and encouraging the women to get out and hustle for votes. The more conservative Republican Party was slower to see the value of a spectacular fight by women vote getters, and it proceeded more deliberately. But finally it fell in line by having its regular women's organization establish headquarters alongside the men workers and the feminization of the campaign bureaus was complete.

Upon the twenty-fourth floor of the Metropolitan Tower the Women's Bureau of the Progressive or Bull Moose Party holds equal sway with the men's bureau across the hall. In fact, State Chairman Hotchkiss of the men's bureau emphatically says that the women's bureau is not to be an auxiliary affair, but will have equal voice with the men in every phase of party management. The managers of the other bureaus have not dared to go so far. The destinies of the Bull Moose women's bureau are presided over by Miss Alice Carpenter, a wealthy club worker of Brookline, Mass., and Miss Frances I. Kellor of Brooklyn, who has already done much good in the way of bettering the lot of women and children, and particularly unfortunate aliens. Miss Mary Dreier of Brooklyn is also doing effective work. Miss Dreier was a delegate to the Bull Moose National Convention at Chicago, and Miss Kellor an alternate. Miss Carpenter has been made a member of the party's National Committee.

Across Madison Square in the Fifth Avenue Building, where the headquarters of the Wilson campaign bureau is situated, there is a busy hive of women on the tenth floor in active charge of Mrs. J. Borden Harriman, wealthy society leader, club woman, and philanthropist. This is the most ambitious

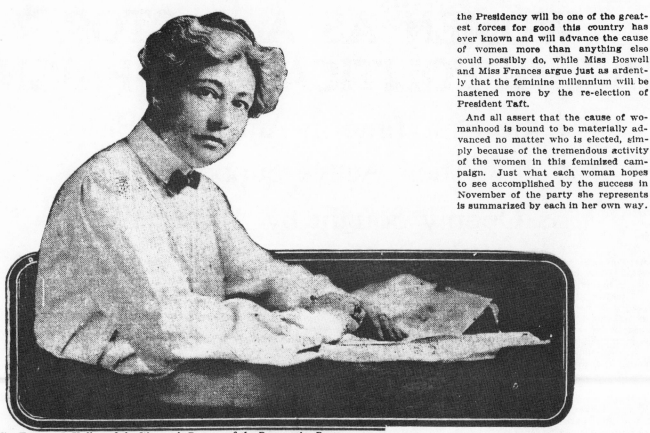

Miss Frances I. Kellor of the Woman's Bureau of the Progressive Party.

the Presidency will be one of the greatest forces for good this country has ever known and will advance the cause of women more than anything else could possibly do, while Miss Boswell and Miss Frances argue just as ardently that the feminine millennium will be hastened more by the re-election of President Taft.

And all assert that the cause of womanhood is bound to be materially advanced no matter who is elected, simply because of the tremendous activity of the women in this feminized campaign. Just what each woman hopes to see accomplished by the success in November of the party she represents is summarized by each in her own way.

bureau of them all in the way of work, for the wives of many of the Democratic National Committeemen have allied themselves with the bureau and are working hard to elect Gov. Wilson.

Mrs. Harriman did not want to be under the domination of the mere men of the Wilson Campaign Committee, so she started the Women's National Wilson and Marshall organization, with these women as active workers: Mrs. Harriman, Chairman; Mrs. A. S. Alexander, Mrs. Caroline B. Alexander, Mrs. A. S. Burleson, Mrs. J. Sergeant Cram, Mrs. Josephus Daniels, Mrs. Joseph Davies, Mrs. J. B. Eustis, Mrs. Thomas P. Gore, Mrs. Frank Lyon Polk, and Mrs. Oswald Villard. They are running their bureau in their own way without any interference from the men, and all confidently expect to elect their candidate. They are making a plea direct to the women of the country on the high cost of living and the tariff.

In the Times Building, on the seventh floor, is the women's department of the Republican National Committee, presided over by Miss Helen Varick Boswell, an organizer of experience and ability, and Miss Mary C. Frances, a well-known writer. Mrs. John Frances Yawger, President of the New York State Republican Association, has charge of the work in the State, and Miss Elizabeth Toombs, as Chairman of the New York City Committee, devotes her attention to the local end of the work.

In one way the women's bureau of the Republican National Committee is better equipped to do campaign work than the other two organizations, because it has been organized for years, and it knows just how to go about to get the best results with the least amount of effort. While Mrs. Harriman and her workers have to organize parades and hold mass meetings to get to the people, and Miss Carpenter and Miss Kellor write voluminously and plead with the women to take an active part in their organization, Miss Boswell and Miss Frances are as well intrenched as the regular Republican machine of which their bureau is an integral part, and it is no difficulty for them to reach just the kind of women who can influence votes, if they don't actually cast them.

While the leaders of the three women's organizations are working to elect three separate candidates and are using somewhat diverse methods to accomplish this result, all admit that they will arrive at the same end in the final analysis so far as the advancement of the cause of womankind is concerned. This, as has already been said, is the putting of new laws on the statute books that will benefit humanity in general and women and children in particular. Miss Carpenter and Miss Kellor argue that this result as well as the emancipation of women will be accomplished quicker through the election of Col. Roosevelt. Mrs. Harriman believes the election of Gov. Wilson to

As Mrs. Harriman Sees It.

"About the most remarkable thing of this whole remarkable campaign," said Mrs. Harriman to THE SUNDAY TIMES reporter, "is the fact that for the first time in American history the active support and influence of women have been openly sought by all the great political parties. What greater proof of the growing power of women in political affairs could be had, and the women everywhere should not fail to understand and seize the opportunity. There are many crying needs for reform in the treatment of women and children in this country, and women, by taking an intelligent interest in the political problems before the country, can do much to help themselves or their more unfortunate neighbors.

"No woman can refuse to consider the conditions which make it possible for little children to be deformed under labor which they have not strength to perform. Likewise conditions which permit children to be sent to work before they have the opportunity to acquire a common school education are of supreme interest to all women. Women should also interest themselves in all measures which have to do with the provision of proper play places for children. The condition of the workingwoman is also the immediate concern of all women, for workingwomen of the country are the mothers of the coming Nation, and unless they are protected, their health conserved,

Miss Helen Varick Boswell, Chairman Woman's Department, Republican National Committee.

and the condition of their lives made endurable, we cannot look forward to a strong and able race of men and women.

"Women should add their influence to those who are struggling to bring politics into the open, to make politics the business of the whole people, for how else can the common interest be promoted? Now these conditions, much to be desired, can be brought about, or at least brought nearer to accomplishment, by a partnership, irrespective of former party affiliations, of all women in the United States interested in the enforcement of measures for the benefit of children, women, and the home.

"We believe that much more will be accomplished by the election of Gov. Wilson to the Presidency than any other candidate, for Mr. Wilson does not promise, he performs. His record in behalf of better laws for wo-

men and children since he has been Governor of New Jersey is but an indication of what he will do if his sphere of influence is enlarged. It was through him that the first law relating to women wage earners ever enacted in New Jersey was put on the statute books. I refer to the law limiting the employment of workingwomen to sixty hours a week. What he has accomplished in behalf of women, children, the home, health, &c., fills a large pamphlet which we issue as campaign literature."

Miss Boswell Is Optimistic.

Miss Boswell, for the Taft bureau, argues that the Republican Party is responsible for the giving of the franchise to women in the voting States.

"It is the Republicans that have passed the best laws for women and children," she said enthusiastically. "We ask women to study the standards of living in this country as illustrating

the wisdom of the principles and the constructive policies of the Republican Party, and to contrast them with the unwisdom and the dangerous go-as-you-please, irresponsible suggestions of the Democratic Party or the will-o'-the-wisp promises of the brand-new Bull Moose Party, and we do not fear the final judgment of the average woman when she accepts the fact of her wider sphere in politics and informs herself.

"Women have always been welcome in the councils of the Republican Party. In every campaign since 1888 the Republican National Committee has maintained a department in charge of women. For the first time the Democratic Committee is following this good and long-established example. From the several parties campaigning appeals will go out to the women of the country. We feel that the Republican Party, with its record of accomplishment, with its greatness of measures and of men, will gather to its support the intelligent, patriotic womanhood of the United States, and we welcome their interest and practical support."

Miss Boswell also outlined the methods of work which her bureau has taken up already.

Miss Carpenter's Bull Moose Views.

Miss Carpenter, for the Bull Moose Party, told of her methods of work.

"We call the attention of the women of the State to the Progressive Party, pledged to the work of the protection of children, of overworked women, and of the home," she said. "We wish to emphasize the fact that the platform must appeal to women who in any capacity are trying to better conditions of life, and we offer to them the medium of a great political party as a means of obtaining legislation, long needed and desired. Our party has already drawn into its ranks as leaders men and women who represent to the public disinterested service, whereby we may know that the pledges they have laid down will be fulfilled. The Progressive Party, as a party, pledges itself to these principles which only individuals in the other parties can do.

"This is a man and woman party. A woman, to belong to it, does not have to be a suffragette. We are all fighting together, and think this new idea in politics will advance our country greatly."

This is the way Miss Kellor sizes up the duties and responsibilities of women in this campaign:

"I believe in the Progressive Party for its splendid tribute to women, the eminently satisfactory way in which the men are working together with us, the utter disappearance of all sham and hypocrisy and sentiment in the battle for the ideals in which we believe. There is an accusation that Mr. Roosevelt is making a bid for the support of the women, and his only interest is to win. This is not true. The whole woman's programme as it is being carried out was suggested to some of the leaders first, and then taken up with him, and it was the full educational plan that appealed to him. He has been won to suffrage through his deeper interest in the perils of the workingwoman and the dangers to children, which some of us have constantly brought to his attention these last two years, and which he dealt with as President.

"Neither did Mr. Roosevelt write the platform, as has been said. That platform was written by groups of specialists—immigration experts wrote one, suffrage experts wrote one, health authorities one, social workers the industrial plank, lawyers the judiciary planks, &c. This is not the platform of one man or one party, but of hundreds of people giving of their best thought and experience.

"One of the real accomplishments is the change of women's interest from the one interest, the vote, to the triple interest—the vote, the home, and women and children. The vote is only a tool—the things to remedy are just as important, and the conditions should be known and the remedies understood. Already the narrow suffrage lines are breaking, women are becoming Progressives and Democrats and Republicans as fast as these two old parties can take them in. Why, the movement is so popular, following the lead of the Progressives, that there are Wilson organizations working for suffrage when Wilson is not on record for it; Taft organizations of women are organizing, just to preserve the party from this new danger. The Socialists are lukewarm on suffrage in Wisconsin, afraid that the conservative and working women's interests will sweep their programme. The Indiana suffrage organization is reported from Chicago to have come over in a body to the Progressives, and the National Suffrage Society is canceling the engagement of speakers, who have become Progressives, and is reprimanding the officers who are out for the cause. It is no longer women for the vote alone, it is women standing for the right and protection of working women, the preservation of children, help to the stranger aliens, insistence on health standards, and, above all, on freedom of thought and action, to do what they think right, and act for the best good. The crusaders' spirit is abroad in women for womankind, and the parties and their leaders are but instruments in the cause."

SANDWICH GIRLS PARADE.

Advertise Ball to be Given by Mrs. Belmont's Association.

Six little sandwich girls marched from the Belmont lunchrooms at 4 o'clock yesterday afternoon and tramped up and down Fifth Avenue and the adjoining streets. They were headed by Miss Mazie Belle Glover and advertised with sandwich boards a play and ball to be given by Mrs. Belmont's Political Equality Association at Terrace Garden on Wednesday, April 9.

The girls were much excited as they prepared to start and Mrs. Belmont, who was on hand to see them off, sobered them down.

"You mustn't laugh," she said, "you must be very sedate on the street or men will speak to you."

Little Miss Glover, who was in a white military frock, carried the Political Equality Association dark blue flag with the name on one side and "Votes for Women" on the other. Miss Elsie McKensie, who has charge of the Junior League of the Belmont headquarters, marched in second place.

The two plays which will precede the ball will be "How the Vote was Won," and "Camp Fire Girls." In their play, the Camp Fire Girls, who are having a care-free time in the woods, come out in pajamas of various hues and give a little dance.

IMPRESSIVE MARCH OF SUFFRAGE 531

Present to Congress Petitions for a Constitutional Amendment.

CAPITAL POLICE EFFICIENT

Women Received by Special Congress Committee—Resolutions Promptly Introduced.

Special to The New York Times.

WASHINGTON, April 7.—The largest delegation of woman suffragists that ever presented the cause of "votes for women" to Congress, marched to the Capitol this afternoon and left for every Senator and every Representative a personal plea for his support of an amendment to the Federal Constitution establishing woman suffrage throughout the country. There were 531 women in the delegation, two from every State, and one from each Congress district, and each woman bore in a small envelope a copy of the petition destined for a particular Congressman.

Though far less elaborate than the spectacular parade of the woman suffragists on the eve of Inauguration Day, to-day's march through the streets from the Columbia Theatre was in some respects more impressive. There was no attempt to-day at allegorical costumes, and floats and dances were omitted. Instead, the delegates after a mass meeting at the theatre, where several women made speeches, marched in a compact group down to Pennsylvania Avenue and along that thoroughfare to Capitol Hill.

Most of the delegates wore white, and that uniformity of costume and the carrying of the yellow flags of "the cause" and individual State flags at the head of the sections representing each State were the only attempts at display. The simpler uniform seemed to produce a good effect upon the spectators who lined the streets. There was no repetition of the horse play that largely broke up the parade on March 3, and the police stationed at intervals along the line of march and the escort that accompanied the closely massed battalion of women had no difficulty in keeping an open passage.

The one cause of friction between the marchers and the police was the wish of the women to march down the middle of the avenue, directly on the car tracks. Finally the police persuaded them to take the right side of the street, but by that time car traffic for many blocks was congested.

At the foot of Capitol Hill, by a previous agreement with the authorities, the two bands that preceded the white-suited battalion halted. The police even refused to permit the parade to be continued through the streets to the right and left of the Capitol building. Instead, the women in narrow column walked up one of the paths through the grounds, reformed before the Capitol, and then, after Senator Lane of Washington had made a speech of welcome on the front steps, they filed into the rotunda.

There a committee of nine Senators and many Representatives from the States that have already granted woman suffrage was waiting to receive them. The members of the committee shook hands with every woman in the parade as she passed and dropped her petition into a box prepared for the purpose. The women then scattered to the various galleries to watch the two houses of Congress.

The meeting at the Columbia was held chiefly for the purpose of rallying the delegates for their march to the Capitol. Speeches were made by Mrs. Beatrice Forbes-Robertson Hale, niece of J. Forbes-Robertson, the actor; Mrs. James Lees Laidlaw of the National American Woman Suffrage Association, and Miss Janet Richards, a well-known suffrage worker.

WASHINGTON, April 7.—Formal resolutions proposing the Constitutional amendment giving women the right to vote were introduced in both Houses of Congress, together with scores of petitions and memorials from various societies and individuals. Senator Chamberlain of Oregon and Representative Mondell of Wyoming introduced the resolutions in their respective Houses.

SENATE HEARS FROM FOES OF SUFFRAGE

Committee for Two Hours Listens to Arguments by Leaders of "Antis."

WASHINGTON, April 19.—Anti-suffragists appeared in force to-day in a committee room in the Capitol to protest to the Senate Woman Suffrage Committee against any Constitutional amendment giving the franchise to women. They expressed regret that only two hours had been allotted them in which to present their arguments.

The committee room was filled—women, with a sprinkling of men. Miss Alice Paul and several other leaders of the suffragist cause had places near the committee table and listened to the arguments. Dr. Mary Walker, who has the statutory right to wear trousers, sat just behind Chairman Thomas.

Mrs. William L. Putnam of Massachusetts read a paper by Kate Douglas Wiggin, author.

"I cannot believe that the ballot is the first, the next or the best thing to work for," she read. "I want woman to be a good home-maker, a good mother and a loyal, intelligent, active citizen, but, above all, to be a helpful, stimulating, inspiring force in the world, rather than a useful and influential factor in politics. It is even more difficult to be an inspiring woman than a good citizen and an honest voter.

Negro Women at the Polls.

"A woman's 'job,' to my mind, is with other women, with children and with men, who next to children are most dependent upon what she thinks and says, and does, and is. I would have woman strong enough to keep just a trifle in the background; the limelight never makes anything grow."

Molly Elliot Seawell, author, told the comittee, in a letter read by Miss Lucy J. Price, that nineteen States could be counted on to vote against an amendment to the Constitution giving women the ballot.

"The first fruits of this amendment," the letter read, "would be to admit negro women to the polls, when eleven States have successfully defied the Federal Government in any effort to admit negro men to the polls."

Miss Price wrote of campaigning against sufrage before the recent election in Michigan.

"They charged me with being in the employ of the liquor interests, of the breweries, and said that, although I was called 'Miss Price,' I was the wife of a saloonkeeper," she said. "That is the position you will put your wives and daughters in if you vote for woman suffrage. They will lay themselves open to just such attacks.

Inevi ab y in Po it cs

"Suffrage would put every woman into politics, although the suffragists say it wouldn't, because some time or other a woman would have to get into politics to help a friend, or a friend of her husband, or to beat an enemy. It's not a pleasant prospect."

Mrs. A. J. George, Secretary of the Massachusetts branch of the anti-suffrage organization declared more legislation to guard women workers had been passed in States where women do not vote.

"What we need," said she, "is not to increase the electorate, but to be specialists in our own line and not afraid of being specialists. The work of women has been fairly successful for the last nineteen centuries. If men have not been what they should, what can we say of the women who trained the men?"

The last speaker was Annie Riley Hale, who said she found faults in arguments for and against suffrage.

The committee on Monday will hear the suffragists.

April 20, 1913

ROOSEVELT CENTRE OF SUFFRAGE HOST

Crowded Metropolitan Opera House Cheers the Colonel's Defense of His Faith.

VOICE OF "ANTIS" IS STILL

Not a Protest Against Call to U. S. Senate to Pass Bill—Pageant Enlivens Eve of Parade.

Col. Theodore Roosevelt, appearing for the first time on the stump as an advocate of votes for women, was easily the lion of the hour at the pageant-tableau given last night at the Metropolitan Opera House under the auspices of ten suffrage organizations. Every seat in the opera house was occupied; every box subscribed for, and hundreds of men and women who felt that they were fortunate to obtain tickets of admission after the S. R. O. sign was hung out, crowded the aisles. When the curtain finally went up twenty-five minutes after the hour set for the prologue to begin, men and women rose to their feet waving American flags and suffrage pennants. Occupying the centre of the stage, on the right of Dr. Anna Shaw, President of the National American Woman Suffrage Association, was the Colonel, smiling and impatient to begin.

The pageant was one of the most remarkable affairs given by the suffragists in this city, and Col. Roosevelt was quick to grasp the significance of it. He asserted that the fact that it was possible to hold such a gathering here in New York was the best proof that "civilization was slowly creeping from the West," assuring votes for women in a short time. The pageant-tableau, "A Dream of Freedom," coming after the addresses was elaborate and imposing. Mrs. Florence Fleming Noyes, as Hope, was the central figure.

After the first demonstration Dr. Shaw took charge of the early meeting, overshadowing the Colonel for a time as she told of the advance that the cause of woman suffrage had made in the last few years. She made the statement that Michigan had been stolen from the advocates of equal rights, and the Colonel leaned forward and clapped his hands and shook his head up and down violently in approval.

When he was introduced as the biggest addition to the cause of woman suffrage in the past year he rose quickly, bowed to Dr. Shaw and advanced to the front of the stage. Never in the many days of his long campaigns was the Colonel in finer fettle. During the two minutes' demonstration which followed he waved his hand in the old enthusiastic way.

Colonel a Ready Convert.

In his address, which occupied nearly an hour, the Colonel went thoroughly into his conversion to the cause, and aimed shafts of sarcasm at those who opposed the movement. A new recruit, he was a master of his topic, and had a ready answer for any objection. The audience was delighted, and frequently broke into applause.

Right at the start the Colonel said he wanted to say ditto to all that Mrs. Shaw had said. And then he began to explain why.

"It is an utter absurdity, it is wicked to condemn a great law-abiding movement because there are a few elsewhere who do foolish and wicked things," began the Colonel. "As Dr. Shaw said, apply to men the rule that none are worthy of the vote because some of them are not and there will not be one of us permitted to vote. No reform has been succesful unless it attracted the zealous spirits who dare and suffer. It must, of course, attract a few whose zeal outruns discretion and even morality, and to hold that against all is more wicked and foolish than the conduct of those against whom the charge is made."

Col. Roosevelt said that he wanted to make his appeal primarily to men, and that he believed Dr. Shaw was right when she said that women were sure to obtain the ballot.

"I don't think the East is going to always lag behind the West in darkness," he said. "I think civilization is coming East gradually. I want to speak to the men who have the right to vote and who are recreant in their duty if they don't see that the women share it with them. I ask every decent, self-respecting citizen who has the right to vote to join the movement to secure for women the suffrage now denied them."

Then the Colonel said he wanted to make it plain that equality of right did not mean identity of function any more between men and women than it did between man and man. And he added that you couldn't draw any line of conduct without leaving some of both sex on either side of it, and that there would be more women on the right side of the line than men. One argument which started a great outburst of applause he made near the end of his address when he said:

A Blow to the Underworld.

"In every community where women have received the vote it has meant so much loss of power to the underworld. Just by so much there has been a loss of influence to the powers that prey. The underworld is predominantly a world of men. Vice and crime are conducted by a portion of the population in which there are ten men to one woman. Every disbeliever in decency will oppose this movement. And when you see men who make a business of that which is foul and base rallying against a cause you may be convinced that it is pretty good common sense to stand for that cause."

The Colonel said that in his last campaign in Michigan he had seen in all the saloons signs saying: "Vote against woman suffrage." He was the first to laugh as he explained that what he had intended to say was that he had seen the signs "outside of the saloons."

Sixty-five years ago, when the suffrage movement started, said Col. Roosevelt, a meeting like that in the opera house would have been impossible.

"At that time," he continued, "you would have found a great number of worthy people, including the very orthodox people, who insisted that the foundation of the family would have been ruined if it didn't rest on the masterful headship of the man. But now we have advanced to a far better ideal, the ideal of equal partnership between man and woman."

The advocates of woman suffrage, said the Colonel, were not asking the East to try anything that was new.

"I never say anything on the stump that I can't carry out when off the stump," exclaimed Mr. Roosevelt, and his audience chuckled delightedly. "Mind you, I don't believe that getting votes for women will cure all our ills and ailments, but I give it as my deliberate and careful judgment that in every State where suffrage has been tried, there has been, as far as I know, no single instance where it has produced damage. And there has been case after case where it has worked for the universal betterment of social and civic conditions."

There were scores of women, the Colonel added, whose faith and ability rendered them as useful as men for the public service, and every argument advanced against woman suffrage today was advanced against manhood suffrage 100 years ago.

The theory of the progressives nowadays, he said, was to so conduct the government that the average man could do his duty without neglecting his home. He added, as the audience applauded:

"Now, all we propose to do is to get his partner alongside of him. I don't say it isn't possible for any number of first-class citizens to be frightened at new ideas. I know that from personal experience, but they get over their fright."

Queens and the Home.

Several questions put to him by Miss Ida Tarbell in a letter, the Colonel answered, adding that he thought she was competent to "vote" if she was competent to tell him why he should vote. Then he added:

"If you ask the finest and most musty old conservative to tell you something dear to his heart, and he knows something about history, he will tell you that the greatest sovereign of England was Queen Elizabeth, that the second most powerful ruler of Russia was Catherine, and the greatest Austrian ruler Maria Theresa.

"What we say," he continued, "is that when you get women like that we should be allowed to use them for the public good in the way that they can do the most good."

The Colonel then said that he had found it of the greatest value to consult women in many of the great problems of to-day. He mentioned the child labor laws and minimum wage and immigration.

"In every such case," he said, "I turn to certain women just as I turn to certain men on other questions, because they can give me the assistance and help I need."

Referring to the coming constitutional convention in this State the Colonel called upon the Progressives to consult and heed the women, saying that he did not believe it was right that half of the 10,000,000 people in the State should decide what was best for all. Then the Colonel took another tack which started applause.

"Conservative friends tell me that woman's duty is in the home," he said. "Certainly. So is the man's. The duty of the woman to the home isn't any more than the man's. If any married man doesn't know that the woman pulls a little more than her share in the home then he needs education. If the average man has more leisure to think of public matters than the average woman has then it's a frightful reflection on him. If the average man tells you the average woman hasn't the time to thnk of these questions, tell him to go home and do his duty. The average woman needs fifteen minutes to vote, and I want to point out to the alarmist that she will still have left 364 days, twenty-three hours, and forty-five minutes."

The Colonel produced a letter from another woman, who asked him if he thought that women would have the same respect of men with the vote. His reply was "Yes, and a good deal more."

"There is no surer sign of advancing civilization than the advanced respect paid to woman, who is neither a doll nor a drudge," he exclaimed. He added that an investigation would show that in the section of this country and in other countries where family life was found to be failing lower, the women did not have the right to vote. To the question "Are women physically capable to enter the political arena?" his reply was: "Yes, wherever you find an honest election. I have already said that in the political arena woman was doing 99½ per cent. of the work she would do if she had the right to vote. To cast the ballot doesn't take the strength of a Hercules. Really, it's difficult to answer that question without seeming humorous."

Those Opposed Silent.

When Dr. Anna Howard Shaw called on the vast audience to adopt the resolution asking the United States Senate to pass the Senate joint resolution to give the franchise to women there was an "Aye" that made the echoes ring, and there was not a sound when she asked for those opposed. If there were anti-suffragists in the house they were silent.

Dr. Shaw addressed the audience as "suffragists or those who soon will be." The sixty-five years that the suffragists had worked, she said, should have brought them to their majority.

"And in all those years," she continued, "there has never been a time when I could say that I was ashamed of these women or the means they have taken to gain their freedom. They have not committed a single unlawful act. The President of the United States, in a book he has written, says that, if there are any part of the people who want to be taken care of I am sorry for them. We women may not be some part of the people, but we are any part of the people. If putting guardians over men has weakened them it has weakened the women of the country and we rebel against the tutelage and guardianship.

"Our sixty-five years of work has earned us the respect and consideration of the people and we protest against continued disenchisement because women in other parts of the world have used acts of violence while we have been patriotic and law-abiding. If any man says that, I want to hurl it in his face. The men would not vote if they waited until all men were fitted, for even in our own country men are still taken by men from the jails and burned alive at the stake."

Pageant Follows $1,000 Gifts.

Contributions were taken, and there

were calls for pledges from the floor. There was tremendous applause from parts of the house when $25 was given for Mrs. Pankhurst. Mrs Mackay in the box of the Equal Franchise Society, of which she is the founder, gave $250. About $1,000 was taken in pledges.

The pageant which closed the evening was short and beautiful. It was given under the auspices of nine different suffrage societies. The curtain went up upon a beautiful twilight scene. Hope (Florence Fleming Noyes) appears, and, descending the stairs that occupy the centre of the scene, lights her torch at the altar of Truth. She is accompanied by the handmaidens of Truth, who dance; and Woman (Pauline Fredericks) appears and wakens her sleeping sisters. They are a motley crew. Justice (Sarah Truax-Albert) appears, and the women and the child climb the stairs to be clasped in her arms.

The States were represented by many beautiful women. There was applause for the enfranchised States, each with a star in her hair. The twilight, which has deepened into darkness, gradually gives way to the dawn and rosy daylight, and Columbia. (Mme. Nordica,) with the Stars and Stripes, descends to the front of the stage, sings "The Star-Spangled Banner," the audience joining in the chorus.

The orchestra was under the direction of David Mannes, many women taking part through the courtesy of the Musicians' Protective Union.

The opera house was crowded as early as 8 o'clock, the hour set officially for Col. Roosevelt to make his apepearance, and there was some confusion in the lobby as men and women hurried to find their seats. Outside the theatre and in the lobby scores of women representing the organizations pushed through the throng calling out their wares—programmes and suffrage pennants. The programmes were all sold some time before the curtain went up, and the last hundred or more went at advanced price.

Baners of the suffrage organizations, strung from the boxes, were the chief decoration. There was also a huge banner of the Progressive Party, in honor of Col. Roosevelt and Controller William A. Prendergast. The Controller had a seat on the platform, and once during his address, Col. Roosevelt turned to address him as a comrade in the party ranks.

The audience fhich the Colonel faced was a mixed one, including many well-known in the social life of the city.

May 3, 1913

SUFFRAGISM AND FORCE

Not to be Wedded in America, Mrs. Blatch Explains.

To the Editor of The New York Times:

There has been a general call to the leaders of the suffrage movement to stand up and be counted as for or against English militant methods, but probably the special challenge to me is based on the fact that I was personally responsible for introducing Mrs. Pankhurst to America. I take up the gauntlet. Here is my confession of faith: I am not a Quaker, nor a non-resistant. Both on my father's side, as well as my mother's, I inherit plenty of the spirit of '76. My own great-grandmother—so the story goes—loaded guns, and if she didn't kill any one in Revolutionary days it was because she was the proverbial bad shot. She aimed to kill her country's enemy. My grandmother, not being a Quaker or non-resistant, taught me to admire the courage, the devotion, the patriotism of my maternal ancestor. As a child I honored her, and I frankly admit I honor her still. And I would not honor her the less if she had loaded guns to gain liberty for women, instead of merely for the men of her time.

But my admiration for the militant women of 1776 does not blind me to the fact that we are living in the twentieth century and not in the eighteenth, and that the manner of pushing our political demands must take into account the conditions of our own time. The adjustments of commercial life are so delicately balanced that public opinion is now against the use of physical force. The tendency in trade disputes, in international disputes, is toward arbitration. Those who use violence, then, are very likely to array against their cause a vigorous public opinion.

Another practical and unromantic argument against militancy is that the highly perfected systems of intercommunication of our time render riot or guerilla warfare impossible of long continuance and growth. Highly mobile armies and navies, highly developed police and detective forces, telegraph, telephone, render victories for violence improbable. The spirit of the reform must honeycomb army and navy as it did in Portugal, or success won't crown rebellion. These considerations have no idealism in them, of course, but they have the counsel of common sense and caution.

Following as they do after men in the demand for political enfranchisement, it is little wonder that women often overemphasize what men have gained through violence. The fact is that scarcely a single wide extension of the franchise during the past fifty years has been achieved by the use of physical force. Not only has the marvelous growth of woman suffrage throughout the world come entirely through the peaceful conversion of the ruling class to the idea of justice, but the extension of the franchise to different classes of men—for example, to the farm laborer in England—has been singularly free from violence, having come usually as a matter of party exigency.

My opposition to even a suggestion of militancy in America does not rest, then, upon any abstract theories in regard to physical force, nor upon the flattering assertion that "American men are different," nor upon the reassuring prophecy that "it will never be necessary here"; my objection to militancy rests upon the substantial fact that in our time the vote has not been won through violence. To suggest militancy in the United States is singularly inept. In our country the final appeal is to the body of the voters. To challenge half the people on the physical plane is as impossible as absurd.

But because I hold such a political philosophy I see no reason for condemning the conduct of the suffrage movement in another land. Surely a little modesty is demanded on the part of Americans. The English battle is not ours. To speak of its leaders, as some do, as "hysterical," as "viragoes," as "insane," is to speak with ignorance of facts or with desire to deceive. Were they such women their movement could be easily crushed. The militants are women of marked intelligence, of exceptional poise, of self-sacrifice and devotion of the highest order. Opposed to them stands a Government that has shown itself weak, vacillating, and false to every pledge. When I utter condemnation, it will be upon the British Cabinet, the fundamental cause of the English situation, that my disapproval will fall. HARRIOT STANTON BLATCH.

New York, May 3, 1913.

May 4, 1913

HELEN KELLER A MILITANT.

Blind Girl Believes Suffrage Will Lead to Socialism.

PHILADELPHIA, May 5.—Helen Keller is a militant suffragette. She believes in the smashing of windows, hunger strikes, anything that will bring publicity to the cause. In an interview given here to-night, the blind girl announced she was a suffragette because she believed the cause eventually would lead to Socialism.

"I believe the women of England are doing right," said Miss Keller. "Mrs. Pankhurst is a great leader. The women of America should follow her example. They would get the ballot much faster if they did. They cannot hope to get anything unless they are willing to fight and suffer for it. The pangs of hunder during their hunger strikes simply are a sample of the suffering they must expect.

"But I am a militant suffragette because I believe suffrage will lead to Socialism, and to me Socialism is the ideal cause."

May 6, 1913

ANSWER ANTIS' ATTACK.

Suffragists Deny the Charge That They Resort to Sex Appeals.

Special to The New York Times.

WASHINGTON, May 12.—Miss Alice Paul, Chairman of the Congressional Committee of the National American Woman Suffrage Association, to-day replied to the charge of Mrs. Arthur M. Dodge, President of the National Association Opposed to Woman Suffrage, that the women in the New York suffragist parade had made their appeal chiefly through sex.

Miss Paul, in her statement, says:

"Senator Poindexter was perfectly right when he said that the anti-suffragists only discredited themselves when they threw undue emphasis upon the question of sex in dealing with the woman suffrage movement. The claim that the movement is based on sex is absurd when we remember that the mass of suffragists to-day are composed of all types of women; old and young, married, single, women of all trades and professions, and women whose lives are devoted to the home.

"It is absurd to believe that the thousands of women who marched with such self-possession in New York last week were all the victims of sex pathology—betrays an extraordinary lack of balance on Mrs. Dodge's part.

"As a wage-earner to-day, woman needs the vote exactly as man does, and for the same reason. As a mother she needs it in order to do efficiently today what it has been her duty in the world to do from time immemorial; that is, to care for the cleanliness and health of her household.

"The truth is that Mrs. Dodge has not advanced one argument against woman suffrage. She has simply rehearsed all the evil she can say of women and blamed it on the suffrage movement and analyzed woman's private virtues in order to contrast them, quite unnecessarily, with public ones. She is taking the same stand that has been taken against every step in woman's advance in the last fifty years. The same dire prophesies of 'woman's departure from her sphere' and the 'loss of all womanly attributes' were made when women asked for education, when they began to take up healthy outdoor exercises, and when they sought freedom of occupation in the business world. The anti-suffragists are afraid of freedom lest it degenerate into license. The danger is always present in a free people, but this country has chosen to brave these temporary disturbances which accompany freedom rather than the mental stultification which goes hand in hand with bondage."

May 13, 1913

CHICAGO WOMEN IN VICTORY MARCH

Suffragists Plan Big Celebration To-day in Honor of Their Springfield Lobby.

MAYOR HARRISON IS GLAD

Mrs. Trout Tells How the Battle Was Won in Long Legislative Campaign.

By Telegraph to the Editor of THE NEW YORK TIMES.

SPRINGFIELD, Ill., June 12.—The only influence employed by the women to secure the passage of suffrage bill in Illinois was the influence of quiet, persistent, educational work.

Mrs. Sherman M. Booth, our executive Chairman, began last Fall studying the personnel of the Legislature. She then attended the Legislature for six weeks rounding up the suffragists. She found little ready-made enthusiasm on the subject. At the end of six weeks she asked me to join her, and for sixteen weeks we have labored together.

During the last seven weeks Mrs. Antoinette Funk, a lawyer of Chicago, has worked with me. We had organized as well as we could in a few months the State into Senatorial districts, and, through our various organizations we brought influence to bear on the legislators from their constituents. We did not decorate the Legislature with suffrage buttons. No one knew who was pledged but ourselves. We used suffrage literature sparingly and only to fit individual cases and distributed it personally. There was no broadcast distribution of leaflets at any time.

We had no suffrage hearings. Arguments were used on the individual members. The uppermost thought was always the fact that votes were all that was needed to pass bills, so we concentrated on votes.

Men kept their pledges and the vote was won in Illinois through the cooperation of Democrats, Republicans, Socialists, Progressive and through the combined votes of so-called "wets" and "drys."

The Legislators treated the question not as a woman's problem, nor a man problem, but as a great human problem. The passage of this bill will help the cause of equal suffrage everywhere and this thought has nerved us through the strenuous work of the past four months. Illinois has lead the way and broken through the conservatism of the great Middle west.

GRACE WILBUR TROUT, President Illinois Equal Suffrage Association.

June 13, 1913

TO INVADE WALL STREET.

Suffragists to Hold Daily Meetings for Month at 86 Nassau Street.

The men of the Wall Street district are to be besieged for a full month by the woman suffragists, beginning next Thursday, at noon, when a meeting will be held at 86 Nassau Street. The Woman's Political Union will open headquarters there, and have a large committee of women on duty for a month with daily noon meetings, to which the men of the district are invited. Mrs. Norman deR. Whitehouse will preside at the first meeting, and Miss Helen Todd will be the speaker.

Among the women who will be on duty at the headquarters will be Mrs. Charles S. Whitman, Mrs. Lionel Sutro, Mrs. Willard Straight, Mrs. Sumner Gerard, Mrs. John Rogers, Jr., Mrs. Emanuel Einstein, Mrs. John Flagler, Mrs. Francis H. Cabot, Mrs. John Winters Branham, Mrs. Sidney Borg, and Mrs. Hobart Park.

April 11, 1914

500 WOMEN CHEER FOR MOTHER JONES

Not a Man Allowed at Dinner Given for Agitator by Six of Her Admirers.

SUFFRAGISTS GET A SHOCK

Guest Says Colorado Mine Owner Ascribed Control Over the Workers to the Women's Votes.

Mother Jones, the agitator, gave women some lights on suffrage at a dinner given for her at the Café Boheme, Second Avenue and Tenth Street, last evening. Not a man was allowed at the gathering.

Mother Jones spoke an hour and a half, and then read a few facts. She told the women they must stand for free speech in the streets, that it was their right, and they must have it.

"But how can we get it, mother?" cried a voice from the audience.

"I have no vote," answered Mother Jones cheerfully, "and I've raised hell all over this country."

The entire roomfull of women shrieked with glee. The dinner was arranged by six women—Katherine Leckie, Marie Jenney Howe, Edna Kenton, Fola La Follette, Rose Young, and Florence Woolston—and the number of guests was limited to 500. There were writers, artists, women of wealth, a few suffrage leaders, and women interested in labor movements and philanthropy.

Mother Jones was kept quietly in a rear room while the dinner was in progress to conserve her strength, but she showed no weight of her 82 years when she went into the big dining room and stood on a chair to speak. The women, standing, gave cheers of welcome. Mother Jones is fond of the frills and accessories of dress. She wore a figured bodice with the dark skirt of her gown. There were ruffles at the neck and wrists; little dingley ornaments at the latter and her white hair was arranged in the style that was known some years ago as a "French twist." In front it had been cut in something of a bang and fluffed over her forehead. There were two little side combs and a glittering ornament was at the base of the twist.

Behind her gold-rimmed, gold-bowed glasses Mother Jones's blue eyes twinkled. She likes to talk, and she does not mind using what she calls classic language. Her talk was more or less of a rambling description of different strikes in which she had taken part, with sometimes thrilling and often amusing descriptions.

"There is going to be no speaking," said Miss Leckie, who introduced her, "and only one talk by the biggest woman in the world. She loves every man, woman, and child in it, and we love her."

Mother Jones started in, beginning with Rome, so it was not surprising that it took her nearly two hours to tell the women all about it. The remarks on suffrage were an interlude and a surprise to many, and she said things about the Colorado women to which some of the guests took exception.

"Some one says I'm an anti-suffragist," said Mother Jones. "Well, that's a horrible crime. I'll tell you something, girls."

The women smiled at that nice little familiar word.

"I'm not an anti to anything that will bring freedom. But I'm going to be honest with you about those women in Colorado. There is no use in throwing bouquets. They have had the vote for nineteen years, and this is what some one who was present at a meeting of mine owners told me. One of the men proposed disenfranchising the women and another jumped to his feet and shouted:

"'For God's sake, what are you talking about? If it hadn't been for the women, the miners would have beat us long ago?'"

There was a gasp of horror from the women in the room, and one woman asked if Mother Jones would not explain that statement.

"You see," said Mother Jones, "the women got the vote without knowing anything about the civic conditions, but now they are waking up, and when the women in America wake up there will be something done. A woman in a comfortable home who is reading her books and amusing her children says to me:

"'Why, really, we didn't know anything about these terrible conditions.'

"'Well,' I answer, 'I was 1,800 miles away and I knew all about it.'

"I don't believe in the rights of women or the rights of men, but human rights. No country can rise higher than its women, and I don't have to see the mother to know what she is. I can tell when I see the man she has raised. And there are not as many good mothers as there should be."

In telling the women to go on with their work Mother Jones said:

"Never mind if you are not ladylike, you are woman-like. God Almighty made the woman and the Rockefeller gang of thieves made the ladies."

Speaking of Mexico, she told of her acquaintance with Villa. "I went over to see Villa, and I was wishing to God that we had two or three Villas in this country."

Mrs. Havelock Ellis was one of the women at the speakers' table with Mrs. John F. Trow, Dr. Gertrude Kelley, and Miss Livinia Dock. Among others present were Mrs. Frank Cothren, Miss Elizabeth Dutcher, Mrs. Mary Ware Dennett, Mrs. Charlotte Perkins Gilman, Mrs. Calvin Tomkins, Mrs. Robert Adamson, Maria Thompson Daviess, Lou Rogers, Miss Knox, and Maude Malone.

May 23, 1914

RAISE "FREE LOVE" CRY.

Antis in a Bulletin Quote the Views of Suffragist Workers.

Special to The New York Times.

WASHINGTON, May 24.—The National Association Opposed to Woman Suffrage, with offices in Washington, issued a bulletin today attacking the suffragists on the ground that they in reality favor "free love." The antis for some time have contended that woman suffrage tended to disrupt the home. In today's bulletin the antis present quotations from the remarks of various advocates of woman suffrage.

"The only way to define a feminist," says the bulletin, "is to quote what might be called the leading authorities on the subject." The bulletin then proceeds:

"Edna Kenton, a famous suffragist and feminist, has declared: 'Nothing invented of man has ever had a more stultifying effect upon the character and morals of women and men than the Christian ideal which St. Paul laid down for women.'

"Jane Olcott, former Secretary of the New York State Suffrage Association, stated in a newspaper interview: 'A man or woman should be free to give love whenever it is natural. Love is volatile, and when it goes I believe it is unmoral for man and wife even to appear to live together, except for the sake of their children. In that case each should be free to bestow love elsewhere by mutual agreement.'

"Marie Jenney Howe, woman suffragist and feminist, has given this as an article of her belief: 'We are sick of being specialized as to sex; we do not put any fence around man. And we merely want to take down the fence that has been put around us.'

"Mrs. Florence Wise, Secretary of the Women's Trade Union League of New York and a speaker on feminism, has contributed this thought: 'I believe only in voluntary motherhood, anyway There are many persons, men as well as women, who are better off without children. Many unmarried women, on the other hand, want children, and there ought to be an opportunity for the expression of their innate mother love.'

"Mrs. Charlotte Perkins Gilman, member of the Congressional Union, has shed this light on feminism: 'Human beings believe their duty is far outside of merely being mothers, even a kitten could be a mother.'"

May 25, 1914

TRINKETS AND SONGS OF THE SUFFRAGISTS

SINCE suffrage has become popular and more or less fashionable the different suffrage societies have spent a good deal of their time answering the hundreds of people who are continually sending in suggestions for songs and suffrage trinkets. There has ever been thought of opening a special "Suggestion Bureau" to handle the letters. The ideas come from professionals as well as suffragists and about one in a hundred is worth while.

Some things have materalized. There is a special soap which has been dedicated to suffrage and from the sales of which the women get a percentage. There is a special suffrage candy and a well-known firm making health crackers has named one variety the "Suffragette." Weird suffrage pincushions flourish in the fancywork shops. A number of things the suffragists themselves have adopted.

There are many songs which have been dedicated to them and which are kept on sale for any one who wishes them. There is a little book in a yellow cover, the "Equal Suffrage Song Sheaf," which has a collection of songs written to old familiar tunes. One set to "Comin' Through the Rye" has this sentimental verse:

Gin a pair meet in the gloaming,
  When the votings o'er,
Gin they plight their troth while homing,
  Who their plight deplore?
And the chorus—
Every Jill must have her Jack, Sir,
  Why should this cause note?
Yet the world calls out "Alack! Sir,"
  On the way to vote.

A song written to the tune of "The Wearing of the Green" begins:

Oh, townsmen, have you heard the cry
  that's lately noised about?
The suffragists and antis turn the city
  inside out—
With meetings here and meetings there,
  'twould turn a sane man's head,
Before it's o'er we men will pass our
  votes to them instead.

One of two songs brought out together on a double card is dedicated to the antis. It is called "A Lullaby—or An Eye-Opener—Which?" It is sung to the tune of "Kentucky Babe," and runs:

Father is not lonely now, Mother with him goes.
Polls her vote and back she comes to mend her baby's clothes.
Close your eyes, my dearie;
Oh, you make me weary—
Or—ope' your eyes and see!

"Women's Rights," printed on a regular music sheet, both words and music written for suffrage, begins: "To the polls the ladies go, and they'll make a lively show, as the baby carriages go marching by."

Serious is "The New America," dedicated to the women of California, written to the tune of "America":

My country, 'tis of thee,
We plead for liberty
Thou hast denied.
Our hearts, like men's, awake
To make thee strong and great!
Within thy Halls of State
Must Mothers stand.

With the suffrage trinkets sold, both to propagate the faith and also as a means of raising money, many suffrage headquarters have suffrage shops. From the national headquarters in New York the supplies go all over the country.

The most popular thing the women have brought out has been "Votes for Women" playing cards. These have the suffrage slogan on the back, and are in the national suffrage color, yellow, with black and white, and in purple, green, and white, which are the colors of the Women's Political Union as well as of the English suffragettes. They are good cards, sell for 25 cents a pack and $2 a dozen, and are altogether the suffragists' "best sellers." A good suffragist will hardly play bridge without her own cards. A popular use is to give a card party and present every guest a pack of Votes for Women cards to take home.

There is pretty fine china with gold decoration bearing the motto "Votes for Women," and Mrs. O. H. P. Belmont has a cheaper ware with the same words in blue, the color of her organization, and sells dozens of little cream jugs, which make attractive souvenirs, for 25 cents apiece, at the suffrage shop connected with her lunch room.

There is Votes-for-Women note paper in different styles, yellow bordered and lettered, and any number of suffrage seals in different colors and designs. The women have their own holly-sprayed ribbon bearing the suffrage slogan for tying Christmas packages, and there were any number of suffrage calendars for the new year.

There are postals and buttons galore, big votes for women umbrellas in yellow and white cambric, which count in with the regalia, sashes, banners, &c. There are suffrage flowers, yellow for the organizations using that color, or purple and white with green leaves.

WILSON WON'T LET WOMEN HECKLE HIM

Tells Suffrage Delegation That Their Fight Can Only Be Won in the States.

NO DISCOURTESY SHOWN

Some Women Didn't Hear President's Friendly Parting Words with Leaders and Started to Hiss.

Special to The New York Times.

WASHINGTON, June 30.—Five hundred women, many of whom are prominent in their struggle for the ballot, marched to the White House this afternoon and assembled in the East Room, where they heard the President say definitely that he thought they should carry their fight to the States instead of asking Congress for an amendment to the Constitution. Though he was asked in several ways for his personal views on the subject, Mr. Wilson did not go further than to say that he thought the fight should be won in the States, if at all. But what he said, taken in connection with the speeches addressed to him, made it plain not only that he would not use his influence for the Bristow-Mondell amendment, but that he was opposed to it.

The meeting in the East Room, which was otherwise of a friendly and informal sort, was marred at its close by a painful misunderstanding. Three set speeches had been made for the women by Mrs. Harvey W. Wiley, Mrs. Ellis Logan, and Mrs. Rheta Childe Dorr, representing the General Federation of Women's Clubs, which indorsed woman suffrage in Chicago two weeks ago. The President replied briefly, and then answered questions from Mrs. Wiley and Mrs. Dorr. At last he said that he did not think it proper for him to submit himself to cross-examination. Mrs. Dorr thanked him for his courtesy; he expressed his pleasure at seeing his callers, and withdrew.

But in the crowded room these courtesies were heard by few. Even women in the front row heard simply his refusal to be further cross-examined. Then he stepped back with his aid, Col. Hart, and the Secret Service men, and the folding doors were shut behind him. Nearly everybody present got the impression that the President, in anger at the rain of questions, had turned abruptly and ordered the door shut in the faces of the women who had called on him. Expectation in some quarters that the delegates would advance in single file and be personally presented increased the feeling of resentment.

When the doors shut with a clang there was a moment's intense silence. Then a single hiss rang out distinctly clear. That, in turn, was drowned by a little round of hand-clapping. After standing a few minutes gazing at the closed door through which the President and his escort had disappeared, the women slowly filed out, many of them vehemently criticising what they understood as the President's discourtesy.

What really happened before the President withdrew was not disclosed until two hours later, when a transcript of the colloquy by a White House stenographer was given out. This transcript set forth the following as ending the President's part in the conference:

"Mrs. Wiley—Mr. President, don't you think that when the Constitution was made it was agreed that when three-fourths of the States wanted a reform, the other fourth would receive it also?

"The President—I cannot say what was agreed upon. I can only say that I have tried to answer your question, and I do not think it is quite proper that I submit myself to cross-examination.

"Mrs. Dorr—Thank you, Mr. President, for the courtesy.

"The President—I am very much obliged to you. It has been a pleasant occasion."

Mr. Wilson today took the position he set forth the last time he received a delegation of suffragists. He said that the Democratic Party, through its convention at Baltimore, had not declared for woman suffrage, and he could not press it upon a Democratic Congress. The women who called on him today were prepared for that statement, and Mrs. Dorr disputed it sharply. She said that since announcing that attitude the first time the President had reversed himself in advocating the passage of a bill favoring the tolls exemption provision in the Panama Canal act, which not only was not indorsed by the Democratic convention, but had been specifically condemned. This argument produced little effect upon the President.

The President's address was as follows:

"Mrs. Wiley and ladies, no one could fail to be impressed by this great body of thoughtful women, and I want to assure you that it is to me most impressive. I have stated once before the position which as the leader of a party I feel obliged to take, and I am sure that you will not wish me to state it again. Perhaps it would be more serviceable if I ventured upon the confident conjecture that the Baltimore Convention did not embody this very important question in the platform which it adopted because of its conviction that the principles of the Constitution which allotted these questions to the States were well-considered principles, from which they did not wish to depart.

"You have asked me to state my personal position with regard to the pending measure. It is my conviction that this is a matter for settlement by the States and not by the Federal Government, and therefore that being my personal conviction, and it being obvious that there is no ground on your part for discouragement in the progress you are making, and my passion being for local self-government and the determination by the great communities into which this nation is organised of their own policy and life, I can only say that since you turned away from me as a leader of a party and asked me my position as a man, I am obliged to state it very frankly, and I believe that in stating it I am probably in agreement with those who framed the platform to which allusion has been made.

"I think that very few persons, perhaps, realize the difficulty of the dual duty that must be exercised, whether he will or not, by a President of the United States. He is President of the United States as an executive charged with the administration of the law, but he is the choice of a party as a leader in policy. The policy is determined by the party or else upon unusual and new circumstances by the determination of those who lead the party. This is my situation as an individual. I have told you that I believed that the best way of settling this thing and the best considered principles of the Constitution with regard to it is that it should be settled by the States. I am very much obliged to you."

"May I ask you this question?" said Mrs. Dorr. "Is it not a fact that we have very good precedents existing for altering the electorate by the Constitution of the United States?"

"I do not think that that has anything to do with my conviction as to the best way that it can be done," replied Mr. Wilson.

"It does not," she retorted, "but it leaves room for the women of the country to say what they want through the Constitution of the United States."

"Certainly it does," said the President. "There is good room; but I stated my conviction, and I have no right to criticise the opinions of those who have different convictions, and I certainly would not wish to do so."

"Granted it is a State matter," insisted Mrs. Dorr, "would it not give the great movement a mighty impetus if the resolution now pending in Congress were passed?"

"But that resolution is for an amendment to the Constitution," objected the President.

Mrs. Wiley—"The States would have to pass upon it before it became an amendment. Would it not be a State matter then?"

"Yes," said the President, "but by a very different process, for by that process it would be forced upon the minority; they would have to accept it."

"They could reject it if they wished to," interposed Mrs. Wiley; "three-fourths of the States would have to pass it."

"Yes," said the President, "but the other fourth could not reject it."

Then came the parting words over which the misunderstanding arose.

BRYAN INDORSES VOTES FOR WOMEN

WASHINGTON, July 16.—William J. Bryan, in a formal statement issued tonight, indorsed woman suffrage, asserting that he would ask no political right for himself that he was not willing to grant to his wife. He also announced his intention of supporting the proposed State Constitutional amendment extending the franchise to women, to be voted upon in Nebraska next November.

Woman, Mr. Bryan said, had proved herself equal to every responsibility imposed upon her, and would not fail society in this emergency. Above all other arguments in favor of giving her the ballot he placed the right of the mother to a voice in the molding of the environment of her children.

"The mother," the Secretary said, "can justly claim the right to employ every weapon which can be made effective for the protection of those whose interests she guards, and the ballot will put within her reach all of the instrumentalities of government, including the police power."

The statement follows in full:

"The voters of Nebraska will, at the election next November, adopt or reject a proposed amendment extending suffrage to women on equal terms with men. As a citizen of that State it will be my duty to participate in the decision to be rendered at the polls. I have delayed expressing an opinion on this subject, partly because I have been seeking information and partly because my time has been occupied with national questions upon which the entire country was acting; but, now that the issue is presented in my State, I take my position. I shall support the amendment. I shall ask no political rights for myself that I am not willing to grant to my wife.

Finds Objections Invalid.

"As man and woman are co-tenants of the earth, and must work out their destiny together, the presumption is on the side of equality of treatment in all that pertains to their joint life and its opportunities. The burden of proof is on those who claim for one an advantage over the other in determining the conditions under which both shall live. This claim has not been established in the matter of suffrage. On the contrary, the objections raised to woman suffrage appear to me to be invalid, while the arguments advanced in support of the proposition are, in my judgment, convincing.

"The first objection which I remember to have heard was that as woman cannot bear arms, she should not have a voice in deciding questions that might lead to war, or in enacting laws that might require an army for their enforcement. This argument is seldom offered now, for the reason that as civilization advances laws are obeyed because they are an expression of the public opinion, not merely because they have power and lead behind them. And as we look back over the past we may well wonder whether the peace movement would not have grown more rapidly than it has had woman, who suffers more than man from the results of war, been consulted before hostilities began.

"Second. It is urged by some that woman's life is already full of care, and that the addition of suffrage would either overburden her or turn her attention away from the duties of the home. The answer made to this is that the exercise of the franchise might result in a change of thought and occupation that would relieve the monotony of woman's work and give restful variety to her activities. And surely the home will not suffer if the mother, 'the child's first teacher,' is able to intelligently discuss with her family the science of government and the art of successfully administering it.

No Lessening of Respect.

"Third. Many well-meaning men and women affirm that suffrage would work a harm to woman by lessening the respect in which she is held. This argument would have more weight had it not been employed against every proposition advanced in favor of the enlargement of woman's sphere. This objection was once raised to the higher education of woman, but it is no longer heard. The same objection was offered each time the door has opened, and woman, instead of suffering degradation, has risen.

"These objections, however honestly advanced, have proved impotent to retard woman's progress. May not the fears, sincerely entertained by opponents of woman's suffrage, be found to be as groundless as those that once forced the widow in Eastern India to ascend the funeral pyre, or as those that now exclude Mohammedan women from the social benefits and responsibilities which the woman of the Christian world shares?

"And are not the second and third objections above stated refuted, to some extent, at least, by the fact that in the States which have adopted woman's suffrage (and in the other nations that have adopted it) there is no agitation for a return to the system under which man has a monopoly of the right to vote? Is it not fair to assume that an effort would be made to correct the mistake if woman's suffrage had really failed to give satisfaction to the people where it has been tried?

"If one were in doubt as to which side of the controversy to take he would be justified in giving weight to the fact that organization and enthusiasm are on the side of those who favor woman's suffrage. Organization is an evidence of earnestness, as well as of a comprehension of the subject. People do not associate themselves together to secure a given end until they have reached a definite conclusion in regard to its desirability and feel that its accomplishment is worth the effort for which it calls. It is quite evident that those who disinterestedly desire woman's suffrage are willing to make greater sacrificos to secure it than those who disinterestedly oppose woman's suffrage are willing to make to prevent it.

Mother's Right to Ballot.

"As for myself, I am not in doubt as to my duty. It is not my purpose to discuss the subject with elaboration at this time, but I desire to present the argument to which I give the greatest weight. Without minimizing other arguments advanced in support of the extending of suffrage to woman, I place the emphasis upon the mother's right to a voice in molding the environment which shall surround her children's environment which operates powerfully in determining whether her offspring will crown her latter years with joy 'or bring down her gray hairs in sorrow to the grave.'

"The Creator has placed upon the mother a burden which she could not shift if she so desired and He has given her the disposition to bear it. Her life trembles in the balance at the child's birth; her active years are given to the care and nurture of her children; her nerve force and vital energy are expended in their behalf; her exhaustless love is poured out upon them. Because the wealth of her existence is bestowed upon them they are a part of her very being—'where your treasure is, there will your heart be also.' When one considers the cost to parents, especially to the mother, of raising a child, it seems impossible that any one would attempt to lead a child astray or rob its parents of the priceless reward to which they are entitled; and yet there are in every generation —aye, in every community—those who are inhuman enough to deliberately lie in wait to make a wreckage of the lives of young men and young women. They lay snares for them; they set traps for them; and the men who ply this ghastly trade for gain are allowed to use the ballot to advance their pecuniary interests. I am not willing to stay the mother's hand if she thinks that by the use of suffrage she can safeguard the welfare of those who are dearer to her than her own life.

Her Weapon of Protection.

"The mother can justly claim the right to employ every weapon which can be made effective for the protection of those whose interests she guards, and the ballot will put within her reach all the instrumentalities of government, including the police power. If she is a widow there is no one who is in a position to speak for her in this matter of supreme importance; if her husband is living she can supplement his influence if they agree as to what is best for those under their joint care; if they do not agree, who will say that only the father should be consulted?

"For a time I was impressed by the suggestion that the question should be left to the women to decide—a majority to determine whether the franchise should be extended to woman, but I find myself less and less disposed to indorse this test. Samuel Johnson coined an epigram which is in point here, namely, that 'No man's conscience can tell him the right of another man.' Responsibility for the child's welfare rests primarily upon the parent; the parent receives in largest measure the blessings that flow from the child's life, if that life is nobly employed, and upon the parent falls the blow with severest force if the child's life is misspent. Why should any mother, therefore, be denied the use of the franchise to safegaurd the welfare of her child merely because another mother may not view her duty in the same light?

Politics Will Not Suffer.

"Politics will not suffer by woman's entrance into it. If the political world has grown more pure in spite of the evil influences that have operated to debase it, it will not be polluted by the presence and participation of woman. Neither should we doubt that woman can be trusted with the ballot. She has proved herself equal to every responsibility imposed upon her; she will not fail society in this emergency. Let her vote! And may that discernment which has throughout the ages ever enabled her to quickly grasp great truths—made her 'the last at the cross and the first at the sepulchre'—so direct her in the discharge of her political duties as to add new glories to her and through her still further bless society."

July 17, 1914

A NATION'S LIFE DEPENDS ON MEN'S FIGHTING EFFICIENCY

By Clement A. Penrose, M. D.

MEDICAL men have studied for centuries the various phenomena of life in its many phases, but have too long neglected the problem of life quality, its protection and propagation, its beauty, and the force of its example. Modern eugenics is a vain protest against existing conditions, in which we hope by careful selection to improve our race material. A crusade for wiser marriages, however, is not nearly as important as the education of parents in the principles of mental hygiene. It is also true that we may have the best of materials, yet create nothing, owing to faulty methods of building. We are probably marring (like the landscape by our billposters) our race quality and general efficiency by these signs of the time, the many "isms," the hysterical cults and rattle-brain theories of our present day, the result of improper training.

We must therefore first protect ourselves, as much as possible, from all these wild leaps in the dark, from all pernicious foreign influences and foolish panaceas, and then determine how we can preserve and cause to develop n our children those qualities which are best for the race. It is only through posterity that we can hope to offset the bad traits we have ourselves acquired, and which we are too prone to excuse, by the adoption of some fallacious idea, in the effort of self-justification. Self, that is the keynote to the present situation; it is the moving spirit in practically every modern movement of any importance. I doubt if ever in the world's history the civilized nations have had a greater need of more unselfish living and teaching, of greater patriotism and love of country and home, than at the present time.

Modern civilization has concerned itself too much with present conditions in its attempted cure of all social evils, by education and various forms of philanthropy, and has considered too little posterity and the great responsibility of race regeneration and preservation which comes to us with every intellectual stride forward more and more clearly as the unselfish mission of advanced culture.

We have in life insurance and in bequests to charitable enterprises, &c., undoubted signs of our awakening to this impulse, which the love of our children, our friends, and country has first inaugurated. There is, however, a broader, more humanitarian outlook, braver than any other, because so unselfish, which is the pride in race and which considers above all the quality of human life rather than the conditions of living. The expression of this is exemplified in the courage of the mother who sends her sons to the war, the father who dies for his home, and the fate of the many heroes who so bravely gave up their lives in the recent tragic disasters on land and sea.

It remains for us, as exponents of the best schools of science, art, and literature, as those who have had the good fortune to grow up under the most modern and beneficial influences, to endeavor to find out, and then teach our brothers, how this race quality can best be utilized, augmented, and handed down to the advantage of posterity and not wasted. The very qualities which make a man or woman desirable in a community are often, unfortunately, those which help to cut short their lives and keep them from giving to posterity that which would be most desirable. Wars too often kill off the flower of a country; epidemics are prone to select the unselfish and neighborly.

Our boasted civilization will come to naught and our philanthropic enterprises in every direction will be futile if we, in the interest of improving the condition of life, neglect to improve the quality of life. This is the great responsibility which rests heavily upon our shoulders today. Unfortunately, there is no evidence, according to the eminent English authority, Dr. Havelock Ellis, that the human race has improved much in quality in the last 100 years; in fact, it is rather otherwise.

Decreasing Efficiency.

In his book, "The Problem of Race Regeneration," he demonstrates that wild philanthropies, often by making people too dependent and by preventing their elimination, which a struggle for existence would necessitate, are actually decreasing the average of human efficiency and lowering the quality of human life. He shows that our increasing population of feeble-minded and inefficient is today the great menace of race regeneration. As he puts it, we must concern ourselves less with the "unemployed than the unemployable," the real danger. In the United States today there is about one mental defective to every 184 normal individuals.

When the quality of human life is lowered in a race, how are we able to lift it up to a higher plane? In but one way, the elimination of the unfit as far as posterity is concerned, by a number of different methods. By unfit I mean both mentally and physically unfit. Biology has taught us three great facts regarding life:

1. The offspring can inherit equally from both parents, but the nutrition of the growing life is dependent solely on the mother.

2. Congenital characteristics are easily inherited, whereas the acquired are possibly so, but not as a rule. For instance, a defective child could receive the most careful modern nursing and education, and all the assistance which money could give it throughout its life, and yet produce little better progeny than one who was more or less neglected. In spite of all efforts, we can do little to better the quality of his life.

3. We know from biology the great law of the survival of the fittest, through the power of natural selection. Should the earth, as an example, gradually cool, in the course of a few years those people who could best stand the cold would survive, and this quality would be handed down to their children.

The earnest contemplation of these three great laws would, I think, give us sufficient argument against some modern tendencies, if nothing else was considered. If a child can inherit half its qualities from its mother and is dependent, while an embryo and infant, for all of its nourishment from her body, how important is it that the mother preserve the mental make-up and physical qualities which make of her a good mother. Otto Weininger says truly in his book on sex and character "that the external characteristics of an individual do not alone determine his or her sex." Some men are more feminine than certain women, some women more masculine than certain men. No matter how we may try to educate or change them, they will preserve those characteristics and greatly influence the succeeding generations.

Competition of Women.

By degrees our civilization, which shows so clearly a lessening of human efficiency, is allowing women with highly developed masculinity to compete with the poorer types of men in many fields of labor. How very glad are these men to have the women work, vote, and support them. An inefficient type of man is generally married by the masculine woman, for the reason that she can afford to marry and will probably have better chances than a more womanly type with such men. History undoubtedly proves that masculine women almost always are attracted to the weaker and effeminate types of men, for instance, Sappho, Rosa Bonheur, and George Sand, &c., who are usually not attractive themselves to manly men.

As the efficiency of the men decreases the masculine type of woman will gain the ascendency She will earnestly put through a number of ill-advised and poorly thought out movements along philanthropic lines, on a par with Christian Science, Dowieism, the anti-vivisection league, &c., supported chiefly by women's influence. She will marry the man of her choice and give to posterity an inferior order of human being, i. e., women too masculine to bear children safely, nourish or rear them properly, and men without the masculine qualities necessary for regeneration, which is only possible when the race is sprung from a normal parentage on both sides.

W. L. George, in an article (Atlantic Monthly, December, 1913) written in defense of the feminist cult, goes so far as to state that "there is no sex and that there should not be any sex distinction." Prof. William T. Sedgwick (NEW YORK TIMES, Dec. 14, 1913) has, in answer to this remarkable doctrine, shown that fortunately this statement would apply only to a minority class and that women and men differ greatly, even in their embryonic life, and are absolutely suited for certain occupations only. W. H. Mallock, in his lecture on socialism, (Public Lecture Bureau of the National Civic Federation, February, 1907,) shows pretty clearly the fallacy of the equality of men without even considering them in contrast to women.

Should present-day conditions continue, however, one can predict very well what will happen in the future. The real womanly type of woman, God bless her! will become as rare as the masculine type of men. When the men of a race are lowered in their efficiency as aggressive fighting men the death knell of such a people has already been sounded. This happened long ago to Egypt, Rome, and Greece. The true cause of their downfall was a decline in the quality of their men, hunt as we may for other reasons.

Every American should read Homer Lea's wonderful military book, "The Valor of Ignorance," which shows only too well the menace now to this country from military inefficiency. The advocates of disarmament and abolition of the military strength of the United States should consider carefully recent statistics before presenting their theories to the ignorant public. In our Spanish-American war fourteen men died from preventable diseases to one killed on the field of battle. In the Japanese-Russian war one man died of preventable disease to four killed in battle. In other words, they were fifty-six times as efficient as we were in avoiding death from preventable diseases. In regard to illness not resulting in death, we sent 170,000 men to the Spanish-American war, 150,000 of whom became incapacitated for some time in one way or another. Japan sent 1,500,000 to their war, of whom less than 20,000 were incapacitated. In other words, 90 per cent. of our men and only one-tenth of 1 per cent. of the Japanese reported to the field hospitals for preventable illness.

A Japanese officer, when asked what they did to deserters from their army, said he did not know, as no one had ever deserted. In one year about 600 men in our army desert to every 10,000, and these all enlist voluntarily. Enlistment in Japan is compulsory.

From this it can readily be seen that more loss of life results many times over from military inefficiency than from the actual loss in battle, and the same can be said of inefficiency in every department of life, the sacrificed usually being of the best element in the nation. Before many decades the Teutonic races will need all of their courage and stamina to hold their ground. May the Almighty help them in their regeneration, or the outlook is very bad. Stewart Chamberlain, in his wonderful work, "Foundations of the Nineteenth Century," shows how important these people are in the world's civilization, what they stand for, what they have done in the past.

More than ever we have need of fighting men in every department of life, and women of the right sort to influence them to do what is right and not, in an ineffectual way, to do the work for them; women who from the cradle to the grave will be the inspiration to mighty effort, and who are worth fighting for. It is time that we got back to the true home as an ideal standard of living. Where the manly father is an example to the stalwart sons, and the womanly mother an example to her gifted daughters; where each member of the family has his respective duties well outlined and does them cheerfully and thoroughly. This would mean simpler living and less complex thinking, the only salvation, in my opinion, for the people of these United States.

The Home Idea.

All men and women carry in their minds, perhaps subconsciously, the image of an ideal home. This is usually small and cozy, on a green meadow with honeysuckle vines, tall trees, and the fragrant aromas from many delightful sources in one's nostrils. The call of a primitive ancestry will not be denied and cannot be entirely obliterated by the intricate mental processes of everyday life.

Although we must agree with the Hindu philosopher, Rabindranath Tagore, that a world without evil and pain is inconceivable, nevertheless a home in which has been created an atmosphere of love and mutual respect, comes pretty close, after all, to being an earthly paradise. A home like this would defy even the machinations of a wily politician, while the men of the family are away toiling for the loved ones. Discord could hardly be sown in such an environment.

But what about the squalid homes of our large cities today, where poverty, ignorance, and discontent go hand in hand? Will families long remain united when the votes and favors of wives and daughters are bartered for, where material gain or preferment of some kind would be the price?

The feminist movement will obviously affect two fundamental elements necessary to the regeneration of the human race, the quality of life itself and the home. It is, like so many movements which arise daily, the result of a wave of mental unrest ever spreading over the civilized countries, and produced by the complexity of modern life.

Too Many Standards.

Where we op . . . se . . . ere
we now have . . . statistics . . . e rural districts
te . . . ne cities.

Three Main Factors.

Well-known authorities agree that the three main factors of our unfortunate prominence in these matters are, first, the reception of so many alien defectives into the country; second, the crowding together of our men and women in the cities; third, the poor bringing up our children are receiving in their homes. We certainly need better fathers and mothers, who will not leave the teaching of their children so much to the schools, a training which Miss E. E. Lynch recently has shown to be such a bad one. Miss

Lynch says that our public schools' sole trend is toward but one point, admission to the high school without regard to individual needs or fitness. As only seven out of one hundred ever get to the high school, the training of the other ninety-three is absolutely inadequate and the children are thrown back on their homes for education or must go to work or run wild on the streets. The training of the high school tends toward the college, and yet only five of the seven go to college. Dr. Frank Crane is right when he says every one should be taught a trade.

What is the result? Whether we consider the social evil, the high cost of living, low wages, infant mortality, or suffrage, the root of all these questions goes right back to one consideration, inefficiency; the inefficient girl who cannot run her home properly, please her husband, or care for her baby, and the inefficient boy who has grown up without a trade, intolerant of all discipline, and who will only work when he feels like it for a salary twice as much as he is worth. So much that is good in our country has been corrupted by vicious foreign influences that it is astonishing that we do not have stricter immigration laws. If we could prevent some of our best women from contracting foreign marriages it might also help.

The idea of doubling the illiterate and mentally unfit vote is most repugnant to the investigator along these lines. That such mothers should yearly add to our already heavy burden is intolerable. The women hold that they will purify politics, but what will politics do for them? Does it improve the men? Will they be proof against its contamination? Alas, I fear not when one sees the effect that it has already had upon them.

Sir Almroth Wright, the distinguished British biologist, says, truly,

that a sure sign of advanced civilization is the observance of those unwritten laws which every man and little boy knows, namely, that it is wrong to leave another fellow in the lurch, to fight one smaller than one's self, or to strike a woman. The militant suffragist, when she resorts to violence against a policeman or public man, is immoral, because, although not perhaps always breaking a statutory law, she is unquestionably breaking an unwritten and unassailable commandment of advanced civilization, which we become aware of the moment we see it violated. In the civilized world there has existed as it were a truce between man and woman, based on the solemn covenant that within the confines of civilization (outside, the rule lapses) the weapons of physical force may not be applied by man against woman nor by woman against man. Under this covenant the half of the human race, which most needs protection, is raised up above the waves of violence. It is this covenant, so faithfully kept by man, that the militant suffragist violates.

A prominent suffragist from New York said "that while she deplored bloodshed, she thought it a good advertisement for the cause." Social degeneracy of this nature can hardly be called a good advertisement of any cause; it has not helped anarchy, and it will never help woman suffrage. Justice Coleridge, although rather favorable to women voting, recognized the immorality in such acts of violence when he sentenced Mrs. Emmaline Pankhurst and Mrs. Pethick Lawrence at the Old Bailey to nine months in jail and to pay heavy costs.

Does the woman who is poisoned by her misplaced self-esteem, and who flies out at every man who does not pay homage to her intellect, do anything really worth while for the quality of her race? She is affronted if the man tells her that the glory of woman for him lies in her powers of attraction, her motherhood, and unswerving allegiance to the ethics of her sex. In the wake of these embittered women come troops of girls, mere children, who are given ideas about their moral, intellectual, and financial values such as men never conceived. Their life programme is to have their husband support them, and give up his time and freedom for many hours in the day, but they themselves must not be asked to give up any of their liberty or subordinate themselves at all to his interest.

A happy outlook for marital bliss in the future if such advice and teaching, so prevalent today in colleges for girls, is accepted.

Never in the world before has woman had such an opportunity to show her quality and unselfishness. Let her give up her ambition and forget her private grievances and refuse to accept the ballot, which only 20 per cent. of her sex want and 80 per cent. are indifferent about or actually oppose. Let her be careful lest, like Lucifer, her pride leads to her downfall.

The suffragist will tell you that women for centuries have led a life of bondage, with suppression of their best possibilities, and are still so hampered that they cannot develop. In a second breath she will say that if she is allowed to work side by side with man she will lift him up to the high moral plane which women enjoy, and not descend to his poor level. Fallacy after fallacy; first, that this continued oppression should have, contrary to the history of nations, produced such a noble creature, and, second, that a woman inheriting, as I have shown, qualities from both parents equally, should perform the same duties as a man, with even less physical resistance, and still not fall to the common level or below it.

The real truth is that in civilized races woman has been made what she is by the reverence of man for her. He has fixed her position in the home and in his heart and given her a standard up to which she must live if we are to preserve any ideals at all in this too material world. Can a woman reform a man by marrying him? Can she uplift a man by doing his work, by undue intimacy with him, by drinking, smoking, and swearing with him? The answer is too apparent to be discussed.

I have been told by men prominent in affairs that in various States the women have resorted to a most corrupt form of lobbying, even threatening public men who have been unkind enough to disagree with them. Instances of this sort of thing we have had right here in Maryland. A foeman worthy of his steel is what any brave man desires. It is unfortunately otherwise with the women in politics, who usually resent any decided opposition.

The excessive abuse of State rights is the cause of more corrupt politics and unfair legislation than any other factor in our Government. The crimes of individuals stand in an inverse ratio to the power of a State to enforce its laws. When one sees what a military Government has done for Cuba, the Philippines, and Panama in a short time, I am not sure but what we should be purer politically if we had a more military form of government. We should certainly be better hygienically.

I believe emphatically in obligatory military training for every able-bodied man in the community, military schools, and the Boy Scout idea, from the standpoint of discipline and physical culture as well as the patriotism it would engender, but for Americans only. Our latest folly is the training of foreign soldiers in our military schools and exposing the weakness of our equipment in this direction to the world's gaze, while we are teaching them how best to overcome us.

Better People Needed.

What we need are better men in civic life and better women in the homes, and better fathers and mothers. I cannot see anything else but the lowering of the efficiency of the race if women do men's work or men women's work. Men's duties and women's should be complementary in the social scheme; like parts of a machine, they run along together better if each is doing its own work well. If there is lack of harmony in the daily routine of life, the fundamental unit of civilization, the home, is utterly disrupted. The actual physical labor done by each is less important.

Our masses need more natural recreation, like the peasants of Europe games, dances, and various forms of outdoor pastimes, only possible when the conditions are as cited above. I have recommended a very good plan to many families under my care, which is to spend a part of every Sunday in the woods, a long walk, with a simple luncheon in some picturesque spot, for the whole family. I believe today that the Children's Playground Associations, thanks to the women, are meeting one of the greatest needs in the community.

The ever-growing tendency for the people to move out into the suburbs shows a revolt against the crowding together in the large cities, and, owing to the distances from places of employment, necessitates more than ever the importance of the mother keeping close to the home. A greater feeling of independence and freedom from petty cares is developed in a rural residence, which more or less dissociates one from the strain and turmoil of the working world when our day's work is done and when we most need complete relaxation. Cowper was right when he said:

God made the country and man made the town.
What wonder then that health and virtue, gifts
That can alone make sweet the bitter draught
That life holds out to all, should most abound
And least be threatened in the fields and groves.

SUFFRAGISTS VOTE TO OPPOSE WILSON

Conference of Woman's Party at Colorado Springs Decides to Work Against His Re-election.

COMMENDS HUGHES' STAND

Wilson's Attitude on Federal Amendment Is Vigorously Assailed by Several Leaders.

COLORADO SPRINGS, Aug. 11.—The National Woman's Party in executive conference here today pledged itself to use its best efforts in the twelve equal suffrage States to defeat the Democratic candidate for President; congratulated the Progressive, Prohibition and Socialist parties upon their indorsement of suffrage for women by national action, and commended the position taken by Charles Evans Hughes, the Republican nominee.

The statement of policy was contained in three resolutions, unanimously adopted, setting forth the attitude of the party.

The scope and policy of the National Woman's Party was discussed tonight by Miss Anne Martin, National Chairman, in addressing an open-air meeting, arranged to announce the election policy of the party during the forthcoming election.

"Our single plank," said Miss Martin, "is suffrage first, the political freedom of women before the interests of any national political party. We ask the women voters to know no party until all the women of this country are free."

"The record of the Democratic Party," Miss Marin went on, "is one of continued hostility and obstruction. President Wilson and the Democratic Party must inevitably lose the West through their unjust denials of freedom to half the people of this country."

The leaders of the Woman's Party had hoped that President Wilson would relent at the last hour, but no message was received showing a change of heart on the part of the Wilson Administration. The two hundred delegates to the convention include about as many Democrats as Republicans. There are also Prohibitionists, Progressives, and Socialists, but the delegates proved on a vote to be suffragists above everything.

At the opening of the session this morning several addresses were made, in which attention was called to the Presidents refusal to favor the Susan B. Anthony Amendment. Mrs. Bertha Fowler of Colorado, in calling the conference to order, termed President Wilsons attitude toward the movement for national equal suffrage as one of "cynical contempt" and political expediency. Women who endorsed the plan to obtain suffrage by States, she said, were "political doormats of designing politicians."

The conference increased the membership of the Resolutions Committee to twelve, which was announced as follows:

Mrs. William Kent, California, Chairman; Mrs. Charlotte Ellis of Arizona, Mrs. Dora Phelps Buell of Colorado, Mrs. Jone Hart of Idaho, Mrs. Bertram Sippy of Illinois, Mrs. Harriet Stanton Blatch of Kansas, Miss Hazel Hunkins of Montana, Miss Mabel Vernon of Nevada, Dr. Florence Manion of Oregon, Mrs. Don Coray of Utah, Mrs. Frances Axtell of Washington, and Dr. Frances Lane of Wyoming.

The committee invited Miss Martin and Miss Alice Paul of New Jersey to meet with it in executive session, and at once began the task of drafting a statement of party policy. They reported the following resolutions:

Whereas, The present Administration under President Wilson and the Democratic Party have persistently opposed the passage of a national suffrage amendment, and

Whereas, Each of the other national parties either by their platform or through their candidates are pledged to the passage of a Federal amendment enfranchising women, therefore be it

RESOLVED, First, that the National Woman's Party so long as the opposition of the Democratic Party continues, pledges itself to use its best efforts in the twelve States where women vote for President, to defeat the Democratic candidate for President, and in the eleven States where women vote for members of Congress, to defeat the candidates of the Democratic Party for Congress.

Resolved, second, That we congratulate the Progressive, Prohibition, and Socialist parties upon the definite stand which they have taken in their indorsement of suffrage for women by national action.

Resolved, third, That we commend the position of the Republican candidate for President, Charles Evans Hughes, for the unequivocal stand which he has taken for human liberty by his indorsement of suffrage for women by national action, and assure him of our appreciation of his statesmanlike position.

Mrs. Florence Bayard Hiles of Wilmington, Del., spoke tonight at the conference. Mrs. Hilles, herself a Democrat and the daughter of Thomas Bayard, Secretary of State under Cleveland, asserted that there had been "gross injustice" shown by the present House Judiciary Committee toward the Susan B. Anthony amendment and the efforts of the women to have it given a fair trial. She concluded:

"The hopeless task of State referendums has taught women the futility of such action and the necessity for concentration on the Federal amendment. Undoubtedly enough States are now won to enable the most skeptical observer to see that the political power already in the hands of women themselves is sufficient to win freedom for all women."

Capital Suffragists Praise Advice.

Special to The New York Times.

WASHINGTON, Aug. 11.—Miss Lucy Burns, Vice Chairman of the Congressional Union for Woman Suffrage, issued this statement tonight:

"The decision of the Woman's Party in the West to devote their best efforts to defeat the Democratic Party will receive the hearty support, both moral and financial, of women throughout the whole country.

"The Democratic Party has for four years treated with open contempt the movement for the enfranchisement of women. They have not only opposed a Federal suffrage amendment, but have refused to allow it to be discussed and voted on by the representatives of the people.

"President Wilson opposed the Federal suffrage amendment without giving it due consideration, in the first place; and now continues his opposition through sheer unwillingness to admit a bad error of judgment and tactics.

"Women will certainly not return to power a party that has denied them justice."

Mrs. Abby Scott Baker, Press Chairman of the Congressional Union and the Woman's Party, made this statement:

"The decision of the woman's party is perfectly consistent. We have always had one plank in our platform, national enfranchisement for women; and we cannot distinguish between the parties which have indorsed Federal woman suffrage, but we will certainly throw our whole weight against the one party which has opposed it. This policy has also the very practical advantage that we can co-operate with all other political parties in helping to drive from power the Democratic Party, the one which has been unfriendly to us."

Crisis in Suffrage Movement

By Carrie Chapman Catt

BECAUSE a real crisis has been reached in the woman suffrage movement and because that fact is appreciated by virtually every suffragist in the country, the emergency-called convention of the National American Woman Suffrage Association at Atlantic City next week will be the most important suffrage event which has taken place for many years. It is intended that a new milestone shall be set from which to measure the distance to the end of our undertaking. When the convention adjourns one week from today, the nation at at large will have awakened to a full realization of that fact, for a new and more powerful campaign will have started to hasten the day when every woman in this country shall have the ballot—and there will be no drones in the army mobilized to push it to a successful conclusion.

Neither the leaders in the movement nor the great majority of the rank and file are laboring under any delusions as to the true status of woman suffrage in this country today. Our victories this year in securing the indorsement of both the political parties have not blinded us to the fact that there is still a tremendous battle to be fought. To be sure, our cause has won all the really important factors of the country—the churches, the principal women's organizations, the chief men's organizations, and recognition by the leading political parties. Moreover, all the leading names in literature, art, philosophy, science, and business are enrolled on our side. But we have not won the reactionaries. We have not won the illiterate. We have not won the powers of evil, and we all realize there must be one final battle between the forces of enlightenment and progress and the forces of ignorance, evil, and tradition. We realize, too, that the time has come for that battle, and that there is no room in our ranks for those who fear the conflict

Mrs. Carrie Chapman Catt.
Photo by W. Burden Stage.

or betray any evidence of showing the white feather.

In our convention next week we shall make over our entire plan of organization. We shall probably revolutionize our entire scheme of organization and work, for it will be necessary to employ new agencies to handle the greatly increased working force that the new campaign will demand.

In the past, our work has been nation-wide, but it has never been conducted with the uniformity that is essential to the final success now within our reach. Our women have been working in hundreds and thousands of separate groups. The time has come now to gather these groups together and set them to work on a shoulder-to-shoulder basis, preserving all the non-partisanship that has characterized this association since its inception forty-six years ago, but giving its movement the additional weight and power of a more compact organization.

There will be renewed enthusiasm at our convention, because every move that is made will be a sign that victory is nearer. There is to be nothing "cut and dried" about the proceedings. Every phase of every subject which concerns our methods, our policies, and our organization will be reviewed and thoroughly discussed. No voice will be silenced, no opinion suppressed, and out of the discussion our organization will rise not only with a clearer understanding of its own powers and policies, but with a more exalted determination than ever to unite in the big drive toward final victory.

This is not a prophecy; it is a statement of fact, based upon the knowledge gathered first hand during the last six months from our workers in all parts of the country. Never before has the spirit of optimism been so contagious among our women, and never before has it been supported by such earnestness and determination. They know that after the long, hard years of struggle their hour has struck. It is as if a tremendous telepathic wave were sweeping the entire country bearing with it to every woman in every State the message that victory is at hand and within our reach.

For years we have been saying that suffrage is coming. We said it because we knew. Today we can say that it is here and that it remains only for our women to make one last determined assault upon the opposition to make our victory definite.

Mrs. Robert Gould Shaw, Daughter and Granddaughter.

Mrs. Shaw Is a Niece of Agassiz, the Naturalist, and One of the Representative Women Suffragists
Belonging to the National Association.

Three courses of procedure lie before us. We can concentrate on the Federal amendment; we can drop the Federal amendment and confine our activities to State legislation, or we can continue the present policy of the National American Woman Suffrage Association and work for both State and Federal action. Because there is a difference of opinion among our women as to which of these modes of attack would be most effective we shall debate that matter on the opening day of the convention. The debate will be three cornered. Mrs. Ida Husted Harper of New York and Mrs. Glendower Evans of Massachusetts will lead the forces of those who believe in concentrating on Federal action; Miss Laura Clay of Kentucky and Miss Kate Gordon of Louisiana will champion the State campaign method of procedure, while Mrs. Raymond Brown of New York and Miss Florence Allen of Ohio will carry the standards of those who believe that we should continue our present policy and work both for State legislation and a Federal amendment. I will not anticipate the result of that discussion.

This three-cornered debate will decide the policy that we are to follow in the continuation of our campaigning, but it will not decide the plan of campaign, nor whether a definite election policy shall be adopted. That is a matter which will be worked out in the remaining sessions of the convention. We shall have the benefit of the best brains in the country in the new plans to be made, as the most represen-

tative women of the United States will be present at the convention. College Presidents, women in high positions, wives and daughters of eminent men, rich women, working women, will be factors in the great democratic gathering whose object it will be to determine the shortest route to political emancipation.

All of these women appreciate that we are passing through not only a national crisis but a world crisis. Already 3,500,-000 lives have been lost in the world's cataclysm. The number becomes the more impressive when it is remembered that the entire population of the American colonies was little more than 3,500,-000. These losses have been the lives of men within the age of economic production. They have been taken abruptly from the normal business of the world, and every human activity, from that of the humblest unskilled labor to art, science, and literature, has been weakened by their loss. Millions of other men will go to their homes blind, crippled, and incapacitated to do the work they once performed. The stability of human institutions has never before suffered so tremendous a shock. Great men are trying to think out the consequences, but one and all proclaim that no imagination can find color or form vivid enough to paint the picture of the world after the war. British and Russian, German and Austrian, French and Italian agree that it will lead to social revolution throughout the entire world. Whatever comes, they agree that the war presages a total change of the status of woman.

Meanwhile, women are taking the vacant places of men in every European country. Hundreds of thousands are making munitions in England and thousands are employed by the German railways.

It is not, however, in direct war work alone that the latent possibilities of women have been made manifest. In all the belligerent lands women have found their way to high posts of administration, where no woman would have been trusted two years ago, and the testimony is overwhelming that they have filled their posts to the entire satisfaction of the authorities.

Men have been frank to acknowledge the heroism and self-sacrifice of these women, but their endurance, their skill, the practicability of their service seem for the first time to have been recognized by Governments as "war powers." That fact has utterly changed the estimate public opinion has placed upon women's work and incidentally upon women themselves. It is reported that hundreds of prominent and influential men who bitterly opposed the enfranchisement of women before the war confess their complete conversion on account of the war services of women. Already three great Provinces of Canada —Manitoba, Alberta, and Saskatchewan —have given universal suffrage to their women in sheer generous appreciation of their war work. Even Mr. Asquith, almost as renowned for his immovable opposition to the Parliamentary suffrage for women as for his position as Prime Minister of Great Britain, has decidedly mellowed his attitude and some declare that he will no longer block the passage of a suffrage bill when the war ends. The significance of the changed status of women in Europe has not been lost upon the men of our own country; nor has the fact been lost upon our women that a colony of the British Empire over our northern border has given the vote to women in a territory nearly as large as that of our own land east of the Mississippi. Americans are not so ignorant of history nor so lacking in national pride that they will indifferently permit the Republic to lag behind the Empire in the spirit of democracy.

So it happens that there is a new star in suffrage circles and a gladsome spirit of coming victory.

In our own country the sentiment for nation-wide suffrage grows stronger daily. With this growth in sentiment has come an increased demand for the passage of the Federal suffrage amendmen, and because women throughout the country are turning to that Federal amendment for relief from their political disabilities it enters into the political campaign this year with an importance it never had before.

The women of six States will vote for President this year for the first time, and those of six others have the Presidential vote. One group of suffragists has made bold claims that it will persuade enough women within these States to vote against the President, because his party in Congress has blocked the Federal amendment, to defeat him. The audacity and novelty of these claims have piqued the curiosity of some and aroused the angry indignation of others. The main body of suffragists have yet to speak.

It was the National Woman Suffrage Association which introduced the Federal amendment, now discussed as though it were a new discovery, and this was done in 1875. It has been introduced in each succeeding Congress, and ardently supported. I do not wish to anticipate the action of the coming convention, but I may speak for myself. I am unalterably opposed to any method which proposes to enfranchise women by partisan methods. The woman's vote should never be mortgaged in advance by any political party. It has been the experience in most extensions of suffrage that the Democrats were more largely responsible for the enfranchisement of the workingman, and the Democratic Party has held the workingmen in large degree ever since. The Republicans enfranchised the negroes, and appeal to them for votes as proper expressions of gratitude. It will be a temptation for some dominant party to enfranchise the women, in order to increase its own voting strength. That is good policy for the party, but bad for the new voters, who should have the right of free choice, without obligation to any party. It is this bigger, more fundamental principle which warns me of the dangers of partisan action.

Nor, in my judgment, is it a quicker route. There are splendid, sincere, big-souled Democrats and Republicans in Congress who want to put the Federal amendment through, and there are stubborn, narrow-minded, tradition-bound Republicans and Democrats who will block the amendment so long as they serve in Washington. I refuse to believe that party power, sordid as it undoubtedly is, has so far lapsed into autocracy that men of brains will bend the knee and vote the way the President orders. I give our lawmakers in Washington the credit of being, in the main, conscientious, intelligent men, not cringing party slaves. If I am right, then the nonpartisan appeal in the long run, though less spectacular, is more compelling, and quite as quick.

What the Atlantic City convention will determine on these points remains to be seen. One thing is certain: The confusion, the criss-cross of diverse views on policies and tactics, will be relieved.

The emergency convention will pass into suffrage history as the starting point of the last lap in the long march to victory.

September 3, 1916

HANG SUFFRAGE BANNER AS PRESIDENT SPEAKS

Carefully Planned Demonstration in the Capitol Fails to Interrupt Wilson's Address.

Special to The New York Times.

WASHINGTON, Dec. 5.—While legislators and gallery spectators looked on in amazement, a large yellow banner bearing the words, "Mr. President, what will you do for woman suffrage?" was unfurled before President Wilson as he read his annual address in the hall of the House of Representatives today.

A delegation representing the Congressional Union for Woman Suffrage staged this sensational incident. Without warning the banner was rapidly strung out along the railing of the public gallery, almost directly in front of the rostrum, from which the President was reading his message.

The affair was carefully planned. This was shown by the fact that at the very instant the banner was unfurled a messenger from the Congressional Union headquarters appeared suddenly at the door of the press gallery of the House and shoved into a doorkeeper's hands more than a hundred mimeographed copies of an article about the banner and the women responsible for its display.

The President caught only a glimpse of the big streamer. Those immediately in front of Mr. Wilson say he smiled just a little, but there was no break in the reading of his address.

James Griffin, one of the assistant doorkeepers of the House, moved quickly from his place on the floor toward the offending banner. Twice he jumped in an effort to haul it down. On a third attempt he was successful. He gave the banner a vigorous jerk, and it was pulled out of the hands of the six women who held it.

Capitol policemen immediately appeared in the gallery doors with the intention of arresting those responsible for the disturbance. This plan was abandoned on orders from the chief doorkeeper.

Here is an extract from the prepared article sent to the press gallery by the Congressional Union messenger:

"A sensation was created in the House today while President Wilson was reading his message when six prominent members of the Congressional Union for Woman Suffrage unfurled a banner over the rail of the gallery directly opposite the rostrum on which the President was standing. In large black letters on a gold background, it bore this inscription:

"'Mr. President: What will you do for woman suffrage?'

"The women who held the banner were Mrs. John Rogers of New York, Chairman of the National Advisory Council of the Congressional Union; Mrs. William Colt of New York, representative on the council from New York; Mrs. Florence Bayard Hilles of Wilmington, Chairman of the Delaware branch; Mrs. Anna Lowenberg of Philadelphia, Vice Chairman of the Pennsylvania branch of the Congressional Union; Dr. Caroline E. Spencer of Colorado Springs, Secretary of the Colorado branch of the National Women's Party, and Miss Mary G. Fendall of Baltimore, who campaigned in Oregon for the Women's Party.

"Officials of the Congressional Union decided on the method adopted today of directing attention of the President to woman suffrage, it was said, because they understood that he had decided to omit all reference to this vital issue in his message outlining his program. Mrs. Hilles, a Democrat and the daughter of the late Thomas F. Bayard, Secretary of State under Cleveland, and the first Ambassador to Great Britain, asserted that today's action 'merely presages our constant and further activities that will never be relinquished until our cause is won.' Mrs. Hilles said:

"'I came here as a Democrat to hear the message of a Democratic President, who within three months appeared before a national gathering of suffragists and told them that he had "come to fight with them." We have listened today to a message to the people of the United States, and not one word as to this recent promise, or a hint as to the method by which it shall be put into action. If, by my presence together with these other women, I can help to register the intense and human interest of millions of women in the Susan B. Anthony amendment, and the desire for immediate and favorable action by the present Congress, our presence here today shall not be in vain; but today merely presages our constant and further activities that will never be relinquished until our cause is won.'"

Members of Congress from the woman suffrage States privately deplored the incident. They asserted that the rank and file of woman suffragists did not believe in such spectacular methods, and the affair would injure rather than help the suffrage cause.

December 6, 1916

96

HOUSE FOR SUFFRAGE, 274 TO 136, EXACT TWO-THIRDS VOTE REQUIRED, WITH CLARK'S BALLOT IN RESERVE

Mann and Sims Save Day for Suffragists—Miss Rankin Leads Their Fight.

Special to The New York Times.

WASHINGTON, Jan. 10.—By a vote of 274 to 136, the House of Representatives tonight adopted the Susan B. Anthony resolution to submit the woman suffrage Constitutional Amendment to the State Legislatures for ratification. The resolution, contended for by suffrage leaders for seventy years, commanded the exact number of votes, two-thirds of those voting necessary to submit a proposed amendment. Speaker Clark, who was favorable to the resolution, did not vote.

The vote was so close that the opposition fought hard against the admission of the vote of Representative Joseph J. Russell of Missouri, who hurried to the Speaker's desk on the second roll call and demanded that he be allowed to vote. The opposition insisted that he was not in the chamber during the roll call. Mr. Russell proved that he had been present, and his vote was counted on the side of the proponents. Not satisfied that they had been defeated, the anti forces led by Representative Saunders of Virginia demanded a recapitulation of the vote; that failed to change the result.

The debate, in which the leading members of both sides participated, with Miss Jeannette Rankin directing the suffrage hosts on the Republican side, lasted five hours. Many women found seats in the crowded galleries. Some were there two hours before the House convened. During the debate women knitted, but the leaders devoted themselves to intently following the argument. Nearly every woman who journeyed to the House carried a knitting bag. Acting under the rules forbidding bags to be carried into the Capitol, the guards seized such appurtenances; only a few succeeded in breaking down the rule.

Had Clark's Vote to Spare.

The vote, making the greatest national victory ever scored by the suffrage cause, came after a very hard and uncertain struggle. Backed by the support given to the resolution by President Wilson, and by the conference of Republican members last night, suffrage champions began the fight with every hope of victory. As it drew toward the close and the leaders saw that Democrat after Democrat had refused to follow the President these hopes began to wane.

The galleries, which had been all animation, suddenly became serious, and some leaders whispered, "We are defeated." The watchers were electrified when Representative Russell broke through the crowd of members surging around the Speaker's rostrum and succeeded in having his vote recorded for the resolution. Victory also could have come through the support of Speaker Clark, who had assured the women that he would be with them if his vote were necessary.

Text of Suffrage Resolution as Adopted; How Members Divided Politically on Vote

Special to The New York Times.

WASHINGTON, Jan. 10.—Here is the text of the suffrage amendment to the Constitution, as adopted by the House today:

Resolved, By the Senate and House of Representatives of the United States of America in Congress assembled, (two-thirds of each House concurring therein,) that the following article be proposed to the Legislatures of the several States as an amendment to the Constitution of the United States, which, when ratified by three-fourths of the said Legislatures, shall be valid as part of said Constitution, namely:

ARTICLE —.

Section 1. The right of citizens of the United States to vote shall not be denied or abridged by the United States, or by any State, on account of sex.

Section 2. Congress shall have power, by appropriate legislation, to enforce the provision of this article.

How the Vote Was Divided

Analyzed on political lines, the vote on the resolution was:

For—Democrats, 104; Republicans, 165; Independents, 2; Socialist, 1; Prohibitionist, 1; Progressive, 1; total, 274.

Against—Democrats, 102; Republicans, 33; Progressive, 1; total, 136.

When Speaker Clark announced the final vote the people in the galleries arose en masse and cheered; members on the floor joined in the jubilation. Representative James R. Mann, the Republican leader, who had left a sick bed to give his support to the resolution, received an ovation along with Miss Rankin. Fully a thousand women congregated on the steps outside the House following adjournment and cheered with all the enthusiasm of collegians after a football victory.

Effort to amend the resolution failed. Representative Merrill Moores of Indiana offered an amendment to refer the resolution to a referendum of the voters, instead of to the State Legislatures. This was defeated, 131 to 272. While this amendment was being proposed a long protest against the resolution, signed by ex-Judge George Gray, Thomas Bayard, Jr., H. I. du Pont, and other citizens of Delaware, was read.

The only other attempt to amend proposed to limit the time for action by the States to seven years. This was defeated, 159 to 246. This amendment was offered by Representative Gard of Ohio, who urged that the same restriction should be placed on this resolution as had been carried by the prohibition amendment.

Vote of New York Delegates

Members of the New York [...] lined up in the final vo[...] [...] front DEMOCRATS: [...] about to Maher, Sullivan, [...] mbarrassed, Ca[...] [...]iss Rankin, who [...]d to be the longest [...] in favor of the resolu[...] [...]ke with great fervor.

Miss Rankin's Plea.

"We are facing a question of political evolution," she said. "International circumstances have forced this question to an issue. Things we have for years been taking for granted are suddenly assuming a new significance for us.

"Today we are mobilizing all our resources for the ideals of democracy. And we are finding that, with all our past wastefulness, we still have limitless resources upon which we can count. We have men for the army, the navy, the air; men for the industries, the mines, the fields; men for the Government.

"But something is still lacking in the completeness of our national effort. With all our abundance of coal, with our great stretches of idle, fertile land, babies are dying from cold and hunger; soldiers have died for lack of a woolen shirt.

"Might it not be that the men who have spent their lives thinking in terms of commercial profit find it hard to adjust themselves to thinking in terms of human needs? Might it not be that a great force that has always been thinking in terms of human needs and that always will think in terms of human needs has not been mobilized? Is it not possible that the women of the country have something of value to give the nation at this time?

"It would be strange indeed if the women of this country through all these years had not developed an intelligence, a feeling, a spiritual force peculiar to themselves, which they held in readiness to give to the world. It would be strange if the influence of women through direct participation in the political struggles through which all social and industrial development proceeds would not lend a certain virility, a certain influx of new strength and understanding and sympathy and ability to the exhausting effort we are now making to meet the problem before us.

"Today as never before the nation needs its women, needs the work of their hands and their hearts and their minds. Their energy must be utilized in the most effective service they can give. Are we now going to refuse these women the opportunity to serve, in the face of their plea, in the face of the nation's great need?

"These are heroic times, and they call for the strength and the courage and the dignity to think and act in national terms. We thought in national terms when we restricted activities by the prohibition amendment a few weeks ago. Why can we not now think in national terms and extend opportunities?

"The girl who works in the Treasury no longer works until she is married. She knows now that she will work on and on and on. The war has taken from

her opportunities for the joys that young girls look forward to. Cheerfully and willingly she makes her sacrifice. And she will pay to the very end, in order that the future need not find women paying again for the same cause.

"The boys at the front know something of the democracy for which they are fighting. These courageous lads who are paying with their lives testified to their sincerity when they sent home their ballots in the New York election and voted two to one in favor of woman suffrage and democracy at home.

"Can we afford to permit a doubt as to the sincerity of our protestations of democracy? How can we explain if the same Congress that voted for war to make the world safe for democracy refuses to give this small measure of democracy to the women of our country?"

Chairman Baker said the President had been ready to approve the amendment for a long time.

"I was in conference with the President three weeks ago," he declared. "He told me the same thing that he told the committee of Congressmen yesterday. The President, the Speaker of this House, hold their positions as a result of the votes of women. Those voters realized that the Democratic Party had stood for the people."

Analyzes New York Victory.

Representative Chandler of New York denied that suffrage was adopted in New York State by the votes of pro-Germans and Socialists. He sought to show that, where the un-American vote was largest, suffrage got the smallest vote.

"The overwhelming victory for woman suffrage in New York City is deeply significant because it is highly symbolic," said Mr. Chandler. "The population of New York is truly typical of the population of the entire world, and especially of the population of the States of this Union. From every State of the Republic men and women of brains and character have gone to New York to live and labor. What is best and bravest in brains and character of the men and women of every State of the Republic is mirrored in the thought and life of the people of the metropolis. Therefore, when the brain of New York City is acting, the people of the Republic are thinking, and when New York City feels sympathy and sentiment, the heart of the Republic is beating.

"When the people of New York City declared overwhelmingly for woman suffrage it was a practical mandate to Congress to take notice that the American people, represented in every intelligent cause in New York City, demanded woman suffrage. The expressed action of the New York City electorate was an exact index of the unuttered wish of the entire American electorate.

"It has been stoutly contended that the victory for suffrage in New York was due to socialism and pro-Germanism; that it was created by disloyal and unpatriotic influences. This contention is utterly groundless and ridiculous. For instance, my district in New York City, in which are located Columbia University and Grant's Tomb, gave an overwhelming majority for woman suffrage, and in this district the vote for Hillquit, the Socialist candidate, was almost negligible. Admitting that every Socialist vote was cast for woman suffrage, and this is a reckless admission, approximately five times as many Democrats and Republicans as Socialists voted for equal suffrage in my district.

"The Ninth Assembly District of Manhattan, located in my Congressional district, is typical of dozens of other Assembly districts in the greater city. In the Ninth Hillquit received 967 votes and woman suffrage 5,911. This general average prevailed in every Assembly district of my Congressional district.

The Result Up-State.

"The results up-State were still more remarkable. The rural counties of Nassau, Orange, Suffolk, Cortland, Chautauqua, and Westchester, located in different parts of the State and inhabited in the main, by pure-blooded, [...] going Americans, voted for [...] a decided majority. T[...] Schenectady, the [...] year[...] su[...]

SUFFRAGE MOTION BEATEN IN SENATE

Attempt to Take Vote on Anthony Amendment on Friday Fails by One Ballot.

Special to The New York Times.

WASHINGTON, May 6.—An effort of woman suffrage advocates in the Senate today to bring about a vote on the Susan B. Anthony amendment to the Constitution failed by just one vote. Senator Jones of New Mexico, Chairman of the Woman Suffrage Committee, who attempted to obtain consent to the vote for Friday, announced that he would call up his motion again on that day.

Senator Jones, who brought up the resolution, move that it be made the special order for Friday. Vice President Marshall ruled that it would require a two-thirds vote of the Senators present to adopt the motion. On the roll call, the motion was lost by a vote of 40 to 21. The vote was as follows:

FOR — Democrats: Ashurst, Beck, Chamberlain, Culberson, Gerry, Hen-Hollis, Jones of New Mexico, Ki, McKellar, Nugent, Phelan, Pit, dell, Robinson, Shafroth, Ja, son, Walsh—20. Repub'' Curtis, France, Gall', son of Califor, Kenyon, Len, la, , , , , , , Fletch-, , ene, Reed, , Smith of dex, , , , , , , , on, Tillman, Tram-, , , ardaman, Williams—16, , illingham, Knox, Lodge, Mc-, Weer, 5. Total—21.

The suffrage advocates are sanguine that they will put the Susan B. Anthony amendment through. They are assured of the support of Senators Cummins, Fall, Frelinghuysen, Goff, Gore, Johnson of South Dakota, Kendrick, La Follette, McCumber, McNary, Myers, Nelson, Owen, Smith of Arizona, Smith of Michigan, Thomas, and Townsend, all of whom were absent today.

May 7, 1918

ANTIS STAVE OFF SUFFRAGE VOTE

Special to The New York Times.

WASHINGTON, June 27.—Facing the charge of obstructing war supply bills aggregating $20,000,000,000, Senate supporters of woman suffrage today receded from their avowed determination to force a vote on the resolution to submit the Susan B. Anthony Constitutional Amendment to the Legislatures of the States, but announced that as soon as the Army and Fortification bills had been disposed of the suffrage issue would be revived and Congress prevented from recessing until the resolution had been brought to a vote.

This action closed a day of bitter debate, which revolved around the refusal of suffrage forces to pair with Senator Ollie James of Kentucky, an "anti," who is ill in a Baltimore hospital. Because a constitutional amendment requires a two-thirds majority, the antis insisted that two pros be paired with Senator James. This meant that Senator James's absence would cost the suffragists two votes, and their most optimistic poll this morning had shown just enough votes to win.

The antis, through Senator Underwood, told the pros that until a pair was arranged with Senator James no vote would be permitted. Carrying out this threat, Senator Reed of Missouri delivered a long speech, after announcing he was prepared to talk "until I see if that pair can't be arranged."

Senator Underwood, warning the suffrage forces that if they refused to pair "it would be a long time until the Senate comes to a vote on this question," urged them, if they wished an immediate settlement of the question, to arrange the pair and take a beating. Otherwise, he said, they must bear the responsibility for delaying the passage of the Army bill and the Fortification bill, which together carry nearly $20,000,000,000 for army equipment and supplies.

Senator Jones, in charge of the suffrage forces, admitted that if the pair were arranged it would mean the defeat of the resolution. Senator Smoot served notice on the antis that, if they persisted, the suffragists would prevent a Summer recess.

Senator Reed then announced his decision to talk until after further efforts to arrange a pair had been made. While Senator Reed discussed the Army bill, both sides to the controversy reorganized. After two hours of conferences

Senator Jones announced that he regretted "that to press a vote now would unduly delay the great supply bills. I think the sentiment of the country is that the suffrage resolution should come to a vote and be passed. I believe it will pass. I, therefore, ask leave to withdraw my motion to set aside the Army bill for discussion of the suffrage amendment, with the understanding that after the Supply bills are out of the way this matter will be brought before the Senate and kept there until it has been disposed of."

Preceding the wrangle over the pair a number of speeches were made on suffrage. Senator Brandegee of Connecticut, an ardent opponent of the measure, declared that "all this talk about striking the shackles from the limbs of enslaved American women is pure and simple tommyrot. American women are not enslaved. All this lingo to the effect that they are is mere frumpery and foolishness. Why, nowadays, a man can't get into a street car without taking off his hat and giving up his seat to a woman."

Senator Williams of Mississippi moved to amend the resolution by inserting the word "white," so that suffrage would be granted only to white women.

"This is an amendment that ought to appeal to any man who is white," said Senator Williams. "We've got to draw the color line. I say to the West, and to the people in California, you have not been through your time of tribulation yet, but you will get it. Do you want to have Chinese and Japanese labor and women admited to suffrage?"

The failure of the Senate to act on the Anthony amendment proved a great disappointment to a large gathering of suffragists and anti-suffragists who had come here to be in the thick of the struggle. Mrs. James W. Wadsworth, wife of the Senator from New York, and President of the National Association Opposed to Woman Suffrage, arrived early and was among the last to leave the Capitol. She was accompanied by a large delegation of women, all wearing the pink rose of the society. They had seats reserved in the Ladies' Gallery, a privilege extended also to their dissenting sisters, who wore yellow and purple badges.

Mrs. Carrie Chapman Catt, President of the National Woman Suffrage Association, was with her supporters the greater part of the day. Mrs. Emmeline Pankhurst, as a guest of the suffrage leaders, sat in one of the galleries. Mrs. Charles Boughton Wood, Mrs. Montgomery of Washington, and Miss Flora Wilson, daughter of James Wilson, ex-Secretary of Agriculture, were prominent in the suffrage ranks. Among Mrs. Wadsworth's supporters were Mrs. Swagar Sherley of Kentucky, Mrs. James Brown Herch of Pittsburgh, and a large following of Washington women of social prominence.

June 28, 1918

WILSON MAKES SUFFRAGE APPEAL, BUT SENATE WAITS

Special to The New York Times.

WASHINGTON, Sept. 30.—In an effort to break down the opposition to the Woman's Suffrage resolution in the Senate, President Wilson went before that body today and urged that it be adopted as a war measure. The appearance of the Chief Executive was entirely unexpected. Its immediate effect was merely to add to the tensity of the battle that has occupied the Senate for five days. The President's appearance, so far as an exhaustive poll of the Senate went later on, appeared to have failed to swing one opposing vote. At the end of the day's debate, Senator Jones of New Mexico, sponsor for the measure, knowing that the suffrage hosts still lacked the strength to win, moved a recess until tomorrow. As the Senate stood tonight, there were sixty-one votes in favor of the suffrage amendment, embracing twenty-nine Democrats and thirty-two Republicans, while against it were thirty-four Senators, comprising twenty-two Democrats and twelve Republicans. Only thirty-three votes are needed to block the passage of the amendment. One Senator, Martin, Democrat, of Kentucky, has been put down as doubtful, with the suffrage leaders counting upon his vote.

President Wilson's address to the Senate was based on the insistence that suffrage for women had become a war necessity. As Commander in Chief of the Army he urged its passage. The President argued that America must show the world that "we wish to lead democracy" and that "professions will not suffice." America must demonstrate, he argued, that she is willing to "give justice to women" as a democratic right.

"Women suffrage is not a party issue," the President declared, "both great parties being explicitly pledged to equality of suffrage for the women of the country." So, leaving politics out of it, the President said there was but one way in which to consider it, and that was from the viewpoint of the war.

Later the President, his voice ringing through the Senate Chamber, exclaimed: "I tell you plainly that this measure which I urge upon you is vital to the winning of the war and to the energies alike of preparation and of battle."

Line-Up Tonight.

When the President left the Senate Chamber speculation was rife as to what effect his address would have upon the opposition to the suffrage amendment. As the day wore on it was found that not one Democratic or Republican Senator seemed disposed to change his attitude. The line-up at the end of the day was precisely as it had been before the President spoke. Suffrage leaders were hopeful, after recess, that with a night to think it over enough recalcitrant Democrats might yield to make passage of the amendment possible tomorrow. But from the temper of Senators as expressed during the day this did not seem likely.

At the end in

October 1, 1918

SUFFRAGISTS OFF IN 'PRISON SPECIAL'

Women Who Have Been Sentenced for White House Disturbances Will Tour Country.

WILL WEAR JAIL CLOTHES

As They Demand the Passage of the Federal Amendment—A Who's Who of the Militant Party.

Special to The New York Times.

WASHINGTON, Feb. 15.—Militant suffragists of the National Woman's Party left Washington tonight on a special train which they are calling the "Prison Special," for a transcontinental tour in advocacy of immediate action on the national suffrage amendment. On this trip the speakers, most of them women who have been jailed for their picketing and other demonstrations in front of the White House, will demand the reintroduction and passage of the suffrage amendment before March 4. Twenty-six of the women who have served jail or workhouse sentences for their demonstrations left Washington on the special.

The itinerary of the prison special will be Charleston, S. C.; Jacksonville, Chattanooga, New Orleans, San Antonio, Los Angeles, San Francisco, Denver, Chicago, Milwaukee, Syracuse, Boston, Hartford and New York. The prison special, after having gone to the Pacific Coast and return, will arrive at New York City at 5:40 o'clock the afternoon of Monday, March 10, and will leave New York for Washington at 12 o'clock the same night.

Duplicates of the prison costumes worn by the women in the Ocoquan workhouse have been made for all those traveling on the special. The costumes consist of shapeless blue calico wrappers, with washrags pinned at the belt. Some members of the party will wear these costumes at every meeting.

There was no outside evidence of the character of the tour on the car, the Railroad Administration having refused to carry the car over its lines if there were any bars or prison insignia on the outside of it.

The New York women making the journey are Mrs. H. O. Havemeyer, Mrs. John Rogers, Mrs. Lucy Burns, Miss Vida Milholland, Miss Cira Week, Miss Edith Ainge, and Mrs. W. D. Ascough. Mrs. Havemeyer was recently imprisoned for taking part in the demonstrations in front of the White House. She has been active in all phases of war work, campaigning for the Liberty Loan and food conservation, was one of the founders of the "Land Army," and the first woman to agitate for military rank for nurses.

Mrs. Roger is the wife of the surgeon, Dr. John Rogers. She has been active in suffrage and in work for public education. She is a descendant of John Alden and Miles Standish. Roger Sherman, an ancestor, was a signer of the Declaration of Independence.

Mrs. Lucy Burns has served more jail sentences than any other suffragist, and has been in charge of all recent demonstrations at the White House.

Miss Milholland is a sister of the late Inez Milholland Boissevain, and will sing "The Women's Marseillaise" and other war songs of suffrage on the trip.

Miss Week, it is explained by the militants, is descended from Scandinavian vikings. Her family were pioneers in this country, tramping across the plains of Wisconsin, where she was raised and educated. She studied art in Paris, and exhibited there.

Miss Ainge of Jamestown, N. Y., was brought up in a family of nine brothers and sisters before she took up suffrage work in New York State.

Mrs. Ascough gave up a career as a professional singer to devote herself to suffrage.

Others on the prison special are: Miss Mary Ingham of Philadelphia, State Chairman of the National Woman's Party, a graduate of Bryn Mawr, Secretary of the National Progressive League in 1912, member of the State Committee of Progressive Party, member of Executive Committee of the National Party; Miss Mary Winsor of Haverford, Penn., graduate of Drexel Institute and Bryn Mawr College, student at Columbia and Harvard, sent abroad by the American Academy of Political and Social Science to study the English Suffrage movement; Miss Elizabeth McShane of Uniontown, Penn., graduate of Vassar.

Mrs. Robert Walker of Baltimore, whose husband is a Captain in the army, formerly Miss Amelia Himes; Miss Gladys Greiner, daughter of John E. Griner, member of the Stevens Railway Commission to Russia, holder of the golf and tennis championships for Maryland; Mrs. Mary A. Nolan of Jacksonville, Fla., who at 75 years of age suffered imprisonment; Miss Willie Grace Johnson of Shreveport, La., of an old Southern family; Mrs. Estella Eylward of New Orleans, studied in Stanford University, studied law in her father's office, and has traveled extensively throughout this country.

Miss Sue White of Nashville, Tenn., State Chairman of the National Woman's Party, member of the D. A. R.; Mrs. A. R. Colvin of St. Paul, State Chairman of National Woman's Party; Mrs. Pauline Adams of Norfolk, Va., wife of noted physician and prominent clubwoman; Mrs. Abbie Scott Baker of Washington, Political Chairman National Woman's Party; Mrs. Raymond B. Hunter of Port Huron, Mich., and Miss Gertrude Shaw of Grand Rapids, both of whom came to Washington to do war work.

State branches of the Woman's Party and special organizers are arranging mass meetings in the cities where the special stops.

SENATE AGAIN BEATS SUFFRAGE

Special to The New York Times.

WASHINGTON, Feb. 10.—To the bitter disappointment of anxious suffragists who thronged the galleries, the Senate today, by a vote of 55 to 29, again defeated the resolution for the woman suffrage amendment to the Constitution. Despite the urgent cabled appeals of President Wilson, the bulk of Southern Democrats declined to support the measure.

The vote means that all hope of adopting the suffrage resolution in this Congress is gone. Senator Jones of New Mexico, in charge of the resolution, admitted that there was no further chance of putting it through, adding that without doubt the next Republican Congress would adopt it.

After the defeat of the resolution Democrats who had supported it did not hesitate to express their keen disappointment. The refusal of the Southern Democrats to comply with the desire of the President, they felt, would mean that the Democratic Party's hopes at the 1920 election were appreciably hurt. Some went so far as to say that the party could not hope to retrieve itself.

"It means the certain defeat of the Democrats in 1920," said one Democratic leader. "The Republicans will adopt the resolution, and the women of the country will give them full credit for it. The Democrats have perpetrated a stupid trick in defeating the resolution."

The vote came after half an hour of debate. Up to the time of the roll call the suffrage proponents held to the hope that at the last minute enough votes would be won over to adopt it. But on roll call it was found that the Senate stood exactly where it did two months ago, one vote short of the necessary two-thirds of those voting. The vote last December stood 63 to 33.

The Vote in Detail.

Here is the vote by which the resolution was defeated today:

FOR THE AMENDMENT.

Democrats — Ashurst, Culberson, Gerry, Gore, Henderson, Johnson, (S. D.) Jones, (N. M.) Kendrick, Kirby, Lewis, McKellar, Myers, Nugent, Pittman, Pollock, Ransdell, Robinson, Shafroth, Sheppard, Smith, (Ariz.,) Thomas, Thompson, Vardaman, Walsh—24.

Republicans—Calder, Colt, Cummins, Curtis, Fernald, France, Frelinghuysen, Gronna, Harding, Johnson, (Cal.) Jones, (Wash.,) Kellogg, Kenyon, La Follette, Lenroot, McCumber, McNary, Nelson, New, Norris, Page, Poindexter, Sherman, Smith, (Mich.,) Smoot, Spencer, Sterling, Sutherland, Townsend, Warren, Watson—31.
Total in favor—55.

AGAINST THE AMENDMENT
Democrats—Bankhead, Beckham, Fletcher, Gay, Hardwick, Hitchcock, Martin, (Va.,) Overman, Pomerene, Saulsbury, Simmons, Smith, (Ga.,) Smith, (S. C.,) Swanson, Trammell, Underwood, Williams, Wolcott—18.
Republicans—Baird, Borah, Brandegee, Dillingham, Hale, Lodge, McLean, Moses, Penrose, Wadsworth, Weeks—11.
Total against—29.

PAIRED AND NOT VOTING.
Chamberlain (for) and Martin (Ky.) (for) with Reed, (against.)
Goff (for) and Owen (for) with Shields, (against.)
Hollis (for) and King (for) with Knox, (against.)
Phelan (for) and Fall (for) with Smith, (Md.) (against.)

An analysis of the vote shows that, had all the Senators who were paired been able to vote, the result would have been 63 to 33, which would have left the outcome just as it was without them—one short of the requisite two-thirds.

Stand of Southern Democrats.

Eleven Southern Democrats voted for the resolution, as against ten when it was voted upon in December. The new advocate was Senator Pollock of South Carolina. Senator Gay of Louisiana was a disappointment to the suffrage proponents. In a speech he told the Senate that, while he had worked to get woman suffrage through the Louisiana Legislature as a State measure, he was opposed to making it part of the Federal Constitution.

"I believe in the right of the States to decide this matter for themselves," explained Senator Gay. He denounced the militants for their attacks on President Wilson, saying they had hurt the suffrage cause.

Senator Ransdell, colleague of Senator Gay, voted with the suffrage supporters. Senator Trammell of Florida, upon whom the suffragists brought particular pressure, even to the point of bringing up a delegation of legislators from his State to urge his support of the resolution, and who received one of President Wilson's cablegrams, stood firmly against it. Senator Martin, the Democratic floor leader, was inflexible in his opposition, even though he was warned by Democratic colleagues supporting the resolution that its defeat might "dig a hole" for the Democratic Party.

The Southern Democrats based their opposition, as before, upon the argument that woman suffrage ought to be disposed of by the States. They feared giving the negro women the vote.

After the resolution had been voted down, Republican Senators began to forecast the attitude of the next Republican Senate regarding it. They calculated upon a gain of three votes in favor, and a loss of one, making a net gain of two; this, with the votes already secure, would give one more than the necessary two-thirds, if the entire Senate voted. The three Senators to enter the next Congress who are known to be suffrage advocates are Mr. Ball of Delaware, who succeeds Senator Saulsbury; Edge of New Jersey, succeeding Senator Baird, and Governor Walsh of Massachusetts, succeeding Senator Weeks. The loss will come with the vote of Mr. Dial of South Carolina, who succeeds Senator Pollock.

The galleries presented a display of Spring millinery fashions, as the Senate assembled. The ushers were careful to separate the militant suffragists, who yesterday burned President Wilson in effigy, from the less belligerent suffragists. The anti-suffragettes were allotted a gallery by themselves.

Preceded by Brief Debate.

The suffrage resolution came up just after 1 o'clock, when Senator Jones asked that it be considered. No opposition was raised. Senator Williams of Mississippi offered an amendment restricting the vote to white women, but it was ruled out of order, as the resolution was up on third reading.

Senator Pollock explained why he would support the resolution.

"For a century and a half we have had the privilege of the vote for one-half of our people and slavery for the other half," he said. "The pending amendment does not in any way interfere with State rights. It will have no effect whatever on the race question. It would not mean negro supremacy in the South. The white women would hold control over the negro vote just as the white men do with the vote of the negro men."

"I will vote for the resolution because I believe in it," said Senator Calder of New York.

Senator Wadsworth of New York, whose wife is a member of the anti-suffragists, did not attempt to defend his vote against it.

Senator Frelinghuysen offered an amendment to the resolution, as he did before, to provide drastic naturalization of alien women.

"I favor woman suffrage when proper safeguards are thrown around it for worthy women," said the New Jersey Senator. "But we face the situation of having too many alien women marrying Americans simply to get the benefits of American citizenship, and this, with our lax immigration laws, becomes a menace."

The Senator's amendment was ruled out of order. He voted, notwithstanding, for the resolution.

After Senator Gay had explained his attitude the Senate voted.

The National American Woman's Suffrage Association in a statement denounced the opponents of suffrage. They placed the blame for the defeat of the resolution upon the Democrats.

February 11, 1919

SUFFRAGE WINS IN SENATE; NOW GOES TO STATES

Constitutional Amendment Is Passed, 56 to 25, or Two More Than Two-thirds.

Special to The New York Times.

WASHINGTON, June 4.—After a long and persistent fight advocates of woman suffrage won a victory in the Senate today when that body, by a vote of 56 to 25, adopted the Susan Anthony amendment to the Constitution. The suffrage supporters had two more than the necessary two-thirds vote of Senators present. Had all the Senators known to be in favor of suffrage been present the amendment would have had 66 votes, or two more than a two-thirds vote of the entire Senate.

The amendment, having already been passed by the House, where the vote was 304 to 89, now goes to the States for ratification, where it will be passed upon in the form in which it has been adopted by Congress, as follows:

"Article—, Section 1.—The right of citizens of the United States to vote shall not be denied or abridged by the United States or by any State on account of sex.

"Section 2.—Congress shall have power, by appropriate legislation, to enforce the provisions of this article."

Leaders of the National Woman's Party announced tonight that they would at once embark upon a campaign to obtain ratification of the amendment by the necessary three-fourths of the States so that women might have the vote in the next Presidential election. To achieve this ratification it will be necessary to hold special sessions of some Legislatures which otherwise would not convene until after the Presidential election in 1920. Miss Alice Paul, Chairman of the Woman's Party, predicted that the campaign for ratification would succeed and that women would vote for the next President.

Suffragists thronged the Senate galleries in anticipation of the final vote, and when the outcome was announced by President Pro Tem. Cummins they broke into deafening applause. For two minutes the demonstration went on, Senator Cummins making no effort to check it.

The vote came after four hours of debate, during which Democratic Senators opposed to the amendment filibustered to prevent a roll call until their absent Senators could be protected by pairs. They gave up the effort finally as futile.

Changes Defeated.

Before the final vote was taken Senator Underwood of Alabama called for a vote on his amendment to submit the suffrage amendment to Constitutional conventions of the various States, instead of to the Legislatures, for ratification. This was defeated by a vote of 55 against to 28 in favor.

Senator Gay of Louisiana offered an amendment proposing enforcement of the suffrage amendment by the States, instead of by the Federal Government. Senator Gay said that from a survey of the States he could predict that thirteen States would not ratify the amendment, enough to block it. His amendment was defeated, 62 to 19.

During debate, Senator Wadsworth of New York, who has been an uncompromising opponent of woman suffrage, explained his attitude as being actuated by the motive of preserving to the States the right to determine the question, each State for itself.

"No vote of mine cast upon this amendment would deprive any of the electors of my State of any privilege they now enjoy," said the Senator. "I feel so strongly that the people of the several States should be permitted to decide for themselves, that I am frank to say that, if this amendment, instead of being drafted to extend woman suffrage all over the country, were drafted to forbid the extension of the franchise to women in the States, I would vote against it. Even though one might be opposed on general principles to the extension of the franchise to women, one cannot logically object to the people of a State settling that question for themselves.

"It seems to me that it is incumbent upon a Senator in considering his attitude on this matter to regard the nation as a whole and to give consideration to the wishes of the people of the various States which have expressed themselves from time to time."

Overriding State Votes.

Senator Wadsworth spoke of the results in Massachusetts, New Jersey, Pennsylvania, West Virginia, Ohio, Louisiana, Texas, Wisconsin, and other States where woman suffrage was defeated at the polls.

"Now the question is," he resumed, "whether the people of these States are competent to settle the question for themselves. There is no tremendous emergency facing the country, no revolution or rebellion threatened, which would seem to make it necessary to impose on the people of these States a thing they have said as free citizens they do not require or desire. Is it contrary to the spirit of American institutions that they shall be left free to decide these things for themselves?

"My contention has been, with respect to an amendment to the Constitution, that, if it be placed there, it should command the reverence and devotion of all the people of the country. The discussion here yesterday makes it perfectly apparent that, in part at least, in a certain section of this country, this proposed amendment will be a dead letter. No pretense is made that it will be lived up to in spirit as well as in letter. That same attitude has been manifest in the discussion of the last amendment to the Constitution, ratified last Winter. Today there are thousands of people all over the United States who are attempting to contrive ways by which the prohibition amendment can be evaded. This attitude shows an utter lack of appreciation of the Constitution as a sacred instrument, a lack of realization of the spirit of self-government."

Senator Smith of South Carolina opposed giving women the right to vote, he said, because to allow it would induce "sectional anarchy."

Signing of the Resolution.

Immediately after its passage by the Senate the Suffrage Amendment was signed. In appreciation of the fifty-year campaign of the National American Woman Suffrage Association, the guests were limited to representatives of that association and members of Congress, and the gold pen used was presented to the national association. The women chosen to represent the national association were Mrs. Wood Park of Massachusetts, who for two years has been in charge of the association's Congressional work; Mrs. Helen Gardener of Washington, D. C.; Mrs. Ida Husted Harper of New York, Mrs. Harriet Taylor Upton of Ohio, Miss Mary G. Hay, and Miss Marjorie Shuler of New York.

Besides Speaker Gillett, who signed the bill, the members of the House present were Frank W. Mondell, majority leader; Champ Clark, minority leader and ex-Speaker, under whom the amendment first passed the House, and John E. Raker, Chairman of the committee which won the suffrage victory in the House last year.

The Senators present at the signing of the bill for the Senate were Albert B. Cummins, President Pro Tempore, who signed the measure; James E. Watson, Chairman of the Suffrage Committee; Charles Curtis, Republican whip; A. A. Jones, Chairman of the Suffrage Committee in the last Congress; Thomas J. Walsh of Montana, Morris Sheppard, Joseph E. Ransdell, and Reed Smoot.

To celebrate the passage of the amendment the national association will give a reception next Tuesday evening at its Washington headquarters to the members of the House and Senate who voted for the resolution and to their wives. These will be the only guests.

Miss Paul, Chairman of the National Woman's Party, issued a statement, in which she said: "There is no doubt of ratification by the States. We enter upon the campaign for special sessions of Legislatures to accomplish this ratification before 1920 in the full assurance that we shall win."

"The last stage of the fight is to obtain ratification of the amendment so women may vote in the Presidential election in 1920," said Mrs. Carrie Chapman Catt, President of the association. "This we are confident will be achieved. The friends of woman suffrage in both parties have carried out their word. In the result we can turn our backs upon the end of a long and arduous struggle, needlessly darkened and embittered by the stubbornness of a few at the expense of the many. 'Eyes front' is the watchword as we turn upon the struggle for ratification by the States."

Prospects of Ratification.

Suffrage leaders say quick ratification is assured in twenty-eight States in which women now have full or Presidential suffrage. These States are Wyoming, Colorado, Utah, Idaho, Washington, California, Kansas, Arizona, Oregon, Montant, New York, Oklahoma, South Dakota, Michigan, Illinois, Nebraska, Rhode Island, North Dakota, Iowa, Wisconsin, Indiana, Maine, Minnesota, Missouri, Tennessee, Arkansas, Nevada, and Texas.

Legislatures now in session are Illinois, will adjourn late in June; Pennsylvania, Massachusetts, adjourn end of June or first of July; Wisconsin, Florida, in session until June 1, cannot ratify, because an election must intervene between submission of amendment and ratification.

Legislatures to meet comparatively soon, or with prospects of meeting soon, are: Michigan and Texas, extra sessions called in June; Georgia, to meet this month; Alabama, to meet in July; Louisiana, possibility of extra session before September; New Jersey, movement for extra session soon; Maine, special session in October; Iowa, special session in January; Kentucky, South Carolina, and Mississippi, meet in January; Virginia, meets in February; Maryland, meets during 1920; Ohio, meets in June.

Today's victory for suffrage ends a fight that really dates from the American Revolution. Women voted under several of the Colonial Governments. During the Revolution women demanded to be included in the Government. Abigail Adams wrote her husband, John Adams, "If women are not represented in this new republic there will be another revolution." From the time of the Revolution women agitated for suffrage by means of meetings and petitions. In 1848 a woman's rights convention was held at Seneca Falls, N. Y., arranged by Lucretia Mott and Elizabeth Cady Stanton as the first big suffrage demonstration. From 1848 to the civil war efforts were made to have State laws altered to include women, and Susan B. Anthony became leader of the movement.

For five years after the civil war suffragists tried to secure interpretation of the Fourteenth and Fifteenth Amendments which would permit them to vote. In 1872 Miss Anthony made a test vote at the polls, was arrested, and refused to pay her fine, but was never jailed. In 1875 Miss Anthony drafted the proposed Federal amendment, the same one that was voted on today. In 1878 the amendment was introduced in the Senate by Senator Sargent of California. It has been voted on in the Senate five times, including today. In 1878 the vote was 16 yeas to 34 nays; in 1914 it failed by 11 votes, in 1918 it failed by two votes, and on Feb. 10, 1919, it failed by one vote. It has been voted on three times in the House. It failed there in 1915 by 78 votes. In 1918 it passed the House with one vote to spare. On May 21, 1919, it passed the House with 14 votes more than the necessary two-thirds.

Foreign countries or divisions of countries in which women have suffrage are Isle of Man, granted 1881; New Zealand 1893; Australia, 1902; Finland, 1906 Norway, 1907; Iceland, 1913; Denmark 1915; Russia, 1917; Canada, Austria England, Germany, Hungary, Ireland Poland, Scotland, and Wales, 1918 Holland and Sweden, 1919.

June 5, 1919

TENNESSEE COMPLETES SUFFRAGE VICTORY; MOVE TO RECONSIDER IS FEARED TODAY; PARTIES SPUR BATTLE FOR WOMEN'S VOTES

AMENDMENT WINS, 50 TO 46

"Antis" May Attempt to Force Fight for Rescinding it.

TWO DAYS LEFT FOR ACTION

Opponents Prepare to Attack Ratification on Constitutional Grounds.

CONVERTED BY HIS MOTHER

Legislator Whose Vote Turned the Scale Is Lionized by the Suffragists.

NASHVILLE, Tenn., Aug. 18.—The amendment extending equal suffrage to American women was ratified today for inclusion in the Federal Constitution, the lower house of the Tennessee Legislature voting 50 to 46 to concur in the Senate resolution adopted Friday, 25 to 4. The action of the House made Tennessee the thirty-sixth State to approve the amendment.

There is still a possibility that the House may rescind its action. At the last moment Speaker Walker, leader of the anti-suffrage forces, changed his vote form "nay" to "yea," paving the way for a motion to reconsider. Under House rules he can present such a motion within the next two legislative days. If today's vote is confirmed, or if the House fails to take further action before adjournment Friday, millions of women will be free under the amendment to vote in the Presidential election next November. Only successful litigation contesting the legal right of the Legislature to ratify the section could prevent them. Steps toward such a test of the provisions of the Tennessee Constitution involved already have been taken by the Tennessee Constitutional League.

First Test Vote a Tie.

Ninety-six of the ninety-nine members of the House were present today, and the alignment, until a vote on concurrence was taken, was a tie, each faction polling forty-eight votes on a motion by Speaker Walker to table the resolu-

tion. On the ballot for concurrence the lineup was 49 to 47 until the Speaker changed his vote. This apparently would give the suffragists an advantage of only two votes, but their leaders declared tonight that members in favor of suffrage, who were absent today, would arrive probably tomorrow morning.

The motion to reconsider may be carried by a majority vote of the members present, and since Mr. Walker can act without a moment's notice, the suffragists have planned to be on hand in full force during the next two days.

Suffrage leaders said they expected no defections among their forces, but as a precaution were tightening their lines tonight, while opposition leaders were waging an active campaign to increase their strength for a final effort.

The end came suddenly. Debate on the motion to concur had been in progress little more than an hour, and there was no indication that a vote was imminent when Speaker Walker called Representative Overton to the chair and took the floor to reply to a suffragist who had charged that special interests were at work to defeat ratification.

"The battle has been won, and the measure has been defeated," Mr. Walker said. "I resent the iniquitous remarks that special interests are here alone against this measure. I resent this on behalf of the womanhood that is both for and against suffrage. I move that this measure go where it belongs, to the table."

Uproar Follows Motion to Table.

Instantly the Chamber was in an uproar. Suffragists clamored for recognition, while a chorus of "Second the motion" came from the antis. Mr. Overton, however, refused to recognize any one and ordered the roll called. The result was in doubt on unofficial tallies. An appeal to the clerk developed that his tally showed a tie, 48 to 48.

Pandemonium reigned. Members left their seats and crowded around the Speaker's stand, many demanding another roll call.

Mr. Overton, who occupied the chair during the remainder of the session, ordered a second roll call, which showed a tie of 48 to 48, and declared the motion lost for want of a majority.

Instantly the anti-suffragists demanded a vote on the original motion to concur in the Senate action. If another tie resulted it meant rejection of the amendment. When the Speaker put the motion hundreds of suffragists regarded the battle as lost.

Member Breaks from "Antis."

The vote at the outset was on partisan lines, but when the name of Representative Harry T. Burn, Republican, of McMinn County, was called, he voted "Aye." The opposition then virtually conceded defeat, for Mr. Burn had voted with them to table the resolution, and his change gave the suffragists the needed majority.

The attitude of other members was unchanged until the name of Representative B. P. Turner, Democrat, of Gibson County, was reached, and he passed. Instantly there was a shout of satisfaction from the antis. He had voted

against the motion to table, and his failure to vote again balanced the opposing forces; but just before the end of the roll call Mr. Turner requested the Clerk to record him as voting "Aye."

Mr. Turner had said repeatedly that he would vote neither for nor against ratification for the amendment.

The suffragists launched an uproarious demonstration before the clerk announced the vote, for there was no question that they had won. Women screamed frantically. Scores threw their arms around the necks of those nearest them and danced, so far as it was possible to do so, in the mass of humanity. Hundreds of suffrage banners were waved wildly, and many removed the yellow flowers they had been wearing and threw them upward to meet a similar shower from the galleries.

There were few tears of joy shed by the suffragists. Some wiped their eyes, but, on the whole, they considered it no time for weeping. Their happiness was far beyond that stage.

A motion to adjourn until 10 o'clock tomorrow morning was offered after the official vote was announced, but in the uproar it was doubted whether any members heard it or whether it was seconded. The Speaker put the question, called for the "yeas" and "nays" and announced gravely that the motion had been carried unanimously.

The announced intention to attack the legality of ratification if the House failed to rescind its action was the subject of conferences held tonight by the suffrage leaders and the leaders of the opposition. The clause of the Tennessee Constitution upon which would be based the test in the courts is Article 2, Section 32. It follows:

"A convention or General Assembly of this State shall not act act upon any ratification unless it is evident that his vote was needed, but in that event would amendment of the Constitution of the United States proposed by Congress to the several States unless such convention or General Assembly shall have been elected after such amendment is submitted."

The present Legislature was elected in November, 1918, and the suffrage amendment was not submitted to the State until months afterward.

The article was adopted in 1870 as a result of the ratification by the Tennessee Legislature of the Fourteenth Amendment in the reconstruction days after the civil war. White citizens of Tennessee were not represented in that Legislature, it is said, and to prevent ratification of amendments by similar tactics, the adoption of the article was one of the first things effected after the whites' civil rights were restored.

The Supreme Court of the United States in deciding recently a case originating in Ohio, held void a clause in the Constitution of that State relating to referendums on amendments. Acting on opinions given by W. L. Frierson, Solicitor-General of the United States, and State's Attorney-General Thompson, Governor Roberts called the present Legislature in extraordinary session to act on the Suffrage Amendment, declaring that he had been assured that the Supreme Court's ruling in the Ohio case served to nullify the article in the Tennessee Constitution.

The opponents of suffrage in Tennessee held that the two cases were not parallel, and that action by the present Legislature would be in violation of the State Constitution, and the fight of the opposition from the beginning has centered largely upon this contention.

The Tennessee Constitutional League, of which Judge Joseph Higgins of Nashville is President, which has prepared to place the case in the hands of the courts, is an organization of attorneys, and includes in its membership both suffrage advocates and opponents, according to a statement by Judge Higgins. The purpose of the organization, Judge Higgins said, was nothing more nor less than to uphold and protect the Constitution of Tennessee.

COLBY TO PROCLAIM SUFFRAGE PROMPTLY

Will Announce Validity of the Amendment on Receipt of Tennessee Certification.

WOMAN'S PARTY JUBILANT

Chairman Wires Thanks to Cox and Harding — 22,000,000 Women May Vote in November.

Special to The New York Times.

WASHINGTON, Aug. 18.—Immediately upon getting the news today that the Tennessee House had ratified the woman suffrage amendment to the Federal Constitution, Miss Alice Paul, Chairman of the National Woman's Party, and other suffrage workers asked Secretary of State Colby to issue the proclamation declaring the adoption of the amendment as part of the Constitution as soon as official notification had been received of the affirmation given by the State of Tennessee.

Secretary Colby said that, while there had been a suggestion that the proclamation should be issued immediately he thought it would be the part of legal wisdom to wait until the State of Tennessee had certified that it had ratified. All arrangements have been made for proclaiming the new amendment promptly. Under its terms the amendment becomes part of the Constitution as soon as it is proclaimed by the State Department.

All the thirty-five States that had previously ratified the suffrage amendment have certified the fact to the State Department, and all that remains to make the amendment effective is the receipt of the official notification of Tennessee's action. It is asserted that the amendment becomes operative as soon as it is ratified by the thirty-sixth State, and that proclamation by the State Department is a mere detail. According to this contention, the failure of the Secretary of State to proclaim the amendment would not prevent its inclusion in the Constitution. However, as no question has been raised formally in this instance, the State Department will wait for formal notification before the proclamation is issued.

The Woman's Party has wired Sue White, its Tennessee State Chairman, to have the certificate of ratification forwarded at once to Secretary Colby in order that he may have it on hand to sign it the moment the time for reconsideration has expired.

No Fear of Efforts to Reconsider.

"We do not fear the results of the efforts to reconsider," Miss Paul said, "but we shall, of course, do everything possible to prevent such action. We are informed by our workers in Nashville that the forces opposing suffrage, as soon as the vote was taken, began attacks on our men to induce a sufficient number of them to remain at home for the next two days in order that the reconsideration measure might be passed and the amendment defeated.

"They are reported to be saying to our men: "You have done everything you need to do now to please the suffragists; all you need to do for us is to stay at home for two days.' We are confident that none of the men who voted for us today will agree to such tactics.

"The vote in the Tennessee House today showed that we had one more vote than the necessary clear majority of fifty, since the two men who failed to vote were strong suffragists. One of them was unable to leave his home because of his own illness, the other was with his wife, who is critically ill. Both of these absent men were Republicans.

"In addition to these two men fourteen Republican members voted for ratification, which means that the Republicans have enlisted on the side of ratification more than a majority of their delegation in the House—a record of which they may well be proud."

The United States Attorney General has announced that no legislation will be necessary to make the Amendment operative, since the Suffrage Amendment is identical, except as to subject matter, with the Fifteenth Amendment, and that Amendment has been ruled to be self-executory and to render inoperative contrary provisions of State Constitutions or statutes.

In regard to legislation providing the necessary funds or machinery for the registration of women and their voting, in the majority of States it has been decided that none will be required. Virginia, New Hampshire, Minnesota, Massachusetts and Mississippi have already passed enabling acts.

The Attorney Generals of Maryland, New Mexico, North Carolina, Ohio and West Virginia have rendered special opinions that no legislation is necessary. The Governor of Missouri has stated that he will call a special session of the Legislature if it is found necessary. The Attorney General of Georgia has announced that there will be opportunity for women to register in October for the November election.

There is still some question as to the necessity for legislation in Alabama, Connecticut, Delaware, New Jersey, Pennsylvania, South Carolina and Vermont.

First Submitted in 1919.

The suffrage amendment to the Federal Constitution, which its advocates have designated "the Susan B. Anthony amendment," was submitted to the several States in 1919. The House of Representatives in January, 1918, adopted the resolution submitting the amendment for ratification. On May 21, 1919, the House readopted the resolution, and on June 4, 1919, it was adopted by the Senate. The amendment was thereupon submitted to the States.

The text of the amendment follows:

Section 1. The right of citizens of the United States to vote shall not be denied or abridged by the United States or by any State on account of sex.

Section 2. Congress shall have power, by appropriate legislation, to enforce the provisions of this article.

Wisconsin was the first to ratify. Its Legislature completed the ratification on June 10, 1919, six days after the resolution submitting the amendment was adopted by the United States Senate. Michigan ratified the amendment on the same day and before the end of the year twenty-one States had taken favorable action. The last State to ratify before Tennessee was Washington, whose Legislature completed the process by unanimous vote on March 22, 1919.

No statement came from the White House today as to President Wilson's view on the action of the Tennessee Legislature, but it was explained there that the President withheld his comment until the pending motion to reconsider in the Tennessee house had been disposed of.

Telegrams of Congratulation.

Secretary Daniels, who had labored to have his own State of North Carolina effect the thirty-sixth ratification, sent the following telegram to Governor Roberts of Tennessee:

Congratulations. The Volunteer State has done itself a lasting honor in insuring the women of America an equal voice in government.

Wayne B. Wheeler, general counsel of the Anti-Saloon League, gave out a statement in which he said that the new Constitutional Amendment made it easier to enforce national prohibition. The statement follows:

The ratification of the Nineteenth Amendment makes the fight to maintain and enforce national prohibition much easier. Not all women favor prohibition, but an overwhelming majority of them favor it, and they will naturally favor a Congress to sustain it and enforce it. Liquor interests have always been aggressively against woman suffrage. The women know it and they will naturally not help an outlawed enemy to be reinstated.

The following telegrams were sent by Miss Paul:

To Governor Cox:

On behalf of the National Woman's Party, representing women in every State of the Union, I wish to express to you our sincere appreciation of your splendid and continued help in the campaign for ratification of suffrage. Your aid has been invaluable in winning today's victory.

To Senator Harding:

On behalf of the National Woman's Party, representing women in every State of the Union, I wish to express our deep appreciation of your co-operation in the campaign for the ratification of suffrage. Your aid has been of great help in winning the large Republican vote in the Tennessee Legislature.

To Governor Roberts:

On behalf of the National Woman's Party, representing women in every State in the Union, permit me to offer our hearty congratulations on your splendid fight for ratification and our sincere appreciation of your continued and able work for enfranchisement of American women.

Miss Paul Issues a Statement.

The following statement was made by Miss Paul, as Chairman of the National Woman's Party:

"The victory of women today completes the political democracy of America and enfranchises half the people of a great nation.

"It is a victory which has been won not by an individual or group, but by all those women who since the time of the Revolution have suffered and protested against the humiliation of disfranchisement and proclaimed the equality of men and women.

"All women of the United States are now entitled to vote in the coming elections on the same basis as men. But our work cannot yet end. Ratification must be protected in the courts against the attacks of its opponents. It must be safeguarded, if possible, by the winning of a thirty-seventh State.

"In certain States, also, provision must be made for admitting women to the polls and providing for their registration in accordance with the law. The Woman's Party at once will get in touch with the Attorney General of each State with the object of aiding in this matter, which we anticipate will cause no difficulty or delay.

"With their power to vote achieved, women still have before them the task of supplementing political equality with equality in all other fields.

"In State and national legislation, as well as in other fields, women are not yet on an equal basis with men. The vote will make it infinitely easier for them to end all discriminations, and they will use the vote toward that end.

"The National Woman's Party, organized in 1913 to secure the passage of the Federal suffrage amendment, has accomplished the purpose for which it was founded. It will meet in convention within the next two months to decide upon its future."

Following is the list of the States that have ratified the suffrage amendment, with the dates of ratification and the political affiliations of the Governor and the majority of the Legislature:

State.	Governor.	Legislature.	Date.
Wisconsin	R.	R.	June 10
Michigan	R.	R.	June 10
Kansas	R.	R.	June 16
Ohio	D.	R.	June 16
New York	D.	R.	June 16
Illinois	R.	R.	June 17
Pennsylvania	R.	R.	June 24
Massachusetts	R.	R.	June 25
Texas	D.	D.	June 29
Iowa	R.	R.	July 2
Missouri	D.	Divided	July 3
Arkansas	D.	D.	July 30
Montana	D.	D.	July 30
Nebraska	R.	R.	Aug. 2
Minnesota	R.	R.	Sep. 8
New Hampshire	R.	R.	Sep. 10
Utah	D.	D.	Sep. 30
California	R.	R.	Nov. 1
Maine	R.	R.	Nov. 5
North Dakota	R.	R.	Dec. 1
South Dakota	R.	R.	Dec. 4
Colorado	R.	R.	Dec. 8
Rhode Island	R.	R.	Jan. 6
Kentucky	R.	Divided	Jan. 6
Oregon	R.	R.	Jan. 12
Indiana	R.	R.	Jan. 16
Wyoming	R.	R.	Jan. 27
Nevada	D.	Divided	Feb. 7
New Jersey	R.	R.	Feb. 10
Idaho	R.	R.	Feb. 11
Arizona	R.	D.	Feb. 12
New Mexico	R.	D.	Feb. 19
Oklahoma	D.	D.	Feb. 27
West Virginia	D.	D.	Mar. 10
Washington	R.	R.	Mar. 22
Tennessee	D.	D.	Aug. 18

The following States defeated ratification:

State.	Governor.	Legislature.	Date.
Alabama	D.	D.	Sep. 2
Georgia	D.	D.	July 24
Mississippi	D.	D.	Jan. 21
South Carolina	D.	D.	Jan. 24
Virginia	D.	D.	Feb. 12
Maryland	D.	D.	Feb. 17
Delaware	R.	R.	June 2
North Carolina	D.	D.	Aug. 17
Louisiana	D.	D.	June 15

The States which have not acted are:

State.	Governor.	Legislature.
Connecticut	R.	R.
Vermont	R.	R.
Florida	D.	D.

The following foreign States and Dominions have granted woman suffrage: Isle of Man, 1881; New Zealand, 1893; Australia, 1902; Finland, 1906; Poland, 1918; Scotland, 1918; Austria, 1918; Czechoslovakia, 1918; Hungary, 1918; Holland, 1919; British East Africa, 1919; Luxemburg, 1919; Uruguay (municipal), 1919; Norway, 1907; Denmark, 1915; Mexico, 1917; Russia, 1917; Ireland, 1918; Wales, 1918; Canada, 1918; Germany, 1918; England, 1918; Belgium, 1919; Rhodesia, 1919; Iceland, 1919; Sweden, 1919.

It is estimated that there are 23,883,566 women of voting age in the United States, of whom about 5,000,000 are aliens. This means that more than 22,000,000 women will be able to vote under the suffrage amendment to the Federal Constitution. The men of voting age in the country are estimated to number 29,577,690, including aliens. About 11,000,000 women citizens of voting age living in States that have not had woman suffrage will be entitled to vote under the new amendment.

On the basis of the 1920 census it is estimated that there are 3,033,273 women of voting age, including aliens, in New York State. The estimated number of men in New York State of voting age, including aliens, is 3,119,773.

About 17,000,000 women are already entitled to vote for President of the United States under State laws. About 7,000,000 already had the right to vote for members of Congress under State laws.

In thirteen States women have the right to vote for President. Barring the States that had previously given full voting rights to women electors, Illinois was the first to grant this privilege. That was in 1913. North Dakota followed suit in 1917, with Nebraska a close third. The others are Tennessee, Rhode Island, Indiana, Iowa, Maine, Minnesota, Missouri, Wisconsin, Ohio and Kentucky.

Two States, Arkansas and Texas, have given women the right to vote in primary elections. Alaska has given women an equal share with men in its government.

WOMEN ARE JUBILANT; ANTIS PROMISE APPEAL

Legal Fight Threatened Over Successful Outcome of Half-Century Suffrage Fight.

Hailing the suffrage victory as bringing added opportunity and responsibility to American women, Mrs. Carrie Chapman Catt, President of the National American Woman Suffrage Association, applauded the Tennessee Legislature in a statement issued yesterday.

"Tennessee has thus closed sixteen years of woman's struggle for the right to have their prayers counted on Election Day," said Mrs. Catt. "The ratification of the amendment is more than a victory for us. In the hour of victory there is but one regret and that is that every man and woman in the nation does not share our joy. Today there are those yet too blinded by prejudice to recognize the justice and inevitability of woman suffrage. But tomorrow we know that we shall work together for the common good of this great nation."

The opposing forces expressed their views through Miss Mary G. Kilbreth, President of the National Association Opposed to Woman Suffrage. She told a TIMES reporter over the telephone from her Long Island home that she was "bitterly disappointed," but declared that all preparations for a legal fight against the amendment had been made, and that the right of the Tennessee Legislature to sit in special session on the measure would be questioned in the courts of that State.

"If the amendment has really been passed," she said, "it means that a blow has been struck at representative government, and that the balance of power between the Federal Government and the States has been destroyed. I cannot believe that the members of the Tennessee Legislature, whom we counted upon have allowed themselves to be swayed by petty politics and failed us. But the legal steps we shall take have been carefully formed, and we shall carry our case to the United States Supreme Court if need be."

Mrs. Frank A. Vanderlip, Chairman of the New York State League of Women Voters, expressed pleasure over the suffrage ratification. She likened yesterday to Armistice Day, saying that to her "the great war and the battle for women's votes were very much alike."

The League of Women Voters, according to statements made yesterday, will continue to function as a national body, devoting itself to urging legislative reforms and educating the new women voters regardless of party lines.

The National American Suffrage Association will pass out of official existence in January, 1922, the two years being allotted for the winding up of affairs. It is expected that the rank and file of its workers and many of its leaders will transfer their activities in the future to the National League of Women Voters. The latter is preparing to meet any attacks which may be made on the new amendment, the New York headquarters stated. It rejects as ridiculous the statement that the next Presidential election may be thrown out as invalid by opponents on account of the women's participation.

"21 PLUS" CLUB WINS.

Topeka Women Voters Register Without Giving Exact Ages.

Special to The New York Times.

TOPEKA, Kan., July 23.—The "21 Plus" Club, which has been organized here as the result of the controversy over the City Clerk's efforts to force women to tell their exact age as a requirement to registration, is rapidly gaining in popularity.

Two Topeka women, Mrs. Margaret Hill McCarter, writer and politician, and Mrs. Lee Monroe, president of the Women's Good Government Club and the Kansas Women Lawyers' Association, walked into the office of the City Clerk yesterday and obtained certificates entitling them to vote at the next primary.

Last week registration was refused to Mrs. McCarter because she declined to give her age. Mrs. Monroe took up the fight and demanded a ruling by the Attorney General. Yesterday he gave his opinion that it was not necessary to give ages other than proof or oath that the registrant was "over 21."

BAR NEGRO WOMEN'S VOTE.

Savannah Judges Refuse Their Vote ——White Women Stay Away.

SAVANNAH, Ga., Nov. 2.—Ballots were refused negro women at the voting places in Savannah today. Many negro women had registered since the suffrage amendment became effective, but the election judges ruled they were not entitled to vote because of a State law which requires registration six months before an election.

No white women presented themselves at the polls.

CHAPTER 2
The Twenties

Emma Goldman, "dangerous anarchist,"
returns to the U.S. after 15 years exile, 1934.
Courtesy Compix.

FINDS 1920 WOMAN SAD, BUT FRIVOLOUS

Marcelle Tinayre Takes the "Golden-Robed Dancer" as Typical of the War Reaction.

SEES MAD DESIRE TO FORGET

But After a Slow Process of Adaptation, the French Writer Pedicts a Saner Womanhood Tomorrow.

By EDWIN L. JAMES.

Copyright. 1920, by The New York Times Company.
Special Cable to THE NEW YORK TIMES.

PARIS, Feb. 1.—"The woman of to-day, in her dancing, pleasure-seeking frivolity, is in a process of adaptation which will bring saner results tomorrow." Such is the thesis of Mme. Marcelle Tynaire, the well-known writer who in an address to a Congress of Women's Clubs today, recalled that a similar condition followed other wars. She says there is no joy in the life of pleasure such as the women of Paris follow today, and she urged men to help them think more sober thoughts and live quieter days.

"Have you noticed," she asked, "that the women of 1920 are not gay? Frantically they exert themselves morally and physically. Never before have they so madly danced in golden and costly robes. Under the colored lights and in the voluptuous surroundings of modern dancing palaces some hundreds of women—always the same women—tango and fox-trot. As in Paris, so in London and Berlin. From the wine shops of the suburbs, where the phonograph takes the place of the orchestra, to the other end of the social scale the silk stockinged and slippered feet are always on the move.

"Never have women worn more jewels and more furs. Never have men worked harder to dress them, perfume them and bejewel them than now when men are scarce and needed for other work. And not only the women of the demi-monde and the newly rich lead this life, but also the women of the people to the extent of their means, now greater than ever, who if they do not find in it happiness find a sort of revenge for past deprivations.

"Never before were there so many kitchen maids in feathers, so many midinettes with frizzled hair and faces rouged, never so many working girls who rush from factory to hairdressers.

"Older women and scandalized men, suffocated by the spectacle of customs which were not of their youth, shake their heads and say that things are not as they used to be. They forget that their grandfathers and grandmothers did the same sort of thing forty years ago.

"However, is it not true that in other days if we were really no more virtucus or wiser than today we were at least happier? Our parents have told us how rapidly after the war of 1870 France repaired her damages and healed her wounds. What was accomplished in defeat we seem not able to accomplish in victory. It seems her soul tried in the great war effort is not yet able to make the less 'sublime but none the less necessary effort. The social ills of today are so vast and so profound, the outcome is so uncertain, that the stoutest hearts are sometimes sad. Halt in her mad whirl the golden-dressed dancer who swings in magic circles as if to escape from herself. Look in her eyes, listen to her laughter, and you will find among her vain thoughts a strange fear, a sentiment of unrest, and almost crazy desire to forget yesterday, tomorrow, and herself.

"But this dancer is not the modern woman. She is only one of the aspects of modern women. Think of those who do not dance, those whom grief weighs down, those who have become heads of families, and those who never will have families. You find among them the same melancholy unrest, but they smother it with the resignation of courage. But in their souls you find virtues the dancer of the golden robe does not possess.

"All women on the morrow of the war are in a process of adaptation, and we see that they have not become completely adapted to a form of life which astonishes them and hurts them."

MARRIED LIFE IS ART, SAYS MISS PICKFORD

Movie Star and Husband Come to New York to Arrange for More Dividends.

SHE LIKES REPUBLICANS

Fairbanks Says He Agrees with Mack Sennett That Matrimony Is "Not a War Picture."

Mary, of the movies, gazed into the depths of the lemonade glass, gingerly captured the maraschino in the bottom, and remarked that although she wasn't a good cook she could boil water, and that while she couldn't sew worth a button she didn't have to, "'cause I can make more money in the pictures."

And husband Douglas Fairbanks, with a picture of what the newly organized United Artists, Inc., is going to offer in the form of dividends, grinned and said he thought that was about right.

Mr. and Mrs. Fairbanks arrived yesterday at the Ritz, after a jaunt across country from Hollywood, Cal. The screen couple invited reporters to the Ritz to sip lemonade and hear all about what's been happening to Mary and Doug these last few months.

The tearful, wistful little lady of the silent drama wasn't a bit tearful or a bit wistful yesterday. She was, you might say, decidedly chipper. After some pictures on the roof, she said:

Calls Married Life an Art.

"How do I regard married life? Well, married life is an art. It is something that must be carefully attended to. Nope, I am not going to write a book or anything else. Everybody seems to be writing something these days. Go into the subway, and it's ten to one that the folks on either side of you, if you've been lucky enough to get a seat, are writing something, or planning to do so. I wrote some scenarios once. The first one was 'Madame X.' I did that for Vitagraph, and I got $25 for it.

"I wrote another immediately after that, but I guess it wasn't so good, 'cause they gave me only $15 for that. I guess that I've written about thirty-five scenarios altogether."

Politics and religion are two things, remarked Mrs. Fairbanks, that are strictly non-interviewable. She did mention, however, that the Republicans were all right and that Douglas was keen for T. R.

"Mother," who was there also, said Mary "is the business brain. I just second the motion she offers," and she went on to tell how much money it takes to bring out a movie. She said there are times when a big staff of extras are camping around Hollywood, when the Pickford-Fairbanks pay roll, leaving Mary's stipend out of it, runs to $10,000 a week. And, again, there are times when Mary's time is worth $100 a minute.

"Married Life: Not War Picture."

Then Doug himself came into the picture. He was a bunch of California tan, gray checks and a grin. He talked as he acts—fast, and full of ambition. Get him on married life:

"Well," he lighted a cigarette as Bill Hart does, "Mack Sennett's just named a picture—'Married Life: Not a War Picture.' Good, isn't it? I agree with Sennett."

Then Doug launched into a full and vivid account of what a rip-snorting time all hands had when they dropped in to pay the Hopi Indians a friendly little visit. He was going strong, telling how the Indians put one over on Dr. Baer—they pitch 'em over a cliff and pray to the Rain God, it seems—when he happened to mention something about Hopi domestic arrangements. Mary set down the lemonade and interjected:

"We've too many servants out at Nevely. Doug's awfully extravagant. We ought to have less, but then I guess we can't. He's always bringing people home to dinner. And just funny people. One day he had an ex-prizefighter, 'Bull' Montana, a dwarf, a Polish immigrant, a tramp and two cats. I don't know why he brought the cats home. Goodness me, we've enough cats and pets out there now. How many? Let's see. Well, we've sixteen Alaskan dogs, twelve cats, twenty canaries, a Jersey cow and six horses."

There was a lot of conversation like that, but, after all, the main thing is that Doug and Mary have come East for a while to elect a new President of the United Artists—formed to handle the output of Fairbanks, Pickford, Chaplin et al.

ELLIS ISLAND DOUBTS WAR WEDDINGS' RISE

Passage of Calder-Siegel Bill Found Illiterate Fiancees Admitted Under Bond.

The passage by Congress of the Calder-Siegel bill exempting from the literacy test soldiers' fiancées arriving in this country, will not mean any unusual increase in the number of those marriages, it was said yesterday at Ellis Island, as the brides-to-be held there because of the literacy test had been released under bonds about two months ago and that since their release some of them had married and as the wives of American citizens were not subject to deportation. The new law will benefit women who are engaged to marry soldiers and who have remained abroad fearing that the literacy test would prevent their entrance into this country.

The brides-to-be who were detained at Ellis Island because they could not read and write were admitted under bond and there was what might have been called "a gentleman's agreement" between the bondsmen and the Government that there were to be no weddings until some way was found to straighten out the tangle. Love, however, was not always daunted by agreements, so some of the women married. In these cases the bonds will be canceled and the case closed.

The case which is said to have influenced passage of the law exempting such aliens from the literacy test was that of Maria Taccomini, a pretty Italian girl who came here to marry Alfonzo Mastrodi, who saw service first with the Italian Army and later under General Pershing, and was gassed at Verdun. Maria could not read the number of words required by law, and although she could write her name, it was simply copying, as she did not know one letter from the other.

Almost every day Alfonzo came to Ellis Island and tried to teach her to read and write. Progress was slow and even the kindly matron did not think the Italian girl would ever possess sufficient knowledge to meet the requirements of the law. One day Alfonzo appeared rejoicing with a letter from Senator Calder saying that this bill would soon be passed.

Another interesting case was that of a beautiful Greek girl, Vasiliki Demopolas, brought by her brother, Demetrius Demopolas of Chicago, so that she might become the wife of Samuel Thedos of that city. The schools of her neighborhood had been neglected because of wars and she was without education. The girl spent many weary months at Ellis Island waiting for the passage of the Calder bill. Finally word came from Washington that all the war brides who could not pass the literacy test should be released for sixty days on bond and Demetrius Demopolas, who had obtained temporary employment in Port Chester, N. Y., obtained his sister's release.

The new law extends exemption for five years. How many illiterate brides will be admitted is speculative.

June 6, 1920

MARRYING COLLEGE GIRLS

NOT so very many years ago the woman who could boast of a college education or a college degree didn't do it. If she did it was upon pain of social obscurity. Confession of education or erudition beyond that of the finishing school or a trip abroad meant the courting of a life spent in a setting which consisted of a lone chair and a bleak wall.

Tradition has it that such young martyrs, sitting with their feet primly crossed, while their less learned but apparently more charming sisters danced the "light fantastic," invariably clothed their ankles in blue stockings. The coincidence of the blue stockings may have been purely accidental, or it may have been the sign of a sacred cult, but at any rate, before very long the term "blue stockings" became anathema to all the desirable young men and the many scheming mammas who sought to entangle them in domestic webs. The wise young thing who knew so much about science and literature was a very lonely young person.

Time passed. Together with the many other changes that occurred came the ever-recurrent changes in fashions. The more popular sister of the learned and very lonely young thing went through the whole gamut of styles, through frills and furbelows and balloons and bouffons. Finally she came to the sensible but not unattractive sports clothes which had become necessary for the new type of recreation. In an endeavor to be different, to give comfort to the masculine eye accustomed to the all white of the seashore and mountain resort costume, some of the more daring and original hit upon the idea of introducing a bit of color into their costume. Either utterly oblivious of the contumely that went with blue stockings or consciously desirous of smashing an old-fashioned convention, the first thing they adopted was the navy blue silk stocking which, they discovered, went exceedingly well with a white frock or a white suit.

Tradition was smashed with a bang. Blue stockings grew popular over night. The college girl became all the "go." That wasn't all. The war came. The girls who wore frills and feathers were left behind. But—the girls who came honestly by the right of wearing blue stockings were asked to go over and help make life pleasanter for the boys in the trenches. As a patriotic duty, the blue-stockinged girls went, leaving an Adamless Eden behind them, so to say.

Once more, as this version has it, scheming mammas put their heads together and not only came to the conclusion that a college education was a necessary adjunct in a young woman's social career, but, what's more, insisted that it was indispensable in the pursuit of the life work of their daughters—which was quite true, irrespective of what the life work was intended to be.

In any event, there has been an almost overwhelming increase in the number of applications for admission to women's colleges. Smith, Wellesley, Bryn Mawr, Vassar and scores of others report that young American womanhood is knocking at their gates.

An idea of the increase in popularity of the colleges may be gained from the following figures given by Wellesley:

1915—732 on application list Feb. 1.
1916—871 on application list Feb. 1.
1917—937 on application list Feb. 1.
1918—960 on application list Feb. 1.
1919—1,099 on application list Feb. 1. List closed.
1920—1,447 on application list Jan. 15. List closed.

A request for an explanation of the increase of students brought forth the statements showing that a variety of causes played a part in the increase. This is one:

"One reason for the increase undoubtedly is the fact that it has become 'the thing' for women to go to college far more than it was ten years ago. The colleges are receiving a great many girls who come primarily because of the enjoyment that they think they will get from 'the life.' Luckily, a good many of these are really good college material. Some, of course, are not, and are not very advantageous to the college. The proportion of these is not yet large enough to be a serious menace—it is certainly nothing like the proportion of the same type in the leading colleges and universities for men; and we are hoping that the examination-only plan of admission may further reduce their numbers.

"The main reason for the increase is, I am convinced, the increasing desire of women to take an active part in the life about them. The fact that they do not need to earn their living makes no difference to them. In fact, some of the students of largest means are the very ones who are taking the opportunities of college most seriously and are planning to go on with professional courses after leaving. I think of several such students recently graduated who are going into the study of medicine, for instance. Those who do not have any idea of a special vocation have the feeling, I believe, that college will give them contact with varieties of people, representing varieties of opinion, tradition, character, and power, which will be valuable for their life as citizens.

"I am glad to say that in spite of the increase of wealth represented we have not seen signs of decrease of the right democratic spirit. The leaders of student opinion and activity are likely to come from the house in which the students do the housework to get a reduction in board. When, in an emergency, the college has to ask students to volunteer as waitresses, or, as this Spring, to help clean up the grounds, the volunteers will include all sorts and conditions of incomes and social positions, working together without any consciousness of difference between the girl who is doing it because she has to earn the extra dollars and the girl who is only helping out because she is needed and has more money than she can easily spend."

The fact that applicants at Bryn Mawr may choose their rooms upon being accepted for admission may have something to do with the unusual number of advance applications received. The registrar there reports that already a number of applications for the year 1931-32 have been received. In a large number of instances these applications are filed by the parent or the aunt of the girl who desires that her kin occupy the same room she did when she was a student.

Another interesting explanation given by this college for the increase in enrollment is the war. To quote:

"The war has undoubtedly, however, had a marked effect in increasing the general interest in women's education. This is probably because of the greater seriousness with which women look upon life and the possibility of usefulness during such a time and also, perhaps, because the need of self-support appears to be more general. The increase in the number of women students may also be somewhat due to the fact that brothers have been called to war and are not in college, and in cases where it is impossible for both brothers and sisters to go, a greater chance is thus given to the sisters.

"There has been a gradual increase for years in the number of women who go to college. There was a sudden spurt during the war and on the whole there seems to have been no decrease since the war is over."

Vassar brings out the interesting information that so great is the advance enrollment for the next five years that the college is virtually closed to girls who are now entering the high schools of the country. The situation there as explained by the registrar is as follows: "Vassar College, by order of the Trustees, limits its enrollment of students to the number that can be housed and cared for within the college. Ten years ago, at the time of the establishment of this rule, 1,000 was the limitation fixed. Slight additional space makes it possible to accommodate a few more than 1,100, though the regulation still reads 'one thousand.' The great argument in favor of this limitation is that increasing numbers of students, resulting in the overcrowding of residence halls, classrooms and laboratories, lessens the value of the college life and experience to each student.

"Vassar makes a single charge to each student for tuition, board and lodging, and, naturally, is under obligation to provide all of these things in proper quality throughout the four years of residence.

"This limited enrollment has led parents to enroll their students in advance, often in their babyhood, and there are between 5,000 and 6,000 names thus enrolled at the present time at Vassar, so that so far as this advance enrollment is concerned the lists are closed for classes of girls who are now entering high school

"The danger of this policy is that Vassar might thus become an aristocratic, one-class institution, admitting only those girls who are so well-to-do that they know so long in advance that they will certainly be able to go to college. In order to prevent this, and to secure the first-class student of limited means, 100 places in the entering class are left open until the last moment, that is, until June preceding entrance, and any who wish may try for a place in that 'Honor Group' of 100 students by competitive examination. It is not unusual for a student to sacrifice her place in the enrolled list in order to take a 'sporting chance' at this Honor Group of 100. It is not impossible that some day the entire entering class will be, as at West Point, selected by competition.

"Although Vassar thus limits her entering classes, we feel here very definitely the increasing pressure for entrance, due to changing social conditions. During the war the applications for admission increased in great proportion. Young women who had up to that time planned to 'finish' at school, then 'come out' into society, suddenly realized their lack of equipment and organized ability to do anything useful in the world. Not only the women's colleges, but the women's departments in co-educational institutions, felt this change of attitude.

"The increase continues. There was at one time a feeling among young women with social aspirations that college was incompatible. They have discovered that the educated woman takes a more important place in every sort of society today than the uneducated one, and they are clamoring for admission.

"The solution, for women's colleges even more than for men's colleges, is not larger institutions, where there will be less intimate relationship between Faculty and students and less supervision, but more institutions. We must have more colleges for women. A raising of the qualifications for entrance and the standards required after entrance does not affect the situation so far as Vassar is concerned. Both of these things have been done, and we are receiving more requests for admission than ever before."

The situation at Smith College, another of the big women's colleges of the country, is the same. Applications for admission are far in excess of the space available. In order to assure their daughters' education mothers are enrolling them at early periods. Perhaps the most forehanded case reported is that of the enrollment of twins of the age of one day.

August 22, 1920

THE DOWNTRODDEN SEX

By SAMUEL SALOMAN.

THREE-QUARTERS of a century ago a small group of determined women, led by Susan Brownell Anthony, began their campaign to make this a "true republic," granting "men their rights and nothing more; women their rights and nothing less." The work of these women and their equally determined successors finally was crowned with success. General enfranchisement of women, the first and foremost goal of the crusaders, was had by methods that will not bear too close inspection. In this the newly enfranchised female citizen enjoyed a distinct advantage over the male. The latter must with his citizenship assume military and other burdens, while his sister is called upon to assume no unpleasant and dangerous duties as compensation to the State for the advantages that citizenship undoubtedly confers. To that extent citizenship to women is all gain and no loss.

In the legal field woman had won substantial victories even before she had achieved the ballot. In this she went far beyond her goal in many of the States. Demanding her "rights and nothing less," that man be shorn of those privileges that trespassed on those of his sister, she won her rights, and a great deal more, and so dangerously trespassed on the legitimate rights of the other sex.

Marriage and divorce furnish many examples of the inequalities of the law as it affects the sexes in this day. There, it will be admitted, the law especially favors woman and is decidedly unfavorable to the man.

Under the laws of many of the States the marriage copartnership is a most unequal and inequitable one, with practically all the burdens and obligations on the male and the profits and privileges to the female partner to the arrangement.

When a man marries he automatically, according to the laws of practically all, if not all, of the States, assumes the financial burdens of his other and supposedly "better half"; he is responsible for all her debts (at least those contracted after marriage) and obligates himself properly and generously to contribute to her support. She, on her part, even if plentifully supplied with the world's goods, is free to give of her means or to withhhold needed assistance altogether should the man meet with misfortune, and the law upholds her in her course.

During a symposium on woman suffrage some years ago before one of the Washington, D. C., organizations, with Mrs. Belva A. Lockwood, sometime Presidential candidate, advocate of "equal rights" for women, as the principal speaker, the point was made by one of the opposition that generally man was compelled by the law to provide for his wife, even if she were in position generously to provide for herself, but that the woman is under no legal compulsion to care for her sick, infirm, or disabled spouse, could even drive him into the streets if she felt so disposed.

In true feminine fashion, Mrs. Lockwood retorted that no real woman could be so inhuman as to act thus under the conditions indicated. It was suggested that no real man would shirk his duty, but the law nevertheless discriminates between the man and the woman, holds the legal club over the man and leaves the woman to her conscience and the more or less compelling force of public opinion.

Recently a friend, an earnest advocate of full political "rights" for women, complained to me that his wife had left his bed and board and had taken up quarters in a neighboring city. He wanted to know if there was any way to compel her to return. I said that he might find some comfort in the legal fact that she was full mistress of herself, that although she had taken the solemn oath during the marriage ceremony to love, honor and obey, the law left her entirely free to honor or dishonor such pledge. I in-

proceeded to pick quarrels over frivolous matters, and eventually left my house after reiterating her demand that I make a division of my property. She has kept away from me, refusing to see me when I called upon her or attempted to do so, refusing to answer any letters from me, keeping absolutely silent, evidently relying upon her stranglehold upon me to compel accedence with her demands. The result is that I cannot borrow or sell to protect myself, the mortgagees are foreclosing, and I will lose everything simply because I fell a victim to the wiles of a woman who I thought had affection for me. The law protects her, and will do nothing for me, and only by a circuitous and expensive course can she be circumvented."

In some few of the States the man has a dower right in the estate of his wife; generally he has no legal claim to any part of her property, while she inherits on his death, will or no will, a definite fraction of his estate. A case that recently came to my attention will show the injustice of the law in that respect.

A friend in the District of Columbia by hard work and denial managed to acquire a piece of real estate. He did as so many loving and considerate husbands do, signed over the property to his wife. She died without will or direct issue, and the property—by the laws of God if not of man his property—automatically went to her sisters, with whom the man had nothing in common, leaving him virtually penniless.

Another howling injustice against the man and in the interest of the woman is the matter of alimony following divorce. It would seem that with divorce—the severance of the marriage copartnership—the obligation of one of the parties to support the other definitely ceases. But generally man still is liable for whole or partial support of one who has no equitable claim on him. In the event that he fails to meet the legal requirement and does not contribute a designated sum to his own "parasite woman" he is branded as a felon and committed to jail, without even the formality of a trial. Some debts are outlawed after a stated period of time.. Not so the debt the man is said to owe to a divorced wife in some of the States, which increases month after month and eventually becomes a crushing liability to the man.

A recent decision by one of the Washington (D. C.) Judges makes

dicated that if the shoe had been on the other foot, if he had left his wife, even if he had good and sufficient reason for such action, the law would regard it as a criminal move on his part, and he could be arrested as a common felon, could be imprisoned if he refused to contribute toward her support and such children as supposedly were born to them.

In the vital matter of property holding the law generally favors the woman and discriminates against the man. Woman's property, as a rule is entirely within her keeping, to dispose of as she desires; in man's real property the wife has an equity, and the man may not lawfully dispose of same without the written

consent of his other half. This law occasionally results to his disadvantage, as indicated by an interesting letter to THE NEW YORK TIMES a few years ago, signed "Elderly Husband." The letter in part follows:

"At present all a young woman has to do is to inveigle an elderly man with real property into a marriage by protestations of affection and those arts so well understood by women, and later making demands upon him and leaving him, thus tying his hands, so far as his real property is concerned.

"Take my own case, for instance. Two years ago I was the owner of considerable property, heavily mortgaged. One day my wife, to whom I had been married but a year, remarked to me, 'I want you to hurry and sell this property and give me my half.' Somewhat surprised, I said: 'There is no half coming to you until I die, and then you can have it all.' Then my wife remarked: 'You cannot sell this property.'. She then, together with her mother, alimony a preferred claim. Thus:

" The payment of alimony is a preferred claim over everything else. When a husband is ordered to pay alimony he must take his medicine and pay or go to jail for violation of the court's order. Better get behind in every other obligation and take the consequences, whatever they may be, than risk the chance of being sent to jail for contempt of court."

The Washington Post of Sept. 13, 1920, thus editorially comments on this extraordinary decision:

" Heretofore it has been the custom in many States for former husbands to avoid the payment of alimony on a variety of excuses. Some have pleaded the insufficiency of their income; others have fallen back upon the claim that their former wives are able to earn their own living and do not need alimony. And there are still others who have disappeared and paid no attention to the court's decree.

" But if Judge Gould's rule is to be adopted generally, an alimony decree will become as gilt-edged as a Government bond—more so, in fact, than a Liberty bond at present, since it will be subject to no discount. It will constitute a first lien upon the earnings and resources of the former husband. He may be forced to wear patched shoes and eat at dairy lunchrooms, but the alimony must be paid when due.

" General adoption of this rule might discourage divorces, so far as the men are concerned, and it might possibly encourage them among the women. With the prospect of an alimony check coming regularly every month, many women might be disinclined to bear with humility and patience the burdens which otherwise they would endure in silence."

In New York the divorcée, your true " parasite woman," had long tyrannized over the man who conscientiously objected to contribute to her support. Some men had carried their objections to the point where they willingly embraced martyrdom in the cause of justice, joining, as a matter of principle, the " Alimony Club," consisting of those confined to jail for violating the court decree.

For a time the statute of limitations prevailed in alimony cases in the Empire State, and it was possible for the man to free himself eventually of such unjust obligation by absenting himself from the State for a stated term of years. Lately, we are informed, the law was changed, and now the decree hangs over his head like a veritable sword of Damocles for all of his days. He now guilty of such form of " con-

tempt of court " is placed with those committing the major crimes, and may spend the balance of his days in a noisome cell in one of the jails for his heinous crime, unless the Judge or the woman relents.

Some members of the female sex, not satisfied with the law as it is, would make desertion and alimony neglect extraditable offenses, so making the man liable to arrest wherever he may be found and extradited with the murderer, the thief, and the other major criminals to the scene of his crime.

As briefly stated in an opening paragraph, citizenship means something more to the male than to the female.

The man, in return for the privilege of voting and holding office and for the protection he gets (oftentimes does not get) from the State, is forced to shoulder grievous burdens and obligates himself to yield up his liberty, his welfare, and his life, if need be, that the State may live. He is liable to jury duty and to all the calls of the State, and is forced at all times to throw aside personal interests for the public business. Every man, when called upon, must assist the police and other of the officials in the discharge of his duty. In the dread hour of war he is called to the colors, whether it suits his convenience of his fancy, and is penalized for refusal.

During the World War 24,234,021 men of military age (between 18 and 45) were forced to register, and 2,810,296 were selected for service to join the 2,000,000 and more who had volunteered or who were in the army and navy on the outbreak of war. And those able ones who were not called to the colors were plainly told that they would have to " work or fight," and to work in what the State had decreed " essential industries."

To the woman citizenship brings with it full protection (with special protection by reason of sex), the privilege of the ballot, of being appointed or elected to positions of honor or preferment. Practically no obligations or duties or burdens are assumed by the female sex in return for the privileges she so gracefully assumes. Generally she is called upon for no public services. And in the nation's hour of danger, all her services are voluntary ones.

In the late war many of the sex chose to play at public work, mainly pleasant, paying a larger salary than the woman had before enjoyed and that many of them ever had hoped for. Though some " patriotically " replaced men in industries, so that he could go to the " front," when

the hero returned the woman almost literally had to be pried from the position she had assumed for the duration of the war.

From the facts set forth it will be evident to one not really mentally blind that at present we have nothing that resembles even-handed justice between men and women; that the scales of the law ever incline in the direction of the " weaker sex," as women had been termed before " emancipation."

But the time has come for a change. With the incorporation of the Nineteenth (Anthony) Amendment into the fundamental law of the land there must be a new alignment of the sexes, a readjustment of the relations of the one sex toward the other.

Men for ages had been penalizing themselves voluntarily in the interest and for the benefit of the other and alleged weaker sex. So long as women were content to acknowledge in effect inequality, to some degree claim dependence upon the other and stronger sex, men willingly assumed what now are felt to be unjust burdens.

But a decided change brought about in the main by woman had come about in the last few years, and men now are beginning to feel that unequal and unjust laws should be swept from the statute books and woman shorn of what she is compelled to admit (if her protestations against inequality are at all sincere), are unjust advantages over men.

It is evident that women cannot be equal and unequal at one and the same time: that she cannot logically and justly claim full independence and at the same time receive those things justly due only to dependents.

Replying to a communication of mine to The Woman Citizen, in which the demand was made that if women insist on political equality they should, to be consistent, be willing to accept legal equality, Rose Young, editor in chief, said in her publication of Dec. 29, 1917:

" There can be no argument between us on the subject of discriminatory legislation in favor of women. Favoritism to one sex at the expense of the other works to no better advantage in economics than in politics, and the goal of the suffrage effort is to do away with these unevennesses all along the line.

" Even though it is true that there are offsetting discriminations against women along the exact line that you cite against men, it remains none the less true that any discriminations against men in favor of women can only react to the hurt of women as well as men. I think that most women have learned this, or are rapidly learning it. Almost all such discriminatory legislation against men is to be attributed either to a sort of makeshift effort to atone to women for the political disability under which she labors or to the fact that society is prone to consider discriminations in favor of women as being added safeguards for itself."

If the latter part of the sentence we have quoted from our very logical and consistent friend is at all true, that disposes of every claim feminists have made. If special consideration must be shown because of sex, it proves that the claim of equality ever advanced by a certain type of women is in no sense a valid one. If, on the other hand, such " discriminatory legislation against men " is to be attributed to a " sort of makeshift effort to atone to woman for the political disability under which she labors," the removal of such disability should carry with it the removal of legislation enacted especially for women.

Our very logical friend in a later paragraph of the same communication goes further toward equality than we dare to when she declares:

" I find myself in thorough accord with your suggestion that women be willing to renounce every privilege gained at the expense of man. Women who are not willing to renounce such privileges have not the welfare of the race at heart, for neither sex can profit at the expense of the other with advantage to the race. Men and women who are truly democratic are trying to move forward today to a plane where both sexes can function fully and freely without either encroaching upon the other."

The marriage relation, because of the changes that lately have taken place in human society, must be reconstituted. It is time that we had a real mutuality of interests in the marriage relationship, a just and equitable co-partnership, instead of the lopsided arrangement that now is too much in evidence.

Man, of course, in the new and expected order, will be expected to be the chief, if not the sole, provider; the woman, on her part, will be expected to shoulder the burden in the event that the man, for any legitimate cause, becomes incapacitated.

Property should be held in common, and the woman, as the man is now, should be compelled to secure the concurrence of her male partner before she is able to dispose of her real property. Man should be given an inheritance right in the property of his wife, as the wife now has in the property of the husband.

The woman, with the man, should be penalized for desertion, or the man in large part freed of the penalties that now attach to him alone.

Alimony award and the penalty that attaches to the man for refusing to heed an unjust court decree has no place in a civilization in which man and woman supposedly are equal. The learned editor of The Woman Citizen gracefully falls into this view, for we have her statement:

" Alimony, I consider, permits of the supremest travesty of justice to be found anywhere in our social institutions, and I am convinced that the woman who cannot fall back on political disability and cannot be exploited industrially, will be easily educated into a pride of economic independence which she cannot know under existing social and political limitations."

All in all, it is to be hoped that the women will not be content with a selfish victory; that they will by their deeds justify their pre-campaign assertions that political emancipation for women is one of the greatest forward steps in the progress of the race.

TALLEY WOULD BAR WOMEN.

Says Their Service in Home is Above That on a Jury.

Sheriff David H. Knott, who supervises the listing of jurors for service in all the courts, has been considering an amendment to the judiciary law permitting him to include women in the jury panels. The Sheriff submitted the problem to Judge Alfred J. Talley of General Sessions, who replied yesterday that a woman's place still continued to be the home and that the law of nature was supreme to the law of men and the political freedom recently accorded her.

"It is my thought that women should be free from jury service," wrote Judge Talley. "They should be exempted because the work which nature has designed for women is of paramount importance to any service which they might be called upon to perform on a jury. Some women may still storm against what they call the inequality of the law, but in their hearts they know that the law of nature is paramount to the law of man. The one is human, finite, fallible; the other is divine, and it is part of a divine plan that woman is destined and qualified for the bearing of the children of the race and for the creation and guardianship of the homes of the world and their maintenance in love and honor."

January 7, 1921

Ankle Curtains for Woman Jury.

SPRINGFIELD, Ohio, Feb. 18.—Keeping the promise he made to women jurors three weeks ago, Judge F. W. Geiger of the Common Pleas Court had "ankle curtains" put up today. The jury box is now surrounded by a beautiful green curtain, and behind this the ankles of the women jurors are shielded from the public gaze.

February 19, 1921

Is There a Decline in American Morals?

By GERTRUDE ATHERTON

The following article is printed here by courtesy of the Forum, and appears in the March number of that magazine.

IS there a moral decline?" How very odd that any one in the United States of America should ask such a question! No country since the world began has had so many moral guardians, self-imposed and legal. I merely touch upon the painful subject of prohibition and drop it. It is, and that is the end of it. (When it isn't—but that is by the way.) Think of the moving-picture censors, who will carefully eliminate from a picture the details of a convict's escape from prison, lest the youth in the audience turn criminal for the fun of breaking out. Think of the towns that are passing laws forbidding high heels, short skirts and transparent blouses. Think of the impending blue laws and the crusade against tobacco. Some years ago, by the way, twelve good women and true of Los Angeles, pillars of the W. C. T. U., called on me and extracted a promise (I was forced to give it or we should all be sitting there yet) that I would not smoke in public any more. Several times there had been front-page "stories" of this sensational breach of morality on my part, and the ignorant youth of the country (according to these good ladies) argued that if I smoked and retained my health and power to turn out a book a year or so, smoking was rather a virtue than a vice. I really gave my promise because I felt sorry for the women—they were so much in earnest, and it was not difficult to guess the large futility of their endeavors.

There is an old, generally ignored statute that any man or woman transgressing the moral code is liable to arrest and imprisonment. There is but one place I know of where this law is sometimes put into effect—Los Angeles, Cal. Some one has wittily said that the reason there is a scandal a day in the Southern California newspapers is because the methodist spirit is constantly at war with the climate. I should say the odds were in favor of the climate (after observations covering some seven months in Hollywood, the centre of the moving-picture industry), but occasionally the stern, uncompromising spirit of methodism triumphs and a delinquent is arrested. Whether it be true, as rumored, that certain men and women have found the law handy for revenge I am not in a position to say.

Let us consider our famous censor of morals in New York. No one can deny the tenderness of his care in suppressing such a book as "Jurgen." Think of the millions that might have been corrupted by reading that book. It is quite as immoral as "The Electra" of Sophocles or "The Turn of the Screw," by our own Henry James; but some things are bound to escape even the vigilant eye of our censor, and when he does happen upon a chance to prove his solicitude for public morality, then he uses his public office for all it is worth. That "Jurgen" is a masterpiece, one of the few in American literature, makes it all the more dangerous. So does the fact that the innocent mind would have to take a microscope to find the naughtiness (plain only to the highly sophisticated, who are beyond any censor's hope). Subtlety rightfully incurs the suspicion of any pillar of democracy. All cards should be on the table. Subtlety gives to think, and much thinking will find hidden wickedness even where none is intended. Save our youth (who are notoriously addicted to subtly written masterpieces) at all cost. So "Jurgen" now costs $50 a copy, and its author, Mr. Cabell, has taken to writing for the Yale Review, which, by the way, brazenly advertises its contributor as the author of "Jurgen." Will not the censor please suppress the Yale Review?

Now let us take what is admittedly the best novel (or chronicle) of 1920—"Main Street." (The Domesday Book, of course, is in a class by itself.) It must have sold a hundred thousand copies by this time, and I hope it will sell a million more. It portrays a small town typical of tens of thousands of small towns in the United States; and what is the impression that remains in one's memory after one has read a dozen or two other novels in bed at night? Is it a mad orgy of dancing, immorality, crime, a repetition of ancient Rome and still more ancient Atlantis? Oh, no! Not by a long sight. It is the history of a people who are sordid, mean and petty, vulgar, common, unambitious, backbiting, ill-educated, suspicious of any attempt, even of amateur attempts, to improve what passes for their minds; smug, conceited and vicious as a lioness bereft of her cubs over any suspected moral lapse. Of course the book is onesided. There are estimable, mentally ambitious, openly or secretly immoral, traveled and broad-minded people in every small town; human nature in its infinite variety, cropping out everywhere from mountain hamlets to desert islands temporarily inhabited by castaways. But in the main it is true; Mr. Lewis has concerned himself with the majority, and

111

"There is a curious superstition that when a nation begins to dance its downfall is at hand."

the majority rules when it comes to atmosphere. There is no evidence in this chronicle of Main Streets of America that the dancing craze, popularly supposed to inaugurate the downfall of nations, has taken possession of our middle class, and is not the middle class the backbone of any nation? Nor is any tendency to indulge in terpsichorean revels observable in the ranks of the famous proletariat, even since wood alcohol has taken the place of straight whisky or the sinister juice of the hop. All communities, even the smallest, have their gay little " bunches," but the bunch is lost in the herd, and the herd chews its cud from birth till death, and regards life with the large bovine gaze of formidable respectability.

Take even this new heterogeneous City of Los Angeles, of which Hollywood, my present place of abode, is a distant (and exotic) annex. The newspapers could not be more sensational if printed in blood, and the casual visitor might be pardoned for believing that it spent its days in one

wild orgy of murder and marital delinquencies. But it is a city of over half a million inhabitants, and under this red froth no Main Street ever pursued the tenor of its way more evenly, had a larger proportion of good, quiet, domestic, ultra-respectable people. Like all large cities, it has its show dens of vice, its " gay bunches," its local and floating criminal element, but, ah!—the majority. You only find its parallel in the great French bourgeoisie. They'll reform, even the newspapers yet.

Of Hollywood I shall write after I have left it, but Hollywood is itself and no other.

That is a curious superstition—that when a nation begins to dance its downfall is at hand. It is true that Rome danced (possibly Atlantis, although authorities are not as exact as they might be), but then Rome also spent long hours in hot scented baths (do our million Main Streets?); they overate and lived for pleasure generally—the small upper class reclining on the bent backs of their swarming slaves—merely be-

cause, having reached the pinnacle of civilization as civilization went in those days, having achieved all that was left in their ken to achieve, they had nothing to do but amuse themselves, and naturally grew so soft and devitalized that they would have been gobbled up in one mouthful by any hardy savage tribe that swept down upon them. Are we in similar case? To use the expressive vernacular of our boys, " Not so's you'd notice it." Even our large cities are only big small towns, as plodding and respectable as the Main Streets in all but those centres of high activity, where people dance for want of other exercise and amusement, and to which flows naturally the frivolous, idle, possibly immoral element with too much money and leisure; an element that has existed in every great city since the beginning of time, and no doubt will continue to exist until its end.

Paris was dancing madly before the war; she had " the craze." Everybody was talking about it. Even the good bourgeoisie, those that dwelt in

Paris, at least, were affected. We all know how she collapsed from internal rottenness on Aug. 1, 1914. There was a time when Spain owned nearly three-fourths of the earth's surface. Was it dancing or brutal stupidity that caused her gradual downfall? Did dancing sink the Armada? Was dancing responsible for the collapse of the old Russian régime, or the same brutal stupidity that distinguished Spain in a century when there was more excuse? The peasants in Germany danced on Sundays, their only day of leisure, and so they had done for centuries; but with the exception of the coarse imitations of Paris vice in Berlin, there was no outbreak of dancing in Germany before the war. They are a heavy-footed race and prefer to eat and grow fat. But they turned the world into chaos.

It is a silly old superstition, and only trotted out when some writer is hard up for publicity and the press for news. If the Main Streets would take to dancing and tune their sluggish blood and brains to action, we should have no " Red menace," no necessity for such disquieting warnings as " Seed of the Sun."

Honor? Is it decaying? Taking a backward glance through history, I should say that the diplomatists of today lie and intrigue pretty much as they have done since the dawn of history—no better, no worse. (Judging from Mr. Wilson's experience at the Paris Conference, it looks as if we were too honorable and honest to survive.) Big Business, Little Business, Yankee horse traders, belong to the same class; in other words, show the same old crooked streaks inherent in human nature. Lenin cynically announces that he will keep his word only when it suits him; but all fanatics have a screw loose—in other words, are unnormal. The vast majority of people grow up under a certain discipline—first of the home and the school, and then of life—are taught that it is wiser to keep your word than to break it. Crooks, even in high places, " get theirs " sooner or later, even if only in being ostracized to a pale where they have no friends and fewer opportunities.

Take it all in all, it seems to me that if the United States of America is conquered by internal or external enemies it will not be from bad morals but smug stupidity.

Mrs. Grundy On the Job of Reforming the Flapper

By HELEN BULLITT LOWRY

YES, and when we were playing truth, all the girls except Jane and me said they had ' put out,' " remarked, serenely, our 16-year-old flapper, at home for a vacation from boarding school.

" ' Put out '! " gasped her puzzled mother. " What does put out mean? "

" Oh, kissed the boys and things like that," explained our flapper, casually, " ' put out ' petting, you know, and—Fan Walker said we'd missed a lot."

That afternoon was Sunday, and two youths called. This particular mother " put out " great quantities of chocolate fudge cake and a pitcher of lemonade. Blindly, she was trying to " put out " something besides her flapper.

Thus struggled this mother against the changing custom of the times, sticking her finger through the hole in the dike to guard from floods the pre-war ideals—ideals of the period when maids had the grace at least to conceal what they " put out " from each other.

So it goes all over the country. Individuals and organizations are struggling, with their fingers plugged in the dike, to hold back the flood of new morals and ethics and dress of our Younger Generation. Others are trying to bale out, with a nice little tin bucket, the waters that were washed in before the wise elders noticed the holes all along the sea wall. All of a sudden Mrs. Grundy is trying to do something about it. All of a sudden you can't pick up a newspaper or attend an educational conference, listen to the man in the pulpit, or join a woman's club without running into somebody that is trying to launch some plan to reform the Younger Generation.

In a general way the plans can be pigeonholed into two groups. There is the plan to chaperon the flappers on automobile rides and dances. And there is the diametrically opposed plan to develop in them self-government. Since the Young Things have got out into the great wicked world, argue the propagandists of the latter school, parents should put the responsibility up to the girls themselves to take care of themselves and keep up the old standards.

One of the most amusing " plans " comes from Brown University. There the student editors of the student magazine have set out to " reform " the girls at their dances, by assuring them through the college press that the boys really prefer the girls who do not take to " petting." One youth recounts in print his experience as he walked on the campus with the girl of his dreams. Just as he was reverently picturing her in the bridal veil, his emotions too holy even to touch her hand, his dreams were crudely dispelled by the lady's announcing practically:

" Here, we're wasting time in this moonlight." Trembling with emotion, she ardently clutched his arm.

The editor sternly informs all flappers who henceforth shall attend Brown dances that men don't like to have advances made—that men yearn for the old-fashioned reluctantly yielding type of female. As no big dance has been held since the editorials were published, it is too early to tell if the reform is " taking."

The Woman's Auxiliary of the Episcopal Church has entered the ring with a nation-wide campaign. It has definite progress to report, even if the result of the Brown University propaganda be still held in breathless suspense. The progress it boasts is that many prominent society girls of the Younger Generation have joined its " meetings for girls " to discuss the problem of upholding standards.

As for the Older Generation, it simply jumped at the auxiliary's idea. In the words of one of the organizers: " Philadelphia sends out a thrilling cry for help. The South is calling to us. Even Boston is frightened." Many a diocese now has a flourishing organization, busy getting groups formed in the separate churches. Unofficially, the Episcopal plan is just this: Some of the most influential society people of each community belong to this Church—in fact, it is the Church which the society aspirant is likely to join as soon as she gets her money —so the upholders of standards organize the most fashionable matrons, and the most influential débutantes and let them make it "smart" again to be conservative. As for the platform of the "movement," it is a large order: "To eliminate indecent dress, painted faces, joy rides, improper dancing, vulgar conversation and swearing."

Educational conferences have their reform platforms, too. When the National Association of Deans of Women held its annual meeting at Atlantic City, early this month, the morals of the college and high school girls were the main subject of debate. And here, too, as among the other debaters, they cut the cure in two, even as the wise Solomon suggested. Some wanted to resurrect the chaperon system; others proposed to develop more and more the idea of student government.

The most vigorous spokesman for the chaperon of yester-year was the Dean of Morningside College, Iowa.

"Although the single code of morals may come into existence, nevertheless it will always be woman who suffers most for transgression," was the way she summed up the impassioned debate. "For this reason women must have the protection of chaperonage."

She denounced the automobile as one of the prime causes of the "riotous license."

What the conference did in the way of action was to pass a resolution urging every high school in the country to have a Dean to look after the morals of the girls and to keep in touch with their outside life—"Dean" apparently being just another name for duenna. The conventional "Whereases" of the formal resolution call attention to the necessity for some wise woman to organize outside activities for the schoolgirls—even as the mother who "put out" the fudge cake.

Stretch forth a hand anywhere in the dark and touch a school—and you will find that some effort is being exerted to find an answer to the problem. I talked with the Dean of a Southern co-educational university, who pins her hopes to student government. She hasn't an ounce of pessimism.

"Help for conditions these days must come from the inside instead of from the outside," was her idea. "You can't tell the college girl of this day, 'You shall not.' But you can say to their student government council, 'Call a meeting and let the girls vote on whether or not they will have cheek-to-cheek dancing. Let the will of the majority decide.'"

This council, by the way, voted out cheek-to-cheek dancing, and so

"The chaperon's place is on the stairway."

did the student government of the Washington Irving High School. To tell the truth, this Southern Dean—or glorified duenna, if you will—points out that many of the girls will be glad enough to drop the more "advanced" methods provided the other girls will do it, too. But as long as the majority goes in for the other new freedoms, it is asking martyrlike qualities of one lone girl to stand out against the custom, under penalty of being dubbed a prude.

"Take the girl, for instance, who seems to have decided that one ought to go much corseted to dances," said the Duenna-Dean. "I've heard that she's called Old Ironsides. But when it is the student council that has passed against cheeking, the others almost hiss 'scab' when a girl persists in that style of dancing."

"The problem of the future for Deans is cultivating leadership among girls who are also popular with boys. You are just wasting your time to create anti-petting leadership in a girl whom nobody is trying to pet."

Also the college girl of today can be aroused to a sense of responsibility toward the future where she hasn't a grain of responsibility to the past. The sorority girls of her particular college voted to stop dancing on Sunday afternoons, lest they jeopardize the privileges of their coming "sisters."

"But as for controlling conditions with chaperons," continued the Dean, "we'd just be wasting our time, because, frankly, the girls no longer care what their elders think of them. Through their fault or our fault, we've lost their respect for our generation. The modern young girl values no censorship under heaven save the public opinion of her contemporaries."

For all that, the Older Generation is trying to mold her. Mrs. Grundy has begun to do something. Why else were glaring electric lights put outside the garages of a Hoboken country club? To chaperon the young things that sit in the cars between dances, explains the shocked Mrs. Grundy. Why else did the Principal of a high school in Pittsburgh ban the use of powder and rouge and lip stick? Why else has the Catholic Archbishop of the Ohio diocese issued a warning against the toddle and shimmy and also against

" bare female shoulders "? And why else should the city fathers of Syracuse positively forbid jazz dancing in public dance places? And the college authorities of the same town forbid hiking army breeches for co-eds outside of the college campus—and right after they had banned smoking, too?

These are general cases—a panoramic view of flapper reform. Try a close up of the reforming of White Plains, that pretty little suburb in Westchester County. That will serve as well as another example to show how reforming the flappers works out in detail.

Reform in the suburb began just six weeks ago, when the most " fashionable " preacher in town preached a sermon about the young people of the high school—about their " immoralities," and about their wicked lip sticks. Everything till then had been going along fairly well in the town. Vice hadn't been discovered. The bridge clubs had flourished, with the feet of the mothers tucked comfortably under the bridge tables. But now the old, serene life was over. A mass meeting was called at the high school, a meeting of mothers and fathers and teachers and students.

A young person, whom one somehow pictures as not quite the belle of the ball, rose to her feet to speak.

" If you mothers just knew what goes on in the dressing room at the dances!" said this young person. " The boys get intoxicated. Last dance I saw one carried down the steps."

A youth sprang to his feet. " That was just a fellow that had come in without paying for his ticket, and the rest of us put him out."

The Chairman rapped for order. The mass meeting continued along these ultra-personal lines, to the vast amusement of the casual spectators.

The next meeting of the parents and teachers was held in private, with practical results. Two hundred mothers decided to chaperon their daughters more closely. " Mothers, take your feet out from under the bridge table, and get on your job of chaperoning again," is the clarion call that has gone out. For chaperons in White Plains recently had become what they are in most other communities. They were the harmless kind that the young persons themselves selected. They had come to resemble that famous

Sunday night sandwich that used to be served in New York before the era of prohibition. They were young things themselves, just married. They weren't supposed to be cramping other girls' style.

" But chaperons nowadays have to be all over the place," explains the mother who has helped organize the new Parents-Teachers' Associations. " The chaperon's place is on the stairway and out where the automobiles are parked."

As for the other result of the movement in White Plains, it is a request from the girls of this high school for a student government council. " Oh," giggled one of the maids when she first heard the news of the student government, " now we can do just what we like!

But that isn't the council's idea. Some of the most influential girls are actually frightened by the notoriety which their dances have attracted. " It's time somebody did something," they say, " to stop the chatter." Being members of the Young Generation, they naturally think of doing that something themselves. So the results of the mass meeting may be called rather practical, when compared to the usual outcome of the dress-reform-for-young-people committees that are being formed in the woman's clubs the whole country over.

The chief difficulty in collecting authentic information about what Mrs. Grundy really is accomplishing is that much of her activity accomplishes nothing. The " reforms " that I have enumerated are selected from a few hundred others, because these happen to be the least impractical.

Last week I chanced on " ladies' day " to be in a club whose bar, with all its paraphernalia, had been made into a soft-drink fountain. The wife of one of the clubmen put her high-heeled shoe on the brass rail. With horror her husband caught her arm. " Let's go into the other room, Lucy," he begged. I remembered the preacher who exposed " conditions " in White Plains had mentioned immorality and lip sticks in the same breath!

Reforming flappers is, so to speak, all over the place—but it's very difficult to know which of the reformers to take seriously.

MAIDEN NAMERS SCORE A VICTORY

Ruth Hale Gets Her Name on Deed Just That Way, Not as Mrs. Heywood Broun.

WILL KEEP HER IDENTITY

Lucy Stone League, With Fifty Members, Men Welcome, Trying to Popularize Movement.

The Lucy Stone League, recently organized for the purpose of enabling women to maintain their maiden names after marriage, scored a point yesterday when the President of the league, Miss Ruth Hale, who insists that she is still Ruth Hale and not Mrs. Heywood Broun, had her own name incorporated in a real estate deed. The transaction is unique in the dusty tomes which record the city's realty transactions.

The property involved is a three-story private house at 333 West Eighty-fifth Street, sold recently by the Drive Realty Company through the agency of M. H. Gaillard, to Mr. Broun and Miss Hale for $28,500. When the time came for the transfer of title Miss Hale declined to go on record as Mrs. Heywood Broun. She maintained that the incident of a real estate purchase did not require her to lose her individuality, and, with the aid of Caldwell, Holmes & Bernstein, convinced the other principals in the transaction that her contention was legal. The deed was made out to " Heywood Broun and Ruth Hole, his wife," and was duly executed and recorded.

Miss Hale said yesterday that the regular organization meeting of the Lucy Stone League would be held next Tuesday night at the Hotel Pennsylvania, when the matter of a constitution would be taken up. The present membership consists of about fifty women, but men are not barred. Miss Hale said that Mr. Broun, who is the dramatic critic of The Tribune, heartily favored the movement and would probably join. Francis Hackett of the editorial staff of The New Republic is also said to be a candidate.

" I have never taken the name of Broun," declared Miss Hale, " and I never intend to, in spite of the antiquated custom which so decrees it. This league was organized to protect women who desire to keep their own names and identity after marriage. All the laws now in force apply equally to men and women and it was only social custom which compelled women to adopt the names of their husbands."

The league was named after Miss Lucy Stone, the first woman in the United States to carry her own name through life, despite the fact that she was married in 1855. Miss Hale recently gave up a trip to Europe because the authorities refused to issue a passport to her under her maiden name.

Women as Fliers Considered.

So many men now have lost their lives in airplane accidents that individual additions to the long list of their names have ceased to cause any really deep emotion except in the minds of their relatives and friends. When a woman is the victim, however, the feeling of pity and horror is as strong as was that produced by the first of these disasters to men, and though there is at present no expectation. that aviation should be abandoned by men because of its recognized dangers, the death of Miss BROMWELL is almost sure to raise in many minds at least the question if it would not be well to exclude women from a field of activity in which their presence certainly is unnecessary from any point of view.

That question is worthy of consideration, but it should not be answered hastily, and especially its answer should not be based on this particular accident, lamentable as it was.

There is little if any reason for assuming that Miss BROMWELL as an aviator was less competent than a man of the same training, experience and ambition or taste. She had made many flights safely, and though there seems to be some evidence of something like carelessness in her preparations for her last flight—some failure to take all possible precautions, that is—there was nothing characteristic of her sex in that—nothing unlike what many male aviators have done, sometimes with like results.

All the fliers are so wonted to the taking of risks, and so frequently do they go aloft when conditions are not perfect and the principle of "safety first" would keep them on the ground, that Miss BROMWELL's failure to have her holding straps in perfect order should not be taken as counting against the capacity of women as a class to compete with men in this new profession.

June 7, 1921

Columbia University

Columbia University at its commencement exercises conferred its annual prize awards for excellence in the arts and sciences. To Mrs. Edith Wharton was awarded the $1,000 Pulitzer prize for her novel, "The Age of Innocence," as "the American novel published during the year which best presented the wholesome atmosphere of American life and the highest standard of American manners and manhood." Zona Gale, author of "Miss Lulu Bett," received the Pulitzer prize of $1,000 "for the American original play, performed in New York, which shall best represent the educational value and power of the stage in raising the standard of good morals, good taste and good manners." The Nicolas Murray Butler Medal is awarded yearly to the graduate who during year has show
in

June 19, 1920

Mrs. Gompers Says Married Women Who Work, Not from Necessity, Take Bread from the Needy

Special to The New York Times.

ATLANTIC CITY, N. J., Aug. 30.— "A married woman who works, not of necessity but from choice, is taking bread and butter away from some one who needs it," declared Mrs. Samuel Gompers, recent bride of the President of the American Federation of Labor, at the Hotel Ambassador today.

"Women whose husbands earn a good living should not seek positions in the business world, and thereby furnish an overplus of labor, which will allow employers to use competitive demand for jobs for the purpose of lowering wages of women who are compelled to work.

"Then, too, the married woman who works without necessity is dividing her interests. A home, no matter how small, is large enough to occupy her mind and time. The home suffers if the wife and mother is in business, and her husband loses something to which a husband is entitled—the whole-hearted interest of his wife. If there are children, it is criminal to leave them to the mercy of the streets. The evil influence of older, wiser and mischievous children leaves its indelible stamp on young minds and increases the number of unfortunates who occupy cells in our penitentiaries. Remember, I speak of the woman who does not have to work. Some mothers are compelled to add to the family coffers. They must be praised, not censured."

"Do you believe unmarried women should occupy political positions?" Mrs. Gompers was asked.

"No, unless schools and hospitals are considered political. I think these and similar institutions should be governed by women. I do not approve of women Mayors."

"Do you think there will be a woman President some day?"

"Never. I would not like to think of one," she immediately replied.

August 31, 1921

BIRTH CONTROL RAID MADE BY POLICE ON ARCHBISHOP'S ORDER

Capt. Donohue's Only Instructions From Headquarters Were to "Look for Mgr. Dineen."

SUPPRESSED BEFORE START

Policeman Testifies That Donohue Ordered Him to Get Mrs. Sanger Off the Stage.

THE TWO PRISONERS FREED

Evidence Lacking, Says Magistrate —Mgr. Dineen Explains Catholic Church's Attitude.

The police suppression of the birth control meeting at the Town Hall Sunday night, which culminated in the arrest of two of the speakers after they had refused to leave the stage, was brought about at the instance of Archbishop Patrick J. Hayes of this Roman Catholic Archdiocese.

The first complaint about the meeting, it was admitted yesterday at the archiepiscopal residence in Madison Avenue, was made at the Archbishop's direction to Police Headquarters by telephone some time before the meeting, and Mgr. Joseph P. Dineen, the Archbishop's secretary, went to the Town Hall before the meeting to meet Police Captain Thomas Donohue of the West Forty-seventh Street station. Captain Donohue, it was learned, did not know why he had been sent to the Town Hall until he met the Monsignor there.

Mrs. Margaret Sanger and Mary Winsor, who were arrested at the meeting when they attempted to speak, by the order of Captain Donohue, were discharged yesterday by Magistrate Joseph E. Corrigan for lack of evidence. Following their release they went into conference with counsel to determine what legal steps would be taken to prevent police interference at further meetings and to obtain redress for the action taken Sunday.

The first American Birth Control Conference, which had arranged Sunday's meeting as a part of the program of a three days' conference, announced yesterday that the meeting would be held on Friday night at Bryant Hall, Forty-second Street and Sixth Avenue. The subject will be "Birth Control: Is It Moral?" and the speakers will be Mrs. Sanger and Harold Cox, a former member of the British Parliament, who had come here from England to speak at the Town Hall.

Archbishop Hayes Invited.

When Mgr. Dineen was told by reporters yesterday that persons who had attended the meeting had recognized him he said: "I was present from the start. The Archbishop had received an invitation from Mrs. Margaret Sanger to attend the meeting and I went there as his representative. The Archbishop is delighted and pleased at the action of the police, as am I, because it was no meeting to be held publicly and without restrictions.

"I need not tell you what the attitude of the Catholic Church is toward so-called 'birth control.' What particularly aroused me, when I entered the hall, was the presence there of four children. I think any one will admit that a meeting of that character is no place for growing children.

"Decent and clean-minded people would not discuss a subject such as birth control in public before children or at all. The police had been informed in advance of the character of the meeting. They were told that this subject—this plan which attacks the very foundations of human society—was again being dragged before the public in a public hall. The presence of these four children at least was a reason for police action."

Mgr. Dineen was asked whether or not the Archbishop would personally discuss his reasons for urging police intervention. He replied: "The Archbishop may make a statement setting forth his attitude in the near future. I repeat that the attitude of the Catholic Church is well known, through pamphlets and brochures made public when this matter came up before. These were written by eminent theologians, who set forth the age-old doctrine of the Church, explaining fully that the Roman Catholic Church could have no sympathy with this so-called movement, so similar as it is to a practice which is against the law of every civilized country."

Told to See Mgr. Dineen.

Asked whether representatives of the Archbishop had got in touch with Commissioner Enright direct, Mgr. Dineen said: "The proper police officials were informed." The instructions from Police Headquarters to Captain Donohue, it was learned from another source, were merely to go to the Town Hall and "look for Mgr. Dineen, who had made a complaint about a birth control meeting."

Officials at Police Headquarters declined to discuss yesterday the details of the complaint against the meeting and the process by which Captain Donohue received his orders. Chief Inspec-

tor Lahey referred reporters to Commissioner Enright, who is out of town.

Captain Donohue's statement at the meeting on Sunday night was that he had acted on orders received by telephone from Police Headquarters. He took several policemen with him to the hall, but did not take any steps to stop the meeting until the hall was more than half filled. Then those inside were locked in and those outside, including Mrs. Sanger and Mr. Cox, were locked out. The arrest of Mrs. Sanger and Miss Winsor was on Captain Donohue's orders. At the police station, the patrolman said that Captain Donohue was the complainant, but in Night Court the patrolman himself, Thomas Gaine, appeared as the complainant.

About 250 persons, including some of the socially prominent men and women who were on the committee on arrangements for Sunday's meeting, were in West Side Court yesterday when Mrs. Sanger and Miss Winsor were arraigned for examination. Robert McC. Marsh, who witnessed the arrests, appeared as counsel.

Evidence Submitted to Court.

Following Mr. Marsh's request for an adjournment of the examination Magistrate Corrigan declared that no complaint had been drawn up against the two women. The clerk in charge of the complaint room, it developed, had, on hearing the evidence of the two patrolmen, refused to draw up a complaint for disorderly conduct on the ground that there was not sufficient evidence. He consulted Magistrate Corrigan, who also said that the evidence was insufficient. The Magistrate ordered an "O-14" drawn up. That is not an actual complaint, but a paper submitting the case to the court for determination as to whether a complaint may be

entertained. Magistrate Corrigan ordered Captain Donohue to be present later in the day.

Captain Donohue was not in court when the matter came up for hearing on the " O-14 " complaint, and Magistrate Corrigan, after hearing two patrolmen testify, discharged the prisoners. Although several witnesses for Mrs. Sanger and Miss Winsor, including Mrs. Ogden Mills Reid, Mrs. Ernest R. Adee and Mrs. Juliet Barrett Rublee, were ready to testify for them, no defense was put in and Robert McC. Marsh and Jonah J. Goldstein, counsel for the prisoners, did not once interrupt the hearing.

"We entered the hall about 8:30 o'clock and stopped the meeting as it was about to start," said Patrolman Thomas Gaine.

"How can you stop anything when it has not started?" asked the Magistrate.

"Well," Gaine replied, "The police captain had instructed me to go and tell Mrs. Sanger to get off the stage, which I did."

Gaine said that the audience had hissed the police. Testimony to the same effect was given by Patrolman William S. Davis, who added: "Miss Winsor was trying to make a speech on birth control." Hisses followed this statement and Magistrate Corrigan and Court Officer Edward Sullivan had to pound for order.

Dismissal Recommended.

"Do you see where there has been any offense committed to cause this action?" Magistrate Corrigan asked Assistant District Attorney Gibbs.

"No I do not," was the reply. "I move to recommend the dismissal of the O-14 complaint on the ground that the evidence is insufficient to cause a drawing up of a regular complaint that would allege violation of any law."

Mrs. Sanger in a statement said yesterday:

"The final session of the First American Birth Control Conference, which we were prevented from holding at the Town Hall Sunday evening, will be held at Bryant Hall next Friday evening. The same topic, 'Birth Control, Is It Moral?' will be discussed, just as it has been in my book, "Women and the New Race," which goes through the mails. This meeting is a free mass meeting, open, just as the one scheduled for Sunday night was, to the public. It is expected that both sides of this important question will be discussed. Harold Cox, the editor of the Edinburgh Review, and myself, will lead the discussion.

"I invited Dr. John A. Ryan of Washington, D. C., one of the leading Catholics of the country, to attend the Sunday night meeting, and offered to defray his expenses if he would attend. Of course, it goes without saying that such a distinguished and learned man would have been given every opportunity to present his views. I also sent an invitation to John Sumner, the leader of the Society for the Suppression of Vice. I am inviting Archbishop Hayes or any representative he wishes to send, to the meeting next Friday night. We hope the Archbishop will attend or be represented, to present the Catholic Church's side of Birth Control.

"My attorney, Robert McC. Marsh, is investigating what rights were violated last evening and what our redress will be.

"The question I am desirous of settling is, by whose authority our meeting was stopped? From the facts presented to me it would seem that Captain Donohue, a recognized officer of this State, was taking his orders directly from some one other than the recognized governmental authority."

November 15, 1921

TWELVE GREATEST WOMEN

Composite List From One Hundred Who Have Been Nominated for Honor—Comment of Chauncey Depew and Others—Why a Scientist Refused to Name Candidates

WHO are the twelve greatest living American women?" When Señorita Graciala Mandujano of Chile put that question to the National League of Women Voters a short time ago she did not know that she was touching upon a profound and delicate subject that would force even strong men to throw up their hands in despair or fear! She has not received a complete or non-debatable answer to her question.

The officers of the National League of Women Voters were stumped by the question. They called on the members of the Women's Joint Congressional Committee to give an American answer to the Chilean question. The committee drew up rules and decided to call in "mere man" to help draw up the list of twelve. Five men were to help answer this perplexing question, with an equal number of women. But it remains unanswered by them.

"Mere man" flinches from the task. Men who have been valorous in battle and whose intrepidity in other fields is undoubted turn away from the task of selecting a list of the twelve greatest American women, and Chauncey M. Depew voiced this universal feeling of man, when, asked by THE TIMES to

draw up a list, he said:

"What will No. 13 say to me—or do to me? Do you want me to ruin my young life after these eighty-eight years of existence? It's a hard job, harder and more perilous than any man ought to tackle, but I'll try it."

Names of more than 100 women have been suggested for inclusion among the twelve greatest, and from about twenty lists submitted by prominent persons the following composite list has been compiled by giving each woman one tally each time she was mentioned in a proposed list:

JANE ADDAMS, settlement worker.
CARRIE CHAPMAN CATT, lecturer and suffragist.
M. CAREY THOMAS, college President.
EDITH WHARTON, novelist.
CECILIA BEAUX, artist.
IDA M. TARBELL, editor and writer.
GERALDINE FARRAR, grand opera singer.
JULIA C. LATHROP, humanitarian.
ANNE MORGAN, philanthropist.
MARY ROBERTS RINEHART, author and playwright.
KATHARINE BEMENT DAVIS, sociologist.
EVANGELINE BOOTH, Commander, Salvation Army.

Leaders in the Lists.

Miss Addams, Mrs. Catt, and Miss Thomas were mentioned on virtually every list proposed, and Mrs. Wharton and Miss Beaux were only a few tallies behind on the list. The others stood approximately the same in the rating by tallies, and in the thirteenth place, just off the list, were at least ten other noted women whose achievements entitle them to distinction among Americans of both sexes.

"It is impossible to do justice to American women by selecting a paltry twelve as those that are greatest," said Miss Mary Garrett Hay in enclosing her list. "Each person who selects will select according to his mental bias and thus will necessarily exclude many women who are eminent in fields of work in which he is not interested.

"The women I have chosen conform to a type that I admire, the kind of woman who is highly educated, progressive, devoted to the ideals of the new womanhood, giving her life to serious work earnestly performed. America may well be proud of the fact that there are so many women of this character in the public eye today that it

is difficult to make a satisfactory choice."

All the lists in this article were prepared with the understanding that the women should not be rated on the list, because some of those who answered the question first pointed out that the task of picking twelve of the greatest women was a job difficult enough, without any attempt to rate them according to the individual's opinion of their comparative greatness. This is Miss Hay's list, compiled in accordance with that understanding:

CARRIE CHAPMAN CATT,
JANE ADDAMS,
M. CAREY THOMAS,
MARY C. C. BRADFORD,
KATHARINE BEMENT DAVIS,
MRS. THOMAS G. WINTER,
ELLA BOOLE,
CECILIA BEAUX,
EDITH WHARTON,
MAUDE WOOD PARK,
AMY LOWELL,
MRS. RAYMOND ROBINS.

Mr. Depew has studied every woman's movement for more than sixty years, and has been an "eyewitness" of every campaign in the long battle for the ballot. After his humorous references to his fear of No. 13 he compiled

MISS JANE ADDAMS

© KEYSTONE VIEW CO.

MRS. CARRIE CHAPMAN CATT

DR. M. CAREY THOMAS
© UNDERWOOD & UNDERWOOD

MRS. EDITH WHARTON

The Leaders in a Composite List of Twelve Greatest Living American Women.

the following list as his estimate of the twelve greatest:

MRS. WARREN G. HARDING,
JANE ADDAMS,
MRS. A. L. LIVERMORE,
ANNE MORGAN,
MARY ROBERTS RINEHART,
CARRIE CHAPMAN CATT,
MRS. RAYMOND ROBINS,
MABEL BOARDMAN,
M. CAREY THOMAS,
JULIA C. LATHROP,
KATHARINE BEMENT DAVIS,
MRS. BALLINGTON BOOTH,
CORINNE ROOSEVELT ROBINSON.

Excludes Politicians.

"First, in my list of the twelve greatest American women, I exclude women politicians, no matter how able their leadership," said Miss Elizabeth Marbury. "I exclude women promoters, no matter how pronounced their success. I exclude women reformers, no matter how sincere they are in motive. I exclude women welfare workers whose service has been chiefly in for-

eign countries. I believe that each of the twelve women should stand pre-eminent in the profession or occupation she follows." Then Miss Marbury named the following as her selection:

EDITH WHARTON, writer.
IDA TARBELL, economist.
GERTRUDE WHITNEY, sculptress.
CECILIA BEAUX, artist.
ELSIE DE WOLFE, decorator.
JEAN H. NORRIS, jurist.
MARGARET ANGLIN, actress.
AMY LOWELL, poetess.
FANNIE HURST, short stories.
MARY GARRET HAY, feminist.
M. CAREY THOMAS, educator.
ANNA MAXWELL, nurse.

Miss Marbury said that she included Miss Maxwell, who, because of her thirty years as director of nurses in the Presbyterian Hospital, is known as the Florence Nightingale of America, as a woman who "has done more to raise the standard of training schools for nurses in this country than any one else." Miss Maxwell was included in other lists, and has been mentioned in

several letters to the editor of THE TIMES.

Miss Lillian D. Wald, Director of the Henry Street Settlement, who was mentioned on several of the lists of the twelve greatest, made up her list of the twelve greatest without comment. This is her list:

JANE ADDAMS,
HELEN KELLER,
FLORENCE KELLEY,
EDITH WHARTON,
ALICE HAMILTON,
MINNIE MADDERN FISKE,
GERALDINE FARRAR,
MRS. HARRY PAYNE WHITNEY,
JULIA LATHROP,
M. CAREY THOMAS,
CARRIE CHAPMAN CATT,
ZONA GALE.

Dr. Robert Underwood Johnson, the Director of the Hall of Fame at New York University, in answering the question of Señorita Mandujano, changed the phraseology of her question and

compiled a list of "the twelve most distinguished American women." This is Dr. Johnson's list:

LOUISE LEE SCHUYLER, philanthropist.
Mrs. SCHUYLER VAN RENSSELAER, poet and art critic.
EDITH WHARTON, novelist.
EDITH M. THOMAS, poet.
CECILIA BEAUX, painter.
ELLEN GLASGOW, novelist.
CHRISTINE LADD FRANKLIN, scientist.
M. CAREY THOMAS, educator.
CARRIE CHAPMAN CATT, reformer.
FRANCES HODGSON BURNETT, novelist.
JULIA MARLOWE, actress.
GERALDINE FARRAR, singer.

Dr. Johnson added that he "might change this list slightly on consideration of other names which do not now occur to me," and that he was "not including wives of Presidents, who certainly are distinguished." He said also that he wished to point out that the separate section for women in the Hall of Fame had been discontinued by vote of the Directors, "and all future discrimination as to sex in the Hall of Fame was abolished."

Miss Annie Mathews, who was chosen at the last election for the $12,000 post as Register of New York County, chose the following for her list:

CARRIE CHAPMAN CATT,
JANE ADDAMS,
EDITH WHARTON,
M. CAREY THOMAS,
JULIA LATHROP,
FLORENCE ALLEN,
MRS. RAYMOND ROBINS,
JULIA MARLOWE,
GERALDINE FARRAR,
LOUISA AMES MEAD,
AGNES REPPLIER,
HELEN BARRETT MONTGOMERY.

Miss Mathews explained that she chose Miss Mead " for her long pioneer work in the cause of international peace." She described Miss Montgomery as " a broad-minded Western woman, with a real vision of what Western women can do for their Eastern sisters, who has attained high honors and responsibilities in the missionary work of the Church," and explained that by the terms Eastern and Western she meant Oriental and Occidental.

Dr. Mary Mills Patrick, for many years President of the Constantinople Women's College and a deep student of woman's activities and problems throughout the world, compiled the following list:

CARRIE CHAPMAN CATT,
MRS. FRANK A. VANDERLIP,
JANE ADDAMS,
FRANCES HODGSON BURNETT,
M. CAREY THOMAS,
CHRISTINE LADD FRANKLIN,
MARY GARDEN,
MAUDE ADAMS,
MARY E. WILKINS-FREEMAN,
MARGARET DELAND,
JOSEPHINE BAKER,
ANNE MORGAN.

Daniel Frohman the theatrical manager, gave his list of women as follows:

JANE ADDAMS,
GERTRUDE ATHERTON,
EVANGELINE BOOTH,
CARRIE CHAPMAN CATT,
MINNIE MADDERN FISKE,
WINIFRED HOLT,
MARY PICKFORD,
IDA M. TARBELL,
EDITH WHARTON,
GERALDINE FARRAR,
MARY GARDEN,
MARY ROBERTS RINEHART.

George Gordon Battle, lawyer and President of the Parks and Playgrounds Association here, said that " it is, of course, obviously impossible to make such a list that will be in any sense complete or satisfactory," and that "the most that one can do is to state the names of twelve living American women who have won distinction in their respective fields of endeavor." This is Mr. Battle's list, as he arranged it, alphabetically:

MAUDE ADAMS,
JANE ADDAMS,
CECILIA BEAUX,
EVANGELINE BOOTH,
CARRIE CHAPMAN CATT,
GERALDINE FARRAR,
MINNIE MADDERN FISKE,
AMY LOWELL,
M. CAREY THOMAS,
AGNES REPPLIER,
LILLIAN D. WALD,
EDITH WHARTON.

"I have selected Commander Booth, Miss Wald and Miss Jane Addams," added Mr. Battle, "as pre-eminent representatives in the line of humanitarian work, to which women are by nature peculiarly adapted and in which they so markedly excel. Mrs. Wharton, Miss Repplier and Miss Lowell have deservedly achieved notable success in letters, Miss Thomas has rendered a great service in the cause of education, the paintings of Miss Beaux have world-wide fame, and all Americans are proud of the accomplishments of Miss Maude Adams, Miss Farrar and Mrs. Fiske on the operatic and dramatic stage.

"If it were permissible I should like very much to add the names of Miss Ethel Barrymore and Miss Mary Pickford to those who have added lustre to our national reputation upon the speaking and the silent stage.

"I know that there are many American women who have earned great distinction and given great service in scientific work, and particularly in the medical profession. I am not, however, sufficiently familiar with this subject to venture any suggestion. Also, there are a great number of women who are striving most nobly for the betterment of humanity in various phases of public life. I have only been able to mention a few of these. There are many who deserve such recognition."

The Rev. Dr. Caleb R. Stetson, Rector of Trinity Parish, compiled his list without comment, as follows:

CARRIE CHAPMAN CATT,
JANE ADDAMS,

EVANGELINE BOOTH,
ANNE MORGAN,
MRS. FINLEY SHEPARD,
IDA M. TARBELL,
EDITH WHARTON,
MARY ROBERTS RINEHART,
M. CAREY THOMAS,
KATHARINE B. DAVIS,
VIRGINIA C. GILDERSLEEVE,
ANNA VAUGHN HYATT.

Most Difficult Task.

"My sympathies incline toward the mother as queen of her sex," said the Rev. Dr. S. Parkes Cadman of the Central Congregational Church of Brooklyn, "and it is impossible for me to select the twelve greatest living women who are also mothers from the multitudes who claim that imperishable distinction. To give life is the supreme function of the feminine sex and upon its sanctity and lawful exercise depend the actual existence and the welfare of all nations."

Mrs. Charles H. Ditson, who has been a close student of the woman's movements and various charitable movements, compiled this list:

EDITH WHARTON,
CECILIA BEAUX,
AGNES REPPLIER,
SALLY J. FARNHAM,
ANNE MORGAN,
CARRIE CHAPMAN CATT,
JOSEPHINE BAKER,
GERTRUDE ATHERTON,
LOUISA LEE SCHUYLER,
EVANGELINE BOOTH,
ALICE M. ROBERTSON,
MINNIE MADDERN FISKE,

"These women are, it seems to me, all great in their particular line," said Mrs. Ditson. The list of truly great women in an all-around sense, I feel, would be even more limited."

As her first choice on the list, Norma Talmadge, the actress, selected the mother of the unknown soldier. Her other selections were:

JANE ADDAMS,
ELLEN KEY,
MARY PICKFORD,
MARY GARDEN,
EDNA ST. VINCENT MILLAY,
CARRIE CHAPMAN CATT,
IDA M. TARBELL,
EDITH WHARTON,
GERALDINE FARRAR,
CECILIA BEAUX,
KATHARINE B. DAVIS.

Dr. S. Edward Young, pastor of the Bedford Presbyterian Church in Brooklyn, selected the following list:

JANE ADDAMS,
LILLIAN D. WALD,
EVANGELINE BOOTH,
MARY ROBERTS RINEHART,
IDA M. TARBELL,
ELLA A. BOOLE,
ISABELLA McDONALD ALDEN,
MAUDE ADAMS,
MARGARET SLATTERY,
MARGARET WADE DELAND,
MARY EMMA WOOLLEY,
ALICE ROBERTSON.

Dr. Henry Noble MacCracken, President of Vassar, subdivided his list, with names under various groups, adding that "this list is partly based on a sense of the value of particular services at this particular stage of civilization. Athletics are important now." This is his list:

JANE ADDAMS, social worker.
KATHARINE B. DAVIS, social worker.
JULIA C. LATHROP, social worker.
MRS. HENRY PEABODY, religious worker.
MAUD BALLINGTON BOOTH, religious worker.
MRS. C. C. CATT, worker for women.
MARY E. WOOLLEY, worker for women.
ELLEN C. SEMPLE, scientist.
MARIETTA JOHNSON, educational reformer.
CECILIA BEAUX, artist.
EDITH WHARTON, writer.
E. BLEIBTREY, athlete.

The Rev. Christian F. Reisner wrote:

"I have found it a very difficult task to select twelve living women whom I considered the greatest.

"In my estimation, it is not necessary for people to have commanding speaking ability or to be even literary prodigies to make them prominent, so I have included Helen Gould Shepard, who has set the world a very good example of very beautiful service.

"When it comes to the stage I have had a very hard time deciding, but have finally included the name of Ethel Barrymore.

"Evangeline Booth, with a frail body, has exhibited rare tact in facing difficult problems as a religious leader, and is well worthy of being placed among the great women.

"Since I have known Margaret Deland from boyhood and have been influenced by her writings, I quickly picked her.

"Mrs. Harry Payne Whitney appeals to me because, while a rich woman, she

has given herself to an arduous task and has excelled only because she has worked hard.

"Mme. Louise Homer is not only a woman of rare gifts, but has cultured a most beautiful spirit which has given itself to mothering a large family of children, as well as scattering blessings wherever she goes. The other names in my list are so pre-eminently great that they need no comment.

"Helen Keller must shame all complainers by her zeal and optimism."

The following is the Rev. Mr. Reisner's list:

JANE ADDAMS,
CARRIE CHAPMAN CATT,
EVANGELINE BOOTH,
IDA M. TARBELL,
M. CAREY THOMAS,
HELEN KELLER,
HELEN GOULD SHEPARD,
LOUISE HOMER,
MRS. HARRY PAYNE WHITNEY,
ETHEL BARRYMORE,
MARGARET DELAND,
MISS LILLIAN WALD.

A famous scientist, who has no trouble sorting out plants and animals, found himself unable to compile a list that he thought satisfactory,

"Some of the women of our country who have done and are doing a great amount of good for the succor and uplift of humanity are making very little noise about it," he said, "and outside of a comparatively small circle are almost unknown. Such a list would, of course, be scorned by people who think only of popularity, notoriety and qualities of that sort."

College President's List.

Dr. Sidney E. Mezes, President of the City College, chose the following list without comment:

JANE ADDAMS,
EVANGELINE BOOTH,
IDA M. TARBELL,
MINNIE MADDERN FISKE,
M. CAREY THOMAS,
MRS. HARRY PAYNE WHITNEY,
ALICE M. ROBERTSON,
CECILIA BEAUX,
MARGARET DELAND,
CARRIE CHAPMAN CATT,
AGNES REPPLIER,
MARY GARDEN.

Miss Cecilia Beaux, whose own name appears on so many of the lists, said that "it is quite impossible for me to make a selection of twelve pre-eminent American women, and I confess I have little sympathy with such methods—in behalf of my own sex—of raising the wind."

June 25, 1922

SEIZE 772 BOOKS IN VICE CRUSADE RAID

Secretary of Society for Suppression of Vice Attacks Three Seltzer Volumes.

Every copy of "A Young Girl's Diary," "Women in Love," and "Casanova's Homecoming" was seized by John S. Sumner, Secretary of the Society for the Suppression of Vice, when, armed with a search warrant issued by Magistrate Edward Weil, he visited the offices and shipping room of Thomas Seltzer, Inc., 5 West Fiftieth Street last Friday.

A summons charging Mr. Seltzer, who is the publisher of the confiscated volumes, with violating Section 1141 of the Penal Code, was adjourned to next Tuesday when the case came before Magistrate George E. Simms in the West Side Court yesterday. The section of the Penal Code specified in the summons deals with the publication and sale of obscene literature.

When asked why he seized the books, Mr. Sumner said he had received a complaint from a source which he refused to divulge. He said he would say nothing more until the case came up in court. Jonah Goldstein will appear as counsel for the publisher.

After packing up the books, Mr. Sumner gave Mr. Seltzer a receipt for a total of 772 volumes and had them carted away by a truckman employed by Mr. Seltzer. Mr. Seltzer alleges that he was not only ordered to open his desk to the vice crusader, but was told that a police patrol wagon would be called to transport the books if the publisher declined to call for his own truckman.

Words were passed between the two men in reference to the question of licentiousness in "A Young Girl's Diary." In signing for the books Mr. Sumner indicated that they were receipted for by the District Attorney.

"A Young Girl's Diary" is the work of an anonymous Austrian girl. Among those who have endorsed the book, according to Mr. Seltzer, are Professor Stanley G. Hall, author of a number of books on sex hygiene; Professor Joseph Jastrow of the University of Wisconsin, Dr. Smith Ely Jelliffe, Dr. Sigmund Freud, Dr. A. A. Brill, Dr. Ira S. Wile, Charles Rann Kennedy, Miss Gertrude Gogin of the Y. W. C. A., and Laura B. Garrett, lecturer on sex hygiene in the New York public schools.

D. H. Lawrence, the English author, wrote "Women in Love," which has been on sale for two years at $15 a volume. "Casanova's Homecoming" is the work of Arthur Schnitzler, the Viennese novelist and playwright.

Brentano's phoned Mr. Seltzer yesterday and said that their copies of "A Young Girl's Diary" had been removed by Mr. Sumner. It was the only one of the three banned books carried on their shelves.

July 12, 1922

Give Me Liberty

By
SALLY FAIRFIELD BURTON

GIRLS are after liberty; they believe in the "as you will" theory. To give the full sensations of freedom, however, there must be an audience to recognize the actuality of the liberation. The negro was a slave as long as the world made him conscious of his chains—until the emancipation proclamation declared him free. That is what the girl of today is worrying about. She has not been really or officially recognized. She is all set for progress, but the conservative male is holding her back. He doesn't see why his sisters and sweethearts and tennis partners should want to earn their livings. His mother didn't, and that is enough for him. If he thinks things out at all, he is apt to become rather sentimental about womanliness and motherhood; but all too often he is contemptuously indifferent. He will not make the emancipation proclamation.

Of course, there have always been working girls in the world, but the bone of contention at present is the girl of fine forebears and superior environment who wants both to work and play. The carefully brought-up daughter can only play with sons of the same sort, and these are the ones who are turning from her, flushed with idealism or dulled by indifference.

"These conservative men will drive me crazy," said one Emancipated Girl, hotly. "They don't understand us at all; and what is more, they don't care. They make me furious!" She flung back her black mop of hair, her cheeks glowing. Slenderly, vividly attractive, for four years she had been the leader of the wildest crowd in the exclusive Rose Manor School and had attended the giddiest of collegiate house parties and proms. Then, to every one's amusement, she went to business school for a year and finally was established in New York, doing secretarial work for a wholesale drug company.

She came to New York with most favorable recommendations of the Scott Fitzgerald-Dorothy Speare type. Every evening she theatred and danced with some one whose brother or sister or roommate had advised him to "look her up, she's worth it." These young men keenly, but with an air of silent indifference, sized her up as a "darned good egg," who knew how to manipulate the latest one-sided, hitch-and-glide dances and to wear long, clinging, dripping draperies. Then toward the end of each evening she casually mentioned her job. Surprise, amusement, consternation, indifference—she could think back upon the various reactions and the expressions on her escorts' faces.

There was one youngster on his way home from prep school who thought she was "throwing some new sort of line," which, of course, means talking some spectacular,

carefully calculated nonsense instead of simply conversing. Running true to form, he pretended to believe it and approve of it, mildly. With simulated interest, he asked her innumerable vacuous questions, but was beginning to doubt the potency of the line when she, aware of his flapperish attitude, changed the subject.

Another boy took it all as a vast joke. Looking across the narrow table at her exotic charm—creamy pallor, scarlet lips, casually disheveled locks—all in accord with the style of the moment, he chortled: 'Job! You with a job? You'd spoil the morale of any office you went in. Say, I'll get you a job in my place any time you want it, 'cause I don't care about this business and I'd just as soon see it go to wrack and ruin. You with a job! That's a knockout. Do you play the typewriter by ear?"

His glance was full of appreciation of his own wit and of gratitude toward the girl for giving him such an opportunity. Hopelessly she shook her head. It was no use telling this gay humorist that she had really taken a business course, that her teachers had given her valuable recommendations, and that her progress had been made without "pull." This witty youth would not understand how seriously she felt the call to work rather than to dance, smoke and "pet" her way through life. She couldn't announce to him that she thought women with nothing to do were spoiling their lives and the lives of their parents and husbands and children by becoming too self-centred and narrow-minded. It had grown disgustingly trite, this talk, but it was true just the same.

She had once attempted to explain it all to a man who had been effusive in his approval of girls' freedom. He had considered chaperons ridiculous and stultifying, pronounced cigarettes and cocktails absolutely comme il faut, and recommended knickers if the wearer's legs were sufficiently good. So the Emancipated Girl had told him of her secretaryship. He had been startled and incredulous, then had casually asked if it were a hang-over from a war stenographic course; if she were writing her father's letters, from 10 o'clock till 1, to stave off boredom. She had become angry and burst forth in a tirade against the hypocritical male who wanted girls to be free in all sorts of little ways that didn't count, but who were oblivious to any desire for real freedom.

"Our little mannerisms of liberty amuse you," she had cried, "but you want to keep us tied up to our mother's apron-strings so that we can really make no progress. If a girl is decently attractive and plays around, you think she ought to do nothing but that. My brother can go out with the best-looking, most charming girls and yet he can earn his living at the same time. I don't see why I can't. You men are selfish, you—" The man had not interrupted her, but she stopped with a small gesture of hopelessness. This

veteran of college proms, of debutante parties and of taxi rides had forgotten for the moment that anger is often more becoming than amiability. It was obviously this becomingness which was reflected in the man's fascinated gaze. He had not even vaguely understood what she meant.

Another Emancipated Girl had arrived in New York, also to become a secretary. Quietly charming and sweet, with a dignified prettiness and a conservative wardrobe, she did not have spectacular recommendations, crowds of well-informed yet inquisitive men seeking her out. Her few school friends introduced her to their intimates and, as she had nothing else particularly to distinguish her, it became generally known that she had a job. The average youths seemed to accept her at her face value. She danced well, played a fair game of bridge, was a good sport, easy to talk to, and yet they felt differently toward her. She was working and, well, it certainly was too bad she thought it necessary to do it.

"You don't know what you're getting into," said one boy who had worked for two Summer vacations. "You may think you are going to like it and keep on liking it, but I bet you're not."

"Well, what of that?" replied the girl. "Men keep on working even though they do get tired, don't they—if they are the right sort? I think girls ought to have a little stick-to-it-iveness, too, don't you?"

"Yes, but—" he answered vaguely. His reactionary prejudices defying expression, he interrupted himself, "Let's dance."

A man four years out of college, much sought after, holding himself aloof, studiously casual and superficial, engaged this working girl in serious conversation one evening. It was that intimate yet curiously impersonal sort of talk that most men fall into occasionally, all about homes and cooking and keeping the light still burning in the window; about love and marriage, everything in a general sort of way. It was rather incoherent and the man kept inserting the phrases, "I guess I'm pretty old-fashioned," and "I don't usually say things like this." Finally he was drawing a picture of an ideal girl. "I think a girl should be able to make a home out of the place she lives in, whether it is a single room or a house with fifteen servants." Ignoring the banality of his remarks, he added, "Also, I think girls should marry young."

"So do I," replied the Emancipated Girl, promptly; "if they're in love."

The man looked surprised and burst forth, "So you admit you're not going into business seriously, as a permanent thing, the way a man would. And must realize that you're not preparing yourself for marriage by writing on a typewriter all day when you ought to be learning to cook." The girl started to explain enthusiastically that she knew how to cook and that she certainly was serious in her work, expecting to go on with it in some form later in life, even if she had to drop it for a

"You'd spoil the morale of any office you went in."

EASTERN WOMEN AGAINST DRY LAW

First 21,000 Votes in Digest's Poll Show 65 Per Cent. Opposed to Volstead Act.

NEW YORK VOTING 3 TO 1

Returns From the Women Also Show Stronger Sentiment for Soldiers' Bonus.

Women of the Eastern States and particularly New York are opposed to the present dry laws, the first 21,000 votes in a poll by The Literary Digest on prohibition indicate. The first returns, according to the current Digest, which gives the first summary of a special poll of 2,200,000 women, show more than 65 per cent. against the continuance and strict enforcement of the Volstead Law. The percentage in the main poll is about 61.5 per cent. the same way.

The first returns from the women on the soldiers' bonus question show a much stronger sentiment for the bonus than the main poll. This showing the Digest calls all the more noteworthy, "since the returns are from nearby States where, as the main poll has shown, bonus sentiment is hardly as strong as in the country at large."

The first women's votes on prohibition are distributed as follows:

	For Enforcement	For Modification	For Repeal
New England States	1,297	1,218	702
Middle Atlantic	3,078	4,842	3,455
East North Central	1,721	1,382	699
West North Central	282	252	158
South Atlantic	721	651	390
East South Central	224	152	70
Scattering	40	78	45
Totals	7,363	8,575	5,520

On the bonus question the first tabulation shows the following results:

	In favor of Bonus	Opposed
New England States	1,393	1,598
Middle Atlantic States	5,765	5,711
East North Central States	2,466	1,252
South Atlantic States	878	475
Scattering	865	443
Totals	11,567	9,879

"It must be taken into consideration, as affecting the continued 'wetness' of the women's poll, that the vote so far comes chiefly from Eastern States, which are commonly considered to be 'damper' in sentiment than are those of the Middle West, Northwest and South," says the Digest. "While New York, in the small returns from the women's poll so far received, gives 1,644 for enforcement to 3,202 for modification and 2,239 for repeal, a total of more than three to one against the present laws, the first few returns from Kansas show 136 for enforcement to 68 for modification and 22 for repeal. The first scattering votes from California, on the other hand, the only Far Western State thus far represented in the returns, show 37 for enforcement to 73 for modification and 44 for repeal.

"While the main poll this week shows a slight increase of 'dry' sentiment, equivalent to at least one-half of 1 per cent., the factory polls continue to be strongly in favor of less stringent liquor laws. The most recent factory poll, taken in a branch establishment of a large automobile manufacturer with branches throughout the country, shows the following result:

For enforcement.................. 171
For modification..................2,170
For repeal........................ 643

"This poll ranks with the 'wettest' of those so far taken, showing approximately 16 to 1 against 'bone-dryness.'

time. She protested that a man wouldn't expect to stick to a job like typewriting all his life, anyway; and, moreover, it was really good training for marriage, because it taught patience and accuracy and such things. But the Ultra-conservative Male was not listening. He was complacently disapproving of her, burbling with sincere self-satisfaction, "I guess I'm pretty old-fashioned, down underneath. I can't understand your point of view at all."

Thus the girl who works and plays comes up against masculine antagonism. Strange to say, it is usually young masculinity that is the most belligerently opposed or the most deadeningly oblivious. They perhaps are subconsciously demanding the traditional heroine, with enough evidences of freedom and modernity to make her interesting and companionable, but still a heroine to play with and protect.

Work and bustling efficiency do not fit into this subliminal picture. Cigarettes and knickers are more consistent with the playfellow rôle than are shorthand books and office frocks. So the Ultra-conservative Male continues to be the despair of the Emancipated Girl because he so utterly fails to understand her, and so the girl continues to hope for recognition.

Combining the four polls which have been taken among factory-workers, the result runs:

For enforcement................ 644
For modification..............4,949
For repeal.....................2,570

"The totals in the main poll on the prohibition and bonus questions, representing about 700,000 votes, are as follows:

PROHIBITION.

For enforcement............271,954
For modification............290,172
For repeal..................146,679

BONUS.

For 344,792
Against 356,167

"Bonus advocates receive additional aid and comfort by the continued strength of the bonus vote in The Digest's special factory polls.

"The Digest's main poll on the bonus has been swinging in the opposite direction. The present tabulation of some 700,000 votes shows a total majority in the 'No' column of over 11,000."

August 21, 1922

Woman Walks Eleven Miles A Day Doing Housework

An experiment conducted recently at Cornell University in connection with the "Better Homes in America" movement resulted in some interesting discoveries on the distance a woman walks in the course of her ordinary household duties in an average private house. In checking up by means of a pedometer it was found that a housewife walked about eleven miles a day doing house cleaning, working in the kitchen and laundry and caring for the baby.

By introducing a tea cart to reduce the number of trips incident to carrying food, dishes and other household articles it was found that the housekeeper's pedometer registered a distance of only five and three-quarters miles for the day, or about half the distance traveled when the conveyer was not used.

The figures represent a saving of four miles a day in dining room and kitchen work and a mile and a quarter a day in the nursery.

October 15, 1922

Public Printer to Pay Women Same as Men for Same Work

WASHINGTON, Dec. 2.—Women in the Government Printing Office here performing the same operations as men will receive equal pay with men, it was announced today by George H. Carter, Public Printer. The order, effective immediately, followed an investigation which showed "unjust discrimination," Mr. Carter said.

Increases from 10 to 20 cents an hour will be given the 215 women affected by the order, and decreases in salaries of about 200 men employes will offset this in part.

December 3, 1922

KU KLUX CONSIDERS WOMEN AUXILIARIES

Klonvokation's Decision Withheld —State Goblins to Elect Future Imperial Wizards.

Special to The New York Times.
ATLANTA, Nov. 29.—Consideration of a resolution disclaiming any connection between the Ku Klux Klan and women's secret organizations of a similar nature occupied the session of the imperial klonvokation of the order tonight in the pavilion on the grounds of the Great American University. This resolution carries with it the penalty of ejection for any member of the Klan who serves in any way with such bodies of women or who aids or abets such organizations. The result was not announced.

The new constitution which adopted provides that the I Wizard hereafter shall be ele grand goblins or State ch shall be no nominees for and each goblin will man in good st lect as his ch will r kl

November 30, 1922

Women Without a Country Are in Straits From the New American Nationality Law

LONDON, Oct. 17 (Associated Press).—Women without a country are becoming numerous here as a result of the new American law allowing American women who marry foreigners to retain their own nationality and providing that foreigners who become the wives of Americans keep their native identity.

Dozens of distracted women have been applying daily at the American Consulate for passport visas only to learn that they have lost their nationality and have nothing to replace it, it was said today at the consulate.

Under the British law, a woman who marries a foreigner automatically loses her British citizenship, and therefore cannot obtain a British passport. If, having married an American, she tries to obtain a United States passport, she is confronted with the fact that she is not an American, because, under the new law, she retains her own nationality. Nor can the American wife of a Briton obtain a British visa on an American passport, because, under the British law, she is British, not American.

The American Consulate is doing everything possible to lessen the inconveniences which the law has brought upon these women. They are asked by the consulate to provide affidavits regarding their birth, marriage and other details.

Complications worse than mere inconvenience may arise from the new law, it is pointed out. For example, if one of these "women without a country" should die on board a ship without possessing the necessary passport, intricate complications over the settlement of her property might arise. In consular circles there is a rather general feeling that the advocates of the new law were perhaps so zealous over their independence that they forgot to consider potential complications.

"But they've got what they wanted," said an official, "and we must do the best we can for them. However, one can't help but reflect that they are 'hoist by their own petard.'"

October 18, 1922

GEORGIA WOMAN, 87, IS NAMED AS SENATOR

ATLANTA, Ga., Oct. 3 (Associated Press).—Mrs. W. H. Felton of Cartersville, Ga., was appointed by Governor Thomas W. Hardwick today to fill the vacancy caused by the death of Senator Thomas E. Watson, until the people elect a successor in November. Mrs. Felton will be the first woman to become a Senator.

Whether Mrs. Felton will actually have an opportunity to qualify and sit in the Senate is doubtful, for her successor will have been elected before the expected special session of Congress in November.

Mrs. Felton is the widow of Dr. W. H. Felton, who served as a Member of Congress for several terms. She has long been active in Georgia politics. Many years before the women obtained the right of suffrage Mrs. Felton managed her husband's campaign and stumped the district in his behalf. She was a friend of the late Senator Watson and supported Governor Hardwick in his recent campaign for renomination. She has served as a member of the Board of Visitors of the University of Georgia.

In announcing Mrs. Felton's appointment, Governor Hardwick said he would himself be a candidate to succeed Senator Watson in the primary to be held Oct. 17.

Mrs. Felton announced she would accept the appointment, which previously had been declined by Mrs. Watson, widow of the late Senator, because of ill health and an aversion to public life.

"The lady I have selected for the appointment," said a statement by the

Governor announcing Mrs. Felton's selection, "is now and has been for many years the warm and loyal friend of the distinguished Georgian whom she temporarily succeeds in this high office. She is my own loyal, devoted and dearly loved friend. She is splendidly fitted to adorn the highest public station in the land, for she wields the gifted pen of a cogent and forceful writer and has all the qualities of heart and head that equip one for broad and constructive statesmanship. She is wise, even beyond her years, and is glorious in the sunset of a splendid and useful life. She is known and loved throughout Georgia, the South and the country as Georgia's foremost woman citizen."

At her home in Cartersville, the new Senator-designate dictated a message to Governor Hardwick, accepting the appointment, "with mingled feelings of personal gratitude and profound admiration for your courage in thus placing, so far as your office allows, a woman in the ranks of the most exalted body in the known world."

"It's going to thrill the nation," Mrs. Felton added. She said it was "eminently fitting" that the position had first been tendered to Mrs. Watson.

Mrs. Felton was born in De Kalb County, Georgia, June 10, 1835, the daughter of Charles and Eleanor Lattimer, the former a native of Maryland. She was married in 1853 to Dr. H. W. Felton, who died in 1909. Five children were born to them, but only one, Dr. Howard E. Felton, survives. He is living in Rome, Ga.

October 4, 1922

CAPITAL WOMEN PROTEST.

They Appeal to Harding Against "Sex Prejudice" In Offices.

WASHINGTON, Nov. 10.—Declaring that "sex prejudice exists in some bureaus and offices of the Government," a committee of women, representing the women members of the National Federation of Federal Employees, delivered to the White House today an appeal to President Harding to take up in his message to the forthcoming extra session of Congress the question of fair play to women in Government service.

"Sex prejudice exists in some bureaus and offices of the Government to such an extent that instances of discrimination against women are constantly being reported to our headquarters," the appeal asserted. "We find that the average entrance salary of women employed by the Government is $200 less per year than the average entrance salary of men; the women are massed in the lower grades of pay, very few occupying the higher positions, especially in executive rank; women are paid less than men for the same or comparable work, some bureaus or offices drawing a dead line for women at $1,200, others at $1,800 a year, and certain high-grade technical or professional positions are almost never open to women."

The appeal asked particularly that the President urge the passage of the Sterling-Lehlbach bill, which, it was said, would erase from the statute books the law of 1870, making women's status in the Civil Service subject to the discretion of appointing officers.

November 11, 1922

APOSTLE OF BIRTH CONTROL SEES CAUSE GAINING HERE

Hearing in Albany on Bill to Legalize Practice a Milestone in Long Fight of Margaret Sanger—Even China Awakening to Need of Selective Methods, She Says.

BY MARGARET SANGER.
President American Birth Control League.

AFTER ten years of incessant agitation and activity the much-discussed question of birth control has invaded the legislative halls of Albany. A bill intended to amend existing laws so that New York physicians may be authorized to disseminate contraceptive advice has been introduced. There will be a hearing on the matter in the Assembly Chamber on April 10. If enacted, we may hope for the beginning of a new era of social welfare and racial hygiene. But whatever the outcome, this bill means that birth control is no longer looked upon, even in the judicial and legislative field, as a topic "obscene and indecent," worthy only of ribald jest and suggestive leer.

No other great problem affecting the welfare of nation and race has been more misinterpreted and misunderstood, even by Americans who consider themselves well informed. Advocates of this doctrine do not beg for mere assent or approval. They ask for investigation and understanding, as the initial step toward support and adherence to their doctrines.

Much of the opposition to birth control has had its source among clergymen and other professional moralists. This ecclesiastic opposition is amazing in view of the fact that the "onlie true begetter" of the whole birth control movement, Robert Malthus, was himself a clergyman of the Church of England. He advocated "prudential checks" on the grounds of austere morality. Our clerical opponents also ignore the fact that many of the most noted champions of birth control today are clergymen. The most noteworthy example is that of the distinguished Dean of St. Paul's, London, William Ralph Inge.

There is a confusion in the public mind concerning the origin of the present movement, which must be distinguished from the so-called Neo-Malthusian movement of Great Britain and the Continent. The Neo-Malthusian League was the direct outcome of the celebrated trial in London in 1877 of Charles Bradlaugh and Mrs. Annie Besant, who had frankly admitted distributing among the English poor thousands upon thousands of copies of the pamphlet of a Boston physician, Dr. Knowlton, entitled "Fruits of Philosophy," originally published in this country in 1833. The Neo-Malthusian League, sponsored by those valiant pioneers, Charles and George Drysdale and Dr. Alice Vickery, soon spread to all countries of the continent, and its doctrines were put into practice in Holland, where fifty-three birth control clinics, approved by the Dutch Government, have been conducted with great success for forty years.

The birth control movement, which has now absorbed the earlier Neo-Malthusian movement, originated right here in New York just a decade ago. While the Neo-Malthusians based their propaganda on the broad general basis of Malthus's theory of population, the expression "birth control" was devised in my little paper of advance feminism, The Woman Rebel, as one of the fundamental rights of the emancipation of working women. The response to this idea of birth control was so immediate and so overwhelming that a league was formed—the first birth control league in the world.

Why She Took Up Task.

With all the flame-like ardor of pioneers we did not at first realize the full scope of this fundamental discovery. At that time I knew nothing of Malthus, nothing of the courageous and desperate battle waged by the Drysdales in England, Rutgers in Holland, of G. Hardy and Paul Robin in France, for this century-old doctrine. I was merely thinking of the poor mothers of congested districts of the East Side who had so poignantly begged me for relief, in order that the children they had already brought into the world might have a chance to grow into strong and stalwart Americans. It was almost impossible to believe that the dissemination of knowledge easily available to the intelligent and thoughtful parents of the well-to-do-classes was actually a criminal act, proscribed not only by State laws but by Federal as well.

My paper was suppressed. I was arrested and indicted by the Federal authorities. But owing to the vigorous protests of the public and an appeal sent by a number of distinguished English writers and thinkers, the case against me was finally abandoned. Meanwhile "birth control" became the slogan of the idea and not only spread through the American press from coast to coast, but immediately gained currency in Great Britain. Succinctly and with telling brevity and precision "birth control" summed up our whole philosophy. Birth control is not contraception indiscriminately and thoughtlessly practiced. It means the release and cultivation of the better racial elements in our society, and the gradual suppression, elimination and eventual extirpation of defective stocks—those human weeds which threaten the blooming of the finest flowers of American civilization.

In our efforts to effect the repeal of the existing laws which declare the use of contraceptive methods indecent and obscene, birth control advocates have been forced to battle every inch of the way. To get the matter before the Legislature of New York my path has led completely around the earth. Our effort has been to enlist the support of the best minds of every country, an object we have achieved even beyond our fondest expectations.

The backbone of the birth control movement has been from the time Malthus first published his epoch-making "Principles of Population" essentially Anglo-Saxon. John Stuart Mill, Francis Place, Matthew Arnold, Thomas Huxley and our own Thomas Jefferson, James Madison, Ralph Waldo Emerson and Robert G. Ingersoll spoke openly in favor of control of the population. Today such thinkers and writers as H. G. Wells, Harold Cox (editor of The Edinburgh Review), Arnold Bennett, Dean Inge, William Archer, Havelock Ellis, Gilbert Murry, Bertram Russell, John Meynard Keynes (editor of The Nation), and Lord Dawson, one of the

King's physicians, and innumerable others in Great Britain speak openly and valiantly for birth control.

It is not without significance that since the inauguration of our agitation in 1913 there has been an immense recrudescence of interest in the persistent problem of population; and a number of new efforts, notably that of A. M. Carr-Saunders, to reinterpret the thesis so brilliantly advanced by that obscure clergyman, Malthus.

Most gratifying to the battle-scarred propagandist for birth control has been the awakening of the Orient. China and Japan for ages have been the notoriously overpopulated countries of the earth, the high birth rate, as always, accompanied by a high death rate, a high infant mortality rate and even acceptance of the widespread practice of infanticide. Famine, pestilence and flood have been the only checks to over-population in China, and these have been regarded even as a blessing by the yellow races. "Yang to meng ping" is a well known exclamation in China—"Many men, life cheap!"

Following my sojourn in China last year, the Ladies' Journal of China, the most influential women's publication there, devoted a special edition of more than one hundred pages to the problem of birth control. In this paper Tzi Sang wrote: "Since Mrs. Sanger's visit public opinion has been greatly influenced, and I understand that some educators are planning to propagate the doctrine in the interior so that our women will no longer be mere machines for breeding children. When the majority of our people know the benefits of birth control and believe that it is the remedy for plague, famine and war in China, then we can adopt the method of asking doctors to pass on their knowledge to women poor in health."

Set Lu, another writer in the same paper, points out that "if we study the actual situation in China we find that unconsciously the Chinese have attempted to practice birth control in a different way. Do we not throw away our babies?" frankly asks this writer of his compatriots. His answer is interesting: "Savages practice infanticide, but civilized people use scientific methods of prevention. Herein lies the difference between a barbarous and a civilized people. No wonder that our civilization fails to make any noticeable advance."

Both in Japan and China, as a result of my visit, and especially as the effect of the attempt upon the part of the Imperial Japanese Government to suppress birth control and to shut its door in my face, the subject of birth control has aroused the deepest and most widespread interest among all classes. In both these great Oriental empires the roots of a permanent birth control movement have struck deep in popular interest, and undoubtedly will exert a great influence toward bringing down the alarmingly high birth rates to the level of those of Western civilization. The importance, the immediate necessity of an autonomous control of the birth rate by the races of the Orient is by no one more emphatically stated than by that eloquent and picturesque writer and traveler, J. O. P. Bland.

Since the first birth control clinic established in this country was raided by the New York police in Brownsville, some years ago, and its founders sentenced to jail as petty miscreants, the whole current of opinion has advanced, not merely in this country but throughout the world. The results of the intelligence tests, the menace of indiscriminate immigration, the fertility of the unfit and the increasing burden upon the healthful and vigorous members of American society of the delinquent and dependent classes, together with the growing danger of the abnormal fecundity of the feeble-minded, all emphasize the necessity of clear-sightedness and courageously facing the problem and the possibilities of birth control as a practical and feasible weapon against national and racial decadence.

●

With the invasion of the New York Legislature exponents of this challenging doctrine may well congratulate themselves that they have won another victory against their opponents. Whatever the outcome of the hearing on April 10, birth control in any event will have compelled serious attention from our legislators. If we can convince the Assemblymen and State Senators that this is a matter which concerns not merely a group of "well-meaning" feminists, but is organically bound up with the biological welfare of the whole community, we shall consider that our efforts have not been entirely in vain.

April 8, 1923

MINIMUM WAGE LAW FOR WOMEN IS VOID

Supreme Court, by 5 to 3, Rules District of Columbia Act Is Unconstitutional.

CONGRESS CANNOT FIX PAY

Justice Sutherland, for Majority, Declares Employer and Employe Must Be Free to Contract.

TAFT GIVES MINORITY VIEW

Twelve States Have Measures to Protect Women and These May Be All Upset.

Special to The New York Times.

WASHINGTON, April 9.—The law passed by Congress fixing the minimum wage for women and minor girls in the District of Columbia was declared unconstitutional by the United States Supreme Court this afternoon. The decision is regarded as one of the most important the court has ever rendered, and indeed a nation-wide precedent, for minimum wage laws are in effect in more than a dozen States, six of which, New York, Kansas, California, Oregon, Wisconsin and Washington, got permission to intervene in the case as friends of the court. No less than 12,500 women and girls in the District of Columbia are directly affected by the ruling.

Associate Justice Sutherland, who delivered the opinion of the court, took the ground that the law interfered with the liberty of contract guaranteed under the Constitution and was also discriminatory in that it favored women, who, the opinion stated, were today fully as able to make contracts as men.

Chief Justice Taft submitted a dissenting opinion in which he held that it was not the function of the Supreme Court to hold a Congressional act invalid merely because these statutes carried out economic views which the court considered unsound. Associate Justice Sanford agreed with Mr. Taft in this dissent. Another dissenting opinion was delivered by Associate Justice Holmes. Associate Justice Brandeis took no part in the case. He once appeared in a minimum wage case involving an Oregon decision. His daughter, Miss Elizabeth Brandeis, is Secretary of the District of Columbia Minimum Wage Board.

The case came to the Supreme Court from the Court of Appeals of the District of Columbia, which once, after sustaining the law, ordered a rehearing and reversed itself, declaring the law unconstitutional in that it restricted the liberty of contract. The action arose when suits were brought by the Children's Hospital and by Willie A. Lyons, a woman elevator operator at a hotel, against the Congress Hall Hotel.

Gompers Deplores Ruling.

Wade H. Ellis, former assistant to the Attorney General of the United States, who appeared for the plaintiffs, said tonight he believed the decision had more profound consequences than any other rendered by the Supreme Court in a generation. Samuel Gompers, President of the American Federation of Labor, issued a statement deploring the action of the court.

The opinion by Justice Sutherland held that the Minimum Wage law of the District did not come within any of the exceptions to the general rule forbidding legislative interference with freedom of contract, in that it did not touch on contracts of public interest, emergency and other considerations of a similar public nature.

"It is simply and exclusively a price-fixing law," he said, "confined to adult women who are legally as capable of contracting for themselves as men. It forbids two parties having lawful capacity—under penalties to the employer—to contract freely with one another in respects of the price for which one shall render service to the other in a purely private employment where both are willing, perhaps anxious, to agree, even though the consequence may be to oblige one to surrender a desirable engagement and the other to dispense with the service of a desirable employe.

"The price fixed by the board need have no relation to the capacity or earning power of the employe, the number of hours which may happen to constitute the day's work, the character of the place where the work is done or the circumstances or surroundings of the employment; and while it has no other basis to support its validity than the assumed necessities of the employe, it takes no account of any independent resources she may have. It is based wholly on the opinion of the members of the board and their advisers—perhaps an average of their opinion if they did not precisely agree—as to what will be necessary to provide a living wage for a woman, keep her in health and preserve her morals.

"It applies to any and every occupation in the District of Columbia without regard to its nature or the character of the work."

Turning to an Oregon statute forbidding the employment of women in certain industries for more than ten hours, Justice Sutherland read that the act was upheld as a measure of protection to the health of women.

Finds No Inequality of Sexes.

"But the ancient inequality of the sexes," the majority opinion continued, "otherwise than physical, as suggested in the Muller vs. Oregon case has continued without 'diminishing intensity' in view of the great—not to say revolutionary—changes which have taken place since that utterance in the contractual, political and civil status of women culminating in the Nineteenth Amendment. It is not unreasonable to say that these differences have now come almost if not quite to the vanishing point. In this aspect of the matter, while the physical differences must be recognized in appropriate cases and legislation fixing hours or conditions of work may properly take them into account, we cannot accept the doctrine that women of mature age sui juris require or may be subjected to restrictions upon their liberty of contract which could not be lawfully imposed in the case of men under similar circumstances. To do so would be to ignore all the implications to be drawn from the present day trend of legislation as well as that of common thought and usage by which woman is accorded emancipation from the old doctrine that she must be given special protection or be subjected to special restraint in her contractual and civil relationships."

The wage standards furnished by the statute were held by Justice Sutherland to be so vague as to be impossible of application with any degree of accuracy. In addition, he held that earnings and morals could not be standardized in as far as morality rests on other considerations than wages. The opinion held the law failed to consider whether the employe was capable of earning the minimum wage specified by the board and that no equivalent was demanded of the employe.

As examples of the uncertainty of the statutory standards the opinion recited that the minimum wage for a woman employed in a place where food is served or in a mercantile establishment is $16.50 a week, and in a printing establishment $15.50 a week, while in a laundry it was $15 a week, with a provision reducing it to $9 in the case of a beginner.

"The feature of this statute, which perhaps more than any other," the opinion continued, "puts upon it the stamp of invalidity is that it exacts from the employer an arbitrary payment for a purpose and upon a basis having no casual connection with his business or the contract or the work the employe engages to do. The declared basis is not the value of the service rendered, but the extraneous circumstances that the employe needs to get a prescribed sum of money to insure her subsistence, health and morals.

"The ethical rights of every worker, man or woman, to a living wage may be conceded. One of the declared and important purposes of trade organizations is to secure it, and with that principle and with every legitimate effort to realize it in fact, no one can quarrel, but the fallacy of the proposed method of obtaining it is that it assumes that every employer is bound to furnish it."

Justice Sutherland argued that the minimum wage law ignored the moral requirement implicit in every contract that the amount paid and the service rendered shall be equal. In principle, he contended there can be no difference between the case of selling labor and the case of selling goods.

Fears Power for Maximum Wage.

"Finally, it may be said," the Court continued, "that if in the interest of public welfare the police power may be invoked to justify the fixing of a minimum wage, it may, when the public welfare is thought to require it, be invoked to justify a maximum wage. The power to fix wages connotes by like course of reasoning the power to fix low wages.

"If in the face of the guarantee of the Fifth Amendment this form of legislation shall be legally justified, the field for the operation of the police power will have been widened to a great and dangerous degree. To sustain the individual freedom of action contemplated by the Constitution is not to strike down the common good but to exalt it; for surely the good of society as a whole cannot be better served than by the preservation against arbitrary restraint of the liberties of its constituent members."

In a long discussion of the validity of the law, Justice Sutherland considered the powers of the Supreme Court in declaring laws unconstitutional.

"This is not the exercise of a substantive power to review and nullify acts of Congress," he said, "for no such substantive power exists. It is simply a necessary concomitant of a power to hear and dispose of a controversy properly before the court to the determination of which must be brought the test and measure of the law * * * but if by clear and indubitable demonstration a statute be opposed to the Constitution we have no choice but to say so."

The majority opinion said a long line of decisions from John Marshall down protected the liberty of individuals to contract on their private affairs. Such restrictions which had been placed on this right, it was held, covered exceptional cases.

Taft Gives Minority View.

The dissenting opinion by Chief Justice Taft, in which Justice Sanford concurred, stated:

"Legislatures in limiting freedom of contract between employer and employe by a minimum wage proceed on the assumption that employes, in the class receiving less pay, are not upon a full level of equality of choice with their employers and by necessitous circumstances are prone to accept pretty much anything that is offered. They are peculiarly subject to the overreaching of the harsh and greedy employer. The evils of the sweating system and long hours and low wages which are characteristic of it are well known. Now, I agree it is a disputable question in the field

of political economy how far a statutory requirement of maximum hours or minimum wages may be a useful remedy for these evils and whether it may not make the case of the oppressed employe worse than it was before. But it is not the function of this Court to hold Congressional acts invalid simply because they are passed to carry out economic views which the Court believes to be unwise or unsound.

"The right of the Legislature under the Fifth and Fourteenth Amendments to limit the hours of employment on the score of health of the employe, it seems to me, has been firmly established."

Chief Justice Taft then referred to decisions in other cases relating to maximum hours of employment. He continued:

"However, the opinion herein does not override the Bunting case in express terms and therefore I assume the conclusion in this case rests on limiting of liberty to contract. I regret to be at variance with the Court as to the substance of this distinction. In absolute freedom of contract the one term is as important as the other, for both enter equally into the consideration given and received. A restriction as to one is not any greater in essence than the other and is of the same kind."

Congress, said Mr. Taft, had taken the view that low wages and long hours were equally harmful upon the health of the employe. He continued:

"With deference to the very able opinion of the Court and my brethren who concur in it, it appears to me to exaggerate the importance of the wage term of the contract of employment as more inviolate than its other terms. Its conclusion seems influenced by the fear that the concession of power to impose a minimum wage must carry with it a concession of the power to fix a maximum wage. This, I submit, is a non-sequitur. Certainly the wide difference between prescribing a minimum wage and a maximum wage could as a matter of degree and experience

be easily affirmed.

"I am not sure from reading the opinion whether the Court thinks the authority of Muller vs. Oregon is shaken by the adoption of the Nineteenth Amendment. The Nineteenth Amendment did not change the physical strength or limitations of women upon which the decision in this case rests. The amendment did give women political power and makes more certain that the Legislative provisions for their protection will be in accordance with their interests as they see them, but I do not think we are warranted in varying constitutional construction based on physical differences between men and women because of the amendment."

Gompers Sees Big Loss to Women.

Samuel Gompers in commenting on the decision said:

"It is regrettable that the Court should have taken away from the women wage earners of the district this sorely needed protection.

"Presumably the Court followed what in its mind is a certain philosophy of government and a certain construction of the Constitution. It is notable, however, that in practically every case of importance involving employment relations and the protection of humanity, the Court ranges itself on the side of property and against humanity.

"The woman wage earners of the District of Columbia are less favorably situated than women wage earners elsewhere. Not only are they less able to defend themselves on the economic fields, but they are absolutely without means of defense in the political field. This is a situation peculiar to this voteless oasis.

"The Supreme Court has declared the Child Labor law unconstitutional, and this new decision taking a proper and needed protection from women is a logical next step in perfecting the doctrine that those who cannot help themselves shall not be helped."

April 10, 1923

Darlings of the Gods

STANDARDS of feminine beauty have changed, according to Frank Lloyd, who has just finished directing Norma Talmadge in her latest production, "Ashes of Vengeance." Quoting Sir William Orpen, the great English portrait painter, as saying that in the last twenty-five years he has not seen a perfect model nor a really pretty woman, Mr. Lloyd suggests that Sir William ought to visit Hollywood. The motion-picture man opines that the Englishman is following false gods when he attempts to measure female loveliness by the old Greek standard.

"Tempus figit—and so do the standards of beauty," says Mr. Lloyd. "The ancient standard of beauty set by the Greek painters and sculptors was naturally influenced by the environment in which they lived. Every few square miles was a kingdom, principality or tribal fatherland, and each of these was engaged in a ceaseless war of defense or aggression. It was a militaristic age and, owing to the primitive weapons

used, a fine physique was indispensable. It is a fact that physically imperfect men were permitted to expire, in order that the Kingdom of Sparta be the home of none other than perfect physical specimens.

"Naturally this idea influenced the standard required of the women. The Amazons were a nation of female warriors. Pallas Athene, the favorite Greek goddess, was worshipped as a fighting woman bearing armor. Brawn was the motive power on which the people relied.

"With the decline of chivalry came the standard influenced by obesity. The famous beauties were buxom. If the beauties painted by Rubens were alive today, they would be taking Swedish treatments, joining physical culture classes and counting their calories in order to reduce.

"Man's instinctive feeling toward woman is one of protection. Bulk and strength does not suggest the necessity of protection. Men nowadays may pause to look at, and perhaps admire, a Junoesque figure—but they know that she does not need protection.

"The beautiful woman of today is svelt and at times petite. Despite the mania for jazz, of which we hear so frequently, a study of the situation will reveal that actually we live in a sane era. From this deduction we must realize that women must be viewed as fem-

inine creatures. The perfect beauty of today is not modeled after Venus, who, by the way, had big feet. The modern woman should not be more than five feet four inches in height. Her figure should be well formed and her features regular. And, above all, she should possess something of which the Greek goddesses never dreamed—personality.

"Ancient painters and sculptors depicted women as cold, beautiful creatures, with no suggestion of personality, the real quality which makes a woman beautiful and attractive.

"If Sir William Orpen could see the hundreds of beautiful girls in pictures he would probably forsake the old idea of feminine physical perfection and progress with the times. I can show him two dozen beautiful girls with perfect figures working as 'atmosphere' in 'Ashes of Vengeance.' There are plenty in other studios as well, and in quantities to make the Trojans and Greeks ashamed of battling so many years for the possession of one woman.

"I can almost imagine the shades of Agamemnon, Achilles, Hector, Ulysses and Menelaus forsaking Mount Olympus and hovering about the peaks of Hollywood's foothills to peer down into the home of the most beautiful women the world has ever known."

July 15, 1923

WOMEN WORKERS INVADE NEARLY ALL OCCUPATIONS

There Is Scarcely a Line of Endeavor Formerly Restricted to Men in Which Women Are Not Making Good Today— Some Instances of Their Success.

ACCORDING to the 1920 census more than eight and a half million women are gainfully employed in the United States, which is to say that of every four working persons in the country one is a woman. These figures, as the Department of Labor observes in a recent bulletin, indicate somewhat the extent to which women have become a factor in a sphere formerly considered not to be theirs.

The last decade shows marked inroads by the women in the trades and professions formerly restricted to men. Increasing numbers of women appear enrolled as apiarists, poultry raisers, dairy farmers, stock raisers, gardeners, florists, fruit growers and nursery culturists, owners and managers of timber plants; operators, officials and managers of mines; mechanical engineers, electrical engineers, civil engineers and surveyors; architects, designers and draftsmen apprentice; engravers, chauffeurs and dentists.

Women doctors have become a matter of course; women lawyers scarcely less so, and women in the ministry, according to the census report, increased from 685 in 1910 to 1,785 in 1920. The Society of Friends has, like the Salvation Army, stood for sex equality from the beginning, and in the United States at least forty sects receive women freely into the pulpits. Recently a conference of the reformed wing of Jewish rabbis passed a resolution allowing women to be ordained on equal terms with men. In England the eloquent preaching of Maude Royden has done much to undermine the prejudice against women speakers in churches. She has permanent access to the pulpit of the Congregational City Temple in London, a right denied her by the Church of England. Here in the United States so recently as 1921 appeared, in a church paper, this communication from a clergyman:

"It would be a terrible thing for the —— Church to ordain women in the ministry, for, besides being unscriptural, it would tend to the feminization of the churches, increase tenfold the occasions for scandal, faction, and unhappy and Satanic church quarreling, and dangerously increase the spread of heresy, schism, error and fanaticism."

Some Professions for Women.

The Women's Activities Exhibition, held last September, under the auspices of the New York League of Business and Professional Women, showed the number of new avenues continually opening. It was not remarkable to find a growing movement among women to own and manage such individual businesses as small specialty shops, book shops, tea rooms, beauty parlors and shops for the sale of confectionery, hand-made jewelry, handicrafts of all sorts; but it was surprising to note the less usual occupations indicated by the exhibition, such as banking, investment, building, insurance and manufacturing.

One woman was selling real estate; in the booth adjoining, her neighbor sold oil securities. Miss Katherine Blanc of Brooklyn, an optician by profession, had an elaborate exhibit, including apparatus for the grinding of lenses. Miss Sarah Barclay De Forest was there, representing the big varnish factory that she owns and manages, and a third Brooklynite, Miss Mary Ryan, represented the large paint business which she took over from her father six years ago and carries on successfully. Other women appeared in their professional rôles of landscape gardeners, purchasing agents, cutlery workers; there was a designer and maker of stained glass; there was even a woman miller, all the way from Kansas.

Mrs. John Wallace Riddle, wife of the United States Ambassador to Argentina, maintains, under her maiden name of Theodate Pope, an architects' office in Madison Avenue, where she employs a staff of men to carry out her ideas. Eleanor Raymond, a Wellesley 1909 girl of the Boston firm of Frost & Raymond, has engaged in the new field of so-called "domestic architecture," combining the arts of landscaping, house-planning and interior decorating.

Last Fall, at the convention of the American Bankers' Association in New York, appeared a goodly number of women delegates; not only cashiers, but managers and even presidents of the organizations that they had been deputed to represent.

Out in Terre Haute, Ind., is a woman who sells structural steel. Mrs. Jean Sharrere places competitive bids on buildings, and, according to the contracts she has won, is proving this to be a good field for women. Her preparation for this work included a thorough study of steel, which fitted her to make necessary recommendations as to quality, price, &c. In cases needing quick handlings, she frequently makes bids, it is said, without any preliminary consultation with the home office in Chicago.

By way of rebuttal of the time-honored tradition as to women's inability to understand machinery, it is interesting to note that a survey of the Patent Office at Washington shows, among the inventions and discoveries attributable to women, an internal combustion engine; also, a block signal system. At the Missouri River Power Plant, which generates electricity for the Kansas City Railway Company, a girl graduate of the mechanical department of the University of Illinois is employed. Miss Clare Nicholet tips the scales, incidentally, at 95 pounds, and among the huge turbines where she works in overalls it is remarked that she "uses waste as deftly as a power puff."

The distinction of being the first woman certified public accountant in Rhode Island and the second in the United States, came recently to Miss Adele Emin of Providence, who passed the examinations held by the State Board of Accountancy with an almost perfect marking. She is employed as "work editor" by an accountancy firm of that city.

In May the newspapers of Washington announced the appointment of Mrs. Harriet De Krafft Woods as Superintendent of Buildings and Grounds for the Congressional Library, the first time that a woman has received an appointment of similar nature.

Out in Vancouver, B. C., has been started a taxicab company, owned and controlled and entirely "manned" by women; many of the chauffeurs were motor corps girls in the war, when they gained their necessary experience. There are several licensed women taxidrivers in Greater New York.

In Massachusetts a short time ago, Mrs. Jennie Crocker of Cliftondale, wife of the skipper of the schooner, "Ruth Martin," applied for a license as master of sailing vessels empowering her to command and navigate any sailing vessel on any waters.

The large department stores offer sundry opportunities for women outside and beyond the usual buying and selling ends of the game. In the personnel department a woman gives special attention to the recreation of the employes, her job being to organize picnics, dances, choruses, clubs, athletic teams and an amazing array of varied activities. Every shop has its "comparison shoppers," who visit the other department stores to observe, and often buy the goods of competing merchants in order that information on prices, assortments, qualities, &c., may be available for the buyers and merchandise managers. Training is not necessary for this work, but it demands a woman with an interest in merchandise, some knowledge of it and good powers of observation. Certain department stores that cater to the South American trade have found it expedient to open a reception room in charge of a gracious, tactful woman who can speak Spanish to visiting senoras and senoritas and assist them with their purchases.

From overseas comes tidings of a woman diver, Miss Naylor, who has been employed to search at Tobermory Bay, in Scotland, for treasure lost by a ship of the Spanish Armada. Miss Naylor frequently makes dives of ten fathoms.

Every moving-picture studio now finds it expedient to employ somebody, usually a woman, to take down notes on the scenes as they are filmed, and make sure that the costumes check up properly from day to day. Likewise, when the final film is run off, somebody has to survey the final product as a whole and make the necessary cuts.

One of the leading hotels in New York employs a young woman as "social directa," her job being to keep the name of the hotel in the public eye continually. This she arranges by sending notices to the society columns of the newspapers whenever celebrities register at the hotel. Likewise, she endeavors to drum up trade for the establishment—wedding parties, receptions and coming-out teas—by calling up society persons who might be in line for such service and explaining the advantages to be obtained at that hotel beyond all other.

Stringing seed pearls seems not much in the way of an occupation; but it is not an easy thing to do. One woman makes her livelihood that way in New York and is employed by the best Fifth Avenue jewelers whenever an especially fine necklace of one of their customers needs restringing.

Another woman has achieved success in making "maquettes," the little cardboard models used by decorators and architects to give an idea of the effect of a particular color scheme and arrangement of furniture.

Two elderly women have achieved independence right in their own home by getting up every morning at 2 o'clock to bake bread for the Woman's Exchange, until 9 or 10 o'clock, when their day's work is over. Before the Volstead act a woman made $300 to $400 a week through the manufacture of a particularly good pineapple conserve, the most important ingredient being rum. An artist, broken in health, retired to Cape Cod and now makes bayberry candles. Two young women cover boxes with attractive wall paper, which find a ready sale.

Among the unusual calls coming to the Woman's Exchange was one asking for a girl to accompany another girl abroad and teach her the social graces. A job in a beauty parlor awaited a young woman versed in physical education who could conduct the correspondence department and answer questions by mail. One young woman, as a result of frequent calls for advice as to how her friends should dress their hair most becomingly, decided to go into the business, setting herself up as a "personality expert," and rendering for money the services that she formerly supplied gratis.

A chain of restaurants last Winter was in quest of a woman of a superior sort who had a simple, practical knowledge of good home cooking on a large scale. Her work was not to be cooking, but to keep an eye on the chefs of the several establishments and see that their product measured up to the best "home" standard.

Perhaps the most unusual job of all is that of a certain old lady on Manhattan Island, who, out of the proceeds of a fund provided by the legacy of another old lady, sallies forth every morning, "Winter and Summer, laden with nuts wherewith to refect the squirrels in Central Park.

WANT MORE NEGRO DOCTORS.

THERE are sixty-five negro women physicians, surgeons and osteopaths in this country, according to figures compiled by the Department of the Interior through Howard University. There are five negro women who practice dentistry in the United States. Other statistics show that the average yearly increase of negro physicians is sixty-three when there is need of an annual increase of at least 450. The average number of additional dentists graduating every year is sixty-three, but there should be 500. The same condition applies with regard to trained nurses, ninety being turned out each year when 600 are needed. Data collected by the university show that more negro physicians and dentists are practicing in the cities of New York, Philadelphia, Washington, Cleveland and Chicago than in the sixteen Southern States combined, where fully 8,000,000 negroes live.

MORE WOMEN LEAVE FARM.

Exceed Number of Men Seeking More Lucrative Fields.

WASHINGTON, Nov. 29. — Larger numbers of women than of men are leaving farms in search of more lucrative fields of endeavor, the Census Bureau says, basing its statement on an analysis of the 1920 census statistics. The enumeration shows the ratio of males to females was higher for farm population than for the total population, despite the fact that the foreign-born element, in which the males considerably outnumber the females, is found mainly in the cities. The sex ratio of farm population on July 1, 1920, was 109.1 males to 100 females, while the ratio for the entire population was 104 males to 100 females.

Of the number of farm dwellers, totaling 31,614,269, males number 16,496,838 and females 15,117,931. Of the total farm population 49.5 per cent. was 21 years and over, 24.7 per cent. between 10 and 20 years, and 25.7 under 10 years. Those 21 years and over numbered 15,632,093. For the country as a whole those 21 years and over comprised 57.6 per cent. of the total population. The farm population, therefore, includes a relatively large proportion of persons under 21 and a relatively small proportion 21 years and over.

The difference in age distribution is declared by the Census Bureau to be due in large part to the fact that the majority of persons who leave the farm to take up their residence elsewhere have reached or passed 21. The largest proportions of children and youth in the farm population are shown for the Southern States and the lowest for the New England States, New York, New Jersey and California.

November 30, 1922

FARMERS' WIVES LEAD HAPPIER LIVES

THE farm woman of today is not a mere drudge. Unlike her sister of twenty-five or thirty years ago, her daily routine of living is not limited to such monotonous tasks as feeding chickens, milking cows, churning butter, cooking heavy meals or taking care of children and housework in between times. True, the cows are still there to be milked, the chickens to be fed, the butter to be churned, the meals to be cooked, but modern inventions have so lightened her burdens that she has time to broaden her horizon.

Red-letter days in her existence used to mean going to church or weekly trips to the village. Her wardrobe, Summer and Winter, generally consisted of one black silk frock for such state occasions as church funerals or christenings. The remainder of her dresses were calico frocks conforming more to comfort than beauty.

Her recreations were few beyond the church-going and funerals.

As a rule, the farm girl of that day married young after a sketchy course at the country school. Her husband was a farm boy and their property consisted of a cow, a feather bed, a fat porker or two and household furniture donated by the families. Sometimes they went to live with their parents or set up their household gods in a cottage by themselves on a plot of the ancestral acres. After a wedding trip to the village they went to work saving money to buy more acres and so on. By thirty—after she had given much of her time to children and hard work—she was regarded as an old woman with the best of life behind her. She was too tired at night to think and gradually stopped with the years.

The farm woman of today has rebelled. She wants for her children schools as good as those city children attend; she wants good roads, frocks that are up to date, a home in which she will not be ashamed to entertain her city friends; books and time to read them. In short, she seeks relief from the drudgery of farm life and time to enjoy its beauty. What is more, she is getting her wants before she is a worn out "old woman" of thirty. If the grandmothers and mothers of many of the farm women of today could pay a visit to the homes in which they used to live they would hardly recognize them.

Has Her Own Car Now.

The average farm woman of today goes to market over good roads in a car. Seldom does she ride in a buggy. Horses are getting to be as much of a farm curiosity as in the city. She has learned to drive her car and takes a spin to town whenever she likes, to go shopping, visit a friend or attend her club meetings.

Nor does she go to town garbed in a calico frock. Her dress has been ordered by mail catalog or purchased in a near-by city and is tastefully made. Her hat is not a result of home millinery, but was purchased at a real millinery store and is in keeping with the season.

Her state occasions no longer consist of funerals and church-going. She has gone far beyond that. A country club, in many cases, is near her home. She goes there when the spirit moves. She attends weekly meetings of her literary or political club and frequently entertains in her rural home.

She is a graduate of the country consolidated school, the township high school, and in many instances the State agricultural school. She knows good books, pictures and music and takes time to enjoy them.

The farm woman of today sees her children getting educational advantages equal to their city cousins. Her daughters are meeting the right sort of young men. Her sons are having an opportunity to choose an agricultural career or that of the professional or business man. Her husband has more time to enjoy life with her.

Milking machines, electric churns, dish washers, sweepers, lights, automobiles, telephones, rural mail delivery, phonographs and other inventions have brought real joy to the farm and taken away the monotony of existence. Motor power for plows, tractors and so forth coupled with good roads and daily knowledge of prices, have greatly helped the farmer too.

All Comforts of City.

A car can be procured in almost any village to reach the adjoining farms. Where the roads are not paved, in many cases they have been oiled to settle the dust. Telephone lines connect farm homes, pianos are in most of them. The majority have their own electric outfits to run farm and house machinery. Cars stand in the farm yard where the wagon and horses used to stay.

Catalogues from city stores find their way readily to the farm women; magazines are easily within her reach and she can get books as often as she wishes from the village library that is a feature of every mid-Western town, no matter how small. She has the vote and, what is more, she is using it. A number of farm women now occupy seats in State legislatures and more of them are making ready to go. A seat in Congress is not out of their vision.

The writer visited a typical mid-Western farm home several miles from a village that was reached by a paved road. The home was a tasteful bungalow, erected according to the wishes of the farm woman. All sorts of labor saving devices were installed to save her time and energy. There was a tennis court. She was Vice President of the village club, Chairman of the Committee on Civics. A rural nurse, through her efforts, visited the country school regularly. Her wardrobe was full of dainty frocks and her children were well dressed.

The farm was one that had been handed down for several generations but was being made to pay more than ever since the head of the house went to the agricultural school and learned to use fertilizers, install more dairy cows and sheep and trim his orchard.

"Fifteen years ago," explained the wife, "we had an average, run-down, middle Western farm. John was discouraged and so was I. We decided to take stock and avail ourselves of the opportunities that the experiment stations offered. We interested our neighbors in getting better roads and more intelligent use out of their vote. We studied our soil and decided to erect a better house and enjoy life before we were too old.

August 12, 1923

WOMEN GET LOW WAGES.

30,000 in Several Trades in State Receive Below $16.

Thirty thousand women employed in the confectionery, paper box, tobacco, collar and shirt industries and in mercantile establishments of the State are receiving less than $16 a week, according to a report made public yesterday by Barnard L. Shientag, State Industrial Commissioner. More than one-fourth of the women employed in these factory industries and more than one-fifth of the women working in the mercantile places are paid less than $12 a week, the report says, adding that many thousands of women wage earners get less than $10 a week.

The report is the result of a study of wage conditions among 80,000 women over 16 years, embracing 278 firms in New York City and 299 in other parts of the State. These wages, the Commissioner said, are being paid at a time when experts place a fifty-five cent valuation on a dollar. The figures were furnished by the employers.

According to the report in New York City in the industries studied, approximately one-half of the women workers received less than $16.25 and a similar proportion upstate received less than $14.25 a week for their services. The Commissioner found that the highest wages paid to women in the trades considered were in the mercantile and tobacco industries. Even in these industries about one-half of the women received less than $17.25.

Commissioner Shientag believes the State should set up machinery for a thorough investigation of wages paid to women and minors in all industries. He urges the appointment of a wage board, with representatives of the employers, employes and the general public to considr the question and to make recommendations for the payment of a living wage.

November 12, 1923

EQUAL RIGHTS MEETING HELD IN CAPITOL CRYPT

National Woman's Party Ends Celebration of 75th Anniversary of Movement.

WASHINGTON, Nov. 18.—As the closing ceremony in its celebration of the seventy-fifth anniversary of the equal rights movement, the National Woman's Party held this afternoon in the crypt of the Capitol a mass meeting at which women were present from every State in the Union.

Mrs. Dudley Field Malone was Chairman and the speakers were Mrs. O. H. P. Belmont, President of the National Woman's Party; Edna St. Vincent Millay and Inez Haynes Irwin.

In her speech Mrs. Belmont said:

"The women of the United States have recently been given the right to vote, but this is only a small part of the equality which still remains to be attained. The Constitution left women in the position in which the old English common law had always placed them—nonexistent as human beings, enslaved as the chattels of men. This condition, with little improvement, exists today in the various States.

"In all States men have greater pay for equal work. In all States men have greater opportunity for advancement in industries and professions, and in all States they exercise control over policies and laws under which women live. Sex, not capacity, is the barrier used to hold woman down.

"The old English common law theory remains the basis of women's legal position in the United States. This condition can no longer be accepted. We are the voting power of one-half of this country.

"We demand that the principle of equality be written into the fundamental law of the land. We demand that an amendment be added to the United States Constitution giving equal rights to men and women in the United States and in every place subject to its jurisdiction."

November 19, 1923

WOMEN WANT TO BE HOSPITAL INTERNES

Women medical students of New York City yesterday launched a movement by which they hope to open the doors of the hospitals of this city sufficiently wide for women to become internes. The movement was set on foot at a tea given at the Y. M. C. A., 410 East Twenty-sixth Street, by the Women's Medical Association of Bellevue College for about thirty-five women medical students, representing the College of Physicians and Surgeons, Bellevue Medical College, Long Island College Hospital and Flower Hospital Medical College.

A committee was appointed to draw up the plans of a permanent organization which will seek to further the interests of women in medicine. Dr. Helen O'Brien of the medical service at Bellevue Hospital was Chairman of the meeting that followed the tea. The plans of the association were outlined by Florence Hulton Frankel of the Bellevue Medical College.

Women who finish their collegiate training find it difficult to obtain further experience because internships are not available to women. They are told by hospital authorities that there is a lack of quarters for women, and for that reason principally they may not be used as internes. Formerly, according to Miss Frankel, they were refused by the hospital authorities, who explained that there were not enough women medical students to warrant the allocation of quarters for women internes.

Miss Frankel said that there were about 125 women medical students in the medical colleges and other institutions in New York City. She said that women had won distinction as physicians and surgeons, and that it was only a question of time before hospitals would make provision for women internes.

The committee appointed to draw up the plans of the organization of women students and its campaign for the admission of women as internes was instructed to have its report ready for a meeting to be held in January.

December 9, 1923

Governor's Boom as "Favorite Son" Will Be Launched at Albany Today.

HUGE OVATION IS EXPECTED

He Will Speak on State Issues and Refer to Washington Scandals.

WOMEN ARE IN REVOLT

Support Smith, but Insist on Choosing Their Own Delegates to National Convention.

Special to The New York Times.

ALBANY, April 14.—Governor Alfred E. Smith will be placed in the running as an open candidate for the Democratic nomination for President at the State convention here tomorrow.

The official launching of the boom for Governor Smith as New York's "favorite son" will be accompanied by a demonstration for him which is expected to surpass any recent outburst of political enthusiasm, if the expressions of the incoming delegates can be credited.

The official business of the convention, which is to elect eight delegates-at-large and eight alternates-at-large to the National Convention, apparently will be only a minor feature of tomorrow's gathering in Harmanus Bleecker Hall. The ovation to the Governor is expected to be the main event and probably will follow the speech by D-Cady Herrick, the temporary Chairman, who is expected to sound a "keynote" which, if it does not furnish a slogan for the Democratic Party in the nation, at least will furnish to a certain degree a platform for the candidacy of the Governor.

Governor to Address Convention.

It was uncertain tonight whether he would be selected as a delegate at large. His personal preference was said to be against this and the question was discussed at a conference with Charles F. Murphy, leader of Tammany Hall; Norman E. Mack, National Committeeman; Herbert C. Pell Jr., State Chairman, and other party leaders.

The Governor will visit the convention and will probably make a speech which, it is expected, will deal principally with State issues and will probably contain an attack on the Republican majority in the Assembly for the defeat of his reconstruction program. It was understood that the Governor would not discuss national issues except for a reference to the recent investigation disclosures at Washington. It is expected that he will devote a part of his speech to an affirmation of the theory of party responsibility and that he will hold that the Republican Party is responsible for the misdeeds of those who held appointment as members of that party.

The only inharmonious note of the gathering so far has been that struck by the Democratic women. They raised the standard ¹ revolt at a dinner in the Hotel Ten Eyck and demanded that they should be permitted to select the four women delegates at large to the national convention. All the women are strong supporters of the Governor and the fight was really aimed at the control exercised by Mr. Murphy and the other men leaders.

Mrs. Franklin D. Roosevelt, whose husband, the former Assistant Secretary of the Navy and Democratic nominee for Vice President, was slated to be one of the four delegates-at-large, led the fight for the women.

"We have now had the vote for four years, and some very ardent suffragists seem to feel that instead of gaining in power the women have lost," she said.

"Their contention is that at first wherever there were groups of political organization leaders gathered together four years ago, you could hear them saying, 'We must be careful what we do—we don't know what the women will do.' Now some of the women have fallen into line and can be counted on just in the way they count upon the men. The others have done nothing, seem to be entirely apathetic and uninterested, and, therefore, can be discounted. A small group have become independent voters and wield a certain amount of influence because both parties realize the independent voter is of importance on election day. A still smaller group is working actively in the parties, trying to realize its hope and belief in the influence of women.

"I have been wondering whether it occurs to the women as a whole that, if they expect to gain the ends for which they fought, it is not going to be sufficient simply to cast a ballot on election day. They must gain for themselves a place of real equality and the respect of the men, and prove that while their one desire is to work with the men, they cannot accomplish the only good which was to be gained from woman suffrage if they work for the men. The whole point in women's suffrage is that the Government needs the point of view of all its citizens and the women have a point of view which is of value to the Government. If they have not, then there is no excuse and no answer to the arguments against woman suffrage.

"Now if we are to gain our position of equality we must not only be on the County Committees in equal numbers, but we must be among the small group of people who make up the tickets which are voted on in the primaries and in the conventions. We must also remember that the great power of the women to make themselves felt lies in their power to help select at the primaries, not only candidates for elective offices, but the officials of their county political organizations. They can choose a candidate, and if neither candidate suits them they can write in the name of some one who seems to them better fitted for the nomination. Even when there is no contest, we women should realize the habit of voting on primary day is an all-important one to acquire for us.

"Now it may be necessary at times for individual women to sacrifice themselves—that is to say, not to accept appointments or positions which are offered them by the men, done without consultation with the women, but to insist that whatever they have, they shall have because their women constituents have decreed it.

"It is disagreeable to take stands. It was always easier to compromise, always easier to let things go. To many women, and I am one of them, it is extraordinarily difficult to care about anything enough to cause disagreement or unpleasant feelings, but I have come to the conclusion that this must be done for a time until we can prove our strength and demand respect for our wishes. We cannot even be of real service in the coming campaign and speak as a united body of women unless we have the respect of the men and show that, when we express a wish, we are willing to stand by it.

"All of us want to work for Governor Smith with all our heart and soul and for the success of the whole Democratic ticket, national and State. We will be enormously strengthened if we can show that we are willing to fight to the very last ditch for what we believe in."

Mrs. Vanderbilt Webb of Putnam County supported Mrs. Roosevelt.

"I feel that the women of the State should realize that as yet they are not considered on an equal basis with the men," she said. "This is natural, but if we are to be of any service to the State our opinions must find expression and be considered. Therefore, I think we should now make it clear that wherever the appointing of women is concerned we wish to be consulted before the men decide things for us."

Miss Annie E. Mathews, Register of New York County, replied to Mrs. Roosevelt and declared that the Tammany organization, of which she is an associate district leader, had always treated women fairly.

Opposition to the selection of Miss Nancy Cook as one of the delegates-at-large developed on the ground that Miss Cook, a prominent member of the League of Women Voters, had been against the Democratic organization. After discussion Mrs. Robert Mitchell of Chemung, Mrs. Roosevelt and Mrs. Grosvenor Allen of Madison Counties were appointed a committee to confer with the men leaders and try to reach an agreement on two woman delegates-at-large to represent the up-State women.

DEMOCRATIC WOMEN WIN.

Party Leaders Concede Their Right to Name Their Delegation.

Special to The New York Times.

ALBANY, April 15.—Up-State women at the Democratic state convention won the principal points in their contention that the selection of women delegates and alternates at large should be made by them rather than by Charles F. Murphy and other men party leaders. An agreement was reached after a committee headed by Mrs. Franklin D. Roosevelt had called on Governor Smith and conferred with a special committee of the State Committee and Miss Nancy Cook of St. Lawrence County, to whom some of the organization women had objected, had withdrawn as a candidate for alternate in favor of Miss Harriet May Mills of Syracuse.

"It was our belief that the women associate Chairmen of each up-State county were best qualified to speak for the women voters of their districts," said Mrs. Roosevelt, after an agreement had been reached.

"After several informal discussions the up-State women were requested to confer as to their choice. At this conference a committee was appointed which met this morning with the subcommittee of the State committee on delegates-at-large to discuss what up-State women should be selected. Miss Nancy Cook, who was one of the women originally named by the up-State women associate county Chairmen, having withdrawn in favor of Miss Mills, the committee presented the names of Mrs. O'Day as delegate and Miss Mills and Mrs. Colbert as alternates, which were accepted by the State Committee. It was also agreed that Mrs. Pfohl should be a delegate and Mrs. Nichols an alternate.

"We feel that the Democratic women of up-State in establishing this precedent have set an example which the Republican Party might follow with advantage if they were wise.

"We go into the campaign feeling that our party has recognized us as an independent part of the organization, and are encouraged accordingly. No better evidence could be shown that it is to the Democratic Party that the women voters of this State must turn if they desire to take a real part in political affairs.

"The Governor has recognized the justice of our claim to be consulted and was a powerful factor in bringing about the very satisfactory conclusion arrived at."

April 15, 1924

April 16, 1924

Bobbing Spreads to All Ages of Women

Fashion Requires the Small Hat, and There's Nothing to Do but Visit the Barber Shop

By VIRGINIA POPE.

IT is a day of commoners. Czars and emperors are no more, and women, queens of the universe, are heedlessly casting from them their crowning glory, all in the name of liberté, egalité, fraternité.

There are two camps, the bobbed and the unbobbed, and a mere hair line divides them. It is not yet possible to express an opinion on which side is the stronger; returns are not in from the country at large, and only a local report can be given.

The hairdressers, barbers, or bobbers, the real executionists in this newest of revolutions, agree that about 70 per cent. of the women in Greater New York have shorn their tresses. The Spring styles brought on a veritable harvest of hair. In preparation for the Easter parade, in Manhattan alone, some 4,000 heads a day were trimmed. In Brooklyn, it is stated, the figure reached 2,000.

Dame Fashion is the Lenin of this red revolution—don't husbands see red when they first behold their wives' bobbed heads? Her decree that the cloche hat is "the thing" to be worn has brought about the downfall of long hair. The edict went forth from her stronghold in Paris. Designers and manufacturers obeyed at once. They pared down blocks that had been made the size of heads plus capillary adornment, and to them they fitted the straw shapes of the coming Spring season. From the French capital to Keokuk the market was flooded with headgear that only the bobbed could wear with comfort.

Women portly and staid tried in vain to put them on. The new hats rested like bell buoys on the crest of their permanent waves. If by dint of exertion they succeeded in forcing one of these helmets down on their foreheads a headache resulted.

"What is to be done?" wailed the matrons to the salesgirls.

"Madame must bob her hair or wear this——" was the inevitable reply as the milliner produced a bonnet of the kind that grandmothers used to wear. There was but one way out—the path to the nearest tonsorial parlor.

Barber Shops Invaded.

Not so long ago the men reclined in their barber chairs, gazing over lathered cheeks at maidens hurrying past the plate-glass window with downcast eyes. They felt secure in their collarless isolation. But times have changed. The up-to-date barber shops now have special chairs for women, and the women, true to the ways of today, take their places beside the men.

"Oh, yes," said the manager of a Broadway hotel barber shop, "we do many ladies here every day. Some come for bobs, some for trims. A beautiful young woman walked in the other day and wanted to have her hair cut off. I shudderingly watched the barber apply his clips to her long black curls. Before the operation was completed I was called from the room. When I returned I looked for the transformation. The girl was nowhere to be seen. I asked one of the barbers and he pointed to a sheeted form stretched out in the chair. On either side of her were similar figures, all with mud packs pasted over their faces. I couldn't tell the woman from the men. Her hair, like theirs, was short. My eye wandered to the tips of her shoes. 'Well,' said I to myself, 'this mannish business has gone to her head. Thank goodness, she can't change her feet.'"

"La Garçonne" was the name given by Paris to the new hair cut. In America we have the boyish—plain, curled or marcelled—the Dutch, the mah jong, the hyacinth, the chrysanthemum, the slave, or clubbed, and the Ina Claire (with a little point running down into the nape of the neck).

Apparently every age has applied names to capillary arrangements. Twenty-five years ago the Gibson girl of flopping hats and feather boas wore her hair in a pompadour with a psyche in the back. One is loath to admit that this outward manifestation of her romantic soul was supported by so mean a thing as a rat! In the reign of Louis XIV. the beauteous ones topped their charms with head-dresses known as coiffure à la Inoculation, à la belle Poule, au Parc Anglais, à la Monte au Ciel, and à la tête au mouton. A la "mutton head" was done by "arranging irregular curls upon springs to cover all parts of the head," and it is greatly to be feared that a certain Harvard sage might willingly adopt the epithet, for this gentleman, instructing at Cambridge, has publicly announced that the flapper with her bobbed hair is more scatter-brained than her long-haired sister.

Bobs and Brains.

How do bobs affect brains? Does wisdom ooze out of the freshly mowed medulla? Then why do men consider themselves brainier than women? And why do bald-headed men proudly point to their shining domes and explain their hairlessness as the result of brain activity?

No, the argument won't stand. Perhaps the sage from Harvard is not old enough to remember that women in the last century who wore their hair short were considered high-brow and were shunned by the men. History cites one case where the cutting of the hair affected a man's strength, but that had nothing to do with his brain, for Samson lost his senses before he did his tresses.

Short hair on women, says the philosophers, means but one thing. It is a badge of emancipation, an outward expression of her freedom of thought and action. The first fearless ones in America who cut their hair en masse were the artists of Greenwich Village (this, of course, excludes the women of a generation or more ago who cut their bangs; they did the job only half way). Conservative women looked with yearning hearts at the hairpinless thatches, but their day had not come. They had to wait for the war.

Women fought beside men, took their places in factories, drove motors. At last they had their longed-for share in the world's burden. But they couldn't carry on effectively when an hour had to be spent in the morning putting hair up in smooth masses and another at night twisting it on curlers. Boldly, therefore, they snipped and cut.

All this was five years and more ago. The girls—at that time they were chiefly young women who cut their hair—triumphantly combed it in public and flaunted it in the faces of the less fortunate. Irene Castle gave them the bucking of fashion when she returned from Europe bobbed.

The furor calmed for a while, and women of uncertain age rejoiced to think that they had not followed their hearts' desire. But now it has been renewed with added vigor, for fashion this Spring has ordered the tailored suit, the straight line and the neat, closely trimmed head that completes the silhouette.

"We don't dictate what women must make wiz their hair," said one of the leading hairdressers in town. "It is ze designers. We have but to follow suit."

The time had come to ask a long unanswered question. "What becomes of the hair you cut off?"

"Ah, ze lady, she guard it as a souvenir of her past glory. It is probablement hidden, tied with a ribbon or put away wiz her love letters in a box wiz ze sachet. We cannot use it." A flash of white teeth. "Ze hair we use come from ze peasant women in Europe. It is cut close to ze scalp.

But that is another story.

Some of the theories advanced for the bobbing epidemic are that it is economical, that it saves time, that it makes a woman look young. The first can scarcely be true, for there is the constant expense of waving, clipping and trimming. And, besides, she must have a postiche, a transformation, a switch, a something to cover up the nape of her neck on occasion.

There is a time-worn notion that the cutting of hair makes it grow in more heavily. But a tonsorial journal has warned that if women continue to cut their hair they will become bald.

The newspapers tell of divorce suits brought because wives bobbed their hair; of suicides on the same ground; of employers who protest; of educators who condemn; of superintendents of hospitals who storm. Yet the world has gone calmly on its way. And the long and short of it is that women will continue to do as they like.

FIRST WOMAN TAKES OFFICE AS GOVERNOR

Mrs. Ross Sworn In and Assumes Her Duties as Chief Executive of Wyoming.

RELIES ON "DIVINE HELP"

Telegrams From All Parts of the Country Bring Congratulations to the New Official.

CHEYENNE, Wyo., Jan. 5 (Associated Press).—A climax to more than fifty-five years of equal rights for women in Wyoming came shortly after noon today when Mrs. Nellie Taylor Ross formally took over her duties as Governor of the State.

Inaugural ceremonies, Spartan-like in their severity and simplicity, marked the induction into office of the first woman Governor of any Commonwealth in the United States.

Calling for "divine guidance," Mrs. Ross, heavily swathed in mourning for her husband, the late Governor William B. Ross, stepped into the place made vacant by his death less than three months ago.

Tears came to her eyes as Acting Governor Lucas, in a brief address, pledged to her the fullest cooperation of the State officials, called upon the electorate of Wyoming to stand solidly behind her and paid a glowing tribute to the virtues of her husband.

Address by the New Governor.

Mrs. Ross addressed the assemblage in the Senate Chamber as "my friends," and continued:

"Owing to the tragic and unprecedented circumstances which surround my induction into office, I have felt it not only unnecessary but inappropriate for me to now enter into such discussion of policies as usually constitutes an inaugural address.

"This occasion does not mark the beginning of a new Administration, but rather the resumption of that which was inaugurated in this chamber two years ago. It is well understood, I am sure, that it is my purpose to continue, as I am convinced it is the desire of my State that I should, in so far as changing conditions will permit, the program and policies then launched.

"I avail myself of this opportunity to acknowledge the gracious consideration shown me by Governor Lucas during the period he served as Executive of our State, and to say that I look forward confidently to that same degree of cooperation with him and with other State officers and with the Legislature that during my husband's term lightened for him the burdens of official life and contributed to his satisfaction and joy in service.

"In approaching the responsibilities of this exalted office I do so with a profound sense of the high obligation it imposes upon me. That the people of Wyoming should have placed such trust in me—in a large measure I feel an expression of their recognition of my husband's devotion to their interests and of his contribution to the progress of the State—calls forth in this solemn hour my deepest gratitude and challenges me to rise to the opportunities for service thus made possible, and to dedicate to the task before me every faculty of mind and body with which I may be endowed.

"Such dedication I now offer to my State, relying upon divine help for strength and guidance."

Country-Wide Congratulations.

Tonight, flushed with happiness and excitement and saddened in turn with the thought of her recent bereavement, the new Governor went through a heap of congratulatory telegrams from persons of all walks of life the country over. Included in the lot was one from Mrs. Miriam A. Ferguson of Texas, who after Jan. 20 will share with Mrs. Ross the distinction of being a woman Governor.

It was a fitting and added tribute to the womanhood of the country that the oath of office was administered by one of the men—Chief Justice C. N. Potter of the Wyoming Supreme Court—who on Sept. 30, 1889, drafted the clause granting equal rights to the women of a State for the first time, at the Constitutional Convention in Cheyenne. A. C. Campbell, another member of the historic convention, witnessed the ceremonies. Old and feeble, Campbell watched with interest the brief formalities in the Senate Chamber.

But the history of woman's rights in Wyoming antedates the constitutional convention by slightly more than twenty years. On Dec. 12, 1869, Territorial Governor Campbell affixed his signature to a measure that gave the women of Wyoming Territory the right to vote and hold office. The measure was not without its opposition when introduced, and a clique of pioneers, headed by Ben Sheck of South Pass, Wyo., bitterly opposed the attempt to enfranchise women.

Sheck, the only surviving member of the first territorial assembly, now a resident of the State of Washington, later regretted his action and during the fight in 1919 to ratify the Federal Suffrage Amendment, he telegraphed Dr. Grace R. Hebard, one of the suffrage pioneers of the State, that he had repented and had not only voted for the measure, but was working actively for its adoption.

Perhaps one of the most interested spectators at today's inauguration was Dr. Hebard, now Doctor of Philosphy at the University of Wyoming. Occupying a seat of honor, she smilingly declared that it was a red letter day for women. Dr. Hebard, together with Mrs. Amelia Post of Cheyenne, and Mrs. Hale, wife of a former territorial Governor, wrote the woman's suffrage clause that was later worked into the Constitution by Justice Potter and his associates. Both Mrs. Post and Mrs. Hale now are dead.

MAY SUE CHAS. E. HUGHES.

Passport Denial to Woman In Maiden Name Stirs League.

The Lucy Stone League, an organization for perpetuating the maiden names after marriage, gave its fourth annual dinner last night in the Butterfly Room at the Hotel Pennsylvania. Three hundred persons were present.

The guest of honor was Mrs. Helena Normanton, who gave a stirring recital of her victory over England's ancient prejudices in gaining admittance to the bar and in retaining use of her maiden name after her marriage to Gavin Clark of London.

At the close of Mrs. Normanton's talk Miss Ruth Hale, President of the league, announced that a league committee had been named to consider the possibility of bringing suit against Secretary Hughes for damages for the infringement of an individual right. The league recently sent a protest to the Secretary over the refusal of a passport to a young married woman under her maiden name.

January 6, 1925

January 21, 1925

'MA' AND JIM TAKE HOLD OF THE TEXAS HELM

By OWEN P. WHITE.

AUSTIN, Texas.

AUSTIN is the capital of a large State of hopeful expectancy. A week ago, when "Ma" Ferguson took her oath of office the place was the throbbing Capital of a State of lurid excitement and away back yonder in 1846, when J. Pinckney Henderson was inaugurated as the first male Governor of the great Lone Star Commonwealth, it was the Capital of a wild State of nature.

In Henderson's time this modern little city, which is now so handsomely up to date that it doesn't sell gasoline on Sunday and handles pedestrians through the medium of automatic traffic cops, consisted merely of an unsightly collection of log cabins, bounded on all sides by vast distances which were adequately filled with bad Indians, bellicose Mexicans and various and sundry other brands of assorted troubles.

In those happy days the men did the fighting, the drinking, the smoking and voting; the women did the work. At least, such is the unholy character of the indictment that a chronicler of the old régime brings against the ladies of that uncivilized period; and naturally one wonders what this same old historian would have thought of the situation if he could have dropped into town last week and taken note of the antics indulged in by the girls when "Ma" Ferguson kissed the Book and picked up the reins of Government.

Doubtless the old sinner would have concluded—and he would have been eminently right about it, too—that the heavy responsibilities of the men of Texas, along with a lot of their lesser and more pleasant vices, are now shared by the women folks, and also it is very likely that he, being a primitive, would have hastily decided that the inauguration of a first male Governor is a very tame, inexpensive and unimportant affair in comparison with the induction into office of a Chief Executive of the opposite sex.

Fashions in Law-Making.

In Pinckney Henderson's day the lawmakers of the great Lone Star State, who now issue their assaults against the free and unrestricted liberties of the people from behind the thick and sheltering walls of the largest red granite structure in America, were well satisfied to divide impartially their official time and their offical patronage between two saloons. This is history, not sarcasm. The members of the first Texas House of Representatives, instead of sitting back in swivel chairs with their feet comfortably silhouetted on the sky line between them and the Speaker, held their sessions—political, pokerish and potational—in an unfinished loft over a well-known drinking place. The Senate likewise functioned and also slept along with a lot of industrious fleas—the fleas being historic, too—in a white-washed attic which surmounted a second prominent filling station. Joint sessions were frequently held on the ground floor at either place, and just a passing glance at the record will furnish us with all the information we need in order that we may form a good mental picture of the character of the festivities indulged in at the Henderson inaugural of 1846.

In that year a liberal old thinker of the name of Baylor sat in dignity upon the bench, and in honor of the occasion, which marked the passing away of the Republic of Texas and the entrance into the American Union of the largest of its States, this learned Judge adjourned his court and told his hearers that no man would be considered drunk on such a glorious day so long as he could pronounce the word "Epsom."

Forty-eight hours later, according to the chronicler, every man who had been implicated in the proceeding was still able to say "Epsom" and thus, with most of the details left to our imagination, but without a single mark to its discredit, has the story of the inauguration of the first Governor of Texas come down to us through the annals of history.

Hendersonian Simplicity Gone.

Likewise, and in a like credible manner, has the inauguration of Miriam Ferguson as the first woman Governor of the State become a matter of record. Her inauguration, however, was not one that was marked by any striking degree of Hendersonian simplicity. Far from it. "Ma" Ferguson may be, and in reality she is, an entirely unostentatious and unassuming woman; but, in so far as everything pertaining to her inauguration was concerned—well, that ceremony was "anything else but." It was just as ornate, just as impressive and just as elaborate an affair as the spectacular inaugurations of a hotly partisan bunch of anti-Klansmen and an enthusiastic crowd of happy Fergusonians could conceive and put over. They did it well, and they did it on time, too. When the moment for the culmination of their hard-won triumph had arrived they were ready for it, and on the stroke of noon the doors to the Hall of Representatives were thrown open and the inaugural party began literally to force its way through a packed mass of humanity that had been uncomfortably accumulating since daybreak.

As the party came slowly up the aisle and mounted the platform a band in the gallery played "The Eyes of Texas Are Upon You"; the crowd screeched out its delirious delight, some women were so happy that they cried aloud over it; a girl in the balcony, wearing a four-gallon hat, a wide smile and a pair of leather chaps, unloosed one cowboy yell after another; the cannon boomed; the newspaper men at the press table smoked furiously, and the centre of it all, the one woman for whom all this disturbance was being created, was very calm, unruffled and unmoved.

Throughout all of the parliamentary engagements, throughout the invocation, throughout the brief ceremonies that accompanied the inauguration of the Lieutenant Governor and during the delivery of a couple of speeches "Ma" Ferguson sat the calmest person in the room. Some of the other people present may have felt some emotion surge, but not "Ma." She was cool and collected to the last, and even when her turn came, even when the retiring Governor, the Hon. Pat M. Neff, in a beautiful outburst of carefully prepared, impromptu oratory, bequeathed to her, as a touching legacy, a white flower, an open Bible and a picture of Woodrow Wilson, she was able not to smile. And then, following this, when she herself, after having kissed the Book and signend the oath of office, told her people that what Texas needed was a long pull, a strong pull and a pull all together, she told it in a way that was remarkable only for its sincerity and simplicity. She delivered her message in just the way that any woman would be expected to deliver such a message who, after many long years lived as a housewife and a mother, finds herself suddenly called upon to turn away from the intricate mysteries of the bread pan and the mixing bowl to take up the even more involved propositions presented by a complicated political situation.

Nothing Fancy About Her.

In other words, "Ma" Ferguson, now Governor of Texas, faced the actual fact of her inauguration and, when that ordeal was over, accepted the congratulations of as many people as could get to her, just as though both of these happenings were mere incidents which had to be encountered and endured before she and Farmer Jim could step out resolutely on the road to their well-established goal.

Photo by the Elliotts.

"Ma" Ferguson in Dress Worn at Inaugural Ball.

Governor Ferguson at Her Desk in the State House at Austin. At Her Left, Jim Ferguson, Her Husband.

On the surface, then, there is nothing fancy about "Ma" Ferguson, and beneath the surface there isn't anything fancy either. Both inside and out Governor "Ma" is just a plain woman, a woman whose instincts are maternal and whose interests and ambitions centre in the welfare of her husband and her children, but when you take that kind of a woman and equip her with a big idea, furnish her with a fighting incentive, push her into the political arena (or any other kind of an arena) and tell her to go to it and develop her idea, something large, exciting and decisive is bound to happen. "Ma's" case was no exception, and it did happen. She ran for office not because she wanted to run but because Farmer Jim couldn't run, and hence she became, because the Klan fight was Jim's fight, the standard bearer of a campaign against the K. K. K. which caused the attention of the entire nation to become centred upon her. She won her fight; that is, she and Farmer Jim working together won it.

Governors' Notable Acts.

Governors at various times and under varying conditions have done large things for the State. J. Pinckney Henderson, for example, almost as his first official act, violated his oath of office by accepting a commission from the United States Government and becoming the leader of the Texas troops during the Mexican War. The Federal Government gave Henderson a sword for his gallantry and the State forgave him for his delinquency. Sam Houston also did so much for his State that it cannot be catalogued here, and in later years Jim Hogg waged a successful warfare against the railroads.

The jobs that the men had to tackle, though, were easy in comparison with "Ma's." All that she has to do is to whip public opinion. With the eyes of Texas upon her, watching her at every step that she takes and checking her up

at every political move she makes, "Ma" Ferguson knows that it is her duty, not only as Governor but also as a wife, a mother and a grandmother, to win vindication for Farmer Jim.

"Ma" resents the statement that Jim was impeached. Regardless of the action taken by the Senate seven years ago, she still believes that the faith of the people of Texas is with her husband —she told me all of this in a conversational chat—and she realizes that the obligation of justifying that faith is now resting squarely upon her shoulders.

"We're on Top Again."

Under these circumstances, then, it is distinctly up to "Ma", to make good. She fully appreciates the situation.

"Seven years ago," she said, in talking to me, "the people said that Jim Ferguson was down and out. But he wasn't. They were just going to begin to get acquainted with Jim Ferguson and they didn't know it. That was seven years ago. Things change every seven years you know and now here we are on top again and with everything, so far as I can see it, harmonious and peaceful."

"Ma's" contract to make good, however, is not one that she is going to tackle alone. In her inaugural address she said frankly she needed help, she admitted her inexperience and asked for the cooperation of the people of Texas. She expects to get that cooperation, but of course it will be to Farmer Jim that she will look for most of her guidance, and it is highly improbable that either one of them will ever allow the other to stray away from the path of good government. Along that path and along that path only, according to "Ma," lies the way to vindication, and the combination of her intuition and Farmer Jim's intelligence—and even his worst enemies admit that he has a head full of it—forms a mixture which, liberally administered to the State of Texas,

will have a very beneficial effect upon it for the next two years.

The first thing that Governor "Ma" did after leaving the inaugural platform was to go directly to her private executive office, seat herself firmly and solidly in the Governor's chair, smile broadly and cheerfully at her husband and say, "Now, Jim, don't you start in by telling me what to do."

"Jim" in No Hurry.

Jim didn't start. Like the sensible man that he has the reputation of being, he postponed offering any suggestions that he may have had in mind until the next day, and "Ma," like the sensible woman that she is, rose from her chair, walked out of the Capitol, stepped into a motor and rode home to rest up a bit and prepare for the festivities of the night. And, believe me, they were some festivities! The invitations which had been sent out, lavishly and liberally, by "Ma's" inaugural ball committee, were about as large and gaudy as the average diploma that is handed to the sweet girl graduate in the country school, and the functions to which they admitted the bearer were fully in keeping, both in size and quality, with the elaborateness of their announcement.

It was proposed to hold three balls in "Ma's" honor, but in reality they didn't hold any at all. What they did have was a large, State-wide, old-fashioned range round-up which brought in thousands of people of three classes: office seekers, rabid anti-Klansmen and ardent Fergusonites. The round-up was split into three droves; two herds were corraled down at the hotels, and the third, the big herd, was run through the chutes up at the Capitol. It must have been a great sight for anybody who could see it. But I couldn't. I got jammed into a corner where I stayed for three hours, and then as soon as I could get out and assemble myself I did so and went home.

"Ma," however, must have fared better than I did because she was at her desk the next morning at 9 o'clock and told all of the newspaper men that she had had a fine time at the ball.

Her Message to Legislature.

"Ma" Ferguson's first official act on her first morning of real work was to sign her message to the Legislature and send it out to be read in both houses. She next granted a pardon to a man who had been thoughtless enough to commit a felony after he had become the father of seven small children, and then, closing her door to the public, she spent the rest of the morning in conferring with office seekers, political potentates and personal friends.

During the afternoon of this, her first day on the job, "Ma" didn't work, but her message did. It was read in both houses, printed in all the papers and widely-discussed. The message is worth it; it covers a lot of ground; it takes up the interesting question of how to put a territorial limit on the predatory operations of a cow tick and suggests to the Legislature that a tax of 2 cents a package be placed on cigarettes, thereby obtaining an income of a million a year—mostly from the students themselves—with which a few more houses can be erected on the campus of the State university. It discusses these things and everything between and, as Farmer Jim remarked the next morning, "maybe after we see how this dose operates on the boys we'll send them in another."

The next day Governor "Ma," after commenting on the fact that news travels rapidly and that the penitentiary seemed to have suddenly filled up with men who had seven children, granted two more pardons; finished moving her household goods into the Executive mansion; had her eyes fitted with a new pair of spectacles and announced to the newspaper men, through Farmer Jim, that she would be ready with a batch of appointments in a few days.

Pardons and appointments are the things that are going to give "Ma" most of her trouble and worry for the next few weeks. In the State penitentiary there are 3,555 potential candidates for executive clemency and within the gift of the Governor there are 400 jobs for which there are, at present, 4,000 applicants. Under the circumstances, then, it is no wonder that "Ma" enters and leaves her office through a private side door. To get in by going through the anteroom would be almost as bad as being inaugurated over again. Every morning and all day long the anteroom is crowded with men and women who are there for a purpose and from 8 till 5 Farmer Jim is on hand to attend to their wants and to stand as a buffer between the public and the Governor.

In regard to the pardon problem "Ma" has already taken that dilemma by the horns and, in good Texas parlance, has bull-dogged it to earth. For four years there has been no pardon board in operation in Texas, but Mrs. Ferguson, realizing that her womanly heart would probably respond too readily to the appeals that are pouring into her office by the hundreds, has appointed one and says that her actions will be guided by its recommendations.

In the matter of appointments also she is displaying a very decided tendency to go slowly, watch her step and listen attentively to the counsel of men who are older in the political game than she is.

She Has Gone Slowly.

And up to the present time Governor Ferguson has gone slowly. She has been in office a week; Texas is still safe; the Treasury hasn't been looted; the gold star in liberty's hand on the top of the Capitol has not been melted and sold for junk and nobody so far has been able to scare "Ma" into doing anything that would indicate that she is a "shadow jumper." She hasn't said anything yet that she couldn't sign her name to and in regard to one or two things she has said practically nothing at all.

One of the subjects on which she has failed to comment, except to say that it was introduced without her knowledge, is the resolution now before the Texas Senate calling upon that body to take some action which will tend to remove the stain of impeachment from the name of her husband.

As already stated, "Ma" resents the use of the word "impeachment" in connection with Farmer Jim's retirement from office seven years ago, but she none the less realizes that it is so written in the records and she wants to see it wiped out. So does the Senate and so does the House and, according to "Ma," so do the people of Texas. By a majority of 128,000 these people elected her to the office for which Farmer Jim could not qualify, and although she looks upon this victory as a popular vindication she says that she is going to make it even more complete by giving Texas a good, honest, economical Administration. In anticipation of this and confident that "Ma" Ferguson is in deadly earnest in her desire to make good, the Texas Legislature is ready, just as soon as it can find how to do it legally, to wipe the record of seven years ago off its books and restore Farmer Jim to his full rights as a citizen of the State, and when that happens "Ma" Ferguson will be completely happy.

WAR MOTHERS ASKED TO REVIVE HOME LIFE

Mrs. H. H. McClure, the National War Mother, of Kansas City, Mo., in an address to the delegates to the New York State War Mothers' Convention at the Hotel Astor yesterday declared that the Government of the country is just as good as the homes make it. Mrs. McClure had come from Washington, where the national charter of the organization was signed by President Coolidge. She told of the work of the national organization during the past year and urged the war mothers to establish homes for disabled veterans.

After her speech $1,400 was pledged to the War Mothers' National Mountain Home at Denver, Col.

Mrs. McClure also urged the war mothers to help create an interest in individual homes. "We are getting away from home life," said Mrs. McClure. "Our greatest mission is in getting back to the old home life and in creating a better understanding between parents and children."

A resolution favoring Defense Day as a permanent institution was introduced by Mrs. William S. Titus, Past State War Mother.

The following officers were elected: Mrs. Mabel C. Digney, President; Mrs. Lottie Haas, First Vice President; Mrs. William Cummings Story, Second Vice President; Mrs. Fannie Smith, Third Vice President; Mrs. Margaret McNally, Fourth Vice President; Mrs. Harold Avery, Recording Secretary; Mrs. Lydia Broderick, Corresponding Secretary; Mrs. M. L. Hodes, Treasurer; Mrs. James Austin Evans, Historian; Mrs. T. Stanton Field, Custodian of Records, and Mrs. Brady Mathieu, Auditor.

WOMEN AT ODDS ON 48-HOUR BILL

Mrs. Franklin D. Roosevelt Urges Passage at Hearing Before Legislators.

MANY WORKERS OPPOSE IT

"Protection Needed From Uplifters," Declares Representative of Brooklyn-Manhattan Lines Employes.

Special to The New York Times.

ALBANY, Feb. 25.—Woman lined up against woman and self-styled uplifters opposed one another at a four-hour hearing in the Assembly chamber this afternoon on bills providing for a forty-eight-hour week for women and minors in industry. Ninety per cent. of the speakers for and against the measures were women.

After listening for two hours to the pleadings of workingwomen not to pass any bill reducing their hours of work on the ground that it would probably mean the loss of their positions and a reduction in their wages, the members of the Senate and Assembly Labor and Industries Committees gave attention for two hours more to other women who urged that the forty-eight-hour bill be passed to protect the health of female workers and give opportunity for their recreation and study.

Shopgirls walked down one aisle and told the committee that the passage of the bill would be one of the worst things that could happen for them. They asserted they were perfectly satisfied to work fifty and fifty-four hours a week, and more if they could, to earn a "decent living." Other shopgirls marched down another aisle and pleaded just as earnestly that the bill be reported out and passed in the name of "humanity."

Mrs. Franklin D. Roosevelt urged the passage of the forty-eight-hour measure sponsored by Senator Mastick and Assemblyman Shonk, Westchester Republicans.

"The one basic thing which we must remember," Mrs. Roosevelt said, "is that women are only women and they need the protection of the Government, because on them depends what the future Government will be. Aside from all the so-called sob stuff which we have heard here this afternoon, I am convinced that a great majority of the workingwomen of this State are really in favor of this bill and would like to see it become law. I can't understand how any woman would want to work fifty-four hours a week if she only had to work forty-eight and could receive the same rate of wages."

Mrs. Rheta Childe Dorr led the opposition, and Mrs. Samuel J. Bens of Utica, long an active member of the League of Women Voters, was in charge of the supporters.

The sincerity of the State Federation of Labor in urging enactment of the bill was challenged by Doris Stevens, representing the New York Branch of the National Woman's Party. She spoke against the proposal as it stands, urging that it be amended to apply to all persons.

"I am not moved by what the employers say regarding this bill," she said. "Of course they want women to work as long as possible because the women are not receiving wages equal to the men, but I am concerned with what the representatives of labor organizations have to say about the bill. I fear their support is rather based on the fact that they would like to see women kept out of industries and thereby prevent them from competing with men."

Mrs. Dorr maintained that if the forty-eight hour week was good for men it was equally good for women.

Mrs. Mary Murray, head of the women workers of the Brooklyn Manhattan Transit Company, told the committee that those who favored the forty-eight-hour legislation were trying to conceal its real purpose by waving the flag of maternity.

"Some years ago they told us that legislation affecting the women working for the B. R. T. would put them on Easy Street," she said. "It put them on the street, all right. What we want most of all is protection from the nonworking and professional uplifters."

Proponents of the bill pointed out that the platforms of both the Republican and Democratic Parties last Fall contained planks endorsing the forty-eight-hour week.

Half a dozen representatives of women collar workers from Troy told the committee that 90 per cent. of the girls and women in the big collar shops were opposed to the bill because they were certain it would mean a cut in their wages. Ada R. Wolfe contended that the working women of the State favored the proposed bill, "despite all that the professional uplifters say to the contrary."

Art in Home Cooking Seen As Aid to Happy Marriages

The raising of culinary activity to the level of an art will go a long way toward making marriages happy and solving health problems, said Dr. J. A. Patton, medical director of the Prudential Insurance Company of America, yesterday.

Men are unhappy because the cooking at home is not good, and suffer digestive complaints, the cause of many ills, because they eat improperly at other places, was the way he expressed it.

"What we need is greater attention to the home dietary," he said. "Men will eat more at home if wives have been taught to regard cooking as an accomplishment as worthy as music. If they eat more good food at home there will be more happy marriages."

March 4, 1925

FIGHT TO PREVENT CHILD MARRIAGES

Bride of 11 Cited in Favor of the "Stop, Look, Listen" Bill.

667,000 WEDDED UNDER 16

Child Welfare Commission and Russell Sage Foundation Issue Statements.

A case of the marriage of a girl of 11 years old was cited yesterday in a statement by the Child Welfare Commission in favor of the "stop, look, listen" bill, which interposes a delay of five days between the application for a marriage license and the granting of it.

The Russell Sage Foundation made public yesterday a preliminary report of its survey of the "child bride" problem, stating that it was found that more than 667,000 women living in the United States today were married before the age of 16 years.

"This century has often been misnamed 'the century of the child'," says the report. "In sober truth, with a quarter of the full term behind us, it must be acknowledged that the twentieth century is no such thing; certainly not when conditions in a country as intelligent as the United States still make possible the marriage of children. Such conditions constitute only a small part of the body of evidence against exaggerated claims of advance in the matter of child welfare, but they are a part which has not yet been developed in any detail."

As an illustration of public apathy on the subject, the report says that in fourteen States it is possible for a girl to marry at an age when she is forbidden because of her youth to become a wage earner.

This situation is largely due, according to the report, to two causes: First, that many States require no better evidence of age than the affidavit of one of the candidates for a marriage license, and that the legal minimum marriageable age is only 12 years for girls and 14 years for boys in New York, New Jersey, Pennsylvania, Kentucky, Louisiana, Virginia, Florida, Maryland, Rhode Island, Tennessee, Colorado, Idaho, Maine and Mississippi.

In support of the bill interposing delay and the bill making 16 years the minimum age of marriage in New York State the Child Welfare Commission made public the following cases:

"A girl of 11 years and 11 months was married by a Justice of the Peace to a man of about 25. The parents not only gave their consent but stated her age falsely. The marriage was fairly satisfactory, but at the age of 20 she was left a widow with five dependent children.

"A child of 12 was married with the consent of her parents to a man of 40. Owing to her neglect of her child she came under the care of the Children's Court. It was discovered that her husband had been married before and that his first wife was still living. The girl was diagnosed as feeble-minded and has since been committed to a State institution. Her child is dependent on the county for support.

"A fourteen-year-old girl, beaten and treated as a drudge by her stepmother and finally married against her will to a boy of 19, gave herself up at a police station one day. The stepmother had arranged the marriage because she had been warned by the school authorities that the girl must attend school rather than work and contribute to an already well-supported household."

March 9, 1925

AID FOR MOTHERS IS WIDELY ADOPTED

THE extent to which America feels its responsibility for the conservation of the home is indicated in a recent study made by the Children's Bureau of the Department of Labor. Formerly, when children needed more support than their own parents could provide, society thought it enough if food, clothing and shelter for them were made available in an institution, or else doled out poor relief intermittently to the struggling parents. Now society recognizes that the child is entitled to maintenance in his own home, if poverty alone is the peril that threatens.

Organized society is, in fact, digging into its purse for the means of preserving homes, and in place of spasmodic giving, is supplying what various States have termed mothers' pensions, mothers' allowances, mothers' assistance funds, widows' compensation, aid for dependent children and so on. Forty-two States have adopted laws authorizing assistance from public funds for dependent children in their own homes, and the District of Columbia, Alaska and Hawaii have made similar provision. It is estimated that approximately 200,000 are thus being cared for wholly or in part.

The need, however, is by no means fully met. Some States, having passed such laws, have failed to put them into practice or have neglected to make available funds necessary for carrying them out. In many States some localities are well looked after, while others are ignored.

A Marked Advance.

The Children's Bureau believes that if the number of home-aided children were doubled, the need would be more nearly met. Still, what progress has been made shows a marked advance over former practices. Mothers' aid, where it is properly administered, means that the family, deprived of its normal breadwinner by death or disability, still has a steady income, carefully adjusted to its particular needs, upon which it can depend. It can arrange its life accordingly, instead of merely existing after the hand-to-mouth manner of those dependent for aid upon spasmodic charity.

The movement is still comparatively young. The first State-wide mothers' aid law was enacted in Illinois in 1911. Before that, several small beginnings had been made. Juvenile courts in some California counties as early as 1906 granted county aid to semi-orphans and others in their own homes. In 1908 Oklahoma started providing school scholarships through its counties for children whose widowed mothers needed their earnings, and Michigan followed this example in 1911. The Missouri Legislature made a definite legal provision to aid mothers of dependent children the same year Illinois did.

The next year Colorado adopted "mothers' compensation" by popular vote; and in the following year eighteen States enacted mothers' aid laws. This early legislation was largely experimental, and most of it has been completely revised. Later laws, too, have undergone change, but the original idea has gained in force, the amendments tending mostly to improve administration, to make the application of the laws more inclusive, and to increase the appropriations available and the size of the individual grants.

In the great majority of States aid is now given not only to widows but also to women whose husbands have deserted their families; women who are divorced, totally incapacitated mentally or physically, imprisoned, or in an institution for the insane, feeble-minded or epileptic. In some States the term "mother" includes a relative or guardian upon whom the child is dependent; in a few, expectant mothers and unmarried mothers are included.

The conditions determining the grant of aid are mainly concerned with the mother's ability to give the child proper care and arrange for his economic needs. The age of the children on behalf of whom aid is given ranges up to 18 years, but generally conforms with compulsory school attendance and with the child labor laws. The amount of the allowance is variable. The grants are not strictly limited, but are based rather on the needs of individual families after all available resources have been taken into consideration.

Maximum grants per child, however, are usually fixed. The great fault of most of the legislation, in the opinion of the bureau, is that the maximum grants have been generally fixed too low. It has been estimated that a minimum of $1,000 a

year is necessary for the maintenance of a mother with three children; yet in thirty-five States $800 is the most that can be granted for such a family, and in twenty States the maximum is less than $480.

When application for aid is made, the procedure is more or less uniform. An investigation is held to determine the character of the home and the amount of aid required. If aid is granted, the family then becomes, in a way, a charge of the administrative agency. Some great, perhaps unlooked-for, misfortune lies behind the appeal, with the result that not only money but also friendly guidance and advice is needed.

It may be that neighbors do not know the family is receiving public aid; nevertheless, a visitor comes at times to help work out the budget; to assist the mother with a problem child, to direct the financing of a new home or the refurbishing of the old, or to help in difficulties of other kinds. Usually once in six months a review is made of the grants, so that the allowances may be adjusted to changing conditions.

Studies made at different times by the Children's Bureau show that the mothers' aid laws, when backed by proper supervision and sufficient funds, have been very constructive measures. Far from developing such a spirit of dependency as older relief measures engendered, the aid is said to make for self-confidence, initiative and the desire for economic independence as soon as possible. Many families, after they have been thus helped to start afresh, have been known to relinquish their grants long before the time allotted.

As a rule, it is found that the family that receives the benefit of mother's aid soon finds itself in a better home.

September 15, 1929

WOULD WED THE BRAINY TO PHYSICALLY STRONG

Boston Alienist Says Educated Families Run Out Because of Equals Mating.

Special to The New York Times.

BOSTON, March 22.—Tracing the fall in the birth rate among highly educated persons to overstimulation of the brain as exercised by the student and the mental worker, L. Vernon Briggs, a Boston alienist, offers as a remedy intermarriage by college graduates with mates of less intellectual calibre.

"It is a medical fact," said Mr. Briggs, "that great mental effort weakens the rest of the human system, in that the greater amount of the blood in the body is drawn to the brain.

"Each human body contains but two-thirds of its veins full of blood, and that blood is drawn to whatever organs are most stimulated. In the case of brain work it goes to the head; in the case of manual labor it is drawn to the head very little, but goes rather to the body.

"The finest family stock in the country can, and frequently does, run out because of too close marriage with those of equal station and equal mental and physical stimulus and intermarriage.

"The greatest good fortune that can come to a family whose every member is a brain worker is the marriage of one of them to a man or woman of lower caste, to a type who uses his or her brain comparatively little, and whose strength, therefore, lies in physical being, for that way will the family name and fame be carried.

"It does not follow that because he or she is not a brain worker that he or she does not make an ideal companion, intelligent and delightful."

March 23, 1925

AIMEE M'PHERSON, EVANGELIST

Mrs. McPherson first achieved national attention in the Nineteen Twenties as the enchanting, blonde evangelist of Angelus Temple in Los Angeles, who, presumably lost while swimming in the surf off Santa Monica, reappeared in the desert near Douglas, Ariz., with a weird story of having been kidnapped.

This event probably brought her more notoriety than any other, but through the theatrical management of her temple, her religious exhibitionism, divorce suits and litigation involving members of her own family and Rheba Crawford, a rival evangelist, she repeatedly found her way into the public prints. She was unique in the realm of evangelism.

Aimee Elizabeth Kennedy was born on a farm near Ingersoll, Ont., Oct. 9, 1890, and not much was known of her antecedents except that her parents were humble and that her mother was a member of the Salvation Army.

In her autobiography Mrs. McPherson told of becoming imbued with religious zeal at the age of 17. She became an evangelist of a sort at that time, but little was known of her until she appeared in California in a battered automobile, with her mother, Mrs. Minnie (Ma) Kennedy, and preached her cheerful gospel.

Called "Miracle Woman"

In 1920 she had made such progress in her calling that she was the chief attraction at a Bronx revival meeting, and she was hailed the next year in Montreal as a "miracle woman"—a faith healer.

After moving to the Los Angeles area, the young woman was surrounded by disciples who gave generously, and she was enabled to found and build the Angelus Temple, an edifice with a seating capacity of 5,000. Not many years after her arrival in California her fortune was estimated at more than $600,000.

Mrs. McPherson disappeared on a spring day in 1926. She was believed to have drowned while bathing, and her followers crowded the the beach at Santa Monica, keeping vigil, chanting and praying.

Mrs. McPherson came back to the world on June 23 at Douglas with a story of maltreatment and even torture at the hands of her captors, but investigation showed that her narrative of wandering about the Mexican desert near Agua Prieta and of leaving the imprint of her French heels on the burning sands was wholly fantastic.

Indeed, those who investigated the case declared that the pastor of Angelus Temple had been the veiled woman who had spent an idyllic ten days in a vine-covered cottage at Carmel, Calif., with one Kenneth G. Ormiston, radio operator of Angelus Temple. Mrs. McPherson resented pointed references to an amorous affair and the suggestion that she had found a new husband.

The closest approximation to the man of her dreams, apparently, came along in the person of David L. Hutton, baritone singer in her choir, whom she married on Sept. 13, 1931, at Yuma, Ariz., after an airplane flight from Los Angeles. Two days after their marriage a suit was filed against Mr. Hutton for $200,000 by Myrtle H. St. Pierre, a Los Angeles nurse.

In 1934, Mr. Hutton, who had wrangled publicly with his wife several times over the affairs of Angelus Temple, of which he had become business manager, sued her for divorce on the grounds of "mental cruelty." She filed a cross suit, saying his posing with scantily clad chorus girls for publicity purposes had humiliated her. Her suit was not heard and the Los Angeles court awarded a divorce to Mr. Hutton on March 6, 1935.

At various times in her career Mrs. McPherson crusaded against New York and Paris night life, and in 1928 made a preaching tour in Great Britain, despite having been denounced by a rival Los Angeles minister then in London as a "twentieth century Jezebel" who was "as dangerous as a man who goes to the schoolhouse to sell poisoned candy."

AIMEE SEMPLE M'PHERSON
The New York Times, 1942

Mrs. McPherson claimed her church had millions of converts and on one occasion, expressing her philosophy, she asserted, "I bring spiritual consolation to the middle classes, leaving those above to themselves and those below to the Salvation Army."

Mrs. McPherson also became entangled with her daughter, Roberta Semple, who brought a $150,000 slander suit against her mother, and finally received an award of $2,000. Miss Semple was divorced from William Bradley Smyth, a ship's purser, and later was married to Harry Salter, an orchestra leader.

Mrs. McPherson's first marriage was terminated by the death of Robert Semple, a Scottish evangelist, to whom she was married at the age of 19. In the Orient both fell ill and Mr. Semple died. Roberta was born shortly thereafter.

The evangelist returned to the United States with her daughter and continued her work. In the South, she met and married Harold McPherson, a grocery clerk, and bore her second child, a son, Rolf McPherson. That marriage ended in divorce.

September 28, 1944

Fannie Hurst Writes of Squalor and Luxury

Her Latest Novel Is Not Distinguished for Its Element of Reality

MANNEQUIN. By Fannie Hurst. 297 pp. New York: Alfred A. Knopf.

MISS FANNIE HURST'S plots are generally better than their working out. This is only another way to say that her imagination (an exuberant one) is apt to set her technique tasks to which it is not quite equal. In "Appassionata" the conception of a beautiful girl, weaned from all idea of marriage or relish for the world, partly by a love of her own intact loveliness, partly by the domestic wreckage she sees about her, somehow stuck in the memory after the book had, not without effort, been finished, and exonerated it from abundant faults of taste and eccentricities of style. In "Mannequin," the novel that follows it at a distance of less than a year, there is even more discrepancy between promise and performance, and extenuations are harder to find. The theme, which is that of a child stolen from a gentle home in infancy and reared in squalor and danger, is promising. Miss Hurst has chosen so to handle it that not one single element of reality, not to say realism, adheres. Amid all the paraphernalia of ashcans, littered fire-

escapes, alley cats, clotheslines and pushcarts that are a mere trick of visual memory, the career of exquisite little Orchid Sargasso, born Joan Herrick, pursues its way back to "priceless patina," "old red brocatelles," "Pomperian bathrooms"—back in fact to the heaven of the interior decorator that Miss Hurst makes her own, with an evenness for which there is no warrant in observed fact.

When we meet Orchid first she is Joan Herrick, the adored baby girl and supreme bibelot in an aspiring apartment on the "wrong side" of Central Park that would make Ibsen's Doll House austere and emancipated by comparison. Her father is a sober and clever young lawyer, whose social possibilities are being discounted in advance by a climbing and managing wife. There are times when we glimpse social satire in Miss Hurst's meticulous cataloging of all Selene's subtle "differences" from her neighbors, her magpie hunt through secondhand shops and auction rooms for little "bits" of brass and glass or scraps of tapestry, her endless juggling with the slender household budget to gratify her esthetic whims. But mostly the satire dis-

appears under an actual relish. Selene is contemplating her first ambitious dinner party:

A formal, seven-thirty, floral-centrepiece, creamed-oysters-incases dinner party. Extra-dry in amber goblets, squab chicken in my darling little Brittany-ware casseroles, and a Nesselrole pudding under pink whipped cream that looks like Sherry's. * * * The trifles were what drove one to frenzy. * * * To remember to telegraph mother to send down her half-dozen silver grapefruit spoons by Brother Ed. * * * To see that Annie remembered the white napkin to be wound around the champagne bottle with just enough of the magic name of Roget on the bottle showing. * * * Yellow candles for the two majolica candlesticks sent * * * on approval from an exclusive importer's shop, and with heartache to be returned the next morning.

Poor Selene's brave attempts to impress meets with a punishment even more condign than the exasperated reader would suggest. Among her investments is a girl found sitting on a bench in the Park, in whom, when tricked out in nursemaid black with "white organdie bows which by a little trick of rolling the edges Selene knew how to make stand upright," possibilities for more social display at slight cost suggest themselves. But Annie Pogany turns out a sullen and dangerous moron. During a quarrel between husband and wife she steals the child, for whom she has developed an unwholesome affection, and carries her off to a secure hiding place among the east side tenements.

It is not easy to find words with which to do justice to Orchid's tene-

ment life. To borrow a phrase from clever Christopher Morley, her immunity from environment is a thing to "wamble" at. No shadow of the speech or manners which are all her conscious life has known falls across her developing exquisiteness. By some miracle of heredity of which Miss Hurst keeps the secret, even her personal habits retain the impress of Central Park (even Central Park West).

Orchid could never bear to let her flesh come into contact with the dirtiness. * * * The flesh of her young body, in a world of sour unfastidious bodies, she kept firm and cool-feeling by letting the water from a faucet run down over her as if she had been a little marble knoll. * * * With her instincts she avoided the contacts with the dirtiness.

A little later, when Orchid, after a scene with a brute of true "abysmal" type, has been rescued and sent as cash girl to the Titanic Stores, Miss Hurst makes some attempt to account for these puzzling immunities.

"The texture of her skin might have helped to explain it. The fine grain of her."

It is an ingenious theory, to be recommended to those who are mak-

ing the complexion of the nation their concern.

Once safely among "fastidious stuffs that her flesh craved" and "sleazy stuffs" that she loves to feel "near the dainty fabric of her own flesh," Orchid's progress toward luxury and exclusiveness becomes a mere matter of yielding to "the intuition that presided over the choice of her adjectives and her blouses."

This leads her not only to a position as mannequin at "probably the most exclusive firm of dressmakers on two continents," and a room where she can now afford to bestow the "little touches her fastidiousness craved," by means of the little "bits" and "few yards" and "subdued prints" of poor Selene's old grab-bag, but to a chivalrous young lover, very near the Innesbrook millions, who asks no more than to sit among the bargains and feel "the creeping sweetness of domestic serenity" gradually enfold him.

Oh, Martin [it is the tenement child speaking], I've an electric stove here behind the screen, and the duckiest aluminium griddle for chops. And lettuce—a whole wet towel of it in my brand new little refrigerator, and the heavenliest strawberries. * * *

Of course there is sterner material to come. A garden party in the more exclusive suburbs, a wild ride home, a drunken admirer to whom even fastidiousness is not sacred, a fatal struggle and a murder trial. over which, as a crowning stroke of invention, the missing father presides. But somehow, all Miss Hurst's intensity, the frenzied and disjointed prayers which seem to have infiltrated from "Appassionata," very much as actresses of limited ability re-echo old successes in new rôles, will not persuade us to take. it seriously. We remember. with some alleviation to our suspense, that no medium has yet been evolved in fiction that will reconcile "Hints to Housewives" with the stuff of tragedy. and that Miss Hurst is not likely to initiate one.

The younger Mr. Weller. on a memorable occasion, hearing a roast leg of mutton called a "swarry" by the footmen of Bath, surmised what the name would be if it were boiled. One is left wondering just what the judges of Liberty, who have awarded $50,000 to "Mannequin" as "the best novel by an American author" written in 1925. would consider a bad one.

CITY'S THRONGS GIVE GREATEST WELCOME TO GERTRUDE EDERLE

Ovation to Swimmer of Channel Outrivals Those to Other Individual Heroes.

SHE IS HAPPY AND EXCITED

Mayor Presents a Medal and Scroll—Coolidge and Smith Send Congratulations.

THOUSANDS PACK STREETS

Showers of Confetti, Flowers and Gifts, and $900,000 in Offers From Stage, Films and Pools.

New York City yesterday welcomed Gertrude Ederle home from her victory over the English Channel with a demonstration that for numbers, noise, spontaneity and variety surpassed any previous reception to a distinguished person. No President or king, soldier or statesman has ever enjoyed such an enthusiastic and affectionate outburst of acclaim by the metropolis as was offered to the butcher's daughter of Amsterdam Avenue, hailed as the "Queen of Swimmers."

Messages of greeting and congratulation came to her from President Coolidge and Governor Smith, giving the welcome a national and State-wide scope.

On land and on water, from the air, and above all else from the heart, the city showered its felicitations upon Trudy Ederle. Harbor craft, with bands playing, flags fluttering and sirens and whistles shrieking, met Miss Ederle when she arrived aboard the Cunarder Berengaria at Quarantine. The city's welcome boat, the Macom, took her off the liner, and steamed to the Battery. The water front symphony of whistles, sirens, fog horns and bells was thunderous.

Crowds Break Police Lines.

From the Battery, the swimmer's progress to the City Hall was a triumphal procession in a renewal of that confetti and ticker tape snowstorm which fell first on Theodore Roosevelt in 1910, and later on such heroes as Marshal Foch and Captain Fried and Lieut. Commander Byrd. Tens of thousands hailed Miss Ederle from the sidewalks, windows and tops of high buildings. At intervals the crowds in the streets broke through the police lines at the curb, and rolled across the street like the Channel surf, to delay but not stop her progress.

After her reception at City Hall, Miss Ederle received a continuous ovation all the way up Lafayette Street, Ninth Street, Fifth Avenue and Fifty-seventh Street to her home at Amsterdam Avenue and Sixty-third Street. Sidewalks and streets were packed. The windows were peopled by cheering, clapping, whistling and stamping thousands, who continued the shower of Manhattan's laurels, confetti and ticker tape.

A detachment of twenty motorcycle policemen led the parade from the Battery. At intervals, where spectators encroached upon the street, they charged the crowds and drove them back to the sidewalks. Following the motorcycle police were ten mounted policemen. Then came the automobile in which Miss Ederle rode with Grover A. Whalen and Dudley Field Malone. Following the automobile marched twelve patrolmen. They were followed by a long line of automobiles carrying members of the Mayor's committee.

10,000 at City Hall.

When the Channel swimmer and the Mayor's committee arrived at City Hall there were more than ten thousand persons waiting in City Hall Park to see and cheer Miss Ederle. As she entered the hall the crowd stormed the doors, but the doors were locked. Many of the Mayor's committee and the press were barred until order was restored.

Following her welcome Miss Ederle and Mayor Walker started to the front steps of the hall to pose for photographers. The crowd launched another tidal wave that upset the photographic battery and engulfed the returning champion and the Mayor.

Patrolman John J. O'Donovan, who had sensed what was coming, picked the swimmer up bodily and carried her back into City Hall. Mayor Walker was rushed inside by two police aids with the technique of football interference, one on each side of him, until he reached a zone of safety. The Mayor escorted Miss Ederle, her mother and other members of her party to his office and Chief Police Inspector August Kuehne sent in a hurry call for an additional 100 police reserves to reinforce the 130 men already on duty at City Hall. Six persons caught in the stampede were injured.

Offers Approach $1,000,000.

Miss Ederle was overwhelmed not only by the magnitude of the city's welcome but by the number of offers of engagements for stage, movie, pool and other appearances. The offers up to late last night were nearly $1,000,000 and most of them are bona fide propositions, according to Miss Ederle's attorney, Dudley Field Malone, who was in charge of arrangements for her reception. Mr. Malone received and made public the message of congratulations from President Coolidge. The telegram follows:

Paul Smith's, N. Y.,
Aug. 27, 1926.

Dudley Field Malone,
New York City:
The President asks that you extend to Miss Ederle congratulations upon her fine achievement and a hearty welcome home.
(Signed) E. T. CLARK,
Acting Secretary to the President.

The letter of Governor Smith, also conveyed to Miss Ederle by Mr. Malone, follows:

New York State
Executive Chamber,
Albany, N. Y., Aug. 26, 1926.

Dear Miss Ederle:
All the people of the State join with me in a hearty welcome upon your return to your own country. You have won distinction for yourself and for the great State of which you are a citizen.

It is a matter of great regret that engagements that I made long ago prevent me from being in the Southern part of the State in order that I could extend a welcome in person.
Sincerely yours,
(Signed) ALFRED E. SMITH,
Governor.

Swimmer Carries Mascot.

Flushed with excitement and beaming with smiles, Miss Ederle entered the Aldermanic Chamber at the City Hall on the arm of Mr. Whalen, Chairman of the Mayor's' Committee that welcomed her. She was greeted on all sides by friends and personal admirers who solidly packed the room, overflowed the chamber and filled the corridor outside the room. Miss Ederle nodded, waved her blue silk handkerchief and tried to wave acknowledgements to every part of the room.

The swimmer's face was deeply tanned and her boyish-bobbed hair was bronzed by salt water and sun. She wore a lavender felt hat, a blue serge coat suit, a Paris blue and flowered silk scarf, gray silk stockings and black patent leather slippers. She carried a doll mascot, which she called "The Channel Sheik," with an imitation rope of pearls around its neck.

In the course of her welcome at the City Hall she received a large bouquet of American Beauty roses, bearing a card inscribed, "The compliments of the Mayor."

When she entered the Aldermanic Chamber, Hector Fuller, official announcer of the Mayor's committee, raised a stentorian voice and called:

"The Mayor's Committee welcomes the champion swimmer of the world, Miss Gertrude Ederle."

The Mayor's Welcome.

This announcement started an ovation which continued while the Mayor and other officials mounted the platform with Miss Ederle, and the Mayor shook hands with her. Mr. Whalen presented Miss Ederle, and Mayor Walker welcomed her, saying:

I have not had the privilege officially, nor personally, to be present at all the receptions that Mr. Whalen has referred to, but since the first of the year my average has been pretty good. If it is necessary to assure you that New York City entirely welcomes you, I do so most heartily. Having had some pride in pluralities, and having thought at one time that I knew something about the proportion that pluralities could attain, I am willing to admit, Trudy, that yours is the biggest plurality ever given.

This is not altogether the day to be facetious. Certainly you know that a Mayor would not be blasphemous. But when history records the great crossings, of course they will speak of Moses crossing the Red Sea, Caesar crossing the Rubicon and Washington crossing the Delaware, but very frankly, your crossing of the British Channel must take its place alongside of those.

The papers have said that upon your entrance to the City Hall you ought to be kissed by the Mayor. I want you to understand that I shall not be held guilty as a defaulter, but at the same time having in mind the fact that you conquered the Channel, and the fact that you might take exception to the contract, I am not going to insist. But if you look over my shoulder at the Mayor's staff, you will see some very attractive young lieutenants who have already volunteered to substitute.

Of course the whole world has its eyes on you. I guess that is no exaggeration, but as the whole world is willing to pay you homage, you are, after all, just a New York City girl and an Amsterdam Avenue girl, and that means more to us in New York City than anything that has ever been visited upon us. We are not only proud, but we are happy, and you have made us happy. I do not know much about this controversy about the tug, but mayors are supposed to be practical. I have this in mind—that the old Channel is still there, and there are a lot of tugs to be hired by any one that wants to try it, and the Mayor will be the first volunteer to refuse to try it. Miss Ederle, on behalf of the City of New York, let me welcome you most heartily and ask you to accept this little memento rrom the city and from the people of the City of New York.

The Mayor then pinned upon Miss Ederle a gold medal commemorating her famous Channel feat and presented her with a "scroll of honor," which he read. The text of the scroll follows:

SCROLL OF HONOR.

The gateway of this the Queen City of the Atlantic seaboard swings wide open to welcome you,

MISS GERTRUDE EDERLE,
Conquerer of the English Channel.

As Chief Executive of New York City, acting not alone for myself but on behalf of millions of New Yorkers, I desire to present as a certification of our esteem, admiration and praise this scroll of honor.

American women, we are proud to say, have ever added to the glory of our nation, even from the time that Betsy Ross first sewed together with patriotic needle the first American flag. There has never been a brave deed adding to the honor of that flag that was not fostered and inspired by glorious American women.

And so our hearts go out to you for the indomitable courage, the skillful grace, the tremendous athletic prowess, which enabled you to be the first girl in the world to swim the English Channel.

From Cape Gris-Nez. France, across to the white cliffs of Dover, England, we followed your unique and successful attempt with full confidence that in your brave heart and stern courage of soul America was assured of another victory in the realm of sport.

You come back to us with the plaudits of the Old World ringing in your ears, but it remains for us, of your native land, to assure you that in true appreciation of your triumph this City of New York stands second to none.

That you may ever be assured of the honor with which we welcome you home I present to you this scroll of honor in the name of our people, and to it we have affixed our signatures and the official seal of the City of New York.

Miss Ederle Replies.

Without hesitation and with as much self-possession as any girl could muster amid such excitement, Miss Ederle responded to the Mayor's welcome as follows:

Well, my dear friends, I have received the most wonderful welcome, and to put it into words, I don't believe there is any word I can find to express how thrilled I am at this wonderful reception. I certainly am proud to bring home the honors for my country, and for the City of New York. It was for my flag that I swam and to know that I could bring home the honors, and my mind was made up to do it.

I wish to thank the Mayor and all the associations and vereins and the German-Americans and the public. I wish to thank them for their wonderful applause and all the thrills they have given me, and now I don't believe there is much more that I can say. I am so thrilled I just can't put it in words. I wish to thank every one in the United States of America. I thank you.

When Mr. Whalen presented Miss Ederle, he paid her this tribute.

Mr. Mayor, it has been my proud privilege for a number of years to escort personages of fame to the City Hall, and in all that experience the reception that was accorded to our Gertrude today is greater than any in the history of New York. There was that human touch that struck the populace and they turned out in millions. It is my privilege to turn over this precious treasure from Amsterdam Avenue to the kind consideration of your Honor.

Under Canopy of Flags.

In the course of the formal reception at the City Hall Miss Ederle stood between Mayor Walker and Mr. Malone

A part of the great crowd in City Hall plaza

under a canopy of American flags. On each side they were flanked by army and navy officers and members of the Mayor's Committee.

Mayor Walker was accompanied by his secretary, Edward L. Stanton and his two police aids, Lieutenants Thomas F. O'Connor and John C. Howard, also Colonel John J. Phelan of the Sixty-ninth Regiment and members of his staff. In the balcony of the Aldermanic Chamber a band played patriotic hymns, and Miss Virginia Choate Pinner sang "The Star-Spangled Banner."

The welcome ceremonies at the City Hall were broadcast by the municipal broadcasting station, WNYC, and relayed to the thousands outside the City Hall by fifty amplifiers installed by order of Commissioner Albert Goldman, head of the Department of Plant and Structures.

Following the ceremonies, Mayor Walker and Miss Ederle and members of the Welcome Committee descended to the vestibule of the City Hall. The Mayor and Miss Ederle walked out to the steps of the building and started to pose for the photographers, but then the crowd surged forward and the police lines broke. The Mayor and the swimmer would have been swept from their feet but for the prompt interference of Patrolman O'Donovan and Policemen O'Connor and Howard.

The sudden upheaval of the crowd catapulted some of those in the front against an iron picket fence at one side of the City Hall steps. The fence gave way, and many were knocked down and trampled upon. Six persons received first-aid treatment and went home. The injured were:

KOHLER, HERBERT, 11 years old, of 322 Carroll Street, Brooklyn; sprained left foot.

MARIA, ANGELINA, 19 years old, of 357 Clifton Avenue, Newark; contusions of the left foot.

GLAVIK, MARIE, 22 years old, of 672 Seventh Avenue, Brooklyn; shock and abrasions of the left leg.

DOBROVOLNY, MARY, 31 years old, of 1,467 First Avenue; abrasions of the foot.

PAPALIA, ADLA, 13 years old, of 600 Thirty-fifth Street, North Bergen, N. J.; overcome by the heat and excitement.

HARBANGER, FANNY, 54 years old, of 1,655 Ninety-second Street, Richmond Hill; syncope.

Miss Ellen Mitchell, 27, of 233 East Ninth Street, was overcome by heat in the press of the crowd, received first aid and went home, after reporting the loss of a watch which she valued at $200.

The injured were treated by Drs. Berry and Petulli of the Beekman Street Hospital. An ambulance from the Beekman Street Hospital was parked in front of the City Hall as an emergency medical station, and most of the injured were taken to it for treatment.

Miss Dobrovolny reported that she had been knocked down by a horse ridden by a mounted policeman and saved from serious injury by quick-witted persons near by. Miss Maria and Miss Glavik were trodden upon before they could be snatched to safety by other spectators who tried to assist them.

Trying to clear the masses of people who pressed right against the barred doors of the City Hall, the mounted police rode here and there among the crowd. Women screamed in fear and men swore in anger.

Police Comment on Crowd.

Inspector Kuehne said the crowd was the most enthusiastic and persistent he had ever seen in his thirty years on the force. He called attention to the large number of women who turned out to greet the girl who was not only the first women to swim the English Channel but a swimmer who had beaten all the records of the men swimmers of the Channel.

"There was an old woman about 85 years old in the front of the crowd which stormed the doors of the City Hall," said Inspector Kuehne. "I was afraid she would get hurt, and tried to assist her to a safer place. She became indignant, and protested.

"'I guess I can take care of myself,' she said, and that seemed to be the attitude of most of the women."

Miss Ederle was surprised and astonished by the warmth of the reception and the determination of the crowd to close in upon her. But she gave heed to the advice of the police and city officials and stayed in the private office of the Mayor with her mother and other members of her party while the police cleared an exit for her through the masses in front of the building.

The Channel swimmer was marooned in the office of Mayor Walker for thirty minutes. Inspector Kuhne asked Police Headquarters to rush 100 more reserves to the City Hall, 100 extra traffic men to Fifth Avenue and Thirty-fourth Street as a precaution against overwhelming crowds there, and another 100 recruits to Fifty-seventh Street and Amsterdam Avenue to take care of the huge neighborhood outpouring.

At 2:30, when a lane was opened through the crowds at City Hall, word was sent to the Mayor's office that everything was ready for Miss Ederle to start the ride to her home. The swimmer and her immediate party hurried out of the hall, posed with Mayor Walker on the steps of the building, and then walked briskly to her waiting automobile. The triumphal ride home began.

"The reception given to that girl was the greatest in the history of the city," said Inspector Kuehne as "Trudy" and the train of automobiles departed. "There has never been anything like it except the greeting that was given to the Twenty-seventh Division, New York's Own, when it returned from France."

Northward from City Hall, the Ederle procession ran into the paper cloudbursts again. The swimmer was bombarded from the curb with "hello" and "welcome, Trudy," and other shouts. At Ninth Street, where the line of automobiles turned west toward Fifth Avenue, a huge cluster of American Beauty roses was presented to Miss Ederle on behalf of the employes of John Wanamaker's by Miss Katherine Rooney.

In Fifth Avenue the procession was halted briefly while Miss Ederle received other elaborate bouquets, one from Altman's, presented by Miss Bertha Yaeger, and one from Saks & Co., tendered by Miss Carolyn Gadony. From Franklin Simon, a large silver loving cup was given to Miss Ederle by Miss Rose Muene, and still another cluster of flowers was presented by Dobbs & Co. Representatives of other stores ran to the car in which Miss Ederle was riding and presented her with gifts.

As "Trudy" and her train passed the Public Library at Forty-second Street the pigeons which nest under its eaves flew out as if to greet her. They circled over her car until she had passed Forty-second Street, and then returned to their perches, having added their tribute to the conqueror.

FEWER WOMEN LAWMAKERS.

122 Elected by 34 States, Mostly Republican, Against 130 Previously.

WASHINGTON, Jan. 2 (AP).—A survey made by the League of Women Voters discloses that 122 women have been elected to the Legislatures of thirty-four States, eleven of whom will take seats in the Senates. In 1925 and 1926 approximately 130 women were elected.

The Republican Party, with eighty-six women legislators, outnumbers the Democrats, who elected thirty-one. Three have no party designation; one is a non-partisan and one an independent.

Connecticut leads all other States, with sixteen women in its 1927 lawmaking body. Wyoming, the first State to grant suffrage to women and the first to install a woman as Governor, will have but one woman legislator.

January 3, 1927

RECORDING CHILD GROWTH.

100 Women Hear Yale Professor on Psychological Experiments.

The association between a child's behavior and its mental growth was stressed by Professor Arnold Gesell, Director of the Yale University Psycho-Clinic, in an address yesterday morning before a group of 100 women who are conducting round-table discussions on parental education, under the auspices of the Child Study Association of America, 54 West Seventy-fourth Street.

In the defective child, he said, a tendency toward a subnormal level of behavior was apparent, while in the superior child an acceleration showed itself. Through tests and behavior norms the psychological status of the growing child may be recorded, he said, from the standpoint of motor development, language, adaptive behavior and emotional life. Hundreds of children have been studied at the Yale clinic, he said, the work being specially valuable in the field of mental hygiene.

Mental growth is most rapid in preschool years, said Dr. Gesell, but it may continue to the brink of old age, the length of this growth varying greatly in different persons.

January 19, 1927

CHESTERTON TILTS WITH LADY RHONDDA

Copyright, 1927, by The New York Times Company.
Special Cable to THE NEW YORK TIMES.

LONDON, Jan. 27.—Gilbert K. Chesterton and Lady Rhondda, one of Great Britain's big business women, debated in London tonight on "The Menace of the Leisured Woman," with George Bernard Shaw in the chair. Mr. Chesterton defended the woman of leisure.

Mr. Shaw warned the speakers that what they said would be broadcast to 8,000,000 listeners and he urged them to be careful.

"Probably at this moment the Postmaster General is listening in," he said. "He is realizing that I am speaking. His horror is probably growing with every sentence falling from my lips.

"It is evident to me that the Postmaster General may call out the guard. If you find an energetic force of military and police breaking into this hall, shattering the microphone and leading me away in custody, I must ask you not to offer resistance. Your remedy is a constitutional one. You must vote against the Government at the next election."

As there was no interference from the military or the police Mr. Shaw proceeded to the business of the evening.

"We are going to have a debate on the subject of leisured woman," he said. "When I was young a debate on this subject would have been impossible for the simple reason that there was no such thing as leisured woman.

Eager for Chesterton's Speech.

"In those days a woman had children to look after. She had a house to keep. Leisure for her was impossible. She hardly had time really to nag her husband as a husband ought to be nagged.

"Nowadays we have changed all that. We have got rid of the house and housekeeper. We have substituted the service flat and the residential hotels. We have got rid of children by birth control."

"After all, the old cares and the old world have been removed from them. I know and understand that it is possible.

"What I do not as yet quite understand, but what I will learn in the course of the next half hour or so, is what Mr. Chesterton is going to say in defense of leisured women.

"It may be that he comes here tonight to advocate the cocktail and the night club and the Charleston. My own private opinion is that if you were to challenge Mr. Chesterton to rise up on this platform and dance the Charleston with Lady Rhondda, I don't believe he would be able to do it.

"Lady Rhondda is the Teller of the House of Lords. Lady Rhondda is also an extremely capable woman of business, and the consequence is that the House of Lords have risen up and said: 'If Lady Rhondda comes in here, we go away.'

"They feel instinctively that if Lady Rhondda started in the House of Lords, there would be such a show-up of the general business ignorance and imbecility of the male sex in the peerage as never was heard of before."

Lady Rhondda in her speech said:

"I am here to put forward a simple proposition, which is that the existence of the leisured woman constitutes a grave menace to modern civilization.

The idle and the irresponsible, she said, were setting the tone. How was one to account for the great clothes shops? They were all full of things for women of leisure to buy and to play. The way to cure the disease was to recognize it, Lady Rhondda went on. The leisured women of today would find that if she could not put things right for herself she could put them right for the next generation.

If she were left as she is today, she might wreck civilization, Lady Rhondda concluded, and it was her business to see that that did not happen.

Mr. Chesterton said he did not think it was a good thing that a couple should have only one child. But if they had only one child they might very well pay some little attention to it. He admitted that there was danger that the leisured woman might turn her attention to philanthropy. She might take up public work.

He took it, he said, that Lady Rhondda did not mean the leisured woman was to be wholly occupied in interfering with the pleasures of other people.

January 28, 1927

PURSUE CAREERS WHEN WED

Nearly Half of Bryn Mawr Graduates Carry On, Report Shows.

Special to The New York Times.

PHILADELPHIA, Jan. 30.—Nearly half of the Bryn Mawr graduates who were pursuing careers at the time of their marriages are continuing their careers along with marriage and apparently making a success of both, members of the Alumnae Association have been informed by Mrs. Leonard Hand of New York, who is at the head of a committee which has just completed an alumnae survey. Mrs. Hand reported that 43 per cent. of the women who replied to a questionnaire had continued their careers after becoming housewives.

"Many of those who had entered a profession did not even abandon their work temporarily," she said, "while others did so for only a short time."

Another fact revealed by the questionnaire is that 70 per cent. of the graduates of the Bryn Mawr Graduate School are holding teaching or administrative positions in colleges and schools throughout the country.

More than 200 alumnae attended the meeting, which was presided over by Mrs. Alfred B. Maclay of New York, the association President.

January 31, 1927

FINDS COLLEGE GIRL AS GOOD AS EVER

The college girl of today is no worse than her mother, in the opinion of Miss R. Louise Fitch, the new Dean of Women at Cornell University, who spoke yesterday at the annual luncheon of the Cornell Women's Club of New York at the Hotel Astor.

"I do not think the younger generation of young women in college are so greatly different from those of my own age," Miss Fitch said. "Perhaps they punctuate their conversation with words like 'golly,' 'darn' and 'devil,' which in former years were considered unesthetic.

"Older women have set younger ones aside too long. We have said they are everything we don't want them to be and perhaps some of them are trying to live up to the opinions we have expressed concerning them. I believe we should teach them principles rather than specific things and then the things will take care of them-

selves. If principles of decency and modesty are instilled in girls, the length of their skirts will take care of itself."

25 Per Cent. Work Their Way.

"The girls who have called on me for advice have been sad, pathetic and sometimes funny," she went on. "Some of them have the best background possible and others none at all. One girl arrived in Ithaca with the clothes she wore and $18 with which to get an education. We found work for her and I think she will pull through the year but I doubt if it is worth the sacrifice. Another girl student and her husband struggled along on $5 a week. Twenty-five per cent. of the girls are earning all or a part of their board.

"There are many girls of the neurotic type and we have psychopathic and ordinary liars. We have 300 girls who must have work. Even from the poorest families I find girls who have never swept a floor or washed dishes in their lives.

"Girls are required to sign a register whenever they go out after 8 o'clock in the evening and also when they return. I am checking up on each girl's social record and the card parties and dances she attends are classified. One girl who did not sign at all was out thirty nights out of the first forty-one and went to New York week-ends.

I refuse to advise girls about their love affairs. If you fail them once in your advice, your influence is gone."

Sees a Rush for Education.

Dr. Frederick B. Robinson, Acting President of the College of the City of New York, said that in every age humanity had fixed its ideal upon something it believed would lead it to salvation and that present-day America had pinned its faith upon universal education. As instancing its growth in the United States, Dr. Robinson said that in 1898 there were 300,000 boys and girls in the high schools of the country. This increased to 600,000 in 1900, 1,218,804 in 1914, and 3,407,801 in 1924, he said.

Counting the training schools, Dr. Robinson said there were about 1,000,000 college students in the United States, whereas, in 1890, there were but 49,000.

"The rich men of the country have decided that their money will not go into the building of cathedrals or the maintaining of armies, but into institutions of learning," he said. "Education is the hope, and universal education the aim of democracy. Most families now expect at least one or two college bred members. Vocational and technical training is essential if we are to continue our industrial progress."

February 13, 1927

The Vivacious Miss Bow.

THREE WEEK ENDS, with Clara Bow, Neil Hamilton, Harrison Ford, Julia Swayne Gordon, Jack Raymond, Edythe Chapman, Guy Oliver, William Holden and others, directed by Clarence Badger; "At the Opera With Saint-Saens"; "The Movie Man"; Jesse Crawford, organist; "Topsy-Turvy Town," produced by Paul Oscard. At the Paramount Theatre.

Judging by the periodical waves of merriment in the Paramount Theatre yesterday afternoon, some of the incidents of Clara Bow's latest picture, "Three Week Ends," found favor with many in the audience. This none too original story was not written by Elinor Glyn, as one might suppose, but by pens in the male fists of Louis Long, Percy Heath and Sam Mintz.

Notwithstanding the nonsensical series of events, Clarence Badger has given expert direction to this subject and consequently it boasts of far better acting than the yarn deserves. It is also especially well photographed and staged.

Miss Bow once again reveals her ability to express herself before the camera. Whether she wishes to spread cheer by her vivacious antics or let a tear or two drop from her large, long-lashed eyes, she is always attractive. She is kept busy throughout this affair and you may see her in one scene covering up her polka-dot bathing suit with a modest but abbreviated garment, and in a later chapter, to carry out the plot, she

does her best to tear off her dress.

Gladys O'Brian (Miss Bow) is one of those hard-working cabaret girls who is sorely tormented during the daylight hours because she can't sleep in the tenement in which she lives. Her father, tall, slender, but elderly, also toils at night, as a watchman. One of the painful moments to Miss O'Brian (and therefore amusing to the audience) is when Pa O'Brian shows himself in his nightshirt just when Gladys's new beau is calling upon her.

Presumably the narrative is chiefly concerned with the good and pretty cabaret dancer's persistence in seeing that James Gordon succeeds in obtaining Millionaire Turner's signature to a life insurance policy. And the fun is at its highest level when Gladys calls upon Mr. Turner herself to have him sign on the dotted line or—be compromised.

Harrison Ford, who has deserted leading male rôles for those of a sedate fun-maker, is not without merit during some of the feverish instants in this photoplay. He affects a vacant stare and, for the nonce, little control of his facial muscles. Neil Hamilton is the sturdy, handsome young man (whether Gladys realizes it or not), who is totally devoid of a sense of humor.

On the surrounding program is "Topsy-Turvy Town," staged by Paul Oscard. Among the numbers in this production is "The Master Clown" (Ferry Corwey), whose antics are highly amusing. Then there is a Vitaphone short film, called "The Movie Man," which afforded some laughter.

December 10, 1928

WOMAN INFERIOR, ASSERTS MUSSOLINI

Play an Important Part as a "Pleasant Parenthesis of Life," He Declares.

SAYS THEY CANNOT CREATE

Should Never Be Taken Seriously— Superior to Man in Physical and Moral Courage.

A woman has interviewed Mussolini about women. Vahdah Jeanne Bordeaux of Paris, author of a life of Eleonora Duse, has gained from the Duce his thoughts and opinions on woman's place in the sun and her relation to man. His views are both flattering and irritating to the sex he eulogizes.

"Women are the agreeable or pleasant parenthesis of life, and considered as such they play a very important part in man's existence," he pronounced at the outset of the interview.

"I do not like the idea of women trying to walk in men's shoes, literally as well as figuratively speaking. Being feminine, women should try to remain so. When forced by circumstances to earn their living, so long as they remain in their proper rôle, they are admirable.

"What should women do? In what field can they shine as man's equal? In anything that is not creative. Women cannot create. In all of the arts, from the beginning of time women have done delicious small things, but when they have attempted gran-

deur they have failed ignominiously. * * * For example, what woman has ever created a great painting?

Just a "Charming Pastime."

"The power behind the throne? No. Woman is not that. No great man has ever been inspired to greatness by a woman's unseen power. * * *

"Men are inspired by ambition or conviction; their desires to accomplish something in the world are purely selfish, and if you could look into the soul of every man you meet in the course of a day, one and all would be the same.

"No vision of a woman would be enshrined there, no thought of other than self, his longings, realized or unrealized; love and hatred, a sense of satisfaction or dissatisfaction; perhaps fear and sadness, and always a sense of aloofness and loneliness. No woman ever penetrates to the soul of a man, despite all things said to the contrary.

"The more virile and intelligent a man is the less need he has of a woman as an integral part of himself. Women are a charming pastime, a means of changing one's trend of thought; but they should never be taken seriously, for they themselves are rarely, if ever, serious. Women love easily, and are tragically serious while intensely interested, but love is a transitory thing, never permanent with them.

"Oh, when it is a question of imagination, women are far superior to men. They are dreamers, idealists, sentimentalists, and innately romantic, exactly opposed to the average man. And they are trusting, confiding little animals.

"When a man tells a woman that he loves her, she makes it a point to believe him, no matter how many times she may already have been deceived. She believes him because she is an idealist, and being loved is an ideal condition * * * She believes him because is romantic, and the state or condition of loving and being loved is a romantic one.

"Then, too, it pleases her vanity to add another scalp to her collection, and if the man is a personage, her ambition is also satisfied.

Advises Men to Flirt.

"What more agreeable than the enthusiasm a woman knows how to awaken in a man?" he continued. "What more charming, thrilling than the first kiss; what brings a more profound sigh of relief than the last?

"Flirtations should be indulged in as frequently as possible up to the age of 40, then a man should settle down to more staple amusements, such as work, sport, and the seriousness of bringing up a family, which in all probability he has left to his wife until feeling the years of discretion upon him, he awakens to the so-called serious 'raison d'être.'

"What do I think of marriage? That it is a necessary institution, a contract to be entered into between a man and a woman for the good of the State, and for that reason it should never be dissolved, so long as they both live. * * *

"Women are inferior to men, but they are courageous, and in all questions of both physical and moral courage they are by far the superior of man * * *

"What mother will refuse to sacrifice herself for her children? The mother always sacrifices, rarely the father * * * In all questions of disease and physical pain, they meet the truth stoically, where men are ready to die from fear.

"Then of course they are decorative * * * and in diplomacy would shine, if only they had the chance * * * And yet, regardless of class, women are all the same, inferior to the men with whom they associate, physically and mentally; superior in courage, loyalty, and their own peculiar sense of honor. Left in their proper relation to man they are all that is delicious, adorable, sensuous. They are, in a large sense, necessary to our physical well-being, as a parenthesis, and in the same sense to our mental.

"Women are to man what men desire them to be—woman is to me—an agreeable parenthesis in my busy life; they never have been more, nor can they ever be less. Today, I have no time to punctuate my life with other than work, but in the past, now the long ago past, when I was free to pick and choose my style of writing, I often found the parenthesis a pleasant way to punctuate."

(Dorr News Service).

March 6, 1927

NEW WOMEN OF RUSSIA TEST LENIN'S THEORIES

They Struggle to Attain the Promised Equality in Industry And Politics, but the Lot of the Peasant Woman Is Little Changed

By ANNA LOUISE STRONG.

THE slow and decorous rise of the women of America and the Western nations to equal rights seems pale and monotonous beside the vigorous picturesqueness of the new women in the older lands of the earth—China, Turkey, Russia and the plains of Central Asia—where women in the revolution of a decade are breaking through bondage hoary with a thousand years of tradition. Nowhere is the vivid contrast between the new women and the old traditions more striking than in the Soviet re-

public, where slumberous peasant custom as ancient as any on earth clashes with determined attempts to introduce marriage laws and sex equality more ultra-modern than even that of America.

I pick up a newspaper in Moscow and note, almost side by side, two items. One says that 50,000 women now hold public office in elective bodies in the Soviet Union. Most of these are members of village Soviets— and some 200 are even Presidents of these local ruling bodies. Twenty county districts boast women Presi-

dents, and seventy-five women are executives on provincial ruling bodies. In fact, says this article, one-fifth of all the members of "city Soviets" in provincial centres (similar to City Councils in America) are now women, though five years ago there were fewer than 4 per cent. of women in these bodies. Such is the result of the campaign to bring more women into public life, a campaign initiated by the Government itself and the ruling Communist Party.

The other item describes elections in the Komi-Permyatski district, near

MME. NIKOLAI LENIN

The Widow of the Former Russian Premier Is Chairman of the Department of Political Education.

the Ural Mountains. "One of the peasant women elected to the Soviet went home weeping, afraid that her husband would beat her for going into politics. * * * The peasant women in general showed a fear of being elected to the Soviets." From which one gathers that it is one thing to have equality and power thrust upon one in a village meeting and another thing to enforce it in the home.

A Comic Opera Plot.

Recognition of the fact that woman's actual status in the average home still lags far behind the freedom and security offered her by law was humorously illustrated in an amateur operetta given in Moscow by a factory workers' club. Surely the plot could have been located nowhere but in the Soviet Union. A petty capitalist, running a small stocking factory with three knitting machines and three charming young operators, is so annoyed by the restrictions of the labor laws, the eight-hour day and the social insurance that he conceives the brilliant idea of marrying his three operators to his three sons, knowing that when once they are members of his family he can make them work all night without interference by any factory inspector. The classic ideals of American fiction in which a shop-girl escapes by marriage to a life of leisure find a rude contrast in this

realistic picture of the ancient family slavery of the working woman.

Many peasant maxims indicate the brutal view of women characteristic of a patriarchal era which never passed through an age of romance or of chivalry. "A chicken is not a bird; a woman is not a person," says one of these. "Long hair, short sense," runs another. "Who doesn't beat his wife doesn't live with her comfortably," is the motto for young husbands.

Set over against these the ultra-modern dictum of Lenin: "No nation can be free when half of its citizens are enslaved in the kitchen." Or this: "Every kitchen maid must learn to rule the State." Or the recognition offered to women by another prominent Communist: "Working women and peasant women are a great power. Without them, and especially against them, we should never win." The contrast between these two sets of maxims indicates something of the clash of forces in the life of Russian women today.

Lenin's Enthusiastic Summary.

The political aims of the dominant Communist group regarding women, and the extent of their fulfilment in law and State action, may be stated in the boast of Lenin: "No democratic country in the world, not even the most advanced, has done one-hundredth part as much for women as we have done in the first few years of

our existence. We have left unturned no stone of those damnable laws of the inequality of woman, the difficulty of divorce and the vulgar, mean formalities that preceded it, of the non-recognition of illegal children. * * * We can a thousand times be proud of what we have done in this sphere. * * * But the more we clear the soil from the old remnants of bourgeois laws and institutions the clearer it becomes that this is merely clearing ground for a new structure, but not yet the structure itself. * * * Woman continues to remain a household slave in spite of emancipating laws. * * *"

It would be easy to find large numbers of women who have taken advantage of their new freedom and who have risen to positions of power and importance in the new State. Mme. Lenin is Chairman of the Department of Political Education; Mme. Trotsky is Chairman of the Committee for Preservation of Art Museums; Mme. Kameneva is head of the Committee on Cultural Relations with other Lands; Mme. Bitzekno is Director of the Cooperative Institute; Mme. Lilina is Director of Welfare Activities of Leningrad Province. Every one knows that the first woman Ambassador appointed by any nation is Alexandra Kollontai, formerly sent to Norway and now to Mexico. Many other highly placed women are doing serious work in the council chamber or at the administrative desk, managing factories as well as Government bureaus. Nor does one hear often in Russia of unwillingness of men to work under a woman chief; there is in the sphere of public work an actual assumption of equality.

Russian Women as Students.

Even larger is the proportion of women preparing for future work of an expert nature. In the higher professional colleges women form 35 per cent. of the students studying for degrees in engineering, medicine, agriculture, pedagogy, economics or art. Even four years ago I chanced to leave Russia on a steamer bearing a group of young women from Turkestan, in the heart of Asia, bound for a year's foreign study in German universities on scholarships provided by the Russian State. Their mothers were still veiled in the harems of polygamous households; they could relate to me tales of wealthy merchants or owners of herds whose households ran to a dozen wives, all strictly secluded. But they themselves, after a coeducational experience in Russian universities, were now bound for the unknown freedoms of Europe, expecting later to return and carry new knowledge and liberation to tens of thousands of their sisters. Yet it is also possible to read in the papers of how some woman of Central Asia was murdered in the street by a religious fanatical avenger "for going unveiled and agitating against the duties of women." So strenuous may the fight for women's rights become in the Soviet Union.

Some younger women do not take their rights with undue solemnity. One remembers in the Peasants' Sanitarium in Livadia a group of giggling Tartar girls, with bright yellow kerchiefs over their brown, oval faces. Only one of the group could talk Russian; she translated the Tartar dialect of the others. They told me with many smiles that men could no longer have many wives and beat them, and that women no longer had to get married in order to be respectable, but could "go to town and study to be doctors." None of these yellow-kerchiefed girls, however, seemed likely to undertake anything so strenuous as a career.

It is quite otherwise with the student women of Moscow. Thoroughly serious and devoted to their labors for their country's future, they scorn such feminine wiles as cosmetics and coquetry and hold easily and obviously a relation of equal comradeship toward the men students with whom they work and whom they occasionally marry. Even in their love affairs they appear to trust to common interests and frank affection to obtain and retain devotion.

Among these students are women who have fought at the front in the civil war. They have risen to be "commissars" of regiments, in charge of hospitals or of political instruction; they have been wounded and rescued from battlefields. And when they relate these experiences they are quite unlikely to mention any special dangers or embarrassments due to sex, but far more likely to dwell at length and humorously on "how hard it was to learn to ride horseback in a hurry when you had to ride thirty-six hours on your first attempt."

Revolution Among Factory Workers.

These are, of course, the exceptions, created by the exceptional conditions of revolution and civil war. Yet today there are thousands of women in universities and factories who are assuming without apparent effort an equal place in political, economic and cultural life. The city women are, naturally, freer than the women of rural districts; the factory women especially have experienced a veritable revolution in all the conditions of their living. There are tens of thousands of them who, before the revolution, lived in ignorance and darkness, crowded in miserable barracks, slaves of husbands and of factory managers. Now they have learned to read; they have even been sent to technical schools; they are beginning to hold little jobs on committees; they find the burdens of motherhood lightened by the social insurance, which gives them four months on pay with extra food and clothing at the birth of a child; which furnishes free day nurseries and is beginning even to furnish cooperative laundries and kitchens.

Dunia was one of these—a textile worker of 39 years in an industrial town fifty versts from Moscow. She told how the year 1919, in spite of hunger and typhus and civil war, was "my year of great joy," since it was "the first year when my husband and two children and I had a whole room to ourselves." Such was the inhuman crowding of factory barracks life before the revolution. The second reason given for her joy was that "it was the year I learned to read and write and my husband respected me as a citizen." Dunia had gone in seven years from the status of a beast of burden to motherhood insurance, day nurseries and scholarships. She is going this year to a scholarship in a special school, expecting to come back as women's organizer for the factory.

"Not all had such good husbands as I," related Dunia. She told of another factory woman whose husband objected to her going to meetings. "He took a chair over his head to beat her back by force. But she picked up the other chair over her head and cried: 'You didn't kill me under Nicholas, and now I'm free,'" thus fighting her way past him to the factory meeting. Dunia added with a wondering comprehension of the vagaries of the male sex: "Yet he was a good revolutionist, only he didn't want his wife to be one." Even today one may read in the newspaper columns on "Workers' Life" that "Comrade ——, although Secretary of the Young Communists, argues against electing women to the Soviets, and is especially bitter about the election of his own wife, whom he beats at home."

A new institution has come into the life of factory women, that of the "delegatka," or woman delegate, who represents five or ten other women in the general meetings of workers which guide the life of the factory. There are about half a million of these delegatkas today, each of them charged with a tiny load of public responsibility, which is designed to educate her and draw her gradually into wider and wider fields of work. Tens of thousands of these delegatkas have already been drawn on municipal commissions of all kinds, housing, health, taxation, social insurance; other tens of thousands are absorbed by trade union work on wage and cultural committees; still others are used by thousands of boards of management in the cooperatives.

A Woman Factory Manager.

An occasional picturesque figure rises to be factory manager. Such was Anna Kulikova, who has worked twenty-seven years in one factory, learning to read and write since the revolution, sent for three years to a special school for "delegatkas" and then progressing through the factory shop committee to a technical school and at last to a job as factory director, with 1,000 workers under her. Like a good housewife she decreased waste, and like a good mother she cares for her flock of women workers, listening to their personal troubles. "To whom but to Anna can one go," said one woman worker, "when one's husband drinks and it is payday and you want to get off fifteen minutes early to get his wages before he does. Anna knows; she'll let you off to get those wages!"

The women of country districts are naturally far more backward than those of the factories, yet even among them the new freedom is available—for those who have will to fight for it. One such was a peasant woman in her early thirties from a village in White Russia who one day harangued a dozen sheepish peasants on the ancient wrongs and the modern rights of women.

"Since the men know we have equal rights they behave themselves," she affirmed, amid the embarrassed grins of her audience. "If a man ill-treats his wife in our village, she goes to the President of the Soviet. By and by a paper comes to her husband: 'If we don't hear from you by a certain day, you are divorced.' * * * Just like that, if the woman wants to leave him. * * * The old family was terrible. For the daughter-in-law who came to the house—what a life! They treated her like a beast of burden.

But for one such ardent feminist as this there are still in the dark and backward villages of Russia dozens of older women who face new freedoms with a sense of fear. A charming old peasant woman, her hair gleaming softly under a white kerchief, sat quietly knitting in the former arbor of the Czar when I asked her what change the revolution had brought to her village.

"Oh, it is all the same, dearie," she answered softly, "all the same. Woman's chief burden is her husband. Family life is dark and bitter as always. * * * Yet I think it is a little better. Men are ashamed to beat their wives so often. Formerly after holidays one could not get up from the beating. [Because of the drunken celebration.] I think also they are afraid. A woman in the next village got a divorce. * * * But not in our village." She paused in mingled awe and horror of the venturesome divorcée.

"It Is Only Recently That Women Have Succeeded in Entering Those Professions Which, as Muses, They Typified for the Greeks."

By MIRIAM BEARD

THE figure of a handsome woman, blindfolded, holding a pair of scales in her outstretched, majestic hand, was used by Man to symbolize the Spirit of Justice long before he admitted any of her sex to the bar or jury duty. And the very college students who most loudly hymned their "Alma Mater" most resolutely kept their sisters from the campus.

Man has always liked to have some woman, especially one about eight feet high and of earnest aspect, to represent his ideas or inventions. At the same time, of course, he anxiously thwarted her attempts to utilize the inventions or pursue the theories. Thus, he wanted women to be illiterate, but to represent the Spirit of Education; he denied them property rights and painted them as the Spirit of Plenty; he refused them the custody of their own children and sculptured them as the Spirit of Motherhood.

He wanted some smiling damsel to typify Architecture for him, but never to build his houses. And, much as he insisted on having his womenfolk meek and shy, he was always portraying them blowing trumpets and leading his armies to war. Indeed, nothing pleased him better than to be painted as Victor, clad in faultless frock coat or toga, with a crown suspended over his head by some Greek-robed Spirit of Triumph, blond and of irreproachable profile.

Frescoes and Photographs

Today man, being only human, is the first to complain when his dreams come true. He sees, in the rotogravure sections of the Sunday newspaper, a great panorama of pictures, showing women in costumes almost as daring as those in Victorian paintings of the "Spirit of Progress," and holding in their hands appropriate symbols: college degrees, baseball bats, rifles, golf trophies and gavels. And he grows indignant—because his allegory walks out of the canvas.

After all, it would be hard to decide between the merits of the two types of pictures, frescoes and photographs. Only a divinity could determine which is funnier, Man's dream of Woman, or Woman as she is. Surely, from the feminine point of view, the height of hilarity is reached by those old-fashioned panels in which haughty, huge ladies, several tons overweight, stroll on clouds, brandish swords and represent the Spirit of Freedom. But then, to a masculine eye, there is equally high comedy in the modern snapshot of some daring American college girl standing on her head at the wing-tip of an airplane, speeding 210 miles an hour—and enjoying freedom.

Rightly appreciated, our Sunday newspapers afford a pageant as varied, as symbolic, as the statues of "Democracy, Liberty and Agriculture" at any county fair. The news columns offer vivid word-pictures of

woman, busy symbolizing the age of modern progress. Débutantes, Dianalike, are shooting elephants; a woman becomes carilloneuse; another is the only feminine engineer in the British marine service; a third applies for a seat on the New York Stock Exchange. Six girls attempt to run a schooner; one is sent as assistant American Consul to Amsterdam. A club is formed in London to enable its members to puff large, black cheroots. A woman writer sails to Nigeria to investigate the background of Primitive Man. American women are winning fame as Judges, evangelists, Governors, restaurateurs; Japanese women are forcing their way into political clubs, and becoming cops, radio announcers, aviators.

One day we read about a little group of advanced feminists who plan to descend on Washington by airplane; this should surprise no one who has seen the old allegorical paintings, in which, since medieval days, winged ladies have

WOMAN SPRINGS FROM ALLEGORY TO LIFE

She Is Actually Doing the Things Which From Time Immemorial She Merely Symbolized

always been depicted in flight, strewing roses or carrying banners. It is a medieval dream realized.

The next week brings reports of the proposal of the New York State Branch of the National Woman's Party to demand the appointment, by the President, of women Cabinet members and Ambassadors. Those who find this surprising need only remember how long woman has practiced for these rôles, silently, on marble thrones, posing as "The State," "The Awakening Commonwealth," or "The Spirit of International Good-Will," in the rotundas or on the ceilings of our State Capitols. It is but an attempt, picturesque indeed, to transform fresco into fact.

When we are through reading the Sunday papers and gazing at the photographic allegories of the modern camera man, we may go for a stroll in Central Park. At once our eye is met by the Victorian prototypes of the "New Woman." At one point stands a bronze lady, typifying the Soul of Music, plucking a lyre and gazing seriously into the heavens. Long after she was cast in metal a woman became an orchestra conductor for the first time. And at the southern extremity of the park we find another figure, rushing along in fluttering robes, leading General Sherman on to Victory—or mayhap, the amiable creature is trying to assist him through the dense traffic at

that point. At least, she reminds us of the women's battalion which so recently fought for General Diaz in Nicaragua.

Other cities, notably Boston, abound with frescoed femininity. They are mostly overgrown and overweight—indeed, a thin woman, to your average painter, symbolizes simply nothing. They adorn domes of State Capitols, public schools, hotels, college auditoriums, banks, libraries, fountains and parks, all with equal propriety. Some pose amid clouds, cherubs and velvet curtains; others sit on thrones; some stand around in graceful groups, pointing to one another.

Tall, fair, ample, dignified, it is apparent that these are but the prototypes of the modern American clubwoman. They are so calm, so efficient. One of them balances in her left hand a book, a compass, a tripod, and with the other hands a flag to Benjamin Franklin. Another is the only woman present in a huge crowd of men—soldiers, miners, Indians, Puritans, men with hoes and pickaxes, signers of the Declaration of Independence. But she is not a bit embarrassed; coolly she unfurls her flag, brandishes a sword and carries a cornucopia of agricultural produce up a stone stairway without dropping a thing.

The titles of these ladies are as elegant as their mien: Spirit of Peace, Spirit of War, Spirit of Night, Spirit of Weebaskus Public

School, Number 609, Spirit of Electricity, Spirit of the Seesawkus Flour and Grain Industry, the Soul of Poesie, the Latin Soul, the Teuton Soul, the Spirit of Alaskan Chambers of Commerce.

How, wonders the innocent beholder, can one tell which of these ladies represents what? This is easy, once you know the rules. In the laps or the ample palms of these generously proportioned and nobly crowned damsels, may be seen a variety of objects: maps, globes, scrolls, arquebuses, chisels and paint-palettes, wreaths, shields, miniature models of houses or ships, books, harps and dynamos. They hold, in brief, everything that Man, their creator, has objected to their using, professionally and in real life.

Man has protested against the earning by modern woman of her own livelihood; yet for years he has placed her laurel-encircled head on his dimes, quarters and fifty-cent pieces. He declared that her sphere was the home, but he put her out in the harbor, in public, as the Statue of Liberty.

Blame the Greeks

Partly the Greeks are to blame. They kept their wives away from the bad influence of the theatre, but used a feminine figure to delineate Tragedy. And though respectable girls were not supposed to appear in public, Victory was displayed as a maiden with wings and Wisdom as another with a helmet. The Greeks called History by the charming name of Clio, while discouraging women from reading any.

Medieval men carried on the tradition. They were frequently vociferous in denouncing the frail sex as vain, shallow, inferior; yet they employed feminine models to typify the very qualities they denied to women in general. When they wished to paint Faith, Hope, Charity, Truth, they personified them as starry-eyed damsels singing in a cerulean heaven.

It is only very recently that women have succeeded in entering those professions which, as Muses, they typified for the Greeks; or have actively demonstrated many of the qualities they embodied for the Middle Ages. Modern woman is the first living and breathing allegory.

At the Women's Exposition, which opened Nov. 9, 1925, at Cleveland, Ohio, it was observed that, of all the hundreds of occupations followed by man, all but thirty-five had today been invaded by feminine competitors. There may be no women miners or pilots of locomotives, as yet, in this country; but there are millions of girls and women in manufacturing, agriculture and animal husbandry, clerical work, trade, the arts and professions. There are women managers of factories, lawyers, bankers, preachers, chauffeurs, insurance sellers, flagpole painters, "switchmen and flagmen on steam railroads."

This report was considered astonishing. But as early as 1910 there

was a noted mural painting in the Cleveland Trust Company building showing a scientist, a woman in cap and gown and another with a lyre approaching a goddess on a high throne, holding a key in one hand and with the other touching a sword and shield. The painting foreshadowed the report.

The spirit of war, no less than the spirit of art, music, drama and literature, is today embodied in actual women. They are no longer content, it seems, merely to lead hosts to battle, bearing trumpet and banner; nor merely to welcome home the victors by standing, in marble effigy, on triumphal arches. They doff wings, don nurses' and canteen workers' uniforms and investigate war for themselves.

In China, where the "new freedom" is rapidly spreading, the serviceability of woman to war is given official recognition. The Kuomintang, always abreast of Western civilization, is said to be sending a women's guard, armed and classified as soldiers, to the front, to serve as nurses and "propaganda-agents." This rumor has alarmed the Northern Ankuochun—and no wonder. Any tourist must feel anxious, too, who has once observed Cantonese girls bossing gangs of dock laborers, with a shrill and scorching stream of apt remarks, each syllable cracking like a whip. It is high time for the Peking army to enroll their own women-folk in self-defense.

Indifferent Calm

One of the great characteristics of all allegorical figures is their air of indifferent calm. It seems to make no difference to their tranquillity whether they are protecting a school child or greeting George Washington, plucking a lyre or symbolizing agriculture at a county fair. And in real life, as well as in painting, women are cheerfully efficient in benevolence as in war.

Peace, faith, charity—for these, in the past, have women posed. And today they are actively engaged, for the first time, in demonstrating these qualities on a large scale. There are four national organizations in this country, with a total enrolment of six million, which are devoted to philanthropic, missionary and temperance endeavors. Social work, community health, civic improvement—in a dozen fields, American women have been the chief donors of energy and time.

Lady Rhondda, one of Britain's captains of industry, at a recent debate, decried the "Menace of the Leisured Woman." Her opponent, Gilbert K. Chesterton, maintained that woman was more to be feared in her activity than in her idleness.

"There is always very serious danger that she may turn her attention to philanthropy or social reform • • • oppression of the poor and interference with human liberty." No doubt Mr. Chesterton, always an ardent admirer of the Middle Ages, would like a return to the days when women employed their leisure, not in social work, but in posing for man-made allegories of charity.

The debate was significant. Already the allegory wears a less placid look. She begins to question herself: "What are these instruments I hold in my hands? Whatever shall I do with them?" And man is wondering what strange thing is this new woman, whom he foreshadowed by his painting and created by his machinery. The modern age thus offers a rare opportunity to enjoy frescoes and photographs together—two excellent jokes.

About Books, *More or Less:*
Women, Supermen, Mobs

By SIMEON STRUNSKY

SPEAKING through the mouth of Zarathustra the late Friedrich Nietzsche strongly urged that in calling upon the ladies one should take a whip along. The admonition has been taken thoroughly to heart by the completest of British Nietzscheans, Anthony M. Ludovici. His "Man: an Indictment" (E. P. Dutton & Co.) resounds with the crack of the lash so lustily wielded on previous occasions in "Woman: a Vindication," and "Lysistrata." Woman might well pray to be spared any such vindications of her own claims or any such indictments of the party of the second part. Mr. Ludovici contends that the trouble with the world today is not the forwardness of the female but the degeneracy of the male, but this will bring little comfort to her heart. The decline of the male is registered precisely in the advance of woman. The victories of feminism are not due in the least to feminine merit, but to the collapse of the enemy front from inner weakness. To recover its health humanity needs a Masculine Renaissance. The male must resume his ancient prerogative, among others, of keeping woman in her place. The Ludovici sjambok descends heavily on masculine shoulders; heavily but only ostensibly. Over the broad shoulders of the male the leather thong bites into softer bodies. Man is only imperfectly indicted and woman is very imperfectly vindicated in the Ludovici formula by which alone may be attained the sex-equality to which progressive women strive:

That method and those means [of sex-equality], as we shall see, have consisted in dwarfing, limiting, and reducing man's claims and prerogatives, in truncating and extirpating his hereditary gifts, in making him timid and hesitating where he should be most intrepid, in sentimentalizing, cowing and debilitating him, and above all in besotting and improverishing his intellect and his body. This method and these means have been man's own invention, man's own deliberate choice.

POLITICS is not the only force in nature that makes strange bedfellows. Or I can think of a better text. It is the ancient anecdote of two boyhood friends from County Clare who settled, one in New York, one in Chicago, and severally prospered. They met, after twenty years, on a railroad platform in Buffalo, one headed for Chicago the other for New York, and foregathered in a train compartment for an appraisal of the America that had been so good to them. The train pulled out and they were still absorbed in appreciation of their marvelous adopted country. Was there any other nation that could even touch American ingenuity and progress? There was not. "Here am I going to Chicago and you going to New York and both of us on the same train." If there are any two more opposite directions in which two passengers could be conceivably headed it would be the ultimate destination of a 100 per cent. Nietzschean like Mr. Ludovici and a 100 per cent. American of the traditional Baptist-Rotary type. Yet Main Street would find itself at home a considerable part of the time on the Ludovici flyer and Mr. Ludovici would experience long stretches of comfort in a Fundamentalist day coach. Mr. Ludovici would be traveling toward the pagan, anti-Christian, Superman, the other would be traveling to Queen Victoria and Mrs. Grundy, and both would speak the same language concerning women. Main Street's ancient grievance against Greenwich Village with its long-haired men and short-haired women is, almost verbatim, Mr. Ludovici's grievance against the effeminate modern man and the unsexed modern woman.

Main Street and the grove of Dionysos join in deploring the breakdown of standards, the confusion of values, the efforts of men and women to set themselves agin nature. Much more eruditely than Main Street the apostle of Nietzsche will demonstrate, with a wealth of anthropological and ethnological data, that men and women are different. Main Street will go back only six thousand years and argue that male and female created he them. Mr. Ludovici can go back ten millions years to the time when the animal female ceased to be oviparous and became viviparous, with formidable consequences.

HOWEVER, it is only fair to recall that part of the responsibility for the present bleak state of things, as Mr. Ludovici sees it, does rest with the male. Woman is only the symptom, the disease is in her mate. She is the clinical thermometer of any number of fevers that beset her erstwhile master, guide, protector, wooer. The list of ailments is very much as it was drawn up by the author of "Zarathustra" himself. Man today is afflicted with ascetic Christianity, with democracy, with humanitarianism. He is a victim of that morbid pity which expends itself on the relief of suffering among those who might well be allowed to suffer without affecting the higher destinies of the race. It is that criminal Christian pity which devotes itself to saving, by the scores of millions, worthless lives. It glories in the shoddy victories of the serums and the vaccines and the sanitations which keep weaklings alive, instead of seeing to it that a race is developed which can snap its fingers at the bacteria without the artificial succor of the antitoxins. Modern humanitarianism, mourns our author, has discarded the salutary example of the farmer who cherishes the wheat and slays the tares; humanitarianism has gone in for the encouragement of the weeds. Be hard, said the rediscoverer of the superman; which at times sounds not very differently from a recommendation to be hard-boiled.

Now it will be immediately apparent to the intelligent reader that the voice of the superman is by no means a voice crying out in the wilderness of 1927. Of the superman and of Nietzsche explicitly we do not hear as much as we used to hear before the war; but phases of the doctrine are very much with us today. The need of combating the Christian sex-phobia as a force contributing to the production of asexual men and asexual women is occasionally stressed. The menace of morbid pity as expressed in the elimination or alleviation of mass suffering finds comparatively few expounders. But the perils, the mistakes, the "breakdown" of democracy constitute the big subject of the day. And the democratic error may be considered basic in the Nietzschean argument. Democracy is that herd, that slave-mass, that aggregation of undermen which has succeeded in imposing its interests, its outlook, its ethic upon the better few. Beyond all there is the direct "breakdown" of democracy in post-war Europe. There is Mussolini and there is the Union of Socialist Soviet Republics. A good many good people who would shiver to think themselves at one with the philosopher of the "blond beast" and the enemy of Christian slave-ethics are not very remote from him in their present acute doubts about the democratic system.

WHEREUPON we once more run headlong into anomaly. The Fascist dictatorship which has taken charge of the Italian herd, the Red dictatorship which has been shepherding the great Slav herd—how much joy would the creator of Zarathustra have taken in them if he were alive today? Very little, I am afraid. The fact that Mussolini takes daily exercise in jumping on the "decomposed corpse of democratic liberty," the fact that Moscow regularly pays its compliments to "democracy" as the tool employed by capitalism for the enslavement of the working masses, would make good reading if not for the ends to which Fascist and Communist dictatorship are directed. Among the things that Nietzsche and his disciples detest most is the State. The State is an instrument of oppression for the chosen few who carry within themselves the seeds of the superman. The State establishes and maintains standards, laws, ethics, conformities of all kind. The State crushes the individual, but the hope of the superman rests entirely in the individual.

And now look at Mussolini! He is not afraid to be hard, like the superman. He lives dangerously, as the superman must always live. He has informed the masses, almost in the words of Zarathustra, that their function is labor and their duty is obedience. But to what end? To the upbuilding of the State. Let the Duce have his super-State and it will, by the Nietzschean definition, be all over with the superman. Supplementing this major vice there are minor afflictions. In the pursuit of his aims what kind of conduct, of morality, is Mussolini prescribing for his people? The old Christian slave morality. The Duce has frowned severely upon certain contemporary tendencies in the direction of—shall we say paganism? In the matter of jazz, cabarets, short skirts and allied phenomena Italy's strong man has shown himself far less open-minded than certain democracies one can think of; where, for instance, a light humor speaks of petting parties, "pash" and S. A.

AS for the other large-scale antidemocratic experiment, Russia, obviously little need be said. It is a denial of democracy for the express purpose of discouraging the superman and lifting up the Nietzschean herd. Readers of Mr. Ludovici's volume will encounter several extremely forceful references to Bolshevism, summing themselves up in the fatal charge that Bolshevism is the logical continuation of Christian principles:

If God [according to the author of the First Corinthians] hath chosen the foolish things of the world to confound the wise * * * and the weak things of the world to confound the things which are mighty, and the base things of the world, and things which are despised * * * to bring to naught things that are, why should it not be my holy duty, says the Bolshevik, to be one of the instruments in the realization of this plan?

From the study of contemporary Italy and contemporary Russia it would thus seem to follow that those of us who have been developing doubts about democracy might look a little deeper into the subject. Mr. Mencken, himself a disciple of Zarathustra, sees the American yokel engaged in imposing his own obscene standards on the few fine spirits who alone are fitted to carry forward the torch of civilization. The eugenist sees democratic humanitarianism engaged in stimulating the procreation and survival of the many "unfit" to the discouragement and suppression of the much fewer "fit." And the student of politics sees brute democratic masses under the manipulation of a few profit-makers or of their own herd prejudices and fears engaged in nominating and electing mediocrity and passing over eminent individual worth. It is all summed up in the tyranny of the mob, as it functions for the suppression of freedom, for the vulgarization of values. This was very nearly the sum of Nietzsche's grievance against the mob.

Yet here is Rome and here is Moscow successfully disposing of democracy and substituting the rule of the strong man. And what satisfaction does the superman gospel get out of it? None that is perceptible to the naked eye. Mussolini exalts the State which Nietzsche hated. He insists that the individual has no reason for being save as a cog in the machine of the State. He has to be reminded of the sacred rights of the individual by no less a champion of the Christian slave morality than the head of the Roman Catholic Church. Moscow discards democracy and with it freedom; insists that the individual poet must think only in terms of proletarian poetry, the individual scientist must develop only proletarian science, and the individual philosophy must find its answer to things only in the class struggle which asserts the superior claims of the Underman to the Superman. It really does seem that if Nietzsche were alive today he would find the freest opportunities for the development of the superman in one of our herd democracies.

COMPANIONATE PAIR ADVISED BY LINDSEY

Denver Advocate of Step Warns Kansas Couple to Take Bitter With the Sweet.

JANE ADDAMS DISAPPROVES

Special to The New York Times.
GIRARD, Kan., Nov. 23.—Mr. and Mrs. E. Haldeman-Julius today made public a letter from Judge Ben B. Lindsey, noted Denver jurist and advocate of "companionate marriage," giving advice to their daughter Josephine, who was married yesterday to Aubrey C. Roselle in what was termed a "companionate" ceremony, and her husband.

"My hearty congratulations upon your marriage," said the letter. "My still heartier congratulations upon your honesty in openly entering into a companionate marriage.

"Make your partnership a 'go' for life, if you can. That is the way to the greatest happiness, and remember happiness is relative; made up of joys and sorrows. Expect some of the bitter with the sweet. Enjoy love to the fullest, but strive for patience, understanding and unselfishness.

"Do not feel that you really own each other without the other's full and free consent or you will encounter the green eyes of jealousy.

"If with such an honest effort your marriage should fail, as most of them under conventional codes are doing, do not frame up the lies, frauds and collusions with or against each other

as is now done in 90 per cent. of our divorce cases that are given the illegal blessing of our silly divorce courts, but insist in your honesty upon a divorce by mutual consent.

"Order your lives by your own individual wishes and not those of age-old greed, tyranny and ignorance. Throw off all such shackles that bind your right to reason and to happiness. Thus you will be joyfully unafraid."

The young couple returned suddenly today to the Haldeman-Julius home to plan for the Thanksgiving day dinner and reception.

Nothing New Says Jane Addams.

Special to The New York Times.
CHICAGO, Nov. 23.—Jane Addams, the settlement worker, said today that instead of companionate marriage young persons should be taught self-control. Miss Addams is the grand-aunt of the former Josephine Haldeman-Julius.

"I never did believe in companionate marriages," said Miss Addams. "Young people should be taught self-control. Companionate marriages are not so new. I know of several right here in Chicago where the parents of the young people helped them out financially till the boy finished medical or law school.

"Of course, it is very difficult for young persons to earn a living right at the start, and I think parents should help them as far as possible that way."

"Just Companionate" Says Bigamist.

Companionate marriage was the way Mrs. Katherine Dornacher Gruber, 40 years old, described her wedded state to Albert Obzut at her trial for bigamy here today.

It lasted only five days, she said, and should be considered companionate and be forgotten. Obzut is one of six husbands the defendant is alleged to have wedded without the formality of divorce.

November 24, 1927

PRESCRIBES 8 RULES FOR COURTSHIPS

Dr. Reisner Declares Marriage Happiness Still Depends on "Joyful Sweethearting."

The Rev. Dr. Christian F. Reisner in his sermon last night in the Chelsea Methodist Episcopal Church, 178th Street and Fort Washington Avenue, gave eight rules for "sweethearting," explaining his belief that happy marriages still depended upon "old-fashioned falling-in-love, joyful sweethearting, and rollicking full-fledged courtship," rather than companionate marriage, free love or eugenics. The eight rules are:

"Keep your heart clean, rejecting excuses for loose morals, so that it can send out rich love as a spring does pure water.

"Practise building an affection capacity by loving your enemies, seeing values in the hateful, and picking beauty out of the ugly.

"Avoid wasting and cheapening love by permitting dangerous liberties, the careless use of sacred tokens of affection and all excesses, however approved by 'experts,' falsely so-called.

"Look upon sweethearting, when safeguarded as above, as perfectly normal and ignore critics and objectors, even though they be selfish parents and then expect the blessing of the Master, who dignified a wedding feast with His first miracle.

"Trust God, dispelling all doubt by remembrance of His love—and believe in folks in spite of faults, and guard against pessimism as florists do against frost, and so keep young in spirit.

"Allow no 'disappointment in love' to sour or crush but find a value in sad experiences and be assured that somewhere there is a mate who will help to sweeten your days, and then determine to find him or her."

THE SWELLING TIDE OF FOREIGN TRAVEL

Americans Who Were Seldom Seen in Europe Before the War Now Make an Annual Trek Across the Atlantic

By EUNICE FULLER BARNARD

IT is Spring in Europe. In the shadow of a Constantinople wall a Turkish policeman dutifully cons his English phrase-book; for has not the order gone out that the oncoming American tourists are to be welcomed in their own tongue?

In hundreds of French towns free information booths for the traveler open up brightly. Chauffeurs at their stands chaff one another in the new-learned English of their union classes. From Ireland to Morocco sumptuous hotels are in building. The Central European powers in economic conference plot festivals and posters to beguile the American interest. Amsterdam paints and hammers for the Olympic Games. This year, as never before, all Europe sets its house in order for the transatlantic guest. Even Soviet Russia opens a travel bureau.

Here in America, at 10,000 steamship agencies, belated seagoers sign. Mail bags bulge with the romantic folders of European tours. Just ahead looms the annual vacation rush to Europe, an event as seasonal, as inevitable, as increasingly popular as the world's series or the college football games.

In 1913, the peak year before the war, some 246,000 people went to Europe from this country in the first and second classes. Last year in those classes and the two newly created ones—"cabin" and "tourist third"—which also carry mainly tourist passengers—322,000 people went over. That is a 30 per cent. increase over the best pre-war year, and about a 50 per cent. increase over the immediate pre-war average. And it has occurred in the face of rates half again as high.

Yet, paradoxically, the new American traveler, the majority type among our 76,000 new seagoers, is concededly a poorer, instead of a richer person than his pre-war brother. He or, more often, she is also younger, a student beginner in one of the professions, who before the war might not have thought of going abroad at all. In the last three years such young people have been crossing for Summer vacations in increasing thousands. Where gilded youth used to go by twos and threes with parents or tutor, youth today, gilded and ungilded, moves Europe-ward in mass formation, sometimes hundreds in a party, with all the enthusiasm of a college cheering section.

"Tourist third"—usually part of the erstwhile steerage, deodorized, glorified and attractively decorated—rings from June to September with lecturers' voices, jazz-band music and college songs. For here, compressed below decks and within the compass of a week, is a kind of intensified college life—instruction, sport and romance in the kaleidoscope of shipboard days. While millionaires move through the spacious baronial halls above, these new oceangoers dance on the crowded main deck, swim in a makeshift pool, eat ample American meals served without flourishes, and sleep in the uncompromising white bunks of a pre-decorator age.

Three years ago when "tourist third" was first thought of as a way of providing polite travel at a minimum rate, fewer than twenty thousand people went that way. The next year there were 44,000, and last year almost 80,000. Perhaps it is not coincidence that makes that figure roughly correspond to the total number of our new tourists in all classes. Certainly "tourist third" does represent the chief new mass movement of Americans to Europe—the thin edge of the wedge perhaps in transforming foreign travel from a leisure class to a popular avocation.

A new industry has blossomed into prosperity, taking students abroad at cheap rates, with college lecturers, hostesses and organized entertainment every day of the way. Already there are so many bureaus of student travel that they are constantly getting their mail mixed up. One of them alone has a thousand agents around the country. All the older, well-known tourist companies have added student departments. Almost over night, student tour-conducting as a vacation business bids fair to rival that of the Summer camp. It has taken its place in the American trend toward organized vacations.

One of the largest and oldest of such bureaus has gained about eight hundred new tourists each year. Starting in 1925 with some six hundred, this year it will take 3,000 across, including students from 265 colleges and universities. From the middle of May to the middle of July it will be sending out over a hundred tours, lasting from one to two months, at a cost between $300 and $785 a person.

⁎

IN its motor buses American boys and girls will roam the Alps and tour the Black Forest and the Pyrenees. Some of them will do twelve European countries and be home again in two months. There is no curbing the ardor of the youngsters. They are eager to see all the sights and to have all the experiences. They may want to dance away the night at a boulevard café in order to be up and ready for early mass at the cathedral.

Last Summer a group of college girls took a trip routed solely to cover the famous European beaches and other week-end resorts. Yet it was their ringleader who, on a casual day in Rome, was found blinking back sudden tears over the Forum.

One of the noteworthy things about "tourist third" is that the young traveler roughing it is more than likely to be a girl. Last June and July, Government officials report, about 60 per cent. of outgoing passengers were women. That was true of all classes, and an uncommon number were traveling alone. Widows, elderly spinsters, wives and mothers taking vacations from their families, and college girls on their own—they make up a growing proportion of the Winter cruise clientele, and, indeed, of the year-round traffic.

The student tours are of widely varying educational value. Some are pleasure junkets. Others include resident Summer study at universities. Still others make their routes illustrative of courses in European history, music, literature, art or geography, given along the way by university professors. Har-

The Beginning of the Vacation Trek.

we have but 250,000, the proportion returning is correspondingly reduced. Into this situation some genius projected the idea of scrubbing up some of the third-class cabins for tourists of limited means.

"Cabin class" started two years earlier, and from the other end of the scale. It consists of former first-class accommodations toned down to an intermediate price range. Whole ships were converted to this service, until today there are almost as many as there are of the first-class—fifty-three as against sixty-one—while some eighty-four liners carry the still cheaper "tourist third" in combination both with first-class and second-class accommodations and with "cabin." By both these new services the American "white-collar" worker has profited.

Through them he has become a recognized new phenomenon in the shops and hotels of Europe—the American of slender purse. A year ago he was resented. To the European mind he was obviously outside the ordered scheme of nature—an American who refused a guide, did not tip, thought hotel keepers thieves and blundered along on his own, seeing Europe with perhaps $200 in his pocket. He violated the major premise on which Europe has proceeded for a century, that all Americans are rich. Slowly, however, the Old World is seeing that it must adjust to him and his needs if it wishes an expanded tourist trade. Already American tourists spend annually some $650,000,000 in Europe. In France alone they spend over $200,000,000, a sum greater than the ordinary exports of France to the United States.

THE very rich go abroad as much as ever, and first-class bookings have shown an almost steady rise since the war. Recently a steamship agent reported that he could have sold fifty more cabins with private baths for his next sailing, but could not get rid of his lower-rate first-class accommodations.

The chief difference in the wealthy American's trip abroad today is not so much one of frequency as of purpose. In the old days, to him, almost as much as to the school teacher, Europe was a shrine, full of historic spots that had to be piously and indiscriminately visited. Today he and Americans generally look at Europe with a more appraising eye. They go there far less objectively, but frankly for the subjective satisfactions.

These satisfactions are as wide apart as their individual temperaments. One man will go over almost solely for the Derby or the Folies Bergeres; another for months of contemplation of the stained

vard conducts a Summer School of Geology abroad. Then there is the fully equipped "University Afloat," which made a world tour last year and will start again next October. Up to date it has received some 14,000 applications from college instructors for places on its Faculty.

The teacher feels the need of going abroad now as never before. Otherwise, when he is lecturing on the battleground of Waterloo he may be tripped up by a bright student who has really been there. Modern-language teachers run across for a month or so of actual experience with the foreign tongue that they have chosen for their specialty, and American education is the gainer.

Older people in other professional ranks are traveling "tourist third" nowadays. On a recent trip were counted an architect, a clergyman, a graduate nurse, a lawyer, a physician, a chemical engineer, a bacteriologist, an author, a banker, an army officer and an office manager. But more of the professional group, probably, go in the "cabin-class" steamers, the other new type of travel. "Tourist third" arose almost of necessity in 1925, after the steerage had been largely emptied by the immigration restriction law. Oddly, the law affected east-bound traffic as well as west-bound. When we had a million immigrants in a year, about a third as many went back in the same period. Now that glass at Chartres. Americans, that is, particularly of the wealthier classes, have begun to use Europe as they use America, without awe or inhibitions. One result of this new attitude in the last few years has been the increase in number of those who go over for special sports or for resort life in general.

Ireland is having a vogue because hunting there is good and relatively cheap. American sportsmen, indeed, maintain a clubhouse there. Norway is more and more a mecca for American anglers and devotees of skiing and other Winter sports, threatening even to eclipse crowded Switzerland in that regard. Some of us cross to play the famous golf courses of Scotland or to watch the tennis at Wimbledon, and there are Americans who follow the races in England and on the Continent. This year a special shipload will go over for the Olympic games.

New resorts and gaming casinos are springing up, supported largely by American patronage. Monte Carlo, Deauville, Biarritz and Nice are coming to be rivaled by resorts at Tangier, in Algeria, and at Zoppot, outside Danzig. One tendency of the new American traveler, according to a tourist agency, is to carry his explorations further afield to the less visited countries, such as Czechoslovakia, Spain and Portugal.

Wether the battlefields of France and the other war scenes have exerted much influence in taking Americans abroad is a moot point. Last year 25,000 of the American Legion made an anniversary pilgrimage, and Gold Star mothers have also been across. But report has it that the battlefield buses are less patronized than in other years: and that more people still visit Waterloo than go to view any other battle site in Belgium.

One new class of tourists consists of delegates to conventions. This year the steamship companies have lists pages long of groups that are going over—religious, educational, industrial, commercial. Since the American Bar Association, the Advertising Club and the Rotary Club held their conventions in European cities a year or so ago, there has been a well-defined inclination in that direction on the part of other organizations.

Perhaps the fastest growing group of American visitors, however, is made up of buyers. Department stores in all parts of the land are now sending their representatives to Paris, while the buyers for New York and Philadelphia shops often make four trips a year. Always they go first class, and ually on the fast ships. In Winter it is said that they comprise 40 per cent. of the first-class traffic.

Many Americans who go abroad can hardly be classed as tourists. There are those seeking health at the foreign spas, and those seeking to quench thirst in the Paris cafés. There is the not inconsiderable group whose members scorn sightseeing and spend their days and night in dancing. card playing and other pastimes they would indulge in at home.

There are gay travelers at Geneva who, if they know that the League of Nations has its headquarters in that city, never go out of their way to see it. There are parties of the same merry genus in Paris who are so self-contained that they may be said to have no contact at all with French life around them. To such folk Europe is only an extension of the American boardwalk. There will always be a good-sized element of them among transatlantic passengers.

The American farmer has joined the globe trotters. He takes his trip in the Winter, after his harvest is in the barn. On the Scandinavian lines especially are seen agriculturists from the mid-West, returning to Norway or Sweden to visit in their native haunts. On the Italian lines go retired merchants to build chateaux and therein lead lives of ease in the old country. In the steerage are itinerant workers; waiters who swing back and forth between Havana and Cairo, and machinists who alternate between Lancashire and New England.

By far the greater number of seagoing Americans come from the Atlantic seaboard, and of the 10,000 steamship agents in the country, most are east of the Mississippi. It is said that three-quarters of all passengers come from the twenty largest cities and the regions close around them.

In spite of all the new urges toward Europe, in spite of the increase in upper-class traffic, in spite of the fact that travel abroad beomes daily more and more of a social compulsion, still the steamship agent is gloomy. With all the new tours and the new passenger classes, his total bookings have never nearly come back to the prewar, pre-immigration restriction figure. He says that, year in and year out, only 30 per cent. of his passenger berthage is occupied.

In his halcyon days before the war, with no more trouble than a little advertising in the foreign-language newspapers, he used to take almost half a million a year back to Europe in the steerage. There they were carried six in a room, where in "tourist-third" there are but two. And 1,800 would cheerfully use the deck space that in "tourist-third" must be reserved for a paltry 600. Indeed, some lines regard "tourist-third" as so expensive that they have dropped it on their express ships.

WHERE else in the world, the agent asks, can one get transportation at less than 2 cents a mile with bed and board thrown in? And in spite of the vaunted European rush, he laments, how small a proportion of Americans really do spend their vacations in Europe! After all the advertising, less than half of 1 per cent.—a figure discouraging to the European shipowner.

Recently, too, the Institute of Foreign Travel analyzed the passports of thousands of Europe-bound tourists of 1926, only to find that but little more than half were citizens of the United States. Ten per cent. were foreign visitors. More than a quarter were immigrants going home for a time, and the remainder were Canadians.

Two reasons, the candid agent believes, work against steamship lines in obtaining the much greater tourist traffic that lies somehow just beyond their grasp. One reason is that most lines are foreign corporations, with little knowledge of American psychology, and with a century-old prejudice against popular advertising, inherited from the days when tourist traffic was confined to the wealthy classes. The second reason is that Europe is not yet mentally or materially adjusted to receive the non-rich American

May 6, 1928

ROOSEVELT PRAISES
WOMEN IN POLITICS

Franklin D. Roosevelt has written an article for the October issue of Woman's City Club Magazine in which he discusses the possibility of having the great mass of the people fed, housed and insured of a little prosperity before the "ravenous appetite" of a few favored industrial corporations has been satisfied, and says this is the leading issue in the Presidential campaign.

"It is greater than the 'noble experiment' which has so ignobly failed," he writes. "It is greater even than the breaking of the chains of superstition and bigotry which have so hampered our progress.

"I think if we look at our civilization today, beginning with a survey of our cities and ending with our national Government, we will see that the greatest defects have come from the fact that all these laws, until very recently, have been made exclusively by men. Here and there this thing or that thing has been improved by women's pleadings, by women's arguments, by women's persistency. But until women were given the vote, never by woman's direct authority or by woman's direct command.

"It is my firm belief that had women had equal share in making the laws in years past, the unspeakable conditions in crowded tenement districts, the neglect of the poor, the unwillingness to spend money for hospitals and sanitariums, the whole underlying cynical attitude toward human life and happiness as compared to material prosperity, which has reached its height under the present Republican Administration, would never have come about.

"It might almost be claimed that the preservation of human life had become distinctly a feminine concern, and that man, with his hereditary warlike instincts, was interested more in its destruction, when necessary for his own advancement.

"I have always believed in giving women an equal share in the making of our laws. I have regarded their entry into politics — for they must enter politics if they are to have a voice in our legislative halls — the most noteworthy step toward securing greater happiness and greater prosperity for the individual that we have ever taken."

October 4, 1928

URGES MARRIAGE CAUTION.

Mrs. Bertrand Russell Advocates "rPeliminary Partnership."

LONDON, Oct. 30 (AP).—Mrs. Bertrand Russell, wife of the Hon. Bertrand Russell, speaking today on marriage at the Guildhouse, where Agnes Maude Royden holds Sunday services, openly advocated "preliminary partnerships" before marriage.

"If you ask women for an honest opinion," she said, "most of them would admit that if they had married the first man that attracted them they would have made the biggest mistake of their lives."

October 31, 1927

NOW THE SIREN ECLIPSES THE FLAPPER

By MILDRED ADAMS

PARIS, endlessly resourceful in feminine inventions, is busily engaged in sending New York a new siren. On the stage and in the subtly lighted salons of the great couturiers, at the races and under the trees of smart midsummer cafés, she takes her graceful way before the attentive eyes of the tourist throng. With her clothes molded to her figure, her draperies that veil line and curve only to accentuate them, her air of knowing much and saying little, her mysterious allure that is at once the oldest and the newest of feminine accomplishments, she spells the death sentence of the flapper.

And the flappers know it. Voices falter in their stridencies and reach for lower notes. Girls from the hinterland clutch at brief skirts in a sudden agony of doubt as to the chic of bumpy knees. And the maidens from Park Avenue register a mental note that smartness has now clothed itself in garments of a fascinating complexity, and that sophistication no longer lies in revealing too much.

Outward indications of the new siren's ascendency have already reached those evening haunts about New York which pride themselves on being most truly informed of the mode. The city's smartest roofs, dinners and dances in Newport and Long Island are thronged with slim loveliness in long tulle gowns that swirl about like the gauzy tails of mermaids. Impish glances and gamin impertinence have given way to a high serenity and a slow seductive languor. Flapper violence and flapper knees are, in the evening, as dead as the Charleston.

But the woman beloved of Paris is more than a thing of clothes and mannerisms, and the eagerness of America to imitate her outward semblance without realizing that it connotes an indefinable inner grace might well evoke that slow, enigmatic smile which is one of her most charming weapons. She knows very well the ways of the world. She has character and background as well as long skirts and a deep-back décolletage. It is whispered that she has brains under her smooth long hair, and that she is not ashamed of having lived a discreet number of years.

Those who welcome her advent say that she challenges the present supremacy of the very young, and that the débutantes who ape her ways are thereby their own severest critics. Optimists go so far as to hope that she may bring the return of good manners, the revaluing of good breeding, and the scornful banishing of flaming youth to the nursery without any supper.

Whether she can accomplish so thorough a revolution as that is a matter for the future to examine and record. At the present moment she is engaged in remodeling the appearance of evening parties. The sirens who haunt smart clubs and débutante dances are a delight to eyes weary of unjustified legs. Clad in gowns that float softly to the floor, they carry themselves with a grace that is as old as Lilith. As long as they do not speak, they entice the imagination into weaving for them the most enchanting of destinies. Speaking is admittedly harder.

TO Europe, the emergence of this new-old feminine type symbolizes the end of the post-war jazz age and the recrudescence of values that for years were crowded out by the nervous tensity of speed and the jeering laughter of saxophones. But that does not mean she has turned back the clock. The siren of 1929 is no more a return to the Trilbys or the Sapphos of the '90s than she is like the Theda Baras of one's childhood movies. She is as modern as the airplane and the backless bathing suit. She is the most versatile thing that ancient tradition and progressive education have yet produced. In her highest development she is a combination of the best of old Europe and young America.

The European mind, visualizing its ideal woman, has never been satisfied with the vapid prettiness that a thousand magazine covers taught America to regard as most desirable. It bowed too long ago before the fascination of Diane de Poitiers, who could not possibly win a drugstore beauty contest. It has known too many Ninons de l'Enclos, it has cherished the wit of

Seductive Languor Has Taken the Place of The Violence of The Young

Mme. de Sévigné and loved the spicy knowledge of Margaret of Navarre. It likes its women poised and suave, wise in the ways of life and willing to accept all its implications. It prefers that they carry an air of class and breeding, and it is even willing that they be savants. It places the charms of character and the beauty of personality far above straight noses and even teeth.

America, on the other hand, is as frank as a child or a Greek in loving healthy physical beauty. Clear eyes and a fine skin, good muscles and white teeth are so thoroughly the accepted ideal that millions of dollars are earned yearly by drops and creams, salts and mineral oils, lotions and pastes and powders warranted to produce them. And along with that adoration of the thing seen goes a distrust of the subtle charm that does not appear on the surface. Thus the quiet reserve of European women is dismissed as snobbishness, and their complex depths are suspected of hiding treacherous and secret plottings.

But a war and a tide of tourist travel have done their best to modify even such powerful things as national ideals and prejudices. American soldiers found French girls fascinating, and wrote home about it. American girls went over to find out what this fabulous new technique was all about. European women took notes from the hordes of clear, frank, outspoken youngsters. Flappers became suddenly aware of nuances and depths they had never known.

•.•

THIS new siren of the Champs Elysées and Park Avenue is the result of that mutual scrutiny. European in her poise, her knowledge of clothes and of the uses of mystery, American in her clear beauty of slim form, her calm directness, she is an enchanting proof that the Old and the New Continents, when they work together, can do better than either of them alone.

In the first place, she is grown up, not in any sere and yellow sense, but because she has been about and knows the world in a way that not even a blasé sixteen-year-old hotel child can imitate. She has an air of cosmopolitan good breeding. She was a flapper when very young, therefore she has been through the noisy and the bizarre

"The Couturiers Never Did Like the Flapper Uniform."

stages, and has relegated sensation to its proper place as a useful stimulant, but a poor food, a spice of life, but apt to produce anemia if mistaken for meat.

She makes no pretense of being pretty in the poster sense of that dubious word. Distinguished, sometimes striking, she is a type that such men as Doumergue and Van Dongen, who barred the flapper from their canvases, might well make every effort to paint. She knows how to stand and to walk, she can move into a drawing room amid her draperies without stumbling over them or kicking the furniture. She has combined American hygienic notions of how to keep a body in good running order with European wisdom about its clothing and its handling. Always well groomed, she is in her more expensive incarnations as exotic as

a piece of rare old porcelain. And always there gleams behind her surfaces that indefinable thing for which Broadway, balked in definition, utters the cryptic "It."

She is afraid neither of brains nor of her own version of what used to be called feminine wiles. Some of her older sisters fled the first, and others sternly forswore the second as unfair tactics. Tradition demanded that the beautiful be dumb and pre-war feminist ethics insisted that charm be carefully hidden so that women might meet men on equal terms. Apparently they were unaware of the implied insult to men. The modern siren is wiser. Brains, she has discovered, are useful in that they make available both wisdom and a knowledge of how and when to use them. Charm is one of those things for which a

"The Siren Turns the Tired Business Man Into a Courtier."

grimy and hard-working world is always grateful.

And so, being thus equipped, she goes serenely about the main business of being a siren. She handles men with the combined skill of both her parental continents. She turns the tired business man into a courtier and makes him like it. Ancient wisdom teaches her to be a confidante, but seldom to confide, to understand rather than to seek to be understood, to charm and delight rather than to demand amusement. Newer, franker ways have abolished any "slave complex" she might have inherited along with that knowledge. She has learned from brothers and schoolmates that men are not angels, but beings very human who prefer flesh and blood to sugar candy heroines. And she has discovered abroad that the best technique of managing them keeps always a reserve of power, and that mystery which suggests untold possibilities is more successful than frankness which knows nothing worth revealing.

So she puzzles the boy friend by leading him away from headlong petting parties into the ancient devious ways of courtship, and she has given up "going blotto" for the more confusing method of holding her liquor well, or saying "no, thank you."

SHE no longer has to bother about smashing tradition or demonstrating her superiority to convention. In this she is the flapper's debtor, for that young person abolished surplus clothes and surplus manners with the same enthusiasm she devoted to acquiring gin and cigarettes. By sheer force of violence she established the feminine right to equal representation in such hitherto masculine fields of endeavor as smoking and drinking, swearing, petting and upsetting the community peace. They need no longer be the subject of crusade. Indeed the incurable flappers who go on fighting for them are as absurd as the good ladies who still carry the hysteric

air of martyrs in the cause of women's rights.

They being won, the new siren may elect to use them or not as she sees fit. She may go on disregarding the old conventions, she may set up new ones as a convenient set of rules which give form and seemliness to the game of life.

It all sounds perilously close to that creature discarded ten years ago, the lady. But this one is no mid-Victorian. She neither faints nor bridles, though if she chose she could probably manage either as well as she manages men and motor boats and polo ponies. It is that adaptability, that perfect sense of familiarity with all the tools of life that is perhaps her outstanding characteristic. Her motto might well be the ancient "All of which I saw, part of which I was." She looks at life with clear wide-open eyes, and likes it.

Her advent in Paris has been hailed with delight by the suave couturiers and the wise producers of plays. The former never did like the straight, short-belted slip which was the flappers' uniform. It gave no scope for his skill, it was too easily imitated by the dozen gross on power machines. Now Lucien Lelong proclaims triumphantly that "the subadolescent figure is obviously absurd, because it is not typical of today's young women," and seizing his shears to prove his point, he cuts and molds in long lines princess bodices and intricate feminine draperies. Jean Patou has definitely ceased to make "girlish" dresses for any but girls. Worth, who ruled the '80s and the '90s, and kept his distinguished list of patrons through the flapper years by heroic feats of preserving dignity in the midst of a hoyden mode, is triumphantly gowning women so that they look neither like clothes horses nor children, but like the fascinating people that some of them are. There is even a rumor that clothes must fit.

The Paris stage has put on clothes. Nudity, rampant in these later years in the persons of hard-working chorus girls who came and went along aisles so close to the audience that no detail of knees bruised from rehearsal or feet soiled by a dirty floor was left to the imagination, has vanished even from the music halls. The Quatr'arts Ball, famous for nothing more concealing than a leopard skin or a fig leaf, bowed this year to the new order of things and put on what might really be called costumes.

Meanwhile the movies, in the very midst of becoming the talkies, have taken time off to help along the revolution. Having spread the flapper broadcast over the globe as the American ideal, they are now bending every effort toward tumbling her off her throne and sending her to join the Gibson Girl and the bicycle built for two. Their most potent tool is the imported heroine with ways that look very strange to Main Street. Starting with Pola Negri, they added the blonde mysterious languor of Greta Garbo, the passionate abandon of Lupe Velez, the Russian power of Olga Baclanova. It confused and fascinated Minneapolis and Galveston, Detroit and Tacoma. It set their men to dreaming and their women to wondering. How many domestic tempests it produced can only be estimated by the trail of

startled ears that came out in the wake of Garbo pictures.

All of this has put the flapper on a starvation diet. Deprived of her models on stage and screen, she could only repeat old tricks and worn out lines. She grew tiresome and irritable, her voice a bit too shrill, her boisterous gayety a little forced. Her impertinences became bad manners, her insouciance mere rudeness. The world tired of her, and she, above all types dependent on the public opinion she pretended to scorn, worked more and more hectically to retain her throne. But the only tools she knew had lost their power. She was doomed to fall by the very forces which had created her.

It is true that in many places she does not yet seem to know that she is dead. Long Beach and Coney Island, Times Square at 5 o'clock and the chain stores at noon bear little evidence of the new reign. Hats that may be bought in head-sizes large enough to fit over long hair, and wisps of chiffon that trail below short hem lines are the only signs. So far the siren rules only by artificial light in somewhat formal gatherings.

WHETHER she will win predominance in all phases of modern existence and at all hours of the modern day is a matter for controversy. Already lovely at evening dances, she will be equally exquisite at afternoon teas and garden parties. But the street, the office, the tennis court, the golf links are a different matter. The beaches show no signs of capitulating, unless the very violence of their nakedness means an emotional protest which presages surrender.

The dream of idealists is that the new style means a real chance to follow the sloganeers and "be yourself." Short skirts and freedom for streets and sports, long skirts and illusion for afternoon and evening. Frankness and camaraderie and gamin impertinence for the golf links, the swimming pool, the swift walk down the avenue, and sirenish mystery, allure, the ancient intricate practice of man-handling for the tea lounge and the shaded corner. It is variety's golden opportunity to step in and banish the monotony of life, to make a change of personality as easy and as pleasant as the shift from tweeds to tulle.

WOMEN SEEK SUPPORT TO REFORM DRY LAW

National Group Meeting at Southampton Hears Present Statute Defeas Its Aims.

Special to The New York Times.
SOUTHAMPTON, L. I., July 27.— The first meeting of the women's organization for national prohibition reform was held yesterday afternoon at Glynne's Garden Theatre, Southampton. The object of the meeting was to present the aims of the organization and to enlist the aid of the residents of Southampton, East Hampton, Water Mill and West Hampton and to gain new members. Mrs. Charles H. Sabin, the acting president of the organization, presided.

In a brief speech before introducing the speakers, Mrs. Sabin explained the reasons for the meeting and said that she had resigned from the National Women's Republican Club in order to devote her entire time to the work of the organization for national prohibition reform. Mrs. Sabin said the present organization was not complete, that it was but a temporary agency to discuss ways to meet the problems brought about by prohibition. She said that many prominent professional and business women throughout the nation already had pledged their support.

Mrs. Sabin introduced Mrs. Cortlandt Nicoll, who is the temporary secretary of the organization. Mrs. Nicoll cited statistics to show that under the prohibition amendment drunkenness had increased. She said that there were only three licensed saloons in Southampton before prohibition, there were now thirty-two speak-easies.

The Rev. Arthur L. Kinsolving, rector of Grace Church, Amherst, Mass., spoke of increasing drunkenness, especially among the youth of the country. Captain William H. Slayton of Baltimore, asserted that prohibition had had just the opposite effect from the intention of its originators, even though their motives were good. He stressed the fact that temperance was gaining in 1917 throughout the nation, but that the amendment, instead of increasing moderation, caused us to lose the progress we had made.

SEVEN MEN ACCUSED IN GASTONIA KILLING OF WOMAN STRIKER

Murder Charges Name Six Mill Employes and Driver of Truck Attacked by Anti-Red Mob.

INQUEST UNFOLDS TERROR

Little Mountaineer Tells How Victim Fell Dying in His Arms as Others Fled Under Fire.

ANOTHER PICKS PURSUERS

Mill Manager Corroborates Story of Shooting—Prisoners Held in Bail for Grand Jury.

Special to The New York Times.

GASTONIA, N. C., Sept. 15.—Seven men were charged with the murder of Mrs. Ella May Wiggins here this afternoon, less than twenty-four hours after she had been shot to death by an anti-Communist mob as she fled in a truck, with twenty-two other textile strikers.

Six of the men charged with the crime are employes in the Loray Mill here. The seventh is the truck driver who drove the death car from Bessemer City, eight miles away, bringing the Red sympathizers to a scheduled Communist rally here, which never took place.

The men are held in $1,000 bail each for the October grand jury term. It is charged that they "did conspire, confederate and agree together to slay and did slay Ella May Wiggins," who was 35 years old and the mother of five children.

The charge means either second degree murder or manslaughter. J. A. Baugh Jr., resident manager of the Manville-Jenckes Company of Pawtucket, R. I., owners of the Loray mill, signed the bonds for his employes.

Mrs. Wiggins was to have been buried here this afternoon, but a call to the undertaking parlor where the body is held asked that the ministers and others be notified that the funeral had been postponed until Tuesday. It was said the textile union wanted time to arrange for a "mass funeral."

The Accused.

Those named in the murder charge were:

I. M. SOSSOMAN, described as a "mill boss."

WILL LUNCHFORD, mill foreman, said to have jumped out of an automobile while the shooting was going on and shouted, "That's enough shooting, boys."

TROY JONES, who recently "threatened to blow up union headquarters" and sued the National Textile Workers' Union for $100,-000 for alienation of his wife's affections.

LOWREY DAVIS, a young mill worker.

THEODORE SIMMS, a middle-aged office man at the mill.

F. C. MORROW, mill worker who drove the car which was in collision with the strikers' truck.

GEORGE LINGERFELT, World War veteran and driver of the strikers' truck.

The inquiry today into Gastonia's second anti-Communist riot within a week was held before a jury of six men sworn in by Coroner J. F. Wallace. The examination of thirty witnesses was conducted by Solicitor John C. Carpenter, who was assisted by Judge N. A. T. Townsend, executive counsel and personal representative of Governor O. Max Gardner.

Major A. L. Bulwinkle, counsel for textile interests, represented the six mill employes among the accused, while R. E. Sigmon, attorney for the International Labor Defense, and H. L. Kiser, a Gastonia lawyer, represented Lingerfelt, the driver of the strikers' truck.

At the end of today's session Solicitor Carpenter announced the coroner's inquiry would be resumed here next Saturday morning.

Mountaineer Gives Graphic Account.

Eyewitness accounts of the raid on the strikers' truck five miles south of here yesterday afternoon were dramatic. Witness after witness told of fleeing strikers being hunted like jack-rabbits as they raced across a cotton field toward the shelter of woods near by.

Every one in the truck at the time Mrs. Wiggins was slain gave his version of the raid. They ranged from youths to elderly men and one was a sullen-faced little girl of 17 who testified that she was married, but that "my husband is in the penitentiary for stealing."

The men arrested this afternoon were identified by several of the witnesses, but the majority appeared afraid to admit that they recognized any one at the scene of the shooting.

Charlie Shope, a weazened-face, blue-eyed little mountaineer, told the most connected story of the shooting. He took the stand in his shirt sleeves. There were blood stains on his shirt and trousers for "Miss Ella May," as he called the slain woman, had fallen into his arms, crying, "Lord-a-mercy, they done shot and killed me!"

"I heard it discussed at Bessemer City Friday night at a union meeting," testified Shope, "that there was a-going to be a big meeting Saturday at Gastonia. We all 'lowed we'd go down there this Saturday and we-all went.

"I 'lowed to hear one of the organizer fellows and I reckon the rest of the twenty-two folks in that truck went for the same reason."

Tells of Pursuit, Attack and Killing.

"Well, Mr. A. W. Williams—he's our organizer—had been a-telling us a lot about what might happen, but we warn't honing for trouble," he continued.

"They said if the law don't protect you, protect yourself, but I warn't prepared for fighting. Nobody in the truck had any guns.

"We got to Gastonia and the mob in automobiles turned us back. They hollered, 'Git going' and we headed for Bessemer City. Then they came a-chasing us and pestering us with cussings.

"'You fellers are going to get shot up,' one of them hollered. To tell you the darned truth I never believed it then.

"Well, sir, we got 'bout five miles away and was a-hitting it up. Mrs. Wiggins and Mary Goldsmith was a-standing by me in the truck. About right then a Essex car came a-whizzing past us and stopped right in front.

"We couldn't stop, so hit it smack in the rear. Then, bang went a gun. Mrs. Wiggins shouted, 'Lord 'a' mercy, they done shot and killed me!' I caught her and Roy Carpenter helped me hold her up.

"I warn't much skeered till I looked out in the field and saw a gang of men with rifles and shotguns shooting every which-away. Some of the boys started running across the cotton patch and the men was a-gunning for them. I reckon there must ha' been forty or fifty shots fired.

"After we got Mrs. Wiggins in a house acros the road I got going home."

Mill Official Backs Strikers' Story.

The only eye witness not directly involved to take the stand was G. R. Spencer, general manager of the American Mills at Bessemer City, which also had much strike trouble during the past five months.

Mr. Spencer testified he was passing at about the time the truck was halted by a collision, that he saw three or four men engaged in shooting pump guns at other men who were fleeing through a cotton patch.

Being himself a member of what the Communists call the "boss class," Mr. Spencer, in his testimony, went far to discount the testimony of the Loray employes who testified that there were no guns and that there was no shooting.

Witness Names Three As in Mob.

W. O. Bradley, a Gastonia Communist sympathizer, who "hopped the truck when the mob turned it back," gave the most damaging testimony. He knew the folks "in the mob" and did not appear afraid to name them.

"There was a feller named Jack Carver who drove up in a car with L. M. Sossoman of the Loray Mill," he testified. "They was there when the shooting was going on. Mr. Sossoman said, 'All right, now boys. Don't shoot no more.'

"Then I saw Morrow in a car with a shotgun. (Morrow was called into the courtroom and identified). I saw him again on the left side of the road in the field holding a gun."

Morrow took the stand and testified that he was accompanied by Simms, David and Jones in the automobile which was in collision with the truck. He denied that they were chasing the strikers and insisted that they were headed for Jenk's Lake, a fishing resort, for a week-end party.

Morrow and his companions testified that they did not have anything to do with the mob, did not hear any shots and did not know Mrs. Wiggins or any one else "had been hurt" until late Saturday night.

Charge Manoeuvre for Crash.

At the scene of the murder, according to the union witnesses, Morrow's car and other cars drove around in front of the truck and blocked it, causing a collision that wrecked Morrow's car and ran the truck off the road. Immediately the mob, riding in about fifteen cars, opened fire, the first shot killing Mrs. Wiggins.

George Lingerfelt, driver of the truck. He is a shell-shocked and gassed war veteran, who is not a member of the union or of the International Labor Defense.

The unionists had asked to hire his truck, he said, and added: "I am in that business and thought I ought to give service." Lingerfelt said that Morrow, in his automobile, deliberately blocked his truck and caused the wreck. "Then they started shooting," he declared.

Solicitor Carpenter explained that Lingerfelt was held because he "was the driver of the other car" in the wreck preceding the shooting. Four doctors testified that Mrs. Wiggins died of a gunshot wound, not from the wreck, and there was no evidence to the effect that Lingerfelt had a gun.

Scene Shifts Today to Charlotte.

Tomorrow the scene of the North Carolina textile workers' struggle moves back to Charlotte, where the courts are endeavoring to untangle the results of previous battles between the Communists, the police and the anti-Communist mobs, as well as to prepare for the retrial of the sixteen strike leaders and Communists on the charge of murdering Chief of Police Aderholt of Gastonia.

Several witnesses still are to be heard in the investigation of the activities of last Monday's mob which flogged Ben Wells, the British Communist organizer, and kidnapped two of his companions. The hearing is being conducted by Judge Thomas J. Shaw.

Eight men accused of a plot to overthrow the State government will go on trial tomorrow morning in the City Recorder's Court.

PICTURES A STRIKE "TERROR."

Engdahl Sees Endeavor to Intimidate Gastonia Trial's Witnesses.

J. Louis Engdahl, national secretary of the International Labor Defense, yesterday issued a statement on the Gastonia strike situation in which he said:

"The events of Gastonia, the brutal killing of the widow, Mrs. Ella May Wiggins; the absolute Fascist reign of terror, prove our contention that the mill owners, the police and authorities are working hand in hand to terrorize the workers and union organizers, to intimidate the witnesses for the defense in the trial of the sixteen strikers that reopens Sept. 30 in Charlotte, N. C.

"They also wish to destroy the foothold the National Textile Workers' Union has gained in the South; but despite this terrorization, this unparalleled rule of brutality, the union and the International Labor Defense will continue to help the Southern workers to get an increase in the wage scale, to obtain a reduction in the general sixty-hour week and for general better livable conditions."

Mob Victim Had Been in New York.

CHARLOTTE, N. C., Sept. 16 (AP). —Following announcement of the plans of the International Labor Defense for a mass funeral Tuesday for Mrs. Ella May Wiggins, victim of a Gastonia mob, it was stated that the union headquarters in Bessemer City and the dead woman's home would be draped in black late today and that a sign was to be placed on the house reading:

"Ella May, slaughtered by the bosses' black hundred, martyr to the cause of organized labor."

Mrs. Wiggins was separated from her husband and had been going under her maiden name, Ella May. Under the name Ella May she was one of a party of strikers who went to New York and other cities in the North and East, on a tour designed to raise funds for the strikers.

CHAPTER 3
The Thirties

Mother Mary Jones, labor leader.

DR. CHARLES ASSAILS WIVES WHO HOLD JOBS

False Ideas of Individuality Break Up Homes and Rob Needy of Work, He Asserts.

Deploring the increasing tendency of young persons, especially young women, to retain their "individuality" after entering matrimony, the Rev. Dr. Arthur L. Charles, rector of St. Mark's Protestant Episcopal Church, Brooklyn, declared yesterday that this mental attitude is directly opposed to the ideal of unity as expressed in the fundamental principles of marriage. Dr. Charles spoke on the subject "Till Death Do

Us Part" at the family forum, conducted under the auspices of the New York State Federation of Women's Clubs, at its Home Making Centre, Grand Central Palace.

In his research through the family clinic, conducted by the St. Mark's Church, Dr. Charles found, he said, that much of the discord among young married people can be traced back to conditions created by such an attitude.

"If these young women would found a home and raise a family, instead of insisting on keeping their jobs and 'living their own life,' they would cease to make home a stopping place and marriage a convenience," the speaker asserted.

Dr. Charles blamed much of present unemployment as well as age-limits in all fields of employment, to young women, who, indulging their selfish desire to remain independent though married, are taking the places of older and needier workers.

March 7, 1930

PLEDGE BUSINESS AID BY SPENDING MONEY

Detroit Club Women Resolve on Effort to Dispel Depression Fear and Bring Out Hoarded Cash.

Special to The New York Times.

DETROIT, Mich., April 14.—Hastening to be among the first to answer the plea of President Hoover for increased activity in the interest of improved business conditions, and proceeding on the theory that business depression is primarily a psychological and emotional problem, more than 200 Detroit clubwomen at a luncheon here today pledged themselves to a program of "spending, that others may spend."

They adopted resolutions to be forwarded to the President urging women to "dispel the psychology of fear and to restore hoarded money to circulation and to all the fields of commerce."

Judge Florence Allen of Cleveland, the principal speaker, asserting that the object of the meeting was "to create a state of mind that will be transferred into action," added that "no one is better able to carry out the idea than the militant woman of Detroit and America."

Showing how the "natural conservatism" of women might react to the detriment of business and general welfare, she said:

"Suppose I have decided to buy an automobile, but because I have this fear of depression I change my mind and keep the money. Many others decide, as I decided, not to buy.

"The automobile manufacturers find it necessary to lay off large numbers of men. The parts manufacturers, deprived of their market, do likewise. The producers of raw materials in turn are forced to cut their forces. The doctor, the grocer, the merchant cannot collect the money due them and we have depression, because those who have money to buy decided not to do so.

"If the trouble is that money is not in circulation, then we must know that the thing to do is not to withhold more money from circulation but to put it back in. You can't cure a man of his ills by giving him more of what made him ill."

April 15, 1930

MASTICK LAW ASSAILED BY WOMEN'S PARTY

Curb on Overtime Will Keep Women From Promotion, Party Leaders Assert.

The New York State Branch of the National Women's party, which is opposed to the Mastick law applying to the employment of women in factories and mercantile establishments, declared yesterday that by abolishing overtime for women working eight

hours a day for six days a week the new statute would prevent them from being hired as executives in mercantile establishments and from winning promotion. The law denies to women equal opportunity with men in earning a livelihood, the statement charged.

Miss Frances Perkins, State Industrial Commissioner, pointed out that permission to work employes overtime was essentially a bonus to those employers who gave workers a half holiday. The new law was framed to correct the decision in the Elite Laundry case in which the highest State court held that employers could work employes overtime on the half holiday, said Miss Perkins, thus nullifying the effect of the shorter work-day.

June 26, 1930

5,000 Women Storm Office To Get 200 Jobs at Capital

WASHINGTON, July 30 (AP).—Five thousand women, many of whom had remained in line all night, today stormed the office of the Civil Service Commission to apply for 200 positions as charwomen in government buildings. The line began forming at 8 o'clock last night.

Several hundred women not in line attempted to "crash the gate." Police were forced to struggle with them before restoring order. There was a silver lining, however, for some of the unsuccessful applicants. Washington matrons, attracted to the scene, took advantage of the opportunity to hire cooks and maids.

Civil service officials said most of the women, many of whom were Negroes, had positions, but were attracted by the $90 a month paid to charwomen.

July 31, 1930

Census Will Classify Women 'Home-Makers'

WASHINGTON, March 20.—For the first time in the history of census-taking, home-making will be classified officially as an occupation, Secretary of Commerce Lamont declared in a radio talk tonight over the Columbia broadcasting system.

"The aim is to give recognition to women in the home who hitherto, unless they had some money-making employment, were reported as having no occupation," Mr. Lamont said.

Illustrating the value of census statistics, Mr. Lamont said that the department had been forced to make its third issue of a document entitled "Market Data Handbook of United States," which, although containing 515 pages of solid figures, had become one of the "books of the month."

"Business men have purchased it eagerly," Mr. Lamont said. "They have plunged into that apparent wilderness of figures as gleefully as they would into a piece of fiction. Thus we see that figures can be extremely vital."

Secretary Lamont characterized the census to start April 2 as ranking among the major tasks of the government this year. It will cost about $40,000,000. Among the new features will be the requirement that as soon as the enumeration of the population of any city or town is completed an immediate announcement shall be made by supervisors.

The unemployment census, to be taken for the first time, will be of greatest importance in economic studies, according to Mr. Lamont. For the first time also the number of radio sets in use will be obtained as well as the value of dwellings.

"The new census of distribution is being undertaken at the insistent demand not only of the merchants of the country but of manufacturers, bankers and business men in general," Mr. Lamont said. "In a country of high standards of living like the United States the marketing of goods is an extremely complex process."

The purpose of the distribution census is to discover where waste can be eliminated.

March 21, 1930

WOMAN DEFIES RIGORS OF ARCTIC EXPEDITION

Nina Demney Is With Russian Party Making Scientific Study in Fridtjof Nansen Land.

FRIDTJOF NANSEN LAND (formerly Franz Josef Land), U. S. S. R., Aug. 2 (P).—In a tiny tent on the northernmost fringe of this remote and desolate Arctic island, which may almost be called the roof of the world, today sat the world's first woman Arctic explorer.

She is Miss Nina Petrovana Demney of Leningrad, and she is 28 years old. She is a member of the Soviet Arctic expedition that arrived here today from Archangel aboard the Soviet icebreaker Sedov.

Miss Demney, ignoring warnings that no woman could survive the rigors and privations of life in the frozen Arctic, insisted upon braving the perils of the Polar regions with the veteran male explorers who compose the present expedition, led by the well-known Professor Otto Schmidt.

While this dispatch announcing their arrival was being transmitted by wireless from the icebreaker across the icy wastes of the Polar ocean to Archangel, Miss Demney, who is second in command of the expedition, was giving orders to the men of a party that is to restore the hut on Cape Flor left thirty-three years ago by Frederick G. Jackson, the first English explorer to chart the former Franz Joseph Land.

Miss Demney will place near the Jackson hut, as a memorial of the present expedition's visit, a red flag of the Soviets which she made with her own hands.

Among the fifty men comprising the crew of the Sedov and the expedition, she is the only woman, but she finds it most natural that women should undertake the heavy labor and exertion of exploring. She is a graduate of the Leningrad Geographical and Topographical Institute.

Miss Demney will remain here with her male colleagues throughout the Autumn and the Winter, mapping, exploring and studying the huge archipelago of Fridtjof Nansen Land, lying within the shadow of the North Pole.

Miss Demney is an active member of the Communist party and secretary of the northernmost Communist nucleus in the world, which was recently established here.

August 3, 1930

EUTHENICS TAUGHT IN VACATION STUDY

Group of Mothers at Vassar Learn the Art of Living Freed From Home Cares.

COURSE LASTS SIX WEEKS

Subjects Which Touch All Phases of Child Care and Family Life Offered at the Institute.

By DOROTHY WOOLF.

Although some people might not consider going to school an ideal way of spending the Summer, the students now attending Vassar's Institute of Euthenics are enthusiastic about it as a profitable vacation for the entire family. For six weeks almost 100 married women living in comfortable dormitories on the 1,000-acre campus are freed from the strain of running a home while they attend classes assisting them to become better housewives and mothers. Those who have brought their children with them are secure in the knowledge that the youngsters are happy under expert guidance in their own Summer nursery and progressive schools connected with the institute.

Week-ends find the husbands of many of the women interested audiences in the classes and eager to give the masculine viewpoint in the discussion groups arranged especially for them. Sisters who are teachers, nurses and social workers and a few grandmothers who are engaged in parent education movements are also enrolled at the institute, and with the fathers and mothers are seeking the answers to the complicated problems of family life today.

They are a more alert group than is found in the ordinary Summer school. They have reached a point in their lives where they feel definitely a need for outside assistance in solving immediate, real and personal problems. Coming from farms as well as suburban towns and large cities, some of them college graduates, others from normal schools, wealthy women and those of moderate circumstances, they represent many different points of view. And the fact that numbers of them who thought their difficulties unique have found other people facing similar situations doubtless is the reason why at evening little groups gather under the trees and in the gardens to continue the discussions begun in the classrooms.

The Courses Offered.

From 8 o'clock in the morning until 3:30 in the afternoon the women take courses ranging from technological subjects like cooking and interior decoration to the more intangible ones of mental hygiene and religion. Though the latter may at first glance seem abstract, the interest of the students in them is decidedly practical. For in approaching religion they came to their instructor and asked, "What shall we teach our children about God?" He countered, "What do you think about Him yourselves?" So they began the class with a study of religious ideas in different ages and countries in order to find out why they believed as they did and proceeded from that to means of teaching these beliefs to children.

Similarly in mental hygiene they inquired, "How can we make our children behave?" and decided that they must first review the learning processes of the mind before they discussed particular problems. In this course, too, they felt that in order to be good parents they must first be mentally healthy individuals and most of them took advantage of the privilege of a personal consultation with a psychiatrist to straighten out their own difficulties.

As mothers they are interested in a class which covers what parents should know about schools and education. This deals with the financing of education as well as giving the women an insight into the changes that have taken place in its method and theory since their own school days, while they have a chance to exchange views with the teachers studying at the Institute of Progressive Education also being conducted on the campus.

Children a Favorite Topic.

Even classes such as that in spoken English, which was offered to aid clubwomen in overcoming their difficulties when addressing large audiences, show that the students are primarily concerned with motherhood. For, when called upon to speak, they usually choose such topics as suitable clothing for children and whether careers interfere with raising a family, though they have been known to consider the psychology of dress and cosmetics and ways of holding husbands.

Although all the courses are practical in their outlook, in none is the gap between theory and application better bridged than in the class on child guidance. In college many of the women were taught that sparing the rod is less apt to spoil the child than its use is to develop psychoses, but when faced with actual problems of behavior in their own children they had become vague about substitutes for spanking. Similarly they may be fully aware that they should be frank and unembarrassed in giving their children information about death and sex, but they have found that this is not always easy in practice.

Theory Put to Practice.

The women have an excellent opportunity to put classroom suggestions into operation while they are still at the institute and under the supervision of their instructors. The two schools for children are their laboratories, where they observe the youngsters at meals and at play. They are at first impressed by the leisurely, calm attitude of the teachers who keep in the background as much as possible while the children make their own decisions about what to play or to do next. Yet closer observation shows that guidance, though scarcely perceptible, is present.

At the table a mother sees that the food a child deliberately drops onto the floor to avoid eating it is replaced with an equal amount, which is more likely to correct this habit than repeated verbal protests.

On the playground her child's activity with packing boxes and barrels at first seems pointless, but suddenly the mother realizes that he is arranging them into a steam engine, thus exercising his ingenuity far more than he does in dragging a mechanical toy about.

Another little boy comes up and starts to walk off with the box that represents the cow-catcher, and both children begin a loud argument. The teacher steps in and settles it quietly by suggesting that they both work on the steam engine, or that the interfering child find another box at the opposite end of the yard.

The child who at home would never go to sleep unless his mother stayed with him may whimper the first night or two that he spends in the dormitory with the rest of the children, but when no one runs to his side at his first cry he quickly outgrows his dependence on his mother and falls asleep as soon as he is in bed.

Thus while the child is developing independence, self-control and creativeness, his mother is learning how to assist him toward these goals. For an hour or two each afternoon she personally directs his play. Teachers are near at hand for consultation when difficulties arise, but in a few weeks mothers have become quite expert in using the methods employed by the school.

At the end of the session each mother receives a written report on her child, which is largely a study of his temperament as seen by outsiders—the teachers who have been in constant contact with him for the past six weeks. It analyzes behavior difficulties he may have and contains suggestions for his future training.

Husbands Come Week-Ends.

But as much in agreement as the mother may come to be with the ideas and recommendations she has received in classes and from the children's schools, she cannot carry them out at home unless her husband is also in sympathy with them. For this reason most of the women are anxious for their husbands to join them for the week-end lectures. These attempt to give a cross-section of the institute's activities and theories, while special problems are brought up in the discussion groups for men.

10,000,000 WOMEN IN 'GAINFUL' WORK

Census Also Enumerates 23,000,000 Housewives, Steuart Says Over the Radio.

47,000,000 BREAD WINNERS

Special to The New York Times.
WASHINGTON, Aug. 31.—Summarizing census data on what the people are doing for a living, William M. Steuart, director of the census, told the radio audience tonight that of more than 122,000,000 people in the United States about 47,000,000 are engaged in bread-winning work. These because of days off, vacations, sickness and part time employment work about 275 days a year, or three-fourths of the time on an average. There are 38,000,000 males and 37,000,000 females between the ages of 16 and 64.

"While the count has not yet been made," he said, "it is probable that about 49,000,000 people told the census enumerators last April that they had some gainful occupation. Some of them were not actually engaged in this occupation at the time of the enumeration, some were sick, some were on vacations and some reported that they could find no work to do, though they were able and willing to work and were looking for a job. There were others who, while they were working, were not working full time, being idle part of the days of the week, or part of the normal working hours in each day.

"It is probably true that under present normal industrial and business conditions there are not more than 40,000,000 or 42,000,000 people in this country who, on a given day, are at work full time on a gainful occupation. Figures indicate that during last April there were more than 2,000,000 people who usually work at a gainful occupation who had no job, people who were able to work and looking for a job but could not find it.

Do Not Work All Time.

The workers, as a rule, do not work all the time. They have at least one day off in a week, usually Sunday, and perhaps have half of Saturday. Many of them have some vacation, perhaps two weeks or a month, and in some occupations more. Some of them are engaged in seasonal occupations, which are carried on only in certain months of the year. Sickness interferes with continuous employment. There are many other reasons why work is not continuous.

"Probably it is safe to say that, on the average, the gainful workers do not work more than 275 days in the year. So it may be said that the

population of more than 122,000,000 is mainly supported, so far as bread-winning labor is concerned, by about 47,000,000 people working about three-fourths of the time. It is their labor—aided, of course, by machinery and by the power applied through electricity, steam or other means—that produces the food, clothing, houses, automobiles and all the material goods that we may possess or enjoy, and supplies the professional and personal services that we may command."

"The largest number of males, about 11,000,000," Mr. Steuart said in speaking over the Columbia Broadcasting System, "are engaged in agriculture, forestry and animal husbandry. These assist in giving employment to about 12,000,000 engaged in the mechanical and manufacturing industries, of which agricultural machinery, fertilizer and numerous commodities required for the conduct of the farm are an important part."

Of those engaged in agricultural pursuits, Mr. Steuart said, there are about 6,000,000 farmers and about 4,000,000 farm laborers.

"About one-third of the total number of workers are engaged in manufacturing or mechanical pursuits, a larger number than in agriculture. It was not always so.

"In the early days of the republic agriculture was the predominant occupation, and if we go back only fifty years to the census of 1880 we find that 45 per cent of the gainful workers were engaged in agriculture, as compared with only 25 per cent at the present time, and that the farmers and farm laborers outnumbered the workers in manufacturing and mechanical pursuits by more than 2 to 1.

"Since then, while the number of workers engaged in agriculture has increased about 40 per cent, the number of persons employed in manufacturing and mechanical pursuits has increased by over 200 per cent. From being predominantly an agricultural people we are coming to be predominantly a manufacturing people."

"In the conduct of business of all kinds, it is necessary to employ large numbers of clerks, stenographers, agents, bookkeepers and messenger boys. These occupations give employment to about 7 or 8 per cent of the total number of workers."

23,000,000 Work as Housewives.

Pointing out that women are now engaging more actively in industry, trade and office work than ever before, Mr. Steuart said that of the 37,000,000 females between the ages of 16 and 64 about 10,000,000 are employed in "gainful occupations."

"In addition to these 10,000,000 women in what we have termed 'gainful occupations,' however," he said, "there are perhaps 23,000,000 housewives engaged in the work of keeping their own homes, most of them doing themselves the major part of the work involved in keeping the home.

"Adding these housewives to the 10,000,000 classified for statistical purposes as 'gainful workers,' the total amounts to about 90 per cent of the whole number of women in the age group under consideration, or practically the same as the percentage of men in gainful occupations."

More than one-third of the population, said Mr. Steuart, or 41,000,000 people, are under 16 years of age, and, of these, 1,000,000 were reported in the 1920 census as having gainful occupations, "principally on the farm helping dad." But the number of workers under 16 in factories, stores and shops is decreasing, he said.

WOMAN MADE HEAD OF RAILROAD LINE

William B. Thompson's Widow Becomes Board Chairman of Magma Arizona Co.

CONTINUES HIS ACTIVITIES

Philanthropic and Scientific Work of Yonkers Capitalist Are Her Interests Now.

Mrs. William Boyce Thompson of Yonkers, widow of Colonel William Boyce Thompson, mining engineer and banker, is the new chairman of the board of directors of the Magma Arizona Railroad, it was learned yesterday. She is believed to be the first woman to hold such a position.

The railroad is a standard-gauge line extending about thirty miles between Superior and Magma, on the Southern Pacific system in Arizona, and its entire capital stock is controlled by the Magma Copper Company, of which Colonel Thompson was president and director. It is in Pinal County, where the mining company has more than 2,300 acres, a smelting plant and large mills.

Colonel Thompson died last June 27, leaving an estate estimated by his associates at between $85,000,000 and $160,000,000, the bulk of which was inherited by Mrs. Thompson and her daughter, Mrs. Margaret Boyce Thompson Schulz. The widow has taken over most of her husband's interests and carries on his philanthropic works. She was elected chairman of the Magma Arizona Railroad Company last week.

At the time of his death Colonel Thompson had spent approximately $9,000,000 on his greatest contribution to science, the Boyce Thompson Institute for Plant Research, Inc., at Yonkers, and had announced plans for enlarging the greenhouses and equipment to push experimentation with plants. Mrs. Thompson, who always was interested in the project, is a director of the institute.

The new chairman of the board of the Magma Arizona Railroad Company was Miss Gertrude Hickman of Helena, Mont. She met Colonel Thompson there when he was a mining engineer. They were married thirty-five years ago. She lives at 1,081 Broadway, Yonkers, and under the terms of her husband's will inherited the family yacht, the Alder. Mrs. Thompson is sailing on the liner Ile de France today for a Winter tour abroad.

October 24, 1930

AMERICAN WOMEN IN CONGRESS

THE recent appointment to the United States Senate of Mrs. Hattie Caraway of Arkansas will give to the upper house of Congress its second woman member, the first having been Mrs. Rebecca L. Felton of Georgia. But while women have found admission to the Senate difficult, more than a dozen have become members of the House of Representatives.

Miss Jeanette Rankin, Republican, of Montana, was the first woman to become a member of either house of Congress, having been elected a Representative in the Fall of 1916 and taking her seat with the Sixty-fifth Congress. She served through that Congress, but was not elected for the Sixty-sixth Congress, which had no women members. In 1920, however, when the Sixty-seventh Congress was elected, it choose another woman member, Miss Alice M. Robertson of Oklahoma. Her platform was expressed as follows: "I am a Christian, I am an American, I am a Republican." In the Fall of 1922 Miss Robertson was joined by another woman member, Mrs. Winifred Mason Huck of Illinois, elected to fill the vacancy left by the death of her father, Representative William E. Mason. She was also a Republican. Another woman member of the same party also joined this feminine bloc, Mrs. Mae E. Nolan, Republican, of California, elected in 1924 as a successor to her deceased husband, Representative John I. Nolan.

The Democratic party first elected a woman member to Congress in 1924, putting Mrs. Mary T. Norton of New Jersey, prominent in politics in her State, into the Sixty-eighth Congress. Mrs. Norton carried over through this Congress, and another Republican woman, Mrs. Edith N. Rogers of Massachusetts, was elected to fill the vacancy left by the death of her husband, Representative John Jacob Rogers.

A newcomer to the Sixty-ninth Congress was Mrs. Florence Kahn, Republican, of California, elected on Feb. 5, 1925, to succeed her late husband, Representative Julius Kahn. In this Congress were also Mrs. Norton and Mrs. Rogers.

© Harris & Ewing.
Mrs. Hattie Caraway.

The Seventieth Congress had two new women members. Mrs. Katherine Langley, Republican, of Kentucky, who had been in State politics a number of years and followed her husband in the House, was one. Mrs. Pearl P. Oldfield, Democrat, of Arkansas was elected to fill the vacancy left by the death of her husband, Representative William A. Oldfield. Mrs. Kahn, Mrs. Norton and Mrs. Rogers were also members of this Congress.

The Seventy-first Congress, beginning on March 4, 1929, had the largest contingent of women members, nine in number. Veterans were Mrs. Kahn, Mrs. Oldfield, Mrs. Langley, Mrs. Norton and Mrs. Rogers. Newcomers were Mrs. Ruth Bryan Owen, Democrat, of Florida, daughter of the "Great Commoner"; Mrs. Ruth Baker Pratt, Republican, of New York; Mrs. Effiegene Wingo, Democrat, of Arkansas, elected to the place left vacant by the death of her husband, Representative Otis Wingo, and Mrs. Ruth Hanna McCormick, Republican, of Illinois.

November 22, 1931

FEW OCCUPATIONS LACK WOMEN NOW
Ten Million Workers Listed

WASHINGTON, July 24 (AP).—The designation, "a man's job," is fading from the American scene. Women, whose province once was little extended beyond the home, have invaded nearly every pursuit in the occupational life of the nation.

Few callings may be found, according to a tabulation by the Bureau of Census of occupation statistics which exclusively belong to men. Among the gainful workers, 10 years old and over, were, for instance, 87 women hunters, trappers and guides.

There were 209 fisherwomen and oysterwomen, 15 foresters, forest rangers and timber cruisers and 95 lumberwomen, raftswomen and wood choppers.

Three plasterers were listed, also 1 plumber, 1 stonecutter, 1 coppersmith, 5 tinsmiths and sheet metal workers and 261 shoemakers and cobblers.

Among the few pursuits women did not invade were the fields of the professional fighter, structural iron work, steam railroad occupations, iron puddling, boiler-making and roofing and slating.

In all, more than 10,000,000 women were gainfully employed, school teachers making up the largest single occupation class next to domestic servants.

July 25, 1932

MANY TEXTILE MILLS BACK NIGHT WORK BAN

French Manufacturers Told 74% of Industry Approves Institute Plan.

Cotton manufacturers representing 23,302,252 spindles, or 74 per cent of the entire industry, have approved in principle the elimination of night work in cotton mills for women and minors under 18 years of age, George A. Sloan, president of the Cotton Textile Industry, announced yesterday in outlining the association's activities to a group of French cotton manufacturers, who have been visiting textile centres in the United States for the last three weeks.

Leaders in the industry are distinctly encouraged by the extent of the support which the proposal has already received, Mr. Sloan declared.

S. Robert Glassford, president of the Association of Cotton Textile Merchants of New York, made a brief address of welcome to the French delegation and outlined the distribution problems confronting the members of his association.

A shortening of terms granted to buyers was discussed by Floyd W. Jefferson, newly elected president of the Textile Export Association of the United States.

At the conclusion of the conference the institute's new-uses work, and particularly its efforts to promote the fashion importance of cotton, were explained in detail to the visitors by C. K. Everett, in charge of the new-uses sections.

Members of the French delegation who called at the institute were Roger Crépy, Roger Crépy, Lille; Claude Delesalle, Delesalle-Desmedt, Lille; Robert Faisant, La Cotonnière de St. Quentin, St. Quentin; Jacques Fauchille, Léon Crépy, Fils et Cie., Lambersart; Léon Foulon, Comptoir de l'Industrie Cotonnière, Paris, and Robert Vandendriesche, Establissment Boudeux et Vandendriesche, St. Quentin.

MOTHER JONES DIES; LED MINE WORKERS

100-Year-Old Crusader in Her Time Had Headed Many All-Night Marches of Strikers.

OFTEN WENT TO PRESIDENT

Lost All Her Family in Memphis Epidemic of 1867 and Miners Became Her "Children."

WASHINGTON, Monday, Dec. 1 (P).—Mary (Mother) Jones, militant crusader for the rights of the laboring man, died at 11:55 last night at her home in near-by Maryland. She was 100 years old.

Mother Jones, who had been confined to bed for more than a year at the Silver Springs (Md.) home of friends, had been barely alive for some time. Yesterday at one time she was believed dead when her heart almost ceased to beat, but the pulse returned.

William Green, president of the American Federation of Labor, said the death of Mother Jones would bring sorrow to millions of working men and women.

"Even though she had been incapacitated through illness and advancing age, her name and her personality had been a great influence in public life and an inspiration to the men and women of organized labor," he said.

"During her entire lifetime she had been in the forefront of labor struggles, cheering and inspiring men and women to fight for the cause of organized labor."

Idolized by Workers.

Mary (Mother) Jones, once an idolized leader of the United Mine Workers of America, was born in Cork, Ireland, in 1830, according to the autobiography she published in 1925. Her father, Robert Harris, a railroad laborer, who, like his famous daughter, was an agitator for better conditions among working people, migrated to Toronto, Canada, when Mary was 7 years of age.

Mother Jones began her career by teaching in a Michigan convent. She taught later in Memphis, Tenn. There she was married to an iron molder, "a stanch member of the Iron Molders' Union." In 1867 the Memphis yellow fever epidemic killed her husband and their four children in one week. She nursed among the stricken until the plague was spent. Then she went to Chicago, where she became a dressmaker.

After the great fire of 1871 had wiped out her business, Mother Jones settled down to what was to be her life work—the betterment of working conditions. Her outstanding activity in the East was at the time of the six weeks' hard-coal strike in September-October, 1900. She was freely used by the miners' organization to exhort the men to stay on strike. She helped to organize marches of miners to collieries for the purpose of closing them down, sometimes marching all night with the men or getting up at 4 A. M. to help dissuade workers from going into the mines. She did not fear armed deputy sheriffs nor the militia. She was usually at the head of the crowd that marched from one town to another.

MARY (MOTHER) JONES.

Sometimes she would talk so fiercely on the differences between capital and labor as privately to meet the disapproval of the more conservative leaders. All capitalists who expressed opposition to union labor were characterized by her as "high-class burglars." It was one of her favorite expressions.

Child labor in the South enlisted her first efforts as a crusader. As a young woman, she had worked in the cotton mills, an experience of which she later said:

"I wondered that armies did not stand forth to free those slaves. Poor men and women and little children worked from morning to night for bread, nothing but bread, no hope of anything better, only the opportunity to prolong their miserable lives. No wonder that very early in life I determined to wage war for the factory people."

Once she "abducted" the members of a helpless family to free them from the bondage of a company store to which they were indebted.

Soon after leaving Chicago Mrs. Jones began to organize women's auxiliaries to labor unions and later affiliated with the United Mine Workers, serving for years as one of its organizers. In subsequent years, however, it was said, she had been a "free lance," going where she pleased and doing what she pleased to further the cause of the miners.

Her activities took her to Montana, West Virginia, the Eastern Pennsylvania coal fields, Southern Colorado, Tennessee and other States. Wherever there was industrial trouble involving the welfare of women and children, Mother Jones endeavored to be there. She went from El Paso to Trinidad, Col., in 1914, at the time of the coal strike in that region, and upon her arrival there was seized by militiamen and deported to Denver as an "agitator."

Opposed to Socialism, the I. W. W. and Bolshevism, Mother Jones stood for years by the principles of the American Federation of Labor. Violence she denounced as "silly." Her views as to how capital and labor could reconcile their differences were set forth in an interview in 1913, when she said:

"If labor would eliminate violence and capital would eliminate injunctions, the battle would be practically over. We could then go sanely to arranging peace. Common sense, uninflamed, could step in. But labor will be violent so long as capital swears out injunctions. Also, the first step toward peace must come from capital. ɪt has more advantages."

Celebrates 100th Birthday.

In one of her last labor exhortations, on her 100th birthday, May 1, 1930, Mother Jones made as vigorous a speech as she did in her prime. The occasion was a little celebration at the home of her friend Mrs. Walter Burgess, with whom she spent her last days, at Silver Spring, Md.

Dressed in her best black silk, she was carried by devoted friends into the farmyard, where she spoke to an admiring group of labor leaders. Among other things, she again expressed opposition to prohibition, which she had been denouncing since 1920.

A few days later she received a congratulatory telegram from John D. Rockefeller Jr., whom she had bitterly assailed during the "Ludlow massacre" in Colorado. "He's a damn good sport," she said. "I've licked

him many times, but we've made peace." At that time she said Mr. Rockefeller had invited her to dinner several years before the incident, but she did not go because people would have said that she "had sold out the workers."

In reciprocation of the greeting sent her by the junior Rockefeller Mrs. Jones wired greetings to his father on July 8 on the occasion of the latter's ninety-first birthday.

One of her last acts evidencing her interest in the coal miners was her gift of $1,000 to John Walker, former president of the Illinois Federation of Labor, who was leading the fight of the insurgent group to oust John L. Lewis, president of the United Mine Workers.

Mother Jones had a distinct aversion for woman suffrage. She said women were out of place in political work, declaring that it had been in part "their sad neglect of motherhood" which had filled reform schools and kept the juvenile courts busy." Her chief contention was that "if the industrial problem were solved men would earn enough so that women could remain at home and attend to their duties."

December 1, 1930

"MOTHER" JONES.

"Mother" JONES was an old woman twenty years ago; spectacled, white-haired, quiet, dressed in black. She might have been a Quaker. She might have been a lay sister, except that she could say "Hell" on occasion with no more effort than she said "eyther" and "neyther." How could she live so long through such violent excitements? "There was a strike going on and I was there," she testified once when there was trouble in Arizona. Her fierce, undaunted spirit, her wit, energy and resourcefulness, made her a salient figure in the great labor troubles beginning with the early '70s. Passionately humane, a hater of injustice, if she fought violence with violence in days that now seem so crude and cruel, it was not from any belief in it. Hers were the methods of the pioneer. She lived to be honored and accepted as organized labor triumphed under a more enlightened public opinion.

Trial by civil and military tribunals, fine, imprisonment were ordinary incidents to her in many States. She didn't hesitate to call a Federal judge a "scab," though she was woman enough to take it back when the aggrieved functionary convinced her that she was wrong. Many worthy persons used to regard her

as a sort of she-devil. Certainly she had strong views at times about the militia, the military police, coal-mine operators. She loved to outwit them. Perhaps she looked on them as perverse or backward children. Her special faculty was the arrangement of what may be called pageants of poverty, processions of the ill-used. In setting miners and their wives on the march, in parades of child workers, she was subtly seeking public sympathy for their cause. Whatever her errors of militancy, she had the good fortune to see labor conditions astoundingly bettered. It is pleasant to think that she and Mr. ROCKEFELLER came to know each other better and to recognize each other's merits.

ᴄ The fiery agitator, the "anarchist" and what-not of legend lived to be respected by Presidents. She will be regretted by all who appreciate a vivid nature, an upright character, a generous heart, a steady and unselfish devotion to the good of others. Her activities in behalf of labor, reaching from MARTIN IRONS to WILLIAM GREEN, make her a sort of symbol of the Sturm-und-Drang period. To think of "Mother" JONES is to think of marching. So American labor goes marching on, but in peace now, mostly, without the conflicts and the losses of "Mother" JONES's prime.

December 2, 1930

AMERICAN WIVES.

Are They Creating a Matriarchy in This Country?

To the Editor of The New York Times

E. B.'s letter on American husbands touches a vital chord in our American sociology which is fast leading our civilization to the rocks of perdition. We all know of the legal serfdom of our men under our domestic relations laws, but our chivalry has created here a glory of women on a style far more grand than in any period in history. This veneration of women has made them all-powerful.

We find the women's organizations in every State of the Union demanding laws for women and children, and in reality gradually rearing a most powerful matriarchy. If any man dares to say anything against this tyranny of women he is at once looked upon as a brute.

The history of civilization seems to show clearly that under a matriarchy men are abused, crime increases, morality is at its lowest ebb, the family life, the home breaks down, and the biological laws governing the heredity of genius is practically checked. In a patriarchy, women are always sheltered and protected. Morality is in a most ideal position, crime is an accident, the family life, the home, is most wholesome and complete, separations and divorces are few and the biological laws governing the heredity of genius become a most fertile field.

See Greece until a little after the rule of Pericles—what genius the Greek patriarchy reared, and see its decline with the greater freedom of women! Look at Rome up to the Punic wars, when under the strict rule of men—there was not one divorce in 525 years (Lecky's "History of European Morals"), and see Rome after the Punic wars, with the greater freedom of women, how the marriage institution and the family life were completely undermined. See the history of Japan up to 1896, when the Taiho code of laws gave women the right to divorce, and we find divorces jumped to 34 per cent the first year and is still about 28 per cent. Before this Taiho code of 1896, when the man had absolute right to divorce, there was hardly ever a divorce. ("History of Human Marriage," by Westermarck.)

The result of the present domestic relations laws will have its most telling effects within the next fifty years. Population will decline. Men will shun marriage. Immorality will become more general.

I addressed the various legislative committees on anti-alimony legislation many times. The glory of women is so deep-rooted in the minds of many of our legislators that the only hope of amending the present domestic relations laws lies in the fact that when a greater majority of our legislators will have suffered its tyranny either directly or indirectly, then we will have a change.

C. R. WILMER.
New York, May 1, 1931.

May 8, 1931

LOW TEACHING PAY IS LAID TO WOMEN

Dr. Elsbree, in Survey, Says Overfeminization Is Cause of Salary Level.

URGES PUBLICITY DRIVE

Columbia Educator Asserts That Public Must Be Awakened to Profession's Importance.

Overfeminization and lack of adequate publicity in the school system have caused a lowering of the teaching standard from an economic point of view, Dr. Willard S. Elsbree, Associate Professor of Education at Teachers College, Columbia University, declared yesterday in a survey on "Teachers' Salaries," released by the Columbia Bureau of Publications.

Dr. Elsbree pointed out that more than three-quarters of public school teachers are women and that this factor has had a definite effect upon salaries. "The presence of such a large proportion of women in the teaching profession has a decided tendency to lower salaries, since women are notoriously paid less for the same work than men with equivalent qualifications," he declared.

Finds Field Overcrowded.

Dr. Elsbree indicated that this "ladylike" profession is already overcrowded. His survey showed that the nation is becoming less and less able to take care of the "annual crop of normal school and college graduates dumped on the education market."

"In New York City at the present time literally hundreds of eligible candidates are clamoring for teaching jobs," Dr. Elsbree reported. "The relative ease with which training standards are being raised in all parts of the country is an indication of the generous supply of teachers. In many States the supply of women teachers already far exceeds the demand for them."

Dr. Elsbree found that there has been a steady decline in the proportion of men teaching in public schools during the past half-century. Beginning with 42 per cent in 1876, men teachers dropped to 17 per cent in 1926, he said.

"At this rate there is grave danger that women will drive men out of the classroom altogether and that in a few more decades the genus male teacher will be extinct," Dr. Elsbree prophesied. "A fifty-fifty ratio between men and women teachers would be ideal, but as this is usually impracticable, it is urged that not less than 25 per cent of the teaching staff in any school system be men."

In addition to the effect of women teachers, Dr. Elsbree found that the lack of strong professional organization and the oversupply of technically qualified teachers also tended to lower salaries. To remedy this, he declared that the teaching profession must resort to publicity in order to acquaint the public of the constant changes in education.

He asserted that "teachers might well take a leaf from the book of business and do a little discreet advertising on their own account," adding that "anything which enhances the teaching profession in the public eye strengthens the teachers' case for higher salaries." In this respect he pointed out that honors, awards, and recognitions of any sort magnify the importance of teaching and "compels public respect."

Profession "Too Modest."

"The teaching profession has been far too modest about its responsibilities and accomplishments for its own good and for the good of society," said Dr. Elsbree. "Teachers have been content to accept the paltry salaries doled out to them by short-sighted boards of education and with nothing more than a little private grumbling have resigned themselves to living within their meager incomes."

If there is to be a "real and spontaneous demand for education," Dr. Elsbree asserted, the public must be "jolted out of its traditional attitude of indifference and awakened to the vast importance of the schools." As long as schools have "no salesmen, no advertising department to proclaim its wares to the public," educators will be underpaid, the Columbia professor maintained.

"The public is too prone to regard school teaching as an easy, pleasant occupation and is inclined to pooh-pooh any suggestion that the work is either difficult or arduous unless specifically pointed out and explained," he said. "A detailed picture of the school teacher's day with its variety and multiplicity of demands would be something of an eye-opener to most laymen."

August 23, 1931

PLANS TO GIVE PRIZE AWAY.

Miss Addams Feels It Belongs to Women's League.

Special to The New York Times.

BALTIMORE, Dec. 10.—Lying on a cot in the Marburg Memorial Building of the Johns Hopkins Hospital here today, Miss Jane Addams revealed that she plans to turn her share of the Nobel Peace Prize over to the Women's International League for Peace and Freedom.

The only two persons permitted by her physicians to talk with Miss Addams were Mrs. Joseph T. Bowen and Mary Rozet Smith, trustees of Hull House in Chicago.

Miss Smith said she had tried to get Miss Addams to indicate "what part of the money would be used for the league" and Miss Addams had insisted that she "feels the award really belongs to the league, and to her only because of her connection with it. No amount of persuasion could sway her from the determination to pass every bit of the money into league work.

"She will, of course, have a great deal to do with the spending of the money, and it is consideration of the uses to which it will be put that is occupying her attention today."

Miss Smith also revealed that Miss Addams virtually has exhausted in Chicago relief work the cash from two other awards given to her this year. One was received from Bryn Mawr College and the other from a woman's magazine.

Miss Addams arrived here yesterday from Chicago and may undergo a serious operation. She is under the care of Dr. Thomas Scullen. Miss Smith and Mrs. Bowen accompanied her from Chicago.

December 11, 1931

The First "Madame Chairman." Perhaps fastidious members of the House will address Mrs. MARY T. NORTON of New Jersey as "Madame Chairwoman." She is the first woman to become chairman of a committee of Congress. To the citizens of Washington, Representative NORTON's committee on the District of Columbia is the most important one in Congress. It makes the local laws for over 350,000 people. If the President is "Mayor of Washington," then Mrs. NORTON is co-chairman of its "Board of Aldermen," for the Senate has a District committee also.

Mrs. NORTON was the first Democratic woman to be elected Freeholder in New Jersey. Mayor HAGUE of Jersey City sent her to the national convention of 1924 as a delegate-at-large. She is the first woman Democrat elected to Congress and has served in the House ever since 1924. Mrs. NORTON secured passage of the law by which the Hudson County maternity hospital is being built. She knows cities and their problems, as Washington will discover with pleasure and other American women will note with pride.

December 16, 1931

GUESTS AT 10-CENT MEAL.

Mrs. Roosevelt and Daughter Are Entertained by Macfadden.

Mrs. Franklin D. Roosevelt and her daughter, Mrs. Curtis B. Dall, editors of the forthcoming magazine, Babies; Just Babies, lunched standing up yesterday. Bernarr Macfadden, the publisher, whose representatives will handle the business end of the new magazine, was host to the wife and daughter of the Governor at the one-cent restaurant maintained by the Bernarr Macfadden Foundation at 107 West Forty-third Street, and they, like the rest of the diners, remained on their feet as they ate pea soup, beef stew, raisin bread, whole wheat apple pie and milk from one of the high white-topped tables.

It was a 10-cent meal, and at its conclusion Mrs. Roosevelt congratulated Kay Hermansen, the institution's chef.

August 5, 1932

FINDS HOMELESS MEN FACE HARD WINTER

Relief Investigators Report 500 Already Are Forced to Live in Flimsy Shacks.

FEW ARE OF VAGRANT TYPE

32,000 Free or Cheap Beds Not Sufficient to Meet the Need, Committee Declares.

WOMEN ALSO A PROBLEM

Y. W. C. A. Warns Unmarried Are Unable to Find Jobs—Federal Workers Aid Drive.

The problem of homeless men will be serious this Winter, according to a study made by the Emergency Unemployment Relief Committee, which said yesterday that more than 500 men already had been forced to find shelter in temporary shacks.

At the same time Mrs. Marie Chase Cole, executive secretary of the International Institute of the Y. W. C. A., informed members of her management committee that the plight of foreign-born unemployed and unmarried women was becoming increasingly tragic, as it was impossible to find work for them.

32,000 Beds Found Not Enough.

In its survey of destitute men, the Gibson committee ascertained that municipal and private charitable organizations have facilities to house 12,000 men and that beds for an additional 20,000 are available in the cheapest type of commercial hotels at 15 to 50 cents a night. Even these have not been sufficient to meet the needs of the homeless men, the survey indicated, and many are forced to find shelter in parks, doorways, subways and rudely constructed shanties.

Three large camps in Manhattan, it was said, reveal how at least 500 men have met the shortage of shelter by building "homes." The camps are at Eighth Street and East River, Riverside Drive and Seventy-sixth Street and on Central Park Reservoir site.

Most of the men who have met the depression in this manner come from the higher type of the unemployed, it was said. Very few of the habitually destitute were found by investigators. The residents included skilled mechanics, manual laborers, salesmen, seamen and men who had cut themselves off from their families in the belief that their absence would lighten the burden for their wives and children.

In reporting on the situation of foreign-born unemployed women, Mrs. Cole said that in September 539 such girls and women appealed to the international institute for employment and relief, an increase of 202 over September, 1931. Mrs. Cole urged on her committee the seriousness of the situation, for while families may apply to the Home Relief Bureau, the International Y. W. C. A. was the only agency to which such single women could turn.

Federal Workers Aid Drive.

Representatives of the army, navy, customs service and other Federal departments in New York City pledged support to the coming campaign of the Emergency Unemployment Relief Committee. The Federal representatives conferred with Bayard F. Pope, executive vice chairman; Peter S. Duryee, executive director, and other officials of the committee, and prepared to organize their departments to participate in the campaign for $15,000,000, which begins Nov. 10.

Last year Federal services in New York City contributed more than $200,000 to the committee's campaign, Mr. Pope announced. Fred R. Shattuck is chairman of the Federal fund-raising group, which is included in the committee's commerce and industry division, headed by H. B. Lamy Jr.

The Salvation Army is cooperating with the Emergency Unemployment Relief Committee, Peter S. Duryee, vice chairman and executive director of the committee, announced. Money raised for direct relief will be distributed to destitute families through the Salvation Army as well as other established family-welfare agencies, as has been done in the past.

October 22, 1932

STILL BAR WOMEN FROM MANY JOBS

Labor Laws of States, in New Compilation, Show Tasks Which Cannot Be Undertaken.

8-HOUR DAY IN SIX STATES

But 47 Require Provision for Seating—Various Bans Include Mining, Quarrying, Shoe-Shining.

WASHINGTON, Nov. 6 (AP).—A revised compilation of labor laws for women, issued today by the Woman's Bureau, shows there are still some jobs a woman can't tackle.

Mining as an occupation for women is prohibited in seventeen States.

Colorado bars them from working in coke ovens. Arizona, Oklahoma and Wisconsin prohibit them from working in quarries.

A blanket prohibition on employment of women on jobs disproportional to strength or detrimental to health obtains in Kansas, Michigan, North Dakota, Washington, Oregon and Wisconsin.

California, Massachusetts, Ohio, Pennsylvania and Washington forbid women to perform tasks involving the lifting or carrying of heavy weights.

Ohio has a list of twenty-three prohibitions against employment of women, among them being baggage handling, bell-hop, blast furnaces, bowling alleys, crossing watchman, delivery service, express driver, freight handling, jitney driver, meter reader, molder, pool rooms, section work, shoe-shining parlors, smelters and taxi drivers. An annotation says an Ohio county court has declared the taxi-driving prohibition unconstitutional.

The compendium shows that thirteen States provide that a woman worker must be provided time for meals, varying from thirty minutes to one hour. Laws requiring some kind of seating accommodations are reported for all States but Mississippi.

"The eight-hour day with the forty-eight-hour week for women in industry has been legally established in only six States—Arizona, California, Kansas, New Mexico, New York, Utah—the District of Columbia and Puerto Rico," the bureau notes.

It adds, however, that only four States—Alabama, Florida, Iowa and West Virginia—"have no law of any sort regulating the hours of work for women."

November 7, 1932

WOMEN AT WORK

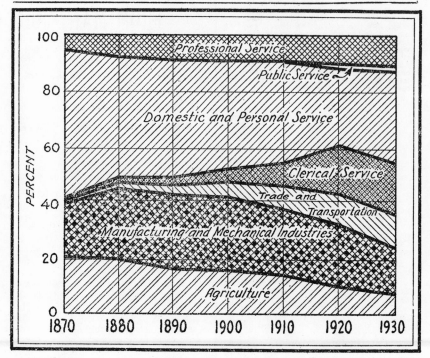

This chart shows the changing relative importance of the major occupation groups for all gainfully employed women 16 years and over. While the actual number in each group increased, the data seem to show a continuous shift in women's employment away from the older agricultural and industrial pursuits toward office, store and professional work, with domestic and personal service somewhat more stable.

In 1870 agriculture claimed 21 per cent of the employed women, but by 1930 it claimed only 7 per cent. In 1870, 20 per cent of all working women were engaged in manufacturing, but the proportion fell to 18 per cent in 1930. The domestic and personal service group shows a drop from 53 per cent in 1870 to 28 per cent in 1920 and then a slight rise to 33 per cent in 1930. The remaining occupations show relative increases. Among the professions, women constitute 78 per cent of all teachers and 98 per cent of all trained nurses.

WOMEN LOSING JOBS FASTER THAN MEN

THEIR NEEDS "EXPLOITED"

Special to THE NEW YORK TIMES.
WASHINGTON, Dec. 12.—Unemployment among women not only is widespread but in many industries is proportionately greater and increasing more rapidly than in the case of men, according to the annual report of Miss Mary Anderson, chief of the Women's Bureau of the Department of Labor.

At the same time pay cuts have forced to new low levels the weekly wages, never high, of women still "on the job," and sweat-shop operators in "gypsy" industries are taking advantage of the desperate need of work among women to exploit them still further Miss Anderson reports on the basis of surveys conducted in all parts of the country during the past year.

In Connecticut, where a study was made at the request of Governor Cross of 7,800 women making wearing apparel, many in typical "runaway shop" were being paid from $4 to $6 for a 48 or 50 hour week, with no record kept of the hours of pieceworkers.

The unemployment census of April, 1930, reported 668,661 women out of work, one-tenth of whom were heads of families, with others dependent on them for support. Of the total number, nearly one-tenth had been out of work for as much as six months and many for more than a year.

In January, 1931, another unemployment count revealed that one-fifth of the women in nineteen of the largest cities in all sections of the country were out of work. In eight of the cities more than that proportion were without jobs. Studies now in progress indicate the existence of conditions even more serious and growing steadily worse.

Employment records of New York, Illinois and other States show a decline in number of women working greater than that among men in a considerable number of industries, and in nearly all the woman-employing industries or groups, particularly in the more highly paid supervisory or executive positions.

A decline also was shown nearly as great as in the case of men from wage levels, which were very much lower to begin with, owing to the prevailing double standard of wages. These wage cuts were vastly greater than the decline in women's pay reported during the same period by Canada.

Wages received by women in New York State who continued to hold their jobs declined 13 per cent and those of men 14.8 per cent between September, 1929 and 1931, and from 1929 to 1932 the decline was 21.5 per cent for women and 22.5 for men, Miss Anderson stated, while in Canada, according to the Minimum Wage Board of Ontario, women's wages decreased only 1.7 per cent.

MEMBER OF ROOSEVELT CABINET

Associated Press Photo.

Miss Frances Perkins.

Frances Perkins, who, as Secretary of Labor, would be the first woman to grace a President's Cabinet, will carry to that post a large understanding and experience of labor and sociological problems that began soon after her graduation from Mount Holyoke College in 1902.

Recommended to President-elect Roosevelt by numerous civic and welfare leaders and women's groups, Miss Perkins's career in the Cabinet will be a continuation on a broader scale of the work she has been doing for many years.

Her appointment to the Washington post was preceded by service in the State Labor Department under Governors Smith and Roosevelt, whom she first met in Albany when both were young Assemblymen more than twenty years ago. She will leave the office of State Industrial Commissioner, having been appointed a member of the commission by Governor Smith in 1923 and chairman under Governor Roosevelt in 1929. Governor Lehman continued her in office when he went to the capital on Jan. 1.

Born in Boston in 1882 of an old Revolutionary family which numbered the fiery James Otis among its members, Miss Perkins began her career in life fortified by courses in economics and sociology.

For a time she taught in a girls' school at Lake Forest, Ill., but abandoned that career when she came under the influence of a group of welfare workers, including Graham Taylor and Jane Addams, at the Chicago Commons and Hull House.

When her teaching years ended, she spent some time at Hull House and then returned home. Courses in economics and sociology at Columbia and the University of Pennsylvania followed, as well as foreign travel. In 1907 she was secretary of the Philadelphia Research and Protective Association.

As executive secretary of the Consumers' League in New York from 1910 to 1912, Miss Perkins took part in many investigations of labor conditions. In 1911 she witnessed the Triangle shirt-waist factory fire in Washington Square, where 146 lives were lost, and was stimulated to campaign for safety provisions in factories.

Head of Board Since 1926.

Later she was appointed director of investigation of the State Factory Commission and in this work she was supported by such members of the Legislature as Alfred E. Smith, Robert F. Wagner and Franklin D. Roosevelt, destined to continue to link their careers with her own for many years.

After serving from 1917 to 1919 as executive director of the New York Council of Organizations for War Service, Miss Perkins was appointed to the State Industrial Commission in 1919 and was made a member of the State Industrial Board in 1923. She became chairman in 1926 and has held this position since.

In the last three years Miss Perkins has had several clashes with the Federal Department of Labor in connection with employment agencies and unemployment figures. She has definite ideas as to how the Federal employment service may be extended, strengthened and correlated with the State employment agencies. For several years she has been an ardent advocate of unemployment insurance.

In 1917 Miss Perkins married Paul C. Wilson, a secretary to Mayor John Purroy Mitchel. They have one daughter, Susanna Winslow Perkins Wilson.

In appearance Miss Perkins is of medium height, with olive skin, brown hair and vivid dark-brown eyes. She usually wears dark clothes and seldom varies from her brown tricorne hat, which is as inseparable from her as Al Smith's brown derby is from his sartorial make-up.

February 23, 1933

Mrs. Owen to Be Envoy at Copenhagen; She Will Be First Woman Named Minister

WASHINGTON, April 3.—Former Representative Ruth Bryan Owen is to be the next Minister to Denmark, and the first woman ever named by an American President to represent this country at a foreign Court. Her nomination may be sent to the Senate tomorrow.

Rumors of the intention of President Roosevelt to appoint Mrs. Owen to Denmark subsided for a time when it was stated that she preferred a State Department appointment to a foreign post, but were revived within the last few days following a dinner given for her by the Danish Minister and Mme. Wadsted.

It is understood that Mrs. Owen's objections to accepting the appointment to Copenhagen, which at first she felt would be for personal reasons impossible, have been overcome by the insistence of President Roosevelt and the cordiality with which her suggested appointment was received in Denmark.

It is said to be the strong desire both of President Roosevelt and the government and people of Denmark to have Mrs. Owen as the first woman named as Minister to a foreign country, a post for which it is felt that she is exceptionally well fitted both by personality and experience. In Denmark she has many warm friends and her arrival in an official capacity is eagerly anticipated, judging by the many letters and messages received in Washington concerning her prospective appointment.

She will take with her to Denmark her two younger children, Bryan, aged 20, who is a student at Rollins College, and her daughter, Helen Rudd Owen, aged 12, who is at school in Miami.

April 4, 1933

MRS. ROSS NAMED DIRECTOR OF MINT

First Woman in That Office Is to Succeed R. J. Grant, Who Will Head Chinese Mint.

Special to THE NEW YORK TIMES.

WASHINGTON, April 26.—Mrs. Nellie Tayloe Ross, former Governor of Wyoming and vice chairman of the Democratic National Committee, was appointed Director of the Mint today by President Roosevelt.

The nomination was sent to the Senate immediately after the resignation of Robert J. Grant, who will become financial adviser in charge of the Chinese National Government's Central Mint at Shanghai.

Active in Democratic national politics as head of the women's organization of the party, Mrs. Ross stumped the country in the last campaign and is one of the best known women in the party.

She became the first woman Governor in the country when her husband, William B. Ross, died in office in October, 1924.

She will be the first woman Director of the Mint.

President Roosevelt also sent to the Senate today the nomination of

© Harris & Ewing Photo.

Mrs. Nellie Tayloe Ross, Named Director of the Mint.

Laurence A. Steinhardt of New York to be Minister to Sweden. He was a member of President Roosevelt's pre-primary advisory board, has been active in New York politics and is a nephew of Samuel Untermyer.

Other nominations today were:

Solicitor of the Department of Labor—Charles Wyzanski Jr. of Massachusetts.
Secretaries in the Diplomatic Service—Cavendish W. Cannon of Utah and James S. Moose Jr. of Arkansas.
Brigadier General, Ordnance Department, Reserve—John Ross Delafield.

April 27, 1933

NEW GUINEA SONGS ARE SOLD FOR A PIG

Woman Explorer, Back, Says Old Tunes Bring High Prices Among the Aborigines.

THEY KILL GIRL BABIES

But Spare Enough to Do All Their Work—'Sweetest' of People, Even So.

Some of the "nicest, sweetest" people Dr. Margaret Mead knows strangle superfluous babies and marry their daughters off at 8 years of age.

She emphasized in an interview the other day at the American Museum of Natural History, however, that these practices grow out of tribal customs and necessity and give an entirely false impression of the general "temperament" of the aborigines of New Guinea.

Dr. Mead, whose studies and books have brought her prominence both as ethnologist and author, spent the last two years with her husband, Dr. R. F. Fortune, living with the Arapesh of the Prince Alexander Mountains, the Mundugumor tribe on the Yuat River and the Tehambuli tribe on Aibom Lake in what was formerly Kaiser Wilhelm Land and is now the Australian mandate of New Guinea.

She returned this week to her duties as assistant curator of ethnology at the museum.

"Strangulation of unwanted babies—and the girl babies are the ones that are unwanted—sounds awfully harsh until you know that it is a question of strangulation or starvation," she said. "It is simply a case of there not being enough food to go around."

Girls Leave Home Early.

The reason for keeping boy babies in preference to girls also has a humane foundation, she explained. The girls are married outside the tribe, whereas the boys stay at home, and, since there is only a limited amount of food, the "gentle savages" prefer to rear children who will not leave them.

The marriage of girls at an early age merely means that the little girl goes to live in the home of her future husband so that she will grow up with him and his relatives and know how to get along with them by the time she is of age to become a wife and mother.

Times Wide World Photo.

THE FIRST DOLL STIRS INTEREST IN NEW GUINEA.

Dr. Margaret Mead, who headed the expedition of the American Museum of Natural History, watches the reaction of a native child. Women of the tribe had to be persuaded that the doll was not a mummified baby.

"There is no such thing as romantic love," Dr. Mead went on. "They simply have no notion of the meaning of such a term. But there is a sweetness, a loyalty and affection within the family group that is charming.

"The little boys and the men have the best of everything. A little girl cannot cry after she is 5 years old and she is taught to bear burdens almost from the time she can walk.

"A little boy, on the other hand, can cry and have tantrum fits and expect all sorts of indulgences until he is 13 or 14 years old. The women do the work and the men are dandies. The women shave their heads and bear burdens, while the men decorate their long hair with peacock feathers and strut about like lords. Beauty is distinctly a male attribute rather than a female."

Song Copyright System.

She went on to describe a system of barter whereby Murik, a village on the coast, sells songs and fashions to inland villages, receiving payment chiefly in pigs, which are the principal item of currency. Murik sells a song or a new style of dress to the nearest inland village, the next village in line buys the rights from the second village and so on.

"If a village did not pay its tribute before singing the 'new' song—which is apt to be from five to twenty years old—there might follow a war," she declared.

Dr. Mead and her husband mastered the native language, she said, but only with some difficulty, "because it has thirteen genders and twenty-six personal pronouns; it is so complex that it takes the natives many years to teach it to their children."

The natives led a communal life, in which every one's property belonged to every one else and in which it was considered outrageous for a man to eat what he had grown himself without sharing it. The reason that pigs constituted the chief currency, she said, was that a pig was one thing that was infinitely divisible.

Florence E. Allen Named Federal Judge; First Woman on Circuit Bench

WASHINGTON, March 6.—President Roosevelt today nominated Miss Florence E. Allen of Cleveland to be judge of the Sixth Circuit Court. She is the first woman to be named to a judgeship of this rank. Miss Allen succeeds Judge Smith Hickenlooper, who died recently.

© Standiford Photo.
Florence E. Allen.

Florence E. Allen was born in Salt Lake City, Utah, on March 23, 1884, the daughter of Clarence Emir and Corinne Marie Allen. In addition to her eminence as a lawyer, she was known as a crusader for the rights of women in professional and public life.

Her father was a teacher at Western Reserve University and later at a Congregational School in Salt Lake City, and began teaching his daughter Latin and Greek when she was only 7 years old. Later she attended New Lyme Institute, Ashtabula County, Ohio, Salt Lake College and Western Reserve, where she received a degree of A. B. in 1904 and an A. M. in 1908.

From 1904 to 1906 she served as assistant correspondent in Berlin for The Musical Courier, a New York publication. While studying for her master's degree she was musical critic for The Cleveland Plain Dealer.

Because women were barred from the law school of Western Reserve, she went to the University of Chicago, then to New York University, where she received an LL. B. in 1913. While studying law here she did legal work for the New York League for the Protection of Immigrants and delivered lectures on music for the Board of Education.

She was admitted to the bar in Ohio in 1914. Her public career began five years later, when she was appointed assistant prosecutor for Cuyahoga County. After two years in this post she was elected to the Court of Common Pleas by the largest vote ever given a candidate for that office.

Judge Allen is a Democrat but both her elections to judgeships were on a nonpartisan ticket. She never married. She served at various times as assistant secretary of the National College Equal Suffrage Association, as a member of the executive board of the Ohio Woman Suffrage Association, and as a trustee of Western Reserve University. In 1925 at Smith College she received the honorary degree of LL. D.

She is a member of the D. A. R., Sigma Psi, Kappa Beta Pi, and the Women's City and the Business Women's Clubs of Cleveland.

March 7, 1934

DIET 'DERBY' AIDS 3 GIRLS.

Bananas and Skimmed Milk Reduce Weight in Experiment.

CHICAGO, May 31 (AP).—Three girls who forsook meat and potatoes for bananas and skimmed milk in a scientifically supervised thirty-day diet derby stepped down from the scales today a total of thirty-two pounds nearer proper weight.

A new sparkle in their eyes and a flush to their cheeks attested that, while they had lost weight, they had gained in appearance, health, energy and spirit.

The diet, supervised by Dr. Herman N. Bundesen, Health Commissioner, started a month ago with the selection of Alice Joy, Felicia Terry and Deon Craddock as the participants.

Today Alice, who was twelve pounds overweight, had lost nine and one-quarter pounds; Felicia, who was twenty-five pounds too heavy, fourteen pounds, and Deon eight and one-half of her twenty-one pounds of excess weight.

Alice submitted to the most rigid diet—six bananas and three glasses of skimmed milk daily for the first two weeks, supplemented the second two weeks by other foods. The two others followed a milk and banana base diet.

"It is perfectly possible for any one to do as these girls have done," Dr. Bundesen said. "A doctor's examination will tell you how much overweight you are. A diet like the ones we followed, recommended by a doctor, cannot fail to rid you of excess pounds. Remember that every pound lost is health gained, beauty added. Dieting to reduce is dieting for health. Our experience with Alice, Felicia and Deon has proved our case."

June 1, 1934

Women Held Best Suited For Monotonous Jobs

LONDON, Aug. 11 (Canadian Press).—Women can adapt themselves to monotonous work with far greater success than men, Dr. Sibyl Horner, home office medical inspector of factories, has concluded in her annual report. Dr. Horner remarked that women alone of the industrial groups can bring themselves to the daily performance of monotonous work without losing their interest in life.

Dr. Horner said the effect of industrial life on the 2,000,000 women and girls employed in it in Great Britain was "good and getting better." But such work, she commented, causes girls to age quickly. Physical attractiveness is early attained and quickly lost, she said.

August 12, 1934

Woman's Many Enemies. MUSSOLINI wants women to give up careers and stay at home to be the mothers of Italy's invincible soldiers. HITLER wants women to stay at home and defer to the general principle of male leadership and domination. But the movement to force women back into the home extends beyond the confines of the new Germany and Italy. The president of the National Association of Women Lawyers is justified in calling it world-wide.

Persons who would be shocked to find themselves in the same galley with Fascism or Nazism are nevertheless playing around with doctrines which, on the subject of woman's place in the world, lend aid and comfort to MUSSOLINI and HITLER. Excited preachments about Technological Unemployment, about the Machine Age and the Scrap-Heap, about a "finished" world, about a doomed world market and a general state of saturation and satiety—all these things slant heavily against women in careers outside the home.

In a world of fewer opportunities and fewer jobs it is inevitable that men should begin to grumble about a pack of women in industry who have no business there. If there is not enough occupation to go round, the late-comers, the women, take on the character of intruders.

September 1, 1934

FIRST LADY FAVORS MEN AS PRESIDENTS

Mrs. Roosevelt Doubts That a Woman Could Win Confidence of Nation at Present.

DISCUSSES MANY TOPICS

Hot Dogs, Banking, Dancing, Textile Strike and Science Among Her Subjects.

A variety of subjects, ranging from the importation of hot dogs to the likelihood of a woman's becoming President of the United States, were discussed last night by Mrs. Franklin D. Roosevelt in her radio comments on current news events.

Apropos of a statement made in Chicago recently by Lillian D. Rock, secretary of the National Association of Women Lawyers, in which Miss Rock said she expected to see a woman President within her lifetime, Mrs. Roosevelt declared:

"I do not think that it would be impossible to find a woman who could be President, but I hope that it doesn't happen in the near future. There are exceptional women, just as there are exceptional men, and it takes an exceptional man to be a successful and useful President.

Not Enough Confidence Yet.

"Though women are doing more and more, and are proving every year that they are capable of assuming responsibilities which were considered to be out of their province in the past, I do not think that we have yet reached the point where the majority of our people would feel satisfied to follow the leadership and trust the judgment of a woman as President. And no woman could, therefore, succeed as President, any more than could any man who did not have the trust and confidence of the majority of the nation; for this is a democracy, and governed by majority rule.

"People say no woman could stand the physical strain, but that, I think, is nonsense, and answered over and over again by women through the length and breadth of the land. No man works harder in the fields than the farmer's wife in her home and on the farm.

"Women have carried the same jobs in factories, even in mines, up to a few years ago; and besides their industrial jobs they have almost carried on the work of the home, sometimes badly, to be sure, but still that work has always been before them when the other work was done.

"The stories of women who clean office buildings all night and go home and get their children off to school, and somehow manage to snatch some sleep during the day, and then go back to work at night and yet keep the home going would seem to indicate that while women may not have as much muscular strength as men, they have as much endurance and ability to bear strain as the male of the species.

Sees Background Lacking.

"Women have not as yet had, however, as many years of background in public life, or as many years of experience in learning how to give and take in the world of affairs and I, personally, would be sorry to see any woman take any position of responsibility which she was not well equipped to undertake and where she could not command the following which she would need for success.

"Some day a woman may be President, but I hope it will not be while we speak of a 'woman's vote.' I hope it only becomes a reality when she is elected as an individual, because of her capacity and the trust which the majority of the people have in her integrity and ability as a person."

Mrs. Roosevelt commented on the feat of Lewis Deane, 15-year-old New York boy who towed a catboat five miles to shore when the boat, with himself and a girl aboard, was becalmed in Long Island Sound last Sunday night. Of the textile strike she said that the situation requires "a desire to cooperate in reaching a fair settlement to all concerned."

Discussing the importation of new-style hot-dogs from France, she said she expected before long to see road signs "advertising hot puppies imported from France, Germany and England."

She also discussed bank-deposit and unemployment insurance, the return of the waltz and two-step to vogue in dancing, Anne Morrow Lindbergh's recent magazine article, opportunities for women in science and the government's appeal to scientists of seventy-one universities to aid in tracing the origin of "ghosts of the air," a deviation in the radio beam that guides aviators.

Mrs. Roosevelt spoke from the NBC studios in Radio City. Her address was the second of a series of commercial broadcasts and was over an extensive network.

NEW DEAL CALLED UNFAIR TO WOMEN

Lower Minimum Wage Scales Denounced by Speakers at Atlantic City Parley.

NEW TREATY IS EXTOLLED

Compact Granting Equal Rights of Citizenship Is Hailed as a Major Advance.

Special to THE NEW YORK TIMES.

ATLANTIC CITY, June 9.—Denouncing discrimination against women, speakers at the Eastern regional conference of the National Woman's party today attacked what they termed "unfair" provisions of the NRA, the economy act and other national and State statutes.

Mrs. Edith Houghton Hooker of Baltimore, author of a digest of Maryland laws, cited a long list of instances throughout the country where women were unjustly discriminated against.

Other speakers declared that the lower minimum wages assigned to women in almost all NRA codes not only reacted unfavorably for the women but pulled down the salaries of the men also. It was said that the economy act provided that when both a husband and wife were working, one of them should be the first discharged in any retrenchment.

The honored guest at the dinner tonight, Miss Doris Stevens of New York, was introduced as the first woman in the world to negotiate a treaty. She told the story of her fight to obtain ratification of the equal nationality treaty by the United States and the twenty-one other American republics, represented at the Montevideo conference.

She said that formerly many American-born women who married foreigners, became widows and wished to return here, but could not bring their children because under the laws they took their fathers' nationality. Now the mother can declare her child a citizen of the United States, Miss Steven said.

Other speakers included Miss Amelia Doetch and Miss Elizabeth Brown, Baltimore attorneys; Miss Gail Laughlin, Portland, a member of the Maine Legislature; Mrs. Sarah B. Cummings and Miss Arabel W. Clark, Philadelphia, who acted as chairman of the regional conference.

Approximately 100 delegates representing the Eastern States from Maine to Virginia are attending the two-day session in the Hotel Madison. The organization was formed in 1920.

Returns Right to Pick A Man or Woman Aide

By The Associated Press.

WASHINGTON, Oct. 9.—The head of a government department again has the right to choose whether he wants a man or a woman in a civil service post.

President Roosevelt has issued an executive order rescinding the December, 1932, action of President Hoover, which decreed certification without regard to sex unless the Civil Service Commission were of the opinion the job could be done only by men, or only by women.

The Civil Service Commission recommended the change, on the ground that they had no legal right to restrict the right of choice of appointive officers.

Their objections were purely legal. But they also pointed out that the Hoover ruling had not helped the women any, a marked reduction having taken place in the number of women appointed after the order was issued.

October 10, 1934

OLD ORDER CALLED A PERIL TO WOMEN

Fannie Hurst Warns Return to Kitchen Is Backsliding That Endangers Equality.

STYLE CHANGES FORECAST

Fashion Group Hears That One Paris Designer Plans Mass Production of His Creations.

The women of this country must not be backsliders if they are to sustain the equality with men they have gained so far, Fannie Hurst, the novelist, told more than 300 women yesterday at a luncheon of the Fashion Group in the Ritz-Carlton Hotel.

"Hitler and other individualistic leaders in Europe are pushing half of their populations back into the kitchen and deciding how the women of their countries are to live," she said. "You hear a lot of patter about women having lost their souls. Hitler and Mussolini seem to think they may have rolled under the kitchen sink."

She contrasted this relegation of women to the background abroad with the opportunities they enjoy here of "gaining the highest government office—not as women, but as the best fitted individuals for certain jobs."

But, she admonished, while women here probably have more of their intellectual eyes open than those anywhere else," they must not permit each other to take their freedom and equality for granted. Women have duties of leadership in some fields and one of these is in preventing war, she declared.

"Woman must secure governmental control of the munitions industry so that the vicious conditions unearthed by the Nye committee will not be repeated. But she is never going to do this by performing the fallacious errand of scuttling back to the kitchen to search for her soul."

Bettina Bedwell, a Paris fashion correspondent, forecast a greater change in women's styles and in the customs of dressmakers than has occurred since 1925.

One leading Paris designer, she said, is establishing a low-priced line of dresses, with the same type of materials he has used in his exclusive gowns, but with the economical features of mass production introduced to bring his creations within the price class of "the 300,000 women, and not only the 3,000 who can pay for grand clothes."

Victor Stiebel, a London designer of women's clothes, explained his ability to design clothes for American women without ever having been here before with the assertion:

"A smartly dressed woman is smart the world over; there are no national distinctions in fashions. Chic is international."

Alice Hughes, fashion writer, presided at the luncheon. The Grand Duchess Marie was a guest of honor.

RAID TRAPS POLLY ADLER

per-
y and
Other wit-
_oena in this
investigation refused
naive immunity.

The police arrested Polly Adler, a notorious middle-aged woman of the underworld, who figured in the Seabury investigation of the magistrates' courts, and three young women in a raid on an apartment at 30 East Fifty-fifth Street, between Fifth and Madison Avenues, at 6:55 o'clock yesterday morning. The Adler woman was charged with keeping a disorderly house, and the three young women with being inmates.

Lawyer Is Reticent.

Magistrate Anna M. Kross in the Women's Court held the Adler woman in $2,500 bail and the three inmates in $500 each. John Duff, attorney for the Adler woman, argued in vain for lower bail. When Magistrate Kross asked who had retained him, Duff refused to tell. The woman was arraigned as Polly Adler, alias Joan Martin.

Later the Adler woman was taken to Yorkville Court and held on the charge of possessing indecent moving picture films, which the arresting detectives said they found in her apartment.

Short, stocky, with heavily rouged lips and cheeks and brightly tinted finger nails, the Adler woman wore an expensive fur coat as she emerged from a patrol wagon in front of Yorkville Court, where a large crowd had gathered to see her. She buried her head in the collar of her coat and kicked and shouted torrid words at photographers who tried to take her picture as she was led into court.

The photographers followed the woman into the court room, but were ordered to leave by Magistrate H. Stanley Renaud, who threatened to impose ten-day prison sentences upon any one who took pictures in court. They were allowed to take pictures in the adjoining complaint room.

Duff said the woman's real name was Joan Martin and insisted that she be arraigned under that name, which was done. He asked that bail be fixed at $500, but Magistrate Renaud set it at $1,000 on the request of Assistant District Attorney Raymond Leo. A hearing was set for March 14.

Court Deaf to Plea.

The attorney obtained a writ of habeas corpus late yesterday afternoon and took the Adler woman from the House of Detention to the Supreme Court, where Justice Philip J. McCook refused his appeal to lower her bail in the prostitution case. Duff asserted that the bail was "excessive, exorbitant and unreasonable," and asked that Justice McCook fix bail "commensurate with the crime charged."

According to Duff, bail in such cases is usually $200 or $300, except when the defendant has a criminal record or the authorities have reason to believe he is about to leave the jurisdiction. His client, he said, had never been convicted of a crime.

"Why should this woman be singled out?" he demanded.

Assistant District Attorney Irving Tell pointed out that the Adler woman had been arrested ten times, although never convicted. He asked that bail remain as fixed because of "the notoriety" of the defendant.

Detective Michaels, who had charge of the police making the arrest, told of watching the apartment and of tapping its telephone wires before the raid. He was not allowed to testify as to what he had heard over the wires, as he said he could not identify voices. He was also prohibited from testifying about a book with names, addresses and telephone numbers of women, found in the apartment.

"The place has a notorious reputation," the detective testified.

When Mr. Tell referred to "the current vice drive," Justice McCook replied that he did not know "of any drive against houses of prostitution." The prosecutor insisted that Magistrate Kross was within her power in fixing the amount of bail, and Justice McCook agreed, dismissing the writ with this remark:

"I shall not interfere with the discretion of the magistrate."

Police Commissioner Valentine made the following comment on the Adler woman's arrest:

"I am very much elated over the arrest of the notorious Polly Adler. She is one woman I wanted to see brought in. The police who have been working on her case have been doing so for the past four months, but they could never get her in the place until this morning. We wanted her as the keeper of a disorderly house."

A woman known to the police "Spanish Rose" was arre_ the charge of prost_ West Seventy-eigh_ o'clock yest_ ider_

March 6, 1935

A WOMAN SITS IN JUDGMENT FOR NRA

By S. J. WOOLF

DOWN on lower Broadway in a building that once flaunted the two-headed eagle of imperial Germany the Blue Eagle of the NRA is now supreme. Through red, white and black marble halls that years ago echoed the footsteps of prospective visitors to the Fatherland tread representatives of labor and industry. On four floors of the old Hamburg-American Building more than 400 lawyers, investigators, clerks and stenographers are engaged in ironing out difficulties between employers and employes and among employers themselves.

At the head is a slip of a woman who now holds three jobs. When Anna Marie Rosenberg was recently appointed Regional Director of NRA, she was already State Compliance Director as well as Executive Assistant of the National Emergency Council. But the loading of extra work upon her small shoulders apparently does not appall her. Despite the fact that she is, as it were, the court of last resort for most of the complex problems which arise in the administration of the codes in New York, she bears her responsibilities easily.

Sitting in what was at one time the directors' room of the old steamship company, she outlined the workings of the new plan that aims at decentralizing the activities of NRA.

"Up to a short time ago," she said, "the enforcement of the NRA code was in the hands of forty-eight State compliance offices. When the decision of the State Director were not satisfactory to the people concerned, it was necessary to go to Washington to make an appeal. The result was long delays. Almost 100,000 cases reached Washington for final adjustment. Although three-quarters of them were settled, it became increasingly evident that a change had to be made in the manner of handling them. The fact that both the violator and the complainant had to appear in Washington worked a hardship on many.

"To expedite action, nine Regional Directors were appointed, whose judgments are final. They have the power to hear cases on the revocation of the Blue Eagle; they can order the removal of NRA labels and direct all litigation over the violation of the code. The State Compliance Directors retain their positions but, except for New York, which handles about 45 per cent of all the cases and has for the time being a Regional Director for itself, the States are grouped in eight regions."

∗ ∗ ∗

MRS. ROSENBERG seemed very small in that large mahogany-paneled room behind whose walls a wireless set at one time flashed secret messages to Germany. She scorns the tremendous roll-top desk built in one corner—uses a flat one set at right angles to the large directors' table. Her democratic manner is in strange contrast with the pompous furniture and decorations left by her German predecessors; it becomes more evident as she makes her way from one floor to another and greets every worker from elevator man to head of department by his first name.

She radiates a spirit of friendliness throughout the organization. The observer feels it as he watches the field inspectors on the first floor listening to complaints; it is intensified on the second floor, where she has her office and where her cheery "Hello!" greets the caller. In the room where a regional board hears cases the visitor gets the impression of governmental assistance rather than officious supervision.

As she explained the intricate workings of the machinery she keeps running smoothly; as she showed letters written with shaky hands by frightened workers telling of abuses in factories; as she opened folder after folder filled with the records of the investigations; as she described how the cases go from one investigator to another until they reach the regional board, she was dealing with matters that are ordinarily within the province of men. Yet one never forgets in her presence that she is feminine.

When she went to Washington, immediately after her appointment, she was ushered into the office of a man she had never met. He gave a start. He had expected to see a large, oldish woman with masculine manners, tailored suit and flat-heeled shoes. Instead he saw a small brunette, her hair carefully dressed, her clothes chic, her whole manner different from that of the person he had expected to see.

Perhaps her personal charm is partly responsible for the efficient way in which she carries on her work. Her serious-minded, white-haired secretary, who was once a Professor of English, might be expected to frown upon her informal way of expressing herself. Yet her

Drawn From Life by S. J. Woolf.
Anna Marie Rosenberg.

speech, her manner, her engaging qualities help her to hold her own against blustering groups of hard-boiled labor men and at the same time manage suave business executives. Her straightforwardness inspires confidence, her informality cuts red tape.

The group around the council table may wrangle at times. She usually preserves her equanimity. Yet, when occasion demands, she can express herself forcefully. She did so recently when a labor man began assailing NRA. In her own words she told him "where to get off." After the meeting he apologized.

∗ ∗ ∗

"I HAVE always been interested in politics and social work," Mrs. Rosenberg told me. "I organized a political club while I was still at Wadleigh High School, although I was but 14 years old at the time. When the war came along I was still at school, but I went to work at the base hospital in the old Siegel-Cooper building, at Sixth Avenue and Eighteenth Street. For

a time I went there for only half the day, continuing my studies the other half, but I soon began to feel that I could do more down there by devoting all my time to my work, so I gave up school.

"I was born in Budapest and had attended the gymnasium there before I came to this country. After the war I returned and continued my studies there for a short time. Then I came back here and looked for a job.

"What have I done? Almost everything. I went into politics. I arranged large public dinners and managed concerts. It was through my work in connection with a dinner for 3,500 clubwomen that I first met Belle Moskowitz. As a result of that meeting I was engaged by several Jewish philanthropic organizations. I also worked in a settlement house for a time. Then I was a public relations counsel for a number of firms that had factories in the South, and I traveled a lot trying to instil new ideas into old businesses.

"It is strange," she continued, "how many active business men keep their noses so close to the grindstone that they are not able to see the changes that are taking place in the world about them. Even today there are many firms trying to conduct their affairs in the same manner they did fifty years ago. They do not realize that the world has progressed, that human relations are different and that workers are no longer slaves.

"My experience as a public relations counsel brought clearly before me the new problems that were constantly arising in the conduct of a large business—not only problems resulting from contact between business and the public but also those arising between employer and employe. Many times I was called upon to solve these problems.

"People interest me. The duties of the Regional Director afford marvelous opportunity for meeting with all kinds. Workers and employers are both in close touch with us, and I like to see and study the reactions of individuals, as well as groups, to the new ideas which NRA has brought to business.

"Last Winter we were called upon to deal with a number of cases of underpayment under some of the codes. We managed to persuade many of the employers to settle claims just before Christmas. Some $50,000 was paid out. I, for one, was curious to discover what was done with this extra money. I made numberless investigations I found that one woman who had never been able to give her children any presents went out and bought gifts for all of them—and, there were quite a number. One man went to Europe to visit his old parents, whom he had not seen for years. Some paid doctors' bills that had been running for a long time. Others bought clothes of which they were sorely in need."

* * *

MRS. ROSENBERG, however, refused to judge the entire results of NIRA in terms of dollars and cents.

"There is something more than money in the world," she said, "and in spite of the fact that in some codes there has been a tendency for the maximum wages to drop toward the minimum, nevertheless, the entire attitude of the workingman has changed."

I mentioned strikes.

"Of course there are strikes," she said. "They are sure signs of an improvement in conditions. The same thing always happens after every depression. Recovery is always marked by labor disputes and a readjustment of wages and conditions. This depression has brought in its wake an entire realignment of these conditions. For years labor had had no chance. Now a new scheme has been worked out under which labor has come into its own. Labor and capital have been put on an equal footing. An entire new machinery has been set up, and its effect is evident upon the workers.

"Men and women who once regarded themselves as little more than slaves have a new outlook upon life. They have lost that cowed attitude. They come into our offices with a new sense of freedom. Right through the ranks there is a new spirit. Labor realizes that it has a place to go to with its complaints; a government which at one time was deaf to the woes of the worker has now set up an agency that has his interest at heart. It has not done this at the expense of the employer, for he too is protected against unfair competition and false claims of unscrupulous competitors. There is increasing evidence that employers and employes are finding in our organization the means of fulfilling the obligations which the National Recovery Act set up.

"I have found that compliance with the codes depends primarily on the support of public opinion, and the support of public opinion depends on the respect that an enforcing agency is able to command. We have made every effort to show all concerned that the NRA is a cooperative organization, ready and willing to see that labor and industry get, each, a square deal."

* * *

AT last I asked the inevitable question about a woman in public life.

"I want to be regarded as a public official," she replied. "The fact that I am a woman plays no part. The other day some girl interviewer asked me my favorite color, my favorite recipe and a lot of similar foolish questions which had nothing to do with my work. I know my house is run just as efficiently as it would be if I were at home all the time. My boy of 14 is away all day at school, so he is not deprived of much of my time. Moreover, I don't play bridge.

"I like theatres, art exhibitions and concerts. Unfortunately, I have been deprived of these. Why, it's five months since I have been to a movie. But the worst of all is that I have to order my hats and clothes over the phone, and that's bad for a woman, even if she is a Regional Director of NRA."

March 31, 1935

WOMAN GAINS

An Observer Declares

By ELLEN S. WOODWARD,
Assistant Administrator, Works Progress Administration

THERE is a tremendous task ahead of us. When the President said that "we must quit this business of relief," that no longer were able-bodied citizens to be allowed to deteriorate on relief but must be given jobs, he meant women as well as men.

It is the task of the women's division of the Works Progress Administration to put approximately 500,000 women to work. These women must be given jobs for which they are fitted, jobs that will allow them to maintain their self-respect and dignity. Instead of being a debit to their communities, they are going to become self-maintaining productive citizens.

Who are these 500,000 women? They are married women who are economic heads of families; they are widows left without resources; they are single women with relatives dependent on them; they are unattached women who have to make their own way. They are 15 per cent of all the 3,500,000 able-bodied unemployed on relief today between the ages of 16 and 65. Statistically this is the problem.

The Human Problem.

Personally, I like to approach this problem in a more human way. I like to think of it in terms of the individual. As I see it, my job is to find a job for Mary Jones who lives in this town or that village, or on a certain street in a large city. Mary Jones is on relief—she has been for six months. But she doesn't want relief, she wants a job. It is our business to see that a job is created for her. We have to ask what she can do. Has she a trade or professional training, or has she never before had to earn a living outside of her home? If she has no training, what can we teach her to do?

These are the elementary questions—the things we have to know about Mary Jones and the 500,000 more like her. Knowing this, we have to develop projects and programs which will provide work opportunities for all of them or as many as our funds will allow. It is a task which requires not only knowledge of the facts but imagination and ingenuity.

We are not entirely novices at this job. During the last year and a half, through the State directors of women's work, we put 300,000 women to work under the FERA work-relief program. The knowl-

177

edge we gained during that experience will stand us in good stead in the much greater task that lies ahead. We know the answers to many questions now and we intend to keep the best of the old program as a foundation for the new.

A Varied Group.

One basic fact we have learned is what a greatly varied group of women we have to deal with. We have discovered that there are more than 250 occupational classifications represented by the women on relief rolls. That means that we must design projects to meet the needs of women whose training, skills and other qualifications for work range from one end of the ability scale to the other.

We must find projects that will provide jobs for the professional worker highly trained in some particular field, for the woman who can do only unskilled manual work, and for all the many types in between. We want these projects to be of the highest social value.

One part of our job now, as in the past, will be to maintain a constant watch to see that women receive equal consideration with men in the assignment of work. We will see to it that the projects planned under the Works Progress Administration have a fair number of jobs for women and that women's projects shall receive equal consideration in the matter of materials and supplies.

The fact that in February of this year 53 per cent of the men on relief rolls certified for work were at work and 53 per cent of the women certified were also working shows that we have already made a record in this respect. The new Works Progress program will afford opportunity to expand projects and to develop new ones which will employ the many women who have been certified for work, but who because of limited funds have not yet had a chance.

Wide Sphere of Action.

Women can and will be employed on almost all types of projects that are to be conducted by the Works Progress Administration. The possible sphere of action for women is far more extensive today than any such program would have been twenty years ago.

A large number of jobs will necessarily be of the traditional variety such as sewing, food preparation and conservation, child care, general home-making and care of the sick simply because so many women are fitted for these tasks. But we also recognize that large numbers of women today are capable of playing an important part in the art, music and drama projects; in library work, in skilled laboratory research, in statistical surveys and in many other specialized activities once considered the exclusive domain of men.

In fact, the plans for women's work will be as many and as varied as our skill and inventiveness will permit, within the boundaries of social usefulness and the limitations inherent in the Works Relief Act itself.

Many valuable suggestions for women's work come to us from every part of the country. It is interesting to note that in some cases these are for projects which have already been conducted on a limited scale, but which we intend to amplify under the new program. One of these which came to my attention very recently was a program for transcribing books into Braille for the use of the blind.

Employment for Blind.

Several such projects have already been successfully operated under the FERA Work Relief program. We have found it possible to employ the blind themselves to do a great deal of this work. This instance is cited only to show the extent of our planning in fitting the job to the person and in making it a thoroughly worth while job as well.

It is hardly necessary to enumerate the 101 useful and desirable services that every community needs, that can be developed under the Works Progress program, and that ordinarily would not be undertaken by private initiative.

Health services in your neighborhood may have been reduced considerably, in some cases to a dangerous minimum, while capable nurses and public health workers remain idle and on relief. The solution is obvious.

There is hardly a limit to the amount of useful work that needs to be done. And we can give thousands of women — at present despondent, feeling that life has cast them aside and society has no need for them — an opportunity once more to use their hands and brains for the common good, to be once more vital and contributing members of society. This is our fundamental aim.

July 7, 1935

Criminal Female Found Deadlier Than the Male

By The Associated Press.

WASHINGTON, Nov. 26.—The female of the species criminal is deadlier than the male of the same tribe, according to J. Edgar Hoover, Director of the Federal Bureau of Investigation.

He revealed today statistics showing that while only 6.9 per cent of the persons arrested in the United States during October were women, these women showed a greater tendency toward murder than the males taken into custody.

"Generally speaking, the tendency of members of the female sex to commit crimes of violence against the person was more pronounced than in the case of the male," Mr. Hoover said.

More than nine out of every 100 women arrested were charged with homicide, he explained, while only eight out of every 100 men were charged with the same offense.

November 27, 1935

Mothers' Autocratic Care Of Children Found Hurtful

The Tendency Toward Matriarchy in Middle-Class Homes Is Now Partly Offset by a Sharing of Responsibilities by Younger Fathers

By EUNICE BARNARD

The American child of a middle-class family is more apt to suffer from a mother's conscientious management than from her neglect, investigators of child problems reported to the joint conference of the National Council of Parent Education and the Progressive Education Association held in Detroit last week. A matriarchy in the home was indicated as at the root of some of our adolescents' troubles.

One remedy suggested for this matriarchial tendency was a sympathetic sharing by the father of the responsibilities of child care. Apparently a swing in this direction has already begun among young fathers, according to a self-survey made by fifty-three college-educated groups in twenty-three States. The survey showed 80 per cent of the husbands cooperating in the management of the children, the majority taking part in their physical care and many also helping with the housework.

Under the Old System

This study was initiated by the American Association of University Women and was carried out by members and their husbands from California to Georgia. The results showing the return of the American father to an active part in the home were hailed by convention psychologists as auguring well for the mental health of the coming crop of youngsters.

The bad effects of the older American pattern of the absentee father and the autocratic mother are all too evident among our high school and college youth, according to Dr. Carolyn Zachry, chairman of the Progressive Education Association's committee on the study of adolescents. For four and a half years this committee has been making an intensive study of the intimate case histories of 800 typical young people in metropolitan areas.

Many of the maladjustments of these youngsters in their 'teens and twenties date back to the typical conditions under which their parents, now in their late forties, have had to work out their lives, Dr. Zachry finds. The father in the middle-class home has considered his proper role that of provider. Thus he has worked long hours at the office, taken his few hours off for necessary recreation, and left home and children entirely to his wife.

Far from failing him, she has been and is a most excellent home manager, the study has revealed. Her whole history has impelled her to throw herself into making a topnotch job of it. For this middle-aged, middle-class mother in her youth had to meet and conquer obstacles. She went to college, per-

© Punch

"Now, now, Madam, remember the timetable—kissing from 5:30 to 6."

haps, when higher education for women was not so popular as it is now. She therefore felt upon her mettle to make as good grades as her brother.

"Running" the Family

Often, too, she went into an office where again she had to prove her efficiency, and she frequently faced the conflict between marriage and a career. When she chose marriage she turned all her trained energies into the home. She took parent-education courses and worried over her children, for whose welfare she was usually solely responsible. She has "run" her family. The results have often been good housekeeping and good health, but they have not always been so satisfactory emotionally, the committee reports.

The typical son of this family is over-docile. He loves his mother, identifies himself with her and accepts here domination happily. The daughter, on the other hand, has her antagonism aroused and usually "fights back." Neither has the emotional security he needs.

The boy, missing his father's companionship, has not had the benefit of a natural masculine ideal in the home, the committee observes. The girl has suffered even more, because her development as a woman and her future attitude toward marriage depend largely on having a satisfactory rapport with her father, Dr. Zachry believes.

Younger parents are not making the same mistakes, this study finds in agreement with that of the A. A. U. W. The younger mother is no longer under pressure to prove her

ability. She is less tense in her family relations and has a less managing attitude toward her children. She is not torn between marriage and a career. Often she is arranging to have both.

Moreover, the young father is not so obsessed with the idea that it is non-masculine to take part in the career of his children. It is the style to want children and to be interested in them. There is a greater recognition that their healthy emotional development depends upon the father's as well as the mother's presence as a working partner in the home, the study finds.

Cooperation between parents was also put at the top of the list among the essentials for a happy marriage by the 1,400 husbands and wives (most of whom were under 40) taking part in the nation-wide group sampling made by the A. A. U. W. "That the belief in cooperation is not merely an academic one is evidenced by the large number of husbands and wives actually sharing responsibility in home life," said Mrs. Harriet A. Houdlette, who reported on this survey to the convention.

What the Figures Show

"Ninety-two per cent of these husbands and wives handle the family's money cooperatively, while 80 per cent take joint responsibility for the management of the children and 60 per cent for the management of the household. Sympathy toward the problems of one's marriage partner was listed in third place as a desideratum of successful marriage by the wives and in fourth place by the husbands."

In three-fifths of the groups reporting, sympathy and cooperation on the husband's part extended not only to physical care of the children but to washing dishes, and in two-fifths of the groups to cooking. More than two-thirds of these professional, college-educated parents are running their homes on incomes of less than $5,000 a year, and only 30 per cent employ full-time maids, the study discovered.

A List of Virtues

Patience, tolerance, understanding, sense of humor and frankness were listed by these husbands and wives as the most necessary qualities for successful parenthood. All of these democratic virtues tallied, oddly enough, with those advised for parents by the experts who lectured at the convention.

"The rigid rules which we used to advise parents to enforce in habit-training were on the wrong track," said Dr. Lois Hayden Meek of Teachers College, Columbia University. "We now recognize that for mental hygiene we must begin habit-training later, and not be too insistent on regular habits without regard for the emotional relation between parent and child. That, after all, is the most important thing."

Similarly Dr. Alice V. Keliher of the Progressive Education Association reported that her studies of youth show that the home must somehow break down the present state of incommunicability between parent and child. "Thus we may work to replace striving for rules and dogmas with sensitivity and joint effort to find a more humane and tolerable family life," she said. "But let us remember that release of sensitivity leading to tolerance and sympathy is in ratio to the security of the individual."

Professor L. Thomas Hopkins of Teachers College, Columbia, added his voice to the general plea for a breakdown of too autocratic family control. "In the past," he said, "the home has too frequently been organized to represent fascism or any other authoritarian way of life. The parents make the decisions; the children accept them. The parents are too fearful that if allowed to make decisions on matters within their interests and abilities children will not make wise decisions. By this parents mean decisions that adults would make under similar circumstances. Of course, children are unable to do this because they are children. However, the fact that adults fix the result denies the democratic process."

WIVES IN JOBS DEFENDED

Miss Kenyon Says Most Must Work for Living.

There is no more logic in removing married women from jobs than there would be in taking away positions from red-headed old men, Miss Dorothy Kenyon, Deputy Comsioner of Licenses, said last night at the annual meeting of the Twenty-third Assembly District branch of the New York League of Women Voters at 870 West 181st Street.

All but an "infinitesimal minority" of the married women gainfully employed worked because they were forced to by economic necessity, she said, adding that it was wrong to pick out the married women as "a special sacrificial lamb" to the need for more jobs. Merit and capacity should determine who should hold jobs, she said.

February 26, 1936

April 22, 1936

A FINE NOVEL OF THE CIVIL WAR

Miss Mitchell's "Gone With the Wind"

Is an Absorbing Narrative

GONE WITH THE WIND. By Margaret Mitchell. 1,037 pp. New York: The Macmillan Company. $3.

By J. DONALD ADAMS

THIS is beyond a doubt one of the most remarkable first novels produced by an American writer. It is also one of the best. I would go so far as to say that although it is not the equal in style or in artistic conception of such a first novel as Miss Roberts's "The Time of Man," it is, in narrative power, in sheer readability, surpassed by nothing in American fiction. "Gone With the Wind" is by no means a great novel, in the sense that "War and Peace" is, or even "Henry Esmond," to name only novels which dealt, like this one, with past periods of time. But it is a long while since the American reading public has been offered such a bounteous feast of excellent story telling. If this tale of the Civil War and the Reconstruction days which followed does not attract to itself more readers than even "Anthony Adverse" I shall be more than mildly surprised.

Miss Mitchell's performance is remarkable on several counts. She spent, we are told, seven years in writing this book. One can readily believe that, and as heartily wish that more young novelists would follow her example. Even so, that a first book should display a narrative sense so sure, so unwaveringly sustained through more than a thousand pages, is little short of amazing. But Miss Mitchell can do more than tell a story. She can people it with characters who are not merely described, but who live, grow older and change under our eyes, as do our friends. At least four of the people in this book achieve a quality of life as vivid as may be caught on the printed page.

"Gone With the Wind" seems to me the best Civil War novel that has yet been written. It is an extraordinary blending of romantic and realistic treatment, as any worthwhile re-creation in fiction of

those years should be. I am not forgetting Mary Johnston's "The Long Roll" and "Cease Firing," nor Miss Glasgow's "The Battleground," of which the first two contained the most vivid battle scenes of the Civil War that have been done in fiction, and the last, though by no means on the level of Miss Glasgow's maturer work, a vivid picture of what the war meant to non-combatants in the South. Nor am I forgetting a more recent book, Stark Young's "So Red the Rose." But that novel, looked at now in retrospect, was more a personal statement, a memorial wreath laid before a cherished tradition and way of life, than it was a work of the creative imagination.

Miss Mitchell's book is more objective in its approach, more in the mood, let us say, of McKinlay Kantor's "Long Remember." It is, however, much wider in scope and filled with a greater vitality. Miss Mitchell, like Mr. Kantor, paints no battle scenes; like him, she chooses a focal point about which swirls the war itself. Many things happen in her book; it is full of movement, but the guns are off-stage. So too are the great figures which the war produced; they are only spoken names, and the things which happened to Scarlett O'Hara and to Ashley Wilkes, to his wife Melanie and to Rhett Butler, are the things which happened to many other lives in that time and place.

The story opens in the plantation country of Northern Georgia, immediately before the war. Most of the action takes place in and about Atlanta, the sprawling new city of the South, a crossroads planted in the red mud and soon a hustling town, rising as the railroads come and cross it east and west and north and south. That choice of Atlanta (Miss Mitchell's native city) as the focal point of her novel was a happy one. It has not been done before in the fiction of the period, and it brings to her book a freshness and vitality of background.

Atlanta, once the war was begun, was

much more the nerve center of the lower South than Charleston, where it was born, or the other older cities, like Savannah and Augusta, which looked pridefully askance at the blustering and arrogant newcomer. There were army headquarters and feverishly busy hospitals, and much of what industrial activity the South could then muster. There too, when the war was over, the brutal and crushing force of Reconstruction closed in most ominously. Miss Mitchell has brought those scenes vigorously before us; the anxious and the bedeviled city leaps to life before our eyes. This is background done with a skill more practiced hands might envy.

But Miss Mitchell's real triumph is Scarlett O'Hara, a heroine lacking in many virtues—in nearly all, one might say, but courage. She is a vital creature, this Scarlett, alive in every inch of her, selfish, unprincipled, ruthless, greedy and dominating, but with a backbone of supple, springing steel. Daughter of an immigrant Irishman who by force of character and personal charm fought his way into the ranks of the plantation nabobs and married a belle of aristocratic family, she was earthily Irish, with but little trace of her mother's gentle strain, and a complete rebel against the standards and taboos of the society in which she was reared. She is a memorable figure in American fiction, a compound of Becky Sharp and of a much better woman, Dorinda of Miss Glasgow's "Barren Ground." But she lives in her own right, completely, and will, I suspect, for a long time to come.

An almost equally vital figure is Rhett Butler, scapegrace son of a Charleston family, cynical and hard-bitten realist (but no more realist than Scarlett herself), who saw the hopelessness of the South's position from the first, and who, as a daring blockade runner, lined his pockets during the war. The remarkable thing about Miss Mitchell's portrait of him is that she has taken a stock figure

Margaret Mitchell.

with a woman as we are told he was with Scarlett could have made her believe that he wanted only her body.

Melanie, whom Ashley Wilkes married, and Ashley himself, are foils for these two. Ashley was the man of honor and the romantic idealist, swept from his bearings and left purposeless when the life he loved and into which he fitted was swept away; he cannot adjust himself to the new time and to the made-over world, as Rhett could, and Scarlett, with her fighting salvage of her father's plantation and her shrewdly managed but unprincipled handling of her lumber business in Atlanta. And Melanie—she is all that Scarlett is not, outwardly Amelia of "Vanity Fair" to Scarlett's Becky, but underneath the shyness, the sweetness, the generous loving heart, a core of courage and determined will which save her from flatness and the milk and water of negative goodness.

These are only Miss Mitchell's most fully drawn characters, the central figures of her story. She has a host of others, excellently if sketchily done. She draws on the whole social fabric of the ante-bellum, war time and Reconstruction South for her people. They are all there, from the field hand and the Georgia Cracker to the Yankee carpetbagger, and she interests us in them all. Her dialogue is good (though I doubt the authenticity of her rendering of Negro speech—it would not, I think, meet with Joel Chandler Harris's approval) and her telling of such events as Scarlett's flight from Atlanta to Tara (her plantation) with Melanie and her new-born child, through the war-swept countryside, is excellent narration. Her style is not distinguished, but if it seldom touches beauty it is a good instrument and serves her purpose well.

Let me end by saying that although this is not a great novel, not one with any profound reading of life, it is nevertheless a book of uncommon quality, a superb piece of story-telling which nobody who finds pleasure in the art of fiction can afford to neglect. He would be a rash critic who would make any prophecies as to Miss Mitchell's future. She has set herself a hard mark to match with a second book, and I hope only that she will not set too soon about it.

of melodrama and romance, even to the black mustache, the piercing eyes and the irresistible way with women, and made him credible and alive.

The battle of wills between these two, set against the cross-current of Scarlett's self-deceiving love for Ashley Wilkes, makes an uncommonly absorbing love story, and one that Miss Mitchell manages to tell with rarely a false note, and which she carries to a logical and unforced conclusion. It is an ending entirely in key with Scarlett's character; if there is any weakness, any lingering doubt in one's mind as to the validity of the final scene between Rhett and Scarlett, it must lie in the motivation of Rhett. One wonders whether a man as deeply in love

MINIMUM WAGE LAW CONSTITUTIONAL; SUPREME COURT SWITCH DUE TO ROBERTS

A 5-TO-4 DECISION

Washington Law Akin to Voided New York Act Is Sustained

ADKINS RULING REVERSED

Hughes Reads Opinion—Sutherland, Van Devanter, Butler and McReynolds Dissent

By TURNER CATLEDGE

Special to THE NEW YORK TIMES.

WASHINGTON, March 29.—By a 5-to-4 decision, the numerical division by which it struck down the New York Minimum Wage Law for Women and Children last June, the Supreme Court today held constitutional a similar statute of another State, the Minimum Wages for Women Act of the State of Washington.

But while the numerical division was the same, the line-up was changed. Justice Owen J. Roberts switched from the "conservative" to the "liberal" side and turned what for fourteen years had been a minority view, into the controlling opinion of the court.

Justice Roberts found sufficient reason today to join with Chief Justice Hughes and Justices Brandeis, Stone and Cardozo in validating the Washington act, leaving Justices Sutherland, Van Devanter, McReynolds and Butler, with whom he had acted in overthrowing the New York law, powerless to do anything but issue a vehement dissent.

Reports of the court's decision, rushed to the Senate floor by a messenger, found that body engaged in a heated debate over President Roosevelt's judiciary reorganization program. Breaking into the discussion to tell the Senate what had happened, Senator Robinson shouted that the Supreme Court had "reversed" itself.

Other States' Wage Laws Spared

Not only did the decision settle the constitutionality of the 24-year-old Washington statute, but it expressly reversed the basis upon which the New York law had been invalidated and the minimum wage laws of fifteen other States jeopardized.

That basis was the decision in the Adkins case, long considered a barrier against the fixing by Congress of minimum wages for women in Federal jurisdiction, and cited as the controlling factor in the adverse opinion in the New York case, even though the latter involved a State law. Senator Robinson told the Senate that the reversal on the Adkins case probably validated the New York law, which was ruled unconstitutional ten months ago.

In the Adkins case the Supreme Court invalidated a minimum wage law for women enacted by Congress for the District of Columbia, a strictly Federal territory. In view of this new ruling of the court, Elwood Seal, Corporation Counsel for the District of Columbia, held tonight that the old law, which was in effect from 1919 to 1923, "is fully effective" and began preparations to re-establish the Minimum Wage Board which administered it.

The court's opinion today, read to a packed court room by Chief Justice Hughes, said specifically:

"Our conclusion is that the case of Adkins vs. Children's Hospital should be and is overruled."

The opinion pointed out that in the New York case the court had not been asked to overthrow the Adkins decision, and therefore could not, while in the Washington case it had been made a vital point by the refusal of the State Supreme Court, in its decision upholding the validity of the statute, to consider the Adkins case as controlling.

Doubt Effect on Congress Fight

With the disclosure of this new attitude of the court on State powers in dealing with industrial reform legislation, speculation sprang high as to its probable influence on President Roosevelt's plan to remake the tribunal with more "liberal" members.

The prevailing opinion was that there was little net effect; that while some of the President's chief reasons for wanting a remodeled court were discounted by the inherent liberality of the decision, the circumstances by which it was brought about, specifically the switch of one justice, added strength to the argument against 5-to-4 decisions.

Removing the Adkins decision from its pathway, the majority of the court said in its opinion that the essential question remaining was whether the need for protecting women by minimum wage standards was sufficiently in the public interest to outweigh the arguments of deprivation of property without due process of law, if set up in the exercise of a State's police powers.

The opinion pointed out that present-day social conditions, which must be considered in reaching a decision, required the "protection of law against the evils which menace the health, safety, morals and welfare of the people."

Close to the 'Public Interest'

"What can be closer to the public interest," the majority then asked, "than the health of women and their protection from unscrupulous and overreaching employers? And if the protection of women is a legitimate end of the exercise of State power, how can it be said that the requirement of the payment of a minimum wage fairly fixed in order to meet the very necessities of existence is not an admissible means to that end?"

The dissenting justices demurred to this line of reasoning. In their opinion, read by Justice Sutherland with an emphasis in striking contrast to his usual placidity, they insisted that the pressure of economic conditions did not change the meaning of the Constitution, the due process provisions of which they construed the minimum wage law to contravene.

Furthermore, the dissenting opinion saw no impelling reason why the Legislature should discriminate between men and women in enacting laws restricting the right to bargain for wages.

Discussion of the case at issue was prefaced by the dissenting justices with an extended discourse on the powers and duties of the Supreme Court in passing upon acts of Congress and the States. They contended the Constitution made it clear that the court was intrusted with the power to determine cases arising within its jurisdiction, "and so long as the power remains there, its exercise cannot be avoided without betrayal of a trust."

"Reasonable Doubt" Issue Raised

The minority opinion discussed, too, the question of the court's rule of resolving all "reasonable doubt" in favor of the legislative branch, which has been raised in recent discussions on the court's activities. The dissenters concluded that a justice's responsibility in deciding a case was upon him and no one else, that his oath was an "individual" oath and not a "composite" one, and that the question of "reasonable doubt" was personal to the justice himself.

This was construed by observers as being in answer both to the arguments of Justice Stone in recent minority opinions of the court, and to certain contentions made by witnesses sponsoring the President's court reorganization before the Senate Judiciary Committee.

As to the Washington minimum wage case, the dissenting justices contended that it violated that section of the Fourteenth Amendment prohibiting States from passing acts depriving citizens of property without due process of law, in that it deprived women workers of freedom of contract—of their right to bargain freely for their labor, without restraint as to the amount they should receive.

Washington Woman Fought Case

The case which brought about this new alignment of the court and the speculation that revolved around it tonight originated with Elsie Parrish, a chambermaid in a hotel at Wenatchee, Wash.

Mrs. Parrish worked in the hotel intermittently from August, 1933, until May, 1935. When her job was ended $17 was offered to her in final settlement for her services, but she and her husband knew that a State board, acting under the State Minimum Wages for Women Law passed in 1913, had fixed $14.30 a week as the minimum for her work. She and her husband sued in the State court for the difference of $216, which she contended was due her under that scale.

After losing in the county court, they appealed to the Washington State Supreme Court, which upheld the law and ordered payment. The West Coast Hotels Company appealed to the United States Supreme Court, and the State of Washington through its attorneys intervened in defense of its law. The decision today affirmed the judgment of the Washington State Supreme Court.

Early in the prevailing opinion Chief Justice Hughes said that the Washington case had necessitated a re-examination of the Adkins decision. He pointed out quickly, moreover, that the New York minimum wage case had come to the Supreme Court on the contention of attorneys for the State that it was distinguishable from the Adkins case, not that this latter suit had been decided erroneously when it was determined on a 5-to-3 decision in 1923.

Way to Reconsideration Is Seen

"We think that the question which was not deemed to be open in the Morehead (New York minimum wage) case is open and is necessarily presented here," read the Chief Justice.

Amplifying his reasons, the Chief Justice said that the importance of the pending question, in which many States are concerned by virtue of similar laws, the close division by which the Adkins decision was reached in the first instance, and "the economic conditions which have supervened, and in the light of the reasonableness of the exercise of the protective power of the State must be considered, make it not only appropriate, but we think imperative, that in deciding the present case the subject should receive fresh consideration."

Mr. Hughes said there was no doubt on the question of principle involved. The due process clause of the Fourteenth Amendment governed the States just as the due process clause of the Fifth Amendment governed Congress. In both the Adkins case and the pending case, the violation alleged by those attacking minimum wage regulation for women was that it deprived them of the freedom of contract.

As to the Freedom of Contract

"What is this freedom?" asked the Chief Justice, reading the opinion for himself and colleagues. "The Constitution does not speak of freedom of contract. It speaks of liberty and prohibits the deprivation of liberty without due process of law. In prohibiting that deprivation, the Constitution does not recognize an absolute and uncontrollable liberty. Liberty in each of its phases has its history and connotation. But the liberty safeguarded is liberty in a social organization which requires the protection of law against the evils which menace the health, safety, morals and welfare of the people."

The Chief Justice cited former language of the court to support the contention that the State had a direct interest in its citizens, their welfare and protection. "The whole is no greater than the sum of all the parts and when the individual health, safety and welfare are sacrificed or neglected, the State must suffer," he quoted from Holden v. Hardy, decided, as he said, nearly forty years ago.

"We emphasize the need for protecting woman against oppression despite her possession of contractual rights," the Chief Justice said.

He quoted from the late Justice Holmes, who dissented in the Adkins case, to the effect that the statute in question did not compel anybody to do anything; and from the late Chief Justice Taft, who also dissented, upholding the justice and the validity of such laws.

Women's Position a Factor

The court held that the Legislature of the State was clearly within its proper sphere when considering the situation of women in employment, "the fact that they are in the class receiving the least pay, that their bargaining power is relatively weak, and that they are the ready victims of those who would take advantage of their necessitous circumstances."

It held that the Legislature was entitled to adopt measures to reduce the evils of the "sweating system," the exploiting of workers at wages so low as to be insufficient to meet the bare cost of living, "thus making their very helplessness the occasion of a most injurious competition."

The Legislature had the right, the majority decision said, to consider that its minimum wage requirements would be an important aid in carrying out its policy of protection. The adoption of similar requirements by many of the other States was cited as evidence of a "deep-seated conviction both as to the presence of the evil and as to the means adopted to check it."

"Legislative response to that conviction cannot be regarded as arbitrary or capricious and that is all we have to decide," read the Chief Justice. "Even if the wisdom of the policy be regarded as debatable and its effects uncertain, still the Legislature is entitled to its judgment."

Burden on Community Cited

The court said there was an additional "and compelling" consideration which recent economic experience had brought strongly into light—the exploitation of a class of workers who are in an unequal position with reference to bargaining power "and are thus relatively defenseless against the denial of a living wage."

The decision held that this was not only detrimental to the health and well-being of the workers themselves but cast a direct burden for their support upon the community.

"What these workers lose in wages, the taxpayers are called upon to pay," said the court.

The relief load, carried even now in the midst of evidences of recovery, was pointed out.

"The community is not bound to provide what is in effect a subsidy for unconscionable employers," the opinion said.

The majority recalled that the court had frequently held that the legislative authority, acting within its proper field, was not bound to extend its regulation to all cases which it might possibly reach. It is free to recognize degrees of harm and restrict its remedies to classes and groups as it sees fit.

Quoting a former decision of the court, the opinion said:

"If 'the law presumably hits the evil where it is most felt, it is not to be overthrown because there are other instances to which it might have been applied.'"

Sutherland Reads Dissent

Almost half of the dissenting opinion, as read by Justice Sutherland, was taken up with a discussion of the general constitutional problem. To this extent it might have been taken as an answer to many of the attacks on the present judicial system as made over the radio, in Congress and before its committees by proponents of the President's plan for judiciary reorganization.

The dissenters upheld the right of the Supreme Court to pass upon the constitutionality of acts of Congress coming within its jurisdiction, and emphasized the duty of a justice to vote according to his own convictions. A justice cannot subordinate his convictions and refuse to pass upon a constitutional question and keep faith with his oath "or retain his judicial and moral independence."

Specifically, answer was given to the suggestion, made by certain Supreme Court justices themselves and repeated in the debate now raging over the court problem, that the only check upon the exercise of judicial power is a judge's own faculty of self-restraint. This suggestion, said the minority opinion, "is both ill considered and mischievous."

Taking up the point emphasized by the court majority, that the question involved should now receive fresh consideration because of economic conditions that have intervened, the minority said that "the meaning of the Constitution does not change with the ebb and flow of economic events."

They urged that if the Constitution stands in the way of desirable legislation, "the blame must rest upon that instrument and not upon the court for enforcing it according to its terms."

"The remedy in that situation—and the only true remedy—is to amend the Constitution," said the minority opinion.

Coming finally to the Washington case, the dissenting justices held that if the Adkins case was properly decided, as they insisted it was, it necessarily followed that the Washington statute was invalid. They termed the law exclusively one fixing wages for adult women, "who are legally as capable of contracting for themselves as men," and held that it would not be sustained unless upon principles apart from those involved in cases already decided by the court.

They contended that the sole basis upon which the question of validity of the act rested was the assumption that the employe is entitled to receive a sum of money sufficient to provide a living for her, keep her in health and preserve her morals, a question, which they insisted, could not be determined by any general formula prescribed by a statutory board.

Furthermore, the minority contended that the clause of the Fourteenth Amendment forbidding a State to deprive any person of life, liberty or property without due process of law includes freedom of contract—a principle "so well settled as to be no longer open to question."

"Nor reasonably can it be disputed that contracts of employment of labor are included in the law," said the opinion.

The dissenters added that the law failed to recognize the rights of the employer and failed to distinguish between the "great and powerful" employer and him of weak bargaining power.

They construed as "significant and important" the fact that all State statutes to which the court's attention had been called referred to women employes, and left adult men and their employers free to bargain as they please.

"The common-law rules restricting the power of women to make contracts have, under our system, long since practically disappeared," said the minority opinion. "Women today stand upon a legal and political equality with men. There is no longer reason why they should be put in different classes in respect of their legal right to make contracts; nor should they be denied, in effect, the right to compete with men for work paying lower wages which men may be willing to accept."

The minority quoted copiously from the prevailing opinion in the New York minimum wage case, contending that the language was exactly applicable in the present case. They contended finally that fixing of wages by public authority, if followed to its final conclusion, would abrogate completely the right of contract so far as wages are concerned.

When word of the court's decision, and the fact that the former majority opinion holding States unable to enact minimum wage laws had been overturned, reached the Senate, Senator Wheeler of Montana was on his feet answering an attack upon the court by Senator McKellar.

Senator Robinson interrupted to refer to what the court had done. Swinging both fists above his head to emphasize his point, Senator Robinson said:

"I would like to refer to' the fact that the Supreme Court has reversed itself in the Adkins case and probably in the New York wage case."

"I am sure the Senator from Arkansas is delighted because they did it," put in Senator Wheeler.

"Certainly, I am delighted," Senator Robinson replied.

Continuing for a moment, Senator Robinson read the concluding remarks of the court in its prevailing opinion today, expressly reversing itself in the Adkins case.

"Fine," interjected Senator Wheeler.

"Yes, fine," shouted Senator Robinson, "but what happens to the thousands of women and children in the great State of New York who are compelled to work unlimited hours in sweat shops and in factories on the basis of the decision resting on the Adkins case? The basis of the decision in the Tipaldo case ought to be reconsidered and reversed."

"Let me say to the Senator from Arkansas," Mr. Wheeler put in, "that I am sure he is very happy that the Supreme Court has seen the light with reference to this case."

"I was made miserable when the Supreme Court decided that Congress could not fix maximum hours of labor and minimum wages for women and children workers in the District of Columbia," Mr. Robinson replied.

"I was made more unhappy when, following that precedent, the Supreme Court said that the New York State law-making power could not do it in the State of New York. I am glad that the Supreme Court has completely faced about and recognized the necessity of overruling its former decision.

"Mr. President, talk about accepting in all cases Supreme Court decisions as binding and being above question! Here is a case where the minority opinion at last after many years becomes the majority opinion."

NAVY ENDS SEARCH FOR MISS EARHART

Flier and Her Navigator Are Dead, Officials Believe— Warships Are Recalled

VAST HUNT SET A RECORD

Aviator Was First Woman to Fly Atlantic—Only One to Cross 2 Oceans by Plane

By The Associated Press.

HONOLULU, July 18.—The United States Navy gave Amelia Earhart up for dead at sunset today, when it announced an end to the vast South Pacific hunt for the aviator and ordered the return of the giant aircraft carrier Lexington to her base at San Diego, Calif.

The carrier, which had sent her searching planes roaring vainly across Equatorial skies for nearly a week, was ordered to proceed directly to San Diego.

Three destroyers, also in the hunt for Miss Earhart and her navigator, Frederick J. Noonan, will return to the Pacific Coast via Pearl Harbor, Hawaii, where they will refuel.

The world-famous flier and Noonan vanished on July 2 on a 2,570-mile flight from Lae, New Guinea, to Howland Island, a tiny isle two feet above the sea.

The naval authorities directing a search that had encompassed more than 250,000 square miles in every direction from Howland Island said they believed they had exhausted every possible hope of finding the missing pair alive.

Flier Greatest of Her Sex

The end of the search for Amelia Earhart and her colleague, Frederick J. Noonan, who vanished into the empty wastes of the south Pacific July 2 on an around-the-world flight, marks the conclusion of the greatest mass rescue effort ever undertaken for a lost plane. The rescue expedition finally included more than 3,000 men, 10 ships, 102 American fighting planes and an undisclosed number of Japanese Navy aircraft.

The attempt of Miss Earhart and her navigator to encircle the world at middle latitudes, never heretofore attempted by air, was to have been her last major flight, it was said.

Miss Earhart was the first woman to fly the Atlantic Ocean, with the added distinction of being the first woman to fly it alone. Also, she was the only aviatrix to have both transatlantic and transpacific flights to her credit. She was the first woman to fly across the United States, both by stages and in a non-stop flight, and on two occasions she established new speed records for women. She set a new altitude record for women and was the first woman to fly— and, by the same token, to wreck —an autogiro.

When Miss Earhart announced last Spring that she planned to girdle the globe along the line of the Equator certain long-range flying experts, who would not permit themselves to be quoted, pointed out the extreme hazards of such a trip, which called for the spanning of 27,000 miles, most of it over regions not frequently flown or mapped for air navigation.

It was pointed out by these experts that such a flight must be made without the aid of regularly established weather and radio beam services, which are now regarded as indispensable to standardized long-range commercial and military flights.

She Realized Hazards

Miss Earhart was known to be thoroughly aware of the difficulties but was possessed of a confidence born of long experience.

Her first attempt to fly around the world met with disaster. On March 17 she and Mr. Noonan hopped off from Oakland, Calif., to Hawaii on the first leg of the flight. They reached Honolulu safely, but when they were taking off on the 1,500-mile trip to Howland Island the plane burst a tire and cracked up. Miss Earhart climbed out of the cockpit and immediately announced that she would have the plane repaired and make the attempt again. The plane was taken to Los Angeles to be repaired.

On June 1 she and Mr. Noonan set out again. This time they planned to fly around the world in an easterly direction, seasonal weather conditions having made a westerly flight impractical. The early stages of their voyage were uneventful. They flew 1,033 miles to Puerto Rico and then 600 miles to Caprito, Venezuela, without incident. After touching in Brazil they made a perfect flight of 1,900 miles across the South Atlantic to St. Louis, Senegal, Africa.

Storms harassed them on the flight across Africa, but Miss Earhart brought the plane safely to Assab, Eritrea. In two long hops they made Calcutta, India, and left for Siam on June 18. On this flight stormy weather forced them back, and after an unsuccessful second attempt, followed by a short rest, they took off for Rangoon, Burma, where they made a successful landing after a rough and dangerous trip.

Surabaya, Java, was reached in short hops. They took several days off in the Javanese city to rest and check their instruments for the flight across the Dutch East Indies and the Timor Sea.

They were in Lae, British New Guinea, in three days and prepared for the most dangerous leg of their journey. Skill and good luck had enabled them to keep to their time schedule with few variations over lands and seas not entirely unknown to regular scheduled flying. But the journey ahead of them was ... ... to make the stoutest hearts quail.

Howland Island lay in the Pacific, north and east of them. The layman, looking at the map, sees many islands, reefs and atolls scattered along the path to Howland Island, but the vast distances make these tiny points of land of little use to the navigating flier and of little hope to the lost aviator. Their total land area represents little more than the area of New York City. The region had never been flown before, and the possibilities of radio comunication had never been tested.

Against the fearful odds of distance, Miss Earhart and her companion could pit only their skill as navigators and pilots and the ability of their plane to fulfill one of the most difficult assignments in the history of flying. They carried a small supply of food and water, together with a large yellow kite to fly as a signal if they came down, a Very pistol and a supply of flares.

Late on the night of July 1, Miss Earhart lifted the big plane from the flying field at Lae and took it out into the unknown. It has not been seen since, unless by some chance natives that might occupy the tiny islands, most of which are believed, however, to be uninhabited.

When Miss Earhart approached Howland Island, various messages were heard from her. The last one was received by the Itasca at 8:44 A. M. [Howland Island time] July 2. It gave her position. A previous message stated that she was running out of gasoline. For several days radio amateurs and some regular stations reported messages that might have been from Miss Earhart's plane, but none of these messages was established as actually being from her.

As the world waited in vain for news of the tousle-headed and boyish appearing young woman flier whom it had taken to its heart as it had taken no other flier except Colonel Charles A. Lindbergh, the oddly contradictory phases of Amelia Earhart's life were recalled. She was 39 years old when she took off on her around-the-world flight and had been in turn a nurse, a research worker, a social worker and a flier. Born at Atchison, Kan., she attended high school in Chicago and was a nurse in Canada during the closing years of the World War.

Always of an adventurous nature, she decided to learn to fly. When her father would not consent to finance her training, she sold some jewelry and her fur coat to pay for her first lessons.

On June 3, 1928, she leaped to fame literally overnight when she hopped off in the monoplane Friendship with Wilmer Stultz and Louis Gordon, two trained fliers, on a transatlantic flight.

They landed safely in Wales and Miss Earhart was immediately enthroned as the first woman to fly the Atlantic Ocean. Although a good pilot, Miss Earhart had been more or less of a passenger during the trip and did not hesitate to give most of the credit to her colleagues.

Her next venture was her greatest. On May 19, 1932, she took off from Hasbrouck Heights, N. J., on the first lap of a solo flight across the Atlantic. On the afternoon of May 20 she hopped from Harbor Grace, Nfld., landing in Ireland the next day.

In December, 1934, Miss Earhart made a solo flight of 2,408 miles from Hawaii to California in 18 hours and 16 minutes. The only other person to make the flight alone was Air Commodore Sir Charles Kingsford-Smith, the British aviator, since lost in a Pacific flight.

The graciousness that Miss Earhart always displayed toward her male colleagues was manifest in her desire to give credit to Frederick J. Noonan, her companion on the around-the-world flight. She insisted that he receive full credit for much of the careful preparation that went into the flight and for his skill in navigation on the voyage itself.

MISS LENROOT WARS ON PUBLIC ENEMY

Head of Children's Bureau Holds
Childbirth Mortality
Can Be Cut

By MILDRED ADAMS
WASHINGTON.

MISS KATHARINE LENROOT, head of the Children's Bureau, will call to order tomorrow a conference the purpose of which is to find ways and means of waging successful war against the needless loss of life in childbirth—an enemy that grows more dangerous as the United States grows older. She will have the aid of doctors of national repute, of public health nurses, of State and local health officers distinguished in their fields, and the support of national organizations that reach into the heart of cities, small towns and country districts. She will have marshaled behind her a body of evidence as to causes and possible ways of attack which has been gathered in two years of study and local demonstration.

The strength of the enemy is indicated by the imposing quality of this new attack. The death rate of women in childbirth is higher in the United States than in most civilized countries of the world. Moreover, it has shown stubborn and terrifying persistence in the face of marked improvement in other fields with which doctors deal. Life has been lengthened, and the span stretched out toward the end, but at the beginning there is still the same too great toll. Too many new mothers die for the good repute or the good health of America. Too many die needlessly; too many take their newborn babies with them. And the country which needs its young to balance the growing force of its old thereby suffers.

THE extent of the problem is indicated by the experience which the Children's Bureau has had in the course of the last two years under funds provided by the Social Security Act. That creaking omnibus of legislation granted $3,800,000 a year "for the purpose of enabling each State to extend and improve, as far as is practicable under the conditions in such State, services for promoting the health of mothers and children, especially in rural districts and in areas suffering from severe economic distress." It gave the administration of the fund to the Children's Bureau.

In the storm of comment, criticism and analysis which accompanied the passage of the bill and the setting up of its gigantic machinery, that modest grant was

Katharine Lenroot—Her job is to help America's children.

Harris-Ewing and Wendell MacRae from "Willingly to School." (© Round Table Press)

generally overlooked. But not by the bureau, and not by the local agencies affected.

The act said "the sums made available under this section shall be used for making payment to States which have submitted and have had approved by the chief of the Children's Bureau State plans for such services." Those plans were to include "financial participation by the State," which meant, for the most part, the matching of Federal funds by State funds.

With the bureau's encouragement, all the forty-eight States, Alaska, Hawaii and the District of Columbia went to work on their local plans, and within an astonishingly short time set up divisions of maternal and child health to carry them out. They had a medical director in charge, and public health nurses to assist. The details of their work varied with local conditions, but they always included "demonstration services in needy areas and among groups in special need." Here they would show what they meant by "proper care" for mothers about to bear babies, and for babies just after they were born.

State programs aroused public discussion and public interest in the local communities they affected. They stimulated the establishment of prenatal clinics and child-health conferences. They acted as a magnet for health officers and nurses, for country doctors used to traveling far and hard in order to reach a distant farmhouse at the vital hour, for trained obstetricians where they existed, and for general practitioners where—as in the majority of cases that had any doctor at all—they were the ones who chiefly assisted in bringing the local babies safely into the world. They gave out knowledge of the best modern practices and they took in—and sent on to Washington for further study—knowledge of local conditions and facilities (or lack of them) as they existed at the time.

"You'd think, to look at these reports, that mothers were cheap in America," said the head of the Children's Bureau. "Over the last twenty years we have managed to reduce infant mortality, and we are making some progress in getting proper care for women before their children are born. But the stubborn figure, the tragic curve that shows little sign of going down, is the one marking the number of mothers that die every year in the process of bearing babies.

"THERE, at the high point of importance, where you would expect medical and social forces to rally to their greatest efforts, they are actually the weakest. At the moment of crisis we still tend to leave it all to nature, as if a modern woman in these high-strung times could safely drop off the trail, have her baby and catch up with the tribe again. Fortunately for those who praise that stoic tradition, there are no sta-

tistics to show how many women died that way.

"But we do know how many die under modern conditions, and it is not a record that sheds any glory on our own country. Out of every 10,000 women who bore babies in the United States in 1934 we lost 59. That is a third more than Norway loses, it is much worse than the record of England and Germany. Out of a list of twenty-five countries reporting on this vital matter in 1934, and ranged in order of excellence, the United States ranks fifth from the bottom. Only Lithuania, Northern Ireland, Scotland and Chile are below us.

"And don't forget, in counting the mothers who die, that with them all too often go their babies. It is true that we have reduced infant mortality—that is, the number of babies who die in the first year of life is notably less than it was twenty years ago. But we have no such shining record with the new babies. We still lose altogether too many just as they come into the world. The death rate of babies on the first day of life has not changed in fifteen years. At that point their mothers die, and they die, too. So that the total loss of life due to conditions of childbirth is even worse than it looks at first sight."

MISS LENROOT makes no claim that the situation which she puts in such emphatic terms is a new one. "We have known that it existed for the last twenty years," she says. "That is what makes it the more disturbing, for during those twenty years we have done a great deal to save life in other fields. Our advances in medical science are matters of common knowledge.

"Sometimes it seems as though the ancient enemies had all been conquered, and the only danger lay in wars, internal combustion engines and the strain imposed by high-speed living. But the weak spots of medical science get no such publicity. Much of the pride we justly take in having lessened the terror of tuberculosis and diphtheria, for instance, is dimmed when one realizes that so basic a human function as child-bearing still takes an inordinate and unnecessarily high toll of life in the United States.

"Fortunately, there are things which we can do about it if we only will. That has been amply proved by the results of measures in effect in sections where public opinion is wide awake, where the right kind of instruction is provided ahead of time and the right kind of care is available at the crisis. Under such circumstances the death rate has been cut at least in half.

"But those model areas are, at the present time, few and far between. The Children's Bureau believes that the time has come to work for their extension over the rest of the country. It is in the hope of finding ways and means of doing it that the Children's Bureau is calling this conference."

CONFERENCE and cooperation form the keystone of the Children's Bureau's work, and the weapon on which its director pins her faith. She is an extraordinary person, this Katharine Lenroot, who directs it so quietly. The third chief of the Children's Bureau, she follows in the able footsteps of Julia Lathrop, who started it, and Grace Abbott, who carried it through the dangerous period that included the wiping out of the Federal Child Labor laws and the vicissitudes of the child labor amendment.

Miss Lenroot has had a hand in the bureau's work for almost the whole of its life. She was graduated from the University of Wisconsin in 1912, served for a year as deputy for Wisconsin's Industrial Commission, and then took a civil service examination for a position as special agent of the then new Children's Bureau. She was appointed in December, 1914, and has been busy ever since in the bureau's work. Her appointment to its leadership in December, 1934, was hailed as a triumph of the merit system.

Even-tempered, soft of speech, tactful as only a woman can be who has learned to walk successfully through the briary path of public service, Katharine Lenroot has about her an almost nun-like dedication to her job. Golden hair that is turning silver, blue eyes that are wide apart, a round face that still dimples when she smiles, betray her Scandinavian ancestry. She is a very practical person, skillful in both the details and the matters of policy which her job implies. A report issued by the bureau this year defines the possibilities, the difficulties and the limitations of her job in a paragraph:

"To investigate, to report and to administer—these are the specific functions of the Children's Bureau. The organization of the bureau is based upon these functions and the services growing out of them which the bureau is called on to give, such as consultation and advisory services to States, localities and organized groups concerned with the health and welfare of children."

IT was as consultant and adviser to the States that the bureau urged local action on the problem of maternal and child health when the $3,800,000 was made available under the Social Security Act. And it was in that capacity that it received local reports and pieced together the picture that gradually revealed the causes lying at the root of the problem.

Lack of money, lack of facilities, lack of knowledge—part of the trouble lies in the familiar and hard-pressed fields of economics and education. Half the babies born in the United States arrive in families that have less than $24 a week to spend, and you can't pay for much prenatal care, hospital care and nursing afterward on $24 a week.

Too much geography, and too few capable people to cover it—that is another difficulty. In certain regions of the country people are spread so thinly that an obstetrician would have to travel by airplane to build up a practice sufficient to support himself.

IN places like that it is the general practitioner, or the country doctor, or the public health nurse (when the community has one), or the midwife, or the grandmother who presides at the baby's birth. And here the records complain that the general practitioners and the country octors don't have enough obstetrical training in medical school to be able to handle difficult cases, that there are not enough properly trained public health nurses to go around. And again the familiar cry, that the public is slow in asking for something vital and valuable which the experts know it ought to have.

These facets of ignorance, poverty and inertia play their stubborn roles in almost all the social tragedies. But there is still more to this story. And there is still more than geography, and the vestiges of pioneer ways and pioneer difficulties. This problem is further complicated by primitive folkways on the one hand and mid-Victorian prudery on the other.

That the primitive folkways still hold sway among the Negroes of the South and the Mexican Indians of the Southwest will not be so surprising to sophisticated New Yorkers as that mid-Victorian prudery still makes a last and powerful stand in this most vital field. It is only a short time since a great metropolitan newspaper considered the word "pregnancy" unfit to print. At this present moment an educational film made under the most careful medical and social auspices to show women the kind of care they and their babies ought to have before and after birth is being held up by the New York censor lest public morals suffer at the sight of it.

CERTAIN lines of attack upon the problem have emerged out of the Children's Bureau work as possibilities. Last April a meeting of the bureau's general advisory committee recommended that work in maternal and child health be extended, and that public funds be granted for maternal care, medical aid and nursing "for all women in need of such care, considering need as including not only economic but also medical needs and lack or inadequacy of existing facilities."

The committee warned that in the development of such a program "the right of the patient to select her own physician should be maintained." In addition, it recommended "that a center or centers of post-graduate education should be established to teach urban and rural practitioners of medicine and nurses the fundamental principles of complete maternal and infant care." All this to be done in "cooperation with the national, State and local medical societies."

●

That is the recommended offensive. It remains to be seen what action will be taken by the conference that meets tomorrow.

January 16, 1938

STORE GIRLS TO GET A WAGE 'NEW DEAL'

Special to THE NEW YORK TIMES

WASHINGTON, Jan. 29. — Girl store workers are about to get their own New Deal, when minimum wage rates go into effect in Utah, Feb. 1, and in the District of Columbia, Feb. 14, the Labor Department said today.

The Wage Law becomes effective, it was pointed out, as a result of the decision of the Supreme Court last March upholding the constitutionality of the Washington (State) Minimum Wage Law, which Miss Perkins said "led to a wave of new minimum-wage legislation and the revival of old minimum-wage laws."

The minimum wage rates prescribed for women retail clerks in the District of Columbia and Utah are the highest, so far as established, outside of Nevada, which has written an $18 weekly minimum into its labor laws, the department said.

On an hourly basis, the District of Columbia minimum wage might be higher than that in Nevada, for the $17 minimum applies to a work week of from 40 to 48 hours or even shorter, whereas in Nevada the $18 need not be paid for anything less than 48 hours.

California has a minimum-wage rate of $16 a week, but the maximum number of hours allowed is 48, whereas, in Utah, the $16 rate is 42½ hours a week and anything above 42½ hours is to be paid for overtime at "time and a half."

"Not one woman sales clerk in the limited-price stores surveyed in 1937 was paid as much as $16.50 a week, the minimum wage for such employes in effect price to 193? " the survey showed.

"Moreover, 98 per cent of the women received less than $15 a week and half of them had earnings of less than $12.50 a week. Three in five worked the full legal limit in the District of Columbia—forty-eight hours a week and averaged only $13."

Highest-paid workers surveyed were in the telephone service. The average weekly wage of office workers in the telephone service was $25.38 and of telephone operators, $22.03. Beauty operators in stores had the next highest average weekly wage, $19.65, followed by non-office employes in ready-to-wear shops, $18.60, and women employes of beauty shops not in stores, $17.80.

Minimum-wage laws for women are in effect in the following twenty-two States: Arizona, Arkansas, California, Colorado, Connecticut, Illinois, Massachusetts, Minnesota, Nevada, New Hampshire, New Jersey, New York, North Dakota, Ohio, Oklahoma, Oregon, Pennsylvania, Rhode Island, South Dakota, Utah, Washington and Wisconsin —and the District of Columbia and Puerto Rico.

Similar bills are expected to be introduced this year to the State Legislatures of Kentucky, Michigan and Virginia.

January 30, 1938

TEACHING THEM HOW TO LIVE HAPPILY EVER AFTER

Colleges Now Offer Courses on Marriage

By EUNICE FULLER BARNARD

COLLEGE boys and girls trooping back to the campus this Autumn will be taught more generally than ever before in academic history how to become good husbands and wives. In the East and West, and even shyly and anonymously in the South, the preparation-for-marriage course is picking its arduous and uncertain way into ivied halls.

Economically, emotionally, physically and philosophically scores of American colleges are offering to instruct their young charges, from football player to curly haired co-ed, how to enter wedlock "soberly, advisedly, and in the sight of God." And the state of matrimony is beginning to be recognized, alongside the political State, as a legitimate subject of research.

More than one conclave of college professors is considering whether some elementary course in marital responsibilities —with or without credit—should not be required of all aspirants for a diploma. Consciously and subconsciously, the idea is gaining ground in the academic mind that an educated person should know some of the basic principles about making a go of his married life.

EVEN in 200 of the more staid institutions whose catalogues still eschew any listing of marriage as a separate subject, some phases of it nevertheless slip into

"Scores of American colleges are offering to instruct their young charges how to enter wedlock."

the curriculum in thin disguise as "Sociology 2A" or "Home Economics 4." Moreover, many a packed auditorium in such colleges will resound this Winter with the voices of visiting experts giving extracurricular lectures on marriage problems.

Meanwhile in more progressive halls the fair Phi Beta Kappa today may turn from microscopes and mathematics to write her major thesis on the "technique of harmony in modern marriage." And the young man on the make may even turn from the boss's daughter to seek his bride among the co-eds who achieve A-plus on the exams on the philosophy of the family budget.

Certainly no new study ever has been greeted with more acclaim by the students. None, perhaps, ever has been so spontaneously and simultaneously demanded by them. Again and again in the past year when a college has failed to grant their petition to provide marriage

courses, boys and girls have promptly arranged their own. A newly vocal younger generation demands that its universal and immediate problem of marriage be lifted out of the smoky atmosphere of the "bull session" into the clearer air of classroom discussion.

PERHAPS some of this new inquiry is due to the postponement of marriage which the depression in many cases has enforced. Perhaps it is owing in part to the new reliance on science that questions once asked in newspaper columns for the lovelorn are now put to the college professor. At any rate, these new youngsters recognize that marriage is one of their big adventures and they want to see what they are getting into. They are beginning to look beyond the moonlight-and-mystery aspects and insisting on advance instruction in some of the prosaic processes by

which living happily ever after is accomplished.

Thus last Spring 800 upper classmen at Michigan State College jammed the lecture hall week after week to hear doctors and professors talk on questions of sex and emotional adjustment in marriage and financing a new home, in a "better husband" series sponsored by the student council. Near by, the co-eds held their own sessions, also arranged by themselves and attended without hope of credit. This Fall student insistance is expected to result in similar lectures at the University of Michigan. With equal enterprise Smith College girls organized last Spring four seminars on physical and psychological aspects of marriage, under the aegis of the Student Association for Christian Work.

TO meet students' "actual present curiosities," one of the plainest spoken extra-

"The main mother-in-law trouble, as college youth sees it today, is between the husband's mother and the wife."

At the moment at North Carolina State College a similar petition signed by 300 students is apparently to be granted, and Duke University, too, is looking forward to a course. Some Catholic colleges hold discussions on the ethical, religious and psychological aspects of marriage. Even high schools are tentatively beginning to offer certain phases of pre-marital instruction, and a commission of the Progressive Education Association is working out textbooks and courses.

LARGELY because of the traditional taboos on discussion of the subject, sex problems are often a student's first and burning interest in the marriage course, but they are seldom his main and permanent one, college professors affirm. His curiosity satisfied by scientific information, he dwells longer on the more vexing questions of emotional adjustment.

"Many college girls have led sheltered lives," said Pro-

years ago among 2,000 undergraduates in sixteen colleges in all parts of the country by Mrs. Ruth W. Beebe for a thesis at Teachers College, Columbia, showed a similar tendency. Among 8,000 questions volunteered by students the most frequent was how to handle the sex drive before marriage. Second in frequency was a group of questions dealing with emotional and economic factors making for marital happiness. Methods of birth control ranked third.

By and large, students are eagerly concerned with all sorts of information which will help them to a successful married life, from how to avoid marital squabbles to how two can live as cheaply as one, pedagogues in various parts of the country agree. "College students have a sincere interest

curricular series in the country was given a year or so ago at Vassar under faculty auspices by a group including a New York gynecologist, a psychiatrist, a physiologist, a sociologist, a home economist and a child-study expert. Half the student body crowded many of the lectures, and when this year the course was printed in book form, some 400 copies were sold on the campus. This Fall, convinced that "every student should have this information," college authorities are taking steps to incorporate much of it into the noncredit hygiene lectures required of freshmen.

But the urge for pre-marital instruction is not confined to women's colleges and to coeducational ones. Though progressive institutions like Sarah Lawrence and Russell Sage in New York and Stephens in Missouri have pioneered with credit courses, some of the conservative men's colleges are just as ardent in the cause. Colgate has a marriage course counting toward a degree. Eighty per cent of Wesleyan seniors flock to an extra-curricular lecture series similar to Vassar's. Dartmouth is reported considering a course.

The first thoroughgoing attempt in the country was the course given upon their own petition for senior men at the University of North Carolina by the dean of the movement, Professor Ernest Groves.

"Our youngsters would snort at the old-time approach to sex problems via the birds, the bees, the flowers."

fessor J. K. Folsom of Vassar. "Some college boys still harbor mistaken notions about sex. They are eager to be straightened out. But after that is accomplished, the interest in sex adjustment is no greater than that in other phases of marriage. For a girl these are usually the problems of the proper balance between marriage and a career and the matter of deciding upon a suitable man or finding him."

AN investigation made two

in, and a wholesome approach to, the problem," said Dr. Robert G. Foster of the Merrill-Palmer School of Detroit. "Fundamentally they want to know how to forestall broken homes."

"Undergraduates want straight answers to practical questions," explained Miss Eleanor Dodge, Warden of Vassar. "They want the behavioristic side: how to achieve the best emotional adjustment in marriage, how much affection to allow beforehand, and so on. They are eager for an ethical point of view, scientifically rather than sentimentally arrived at."

"Not one student question in

189

six deals exclusively with sex, so far as my experience goes in forums of older students all over the country," Dr. M. A. Bigelow of Teachers College asserted. "On the contrary, the older girl is apt to be most concerned over the mother-in-law problem—what to do about her sweetheart's fixation on his mother."

AGAIN and again professors emphasized this point. Apparently the old mother-in-law joke should be reversed. The main in-law trouble, as college youth sees it today, is not between the wife's mother and the husband but between the husband's mother and the wife.

Another problem which apparently disturbs both boys and girls is that of the wife's working after marriage. They see cogent arguments on both sides and they want help in coming to a solution which will be satisfactory both economically and emotionally.

Women post-graduate students especially often express regret that they had not come earlier to see the advantages of wives' working, Dr. Helen Judy Bond of Teachers College said. Frequently a woman says she has failed to marry because the man in question could not support her in the style to which her own earnings had accustomed her. Now she is sorry that they did not marry and both continue working.

In general the newer college courses try to meet student questions squarely. Rarely is there pussyfooting. The zealously inquiring students will not accept it, college authorities admit. "Our youngsters nowadays would snort at the old-time circuitous approach to sex problems via the birds, the bees and flowers," said one dean. And this prophecy was borne out at Syracuse recently when many students protested that the marriage course was too vague. This Fall it is expected to be revised on franker lines.

In the most pragmatic approach of all for youngsters still in college, several professors advise students on the vagaries of the marriage market, and a few are working out tests for finding the ideal mate. For the college girl especially this is often the most pressing problem, Professor Folsom indicated. "It is difficult for her to figure out whether to marry a certain individual," he said. "She does not know how to gauge the possible conflicts that may arise from the differences in their temperaments and backgrounds. Sometimes, though she is able and charming, she has not found any man to whom she can look up."

THIS is the typical problem of the college woman, who even today does not have so high an expectancy of marriage as her less academically inclined sister. Here again some of the new courses bring statistics to her aid. Go West, young woman, is the burden of their song. Go also into professions other than the usual school teaching and library work where there is a shortage of men. And considering her own presumably unusually high intelligence she would better not be too insistent on finding an equally intellectual mate.

They marshal figures, too, to show her that she will do better to accept her best offer in her early twenties. For her brother collegian, at least by implication, the courses are often even more insistent on early marriage, this time as a life preserver. For married men of 30 and upward, they point out, the death rate is less than half that of bachelors.

On the chances of marital happiness for two people of different political and social beliefs, nationality, race or religion the pedagogues are apt to be noncommittal, merely pointing out the additional hazards. In general they dispute the old idea that it is good for "opposites" to marry. But as to precisely who should marry whom, the professors have to admit that they are still uncertain.

Despite the swift triumphs of marriage study, the doctors still disagree on how far it should be accepted as work counting toward a liberal-arts degree. At one end of the scale is a college like Russell Sage which requires all juniors to take a comprehensive marriage - and - home course taught in collaboration by professors of sociology, biology, home economics, fine arts and physical education. At the other are the more conservative institutions which contemplate offering little earmarked diploma fare in the subject aside from a more or less historical course in family sociology.

President MacCracken of Vassar, for example, plans to keep the marriage course as such wholly extra-curricular. "In the older Eastern colleges," he said, "I fail to foresee much extension of the orientation course and the break-up of traditional departments, which has been elsewhere the fad. We still believe it sounder to give a single discipline thoroughly than a superficial knowledge of many fields. A student who is especially interested in the family now as always can gain a thorough knowledge of sex and reproduction in the physiology course; of family relations in sociology; of budgeting in economics; of child study in psychology.

"THE average student's curiosity about marriage can be met in great part through good books. We need a sound bibliography on the subject, a few lectures and informal clinics organized to meet individual requirements. Thus a student with a morbid interest may be referred to the mental hygienist; another with a different problem may go to the college physician; still another to the Professor of Religion."

Nevertheless Professors Bigelow and Bond in an extensive survey of the situation throughout the country see "much evidence" of a trend in the opposite direction, toward an interdepartmental marriage course open without prerequisite to upper classmen. Professor Groves is still more sanguine. Because of impatience with marriage failures and the interest of young people in the subject, regular marriage courses will be a commonplace within a decade, he prophesied recently.

WOMEN SHOW GAIN IN STATE OFFICE

Their Numbers Reduced by On[e] in Congress, They Nevertheless Did Well in the Vote

STRONG IN NEW ENGLAN[D]

Mother and Daughter Won i[n] Connecticut—Several Ran fo[r] Post of State Secretary

By KATHLEEN McLAUGHLIN

Feminists disconsolate over election bulletins from Washington, where they will have one less Congressional Representative next session, will find more cheering news in a check of State results, not yet complete. New England areas, particularly, registered a benevolent attitude at the polls toward women office-seekers, and thus the Legislatures of the country's Northeast section will include next January a gratifying quota of women.

In New Hampshire, with a whacking total of fifty-seven women nominees among those aspiring to the next "General Court," the outcome remains in doubt because the checking of the ballots was discontinued over the Armistice Day holiday. Connecticut, which in 1937 had fourteen Republican and four Democratic women in its General Assembly, elected nineteen on Tuesday, including one Socialist.

Vermont maintained its Republican tradition by electing one woman State Senator and twelve women Republicans to the House, in addition to electing two women running for the House as independents, for a total of fifteen. Massachusetts elected one Democrat and one Republican in the House, and Rhode Island returned three women to the House and elected one woman as State Senator.

New York State, where competition for nomination was much more intense, retained its lone woman Senator, Mrs. Rhoda Fox Graves, and its single Assemblywoman, Miss Jane Todd, both Republicans. Each received a large plurality over her masculine opponent.

New Jersey emerged from the campaign with five women members in its Assembly, four Republicans and one Democrat. Mary Smith, Olive Sanford, Mattie Doremus and Constance Hand are Republicans, and Teresa Maloney a Democrat.

Both Mother and Daughter Win

Connecticut has no feminine State Senators and Massachusetts lost the

190

only one serving in its present session. Miss Sybil Holmes, Republican. Vermont elected Miss Flora Coutts of Newport, Republican, but defeated Miss Vanessa Huffnail, Democratic nominee. The Rhode Island State Senate acquired Edith C. Logee, Republican, the first woman in its membership in five years, who won by a plurality of 284 over her male opponent when Burrillville went Republican for the first time in thirty-four years.

A mother-daughter team was entered on the official roster of Connecticut, where Mrs. Sara B. Crawford of Westport was elected Secretary of State and Mrs. Sara Crawford Maschal of Norwalk won a seat in the lower house of the Legislature.

Mrs. Gertrude Smith of Farmington, Republican, who will be among Mrs. Maschal's Assembly associates, is the widow of Herbert Knox Smith and the daughter of the former Republican Senator from Illinois, Frank L. Smith.

At Washington, Illinois will have the only new feminine Representative—County Judge Jessie Sumner of Milford. Miss Sumner is the feminists' 50 per cent consolation for the loss of the seats held by Mrs. Nan Wood Honeyman of Oregon and Mrs. Virginia Jenckes of Indiana. With Mrs. Edith Nourse Rogers of Massachusetts, Mrs. Mary T. Norton of New Jersey and Mrs. Caroline O'Day of New York, she constitutes the quartet which proves that the day of the woman member of Congress is not yet over.

Woman Judge Wins Seat

Back in the Winter of 1930-31 there were nine women on the floor of the House, the record in Congress to date. Included were the famous "three Ruths"—Ruth Baker Pratt of New York, Ruth Hanna McCormick (Simms) of Illinois, and Ruth Bryan Owen (Rohde) of Florida; and Mrs. Rogers, Mrs. Norton, Mrs. Florence P. Kahn of California, Mrs. Katherine Langley of Virginia, and Mrs. Pearl Oldfield and Mrs. Effiegene Wingo of Arkansas, the latter three appointed to fill out unexpired terms as the widows of Representatives.

Miss Sumner will be the first woman in the Illinois delegation in Congress since Mrs. McCormick's time. A year ago she was unknown in politics. By a whirlwind method of campaigning, she has since become the first woman county judge of Illinois and now is the youngest woman member of Congress to represent her State. She is 38 years old.

Last December she defeated two men opponents for the judgeship left vacant by the death of her uncle, and in April again defeated two men for the Republican nomination for Congress. She is an alumna of Smith College, the University of Chicago and Columbia, and was the first American woman to specialize in law at Oxford.

In the old red brick courthouse at Watseka, seat of Iroquois County, she lifted her head yesterday from her desk and retorted to a query: "What'll I do in Congress? Oh, the best I can."

Women were victors in several important instances in the contests for important State posts. Thus in Arizona, Mrs. Ana Frohmiller was elected on the Democratic ticket to her seventh consecutive two-year term as State Auditor. She supervises the writing of about 250,000 tax warrants a year, involving $17,000,000.

In Idaho, Mrs. Myrtle Enking won an overwhelming victory over Mrs. Helga M. Cook, another woman who began the race for State Treasurer on a write-in vote when the Republican party entered the primaries without a candidate. Mrs. Enking will start her fourth term in January. And in Oklahoma, the "vote-getting grandmother," Mrs. Mabel Bassett, was the winner for the post of Commissioner of Charities and Corrections, for her fifth 'erm of four years each. She is a Democrat.

But the office of Secretary of State appeared to lure women aspirants more than any other. Confusion is apt to result in New Mexico, where Mrs. Elizabeth F. Gonzales, mother of twelve children, who served two terms in the post, was succeeded by another woman of the same name, Mrs. Fidel C. Gonzales, Democrat, defeated Mrs. Fern Veilacott in the race for Secretary of State. She is 38, a graduate of the Normal University in Las Vegas, and member of a well-known family of Southern Colorado.

Two women competed for the same office in South Dakota, where the incumbent, Miss Goldie Wells, was defeated by Miss Olive Ringsrud, a niece of the first Secretary of State of the Commonwealth.

Mrs. Katherine A. Foley, a Democratic State Representative, ran for Secretary of State in Massachusetts, but was defeated. Mrs. Emily Edson of Portland, Ore.; Mrs. Marguerite McGrew of Kansas, and Miss Rita Murphy of North Dakota were other contestants for the office. All are Democrats.

November 12, 1938

Mrs. Roosevelt Indicates She Has Resigned From D.A.R. Over Refusal of Hall to Negro

WASHINGTON, Feb. 27.—Mrs. Franklin D. Roosevelt indicated today that she had resigned from the Daughters of the American Revolution in disapproval of the national society's refusal to permit the appearance in Constitution Hall of Marian Anderson, Negro contralto, for whom Howard University is seeking to arrange a concert in Washington.

She would "neither affirm nor deny" that the D. A. R. was the organization from which she had announced in her newspaper column she intended to resign rather than by continued membership seem to acquiesce in a policy of which she disapproved. She said she thought it the prerogative of the organization in question to make any announcement on the subject.

Neither would she answer directly a question as to whether the policy in question was the exclusion of Miss Anderson from the society's auditorium, nor comment upon the decision of the society in the matter. However, she said she had joined the society "by request" soon after taking up her residence in the White House.

She said she deplored the fact that Miss Anderson might not be heard in Washington, and so had telegraphed James E. Scott, Negro, treasurer of the Marian Anderson Citizens Committee. Her telegram which she confirmed, was as follows:

"I regret exceedingly that Washington is to be deprived of hearing Marian Anderson, a great artist."

At the D. A. R. offices it was stated that Mrs. Henry M. Robert, president general of the national society, was out of town; her secretary at home, ill, and that if Mrs. Roosevelt's resignation had indeed been submitted, it was yet in the unopened mail accumulating on Mrs. Robert's desk. No such communication thus far has been received by any national officer, according to members of the clerical staff, and the resignation, if submitted, awaits Mrs. Robert's return.

Criticism of the D. A. R. for barring Miss Anderson from Constitution Hall, and of the Public School Board for sustaining the refusal of Dr. Frank G. Ballou, the Superintendent of Schools, to permit the use of the Central High School auditorium for her proposed concert, has crystallized into a petition for protest which will be published on Wednesday at the next meeting of the school board.

Declaring that "snobbery is back of this," Charles Edward Russell,

D'Arlene

Marian Anderson

liberal writer, commented today that the D. A. R. and the District School Board "have given Hitler, Goebbels and the Nazi press of Germany a very happy half hour."

Oswald Garrison Villard, Donald Ogden Stewart and Dr. Vincent Nicholson of the Society of Friends are among those who have joined in a protest for presentation to the school board, which is said to have been signed by more than 5,000 men and women.

Professor Doxey Wilkerson of Howard University said that Constitution Hall had been engaged by others for April 9, the night on which it was planned to present Miss Anderson, but that subsequent attempts by the university's School of Music to obtain the hall for either April 8 or 10 also had been "turned down."

Regulation Is Cited

A request for the use of the Central High School auditorium was then made, and disapproved by Dr. Ballou, from whose decision appeal was taken by a group of citizens at the Feb. 15 meeting of the school board. Five members of the nine board members voted to sustain Dr. Ballou's refusal of the high school auditorium; one, Colonel West Hamilton, a Negro, voted against it, two members of the board were not present at the meeting, and one left before the vote was taken.

In 1936 and again in 1937 the use of the Armstrong High School auditorium was granted by Dr. Ballou for a Marion Anderson recital, but Armstrong is a Negro school. The dual (white and Negro) school system provided by law for Washington was one of the reasons on which Mr. Ballou based his refusal of the use of the Central Auditorium, and in support of the other he cited the profit issue involved, quoting the following regulation:

"Use of school facilities will not be granted to any organization for any purposes which will result in a financial profit accruing to the organizations to which such school facilities have been granted."

Mrs. Robert Is Silent

By The Associated Press.

WASHINGTON, Feb. 27.—In Phoenix, Ariz., Mrs. Henry M. Robert, president-general of the D. A. R., declined to comment about the reported resignation of Mrs. Roosevelt.

No Word Received by Registrar

By The Associated Press.

BOSTON, Feb. 27.—Mrs. Frank Leon Nason, registrar-general of the Daughters of the American Revolution, tonight said she had not received any statement from Mrs. Franklin D. Roosevelt relative to resigning from the D. A. R.

She indicated to newspaper men that the resignation of a member would come to her.

Singer Extols Mrs. Roosevelt

Special to THE NEW YORK TIMES.

SAN FRANCISCO, Feb. 27.—"I am not surprised at Mrs. Roosevelt's action," said Marian Anderson today," because she seems to me to be one who really comprehends the true meaning of democracy. I am shocked beyond words to be barred from the capital of my own country after having appeared almost in every other capital in the world.

"My manager in New York is arranging an outdoor concert in Washington on April 9, free to the public."

Her Manager Attacks D. A. R.

Mrs. Roosevelt's reported resignation from the D. A. R. was characterized yesterday by S. Hurok, Miss Anderson's manager, as "one of the most hopeful signs in these troublesome times for democracy." Mr. Hurok's statement continued:

"The D. A. R.'s un-American, unconstitutional restriction upon Marian Anderson is a plain instance of the charge, often repeated, that they have not yet begun to understand the true meaning of American democracy.

"By her action Mrs. Roosevelt has shown herself to be a woman of courage and excellent taste. I applaud her."

Throng Honors Marian Anderson In Concert at Lincoln Memorial

Estimated 75,000, Gathered at Monument to Emancipator, Rush Toward Negro Singer at End—Ickes Introduces Her

WASHINGTON, April 9.—An enthusiastic crowd estimated at 75,000, including many government officials, stood at the foot of Lincoln Memorial today and heard Marian Anderson, Negro contralto, give a concert and tendered her an unusual ovation. Permission to sing in Constitution Hall had been refused Miss Anderson by the Daughters of the American Revolution.

The audience, about half composed of Negroes, was gathered in a semi-circle at the foot of the great marble monument to the man who emancipated the Negroes. It stretched half-way around the long reflecting pool. Miss Anderson was applauded heartily after each of her numbers and was forced to give an encore.

When the concert was finished the crowd, in attempting to congratulate Miss Anderson, threatened to mob her and police had to rush her back inside the Memorial where the heroic statue of Lincoln towers.

Even there, well-wishers threatened to overwhelm her, and the prompt action of Walter White of the American Association for the Advancement of Colored People, who stepped to a microphone and appealed to the crowd, probably averted a serious incident.

Secretary Ickes, who granted Miss Anderson permission to sing at this site, sat on her right on the monument's plaza, just above the specially arranged platform from which Miss Anderson sang into six microphones that carried the sound of her voice for blocks and over radio channels to millions throughout the country.

Next to Secretary Ickes was Secretary Morgenthau and on Miss Anderson's left sat Representative Caroline O'Day of New York.

Among the others on the plaza were Senators Wagner and Mead of New York, Justice Black of the Supreme Court, Senator Barkley, majority leader of the chamber and Senators Clark of Missouri, Guffey and Capper. Representative Mitchell of Illinois, a Negro, was among members of the House present.

Miss Anderson wore a tan fur coat with a bright orange and yellow scarf about her throat. She was bareheaded. Her mother was present.

In introducing Miss Anderson, Mr. Ickes referred to the Washington Monument at one end of the reflecting pool and to the Lincoln Memorial and in an implied rebuke to the D. A. R. remarked that "in our own time too many pay mere lip service to these twin planets in our democratic heaven."

"In this great auditorium under the sky all of us are free," the Secretary asserted. "When God gave us this wonderful outdoors and the sun, the moon and the stars, He made no distinction of race, or creed, or color."

In a few brief remarks at the end of her concert Miss Anderson said:

"I am so overwhelmed, I just can't talk. I can't tell you what you have done for me today. I thank you from the bottom of my heart again and again."

The singer was conducted to the platform by Mrs. O'Day, who was born in Georgia, and Oscar Chapman, assistant Secretary of the Interior, who is a Virginian.

There has long been a rule that no photographs of the Lincoln statue can be taken from within the sanctum where the statue stands. This was broken during the confusion following the concert. Photographers took pictures of Miss Anderson making an appealing gesture to the figure of Lincoln.

After beginning with "America," Miss Anderson sang the aria "Mio Fernando" from "La Favorita" by Donizetti, Schubert's "Ave Maria," "Gospel Train" by Burleigh, "Trampin'" by Boatner, and Florence Price's "My Soul Is Anchored in the Lord." She was accompanied on the piano by Kosti Vehanen.

Ickes Scores the "Too Timid"

WASHINGTON, April 9 (P).—Secretary Ickes, in introducing Miss Anderson at her concert, did not mention by name the Daughters of the American Revolution. He lauded Thomas Jefferson and Abraham Lincoln for stressing equality of opportunity, and added:

"There are those, even in this great capital of our democratic Republic, who are either too timid or too indifferent to lift up the light that Jefferson and Lincoln carried aloft."

Miss Josephine Roche, former assistant Secretary of the Treasury, and Miss Katharine Lenroot, chief of the Federal Children's Bureau, were among those on the platform.

February 28, 1939

April 10, 1939

Dorothy Thompson

For many years Miss Thompson was a successful commentator, mainly on international affairs. A magazine article about her once said: "Dorothy Thompson is perhaps the only person in the United States who makes a career out of stewing publicly about the state of the world."

Miss Thompson's influence was at its greatest just before World War II. Her column appeared in 170 newspapers and reached about 8,000,000 readers. She also contributed a monthly magazine article to Ladies' Home Journal, which had about 3,000,000 readers, and she was heard by 5,000,000 listeners in 1938 and 1939 over the radio stations of the National Broadcasting Company.

Her newspaper column, "On the Record," appeared for twenty-two years. It was discontinued in August, 1958. At her death she was still writing for Ladies' Home Journal.

In 1959, Miss Thompson was active in the American Friends of the Middle East, Inc. This organization urged, among other things, that Americans refuse to commit themselves in behalf of either Israel or the Moslem countries in the Middle East. Miss Thompson was president of the American Friends of the Middle East in 1956.

Interviewed Hitler

Early in her career she obtained an exclusive interview with Hitler. She wrote: "When I finally walked into Adolf Hitler's salon * * * I was convinced that I was meeting the future dictator of Germany. In something less than fifty seconds I was quite sure that I was not."

After she had been proved wrong, Miss Thompson, who was then with the Berlin bureau of the now-defunct Philadelphia Public Ledger, expressed her opinion of Hitler and his regime with such vehemence that she was expelled from Germany as soon as Hitler came to power.

She continued her crusade abroad, with her pen, her speeches and, in one notable case, with laughter. That was in February, 1939, when she was "covering" a German-American Bund rally in Madison Square Garden. Her guffaws at speakers all but disrupted the meeting. She was finally escorted out by the police, for her own protection, but the exploit drew international attention.

Miss Thompson was born in Lancaster, N. Y., on July 9, 1894, the eldest child of Peter and Margaret Thompson. Her father was a Methodist minister who had struggled to bring in an income that at times barely exceeded $500 a year.

As a child Miss Thompson was sent to live with an aunt in Chicago. She attended Lewis Institute there and went on to Syracuse University, where she received a scholarship as the child of a Methodist clergyman.

At Syracuse she became a strong feminist, and after her graduation in 1914 she went to work for the Woman Suffrage party, first as a clerk in its Buffalo office and then as a stump speaker and organizer.

By establishing somewhat vague connections with the American Red Cross immediately after World War I, Miss Thompson managed to reach

Miss Thompson

Europe, where she quickly became successful as a freelance newspaper correspondent. She had had no previous experience in newspaper work. She was later made Vienna correspondent for The Public Ledger.

Her Books Listed

When the followers of the deposed Emperor Karl of Austria tried unsuccessfully to re-establish him on the imperial throne of Austria-Hungary in 1921, Miss Thompson managed to get an interview with his mother, the Empress Zita. Miss Thompson's reputation was then established and she blazed her way through Europe, as John Gunther said, "like a blue-eyed tornado."

Miss Thompson wrote several books, including "Listen, Hans," "The New Russia," "Political Guide," "I Saw Hitler" and "The Courage to Be Happy."

In 1938, Miss Thompson won a gold medal from the National Institute of Social Sciences "for distinguished services to humanity" and an achievement medal from the American Woman's Association. She served as president of the American PEN Club, a writers' group, from 1936 to 1940 and was president of Freedom House in 1944.

Miss Thompson was married to Josef Bard, a Hungarian writer, in 1923. They were divorced four years later.

While Miss Thompson was head of the Berlin bureau of The New York Evening Post, now The New York Post, she met Mr. Lewis at a tea given by German Chancellor Gustav Stresemann.

Miss Thompson and Mr. Lewis were married in London in 1928. This marriage ended in divorce in 1942. The next year Miss Thompson was married to Maxim Kopf, a painter and sculptor. He died in 1958.

February 1, 1965

A GLANCE AT THAT AWFUL THING CALLED GLAMOUR

By B. R. CRISLER

POSTERITY'S final verdict may conceivably be that the art of the motion picture died some time in the late Nineteen Thirties of a self-administered overdose of glamour. Like the internal corruption which gradually ate away the foundations of Byzantium (some future historian may write) glamour was not an overnight growth but ripened slowly into the monstrous perfection it finally achieved through the activities of those painstaking pygmalions—the Max Factors and Gilbert Adrians of Hollywood's make-up and wardrobe departments. By 1939, the pace of being glamorous had become so terrifically professional that only one successful amateur was left, and she was at last driven to exile herself on a semitropical Elba in mid-Atlantic, to escape from the ever-present reminders of her rarity.

Apprehension in a haystack, or Robert Montgomery and Rosalind Russell in a situation from "Fast and Loose," now at the Criterion.

In that climactic year, the historian may learnedly point out, a brunette from Hungary was the chief embodiment of the glamour myth, for no good reason except possibly that a blonde from England had been the reigning queen of the previous year. These frequent changes of favorite, demonstrating the essentially polygamous nature of public taste, were delicate matters, customarily made known through an announcement from the Columbia University senior class that Miss So-and-So had been chosen that year as the ideal companion with whom to be shipwrecked on a desert island. This curious result of the higher education among a group which might better have been expected to choose good books, such as Shakespeare and the Bible, for such a desperate eventuality, was likewise—as the commentator may point out, parenthetically—a proof of woeful ignorance as to just how much desert island movie glamour can stand.

For in the movies glamour is strictly an applied art: a beauty not even skin deep which melts in the sun, streaks in the rain, grows straight and stringy on damp days, peels and rubs off—a mask to be removed at night, exposing the tired, all-too-human tissues beneath. And this, precisely, is the basic fallacy of the glamour concept: that it violates the most fundamental canon of what remains, after all, an inescapably naturalistic art. Hollywood's denatured dream girls are, of necessity, spiritually static, with no more "soul" than a geisha. With the make-up man constantly standing by to pat the perspiration from her face and with "wardrobe" dancing attendance to guard her gown (specially designed to minimize anatomical defects) from wrinkles, she is as far above the plane of mortal infirmities, and consequently is as uninteresting, psychologically, as a statue in a museum. Even as a work of art, she is very second-rate, a Mona Lisa as phony as the scenery among which she reclines on a wrinkle-preventer, waiting for the next "take."

When Miss Hedy Lamarr, Columbia's current crush, arrived from Europe last year, there was no indication, either in photographs or stories, that here was the wave-born Aphrodite of our day; there is no record that she caused a single ship news reporter to dream of leaving his wife and kiddies. Her fashions were a little extreme; her face was arranged according to her own imperfect, home-made plan; looking back today, only the expert could recognize in her the voluptuous siren in whom a senior class this year perceives the perfect desert island companion. But it is glamour which ruins actresses, making them vain and consequently lazy. It was the glamour concept which dated Dietrich, caused Darrieux to overdo, threatened Lombard till she defied it, let her hair go straight, acquired a sense of humor.

The men catch it too, of course. Gable has managed to survive the pinning back of his ears with adhesive tape for full-face shots (in which he was said to suggest an angry elephant); it remains to be seen whether Robert Taylor will live down his artificial widow's peak. But it is significant that two of the most popular stars of the current year are Mickey Rooney and John Garfield, whose faces are always greasy and who have the look of being more comfortable that way. Perhaps a new generation will reclaim the movies from the beauty-parlor industry and the hairdressers of America and restore it to the people. Only time will tell.

March 12, 1939

Girl Graduates Are Heartened In Job Outlook

But Optimism Is Tempered by View That Situation Still Is 'Pretty Difficult'

By ANNE PETERSEN

The preference for youth in the employment market and the wide public interest in job difficulties of young persons are two advantages the girl graduate possesses as she sets out to hunt a job this Spring. But they are about the only encouragements held out by women leaders in an employment field still, they believe, discouragingly depressed.

Most optimistic among them was Mrs. Chase Going Woodhouse, director of the Institute of Women's Professional Relations at Connecticut College, New London, who has visited a number of college placement offices recently.

"They left me with the impression that June graduates are finding openings more readily than was true last year," she reported. "Certainly they are more optimistic about jobs, more interested in planning for future work. I found very little of the attitude of 'Why bother? The best thing to do is to get married,' which was fairly prevalent some two years ago.

"The facility and imagination with which young college women are using the occupational information our institute collects would force even a professional pessimist to be a bit optimistic for their future."

Jobs Essentially for Women

Trends in business which are opening new jobs that have not had time to become labeled men's jobs give promise to a certain number. This is especially true, she pointed out, in the consumer service departments of retail and industrial concerns where women are the consumers, and where women are profitably employed to translate a feminine viewpoint into industrial services, design and distribution.

A second aid the jobseeker has in entering the competition for work is found in a combination of skills which men are not likely to possess, such as secretarial training in addition to her specialty, whether it is economics, chemistry or language ability.

The barriers which are being imposed against the employment of married women and of older women work, to some degree, to the advantage of the young graduate, it was pointed out by Miss Lena Madesin Phillips, president of the International Federation of Business and Professional Women.

"The lines are tightening against married women and older women

in business," she declared. "Three employment agencies recently refused the application of a young married woman, aged 27, although she had the highest letters of recommendation. Another instance is that of a married woman with a fine business record, who has tried vainly to return to the job she formerly held. While this trend works to the disadvantage of women generally, it does leave the field open for young college girls."

Although the general situation is still "pretty difficult" for any jobseeker, Miss Phillips pointed out that there was real improvement in the psychological approach to job-hunting. Realizing that the depression is not a temporary matter, girls are not satisfied to wait for it to improve.

"They have come to see more clearly than ever that they can't follow the old routine of job-hunting, but must create a new opening for themselves and search about for new community services they may render. Any young woman coming out of college would do well to make a brief survey of her town," she advised, "and discover what work women would gladly pay to have done for them, which is not now being done commercially."

The superior training of colleges today gives this year's graduates a decided edge on the experienced worker in the employment game, according to Miss Ollie Randall, assistant director of welfare for the Community Service Society. "Lack of experience is not nearly so great a hindrance to young people today as their age is to older workers," she said. "But jobs are limited, no matter which group you belong to, and even more limited than last year, from my observations. However, when an opening does appear, it is the young person who is given the opportunity.

"The reason is not only that youth is a great asset in all types of employment, but also because young women who have had the benefit of our modern educational system are preferred over those who have been trained under earlier methods. The educational requirements for such fields as social work, nursing, and some branches of teaching have increased considerably in recent years, and no quarter is given those applicants, however experienced, who come without bearing degrees."

Employment Through Education

The humanizing influence of the depression in waking public consciences to the employment needs of youth was stressed by Mrs. Rudolph M. Binder, newly elected president of the New York City Federation of Women's Clubs. Education today, she believes, tends to equip young women to become self-supporting in ways unthought of a generation ago.

"Nevertheless, the situation is desperate for both young and old, today; and we should guard against the development of relief-mindedness among the unemployed. Unemployment is one of the questions which the federation should study more carefully, with the thought of giving still more support to agencies which are looking for constructive answers to this difficult question."

May 14, 1939

Democratic Ideal Urged on Mothers

Organized Drive Will Seek Pledges to Guide Youth In Nation's Philosophy

Mothers throughout the country will be asked today to pledge that they will teach their children democratic principles in observance of the twenty-fifth anniversary of Mother's Day. The drive, launched by the American Mothers' Declaration, will attempt to obtain 5,000,000 signatures within the next two months through the cooperation of women's clubs.

Mrs. Carrie Chapman Catt is honorary chairman of a group of twenty-two women from various States which is sponsoring the movement. Mrs. William Dick Sporborg is chairman.

Mrs. Otelia Compton, American Mother of 1939, it was announced yesterday, will be among the first to endorse and sign the declaration, which reads:

"Thankful for the benefits of a free country, I, an American mother, will do my utmost to help my children understand, cherish and guard the five freedoms upon which this nation was founded: freedom of speech, press, assembly, worship and petition. I will teach my children by my own example that they should respect the rights and opinions of others if they would defend their own, and thus preserve our heritage of liberty against any and all doctrines opposed to the traditions of our nation."

The signatures will be presented to officials at the Court of Peace at the New York World's Fair.

A second observance today will be the celebration of Mother's Peace Day, supported by the Women's Division of the American League for Peace and Democracy, which has announced that a parade of mothers for peace will be held in Cleveland.

May 14, 1939

SHALL WIVES WORK?

Whether married women should work is again an issue. Many of our State legislators say they should not.

By KATHLEEN McLAUGHLIN

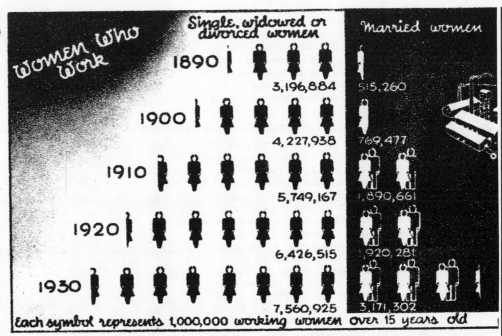

Women Who Work — Single, widowed or divorced women / Married women

1890   3,196,884   515,260

1900   4,227,938   769,477

1910   5,749,167   1,890,661

1920   6,426,515   1,920,281

1930   7,560,925   3,171,302

Each symbol represents 1,000,000 working women over 15 years old

THIS has been a punishing year, in our legislative halls, for the good old institution of wedlock. There aren't enough jobs, and the newest and brightest solution advanced by an astonishing number of elected representatives of the people is to forbid married women to work if their husbands have jobs.

So hot has the fight become that the National Federation of Business and Professional Women's Clubs, in its recent national convention in Kansas City, designated the problem the most serious confronted in twenty years. The federation went after it, hammer and tongs, and will be carrying the fight to the legislators when they next convene. For although legislation to keep married women out of jobs was defeated in nearly every instance at the last series of legislative sessions, the battle continues.

Technically, the attack has been on both sides of the marriage partnership. In almost all the bills the attempt has been made to bar "husband or wife" from public office when wife or husband already has a job. But there is no further effort than that to veil the issue; it is aimed at working wives, and it is intended to open their jobs to the men. Yet one of the most disquieting factors to the women concerned has been the acquiescent attitude of their younger—and unmarried—sisters and associates, who obviously expect to benefit from any such legislation.

DURING last Winter's sessions, twenty-eight State Legislatures received bills discriminating against married women workers. In several instances the forces of opposition to these bills were "saved by the bell" of adjournment. But they look with foreboding toward the next sessions.

Their foreboding is not without reason. Something like the fanaticism of the Huey Long "share the wealth" proponents has gleamed in the eyes of the vote-courting solons since one of them sprang the first of the "share the jobs" bills, following publication of the summarized findings of the Biggers report on unemployment. Their interpretation of that report—wholly inaccurate, in the opinion of feminine

units—was that an increasingly disproportionate number of married women have been invading the labor market during the past few years.

From this springboard the legislators dived with joyful eagerness into the scramble to write the first statutes to reverse this situation. Their attitudes in arguments in committee rooms and in legislative halls implied unmistakable conviction that they had stumbled upon the cure-all and end-all of the depression. There was much quoting, in stentorian tones, of the assertion of an economist of national reputation, to the effect that "unemployment would drop by a full million tomorrow" if working wives were fired.

IN the main, all the bills purport to reduce unemployment by plucking married women out of jobs closest to the jurisdiction of the Legislatures, i.e., public service, and making their positions and salaries available to single women or to men, married or single. The supposition is that by handing over the affected jobs to the currently unemployed, relief rolls will presently be seen to be dwindling rapidly.

The salient paragraph of a typical bill submitted in Minnesota read:

It shall be unlawful for a husband and wife to work for the State, county, city or any other subdivision of this State or any combination thereof, if their combined income for their services exceeds $120 per month; provided, however, that military service in the National Guard shall not come within the provisions of this act. Any violation of this act shall be a misdemeanor.

One of the Massachusetts measures stated that "No married woman shall be employed by the Commonwealth, nor by any county, city, town or district, unless

she establishes to the satisfaction of the employing official that her husband is earning less than $3,000, or that she is living apart from her husband for justifiable causes." California legislators were asked to pass a measure which would have barred from employment "any married person whose spouse earns more than $1,500 in any public office or private employment, including persons, firms or corporations."

Stern provision is made in various bills for the dismissal of any working wife who cannot bolster firmly her claim to dire need of her job. Some—as in Connecticut—would establish a commission of three, before which a culprit could be haled for submission of data as to her bank balance if any, and her husband's; affidavits as to the total amount of her mate's earnings; and sworn statements as to any supplementary income, whether from the butter and egg money, Christmas checks from home, or a ticket on Hotheels in the fourth at Belmont.

AUTHORS of many bills wrote into them, as evidence of their practical approach, some escape provisions for those women incautious enough to have married unsuccessful husbands. In those presumably rare instances in which the family income is admittedly below par, wives might continue working until and unless their husbands' earnings were shown to be "adequate." The most confusing spread was discovered in the sums indicated as "adequate" in various parts of the country.

In Utah, it developed, $800 constitutes a sufficient annual income and debars a wife from gainful employment. In Wisconsin, one measure set the total at $2,000, with $400 additional for each dependent child. But in Massachusetts, a wife still could work if her husband earned as much as $3,000 a year. The Texas Senate adopted a House concurrent resolution, now in effect, under which a man and his wife are prevented from working for the State if their combined income exceeds $175 a month.

SCARCITY of jobs explains the flood of attempts to restrict the employment opportunities of a section of the American public, despite the lurking question mark as to the constitutional rights of individuals involved. The situation is further affected by the wholesale retrogression of women in some European countries, notably Germany and Italy, within recent years, where Hitler and Mussolini have in large measure barred women from public life and confined them to the domestic. There are always and everywhere wistful adherents of the old and revered tradition about women's proper sphere. Anything that would restore lovely woman to her former niche in-

Anton Kamp—Black Star

The growing ranks of working wives are shown in the chart. In 1930 approximately six times as many married women were gainfully employed as in 1890, while in the same period the total of single, widowed and divorced women gainfully employed increased about two and one-half times.

side of the four walls of her own home must in consequence revive the old days and the old order, they feel, resolutely ignoring the altered routine of today's homes, the mechanization of some household tasks and industrialization of others, and the enforced partial leisure of many women.

THE number and severity of the "anti-working-wives" measures took the majority of women by surprise. First, there was only incredulity or mirth; laughter died as the multiplication of bills indicated the extent of the epidemic, or else was directed into a campaign of satire. Sometimes the intended victims managed to turn a neat burlesque on the lawmakers.

There was the bill submitted in Massachusetts by Mrs. Leslie B. Cutler, stipulating that public service jobs should be prohibited in that State to "married men whose wives have sufficient income to look after them." The solons did not think it was very funny.

Members of the National Federation of Business and Professional Women, the organization which is concentrating the greatest amount of time, money and effort in the battle against the bills, turned mountebanks and staged take-offs on the hearings, as the legislative sessions closed. Salt Lake City set the pattern and the precedent, in a frolic held there by some of the community's most prominent women. In judicial robes and wigs and "solemn owl" spectacles, they naughtily aped the pomposities of their legislative representatives through the proceedings on the bills, while the audience howled and applauded.

Mrs. Cutler's technique did not go unnoted, and in consequence, the reintroduction of "anti-working-wives" legislation in the fu-

ture is expected to draw a cross-barrage of burlesque bills. Drafted with tongue in cheek, they are based, their originators contend, on logic equally sound.

Thus a bill to oust employed married women may be followed by a bill to deny employment to the sons of wealthy men "whose fathers are amply able to provide for them"—or even to dismiss the wealthy dads themselves. There will be bills aimed at brothers and sisters of men whose earnings exceed $2,500 a year, and others making a gigolo of any man who contracts marriage with a girl whose resources make it unnecessary for him to work.

WITH experience of showmanship acquired in many State capitals during the last twenty years for divergent causes, the chairmen of legislative departments of the large organizations taking part in this fight promise to trot out a host of other satirical stunts. They will not be able to count too heavily on a solid feminine front in their warfare, however. There will be individual opponents like Miss Florence Birmingham of Boston, who has run a one-woman campaign against employed married women for a couple of decades.

The most significant unit of dissent will center in the college graduates and the high school girls of this Summer, and those of the last several years, who have not yet found a place for themselves in the world of business. There is a sullen, resolute attitude among a number of this generation, who hold that every one is entitled to a chance, and that a woman who has both an employed husband and a job should be made to yield the job which may mean growth and happiness and a chance at life

for some girl. They can't be laughed off or argued down, even when challenged by the point that a law that operates for them today as spinsters will operate against them tomorrow as wives. The future, they feel, will take care of that.

Fixations in jobs decrease efficiency, the younger women argue, and it is only fair that a woman who has had a living from a certain position for a number of years should relinquish it to some one who needs the salary even more. Views of this sort are shared with enthusiasm by men and women on the relief rolls, hoping for jobs.

IN refutation, Miss Mary Anderson, chief of the Women's Bureau of the Department of Labor, takes up the facts she has compiled since the release of the Biggers report. Her office is now the source of the greatest mass of information on the situation, and the hub of activity in opposition to the "anti-working-wives" bills.

Of the men reporting themselves unemployed in the 1937 registration, Miss Anderson says more than one-third were laborers, whereas less than one-twentieth of the women were so classified; and 18 per cent of the men were skilled artisans, as against less than 1 per cent of the women. The number of jobs interchangeable between the two groups is necessarily small.

Of all gainfully employed women in 1930, at the time of the last census, 3,071,302 were listed as married. Today no one can say accurately what the number of employed married women may be. In 1930, even, those whose marital status was unknown were placed in the "single" columns, and many who designated themselves as married were either widows or deserted wives. Many

others described themselves as earners, although jobless at the time.

Types of employment vary so widely between men and women, Miss Anderson emphasizes, that wholesale firing of the women cannot provide employment for the men in large enough volume to make a dent in the unemployment problem. Her figures show concentration of women workers in a few lines unsuited to male workers. About one-third of all women employed, she reports, are domestics. The smallest percentage of women hold the jobs requiring the greatest skill and training, such as bookkeepers, stenographers, secretaries, file clerks and professional women—the group against which the "anti-working-wives" measures would operate most disastrously.

STUDIES made by Federal and State Labor Departments over a number of years reveal the increasing tendency of married women to take jobs, Miss Anderson says, in order to support dependents outside their own families, rather than to purchase luxuries for themselves. According to Miss Earlene White, president of the National Federation of Business and Professional Women, a recent study of members of her organization shows that among 12,000 replying to questions, about half support entirely or help to support persons other than themselves.

While the United States, long advertised as a paradise for women, inches slowly in the direction of restrictions on their "lif liberty and pursuit of happiness," Argentina has just executed a gallant flourish in the opposite direction. It has adopted a law prohibiting the dismissal of any one from any job on the ground of matrimony.

Journalism Jobs Won by Women

Columbia Survey Finds 41 of 43 Graduates Placed Over A Three-Year Period

Of the forty-three women who were graduated from Columbia University's Graduate School of Journalism during the last three years, forty-one have found employment in journalism and only one has been without a job, it was announced yesterday by Professor Eleanor Carroll. Although the graduates came from nineteen States and three foreign countries, she said, exactly half of the positions they subsequently held were in New York.

Professor Carroll reported that the average weekly salary for women in the class of '37 was $34.83, in the class of '38, $30.96, and in the class of '39, $25.02.

"The youth of the wage earners must be kept in mind," she explained. "The average age is under 25. The fact that journalism is a profession proverbially badly paid save for the glittering exceptions has bearing on the figures."

The women graduates, who in each class averaged about one-quarter of the total enrollment, held twenty-three jobs on newspapers, twenty-one on magazines, sixteen in publicity and three in radio. Professor Carroll noted that magazines annually recruited the graduates best fitted for that field and that publicity was an expanding occupation that offered the lure of quick opportunity and good pay.

Professor Carroll said there was no difference in the school's basis for selection between men and women applicants. In both cases, she added, the deciding factors are aptitude for journalism, academic record, personality, health and "the intangibles which in class formation make for rich and varied total experience."

The preponderance of applicants who have majored in English while at college, she continued, is viewed by the school as undesirable, because different subject-matter is becoming increasingly the basis for employment in journalism.

Professor Carroll pointed out that a high academic record as an undergraduate offered no guarantee of exceptional achievement in the school.

"The total number of women who had extracurricular journalism and newspaper experience before they came to the school is high," she declared.

Job Study Puts Daughter First In Family Aid

Labor Bureau Survey Shows How Women's Wages Are Earned and Spent

By ANNE PETERSEN

Just where the money goes that working women earn is a question that finds an answer in a newly published study made by the Women's Bureau of the Department of Labor. Much of it goes to help support their families, whether they are single or married. Further, says the bureau, their working years are long enough to justify preparation for positions of responsibility both by schools and employers.

To reach these conclusions, the bureau has taken samplings of families in which there are working women and analyzed their economic circumstances and the sources of the family exchequer. Two sections of the country—Cleveland, Ohio, and the State of Utah—supplied the family statistics on which the report is based.

Numerically speaking, the most important contributor to family funds is the unmarried daughter, says the bureau, in both normal families and broken or composite ones.

Women are drawn into employment out of financial need, the figures show, whether they are married or single; and, as a result, their wages are not casual sources of family support, but "supporting pillars" in the homes studied.

Although women form the weaker economic link in family fortunes because of their lower earnings compared to those of men, their sense of responsibility may often be stronger, the report indicates.

Daughters the Chief Pillar

"Unmarried daughters may be the sole support in normal as well as broken families, or they may have the sustaining advantage in a normal family of a father who carries the chief responsibility for family support," says the bureau in leading up to this conclusion. "Even so, very few daughters keep their entire earnings, no matter how limited, for their own use. In families with unmarried sons and daughters, daughters supply more of the family supporting income than sons supply, though earning less than their brothers earn."

As is to be expected, the family environment of three-fifths of the women earners was definitely not the ideal and normal group of father, mother and children. The households in which women workers are found were once normal, but have been visited by misfortunes in the loss or the incapacity of the traditional breadwinner.

"Homes without fathers, or with disabled or aged fathers and husbands; homes without either parent; homes to which married son or daughter, or sister or brother and their children, or father and mother have come when their own homes have collided with misfortune or disaster; homes whose duties for mother and homemaker are over—such is the family environment of the majority of wage-earning women," as described in the report.

Cousins and Aunts Included

The woman working in these families may be daughter, daughter-in-law, sister, mother, wife, cousin or aunt, or any one of the other varied relations to the head of the family.

The largest single group among broken families from which women workers come is the family without a father. In this group, says the report, "the daughters are the women earners in over half the families. In Utah, the mothers are sole women earners in about three-tenths of the families without fathers, as compared to one-fifth in Cleveland, and mother and daughters are earners in nearly one-tenth of the fatherless families in both communities. Broken families with only the father and a daughter at work are relatively few.

"The single daughter living at home is numerically most important as an earner when all families are grouped, for from three to four in every ten women have this status. Three-fourths of such daughters are under thirty years of age."

Wives' Earnings Substantial

Joint earnings in families in which the two at work are father and daughter are, as a rule, higher than those in which the two working members are husband and wife, the study discloses. Wives seek employment to supplement the low annual earning power of their husbands due to irregularity or uncertainty of their work, and also to meet the demands of relatives for financial assistance.

In about one-third of the families surveyed, the wife's or mother's earnings comprise one-half or more of all contributions to the family, and in a larger proportion of families they form from a fourth to a half of all contributions.

Regarding the continuity of employment among the women studied, the bureau found that about half the women have worked ten years or more, with a fourth working at least fifteen years. Between two-fifths and one-half have uninterrupted histories at their jobs. "With this proportion giving long or continuous service to industry," the report concludes, "women cannot rightfully be refused positions of responsibility on the ground that their service to industry is too short in duration to warrant training."

SPINNING ENDLESS YARNS

Serials on Family Life Triangles and Romance Saturate the Air

By ORRIN E. DUNLAP Jr.

THE American air in the daytime is saturated with family troubles, joys and sorrows. Educators are heard to protest that there are too many throbbing serials; too many trivial triangles of love and romance. Parents and teachers complain that radio from morn to night is out of balance. They want more music and news.

Only recently 600 Westchester clubwomen unanimously voted to urge the broadcasters to electrify fewer love dramas, described as an "insult to intelligent women," and concentrate on more programs dealing with home making and child training. Also mothers want fewer contests as bait, fewer calls flashed to children urging them to send in box tops or wrappers.

But there must be some reason or method in the madness of it all. Radio in the United States is said to be built upon the public wishes. The broadcasters assert that they cater to the listeners; that they give them what they want. Their letters are the applause and criticism that form the yardstick of public taste. In fact, listeners are told that through their approval or disapproval they have the power to hold programs on the air or push them off. Ask a radio showman why so many sentimental serials are broadcast and he answers, "Because the public likes them; listeners are engrossed."

* * *

WHERE do these endless serials come from? Ask Elaine Sterne Carrington, who writes two of them, "Pepper Young's Family" and "When a Girl Marries," both heard five times a week and calling for 20,000 words. They trip out of everyday life. They are not based on the imagination, but upon the simple events and experiences of life.

How do you account for the popularity of the daytime serial? Mrs. Carrington was asked.

"A great number of people, especially women at home in city and on farm, are lonely," she replied. "To them the people in the serials become real people who talk to them. They become wrapped up in their ups and downs; their troubles become real and become theirs too. Before they know it they find themselves living along with the radio family. They rejoice and sorrow with them. They find their problems are the same as those of the people who dwell on the wavelengths, and when their problems are solved the listeners' may fade too. Radio becomes a mental uplift, also a mirror of life to them; they are made more a part of the world, and each day they keep a rendezvous with these unseen neighbors who come along to visit and to interrupt time which otherwise would be humdrum and empty."

* * *

"LISTENERS are child-like in their belief of the radio story," continued Mrs. Carrington. "They become part of it. They are pulling for the character to come out on top."

How can you write two serials without mixing the stories, and where do you get the ideas? the interviewer asked.

"The trick, if it may be called a trick," she replied, "is to let the listener hear his or her own problem solved. They learn without being taught; unconsciously they learn without being lectured through a cut-and-dried script. Dialogue is the keynote. On the radio as in the theatre, the basic ideas plus good dialogue is everything.

"My suggestion to those who want to write for radio is to look around their own home and into their own lives for the things they know and understand best. It is from such stuff that serials are made. But radio time is fleeting; and the ever-hungry microphone consumes one page of dialogue in a minute. A 15-minute story calls for twelve pages.

"It is important to remember that the story must be one that tugs at the heart, for this is the element that brings the listener back day after day. The situation must be one which they experienced. It's the common things in life and simplicity that are the driving force of the serial.

"The secret of writing two shows at once without conflict of characters and plots is to completely shut the door on the one group as soon as their tale of the week is finished."

* * *

AMERICAN families seem to have five "big" problems in common, Mrs. Carrington observes, based upon the mail she receives from all parts of the country. She lists them as follows:

Should the 16 or 17 year old boy or girl be permitted to use the family automobile?

Should children be given an allowance or be paid for chores such as cutting the grass, shoveling snow or milking the cow?

Should youngsters be given a latchkey or should the family sit up and wait for Johnny to come home? (This question pertaining more to boys.)

How late should the 16 or 17 year old Mary stay out in the evening?

Why cannot a boy decide for himself whether he is to go to college or go to work. For example, if a young man wants to be an airplane pilot why should his parents insist that he follow in his father's footsteps in the grocery store?

Following the formula "write about something you know," Mrs. Carrington works three weeks ahead of the broadcasting schedule. She completes the episodes for the ensuing week on Thursday nights. Until Monday she forgets radio.

* * *

IN planning for the broadcasts, first she lays out the yarn's general scheme or the direction it will follow for a year. This is broken down into a monthly synopsis and a day to day outline. Then it is time to put the words into the characters' mouths.

"Monday morning I start to dictate about 10 o'clock and I keep at it until midnight," explained Mrs. Carrington. "I do take time out, and have an occasional nap. I may cover two or three episodes a day. When five are finished they are typed and overhauled by numerous corrections. It's all sort of a seance. While dictating I see the whole affair acted; the lines spoken. Interruptions are disastrous."

* * *

IN no category of broadcasting is so much repetition tolerated as in the serials. A number of sketches are broadcast on both the morning and afternoon air, and one New York station devotes two hours nightly in repeating from recordings sketches heard earlier in the day on the networks.

No end of characters created by radio are traveling down the wave lengths. On and on they go from morning until night, running from family to family, from the O'Neills to Billy and Betty, and from "Stepmother" to "Big Sister" or "Manhattan Mother," from Lorenzo Jones to Young Widder Brown. The "theatres" in which these actors fall to earth to stalk the home stage are envisaged as the kitchen, where the audience may be cooking, ironing or dishwashing; or the listener may be waxing the floors, making the beds, rocking the cradle, sweeping the carpets, washing the windows, or the baby. The daytime audience is visualized as made up of busy people. Nevertheless, the cry is heard from city clubwomen that daytime radio is dull, blunt and all one-sided.

A survey of daytime radio programs is being planned by the Women's National Radio Committee, according to a decision reached during the past week, "to determine whether daytime broadcasts actually interest home women and shut-ins, for whom they are particularly designed."

"Members of our listening groups have complained at the monotony of being obliged either to listen to one 'talkie' or serial after another, or else turn off the radio," said Mrs. Samuel Kubie, who will serve as chairman of the Daytime Programs Committee. "They also contend that many of the daytime programs are an affront to the intelligence of the home-woman who has a wide range of interests.

"While these complaints have prompted the survey, we are starting it without preconceived prejudices. The women who have written to us may represent a minority of the daytime audience. On the other hand, however, although a volume of fan mail has in all probability been responsible for continuance of some of these programs which have been on the air for several years, does writing in for leaflets or information and premiums really constitute approval of the program itself! That is what we want to find out."

February 11, 1940

WILLKIE SPEECHES ON LABOR ASSAILED

Tobin Says Candidate's Talk at Pittsburgh Proved Him 'Master Legal Trickster'

WOMEN JOIN IN ATTACK

Take Umbrage at Remark That Labor Secretaryship Is a 'Man's Job'

Wendell L. Willkie's recent speeches on labor drew sharp retorts yesterday from President Roosevelt's supporters. Daniel J. Tobin, chairman of the labor division of the Democratic National Committee, asserted that the Pittsburgh speech showed the Republican candidate as a "master legal trickster." A group of women associated with the Norris-La Guardia Committee of Independent Voters took umbrage at Mr. Willkie's remark that the Secretaryship of Labor is a "man's job."

In a statement issued through the Democratic National Committee, Mr. Tobin repeated charges made earlier that subsidiaries of the Commonwealth and Southern Corporation that Mr. Willkie formerly headed had employed labor espionage agencies and purchased guns and tear gas shells and that Ernest T. Weir, chairman of the Republican Finance Committee, was fighting the National Labor Relations Act in court.

He also accused Mr. Willkie of planning to bring about the collapse of the act by leaving enforcement to local communities.

"Height of Futility"

"To favor the principles of the National Labor Relations Act and yet to favor in the same breath the local administration of those principles—that is the height of futility," Mr. Tobin continued. "For Mr. Willkie must know from experience that if the enforcement of that act were left to the local communities, then the whole act would collapse."

Mr. Willkie's remark that a man should hold the job of Secretary of Labor was interpreted by women at the Norris-La Guardia committee as an attack on women in public office as well as on Miss Frances Perkins, who has held the office through Mr. Roosevelt's two Administrations.

Those who joined in rebuking the Republican candidate for making it were Dr. Emily Hickman, history professor at New Jersey College for Women; President Kathryn Starbuck of Skidmore College; Mrs. Henrietta Roelofs, secretary of the public affairs committee of the national board of the Y. W. C. A.; Mrs. Geline MacDonald Bowman, past president of the National Federation of Business and Professional Women's Clubs; Gertrude Ely of Bryn Mawr College, and Josephine Schain, chairman of the National Committee on the Cause and Cure of War.

Women to Speak in West

Plans for an invasion of the Middle West by a group of women speakers were announced by the Women's Division of the Democratic National Committee. It gets under way this week, the speakers concentrating on Illinois, Ohio, Iowa and Nebraska. The invaders include Mrs. J. Borden Harriman, Minister to Norway; Mrs. Ruth Bryan Owen Rohde, former Minister to Denmark; Mrs. Anthony J. Drexel Biddle, wife of the Ambassador to Poland; Mrs. Nellie Tayloe Ross, Director of the United States Mint, and Miss Helen Gahagan, screen actress and national committeewoman from California.

October 6, 1940

Clare Boothe Talks About Her Writing

The Author of "Europe in the Spring" and "The Women"
Discusses Her Methods of Work

By ROBERT VAN GELDER

CLARE BOOTHE said that she doesn't like most people. "I have a few friends with whom I spend most of my time." It was 5 o'clock in the afternoon and Miss Boothe ordered a pitcher of hot water, a lemon and a knife. She cut the lemon, squeezed the juice into the hot water and drank it.

She said that she found the idea for her first successful piece of writing one night after she had kept Henry R. Luce, her husband, waiting for half an hour outside the ladies' room of a night club. "When I came out he asked what had kept me and I told him that I had been talking to the girls. So he said, 'What about?' Not casually. He wanted to know. It was the first time his mind ever had turned upon this subject and he is a man with great curiosity. When he wonders about something, he wants answers. So I thought about what we had said, trying to pass the gist of it on to him, and it struck me—actually as a surprise, though, of course it shouldn't have been—that all we had talked about had been utterly impossible tripe.

"That week-end we were going to White Sulphur, and were no sooner there than my husband was called back to the office. I still was thinking about the women in the ladies' room and beyond them to some unmitigated heels it had been my misfortune to know, and so, while I was stranded there at White Sulphur, I mentally, and with pen and ink, gathered some of these heels around a bridge table, set them to talking, and let it run. I wrote for three days, with no outline, following the very simplest story, and at the end of three days had the play, 'The Women,' all down.

"I suppose that it wouldn't have been hard to tell that there was no outline. With the best will in the world, you can't hand the plot much; it was very—well, indistinctly plotted. But I think it caught the people—as I knew them."

She works, by habit, swiftly, using "pen and ink, because my handwriting is so bad that it is a chore to read back over it. When I use a typewriter I keep reading, over and over, the last few lines that I've written and that holds me up." She does not cherish her original drafts: when a theatre producer asks for a few scene changes, she is apt to turn up with the play almost entirely rewritten. But all of the rewriting must be done by herself—no managerial hand is allowed to insert a few lines—and she guards this right to complete authorship jealously. "I believe I prefer to write books, because a book is your own—every one hasn't been at you with suggestions and advice."

She said that she was a natural "night writer," but had to change around after her second marriage "because if I'd gone on working at night I never would have seen my husband, who works very hard all day and has a chance to relax only in the evenings." In order to obtain the privacy necessary for writing, "I either have the telephone cut off, if I'm here in New York, or if I'm in Greenwich I leave word that I'm at the golf course or in the swimming pool or out in a boat, or something—any activity that can be understood to be worth-while and interesting."

She said that she has just about given up worrying about plots. "In 'Margin for Error' I had the same man killed twice and thought that finally I had concocted a really good situation. Of course it wasn't very long before I learned that this is one of the oldest devices known to detective-story writers—and readers. So now I'm just using plots as they come. The newest thing I'm working on is simply the story of Tristan and Isolde so far as basic plot structure is concerned."

Miss Boothe said that when she was a child she knew that she was going to be an actress or a writer—"it wasn't a plan; I simply was certain that I'd be one or the other." When very young she was given a chance as an actress, "and I played the part so badly that I knew there was no hope

Clare Boothe.

there." "I married and lived for quite a few years among people who had no possible interest in books or writing—didn't know anything about them or want to. And for a long time I forgot my own interest. But when I had my divorce my only thought was, 'What magazine will I go to work for?'—it was as natural as that—and I managed to get a job on Vanity Fair."

She wrote three plays that went unproduced. Then "Abide With Me," a study of a young woman married to a dipsomaniac, was brought to Broadway and died writing, penned by a great liberal a very few performances. "The Women," produced in 1936, was by no means raved about by the reviewers, but it developed as a lasting hit. "Kiss the Boys Goodbye," two years later, also had to meet some very sharp criticism, and also became a popular success. "Margin for Error" had less of a rough ride, but neither was it so successful.

Miss Boothe's "Europe in the Spring," a racing mixture of first-rate journalism and entirely justified preachment, was the result of a decision made last February to "go to Europe and see about the war." To obtain permission to use her passport she had to travel as a journalist so she signed a contract with a magazine. On her return here in June she wrote a 10,000-word article and sent it to Life, which is published by her husband. "The editor sent it back with a note saying that Life was a magazine, not a book publisher. And by then I'd found that I had a lot more to say than I possibly could get into an article, so I went to the country, worked furiously for six weeks and emerged with the book."

The book has had—as the plays never did—both good notices and a fairly satisfactory sale. It was written for, and should have, a very large audience. Analysts in plenty have, with more or less dryness, called attention to that lethargy, that apparent sense of endless time ahead, that checked and strangled the war effort of the democracies in Europe so that they seemed like lazy bankrupts waiting for the sheriff, helpless to make more than a spasmodic, instinctive effort, as the inevitable force closed down upon them.

Miss Boothe is, if anything, a made analyst, but surely she is a natural dramatist. And effectively, as a dramatist should, she gives point for the mass of readers to that main lesson learned at first hand in Europe last Spring—that there is no time, that the years of preparation are running out, that action cannot be delayed if it is to have meaning.

WRITERS PICTURE BOOM TOWN RISKS

Daniels and Four Others Tell House Inquiry on Migrants Defense Housing Is Poor

'LUCK' IN NO EPIDEMICS

Some Witnesses Say Workers Are Not Spending Wildly— Forced Saving Weighed

By BYRON DARNTON
Special to THE NEW YORK TIMES.

WASHINGTON, March 24—A group of newspaper and magazine investigators told a Congressional committee today about conditions they had observed at defense centers in the country where cantonments and industrial plants were being built. Their reports were far from cheerful.

Among the things the committee heard were these:

It was largely a matter of luck that there had been no serious epidemics during the Winter.

Housing generally has been frightful.

In many defense towns no pretense has been made of enforcing compulsory school attendance.

Moral conditions in many places are at the usual boom-town level.

Respectable residents of the defense boom towns are becoming sensitive over the amount of public attention they have received; they fear that outsiders think they all live in rough, tough places where sin runs rampant and liquor flows in the gutters.

Jonathan Daniels a Witness

This testimony was heard by the House Committee Investigating Destitute Migrants, headed by Representative Tolan of California. The witnesses were Jonathan Daniels, editor of The Raleigh News and Observer; Samuel Grafton, New York Post columnist; Miss Katherine Smith, reporter for The Washington Times-Herald; Duncan Aikman, national correspondent for PM, and Pare Lorenz, of McCall's.

Mr. Daniels told the committee that the fact that no epidemics had developed was proof that "once again America's luck has held."

"Thousands of men—and women and children, too—were pulled into little towns, some of them without any sewage facilities, most of them without adequate housing, health and feeding facilities, not to speak of school and recreational opportunities," Mr. Daniels said.

"Undoubtedly the boom towns of this defense spending are like the boom towns of the past. There is the same crowding of the beer joints, the same pressure on facilities of bed and board. There are the same camp followers in them.

"I have been impressed with the strength and ingenuity of the folk; indeed, most of them seemed to me from Maine to Texas to look and seem as I have imagined the pioneers. Not many of them felt sorry for themselves. But a good many of them did keep a sense—sometimes a saving sense—of economic insecurity in the midst of boom jobs and boom wages."

Grafton Found Prudence

Mr. Grafton said that many New England business men had told him that this was not a "spending boom" like that of the World War. There were no evidences of a "silk shirt era," he reported, although some of the young people, now holding jobs for the first time since they left high school, were letting their money slip through their fingers.

Members of the committee wanted to know if some form of compulsory saving should be set up for men drawing big wages on defense jobs. Representative Osmers of New Jersey, for instance, suggested special social security payments by such workers and their employers and increased government participation, so that unemployment insurance payments might be kept up for as long as six months after the boom had burst. Some of the journalistic witnesses thought that might be a good idea.

Mr. Grafton said that it was necessary to set up some sort of Federal emergency fund to deal with the social problems that would arise with the end of the boom.

"You have to look forward," he continued, "to the day when it will be necessary to send agents into some of these communities just as Red Cross agents were sent to starving European countries after the last war."

Lorenz Urges Planning

Mr. Lorenz advocated more careful planning of community services before construction got under way in rural and semi-rural defense centers.

"If the Army can expand 680 per cent and still provide clean water for the troops to drink and sewerage services," he said, "then I don't see why the same facilities cannot be made available to the army of workmen that go into backwoods areas to work on defense construction jobs."

Decent planning, he declared, would speed the defense program, for it would mean the providing of roads for better transportation and of health safeguards which would obviate delays caused by sickness.

"The greatest social problem arising from defense migration," he continued, "is the public health problem. And yet our greatest defense concentration points have been in the very areas of the South where health provisions are the barest."

Mr. Lorenz said he realized that planning was a "dread word" but he thought a little of it would accomplish wonders. He suggested that future contracts with construction companies carry clauses requiring the contractors to provide decent housing and health facilities on jobs undertaken in areas where such facilities did not exist.

Daniels Puts Onus on All

Mr. Daniels pointed out that the call for speed had been persistent and that proper planning had been impossible in many instances.

"In general," he said, "the responsibility for the conditions which existed in the first push of defense belongs to the whole American people, who demanded such a push and demand it still. Sometimes undoubtedly military officials seemed to act less in preparation of communities than in surprise. I remember one official of a defense-inundated town said to me:

" 'We didn't have any more idea of this happening that a hog has of Sunday.' "

In many communities, Mr. Daniels said, the authorities were worried so much about what to do with migrant children who appeared voluntarily to attend school that no effort was made to get the truants into the classrooms.

"There has been no time or facilities," he explained, "to take care of children coming into the world, not to speak of the children going into schools. In one military area a count by qualified investigators disclosed that fifty-eight women had arrived who were expecting babies within three months, without plans—or proper place—for their arrival. The health officer in Monterey County, California, said not long ago, 'No woman has had her baby in the street yet, but a good many births take place under very undesirable conditions.' "

Aikman Tells of High Hopes

Mr. Aikman told the committee that in recent months he had traveled 12,000 miles about the country, talking to many defense workers and aspirant defense workers. Many of them seemed to think, he said, that the defense program was a sort of restoration of the frontier, because it seemed to be a provider of boundless opportunity. But he considered it a "phony frontier" because it meant three-month or six-month jobs, or, at the best, two-year jobs.

He agreed with some other witnesses that employers in some cases preferred migrant workers to home town workers on the theory that they were harder to organize into unions and might go back home when the boom was over.

Miss Smith, who investigated living conditions at Charlestown, Ind., where a powder plant is being built, said that workers' wives were in terror about the approaching Spring thaw, because they were getting shelter in all sorts of shacks in communities that had no sewerage systems.

CHAPTER 4

Women and World II

Representative Jeannette Rankin telephones
from the House cloakroom after she
was booed and hissed for casting her vote
against war with Japan, December 8, 1941.
Courtesy Compix.

HUNDREDS MARRY TO ESCAPE DRAFT

Manhattan License Bureau Has Busiest Day of Year as Couples Form Line

BROOKLYN TURNS AWAY 300

Queens Sets Record for 1940 —Staten Island Has a Rush —Men Between 21 and 28

As Congress continues to debate the merits of conscription, hundreds of young men have decided they prefer marriage to the draft. As a result, yesterday was the busiest day of the year at the Manhattan Marriage License Bureau.

In Brooklyn the Marriage License Bureau was so crowded that ten policemen and a sergeant had to be called out to maintain order. The bureau in Queens set a new record for the year and in Staten Island the number of licenses issued was far in excess of normal.

"This is the biggest day we've had this year," reported Julius J. Erosen, chief clerk of the Manhattan bureau.

"And," he added, "I hear most couples talking of the proposed draft now pending before Congress. I think it's the reason for this large crowd. We've had fifty to sixty more couples down here than usual and we were able to take care of all of them and send everybody home happy.

"At 8:30 this morning there was a line of forty couples waiting for the bureau to open. When the bureau closed at 1:45 P.M., 188 marriage licenses had been issued and seventy civil weddings had taken place in the city chapel."

In Brooklyn the line of applicants began forming at 7:30 A.M., an hour and a half before the office opens. At noon, when the office closes, 250 couples had obtained their licenses and 300 other couples were turned away and told to come back next week.

The bureau office in Queens was kept open an hour beyond closing time to accommodate all of the couples. Of the 139 males who took out licenses in that borough 130 were between 21 and 28 years old.

Dispatches from other cities told of similar increases in marriages. In Chicago, The United Press said, twenty-four clerks were added to the staff of the county clerk to accommodate more than 600 applicants for licenses, and despite this added staff sixty couples were turned away. At Philadelphia, twenty clerks were added to handle 247 applications, and at Columbus, Ohio, the rush was described as greater than in June, traditional month of weddings.

August 11, 1940

YOUTH LOOKS OVER HOMESPUN VIRTUES

Honesty, Fidelity and Justice Elicit Both Huzzahs and Heckling in Air Forum

The homespun moral principles of honesty, fidelity, love, equality and tolerance came in for a round of applause tempered with a bit of heckling last night when "youth" took over "America's Town Meeting of the Air" broadcast from Town Hall. Two young men and two young women, all in their twenties, saw youth strong in its desire to achieve the American ideal—"the democratic moral code"—but admitted there was confusion in the ranks of the young on the matter of method.

Participants in the debate on "What Is American Youth's Moral Code?" were, in their speaking order, Jean Sarasy, third-year student at Stephens College, Columbia, Mo.; Mary Draper, a senior at Vassar College; Melvin Evans, clerk in a Forty-second Street bookshop, and Stanford Bissell, president of the Young Men's Board of Trade of New York.

Miss Sarasy opened the hour's forum with a speech calling for reaffirmation of the homely virtues of "honesty, tolerance, fidelity, justice, self-respect, and duty to those around you." Terming these "permanent principles" that young people learned from their elders, she urged that they be restored to a prominent role in the social scheme by training better mothers to educate better children.

Calls Careers Secondary

In essence, she urged that women stay in their homes and do a better job of rearing their children. Careers, she said, should be only a secondary consideration. This point of view was later challenged by Miss Draper.

Mr. Evans affirmed his belief in "the democratic morality," but charged that it has been degraded by the adults of today's world.

"We are still trying to pour the new civilization into the old moral bottles," he asserted, pointing out that modern youth is faced with the fact social equality does not exist, that "justice, moral and legal, is beyond the reach of great groups of us," and that "special privilege often defeats common weal."

The bookstore clerk, formerly a student at the University of Pittsburgh, closed with the challenge: "Shall we live our moral code—or will we ride Nietzsche's wild horse?"

Mr. Bissell, confessing that he could not follow Mr. Evans's "philosophical reasoning," said he agreed with the latter that morals are "the laws of nature, which are as definite and unvarying as the laws of mathematics."

As the basis of his code, he laid down the precept that each man should be free to do that work for which he is best fitted, adding the suggestion that "censorship and monopoly, taxes and strikes, and government relief" hamper the realization of this freedom. He declared that there should be no compromising of this freedom merely to cope with "the expediency of the moment."

Miss Draper asserted that women should take their place "on a par with men." After quoting statistics to prove that working women can run healthy, happy homes, she averred that women should strive to do things outside the home that will help men "to build a world that makes more sense."

Queries on Home and Job

In the question period following the speeches, Miss Draper came in for a good deal of interrogation—largely from the males in the audience—on the advisability of a woman running both her home and a job. She contended that both could be accomplished simultaneously without detriment to either until the question came: "Do you think a woman could be both the President of the United States and a mother?"

"You've got me there," Miss Draper replied. "If a woman ever got to be President, I think she'd have to concentrate on that."

Miss Sarasy, who stanchly upheld religion as the basis of morality, was asked whether an atheist could have a moral code. She agreed that he could have "good principles."

In response to another query, Mr. Bissell asserted that "education today does not train us to think straight."

George V. Denny, Town Hall moderator, listed as the "prize question" of the evening a query from a City College freshman. The question, "Do you think a moral code should be based on a given economic situation or should economic conditions be adapted to a moral code?", was not fully answered from the platform.

November 21, 1941

'I'm Following You'

By Helen B. Sweedy

"I'M following you." Depending on his choice of a mate, a soldier hears these words from the lips of his wife with elation or with uneasy doubt. Of course, some of the married-on-leavers are still too bewitched to guess the effect of uncomfortable living conditions on the tempers of brides. And surprises are often in store for the long-married man, when the trials and uncertainties of Army life are suffered by the woman he thought he knew so thoroughly.

Recently a great deal of space has been used in the public prints exhorting the families of service men to stay at home. The reasons given — congested living quarters, travel space used for non-military purposes, unsatisfactory schooling and health hazards for children—all are valid. Camp sites were chosen to meet military needs and naturally without regard for migrating families. In isolated areas women may expect no help in finding housing or work—if either is to be had. Even communities well adjusted to the demands of a peacetime Army find it hard to cope with the enormous expansion since 1940.

THE problems to be solved for families near an Army base shift and change with the personnel. The outgoing group may have been "Regular Army"—in which case the wives are old hands at following their husbands, and need no help in making adjustments. The incoming group may be primarily enlisted or drafted men of an age to have family responsibilities. Then the agencies find themselves buried in requests for information.

Admittedly it is these families who make the headaches. A newcomer to Army life must first have help in finding her soldier among the thousands, then she must find a spot to live in. Next, if she is empty of pocket, she must have a job. If the camp is near well-established communities there may be work for waitress, laundress, domestic or sales-clerk, or jobs in war industries. Perhaps there may be opportunities in post exchanges or in camp laundries.

If the family has enough to live on, the wife must fill in time, because a soldier does not keep bankers' hours, and his moments at home are extremely limited. The USO has reading, writing and handicraft rooms, gives "married couples" dances and picnics, and encourages women to cook and serve simple luncheons to themselves at cost. Many wives with time on their hands work for the Red Cross, making bandages, driving, knitting and sewing.

BLISSFUL in our ignorance of the difficulties to be encountered, we wives of the new civilian Army set off—the adaptable and the unadaptable, the placid and the tempestuous, the saver and the spendthrift. We realize only that this move may be the last one in this country, and though we have been branded "selfish" for thus following the natural desire to be near our husbands as long as possible, our soldiers must share that epithet. Reluctant as they are to see their wives let in for lowly quarters and lonely hours, they are undeniably pleased when stern orders are ignored and the train pulls in with that one particular woman on it.

That glorious reunion on the station platform is, to be honest, the fleeting honeymoon moment. After that comes the mad flight to find accommodations, for more often than not your husband has lacked time and transportation to house-hunt. If it is your first experience in trying to live near an Army camp, you doubtless will have a picture in your mind of a "suitable" place. After a few hours of finding nothing at all, you will gladly settle for a bed, and you will wearily hope that it's clean.

ARMY wives, who share hopes and fears as well as more material items like spare rooms and groceries, form friendships that survive changes of station. This Army is peripatetic, and if you are following your husband you must be ready to move — either to another camp or, when the last and dreaded order comes, back home. You live in suitcases, and many a wife shies from taking the last thing from the last bag because that is a sure sign that Daddy will come home with orders to move.

It can happen with a week's notice, or none. So to take a few lares and penates with you may be a brave gesture, but to take none and make the best of what's available is far more sensible. Think of all the worrying you don't have to do over lost crates and trunks!

Thus we try, we wives of this huge new Army, to be what our men think we are, to meet with good grace a few discomforts which are nothing compared to the changes and responsibilities they face. We try not to be spoilsports and crybabies and to keep worries to ourselves. We learn to get along with our neighbors. Incorrigible flirts learn that they embarrass their husbands and their husbands' mates alike.

WHY do we submit to this course of sprouts—and embrace it gladly? The reason is universal, and one needs only to quote one girl to speak for the colonel's lady as well as Judy O'Grady. In answer to the question, "Why do you think it's worth while to follow your husband?" she said, "How do Tom and I know how long we can be together? He might be ordered overseas next week. So we figure that even a few hours are better than nothing. When he's sent over, I'll go back and get a job. But until that happens I'm going wherever he goes." Then this young girl in the USO club put a finishing daub of paint on the wooden bowl she was decorating, stored it away and was off to meet her soldier.

Our merit badge is a "Gee, I'm glad you're here, darling!" As long as we get that response I'm afraid no amount of outside moaning about "selfishness" will hit us very hard. Of course, if Uncle Sam says, "No more," that will be different. Till then, boys, we're following you.

October 3, 1943

Soldiers Are Told Status of Alien Brides

WASHINGTON, March 30—Although the Army reports that comparatively few United States soldiers stationed in foreign countries are marrying aliens, the United States Immigration and Naturalization Service and the House Immigration and Naturalization Committee have received several letters from alien brides of American soldiers asking for a definition of their status.

Girls who are citizens of another country and married to United States citizens may enter the United States as non-quota immigrants provided they meet the regular requirements for such immigration. One is that they should be not likely to become public charges.

If the American soldier dies, however, his alien widow cannot enter this country free of the quota. If the petition for her entry was filed before his death, it is then revoked.

On the other hand, alien husbands of United States citizens, for instance Australians who marry American Army nurses or Wacs, are not allowed to enter this country outside the quota. They receive a preferred status under the quota.

Since 1922 an American woman cannot lose her citizenship by marrying an alien, nor can an alien woman gain such citizenship by being married to an American. However, most countries still extend their citizenship to alien women who marry their citizens, according to Edward J. Shaughnessy, special assistant to the Commissioner of Immigration and Naturalization.

A child born outside the United States, one of whose parents is not a United States citizen, can inherit citizenship only if he lives five years in this country while he is between the ages of 13 and 21.

March 31, 1944

Marriage Banns Across the Sea

By ISABELLE MALLET

A BIG ship edges alongside a New York pier, the rails lined with the girls GI Joe didn't leave behind him. Eighty excited war brides are entering America for the first time and on the pier there is a flurry of preparation. A harassed naval officer says, "They're prettier than the last bunch"; a trim Red Cross official hopes her list of expected arrivals checks with the bright faces crowding the decks.

Everywhere is an air of expectancy—and some apprehension, for the foreign girl whom GI Joe married abroad is coming to live with his family until the shooting stops, and ahead of her lies a real test of wartime romance. Four hundred such war brides have already arrived in New York from Italy, Algiers, Morocco, Wales, Scotland, Ireland, England, Iceland, Burma.

Streaming down the gangplank, with or without babies, the wives register everything from bewildered apprehension to slap-happy confidence. They find plenty of welcome waiting on the pier. Each one is expected and her support is undertaken (in writing) by her waiting American in-laws. While the Red Cross ship-meeting committee checks the wives, nurses' aides keep a competent eye on the babies, photographers catch close-ups of hopeful smiles, the canteen workers serve hot coffee.

The atmosphere is businesslike but friendly. The Red Cross routes most of the arrivals on to their new homes all over the country. But some in-laws have come to meet the ship and wait in nervous huddles beyond the customs barriers. An apple-cheeked Irish girl, piloted by a Red Cross worker, approaches a group of solid Brooklyn citizens, asks incredulously: "Are you Jim's family?" and is immediately surrounded. As the family moves off, they are discussing Jim's size and weight as a baby. The first step in the long process of assimilation has begun.

In spite of dire prophecy on both sides of the ocean, this process worked out 80 per cent successfully after the last war. World War I brought over 8,000 foreign daughters-in-law, French and German wives predominating. By 1925 it was estimated that four out of every five of our immigrants-by-marriage had vanished into the normal stream of American life without a ripple to show for it. The unlucky 20 per cent failed, according to the War Department, because of "national and cultural differences." So far World War II statistics are more encouraging. Red Cross Home Service reports out of the 400 wives admitted through New York, only one needs a round-trip.

MOST of the marital pioneers come here against the advice of parental and religious authority in their native lands. Back home they were warned against the hazards of war-widowhood in a strange country. "But," say the majority of brides interviewed, "our husbands insisted that we come. They wanted us to be with their own families—safe in America." Some admit frankly they were afraid of being forgotten by new husbands moving up to European fronts. "So I thought I'd better remind him that I'm part of his family now," says a matter-of-fact Welsh girl. "I'll be waiting for him in his own home when the armistice is signed."

Most of these young women come from countries where war is a first-hand experience. America seems like Arcady to nerves strained by bombs, blackouts and invasions. So the wives determine to get here, correspond briskly with their American in-laws, arrange the necessary formalities and arrive with a little star-dust in their eyes.

IN spite of the star-dust, most of them carry a useful equipment of home-making ability. Even in the excitement of arrival they speak of definite plans. An Icelandic bride—tall, regal, golden-haired—on her way to Chicago says she "wields a competent needle" and plans to be the family dressmaker. A Scottish lassie talks proudly of her Cordon Bleu accomplishments and hopes her mother-in-law in Louisiana will let her preside in the kitchen. An Italian girl has learned English, studied hair-dressing, hoping to become a self-supporting member of her new family.

Do these entangling alliances spell menace to the American girl waiting at home for her GI? The figures are not alarming in proportion to the number of men overseas. An English wife, former canteen worker in Africa and England, who has met hundreds of GI's, volunteers this information: "American soldiers talk and read more about home than any of the other fighting men. GI's don't pay serious attention to outsiders when they're homesick. And American girls are fearfully clever, aren't they? They write so many letters, their men are always homesick."

In any case, GI Joe has invited his girl to come and spend a lifetime with us. It is part and parcel of our national tradition to help her settle in.

November 26, 1944

FAITHLESS WIVES DECRIED
Opera Star, Back From Camp Tour, Urges Head Shaving

Faithless wives of fighting GI's are "the greatest criminals in the world," and ought to have their hair shaved off just as was done to women of Nazi-dominated countries who fraternized with the enemy, Miss Grace Moore, opera star, declared yesterday at La Guardia Field on her return aboard an Army plane from a two months' United Service Organization camp shows tour in Europe.

She also criticized prominent artists, who neglect to offer their services for GI shows.

Miss Moore was equally bitter about sweethearts who jilt service men after promising to wait their return, and said that these, too, should be punished.

"These women are contributing as much to the seriousness of fraternization in Germany as any other element," she asserted. "The boys become bitter and disillusioned. It makes it tough for all American women. The women who have not been true are driving their men into the arms of European women."

July 28, 1945

London GI Wives Storm a Hall; Protest Delay in Coming to U.S.

'We Want Ships' and 'Our Husbands,' They Shout—Tumult Drowns Out Speaker—Commission Studies Problem

LONDON, Oct. 11—Comdr. Herbert Agar, special assistant to Ambassador John G. Winant at the United States Embassy, had the unenviable task at a stormy meeting here tonight of explaining to hundreds of excited British wives of American service men the reasons for the delay in sending 40,000 of them to join their husbands in America.

Above high-pitched interjections of "why a priority for film stars,"

he told them that they were not "completely lost and forgotten people" and that officers assigned to study the problem have arrived in Britain and have already received statistics for an investigation.

The American Embassy announced that the mission was headed by Howard K. Travers, head of the visa section of the State Department, with two representatives of the War Department and one each from the Departments of Justice and Health.

'FORGOTTEN WIVES' MARCH IN LONDON

Wives of American service men parading yesterday before the United States Embassy during demonstration in which they demanded transportation to this country. *Associated Press Radiophoto*

They are expected to return to Washington with their report in a week.

Nearly 1,000 women, many with babies in their arms, queued up outside the Caxton Hall hours before the meeting, sponsored by the Married Women's Association, began. They had come from all parts of the country. The small hall was full to overflowing and many of the young women tried to rush the police barrier when admission was no longer possible.

Mrs. Catherine Domer of Sale, Cheshire, wife of First Lieut. Terence Harry Domer of Youngstown, said:

"I don't know what will happen. The police won't allow a queue of more than 200 outside the hall. All we aim at is to get our grievances heard. I am fighting for less lucky people than myself. Many other brides have babies, are desperately hard up and are uncertain about the future."

Hundreds of the wives who could not get into the meeting stood outside the doorway chanting "We want ships." Later they marched through London's West End to the United States Embassy, where they paraded up and down shouting, "We want our husbands" and "We want transport."

Inside the hall Commander Agar was received with a burst of applause.

"I do not know that there is an answer that is going to satisfy anybody," he said. "It would be very unfair and dishonest if I did not say that. A lot is being done, but in terms of what you want to hear—the date when you can go home—there is no answer."

Cries of dissent drowned out Commander Agar when he attempted to remind the women that they had signed a statement before marriage regarding transportation to the United States.

Nearly all the women had something to say, mostly all at the same time, when questions were invited.

Eighteen-year-old Mrs. Louis Sherman, whose husband is in Milwaukee, held a young baby high above her head and asked why a percentage of wives could not be sent along with the homegoing soldiers.

Commander Agar, whose reply was barely audible over the tumult, said that the troops had to be sent home first.

The excitement died down when Commander Agar concluded with the compliment: "You have been reasonable and sincere. I thank you for your kindness."

However, the young women surged toward him as he tried to leave the hall. Finally he left by a side door.

The chairman of the meeting, Mrs. F. Howes of Manchester, speaking with an American flavor in her Lancashire accent, said:

"We are not an official body. This is not a protest meeting, we are just a group of girls who are feeling pretty sick."

A resolution was adopted expressing the belief that the marriages could play an important part in strengthening goodwill between American and Britain and urging that immediate steps be taken to provide transport. The resolution will be sent to the United States mission now studying the problem.

One of the women, 21-year-old Mrs. J. R. Kaffler, whose husband is now demobilized in Philadelphia, short-circuited the American Embassy, which announced that there was "no hope of immediate amelioration," and wrote to President Truman. "There is enough unhappiness in this world without making any more," her letter said. "We are trying very hard to get to our husbands. If you can help, we will be very grateful."

Many of the wives said they were receiving letters from their husbands chiding them because of the belief that their wives were not really trying to join them.

U. S. TO ALLOT SHIPS FOR GI BRIDES SOON

Hope Held Out to Girls Waiting in Europe—Officials Study 2 Stowaway Cases Here

Large-scale transportation in the near future of GI brides and their children from Europe to the United States was assured yesterday by the Immigration and Naturalization Service as it investigated the cases of two British stowaways —a GI wife and a sweetheart— who arrived Sunday aboard two troop transports.

Meanwhile the Navy, which had denied the presence of one girl when the Europa docked here Sunday, revised its story and admitted, to no one's surprise, that she had stowed away on the transport. The girl, Miss Kathleen Sybil Moody, a 19-year-old waitress, was turned over to immigration officials and will be held on Ellis Island until her case is decided.

The girl who was smuggled into Boston along with her 8-months-old son, had better luck, however. The Immigration Service paroled her for thirty days in the custody of her husband, Ralph J. Maresco, 25, a discharged service man from Corona, Queens. They were reunited in Boston and will come here today.

Decision Expected Soon

Discussing the two cases, a spokesman for the Immigration and Naturalization Service declared at headquarters in Philadelphia that the entire question of GI brides was expected to be settled soon. The important issue, he said, was to convince the 50,000 girls awaiting shipment in the United Kingdom and Europe, along with their 30,000 children, that they should not try to enter this country unlawfully.

He disclosed that a special commission, made up of representatives of the War Department, State Department and Immigration Service, had conducted a special study of the problem last month. As a result of their findings, he continued, two centers have been opened in London and Paris, and the required personnel is now being employed to process 300 alien dependents of American service men daily, beginning about Dec. 1.

After immunization precautions

by the Army and the United States Public Health Service and the issuance of immigration visas, they will receive transportation to the United States as soon as it is possible, it was explained.

Total Put at 100,000

In Washington, The Associated Press reported an estimate that as many as 100,000 service men may have married girls in foreign lands, including Australia and New Zealand, as well as Europe. No officials wanted to guess how many of the brides eventually would come to this country, but so far 22,000 have applied for permission to enter the United States. Beginning in January, The Associated Press reports, from 6,000 to 8,000 service men's brides are scheduled to enter the United States each month.

Referring again to the stowaway situation, the Immigration Service spokesman said that since heavy redeployment began, eight boys and three girls, including two who arrived Sunday, had stowed away on transports. There also have been a few other cases. Permission has been granted for one of the boys to remain here and the cases of two are still pending, but five of the boys have been deported.

Force of Precedent Feared

The girl, a Scottish bride of an American serviceman, was permitted to remain in this country with her husband, a precedent officials feared might encourage other foreign brides.

As for the two most recent stowaways, their cases will be decided on their own merits as there is no set policy, it was explained. Not much was known about the girl in New York, and it was said that she would be kept on Ellis Island until a hearing was held.

Navy officers, reversing themselves completely, told all they knew about Miss Moody, the sweetheart of a soldier who also was on board the Europa. Miss Moody, the Navy account said, boarded the transport by climbing up a hawser at the stern of the ship as the vessel lay anchored in Southampton. The Europa sailed at 12:30 P. M., Nov. 19, and the stowaway was discovered at 9 P. M. that evening when the ship was about 150 miles out of port. She was confined in a stateroom under guard for the rest of the voyage.

Miss Moody explained her act, according to the Navy, by saying she was "engaged" to marry an "Army man" and wished to come to the United States for the ceremony.

Three other British war brides entered the United States yesterday, but they came legally aboard a Pan American Airways plane from Hurn, England, which landed at La Guardia Field.

October 12, 1945

November 27, 1945

The American Woman? Not for This GI

He says she asks much but gives little and her European sister is much nicer.

By VICTOR DALLAIRE
Former Correspondent of The Stars and Stripes

EVEN the Army's vast statistical organization could never compute the number of man-hours spent by our troops gaping at the bicycled beauties of Paris, Rome, Brussels or the Riviera, or the number of words expended by them in barrack and battlefield discussion of foreign females as opposed to the girls they left behind them.

There were girls in England, of course, but they were much like American girls despite corded cotton stockings and peculiar British ways of saying and doing things. And there were girls down in Africa, a few French, Italian and Spanish and a good many Arabs. The European girls in Morocco, Algeria and Tunisia were too few and too tied down by provincial conventions to make much of an impression on the Yanks. If a soldier invited one of them to a movie he found that the invitation included the rest of the family.

In those early days, the remembrance of wives and sweethearts in America was still strong. Homesick soldiers used only pin-up terms to describe the girls back in the States. The poorly clad and unapproachable females south of the Mediterranean had to compete with these dream girls and usually came out a poor second in any argument.

IT took Rome or Paris to teach many of us that Italian and French girls could be just as well dressed and pretty as Americans. It took only a few Wacs and a few days in the United States to convince me that they were nicer in a lot of other ways.

Some of us used to sit in a cabaret on the Rue Washington of Paris last summer and compare the French girls and the American Wacs who visited the place. The American girls would insist on a loud and full share of the conversation with their escorts while the French girls would let the men do most of the talking, adding only a word or two now and then to show their interest. Or they would go into appreciative peals of laughter at the right moments. The over-all impression we gathered was that the Americans looked on their boy friends as competitors while the Parisiennes seemed to be there for the sole purpose of being pleasant to the men.

When I came back to this country after a more-than-three-year stay in Africa and Europe, I found that loudness and rudeness are not the exclusive properties of the American women in uniform who went overseas. Being nice is almost a lost art among American women. They elbow their way through crowds, swipe your seat at bars and bump and push their way around regardless. Their idea of equality is to enjoy all the rights men are supposed to have with none of the responsibilities.

The spectacle of a woman in a smartly tailored business suit on the Champs-Elysées of Paris is unthinkable. The business amazon would not fit into the feminine pattern in France or Italy. While American women insist on a big share in the running of things, few European women want to be engineers, architects or bank presidents. They are mainly interested in the rather fundamental business of getting married, having children and making the best homes their means or conditions will allow. They feel that they can best attain their goals by being easy on the eyes and nerves of their menfolk.

The franchise was given to Frenchwomen when I was in Paris last year, but none of them gloated. They trooped to the polls as they trooped to the markets. The women felt that running the Government was chiefly men's affair even if men were running it badly. It will be hard to jolt them out of their quaint idea that home, husband and family have a No. 1 priority.

AMERICANS have long looked on Paris as the capital of sin, especially that type involving females, and there is little doubt that they'd have to comb the United States to dig up more than half a dozen rivals to Pigalle—the Pig Alley of GI fame. And though lack of female clothing is more noticeable in the Folies Bergère or the Lido than in many of our night spots, such places are as foreign to most Frenchwomen as the Hollywood version of life is to most Americans.

Although the amount of thigh displayed by a veloiste in Paris or on the Riviera would cause a New York cop to grab his summons book if he weren't too stunned to act, the girl on the bike is usually out on a routine mission to market. Her idea of the amount of flesh to be shown during off-beach hours is more liberal than that of her American sisters, a fact that has caused both military and civilian tourists to draw all sorts of conclusions.

Barring the exceptions whose ranks were swelled by war and the terrific pulling power of American cigarettes and chocolate, the girls in Europe are essentially honest and virtuous. They lead simple lives, filled with hard work and the prospect that war every generation or so will undo everything they have done. Despite the terrible beating many women in Europe have taken, I heard few complaints from them and rarely met one, either young or old, whose courtesy and desire to please left anything wanting.

SINCE returning to the United States I have listened to more beefs about lack of nylons than I heard from European women over the destruction of their homes and the slaughter of their husbands and sons. They felt their sorrows keenly, but they've learned to take the good with the bad and to be ever hopeful of something better. Americans have raised all sorts of monuments to the pioneer mothers who uncomplainingly carved homes out of the wilderness. If masonry were to mark the same sort of heroism in Europe, the Continent would be as studded with statues as it is with fortifications.

Very likely,

times make the woman, just as they make the man. Italian, French, Belgian and English women put up with things and did work that made the work of our lady riveters look like play. Under similar circumstances, American women might perform similarly, but they seem to have lost more than they gained in their struggle for equality.

ONE of the sturdiest women I ever met was Mme. Quilicci, a Frenchwoman who lived in Bastia, Corsica. When Mme. Quilicci returned to that bomb-battered seaport she found that two American soldiers had taken over her home. I was one of them and I had my muddy boots parked on her ragged counterpane when she came into the apartment.

She stood there in the doorway, a dumpy woman of 40 flanked by her two children. Accepting fate, after a silent moment or two she turned to go. I stopped her and explained that there was plenty of room for all of us; that Luigi and I could move into one room and she could have the rest of the house for her family. She finally agreed and set about transforming the waterless, battered apartment into a home.

BY all the rules of war, except that we had neglected to go through the necessary paper work, the apartment was ours. It was vacant when the Americans moved in and therefore could be requisitioned for use by the military. Luigi and I requisitioned it simply by moving in, always intending to go down to base section to see about it, if ever we had the ambition and cared to take the risk of being ranked out of our home by some officer. When Mme. Quilicci returned it was automatically removed from the list of requisitionable properties.

Madame had moved out of Bastia after American bombs had killed her husband and two oldest boys. She hid out in a mountain village until long after the bombings had rolled away to the north, and she returned only when she felt that Noel and Pascal would be safe. She didn't expect to add two full-grown Americans to her family. I don't believe she was overpleased at first, although she never acted in any way to make us think we were not the most welcome visitors on earth.

IT wasn't long before Mama Quilicci, as we soon began to call her, was completely happy and hard at work. At 6 o'clock every morning she would put on her widow's shawl and go out on a four-hour foraging trip. She didn't find much, perhaps just an apple or two, a piece of meat or fish the size of a dime hamburger, and a bundle of faggots for the fire. But she was all smiles when the two kids had something to eat, if only enough to keep them alive until the next day.

Luigi and I began bringing home loot from the Army mess, at first just enough for Noel and Pascal, but pretty soon a supply for all of us when we found out what Mama Quilicci's cooking could do for C rations. Inside of a month Grand'mère Quilicci and a wall-eyed little niece moved in. Mama was happy. She had a home. Luigi and I were as much a part of the family as if we had been born into it.

I can't think of a time when Mama Quilicci wasn't eminently polite and helpful, although I imagine both of us were somewhat of a burden with our strange insistence on clean shirts and pressed pants. She did all of our laundry and wouldn't take a sou for it, saying that we were like her own. She discovered that I had grown fond of a particularly vile kind of goat cheese which I called "fromage du chèvre mort." Somehow or other she would get hold of some which she would serve with a pleasing fanfare of chatter and holding of noses. One time I mentioned that I was looking for a Corsican vendetta knife as a souvenir and she produced one as a gift a couple of days later. It was long after that I learned she had walked sixteen miles into the hills to find the knife.

EUROPE is filled with Madame Quiliccis, both old and young. They don't fret and fuss about lack of luxuries, and their ideas of daintiness and sanitation in many instances are as basic as their knowledge of how to get along with men. Parisienne or peasant, they ask for little but give much. American women demand much but give little.

For a long time I was with the First French Army before the Belfort Gap in eastern France. I used to watch the little French girl ambulance drivers go out to pick up the wounded under road and battle conditions that would have given our men drivers a lot to think about. Many of them didn't come back, but the ones who did would soon be sporting a flower or a bright scarf to show that they were just girls after all, despite GI uniforms, clod-hopper boots and mud. Like their sisters in Paris and the Riviera, they knew that their appeal lay in feminine curves and ways and not in their ability to jockey an ambulance.

I was in Italy last summer, three months after the war in Europe had ended, and I saw Italian women rebuilding highway bridges. They carried baskets of wet concrete and rock on their heads that would have floored an American male, but most of them sang while they worked. Jeeping from Rome to Nice, we picked up three girls on the highway above Genoa who had walked over a hundred kilometers to exchange the olive oil of San Remo for the flour of Genoa. Their feet were sore and blistered from walking in sandals made of old automobile tires, but they laughed about the "great oil route" from San Remo to Genoa.

THE women of Germany were at first sullen and then friendly to the point that non-fraternization collapsed and GI's wrote back to their friends in France that the fraeuleins were nicer than the mademoiselles. Many German girls soon let their desire for American rations overcome their original resentment of the victors. But most of them set to work in the fields or in the rubble of their houses, moved by the age-old urge to have some sort of family life.

Back in 1944 some of us used to take American magazines over to a near-by French Army camp. We'd show the French soldiers the pictures of movie and stage queens and tell them that all American girls were like that. If the French soldiers wanted us to, we'd say, we'd arrange to come back after the war and see that they got over to the United States.

After three months in this land of challenging females, I feel that I should go back to France and tell them that they're a heck of a lot better off where they are, just in case some of them believed us and are still waiting.

March 10, 1946

Yank on a Pedestal

With all his faults the American husband is tops with brides from across the sea.

By LEE E. GRAHAM

MORE and more women in the United States may be divorcing their husbands, but as far as the war brides now in this country are concerned, the American male is a marital blue-ribbon winner. Within the past year about 60,000 war brides have landed on these shores with their best clothes, their children and their timid dreams of the future. They have come to know the Yank—as they call him—and have had a good chance to compare him with the husbands they might have had at home. How does he measure up?

To get the answer to that question I interviewed a sample group of brides—mostly from England, France and Italy—at English Speaking Union meetings, at International Institute teas and in private conversations over the telephone. Their comments on the American male make him sound like the ideal man. Below are six questions put to the war brides and their composite answers:

Has the European male better manners?

ONLY superficially, say the wives-from-across-the-sea. True, the European seldom forgets his Emily Post manners; he doesn't shove people as much in crowded places, and he rarely sits down on a train while a woman stands. But the veneer is thin, they say, for he lacks the deeper consideration of the American, who will go shopping for groceries and carry home clumsy packages, dry the dishes after dinner, push the baby carriage on his day off, and even fix his own breakfast while his wife stays in bed. No self-respecting European will do these chores, the girls say, except in an emergency—and certainly not when his friends are around.

"The way the American men put themselves out to please you here—I should think all the women would be spoiled," said a bride from Birmingham, England.

Is the European closer to his family?

ACCORDING to the English girls, there is little difference between the family habits of their countrymen and ours, except that their men are less demonstrative and fonder of going to pubs and clubs. The Italian girls say that their men, while extremely devoted husbands and fathers, are more jealous than Americans and exact greater obedience from their wives and children.

The most generous appraisal of American men come from the French girls. As one Latvian-born bride, who had lived in Paris eighteen years, said, "They [Frenchmen] just do not love the wife like here." The French woman must ask her husband's permission to do many things; she wouldn't dream of wearing clothes that her husband disliked; and she often sits alone at night while he goes out to a cafe. It's true that he more rarely asks for a divorce but, the French girls say, he is more openly unfaithful.

WITH the American, on the other hand, it's a 50-50 proposition. He seldom makes decisions without consulting her; he wants her companionship outside the home; he allows her the utmost freedom of action; he expects less domestic skill from her, and is quite contented with dinner via a can-opener. When he falls in love with another woman he is quicker to admit it and ask for a divorce. The French girls see him as a man who cares deeply for his children and provides for them well, but gives his wife full charge in bringing them up. However, he doesn't want her to spend too much time on them. If she does, he may sulk and feel neglected

Is the European more of a ladies' man?

THE war brides say that the European bachelor is spoiled—the ratio of men to women is too much in his favor. According to the French brides, their beaux (when they could find one) were rude, expected many favors for buying just one drink and often let them go home alone at night. When the Yank first arrived overseas they soon discovered that he was more considerate. He usually brought flowers or candy or food when calling for them, took them out to all the places they wanted to go and spent his money freely.

They hold that the Continental's approach is more flowery and subtle, the Yank's line of talk more direct and sincere. "You know where you stand with an American—with a European you can never be sure," one English girl said.

To the war brides, one of the most surprising things about the Yank is the easy way he falls in love and proposes marriage without a thought of the girl's reputation, dowry or family background. When it comes to choosing a wife, the European thinks it over carefully, considers the opinions of his family and puts a greater emphasis on chastity.

Is the European less of a materialist?

THE young women agreed that he does spend less time worrying about money. To begin with, his marriage has a certain financial stability supplied by his wife's dowry. Traditionally, he works more slowly and thoroughly, concentrating on quality rather than quantity. He lacks the ambition of the American, who imagines that he can be

President. The European is also less concerned with keeping up with the Joneses.

Does the European spend his leisure in a more mature way?

THE girls agree that he does. They observe that the American male amuses himself like a restless little boy who has never grown up. He reads the comic strips, plays silly games with his children, likes Western and whodunit movies, enjoys wild gags and practical jokes, goes mad at prizefights and baseball games, drinks more for the effect than the taste, prefers poker and gin rummy to conversation and savors ice cream as if it were a vintage wine.

The European male is less intense about having a good time, and relies less on commercialized entertainment. He attends more repertory theatres, concerts and operas. And he is perfectly happy to sit for hours in a cafe over one brandy or a game of chess.

Nevertheless many of the wives say it was more fun going out with a Yank. These were some of their reasons: "My husband usually asks me where *I* want to go." "He doesn't object if I have an extra drink." "He doesn't mind waiting patiently while I go window-shopping." "He has a car and he likes to travel around in it." "He doesn't get angry if I dance more than once with one of his friends." "He doesn't spend money like a show-off." "He treats waiters as if they were his equal." "He doesn't flirt with other women while he's sitting with me."

How does the European differ from the American in his appearance?

THE war wives say that the Yank, despite his resemblance to his European brother, is recognizable anywhere. Why? He wears flamingly gay neckties. He walks in a cocky, energetic way. He slouches when he sits, with his feet up on a desk or flung over the arm of a chair. He loves comfort so much that he may wear sports clothes on formal occasions. (But because he is taller and huskier he looks right in them.) He orders milk in restaurants—a thing no European would do unless he were an invalid. When he plays games, he untucks his shirttail, and he dotes on jackets which do not match his trousers. All these things give him that casual, collegiate air, say the brides, which makes him look still young at 45.

THE European is much more dignified and deliberate in his appearance. His clothes are darker, somewhat heavier and more conservative, and he pays greater attention to how they fit. At all times his cravats are subdued. He puts elegance ahead of comfort, formality ahead of play. He is a man at 18, from which time on he takes himself pretty seriously.

Unfortunately, the wives say, real sartorial splendor is limited to the European of upper class. Only in the United States is it possible for a bootblack to look like a bank president. And they also believe that only in the United States can a bank president be treated with respect should he happen to look like a bootblack.

P. S. The high favor in which the war brides hold the Yank evidently is not limited to the particular group interviewed. For, of all the marriages of our men to girls-across-the-sea, only 5 per cent so far have ended in divorce. Which is not bad when compared with our all-American divorce rate of about 1 in 3.

April 13, 1947

PREPAREDNESS AID SEEN IN NURSERIES

Dr. Sockman Holds Progress of Day 'Group Action' Is Help to National Program

SPEAKER AT CONFERENCE

Hear of Association Appeals for Support in Movement as Vital to Social Needs

The progress of "the group action and individual enterprise" of day nurseries throughout the country is an important link in the nation's preparedness program, the Rev. Dr. Ralph W. Sockman, pastor of Christ Methodist Church, told delegates to the second annual conference of the National Association of Day Nurseries that opened yesterday at the Hotel Waldorf-Astoria.

The theme of the conference was announced by Mrs. Ernest F. Eidlitz, president of the association, as "For Children and Democracy" in her annual message delivered at the opening of the session. She said that the association held the view that day nurseries are "essential social instruments deserving voluntary private support."

Reminding her associates of the importance of making their programs "flexible enough to meet current community needs," Mrs. Eidlitz declared:

"If our answers to the problems we face are forthright and honest, we can withstand alarums from abroad. The children we serve will adapt themselves to a changing world. They are now growing in strength and understanding, learning to live coöperatively. They will soon be men and women. In time they will mold their world to their purposes."

Dr. Sockman commended the organization for its work "in its wider settings as a link with preparedness. The day nurseries will maintain the morale of mothers in the home. They will keep alive the long view that the child is the first line of defense," he said.

During the afternoon the delegates took part in separate group discussions, dealing with day nursery services in general, as well as the particular phases of programs relating to the admission of more children; the services provided for both pre-school and school age children, and for foster day care for children under two years of age.

Mrs. Francis T. Boyd, chairman of the conference, announced that discussion groups will meet this morning and at luncheon.

November 14, 1940

WARTIME TRAINING OF WOMEN BACKED

A substantial number of voters—nearly one half—favors the idea of training women now for wartime work, a survey by the American Institute of Public Opinion has shown, according to Dr. George Gallup, its director.

The question was raised by Mrs. Franklin D. Roosevelt, who declared at a Woman's Congress meeting, "I imagine the time is coming when we are going to have to face this question. There have been many requests to the government that some specific training be given to women and girls in national defense, but so far it is a topic that officials shun like the plague."

The question asked by the institute was:

"Would you be in favor of starting now to draft American women between the ages of 21 and 35 to train them for jobs in wartime?'

"Yes 48%
"No 52%

"Only one person in sixteen (6 per cent) expressed no opinion on this issue.

"These results confirm earlier indications of an intense desire among the American people to help push the defense program in every possible way.

"An interesting sidelight in today's study is that woman voters are substantially more in favor of the training-for-women idea than men are. Among women between the ages of 21 and 35 — those who would be affected — the suggestion is approved by a majority.

	Approve women's training program	Disapprove
Men voters	44%	56%
Women voters (total)	52	48
Women vot. aged 21-35	54	56

The greatest desire to have women share defense training with men is found in the lower income group. Voters in this level, comprised of families earning $20 a week or less, are in favor of the drafting of women (55 per cent), whereas a majority of those in the middle and upper income level oppose the idea.

	Approve Women's Training Program	Disapprove
Upper income voters	41%	59%
Middle income voters	44	56
Lower income voters	55	45

"Voters in favor of a training program have two chief reasons—first, that in modern 'total' warfare it is essential that women be trained for emergency work, and, second, that women should share equal responsibility with men in defending the country.

"Those opposed to the draft idea argue that it is not necessary at this stage to train women for war work, that a woman's place is in the home and that any such step would smack of dictatorship. 'Sounds too much like Hitler,' is a typical comment from this group."

December 18, 1940

WOMEN WORK NIGHTS AT WINCHESTER ARMS

Connecticut Permits Emergency Hiring to Make Cartridges

HARTFORD, Conn., April 16 (AP)—Governor Robert A. Hurley stated today that at the War Department's request he had granted to the Winchester Repeating Arms Company of New Haven the right to employ women on some types of night work which would enable it to attain a production goal of 17,000,000 small arms cartridges weekly. It now produces 11,000,000 cartridges a week.

The Governor said that similar authority would be given to the Remington Arms Company of Bridgeport under an emergency provision of a State law which empowers the Governor to waive the 10 P. M. limit set on women's night work.

NEW HAVEN, Conn., April 16 (AP)—Albert F. Snyder, Winchester superintendent of personnel, said that the Governor's action would result in the employment of more than 250 additional women. The company, he added, was particularly desirous of establishing a night shift of women for cartridge inspection, which he termed "a natural woman's job."

April 17, 1941

NATION'S WOMEN HOLD ONE FACTORY JOB IN 4

Food Manufacturers Lead Country in Total Employment

Special to THE NEW YORK TIMES.

WASHINGTON, Aug. 27 — Of every 100 persons engaged in manufacturing at the end of the 1940 census, seventy-five were men and twenty-five women, the Census Bureau stated today.

In number of persons employed, manufacturers of food and kindred products led all industries with 1,355,157 persons, of whom 982,653 were men and 352,504 were women.

Factories in the textile and fiber products industry group had 1,237,630 employes, of whom 711,266 were men and 526,364 were women.

The iron and steel industries had 1,227,390 employes, or 1,133,654 men and 93,736 women.

Women employes outnumbered men in only two industry groups—tobacco manufacturers and apparel and other finished products made from fabrics and similar materials. Of 99,418 employed in tobacco manufactures, 62,374 were women and 37,044 were men. The apparel industries group employed 925,657, or 648,006 women and 277,651 men.

August 28, 1941

FINGERNAILS: Cutting Suggested

In THE NEW YORK TIMES magazine of Oct. 19 there appears a picture of a girl examining bullet casings. It seems to me that greater efficiency and speed would result if women in such work reduced the length of their varnished fingernails and temporarily left off rings. A pianist or violinist whose work demands fingers as skillful and sensitive as possible knows enough to pare his nails and to free his hands of all restriction. Long fingernails may give the impression that the individual does little or no work with the hands, but would it not be only common sense to give up this useless fad in favor of increased efficiency?—ELFREDA C. SAMUELS, Syracuse, N. Y.

October 26, 1941

Mass exodus—3:45 P. M. closing at the Navy Building.   *Much of the work in Washington is routine, as at home.*

Girls' Town—Washington

The Capital has been captured and subdued by an army of young women workers, 80,000 strong

By SALLY RESTON
WASHINGTON.

APERT little stenographer at the Navy Department remarked the other day that the men may have made this war but the women are running it. And judging from the appearance of the capital these days there is something in what she says.

For wartime Washington is a girls' town. It is a postman's nightmare with 2,300,000 letters going out and coming in every day. It is the headquarters of a mechanized army of typists and filing clerks whose battle dress is a pair of saddle shoes, a sweater and skirt, and a long bob. This army isn't going to win the war, as the youngster at the Navy Department suggested, but winning the war without it would be quite a trick.

When France collapsed in June, 1940, the Federal Government not only called for young men who could fly an airplane at 400 miles an hour, but also issued an urgent plea for young women who could

operate a typewriter at forty words a minute. "Help wanted" notices were posted by the Civil Service Commission everywhere from the big-town postoffices to the cracker barrel at Tompkins Corners, and ever since then over 2,000 girls have been arriving in Washington every month.

THIS adds up to a considerable number of girls and a considerable number of problems. In June, 1940, when a Washington stenographer still had room to powder her nose, there were 53,038 women employed by the various government agencies here. One year later there were 77,-774, or 24,736 newcomers, on the distaff side, and officials admit that in the last five months over 10,000 more have arrived.

Most of these new employes were crowded into the expanding defense agencies—over 8,000 were put to work in the War Department alone during the first

year of the emergency—and had to compete not only with one another for jobs and rooms and food (and dates!), but also with hundreds of other girls who were being employed simultaneously by the British Supply Council and various other Allied missions.

These new national defense recruits, like the young men of their own generation being drafted into the new United States Army, came from all over the country. On the whole, they are a pretty unsophisticated lot. They're not as slick as the white-collar brigade in Wall Street, partly because many of them are away from home for the first time and partly because they are younger than the typical New York stenographer. In general they range from 18 to 25 years of age, and in general they have more social and economic problems than their counterparts in New York.

THEIR reasons for coming to Washington are fairly clear. They didn't come down here to beat Adolf Hitler; and they didn't come with any great understanding of the fundamental conflict between the ideals of the youth of Germany and the youth of this country. They came to get a job. They came to get between $105 and $120 a month, because many of them are helping support their families at home. They came for security, because after a six-month probationary period in the government service it's pretty hard to get fired. And they came for adventure just like the stage-struck youngsters who go to Broadway in New York.

It was inevitable that these girls would change the character and atmosphere of Washington. The Federal Triangle at 5 o'clock in the afternoon looks more like a college campus after 3 o'clock classes than the center of the nation's capital. These youngsters are turning the fashions of this city upside down. All the old rules for formal street clothes are off. Washington women are learning to go hatless and like it.

Normally, Washington was a formal city in its appearance and in its living habits. It was a leisurely community, jealous of its social protocol and proud of the planned beauty of its parks and its fashionable mansions. But the girls from Tompkins Corners have changed all this. They do not share the permanent Washingtonian's respect for L'Enfant's plan for the perfect capital. They eat their sandwiches on the Supreme Court steps if they feel like it, and every sunny day they gather in Lafayette Square across the street from the White House and scatter their lunch boxes on the grass.

They have even crashed the most formal executive agency in town. Until recently the financial experts in the beautiful new Federal Reserve Bank Building used to eat lunch in the solitary splendor of their pine-paneled dining rooms. Now every noon they have to crush their way through a long line of stenographers and clerks from the War Department who stand four deep in the marble halls.

Business goes out of its way to meet their needs. A few months ago a busy stenographer with a run in her stocking couldn't get to a store to buy a new pair before closing hour. Now many of the smaller shops are staying open at night, and every Thursday the big department stores keep their doors open until 9 P. M.

IF a new pair of silk stockings were all that was troubling the Washington stenographer, everything would be fine. But there are two main problems which every new business girl in Washington has to solve. First, she must adjust herself to a dull, mechanical job and a completely new conception of her place in the government's service. And secondly, she must

Evening out—There aren't enough men, so a date is highly prized.

adjust herself to the chaotic living conditions peculiar to Washington alone.

Most of the trouble these girls are having here is the result of misapprehensions before they leave home. It is not their fault, nor can the government be blamed. But when they receive an urgent telegram from Washington asking them to join the staff of the War Department or one of the other defense agencies, their expectations run high.

The new jobs are the envy of all the stenographers in the office back home. The girls believe that they are going to Washington to do secretarial work in the office of a general or some other executive. Many of them are told to report for work in forty-eight hours. Others with more luck are given anywhere from four to ten days to find money to pay their railroad fare, pack their bags and say their good-byes. They arrive in Washington eager to meet their new boss and get to work.

And what do they find? Wartime Washington, fighting for time against Hitler's armies, has discovered that secretaries' work can be mass-produced as well as tanks and machine guns. Private secretaries have been cut down to a minimum and what is known as "the pool" has taken their place. The girls often are permanently assigned to one of the big department pools, sharing a room with seventy-five other young typists. Or they may be put to work in a big room at the War Department where fifty girls run machines punching out holes in an endless stack of Army cards. Hundreds of girls are needed in various other pools, to stuff envelopes, to operate mimeographs, addressographs, and the complicated and laborious machines which imitate print. One out of every four or six girls may act as supervisor, directing and reporting on the group's output.

Of course, in the new expanding defense agencies some of the stenographers are getting jobs as private secretaries and doing important and exciting work. But these positions are the exceptions, and for the majority the problem of adjustment to the new work is much the same as that of the skilled laborer who suddenly finds himself on the assembly line of modern mass-production.

ADJUSTMENT to living conditions in Washington, the second great problem of the girls, is made difficult by the fact that all the small apartments in the capital were occupied long ago. Of course, there are plenty of rooms available on the outskirts of the city; but, with uncertain hours of work, much overtime and transportation to be paid, these accommodations are not attractive.

In the areas convenient to the Federal Triangle, therefore, the conditions are appalling. Girls are living three and four to a small room, waiting in line for bathroom facilities. Some of them are developing claustrophobia. For example, a young girl went into the Y. W. C. A. last week and asked if she could find a place to stretch and rest for a little while. She said she had been

climbing over other people's desks at work all day and over her room-mates' shoes and suitcases all night.

The scramble for rooms so far has been limited by law to those areas where rooming houses are allowed. But now the shortage of accommodations near the Federal Triangle has become so acute that there is a movement on foot to lift the restrictions on rooming houses in the more fashionable residential areas. This movement is being opposed by the property owners.

ASIDE from the shortage of living quarters there is the high cost of everything. Even before the boom days Washington had been, by all odds, the most expensive town in the country, as the Department of Labor cost-of-living index shows. And so the girls are finding that their expenses here are almost twice as much as at home. A 20-year-old stenographer from Detroit who was only making $80 a month at home is getting $105 here, but her room and board in Detroit cost her only $28 a month and here she pays $20 for her room and $20 for her food. And a peanut gallery seat at the movies here costs her more than she paid for the best seats at home.

These financial problems are serious indeed for those girls who are trying to send part of their pay check to their families each month, and for those who, having their first experience of living away from home, are bewildered by the need for budgeting.

If a girl in her twenties has a date waiting outside the office door at 5 o'clock in the afternoon, it doesn't really matter what has happened at work that day; it doesn't matter too much that her living conditions are not ideal. But Washington girls have to worry more than others about their social life. Washington can't take care of all those 2,300,-000 letters in the ordinary way and some of the girls have to work at night. A government stenographer working the last shift is likely to be stood up if she expects to meet her boy friend on Constitution Avenue at 7 A. M. Moreover, there aren't enough men to go around. The Bureau of Census statistics show that in April, 1940, before these 35,000 stenographers arrived, there were only ninety-one men

in the District of Columbia for every 100 women—a disparity equaled nowhere else in the country.

SEGREGATED in the pool system as the majority of these girls are, they have little opportunity to meet the eligible young men around Washington. The 10,000 new stenographers in the War Department feel the problem most keenly because Army tradition and discipline forbid all informal conversation between the officers and their employes.

What then is being done about these girls and their problems? What is the government doing to alleviate the situation? How much are the private agencies doing? And what is the end of their social and economic problems?

The government has financed a new dormitory in the center of the city and the Defense Housing Registry plans to issue a new call for more rooms this Winter. Some of the government departments are trying to relieve the monotony of the dull jobs by alternating one week of typing with one week of work on other machines.

The Y. W. C. A. and the churches are actively concerned about the social side of the girls' lives and are using their buildings as rallying points for the day and night workers alike. They are doing all they can to bolster the morale of the youngsters.

But all this is not answering the long-term question of what in the end is going to happen to these young women. If the defense program goes on for years, a great deal will be sapped from their lives. Most social observers here are of the opinion that just as there were thousands of unmarried women in the capital after the last war, so, too, after this one there will be left a new generation of spinsters, living one day on their hard-earned government pensions.

VOLUNTEERS SOUGHT TO CARE FOR CHILDREN

Lack of Them Seen Keeping Mothers Out of Defense Jobs

NEW BRUNSWICK, N. J., Dec. 18 (AP)—Mothers are justified in not accepting defense work unless full-day care is provided for their preschool children, Mrs. Phyllis B. Davis of the New Jersey Extension Service, New Jersey College of Agriculture, Rutgers University, said today.

"Let it not be said that the greatest democracy in the world can not or will not take care of its children in wartime," Mrs. Davis said, after a conference of representatives of State groups on child welfare and parent education.

"Many more women would be glad to put their services at the disposal of defense projects if adequate care were guaranteed their children," she declared. "Those who are concerned with the welfare of children should not rest until every pre-school child is cared for during factory shifts and every elementary school child of a working mother provided with a hot lunch and after-school supervision.

December 19, 1941

RULES GIRLS, 16, MAY WORK

Miss Perkins Grants Exemption on Some Government Orders

WASHINGTON, April 23 (AP)—Manufacturers furnishing some products under government contract may employ girls as young as 16, under a Labor Department ruling made public today.

Secretary Perkins, at the request of the War Department, granted an exemption from a provision in the Walsh-Healey Public Contracts Act, lowering the age minimum from 18 in about fifteen manufacturing lines. Girls under 18, however, may not be employed more than eight hours a day nor between 10 P. M. and 6 A. M.

Industries to which the exemption applies include food processing, arms and ammunition, electrical manufacturing, plastic products, safety appliances, machinery and allied products, converted paper products, fabrication of metal products, chemical, drug and allied products. The exemption does not apply to the manufacture of wearing apparel and allied products and textile products.

PLAN FARM JOBS FOR MANY WOME[N]

Ten Western States Discu[ss] Registration of 'Farmerette[s]' for Special Tasks

OREGON MAPS A SURVE[Y]

California Losing 'Okies' Sin[ce] Pearl Harbor—Shortage in Labor Becomes Acute

Special to THE NEW YORK TIMES.

SAN FRANCISCO, Jan. 5—A[l]though farm placement leaders o[p]pose making "work horses" out o[f] women, the "farmerette" is goin[g] to have an important spot in th[e] wartime agricultural program, [it] was indicated today at a regiona[l] conference of employment and so[ci]al security officials of ten West[-]ern States.

Oregon is setting the pace fo[r] the nation with plans for a house[-]to-house canvass next month of it[s] women power. Twelve thousan[d] volunteers, working on a precinc[t] basis, will interview women to as[-]certain their skills or capabilitie[s] as defense or agricultural em[-]ployes. L. C. Stoll, Federal Em[-]ployment Service director for Ore[-]gon, estimated that by Feb. 1[5] about 300,000 women would be reg[-]istered.

The Oregon plan for registering and classifying all women was termed "sound" by Fay W. Hunter[,] chief of the farm placement station of the Federal Employment Service. The classification, he said[,] would enable their use in many phases of agriculture.

Like other spokesmen, he explained, this would not mean that women would be asked to go into the fields to do men's work. Rather, they would be employed in greater numbers than ever before in canneries and in sorting and packing fruit; in short, "for the type of work they can do."

Shortage of Labor Predicted

Women are to be recruited for agricultural pursuits because, according to the Department of Labor, the farms of America this year will require 300,000 manyears of labor more than they did in 1941.

Part of this shortage, Mr. Hunter said, resulted from the leaving of farms by defense workers, part from the increasing flow of agricultural products to Allied nations and part from the fact that since more people are working, they are living better and are buying more food, thus creating a greater demand.

California, as one of the Pacific Coast States exposed to possible attack by Japan, has a peculiar problem of its own. A shortage of farm workers was threatened even in 1941, in spite of the increasing numbers of "Okies" and "Arkies" arriving from the Great Plains States.

Farm operators actually welcomed these friends and relatives of the penniless migrants of a few years ago, who were driven to the "promised land" west of the Sierra Nevada by dust storms and crop failures. Although many of the new arrivals went to work in Southern California's aircraft factories, thousands were still available for farm work.

Pearl Harbor Turns Tide

But when the Pacific Coast began receiving its wartime blackout orders and when posters giving instructions as to what to do during air raids were nailed up in some of the rural farm camps, the "Okies" and "Arkies" turned back eastward toward their old homes in large numbers. The tide has so alarmed some farm associations, especially in the great lettuce-growing Salinas Valley, that they have appealed to the Farm Placement Service for aid in finding workers.

Filipino labor which used to work the lettuce fields has mostly gone elsewhere; some to San Francisco and industrial suburbs like Vallejo. Mexican workers succeeded Filipinos, but the Mexicans have gone home.

There have been suggestions in California and elsewhere for the importation of alien workers, such as Mexicans, in large numbers, but Mr. Hunter said that there is "no reason to import aliens when there may be areas in the United States where workers are available."

"We must utilize all local labor resources before any request is made for importation," he added. "We want to utilize local labor, women, students and others."

The regional conference, which continues tomorrow, will be followed by one at Memphis for the Southern and Southwestern States next Monday and Tuesday.

Real Farm Work Is Done by Girls

Students Garner Crops as Part of Plan to Replace Men in Services

Garnering crops on Columbia County farms is a favorite vacation idea for a group of young women from some of the East's exclusive finishing schools and colleges, who are serving their country the hard way. Stiff and sunburned at the beginning, they stay long enough to harden up and enjoy the work, their supervisors report, and are soon able to top off a day in the fields with a baseball game, a barn dance or a swimming party.

find enough itinerant labor for this first wartime Summer.

Organizers were Mrs. Charles Coe Townsend and Mrs. Frank B. Washburn, whose Summer homes are near Germantown. One of their advisers is Miss Ida H. Ogilvie, who helped to organize farmerettes in the first World War, and has employed women for farm work ever since.

Wages were set at the scale prevailing in the locality, the season beginning with strawberries at 4 cents per basket and cherries at 10 cents for a four-quart basket. Patriotism rather than the moderate wage was stressed in recruiting.

Almost all of the group, Mrs. Washburn reports, are able to earn the $10 weekly charged for "board, breakfast, box luncheon and dinner." The hardest workers make a few dollars over this amount.

Housed in the Clermont Inn at Clermont and in tourist cabins near by, the group includes, among others, students from Brearley, Chapin and Spence Schools, Wellesley, Smith, Vassar and Mount Holyoke Colleges. Supervision of the day's schedule is in the hands of Miss Christine Davis and Miss Margaret Haskins, both of the Brearley School. In berry picking time they arrange for a 5:30 A. M. breakfast, because berries are picked better in the early hours, and at 6 the girls are off in the farmers' trucks, with their lunches in a bag, returning at 3 and 4 in the afternoon. Saturday is their one free day.

One of the extra responsibilities they have assumed is to write to the service men who have left the farms where the girls are now

The New York Times Studio

Columbia County's bean crops are picked by students on vacation.

The girls, who total 100 "hands" on a weekly schedule, were invited through their schools to join a Farm for Freedom group, formed at the request of thirty farmers who were doubtful of being able to

The plan, however, is not essentially money-making; and all the girls are financially responsible for their board and lodgings, even when rainy days cut into their earnings.

working. "There are at least fifty such men," Mrs. Washburn said, "and our idea was to bring home to the girls through these letters the connection between the work they do and the war."

FARMERS FOR FREEDOM AT CLERMONT, N. Y.

Lunch comes out of a bag and is eaten al fresco to save time.

Farmhands for the Summer, they go bicycling after work.

TIN SCOUTS FIND WHERE DRIVE LAGS

Women on Collection Trucks Feel Campaign Is 'Not Taken Seriously Enough'

Volunteers Make Notes for an Educational Follow-Up— 261 Tons Day's Yield

A corps of New York City housewives, 225 strong, rose with the dawn yesterday, boarded 175 Department of Sanitation trucks, and took a peek into the "backyards" of their sleeping sisters. What they saw explained, in part, the lagging contributions to the tin can salvage drive.

Volunteers from the Office of Civilian Defense and from the American Women's Voluntary Services, the women were out to get a first-hand view of the collections. Their tour of inspection started at 7 A. M. from fifty department garages, was highlighted by a ten-truck caravan down Fifth Avenue, and ended when the yield of those trucks was delivered to the city dump.

Hoisting themselves in pairs beside the driver of each truck, the volunteers began their sidewalk tour of the city. Armed with notebooks and pencils, they noted buildings, jotting down the presence or lack of a collection and the condition of the cans. From this information, the New York City Salvage Committee expects to conduct a house-to-house educational campaign.

Drivers Are Praised

Mrs. Eustace Seligman, an OCD volunteer, was full of praise for the drivers and their helpers.

"They helped each other and the building people, too," she declared, adding ruefully, "the trouble is, the cans are not put out early enough. We had to go back to some places as many as five times."

"The people aren't taking it nearly seriously enough," was the reaction of Mrs. Ethel S. Nathanson, who is Manhattan salvage chairman for the A. W. V. S.

"Where I went only 10 per cent of the cans were properly processed," declared another OCD worker, Mrs. Boris Artzybasheff.

The only words of praise had to do with the New York Infirmary for Women and Children and the Booth Memorial Hospital, both of which, it was reported, had "four barrels of cans each and all in perfect condition."

Mrs. Trulock Gets Reports

Most of these impressions were relayed to Mrs. Guy Percy Trulock, newly appointed chairman of the tin can salvage division of the New York City Salvage Committee, when she arrived to escort the caravan.

Mrs. Trulock, who led the caravan in the car of Philip Wohlfit, West Side Superintendent of the Sanitation Department, expressed the opinion that the collections, which had been the first of a new weekly schedule to replace previous bi-weekly ones, had "gone up very perceptibly."

This statement seemed a little optimistic, however, when results of the collection were announced later in the day at headquarters of the salvage committee. City collections for the day amounted to 261 tons, as compared to a total of 681 tons for last week's two-day collection.

A spokesman for the committee pointed out that the earlier figure covered what had been gathered in the course of two weeks, while yesterday's yield was the result of one week's accrual. The total for the city since March 11 now amounts to 7,918 tons.

FASHIONS FOR 1943 FEEL WAR EFFECTS

All Energies Now Center on Conservation in Keeping With Our Vast Program

BUT LOVELY STYLES STAY

Suit, Essential to Duration Wardrobe, Is Designed on Svelte, Trim Lines

By VIRGINIA POPE

Now in 1943, the curtain rises on a style scene that differs widely from that of a year ago, when we were still in a period of lavishness. The vastness of the war program is making itself felt now and all energies are focused on conservation. This is an all-important motif in the minds of those who create the clothes women will wear for the duration.

Prophecy on the outline of fashions to come during the next several months is not too difficult, after readings of the current style barometer. It is the details—dependent on the creative talents of American designers—that involve speculation. For their importance grows consistently, in the mode of World War II, and American inventiveness keeps pace.

In April of 1942, the government's L-85 regulation was devised to save materials through control of the cutting of wearing apparel. With astounding ingenuity, the country's designers complied with its restrictions. To them the limitations imposed were an asset rather than a hindrance. They evolved a new silhouette—one that will go down in fashion history as the "duration" silhouette. It is sleek, slim, functional, expressive of active American womanhood.

Desires Not Neglected

While conforming to the law, designers have not neglected a woman's desire to be feminine and attractive. They have supplied countless softnesses, superimposed upon the restrained silhouette of suit or dress. The fashion picture of 1943 will encompass two extremes; the severity of the functional and the feminine charm of the "off duty" costume.

The suit is the essential of a duration wardrobe. Svelte and trim, it affords the opportunity to be well dressed from morning till night. Lines are slender, with a bare allowance of fullness in the skirt to provide for a comfortable stride. The length permitted brings the average hem some seventeen inches from the ground. Jackets may be twenty-five inches long. But save in classic tailored suits, designers have not taken advan-

tage of this allowance. They are showing models that come barely over the hip. Waist-length jackets and boleros are equally a part of their Spring and Summer planning.

As a conservation measure, more and more jackets are designed without collar and revers. Some jackets have no collars, and rolled revers. Where there are collars, they are frequently rounded to conform with the dressmaker softness which figures importantly for Spring. Wool on wool may not be used, so pockets used decoratively may turn out to be just flaps. To take the place of accustomed decorations there are welt seams, cordings, fringes and rickrack edgings. Buttons play an ornamental role.

Two-Color Suit a Favorite

The two-color suit, with the jacket of a bright and the skirt of a dark shade, is a favorite. Many are shown with printed crepe blouses. Realizing that women want to practice economy measures designers offer them the opportunity to change the character of their suits with a wide selection of blouses. For the tailor-made occasions, there are classic crepe shirts; for frivolous hours a suit can be dressed up with an enchanting frilled blouse with a froth of pleated ruffles or lace.

Next to the suit in popularity is the two-piece, which has the same easy-to-wear characteristics. This season finds it in soft dressmaker versions in woolens and crepes, as well as in shantung and faille. It is enhanced with lingerie touches, crisp and fresh as the first chirp of the northbound swallow.

Part of the effort to keep women pretty are the ruffles and frills that accompany suits and dresses. New are collars and cuffs of plaid and checked gingham, as well as flower-sprigged calico. These are labor-saving when it comes to washing and ironing. Feminine pink in collars, hats and gloves will charm the masculine eye.

Coats follow the economy trend in saving of materials. There are chesterfields in single and double-breasted versions, and coats that hang in slim, tubular lines. Here again style is achieved with a minimum of fabric.

Of dresses one can say that their charm lies in their detail—in seaming, tucks and pleats developed with infinite care and thought. Daytime necklines are apt to be high, this to contrast them with the low decolletages of the formal afternoon and informal evening models. Among the smartest of the functional frocks are the shirtwaist type with moderately flaring skirts that button from trim collars to hemlines. The coat dress of wool is practical; it can go anywhere. We've seen it with double-breasted fastening, with a deep overlapping front buttoning at one side, and with softly gathered skirt and white collar and cuffs.

Simulated Bolero Dress

Strictly in conformance with wartime regulation is the simulated bolero dress. For the young of figure it is destined to be a winner. A blouse is suggested by lingerie or plaid, checked or striped

FASHIONS CAST SLIM SHADOWS

A characteristic "duration" silhouette. A classic, one-button woolen suit in gray and white bankers' stripe. The 56-inch skirt sweep, 24½-inch jacket length, and hem 17 inches from the floor, all are less than regulations permit.

silk; or the bolero may be made of embroidered crepe, the rest of the dress of a solid color. Another

frock that will "go to town" looks as though it were shirtwaist and skirt, but is in reality all-in-one.

It may have a bodice of black and a skirt of "potent" pink crepe, or a blouse of printed crepe and a skirt in a shade that picks up a color in the pattern; or this may be reversed.

More than ever, designers are thinking without geographic restrictions this season. They are offering styles that can be worn by the bride who follows her husband to the South or West, and that will be equally adequate to meet requirements in the North. They are thinking in terms of a long-run engagement—styles that will hold their own for the duration and do it with grace.

Now we come to a new member of the fashion family—the dressy afternoon and informal evening frock. It is essentially pretty. Generally it has an important neckline cut in a low V, or in a wide rounded curve. It may be edged with a lei of ruching, or outlined with the delicate filigree of transparent lace. Perhaps it is framed with a cloud of soft ruffled chiffon or net, in which nestles a pink bow or rose. The sleeves merely cap the top of the arm, or they may be long, finishing in some sort of a frill. The most striking of all the new sleeves has a deep pleated lampshade ruffle of lace, set onto the cap sleeve of a black crêpe dress.

Distinguished designers are showing street-length dinner dresses of utmost simplicity with draped body lines and very short sleeves (an excellent foil for jewels). This design will be translated into prints, come Spring and Summer, to be worn under a coat of bright shade. In direct opposition to this stark simplicity is the dress having a diaphanous embroidered blouse with a black skirt.

Formal gowns are not visible in the quantities of former years. Physical discomfort in night travel about town makes it less desirable to wear skirts that touch the ground. Yet, there are lovely evening gowns to be had. Sophisticates will wear columnar silhouettes with skirts that may be cut with utter plainness, or be skillfully draped.

Young things will waltz in full and flimsy skirts of net or marquisette, for these diaphanous ma-

terials have not been placed on the don't list when it comes to ample hem lines. The young will court, and have, generously low décolletages. Sophisticated women will wear gowns with semi-low necklines and covered shoulders. The collections reveal a continued endorsement of beading, but its sparkle is dainty.

Items of interest noted as designer collections were reviewed are: Lapels covered with flowers of colored ribbons on dresses and blouses and made with cut-out and appliquéd flower print designs; beading lightly used in flower ornamentation; sequins delicately heightening the patterns of prints; sparkling buttons on woolens and satins; mother-of-pearl coster buttons employed as decorations on suits and dresses.

Here and there is an attempt to revive Empire lines. Occasionally a tendency to place fullness at the back of the skirt was noted. Trouser pleats provide fullness for skirts of dresses and suits. Shepherds' plaids and blankers' stripes are liked in woolens. Gabardine is still a favorite in soft tones in tailored suits and dresses; shantung—though not much of it—makes smart dresses; faille is once again a Spring favorite. Colors: Black and navy in the lead, with gray coming in strong. Beige is liked. As a part of the bright picture there are maize yellows, soft greens, lavender, red in coral and brick tones, and spice browns.

While there are ample marials to provide women with good-looking and suitable styles, it is not always possible for manufacturers of wearing apparel to obtain a steady supply of them as in the past, owing to a shortage of manpower.

American designers who have taken two big hurdles since the beginning of the war with flying colors—namely, the fall of Paris as fashion center of the world and the restrictions of the L-85 regulations—are now facing a third, the price control placed upon manufacturers by the maximum price regulation 287. This they will deal with in the new year with the fortitude shown in the past. They know that it is their responsibility to hold for New York its recently won position of fashion center of the world.

January 2, 1943

IT'S A WOMAN'S WAR, TOO

Reports from several community defense councils that there is a serious shortage of volunteer consumer consultants to answer questions posed by ration-stunned homemakers who come to these centers seeking information are verified by Dr. Persia Campbell, consumer chairman for the Greater New York CDVO. Dr. Campbell declares that her office needs "all of the volunteers we can train in this line," and that 100 could be placed immediately if they could be found.

✦✦✦

The "recurrent tide of isolationism" is the subject of the latest

educational broadside that has just been issued by the National League of Women Voters. Quotations from representatives in Congress, cited by the league, indicate that this sentiment is again rising. The broadside urges its readers to regard this trend as a threat to constructive post-war planning on a basis of reciprocal international benefit.

✦✦✦

In many parts of the country it is reported that women to win their place in industry are being com-

pelled to combat union restrictions as well as a lingering reluctance on the part of management to give them jobs. One employment official noted recently that a heavy industry union in Washington State has finally lifted its ban against women in its membership, although insisting that they await their turns for advancement by strict observance of their seniority rating.

Women in the armed forces are being honored today by a special tea dance in their Y. W. C. A. Hospitality Center, Fifty-third Street and Lexington Avenue. Some 400 service men have been invited to attend. Members of the military auxiliaries are proving somewhat more of a problem to entertain than their opposite numbers in the masculine corps, recreation officials comment whimsically.

Officials in charge of the National Youth Administration's training centers report that enthusiasm for service with the Waves, Waacs, Wafs, etc., is the reason for a slackening enrollment of young women for industrial trades studies. To overcome this obstacle the NYA is inaugurating a course in radio, which its sponsors point out may be used in the military services.

January 3, 1943

WOMEN TAKE POSTS AS UNION LEADERS

Within the last year fourteen women in the New York area have given up jobs in private industry to take on full-time paid union work with the United Electrical, Radio and Machine Workers of America. In addition, about 17 per cent of the union's national staff now are women, as against 2 per cent a year ago, Miss Ruth Young, executive secretary, disclosed yesterday.

For the first time in history Local 16 of the United Office and Professional Workers of America has a woman president. The Book and Magazine Union also is headed by a woman.

These instances, observers say, are indicative of a general trend to encourage women to prepare for union leadership. Miss Mary Anderson, director of the Women's Bureau, Department of Labor, revealed Tuesday night at a meeting in Essex House that the number of women union members in this country has reached the 3,500,000 mark. One and one-half years ago, she said, the total was 1,000,000.

Because the largest proportion of women war workers are employed in the electrical field, the electrical workers report that more than 30 per cent of its membership is on the distaff side. This doubles the figure for a year ago, and the ratio is expected to go as high as 50 per cent in the next twelve months.

Aid Community Projects

Proportionate to the increase in feminine members is the increased interest in community activities outside the shops, Miss Young added. The union has cooperated with Y. W. C. A. groups to establish weekly dances in various sections of New Jersey for young girls working in "swing shifts," who would otherwise have no place to go when they come off the job in the small hours of the morning,

and also is acting jointly with local defense area governments to set up additional day nurseries.

More and more "white collar" women are applying to locals for leadership training, the Office and Professional Workers headquarters finds. Four women are now on the general executive board.

Only now are women assuming real responsibility in the activities of the American Communications Association, according to Miss Josephine Timms, international secretary-treasurer, although for some time about 70 per cent of the membership has been feminine.

Young girls are rapidly becoming "shop stewards," or committee members, and are moving into other leadership positions as men leave for the services. There are now six women organizers, where there were none before, Miss Timms said.

Local 259 of the United Auto Workers has noted a "tremendous influx" of women in the last four or five months, and finds these new members are playing an active part in the union. In some cases they are even "more enthusiastic" than the men.

"Women are particularly interested in studying and promoting legislation concerning price control and rationing," Albert Fischer, secretary-treasurer, declared.

Mr. Fischer said that women would like to remain in industry after the war, but that they hesitate to commit themselves to do so. Among the younger girls "there is a terrific desire to remain," Miss Gretel Spiro, educational director of the Furrier's Joint Council, asserted.

Most of the women who have joined the Federation of Architects, Engineers, Chemists and Technicians are so new at their jobs that they are more anxious to establish their skills and improve production methods than to foster union activities as such, in the opinion of Beryl Gilman, director of the war production department.

Miss Helen Blanchard, vice president, announced that the Women's Trade Union League will begin a course Feb. 17 to train women for union leadership.

February 5, 1943

IT'S ALL 'MANPOWER'

Jobs Are Jobs, Says Director McNutt, Whether Women Hold Them or Men

By KATHLEEN McLAUGHLIN

WASHINGTON.

ASK Director Paul McNutt of the War Manpower Commission about the problems of womanpower, and he retorts tersely that there aren't any. Rhetorically, he is correct. For Mr. McNutt stands now where the suffragettes of yesteryear once stood, in his firm contention that women are people, and that jobs are jobs. Ergo, there's a manpower problem, but womanpower is indistinguishable from it.

This point of view is similar to that of Senator Warren Austin and Representative James Wadsworth, sponsors of last week's abruptly submitted National War Service Act, which proposes the drafting of women equally with men for essential war work. Neither Mr. McNutt nor the sponsors of the bill support the notion that women as workers should comprise a segregated or special group to be considered apart in meeting the main issue of yawning vacancies in factory and farm categories.

Director McNutt, however, rejects the plan for compulsory registration of women between the ages of 18 and 55 which is basic in the Austin-Wadsworth measure. "It would be a staggeringly expensive thing," he argues, "and needless. At the present time we think it would be destructive of morale. The data would be out of date before it could all be used, so that it's foolish to consider it at all. What we have concentrated on, and what we have already begun to do, is to register women locally, in those areas where real industrial congestion exists. It has been going along nicely, so far."

He concedes that to expect uniform efficiency from local supervisors of such registrations in all areas would be anticipating the impossible. When and if the individual routine bogs down, he is prepared to send in "a bolster" from Washington, in the person of some representative of the Manpower Commission qualified to step up the procedure.

No detrimental effect on women workers will follow enactment of

the President's executive order for a forty-eight hour work week, Director McNutt predicts.

"The health of women as well as of men workers is of prime importance in attaining peak production," he said. "Of course, the possibility of the longer hours affecting women will be watched carefully."

In support of his conviction about the ability of women to endure, under the new order, the Manpower Chief cited the case of an 80-year-old woman acquaintance who is "hale and hearty" notwithstanding a sixty-hour work week.

A "net" of 1,900,000 American women will be added to the nation's payrolls, he estimates, in compliance with the order, adding that he believes it will curtail migration of workers of both sexes.

"One of the purposes of the order," he commented, "is to keep migration of workers at a minimum and thereby utilize the local labor supply to the fullest."

He is almost serenely sure that in every area where additional women workers are needed, a full complement of feminine employables will be found, without importing any from outside. Even Buffalo, where a call went forth several days ago for 30,000 more women for war work, should be able to produce that many without recourse to migratory groups, he insists.

Migration of women war workers is an eventuality which he hopes will never come to pass, because "it involves so many problems." Far more than men who roam from place to place in search of work, he indicates, women workers must be supplied with adequate housing, transportation, police protection in questionable areas, and other facilities men can and do dispense with on occasion.

"We still have a vast number of women unemployed who are capable of working," he emphasizes. "We shall have to get to the bottom of that reserve, and we'll fill the jobs. There are many women who have children over 16 who could take war work and who

219

would help greatly if they would. As a matter of fact, there are jobs of one kind or another open even for the older women and the physically handicapped.

"As for mothers with children of school age, plenty of discussion is going on about methods of day care—but that's a large subject."

Woman's Land Army

Well, then, what about a woman's land army? Mr. McNutt takes seriously the suggestion that women might gravitate in large numbers to rural areas from nearby communities, although he is not so sure that farmers would accept this solution of their labor quandaries.

His agency, he points out, will no longer have supervision if a woman's land army is organized, for what he terms "a very practical reason." Inability to get sufficient appropriations to finance the administration of such units, he discloses, prompted his recent announcement that all agricultural labor problems henceforth would be the responsibility of the Food Administration and the Secretary of Agriculture, Claude R. Wickard.

Mr. McNutt sees no necessity for establishing a women's division of the WMC through which to cope with women workers as a separate entity, and takes occasion to make it plain that Miss Charlotte Carr, who has just joined his staff in the capacity of assistant to Fowler W. Harper, deputy director, will deal with men's work as well as with women's.

OFFICE JOBS WENT MOSTLY TO WOMEN

They Took 70% of Posts Left by Draftees in 1942—Few Men Over 45 Hired

Roughly 70 per cent of the office positions vacated here in 1942 by men leaving for the armed services were filled by women, while relatively few replacements were made by hiring men over 45 years old, according to a survey just completed by the New York chapter of the National Office Management Association.

The study, covering thirty-two companies with an average of 1,000 employes in their New York offices, showed that most of the concerns had satisfactorily used women throughout the entire organization, while others limited them to certain departments.

Several reasons were given for the small percentage of older men taken on, chief of which was the fact that these persons are not suited by nature to clerical work.

Although most companies have found that women, after a reasonable period of training, are as efficient as the men whom they replaced, about 80 per cent of them have limited these new employes to non-supervisory positions, it was found.

More than 70 per cent of the answers showed that the majority of such replacements are made with women from outside the organization, yet only five out of twenty-eight companies found it necessary to inaugurate special training courses. One concern, however, reported it had instituted a $60,-000 training program, amounting to about $1,000 for each woman.

In answer to the question as to which jobs they expected would require the greatest number of women replacements during the coming year, personnel directors included the following: Accountants, bookkeepers, buyer's assistants, purchasing clerks and tabulating operators.

February 14, 1943

Coast State Orders Equal Pay
OLYMPIA, Wash., March 10 (P) —The Legislature, after Senate approval yesterday, sent to Governor Langlie a measure making it unlawful to pay women less than men for the same work.

'I Worked on the Assembly Line'

By Lucy Greenbaum

BUFFALO.

MUCH talk floats around about women in war work, some of it official, a lot pure hearsay. To try to find out what the feminine score is in the war league I worked on the assembly line of a large aircraft plant for a week. Role—riveter. Only a few plant officials were in the know.

Entering a war plant is like visiting a strange, jangling world. It is mechanized bedlam to a civilian when for the first time he finds himself in a room that stretches long and wide, with thousands of workers stirring around him and noise crashing against his ears—a world where men and machines join forces in creating for combat, where stress is on speed and precision and sound measures out the beat of progress.

Long aisles ring loud with the staccato smash of hammering, drilling and riveting —the labor pains of a plane. Noise hits from scalp to arch in this city built on cement. Rivet guns beat at the forehead like a thousand woodpeckers. Vibrations catch every tooth. All the old cavities throb.

Fantastic factory shapes sprout from the cold floors. Iron and steel giants tear apart aluminum pieces, beat form into unshaped metal strips. To the rhythm of the din move rows of facile fingers, building up the finished weapon of war from a mass of prefabricated parts at one end of the shop floor.

Promise of the power to come whirls out from the machine shop—sheet metal, electrical and cowling, wing, tail and fuselage departments. They centralize to create the plane that sprawls in lazy majesty at the other end of the floor.

Fluorescent bars spray theatrical aura over the season's noisiest and biggest drama. They shine through the network of air hoses that shoot down from the ceiling to meet the rivet guns. They light up the maze of jigs and fixtures that clasp parts all down the line.

To this stage of steel the workers bring life and in turn receive the reward of inner satisfaction that accompanies all handiwork. Their faces lack the stamp of one town. They are the rugged countenances of people who left behind them only a few months ago the Green Mountains of Vermont, the wheat lands of Dakota and cotton fields of Alabama.

"Once women overcome the fear of handling tools, they become as expert as men."

The hardened, reality-lined faces of men and women who labored in Buffalo's peacetime factories contrast with the soft, smooth complexions of suburban housewives and social registerites Urban, rural, hilltop, lowland, mountain, plain— all communities are represented. The whole nation speaks out in the accents— Michigan school teacher, New York City model, Buffalo garden-clubber, Smith College graduate, Philharmonic violinist. All have lived different lives in scattered spots of the land.

But now they have this in common— they rise in darkness to drive to work. Those who come twenty miles think of the unfortunate souls who drive forty miles. The latter remind themselves that others spread eighty miles behind them each way daily.

My first day began long before sunrise as a Chevvy slithered along icy roads. It was 6:45 A. M., the darkest hour before a hopelessly gray dawn. The driver expertly swung the shared car out of a spin. "This isn't anything," he reassured five passengers. "Remember last Winter when we skidded into the ditch four times trying to get to the plant?"

The car careened away the fifty minutes to the factory and the passengers bantered, the jocular exchange of people who do not know each other very well but are drawn together by an emergency. One of the girls drew teasing about her coming marriage to an Army private. "Save me the longest kiss at the wedding, will you, Kate?" asked the driver. The man in the back seat said he would settle for four short ones.

Suddenly in the distance shone long squat rows of square blue eyes, steady in their glare. "That's the plant," pointed out the driver. "Curtiss-Wright No. 2."

Flivvers and streamliners jammed wide roads that led to the magnetic blue light. Daylight to the graveyard shift, it glowed jewel-blue to the 8 o'clock trick. Cars crawled past the modernistic plant, magnificent in its massive lines, as only factories of war are. They slowed up by the nursery, where shadowy shapes—parents coming to work—hustled in sleeping children. Slower, always slower, they approached the mammoth parking lot.

Through acres of snow we plowed before the driver swung into an endless row.

Lights from oncoming cars flickered in scattered directions. They played on empty automobiles of the third shift, covered with snow that sifted down during the night. As we stepped out of the car the weather cracked us in the face. Over the slippery ground, whipped along by the wind, we raced. Even the tired face of the girl who staggered into bed at 2 A. M. after a night's dancing was stung to life, reddened by the cutting wind.

As prelude to a day's work we flashed identification cards at guards in the tunnel entrance, shook off the shivers and our coats before grabbing a quick cafeteria breakfast. Then trudged up steps to the shop floor, sardined by a crowd of subway rush-hour size.

The plant lay silent as they rushed it. For a five-minute period the graveyard shift cleans up tools; the newcomers punch the time clock. The quiet strikes an unnatural state. But in five minutes it has gone, and, once disappeared, it seems never to have been. Twenty-four hour motion moves in.

A handsome Irish foreman suggested in a kind but firm voice: "Put all your hair under your hat." A girl, leaning down to pick up a screw driver had been partly scalped a few weeks before when her hair caught in the whirring drill of the girl next to her. A brawny supervisor pointed to an attractive girl, boomed, "That's your partner." I was in. Panel Department, Nose 1 B, L & R. Tails, Outboard Skin, Nose Bulkheads, Match Angles.

LIFE pulsed around the skin (the aluminum frame), the stringers (horizontal ribs that ran inside the skin), the bulkheads (vertical ribs inside), flush rivets (to be driven parallel to the skin) and brazier rivets (ones that stood out on the skin surface). The skin was shaped like the hull of a boat. What it added up to was the wing section of a P-40, the fighting Curtiss Warhawk.

With no apology to Emily Post, my riveting partner, a veteran of eight months, screamed, "Hello." She owned the clearest hazel eyes this side of a rivet. She was 23 and had a 3½-year-old son. While working at the factory, I shared her double bed, lucky to get even half a one in this Queen City of the Lakes, her crown thorny with housing problems.

"We'll start

on the stringers," she shouted. The rivets on the straightaway stringers shot in like a flash, but on bulkheads you twisted your body around the jigs like a contortionist. You tapped twice if the rivet was right, once, if more shooting was needed. You don't dare use your voice. All

strength is needed for riveting. No wonder the training school nurse asked whether you ever had epileptic fits or St. Vitus's dance. The rivet gun shakes you up and down, in and out, around and around, as it plays counterpoint to the beat of surrounding guns.

THE first day at training school I smashed a rivet with the wrong end of the hammer. At the plant I tripped over benches, broke nails in loosening screws, tangled with air tubes. All signs pointed to a potential bottleneck. But in two days I felt like an old hand. I could hold the bucking bar against the rivet without feeling I would be thrown clear through the near-by tool crib.

Riveting is not the hardest nor is it the easiest work done by women. It is the operation, however, performed by most, as it constitutes 70 per cent of assembly work. Airplane rivets are not "hot," like those in building construction. They are tiny, the size of a small screw. There are 50,000 of them to a wing.

Two workers make a riveting team. One shoots the gun, applying the pressure, as my partner did. The other stands on the far side of the rivet, holding a bucking bar, the size and poundage of a paperweight. I had to manoeuvre the bar against the rivet, flattening it out as it shot through the hole.

Both gunner and bucker are responsible for good or bad rivet heads. If the bar is not held parallel to the skin, the rivet will splay out and the job will be a bad one. Or if the rivet is driven too much or the hole is crooked or is countersunk too unevenly, the rivet must be drilled out. That takes time. And time is the stuff of which victory is made.

YOU toil and sweat at 60 cents an hour (beginners' rate) and decide that it is far easier to march eight hours straight than to stand in one spot for the same length of time. You give out a muted "damn" when you first miss a rivet. But after you catch on to the trick of holding the bar square, you think about that wing and the plane on which it will go and the pilot who will fly it and how many Japs or Germans he will knock out of the sky.

"This really ain't much harder than messing around a kitchen," said one woman. An electric motor drill does remind one of an electric egg beater. Once women overcome the fear of handling tools they become as expert as men. This on the sworn word of foremen. They must learn the language, they must feel at home in the labyrinth of machines. That isn't too easy.

Between rivets there is the chance for a furtive eye to roam over the shop. In the distance men create the enormous Curtiss Commandos. Nearer at hand, a hulking man tosses a spitball in the direction of a pretty girl. Or he smiles at some special, slender riveter. (No delay to production are these assembly-line antics.) Occasionally the masculine ego takes other outlets. One woman told of a resentful partner who speeded up his work the first two hours just to wear her down. He eased up when she was too exhausted to move.

BUT women walk down the aisles without feeling eyes focus on them too steadily. They are free to visit personnel counselors in their booths on the floor. My riveting partner campaigned for new stools after the girls in the department, who sit when they hold the rivet guns or drill and countersink holes, had been snagged by splinters a sufficient number of times. Through the counselor she obtained a hearing and eventually new stools.

In spite of the noise handicap, clipped conversation shortens the work day, syllables punctuated by the tattoo of rivet guns. "I'd love to work over there," a girl screamed wistfully, eyeing the adjacent fuselage department. It was lucky the foreman did not hear her. The two departments had a feud on outracing each other toward production goals. "Where did you come from?" yelled a woman, new to the line herself. "How long were you in training?" shouted another. An elderly woman wanted to know if I liked the work.

Cattiness crept in as well as curiosity. One confident girl, nose tilted high, sauntered up. "Your rivets are too high," she announced. "I'll help out." My partner would not let her. "I don't like that girl," she said later. "No one else ever does anything right, except her."

ALTHOUGH they are required to buy standardized light blue uniforms before they are permitted to enter the factory, the women wear chiefly their own slacks, of warm corduroy and flannel. Blouses hide under serviceable sweaters. Maroon caps, furnished by the training school, share popularity with bright bandannas under which bloom many an artificial flower.

"Yes, the girls show a desire to glamourize," said the only woman administrative assistant. "If they weren't interested in dress I'd be worried."

Supervisors complain that women waste too much time; that they refuse to obey safety rules; that they band together more than men. "They can do their work and still things come a-cropping into their minds," said one. "They keep up with everything that happens. They want to know the reason why Susie Jones is making three cents an hour more than Mary Smith."

Just as some dress to kill, and others look to utility, so do some women work diligently, others take their time. They are as good or as bad, as lazy or as conscientious, as American womanhood. "We got all kinds here," my partner summed it up.

One habit common to almost all, and pardonable, is watching the clock the last hungry minutes of the morning hours. To the factory worker lunch brings not food alone but half an hour of relaxation and music. Either the factory band or orchestra or recordings reverberate through the crowded cafeteria, whose walls are lined with colorful scenic paintings.

By a stroke of luck space opened up for us to put food-laden trays on a table near the orchestra which was hemmed in by masticating jitterbugs. Men of the engineering department blew trombones, beat drums and slid notes around saxophones. For their jive they earned the same rate of pay as on regular jobs.

Shoulders of youthful riveters moved in the spirit of "Five by

Five." A cafeteria worker, blues singer on the side, recalled, "I Had the Craziest Dream." An orange-haired, blue-jacketed man munching a red apple gazed at her speculatively. Between bites he hummed the tune along with her. As the orchestra swung into "How I Miss You," the girl sitting across the table wailed, "Of all the songs to play!" Desperately she jabbed her fork into a piece of pumpkin pie. Pumpkin pie, incidentally, is the favorite of workers, according to officials who are surprised to find that for once people like a food that is good for them—pumpkin is a vegetable.

EATING does not stop or begin with lunch. Jaws move round the clock. "He brings his lunch from home," said one stocky riveter of another. "And about 9:30 he gobbles a couple of sandwiches. Then he tears off to the cafeteria at 11:06 and puts down a hot meal. About 2 he polishes off some more of his sandwiches and at 4, he jams in a piece of pie. Then he goes home for supper. I don't see how he does it." "Has a waist as thin as an embroidery hoop, too," he sighed.

A SIGN of supreme sacrifice is the offering of a piece of candy or gum. Both are rationed and one hits the jackpot only by racing to the machine soon after the vender has supplied it. Otherwise the result is the return of the nickel. My partner always wrapped her chewing gum up carefully while she ate lunch, then bawled the dickens out of another girl for carelessly throwing it out with the lunch debris.

Marching back to the line, people waved. A girl with bandaged ears explained, "frost-bitten." One woman stopped to ask my partner a personal question about her husband from whom she was separated: "Do you think I should see him? It would look funny if the kid should ask and I don't know where he is."

So also it went in the rest room where during a fifteen-minute relief period the women ganged up to peel oranges, close heavy eyes, exchange flash news of a per-

sonal nature. Talk hummed on a major note. "It was princesse style with a long veil." "Yeah, she finally got married. I nearly fainted."

The last was said proudly, as well it might be. Even The Aircraftsman, published weekly by the A. F. of L. union, emphasizes the shortage of men. An item on the woman's page asks: "Who do the gals make up for? Are there really some single men in the plant? Or are some married men eligible?" In the company paper, The Curtiss Wright-er, a complete woman's page carries headlines slanted toward male-deprived femininity. A column, "Curtiss-ies," features such rationed news as: "Why is Mary Burns so interested in flying weather recently? Would a certain pilot have anything to do with it?" And, "What dissolved the beautiful romance between 'Jelly Bean' Cayne and Tom Schiesel?"

THE average woman's American dream of a vine-covered cottage enclosing white kitchen is far from forgotten. It wafts out in songs hummed at machines, in casual chatter. The women are the first to defend their positions at the plant. They admit they enjoy the weekly pay check ranging from $45 to $55 (benefit of overtime and bonus). They hint that a civilian's life is not too happy a one these wartime days. But the majority want to return to homes temporarily broken up, expect to marry men now fighting or want to find some hero and get married (still a theoretical state of bliss to many) as soon as war ends.

A small minority expect to keep their jobs, newly earned by grace of Axis aggression. These are mainly women formerly employed in factories and those who held jobs they did not like. One hefty girl slung pre-Pearl Harbor hash. She found customers more difficult to cope with than rivet guns. But if a man wants her job after the war, he can have it, she said. Most of them feel thus.

BUT until there is peace they are content each day five minutes

before quitting time to tuck tools away. "Let's go home and rest an hour and then go dancing tonight around the corner," suggested a lively riveter. She added, "We all dance with girl friends around here."

"I'm going home to the baby," said the mother of a two-and-a-half-month-old girl. "I see her little enough. She's going to start calling my mother 'mother' pretty soon." An elderly woman who lived thirty-five miles away complained, "You can't go out any more nights. No gas." One girl confessed, "I'm getting to know my family. Nothing else to do."

For fourteen hours the factory lay far behind all of them. Then came another dawn with a moon glistening on snow. And a third one, cold and gray again. For them the dawns go on and on. For me there were only a few.

On the last day as I stumbled out of the plant, the foreman, one of the few who knew I was temporary tribulation, motioned to me. "Couldn't you stay here?" he asked. "We need women." To limbo immediately were lulled memories of backache from bending over the skins, sore throat from outshouting machines.

I walked away feeling I had left an important job half done. Voices rang clear as I punched out for the last time, turned in the pass. The mother at the door of the child nursery, picking up her son after work, as she said amazedly to the woman in charge: "I don't see how you make Marvin eat cereal. He spits it up when I give it to him at home." The Texan supervisor, in charge of the panel department, who served twenty-eight years in the Army: "I was the first one to put women in and I'm proud of it. Working in a factory is harder than being in the Army. They're doing very well."

And making me feel less like a heel for leaving, the kindly tired voice of the superintendent of the training school where the women are weeded out: "Stay where you are. We need the newspapers." He added slowly, "The women won't stay in the jobs after the war. But they'll be better off for having worked in a plant. They'll know what it means then, when we say this is a free country."

SAYS WOMEN RAISE ABSENTEEISM RATE

Miss Perkins Finds Men in War Plants Are Away From Jobs Only Half as Much

ACCIDENTS A MAJOR CAUSE

Minor Illness, Another of the Primary Factors, Can Also Be Reduced, She Remarks

Special to THE NEW YORK TIMES.

WASHINGTON, March 5 — Absenteeism among women working in war industries is twice as great as among men, according to Secretary Perkins.

Younger women are absent much more than older women, the Secretary of Labor said today. Hence she considered that it is important for personnel offices to hire not young women solely, but a number who are 45 or more, who tend to be a markedly dependable group.

Women, she said, are more affected by cumulative fatigue than men, are more tied to household affairs, more susceptible to indigestion, and many of them not so accustomed to work habits. Nevertheless they tend to be more "tractable" on their jobs, according to their foremen. Although some younger women insist on Veronica Lake coiffures, they abide by most other safety rules for dress.

Accidents a Big Factor

Between 80 and 90 per cent of absenteeism is due to industrial accidents and illness, Miss Perkins said. Accidents, she remarked, are 90 or 95 per cent preventable, and much minor illness can be avoided. Improved working conditions will help in both cases.

Even secondary causes of absenteeism: transportation difficulties, shopping and household management problems and unfavorable shifts can be alleviated by action within a plant itself, she went on.

Educational campaigns by the Labor Department, unions and employers will tend, she said, to banish psychological causes of absenteeism; a worker who has been bored doing monotonous work will respond with interest if he realizes that he is "making the tool which makes the tool which makes the tool."

In other words, absenteeism is an old industrial story with a new war twist, she said; and it is nothing that a campaign can't lick. Since many causes are curable, she made these suggestions to war plants:

1. Place one person in charge of absences.
2. Have untoward absences reported to him.
3. Analyze the causes of absences.
4. Discover which ones management or labor, or both can remove.
5. Keep absenteeism records which are standard with those kept by other factories.

Advocates Standard Orders

Few employers, the Secretary declared, keep records of absenteeism or keep the same kind, or even agree on the definition.

Besides accident prevention installations and campaigns she suggested that a good canteen, superior sanitation, rest periods and welfare service helped reduce absenteeism.

In the aircraft industry 6½ per cent of the working time is lost by absenteeism, according to a survey made by the Bureau of Labor Statistics. In normal times about 4 per cent of the working time is lost in this industry.

A recently published survey made by the bureau shows that 7½ per cent of the working time in shipyards was lost by absenteeism. Miss Perkins pointed out that in the last war, however, a similar study showed absenteeism causing a loss of 18 per cent of working time in shipyards. Stabilization agreements and less competition on the labor market are largely responsible for the lower absentee rate during this war, she said.

March 6, 1943

'Occupation: Housewife'
—No Amateur Job

Once upon a time the words meant an easy occupation or no occupation. But now—

By Anita Brenner

"OCCUPATION, HOUSEWIFE" is what the census-takers used to scrawl, meaning Occupation, None. And there were uncounted hundreds of people working to make the entry mean, at least, Occupation, Easy. All the convenient markets were smilingly full; the deliveries quick. The lady of the house could tackle her principal business—meals —with the gaudy temptations of the cookery pages floating through her imagination, and not much more curb on her creations than the prejudices of her family and the amount of kitchen talent at hand.

The food news urged upon her a symphonic variety of items, some exotic delicacies, some old reliables flooding the market at favorable prices. She could depend, for speed, on cans and prepared mixes and frozen foods, and she could at ten minutes' notice be bountiful with eggs (at 35 cents a dozen) and coffee with cream, and toast with butter; while for her parties she could choose grandly from the products of the whole round earth, not even conscious of the thousands of miles on rubber, or in refrigerated trains, or in the holds of safe ships, between production and her table.

There were armies of experts devoted to doing away with her drudgeries, producing new and better labor savers, new and better household beautifiers. There were servicemen to cope, almost immediately, with accidents and breakage. Fuel companies took it upon themselves to keep their customers automatically supplied. Stores were anxiously solicitous to please in every detail—the exact shade, the perfect texture, the quality, the hour of delivery; while in the magazines and newspapers, writers tortured their imaginations for new and better recipes, arrangements, ideas—all to save the housewife work, thought and trouble.

Her difficulties were either money or minor. Being a housewife no longer meant the old-fashioned list—hard work, thrift, ingenuity, skill; other qualities came first, intangibles such as attractiveness, being a good companion, a pleasant hostess, an intelligent listener. Any amateur, with a little practice, could meet the specifications, and any reasonably competent Mrs. could get through her chores with plenty of time left for clubs, sports, other occupations. Her ornamental qualities might bear some strain when "mother" was added to housewife, but living was designed to take hard work and inconvenience out of that job, too. The tons of literature offered to mother talked chiefly of behavior and attitude; problems seemed mainly psychological.

IN those far-off days—could that have been not much over a year ago?—"housewife" was a comfortable word. Young girls looked forward to the day when they could apply it to themselves. Matrons relaxed by exploring the bright suggestions of the women's magazines for more to do and buy. The transformed attic, the smartened sunporch, the ugly window framed into a picture, the twirls of chintz, the tropical fish-tanks set into bathroom walls, the spun-glass draperies, the tricks with chromium and aluminum and plastics, the indoor gardens. And the dream-kitchen, with its automatic dishwasher, its precise docile stove, its rows of electrical gadgets, and next month probably, its frozen-food unit and its chemical trays for growing ever-fresh vegetables.

Quaint memories. All that now seems as gone as Grandma's girlhood. Grandma's household encyclopedia read, as a matter of fact, less quaintly than ours now, with half the recipes obsolete and the rest needing to be manoeuvred. (If you wait long enough, everything comes back in style, including long woolen underwear.) So Aunt Sophronia's book for brides, published in 1870, offers that recipe for carrot pudding that Englishwomen have been hurrah-ing; describes how to use meat to

The housewife as a business woman—A scene (somewhat exaggerated) in the American kitchen, 1943.

the last ounce (and make soft soap out of the drippings); how pots and pans are scoured without steel wool; how to do home dry-cleaning; and how to make coffee without wasting even the aroma.

There are instructions too against every conceivable emergency: the right technique for getting a safety pin out of a baby's throat; how to handle a hysteric ("with firmness and not too much sympathy"); what to do for a person struck by lightning; the most reviving drink for laborers; and even, just in case, "how to cure a felon" with a blister of Spanish fly and bread-and-milk poultices.

BUT alas! There are no instructions in Aunt Sophronia, or in the very newest housewife's handbooks, on how to give first aid to the plumbing. Nor is there any homely advice on how to oil, clean, and repair your washing machine. Nor on how to take apart and put back into service a faulty electric iron. Nor on how to diagnose a smoking vacuum-cleaner motor. Nor on how to make a fireplace throw the maximum amount of heat, nor on how to measure cubic space and heat loss, to determine the minimum fuel needed. Nor on what vitamins and calories must replace such butter, meat and

canned fruit juices as must be left off under rationing.

There are no logarithmic tables by which to measure the points of a can of tomatoes against the food and ration value of two envelopes of dehydrated soup; nor is there any light on how to balance the compactness and ration value of frozen foods against the extra work and expense of fresh. There is no formula for arranging the hours of the day to make room for all that Occupation, Housewife, has come to mean and still allow time for other work.

THE job of housewife is not an amateur job any more. It means at the very least Occupation, and demands a list of skills that ought soon to give it the status of a profession, or anyway of a trade calling for trained, experienced operators—like that of

offset, stripper, centerless grinder, commi-butcher, jig-maker, decoder, chocolate stroker, or other mysterious callings mentioned in the employment ads. Universities are now offering wartime courses "For Women Only"—confidential crams on How to Cope.

The list of subjects being taught in the university classes for emergency household management has not been announced, but if a housewife designed the course it surely includes: mechanics, automobile and household; electrical engineering, carpentry, plumbing, advanced mathematics, dietetics, nursing, pediatric principles, applied diplomacy, and news analysis.

MANY of these subjects are being learned by housewives now, as the progressive educators advocate, "by doing." You plead and coax a repair man to your particular emergency, then stand by and ask questions like a child of 6 and next time—well, next time it is a different problem and a different repair man unwillingly being professor. You juggle your meal plans and your calories and vitamins and ration points and arrive at a neat schedule. And then you arrive at the butcher shop where a harassed man looks sadly at what isn't in his refrigerators, and apologizes

for the prices of what is. Maybe the curriculum ought to include Foraging: Beginners' Class.

But there is one subject in the housewife's new curriculum that she studies daily and daily finds herself failing at. That is news analysis. The paper has become something that must be read with serene and minute care. Impending storms around some particular food or household item gather, outside of the news, for weeks and months: remarks dropped by the grocer ("We're running low on this, better get some more * * *" or "Sorry, we couldn't get any this week"); rumors ("They're going to limit us to three dresses a year"); or indirect news, in disputes between bureau heads about who is to blame for the crisis in, let's say, baby-pants.

Throughout the roller-coastering, your experience with, for instance, sugar and then coffee doesn't seem to stand up very well; it takes time to get the hang of the news and see where it seems to be going. Besides, each crucial item becomes all entangled in moral questions: instructions to buy or not to buy, so that you hesitate, guiltily, to buy anything, for fear you may be helping a hoarding rush or operating in some black market, since you know well enough from

what tradesmen say that black markets have taken in a great number of things. And when you look at costs you imagine that you know one reason for the rubber shortage—an immense amount of it must have gone into price-ceilings.

So Occupation, Housewife, becomes a state of mind that goes from irritation to annoyance to alarm and then to relief and graduate philosophy, for most of the bogies turn out to be merely inconveniences. At this point your graduate philosophy is needed chiefly for coping with the admonitions and instructions handed down to you by officials. You are told to go back to the washtub and simultaneously to rush to the nearest United States Employment Office and register for war-plant work. You are warned that if those 5,000,000 women needed to man production don't materialize voluntarily, you, and certainly your maid (if you are fortunate enough to have one), will be drafted for some occupation more essential than housewifery.

BESIDES, you are to expect that, if the man of the house isn't in uniform already, he probably soon will be, so in any case you'd better find the magic formula for handling Occupation, Housewife, in tandem with Occupation, payrolled. You are assured that there are adequate facilities for child-care, while at the same time you discover that schools, recreation centers, camps have cut their scope because of no funds, personnel or transportation. And some professional conscience on the radio, or in the press, admonishes you in the name of all that is holy that housewifery and motherhood must always remain your full-time job.

Still . . . in the next breath of news some place is being bombed; households are being blotted out, not just shaken up and inconvenienced and irritated. Women in other countries are having to combine housewifery with fire-fighting, sabotage, guerrilla sniping. And in many other places they cannot even fight back, nor help to fight in any way; total war has made numb, caged animals of them. Oh, yes, here "housewife" is still a very comfortable and reassuring word.

MAID'S LORGNETTE IS ON THE BOSS NOW

Judy O'Grady, Unionized, Will Give Careful Consideration to Your Request to Employ Her

UNION FIXES HER TERMS

CIO Units in Baltimore and Washington Aim to 'Protect and Dignify' the Servant

WASHINGTON, July 3 (AP)—Now comes the housemaid with a union card.

She asks a 48-hour week and, Sundays off, union pay, steady work and, for the health certificate she must show, she wants assurances of her employers' good health.

The United Domestic Workers Union (CIO), a new figure in the nation's labor picture, has been organized in Baltimore and Washington to "protect and dignify" the maid, the cook and other household employes.

Housewives have viewed this development with mixed feelings, but national women's organizations, which have been working toward standardization of working conditions in the household employment field, look upon it as a possible solution to the rapidly growing "servant problem."

Leaders of these groups contend that if household workers get a better wage and hour set-up and some of the benefits afforded workers in other fields, and if the stigma of servant—whether real or fancied—is removed, fewer may be inclined to drift from one household to another or to war jobs.

Now a housewife may offer to let the maid wear her mink coat on days off or hold out other hitherto undreamed of inducements. For, while it may be hard to get a sirloin steak these days, it's just as hard to get a Susie to cook the steak.

Better Jobs Lure Maids

For Susie, Mary, Agnes and hundreds of other ex-maids are finding jobs in the war plants, restaurants or shops which frequently pay them more per hour than they used to earn in an entire day.

Besides this they have their evenings free and Sundays off. They have better social standing among their friends, protection on their jobs, insurance when they are let off.

Mrs. Jean Collier Brown, formerly with the U. S. Women's Bureau and former consultant of the Y. W. C. A.'s national board on household employment problems, was the organizer of the Baltimore union, first in this field, early last year. Its present members, Mrs. Brown says, all are Negroes.

The Washington group, which includes both white and Negro members, was established in December.

The union says that in placing workers priority is given to households where both husband and wife are employed.

The Union's Pay Scales

Here are the union's pay scales: In Baltimore day workers receive $3.20 for an eight-hour day. Full-time workers receive $15.50 for a forty-eight-hour week.

In Washington workers receive 50 cents an hour for an eight-hour day; $20 a week for a forty-eight-hour week, or $15 for inexperienced workers or those who do not have much responsibility on the job.

In all types of employment overtime rates are fixed at 50 cents an hour. However, in full-time work overtime is payable only after the forty-eight hours have been put in, rather than on a daily basis, giving leeway to the employer to substitute additional time-off during the week in lieu of extra wages.

In Washington members may work ten hours a day in homes where the employers are themselves working, providing they work on a five-day week.

Mrs. Marion Davis, an organizer of the Washington group, says:

"We have tried to impress upon our members that a good job is a job that lasts. The organization of domestic workers should result in an attitude of mutual respect between servant and employer which is of prime importance in a well-run home."

Child Care Funds

WASHINGTON, July 7—The Senate passed, by a vote of 61 to , and sent back to the House today legislation authorizing $200,-000,000 more for community facilities under the Lanham act. The actual appropriation, however, was cut later in the day to $50,000,000, and the Second Deficiency bill, which provided the reduced appropriation, was tied up by Senate and House disagreement over other provisions.

Under the enabling bill adopted by the Senate, the child care program, which has been administered under the Lanham act by the Federal Works Agency, would continue to be administered by this agency, but with two provisions.

First, the Senate amended the measure to insure that no grant be made for the operation or maintenance of public schools without prior consultation with State departments of education and the United States Office of Education.

Second, it was stipulated that none of such funds be used for the operation of day care or extended school services for children of mothers employed in war areas and when the War Area Child Care Act becomes law."

In other words, if the Child Care Act, known also as the Thomas bill, should be adopted by the House, administration of the war program for child care would pass from the Federal Works Agency to the Federal Security Agency, or more specifically, to the Children's Bureau and the Office of Education.

The War Area Child Care bill has been adopted by the Senate and is being considered in committee in the House.

Meanwhile, the Senate, acting on the Second Deficiency bill, cut the Lanham Act appropriation of 200,000,000 to $50,000,000 and failed to vote funds for the Thomas bill. Even if the Thomas bill should get out of committee and be adopted by the House before the impending recess, there would therefore be no funds to administer it.

It is believed, consequently, that further legislative action on the War Area Child Care Act will wait until fall. The children of working mothers in war areas, provided the 50,000,000 fund is finally approved, will be cared for much as they have been this past year, by the FWA, but some consultation with educational authorities will be involved.

The FWA estimates that 1,000,000 children of war working mothers will need care by September.

CHARM BY UNCLE SAM

Thousands of Girls in Capital Train to Be Hostesses to Service Men

By AUDREY ANDERSON

WASHINGTON.

PERHAPS the recent song lament of the lonely sailor, "Aint I Ever Goin' to Get a Bundle of Charm?" spurred a government agency to open a charm school. Whatever the reason, results have proved more than satisfactory. Over 30,000 young women in the nation's capital have been tutored under expert guidance in the art of personal grooming, the qualifications of a good hostess and the essentials of military security, and are now prepared to act as dance hostesses to service men under the sponsorship of the OCD.

Working on the theory that a soldier or sailor on leave will seek the level of the girl in his company, the War Hospitality Committee of the Recreation Service, Inc., has undertaken the training of 75,000 girls in the charm school course. Standards of conduct, appearance and entertainment of the uniformed men and their hostesses are thus kept high, and the amount of military and naval information given out is correspondingly low.

Twelve agencies cooperating with the OCD in giving this charm course, before allowing the girls to participate in the activities of service centers, include: the Y. W. C. A., the Jewish National Welfare Board, USO-National Catholic Community Service, USO-Y. M. C. A., USO-Salvation Army, Masonic Service Center, Federation of Churches, and other church-sponsored agencies. Here the future hostess is given advice on careful make-up—

the correct shade of powder and lipstick, the discreet use of mascara or eye shadow to bring out the sparkle in her eyes, ways of emphasizing her best features and subduing those not so attractive. From a well-known hairdresser she receives tips on the care of her hair.

Clothes and Dancing

Under the guidance of authorities on social behavior she brushes up on her dancing and etiquette. Through the eyes of fashion experts she learns to select the type of clothes service men like best, and by modeling in a self-staged fashion show she acquires ease and poise in wearing them. Evidently the boys show a marked preference for "feminine" styles, for the girls are not allowed to appear in slacks, socks or sweaters and skirts. However, the too-dressed-up girl is as out of place as if she wore a pair of overalls borrowed from a farmerette. Sloppiness is not tolerated; neatness and good grooming are the keynotes in dress. A cotton frock, if it is as spick and span as an escort's uniform, can be the perfect attire for an informal dance.

The potential hostess listens to a lecture on the qualities of a perfect hostess. In that capacity her conduct must be above reproach at all times. She must be polite and friendly to all her guests at the sponsored dances. She should not spend too much time with any one man, neither should she congregate with her sister hostesses to talk, dance or play ping-pong.

Any girl who thinks she can take advantage of the Service Men's club as a dating bureau is likely to be disillusioned, for no hostess is permitted to leave with a date during the evening. And the girls know better than to attend one of the affairs with the preconceived notion of making a future date with one of the soldiers or sailors, then leaving. Her duties re bound within the walls of the club room and the square of the dance floor, and they are as specific as those of the Red Cross worker or the AWVS volunteer.

One stringent rule the young women follow closely is that of not receiving or giving any military information. To each girl is given to study a government-issued booklet, "A Personal Message," which cites the dangers of loose talk and the drastic results of passing on even apparently "harmless" gossip. As soon as any service man, consciously or unconsciously, begins to talk about troop movements, boat departures or equipment, the hostess tells him gently, but firmly, that it is against the rules for her to listen. What the girls do listen to is talk about the boys' homes, their parents and their friends. The men find it relaxing, too, to spill their worries about whether the girl back home will write regularly, and whether she'll wait for them to return.

Girls from every State in the Union come to the charm school. The shy little girl from Iowa, who works as a file clerk for the OPA, the tall, gauche young woman who came from Texas with nothing to recommend her but an ability to type sixty words a minute, the sturdy farm girl from Minnesota who carries messages through the labyrinth of the Pentagon Building —all emerge on the dance floor and in the club rooms as typical of the American girls service men want to spend their free time with.

August 15, 1943

CHILD CARE UNITS IGNORED BY MANY

Child care centers and nursery schools, set up for the benefit of working mothers in areas where Government contracts have put hundreds of thousands of women on industrial payrolls, are standing idle, or are only partly utilized, a

July 8, 1943

survey of manufacturing cities showed yesterday.

Officials in New York, Detroit and on the Pacific Coast, where a manpower shortage has forced employers to canvass for ever-increasing numbers of women war workers, agreed that the program, established by local initiative and by funds supplied under the Federal Works Agency, so far has proved only in part successful.

Ignorance of the facilities provided to care for children while

mothers work on the assembly lines was the explanation most generally offered. But other elements also have hampered the working of the nursery schools, officials said. Among these were lack of adequate transportation, jurisdictional squabbles, which in some instances slowed down the start of operations, and the objections of mothers in some sections of the country to what they characterize as "Sovietized nurseries." In New York, less affected than some other cities by mushrooming war industry, Helen M. Harris, executive director of the Mayor's Committee on Wartime Care of Children, estimated that between 8,000 and 10,000 children now were being cared for by all agencies, public and private. She pointed out, however, that due to their limited hours of service, many fail to provide for the needs of mothers who work long hours in war industry.

With the opening on Oct. 1 of three day nurseries, and of still another on Oct. 8, the committee will bring to twenty-four the number of day care centers which it is helping to finance, Miss Harris said. Miss Harris added that the committee hopes to double its present facilities for 1,570 children before long.

Despite increased opportunities, however, thousands of working mothers in New York are making no move to place their children in centers, she revealed. Ignorant of the existence of convenient nurseries, they often leave their youngsters in the care of an aged grandmother or a watchful neighbor. In other neighborhoods there are not sufficient centers to meet the demand for care.

The mounting number of inquiries answered by the committee's counseling service — which have almost doubled in the last month—indicate that parents are becoming increasingly interested in the use of the care centers. Miss Harris indicated that the opening of school is also partly responsible since children often can no longer be left in charge of their older brothers and sisters.

In Detroit, where an estimated 200,000 women are currently employed in war industry, Warren E. Bow, Superintendent of Schools, said that the Board of Education has set up twenty-three nursery schools

Disputes Over Supervision

Despite the fact that the existing schools are not being used to capacity, Mr. Bow said that progress was being made and the attendance was rising gradually as more working mothers learned that facilities were available in their neighborhoods. The program originally got away to a bad start because of disputes over jurisdiction and supervision. Several agencies sought to control the schools before the city stepped in and placed the responsibility with the Board of Education.

More than 600 child-care centers now are in operation in areas of "acute labor shortage" in the three Pacific Coast States, it was disclosed by Mrs. Mary H. Isham, regional supervisor of war public services of the Federal Works Agency in San Francisco.

Located largely in aircraft and shipbuilding regions, 329 of these are nursery schools and the rest are centers for children of 6 to 14 years.

In general the nursery schools are about two-thirds filled but this fact, according to persons familiar with the situation, is not conclusive evidence that the number is adequate to meet the needs of war-working mothers who have no other place to leave their children.

Dr. Herbert R. Stolz, who operates the Oakland program for the Board of Education and who has sixteen nurseries going, believes that unless a center is placed about every five blocks the transportation problem will be too difficult to attract many mothers who otherwise would take advantage of the centers.

September 24, 1943

RISE IN BIRTHS SPEEDS BABY-CARRIAGE TRADE

WPB Authorizes Making of 693,700 Vehicles in 3 Months

WASHINGTON, Aug. 20 (AP)— The wartime increase in babies brought from the War Production Board today an order for increased output of carriages, walkers, strollers and sulkies.

Expecting that this year's births would total the largest ever, WPB authorized the manufacture of 693,-700 baby vehicles of all kinds in the last three months of this year —an increase of about 50 per cent over the present rate. Of the total, 349,000 will be carriages.

The birth rate has been increasing ever since the start of the war. It advanced from 18.9 a thousand population in 1941 to 20.5 last year, when about 2,800,000 babies were born.

August 21, 1943

From the Lathe To the Hearth

Mrs. Fisher answers the question: 'Will women in industry return to home-making?'

By Dorothy Canfield Fisher

AGES and ages ago two hairy, gnarled old hunters sat at the mouth of the tribal cave and talked. What did they talk about? A subject that has worried every generation—the disastrous changes in women's attitude toward life. If only, they told each other—if only this new-fangled notion that women had about tilling the ground could be done away with, everything would be all right, just as life used to be when mother stayed inside the cave, as mothers should, and kept the fire going and was always there when her menfolks wanted her.

"The big mistake," said one grizzled ancient, shaking his matted head, "was to let the women ever get started on growing things to eat. It'll absolutely ruin home life. All there is to it is that it gives 'em a chance to leave the cave and gad! It's animal fodder anyhow—grains and vegetables—strawy trash! I'll eat a deer all right, hide and hoofs; but I'll be danged if I'll eat what the deer puts into his stomach. I'm a man! Meat, gristle, liver and lights and entrails, especially entrails, that's the food that makes men. That's what made our fathers the grand specimens they were."

"Yes, I hate to see the good old ways breaking up," conceded the other. "But there's something to the idea of having rations to fall back on when the hunting's bad. Meat spoils if you try to keep it too long, and grains don't."

"That's woman's talk," cried the first, testily. "You mark my words, once let women get their food some other way than by having a he-man bring in meat to them, there'll be no living with them. They won't take care of the children! They'll try to boss us. We'll always have to eat a mixed diet, our good meat all tangled up in our insides with deer food, and then where'll we be?"

LIKE the refrain of a folk ballad, this question, "Then where'll we be?" comes echoing down the ages. The First World War heard a flip modern paraphrase of it from soldiers about soldiers, "How you gonna keep 'em down on the farm after they've seen Paree?" Now it runs (once more about women), "How you gonna keep 'em in by the hearth after they've worked on a lathe?" More literally, more soberly expressed, the question runs, anxiously, "Will modern women, now going into industry, be willing to go back to the hearth to resume their role as home-makers when the war is over?"

228

Let us give a first answer to this question in the Yankee way by asking: "What do you mean 'home-makers'?" What is done by a woman to earn that golden, hyphenated title of honor changes with every generation. Not by her will, by the nature of things. For our eighteenth-century colonial forefathers a home-maker was a woman who—always inside the home—manufactured all that her big family clan needed in the way of textiles; dried, canned and salted much of their food; who provided all the nursing care and almost all the medical care the family got; who cut and sewed together their clothes; who, if one of the numerous tribe lost his mind, somehow took care of the insane person (still always inside the home, no matter how trying this was to the others); who taught the little boys most of what learning they had and gave the girls all the education they ever received; who was responsible for the care of all the old folks, bedridden and dying in the midst of family life, because that was the only place she could put them.

SUCH was the home made by your great-great-grandmother and dearly cherished in the boyhood memories of her son, your great-grandfather. Such was the hearth beside which, in his old age, he insisted he thought women ought to have stayed, day in and day out, just as his illiterate devoted mother did. Yet he would have been horrified if his wife had provided such a home as that one really was, if she had stayed closely beside such a hearth. That home was fly-infested, typhoid-fever breeding, superstitious, narrow-minded; its few dark, crowded rooms were constantly full of the groanings of infirm old age and the wailings and smells of infancy, mingling with the whoops of children underfoot all of their waking hours; it was full of senseless hampering prejudices, cruel a good many of them, based on total ignorance of what we consider enlightened or civilized standards of living.

Yet your great-grandfather did well to cherish the memory of it dearly, for it was a good home, as any place is a good home where a good woman lovingly does the very best she can with the raw material of life available to her as a home-maker. Where he did not do well was in allowing an association of ideas to grow up in his mind which confused the basic and immortal character of loving and creative home life with the ever-changing details of earning a living and providing food, clothing and shelter.

THE concern now felt about whether women who have had the experience of industrial employment will "go back to resume their role as home-makers" is based on the idea that, unless they go "back," no homes will be made. But what generation ever went back—except those stricken by the calamity of a return to dark ages? Women were, according to the learned historians of humanity, the first of our race to learn how to plant and cultivate grains and root crops. This knowledge certainly made them more independent of their menfolks. But did they ever refuse to share with their families the excellent new food they had learned how to produce in an abundance that seemed never-failing compared to the haphazard irregularity of hunting? On the contrary, they used their new skill to make homes far better than men had ever had before.

Why should we fear that precisely from 1943 on women are going to stop thus acting according to one of the deepest human instincts? Judging from the unbroken tradition of the past, whatever it is that women today are learning and seeing and doing in the industrial world will be reflected in a home life modified to fit the people who will be (as people always have been) dependent on good homes for their happiness. The plain, double-barreled fact is, first, that women will not go "back" to resume their roles as home-makers; and secondly, that the husbands and children of the years ahead would not like it a bit if they did. Women will go forward to share with those they love—not exactly in the old way; who ever has done this?—whatever rewards come to them with their now industrial, commercial and professional skills.

CAN anyone foresee what rewards (other than more cash in hand) may come to women who have been, or still are, wage-earners? I'll hazard a guess that they will be psychologically closer to their husbands and grown-up children than the women of yesterday who knew only the inside of their own homes; hence that they will understand them better, hence that their loving services for them will be more intimately right.

We are so accustomed to the dark gulf of total ignorance about each other's life work which since the beginning of the industrial age has separated all men from all women who are home makers and nothing else that we do not feel the tragedy of it. We as-

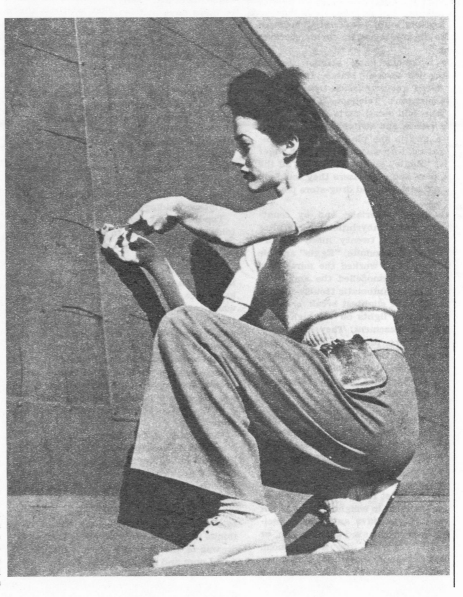

sume that it is in the nature of things.

Yet earlier generations of American men were not thus separated from their women. When the father went for his daily earning-a-living work to the fields around the home or into his own carpenter or shoe shop in the wing of the house he did not vanish into another sphere, as does the jobholder of today, spending the best hours of his every day in work literally unimaginable to the old-time father as to the commuter or jobholder of the modern world.

The pre-industrial father was physically near enough to his home to know what was going on there. If he were greatly needed, say to help care for a sick baby, he could step aside at intervals from his twelve or fourteen hour working day to share in an emergency. The eight hours plus time for getting there and back working day of the modern worker constitutes far more of a literal separation from his family, and infinitely more of a psychological barrier. Never till industrialism drove its great wedge between men working away from the home and women working inside the home was there in our country the yawning crevasse we take for granted between husband and wife.

PERHAPS that strange and unnatural kind of home life may vanish with the more complete utilization of women in industry, commerce and the professions. If all the population of our country, not only a little more than half as at present, does its full share of modern productive and necessary work, the work may get done in much less time. This would coincide with another trend of industry—the cutting down of human work-hours needed — by rapidly increasing utilization of the machine.

If so, there may be ever so much more home life—real home life, with the whole family together—in the future than we have dreamed of. With both husband and wife occupied outside the home for a shorter part of the day, the children may see more of their fathers than for a hundred years; wives may no longer be shamed (as so many fine modern women are) by feeling themselves excluded like ignorant minors from all the important business and professional questions which concern their husbands. In those days mother may have vastly more molding influence on her grown-up sons and daughters because, on the day when they begin to earn their living, they will not step out into life leaving mother behind them, in another century.

It may be that future generations of families, united by first-hand experience in job-holding and wage-earning effort carried on by both husband and wife for a shorter period of each day, will have much more free time for enjoying home life together because the husband will have more time at home, instead of having all the time at home left to the wife. They will, perhaps, look back with wondering compassion on the traditional husband and wife of our period, who, in so many cases, separate after a hasty suburban breakfast and meet again for a late dinner, totally unable even to imagine what in the world the other has been doing all day long.

I DOUBT if that child of the future will have any nostalgic yearning for the early twentieth-century home, dear as that has been to us because, like all good home life, it is associated in our minds with that certainty of parental love which is the essence of homemaking.

Nor will the young people of the future, immersed as we hope they all will be in the idea of federation as the way of life rather than totalitarian one-person domination, probably find anything amiss with a family life based on the same idea as that which is the living core of our beloved nation—a joining together in mutual effort, forbearance and helpfulness of equals. There will not be—we hope—anywhere on the globe human beings brought up to believe in the dog-ideal of unquestioning, implicit obedience to any other human being. Willing, intelligent cooperation with others who have had equal opportunities for development is the conduct they will recognize as right.

Imperialism, colonies kept dependent by being kept economically backward, authoritarian paternalism (no matter how benevolently intended), such are the forms of human organization we devoutly hope we will have left behind us forever, if we survive and win the war. Why should we fear to leave them behind us in family life?

SAYS UNIONS FAIL TO ABSORB WOMEN

Miss Christman Asserts They Will Be Problem After War Unless Policy Is Changed

Special to THE NEW YORK TIMES.

WASHINGTON, Jan. 31 — A warning that unorganized women workers will be a hazard to men unionists after the war unless trade unions take a more constructive policy toward women workers was issued today by Miss Elizabeth Christman in the bulletin of the Women's Trade Union League.

"Chiefly as a result of the war thousands of women who have had no part in the battle for union recognition suddenly find themselves as trade union members," said Miss Christman, executitve secretary of the league. "Unions have taken in new members so fast that less than normal attention has been given to educating new workers in trade union principles. This omission has been especially serious not only because women constitute such a large proportion of new workers but also because many women lacked prior industrial experience and so had not the slightest conception of the importance of organized activity in obtaining fair treatment for workers."

In the face of this situation, Miss Christman said, some local unions in contract negotiations "have used women's wage rates as a pawn to be sacrificed in favor of other, seemingly more important objectives."

She further said that "when an agreement with the employer cannot be reached and a case is taken to the National War Labor Board unions have not been insistent on obtaining fair wages for women workers."

"Usually their request is limited to 'equal pay' for women on 'man's jobs'; they have done almost nothing in board cases toward elimination of notorious differentials against women on so-called 'women's jobs'," she said. "The wage differentials in effect today not only are bound to discourage women's full participation in local union activities but tend to alienate many women from the entire labor movement."

Miss Christman prophesied many thousands of women now in war work will remain in industry after the war, but if present trade union policies are continued may drop out of the unions.

WOMEN FACE BIAS AS ROOM TENANTS

Survey Finds Men Preferred for Variety of Reasons Throughout Country

Special to THE NEW YORK TIMES.

WASHINGTON, April 21—The fact that women quite generally are not desired as roomers, for reasons that are fairly uniform, is stated in a report today by the Women's Bureau on the housing of women war workers.

At least one-third of the critical areas, including all the larger congested zones in forty-four States, were represented in the survey on which the report was based.

Under a caption, "Men Tenants Preferred," the Women's Bureau listed six reasons for women being less desired than men:

Washing, ironing, cooking privileges sought.

At home more, disturbing family life.

Entertain more, especially men friends.

More critical of quality of service and accommodations.

Too great a responsibility.

Less profitable; can't pay so well as men.

"This aspect of the housing problem changed somewhat with the departure of men tenants for military service, and landlords were left with vacancies," the Women's Bureau said. "Women in war industries, now earning good money, began to be tolerated as revenue-producers."

However, this trend was said to be counter-balanced by another—families whose economic situation improves become less inclined to take roomers.

"This fact darkens the housing picture even more for the unattached, employed women, against whom a definite prejudice to her tenancy already prevails" the report states.

The Women's Bureau concludes that for most of the employed young women it seems likely that group living must be the answer, both during and after the war, either in supervised residence halls and clubs or in rooming and boarding houses, especially for younger employes in the lower income groups.

April 22, 1944

3 NEW DEMOCRATS STIR CAPITAL HOPES

Much Is Expected of Women Recently Elected to House in East, West and Midwest

MRS. WOODHOUSE LEADS

She Held Connecticut Office —Mrs. Douglas and Helen Gahagan Are Promising

By KATHLEEN McLAUGHLIN

Special to THE NEW YORK TIMES.

WASHINGTON, Nov. 11—Informal comment in the capital on the new feminine acquisitions in the House of Representatives is almost universally approving of the caliber and background of the three Democrats who will take their oaths on Jan. 3.

Unquestionably the palm for prior experience and preparation for a legislative post among the three goes to Mrs. Chase Going Woodhouse of Connecticut. As a former Secretary of State of that Commonwealth and a long-time active campaigner, Mrs. Woodhouse enjoys seniority in party activities and in association with legislative groups which should make her a valuable and effective Representative.

Although her professional life has focused largely on women's affairs, through her interest in the development of wider fields of opportunity for her sex, she is by no means restricted to that scope either in ability or in perspective. As a professor of economics at the Connecticut College for Women, in New London, and as co-founder

with Mrs. Jouett Shouse of the Institute for Women's Professional Relations, she has functioned as an executive, as a business woman, as a lecturer and as a politician, and is versatile enough to work smoothly on legislative committees.

Mrs. Emily Douglas' Campaign

International affairs have long been an especial interest of Mrs. Emily Taft Douglas of Chicago, daughter of the late sculptor, Lorado Taft, and wife of Marine Capt. Paul H. Douglas, formerly a professor at the University of Chicago.

It was her husband's departure for the Pacific that stimulated Mrs. Douglas' interest in the Congressional race, which she entered as a novice, contesting against the experienced incumbent, Representative Stephen A. Day.

Her sizable majority was built up in part by small groups down-State who campaigned vigorously in that normally unfriendly territory, telling about her keen grasp of world affairs and her resolute opposition to isolationist factions as chairman of government for the Illinois League of Women Voters.

Mrs. Douglas cherishes a special interest in the affairs of service men and of their families. Unable to obtain any household help, Mrs. Douglas ran her State-wide campaign for Representative-at-Large while keeping house for herself and her small daughter.

Mrs. Helen Gahagan Douglas of California comes to Congress under the same handicap suffered by Mrs. Clare Boothe Luce, Republican, in the preceding session. Because both have been public figures and have built up reputations in other fields, superior performances are expected in Washington.

Helen Gahagan Has Varied Life

As Helen Gahagan, Mrs. Douglas starred on the concert stage and in legitimate theatre productions. She was first stirred to action when she encountered Nazi tyranny on its home ground, and broke a concert contract in Germany.

Returning to this country, she saw at first hand the misery and

suffering of the "Oakies" in California, and promptly organized with a number of her friends to provide relief, including a huge Christmas party for the youngsters.

Thereafter she concentrated on political activity, becoming national Democratic committeewoman from California, and proved herself so successful a campaigner that she rapidly acquired backing and support for more ambitious posts. In her race for the nomination and for election as Representative, she had the enthusiastic approval and support of her predecessor, Tom Ford, who yielded his seat after twelve terms in Washington.

Mrs. Douglas is expected to espouse labor interests and to continue her record as a liberal in various fields, also giving emphasis to the objectives of service men and women and supporting administrative measures.

Although developments on the floor of the House eventually dictate the success or failure of a legislator, women who are particularly concerned about obtaining qualified representatives in Washington are well pleased with their prospects for the Congress of 1945-1946, especially since the holdovers, one Democrat and five Republicans, will have acquired additional seniority on important committees.

Mrs. Edith Nourse Rogers of Massachusetts is next to the ranking Republican member of the Foreign Affairs Committee of the House. Mrs. Mary T. Norton, Democrat, has been for some years chairman of the House Labor Committee.

Mrs. Frances P. Bolton of Ohio has served for the last two terms on the Foreign Affairs panel. Miss Jessie Sumner of Illinois has spent the same length of time as a member of the Banking and Currency Committee. Mrs. Margaret Chase Smith of Maine moves up on the Naval Affairs Committee, through the defeat of the ranking Republican member, Melvin J. Maas of Minnesota.

Mrs. Clare Boothe Luce of Connecticut remains on the Military Affairs Committee, to which she was assigned two years ago.

November 12, 1944

Rules are Flexible

By Catherine Mackenzie

BILL is 2 years old. His father is in the Pacific. His wage-earning mother protests to this department that "the books" are written for mothers who stay home with their children. They must be, she says, because all the procedures on which she once boned up so diligently aren't of the slightest use now that she has a job and the only times she sees Bill on weekdays are at breakfast and at dinner time.

declares, or what she once visioned of an orderly routine for Bill, she feels that he needs to be with her even while she has her meals — anyway he is with her!

If you wonder why this mother bothers

"For example," she goes on, "that nice idea about a child eating by himself and not coming to the family meals until table manners are under control. Well! Billy won't stay away from the family meals. He screams if I try to make him. He's all over me, and all over the table too!" And no matter what the "books" say, she de-

about a few departures from the "books," the answer is that all her relatives say she's "spoiling" Billy. Everything in her life has changed since she planned the sequence of his days and hers; her own good sense tells her that she must vary the "rules" to fit these changes. But the social pressure has not changed.

IF these mothers weren't so often physically exhausted maybe they could more easily "take" public opinion or leave it alone. Hardier souls among them manage to do this. Earlier comment on this page quoted the mother who gave a lot of extra time to her 5-year-old's bedtime demands when his father went in the Army; answering the calls from upstairs, sitting by his bed, telling extra stories until he went to sleep. "Sure, I was told I was 'spoiling' him," she comments now, "but as I said then, I figured he missed his father and needed that much extra attention from me. He's all over that now."

The mealtime upheaval hit her family too—with double force, because one child was 5, the other was 2. Once upon a time she breakfasted in peace—she had the whole day to spend with the children. Now she gets to an office at 9 A. M., and they all breakfast together. "But I made a rule," she says, "that nobody could climb in my lap until I have my second cup of coffee. By that time they're both in my lap!"

Another challenge hard for a tired mother to take at the end of the day is, "They don't do that when you're not here." The implication is that it is only you, his loving mother, who rouses a demon in Danny's infant breast. Well, experts say that this is natural, that it is Danny's young way of saying he needs his mother, and some mothers meet it by putting in a little extra time with a child whenever they can—if it is only when getting dressed together. Readjusting bedtimes to their own working hours is another device for giving more time with the children—an hour or so later doesn't matter, mothers say.

Many of the mothers polled on this subject keep special times for the children on week-ends. "Saturdays I spend with Ellen" has been one mother's stock answer to invitations for years. Trips and excursions are on most week-end schedules; the mother of two children sets aside two hours on Saturday to do things with the older boy, "things," she says, "that Peter needs, that Billy can't enjoy." Mothers of older children keep in step with hobbies and bring home things bearing on them—magazines with color pages of airplanes, or the ballet, or stamps or stars. (One mother thinks that presents can be overdone and tend to put "mummy" in the category of the indulgent rich uncle.)

DR. MYRON E. WEGMAN, director of training and research in the Bureau of Child Hygiene of New York City's Department of Health, says that this topic is one calling more for "reassurance" than for specific advice. "If a mother remembers that first things must come first, that the child needs security and the type of routine that lets him know what to expect without trying to stick to alarm-clock regularity she'll be able to work things out for herself."

There are too many factors involved to fit any formula, he explains, and anyway, "Some things are not 'in the book.'" When a child knows that he is loved and cherished and can count on definite times for companionship, Dr. Wegman says, his mother's eight-hour absence won't hurt their relationship.

If any parents have worked things through, yet sometimes go home at night so tired that the children get on their nerves, well, as a father, Dr. Wegman understands that too. He thinks that parents should realize that the reaction is "perfectly understandable," and that they aren't the only ones. Maybe this is the most needed reassurance of all.

August 27, 1944

Part-time Nurseries

By Catherine Mackenzie

PARENTS say, "He knows better. I have told him again and again." In the first five years of life, as Dr. Arnold Gesell long ago pointed out, a child has more to learn than ever again in the same period of time.

As parents well know, this intensive learning process includes a lot of things a child must not do. The fewer his companions and the more he is alone with adults—especially if he is shut up in a small apartment and has to be reminded of the people downstairs—the more a child is apt to resist an incessant barrage of "do's" and "dont's." The brighter a child is, says Dr. Ruth Wendell Washburn, the more apt he is to put up a fight. "Probably not again until adolescence do children's wills and parents' more often come to grips," she writes in a monograph published by the Society for Research in Child Development.

A WELL-RUN nursery group often offers a solution, but the cost is high, and this is where Dr. Washburn's monograph comes in with the suggestion of a part-time nursery program. In this publication, "Re-education in a Nursery Group; A Study in Clinical Psychology," she reports on the seven-year trial of part-time attendance in the "Nursery Group" at Yale University's Clinic of Child Development, first established by Dr. Gesell in 1911.

Dr. Washburn does not suggest this part-time pattern as a substitute for existing patterns in nursery education, but she thinks that the findings at Yale bear on the current problem of making good nursery education available to every child.

The staff found, for example, that a morning or two spent by the child in the nursery (sometimes much longer, of course), and a chance for parents to see their child in a group and to talk with the staff, helped to iron out many difficulties. There were real problems, requiring professional help, but, says Dr. Washburn, often mothers needed only reassurance

(sometimes, alas! they had been reading too much about abnormal behavior). Sometimes the difficulties were based "on merely not knowing" how young children behave.

"Is that enough food for children of that age to eat?" asked one mother. "If so, I have no feeding problem. My child will eat as much as that any day."

The nursery staff were well aware of the difference and greater difficulty in applying at home the routines a child accepted in the nursery, yet over and over they found parents in search of procedures, and unaware, as Dr. Washburn repeatedly points out, that it is not what you do, it's the way you feel, that is of the first importance.

DR. WASHBURN has incorporated a great deal of this experience in her own book, "Children Have Their Reasons" (Appleton-Century), in which she emphasizes that it is "insight," not rules or ready-made methods, that makes for successful upbringing.

In the present scientific report she not only suggests a part-time nursery program as a means of bridging the gap for every child, but outlines a working plan at reasonable per capita cost, which would retain the values of small groups and trained staff considered sound in nursery education.

Dr. Washburn submits that if a school district has, say, fifty children of nursery school age, a part-time system could be evolved to give each child about one day a week in the nursery group, and to afford a one-hour talk with each mother two or three times a year.

Since many mothers feel that "a full school week is too much for a child under four and a half years old," and other mothers would not want to take a small child to school every day, she thinks that this arrangement would be satisfactory for many families.

Nursery schools offer the best possible opportunity for parent education, says Dr. Washburn, who knows from experience "the isolation of many young parents who have no one to talk to, no standards by which to judge the behavior of their child." The opportunity for "talking things over" with people trained and experienced in working with young children comes at the head of the list, she says, in ironing out normal difficulties encountered in a child's first five years.

She quotes one young mother who paused in a long recital to explain, "It's heavenly to feel that there is someone who is paid to listen to me talk about the baby!"

December 3, 1944

JOBLESS WOMEN PUT AT HALF A MILLION

Miss Hickey of WMC Advises Those Who Want to Continue Working

Special to THE NEW YORK TIMES.

WASHINGTON, July 18—Margaret A. Hickey, chairman of the Women's Advisory Committee of the War Manpower Commission, estimated today that at least a half million women were unemployed as a result of cutbacks.

Miss Hickey named as areas of "substantial surpluses" Detroit, Brunswick, Ga., St. Louis, and Portland, Ore., and asserted that greater dislocations were inevitable. She was referring only to women who have been working and who want to continue working—not to those who will voluntarily reassume the role of housewife.

"Throughout the country there is a growing uneasiness about women's unemployment after the war," said Miss Hickey. "There are even a lot of people who are trying to find ways of denying employment to women. Women should not wait until a sign is up which says, 'No women wanted'. They should start swinging on the subject of full employment right now."

Miss Hickey said she would go to England soon to study with the British government and cooperating private agencies measures being used there to solve the problems of shifting women from war production to civilian jobs and fitting them into the general reconversion of industry.

She will also study their policies on the training and utilization of woman-power to the best peacetime advantage. She hoped to be able to obtain information which might help in guiding this country.

"Are women going to be sitting on benches in the employment offices when they ought to be learning new skills?" she asked. "Are they going to be using up their war-time savings frantically looking for jobs?"

She maintained this country should be moving to prevent major dislocations when the war ends. She recommended four measures: full employment legislation; expansion of the employment service to include counselling as well as placement; continuance of Federal aid training programs equally available to women and men; and the widest application of the equal pay principle, including legislation on it.

July 19, 1945

SURVEY IS STARTED OF CHILD DAY CARE

Welfare League Seeks Data on Needs in Face of Plan to End FWA Aid Oct. 31

An immediate nation-wide survey of needs for day care of children was started yesterday by the Child Welfare League of America. Recognizing an emergency in the termination by Oct. 31 of Federal Works Agency assistance to centers for children of working mothers, the League's executive director, Howard W. Hopkirk, called on 700 member agencies and affiliates in forty-three States for prompt and accurate reporting on the present day care in centers or nurseries, and in foster homes, and for an estimate of needs so far as these can be anticipated, as of Nov. 1.

Mr. Hopkirk urges early reporting from communities in which the day care need is especially apparent, "so that an up-to-date and correct picture of the situation may be presented to the President, who has power to continue such programs beyond Nov. 1, if he finds proof that an emergency exists."

"Post-War Brief No. 1," issued from the league's headquarters 130 East Twenty-second Street calls for, in addition to numerical count of all children needing care, data on peak loads, and the number of boys and girls involved in centers receiving FWA aid should be closed, such information as:

"Are children still receiving day care under independent arrangements which lack suitable auspices?"

"Are newspaper advertisements reflecting any use of such independent facilities?"

The day care of children outside of their homes has been a concern of the Child Welfare League for twenty-five years, Mr. Hopkirk explained yesterday, in an interview. Pointing out that in every generation mothers have worked for a living, he said that wartime mobilization of women in industry has only intensified a long-existing need.

Speaking of day care facilities as poorly developed before the war, often hastily improvised since, Mr. Hopkirk said that the welter of services found to exist has convinced the league "the time has come for such planning by the Federal Government as will facilitate development of day care of a quality consistent with American standards of child welfare."

National planning, for day care, and strong leadership from some central agency, such as the Children's Bureau, is urged by Mr. Hopkirk. "Day care," he said, "is closely related to wages women receive, fluctuating demand for women in industry and other lines of employment, and the cost of living. The war has shown that such factors cannot be effectively dealt with solely within the borders of individual counties or States. When the welfare of the country demands employment of large numbers of women we now know that many of them will be mothers whose children require day care. If we fail to assure good service to the children and their mothers, industry and the national welfare will suffer. It is hardly American to leave a mother, too often poorly paid, to shift for her child, without some minimum guarantee of community service and some subsidy for the child's care."

August 23, 1945

PRESIDENT URGES CHILD AID CONTINUE

Special to THE NEW YORK TIMES.

WASHINGTON, Aug. 27—President Truman has asked Gen. Philip Fleming, Administrator of the Federal Works Agency, to present to Congress, as soon as it reconvenes, the problem caused by termination, announced for Oct. 31, of the Lanham Act Fund to child care centers.

The President said he had instructed the FWA Administrator "if possible to obtain authority to continue the centers," which he called necessary for the working wives of service men.

Protests against the closing of the nursery schools, coming from communities all over the country, had asked continuance, by Presidential directive, and had emphasized that many service men's wives had to keep on working until their husbands returned.

The statement by President Truman explained that appropriations recently made for child care centers "were based on the understanding that such assistance would be terminated when women workers were no longer needed for war production." It told, too, of "local communities not yet able, immediately, to continue needed centers without assistance," and pointed out that "a typical situation is that in which mothers, who are the wives of service men, must continue to work until their husbands return from overseas."

Fleming Adhered to Policy

Keeping the promise of war-end termination of Federal aid to child care, General Fleming, by Administrative order, had set a closing date three months after the end of actual combat.

Mothers who organized to protest here, pointed out that funds still were available to continue the centers. Underlying General Fleming's order was believed to be the fact that, as a construction agency, the FWA seeks to concentrate on actual building activities now that materials are becoming available.

All Federal agencies concerned with child care were canvassing immediate and long-range possibilities today in the hope that Congress would take some action which might tide the care of children of working mothers through reconversion. Longer-range legislation, such as the Pepper bills for nursery schools and enlargement of welfare grants, also was being discussed. The Office of War Mobilization and Reconversion was considered the logical agency to direct a reconversion child-care program if the FWA undertakings were terminated, with long-established child-care agencies such as the Children's Bureau and the Office of Education in charge.

Expediency Is Scored

Miss Katharine F. Lenroot, chief of the Children's Bureau, in an interview just before the Presidential action, said that the present nursery school situation "shows up the problems created when measures that have important human implications are developed simply on the basis of war need."

She pointed out the object of the present child care program, under the law, was "to expedite war production" with the welfare of children secondary; and that the previous FWA program was to give employment and not to meet the needs of children.

She urged a swift review by Federal and State governments and by communities of "those aspects of the war related to living conditions and the welfare of people" so as to "meet the stiff needs of reconversion" and carry on into peace-time work.

August 28, 1945

Mothers Take Jobs to Meet Family Needs Just as the Fathers Do, Survey Discloses

By CATHERINE MACKENZIE

The plain fact that mothers work for the same reason that fathers do—to get money for children's shoes, and shelter, and doctor's bills, and to save for their education—is one finding offered by Mrs. Zilpha C. Franklin, director of information, Federal Security Agency, in a review of recent studies issued yesterday by the Child Study Association of America, 221 West Fifty-seventh Street. Neither wartime concern with "working mothers" nor a drop in their employment alters the actual set-up of American family life nor the need of mother's wages, according to this analysis.

Reviewing the double load of job and home-making carried by many more women than usual since 1941, Mrs. Franklin points out that for decades wage-earning among women has been steadily on the upgrade, that the "spectacular increase" in the proportion of women in the labor force (9 per cent) in the last four years has been a change in pace, not in direction. The tempo of family evolution changed during the war, she says, not the tune, and by and large, mothers go to work because they need money, "they need it, often desperately, because our American 'standard of living' has outstripped our family purchasing capacity." An increase of lunch-box packing mothers in wartime should not obscure this fact, Mrs. Franklin submits, offering her conclusions in the quarterly Child Study.

When the double task of home and job becomes too back-breaking, the writer says, most women unhesitatingly chuck the job—of two million women who quit work during the war 95 per cent gave "home responsibilities" as the reason—but she finds "a surprising number, particularly of the younger women" to be clear-headed and articulate on what they are going to do about it.

"The right to have a family and to bring up children in decency and health" is the one right, Mrs. Franklin declares, which most of them value most deeply and express frankly: "They want to marry young and, if necessity dictates, they expect to keep on working until they can afford a family."

As one indication of this determination, Mrs. Franklin points to the situation of young married couples where the husband goes to school while the wife works. Thanks to the GI Bill of Rights and to the earning capacity of the young wives, these couples see no reason to postpone marriage, she submits.

One of the few things that seem certain as we look ahead, in her view, is the likelihood that we shall not "return to self-contained, home-made subsistence living." She thinks that mothers will continue to put shoulders to the wheel, when need be, and, of the parents of today and tomorrow, declares:

"For better or for worse women have been declared in on this partnership. They will see that they and their children aren't pushed around—or know the reason why. And that is one of the very few really sure and really hopeful certainties of the all too uncertain future."

In this appraisal, "Working Mothers—Where Do They Go From Here," Mrs. Franklin has drawn upon surveys made by the Women's Bureau, Department of Labor; the Federal Security Agency, and Bureau of the Census.

November 20, 1945

DROP IN WOMEN WORKERS

Decline of 2,000,000 in Industry Since V-J Day Reported

Many women workers still hold their jobs in heavy industry, although the total is down 2,000,000 since V-J Day, Miss Frieda S. Miller declared yesterday. The director of the women's bureau of the United States Department of Labor spoke at the twenty-fourth annual fall conference of the New York Women's Trade Union League in the Hotel Roosevelt.

In analyzing the position of women workers since the war, Miss Miller said the drop of 2,000,000 included many who left their jobs voluntarily, but that 60,000 were seeking re-employment.

Miss Mary Van Kleeck, director of industrial studies of the Russell Sage Foundation, also addressed the 110 delegates.

October 13, 1946

STATES EASE LAWS AGAINST WOMEN

Moves to End Discrimination Since 1938 Are Reported by Labor Department Bureau

WASHINGTON, Feb. 19 (U.P.)— Inspired partly by the wartime manpower shortage, some States have erased many "lingering discriminatory laws" against women, the Women's Bureau of the Labor Department reported tonight.

Women's freedom from "the handicap of obsolete laws" is much closer as a result, the bureau said in a report on the legal status of women. It said that three States lifted barriers to women's holding public office and that only "minor discriminations" remained in some States against such appointments.

These other steps have been taken since Jan. 1, 1938:

1. Seven States extended jury service to women, so that women now are barred from jury duty in only sixteen States. Five other States extended eligibility of women for jury service.

2. A Georgia statute gave a wife full right to her personal earnings, free from the claims of her husband.

3. Florida, North Carolina and Pennsylvania abolished obstacles to married women's freedom to exercise general powers of contract.

4. North Carolina repealed a law which required a married woman to obtain her husband's consent and observe prescribed court procedure to engage in business of her own account.

5. New Jersey passed a law stating that rights to hold office or employment could not be denied or abridged because of marital status.

6. Laws of family relations and of property rights were modernized in several States. Revision of these laws and extension of jury service undoubtedly stemmed in part from the manpower shortage during the war, the bureau said.

•

Measures were introduced Monday in both the House and Senate calling for a policy of no discrimination on the basis of sex except when reasonably justified "by differences in physical structure, biological or social functions." The measures also would create a commission to study and report to Congress and the President on the legal status of women and local discriminations.

WOMEN GUARDS REPEL FAIR 'PARACHUTISTS'

Pop Away at 'Invaders' With Rifles Loaded With Blanks

A squad of "sharpshooters," members of the Green Guard of America, Inc., a volunteer women's group dedicated to the defense of the United States, "successfully" defended the World's Fair against an invasion of four parachutists yesterday afternoon.

The "invasion" occurred at the Fair's parachute jump in the Amusement Area when four white-uniformed concession attendants obligingly rode two 'chutes to earth as the women popped away at them with rifles loaded with blank cartridges.

Commander James Strong, operator of the jump, declared that although the women's zeal was beyond criticism their marksmanship was not.

"It's a good thing for everybody," he added, "that those rifles were loaded with blanks, because there was quite a crowd standing around here."

Before the "invasion" the sixty members of the Green Guard had a try at parachute jumping.

The guard's national headquarters is in Washington.

August 25, 1940

MRS. HOBBY NAMED DIRECTOR OF WAAC

President Establishes Corps by Executive Order After Signing Rogers Bill

Special to THE NEW YORK TIMES.

WASHINGTON, May 15—Secretary Stimson announced today that Mrs. Oveta Culp Hobby, wife of the former Governor of Texas and at present a War Department publicity executive on a per diem basis, has been appointed Director of the Women's Army Auxiliary Corps.

Word of Mrs. Hobby's appointment came after the White House revealed that President Roosevelt had signed the Rogers bill authorizing the WAAC and had issued an executive order establishing the corps.

The War Department announced that recruiting for officers for the Women's Corps would begin in two weeks and that general recruiting for WAAC members would be opened in about three months. Candidates for the first Women Officers Training School will be able to apply through local recruiting offices and will commence training at Fort Des Moines, Iowa, within two months.

In the executive order President Roosevelt directed Secretary Stimson not to enroll more than 25,000 women in the initial organizational drive and put a temporary limit of 100 on the number of units in the corps. The bill permits a total of 150,000 in the corps.

Although the War Department did not reveal details of the new organization, it was understood that the Air's recruiting quota will be 12,200. Of these, 9,000 will be trained and organized into about forty companies for air raid warning service. The remainder will be assigned to duty at Army posts as typists, telephone operators, clerks, laboratory technicians and similar jobs.

The War Department pointed out specifically that WAAC members will not be used to replace civil service employes now working for the department.

Mrs. Oveta Culp Hobby   Harris & Ewing

Mrs. Hobby, the 37-year-old mother of two children, came to Washington a year ago to organize the Women's Interests Section of the Bureau of Public Relations of the Army.

The War Department announcement said that last September Mrs. Hobby, at the direction of Chief of Staff Marshall, began work on the planning of the WAAC, pending its authorization by Congress. She and a skeleton staff, including Mrs. Genevieve Forbes Herrick as publicity representative, are already established in the WAAC office.

Mrs. Hobby's appointment as director of the WAAC had been opposed by representatives of Negro groups here on the basis that her Southern background would not guarantee fair treatment for Negro women wishing to enlist in the corps.

The National Negro Council and the National Council of Negro Women announced today that they would ask Secretary Stimson to appoint Mrs. Mary McLeod Bethune, Negro educator, as an assistant director of the auxiliary.

Mrs. Emily Newell Blair has been named to succeed Mrs. Hobby as head of the Women's Interests Section.

May 16, 1942

'Yes, Mam,' 'No, Mam,' Says a WAAC to an Officer

By The Associated Press.

DES MOINES, Iowa, June 24—It probably will be "Yes, mam," "No, mam," and "Right away, mam," in the Women's Auxiliary Corps of the Army.

Obviously, the "sir" which every private and officer learns to use in addressing a superior officer is hardly suitable for the women forces.

Until the first officers are commissioned they will be addressed as "Miss" or "Mrs." as the case may be.

June 25, 1942

NINE OF TEN WAACS ATTENDED COLLEGE

Proportion of Graduates at Ft. Des Moines Corresponds to Those Asking to Go Overseas

By The Associated Press.

FORT DES MOINES, Iowa, July 24—Nine out of ten of the white officer candidates at the Women's Army Auxiliary Corps school are college graduates, two-thirds of them have taught school or held clerical positions and 10 per cent are 40 or older.

Only 1 per cent have never been employed, while 12 per cent have had experience in professional positions, 10 per cent have been in business jobs. Three per cent held technical posts.

Statistics supplied by the school on 335 of the 404 white officer-candidates showed that 296 of them were college graduates and that some held advanced degrees. The other age classifications are 21 to 25 years, 55 or 16 per cent; 26-40, 107 or 32 per cent; 31-35, 90 or 27 per cent, 36-40, 49 or 15 per cent.

Information on the other white officer-candidates has not been compiled.

Of the forty Negro candidates, 77½ per cent are college graduates and one has a higher degree.

Ninety per cent of the WAAC's want overseas service, Army men said after the first 700 members of the Women's Army Auxiliary Corps had been interviewed and classified according to their capabilities and experience.

"Few of them want easy assignments," one officer said. "They really want to play an active part in winning the war. Ninety per cent want to go overseas."

July 25, 1942

A PRESENT FOR THE AXIS FROM THE WRENS

Members of the Women's Royal Naval Service wheeling a torpedo into position
The New York Times, passed by British censor

WOMEN NAVY CORPS WILL ENROLL 11,000

By NONA BALDWIN
Special to THE NEW YORK TIMES.

WASHINGTON, July 30—President Roosevelt signed today the bill authorizing the Women's Reserve in the Navy, and the Navy Department at once announced details of the new organization in which 1,000 women will become commissioned officers in the Navy for the first time in history.

The first limit on the reserve will be 11,000 members, about the same as the total number of yeomanettes who served as enlisted personnel in the last war. There is, however, no Congressional limitation on the number who may eventually be drawn into the reserve to perform a multitude of administrative and technical tasks on naval shore stations within continental United States.

The Navy said that the officer quota will be filled before recruitment of enlisted personnel is started. The selection of officers and officer candidates, designated under regulations as women appointed for volunteer emergency service, will begin as soon as final plans are completed by the Navy with the assistance of the Advisory Educational Council.

Gives Ready-Made Name—WAVES

Observers here noted with joy the long title under which women will get their commissions, for the capital letters provided a ready made name, WAVES, for members of the reserve. Heretofore even Rear Admiral Randall Jacobs, chief of the Bureau of Naval Personnel, had been unable to think of an appropriate name that might be derived from the initials of the official name of the organization, Women's Reserve in the Navy.

Some officers will be commissioned directly and assigned to administrative duties in connection with the training program. The remainder will be commissioned as officer candidates and put through an indoctrination course soon to be established at an Eastern women's college.

The Educational Council which has been working with the Bureau of Naval Personnel on plans for the Women's Reserve is composed of seven representatives from the various naval districts and headed by Dean Virginia Gildersleeve of Barnard College. Mildred McAfee of Wellesley has been a member at large with an office in the Navy Department and it appears certain that Miss McAfee will become lieutenant commander of the reserve at the induction ceremony set for Saturday.

Other members of the council are: Ada Comstock, president of Radcliffe College; Mrs. Thomas S. Gates, wife of the president of the University of Pennsylvania; Dr. Meta Glass, president of Sweetbriar College; Alice M. Baldwin, dean of Women's College, Duke University; Alice C. Lloyd, dean of Women at the University of Michigan, and Mrs. Malbone Graham, professor, author and lecturer from Santa Monica, Calif.

Navy spokesmen, outlining the procedure which candidates must follow, stressed that they must first submit a written request for a preliminary application blank, stating their age and educational background, to the Director of Naval Officer Procurement for the Naval district in which they reside. These offices are located in Boston, New York, Philadelphia, Washington, Richmond, Va.; Charleston, S. C.; Miami, New Orleans, Chicago, Los Angeles, San Francisco and Seattle. A college degree is almost mandatory for a person seeking a naval commission.

The group of officers chosen for administrative work will be nominated by the various directors of Naval Office Procurement and the Bureau of Naval Personnel will issue the commissions after viewing the recommendations.

About 300 other women will be appointed in appropriate ranks on a probationary basis and given one month's instruction in the Reserve Midshipmen's School. Those who complete this course will be commissioned to perform technical duties and then assigned to active service or ordered to special schools for training that will qualify them for technical billets.

All other women candidates for commissions as officers will be enlisted as apprentice seamen in Class V-9 and given an indoctrinal course lasting one month, following which those who qualify will become Reserve Midshipmen and undergo additional training to fit them for assignment as specialists. Upon completion of the latter training, they will be commissioned Ensigns in the Woman's Reserve.

HIGH STANDARDS SET FOR NAVY WOMEN
By NONA BALDWIN
Special to THE NEW YORK TIMES

WASHINGTON, July 31—Strict educational requirements for women desiring to become officers or officer-candidates in the Women's Reserve were set forth today by the Navy Department along with an official announcement that Smith College would be the training center for officers.

About 900 WAVES, as the potential women reservists are called, will report during the first week of October at Smith.

By that time the commanding officer of the WAVES probably will be Miss Mildred H. McAfee as Lieutenant Commander. Her induction has been postponed from tomorrow to next week.

Educational standards set by the Bureau of Naval Personnel require that all applicants for commissions or appointments as officer-candidates possess a baccalaureate degree from an accredited university or college, or in place of a degree, completion of two years' work leading to a degree.

In addition, they must have had not less than two years' professional or business experience in fields that will fit them for administrative or technical positions in the naval service and must have had not less than two years of mathematics in high school or college.

A small group of officers will be named soon to serve in administrative positions in connection with the appointment and training of women reservists.

About 300 others will be appointed in a probationary status, ordered to Reserve Midshipmen's schools for a month of indoctrination in naval discipline and customs and then, if deemed to be officer material, they will be commissioned and sent to technical billets or to special schools for technical instruction.

Members of these groups must be citizens of the United States, not less than 21 years of age or over 50, pass physical and aptitude tests, have no children under 18 years of age and be of good repute in the community.

Those appointed to fill technical positions, if unmarried at the time of their appointment, must agree not to marry prior to the completion of training courses in technical schools.

All others desiring to become officers in the Women's Reserve must enroll in Class V-9 as officer-candidates and meet the same requirements as the first two groups except that they must be not less than 20 years old and under 30, must have no children and, if un-

July 31, 1942

married, must agree not to marry prior to completion of their Reserve midshipmen training.

They will be enlisted as apprentice seamen and an indoctrinal course of one month will determine whether they will qualify as Reserve midshipmen. Those who qualify will receive additional training to fit them as specialists and then be commissioned as ensigns and ordered to active duty.

Those who do not qualify for commissions may transfer to enlisted ranks if they desire and are found acceptable.

Special Qualifications Sought

Especially desired as candidates for commissions are those who have majored in such subjects as civil, mechanical, electrical, radio or aeronautical engineering, electronics, meteorology, astronomy, metallurgy, physics, mathematics, business statistics and modern foreign languages.

Considered as desirable are those who majored in industrial or chemical engineering, chemistry, geology, geography, mineralogy, psychology, architecture, government and political science, history, library science, English, journalism, economics, business administration, finance, commerce and transportation.

Also desired are women, otherwise qualified, who have had experience as supervisors of cable, telegraph, telephone and radio commercial offices; maintenance women and operators of teletype, simplex and multiplex transmitting machines; licensed radio operators, lexicographers, amateur cryptanalysts, instructors of touch-typing and typewriter maintenance, statisticians, instructors in the use of file systems, demonstrators and operators of business machines such as sorting, punch card machines, etc.

Also junior executives, superintendents, supervisors, section leaders, personnel supervisors, etc., of banks, finance and insurance companies, brokerage offices, large retail and printing establishments; bookkeepers and accountants, executives of circulation and linotype departments of newspapers and librarians.

Applicants for appointment as officers and officer candidates must submit a written request for a preliminary application blank to the director of naval officer procurement in the city or naval district in which the applicant resides, stating their age and educational background. Blanks will not be issued to those who call in person.

When these blanks have been filled out and returned, selection boards will sit in each district to review them and require those who seem qualified to appear for interviews, aptitude tests and physical examination.

A properly authenticated transcript of the applicant's college record and three letters of recommendation as to character and experience from responsible citizens must be submitted upon a report for an interview.

A native-born applicant must submit an original or properly authenticated copy of her birth certificate, baptismal certificate or an affidavit from her physician or parents.

A foreign-born applicant is required to present a certificate of naturalization of her parents during her minority together with an affidavit of a parent attesting parenthood.

At Smith the Navy has leased one classroom building and three dormitories and has obtained the use of the alumnae gymnasium, playing fields for drill and recreation purposes and other necessary facilities. The Northampton Inn has also been leased.

Male Naval officers will serve as instructors of the first class, which will include women understudies for each instructor.

Upon completion of their indoctrination and training, the understudies will become officers and instructors, some at Smith and others at new training centers, including a school for enlisted personnel of the Women's Reserve to be opened about Nov. 1 at a site to be selected in the Midwest.

The regular Fall session at Smith College will start on Sept. 14, two weeks before the first Navy Class begins training.

August 1, 1942

Army Will Keep Nurses Who Wed, Reversing Rule

WASHINGTON, Sept. 25—A complete reversal of Army Nurse Corps tradition was announced today when the War Department ordered that no nurse would be permitted to resign from the service because of marriage. It had been a rule of the corps since its founding that no married nurses would be accepted in the corps and that all who married on duty must resign.

The reversal was caused by a growing shortage of nurses and the resignation of 224 last month. Under the new War Department order, effective Thurs-

day, members of the corps who marry will, at the discretion of the surgeon general, be continued in active service for the duration of the war and six months thereafter.

Nurses who entered the service before Dec. 27, 1941, and therefore did not sign a pledge not to resign during the war, will be permitted to leave the service only if replacements can be found, and the War Department doubts that there will be replacements.

September 26, 1942

DUTY IN ENGLAND FOR NEGRO WAACS

General Says They Will Help to Entertain Soldiers of Their Race Stationed There

---

WILL ALSO DRIVE CARS

Secretarial Tasks Scheduled for Women Aides With U. S. Army Contingents

---

Wireless to THE NEW YORK TIMES.

LONDON, Aug. 15—The Army plans to send many Negro Waacs to England to perform duties such as car driving and secretarial work and also to provide companionship for the thousands of Negro troops here, Lieut. Gen. Dwight D. Eisenhower, commander of American forces in the European theatre of operations, announced today.

The presence of Negro soldiers in England, where only a few Negroes have been before this time, has caused complications that General Eisenhower discussed frankly at a press conference today. General Eisenhower emphasized that "we are giving Negro troops equal status in the military field." Some of the English, moreover, have accepted them socially on the same basis as other American fighting men.

General Eisenhower explained that Negroes were here because they comprised about 10 per cent of the United States population and he believed that all segments should be represented on the fronts. In addition he said that Negroes were performing essential duties. They have, however, been without the companionship of other Negroes. The residents of smaller English towns where they are stationed have entertained them in homes and have extended various sorts of hospitality.

Frankly recognizing the problem, the Army is attempting to deal with it on a sensible and practical basis, the general stressed. In the larger cities, like London, where in the nature of things there is less home entertainment of soldiers, Negroes on leave wander disconsolately, one of them remarking: "There's no hot music and none of our girls."

Other soldiers also complain of the lack of swing music.

August 16, 1942

ARMY RANK AND PAY SET IN NURSES' BILL

Johnson Measure, Before the Senate, Reported to Have War Department Backing

---

PROPOSAL GOES TO HOUSE

Five Per Cent Rise Is Provided for Those in Ranks After Each 3 Years of Service

---

Special to THE NEW YORK TIMES.

WASHINGTON, Oct. 2—The latest in a series of bills introduced in Congress to increase the pay of women serving in various branches of the armed forces was presented to the Senate today when Senator Johnson of Colorado proposed that the superintendent of the Army Nurse Corps be made a colonel, with equivalent pay, and that the pay scale for other officer nurses be adjusted to that of the Regular Army.

It is understood that the Johnson bill represents the version of pay-increase legislation looked upon most favorably by the War Department. At least one other bill to accomplish this end has been introduced in the Senate, while Representative Edmiston of West Virginia introduced a bill similar to Senator Johnson's in the House and Representative Eberharter of Pennsylvania has proposed a general increase for both Army and Navy nurses on a different basis.

The Senate has on its docket a bill to increase the pay of Waac Auxiliaries, now based on a $21 a month minimum, to meet the Army scale.

Under the Johnson bill, Colonel Julia Flikke, head of the Army Nurse Corps, would receive the pay of a regular officer of that rank. She now holds an appointment as colonel in the temporary Army of the United States, but her right to the salary has been denied by the Controller General.

The upward shift in rank and pay would give to assistant superintendents of the Nurse Corps the relative rank of lieutenant colonels; directors would correspond to majors; assistant directors to captains; chief nurses to first lieutenants, and head nurses to second lieutenants. Their pay would be that of an Army officer of corresponding rank who is unmarried and without dependents.

In addition to this basic revision, nurses would get a 5 per cent pay increase after each three years of service.

October 3, 1942

NURSE DRIVE BEGUN BY WOMEN'S CLUBS

Federation Hopes to Recruit 20,000 Students and to Give Training Scholarships

Special to THE NEW YORK TIMES.

WASHINGTON, Oct. 8—A large-scale drive to increase the country's supply of trained nurses through the recruitment of 20,000 student nurses to whom special scholarships may be made available was announced today by Mrs. John L. Whitehurst, president of the General Federation of Womens Clubs, herself a graduate nurse.

The double drive to recruit young women for nursing training and to provide them with $250 and $500 scholarships through the 16,-500 local women's clubs will get under way simultaneously, Mrs. Whitehurst said, explaining that they were both part of the war action program of the federation.

The object of the campaign is to relieve more young nurses for military service by providing a supply of new nurses and at the same time to reassure civilians that proper health standards will be maintained on the home front.

The campaign, which is to be started immediately, is expected to be stimulated through the award of war bonds and special certificates to individual women and clubs that show the best records in getting money for the scholarships and in persuading girls to take the training.

"The General Federation of Women's Clubs, with over two million members, should be an important factor in meeting America's dangerous nursing shortage," Mrs. Whitehurst said. "We can render an invaluable service in helping the American Red Cross and the National Nursing Council for War Service to secure young women for training, to persuade eligible, inactive nurses to return to the profession, to help recruit part-time nurses for hospitals, and sponsor classes in home nursing and nurses' aides."

As a stimulus to the campaign, the General Federation is offering the following awards:

A $100 war bond to the chairman who gets the greatest number of scholarships in States with more than 100 member clubs; a $75 war bond for the winning chairman among States having from fifty to ninety-nine clubs; a $50 war bond for the winning chairman among States having less than that number of member clubs; a $100 bond to the woman, whether a club member or not, who obtains the greatest number of recruits; a special certificate to every woman who gets a recruit, and a special certificate to the group or organization which sponsors all four parts of the federation's war nursing program. Those four parts are recruiting, scholarships, first-aid classes and home nursing classes.

Mrs. Whitehurst also asked member clubs to fly a service flag bearing a star for each member who has entered either the Army Nurse Corps or the Navy Nurse Corps.

The War Department also underscored the urgent need for nurses

RECALLED BY ARMY

Major Julia Stimson
Associated News

today when officials confirmed the recall of Major Julia Stimson, retired, former superintendent of the Army Nurse Corps. Major Stimson has been assigned to a special three-month detail of duty during which she will travel around the country in the interest of recruiting more nurses for the service. The Army is seeking 2,500 new nurses a month and has authorized the expansion of the Nurse Corps to about 30,000 members.

October 9, 1942

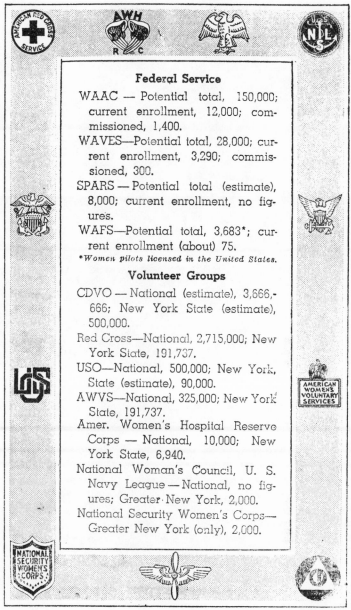

Federal Service

WAAC — Potential total, 150,000; current enrollment, 12,000; commissioned, 1,400.

WAVES—Potential total, 28,000; current enrollment, 3,290; commissioned, 300.

SPARS — Potential total (estimate), 8,000; current enrollment, no figures.

WAFS—Potential total, 3,683*; current enrollment (about) 75.

*Women pilots licensed in the United States.

Volunteer Groups

CDVO — National (estimate), 3,666,-666; New York State (estimate), 500,000.

Red Cross—National, 2,715,000; New York State, 191,737.

USO—National, 500,000; New York, State (estimate), 90,000.

AWVS—National, 325,000; New York State, 191,737.

Amer. Women's Hospital Reserve Corps — National, 10,000; New York State, 6,940.

National Woman's Council, U. S. Navy League — National, no figures; Greater New York, 2,000.

National Security Women's Corps—Greater New York (only), 2,000.

The New York Times

December 13, 1942

Says Waacs Retain Femininity

WASHINGTON, Jan. 4 (Æ)— American women are not losing their femininity by training in the Waacs, Mrs. Frances Bolton, Ohio's first woman member of the House, said today. Just returning from a trip to the West Coast, Mrs. Bolton told a meeting of the Washington branch of the League of Republican Women: "There are former judges and women with no previous training of any sort, but all are responding beautifully to Army training. And they are retaining their femininity to the last degree."

January 5, 1943

MOTHER AND SON JOIN THE ARMY TOGETHER

Mrs. Thomas W. Streeter

Theodore L. Carlson (left), 19, of Chicago, becomes a private and his mother, Mrs. Maggie I. Carlson, 42, is inducted as an auxiliary in the Waac by Captain John A. Andre, Army recruiting officer, in a ceremony at Washington. Marian L. MacAdam, Waac recruiting officer, looks on. — Associated Press Wirephoto

WASHINGTON, Oct. 9 (AP).—A mother and son joined the armed forces at the same time today.

Mrs. Maggie I. Carlson, 42, of Chicago, was sworn in as an auxiliary in the Waacs at the Army recruiting station, while her son, Theodore L. Carlson, 19, took the oath as a private in the Army.

They then separated, Mrs. Carlson leaving for Fort Des Moines, for training, while Theodore departed for the quartermaster replacement training center at Camp Lee, Va.

Mrs. Carlson, a widow, said she thought it was the duty of every youth of 18 or 19 to enlist and said she encouraged her son to take these steps. She was born in Copenhagen, and was there when the Germans invaded Denmark in 1940.

October 10, 1942

WASHINGTON, Jan. 27 (AP)— Lieut. Gen. Thomas Holcomb, commandant of the Marines, announced today the establishment of a women's reserve. The women are to relieve trained marines for combat duty. General Holcomb said that the reserve was still in the "planning stage" and applications would not be received before Feb. 15.

Informed persons said today that Mrs. Thomas W. Streeter, attorney, of Morristown, N. J., would head the reserve. There was no confirmation of this report from official sources.

She has a pilot's license and is active in the Civil Air Patrol.

The women marines will have no official abbreviated name such as the Waves, Waacs and Spars of the Navy, Army and Coast Guard. Their full title will be United States Marine Corps Women's Reserve.

Mrs. Streeter and her mother, Mrs. Mary L. C. Schofield of Peterboro, N. H., annually present the Cheney Award for bravery in the Army Air Corps in memory of Mrs. Streeter's brother, Lieutenant William H. Cheney, who was killed in Italy in the first World War.

EQUALITY DEMANDED FOR SERVICE WOMEN

Federation Draws Up Ten-Point Federal Legislation Program

Equal status for women and men in the armed services was advocated yesterday at the conclusion of the mid-year meeting of the National Federation of Business and Professional Women's Clubs, Inc., at national headquarters, 1819 Broadway.

The suggestion that Waves and Spars serve abroad when needed; the granting of equal compensation to all women in the armed forces in case of injury or death and the permitting of payment of allotments for dependents to members of the Waacs, Waves and Spars, were made in a ten-point program of Federal legislation advocated by the Federation. It is being sent to the six women members of Congress, Miss Alice L. Manning of Salt Lake City, national legislation chairman, announced.

The other points include:

Legislation which would permit women physicians to serve in the Medical Corps of the Army and Navy.

Jury service for women, which would authorize active support of Federal legislation permitting women jurors to serve in Federal courts.

Opposition to discriminations against women in any form, which includes the positive support of all government action regarding equal pay for equal work.

Equal Rights Amendment.

Adequate appropriations for the Women's Bureau of the United States Department of Labor.

Aids Waac Enlistments

Magazine advertising to spur enlistments in the Women's Army Auxiliary Corps has been scheduled in selected weeklies by N. W. Ayer & Son, Inc., Philadelphia. Copy will take the form of a letter from a father to his daughter, who has asked the advice about joining the corps. It reflects the attitudes of men who responded to the nation-wide survey conducted jointly by the United States Army and the agency, which resulted in the conclusion that "a woman seldom if ever makes a major decision except with the approval of, or in defiance of, a man."

March 30, 1943

House Passes the Smith Bill For Waves' Overseas Service

WASHINGTON, June 8 — The House today passed the bill of Representative Margaret Chase Smith, Republican, of Maine, allowing Waves assignments overseas, raising their maximum rank from lieutenant commander to captain and entitling them to allowances for dependents such as Navy men receive.

Representative Melvin J. Maas, Republican, of Minnesota, added an amendment removing any limitation on the number of Waves commanders. The bill had stipulated fifteen.

Similar legislation introduced by Representative Maas had been vigorously opposed several weeks ago particularly by Representative Beverly M Vincent, Democrat, of Kentucky. The Smith bill, however, was not debated.

Rear Admiral Randall Jacobs, Chief of the Bureau of Naval Personnel, testified last week before the House Naval Affairs Committee that the Navy Department preferred not to have the number of Waves commanders limited, because Waves administration would be less flexible.

Mrs. Smith who approves the Maas amendment, said she did not foresee any opposition for her bill in the Senate, although she has not yet queried members of the upper chamber regarding it.

Differing from the more broadly constructed Maas bill, the Smith bill stipulates (1) there shall be only one captain in the Waves (2) Waves "qualified to fill an available billet in the Navy Department proper in Washington" shall not be sent overseas; (3) no Wave who entered the Naval Service prior to enactment of the bill shall be assigned to overseas duty without her consent; (4) none may serve aboard ship or in combat aircraft; and (5) in entitling Waves to the allowances or benefits provided Navy men with dependents, Waves' "husbands shall not be considered dependents."

WASHINGTON, June 8 (P)— Mrs. Franklin D. Roosevelt today denounced as Nazi propaganda any stories of moral misbehavior among members of women's military units and reiterated her belief that women should be permitted to serve overseas.

The First Lady told her press conference that since there now are four divisions of the Women's Army Auxiliary Corps that mean that four divisions of men were released for combat duty and naturally the Germans do not like that.

"Do you suppose we'll ever get over believing Nazi propaganda?" she asked. "It's extraordinary the way we fall for it all the time."

June 9, 1943

WAACS NOW IN ARMY; NAME BECOMES WACS

President Signs Bill Ending Their Status as Auxiliaries

Special to THE NEW YORK TIMES.

WASHINGTON, July 2—The bill making the Waacs an Army rather than an Auxiliary Corps was signed by President Roosevelt today.

Under the new law the officers of the Wac will have real, rather than comparable rank. They will have military authority over men soldiers specifically put under their command and thus will be able to command their own training centers and undertake a wider variety of operational jobs.

The members of the corps receive the same rights and benefits as the enlisted men of the Army under the act, and the size of the corps is no longer limited but will be determined by the President. The age limit at the time of recruitment is extended, so that the corps may now accept recruits between the ages of 20 and 50.

Present members of the Waac must re-enlist within sixty days, at which time the Auxiliary Corps will be dissolved. The old Waac will continue to function until the new Wac can take over.

Colonel Oveta Culp Hobby, director of the Waac, has not yet been sworn in as a colonel in the United States Army and the director of the new Army Corps.

It is believed that she will function as head of both units during the overlapping period before the old auxiliary can be disbanded.

July 3, 1943

WOMEN ON THE MARCH

Uniformed Services, Proving Invaluable In War, Will Be Greatly Expanded

By ELEANOR DARNTON

WASHINGTON.

WOMEN are being moved up faster and further in the uniformed services of this country than has ever happened before in history, and more is being demanded of them by the armed services than has ever before been demanded of women in war. All of which is happening because they are needed and because, rank and file, they are doing a good job, revealing unsuspected abilities, efficiency and, given the chance, heroism.

They are serving in the Waacs, the Waves, the Wafs, the Spars, the Marine Reserve and in the medical and nursing corps of both the Army and the Navy. Their number runs over a hundred thousand now and will easily be double that before the year is out. Among them so far they boast, on the Army side, three colonels, eighteen lieutenant colonels and forty-one majors, and on the Navy side one captain, three commanders, eight lieutenant commanders, and there's one major of marines.

WACS

Probably we are all most conscious of the Wacs, perhaps because they outnumber all the rest —there are 67,000 now—and because they are something of a young, upstart organization, newly proving themselves each day. Recently a law was passed to give them regular Army rather than auxiliary status. Officers will hold commissioned rank rather than relative rank, and can command the men assigned to them.

We are not as familiar with the jobs the Wacs do as we are with their disciplined chic, the Army rather preferring to hide such enlightening details under a bushel, where they will presumably be safe from enemy eyes. It was thought at first, even by the Army, that the Wacs would be doing only a few essentially routine odds and ends, such as filing, typewriting and chauffeuring. They have branched out now into more than 142 Army jobs, having become everything from weather observers, cartographers, radio mechanics, medical technicians and mechanical, structural and electrical draftsmen. Twenty-five of them are now serving in highly technical jobs with the Army Air Force, 200 are working in the Ballistic Research Laboratory.

Eight Army schools have admitted Wac officers for specialized training. Now that the corps has been admitted into the Army the women soldiers are looking with covetous eyes on the 406 Army jobs which it has been determined they can fill. At the present time approximately a million men are engaged in filling these jobs.

The Wacs have proved their worth at the 170 Army posts where they have been serving in this country and overseas to the point where 600,000 requests for their services from commanding officers are now on record.

ARMY NURSES

The Army Nurse Corps is much the senior part of the Army, being 43 years of age this year. This corps has not yet caught up with the infant Wac in certain privileges since, among other things, its officers have only relative rank. One of the disadvantages involved in such a situation, according to Colonel Florence A. Blanchfield, superintendent of the Army Nurse Corps, is the confusion of interpretation of such rank.

In March, 1942, for instance, President Roosevelt appointed Julia O. Flikke, then superintendent, a colonel and Florence Blanchfield a lieutenant colonel. But the Controller General ruled that there could be no legal woman colonel in

Women pilots boss Jackie Cochran.

the Army and issued Colonel Flikke the pay of a major and Lieutenant Colonel Blanchfield the pay of a captain, until the act of Dec. 22 established their rate of pay along with their rank.

Though the exigencies of war may catch up with them, the Army does not send nurses to advanced bases where living conditions are so difficult that the problem of looking after the welfare of the nurses would add an unwarranted burden to the commanding officer. On these fronts, Army corpsmen trained by nurses take over the first care of the wounded until evacuation behind the lines is possible.

Women are serving in the Army outside of the Wacs and the Nurse Corps. There are two majors in the Medical Corps—Major Margaret D. Craighill and Major Margaret Janeway—and Major Emma E. Vogel is director of physical therapy aides and Major Helen C. Burns director of hospital dietitians.

NAVY NURSES

The approximately 5,000 Navy nurses serve under Captain Sue Dauser. Three commanders and six lieutenant commanders head the corps. They serve at base hospitals and on the hospital ships, which are really floating base hospitals. The Navy tries to keep its nurses away from the front. All combat vessels are staffed with masculine medical personnel and hospital corpsmen, but there were thirty-one nurses at Pearl Harbor and thirteen on the hospital ship Solace, all of whom saw action. Five nurses were captured at Guam, more in the Philippines; five have been released, two are still missing.

Eight women physicians have been commissioned lieutenant (j. g.) in the Navy and sixty-eight women are serving as medical technologists with commissions either as lieutenant (j. g.) or ensigns.

WAVES, SPARS, MARINES

The Waves, Spars and women Marines are based far from the fighting fronts at present, much to their apparent frustration. The bill which would have permitted them to serve overseas, after having passed the House of Representatives, has not yet been reported out of the Senate Naval Affairs Committee and so probably will not be acted upon before the impending Congressional recess.

The girls are disappointed because they would like at least to be storekeepers in Puerto Rico or radio operators in Iceland—jobs they know would serve the Navy well, releasing men for sea duty and no nonsense about it, aside from the understandable and more romantic urge to get nearer combat and the far edges of the earth.

The approximately 20,000 Waves who serve under Lieutenant Commander Mildred H. McAfee expect to become 47,000 by the end of the year. Unlike the Wacs, they are neither an auxiliary nor a separate corps within their service. They just do any job they can do, or can be trained to do, anywhere (except overseas), that will release a man for sea duty.

The lady Leathernecks under Major Ruth Cheney Streeter number approximately 3,500 but expect to reach a strength closer to 20,000 during the next year. They replace Marines as needed, much as the Waves replace Navy men. Like the Waves, they are specialists in such things as parachute rigging, radio and communication and instrument repair.

The 3,000 Spars of the Coast Guard, commanded by Lieut. Comdr. Dorothy C. Stratton, expect to grow this year to 5,000 and, like all the others, are itching to be storekeepers in Greenland.

WOMEN FLYERS

The smallest, youngest group and the one which probably will see the quickest expansion in the near future is the group of women who are flying for the Army Air Force. Miss Jacqueline Cochran, who has just been named to the new post of director of women pilots, has been running the training course which is expected to add 400 more fliers this year to the 150 already flying for the Women's Auxiliary Ferrying Squadron. These Wafs, previously under the direction of Mrs. Nancy Harkness Love, who is now an executive on the staff of Col. William H. Turner, commanding officer of the Ferrying Division, Air Transport Command, may serve as the nucleus of a staff of women pilots who will be employed in courier and instruction service and a large variety of jobs in general. They are not military personnel but are civil service employes, under contract. They have no rank, no street uniforms, no special benefits.

July 11, 1943

ONE WAC IN FIVE IS WED

Most of Their Husbands Also in Service—Average Age 24

WASHINGTON, Sept. 24—About 18 per cent of the members of the Women's Army Corps are married, the majority to husbands who also are in service, and an undetermined but probably much higher percentage is engaged to marry soldiers, sailors or Marines, according to personnel statistics released by WAC headquarters.

The average Wac is aged 24. More than half are high school graduates, a fourth have attended college and many are holders of graduate degrees.

Most of the married and engaged Wacs have indicated to personnel officers that their reason for joining the corps was to help get the war won as soon as possible. Many also said that they felt more in common with husbands and fiancés as wearers of the Army uniform.

September 25, 1943

URGES DRAFT OF NEGROES

Council Says 500,000 Illiterates Would Obviate Fathers Going

CHICAGO, Nov. 21 (AP)—A meeting held under the sponsorship of the National Negro Council today urged "utilization of 500,000 single Negro illiterates before drafting pre-Pearl Harbor fathers for noncombat service."

A resolution, which was adopted, asked that the Government make provision for primary education of the Negro illiterates.

The council asked President Roosevelt to issue an executive order "prohibiting the War Department from its present undemocratic policy of segregating and discriminating against a million Negro soldiers by denying Negroes combat service and relegating them to engineer labor and miscellaneous divisions."

The group urged a higher quota of Negro nurses in the Army, admission of Negro women as Waves and Spars and defeat of the Senate proposal for soldier voting "unless perfected to protect the right of Negro soldiers to cast a ballot in the Southern poll-tax States."

November 22, 1943

WAC ENLISTMENTS ENDED

Score System Is Set for De-mobilizing of Corps

WASHINGTON, Aug. 30 (U.P.)—The Wacs have halted enlistments, already stopped by the Waves, Spars and Women Marines.

Col. Westray Battle Boyce, Wac director, said that the corps would be demobilized on a proportionate basis with men. The critical score of 44 points, now needed for discharge, will be lowered from time to time, and a point plan for release of Wac officers is under consideration.

Whether the Wacs will be continued as a peacetime adjunct of the Army is up to Congress. It will cease to exist six months after the end of hostilities is formally proclaimed unless specifically authorized to continue.

August 31, 1945

Special to THE NEW YORK TIMES.

WASHINGTON, Oct. 15—A bill to set up quotas entry of the foreign husbands of service women married abroad during this war was unanimously approved by the House today and sent to the Senate.

This legislation would put the husbands of Wacs and of Army and Navy nurses on the same basis so far as the immigration law is concerned as GI wives.

October 16, 1945

WOMEN GET PLACE IN U. S. MILITARY

Truman Signs Bill Setting Up Permanent Units of Wacs, Wafs, Waves and Marines

WASHINGTON, June 12 (AP)—Women got a permanent place today in the Army, Navy and Marine Corps.

The White House announced that President Truman signed on his Western trip legislation giving it to them.

Under the bill's terms the Wacs will have a maximum strength of 1,000 officers and 17,500 enlisted women. The Waves and Marines will have 1,000 officers and 10,000 in the ranks.

This compares with a peak of 100,400 women in the Wacs and 97,800 in the Waves and Marines during the war. They were enlisted then under wartime authority, which will expire six months after the official end of hostilities.

A joint Army-Navy-Air Force announcement said it is planned to build up to the following strengths at the end of two years:

Army—500 officers, 75 warrant officers, 7,500 enlisted women (present strength 875 officers and 6,000 enlisted).

Navy—500 officers, 20 warrant officers, 6,000 enlisted women.

Marines—100 officers, 10 warrant officers, 1,000 enlisted. (The present Navy and Marine components together total about 425 officers and 1,800 enlisted women).

At the outset the women will be enlisted in the Navy and Marine Corps from among those who served during World War II. Enlisted women for the Wacs and Wafs (women's air force service) will come first from among present members and later from former service women or women with no previous service.

The present directors of the Army, Navy and Marine women's groups are expected to remain in those posts. A director of the Wafs will be named later.

June 13, 1948

CHAPTER 5

The Postwar Period

*Eleanor Roosevelt
at the United Nations, 1959.*
Courtesy Compix.

Books of the Times

By JOHN CHAMBERLAIN

WHERE has Philip Wylie been all these years? Here he is, ringing out the old year and blasting away already at the new, with a book which sounds like a regurgitation of everything that has been said about our civilization by every jaundiced Jeremiah from Count Keyserling (remember him?) to the thirty-odd contributors to Editor Harold Stearns's manifesto of the early Nineteen Twenties, "Civilization in the United States." "Generation of Vipers"* is what Mr. Wylie calls his own atrabilious opus, and he spares no one.

Philip Wylie

We are, he says, a bunch of hypocritical, lying, cheating, sex-crazed, advertisement-doped, puling, whimpering, soft, insanely governed, diseased and tottering imbeciles. We condemn our women to lives of useless dilettantism, and then hand over all our money to them to spend on silly gadgets for kitchen, bathroom and the sort of activity beloved of the cartoonist Helen Hokinson. That makes us a matriarchy, which Count Keyserling was telling us back in 1928 or thereabouts, only Mr. Wylie, who remembers Al Jolson's "Mammy Songs," prefers to call the phenomenon "Momism." If Mr. Wylie wants really to discover just how original he is, I would refer him to Thomas Beer's chapter on "The Titaness" in a book called "The Mauve Decade." Mr. Beer said it all before him.

When it comes to our moving pictures, they are, of course, puerile. So, too, is our popular magazine literature. In the movies and the magazines the heroine is always Cinderella, and she always gets her prince. But the American Cinderella lacks the hard-working virtues of the mythological drudge, and the prince turns out to be just another dope who wants to subsidize "Mom" to a life of bridge-playing and petits fours. Somehow, Mr. Wylie's case against the movies and the magazines sounds like Waldo Frank writing in "Our America" back in 1919.

As for our "business civilization" Mr. Wylie blasts it for its idolatry of mass production on the one hand and its yen for monopoly on the other. Well, I remember a book by James Truslow Adams called "Our Business Civilization," and I recall a figure named George Babbitt. I also remember the forty thousand—or was it only forty?—Frenchmen who came to this country in the Nineteen Twenties and returned home to produce diatribes against "Fordism." We have been called Philistines before this, and doubtless we will hear the charge again.

Our attitude toward sex gives Mr. Wylie the

*GENERATION OF VIPERS. By Philip Wylie. 318 pages. Farrar & Rinehart. $2.75.

screaming meemies. He thinks we are a lecherous, adulterous bunch who pay mere hypocritical homage to the precepts of the Sunday schools. On the other hand, our inhibitions supposedly encourage sex insanity. Do I catch a belated echo here of a score of essays published in the old days of the Calverton-Schmalhausen symposia on "Sex and Civilization," all written under the tutelage of Havelock Ellis? I do indeed.

Americans, of course, exalt mob-thinking and mob-standards. So says Mr. Wylie, and so said a gentleman whose name I have forgotten who wrote a book fifteen years ago called "King Mob." The common man, according to Mr. Wylie, is a blithering moron. "Common people," he says, "vote fools into Congress and the State Legislatures. It is common people who fill the insane asylums. Common people massacre each other on our highways. Common people, mostly, fill our penitentiaries." Well, I am not one to worship the mass, as mass, but Al Capone seems to me decidedly uncommon.

Naturally, in Mr. Wylie's broadside charge, the professors in our universities are blown as high as a whirlwind could carry a mortarboard hat. And the ministers of the Gospel are mostly cast in the role of the Elmer Gantry. Our military men are treated as blooming Gamelins. There ain't nobody who is worth the money to pay for the chemicals in his carcass, if Mr. Wylie's book is to be accepted as a true bill.

But is it a true bill? By judicious selection one may discern trends in our civilization to lend the color of truth to almost any generalization about business, sex, the church, the moving pictures, the arts, the doctors, the soldiers and the statesmen. But, as an inveterate reader of THE TIMES's own topicker, I have long since learned to pick up the world almanac or the statistical abstract whenever some one comes along to slay us with a "truth" which is arithmetically impossible.

But People Are Decent

I can't say that Mr. Wylie's prophecies won't come true; maybe our civilization will be wiped out if we can't learn to live together in the world. All I can say is that I've been listening to authors of Mr. Wylie's stripe for twenty years only to be surprised by the countless number of human beings who simply behave decently even in the face of the Jeremiahs. Maybe it's because I don't get around enough. But it sounds to me as though Mr. Wylie were suffering from the results of a sedentary life. Here he is urging us to "drive roads to Rio and to Moscow and stop spending all our strength in the manufacture of girdles: It is time that Mom's sag became known to the desperate public." The advice may be good, but coming from an author who writes in a garden in Miami Beach it sounds like the "truth" about sin as explained by the repenter who knows that he will backslide the minute he gets off the mourners' bench.

January 2, 1943

Women Have Changed

By ELLEN D. STRUHS

TO the topsy-turvy world of women's fashions the year 1946 is a "year of curves," and hips—which seemed all but extinct during the lean war years—are being worn again. An attractive aspect of this latest style note is that, in order to be de rigueur, no woman need acquire hips the hard way. If she lacks curves but has $2.98, the department stores stand ready today to supply her at once with counterfeit hips of buckram—"hip pads" they're called in the trade—that can be sewn into any garment as easily as men's shoulder pads.

Underneath the camouflage, however, are women's figures really changing?

The story is told of a certain anatomy professor who, when one of his students complained that the class text was at least ten years old, replied amiably: "Young man, there have been very few new bones added to the human body in the last ten years." The professor would seem to have voiced an unassailable truth, yet a glance at the history of the feminine form yields the inescapable conclusion that women have changed—and markedly.

CONSIDER the "best" modern style in feminine figures—the ideal modern. According to the director of one of the largest model agencies, she has a 34-inch bust, 24-inch waist and measures 34 inches around the hips—all subject to very minor variations. Venus de Milo, by contrast, would seem a country cousin with a 37-26-38 figure.

The American woman of today is a different woman from her kin of half a century ago. She is taller, for one thing, and she has broader shoulders, narrower hips and—sad to contemplate—a wider waistline. These observations were painstakingly arrived at by anthropometrists who toured eight States and measured 14,698 examples of American womanhood during the years 1939 to 1941.

Their conclusions were published recently by the Department of Agriculture—which one had imagined concerned itself with other matters—and included a report on the measurements of the "mean" American woman. Mean or not, her height is 63.16 inches in her stocking feet, her bust measurement 35.62 inches, her waist 29.15 inches and her hips 38.82 inches. These measurements, incidentally, have been accepted as standard for the so-called 34 size, which corresponds to a 16.

The Museum of Natural History has also been looking into this fascinating subject. Its experts found, by comparing the measurements of college women of around 1890 and their college daughters of around 1920, that the daughters were 64.8 inches in height as compared to their mothers' 63.6 inches. And, correspondingly, college daughters were heavier, larger in the waist but relatively narrower in the hips.

WHAT has wrought this change in women? Style, of course, has distorted the appearance of the female figure considerably and arbitrarily during the years, as can readily be seen by looking through the pages of old fashion magazines. At the same time, through ubiquitous and clever advertising, women have simply become several times more beauty-conscious than they ever were before.

But there are other considerations. Women today are much more athletic than their mothers were. Knowledge of vitamins and consequently better, more scientific nutrition have done their share. And finally, not to be overlooked is the fact that today 18,288,000 women are working. That means they are away from home all day; they are out of the kitchen, where they were once tempted to taste and sample and indulge in snacks at odd hours. In short, both by accident and design, women have come to the point where they no longer let the world have fun at their "expanse," and they have spent a good deal of their time doing something about it.

THEY have done a good job.

The average American woman cuts a good figure. What's more, she keeps that figure longer. Size 14 is as popular today as the "perfect 36" was in former years. Fifty per cent of all the patterns sold in the stores today are 14's and 16's and there is no age limit to those who buy them. Furthermore, the demand for smaller sizes is increasing all the time rather than slackening.

The evidence shows, then, when you look back over the past forty or fifty years that women haven't been content to sit back and wait for improvement by the slow process of evolution. They have given nature an assist, and there's no telling what may happen to them next.

March 10, 1946

Dilemmas the Modern Woman Faces

MODERN WOMEN: The Lost Sex. By Ferdinand Lundberg and Marynia F. Farnham. 497 pp. New York: Harper & Bros. $3.50.

By MARGARET MEAD

THIS is a disappointing book, although the central theme is sound enough. Briefly, it is contended that society is at the present time profoundly disorganized, that the disorganization expresses itself in the large number of neurotic personalities among both men and women, but that the state of women is crucial because women as mothers transmit the psychological disorientation to the next generation. Dissatisfied and neurotic women who are accorded no dignified and prestige-giving role in modern society, but instead are left to choose between a practically empty home and an equally empty life in industry, are depicted as being the type of mother who will reject, dominate, overprotect or overstimulate their children in an attempt to right the balance in their own disordered lives.

The chapters which describe the psychological plight of the modern woman and those aspects of the plight of the modern male which disqualify him for the role of patriarch (a role for which the authors have a great enthusiasm unsupported by any real documentation) are written simply, with explicit recourse to rather traditional Freudian concepts, clearly stated. The doctrine that women are to be regarded as potentially equal to men (rather than complementary to men) is assailed with fervor and, in the appendix, with something beyond mere assertion.

The authors suggest as remedy various measures, primarily governmental, to raise the status of women as mothers: child subsidies, honors for mothers, a government department devoted to the home, turning the field of teaching over to married women as an appropriate area for the part-time activity of mothers. Also suggested is a general encouragement of women to make their contributions to culture in the field of nurturing activities—if they must make such contributions rather than just bearing and rearing children, which the author would prefer.

ALTHOUGH the authors continually refer to clinical data, none are presented; so that what we have, in these sections of the book, are a series of insights, sympathetically stated, with a regard for abiding human values. Taken together, they add up to about a hundred pages which show fair consistency and gentle wisdom.

But there are almost 400 pages more, in assorted styles and moods, which suggest that the book had not two authors but four or five, or that it was written over a long period of time during which the mood of each changed markedly. There is a long razzle-dazzle trip through European history, in which the Copernican revolution is cast as villain. Man, robbed of his cosmic significance, is psychologized in strokes which make up in boldness what they lack in detail or thought. There is a concerted attack in almost, but not quite the same, jumpy, headline type of style, on every modern ideology: Leftist, Rightist, Socialist, Communist, feminist, and Protestant. (All of these are seen as motivated primarily by hostility.) There are sections of cross-cultural comment, avowedly based on anthropological research; but actually the viewpoint of the book is limited to Western Europe and America, with only a comment or two on the Orient and some sweeping generalizations about human culture in general.

Perhaps most puzzling of all are the sixty pages devoted to a savage attack on the feminist movement. Yet the authors have already asserted that all the disasters which confront us (including wars, neuroses, and the destruction of the home) are themselves due to changes in belief and technology which have been developing since the Renaissance. They state, explicitly, that women's battle for "rights" was as empty and as understandable as men's battles for political rights to compensate them for their loss of spiritual status. Given this historical interpretation, it seems rather unfair to hit with every verbal missile in the dictionary the helpless and mistaken victims of a movement which began centuries before the authors were born.

First to label a group as victims and then excoriate them as false prophets and criminals, reveals a confusion which runs through the whole book. Granted that the home transmits either the good or the bad, the adjustment or the maladjustment in society, one cannot present simultaneously the theory that historical processes are inevitable with the theory that the cause and cure lie in the individuals who are the victims of those very processes. Hence the weak conclusion. After a crack at the atomic physicists, whose attempts to prevent war are characterized as "frenzied behavior," the cure for a world condition (which has been delineated in terms that are lurid and extreme) is presented as governmental measures to increase the dignity of the home and persuade people to have more children.

A central theory which would tie together the processes of history, the behavior of individuals, and suggest ways in which human beings, using the potentialities of both men and women, could take their own destinies in hand, is lacking.

January 26, 1947

Female of the Species

ADAM'S RIB. By Ruth Herschberger. 221 pp. New York: Pellegrini & Cudahy. $3.50.

By EDGAR BROOKE

THIS "Defense of Modern Woman" arouses uneasy speculation about the emphasis we have placed on exhibiting a sense of humor. The question arises, Have we overdone it? The reader who receives the full impact of Ruth Herschberger's lunges with the blunt instrument of her wit will be forced to vote in the affirmative. He will also find her habitually guilty of the crimes against logic of which she accuses others. On page 8 she is sarcastic about the acceptability of deducing sexual facts about human beings from traits observed in primates; on page 126 she endorses the scientific value of precisely this method. Can it be that in one instance the findings oppose her own views and support them in the other?

"Adam's Rib" is apparently the product of Ruth Herschberger's irritation after reading a number of "popular" and scholarly works on the sex life of women. As the self-appointed champion of her sex, she attacks the scientists for their errors. The outcome of the conflict is clear: the battered figure pinned to the mat is that, alas, of Miss Herschberger.

Round One: Robert M. Yerkes, in "Chimpanzees, A Laboratory Colony," concludes from thirty-two days of controlled experiments that males are sexually aggressive, whereas females are "receptive." Miss Herschberger takes this as a libel and attempts to scotch it by conducting an imaginary interview with Josie, one of the female chimpanzees who took part in the experiments. Josie states flatly that she is just as sexually dominant as any male. This satisfies Miss Herschberger. The necessity of broad sampling has been established and Miss Herschberger should have interviewed at least several hundred female chimpanzees.

Round Two: Amram Scheinfeld in "Women and Men" declares that no woman can force a man to make love, but that the reverse is possible. Miss Herschberger rejoins indignantly: "In general the woman must be predisposed or dyspeptic enough to be overcome." This alibi of indigestion is a foul blow and Miss Herschberger should be disqualified.

Round Three: "Why is woman persistently regarded as a mystery?" Miss Herschberger briskly presses the attack. "It is not that she has labored to conceal the organic and psychological facts of her constitution, but that men have showed no interest in exploring them." This arresting statement will cause many readers to dissent and certainly to raise eyebrows.

American girls, Miss Herschberger cries, are taught to arrange flowers, to shun exertion, to be gentle, modest and dignified. They are forbidden to give in to excitement. Is it any wonder that they faint so often while watching basketball games? That they think their sexual inclinations are indecent? The modern girl, Miss Herschberger concludes gloomily, is unfit for love. . . . Would some maladjusted female like to take it from here?

August 1, 1948

SEMINAR TO CONSIDER PROBLEMS OF WOMEN

The opening lecture in a seminar on "Women in Today's World" will be held at 8:30 o'clock tonight at the headquarters of the auxiliary council to the Association for the Advancement of Psychoanalysis, 220 West Ninety-eighth Street.

Dr. Joan Harte, psychoanalyst, will discuss the problems of combining career and motherhood, the pressures faced by unmarried women, cultural pressures and conflicts from childhood through adolescence and the role of women as wives and mothers. Subsequent meetings will be held next Wednesday, Feb. 18 and March 4 and 11.

In an interview this week, Dr. Harte discussed the problem of the wife who had satisfactorily combined a career with her marriage, but did not know if it was advisable to continue after she had children. The psychoanalyst explained that "attitude" was all-important. If the mother gave up her career because she felt she ought to but did not want to, she might be doing the children more harm than good.

"In giving time to children, it should be remembered that the quality of the time spent is more important than the quantity," Dr. Harte said.

"Attitude" is equally important in a woman's approach to volunteer work. If she believes in what she is doing and is not just doing it because "all of her friends do," she can do a lot of good for those she comes in contact with as well as herself. If she secretly considers it a chore, she isn't helping anyone and it will probably show in her work.

It is Dr. Harte's belief that the well-adjusted woman who lives up to her own potentialities and has stopped comparing herself with others, can gracefully make any transition demanded of her.

END CONFORMITY, STEVENSON URGES

Encourages Smith Graduates Not to Echo 'Tribal Refrain' as Wives and Mothers

By EDITH EVANS ASBURY
Special to The New York Times.

NORTHAMPTON, Mass., June 6—Adlai E. Stevenson gave advice on how to be a wife and mother in addressing the graduating class of Smith College today.

Among the graduates was Miss Nancy Lewis Anderson, who will be married to Adlai Stevenson Jr. June 25 at her home in Louisville.

Mr. Stevenson told the seniors that, statistically, most of them were destined for "the humble role of the housewife," whether they liked the idea or not at the present.

"When the time comes, you'll love it," he said.

The principal speaker at the college's seventy-seventh commencement, Mr. Stevenson expressed the hope that as wives and mothers, the graduates would "not be content to wring your hands, feed your family and just echo all the group in tribal refrains."

Decries Conformity

Decrying the trend toward specialization and conformity, he urged the young women to combat it.

"This assignment for you, as wives and mothers, has great advantages," Mr. Stevenson said. "It is homework, you can do it in the living room with a baby in your lap, or in the kitchen with a can-opener in your hands. If you're really clever, maybe you can even practice your saving arts on that unsuspecting man while he's watching television.

"And, secondly, it is important work worthy of you, whoever you are or your education, whatever it is, even Smith College, because we will defeat totalitarian, authoritarian ideas only by better ideas; we will frustrate the evils of vocational specialization only by the virtues of intellectual generalization.

"You will have to be alert or you may get caught yourself—even in the kitchen or the nursery—by the steady pressures with which you will be surrounded."

Somewhere along the line, Mr. Stevenson said, while institutional reforms were being achieved in the last fifty years, too much importance has become attached to the well-adjusted citizens who fit painlessly into the social pattern.

"While I am not in favor of maladjustment," he continued, "I view this cultivation of neutrality, this breeding of mental neuters, this hostility to

February 4, 1953

248

Associated Press Wirephoto

STEVENSON GOES TO SMITH: Adlai E. Stevenson, Democratic Presidential candidate in 1952, was principal speaker at seventy-seventh commencement of Smith College, Northampton, Mass. With him are Janice P. Carlson, left, of Minneapolis, Minn., president of graduating class, and Sallie McFague of Milton, Mass., president of college's student council.

eccentricity and controversity with grave misgiving.

"One looks back with dismay at the possibility of a Shakespeare perfectly adjusted to bourgeois life in Stratford, a Wesley contentedly administering a county parish, George Washington going to London to receive a barony from George III, or Abraham Lincoln prospering in Springfield with nary

a concern for the preservation of the crumbling union."

In addition to well-adjusted conformers, the guest of honor said, this century needs "more idiosyncratic, unpredictable character—that rugged frontier word "ornery" occurs to me—people who take open eyes and open minds out with them into the society which they will share and help transform."

Mr. Stevenson warned the graduates that they would find it much easier to conform.

"Tribal conformity and archaic dictatorship could not have lasted so long if they did not accord comfortably with basic human needs and desires," he observed.

This fact was recognized by Hitler, the Fascists and by Communists who are "busy brain-

washing all over Asia," he added.

In this country, too, Mr. Stevenson said, there are some leaders "who certainly have a brainwashing glint in their eye when they meet with an unfamiliar idea."

Consultation Before Speech

Before beginning his prepared speech, Mr. Stevenson confided to the audience of more than 5,000 that he had consulted with his sons, his prospective daughter-in-law and other students concerning it.

His sons told him that, as the father of three sons and no daughters, he had "no qualifications whatever to speak to a graduating class of a woman's college," Mr. Stevenson revealed.

He was also advised to avoid mentioning "the challenges of life" or "the great responsibility that confronts you," he added.

"That, of course, to a politician, was tantamount to an injunction of silence," Mr. Stevenson commented. It was further suggested by students that he discuss ideals, "but no exalted nonsense," and that he speak wisely, spiritually and wittily.

"When I told my son this," Mr. Stevenson said, "his final word of advice was—decline the invitation."

Bachelor of Arts degrees were conferred on 429 members of the Class of 1955, advanced degrees on forty-two and honorary degrees on seven women.

Marianne Craig Moore, Brooklyn poet; Erica Morini, New York violinist, and Irita Van Doren, literary editor of The New York Herald Tribune, were among the recipients of honorary degrees.

June 7, 1955

Small Town Peep Show

PEYTON PLACE. By Grace Metalious. 372 pp. New York: Julian Messner. $3.95.

By CARLOS BAKER

THIS is the earthy novel of small-town life in New Hampshire which sprang into the news some weeks ago when the Gilmanton School Board dismissed young George Metalious from his position as principal of the local grammar school. "They told me it was because of my wife," said Mr. Metalious. "They don't like her book." Later, the school board said they had dismissed the young teacher for reasons of their own, which had no bearing on the novel. The author herself still insisted that word had got around Gilmanton that "Pey-

Mr. Baker is chairman of the Department of English at Princeton.

ton Place" was a real shocker: "People suddenly decided that George is not the type to teach their sweet innocent children."

Whatever the merits of the Metalious case, the novel lives up very fully to its advance billing. It opens on a warm autumn day in the Thirties with a comparison between Indian summer and a woman ("Ripe, hotly passionate, but fickle, she comes and goes as she pleases"). What follows is a carefully calculated exposé of the comings and goings of a large cast of typical characters in a small New England town until another Indian summer some ten years later.

We learn that life behind the scenes in New Hampshire is not widely different, fictionally speaking, from life in Winesburg, Ohio, Hecate County, Conn., or Gibbsville, Pa. It is only (if that is possible) a little "riper," a little more "hotly passionate," a little more frankly detailed—and, perhaps, a little more widely inclusive than the

small-town chronicles of Messrs. Sherwood Anderson, Edmund Wilson and John O'Hara. The late Sinclair Lewis would no doubt have hailed Grace Metalious as a sister-in-arms against the false fronts and bourgeois pretensions of allegedly respectable communities, and certified her as a public accountant of what goes on in the basements, bedrooms and back porches of a "typical American town."

Mrs. Metalious, who is a pretty fair writer for a first novelist, comes and goes with the Indian Summer air of an emancipated modern authoress who knows the earthy words and rarely stints to use them. Samples of the adventures in store for readers of "Peyton Place" would include the following: Successive violations of a 14-year-old girl by her stepfather, leading to an abortion sadly performed by the town's admirable doctor. A murder in a "shacker's" hut with secret burial of the remains in a sheep pen. A suicide

in a bedroom closet: A carnival accident which amputates a young girl's arm. A high-school seduction in which the girl is bought off by the boy's rich and corrupt father. The seduction of the local dress-shop proprietress by the village schoolmaster. The deflowering of her nubile novelist-daughter by an erotically expert New York literary agent. A lengthy hard-cider binge in a locked cellar involving among others the town handyman who imbibes as a protest against his wife's multiple adulteries. The strangling of a pet tomcat at the feet of a dead spinster by a neurotic boy who has retchingly peered through a backyard hedge at the amorous activities of a neighbor couple.

If Mrs. Metalious can turn her emancipated talents to less lurid purposes, her future as novelist is a good bet. Another good bet is that the citizens of Gilmanton, N. H., can look forward to a busy Indian summer of open or surreptitious reading.

September 23, 1956

Pope Pius Calls Woman Creation's Masterpiece

CASTEL GANDOLFO, Italy, Oct. 14 (Æ) — Pope Pius described woman today as creation's masterpiece. He said her "sublime mission" was maternity and deplored the fact that in some countries women worked in heavy industry.

Speaking by radio from his summer residence here to several thousand Italian women, members of the Italian Feminine Center meeting in Loreto, the Pontiff declared the physical and moral make-up of woman demanded discrimination in the kind and amount of work she should do.

"The concept of the woman of the shipyards, of the mines, or heavy labor, as it is exalted and practiced by some countries that would want to inspire progress, is anything but a modern concept," he said. "It is, on the contrary, a sad return toward epochs that Christian civilization buried long ago."

October 15, 1956

MAN TELLS WOMEN THEY LACK RIGHTS

By EMMA HARRISON

There has been more progress made in the United States against racial prejudice than against sex prejudice a leading psychologist said yesterday.

Racial discrimination has become Page 1 news, while prejudice directed against women is hardly recognized as a problem, Dr. Goodwin Watson, Columbia University psychologist, declared.

He cited President Eisenhower as a bearer of the "typical masculine" attitude toward the question of sex prejudice.

Recently when questioned at a news conference on why he had not been active in attempting to wipe out discrimination based on sex, President Eisenhower answered with a "typical masculine parry," the psychologist charged. The President said it was hard for a "mere man" to believe that women did not already have equal rights.

Dr. Watson said it was not hard for him to believe this, though. He spoke to a meeting of the International Council of Women Psychologists, held in conjunction with the American Psychological Association's sixty-fifth annual meeting.

Top prestige jobs are considered suited for men only, he said. Women are thought capable of heading the Parent-Teachers Association or the Red Cross, but not a bank, factory or nation, he observed.

The effect is the hardest on women when they reached the close of the period of reproduction, the psychologist said.

"Restlessly they turn to beauty parlors, to community organizations, to alcohol, to churches and to psychotherapists, but in this culture, no really satisfactory solution can be found," Dr. Watson declared.

The most obvious loss comes from the "unutilized ability of women," he continued. He said it might be well to note that 40 per cent of the "distinguished members of the Academy of Sciences in the Soviet Union are women."

August 31, 1957

Will Success Spoil American Women?

A European sees our men as an 'oppressed minority'—but the girls' victory is Pyrrhic.

By AMAURY DE RIENCOURT

THE American woman is a major problem today. The most hackneyed cliché, forcefully stated by amazed European men and resentfully acknowledged by American men, is the alarming ascendancy of the female sex in the United States. Writers and novelists, sociologists, historians, clergymen, psychiatrists, all have their pet explanations. Being mostly men, they are usually careful to conceal their findings behind a screen of impenetrable scholarship or of burning satire for fear of arousing the formidable anger of American womanhood. I will venture to discard all screens and, at the risk of arousing the sleep-

AMAURY DE RIENCOURT is a French writer (and bachelor) who knows America and Americans well; he has traveled in forty of our states, and resides here for six months each year. He wrote "The Coming Caesars."

ing dragon, will tread on sacred ground, facing the problem squarely—that is, simply and seriously.

Let us first of all look at the general picture. Statistics tell us quite plainly that women own almost three-quarters of all assets in the United States (more than $100 billion in common and preferred stocks, almost $60 billion in savings accounts, roughly $70 billion in Government bonds, etc. . . .). This is largely the result of the fact that women outlive men by an average of six years (there are seven million widows as against only two million widowers) and therefore inherit the bulk of their deceased husbands' wealth (75 per cent of all life insurance death benefits go to women).

Controlling the purse strings, they are in a material position to exert untold influence on American politics and the American way of life. And we

might just as well start pulling this particular thread out of the fabric of man-woman relationships in the United States. One thread will automatically come out with another and we will soon get at the truth.

The American man works hard, plays hard and dies younger than his mate. Perhaps the best explanation of this fact is that most of the technological progress made in the past half-century has been devoted to easing woman's burden of keeping house and rearing children rather than lightening man's load of work. Technical improvement in the industrial plant, on the farm or in the office is designed to increase productive efficiency, not to ease man's work; he is automatically expected to produce more. But technical improvement in the home is pure benefit and is not balanced by an increase in production. Thus, women have more time on their hands, more unspent energy—they have real freedom while their mates are more than ever tied to their business. Surplus time, energy and freedom amount to a surplus of power. And soon enough, women start to look around for ways and means of exerting this immense power which men have let slip out of their hands.

While men are busy at work in the field of economic production, women get busy shaping the demands of consumption. (As early as 1933 Charles and Mary Beard estimated that women bought almost three-quarters of all

250

manufactured goods.) The American woman has, of course, the last word in the choice of housing, furniture and interior decoration, children's consumption, food, and everything that pertains to herself. But that is only the beginning. She dominates completely the cultural and entertainment field—music, art galleries, education, movies and the theatre, magazines and books. She regulates completely the social life of the family and is the mainstay of religious and welfare activities. She is now in the process of invading man's last preserve—more than half the time she chooses the man's own clothes. What is left to the husband's free choice except his favorite brand of cigars?

This over-all picture must be qualified. Woman's power does not exert itself uniformly through life; it has its ups and downs. The first years of married life are not an unmixed blessing for her, even though she has usually trained her husband to wash dishes and change diapers. The young couple's financial means are limited and kids have to be raised. While the young husband works hard and looks for promotion, his wife is busy rearing a young family and keeping house within the limits of a narrow budget.

BUT years go by and things begin to change. The husband's salary inches up gradually and he brings more money home. The children grow, go to boarding school or college. The husband works harder and, if he is the slightest bit successful in his career, becomes fascinated with it. Work becomes his whole life, involves all his thoughts, absorbs all his energy. On the other hand, his wife has more money to spend and more time now that the children are almost adults and are becoming independent. This is when feminine ascendancy really starts.

So far, feminine influence has been exerted chiefly at home, that is, indirectly. But now it begins to be exerted directly through social channels. The wife joins the local women's club, participates fully in the life of the local community. And because community life is in her hands, education is also. It is through the educational process itself that the American boy learns from the very beginning—first at home, then at school—that women belong to a superior species. It is largely thanks to his mother that a man's wife later on finds he is an adaptable and domesticated being she can push around to her heart's content.

Meanwhile, whereas the man's interests have become more specialized in his particular field of production, and his outlook narrower, his wife's interests become broader. She has plenty of time to read books of general interest while "hubby" concentrates on business reports or technical analyses. She becomes more cultured, more interested in the world at large, in politics, literature, painting, music. She imposes her views—acting not merely as a housewife but as a member of a social group, a well-organized and most powerful lobby—on society as a whole. She is more society-conscious and less individualistic than man, more disciplined. And women now outnumber men.

This numerical superiority is important. The Census Bureau estimated in 1956 that there were roughly four and a half million more women than men of voting age. Their actual vote increased 39 per cent from 1948 to 1952 as against an increase of only 16 per cent in men's vote; and the trend has been continuing ever since. The Metropolitan Life Insurance Company has conjectured that women may very likely have outvoted men for the first time in 1956.

All these elements add up to give women an almost unchallengeable supremacy. By the time he has reached middle age, the man realizes that it is too late—he can no longer recapture the power that has slipped out of his hands. He has become a member of an oppressed minority. And the vicious circle whirls around again. Disappointed, he seeks refuge in business, where he can regain part of his former self-confidence and self-esteem. He goes to conventions, attends his own men's clubs and attempts to preserve the illusion that he is still in control. But it is pure

illusion: being a mere producer, he is at the mercy of his discriminating client, the consuming public—that is to say, women.

THE result is that, as a human being, the American man finds himself in an increasingly inferior position from which he can no longer escape—largely because he no longer wishes to escape. Unable to step out of his narrow specialization and broaden his outlook, unable truly to free himself from the daily pressure of business competition, he can no longer develop that most masculine of all qualities, mental creation (the natural counterpart of women's physical creation), in an atmosphere of complete freedom.

He lacks ideas and inspiration, has little time to make basic discoveries in any field because he has no time to dream or contemplate or fiddle around — he must work at something tangible, not daydream. The pressure of social taboos, which he has been taught to accept from early childhood, will not allow him to "waste" his time in apparent idleness while his wife is waiting impatiently for her dishwasher or her mink coat. And, of course, social standards are mostly set by women.

And he has been repeatedly taught and now believes implicitly that to give and to give endlessly without expecting anything in return is a sign of masculinity. He has become the oddest of all creatures, a volunteer for slavery.

THIS is where an internal threat to freedom exists, worming its way into the very heart of our society—in the fact that feminine ascendancy tends to promote a social conformity which binds man and prevents him from developing his own specific personality. If the feminine instinct for security, social respectability and comfort is allowed to stifle the rather uncomfortable but necessary masculine instinct for risk and creative originality, our culture is threatened with sterility and our society with decay.

The man as husband then becomes a mere tool in the hands of socially ambitious woman, the instrument that will allow her to compete socially with other women. Drowned in a deluge of cocktail and dinner parties, numbed with needless gossip, unable to free himself from social entanglements and often exhausted by a strenuous business life, he is compelled out of sheer lassitude to conform to all the taboos and standards set by women.

All this has come about through an extension of the belief in the democratic equality of all men, to the radical conception of the equality between the sexes. Whereas European societies still believe in a fundamental inequality between the sexes and between age brackets, in man's inherent superiority over women and parents' superiority over children, American society has turned its back on such "old-fashioned" views. American society as a whole believes now in a complete equality between the sexes—one which automatically favors the women since they have the right to vote but not the duty of going to war, the right to financial supremacy but not the obligation to work for it, the right to all the traditional privileges of womanhood but none of the compensating and outdated inferiorities—except the inescapable physiological ones.

Strange as it may seem, this odd situation is not new to history; it has happened before. A crotchety old Roman philosopher, Cato the Elder, warned his fellow men 2,000 years ago, in political circumstances very similar to ours today, "From the moment that they become your equals, women will be your masters." Today, the American woman demands and she gets; and in the end she herself is not quite certain that it should be so. A woman who has her way in everything tends to despise the provider of all things—and the American woman now has undoubtedly lost too much respect for the man who made her a present of equality.

THE impact of the American woman's ascendancy on politics is startling. In any society, but especially and more directly in a democratic one, the professional politician courts only one mistress, public opinion. And women *are* public opinion in the United States. Man will attempt to exert his influence directly in special circumstances, whenever his particular field of activity is directly concerned. He will influence politicians as a farmer, a banker, a member of a particular labor union, but rarely as a plain citizen. He will look for specific results in his own field.

Women take a broader view of things and will look for general results on a national scale. Being essentially unspecialized, they take an interest in the whole picture. And since man operates best as an individual and woman as a member of a social group, public opinion, that elusive, unpredictable and highly emotional entity, is fundamentally feminine.

Any experienced politician or lecturer knows the difference between a masculine and a feminine audience. In my own case, several years of lecturing all over the United States have left a lasting impression—that of the contrast between, say, a Rotary Club meeting where business men exchange jokes and then come down to business, listen to the lecture and ask pointed questions in their own field while displaying a remarkable lack of interest in broader problems; and the local women's club meeting, more solemn and stiff with self-consciousness, but more attentive and at the same time less interested in the lecture itself than in the personality of the speaker.

MEN, more analytical, want new facts, new elements of knowledge—or humorous entertainment. Women want to see a new personality and will believe in his ideas to the extent that they believe in him as a person. The political consequences were clearly stated last year by Bertha S. Adkins, assistant chairman of the Republican National Committee: "There is no question," she said, "that the woman's point of view is more subjective and personal. Women are more concerned about the honesty and integrity of the candidate, and they often react emotionally to his personality."

To this we can add Carl Jung's statement in his "Two Essays on Analytical Psychology" that "personal relationships are as a rule more important and interesting to [woman] than objective facts and their connections." There can hardly be any doubt about it: as a

Drawing by Wm. Steig.

general rule, men are interested in new ideas, women in new people.

This explains, in turn, the peculiarities of the American political system which baffle many Europeans. John Gunther has pointed out in "Inside U. S. A." that "most American politicians—or shall we say most Americans are much dominated by women." Feminine ascendancy in the United States has resulted in a steadily rising interest in individual personalities as against political parties, ideas and programs. Public opinion increasingly believes in ideas only to the extent that it has faith in the man, and not vice versa.

Feminine intuition now has the upper hand and is putting man's logic to flight. Public opinion swings emotionally from one extreme to another, making long-range planning exceedingly difficult. Far-seeing, cool-headed statesmanship becomes almost impossible and has to give way to day-to-day politics, to courting a mercurial public opinion.

Whenever a great crisis, easily predictable and avoidable, occurs, feminine emotionalism takes over and looks, not for articulate programs and ideas to cope with the crisis, but to one man, to a public father, a magician in whom women pour all the faith, love and devotion they have withheld from husbands and fathers. And the danger is that, to this one man, they will deliver all their husbands, fathers, brothers and sons since they are all theirs to deliver.

AND now we come to the meat of the whole matter: What is to be done about it? How can the American woman hand back to the American man the power she has, unwittingly, usurped?

In many ways the American woman today is the most attractive and intelligent woman in the world, although by no means the happiest. Because she is intelligent, she is uncomfortably aware of the fact that her predominance is unjustified and even dangerous, and she would probably be quite willing to set matters right, if only she knew how.

The answer lies in the very nature of her matriarchal predominance: she dominates her husband as a wife only because he has been dominated before by his mother. And as a wife, she can no longer set matters right. A mature man no longer changes. But, as a mother, she can influence her son, and help him to see womanhood in its right perspective.

First of all, she should help her son to "grow up" to adulthood rather than attempt to stunt him and make him into one of the "boys" who remain perpetual adolescents and whose main object in life is to be "popular." She should see in him a human being who is potentially more individual than she, and to whose creative potential everything should be sacrificed—including her own power and influence over him.

BUT more important still, she should display a certain respect for her husband in front of her sons so as to enhance his masculine prestige in their eyes. Children must see in their father an ideal of virility to look up to rather than an object of ridicule to look down upon. Women can only be good mothers to their sons by being, or giving the appearance of being, good wives to their husbands. They can at least pretend that they accept as a generous gift from men what they have in fact come to regard as their due.

It is a great sacrifice that, I am sure, most American women would be glad to make for the sake of a better future.

"Joan of Arc was a woman! Madame Curie was a woman! Sarah Bernhardt was a woman!"

Marilyn Monroe

Actress Enjoyed Immense Popularity but Said She Was Seldom Happy

The life of Marilyn Monroe, the golden girl of the movies, ended as it began, in misery and tragedy.

Her death at the age of 36 closed an incredibly glamorous career and capped a series of somber events that began with her birth as an unwanted, illegitimate baby and went on and on, illuminated during the last dozen years by the lightning of fame.

Her public life was in dazzling contrast to her private life.

The first man to see her on the screen, the man who made her screen test, felt the almost universal reaction as he ran the wordless scene. In it, she walked, sat down and lit a cigarette.

Recalled 'Lush Stars'

"I got a cold chill," he said. "This girl had something I hadn't seen since silent pictures. This is the first girl who looked like one of those lush stars of the silent era. Every frame of the test radiated sex."

Billy Wilder, the director, called it "flesh impact."

"Flesh impact is rare," he said. "Three I remember who had it were Clara Bow, Jean Harlow and Rita Hayworth. Such girls have flesh which photographs like flesh. You feel you can reach out and touch it."

Fans paid $200,000,000 to see her project this quality. No sex symbol of the era other than Brigitte Bardot could match her popularity. Toward the end, she also convinced critics and the public that she could act.

During the years of her greatest success, she saw two of her marriages end in divorce. She suffered at least two miscarriages and was never able to have a child. Her emotional insecurity deepened; her many illnesses came upon her more frequently.

Dismissed From Picture

In 1961, she was twice admitted to hospitals in New York for psychiatric observation and rest. She was dismissed in June by Twentieth Century-Fox after being absent all but five days during seven weeks of shooting "Something's Got to Give."

"It's something that Marilyn no longer can control," one of her studio chiefs confided. "Sure she's sick. She believes she's sick. She may even have a fever, but it's a sickness of the mind. Only a psychiatrist can help her now."

1953: Miss Monroe as she appeared in a scene from "Gentlemen Prefer Blondes."

1959: She portrayed a member of all-girl band in film "Some Like It Hot."

In her last interview, published in the Aug. 3 issue of Life magazine, she told Richard Meryman, an associate editor:

"I was never used to being happy, so that wasn't something I ever took for granted."

Considering her background, this was a statement of exquisite restraint.

She was born in Los Angeles on June 1, 1926. The name on the birth record is Norma Jean Mortenson, the surname of the man who fathered her, then abandoned her mother. She later took her mother's last name, Baker.

Family Tragedies

Both her maternal grandparents and her mother were committed to mental institutions. Her uncle killed himself. Her father died in a motorcycle accident three years after her birth.

Her childhood has been described as "Oliver Twist in girl's clothing."

During her mother's stays in asylums, she was farmed out to twelve sets of foster parents. Two families were religious fanatics; one gave her empty whisky bottles to play with instead of dolls.

At another stage, she lived in a drought area with a family of seven. She spent two years in a Los Angeles orphanage, wearing a uniform she detested.

By the time she was 9 years old, Norma Jean had begun to stammer—an affliction rare among females.

Her dream since childhood had been to be a movie star, and she succeeded beyond her wildest imaginings. The conviction of her mother's best friend was borne out: she had told the little girl, day after day:

"Don't worry. You're going to be a beautiful girl when you get big. You're going to be a movie star. Oh, I feel it in my bones."

Nunnally Johnson, the producer and writer, understood that Miss Monroe was something special. Marilyn, he said, was "a phenomenon of nature, like Niagara Falls and the Grand Canyon.

"You can't talk to it. It can't talk to you. All you can do is stand back and be awed by it," he said.

This figure in the minds of millions was difficult to analyze statistically. Her dimensions—37-23-37—were voluptuous but not extraordinary.

She stood 5 feet 5½ inches tall. She had soft blonde hair, wide, dreamy, gray-blue eyes. She spoke in a high baby voice that was little more than a breathless whisper.

Fans wrote her 5,000 letters a week, at least a dozen of them proposing marriage. The Communists denounced her as a capitalist trick to make the American people forget how miserable they were. In Turkey a young man took leave of his senses while watching "How to Marry a Millionaire" and slashed his wrists.

There were other symbols of success. She married two American male idols—one an athlete, one an intellectual.

Her second husband was Joe DiMaggio the baseball player. Her third and last was the Pulitzer-prize winning playwright, Arthur Miller.

She was 16 when she married for the first time. The bridegroom was James Dougherty, 21, an aircraft worker.

Mr. Dougherty said after their divorce four years later, in 1946, that she had been a "wonderful" housekeeper.

Her two successive divorces came in 1954, when she split with Mr. DiMaggio after only nine months, and in 1960, after a four-year marriage to Mr. Miller.

She became famous with her first featured role of any prominence, in "The Asphalt Jungle," issued in 1950.

Her appearance was brief but unforgettable. From the instant she moved onto the screen with that extraordinary walk of hers, people asked themselves: "Who's that blonde?"

In 1952 it was revealed that Miss Monroe had been the subject of a widely distributed nude calendar photograph shot while she was a notably unsuccessful starlet.

It created a scandal, but it was her reaction to the scandal that was remembered. She told interviewers that she was not ashamed and had needed the money to pay her rent.

She also revealed her sense of humor. When asked by a woman journalist, "You mean you didn't have anything on?" she replied breathlessly:

"Oh yes, I had the radio on."

One of her most exasperating quirks was her tardiness. She was, during the years of her fame, anywhere from one to twenty-four hours late for appointments. Until lately, she managed to get away with it.

Her dilatory nature and sicknesses added nearly $1,000,000 to the budget of "Let's Make Love." The late Jerry Wald, head of her studio, simply commented:

"True, she's not punctual. She can't help it, but I'm not sad about it," he said. "I can get a dozen beautiful blondes who will show up promptly in make-up at 4 A. M. each morning, but they are not Marilyn Monroe."

The tardiness, the lack of responsibility and the fears began to show more and more through the glamorous patina as Miss Monroe's career waxed.

Speaking of her career and her fame in the Life interview, she said, wistfully:

"It might be kind of a relief to be finished. It's sort of like I don't know what kind of a yard dash you're running, but then you're at the finish line and you sort of sigh—you've made it! But you never have —you have to start all over again."

August 6, 1962

FAMILY LIFE HELD UPSET BY MOBILITY

Transient Areas Are Reported Increased by the Advance in American Industry

PHILADELPHIA, Pa., Oct. 3—The mobility of American families, which in some areas change their residences at the rate of six times a decade, was described here tonight as one of the four prime factors undermining the stability of the American home.

Speaking at the Middle Atlantic Regional Conference of the Family Service Association of America, Dr. Eduard C. Lindeman, Professor of Social Philosophy at the New York School of Social Work, listed the other three factors as follows: economic insecurity, lack of education for family life and emotional disturbances precipitated either by internal family elements or by unrest in the world.

Dr. Lindeman linked the rise of mobility of American families to the increase of industry. People, he said, go where jobs are available.

27,000,000 Changed Homes

"During the last war, 27,000,000 families changed their residence," he said. "In other words, industry produces an unstable family, unstable with respect to place or locality. Unstability may lead to psychological or emotional instability unless we learn how to service unstable families."

To meet the causes of family breakdowns, Dr. Lindeman suggested that the individual who seeks to strengthen family life should support a varied adequate program for family life education and casework service in each community.

His remedy also included working to establish and maintain a stable economy for the country, working for adequate housing, and giving time and energy to the problems of world understanding and peace.

"In a society which commands its young men to go to war periodically and destroys untold quantities of wealth which might have contributed to an elevated standard of living and destroys all the normal processes of life in order to concentrate upon killing other individuals, it will not be possible to maintain good families," he said.

More Help for Aged Urged

At an earlier session of the two-day conference, which opened today, Frank J. Hertel, general director of the association, estimated that far more adequate provision for help to older persons in meeting personal problems will have to be made than is in view at present.

In planning for persons 65 years of age and older, communities have concentrated largely on the problems of financial support, he said, adding that lack of financial resources was only one of the needs facing the aged. The others, he went on, are lack of family ties, declining physical strength, unsuitable housing and a need for recreation and fresh interests.

Mr. Hertel suggested two immediate steps that could be taken to solve these problems:

Family agencies, locally, should give leadership in the community-wide planning which will uncover the kinds of problems facing aged persons and suggest kinds of resources and skills required to meet the problems.

The association should give leadership in nation-wide planning to meet the needs of the aged.

October 4, 1947

Name Changes for Women

Some, It Is Said, Would Like Privilege of Keeping Identity

To the Editor of The New York Times:

Henry Waldman in his letter in your issue of Sept. 16, captioned "Changing Names Not New," misleads your readers when he states that "provision is made by statute in New York for the issuance of a formal court order granting leave to assume a new name." One is, therefore, led to believe that resort to court is necessary in New York, whereas the legal findings are that such a statute is only regarded as an expedient in establishing a new name.

I base my statement on research which was done several years ago by the Lucy Stone League, the organization which established legally that it was not necessary for a woman to take her husband's name at marriage. The law then read (and I find no evidence of it having been changed): "The nomenclature by which you are commonly known is your name." Since notification to business associates and friends is slow and difficult, it was believed that the stamp of court approval would give emphasis to the process. But such a step is decidedly not necessary.

In his discourse on names Mr. Waldman has overlooked the phase of the subject affecting those who wish to continue the use of their names. He ignores the implications of wanting not to change one's name. Women can change their names as often as they change their husbands, but let one of them want to keep her original name while making the husband change-overs and she causes quite a stir. It comes as a complete surprise that she might have a deep attachment for the only thing she has worn continuously from birth.

It is actually a breach of civil rights for organizations such as the Waves, Wacs, and other agencies arbitrarily to oblige women to change their names at marriage as they are now doing. The New York City Board of Education has softened its attitude toward the confusing practice, and the Passport Bureau has for many years allowed women passports in their own (maiden) names, although it is still not unusual for a prejudiced clerk to mak his own rules.

As Mr. Waldman points out, imitation is the sincerest form of flattery: many women believe it would be pleasant to imitate men in—among other things—the enjoyment of such privileges as keeping their identity.

JANE GRANT.
New York, Sept. 17, 1948.

September 27, 1948

FAMILY LIVING: FIRST AIM OF HOME DESIGN

By FREDERICK GUTHEIM

In 1950 It Should Influence Individual Items as Well as Over-All Plans

THE second half of this century may well be marked as the time when the unique type of family our industrial society has created began to use the resources of industrialism to the full to make itself homes and communities designed for its needs.

If so, it can be said that housing has come of age. It can be said that the politics of urbanism, city planning; the newest of our large industries, the home-building industry; and our most characteristic design expression, the home furnishings industry, have settled into a long job of building a new environment for the new American family.

It will then follow, too, that the social problems of our time, the most characteristic of which are embedded in family tensions and maladjustments and result in divorce, delinquency, and personal insecurity, will begin to wane in an environment designed to stimulate and support family life and individual fulfillment.

Even against the background of prevailing uncertainties, the home-builder is still building houses at a greater rate than ever before. This phenomenal building boom

PRIVACY RETAINER

Ben Schnall
Vertical louvred fence encloses terrace. Leo Fischer, architect.

reflects the increased number of families in our population, the larger number of small families and the migration of families, from farm to city and from central city to suburbs.

The building boom also reflects changing ideas of what families

need to live well and happily. Among the features of the 1950 house are the all-on-one-level plan, the free-standing suburban home on a half-acre or larger lot, the house oriented to its own private garden with service facilities (kitchen, etc.) facing the road, and with emphasis on outdoor, informal living.

The great demand for new homes has given us a "seller's market" during the last five years, and that kind of market should prevail in the period immediately ahead for most homes of moderate price. It will probably mean continued high prices, perhaps higher prices.

But this seller's market is at odds with the other major characteristic of the housebuilding business—the new emphasis on design. What are the fundamentals of good housing design as we see them today? They begin with sufficient interior space.

The next fundamental characteristic of good housing is a reasonable choice among dwellings of different prices or rents, sizes, and characteristics.

Reasons for Variety

At this point we might take a look at some reasons why we need a diversified rather than a standardized supply of new houses. Several years ago the Women's Foundation, 10 East Fortieth Street, called a conference of leading experts on family life to consider what should be done to get better houses. This three-day meeting and reports of numerous committees set up at the conference was summarized in a pamphlet, "Houses for Family Living."

The first major finding of this pamphlet was that, while a new type of family had appeared in recent years, there was no such thing as an "average" family. Each normal family passes through four clearly defined stages:

(1) The Early Years, the two or three years between marriage and the arrival of the first child, a period devoted mainly to learning how to live together and mastering the household arts.

(2) The Crowded Years, the period lasting usually for twelve to fifteen years until the youngest child has gone to school, when the life of the family is dominated by the needs and personality of the pre-school child.

(3) The Peak Years, the years of the teen-ager, of big appetites

and gangs, of adolescence and courtship, with peaks in family health and income, continuing until the last child has left the home.

(4) The Later Years, that steadily lengthening period now amounting to fifteen years or so, when the couple are again alone.

The second important finding of this pamphlet was that there was no "ideal" house. A dwelling that might be suitable to family living requirements at one stage in the development of a family might be outgrown and unsuitable at another.

The pamphlet was obliged to conclude with a statement of design objectives, among which the most important seemed to be flexibility—the characteristic that would allow the house to be changed to meet changing family living requirements.

Towards Greater Flexibility

Flexibility embraced the design of the house, the interiors, the furniture and the equipment. Along with flexibility, a diversified supply of housing, into which families could move with reasonable freedom as their needs changed, stood at the top of the list of requirements.

In this review so much time has been spent on the design of houses because that is the beginning of any logical consideration of the furnishings and equipment that go into them, on the one hand, and the design of the communities in which they stand on the other. All three factors are interrelated and inseparable in considering what makes good family living environments.

If the house is designed to provide minimum, although adequate space, then we must begin any plan for furnishing it with the idea of making the most of the limited space available. That is the normal problem today in most households.

Interior design begins by thinking of the house as a pattern of spaces to accommodate various activities, not as a series of "rooms" for limited and specialied use, each of which requires specialized kinds of furniture and equipment of its own.

Chair of Many Uses

From this philosophy of design we get the anonymous chair, that is equally at home in the kitchen or the parlor, the bedroom or the dining room. We get the colorful

and cheerful living-kitchen that is often the biggest and best room in the house, and certainly the one lived in most by the servantless family with children. We get a new appreciation for light weight as a desirable characteristic of furniture design.

We want space-conserving furniture that stacks, that folds up that stores easily, that can be converted for many uses. We want lamps that adjust to various heights, that shine directly or indirectly as we wish, that can be moved about the room. We want attractive, durable, easily cleaned and long-wearing surfaces for walls, floors, work surfaces, and furniture.

We want equipment that helps us get through the working part of the homemaking day and leaves us leisure time in big enough blocks to do things with it that really count, that bring home additional money or that bring satisfaction in community service or creative enterprises.

Houses Into Homes

These are some of the ways in which well designed, well equipped houses can help fathers, mothers, and children who are trying to live well as a family in a world that is often hostile to their aspirations, that separates them in work place, household and school for most of the day, and crowds them together in houses that generate irreconcilable conflicts for much of the limited time they can be together.

If conceived from the beginning with such flexible living in mind, the design of houses and their furnishings and equipment will make such living easier and more workable. There will be less feeling that the interior decorator's job is to make good on the shortcomings of the house itself. Fewer people will be asking how to make small rooms look bigger; and more will be demanding that they be big to begin with.

At this point we can begin to see the design of the house and the design of its furnishings and equipment working together as a team. We can also see in such designs that the important thing is the ability of a family to live up to its best possible standard.

The homemaking job is a bigger one than we have recognized, and it is a job that the whole family must tackle together if much progress is to be made.

If family living is the keynote to the design of our homes, and if this design must embrace this principle affect everything from the shape of an ash tray to the character of a planned metropolitan region, then we need more understanding of what must be done. The designers, whose decisions are increasingly decisive as more and more of us find ourselves in "designed" communities, must show a greater awareness of living needs. Producers and manufacturers must come to terms with their market.

And families themselves, those who wish to educate them and those who would speak for them must be more realistic and articulate in their demands.

September 24, 1950

Single Standard of Responsibility

To THE EDITOR OF THE NEW YORK TIMES:

Your up-to-date editorial on women as partners notes that the fight for women's rights is not quite won, but enough so to warn that "women must now recognize their responsibilities" and act accordingly. Yet their "primary responsibility must continue to be the home."

We agree. But are we not saying, "yes, go swim. But don't go near the water. Take on yourself civic and economic responsibilities while also you wheel the baby, do the dishes, restyle your clothes, get Johnny a nourishing lunch while baking for John a be-deviled cake, study the Sunday school lesson, read up on foreign policy, meantime not forgetting the daily dusting and two dozen other small drudgeries, and finally firmly resist fragmentation"?

Are housekeeping and home-making the same thing?

The Princess Elizabeth is universally credited with being a good mother. But she does not wheel the baby or supervise its play. What is good enough for the Princess is good enough for the American woman. We need the best of day nurseries with trained personnel in every district. Once there were no public schools. When that revolutionary idea was broached, a town Selectman up this way said he would never vote to use public funds "for the education of shes." But he did.

Women with a divine afflatus for engineering may be just as frustrated by domestic tasks as a male engineer. Let's have children, homes in which husband and wife cooperate, and responsibilities fitted to the talents of all persons, whether they be male or female. That means more and better day nurseries.

FLORENCE L. C. KITCHELT.
New Haven, Conn., Oct. 1, 1951.

October 9, 1951

The American Family: What It Is—and Isn't

It is dedicated, first of all, to individual happiness -- not to replacing population.

By KINGSLEY DAVIS

NEARLY all social commentaries on America, foreign and domestic, tend to touch upon the American family as if it were a universally understood and somewhat disreputable institution. Bewildered foreigners especially, reading our popular novels and magazines, picture the American family circle as an assemblage of delinquents and neurotics—flying apart at the seams under the influence of TV, Kinsey Reports and divorce-court scandals. Considering the distortions about our family life circu-

PRIVACY—"The newly married couple strives to live apart from the in-laws."

lated at home, it is not surprising that few Americans are equipped to deal with the opinions that are held abroad —that the American family consists exclusively of wild adolescents, domineering wives and henpecked business men, escapists all from solid home ties. This hardly speaks well for our side of the world debate over democracy's future.

Perhaps, therefore, it is wise to give Americans some factual ammunition

KINGSLEY DAVIS is Director of the Bureau of Applied Social Research at Columbia.

with which to counter such unflattering and damaging misconceptions. In doing so, I shall have to speak of the average American family, although of course no such family actually exists. All our families are average in some respects, but none is average in all respects. The picture given here is accordingly synthetic, but it is drawn from the best information available and should modify some false notions that even Americans entertain about themselves.

First of all, let us note that the American family is extremely "marriage-centered." Except in certain classes such as the ultra-élite or the immigrants from peasant countries, it is built around the married pair, the other kin not counting for much. The newly married couple strives to live apart from the in-laws, not because Dorothy Dix advises it but because certain conditions, such as our extraordinary geographical mobility and our perpetual social climbing, favor it. The Census Bureau finds that one-fifth of the native population lives in a state different from that of its birth, and that one out of every five adults changes his residence each year.

Since it is usually only the immediate family that moves, this migratory tendency drives a wedge between the young couple and their respective parental families. An additional wedge is driven by the fact that the young pair often occupy a class position different from their parents. One community study found, for example, that less than 10 per cent of the professional men had fathers who were in professional pursuits, and that only 39 per cent of the skilled workers had fathers in skilled trades. The expansion of the professional and commercial occupations in our economy, plus a higher birth rate in the lower occupations, has produced a current of upward social movement never before equaled. As a result the young couple often find themselves differing from their parents not only in age but also in class position, culture and standard of living.

THE segregation of the immediate family from other relatives, though

LA FAMILLE AMÉRICAINE

AS OTHERS SEE US—"Every European knows that the American family consists of wild adolescents, domineering wives, henpecked business men and neurotic personalities."

characteristic of all industrial societies, has gone further in America than anywhere else, and affects every aspect of our family life. For instance, our ideal, in contrast to that still prevailing in Asia and to some extent in European and Latin-American countries, is that young people should have the privilege of picking their own mates without parental interference. The founding of the new household is thus put squarely in the hands of the potential marriage partners themselves, though they are young and often incapable of making an intelligent choice.

This freedom of choice accounts for the strong interest we take in courtship, in the trials and tribulations of "winning" a mate. In fact, the process of mate selection is part and parcel of our competitive social order, with individual initiative getting a free hand. Our movies, short stories and novels deal incessantly with this adolescent competition—so much so that the foreigner justifiably reaches the superficial conclusion that we are a nation of mental adolescents.

WE even have college courses designed to help young people choose a satisfactory mate. Indeed, the sociologists and psychologists of America, always anxious to be practical, have devised tests which prospective couples can take and from which their "marriage and prediction score" can be computed. But, let us hasten to add, America is still ruggedly individualistic; if a young couple have a low score, no governmental or parental edict can prevent them from going ahead and marrying anyway. All they need is a strong attraction for each other, however temporary and misguided it may be.

This brings us to another trait which often astonishes foreigners — namely, our firm belief that the purpose of marriage is happiness. We have ponderous tomes on how to achieve happiness in marriage, as well as tests designed to measure our "material happiness score" and to determine what it is about mates that proves annoying. Marriage partners are sometimes asked to rate themselves on a seven or five point scale: "Extraordinarily happy, decidedly more happy than average, somewhat more happy than average, about average happy," etc. Other traits of the couples are then studied to determine what factors lead to happiness or unhappiness in marriage.

All of this, you will say (especially if you are a good American), is innocent enough. Why shouldn't young people choose their own mates, and why shouldn't they be concerned with happiness? Well, I certainly have no objection. I am simply describing some salient features of our family system. But one should realize that the salient features are all connected. The preoccupation with courtship and the cult of marital happiness not only reflect the degree to which our family is "marriage centered," but they are also integrally related to other features which some groups at least find objectionable, such as our low birth rate, our young age at marriage and our high divorce rate.

IF marriage exists for the purpose of individual happiness, if it is entered into and maintained because of personal attraction, the decision to have or not to have children will be made by the couple themselves in terms of their own wishes. They may be so happy

together that children would seem an interference.

Most couples, however, decide that children—though not many—will be an adjunct to their happiness. Consequently, the great reduction in the birth rate has come, not from childlessness, but from the desire to have only one, two or three offspring. In America the large brood has become virtually extinct. The rate for births of seventh and higher orders has dropped 60 per cent in the last three decades, and even during the recent war and post-war baby boom, the rates for the higher orders continued downward. The average wife in the United States has, during her lifetime, about three offspring, barely enough to replace the population.

Although this statement may seem questionable in view of the recent baby boom, the truth is that the spectacular increase in births during the Nineteen Forties was a result of temporary causes and must itself therefore be temporary. The Nineteen Thirties represented a depression decade during which people postponed getting married or having children. In the four years 1930 through 1933, for example, approximately 800,000 marriages did not occur which normally would have occurred. After that, except for 1937, the number of marriages continued to be below normal until rearmament got under way in 1940. Then the concurrence of both business improvement and the military draft not only brought about many marriages that had been postponed but also induced many to marry earlier than they normally would have done.

The result was the mightiest wave of marriages the country had ever witnessed. During the 1940 decade the number was approximately 3,670,000 above normal. Since these were in part marriages "borrowed" from the future, we must necessarily expect a marriage rate below normal in the Nineteen Fifties, even if times are good.

THE number of new marriages affects the number of births, especially first births. But in addition, independently of fluctuations in marriages, the birth rate changes with war and prosperity. During the depression, for instance, many married couples postponed having children. In the Nineteen Forties these couples not only had a sizable portion of the children they had post-

257

poned but also the new couples resulting from the extremely high marriage rate had offspring earlier than they would ordinarily have done. The net result was a temporary but impressive rise in the birth rate, made up principally of first, second and third births.

Such a temporary rise does not mean that couples have suddenly changed the number of children they want ultimately to have, but simply the time when they want to have them. Having had two or three children in the Nineteen Forties, they will tend to have few in the Nineteen Fifties. The birth rate must inevitably decline again; in fact, in 1950 it was one-tenth lower than in the peak year of 1947.

WITH the small number of children and the tendency to live apart from in-laws, the American household has been getting steadily smaller. Most old people, whether still married or widowed, like to maintain a separate place of their own, a feat made possible by high real income in America. Thus in 1940 the median number of family members living together per household was 3.15, and by 1947, despite the rise in the birth rate, the number dropped slightly to 3.07.

In some countries a low birth rate is achieved partly by the postponement of marriage. In our country, despite popular belief to the contrary, people are tending to marry younger. In 1890 the average male first married at the age of 26.1, but in 1947 he married at the age of 23.7. The average female married at the age of 22.0 in 1890, but by 1947 she did so at the tender age of 20.5.

THE gradual lowering of the age at marriage since 1890 apparently reflects the changing character of wedlock among us. With increased employment of women, the old notion that a man must be economically established before marrying has been abandoned. Even college students claim the right to matrimony. With scientific birth control and growing social benefits for children, a young marriage does not necessarily mean a burden of more children than can be supported. Finally, marriage is not nearly so irrevocable as it once was. If the initial venture turns out to be irksome, divorce is easy to obtain.

The divorce rate has risen to the point where, on the average, one out of every four marriages is ending in legal dissolution. Indeed, the rate has risen so high that, with the extension of average life-expectancy, divorce has temporarily replaced death as the main way in which marriages end.

The rising divorce rate is not exclusively an American phenomenon. All other urban-industrial countries are experiencing a rise also. During the last forty years the rate has climbed more rapidly in Great Britain, Sweden, the Netherlands, Denmark, France and several other countries than it has in the United States, although, to be sure, the rate was lower in these countries to start with and the United States still leads them.

IF we still lead most of the world in divorce, it is because our conception of the family has changed more radically. To the extent that we base marriage on personal attraction and value it for the happiness it brings, we feel that it has no excuse for being, once such attraction is gone and the two parties are unhappy together. To the extent that we view it as a companionship to be experienced by the young, we cannot regard it as a fixed status, for companionship cannot be forced. To the extent that we have taken the economic functions from the family and have absorbed women into the labor force, the dissolution of marriage brings no overpowering financial loss to either party and no disruption to the production of goods. Only the children suffer; but, as already mentioned, there are fewer children now.

OUR rising frequency of divorce has not meant, as is commonly assumed, a corresponding increase in the number of broken families. The proportion of broken families depends not only on legal divorce but also on separation, desertion and death. Although figures on separations and desertions are impossible to get, there is reason to believe that they have been somewhat displaced by divorce.

Something else which also served to reduce the number of broken families is the increasing popularity of remarriage. Census figures show that in 1940 the proportion of remarried women among those previously widowed or divorced was about one-sixth greater than in 1910. Approximately 75 per cent of those procuring divorces during the five years from 1943 to 1948 were already remarried in 1948; and of those divorced earlier (between 1934 and 1943) approximately 86 per cent had remarried by 1948.

In view of these facts, the hue and cry about the children orphaned by divorce is rather louder than it should be. Not only are few children involved in relation to the total number of divorces, but most of them soon become parts of a complete family again (one that is often better adjusted) when one or the other parent remarries. Divorce is certainly not easy on children, nor is it easy on the adults.

BY way of summing up, suppose we see what happens to the average American couple in the successive stages of marriage, parenthood, and old age. We have already noted that couples marry earlier than they did sixty years ago, and we can add that the average gap between the husband's and the wife's age, three years, is about one year less than it was then. Despite the use of contraception, the average parents wait only about one year to have their first child and they have their subsequent children rather close together — about two years apart. The average couple who bear any children at all have as a rule only three, because they prevent the birth of more children.

This means that the parents have generally finished their reproduction within five or six years after their wedding. Due to an early marriage and rather rapid childbearing, they reach this point at a very young age—an age much earlier than people ended reproduction in any previous civilization. In fact, the typical mother in America bears her final child at about the age of 27 years.

Since women in the United States now live seventy years on the average, and men sixty-five years, the normal mother has completed her childbearing long before the midpoint of her life. Because her children tend to marry early, the average parent today has a long period of life remaining after her last child has left home. Whereas in 1890 the average parent did not even survive to that point, both parents today tend to live eleven years after their last child has married, and the mother, in case she survives her husband, on the average lives about twenty-four years after that event.

These changes are revolutionary in their importance. The modern couple, for instance, face a situation in their declining years which few couples had to face in past times. They must somehow adjust to life without their children, a life often lonely and pointless. Frequently they sell their house and move to an apartment; sometimes they feel unwanted. Finding the adjustment hard to make, the breadwinner often faces still another painful change—retirement. The problem of the empty household thus merges with and makes more difficult the other trials of old age.

THE modern American family is thus a new model, radically different in many ways from the old. Like any other variation of this ancient social institution, it has its stresses and strains, its human problems. At the same time it has solved some of the old problems. Though exposed to a high risk of divorce, it suffers less from dissolution by death and desertion. Though often provided with too few children for satisfaction, it gives its young a better and less restrictive upbringing. Though frequently characterized by a bleak old age, it achieves more companionship and democracy than its predecessor.

On the whole it is far better than the patriarchal mode of peasant-agricultural countries, far better than the *mariage de convenance* of the European upper classes, and far better than the concubinous polygamy of Latin America. Foreign misconceptions of our family life are based on superficialities which the American who knows the facts can repudiate.

BIG FIELD OPENED BY HOME ARTISAN

$4 Billion Sales in Prospect in 1954 as Result of Trend Back to Family Circle

By ALFRED R. ZIPSER Jr.

Americans will spend almost $4,000,000,000 this year on products they spurned or bought in negligible quantities only a few years ago.

The booming new market—or markets—spring from the flight of families from motion picture theaters, night clubs and other often costly outside activities back to the pleasures of home.

Psychologists and high-priced market analysts have various theories to account for the fact that the American as well as the Englishman now considers his home his castle. Some say that television is the principal agent in the revival of real family life that seemed almost extinct in the Roaring Twenties, Depression Thirties and War-Torn Forties. Others maintain the phenomenal increase in the number of new families and babies in recent years is the principal factor.

Groups of business men have no theories about the Stay-At-Home Fifties. They are too busy making money hand over fist as a result of demand for their products used in the home or for some purpose that contributes to family life.

The principal beneficiaries this year will be manufacturers and storekeepers who serve the seemingly insatiable "do-it-yourself" market. This is expected to run to about $3,500,000,000 in 1954.

As early as 1948, millions of veterans, established in new homes, found they could not watch television all the time. The family dwelling needed repairs or improvements. The first impulse was to call a carpenter or other craftsman. These persons offered to do the wanted jobs at prices far higher than the happy home owner could pay or else told him that they might get around to the work three weeks from some odd Wednesday.

The man who pays the family bills, sometimes called the head of the house, retired to his basement and undertook what he thought was a dreary chore. He found that few things compare with the satisfaction felt when gazing at a more than acceptable product turned out with one's own hands. A new market was born.

Manufacturers who make electric saws, drills and other power equipment and stores that sell them are hard put to keep up with orders from the growing legions of "cellar mechanics." Paint manufacturers report that the bulk of their sales are made to people who paint their own homes.

Paint Industry Sees Trend

The paint industry, quick to see the trend early in the game, has not only promoted home painting vigorously but has simplified it to the point where any-one not mentally deficient can do it successfully.

The home owner in the suburbs has found that he does not have to lay out a week's pay in a fancy New York night club to be entertained. He has discovered that a neighborhood party in his own finished basement can be twice as much fun.

The asphalt and plastic floor and wall tile industry and lumber and plywood operators stand ready to help him at a price. Their cash registers tinkle at a more than satisfactory pace. Lumber producers and yards have come to depend more and more on purchases by home craftsmen.

The renaissance of home life has poured dollars into businesses that are considered "big" by their officials but would be considered small by any minor vice president of the United States Steel Corporation. One of these is the home games industry.

Five years ago this industry took in about $6,000,000, according to Robert B. M. Barton, president of Parker Brothers, Inc., and a former president of the Toy Manufacturers of the U. S. A., Inc. This year the total volume should be more than $24,000,000, he predicted.

Others in the home games industry say Mr. Barton's predictions are as conservative as his nature. They are convinced that $55,000,000 worth of home games will be sold this year.

Mr. Barton says his concern is the world's largest manufacturer or "publisher" of proprietary games for the home. He defines proprietary games as those that require some skill on the part of the player. His company markets about 200 adult games, including Monopoly, Keyword and Clue.

The suppliers of these proprietary games get new ones from two sources, Mr. Barton reported. They maintain their own development departments, which come up with new games. Also, they take a new rough idea of an inventor and "edit" it so that it is marketable. The companies then put a price on it and sell it through stores. The inventor receives royalties from sales. This procedure makes them "game publishers," Mr. Barton said, since they work exactly like book publishers.

Inventors of new home games are flourishing. Some months, Mr. Barton's company gets as many as 100 new ideas from hopeful game designers seeking to cash in on growing demand.

Example Is Cited

Another group of small business men flourishing as a result of the return to the home are manufacturers of equipment used for picnics and other outdoor gatherings of the family unit. A typical example is the Hamilton Metal Products Company.

In November of 1947 the company had $90 in the bank and $90,000 outstanding in accounts payable and payroll charges. Its two principals Herbert Piker, president, and his brother, Myron Piker, executive vice president, were afraid the end was in sight.

Myron, who describes himself as "absolutely the worst officer in the United States Naval Reserve during World War II," hated to see the 41-year-old family metal working enterprise founded by his father fail. It had floundered around making lunch boxes, fisherman's metal containers, tool boxes and similar products without much success until the crisis in 1947.

On borrowed money, the Piker brothers took a carefully insulated metal box and hired an industrial designer to cover it with plastic tartan designs. They called their products Skotch Koolers and promoted them widely as ideal picnic refrigerators. The doleful financial straits of 1947 now are a half-forgotten nightmare.

Thousands of families, finding that picnics are not necessarily family events that went out with the bustle, have bought the items Hamilton turns out. Last year the company earned more than $4,800,000. This year it is shooting for a minimum of $7,000,000.

Most of the money being poured out by people who make their homes the center of their lives is being garnered by many small companies like Hamilton and Parker Brothers. But big companies like United States Plywood, Johns-Manville, Aluminum Corporation of America are beginning to devote more and more attention to reaching the home market.

March 7, 1954

Why They Are Marrying Younger

Uncertainties about the future might normally be expected to delay marriage. Today, paradoxically, they are the very thing causing Americans to marry early.

By SIDONIE M. GRUENBERG

I WENT to a wedding recently that was like many weddings these days: the groom was a graduate student, the bride a college junior, and both were going back to the university after their honeymoon. The occasion was unusual in one respect: the bride's mother, too, had married in her junior year and had gone on to get her degree but only by keeping her marriage secret. If the college authorities had known that she was married, they would have had no choice but to expel her.

"We were made to feel like delinquents for marrying at the age of these kids," the bride's father said. "But these youngsters are going into housekeeping right on the campus, and not in one of those Quonset huts either. There's a brand-new garden apartment dormitory for married students, even those with families."

This wedding dramatized for me the great changes we have witnessed in a single generation. Not so long ago girls were expelled from college for marrying; now girls feel hopeless if they haven't a marriage at least in sight by commencement time. Actually, the change has been coming on for

SIDONIE M. GRUENBERG is editor of the "Encyclopedia of Child Care and Guidance," and a former member of the Child Study Assn. of America. She wrote "We, the Parents."

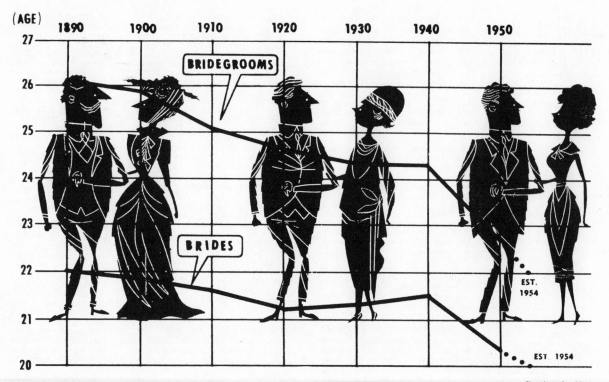

(AGE)

| 1890 | 1900 | 1910 | 1920 | 1930 | 1940 | 1950 |

BRIDEGROOMS

BRIDES

EST. 1954

EST. 1954

Drawings by Ajay.

WEDDING BELLS—From 1890 to the present, they have shown an increasing tendency to ring early, as this chart indicates.

more than half a century. In 1890 the median age for men at the time of a first marriage was 26.7 years; now it is about 22.5 years. In the same period the median age for girls has dropped from 22 to about 20. And the descent is continuing.

In 1900, fewer than half the young women between 20 and 24 years were or had been married; by 1940, a little more than half the girls of that age group were married. Now more than 70 per cent are married.

Young people are also having their babies earlier. Today, 30 per cent of the mothers of "first" babies are 19 years old or under. Fifteen or twenty years ago the youngest third of mothers having their first-born were 20 to 24.

Furthermore, couples are having their babies closer together. While there are no direct statistics as to spacing, it is clear from observation that the two- or three-year interval once considered a protection against the exhaustion of childbearing is no longer observed. Medical science, hospital deliveries, pre-natal and post-natal care have largely taken the hazards out of childbirth. In the last twenty-five years there has been an 80 per cent decline in the maternal death rate.

Young parents are deliberate about wanting their families while they are still young and wanting the children close together. They don't want two or more "only children" growing up years apart. "We had ours fourteen months apart on purpose," said one mother. "It will be hectic for a while

but when we're through with the diapers we'll have two children instead of only one."

All this youthful marrying and family-building can no longer be ascribed to World War II, although the war undoubtedly shook up some old habits of thinking. The 1947 peak of the war-baby boom was long past when 1952 produced a record of 3,824,000 new babies. And 1954 topped 4 million.

Why are young people plunging into early marriage and family life? Prosperity is part of the answer. Certainly marriages were most delayed during the depression of the Thirties. There is also a new attitude toward the financial responsibilities of marriage. At a time when a young man could look forward to earning enough to support a family by his middle twenties, it was reasonable to expect him to wait until then to marry. In our scientific age, however, education for highly skilled occupations and for the professions is more and more prolonged. Today young men must also expect to interrupt their studies and jobs for military reasons. Therefore, to wait until they are well established financially no longer seems reasonable.

Under these circumstances, we have to recognize that some of the traditional obstacles to early marriage are no longer valid. The prejudice, for example, against parents' helping a young couple has all but vanished. In the past, the break-up of a "subsidized" marriage could be lightly explained by saying that the young people could not stand on their own feet. Today, with so many parents helping out, with

varied results, we may no longer fear inevitable disaster.

Also, as more and more women and girls work and train for work, the wife's contribution to the family income becomes less and less humiliating to the young husband. Both partners to the marriage accept the chance that the bride will have a job. So do their respective parents even the father of the bride, whose traditional role once was to demand, "Young man, what are your prospects?" In many cases it is the bride who has the only job in the family; the young man working for his advanced degree cannot always support himself, let alone a wife.

For the boys, the case for early marriage is clear enough. But what of the girls? They undertake, on the whole, the harder share. Several generations of working women have almost eliminated the idea that marriage is synonymous with a meal-ticket. They accept and even welcome the work they are trained to do. Nor do they have to bear the whole burden of the household, for today's young husbands do their share of the housekeeping, the marketing and, when babies come along, of baby care as well.

But, when the babies do come, as they do early and close together these days, the young mother is likely to be hard pressed. She must often get along on a skimpy budget, with no relatives or paid help to assist her during the day, and with little reserve in funds or energy to meet illnesses or other emergencies. These are the prospects of girls who marry young and marry young husbands. Why do they do it?

A girl also has sexual needs and as strong a wish for secure emotional relationships as her young man. In addition, the well-known statistical fact that males are fewer than females in this country tends to push each girl into desire for early marriage. Young men who go into military service may want to marry first to be sure of their girls; but, when they don't, they all too often come back with a bride from another part of the country or from overseas. A girl who hasn't a man in sight by the time she is 20 is not altogether wrong in fearing that she may never get married.

And so they marry—some more and some less successfully. Their parents often help, much as farm parents used to set up young couples with a few acres and a cow. But today the help is likely to come in cold cash and the young couple's dependence is more obvious. With or without help, however, they undertake a great deal and on the whole they manage with considerable courage and resourcefulness.

THE young people begin their families by the same logic that nudges them into early marriage: if there is no certain future to wait for, what's the use of waiting? Important as the economic arguments are for postponing building a family, the uncertainties that confront young people are more persuasive. Few generations have been so aware of forces beyond their grasp that can sweep away in a single night all possessions, plans and hopes. In a world that buffets them about, they feel deeply the need for something that they can do themselves, for something they themselves have created. Thus, paradoxically, the very uncertainties of the future drive young people toward early marriages and young families.

"What I feel most about living is its impermanence," a young woman told me. "The only happiness we can count on is what we make for ourselves and our children."

THOUGH not often so articulate as this, vast numbers of young people are turning intuitively to those timeless sources of inner strength, the family and the home. They are putting their faith in less material, and perhaps more enduring, values—spiritual values, if you like. Many who have lived in apartments want to live in a house a surer symbol of home. They are making the most of today, gathering closely the joys and satisfactions they themselves can make out of human relationships centering in the home.

It seems to me significant that in young families today the father is no longer the detached provider, depended upon only to make financial decisions or to help occasionally with "discipline." Thanks largely to the shortened workweek, he is an active member of the family for many more hours than his father ever was. And his participation extends far beyond the household skills, beyond bathing the baby or shopping at the supermarket. He knows his children intimately from their first hour home from the hospital, and he shares his life with them more than fathers have done since the American family moved away from the farm.

DISCUSSING the trend toward early marriages inevitably raises the question, how early is early? The same arguments that have been used for the marriage of men in their early twenties and for girls in their late teens have also been used by boys and girls much younger. Indeed, high school marriages are far from rare. But, under modern conditions, these adolescents cannot acquire the maturity and experience essential to meet the obligations of marriage and parenthood. This age level involves entirely different problems.

For the young couples I have been considering, the balance seems to be well on the credit side. With an early start and an increasing life expectancy for their elders, many of the children being born these days will have both sets of grandparents and even some great-grandparents to share love and wisdom with them. As to their future, as one young engineer father said, "Nobody's future can be guaranteed. But we hope that out of a good family life our children will get a sort of built-in balance-wheel in the form of inner strengths to deal with whatever life offers or asks of them."

January 30, 1955

Happy Marriage Held Best Legacy to Youth

By DOROTHY BARCLAY

The best legacy parents can leave their children is the example of their own happy marriage, an Indiana physician declared yesterday. He spoke at a symposium on "the family in pursuit of happiness," arranged by the Planned Parenthood Federation of America and held at the Waldorf-Astoria

Hotel. The speaker, Dr. D. Stanley Houser, and nine other participants in the all-day conference stressed the varying responsibilities of the individual and of community agencies in making happy family life possible.

A happy marriage is largely dependent on the reasons the couple had for marrying in the first place, according to Dr. Robert W. Laidlaw, chief of psychiatry division, Roosevelt Hospital. Among the "wrong reasons" he included sex attraction alone; the influence of "glamour," social position and financial status; attempts to escape from unhappy home situations or the desire to avoid spinsterhood.

The only sound, mature basis for marriage, he said, is "deep mutual love plus proven compatibility in major areas of living."

The family doctor has opportunities for timely counseling of young couples and should take more advantage of these, members of the panel agreed. Dr. Houser described the sort of advice he offers when young persons come to him for premarital examinations and later for prenatal attention. He makes the following recommendations to every pair about to be wed:

¶That at least once each day they will sit down together at an attractively set table and eat an unhurried meal.

¶That they will plan to spend one evening out together each week.

¶That they will spend one quiet evening at home together each week, reading, watching television or engaged on some project that is not a chore or obligation.

¶That they will join a religious organization, take an active part in its program and make new friends among the young married group there.

¶That they will place the material things in life second.

¶That they will start a family when, as a couple, they are emotionally ready for it.

¶That they will realize sex life is only one part of their total married life.

When to Have Children

There are sound and unsound reasons for having children just as there are for marrying, Dr. M. Robert Gomberg, executive director of Jewish Family Service, declared. The right time to have children, he held, is when one has finished with the business of one's own growing up, when "the need to take" has given place to "the need to give."

Pierre S. du Pont 3d, secretary of E. I. du Pont de Nemours & Co., said business men have good economic as well as humanitarian reasons for supporting Planned Parenthood. Other speakers discussed the role of the church, the clergyman, the court and social agencies in helping families develop in wholesome fashion.

They included Dr. Frederick Osborn, executive vice president of the Population Council; Rabbi David Wice, Dr. Virginia N. Wilking, assistant director, Pediatric Psychiatric Clinic, Babies Hospital, Columbia-Presbyterian Medical Center; C. Edward Harrison of St. Philip's Protestant Episcopal Church, Justice Hubert T. Delany of the Domestic Relations Court, and Miss M. Josephina R. Albano, chief, social work section, Pan American Union.

May 6, 1955

Housework Is the Road To Boredom

By CYNTHIA KELLOGG
Special to The New York Times.

MINNEAPOLIS, Minn., June 29—A state of mind that many a woman is acquainted with, though she rarely confesses it to other women, to her husband or to her children, was mentioned out loud at meetings here today. It was boredom.

The sessions were held at the forty-sixth annual meeting of the American Home Economics Association. The conference opened here Tuesday at the Minneapolis Auditorium.

Studies have shown that many women are bored in their role of homemaker, and that their boredom is a primary cause of home disruption, Dr. Jennie I. Rowntree of the University of Washington said. A bored woman concentrates on herself, she continued, and escapes from household tasks to recreation, outside work or soap operas.

Dr. Rowntree believes that homemaking education may be to blame for it sets housekeeping standards so high that they are unrelated to real life, it gives directions for doing tasks without giving the reasons why, and it discourages experiment.

Boredom often masquerades as fatigue, according to Dr. Jean Warren of the New York State College of Home Economics at Cornell University. In her talk at the conference she urged that research be done on the subject of boredom.

Boredom and Fatigue

"It has been discovered in studies at Cornell that no housework is really physically tiring, except taking care of a baby, but still women tell us they are fatigued," Dr. Warren said in an interview.

One reason for this, she continued, may be that the woman's housework experiences that she had as a child, when perhaps she did chores that her mother didn't like to do, make her dislike such tasks. Today, when she does them, she gets tired, Dr. Warren added.

Loneliness may be another cause. Or, particularly in the case of career-woman-turned-homemaker, the tiredness may result from feeling left out of other activities because she has to stay at home with her child.

The mature woman accepts the fact that housework may bore her at times, Dr. Warren continued. But the woman who is continually bored with her chores should do something about it. What? Dr. Warren listed these measures:

¶Be experimental. Try different ways to do a job. This may result not only in finding a quicker method, but also make the chore more interesting.

¶Get some help. For most women this means calling on the husband and children. "You will have to make up your mind that the job will be less efficiently done, but it will be more enjoyable and less lonely," Dr. Warren said.

¶Don't do things you don't like. If there are foods you don't enjoy preparing, substitute others for them. If you don't like making beds, get the family to make their own.

¶Alternate disliked tasks with enjoyable activities. "We found that many women dawdle over a task they hate, but if something they enjoy lies ahead they can hustle and get the job done," she explained.

Frustration may be the cause of boredom in women today, according to Dr. Stanley E. Fowler, associate professor of child development and family life at Mississippi Southern College. He added:

"Women are frustrated because men don't give them credit for doing housework any more—they feel that equipment does all the work in the home." Since the woman does not receive approval for her work, she feels inadequate and unneeded. She becomes frustrated also because, in this age of cake-mixes, she does not have as much opportunity for satisfaction in creative tasks.

To help lift the pressure of frustrations Dr. Fowler recommended that women:

¶Accept reasonable housekeeping standards—"don't be a fanatic about dust."

¶Don't put the emphasis on things in the house but on family relationships that make it a home.

¶Stop expecting immediate rewards. They don't come every day, as the child is sent off to school, but twenty years later, when he graduates from college.

Eight Reasons Why Marriages Go Wrong

By JAMES H. S. BOSSARD

APPROXIMATELY 11 per cent of marriages in the United States take place in June. This month some 350,000 men and women will be united in holy matrimony. The distressing part of the story is that at least 80,000 of these people—40,000 couples—face the statistical certainty of divorce at some point in the years ahead.

Never has so large a proportion of our population been married. And the chances of a person getting married in the United States are greater than they are in other countries of the Western world. But the chances of these American marriages failing are also greater than chances of the same sort of failure in other nations. Currently, our annual toll of divorces and annulments approaches 400,000. In recent years, the number of divorces has ranged between one-fourth and one-third of total marriages. In selected cities, the divorce rate at times equals or exceeds one-half the marriage total.

Yet divorce is only one index of family disorganization. Almost 2,000,000 married persons are separated—temporarily or permanently—because of marital discord. And surveys reveal that one-fifth or one-sixth of all couples living together think of themselves as unhappy and that an equal number can report only "medium happiness."

For almost half a century, as a university teacher and student of family life, I have watched this situation develop and spread. From my studies and observations, I have come to think of the following factors as the chief hazards to matrimonial happiness for American youth.

I

MANY people marry too young. The average age at which men and women marry for the first time has been dropping since 1890, and since 1940 has dropped sharply. It is now about 22 for men; about 20 for women.

Yet we know that readiness for marriage is more than a matter of years. Experts speak of a physiological age, a sexual age, a vocational age and the age at which a degree of emotional maturity is reached. Each of these stages of development has its own im-

JAMES H. S. BOSSARD is Professor of Sociology and William T. Carter Professor of Child Development at the University of Pennsylvania. He is also Professor of Sociology in Psychiatry at the university's medical school.

Sculptures by Moissaye Marans.

"The family has historically been the moving force for the perpetuation not only of the race, but of civilization in its entirety."

portance, but emotional maturity—the extent of a person's capacity to deal with life on a normal adult level—is perhaps the most important. Furthermore, adult behavior in marriage is possible only if paralleled by adult behavior in business and industry and citizenship. These qualities of maturity come as by-products of experiences in living, for which there is no substitute. Now,

with the lowering of the marriage age, the extension of the required education period, and with so many more young people going on to college, it is evident that an increasing number of couples pass from the sheltered life of the schoolroom to the stark realities of a job and a wife or husband, and perhaps a child, with little or no intervening experience.

Consider how this works out. Yesterday *he* was a campus big wheel, living at the Epsilon Chi Omega house. *She* was one of the dating favorites

at dear old Siwash. Now they are living in a two-room flat in a large city. It is hot. Today his boss was unreasonable, and the gadget in her kitchen wouldn't work. That night he muses: "If this dame hadn't chased me, I'd still be in clover." And she sulks herself to sleep with memories of last year's junior prom. It is a big transition for these two, on many fronts, in too short a time.

II

MODERN patterns of courtship do not make for wise choices of matrimonial partners. The current premium is upon success in party-going, dancing, sports, petting and use of a patois which in my day was called "a good line." There is, in other words, an impersonality about present-day adolescent courtship similar to what one finds in more adult aspects of social life. We go to a cocktail party or re-

ception, observe all the niceties, say the acceptable, innocuous things and by skillfully avoiding any controversial subject create the impression of being "nice," "adjustable" and having "a pleasant personality." All this, in courtship as in more mature social life, involves a kind of social maneuvering, little of which touches upon or reveals those qualities which matter so much if the couple is going to live happily together for the next forty or more years. When one thinks in terms of a lifelong union, being a good mixer and having a presentable pair of legs are somewhat less important than what one thinks about God, money and a crying baby.

III

INTERMARRIAGE between cultural groups can be a strain on both parties. This is the inevitable price we pay for the heterogeneity of our popu-

lation and the diversity of our cultural strains. Among such marriages, the most important in their effect are those between members of different religious groups.

The number of interfaith marriages is large, and it is increasing. Recent studies show that half of marriages involving Roman Catholics are mixed marriages, valid or invalid, and that the percentage has been increasing steadily since 1910. A study made for the United Lutheran Church shows that 58 per cent of its members marry outside of their church and that there has been a marked increase in such marriages since 1936.

Mixed marriages are looked upon with disfavor by the leaders of all organized church bodies. The Central Conference of American Rabbis has declared that mixed marriages "are contrary to the tradition of the Jewish religion and should therefore be discouraged by the American rabbinate." The attitude of the Roman Catholic Church is definite and uncompromising; it considers invalid any marriage involving Catholics that is not solemnized in a religious ceremony under prescribed conditions. Within the last two decades, several Protestant denominations have been taking an increasingly firm stand on mixed marriages.

●

I T is unfair to argue, as is sometimes done, that the concern of the church is purely one of self-interest, growing out of fear of losing members. It is true that persons contracting mixed marriages tend to drop away from their respective churches and are somewhat less concerned than usual with the religious rearing of their children. But there are other reasons for the attitude of the various churches. Their leaders, for example, have long known what recent sociological studies verify.

Three such studies (Landis, Bell and Weeks), covering a total of 24,184 families, show that there are approximately three times as many divorces or separations in Catholic-Protestant marriages as there are when the marital partners are of the same faith, and about four times as many when a Catholic father is married to a Protestant mother. And here again the story of marital unhappiness is far larger than divorce and separation statistics show.

Contemporary youth tends to be impatient with the verdict of experience concerning mixed marriages. "We are broad-minded," they say. "We are quite willing to respect each other's religious beliefs. Besides, religion is not as important as it used to be." What these young people overlook is the real nature of religion and its role in life. Religion is not merely a set of beliefs; it is a way of living and of thinking. Roman Catholicism is a culture pattern, as we sociologists put it; so is Judaism, or Methodism, or being an Episcopalian.

●

E ACH religion has its distinctive set of values, as well as its forms of worship, and these reach over and express themselves in the minutiae of the daily lives of their respective adherents. Eating fish on Friday is not a mere be-

ANOTHER AGE—A detail from a painting, "Family Group," by Eastman Johnson.

lief; it is a dietary institution. The observance of church holidays involves the organization of a family's leisure time.

Perhaps the real wonder is not that mixed marriages often fail, but rather that so many succeed. An old Chinese maxim has it that every boy should marry the girl who lives across the street from him. The meaning is still clear: people of the same background and circumstances are most likely to find marital happiness with each other.

IV

A MARKED emphasis on the romantic motif is hazardous in marriage. As currently interpreted, this means that a person marries solely for love, that marriage is the final realization of romantic attraction. It might be called the Hollywood concept of marriage, since the movies have done much to foster the lushness of its appeal.

To speak of emphasis upon romance as a pitfall to successful marriage is apt to cause misunderstanding. Surely, the critic will say, there is nothing new or unusual or alarming about love. And one must agree completely and wholeheartedly. Strong emotional attraction between persons of the opposite sex is as old as the human heartbeat and is one of the things that makes the world a brighter place in which to live.

The question that is raised here is the acceptance of romance as the primary, and often the sole, basis of marriage selection and maintenance. In the old days, marriages were arranged on the basis of more practical considerations, such as the judgment of parents and kinsfolk, the exchange of financial agreements, or the promotion

of a career. In addition to these considerations, there was usually a long period of courtship during which the prospective mates and their respective families learned to know and test each other's mettle, for what people in other cultures know, and what we so largely ignore, is that marriage is not only the union of two individuals but also of two kinship groups.

I certainly do not advocate that romance as such should not be included in the ingredients of a happy marriage. My point is simply that romance alone is not enough.

In this respect, it should also be noted that sex in marriage means more than physical attraction or the sequence of romantic glow. Sex adjustment is a deep and pervasive achievement, often made slowly and on the basis of many factors. It involves a deep rapport between two people, the sort that can come only with mutual respect, reciprocal understanding and a sharing of common interests, and it is something quite different from the sentiment engendered by a trim ankle, a chic look or a conspicuous bosom.

V

A MARRIED person who seeks individual development of his or her personality is courting trouble. To these people a good marriage is one that contributes fully and freely to the personality development of each; a poor marriage is one that hinders such development. This sort of emphasis, of course, is but a phase of a much larger ideological pattern.

Many children encounter the pattern early in their school careers, when they are encouraged to "express themselves." Later on, they express what they have

been taught in freedom of choice of their mates, often with complete disregard for the advice or admonition of parents, kinsfolk, pastor or priest. After marriage, this philosophy is maintained. Almost from the beginning, many husbands and wives organize their lives on an individualistic basis. The employment of married women, so widespread today, has enforced the trend.

One wonders if the advocates of individualism as a basis for marriage are aware of the logical consequence of such behavior. It is this: when one marries for personal happiness and fulfillment, then one must leave if his goal is not realized. If living with Jane Brown is essential to one's fullest personality development in 1956, what happens in 1957 when only Mary Smith can serve as the developing agent? If personality development is the sole base for marriage, then obviously when the base disappears the marriage is over

VI

P ARENTHOOD is underestimated as a force in marriage. Less than five per cent of the space in current literature on family relations refers to the matter. Yet married people do have children—six out of every seven couples, in fact, and most of the others wish they could.

Our whole culture is guilty of this detour around the subject of parenthood. The family has historically been the moving force for the perpetuation not only of the race, but of civilization. Yet marriage clinics today deal only with the problems of husband-wife relations. American business, which has engulfed a liberal proportion of married women, considers parenthood an incident. Housing developments and rental offices often ignore children completely.

The lack of attention to the matter of parenthood in sociological writing is supplemented by instances of parents who themselves ignore their offspring. The children who get up and cook their own breakfast, or go without, while Papa and Mama sleep off a hangover brought on by the country club dance, are symbolic and not too exceptional. It is time, in fact, to remind young marrieds once again that the family is the connecting link between successive generations; that this indeed is the basic purpose of the family and that other functions relevant to it are secondary and incidental.

VII

P RESSURES to strive for higher social position strain family life. The popular democratic ideology about social classes in the United States today is strange and paradoxical. First, we are told that there are no social classes and that to recognize them or even speak of them is undemocratic. Second, as the Fortune magazine and other polls have shown, most people think of themselves as middle class. Third, most of us are breaking our necks, figuratively speaking, to rise in this "classless" society. Here is a weird mixture of fancy and fact which gives rise, among other things, to a mad scramble for status and advancement up the ladder.

From this scramble grow many problems bearing on family living. The show girl who marries the banana king's heir makes the news, but a whole host of less spectacular cases go unnoticed. In an open-class system, many ambitious parents nourish the hope that their children will "marry up." Others have done so, why not theirs? As a result, they develop the notion that no mate is quite good enough for their son or daughter. If only they had waited: tomorrow would have been better. Betty Smith's novel of a few years ago, "Tomorrow Will Be Better," poignantly pictures all this among lower-class folk.

Pressure by parents upon children to marry up is only part of a much larger story. Socially ambitious wives put their husbands on the griddle, forward-looking husbands do the same to their wives and many growing children give both parents the full treatment. This striving for status in our "classless" society is an individualizing process in which husband, wife and children tend to climb separately. Certainly nothing about the process fosters the development of familism.

VIII

THERE is far too little emphasis upon the family as a group. Perhaps no civili-

zation in the world has ever formally educated so large a proportion of its young people in the area of family living as has ours—at the university as well as the secondary school level. But most of the emphasis has been upon how to get married rather than on how to stay married. Actually, a family is a project in group living. Its stability requires an emphasis upon group values rather than on the individualistic forces now so widely stressed.

Personally, I am convinced that there are techniques in group living whose nature can be identified, whose importance can be demonstrated, and whose use can be taught. For a number of years, Dr. Eleanor S. Boll, my research associate, and I have studied the relatively formal family procedures centering around holidays, natal days, vacations, family meals and the like. We have come to speak of these as family rituals, meaning prescribed family ways of doing things together which build up a feeling of rightness and happiness through participation.

By nature, ritual in family living is the same as ritual in religion, and the history of religions shows that those with the most elaborate and pervasive rituals are those that best retain the allegiance of their members. It is really very easy to understand this; all it means is that people can best be held together by doing things together.

* * *

THERE are no short or easy solutions to the marriage problems of the American people, no wonder drugs to cure our social ills. Success in family living is not assured by inheritance, legislative fiat, priestly blessing or parental strictures. As in other aspects of life, it must be earned through sound judgment, effective techniques and time-proven values. There are no other ways.

A SCIENTIST LOOKS AT SUBURBANITES

Species Is Found Centered on Child and Home With Mother the Chauffeur

By DAMON STETSON
Special to The New York Times.

DETROIT, Sept. 9—A sociologist from Northwestern University lowered his microscope today on the family in suburbia.

Dr. Ernest R. Mowrer found the species characterized by a child-centered and home-centered life in which the mother was the chauffeur and the father an after-work handyman.

Perhaps the most characteristic feature of life in the newer suburbs, he said, is the loss of class distinctions that function in the city. But he concluded that such class distinctions tended to reappear as the neighborhood grew older.

"In fact," he said, "homogeneity and social integration seem to be characteristic of the initial stages of suburban life succeeded later by diversity and anonymity so typical of the urban community."

Dr. Mower made his observations in a paper presented on the last day of a three-day meeting here of the American Sociological Society. The report was based on a study of the Chicago area.

Children Are Basis

The development of the suburban family, Dr. Mowrer reported, is initially based on a conviction that life in the suburbs will be good for the children and that it can be surrounded with greater physical conveniences than in the cities.

"There is little doubt," he said, "that parents indulge and pamper their children as never before, and that the open spaces of the suburbs seem to offer greater opportunities for such indulgence."

Most suburban couples have lived either in older suburban neighborhoods or in the central cities before moving to the newer suburbia, usually after the birth of the first child, he said. The mean family size of the suburban species, he explained, is 3.8, slightly above the United States mean of 3.6.

The suburban husband is about 40 years old and probably

has gone to college. He is most likely to be employed in a managerial or executive capacity.

"The two roles which most eloquently characterize suburban life of adults," Dr. Mowrer said, "are the role of the chauffeur, which the suburban wife plays, and that of the handyman, which the husband plays."

Roles Are Flexible

The sociologist took note, too, of the flexibility of roles, which he called characteristic of suburban life. The husband often performs feminine household functions such as feeding and diapering the children, he said, while the wife performs masculine functions such as shoveling snow.

"There is probably no place in contemporary life," Dr. Mowrer said, "where the equalitarian pattern is more prevalent than in the new suburbs."

Socially, he said, the suburban family is home-centered, employing a sitter on an average of only four hours a week in order to go out. What the urbanite achieves vicariously by sitting in a night club, Dr. Mowrer said, the suburbanite achieves by participating in organizations of his community.

Everybody knows everybody else in the suburban area, he said, and discussion of personal affairs becomes a common interest.

Discussion in the Present

But it is not the gossip heard on the party line of rural life, he observed. Rather, it consists of items about the children on the school bus and almost always has to do with the present, not the past.

At first, suburban communities have a high esprit de corps, Dr. Mowrer said. People share transportation, exchange tools and horticultural know-how. There is an early intimacy and cohesiveness among families.

But, he added:

"The initial stage passes shortly as the individuals become identified with specialized activities of the larger community. The symbols of status reassert themselves and class distinction again appear. Intimacy of association is slowly dissipated except for small clusters, each individual becoming absorbed into multi-differentiated groups of the large community.

"Eventually, even this stage passes into a stage of secondary relations not unlike that in apartment house areas of the city * * * the suburban becomes urban both with respect to the family and the community, although the single dwelling still remains as a symbol of the suburban vision."

June 24, 1956

September 10, 1956

More Couples in U. S. Live Alone and Like It

WASHINGTON, July 5 (AP)—More married couples are going out on their own instead of living with relatives.

The Census Bureau reported today that as of last March about 1,200,000 of the 38,900,000 married couples in the United States did not maintain their own households. This compares to about 2,000,000 who "doubled up" in the households of others in 1950 and nearly 3,000,000 ten years ago, the bureau said.

The report said the nation now had 49,500,000 households, an increase of some 6,000,000 over 1950.

The figures showed a drop of 1,000,000 since 1950 in the number of rural farm households, now 5,200,000, and an increase of 7,000,000 in nonfarm households, now 44,300,000.

July 6, 1957

'ALIMONY DRONES' DECRIED IN COURT

Justice Hofstadter Terms System 'Perverse' in Era of Woman's Equality

A New York State jurist called yesterday for a system of alimony awards that would not "convert a host of physically and mentally competent women into an army of alimony drones."

Supreme Court Justice Samuel H. Hofstadter declared the time had come for the courts to recognize that the modern married woman was no longer the Victorian who was "something better than her husband's dog, a little dearer than his horse." She is now the equal of man, socially, politically and economically, he said.

"Why should ex-wives and separated women seek a preferred status in which they shall toil not, neither shall they spin?" the justice asked.

In ruling for an increase in alimony payments from $12 to $20 a week to a woman, the court withheld details of the case before him, but he took the opportunity to offer some acid opinions about the "perverse system" of alimony payments. Justice Hofstadter called it unjust in concept and faulty in application.

Alimony should not be a reward for virtue nor a punishment for guilt, he contended. In most cases, he said, neither party is at fault or both are at fault in some degree.

The justice agreed that a woman who has contributed to her husband's career might rightfully be entitled to a share of his gain. Courts should also consider as a rightful claimant a woman who has spent so much time caring for home and children that she has had little chance to learn job skills, he observed.

But he put in a different category a young woman who "has remained alien to her husband's interest," asserting that alimony was never intended to "assure a perpetual state of indolence."

Under the present practices, Justice Hofstadter maintained, some women receive too little, others far too much for their own good and that of society. He said that alimony payments should be based on the wife's actual financial needs less her current assets and earning potential in relation to her husband's capacity to pay.

February 1, 1957

The Trouble With 'Togetherness'

By CHARLES FRANKEL

NOTHING is more important in the history of mankind, it has frequently been said, than the invention of a new phrase. "We hold these truths to be self-evident"; "Workers of the world, unite!"—such phrases light up men's souls, reveal a simple order underlying all the complexities of human life and melt a thousand hesitations into one great certainty. The word that seems to be lighting up our souls today is "togetherness." At any rate, it has begun to kindle a low, sullen flame in my own soul.

It is not easy to stand up and be counted as an enemy of togetherness, and I approach the subject with fear. Togetherness is a friendly condition, and no one likes to make a principle of unfriendliness. It is also a strenuous condition, and no one likes to admit he cannot keep up the pace. As an advertising slogan, togetherness conjures up the image of a husband tossing his wife sportily in the air, their children in the background apparently not at all disturbed that father and mother will hurt themselves while they are having their fun. To suggest one's unfitness for this acrobatic image of domesticity comes close to a confession of cowardice.

And yet I venture to make the churlish suggestion that togetherness is becoming something of a nuisance. Lassoing an adverb and making it do the work of a noun is bad enough. But one can detect the workings of the cult of togetherness not only in the family but in our approach to education, community affairs, business and politics, and in the longing which many of our most serious social thinkers permit themselves for other social orders more tightly knit than our own. Togetherness has done more than catch the family at certain curious moments of rapture; it seems to speak for the budding notion that one can turn all of America into one big family. At this point one's mind jibs and one's instincts revolt.

TO deal with first things first, consider the sly, subversive theory of the family which the creators of togetherness are trying to put over on us. Until the sloganeers had their vision, the notion that a solid family life was based on togetherness would have occurred only to a spinster raised in an orphanage.

CHARLES FRANKEL is Professor of Philosophy at Columbia University and a veteran of years of service on a variety of committees.

Drawing by Abner Dean.

MODERN LAOCOON—Togetherness, practiced simply for its own sake, can be something of a family problem.

As every child knows, the real secret of family life is a little separateness. Few families have ever got along if their members did not occasionally have a chance to be alone. Sister playing records in her room, Junior in the attic, Father in the kitchen, Mother in the city—on these small, lonely things a solid family life is built. These are the only things that keep the members of a family from boring one another silly when they get together.

I dwell on this elementary axiom of family life because it reveals the trouble we get into when we start toying with the English language. "Together" is an adverb, and an adverb describes a way of carrying on a specific activity. Put a suffix on it, and make it designate a thing in itself, and madness beckons. When two people get married, they do not (I hope) seek togetherness. They seek each other. And they are likely to find togethering

(we may as well make it a verb, too) something of a burden unless they find something to do together, and something that is worth doing for its own sake.

In short, the word "together" raises three elementary questions: Together with whom? Together for what purpose? Together how much? "Togetherness," in contrast, puts such finicking questions out of the way, but it is really not unreasonable to suggest that they should be asked and answered. Dante, who was no amateur in these matters, was much struck by the fatuity of Paolo and Francesca, who wanted to do nothing but just be together forever. He gave them their wish, and they found themselves in hell. Their sin was to convert an adverb into a noun, and our advertising men should take note.

The point is worth making because

togetherness has not stopped with an assault on English syntax and a libel on the American home. It has wormed its smiling way into our other affairs as well. More than a century ago Alexis de Tocqueville noticed the peculiar aptitude of Americans for forming associations. "As soon as several of the inhabitants of the United States have taken up an opinion or a feeling which they wish to promote in the world," he observed, "they look out for mutual assistance; and as soon as they have found one another out they combine."

Togetherness carries this old habit to a new height of refinement. It makes it unnecessary for a man to have "an opinion or a feeling * * * to promote in the world" in order to wish to form an association. Indeed, if a man has any social conscience at all, he will try to keep his pet ideas and deep feelings under control, for everyone knows what these can do to the harmony of a group. Tocqueville's mistake, in short, was to assume that

there has to be a purpose behind an association. It shows the errors to which a shallow rationalism can lead.

The story of American education, for example, is a tale of an earnest search for togetherness—for ways of adjusting the parent to the teacher, the teacher to the child, the child to the group and the group to—well, to the maxim that it is good to be a group. I recently heard the consummate expression of this ideal from the mouth of a school administrator expressing his doubts about the acceleration of bright children. "One of the things a child must learn in school," he said thoughtfully, "is how to bear fools gladly." When one thinks of the ingenious new steps that might still be taken in American schools to better fulfill this ideal, the imagination is staggered.

OF course the American school system has had to do a job that no other school system, at any rate until recently, has quite had to do. The emphasis on "training in the habits of democracy" and "adjustment to the group" which can be found in most American schools is, partly, a response to the necessities of a democratic and mobile society. But it can be said of American schools that they have met necessity much more than halfway. In fact, they merely mirror a more general attitude. In community affairs, in universities, in business and in politics, togetherness has also made its presence felt. It has raised a new institution to a position of dominance in American society. This is the committee.

A camel, it has been said, is a horse designed by a committee. Such surly complaints reveal a misunderstanding of the purpose of committees. As any expert on "group dynamics" will tell you, a committee is fundamentally misunderstood when it is regarded merely as a technique for accomplishing a job that no individual can do alone. If this were all that a committee is, there would be no reason for forming all the committees we do form to do jobs that some individual *could* do alone. A committee—I abbreviate

APARTNESS—Men need a certain disengagement from today's pressures.

the latest theories—is a social process. More specifically, it is democracy in action.

THIS sobering thought puts everything in a new light. The value of a committee is that the people on it get to know each other; they learn habits of patience and tolerance; they get a sense of participation and usefulness; most remarkable of all, they learn to think as a group. In short, a committee exists to bring people together, and when this process really takes, the results are unmistakable: a successful committee spawns more committees.

Of course, in order to hold this theory, one must make a number of arbitrary assumptions: for example, that whenever people get to know each other they will also get to like each other; for another example, that the "patience" and "tolerance" displayed by the good committeeman are not really just drowsiness; for still another, that groups think. But any really creative theory must make some new assumptions, and these assumptions are certainly more interesting than most. In fact, if we have any problems with them we can form a committee to iron them out.

In this connection, it is comforting to know that American business is in the stream of things. If that ob-

server of American folkways Mr. William H. Whyte is right, the magic words in business circles today are "the organization," "the team," and, of course, that blood brother of togetherness, "belongingness." As one bit of evidence, Mr. Whyte offers a documentary film put out by a chemical company. As the camera focuses on the young men in the laboratory, the voice on the sound track rings out: "No geniuses here; just a bunch of average Americans working together." One might wish for a little less candor, but it is reassuring to know that American business is not insensitive to the deeper currents of improvement in American life.

BUT probably the most interesting expression of the policy of togetherness can be found today in the area that used to be known as politics. The bitterness and animosities that were present as recently as 1954 have been diluted, and this is surely a good thing. But it would be a euphemism to say that our former disagreements have been replaced by what have come to be known as "areas of agreement." A more exact description would be that they have been replaced by areas of happy obscurity. The peculiar merit possessed by most of the pronouncements that come from the committees by which we are increasingly governed

is that they move on a level of discourse which makes both consent and dissent irrelevant intrusions. This promotes togetherly feelings.

Nevertheless, it may be that there is still something to be said for the words which the now fashionable critics of modern society have made just a little unclean—words like "loneliness," "isolation," even "anonymity." Doubtless one can get too much of these things. But a certain disengagement from the pressures of one's time and place and neighbors is probably necessary for most really creative work, and is also very useful if one merely wishes to play.

FORTUNATELY, as in many other areas of American life, our practice is probably not quite up to our professions, and we are not yet all as togethered together as our present rhetoric might lead an unwary observer to suppose. But with all the talk about the need for "belonging," it seems worth while to point out that there are certain special privileges, such as the privilege of being left alone, which life in a modern society makes possible, and which men in the past fought rather hard to procure.

It was Tocqueville who observed that in a democratic nation, where power is diffused throughout the community, all individuals are powerless if they do not learn voluntarily to help one another. "Among the laws that rule human societies," he wrote, "there is one which seems to be more precise and clear than all the others. If men are to remain civilized or to become so, the art of associating together must grow and improve in the same ratio in which the equality of conditions is increased."

BUT one may reasonably ask whether we might not still be allowed to take a jaundiced view of togetherness when it has no explicit purpose except togetherness for its own dear sake. Being together with others is an unavoidable fact of life. Sometimes it has its advantages, sometimes not. But when we turn it into an obsessive ideal of the good life, it is not even a necessary evil. It is just a bore. It would be nice if we could all come together in agreement on this point.

A Woman's Place Still the Home, Students Insist in Recent Survey

A WOMAN'S place, debated with verve by feminists, suffragettes and freethinkers of a bygone era, is crystal clear to their emancipated descendants.

A study of more than 1,000 high school and college girls disclosed that 80 per cent considered stoking a home fire preferable to blazing a career. Their place, they insisted, is the home.

The study was undertaken by the Department of Rural Sociology of the State College of Washington. The results are reported by Dr. LaMar T. Empey, Associate Professor of Sociology at Brigham Young University, in the latest issue of the magazine Marriage and Family Living.

Contrasting the attitudes of these girls with those of a similar number of high school and college boys, the study found that women felt a greater responsibility toward maintaining family serenity than men.

When asked, "If you knew that the person you loved most was opposed to your taking the job most to your liking, would you still accept it?" 55 per cent of the college women, compared with 17 per cent of the college men, said "no."

In reply to the question, "What type of work do you prefer?" 75 per cent of the girls gave a preference for "work involving relationships with people." Only 30 per cent of the boys preferred such work. They were more inclined to "work with things" and "work with ideas."

The study noted "a growing tendency for young women to view their role as a dual one, that of preparing for marriage and a productive occupation."

BAN ON TESTIMONY BY WIFE AFFIRMED

Supreme Court, in Upsetting a Conviction, Says Rule 'Fosters Family Peace'

Special to The New York Times.

WASHINGTON, Nov. 24— The Supreme Court reaffirmed today the ancient rule that wives may not testify against their husbands, even voluntarily.

Justice Hugo L. Black, writing for a unanimous court said the rule was designed to "foster family peace." Having a spose give adverse testimony in a criminal proceeding, he said, would "be likely to destroy almost any marriage."

The issue was a rule of evidence for the Federal courts only, not state courts. The Government had asked the Supreme Court to let a wife testify when she wanted to, even though she could not be compelled to do so.

Justice Black indicated a reluctance to change so broad a rule in the context of an individual case. He said any needed change would be better made by Congress or in a general revision of rules by the court under its authority to promulgate rules for the Federal courts.

The newest member of the court, Justice Potter Stewart, concurred in a separate opinion —his first since joining the bench Oct. 14. The case was argued that day.

Justice Stewart indicated that he personally would like to junk the entire rule and let a spouse either be compeled to testify or come forward voluntarily. But he suggested that the present case was not an appropriate one for this decision.

The case was a Mann Act prosecution of James Clifton Hawkins, of Dogpatch, Okla! Hawkins was convicted of taking Lola Fay Moudy, 17 years old, from Arkansas to Oklahoma in 1955 to engage in prostitution. He received a five-year sentence.

In the trial the Government attempted to prove that Hawkins had taken Miss Moody to one "Jane Wilson" for instruction as a prostitute. His wife, from whom he was separated, took the stand and identified herself as "Jane Wilson."

The common law rule, developed in England and applied at first in the United States, made husband or wife incompetent as witnesses for or against each other in criminal cases.

In 1933 the Supreme Court changed the rule to let either spouse give testimony favorable to the other. In the light of reason and experience, the court said, the complete bar could not be justified.

But Justice Black wrote that the same could not be said of testimony against the spouse, unless the one who was the criminal defendant gave permission for the other to testify. The witness is qualified under such circumstances.

He said the interest of the courts in promoting happy matrimoney weighed against the interest of getting testimony. And he suggested that voluntary testimony against a spouse might engender "more bitterness" than compelled testimony.

Justice Black said the majority of states still had the exclusionary rule. Others, he said, had put on some limitations, and he left the court free to do so in future.

Kenneth R. King and Byron Tunnell of Tyler, Tex., argued for Hawkins and Kirby W. Patterson for the Government.

Freud Is Viewed As Aid to Child

Psychologist Says Scientist Did Much to Advance Education

By WALTER C. LANGER
Psychological Consultant to Commission on Human Relations.

I saw Freud frequently in those trying days after Hitler came to Vienna in 1938, and I accompanied him on his trip into exile. Now Freud is dead. His long years of research have come to an end. Attempts are being made on all sides to judge the man and his contributions to science and to culture.

There are those who openly express their admiration and their indebtedness—rate Freud with the greatest thinkers of all time: Aristotle, Newton, Pasteur and Darwin. There are others who consider him little more than a flash in the pan—a sensationalist who enjoyed stirring people up by tearing down the things the cultured prized most highly—in short, an iconoclast.

It is not easy to evaluate the contributions he has made to modern thought. The shock of his death is still so close upon us that it is difficult for me to think of him apart from his work. To do so will require the perspective that time alone can give. Nevertheless, some of his discoveries are of such tremendous significance to education that we should give them especial attention at this time.

It was Freud who showed that we cannot hope to educate children by a preconceived formula. It was he who indicated that we cannot understand the behavior of the child apart from underlying motives, and that these motives are often veiled so completely that the individual himself does not know just why he acts as he does—in fact, the acts may be just as unpleasant to him as they are to those about him.

He also did much to save the problem child and the delinquent from social ostracism by showing him to be an unfortunate individual who, due to environmental forces and cultural pressures, had not been able to achieve a satisfactory adjustment.

Freud's name has been most often associated with the topic of sex. Critics have seized upon and distorted this part of his work until it is difficult to recognize his real contributions.

It is true that Freud jolted our culture out of the dogmatic slumber of the Victorian era. Sex was brought into the light of day and thought of as a perfectly natural function—a valid field for study and discussion which no longer had to be concealed because some people thought it was filthy and indecent. This breaking of tradition would probably have been sufficient to bring a storm of protest on Freud's head, but he did not stop there. His studies of people had convinced him that the sexual instinct was one of the powerful forces which determined behavior and personality development, and that it could not be shut off from expression without having detrimental effects upon the adjustment of the individual.

These findings have had a tremendous influence upon education and all phases of child training. Today sex is a suitable subject of study and is included in the curricula of many of our enlightened schools. Wholesome attitudes are developed in the children by treating sex as any other natural function to which the individual must adjust if he is to live within the boundaries laid down by the culture.

Infant training, instead of being a series of taboos and prohibitions of activities which we adults have outgrown, has become more tolerant, patient and understanding guidance of the child's needs into more acceptable forms of expression. We all know that the child's education does not begin when he first steps into the classroom. It begins almost at the moment of birth. Nursery schools have sprung up all over the world to assist parents in guiding and understanding their child's behavior.

Freud made many significant contributions to education, but even more important has been the new point of view about child life which Freud's discoveries have helped teachers to take. No longer is the child treated as a piece of clay to be forced into the mold of the culture at all costs. From the Freudian point of view, the individual as a person is invaluable. He has certain inner demands that must find gratification in some adequate form if he is to live a happy and useful life in his society.

New Problems for Teachers

When socially acceptable forms are denied he finds himself forced to seek outlets through unsocial behavior of one kind or another. The result is that the teacher can no longer regard Johnnie's spit-ball throwing in the classroom or Mary's vomiting when she is asked to do something unpleasant as behavior designed by the individual in order to annoy her. She must now take into consideration the fact that the child does not know why he or she is behaving this way; that the motives underlying these behavior patterns may be buried in the unconscious far beyond the reach of the child's control.

Instead of attempting to prevent such undesirable forms of behavior through punishment, the enlightened teacher now tries to enlist the cooperation of the child and of all who know him in an attempt to discover the unconscious motives which force him to act this way. Since this is often a difficult problem, child guidance clinics have been established in many school systems where experts strive to help the child to a more satisfactory form of adjustment.

In a way Freud's death was timely; the things he had fought for throughout his life—truth, freedom of thought, and the dignity of the individual—were being destroyed through Europe or were losing ground in his native Europe. His death is almost a symbol of the passing of the intellectual Austria and Germany he had loved so well. It should be the occasion for teachers in our democracy to resolve to carry on in his spirit of making understanding and insight a goal in all human relationships.

October 8, 1939

Plea for Mothering

A Right of the Child Which Is Ignored by Modern Science

Infant care has become "a highly mechanical procedure," with attention focused on formulas and cleanliness, while the baby's mental functioning is completely ignored, Dr. Margaret A. Ribble asserts in "The Rights of Infants," a study of hundreds of babies and their parents, published by the Columbia University Press. Dr. Ribble holds that "our highly impersonal civilization has insidiously damaged woman's instinctual nature and has blinded her to one of her most natural rights," and warns that the natural impulses of an infant cannot be summarily dammed up or snuffed out when their expression becomes inconvenient for adults.

Hygiene Overemphasized

She further charges that food and general hygiene for babies have been overemphasized by modern science to the complete exclusion of emotional and social reactions. As a result the child is actually thwarted in his mental development. Poor relations with parents leads to reactions that tend to become the basis of adult personality disorders.

What infants need is more of the old-fashioned "mothering," thinks Dr. Ribble, adding that the rocking chair and the cradle should never have been discarded. "Mothering includes the whole gamut of small acts by means of which an emotionally healthy mother consistently shows her love for her child, thus instinctively stimulating his psychic development."

Obviously, feeding, bathing and all the details of physical care come in, but in addition to these duties, which can easily become routine and perfunctory, Dr. Ribble means by "mothering" all the small evidences of tenderness—fondling, caressing, rocking, singing and baby talk. All these have a deep significance.

Her studies convince Dr. Ribble that breast-fed babies tend to trust their mothers. Consequently they are easily led and directed. "Breast-feeding is of the very essence of mothering and the most important means of immunizing a baby against anxiety."

January 30, 1944

WOMEN RECEIVE ADVICE

Citizenship Committee Urges Careful Child Training

Besides fulfilling her own responsibility as a citizen, the housewife contributes to the training of her children as good citizens by interesting herself in local government problems, according to a report made public yesterday by the committee on citizenship in the home of the Woman's Foundation.

"If a child does not learn to live as a good citizen in the family there is little reason to expect that he will pick up the art by some miracle upon reaching the age of 21," the report pointed out. One aspect of citizenship—promotion of good government in one's own community—can be taught better by example than merely by "fine phrases," it was asserted.

The report urges women to work actively for civic betterment through political parties, nonpartisan groups and independent means, such as writing directly to public officials. "Unless your community is perfect in the way its affairs are handled, there are many opportunities for this kind of action," the statement noted. "The danger of becoming known as a bothersome busybody can be avoided by being sure of your facts and being convinced of the importance of your purpose," it added.

The report was prepared for the foundation by a committee of ten, under the co-chairmanship of Dr. Robert G. Sproul, president of the University of California, and Dr. George B. Cutten, former president of Colgate University.

Healthy Outlook

By DOROTHY BARCLAY

AN infant wriggling with delight at the amazing game of peek-a-boo; a 5-year-old fascinated by mysterious doings of repairmen down a manhole; a group of teen-agers decked out according to some new fad which older eyes find thoroughly unattractive. Parents—or for that matter any

adult who sees the life around him—often observe youngsters in situations like these. It's doubtful, though, that the elders looked upon them as steps in a logical, charted course of healthy personality development.

At the Midcentury White House Conference on Children and Youth, as we've reported before, emphasis was on investigating what factors go into building this much-desired force, the healthy personality. Before the delegates who attended even began thinking out their plans, a fact-finding committee was hard at work, drawing together from endless sources material they felt it important to bring to the attention of the American people. (A 170-page digest of their report was available to delegates and the full version is scheduled for publication within a few months.)

IN the opinion of a number of experts we talked with at the conference, one section of the report was of special importance to all adults concerned with children—an outline of personality development worked out by Erik H. Erikson, a psychologist and practicing psychoanalyst who has had plenty of personal experience with children. During the months since the conference we have heard this material referred to time and again. When it was brought up yet once more at the Child Study Association's annual conference less than two weeks ago, we decided to try presenting the essence of it to our readers.

As Dr. Barbara Biber, of the Bank Street College of Education, pointed out at the C. S. A. meeting, Dr. Erikson's central theme is that for each stage of development in a child's growth there is a characteristic problem he has to work out, a sort of continuing life challenge. How he works out each one of these and how successful he is at finding a solution will determine his basic style of life and his attitudes toward himself and others.

WHEN we discussed the topic with Dr. Helen L. Witmer of the School of Social Welfare, U. C. L. A., who directed the fact-finding staff for the Midcentury Conference, she emphasized the value of the outline in presenting concrete suggestions not only of what boys and girls need at different ages but why. "Instead of just the general 'Be kind to children' idea," she said, "the Erikson material is specific about the key problems of each developmental period and why certain attitudes are particularly important at special times."

The fact-finding digest points out that there's no one authoritative theory of personality just now, nor even several consistent, fully developed ones from which to choose. But Dr. Erikson's outline, the fact-finders held, "has the merit of indicating at one and the same time the main course of personality development and the attributes of a healthy personality."

And what has all this to do with the game of peek-a-boo, teen-age fads and the rest? The tie-up is simple and direct. Each is a specific example of what goes on during different stages of growth and is significant to personality development. The healthy, mature individual, Dr. Erikson holds, has acquired a sense of trust, of autonomy (self-reliance and a will of his own), of initiative, accomplishment, identity, intimacy, a parental sense and a sense of integrity. The first six, developing in the order named, would seem to be parents' particular concern; the last two are not likely to develop fully before adulthood.

During the baby's first year, developing the sense of trust is the key step in his personality development. The measures repeatedly recommended by child-care specialists — feeding baby when he is hungry, comforting him when he cries, protecting him from sudden shocks, keeping him warm and dry and close to mother —all help to build this feeling. But obviously it's not accomplished all at once.

THE baby's trust-mistrust problem is symbolized in the game of peek-a-boo. There is a slightly tense expression on the baby's face when the object goes away; its reappearance is greeted by wriggles and smiles. Only

gradually does a baby learn that things continue to exist even though he does not see them, that there is order and stability in his universe. Peek-a-boo proves the point by playful repetition.

Once trust is established the struggle for autonomy—independence—begins, sometime after the twelfth to fifteenth month. Parents know all too well this "get into everything" toddler stage. Perhaps, the digest suggests, if these little tykes are to develop the feeling of self-reliance and adequacy they need, the most constructive rule a parent can follow is to forbid only what really matters, be clear and consistent about it and scrupulously avoid shaming the child or giving him cause to doubt his own worth.

The 4 and 5 year olds, developing their sense of initiative, want to find out how other people live and work and would like to share their activities, actually and in their play. At this point parents would do well to avoid the constant "no," allow much leeway and provide plenty of encouragement for the enterprise and imagination youngsters show.

*B*ETWEEN the ages of,

roughly, 6 to 12, the sense of accomplishment is in the making. Away with the grandiose projects of the 5's, this youngster wants real tasks that he can carry through to completion. Adults should help him find them.

Developing the senses of identity (Who am I, anyway?) and of intimacy, the capacity for close, warm relationships with others, occupies teen-agers, as every parent knows. Trying to find comfort through similarity can lead to the kind of stereotyped behavior, dress and ideals some parents find so hard to take. The difficulties involved at this particular stage are reflected in the amount of concern mothers and fathers show about their boys and girls and the myriad books written to provide understanding and offer encouragement and help.

Parents who are up-to-date on current ideas of child rearing will not find anything startling in the recommendations that this outline presents for each stage. Rather it should be comforting to them to find that the courses suggested are pretty much those loving and emotionally adjusted mothers and dads follow spontaneously.

Homogenized Children of New Suburbia

By SIDONIE M. GRUENBERG

A YOUNG man who had attended an exclusive preparatory school and an Ivy League college felt that his horizon had been restricted because, during the years of his education he had met only the sons of bankers, brokers, executives, lawyers and doctors. He determined that, when the time came, *his* children would go to public school.

The time came. The young man and his wife moved out to the suburbs where their children could get fresh air and play space, go to public school and grow up with children of all kinds. "And whom do my children meet?" he asks. "The children of bankers, brokers, executives, lawyers and doctors!"

Despite the drawback that depressed this particular parent, the suburb into which he moved had certain things in its favor, besides the obvious attraction of lebensraum. It was a town, one of the older suburbs. It had grown up gradually over the years with its own schools, churches and deepening civic consciousness until it had developed into a real *community* with traditions of its own.

New Suburbia is something else again. Around every major city from the Atlantic to the Pacific the new suburbs have been springing up like mushrooms in a damp season. They are sometimes created by dividing large estates—as on Long Island, in Westchester County and in areas around Chicago, Detroit and Los Angeles. More often the new suburbs are built on what had been until recently empty acreage. Whether in California or New Jersey they are typically "prefabricated" in all their details and the parts are suddenly assembled on the spot. Unlike towns and cities and the suburbs of the past, they do not evolve gradually but emerge full-blown. They are designed and constructed by corporations or real estate operators who work on mass-production principles. A hundred or a thousand houses open their doors almost simultaneously, ready for occupancy.

S INCE there has been an acute shortage of dwellings in all urban areas for

SIDONIE M. GRUENBERG is editor of the "Encyclopedia of Child Care and Guidance," and a former director of the Child Study Assn. of America. She wrote "We, the Parents."

Drawing by Roy Doty.

"New Suburbia families are in danger of becoming as alike as the houses they live in."

well over a decade, these housing developments serve an immediate need for thousands and thousands of families. The mass development of small houses has meant that vast numbers of families have had the chance to get out of small apartments in crowded cities into homes of their own. They may not intend to spend the rest of their lives there, but for the time being fathers, mothers and children all have a stake in making the home as attractive as possible and in keeping it in good repair. It is "home," far more than a rented apartment in the city could ever be. And surrounding even the smallest jerry-built suburban home is a piece of ground on which to have a garden or to place a sand box or a swing.

But the new suburbanites take what they can afford and can get. And they pay a subtle psychological price. For one thing, the new suburb is a community only in the sense that it is an aggregate of dwellings—often identical houses. It may in time become a community, but not yet. No one has grown up in it; it has no traditions. We really don't know what effect it will ultimately have on children; we can only conjecture.

The families of New Suburbia consist typically of a young couple with one or two children, or perhaps one child and another on the way. The child living here sees no elderly people, no teen-agers. Except on week-ends and holidays he sees only mothers and

other children of his own age. This dearth of weekday variety was remarked on by a woman who had moved to a new suburb and returned after some months to visit friends in her former city neighborhood. "Though I have lived in the city most of my life," she said, "I was actually startled to see such a variety of people, of every type and age. It seemed so long since I had seen old people and high school kids, since I had seen men around in the daytime!"

IF Old Suburbia is lacking in a variety of work going on that boys and girls can watch or actively share in, it at least has a garage, a movie theatre, a shoe repair shop. In New Suburbia there is often nothing but a supermarket and a gasoline station. In Old Suburbia children grow up seeing people of all ages and playing with children older than themselves—from whom each child normally learns the ways and customs appropriate to the age into which he matures day by day. In New Suburbia the children are likely to be nearly of the same age. In Old Suburbia the fathers take the train to the city each day, leaving the car with the mothers. In New Suburbia there is often no railroad station, so the fathers drive to work in their own cars or by "car pool." The mothers remain with the house and yard and children.

The children growing up in New Suburbia run the danger of becoming "homogenized." In many of the new suburbs the white child never sees a Negro. In others the Jewish child never plays with any but Jewish children. Some of these suburbs are virtually all Catholic. In others there are no Catholics. Even without racial and religious segregation—and in these new developments groups tend to segregate themselves to an alarming degree—the pressure to conform is intense, and stultifying.

CHILDREN derive their models primarily from their parents. Where the parents live in an atmosphere of general conformity the children will select their friends and associates from among the like-minded, from those who act and speak and judge everything as they themselves have always done at home. And growing up without meeting older children is not conducive to children's dreaming and planning for their own future. Better than the home or the school, older companions challenge the child to try himself out in many ways, to discover the range and variety of his capacities, as well as his limitations.

Moreover, in this atmosphere children are likely to picture the good life in terms of uniform, standardized patterns; and that tends to block invention and experiment. Because nothing out of the way ever happens in these quiet, sanitary and standardized surroundings, one wonders what will arouse the imagination of these children. What spiritual equivalent will they find for the challenge and inspiration that an older generation found during childhood in city streets, on farms, in market towns?

In one new Eastern suburb with a population of 30,000, there is no high school. There is not yet any *need* for a high school. One may wonder how these young children, lacking many of the normal associations, will ever fit into a high school. One wonders, too, how large a high school such a town will eventually need. Between the parents who are newcomers — and therefore typically lacking in civic initiative—and those who hope to move away as soon as their finances are more secure, the children live in an atmosphere of transiency. Will any of these children grow up there, or will the families, one by one, move away as the children near high school age?

Many of the mothers in these new suburbs have had considerable training in offices or shops and some have a degree of executive ability. In new Suburbia they find no outlets for their talents and energies and they tend to focus all their efforts upon their children. Everything that the mothers do, all the little chores, tend to take on disproportionate significance, so that the children feel the pressures while the mothers cannot help feeling frustrated and discontented. This does not mean that they are unhappy with their homes and their children, for they have, essentially, what every woman wants; but they are confused and often feel that there is something lacking in the lives they lead. At the same time, their children cannot help but get a picture of adults as being constantly concerned with trivialities.

Some of the other obvious shortcomings of the new suburbs are incidental to their very newness. In time, a church will be built, perhaps several. A meeting place or assembly hall will rise. In some new suburbs the school from the very first offers a meeting place for parents. But the important question, it seems to me, is how the parents can keep the benefits of new Suburbia without paying too heavy a price.

The first important step has been taken once parents become aware of the spiritual lacks in their new way of life. They do not have to give up the fresh air and the safe play space and go back to the cities. Once they realize that they can enrich and strengthen their children's lives effectively only if they succeed in making their own lives satisfactory, they will find the way.

Here are some of the things that parents can do—things that have in fact already been done here and there.

Individual parents can make an effort to get their sons and daughters into other types of homes, exchanging visits with old friends, perhaps, or with children's cousins. They will recognize the value of inviting old friends and relatives to their home for longer or shorter periods of time—a teen-age niece or nephew, acquaintances with different backgrounds and experience. If a grandmother or grandfather has come to live with a young couple, this should not be looked upon as an unmitigated tragedy. It might even be an advantage to other families to

RARA AVIS—Oldsters are likely to be a curiosity in new Suburbia.

know a three-generation family for a change. As city children are given the benefits of trips to the country to see trees and flowers, farms and animals, and as country children are brought into the city to see factories, wharves, museums and railroad stations, so children from new Suburbia need trips to both city and country in order to become familiar with the world in which they live. Cooperating with one another, mothers can arrange trips that are rewarding and enriching, to themselves as well as to the children. One might take care of the toddler while others take the school-age children on an excursion.

MOTHERS can, and often do, cooperate with one another in order to give each one time to herself, a chance to read or a change of scene. Sometimes they do this by taking turns at supervising a group of children on the playground, sometimes by inviting a child or two to the house for a day.

No mother need feel ashamed when she has the perfectly natural feeling that she'd like a change once in a while. She actually needs it if she is to have a perspective on her family and its life, if she is to see the benefits as well as the lacks in the agencies and institutions of the place in which she and her husband have chosen to live. By enlarging her own contacts with others, she takes pressure from the children and becomes a better parent. As well as "exchanging" children once in a while, mothers can also exchange magazines and books until they have the beginnings of a library.

VARIOUS activities can be organized around the school for the benefit of the entire community. The most obvious ones, of course, are "educa-

tional," such as study groups, public meetings, parent-teacher organizations for considering matters that specifically affect the schools and the children. But recreational projects, dramatics and other amateur entertainments that can bring whole families together will suggest opportunities for further forms of cooperation — choral singing, musical affairs, art classes, carpentry classes, and so on. As the children get a little older, mothers—and fathers too—might start some new enterprises that will bring other kinds of people into the community. The main thing is that more parents should be aware that they have not now a real community—merely an aggregation of homes.

It is not unreasonable to expect some wholesome effects upon children who see their parents exploring their surroundings, adventuring and pioneering with confidence, instead of remaining shut in upon themselves and the circumstances into which they happen to have drifted. Parents *can* do a new kind of pioneering by creating communities which are entirely different from, and in some ways better than, any they have known before.

IN the meantime, those who are responsible for new housing should give more thought to the kind of living our vaunted civilization considers decent for ordinary people and their children. Some of the best planning of new cities has been carried on by industrial establishments for the purpose of furnishing houses and all the necessary facilities and service for a complete community. In one project that I saw recently in Canada, a church, schools, parks and playgrounds, offices and stores were laid out before any of the houses were built. Other planners try to provide for the many kinds and grades of workers the industry will need as well as for the variety of services the families will need. No planning can anticipate all the needs that may arise; and every community will be sure to create new problems. But it is necessary to study the best of the company towns as well as the best publicly initiated housing projects, both in this country and abroad, if we are to evolve workable patterns in which the first consideration will be opportunities for the growth and development of children and for the enrichment of family living.

When Boy (Age 12) Meets Girl

By DOROTHY BARCLAY

OUT in a Connecticut suburb not too long ago a girl of 12 nose powdered, lips lightly rouged, strapless "formal" meticulously padded out- sat tensely at home waiting for her 13-year-old escort-of-the-evening. Her tenseness was understandable. Not only had she been waiting since she was 11 to be asked for a "date" (and a year is mighty long when you're that age) but her gallant was now more than an hour overdue.

The youngster's obvious concern was now being shared by her mother and dad. "Maybe Jack's ill," the mother suggested. But a call to his home revealed he'd left for the party long since. "Maybe he didn't realize he was to pick you up," offered dad. "I'll drive you down." And he did.

In the corner of a living room arranged for dancing Jack stood with a crowd of other boys, his face redder than even an unaccustomed starched collar could account for. "Oh, Hi," he said miserably to his chosen companion for this festive evening. "Hello," she replied. This was the extent of their conversation that night. By 11 P. M. at least one girl was convinced that she was a Failure with Men, that Boys are Not to Be Depended Upon, that dances are really no fun.

Incidents like that have been happening ever since young people's parties began, and many a dusty novel delineates the mixed feelings of 16 and 17-year-olds in a similar situation. Are the ages of the miserable young pair all that has changed? Over a hurdle of disappointment at 12, will our young friend be happier and more relaxed in her relationships with boys at 16 or 17? Or has perhaps this hurt gone deeper because it occurred so early?

FROM time to time over the past year or two, parents' groups (from Charlotte, N. C., to Neenah, Wis.) have written to ask what other communities are doing to peg the continually dropping age at which formal "dating" begins.

"We parents do not in any way wish to stop our children from 'growing,'" one group chairman wrote. "We do not think there is anything wrong with dating and formal dances in themselves. It's just that the children are being introduced to them too young. At sixth and seventh grade, youngsters have enough changes to adjust to in themselves and in school."

Although parents of many pre-adolescent boys and girls have expressed concern in this way for some time, many others, looking on pre-adolescent dating as "cute," or "harmless" or "just for fun," have given it all-out support.

School systems by introducing social dancing instruction for sixth-graders—and in some cases arranging school-sponsored evening dances at this level—have apparently given the early dating trend an endorsement. Through it all the child development specialists have been comparatively quiet.

Now in the latest issue of Child Study, quarterly journal of the Child Study Association

of America, one speaks out strongly against the current course. Mrs. Selma Fraiberg, child therapist and instructor in the Department of Psychiatry, Wayne University College of Medicine, in a piece on helping children develop controls, states her belief that "if the adult world withdrew its support, or its indulgence, of precocious dating activities in early adolescence, we would find the scale of such activities greatly reduced."

And reduced it should be, she feels. "The pressure upon youngsters today to accelerate their heterosexuality at a pace which is not geared to emotional readiness * * * can be damaging."

We took this topic up with a group of leaders active in the parent education program of the United Parents Association. Trained, qualified, they knew the problem first hand from their work throughout the metropolitan area. They did not agree on every detail of the situation. "Who or what is responsible?" Dr. Morey L. Appell asked. "The parents? The youngsters? The culture? A genuine acceleration of physical—and therefore social —growth? Differences of opinion abounded here.

Most, however, did agree on

this; junior high school youngsters are not ready—as a group—for a formal dating pattern. Some may be. Girls are likely to be more mature than the boys and the "socially aggressive" ones may be pushing others to follow a pattern pleasant only to themselves.

FROM direct experience with youngsters at camp Mrs. Mildred Brody held that the early "dating" pattern is largely imposed from the outside. When the girls she works with first learn that there will be co-ed activities on Friday nights, she said, the "successful-with-boys" type invariably wants the proceedings to be on a "date" basis. As the summer goes on, however, more relaxed activities are preferred.

Dances that are strictly dances are a frost with most of the youngsters, she reported. A successful evening party offers an opportunity for dancing for those who want it, but also provides a place for quiet games and (in camp) a "canteen" with plenty of food available as well as surroundings appropriate for the intense discussions likely to spring up among little knots of boys or girls. When there is no pressure on the children to dance, she reported, they may

try it. But there is sanctuary in games or eating for those who are not interested or ready.

PARENTS must think out for themselves what this means to their own young. They should not let themselves be pressured into accepting a pattern for their children just because "everybody else is doing it," Mrs. Mildred Rabinow declared. The measure should not be what others are doing but what is right for the individual child. Is he or she really ready for this kind of experience? Does he understand what is involved? Are the children interested in each other, or is dating a meaningless game where Joe "takes" Sandy because George said it would be a good idea and Sandy (aged 12) accepts his invitation because "having a date" is the measure of social success in her classroom?

Boys and girls should indeed be helped to be more comfortable with one another. The aim may be achieved far more readily, though, by promoting casual boy-girl activities anything from square dances to skating parties and taffy pulls in which pre-adolescents can feel at ease and have real fun.

January 23, 1955

The Co-op Nursery Comes of Age

By DOROTHY BARCLAY

WE'VE heard educators say more than once and sometimes wistfully that it takes fifty years for a new development in their field to grow strong enough for general public acceptance. If that is so, the cooperative nursery school movement appears to be running just about on schedule.

Next year will mark the fortieth anniversary of the founding of the first co-op nursery in this country by a group of twelve faculty wives at the University of Chicago. If similar parent activity is as widespread for the next ten years as it has been for the last, we can look forward to the movement's "coming of

age" when it hits its half-century mark. All signs seem to indicate that it will. Last fall, for instance, the University of California at Los Angeles offered a one-day conference on cooperative nurseries. Anticipated attendance was 125. Final registration was over 550.

The co-op set-up cannot be neatly categorized. It varies with the interests, the resources and the needs of the parents who organize the venture. But generally speaking, parents are responsible for business administration and finance and, under the direction of a trained teacher chosen by themselves, take some part in setting up and maintaining facilities and in working with the children.

No doubt all sorts of sociological reasons could be cited

for this development the bumper crop of babies, the migration to the suburbs, shorter working hours for fathers, the development of the nursery school movement generally.

*I*NDIVIDUAL parents, though, are not too interested in Broad Social Trends. Those who have been active in the co-op movement have had for the most part only one aim in view: They wanted what would be good for their youngsters — and they were willing to work for it. What they didn't realize, and what is only now beginning to be generally recognized, is that they as individuals get many satisfactions from the work beyond the pleasure of seeing their own children happily occupied. Many co-ops are old enough now to have "graduated" scores of parents into other community work just as they have "graduated" their youngest members to primary and secondary schools.

Just what does the co-op experience mean to those who take part? Group members throughout the country have been talking this over among themselves. Here is the way some of them in Los Angeles see it:

A MOTHER who works actively in the nursery school gets a deep understanding and realization of her own importance to her child's development. She finds acceptance in a friendly group of parents who face problems and questions similar to hers. Watching and working with many children the same age as her own, she finds that neither her child's difficulties nor his accomplishments are unique. She learns much about working with children by observing a skilled teacher and gets helpful guidance from the teacher when she wants and needs it most.

The cooperative nature of the venture, the "taking of turns" by all mothers in helping out, gives each one some free time away from her daily routine, relaxation from some of the daily tasks of child care and an opportunity to develop her own interests (or devote herself to younger children) without interruption.

Fathers, too, play a vital role in cooperatives. They are most commonly thought of as lending strong backs and good

right arms to the tasks of setting up the playroom and building equipment but other less materialistic satisfactions are there for them too. Taking part in school activities gives them a chance to see their children in action outside their own home. Their contact with other fathers, discussion of their children with other men, provides an opportunity for reaching masculine acceptance of the fact that "kids are what they are" and masculine understanding of the sometimes mysterious (as described by their wives) Responsibilities of Fatherhood. As men of the community, not only as fathers, they find satisfaction in participating in a group endeavor of real worth.

One aspect of work in cooperatives that has received very little attention, though, has been the personal growth that results when parents and teachers of different backgrounds, different temperaments and different points of view hammer out a real and honest working partnership.

*I*N the early years of the movement and in the early stages of many projects there have been teachers who felt that parents had nothing to offer the children's program except extra hands and feet to relieve the teacher of some tiresome chores. "Treat parents like human beings and they will take over your school," at least one teacher has said. Similarly there have been and still are parents who consider the teacher's honest efforts to build a good program "dictatorial" or "overbearing" no matter how democratic the teacher has

tried to be. And there have, of course, been some parents who held similar negative thoughts about other mothers and dads.

The nursery school divided against itself cannot stand, however. The success of a continually growing number of co-ops proves that all factions, as they work together, can grow in new understanding and respect for the contributions of the others.

Some colleges are now including in their nursery school teacher training programs, courses in working with parents as well as with the young. Perhaps the cooperative nursery schools will lead the way toward finding the keys to closer parent-teacher cooperation at every school level.

*P*ARENTS interested in reading more about co-operative nursery schools might like to look over "Parent Cooperative Nursery Schools" by Katharine Whiteside Taylor, $2.85 from the Bureau of Publications, Teachers College Columbia University, New York 27. Other publications newly revised by successful groups include:

"A Preliminary Guide for Cooperative Nursery Schools," $1.25 from the Los Angeles Council of Cooperative Nursery Schools, 1626 North Genesee Avenue, Los Angeles 46, Calif.

"Our Cooperative Nursery School," $1.50 from Silver Spring Nursery School, Inc., Silver Spring, Md.

"A Nursery School Handbook for Teachers and Parents," $2 from the Sierra Madre Community Nursery School Association, 701 East Sierra Madre Boulevard, Sierra Madre, Calif.

February 27, 1955

The Markets—
Black and Gray—
in Babies

By MARYBETH WEINSTEIN

EACH year the fates of about 20,000 children are decided by persons who give them or sell them to couples they know only casually, if at all. The prevalence of such irresponsible gray- and black-market placements, in view of the effect that ill-chosen homes can have on the children involved, has become a problem so serious that it is being examined by a Senate subcommittee. Headed by Senator Estes Kefauver of Tennessee, it conducted a hearing on adoption abuses last summer in Chicago and again this month in Miami.

The increase in independently arranged adoptions—there are as many children adopted by non-relatives each year without the protection of an agency as with—is blamed by some on the adoption agencies themselves; their requirements and "red tape." Others say that demand is the prime factor and point out that, while adoptions in this country have increased more than 80 per cent in the last ten years, there are at least ten times as many couples who want to adopt infants as there are agency babies to be adopted. Still others indict antiquated state adoption laws, state religious requirements and the inadequacy of authorized services to women pregnant out of wedlock.

Adoption agencies were, of course, founded to find homes for children, not children for homes, and this, the agencies feel, must continue to be their role and responsibility. If a couple goes through agency channels, their experience may be something like this:

Mr. and Mrs. A. of New York City, happily married four years but childless, called for an appointment at a nonsectarian adoption agency. (Had they been Catholic or Jewish, however, they would have been referred to an agency sponsored by their particular faith.) They were invited to a preliminary group meeting attended by other childless couples. Here they found that their ages (she was under 35, he was under 40), citizenship, income (modest but adequate for their needs), health and reasons for wanting to adopt seemed to fit the agency's more obvious standards, so they asked for a private interview. During the next five months they filled out questionnaires, were interviewed separately and together several times, had their doctor send a report on their sterility and general health, gave five references including their clergyman—all of

---

MARYBETH WEINSTEIN, of The Times Magazine, interviewed many specialists in the child welfare field to gather material for this article.

whom were visited—and were themselves twice visited at home.

BECAUSE they were not particular about the sex or age of the child, they did not have to wait as long as some do. Within a year of their winning final approval of their qualifications, the agency telephoned to say it had a baby boy for them to consider. He had been surrendered to the agency by a young unwed mother who had gone there for help shortly before the child was born. Her surrender of the baby, however, had been accepted by the agency only after she had seen the child and was sure her decision to give him up was best for both of them.

The boy had been placed in a foster home and had been observed by a pediatrician for a few months. His health was good and his I. Q., based on tests and the educational attainment of his natural parents, was judged average or above. His eyes were blue, as were Mr. A.'s and, like Mrs. A., he was small-boned and wiry.

When they took the baby, they paid part of a fee ($250), which had been set according to their income. The rest was to be paid at the time of adoption. Then the "trial period"—a year under New York State law—began, during which the agency was there to help if any problems should arise and the child could even be returned to the agency's care if things did not work out well.

When the year was up, Mr. and Mrs. A. filed a petition for adoption, appeared in court with the child and a representative from the adoption agency, and by decree became the boy's parents, just as though he had been born to them.

By contrast, getting a baby through the black market seems simple indeed. A child is bought and no questions are asked. Selling a baby is not a crime in thirty-four states and every state but one will grant a decree that makes the adoption as legal as any arranged by an agency. But this is what happened in a typical case described at the Senate hearing last summer.

Mr. and Mrs. B. of New York City heard of a lawyer in Chicago who could get a child for them in a hurry. They telephoned, were told they would need $3,000 cash—to cover the lawyer's and the unwed mother's "expenses," and should be ready to come to Chicago within the month. On the day the mother left the hospital, the couple arrived, received the baby, and the lawyer pocketed most of the money.

That same day they went to court with the lawyer and filed a petition for adoption (delay was waived for out-of-

staters' convenience). They were home in New York by nightfall. All that remained to make the child legally theirs was a report to be sent later by an investigator they themselves could choose. (This system in the Cook County court was drastically tightened at the time of the Senate's preliminary investigation.)

BUT some weeks later, Mr. and Mrs. B. discovered that the child was defective. They promptly returned him to the lawyer, who in turn thrust him into the arms of the unwed mother, although she had hoped to keep the child a secret and was totally unprepared to take care of him.

Although such black-market placements offer the child no protection and can bring heartache to both the mother and the adoptive parents, black-market operators insist their motives are of the best. A Canadian who used to smuggle "pink parcels" and "blue parcels" to the United States testified before the subcommittee: "I just thought, well, give them a nice home—if a broad, I mean a little girl, has a baby and she can't even take care of herself, how the hell is she going to take care of a baby?"

A similar sentiment, untarnished by mercenary motives, is the bedrock of the gray market. This is a more common type of arrangement by which a child is placed in a home by a housewife, lawyer, minister or doctor—with kindly intentions and without profit.

Social workers deplore both methods. They say that even if the gray- or black-market home turns out to be a good one, and even if the child is all the parents could hope for, there are legal safeguards that should not be bypassed.

A MOTHER, for example, can recover a child if her consent was given under "duress"—and this could include indebtedness (that is, if the only way she could meet her medical expenses was to give up the baby to a couple eager to assume the bill) as well as "ether consents" (in which the mother is made to sign immediately after childbirth). If a child is born in wedlock, the surrender must be signed by the husband, too, even if he is not the father of the child (there have been several cases of doctors unwittingly placing babies whose mothers had said they were unwed). Furthermore, since the names of the adopters in gray- and black-market arrangements are usually known by the natural mother, and through her by others, blackmail is a very real threat.

The Senate subcommittee is currently investigating still another system that has even more dangers—the system whereby an unwed mother registers at the hospital as the wife of the "adoptive" father and no adoption proceedings are ever entered. In one case in Alabama the parents were killed in an automobile accident and the child inherited nothing—his birth certificate was proved to be a fraud and he had no adoptive claim, either. "Even if the secret is never discovered," said Mrs. Henrietta Gordon of the Child Welfare League of America, "the parents live in fear. This does not create the security a child needs in a home."

WHY, then, despite the emotional and legal risks, do so many couples turn to the black or gray markets rather than to an adoption agency?

One important reason is that state laws require that a child be placed "wherever practicable" with a couple of the same religion as that of his natural mother. The black market gets around this by having the natural mother say her religion is that of the couple, but agencies, to be on the safe side and because there are so many couples to choose from that it is "practicable," follow the law to the letter.

How does this work in practice? For one thing, there are many Jewish couples who want to adopt but extraordinarily few Jewish children to be adopted. The Jewish agency in Rochester, N. Y., for example, receives up to fifty applications from couples each year but has had only eight children of Jewish mothers in the last five years. Christian-Jewish or Catholic-Protestant couples have even less chance of adopting through an agency— except in Delaware, where only one adoptive parent must be of the same faith as the child's mother.

"The law is the law and the law implies that a child is born with a religion," said one agency director. "It does give one pause, though, to realize that foundlings are simply dubbed Catholic, Protestant or Jewish, depending on whose turn it is."

ANOTHER source of public misunderstanding and criticism of agencies is the zealous concern of some of them for "matching" parents and child. One agency went to great lengths to find a Hungarian home for a toddler of Hungarian extraction; another refused an anthropologist who wanted to adopt three hard-to-place children of mixed racial origins. Critics also wonder, since there are apparently happy non-adoptive families in which the parents are of only average intelligence and the child is gifted, or vice versa, why agencies try to avoid this.

In answer, agencies cite a study of 200 adoptive homes that was made at the Clinic of Child Development at Yale seven years ago by the late Dr. Catherine Amatruda. Of one hundred independent placements only forty-six were rated good (parents and child were happy and right for each other), twenty-six were rated fair and twenty-eight, bad (maladjusted child, neurotic parents or worse). The one hundred agency-matched placements scored better. Dr. Amatruda rated seventy-six good, sixteen fair, eight bad. How one hundred natural families might have scored is not known.

Another danger to children placed independently was pointed out in a study made by the California Citizens Committee on Adoption. One out of every five children so obtained was never legally adopted or was shunted to several couples before finding a permanent home. Only one agency baby in one hundred was not adopted by the couple that first received him.

THE criticism that agencies find hardest to take is that they have "too few children" for adoption. They feel the real tragedy is that there are children in need of parents and that there are many who are hard to place because of race or age or handicaps. Then, too, half the children who are adopted by non-relatives each year were claimed by the black and gray markets in the first place.

"But what about all those children in the institutions?" critics ask. Some have even accused social workers and religious groups of withholding thousands of children for fear of losing jobs if institutions become untenanted.

Unfortunately, many of these children are not the ones there is a clamor for—they are the older, non-white, disturbed or severely handicapped ones. Some, of course, are in foster care only temporarily. The Welfare and Health Council of New York City has just completed a study of 4,021 of the 14,585 children in this city

From a lithograph by Kaethe Kollwitz

without homes. They found that for one-fifth of these (773), adoption would be a sound plan—the whereabouts of their parents is unknown or their parents cannot or will not take care of them. But of this group, only 141 are legally free for adoption.

These figures are similar to those uncovered in a Los Angeles study. Both show that the number of adoptable institutionalized children is small. But both show, too, a crying need for legal measures and casework to free and find homes for some of them.

ALTHOUGH agencies get the brunt of criticism for the number of couples who are turning to the black and gray markets, many state laws, or lack of them, actually encourage independent arrangements. Delaware is the only

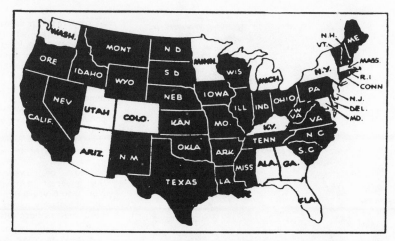

States shown in black are those where there is no criminal law against "baby-selling."

state that will not grant an adoption decree to a couple who obtain a child on their own.

And, although most states require an investigation of the home where a child has been placed independently, this study is made after the adoption petition is filed. Except in New Jersey, where non-agency couples must file right away, this is from six months to a year, by law, after the child has been living in the home. The report would have to be extremely unfavorable for a judge to decide the child would be better off uprooted.

Even more important, selling a baby is not a crime in most states and in the fourteen where it is, prosecution is difficult. Every black-market operation yet uncovered has been interstate and there are no Federal adoption laws.

In addition, although most states require that maternity homes and adoption agencies be licensed, some, like Oklahoma, impose no penalty if they operate without licenses. As a result, a maternity home near Oklahoma City, lacking even sanitary facilities, blatantly advertises shelter to unwed mothers and barters babies for cash, and nothing can be done about it.

THE reason unwed mothers go to such black-market operators or accept gray-market help is that authorized services for them—shelter, medical care, funds—are grossly inadequate and the assistance that is offered is unpublicized or sometimes couched in such delicate terms ("for troubled young women") that it is overlooked. Black-market operators, on the other hand, are on the alert for girls who are pregnant out of wedlock and are ready to provide, sometimes handsomely, for their immediate financial needs. Ernest A. Mitler, special counsel to the Kefauver subcommittee, feels this imbalance in proffered help is the root of the whole problem.

NEBRASKA is the only state with a publicly supported maternity home. All other shelters—with the exception of the commercial ones, which may charge the mother as much as $1,000 if she doesn't give up the baby—are supported by the Community Chest, endowments and other voluntary contributions. This money is insufficient for the space and staff that are needed.

If an unwed mother tries to get public financial aid, she runs into stringent eligibility requirements—her own financial resources (which may mean inquiries sent to her family or at least to her home town) and local residency of six months to a year (though she may have fled to a different town or state). One of the subcommittee's witnesses told how this deadlock caused her to turn to the welcoming black market.

All adoption agencies offer complete confidence and counseling to unwed mothers and will help them arrange for shelter and medical care. But only five agencies, four on the West Coast and the Louise Wise Services in New York City, can provide these services themselves, with the additional advantage to the girl that she need tell her story only once and can work with one caseworker all the way through. Agency help, of course, in no way obligates her to surrender the baby for adoption.

IF, however, a girl doesn't know where to turn, or doesn't find a social agency that can help her or whose help she can accept, the vicious circle rolls on: for want of children, agency waiting lists grow; in limiting waiting lists, rejections grow; for want of hope, couples go where, for want of knowledge or services or funds, half the unwed mothers go.

To break this pattern these suggestions and efforts have been made:

(1) Adoption agencies should continue to examine and evaluate their

standards and practices and, with better financial support, expand their facilities. A number of practices have already been altered. The average couple's wait has dropped from two or three years in 1948 to one year in 1955.

CHILDREN who were formerly considered unadoptable are being placed because agencies have found there are couples who, having a choice, are eager to love a blind or lame or epileptic child, just as they would love a handicapped child of their own. Special efforts are being made, too, to recruit homes for non-white children. Other developments are that babies are being placed younger than agencies once thought advisable and agencies in a few states are pooling information about available couples and children.

(2) Steps should be taken to see how many children in institutions and foster homes need adoption planning. The recent report of the Welfare and Health Council of New York City showed that rearing even the sample 20 per cent who could be adopted, if surrenders were obtained and homes found, costs the city at least $1,000,000 each year. Allocating funds for similar studies and follow-up case-work would be worth while to communities even financially, to say nothing of contributing to the security and well-being of the children.

(3) Better and stronger laws are essential. Because some Federal control seems necessary, Senators Kefauver, Langer of North Dakota and Thye of Minnesota have prepared bills to make it a Federal offense to transport or entice a mother or a child across state lines for black-market purposes.

SENATOR KEFAUVER is also considering a more sweeping proposal that would make all irresponsible interstate placements a Federal offense and would require an investigation before a child is taken to a home, as is done in England. These measures, of course, would have no jurisdiction over in-state abuses.

(4) Services to unwed mothers should be improved, expanded and better publicized. Local requirements for public financial assistance

also should be made more flexible. In Cincinnati, as a result of citizens' efforts, nearly 90 per cent of unwed mothers are reached by authorized agencies and the black market has been virtually wiped out.

"It is good to know," one agency director said, "that in this Century of the Child there are more people who want to adopt than there are children in need of homes. It's a curious twist that this has made our task just that much harder."

November 27, 1955

'ABSENTEE PARENTS' CALLED CRIME CAUSE

ST. LOUIS, June 6 (Æ)—Ellsworth Bunker, president of the American Red Cross, told national convention delegates here today that "absentee parents" were the chief cause of juvenile delinquency in this country.

Mr. Bunker spoke on the last day of the three-day convention that was attended by nearly 5,000 delegates.

He said that parents who were "unwilling to undergo the discipline of making a home and of bringing up children" probably were a "major cause of the nation's present youth problems."

In telling Red Cross workers to adapt their programs to the changing times, Mr. Bunker pointed out that the "average urban family" remained in one location only a little more than two years.

"What effect does this have on children who are thus prevented from putting down any real roots in school, church and community?" he asked.

Mr. Bunker said he thought the concept of "saving and thrift" had been almost forgotten in this country because of "high pressure salesmanship." A large part of the population, he said, "now lives with its income committed for years in the future."

MOTHERLESS—Right, an infant monkey, in the early stages of an experiment at the University of Wisconsin, clings to an artificial "mother." Below, a full grown monkey so reared huddles withdrawn and fearful in his cage.

The Troubled Monkeys of Madison

By LEONARD ENGEL

MADISON, Wis.

SIX years ago a group of researchers at the University of Wisconsin Primate Laboratory succeeded in raising monkeys taken from their mothers almost at the moment of birth and transferred to wood-and-wire "surrogate mothers," contrivances that could supply food and a certain amount of protective comfort. Originally, Dr. Harry F. Harlow and his colleagues at the Primate Laboratory undertook the experiment in order to trace the development of an infant's affection for and reliance upon its mother. Many psychiatrists and students of animal behavior have held that

LEONARD ENGEL is a freelance who specializes in scientific subjects.

this relationship is associated primarily with nursing and the satisfaction of the infant's hunger.

Dr. Harlow's experiment attracted wide attention because the infant monkeys became especially fond of one of the forms of "mothers" provided—those covered with soft terry cloth. Even though they might have to go to a bare-wire "mother" to get milk from a nursing bottle, they returned and clung to the cloth-covered mothers for hours on end. Similarly, when the infant monkeys were frightened they ran to the cloth-covered figures for comfort or "protection."

In some ways, in fact, it appeared that the cloth images seemed as though they might

be preferable to natural mothers: they were always available and they never scolded and never cuffed or rejected the infant, as real monkey mothers sometimes do.

But strange things have happened since.

To date, Dr. Harlow and his colleagues have raised more than 100 monkeys—the rhesus species used in polio work—with the aid of these "surrogate mothers." They have proved to be, however, among the queerest monkeys ever. Now 2 to 6 years old, they are almost entirely asocial. (Rhesus monkeys normally mature at 3.)

A few rage at passers-by from their cages in the laboratory headquarters, a yellow brick building near the university's campus in Madison. Others direct their aggressive feelings inward, biting and mauling themselves. Many more present an unnerving picture of patient apathy. Hour after hour, they sit in strangely contorted positions or huddle in the corners of their cages, seeming to see nothing, seeming to hear nothing.

STILL others, raised in pairs from shortly after birth, clasp each other, unmoving. They reminded me of mentally ill children I had seen in a visit to a Chicago hospital a few days before.

Normal monkeys are highly social creatures with complex behavior patterns and strong group ties. The surrogate-reared animals are strikingly deficient in both respects. For example, monkeys ordinarily spend a great deal of time in cleaning and grooming their fur. Surrogate-raised males seldom groom themselves at all and surrogate-raised females spend far less time at it than females reared in a monkey family group.

A feature of the Wisconsin laboratory is a large playroom "jungle," containing an artificial tree and other play objects and enough space for a number of monkeys to use the room at once. When family-reared animals are let loose in the room, they quickly develop an integrated pattern of play involving all the play objects and all the monkeys in the room.

NOT so the surrogate-reared monkeys. Their play remains at an infantile level. Encounters between them have an almost accidental quality, as though one monkey didn't know what to do when it met another. Attempts to breed the surrogate-reared monkeys have also been wholly unsuccessful; these monkeys—male and female—simply don't know how they are supposed to behave when mating season starts.

"Growing up to be a monkey," Dr. Harlow observes, "is an intricate process involving both ties of feeling toward other monkeys and the learning of monkey behavior patterns.

"The surrogate mother can meet the infant monkey's need for an object of affection. But it cannot teach the infant to groom itself, as the real mother does. Nor can it replace the mother and other members of the monkey group, young and old, in furnishing the variety of stimuli the young monkey needs to form ties with other monkey individuals and to learn to make its way in the monkey world.

"The surrogate cannot carry the infant beyond the earliest stage of psychological development, the attachment of the young infant to its mother. In fact, the surrogate is too good an object of attachment. The real mother helps the infant grow up by rebuffing it and turning its attention elsewhere, when the time comes for the young monkey to begin striking out on its own."

In an effort to define the separate contributions of the mother and playmates to the shaping of the young monkey, a group of Dr. Harlow's associates carried out a long experiment with four monkey infants raised by their mothers and four reared with the aid of the wood-and-wire surrogates.

Beginning sixteen days after birth, each baby monkey was permitted to spend two hours a day with a companion in a playroom containing toys, food platforms and manipulation devices. Surrogate-raised infants were paired only with similar infants; monkeys reared by their mothers with mother-reared monkeys. The mothers were excluded from the playpen.

At first, differences between the two groups of monkey infants were not great. But pronounced differences began to appear as the monkey babies

became older, and then the differences became progressively greater.

AT 120 days of age, integrated play utilizing all available objects and playmates was well established among the mother-raised monkeys. At 180 days, such play was still almost nonexistent in the surrogate-raised infants, but their early contact with playmates had accomplished something; their social responsiveness was considerably greater than that of monkeys with no early contact with other monkeys at all.

Various procedures have also been tried to see whether exposure to more normal monkeys might not help the surrogate-raised animals to learn to behave like monkeys.

In one experiment, eighteen 3- and 4-year-old surrogate-raised monkeys were placed for two months on the monkey island in the Madison zoo. Social grooming and other social responses greatly improved, but none of the eighteen became wholly normal animals. No breeding occurred, although the island's population included sexually active monkeys.

AS surprised and disappointed as anybody by the ultimate outcome of the experiment, Dr. Harlow says:

"The unhappy surrogate-reared monkeys at the Primate Laboratory plainly have many lessons to teach. Without intending to, we have created a laboratory model that can help identify the origin of much mental illness, especially in children.

"In any event, the surrogate-reared monkeys make dramatically clear the critical role of the mother in helping the infant to grow emotionally and in starting the infant on its way. In monkeys, as must also be the case in man, motherhood is not yet dispensable. Nor is contact during the formative years with an adequate range of other individuals, including playmates."

A look back in wonder

By RITA KRAMER

ARE permissive parents to blame for the violence of some of today's campus protesters? Many consider this nation's extremist youth an impulse-ridden generation, too impatient to work toward long-range goals and with no respect for authority or for the past, and a number of recent articles have suggested that the trouble is that, in Stewart Alsop's words, they were "Spocked when they should have been spanked."

Recently, a Long Island reader wrote to this magazine:

It's becoming more and more tiresome and disturbing to read accusations by psychiatrists and psychologists that middle-class parents, because of their false interpretation of Freud (i.e., extreme permissiveness) are to blame for today's way-out, violent, NOW generation.

What they neglect to mention is this: who originally interpreted Freud to these misguided middle-class parents? Who wrote volumes of permissive advice? The child-rearing "experts," of course. I know. I used to read them.

ALL right, what were "the experts" advising parents back in those dear dead days when presumably children still wanted to grow up to be firemen and nurses, not revolutionaries? To find out, we dipped into the pages of some of the mass-circulation women's magazines of the mid-forties to mid-fifties that told millions of mothers how to handle their children.

Children's diseases were still dangerous and a regular summer feature article was the dangers-of-polio piece. A "problem child" meant one with diarrhea. By the late forties almost all the articles on children dealt with emotional development, and psychiatrists and psychologists had replaced

Rita Kramer has written on many facets of child development.

pediatricians as the authors of most of them.

In 1945, the Woman's Home Companion was advising readers of its Child Guidance Series that "when your child has a tantrum . . . lies down on the floor, bangs his head and screams, or may kick and bite, scratch and cry . . . it is a perfectly natural thing for him to do. In most cases the reason for the tantrum lies not with the child but with the adult. He makes an issue over some insignificant situation and the child objects." The doctor-author tells parents to deal with tantrums by preventing them. "Divert the child by saying 'Let's go out and play' or by starting a favorite game." What if it doesn't work and Junior prefers to throw himself on the floor, kick and scream? "My advice," the doctor says, "is to do nothing at all." While the screaming and kicking are going on, he offers parents the comforting thought that, after all, "no tantrum will go on indefinitely," and when it's all over, he cautions, "Don't scold or punish your child. Try to make him happy, do what he is interested in. Punishment will only harm his development."

Nowhere in this glib statement is the kind of punishment that will harm a child's development distinguished from the kind of discipline the lack of which will *also* harm a child's development. There must have been a good number of mothers who put down the Companion with the idea that interfering with any discharge of impulses on their child's part would "harm his development."

The following month a lady Ph.D. was telling them, in a Companion article on "When Your Child Won't Obey," that "the child who has strong drives is more resistant to learning your ways, more forgetful and consequently more likely to be disobedient. It is essential that his impulses be patiently redirected rather than broken, for in them lies the secret of courage, scientific curiosity and boundless energy." We can't really blame a mother who, reading that, is afraid that if she says a firm "no" and stops her tyke from turning the sugar bowl upside down and pouring its contents on

the floor, she will be depriving the world of a future Nobel-Prize-winning scientist.

The emphasis in these articles always seems to be on not breaking a child's will—assumed to be a very fragile thing—rather than on teaching him to control it. A psychologist writing about the bossy, belligerent child (whom she defines as "the one who must always be the marine while the others must be Japs") says he may be suffering from overstrict discipline. Nowhere is it even considered a possibility that he might be suffering from understrict discipline.

To some extent, this seems to have been an expression of the *Zeitgeist*. All during the war we had talked about freedom, and after the war we were full of plans for building a better world. And it was going to be a world of participatory democracy. When the Companion's child-guidance expert advises mothers whose children are deliberately breaking dishes or rules that "what the child really needs is a lessening of demands" what she has in mind is that "If a parent succeeds

in getting strict unquestioned obedience he has a child better adapted to live in a Nazi society than in a democratic one . . . We want children who will choose to cooperate with others, not those who are subservient to the arbitrary personal command of an adult."

The idea that the instinctual side of behavior should be given a freer rein went beyond tolerance

WHEN PERMISSIVENESS WAS IN FLOWER—Time was, parents were told that tantrums were "perfectly natural . . . do nothing about them." Now experts suspect this produced our tantrum-prone rebels.

to active encouragement. A psychiatrist writing about thumbsucking advised parents "If a very young infant has trouble in getting his thumb into his mouth, and seems to be distressed, it's a good idea to help him."

THE great age of clay and fingerpaints was dawning, perhaps in reaction to past restrictions. Everyone seemed to have the idea that undesirable behavior was a sign that what the child needed was "a picnic, a long hike in the country . . . clay to punch, finger paints to smear, etc." Their grasp of the facts of urban family life seems to have been weak. The prescription of picnics and hikes for discipline problems by the authors of articles like "When Your Child Won't Obey" seems about as relevant to many city readers as those schoolbooks about Dick and Jane, their picket-fenced yard and their dog Spot must have seemed to their children.

A 1945 Ladies' Home Journal article on "Preventing Children's Problems" warns parents against "undermining his sense of security by making him feel that our affection for him depends on how well he performs" and advises them to "find something to appreciate and don't hang on his mistakes." Another writer says, "The child needs constant encouragement. Whatever increases the courage of a child is helpful — and whatever discourages, harmful." One wonders how this was interpreted. Never criticize? Never correct? Praise him or else keep quiet? Is the kind of confidence a child would get from treatment like this a realistic basis for meeting the outside world on its own terms?

When the experts advice is least ambiguous, it is liable to be most contradictory. For example, on the subject of how to handle children's fears, Expert A writing in the Journal in September 1946, says to "handle fears, especially ones which seem in danger of being fixed or prolonged, as you would any bad behavior—as something never to be rewarded by attention or affection." But here is Expert B, on the same subject, in a later issue of the same magazine: "It's better to give him sympathy—to make him

feel he isn't facing his fears alone." Who is a parent to trust?

And while one Journal writer tells us the American Mom is a menace ("She is not mothering her son—she is smothering him"), another writes, "I question whether 'moms' exist in significant numbers. There are more youngsters who suffer from neglect because their parents are too busy with their own pursuits than from overattention." Pity the poor mother who reads both articles, immobilized outside her son's door, not knowing whether she should go in and try to give him more attention or go away and get off his back.

Parents of gifted children were being given equally conflicting advice. A writer for this magazine reported: "For each educator who recommends acceleration there is another who holds that such practice can lead to maladjustment." She also informed readers that while "a bullying youngster may have a domineering, overstrict father . . . in another child bullying may be traced to weak, overindulgent parents."

SOME of the advice that was being given in the forties has a vintage flavor today. Comparative strangers called Daddy were returning to many families, and mothers were advised to "avoid shifting your entire attention suddenly to your husband," as well as to try to keep the kids' clutter down. "The Battle of the Bulge hasn't prepared him for the Battle of the Bathroom."

What drove parents frantic in 1946? Then as now, listening to an adolescent girl on the telephone. The vocabulary has changed (did anyone ever really say things like "What a heaven man — he's simply atomic — but definitely"?) but Companion's advice to parents in this situation is probably still valid: "Close the door and try to concentrate on a good book."

Another cause of parental anguish that sounds familiar was "those dreadful programs." But it wasn't television. "Every afternoon from 5 to 6," we read in 1947, "some 5 million children sit before a

magic box in their homes. Deaf to everything else, their attention is riveted on the sounds pouring from the radio." Parents are advised that when the programs are too exciting they should recommend a good book or send the children outdoors to play — advice that was probably as effective then as it is now — but they are also reassured that "these youngsters of the radio age may have developed brand-new habits of concentration." We are told that in their radio programs the kids of the late forties "meet the most exciting characters: cowboys and air pilots, savages (savages?) sea captains and G-men." If that doesn't make you feel old, you are probably well under 40 and shouldn't be reading this piece at all.

The experts gave it to parents straight from the shoulder on the radio question. "There's no escaping the fact that radio has won our children." (Little did they know what was coming!) On the whole, their advice was to make the best of it, to listen with them to some of their favorite programs, and to try to "widen the areas of their appreciation."

You don't realize how much older the young have gotten until you look through the articles about Our Youth in the postwar years. Idealism took the form of campaigning (very politely) for world government; teen canteens were going to help solve the problem of juvenile delinquency, and parents were told, in an issue featuring ads for the year's biggest movie — "The Best Years of Our Lives" — that "today children are assailed on all sides by sexual suggestions and excitement." You look through the illustrated stories, the photographs accompanying the articles, the ads for Ipana and Mum. Everyone is clean and wearing clothes. Lots of clothes. After a while, you get the feeling they're all wearing the same clothes. The picture-of-the-month starred Lassie, and Herbert Hoover was writing about "The Miracle of America" in the space that current magazines devote to the miracle of the pill.

Whatever passed for "sexual suggestions and excitement" twenty-two years ago is hard to imagine getting waxed up about in a time when kids know about—even if they haven't read or seen—"Portnoy's Complaint," "The Story of O," "I Am Curious (Yellow), "Geese", and the New York Review of Sex.

It may not have been as exciting a world to grow up in, but it seems to have been a less pressured one. In 1946 it was felt that "a child should have mastered the essentials of reading by the end of the third grade." Today, parents are more likely to feel he had better have mastered them by the end of his third year if he's going to get into nursery school. One is almost touched by the proselytizing tone of 1940's articles *selling* parents on the idea of nursery schools for their young.

ADVICE to parents of teenagers from the Companion in 1947: "Avoid the I-simply-won't-put-up-with-it tone. Ask what *they* think is reasonable; accept their plan if you can."

In that same year, an article by an up-and-coming pediatrician-author named Benjamin Spock urged "brotherhood on a planet which will soon be destroyed unless there are enough friendly people to prevail." Part of his prescription for raising friendly people: instead of letting a fight develop and punishing the malefactors, "Try to forestall trouble or suggest something else to do."

The emphasis on preventing the outbreak of hostilities is understandable in a world so recently ravaged by hostility, but one wonders if diverting children is always the best thing—if perhaps their education shouldn't also include some lessons in the consequences of certain kinds of actions. How else will they learn to avoid destructive behavior for themselves when we're no longer around to change the subject for them or take them on a picnic? It's perhaps in this sense that children "brought up by the book" in the late forties were "overprotected."

Many family problems of

the middle to late forties were those of the veterans with wives and children going back to school on the G.I. Bill, living in quonset huts and trailers, or sometimes with inlaws. The Journal advised mothers to "Relax with your baby. In these days of housing shortage, crowded living quarters may be a constant source of irritation and upset to the busy mother. When mother and father have to get along in one room, or when families are doubled up so that privacy is impossible to achieve, the wear and tear on nerves may be severe. In doubled-up families there are only too often conflicting opinions about how to care for the baby."

These were the years when "reliable nurses demand 50 cents an hour," when an article on "junk" could only refer to old things found in an attic, and one on "Possible Presidents" included Harold Stassen and Robert A. Taft. And the Journal described "an excellent small home for $3750."

In facing articles in September of 1947 two authors tell "Why I *Like* My Parents" and "Why I *Can't Like* My Parents" (italics theirs), as though the most important thing for parents was to be popular. Needless to say, the reason the second author couldn't like her parents was because they were too strict. And in another issue of that same year we find that "the girl who goes wrong is the girl who is seeking love, which she has not found in her home." Over and over we hear about the child's needs. And "love" is never very clearly distinguished from indulgence.

In 1948 a Journal child-care expert wrote: "The child should have many opportunities to express his feelings, even when they are hostile. These feelings will be less disturbing if they are fully expressed." And a pediatrician counsels, "Avoid making direct suggestions or requests which give the child an opportunity for overt refusal. Instead, offer a choice of desirable behaviors. Instead of

announcing that it is naptime, ask him if he wants to nap with Teddy Bear or Fuzzy Elephant." Again, one wonders how this advice was taken. How, exactly, are hostile feelings "fully expressed"? Does anything go? And how, one wonders, will the child ever be able to cope with external demands in school or later at work if he is given the idea that all choices are his, and the expectation that all of them will be "desirable."

Other words of advice from the Journal in the late forties: "The cause of behavior problems in children often proves to be a lack of love or understanding on the part of the parents." "Try to understand him if you can, but when you can't understand him, let him alone."

THROUGHOUT these articles, the emphasis is on what "parents should" or "parents shouldn't" do. For better or for worse, the emphasis has definitely shifted from the "children should do this or that" of an earlier moralistic age to "parents should do this or that." One occasionally suspects the children might have been better off with parents who were less informed but more secure.

The New York Times Parent-Child editor reported having heard about "one mother who won't even change her two-and-a-half-year-old's diapers without asking him first if he wants her to."

In 1950 the Companion is telling us "There's a powerful new magic in the air. Any afternoon from 5 o'clock on you are likely to find your children in front of that magic box." This time, the magic box is a TV set, but the problem is the same: how to help youngsters organize their time so TV doesn't eat up all of it, and how to be selective about what they watch.

Now the war that fathers are coming home from is Korea, and parents are concerned about brutality and sadism in comic books. The comedy seems to consist mostly of half-naked girls being beaten, whipped, strangled, choked or treated in similarly impolite ways.

Teen-agers were already thought of as a problem for parents in 1950, although they had a long way to go yet before taking over the front pages. According to a writer for this magazine, a 1950 study of 15,000 high school students found only 10 per cent of them felt "There is a barrier between me and my parents." Obviously, they hadn't heard about the generation gap yet. And according to a writer for Companion, "The hardest part in learning to get along with young people is to make the first real contact—to break through the cellophane." How to make contact? "Ask their opinion on current topics. Controversial subjects, in particular, interest young people. You will be refreshed by the phrasing of their answers and often astonished by their penetration and wisdom." (Up against the wall, Woman's Home Companion!)

Another 1950 article, entitled "Be Popular with Your Daughter," advises mother, "Unless you have a sprained ankle, go upstairs and get your knitting bag yourself" instead of expecting daughter to get it for you. "Being undemanding will pay dividends in daily harmony." What price daily harmony?

THE emphasis is on the need for patience, understanding, letting the child go at his own pace, making everything from mealtimes to learning "fun." Nothing suggests that maybe not everything in life can be fun.

This approach seems to have peaked in the years around 1950, when this magazine informed us that while permissive parents reported more damage to the living room furniture, that their children interfered more with adult privacy, and that they didn't mind very well, "they were convinced, along with most child specialists, they were rearing their children in a way that would produce the best results in the long run."

In a 1951 McCall's article co-authored by Dr. Frances L. Ilg of the Gesell Institute, titled "At 2½ They're All Little Tyrants," we are told "to get along with her (or him), try to let her go at her own speed, in her own way, as much as you can. She can't be forced. If you scold or make an issue of discipline, you won't win your point; you only start a battle of wills that may last a lifetime. But if you treat her like a queen, if you bow and scrape, with humor and whimsey, chances are pretty good that you'll both have a wonderful time. If she wants to take her galoshes to bed with her, let her. . . . When you can, set the stage so that she will think she's boss."

The philosophy of not thwarting the child finds one of its most fascinating spokesmen in the author of a 1951 Journal article called "Never Correct Your Child's English," who advises, when a child uses or pronounces words incorrectly, "Don't correct him — he is not looking for criticism. He is making an experiment in communicating an idea; and unless you are intent on wrecking his self-assurance, accept his idea and his new word with dignity and keep your superior knowledge to yourself."

The author of this remarkable advice goes on to say "Continued correction is likely to produce loss of security. The result may be hidden for many years. It may not mani-fest itself until your child is an adult and has to visit a psychoanalyst.

"Perhaps," he adds, "you have never heard of neurotic children, but believe me, they exist." Yes, and one of them even now is probably penning the next great American novel, shocking us all with *his* complaint, which is of course that *his* mother was always correcting his English.

But in the early fifties the pendulum is already starting back in the other direction, toward a less permissive approach to bringing up baby. A later 1951 Journal article — "My Children Won't Obey" — describes a mother who "wanted free, untrammeled children who were not silent and repressed. She had a fear that if she used any strict discipline, the children would develop 'inferiority complexes.'" Well, we have a pretty good idea where she got *that* idea! Anyway, we are told these children, who do a lot of screaming, fighting and having temper tantrums, are so awful that their own father has "even wondered if the children might be abnormal." The author's diagnosis of the situation: "With all her good intentions and child-training reading and trying to follow progressive books, her children have developed such bad qualities that nobody seems to like them—not even their parents."

But by now the new message of the fifties is clear: a return to discipline. A 1952 article in this magazine titled "How Far Permissive Attitudes?" quotes one authority as saying "too extreme a permissive handling of infants and children may be as disastrous in effect as rigid control." Another says, "Children need limits and definite rules." And a third adds, "Limitations and responsibilities are as necessary to a child's social adaptation as is early fulfillment of his basic needs."

The postwar babies were already in grammar school (they're in college now, in case you haven't noticed) when the Journal printed these words for parents in 1953: "In their zeal to avoid harsh, rigid rules, some parents have abandoned all efforts to establish discipline. In these families, the tyranny of the parents has been supplanted by the tyranny of the child. Children need authority, as long as it is reasonable and kindly." Oh.

In the early fifties Dr. Spock wrote in McCall's, "There are many conscientious parents today who are afraid to give their children clear guidance. They think modern psychology preaches that children's freedom must not be cramped. This is a misunderstanding. There is a big difference between not forcing a child to do something that's unnatural for his age and letting him get away with murder."

In 1954 Dr. Spock began writing a monthly column for the Journal, and one looks in vain for the mythical overpermissive Dr. Spock, who on this charge at least seems to be more sinned against than sinning. The earliest edition of his book may have bent over backward to encourage parents to relax some of the rigid ideas of the twenties and thirties on feeding and training, but by the mid-fifties he was telling parents "a child needs to feel that his mother and father, however agreeable, still know how to be firm.

"Firmness," says Dr. Spock in 1956, is one of the aspects of parental love." And thus the age of tyranny of children seems to be drawing to a close.

TODAY most child-caare authorities advocate what sounds like a middle ground between the rigid schedules of the twenties and thirties and the laissez-faire policy of the forties and early fifties. Be kind but firm, we are told. Understand your child, but don't let him become a tyrant. How good is *this* advice? We'll have to wait for some time around 1984 to see. ■

Ph.D.s in the Kitchen

Survey Indicates the Difficulty Encountered By Women Attempting to Enter College

By BENJAMIN FINE

Difficult as it may be for the returning veteran to enter the overcrowded colleges and universities of this country, the situation is far more serious for the potential women students. Co-educational and women's colleges in all parts of the country report record enrollments; thousands of qualified women applicants are being turned away because of insufficient facilities.

A study of thirty typical institutions, conducted by this department, reveals an unprecedented condition—never before in their history have women's and co-educational colleges been swamped with so many women candidates. Not only the big name institutions but even the lesser known colleges are finding it virtually impossible to admit all competent students. In many instances the September rolls have been closed at this early date.

As in the case with the men's colleges, housing is one of the chief bottlenecks in the women's institutions. Filled to capacity, the colleges cannot expand their dormitory quarters nor provide additional living facilities. Many of the housing projects supported by the Government are restricted to veterans and thus do not help the women's colleges.

Probably one of the most important reasons why women are finding it difficult to get into college is that veterans receive priority in most institutions of higher learning. Many colleges report that they are putting aside most of the vacancies for the veterans, even though it may mean that civilians, men and women alike, are to be kept out.

Sons and Daughters

Despite the fewer opportunities for women to get into a college or university, more women are applying for higher education than ever before, THE TIMES survey disclosed. Several college presidents suggested that the GI bill, which provides free educational opportunities for the veterans, is partly responsible for the greater number of women who are seeking admittance. Because the veterans do not have to pay for their college education, many families can now afford to send their daughters to a college or university, using the funds that would have gone in normal times for their sons.

Women's colleges in particular report record enrollments and unprecedented applications from women. In some instances the number of applicants has increased as much as 100 per cent over previous years. Such well-known institutions for women as Bryn Mawr, Mills, Randolph Macon, Mount Holyoke, Vassar, Sweet Briar, Bennington, Smith, Wilson and Welles-

ly report that they are receiving more applications this spring for September than ever before in their history. Thousands will have to be turned away.

Typical of the overcrowding of women's colleges is the situation at Mount Holyoke. Applications are running more than 20 per cent ahead of those on file at the same time last year. Requests for admission to advanced standing have been so heavy that the list for the coming year closed Feb. 1. Enrollment for the present year is 1,149; the normal peacetime figure is 1,000.

Applications Doubled

Similarly, the New Jersey College for Women reports that it has on hand twice as many applications for fall admission as it had a year ago. Because of the large number who are applying, several hundred will have to be turned away for lack of space. Further South, Newcomb College, women's division of Tulane University, reports that it has received 100 per cent more applications this year than in previous years.

At co-educational as well as women's institutions the crowded conditions prevail. At the University of North Carolina 600 women students have been rejected thus far for the Fall quarter—the largest number the university has ever had to turn away. Women students at Bucknell University face an unusually difficult problem. Because of the lack of civilian men, Bucknell admitted an average of 200 women students during each of the war years as compared with a pre-war admission of 130 women each year. The university took over the men's fraternity houses as residences for women.

With men students returning to the campus in large numbers, the fraternity houses are being turned back to the men. As a result the university expects to admit a maximum of forty women next September—only a small percentage of those applying. What will happen to the women who are rejected at Bucknell? Unfortunately, many will find, when applying elsewhere, that a similar situation exists on almost every campus and that former men's quarters which were turned over to women are now being reconverted to men's dormitories.

Whether it is a small New England college, a large Midwestern university, a Southern institution or a college in the Far West, the story is the same. For example, Colby College in Maine reports that three times as many women are applying for admission now as in the past. For the spring term 137

men were accepted, but not one woman. The number of available dormitory rooms limits the women students who can be admitted.

Most women's colleges have a fixed enrollment and find that they cannot expand as much as the co-educational or men's institutions. Smith College is a typical example. Enrollment is limited to 2,000 undergraduates. Although the number of applicants for the incoming freshman class in September is higher than ever before, the size of the college will not be increased.

Similarly, applications for admission to Wilson College are topping all previous figures—thus far there has been a 100 per cent increase over the record-breaking total of last year. However, enrollment will be the same next fall as it has been in the past; the student body is limited to 400

At Oakland, Calif., Mills College is experiencing the same type of record-breaking demand for admittance as are the Eastern institutions. For this semester 35 per cent more applications have been received than for last year; on the basis of present trends, the college reports, competition for admission will be even greater than in the past few years. Hundreds of applicants will be turned away.

Because of the housing situation Marietta College is discouraging applications from women. Sixteen women were admitted this semester as compared with 263 men. Although up to now Marietta has not given priority to men students, this policy is being changed because of lack of housing for women. Campus housing facilities have been given over entirely to women, but they are now filled to capacity.

Priority to Veterans

For the first time in the 100-year history of Marshall College in West Virginia, the enrollment of full-time first-year male students outnumbers women six to one. Boston University reports that three times as many men students were admitted this semester as women students. Co-educational institutions, giving top priority to veterans, are taking the men students at the expense of the women. That is one reason why the students are flocking to the women's colleges.

During the past few years there has been a consistent increase in the number of women students seeking admission to Indiana University. This term 350 women could not be accommodated because of the overcrowded housing situation. The University of Illinois is discouraging women from enrolling because of the lack of room.

Judging from the reports of the college and universities reached in the survey, the situation for women students will remain critical for the next year or two. Many educators are confident that constructive action will be taken once the problem becomes generally known.

April 14, 1946

Class of '34 (Female) Fifteen Years Later

784 graduates report on themselves. They're glad they went to college but are not sure why.

By JOHN WILLIG

THIS month a new crop of women college graduates, diplomas in hand, start off on the road from campus to career; this month, too, another group of college women return to the campus at a time marking a significant milestone in their lives—their fifteenth class reunion.

These are the graduates of the class of 1934, and the great depression; the "college girls of the crisis." Commencement orators of fifteen years ago commented on their "serious attitudes," their "sense of responsibility." As a result of the economic drought and social upheaval shadowing their college years, they could be expected to lead more useful lives, develop into more interesting women, it was said.

Today most of these women are nearing the critical forties. Does life begin in the next two or three years? What adjustment have they made to the ever-recurrent problem of marriage versus career? How has their college training helped them in their life today? And what kind of women are they?

THE following report is based on questionnaires sent to graduates of the class of 1934 of the Seven Associated Colleges—Barnard, Bryn Mawr, Mount Holyoke, Radcliffe, Smith, Vassar and Wellesley. Of 1,654 graduates, about 47 per cent replied, a total of 784. Here is part of the answer to those "stalwart hopes and gentle tears" of commencement 1934, as one class poet was moved to write. Today's graduates, looking to the future, might well scan the record.

The outlook in June, 1934, was bleak. "Support yourself temporarily by any kind of honest work you can find," one woman educator advised. And they did, although it was almost a year before the average graduate got a job. What happened was this: 50 per cent began the job-hunting round immediately; 20 per cent went to work after beginning graduate study, or combined work and study with night

JOHN WILLIG, of The Times Sunday staff, used both accounting machines and typewriter—during the course of five months—to analyze the response to the lengthy questionnaire on which this article is based. He was Sunday editor of the Mediterranean Stars and Stripes during the war.

courses or part-time teaching positions; 13 per cent postponed making a decision and simply went on with their education, half of them never joining the labor force; 8 per cent took business courses to get jobs, and 9 per cent presumably went home and got married or retired.

About one in every four of the graduates found jobs in offices as file clerks, typists, secretaries and general help. Teaching took 24 per cent, sales work 10 per cent, social work 9 per cent and miscellaneous 29 per cent, this last including jobs that ranged from domestic to giving tennis lessons and acting as hostess in a restaurant. Financially, they did not do badly. The graduate worked an average 5.5 years, until 1940 or 1941, before marriage or children ended her earning days, and reached a top annual wage of $1,927—approximately $37 a week. More impressive is the average wage today of those who have continued work without the interruption of marriage, the so-called "career" women of 1934. They are earning an average $3,790, or about $72.50 per week.

FOR most of the class of '34, however, a job was only a stop-gap before marriage. By the fall of 1938, approximately 4.16 years after commencement, the average graduate was married. And two years, nine months and eighteen days later, on the average, she had her first child. The average age at marriage was 25. About 35 per cent of the graduates were married after 25, about 20 per cent before or within one year of commencement and 45 per cent at the ages of 23, 24 and 25.

Today 82 per cent of the class is married, and happily, too. Less than 7 per cent have been divorced (half of them are remarried). From a national view, it could be expected that about twice this percentage of the marriages would have been broken.

How did they marry? Forty per cent married business men; 30 per cent doctors, lawyers and teachers; 12 per cent engineers and scientists; 5 per cent artists, writers, musicians and theatre workers; 5 per cent Government employes, including members of the armed forces, and 8 per cent miscellaneous, in which category are ministers, farmers, factory workers and the specialized job holders. They married well, if one can believe that wives know what their husbands make. Average

annual wage of the husbands, 83 per cent of whom are college graduates, incidentally, comes to something more than $9,800.

Domestically the class is just beginning to emerge from the blanket of babies into the nursery school and PTA world. Of those with children, and 88 per cent of the married graduates have them, about 30 per cent are currently busy with babies. Another 35 per cent have children about ready or attending nursery school, and 35 per cent have children in the grammar or secondary school ages. It may be in line with the national trend, but these college women are reproducing more than is popularly believed. The married graduate has already had, on the average, 2.16 children.

SOCIALLY, life for '34 revolves about the home, the bridge table and her clubs. Approximately 50 per cent mention "visiting with friends and being visited," "informal gatherings," and "friends to lunch or dinner" as their chief social activity. One in every four (25 per cent) lists

Ten per cent find chief diversion in clubs.

bridge as a major diversion, and about one in ten (10 per cent) clubs. The remainder is divided among sports, church work, dancing, concerts and the theatre. Among the individualists, one gets most pleasure from telephoning, one from television, and three from drinking.

IT is probably no surprise to the married women that they drink more intoxicants than the single women. The married graduates who drink, whether "moderately," "rarely" or "only on special occasions," comprise 75 per cent of their group, and average 5.6 cocktails a week. Her single sister, of whom 65 per cent drink, puts away only 4.2 on the average. Altogether, 38 per cent of those who drink usually have one before dinner (3 per cent drink wine), while on the opposite side, 25 per cent average one or less drink of any kind during the week.

Two out of every three of the class smokes, but here the single woman outdoes the married graduate. The single smoker consumes about sixteen cigarettes a day, a married woman thirteen.

Culturally, '34 combines high-brow musical tastes with middle-brow liking in literature. Her magazines are mostly of the "quickie" variety where time and thought are concerned; her books more on the light than serious side. She buys on the average, five magazines and reads about thirty-nine books a year. Only one out of five belongs to a book-of-the-month club. She mentions Time, The New Yorker and the Reader's Digest more than any other individual magazines, and about one in six mentions whodunits and mysteries as among her reading interests. Radio-wise, two out of three prefer symphonies and opera to any other program; one individualist, a low-brow by her husband's standards, admits a preference for soap operas, and only one out of forty indicated a television set. As for movies, '34 is disinterested. The married graduate sees an average 1.2 a month, the single graduate about one-third again as many.

OF much more significance is the disinterest that the class expresses in organized religion and church-going. Only a few more than one-third of the graduates (34 per cent) attend church regularly, whether Catholic, Protestant or Jewish, although about 85 per cent claim the affiliations. About one-half of the group are off-

Forty per cent go to alumnae meetings.

and-on churchgoers, and 16 per cent never go at all. For husbands, the pattern is the same. Two out of three go seldom or not at all, and only one-third attend regularly.

Why the lack of interest? Most numerous were such remarks as: "Don't feel the need for organized worship"; "don't believe in formal religion"; "no service I've ever heard has contributed to my spiritual growth"; "has an untimely approach to current life"; "offers nothing"; "uninspiring sermons." Such remarks account for 32 per cent, or one of every three reasons given for non-attendance.

Among other reasons: "small children" and "tied down by household"—20 per cent; "too busy," "only free day to relax"—18 per cent; "not interested"—15 per cent; "agnostic" and "atheist"—10 per cent; "too lazy" and "too much (or too little) church-going in childhood"—5 per cent.

THE class is almost as negative in its approach to politics. Although about 70 per cent of the graduates consider that college has given them a political awareness, only about 20 per cent take part in politics other than voting. And most of it is in connection with the League of Women Voters, membership in clubs or committees having to do chiefly with school problems. In political registration, Republicans outnumber Democrats almost three to one. Fifty-five per cent of the class is Republican, 20 per cent Democrat, 15 per cent Independent, with Liberals, Progressives, American Labor party members and Socialists making up the balance. And whether it's lack of time, interest or merely intuition, only about 15 per cent of the wives quarrel, disagree, argue or discuss politics with their husbands.

They are more vocal about their classmates. About 40 per cent of the class regularly attend alumni functions of their colleges, but almost all enjoy reporting on classmates seen after a lapse of time. Here are some typical impressions:

"How little they've changed!"

"How the big shots have faded, and the mousier ones become interesting."

"Their improved appearance, poise and maturity."

"How tired we all look!"

"Their failure to fulfill their promise."

"How the married envy the single girls, and the single the married."

"How easy it is to pick up college friendships."

"How little in common we have any more."

"Their hats!"

"How bogged down they are in domesticity."

"How most seem to feel they have missed the boat, and should have achieved more."

"Their apathy concerning intellectual and world affairs."

ALTOGETHER, 34 per cent were impressed by their alertness, adjustment to life, attractiveness and general improvement; 33 per cent remarked about their stagnation, standardization, domesticity, frustration and lack of change except for appearance; 10 per cent commented on how aged or how youthful they looked, with the "how they've aged" a two-to-one favorite; 10 per cent were struck by the number of interests outside the home, and the remainder commented variously on how much remained in common, how little remained in common, how enduring college friendships were or weren't and how the glamour girls had become dowdy or dull, and vice versa.

Whatever '34 thinks of '34, however, 97 per cent of them would go to college again. Only one graduate in five would change to a co-ed school, and about one in seven doesn't know. But twice as many of the single graduates would make the change, given the opportunity, as the married graduates. Does the class plan to send its daughters to the same colleges? Only 30 per cent give a positive answer; 37 per cent will leave the choice of college to the children, 17 per cent are undecided and 16 per cent say no.

THE class is about evenly split on what they consider the greatest benefits derived from their college training. "Intellectual curiosity," together with "the general background of knowledge and culture" and the "ability to think" and "organize ideas," polled 27 per cent and 26 per cent of the vote, respectively. Self-confidence, poise and the independence gained by "the living away from home" won 13 per cent of the vote. In order came "getting along with people"—11 per cent; "tolerance"—9 per cent; "friends" and "social contacts"—8 per cent; "easier living because of degree" or "prestige" because of degree—3 per cent, and "sense of community responsibility"—3 per cent.

Although the class is almost unanimous in agreeing that college was a good thing, about one in five would make some changes in the liberal arts program, either with additional courses or by shifting emphasis and attitude toward the graduate's future.

"All [college courses] gave me culture," says one, "but they did not prepare me for the life I lead now." "None actually prepared me for life," says another. "Only those benefited who planned an academic career," says a third, and "college prepared me * * * for something I am not, and left me woefully lacking in knowledge I now need; it seems to me college prepared me to be another female college professor." The general tone of the comments is summed up by one graduate: "I have discovered in most of my friends and, I must admit, in myself, a feeling of frustration and of having been prepared for something better than the monotonies of dusting, sweeping, cooking and mending."

THE most obvious remedy, say these women, is more practical training, while a few would go to college again at a later age. Courses in cooking, dressmaking, household management, child care and psychology, even in entertaining and "how to have a dinner party," are among the suggestions. One says: "I wish college had given me: (1) a much better social sense; (2) experiences with Negroes, the underprivileged and other classes of people; (3) arts and crafts skills. I now crave to express myself and lack knowledge of the mediums; (4) a thorough-going psychoanalysis and re-orientation of personality; (5) training in practical skills, such as typing, handling finances, etc., and (6) a feeling of responsibility for the world and better understanding of religion."

Illuminating, too, are their replies to the question of marriage versus career. Of the married group, 88 per cent consider marriage more important than a career. About 10 per cent believe the two are equally important or that it depends on the person involved, and 2 per cent "don't know."

Can the two be combined? About 87 per cent think so, provided variously that (1) the children are well along in age; (2) the woman has the energy and the talent; (3) the husband is cooperative and understanding; (4) the career is a part-time one or one that can be carried on at home; (5) there is enough money to secure adequate household help, and (6) the career is kept subordinate to marriage. And they believe so in that order of importance so far as the conditions are concerned. Of the 13 per cent who replied in the negative, opinion was about equally divided—half thought that marriage itself is a career, and half that one or the other would suffer if one tried to combine them.

MORE than 20 per cent of the wives, however, feel that they have sacrificed their careers to marriage. And although only one in six of these say they ever have regrets about the matter, the number who complain about the dullness of the domestic life and the monotony of family routine is much greater.

"Frustrating drudgery, far from creative"; "a frustrating experience to be done with as quickly as possible"; "a satisfactory job, but it can be very lonely, and if you have intellectual interests, very dull"; "this program won't last forever, I hope," are typical comments.

Some of the women have found the solution to the boredom of household tasks in outside work. About 12 per cent of the married graduates, half of whom have children, are working full time today. Only 4 per cent, of whom 90 per cent have children, have found part-time jobs, which most of the class considers the ideal solution. "To find a part-time job, even in teaching, where the need is supposed to be great, is extremely difficult," says one, expressing the general sentiment.

Drawings by Juana Merino.

The girl of '34 has become "a woman married 11 years, her own housekeeper, Republican in politics and convinced of superiority of marriage to a career."

OF those who have found such jobs, however, most have found them teaching in nursery schools. Others work as decorators, work in clinics and other social agencies, or in offices. A few do such individual jobs as literary agent, beauty counselor, researching for writers, book designing and newspaper reporting, and giving music lessons. A few find release helping their husbands in their work during the evenings.

By far the greatest number of the class, however, finds its only break from routine in the activities of the women's clubs, with their luncheons, bridges and study groups. Only one in three does any volunteer social work or community service beyond PTA or other such group, and much of the work done consists only of aiding the yearly Community Fund or Red Cross drives.

The class would like to do more. "I do look forward to part-time volunteer work when my children are older"; "there isn't much time for civic groups—that will have to wait"; "ask me five years from now."

WHETHER '34 ever will begin its "outside" life is a question for the future. Certainly, with 65 per cent of the married graduates still busy with pre-school children, babies and housework (only 25 per cent of all wives have one or more full-time domestics) there is little time for outside interests today. Yet from the evidence there is a recurrent feeling of dissatisfaction and frustration among many members of the class, by no means a majority, however. Their apologies and regrets for "dull," "unintellectual" lives is probably more a matter of training than fact, for they are still thinking in the pattern of their day—when marriage was considered, by the educated woman, a "frustrating drudgery." The note was sounded recently by Dr. Mildred McAfee Horton, retiring president of Wellesley, in an address to alumnae of these same colleges:

"College failed to teach these women that most people accomplish most in the world by working through established social institutions, and that the family is entirely respectable as a sphere of activity."

June 12, 1949

Harvard Law Will Admit Women First Time in School's 132 Years

CAMBRIDGE, Mass., Oct. 9 — Starting in the fall of 1950, the Harvard Law School, for the first time in its 132-year history, will admit qualified women applicants.

"Women have come a long way in the law since they were first admitted to membership in the American Bar Association in 1918," said Dean Erwin N. Griswold, in announcing the decision to admit women students.

"Opportunities for women in the law are still limited," he added, "and the faculty is well aware that many able men are turned away from our doors every year. It is our expectation that we will admit only a small number of unusually qualified women students for the present, at least."

Candidates for admission to Harvard Law School must be college graduates.

As a result of the Law School's decision, all branches of higher scholarship are now to be open to women at Harvard University. The Harvard Medical School conferred the M. D. degree on a woman for the first time last June.

The Graduate School of Business Administration does not admit women, but the management training program at Radcliffe College, under the direction of Harvard Business School faculty members, provides graduate training for women in business administration and personnel work.

The Harvard Divinity School accepts no women as candidates for degrees, but they may study the history and philosophy of religion there.

About 1,350 women who have studied in graduate schools are among the 90,000 Harvard University alumni.

Harvard Law School, founded in 1817, is one of the last law schools in the country to admit women. The step was requested by the school faculty and approved by the governing boards. Standards of admission will be the same as for men, with graduation from an accredited college a basic prerequisite.

A woman teacher preceded girl students into the hitherto masculine precincts of the law school. Soia Mentschikoff served as visiting Professor of Law in 1947-48 and 1948-49.

Harvard's Law School became nationally famous as a training ground for lawyers under the direction of Dean Christopher C. Lingdell, who introduced the case method of study. He guided the school's development from 1870 to 1895.

As a result of the removal of the law school barrier, women graduate students can pursue advanced courses--at either Harvard or its affiliate, Radcliffe College—in the arts and sciences, engineering, law, medicine, public health, dental medicine, architecture, education, public administration and business management.

Women desiring to study the natural or social sciences are accepted in Harvard classes as students of Radcliffe College, both in graduate and undergraduate courses.

The Harvard school of Public Health awarded its first degree to a women in 1936 and women have been trained in architecture since 1942.

WOMEN HELD FACING EDUCATION PROBLEMS

Three men, all college presidents, told 150 college-trained women yesterday that while women had made great strides in education, they still faced many problems.

"Young women are turning away from political and social issues into the realm of philosophy where they can have new ideas without becoming dangerous," said Dr. Harold Taylor, president of Sarah Lawrence College at Bronxville, N. Y. Dr. Taylor discussed "Moral Values in Education" at the annual luncheon meeting of the New York City Branch of the American Association of University Women.

Noting a "new role for women," which demands that they conform to these uncertainties of modern life by marrying younger, he urged that colleges devote more attention to the younger woman, providing more chances for individual development in the first two years of college.

Dr. Peter Sammartino, president of Fairleigh Dickinson College, Rutherford, N. J., remarked the need for women educated to fill useful positions in the world.

Denouncing the "double talk in academic circles" about liberal education, which he said often "rewards indecision with a bachelor's degree," he proposed that general and career courses be combined to produce "the kind of working workmen the country needs."

Dr. George N. Schuster, president of Hunter College, pointed to the difficulties of young women training for careers. "The country wants young ladies who can graduate from college, can type, spell and take a job as a secretary," he said. This is a hard time for young women who want to make their way in a scholarly field."

Refresher Course

Women past 40 years old will have an opportunity to brush up on dormant office techniques beginning Sept. 17. A refresher course is being offered at that time by Greenwich House, 27 Barrow Street.

The course is designed for women who have been out of the labor market for years and who wish to return to office jobs. Training will be given in typing, stenography and bookkeeping.

Counseling will assist applicants with special problems.

Fees are being kept to a minimum, scaled to the individual ability to pay.

Registration will be from Sept. 10 to 13 at Greenwich House. Applicants may also register by phoning Frances Consolo Mostel, director, at CHelsea 2-4140.

September 5, 1956

COLLEGE IS CALLED NO MARRIAGE BAR

Special to The New York Times.

BOSTON, June 24 —The high attrition rate at women's colleges was attributed tonight to women's fear of missing marriage.

Dr. David Riesman of Philadelphia, a social scientist, presented the view in a speech to more than 800 delegates to the seventy-fifth annual convention of the American Association of University Women.

In spite of "good statistical evidence" that women can earn their degrees and still find a husband, a third or more drop out after the freshman year, Dr. Riesman said. He recently was appointed Henry Ford 2d professor of social sciences at Harvard University.

Dr. Riesman said that if "the romance of far-flung possibly unmarried careers attracts few college women, it should also be noted that the images held as to the ideal spouse have departed quite widely from the dreams of romantic love that were popular a generation ago."

The social scientist expressed confidence that an education could be given women that would prepare them for the highest and best eventualities of marriage and career, "while also helping to sustain them if it turns out that family life alone does not prove wholly absorbing."

Even a Ph.D. Can't Escape The Kitchen

NO matter what she may learn today, a woman should never forget that first she is a woman. This is what the current articles on the woman-in-the-gray-flannel-suit versus the one-in-the-gingham-apron seem to boil up or down to.

Latest evidence on the subject is a report from Radcliffe College on a group of women who possess the "highest" of higher education. They hold Ph. D. degrees, granted to them by the college from 1902, when the institution first offered the degree, to 1954.

The report concerns itself with the progress these women have made in their professions. The results, it found, often were disappointing for "* * * few have achieved a position of commanding distinction and leadership."

Why? Most of the women's comments indicate that their sex got in the way of their being scholars.

While the male Ph. D. could retire to the "ivory tower" of research and thought, many of the women declared that they could not—they had the housework to do.

In the academic world, domestic responsibilities interfered often to the point where the woman had to give up her work. Some of the reasons: her husband moved from one college to another and she could not duplicate the position she left in the new location; the university refused to hire husbands or wives of their faculty members; servants were unavailable to run the home while she worked; there was no opportunity for part-time work in the college or town.

The single woman had her problems, too. While they did not prevent her from holding a job, they kept her from accomplishing the extra work that would advance her in her field. Her reasons: she had to housekeep, her budget did not permit a servant even if one could be found, she had an aged relative who took her care and time, correcting papers and advising students ate up the extra hours, she had to spend more attention on her dress than a man, she had to entertain. While some might be termed "alibis," all can be traced to the fact that the Ph. D. was a woman as well as a scholar.

Other Opportunities

Work in the academic world predominated in the professions these women chose. At least half of those so employed believed they were discriminated against because of their sex. They had difficulty in getting a job—then in getting promoted. Their salaries, he said, were less than those of male colleagues in the same positions.

All this was true to a lesser extent of the women in other fields, those working in museums, Government offices, laboratories, publishing concerns. The report noted that in the fields of natural sciences (astronomy, physics, etc.) and social sciences (economics, psychology, etc.) there were more attractive opportunities for work for women than in the humanities (literature, classics, etc.) which often lead to teaching .

It takes a better-than-average student to qualify for a Ph. D. And, the report indicates, it takes a better-than-average woman who once she has the degree, to pursue a career in the profession. She is badly needed in the professions, particularly in the academic world. According to one of the women mentioned in this study, to achieve success in the professions, the woman must:

¶Have a really powerful drive to continue her work.

¶Realize that she has at least two jobs to do—in the home and in the profession. She needs to be tough, physically and mentally.

¶Have a cooperative husband (preferably not in her own field) who is in favor of her working. She must, however, be prepared to give up her job if his work takes him elsewhere.

¶Realize that, if she has children, she may have to give her work up or continue it irregularly. During this period it will take extraordinary interest and will-power to keep up with developments in her field.

March 20, 1956

Two versions of the American clubwoman —Mrs. Banning's and the caricaturists'.

Mary Gibson

Drawing by Mary Gibson.

Inquiry Into Women's Clubs

The charge that 'they don't do anything' is denied, but a lag between purpose and attainment is found.

By MARGARET CULKIN BANNING

THERE are more than twelve million clubwomen in the United States and, considering their vast numbers and their avowed purposes, they are not sufficiently effective. It is possible that, in spite of their increasing activity,

MARGARET CULKIN BANNING, though best known for her fiction, has produced many books and articles on American life and American women. An active clubwoman, her membership; range from the American Association of University Women to the Tryon Riding and Hunt Club.

their influence is really diminishing. The signs point that way.

City fathers are less afraid of the women's clubs than they used to be. Political parties show a decided tendency to keep women off by themselves in separate female organizations. Men are rarely proud of the fact that their wives are clubwomen. Children do not boast to their friends that their mothers are clubwomen. Young girls and many attractive women shy away from joining women's clubs for fear it may type them, or make

them less interesting to men—this in spite of the torrent of good information which is poured out at club meetings, and which should make a woman's conversation fascinating. Even a clubwoman herself usually likes to think that she is rather different from most of her fellow members, as if all the rest were a little queer.

YET women's clubs in America are extremely important, both as an economic factor and as an educational influence. They supply a good deal of the bread and butter for hundreds of lecturers, among whom are some of the most intelligent and informed men and women in the world. They pay enormous sums in rental for the use of auditoriums. They own large chunks of real estate in cities and towns, and a good deal of valuable furniture has been bought for or bequeathed to some of their many headquarters. Chickens by the millions are cut up for their salads and their patties.

Financially they seem to be doing all right. So much so that several leading magazines for women and even general magazines employ special editors to suggest and organize program material for them, and to make the work of many a club president about as arduous as feeding her family out of tin cans. The press and the radio offer facilities for women's club conferences and panel discussions.

As customers they are also important. The fashion editors devote much space to what are called "platform clothes." Some of these are very handsome and some of the women who wear them are really beautiful. And yet a caricature has swept this country and is firmly fixed in many a mind, especially in men's minds. It is the figure of a woman tottering on ankles which are too small to bear her body with ease, wearing a pretentious or absurd hat, and talking about matters which are unrelated to her setting, or on which her opinion will have no possible effect. What young girls, and women with major jobs, and most men believe, as they grin at the sight of that caricature, is that being a clubwoman is a compensation, something a woman goes in for when she has nothing else to do, or when she has ceased to attract men.

IT is interesting to note that the housewife is not so subject to caricature. She may look ridiculous at times, but no one wants—or dares—to make fun of her. The working girl or woman is not mocked, even when her capacities are challenged. Of course housewives and working girls are often members of women's clubs. The odd thing is that a woman may seem more admirable — and desirable — in a smock or a kitchen apron or overalls than the same woman will when she attends a club meeting.

THE reason for stating this and drawing down inevitable fire is that the matter seems serious. We have developed in this country almost innumerable organized groups of women, who band together ostensibly for the most useful and noble purposes. They are good women. They are smart women. They are informed women. Their clubs run smoothly. Why, then, are they mocked and so often discounted? The whole machinery of these clubs costs too much and the women, taken singly, are too valuable as citizens for this to be tolerated. Further, enor-

mous effort goes into the management of these clubs and we should not waste woman-power in this period of American history.

Yet much power is being wasted. Otherwise, why, in spite of all the lectures on foreign policy which are given to women, and despite the large number of women's groups which study international relations, is it true that an influential woman in American diplomatic circles is a curiosity? Why, after women have had organizations for twenty-five years which have made it their concern to give women political education, is a woman mayor in some remote small town still national news? Why, though endless woman-hours have been devoted to the consideration of juvenile delinquency and committees have been set up in thousands of clubs to work against it, were American children terrorists all over the country on last Hallowe'en, and why do judges finally indict parents for the bad conduct of the children? Perhaps they should indict the women's clubs too, which stated they would do something to check delinquency.

APOLOGISTS have said that the span of women's club existence is not yet long enough for much accomplishment, and that it is only a short period in comparison with the centuries in which women had few rights and little personal freedom. That sounds well, and up to a point it is true. But when one looks at what other organizations have done in the past quarter century, it doesn't stand up as a sufficient excuse.

The clubs ask for more time, for a few more decades or generations to accomplish their purposes. But can they have it, as things are going? Is the request a cover-up for lack of achievement? One of the most sharply critical literary men in this country said that he found more intelligent persons in women's clubs than in any other group. The woman material is good. The fault seems to be in what the clubs do with that material.

Women's clubs consume time and energy in prodigious quantities. In committee meetings which must be counted by millions, in listening to lectures, also in inner maneuvers for personal place and advancement within organizations, one cannot possibly measure the time which is absorbed by club work.

From all this effort there is distilled much parliamentary knowledge, considerable technique in group management and a vast assortment of information about many subjects, particularly those related to human welfare. There is also a measure of prestige resulting from the endless procedure of women's clubdom. Or is it nuisance value? The Congressman will not refuse to see a delegation from a large women's club in his district, but he may be derisive

before they arrive and refer to them as "old girls" and "do-gooders" after they have left.

A CERTAIN amount of derision often has to be endured to put over a good cause, and it does not hurt the cause. The first suffragists and the pioneer clubwomen knew that. They braved criticism as well as mockery when they first went out of their homes to hold female-attended meetings, bore down hard on cor-

---

EMANCIPATION

"Sorosis," the first American women's club, was founded in 1869 "to bring together women engaged in literary, artistic, scientific and philanthropic pursuits." Twenty years later there were still less than a hundred women's clubs.

Today, as a result of greater freedom from household drudgery and the widening interests of women, there are 2,000 separate women's groups in one national federation alone.

---

rupt legislative bodies, demanded a vote, got a vote, established garbage collections, put the bite in a pure-food law, insisted — because they knew it was wicked to do otherwise — that children stay in school until they were 14. They drove the panderers to vice out of many a town and in certain temperance societies they marched on saloons and broke bottles. They were mocked.

THE thing that may be wrong today is that nobody is afraid of a clubwoman any more! Somehow, down through the years of perfecting her organization, getting the clubhouse and raising the dues, she has lost authority. The more women spend on themselves and platform dues, on modernizing clubhouses and cultural programs, the less they seem to count as an active force in this country.

"These women's clubs don't do anything!" is a statement often made. It is not true. But it is true that there is a great lag between purpose and accomplishment in many women's clubs. Not in all of them. But often the formal program, or the social life attendant on the meetings, bogs down the purpose of the organization. The members forget the purpose of the occasion or of the food. They have neither the clarity nor the wit to admit and remedy that, and in carrying the banner of a social purpose which they do not achieve, they falsify themselves.

That soon becomes obvious and mockery sets in. Much of it exists even within the clubs, eating cynically away at the structure. If it increases, sooner or later many clubs will collapse or shrivel away. Certainly they will not be able to seed themselves in a new, practical and busy generation.

THE thing that clubs should do—though they probably will leave it to be done for them—is to inspect their purposes and achievements and take honest stock of themselves. Why do they exist? For the purpose which brought them into being? Or has that purpose been changed by the times? Have they functions? Should they fold up and save time and woman-power? Can and will they achieve their purposes and let the chips fall where they may?

E. L. Waldo divided women's organizations into seven categories. They are the patriotic, educational, business, political, religious, reform, rural and general. There is very little criticism of the rural clubs. Those county clubs of farm women, working for State fair exhibits, breaking up the loneliness of farm life, tasting the delight of a city banquet once a year, are worth every grain of energy that goes into them.

The League of Women Voters made a superb start in educating women in the proper use of the ballot and in methods of political criticism. In places and on occasions it is powerful as a critic of government, but almost certainly it is not wielding the full influence it could have. The National Federation of Business and Professional Women's Clubs does fine work among its own groups in many communities, but it has a very guilty conscience because its hundred thousand members are only a small percentage of its potential membership and for this there is a reason. It does not attract enough young women, nor do city business women work together with business women in smaller places.

RELIGIOUS and reform groups, unless parochial, when they do local tasks with diligence and devotion, have also diminished in influence. The General Federation, with all its technical members, counted in job lots, and with all its excellent paper and organization work, suffers from lack of efficacy and is often discounted.

If every women's club were to go out of existence tomorrow, would it make much difference and would this country be worse off? The answer is definitely yes. There are deep human reasons why women's clubs are necessary, and why, if they were abolished at a stroke, they would soon sprout again. It is not only on farms that women lead lonely lives. Women who work at office jobs also seek companionship in clubs. They seek the sense of security that comes from being an acknowledged and enrolled member of a group, and not just a human stray.

ALSO, women more than men, are bothered by their consciences. The woman of middle age, whose housekeeping job has lightened, whose children are not so demanding as they were, feels guilty if she isn't doing something useful. So she wants her club to have a purpose, and if she must fool herself into thinking she is performing a social service when she listens to a lecture on world affairs, she is not dishonest in intention. The unfortunate thing is that she doesn't fool herself very long and usually never deceives anyone else. To the caricaturists she is absurd. They see her laziness, her avoidance of extra work and trouble, her delight in the salad and pink ice cream, her vanity in the new hat, which keeps her mind from dwelling on the problems of the world.

The caricaturists do not see the brains for the hats. Nor the actual loneliness behind the smugness. Nor the haunting desire for a better world behind the vapid resolution to support something. Caricatured or not, these are good women for the most part, and of good intention.

TO defeat the caricature and to make it absurd in its turn, clubwomen must analyze their purposes and honestly follow through on them. If they want a social club, for companionship, let it be one without pretense. If some women want a club, as men often do, to meet semi-strangers, rest their feet, play a game of bridge, have a smoke or a drink, let their club be that and only that.

But if, as is usually true, women feel that in order to live with their consciences they must belong to organizations which work for improvement and betterment, let them work at it. This was the tradition which established early women's clubs in America. It is a heritage which is being dissipated as clubwomen do not follow through to the ultimate ends of their avowed purposes. That is the way and the only way to gain public respect. The comic woman is functionless and futile. The American clubwoman never intended to let herself become such a person and she should not let it come to pass.

April 6, 1947

Women as Ministers: The Pros and Cons

By the Rev. LYMAN RICHARD HARTLEY

SHALL women be ordained as ministers? Tomorrow at its annual meeting the New York Presbytery will vote on that question. And next month at the General Assembly in Grand Rapids, Mich., the Presbyterian Church in the U. S. A. will decide by the vote of its 276 Presbyteries whether women shall be ordained as regular bishops and pastors.

LYMAN R. HARTLEY has been pastor of Fort George Presbyterian Church in Manhattan for thirty-one years. His church is among the first to have women serve as elders and deacons.

(In the Presbyterian Church the terms bishop and pastor are synonymous.)

"Be not the first by whom the new is tried, nor yet the last to lay the old aside," is considered a conservative, middle-of-the-road procedure. The Presbyterian Church is regarded as a conservative middle-of-the-road church. What will its decision be in this matter?

Whatever it is, it certainly will not be "the first by whom the new is tried." Not only do the Society of Friends (Quakers) and the Salvation Army accord this right to women, but the Methodist and Congregationalists allow it, and the Baptists have no set rule as a denomination, each congregation being a law unto itself in this matter.

Nevertheless, what the Presbyterians do will without doubt influence the other denominations which have not yet acted on this question, if for no other reason than their traditional conservative procedure.

So far the vote of Presbyteries over the nation has been close. What the New York Presbytery does tomorrow should have considerable influence on those other Presbyteries not yet voting, since it represents the greatest city in the world and cosmopolitan opinion. A few days ago I was assigned without personal preference to present the negative side of the subject in a pre-vote debate at an open meeting of the New York Presbytery. Here I summarize both sides as I see them and state my personal preference.

LET me first present the main reasons

advanced against women in the ordained ministry.

The first is a matter of women's emotional balance, which many feel is not as stable as men's. They believe that the record of women in public life, especially in politics, sustains this judgment. The word "globaloney," coming at a time when it did, was an emotional blurb that had its natural emotional reaction in the life of the woman who uttered it.

Now the pulpit has lived through a century of overemotionalism, say the folks who feel that today restrained and accurate teaching is desperately needed. The world sits on a powder keg, and not sparks but sober and judicial advice is needed. This they feel, by and large, and with exceptions, men can better deliver.

At the Presbytery meeting I joked about how a woman pastor might come home from church with a couple of elders to dinner. Who else, under the economic status of an average minister (not yet like the teachers under the wing of AFL),

ment for those who believe each admonition of the Holy Writ is timeless in its application, are such passages as I Timothy, ii, 11-12, "Let the women learn in silence with all subjection. But I suffer not a woman to teach nor to usurp authority over the man."

THOSE who favor women being admitted to the regular ordained ministry have very different ideas. They take the negative arguments and pull them to pieces. Women, they say, have in a short time of greater freedom taken their place by men in fields where emotional balance and discretion are prime considerations. They practice as famous physicians, they work as famous scientists, they sit as judges, are Congressional Representatives and will soon get their full political rights to occupy the nation's highest office. It is an insult to her whole species to say a woman cannot keep a confidence as well as a man, say both men and women of the affirmative.

Drawing by David Shaw.

WOMAN IN THE PULPIT

—Or would it be like this?

could or would be there to greet them at the parsonage door but a beruffled husband, hot and anxious from his vigil over the kitchen range, stamping his delicate number twelve shoe when he got the good parson alone because the post-service meeting had taken longer than the roast lamb to get done?

This may be an exaggeration, like the musical moment before the sermon for the preacher to powder her nose, but what about the young married pastor and her children? Must the church be closed for three months for a number of years while the pastor gets her own little flock? Or will the vows of celibacy be ordered as in the Church of Rome? Even birth control has not been developed enough to synchronize births with the summer vacation.

Others think that there is a feminine overbalance in the average congregation now. They feel that women pastors would so feminize the church that men

would frequent it in even smaller numbers. Women will listen to men "tell them off" for their sins, but men will not seriously do the same for women. A man who has been taken over the coals on Saturday night or Sunday morning in his own house by the little lady will not lightly enter a church to hear another woman continue the rebuke. For that matter, say these folks, neither will a woman sit and let another woman preach to her for half an hour with no chance for rebuttal.

AGAIN, the inability of women to keep confidences is advanced by those who think that even a pastor, be she of the feminine sex, would flit from home to home like a busy bee with "the dirt" instead of pollen and what would germinate in no time might not be rosemary for remembrance but poison ivy for the congregation.

Of course, the most conclusive argu-

Of course, there are physical difficulties in connection with motherhood, but these are gradually being overcome as in the case of school teachers.

As for the female overbalance in churches it might be that a few attractive personalities with goodness and eloquence plus personal charm would attract many more men than now attend. Perhaps that is just the reason for any real imbalance in the sex proportion of attendance. Who can say that every male preacher does not exert any personal magnetism he possesses? And, in fact, some overplay this appeal shamefully, as some women might do also.

THERE is a strong point made by those who say that God combines the virtues of both mother and father. It might be that a woman could better depict the former. Just as in the home the balance of family influence is disturbed by removal of either mother or father, the church may be lacking that balanced ministry. Perhaps, say those who believe this, the heavy hand of punishment would be modified in the preaching, by the wooing and winning side of God's love, as the mother's patient understanding in the home sometimes tempers the father's stern unyielding discipline.

As for the scriptural admonitions against women speaking in churches, we must distinguish between timeless truth and local admonition. Again and again Jesus brought the commands of Moses up to date.

WOMEN kept veiled and silent in many other places than the synagogues in the time of Paul, but today they are vocal in all these other spots such as the forum, the market place and the theatre. "Time makes ancient good uncouth." Why not admit them to the pulpit also?

To these protagonists there is one practical reason advanced for ordained women pastors. Many if not the majority of women are home all day. Male pastors are not too welcome or in place visiting these mothers and housewives in the daytime. Their husbands, away at business, at times resent it. But women ministers and pastors could do so and get close to the problems besetting the housewife, counseling her with the knowledge and understanding of a woman's point of view. How fine, too, her tender touch in sickness or in emergencies where a man, no matter how well trained in theology and good intent, would be fumbling and awkward.

I have tried to express the opinions of both sides as judicially as possible. I cannot keep a gleam of humor out of my eye when I speak for the negative. I feel that women get what they want, given time, and will get the privilege of the pulpit and the pastorate in the Presbyterian Church as they got the vote in the affairs of the nation.

Of course, the same arguments hold in the case of Negroes from the South and immigrants from the underprivileged sections of the world. We deny them equal rights because they do not prove they have the requirements that can and will only come to them by the possession and use of those rights.

THE vote in the New York Presbytery will not be so close, I predict, as it will in the whole country, allowing for the backward sections. Women may not win this year, but win they will, and God bless them. But also, God keep too many of them from taking up this new field all at once. Letting folks learn new things, even democracy, is a necessary nuisance. It's like the baldish head I am just beginning to acquire. It's not a pleasant process and some think not a nice thing to have put on us, but I'll fight to keep it.

April 13, 1947

WOMAN PROFESSOR NAMED AT HARVARD

Miss Cam, First of Sex With Full Rank, Will Fill Chair Endowed by Zemurray

Special to THE NEW YORK TIMES.

CAMBRIDGE, Mass., April 15—Miss Helen Maud Cam, lecturer in history at the University of Cambridge, England, became today the first woman to be appointed to a full professorship at Harvard University. The announcement was made jointly by Harvard and Radcliffe College.

Assuming her new position in the fall, Miss Cam will give courses in medieval English history for both Harvard and Radcliffe students. She is regarded as an authority on English constitutional history.

Miss Cam will be the first holder of the new Samuel Zemurray Jr. and Doris Zemurray Stone Radcliffe Professorship. This appointment, open to women scholars, was endowed by a $250,000 gift by Samuel Zemurray of New Orleans, president of the United Fruit Company.

Samuel Zemurray Jr., a graduate of the Harvard Business School, died in action during the recent war. His sister, Mrs. Doris Zemurray Stone of Costa Rica, is a graduate and trustee of Radcliffe.

Miss Cam was born in England and attended the Royal Holloway College of the University of London, where she received her Master of Arts degree in 1909. From the University of Cambridge she received the degree of Doctor of Literature. She was a fellow in history at Bryn Mawr College in 1908.

962,000 U. S. WOMEN SET UP IN BUSINESS

Not for 'Pin Money' but to Help Meet High Cost of Living, Miss Todd Reports

Nearly 1,000,000 women throughout the country are in business for themselves, Miss Jane H. Todd, Deputy Commissioner of the State Department of Commerce and chairman of the New York Woman's Council, declared yesterday. Census Bureau statistics list 962,000 women as "proprietors, managers and officers," she reported.

The high cost of living and need to bolster the family budget accounts for a great part of the increase in women who want to make "necessity money" rather than "pin money," Miss Todd said. She termed the expression "pin money" outdated. Women who try to supplement their incomes by making extra money out of home talents, such as cooking and sewing, no longer do this for "that fur coat."

"Women nowadays," Miss Todd said, "go into business because they want to send junior to college or want a new ice box." Since the State Department of Commerce has published its booklet, 102 Ideas on "A Business of Her Own," 750 requests a day are being received at Woman's Council headquarters, 342 Madison Avenue, including those from European countries, Alaska and Hawaii.

Most requests come from women 35 years old and more. An increasing number are received from farm women who want to market their talents for knitting, crocheting or cooking. The department steers them into productive channels, Miss Todd said. Many women held jobs during the war, so that there were two pay envelopes for the family budget, she noted. However, there has been a decrease of women in employment of 2,000,000 since 1945.

Four times as many women are going into business as in 1930, Miss Todd said. And the occupations they select are as varied as one can possibly imagine, she added. Of 451 types of jobs classified by the Government, women are active in 442.

Among "strange occupations" Miss Todd cited the service developed by a farm woman in Rochester, N. Y., who told the department she always "had a knack with flowers." Now she makes funeral wreaths and takes orders for them, also placing them regularly for patrons on the graves in a near-by cemetery. Another woman went into the tombstone business, selling patent medicines on the side.

April 16, 1948

In Ithaca, N. Y., two grand-mothers opened a business titled, Grandmothers, Inc." Today they have a flock of partners, all grand-mother, Miss Todd said. "These oldsters do baby-sitting for the youngsters of campus GI wives at Cornell University, read to chil-dren and do mending. But they charge extra for mending, even while baby-sitting."

Nor are all the businesses wo-men enter strictly on the feminine side, the Deputy Commissioner re-marked. One woman runs a men's clothing shop, another a bowling alley, a third a trucking business. One "discriminating lady" just opened an exterminating service. And still another woman, who had "smoke in her eyes" about want-ing to go into business, now man-ufactures cigars. When women go after that "necessity money," they are really serious, Miss Todd said.

September 18, 1948

DR. RUTH BENEDICT OF COLUMBIA DIES

Professor of Anthropology Led Study in Behavior Patterns— Defeated Racist Theories

Dr. Ruth Fulton Benedict, pro-fessor of anthropology at Colum-bia, died yesterday at New York Hospital of a coronary thrombosis at the age of 61.

A specialist in the study of be-havior patterns, Dr. Benedict had spent the summer in Europe in connection with one of the most comprehensive research under-takings of her career. She was di-rector of a project, Research in Contemporary Cultures, supported by the Medical Services Branch of the Office of Naval Research and Columbia. In addition to giving a two-week seminar on education for the United Nations Educational, Scientific and Cultural Organiza-tion in Czechoslovakia, she visited Poland, Belgium, France and the Netherlands.

On May 2, 1946, Dr. Benedict was one of four recipients of American Design Awards of $1,000. The citation accompanying her award said in part that she "had endured much hardship in her chosen task in order to give to the world an understanding of its dif-ferent citizens through studies of various civilizations of all races." The American Association of Uni-versity Women gave its Achieve-ment Award of $2,500 to her in June, 1946.

Helped War Propaganda

Dr. Benedict's anthropological studies have been frequently cited by the opponents of racist theories and racial discrimination. During the recent war her researches guided morale and propaganda of-fensives in both Europe and Asia.

Born in this city, Dr. Benedict was graduated from Vassar College in 1909 and spent a year in Europe, where she lived in the homes of Swiss, German, Italian and Eng-lish families. Upon her return to this country, she settled in Cali-fornia, where she first became in-

DR. RUTH F. BENEDICT

terested in the Japanese, Chinese and Korean population groups and their problems.

In 1919 she began her study of anthropology under the late Prof. Franz Boas. Upon receiving her Ph.D. in anthropology in 1923, she joined the Columbia faculty as an instructor. She became an assist-ant professor in 1930 and was an associate professor from 1936 until this spring, when she was named a full professor.

Studied American Indians

In the course of many field trips, Dr. Benedict made extensive studies of the Pueblo Mission, Pima, Apache and Blackfoot In-dians of the American West.

Her works include "Patterns of Culture," "Scientific Papers," "Tales of the Cochiti Indians" and "Zuni Mythology." "Races of Man-kind," a pamphlet she wrote in association with Dr. Gene Weltfish, lecturer in anthropology at Colum-bia, was published by the Public Affairs Committee in 1943. Her most recent books include "Science and Politics" and "The Chrysan-themum and the Sword," a study of the Japanese.

September 18, 1948

LABOR'S PROGRESS IS HAILED BY TOBIN

Further Gains Still Necessary for Good Living Standard, U. S. Secretary Declares

Special to THE NEW YORK TIMES.

WASHINGTON, Sept. 3—Secre-tary of Labor Maurice J. Tobin in a Labor Day message today, noted labor's "great progress," but in-sisted still further gains were nec-essary to guarantee a good stand-ard of living for all.

He said more workers should be placed under the protection of the Wage-Hour Law and urged enact-ment of a "fair" labor-manage-ment relations law "so that road-blocks may not be put in the way of the efforts of lowly paid work-ers to organize." Old Age Insur-ance provisions should be improved, he added.

The Secretary said workers, through a movement that started "almost before the ink was dry on the Constitution," had obtained better living conditions, and "they have contributed to the prosperity of all other economic elements in the country through increased pur-chasing power."

Sweatshop Called "Cancer"

But, he declared, the sweatshop remained a "cancer" threatening the country's economic health. It persisted in many areas in the country, and, by dragging down wages and maintaining a high work week, brought "adverse ef-fects upon the whole economy," he said.

"We need more decent standards for workers and fair competition for business managers," he de-clared.

Frieda S. Miller, Director of the Women's Bureau in the Depart-ment of Labor, in a holiday report said more than 18,500,000 women now held jobs in the United States. They made up, she said, 29 per cent of the country's total labor force.

For these women, Labor Day took on significance as a "planning day" when they took stock of "un-finished business" in the field of social and labor welfare. Miss Miller said, asserting "the matter of equal pay" was the woman worker's most urgent unfinished business.

"Beneficial to women workers in all kinds of employment equal pay and the legislation giving this principle force are currently in the foreground because of growing recognition of the importance of sound wage policies," the bureau director declared.

Thirteen Equal Pay Areas

Miss Miller noted that Maine, California, Connecticut and the Territory of Alaska had passed equal pay laws since the first of this year. This brought to thirteen the total number of "equal pay" states and territories in the United States. Women workers in thirty-six states, however, were still with-out "such legal standards," she said.

In a third Labor Day message, George Meany, secretary-treasurer of the American Federation of Labor, urged workers and "all other Americans" to take more ac-tive interest in politics.

"The enactment of the Taft-Hartley Act and the anti-labor laws in some of the states, plus the pronouncements of the United States Supreme Court making clear that labor must look to the legislative bodies and not to the courts for relief from injustice, has jolted us into an awareness of the vital importance of intelligent and effective use of the power of the ballot," said the AFL official.

Citing the establishment of Labor's League for Political Edu-cation, Mr. Meany said labor's job of political education had only started and the road ahead was "long and rocky."

September 4, 1949

Case (By One of Them) For Women Lawyers

They have overruled male objections and doubts and proved their worth as attorneys and judges.

By DOROTHY KENYON

"**M**ALE and female minds are not alike and should not be treated the same educationally." For this reason, Charles W. Eliot shrank from taking "the responsibility of introducing the education of women in Harvard College." If there were a rising tide in favor of higher education for women, which he strongly doubted, Dr. Eliot had only to say that "if the tide rose high enough it would rise over Harvard." These things were said in 1878.

That tide has risen and, as Eliot so brilliantly foresaw, has overwhelmed the most sacred ramparts of his beloved Harvard. Its citadel of law, the most conservative, the most powerful of the professions, and the last refuge of the male, will be opened to women students next fall.

How has this come about and what would Eliot think of it were he with us now? The subject is worth exploring if only to ease those hurt males (among them a few young gentlemen of the Harvard Law School, class of '50) who still see things as Eliot did and find it difficult to accept the inevitability of the tide.

THE tide, these unhappy ones say, is really a mere trickle. By census count in 1940 there were 4,187 women lawyers in the United States, probably a not appreciably larger number by now. Is not this total a proof of failure rather than of success? Why bother about it?

For partial answer let Eliot speak again, for Eliot was a great man and capable of learning by experience, a rarer attribute than you might think. Considerably later in his life (at my graduation from Smith College, to be precise) he was gracious enough to observe that, contrary to his expectations, the experiment of higher education for women had not proved an utter failure and that women were demonstrating that they could make excellent *assistants* to men. Having a family

---

DOROTHY KENYON began practicing law over thirty years ago. She has since served as a municipal court judge and as U. S. delegate to the League of Nations and U. N. Commission on the Status of Women.

---

consisting entirely of brothers, none of whom I had the faintest intention of ever assisting in any shape or manner, this speech made a profound impression upon my youthful mind and in fact may be said to have been responsible for my unorthodox behavior ever since.

THIS slight shift in Eliot's position in his later years, his walking backward into the future, as it were, gives me hope that, had he lived, he might now understand the present tide and even approve it. Particularly might he have done so if he had learned of certain scientific tests recently concluded whereby it has been demonstrated that, of the five essential traits of a good lawyer, women may possibly excel in all five. None of this information existed in 1878, of course. The great experiment of higher education for women was as yet largely untried; history and science had not yet spoken, and women lawyers, if Eliot thought of them at all, must have seemed to him like a bad dream.

Not that there weren't any at that time. The first woman lawyer had appeared on the scene in 1869. She was rather triumphantly admitted to practice in the State of Iowa under a statute conveniently interpreted to include her under the description of "white male person." By 1870 there were five women practioners in a numbers of states and the movement was definitely under way. But things were not easy. Myra Bradwell, for instance, who was refused admittance to the bar in Illinois solely on the ground of her sex, carried her fight to the Supreme Court of the United States in 1872; but her application was denied on the ground that it was wholly a state matter.

And so the fight went on all over the country until, in 1920, the battle of women for the right to practice law was finally won in all states.

Meanwhile another dragon arose among the universities. People were beginning to go to law school, instead of learning law by reading it in law offices. And women wanted to go too. The pioneer in the East in this field, I am happy to say, was New York University. (Guess where I graduated, and my aunt before me!) In 1892 New

Portia must still work harder to compete.

York University Law School opened its doors to women. It is not without significance, I think, that out of its 800 or so women graduates at least seven of them have served as judges, one of them in the highest judicial position occupied by any woman in the United States (Judge Florence Allen of the United States Court of Appeals, Sixth Circuit).

NEXT came Cornell. Finally, at the conclusion of World War I, Yale gracefully succumbed and has now forgotten that she was ever on the other side of the fence. In the late Twenties Columbia also made a graceful capitulation and admitted women to all its regular law courses.

Bar associations proved to be a peculiarly pesky kind of dragon. Important to the practising lawyer because of their frequently admirable law libraries as well as their opportunities for contacts with fellow-craftsmen and work for the common good, they also occasionally fancied themselves as private clubs and the prospect of women members was in many cases anything but agreeable. Perhaps the greatest battle took place in the Bar Association of the City of New York.

For years an agitation to admit women had been carried on within its sacred precincts by a group of fearless members (among them the beloved C. C. Burlingham), who sought to help these newcomers in the field of law in their fight for recognition. The clubhouse, practically closed to women, had a law library, one of the best, which was open to women for only one day a year. Just what lay back of this particular rule has never been clear to me. It could hardly be because the velocity of thought of the female was supposed to be three hundred and sixty-five times that of the male.

The opponents of change were gradually forced to their last stand. Nothing short of Elizabeth Arden or Helena Rubenstein powder-rooms were worthy of ladies of such note. Alas, there were no such facilities. Eventually the matter was sensibly resolved; women were admitted in 1937 and the powder-rooms, parenthetically, are greatly improved.

While this was going on, women, nothing daunted, were studying in whatever law school they could get into, graduating and trying to get jobs in law offices. Being that fearful thing in the law, a novelty without precedent, they found themselves somewhat less than welcome. But they accustomed themselves to having to work twice as hard as their men colleagues in order, an an eminent jurist has said, to get half as much recognition. Many got discouraged, of course, and dropped out of the ranks. But the hard core stuck and made good (whether in government or private practice, as associates in large firms or in their own offices), brilliantly good in many instances.

The range and variety of their work under these circumstances is impressive.

Rather than fitting themselves into a narrow groove, as some of our Harvard young gentlemen would have us think ("sociology and domestic relations counseloring" are the smug phrases they use), these women are spreading their work, just as men do, all over the lot.

THE real bottleneck nowadays remains the law office. It is to the lawyer what an internship is to the doctor; a sina qua non for the development of skill. The better the law office, the greater the chance for development of skill. Many a promising young legal mind is stopped in her tracks by the reception she receives in the average hard-boiled law office. "What use can we possibly make of you? You'd make a fool of yourself and us in court. We can't work you late at night as we do the boys. What would the clients say? You may be a disturbing element, falling in love with people, and vice versa. We'll have to stick you in a law library, out of sight. In the unlikely contingency that you turn out to be good, you'll probably marry as soon as we've finished training you and we'll have had all our trouble for nothing. Thank you, no, we'll play safe and take a boy."

IT'S a lucky and a nervy girl who can break through these barbed-wire entanglements and serve her law apprenticeship in an even reasonably good law office. It is still the rare exception to crash the gates of the gilded firms, the law factories that possess a monopoly of the big-business clients.

I well remember the brilliant young editor-in-chief of The Law Review of a fine law school, who, long after all the other honor students (boys) of her class had been signed up by these gilded firms, was still drearily making the rounds and peddling her highly superior wares in a market that wanted none of her.

Occasionally, of course, the fears of the traditionalists are to a certain extent realized. Girl law clerks, being human, have been known to fall in love, and vice versa. A friend of mine started her clerkship in the firm of two highly eligible bachelors. In no time both proposed to her. Since she could not marry both (polyandry being unknown to our culture), she was forced to choose. And, having chosen, it seemed the part of wisdom to resign her clerkship. Thus her career ended rather abruptly and a good lawyer was lost through no fault of her own.

HOWEVER, she was not permanently lost. After a brief bout with maternity, and after marrying off the other fellow, she came back to practice law with her husband. This is a common procedure. There are many husband-and-wife law teams, and they work extremely well.

Fears as to women making fools of themselves in the courts have proved quite groundless. There are plenty of fools in our courts, of course, but they are not all women. In fact, women have done rather surprisingly well in this field. Given a clear head and a reasonable amount of training and assurance, they seem to have a flair, a sixth sense (can it be our old friend intuition?) which makes the difference between persuasion and the reverse, between success and failure.

Gone are the days when a woman lawyer shocked the court by appearing in close-fitting trousers; gone even is the shock of the plea which, as solemnly announced by the United States Court of Appeals for the Second Circuit, was probably being made for the first time in history — a plea for adjournment on the grounds of pregnancy. All these things have passed into history, and the woman lawyer, neat, adroit and eloquent, is not exactly a common but is at least an occasional and a sympathetic figure in all our court rooms.

ARE we really miscast as lawyers? There is a growing school of thought, including such an eminent authority as Judge Jerome Frank, that regards the entire field of law as feminine rather than masculine. If the subject-matter of law is human relations, the rules of conduct of human beings in society, can it be that law is peculiarly women's field after all—women who are supposed, if nothing else, to be experts in human relations, women who are the lawgivers, the prosecutors, the jury, the judges of their young, mediators of disputes to tax the wisdom of Solomon, diplomats of the first water and, proverbially, speakers of the last word?

The Human Engineering Laboratory of Stevens Institute of Hoboken, N. J., gives surprising confirmation of this theory in a study which it made a few years ago of the primary characteristics common to various professions. In the case of lawyers it found five important characteristics: a subjective personality, capacity for inductive reasoning, an aptitude for accounting, a large English vocabulary and creative imagination.

"Women," said the report, "were bound to be, on an average, more definitely 'subjective' and therefore more the professional type than men, and to rank higher in accounting aptitude. There is some evidence, although it is not conclusive, that women average higher than men in inductive reasoning. Inductive reasoning is defined as the gift for sensing relationships, for integrating facts, for generalizing.' Such a gift might be that characteristic of women known as intuition."

THE report concludes that "in every aptitude of the lawyer which the laboratory can measure women average higher than men." It winds up by advising more women to consider the bar as a career and reassuring them as to their capacity for success at it.

Yes, the small number of women lawyers means nothing except as it dramatizes the fact that the going has been tough and that the struggle for recognition is scarcely over. Most of us forget what headway women lawyers, with all their handicaps, have already made. Five members of the Federal judiciary, headed by Judge Allen of the United States Court of Appeals; two Federal District Court judges; a Customs and a Tax Court judge; state court judges; mayors of cities; legislators; Federal, state and city commissioners; city solicitors and attorneys—the list is legion. To say nothing of the private practitioners.

Years ago my lawyer father said the words I should like to hear everybody use today. Holding tight to his hand and skipping to keep up with his long stride, the little girl that was me suddenly popped this question out of nowhere to him:

"Can girls be lawyers, father?"

And he answered, smiling: "Why not, my dear?"

February 19, 1950

The Verdict on Women Jurors

A weighing of the evidence brings a judgment in their favor from judges and lawyers and, a bit reluctantly, the male jurors.

By GERTRUDE SAMUELS

THAT reverberating phrase—"twelve good men and true"—is being modified, more and more, by the parade of good and true women into the jury box. Some of the nation's most publicized cases recently point up this dramatic shift. The first Hiss trial was before ten men and two women of the jury; the second before eight women and four men. The first Coplon trial came before four women and eight men; the second trial before six women and six men. Eight women and four men sat in judgment of the eleven Communists in New York; nine mothers and three fathers were in the jury box for the Carol Paight "mercy killing"; for the complicated Tucker auto "fraud" trial in Chicago, six women shared the jury box with six men.

What is woman's worth in the jury box? No true estimate can be made without first looking at the classical picture of the woman juror as conjured up by man (reared as he is on large doses of self- or mom-administered ego). It is a picture tenderly reminiscent of man's general estimate of the "weak" sex, viz., that women are vulnerable to Websterian eloquence; sentimental with witnesses; bewildered and confused by the judge's charge; subjective and emotional during court altercations; unable to differentiate between argument and fact; stubborn and uncompromising in the jury room when jurors are trying to arrive at a verdict; inclined to follow their foolish hearts instead of their heads.

And in sober fact some do.

BUT the verdict, inescapable and overwhelming, of male judges, lawyers and jury officials shatters the whole tender catalogue. There is, those men tell you bravely, virtually no difference in performance between men and women jurors. The great majority serve "as well as men, and sex has nothing to do with it." Women, it seems, enjoy and understand jury work, are attentive and conscientious—and they are just as unpredictable as men.

In fact, this latter quality has caused more than one lawyer to wince. Some time ago, when John M. Kelley, the United States attorney who prosecuted Axis Sally, Mayor Curley and Judith Coplon, was trying a case in Wisconsin, he thought he had one juror who was definitely going to vote his way.

"It was a mixed jury, and she was the kindly, matronly type," he recalls. "She had a way of smiling encouragingly at us, hanging on our words, nodding approval. The jurors filed into the jury room, and for hours we waited and worried. Finally, they came back, a hung jury—11 to 1. She was the one who held out against us. And that," he added, "sort of ruins your idea of the ability to judge jurors."

Women, moreover, are "difficult to fool," especially where a woman's veracity is concerned. They appear to be less moved than men by the large, glistening tears and beautiful orbs. They are largely embarrassed or bored by musical flights of oratory, preferring quiet documentation of evidence (this apparently goes for men jurors, too). And they are often slower to arrive at verdicts "because they are less opinionated than men" and because they have an innate sense of justice.

LAWYERS for litigants in accident and negligence cases freely admit that they don't like to have women in these juries because they fear "pinch-penny verdicts." Jury officials confirm this view; they tell of women's frequently hard arguments with men to arrive at just verdicts on negligence or accident cases. Mrs. Marion P. Johnson, a widow and script reader, who has served on Federal juries for the past eight years, says of the male attitude in damage suits: "The men will take the position in an accident case, 'Well, the Government has lots of money anyway, or a corporation, if a corporation is being sued, is insured anyway, so let's be generous, why be strict with one individual?' And we argue that even if they had ten times the money, they shouldn't pay damages if they're not guilty."

On those exclusive panels—the grand jury—so well does women's performance compare with the men's that "their presence as women goes unnoticed in the jury room," except when sex crimes come up. Then the grand jury foreman may announce that an unpleasant rape case is about to begin. The women may excuse themselves for the case. But they often remain.

Sometimes ruefully, the men make the most shattering admission of all: that women jurors are far less sentimental than the allegedly stronger sex. Some male sources, who shall be nameless, incline to the bold view that women jurors are no more emotional than men jurors; in fact, that women are no more emotional than men, period.

THESE sources, however, draw the line at implying that women show a superior talent for jury duty. (Come to think of it, no woman aspires to that much emancipation.) But it is agreed that, since women have fewer commercial prejudices and intellectual calluses, they "make fewer prejudicial judgments." Judge John Clark Knox, Chief Judge of the United States District Court for the Southern District, who once had his doubts about women on juries, reflects philosophically:

"When it was first made possible for women to sit, I was frankly not enthusiastic. It was my thought that they had little or no business experience and it might be difficult for them to understand commercial matters. I also thought that women in personal injury cases might be unduly sympathetic—that seeing a man in court maimed or on crutches might influence them so that they wouldn't weigh sides objectively. But women's service has proved to be satisfactory and intelligent. What do I mean by intelligent? Well, no judge can try a case without having some idea of what the verdict ought to be. If the jury's verdict approximates that idea, you think that's a pretty good verdict. Therefore, it's an intelligent jury!"

Naturally, not all lawyers and jurors agree with Judge Knox' revised estimate of the woman juror. And a minority opinion goes like this:

Women are sentimental. In divorce actions involving adultery, "women are unfair—ruthless to the other woman and more indulgent to the man involved."

In sex crime cases women are "too tough" because, by indirection, they sense the threat to the security of their homes. In negligence cases, particularly those involving children or the loss of a mother or father, they are deeply affected

Drawings by Doug Anderson.

Women jurors often are slower to arrive at verdicts because they are less opinionated than men.

by an emotional appeal and, despite the court's admonition to weigh the facts only in accordance with the law, they let their sympathies have right-of-way.

But the critics of women jurors say their "worst offense" is their failure to reason abstractly. Accordingly, they fail to weigh the entire testimony and fix instead on one facet, magnify it disproportionately, and make the evidence turn on that. Or, acting on "intuition," or a "hunch," they refuse to take the evidence as presented on the stand.

AN example of this was a murder case of some years ago, in which a common-law husband and wife who witnessed the crime testified. Because these witnesses had not been lawfully married, the two women of the jury refused to consider their evidence. Their reasoning was: The couple were not formally married, so they couldn't tell the truth.

Yet even lawyers who have reservations about women jurors—and more than one declare that they are "chargeable to human nature in both sexes"—like them on a jury, although for the most ambivalent reasons. Some want them simply because they meet the qualifications of good jurors; above all, have perception, stability and, as one judge puts it, "a seriousness and emotional steadiness that will not allow prejudices to run away with judgment." Then there is the Whistler-portrait school, which insists that women are more responsive to their emotional appeal. Or, as one jury official puts it: "You get a good-looking lawyer on a criminal case and he wants women on the jury, but definitely. He knows all he needs is 'one good juror.' He'll learn her name, call her by name during a trial, ingratiate himself, and he's sure he can swing the case."

BUT this personal, or psychological, approach is the exception to the rule. In general, lawyers do not change their trial tactics because they're facing women in the jury box. They may be a bit more deferential so as not to offend the women, and the women sometimes feel "patronized" by counsel's efforts to make legal points painstakingly clear. But as a whole about the only real change in courtroom strategy over the years, trial judges say, is a swing away from old-fashioned hortatory eloquence to cool documentation, even bordering on the unimaginative.

No assaying of women jurors would be worth a peppercorn without some special attention to the views of the men jurors who serve with them. Theirs is a verdict that bears no resemblance whatever to the "battle of the sexes," past or present. No male juror, for example, was heard to say, "Woman's place is in the home." On the contrary, the men seemed extraordinarily anxious to have more women on jury duty all the time. (Could this be the passing of the proverbial buck?)

THE views of one architect, who has served on three or four petit juries and the grand jury, are typical: "I'm not one of the noble kind, and jury service is a chore which I'd do my best to duck. Women conduct themselves as well as men. But you also have a very strong feeling that, because women aren't compelled to serve on the same basis as men—that is, they can volunteer, while we're compelled to serve when called—the girls are out for a good time and the $3. I don't know of any women who are serving out of civic duty, but, of course, I don't know 'em all. Juries need people—men or women—with active minds who are in daily contact with people. And that," he added darkly, "goes for retired business men, too, who get into it as a hobby or pastime."

To this — and to all the pros and cons about their days in court—the women jurors have some reflections of their own.

ONLY twenty states have a compulsory form of jury duty; ten states, all Southern, bar women altogether from jury duty, presumably as unbecoming to their sex; and eighteen states, including New York, follow a "voluntary" service for women, allowing them to refuse jury duty simply on the basis that they are women. That this is an excuse widely used is evident from a survey of potential women jurors by the New York County Jury Division. Of those claiming exemption, 83 per cent gave the reason: "As I am a woman I do not want to serve." Thus volunteers often see themselves as pioneers blazing a trail of good citizenship.

To the question: Why do they volunteer? the women answer: Why not? They call jury service a "beautiful example of equality in the law," but they would prefer it be shared on an equal basis with men and subject to the same rules. Not that women don't heartily agree with the men on their generally good and conscientious service. But they deplore the weak sisters who might be rooted out by a strict selective system.

ONE woman juror recalls, for example, the trial of a man who had shot a policeman. The judge carefully explained that his charge could not include the defendant's background because it would prejudice them. In the jury room—five of the twelve jurors were women—the jurors wholly misinterpreted this point in the charge. The men argued for acquittal and the women allowed themselves to be persuaded. They were deeply shocked when the judge delivered a harsh reprimand, calling them a poor jury. The defendant, he said, was one of the worst criminals and, fortunately, was wanted in Brooklyn on several other counts.

Other women jurors cite petty reactions, born of ignorance, like that of one woman who told a fellow-juror—and carried out her threat—"I'm voting no on this case because you voted no on the other case on which we served together." And many have sat in jury boxes with women who appear to have had the experience and intelligence of an eighth-grade student.

For the "hobby or pastime" criticism the women have a logical answer. At the most, the number of women jurors or men, too, who serve as a hobby, for the love of scandal or sensation, or for the fee ($3 a day in county and municipal courts; $7 in Federal courts) appears negligible.

WOMEN are especially articulate about the lack of preparation for the techniques of what should go on in the jury room. Many resent the "open vote" procedure as exerting pressure on the inexperienced. And many are also bitter because of the number of times jurors are called, go through all the motions of being impaneled, accepted, sworn in, seated in the jury box and ready to hear a case, only to be informed that the case was settled out of court. This procedure—costly to the government but rewarding to a certain class of lawyers who thus collect high trial fees—"certainly leaves you with a frustrated feeling about the high honor of jury service."

Perhaps the deepest impression that women jurors make on one another is the large measure of sincerity that they bring to their service. As Mrs. Thelma Dial, forewoman at the Communist trial, puts

it: "Most of the women who are serving are housewives and as a rule they're not as tired as the men; they have a little more time to think things out in a relaxed way, and those of us who came home nights could do this." And another juror observed: "You'll find a woman who looks mousy will fight like a tiger in the jury room."

The jury system is one of the really great achievements of English and American jurisprudence — the layman's contribution to the administration of justice, and one which must be improved on if freedom is to endure. You are told that better juries and more balanced verdicts cannot be produced unless and until (1) fewer exemptions are granted to men, and (2) women are brought into the jury system on a compulsory basis in all states.

SUMMING up, as the saying goes, the performance of women jurors compares well with that of men jurors. The best evidence of this is in the ways their views actively supplement the men's, bringing more balanced verdicts. Bad jurors—of both sexes—apparently will always be with us, since their names are drawn willy-nilly with the rest from the court drums. But their numbers are dwindling as jury commissions strive to weed out the unintelligent, the biased, the pastime-hunter and the "professional."

For their part, women view jury service as the process of growing into full adult citizenship. Assemblywoman Maude E. Ten Eyck, who has been trying to persuade the Legislature in Albany to make jury service compulsory for women except in hardship cases (minor children, illness in the home, etc.), says: "As women are accustomed to running their own homes, I feel they are worth while sitting on juries for many of the cases in our courts."

The reporter rests.

First Lady of the U. N.

Mrs. Roosevelt, delegate and chairman of the Rights Commission

By ELIZABETH JANEWAY

LAKE SUCCESS.

OUT at Lake Success, where the General Assembly of the United Nations is meeting, the subject of freedom and human dignity is debated by one of the committees in terms of the long-range obligations of the Governments of the world. This is Committee Three, the Humanitarian, Social and Cultural Committee, which has to deal with that fundamental document known as the Covenant on Human Rights, and to issue to the U. N.'s too-little-known Commission on Human Rights further directives on what the covenant is to include and how it is to be implemented.

Tickets for the sessions of the Political Committee — where the Korean questions are debated — are hard to come by. The press section in committee room No. 1 is filled by the reporters assigned to the United Nations and by Washington correspondents who have flown up to cover the political fireworks. But Committee Three plays to an audience of the general public. College students, groups of sailors, housewives and boys and girls from high schools fill the seats, while here and there an observer from an interested organization thumbs through papers and takes down notes.

About the long oval table in the center of the room sit the delegates from the member nations—every one of the United Nations is entitled to a representative on each of the six committees of the General Assembly—with their advisers two and three deep behind them. The debate goes on in English, French, Spanish, Russian or Chinese, and visitors and delegates alike duck their heads into and out of the headphones that bring them a simultaneous translation.

THE eyes of the visitors move about the circle of faces, pausing at the delegate from the Soviet Union, at the Indian representative in her graceful sari, at the Yugoslav or the Chinese. But in the end they come back and focus on the face they know best, the one that they have most probably come to see,

ELIZABETH JANEWAY is author of "The Question of Gregory," about wartime Washington, and other novels with current themes.

the face of the representative of the United States whose name is Mrs. Franklin D. Roosevelt.

Everyone knows what she looks like: she looks like your favorite aunt. Her clothes and her coiffure both express the truth that it is a great nuisance to be fashionable, and also a nuisance to be at odds with fashion. Her mannerisms are those of a younger and much less important woman. They are endearing because they betray that she is shy and that she is determined to pay as little attention as possible to the distraction of her shyness.

The apologetic little laugh, which occasionally breaks her speeches, is maddening to unsympathetic ears. It is a relic of her past. Once, it can have been her only refuge when confronted with a world which was not as good as she would have liked it to be. The world is still not as good as she would like it to be, but now she has other resources with which to meet it. The laugh is a habit that her mind but not her body has outgrown. Enormously inappropriate to the present, it is a reminder that the only member of the United States delegation who has served at every session of the United Nations was once a sheltered upper-class woman who disliked and dreaded public appearances.

MRS. ROOSEVELT is the chairman of the Commission on Human Rights whose work on a draft covenant is to be considered by Committee Three. This is a body appointed by the Economic and Social Council of the U. N. (not to be confused with Unesco, which is a separate but affiliated body with its own delegates). The first duty of the commission was to draw up a Declaration of Human Rights, and this it has done. After some two years of struggling over the principles of contemporary ethics and the minutiae of wording, the Universal Declaration of Human Rights was accepted by the General Assembly in December, 1948. The principles of the declaration have already borne fruit, for both the Indian and Indonesian Constitutions have modeled themselves after it, and it has been referred to in decisions by the Federal courts of the United States.

This, then, is Mrs. Roosevelt's biggest job: to bring down to earth the ideals of the Declaration of Human Rights and contrive, by the lengthy process of discussion and compromise, by bickering and by vote, to get them woven by her committee into an implementation which will be accepted by the United Nations as a whole and by each of the nations singly.

At her job she is untiring. When she first sat as chairman of her commission, she was unfamiliar with parliamentary procedure and was inclined to think common sense an adequate

substitute for Robert's "Rules of Order." This was a naive, if good-hearted, view. She has since got over it and is quite capable of quoting the procedural rules of the United Nations from memory.

She quoted them last spring with great firmness to Mr. Tsarapkin, the Russian delegate, who appeared briefly at the first meeting of the session of the Human Rights Commission.

IT was Mr. Tsarapkin's not unexpected desire to have the delegate from Nationalist China expelled and a representative of the Chinese Communist Government seated in his place. Mrs. Roosevelt ruled that he could present his resolution only on a point of order, which she then overruled on the grounds that, since Dr. Chang had been confirmed in his place by the Economic and Social Council, he could be removed only by this body and not by the Human Rights Commission itself.

She quoted to Mr. Tsarapkin the rule by which he could appeal to a majority of the commission to overrule the chairman's decision. The vote sustained her, and Mr. Tsarapkin, who consistently addressed Mrs. Roosevelt as "Mr. Chairman," launched into a passionate oration. This accused the Nationalist Chinese of numerous crimes, the American Government of aiding and abetting them, and Mrs. Roosevelt specifically of using her position as chairman of the group for political purposes.

In the middle of this denunciation Mrs. Roosevelt's gavel came down with a crack, and it was seen that she could lose her temper with great effect. "I am sorry, sir," she said. "We are now going to proceed with the election of officers. This is no place for propaganda speeches and I must ask you to draw your remarks to a close."

The formality of her speech was matched by the fury in her voice. Then, in a moment or two, she regained her composure and, on Mr. Tsarapkin's request, allowed him to continue to the end, when he and his Ukrainian colleague walked out.

AT the General Assembly Mrs. Roosevelt is able to divide the work to be covered at this session with the distinguished Negro lawyer, Mrs. Edith Sampson, who is also a delegate to Committee Three. Still, the volume of what she must get through is enormous. Mrs. Sampson herself says that she has learned from Mrs. Roosevelt the techniques of concentration and of program-

ming that enable her to handle her responsibilities.

In the daily meetings of the United States delegation Mrs. Roosevelt does not confine her attention to questions before Committee Three. She is au courant with the problems of the Budgetary, Economic, and Political Committees and does not hesitate to comment upon them.

These "briefing" sessions take place before and after meetings, and Mrs. Roosevelt's day will often include a morning session at the United States delegation's offices in New York, continuing in the delegation car on the way to Lake Success, two commission meetings at U. N. headquarters and further discussion in the late afternoon before she goes to a dinner, where she is likely to speak on her work at the United Nations.

NOR are her lunch hours periods of relaxation. The U.N. staff, which used to assemble in awe to watch her pass in the corridor, has got used to seeing her hurry into the delegates' lounge, drop a stuffed briefcase on the most convenient chair and plunge on through toward the cafeteria, where she stands in line to be served, holding her own tray and waiting her turn. Then, if she has time, she will return to the lounge (she has no other office at Lake Success) to meet and talk to a group of students or the members of some organization before the afternoon meeting of the commission. Now that she has added a daily radio program to her schedule, her closest friends are awestruck at the scope of her activities.

This is part and parcel, however, of what she considers a vital part of her job. She is out to cure the country, so far as it is humanly possible for her to do so, of its ignorance about the United Nations and particularly about the great question of human rights. The indefatigable energy which sent her, when she was First Lady, down mines and into hospitals now dispatches her to every speaking engagement she can manage to squeeze in. Convinced, devoted, tireless, endlessly available, she is a symbol of hope for progress throughout the world.

SHE does not particularly like to be a symbol and, indeed, denies that she is one in her own right. "All that," she says, with a touch of embar-

Mrs. Roosevelt explains the workings of the United Nations to a group of visitors at Lake Success.

rassment and distaste at the mention of her prestige, "all that is because people associate with me what my husband meant to them." For herself, if her work could be done as effectively without it, she would be glad to dispense with any symbolic value she may have in the world's eyes.

Mrs. Roosevelt not only believes that privilege is morally wrong; she actively dislikes to be, herself, in a privileged position. Such a feeling is sometimes confused with modesty, or even humility, but it is in truth something much closer to pride; to the kind of pride which believes that using advantages is a sign of weakness, and that to start even with the world and still win out is the greatest achievement possible to a privileged person.

Not that Mrs. Roosevelt denies the usefulness of prestige. She has not always agreed with the instructions from Washington to the United States delegation, and she has carried her arguments to the Secretary of State and to the President on more than one occasion. When she arrived in Paris for the General Assembly late in 1948 she discovered that the United States position on Spain was one with which she disagreed. She presented her arguments against a softening at that time of our attitude toward Franco with great cogency. Senator Austin reported them to the American Government and the United States position returned to its original stiffness.

SHE is alert, too, to the uses of the advisers who sit behind her at meetings. Soviet Foreign Minister Vishinsky once launched into a lengthy speech which included a listing of what he described as American concentration camps. Mrs. Roosevelt noted them down and handed the list to one of her aides who rushed out to phone Washington. By the end of Mr. Vishinsky's oration Mrs. Roosevelt had a report from the Army on the locations mentioned—which had been prisoner-of-war camps, most of them closed.

In her own commission she has used a simple maneuver to cut down the length of speeches. "Have you ever noticed," she will remark with an air of ingenuousness to a long-winded speaker, "about when it is that people begin to remove their headphones? It takes about ten minutes of any speaker's time." Yet her attitude in the chair is one of generous encouragement. "Yes? Yes?" she will say, as if this at last—whatever the subject, whoever the speaker—were bringing her final clarification. "I felt as if she had been waiting all day for me to speak," one delegate said.

THE Russians, of course, with their invective, their accusals and their stereotyped denunciations, are a special problem. By the end of the 1949 session of the Commission on Human Rights Mrs. Roosevelt had more or less worked out a basic formula for dealing with them. Whenever she could ignore the rhetoric and charges with which they prolonged the debate she did so, and spoke merely to the point of whatever their actual suggestions for the drafting of the Covenant might be. She had certainly begun her work at the U. N. by attempting to meet the Soviet delegates halfway, but by 1949 she was ready to state publicly that she would never again try to compromise with them.

As for the Soviet Government itself, it had definitely changed its expressed opinion of Mrs. Roosevelt. The Russians began by calling her nothing worse than a "school teacher" (she replied that she was proud to be regarded as a member of the teaching profession), and even two years ago they were willing to appeal to her, in the name of her husband, to cease advocating "imperialism." Such temperance has stopped, however, and Izvestia later referred to her as a "hypocritical servant of capitalism . . . a fly darkening the Soviet sun." In Paris, late in 1948, a Russian delegate was heard to mutter some words in the heat of debate which seemed to characterize Mrs. Roosevelt as a meddling old woman.

AN observer was forcefully reminded of Stalin's projected plan for dealing with Lenin's widow, Krupskaya. That unhappy lady was more inclined to Trotsky's view than to Stalin's and for some little time made no bones about saying so. "If that old woman doesn't shut up," Stalin is said to have remarked, "I'll appoint someone else Lenin's widow." There is no doubt he would like to have the power to appoint someone else Franklin D. Roosevelt's widow.

Actually Mrs. Roosevelt herself is undoubtedly pleased to have Mrs. Sampson, a younger woman, associated with her and has said that eventually she must withdraw. But in the meantime she must speak for the United States in Committee Three and on the Human Rights Commission. This

is not always simple. As United States delegate, of course, she must always remember those operative words, "two-thirds of the Senate." A covenant on human rights which is not ratified by the United States Senate will not be a covenant at all, either to America or, practically speaking, to the world at large. No one west of the Iron Curtain can doubt Mrs. Roosevelt's firm adherence to the humanitarian statements of the Declaration of Human Rights. But it is just this adherence to principle which makes her advocate practical compromise.

THE United States point of view has thus far excluded from the Covenant of Human Rights economic and social rights, such as the promise of unemployment insurance or material benefits. It has, moreover, restricted very sharply the bringing of petitions for redress against violators of the covenant. Such petitions cannot be presented by distressed individuals, or by organizations representing them, no matter how large a group the organization represents. They can be brought only by national Governments signatory to the covenant.

This puts a wronged human being, whether he be a Czech Democrat, a South African Negro, or a California Japanese subject to the Alien Land Law, in the position of having to discover another national Government willing to bring a case in his behalf against his own Government. To many, such restrictions seem to narrow the covenant to farcical limits; and worse, to invite the bringing of cases as political propaganda. Why does Mrs. Roosevelt support such a position?

MRS. ROOSEVELT recognizes both the force and familiarity of this criticism. But she replies on pragmatic grounds. If individual, or even organizational, petitions were permitted, she says, any apparatus for dealing with violations under the covenant would be swamped. "As it is," she points out, "we have letters from people complaining about their rent being raised."

Mrs. Roosevelt goes on to say that she sees this covenant as a first covenant; as a step to be taken so that more can follow. Let us get this covenant ratified — and here the words "two-thirds of the Senate" almost appear in the air over her head—let us take this first step, and then we can go on to work on covenants which can include social and economic rights; to plan for the acceptance first of organizational petitions and then of individual pleas.

Thus she and her critics meet head-on in this ancient philosophic dilemma of ends and means. Mrs. Roosevelt is for means, for the pragmatic approach so typical of American thought. She is for action. Let us do as much as we can, she believes, and, if we cannot do all we want at once, what we do will be better than nothing. Surely we can win the trust of the oppressed millions of the world by honest effort in their behalf, even though our accomplishments at first must be disappointing.

IN the formulation of public policy Mrs. Roosevelt will never play the role of Caesar's wife and be content to keep herself above criticism by folding her hands and sitting still; and to expect her to prefer her value as a symbol above the human effort of hands, heart and head is to misjudge her entirely. She is at bottom an optimist who believes that "there can be an infinite variety of method, but the objective everywhere is the same. How can you build a world in which all men get a chance for full development of themselves as individuals, and for a better surrounding in which to achieve that end?"

It is because she is an optimist that she is willing to move slowly—she is convinced that the desired end exists ideally, waiting to be achieved. It is because she does actually believe in progress that she can see, in the perspective of her view, this Covenant, and, later, more liberal covenants, as steps toward an ultimate goal.

205,000 U. S. NURSES ARE NOT WORKING

Third of Profession Inactive, Association Says—Better Pay in West Lures Many

Almost a third of the registered nurses in the United States were not working at their profession when the nation began its post-Korea speed-up in mobilization and preparations for civil defense, the American Nursing Association reported yesterday.

This "inactive reserve" accounted for 205,000 of a total of 506,000 registered professional nurses in 1949, it was disclosed in the new edition of the association's "Facts About Nursing."

Describing this reserve that the country might draw upon, the report said that 87 per cent of the inactive nurses were married. A third of them were between 20 and 29 years old and 38 per cent were from 30 to 39 years old.

In 1950, the association estimated in answer to a query, the number of active nurses increased to 322,000.

About 100,000 students were enrolled in schools of nursing in 1950, as compared with 127,000 at the end of World War II. Three thousand of those enrolled last year were Negroes, compared with 2,300 in 1946.

Although most of the figures in the report were for 1949 or the first six months of 1950, the association suggested that they offered necessary basic data "in view of the urgent need for mobilization of nursing resources for both military and civilian services."

New York State had the most registered nurses in 1949, 68,000, with 44,000 active. By August, 1950, the total had declined to 66,000, the New York State Nurses Association said.

California, with 59,000 nurses and 33,000 of them active, was second. The report, in fact, indicated a definite movement of nurses to the West, and, to a lesser degree, to the South, particularly Florida.

Explaining the marked attraction of the West for nurses, Miss Annie Laurie Crawford, assistant executive secretary of the association said: "They're a little farther advanced out there in their thinking, their programs and their pay checks—and nurses, angels though they may be, do follow the pay checks."

The monthly pay checks for hospital nurses living outside averaged $226 in the Pacific states. The national average was $211. In the New York-New Jersey-Pennsylvania area it was $206; in New England, $191. Public health nurses averaged $282 in the Pacific states, $225 in this area and $211 in New England. The Pacific averages for industrial nurses and office nurses were higher, too. In addition, the forty-hour week was more prevalent in the West than elsewhere.

Women Bankers

In few fields have women been more successful than in banking. They have long demonstrated their ability to handle many phases of this complex business. As a result, their progress has been rapid. Ninety-six women are now presidents of banks; twenty-five are board chairmen and six are in the "owner or partner" end of banks. The Association of Bank Women recently announced that of 6,013 women who hold offices in banks, 337 are vice presidents and several thousand junior officers.

May 5, 1951

Elizabeth Gurley Flynn Faces Jail After Double Contempt at Red Trial

Elizabeth Gurley Flynn, Communist party national committee member, was cited twice yesterday by Federal Judge Edward Dimock for contempt for refusing to answer questions under cross-examination in the Communist conspiracy trial.

Judge Dimock imposed thirty-day sentences to run concurrently. When defense counsel pleaded that Miss Flynn's immediate imprisonment would work a grave hardship in the preparation of her defense, Judge Dimock postponed serving of sentence until after Miss Flynn has completed her testimony.

Miss Flynn, who has been on the witness stand for twenty-six days in the seven-month-long trial, is one of thirteen secondary Communist leaders charged with conspiracy to teach and advocate violent overthrow of the Government.

Judge Dimock told Miss Flynn she could purge herself of the contempts by answering the questions before she completes her testimony. The witness said that as a matter of principle she doubted that she would ever answer the questions.

The contempts developed when David Marks, special assistant United States Attorney, asked the witness to identify two individuals he named. She refused and charged that the Government was attempting to make her a "stool pigeon" by identifying individuals as Communists.

Miss Flynn balked for the first time when asked about a Clara Bodian, not further identified by the Government. Mr. Marks asked: "Did she ever participate in the meetings of the National Women's Commission of the Communist party?"

"I can't answer that question," the witness replied.

"Do you refuse to answer that question?" Judge Dimock asked.

"I invoke my rights under the First, Fourth and Fifth Amendments."

"I direct you to answer the question."

"I'm sorry, I can't answer it."

The jury was then excused and United States Attorney Myles J. Lane asked the court to adjudge Miss Flynn in contempt. Judge Dimock immediately held Miss Flynn in contempt and imposed the thirty-day sentence.

When defense counsel tried to delay immediate imposition of the sentence, Judge Dimock said he saw "no reason why we should delay," adding that "it was unrealistic to postpone commitment — the purpose of commitment is to obtain the answer."

The jury was then recalled and Mr. Marks continued his cross-examination. A half hour later the prosecutor asked Miss Flynn: "Do you know Lou Diskin?"

Again Miss Flynn refused to answer when directed by Judge Dimock, and in the absence of the jury she was cited for the second contempt.

"I'm very sorry, but I cannot identify people as Communists," she said, and again invoked her Constitutional privilege, basing her refusal to answer on her desire "not to degrade or debase myself by becoming an informer."

At the end of the court session, defense counsel said it was important to be able to confer with Miss Flynn nightly while she was still on the stand. Judge Dimock said he was "impressed" by the argument and postponed the commitment. Miss Flynn has been free in $10,000 bail.

November 20, 1952

Mrs. Luce Is Sworn In as 'Ambasciatrice' to Italy

Special to The New York Times.

WASHINGTON, March 3— Mrs. Clare Boothe Luce took the oath of office today as Ambassador to Italy. The former Republican Representative and playwright was sworn in by Fred M. Vinson, Chief Justice of the United States, in the office of John Foster Dulles, Secretary of State.

Mr. Dulles, confronting a battery of photographers, reporters, newsreel and television camera men, and an audience of officials and well-wishers estimated at about a hundred, observed that Mrs. Luce would be the first woman in the United States diplomatic corps to hold a post of such responsibility.

"The President and all who know you," the Secretary said, "realize that you will not only discharge your new responsibilities well, but will go even beyond that."

Mrs. Luce, who is the wife of Henry R. Luce, editor of Time, Life and Fortune, said after the ceremony that it was "naturally a very high honor and great responsibility to represent the United States in Italy, especially at a time when Italy and her decisions count so heavily in the world's scales."

"I hope with God's help successfully to pursue the continuing mission of American Ambassadors —to strengthen our bonds with Italy—economic, political and spiritual, which have knit us so closely together since the time of Christopher Columbus," she declared.

Among those on hand to congratulate her were Alberto Tarchiani, Italian Ambassador to the United States, who said that Mrs. Luce would be called "Ambasciatrice," which in Italian is Ambassadress, rather than Mme. Ambassador.

"I hope its the worst I'll be called," Mrs. Luce replied.

Mrs. Luce's only predecessor as a "madam ambassador" in the United States diplomatic service was Mrs. Eugenie Anderson, who was named Ambassador to Denmark by President Truman.

Mrs. Luce is scheduled to arrive in Rome in April and thus will be on hand for the Italian elections, set for May. She will succeed Ellsworth Bunker as United States Ambassador.

The White House announced this afternoon that the President would send to the Senate tomorrow the nomination of Douglas MacArthur 2d as counselor of the State Department. He would succeed Charles E. Bohlen, whose nomination as Ambassador to Russia is pending before the Senate Foreign Relations Committee.

Mr. MacArthur is a nephew of General of the Army Douglas MacArthur and, like Mr. Bohlen, is a career diplomat. He is now special assistant to Gen. Matthew B. Ridgway, Supreme Allied Commander in Europe. He was born in Bryn Mawr, Pa., on July 5, 1909, was graduated from Yale University in 1932 and entered the Foreign Service on Oct. 1, 1935. Mr. MacArthur's appointment had been forecast recently.

March 4, 1953

WORKING MOTHERS CALLED HARMFUL

Catholic Conference Warns on 'Millions' of Women Who Help Destroy the Home

By GEORGE DUGAN
Special to The New York Times,

NEW ORLEANS, March 26— A high proportion of working mothers were accused here today of acting to destroy the American home.

A resolution approved at the closing session of the three-day National Catholic Family Life, Conference asserted that "untold millions of married women are actually helping in the destruction of the very homes they seek to serve", by obtaining employment on the "frequently false plea of economic need."

The conference was also critical of young married couples who postpone having families on the ground that they need time to pay accumulated bills.

Delinquency Link Seen

Mothers who "desert" their homes and leave small children uncared for while they compete in the labor market were cited as contributing factors in the increase of juvenile delinquency.

However, to the many widows and women in the lower income brackets who are forced to seek work outside the home the delegates offered "our prayers, our sympathy, and the hope that society will not only recognize their plight but will take active steps to help them in their economic need."

The resolution noted that working women had played an important role in advancing the wealth of the country, but asserted that, "the price in the shape of moral and spiritual ruin is much too high."

Other resolutions reaffirmed pleas for a Government-sponsored national family welfare program, urged wide establishment of parish and other credit unions and approved the organization of "consumer economic" courses to provide for families information on how to lead a "balanced economic life."

The conference closed tonight with a family Holy Hour and ceremony of renewal of marriage vows in St. Louis Roman Catholic Cathedral. Catholic Mother Awards were presented to three members of the archdiocese, Mrs. Philip Cazale, mother of seven children, four of whom are nuns; Mrs. J. Andrew Bahlinger, mother of nine children, two of whom are Jesuit priests, and Mrs. Ethel Johnson Young, mother of four.

March 27, 1954

ATTITUDE OF U. S. ON WOMEN SCORED

Education and Use in Jobs Are on 'Contingency Basis,' Federal Parley Is Told

By BESS FURMAN
Special to The New York Times,

WASHINGTON, March 10— A woman anthropologist told a Labor Department conference on womanpower today that women still only partly "participate in the main stream of American society."

Dr. Florence Rockwood Kluckhohn of the Harvard University Department of Social Relations said that American women were educated and employed on a "contingency basis" to be ready to work "in an emergency which the men hope won't happen."

"This is psychologically ridiculous," she declared in a panel discussion on "Horizons for Women."

The discussion followed a speech by the Secretary of Labor, James P. Mitchell, and Dr. Kluckhohn made it clear that her comment had reference to the speech.

Mr. Mitchell predicted that women would be asked to do jobs in which they had little chance today.

"As we move into the atomic age," he said, "we feel our nation's work force is not adequate in terms of skills to meet the demands to be made on it."

Planning Called Duty

He asserted that there were few skilled women in the work force and prescribed it as a duty to plan for the wisest use of womanpower in the future.

"Besides the 20,000,000 women not at work," he added, "there are 11,000,000 more women available for work in case our economy has to expand for a national emergency."

Dr. Kluckhohn spoke directly. to this point, referring to it as "what we have heard here today." She said that American women were educated "on the assumption they may have to

support themselves or work if the country goes to war."

She took issue with Dr. Leo H. Bartemeier, the psychiatrist on the panel, who said that the larger proportion of women with small children who worked were "stimulated by neurotic competition."

He declared that these women "rationalize their neurotic competitive demands by a belief that the material things they earn are a benefit to their children."

Mothers should not be separated from small children, he asserted, and should be at home to welcome school-age children

Contrasting Viewpoint

Dr. Kluckhohn contended that children were better off when mothers got out of the isolation of the home, at least part of the time.

She declared that men should cease to sentimentalize the mother role by putting it on a pedestal.

Marie Johada, director of the Research Center for Human Relations, New York University, said that she was. in such complete accord with Dr. Kluckhohn that she would merely add a few points.

Women, she said, are forced into four categories, mother and housewife, career woman without family, working woman with family and, "the most tragic, women who make no contribution in any field."

She added that the first three roles had their satisfactions and frustrations, but that "we should move into the fourth field and help those women have lives that make sense."

She held that "the unmarried woman who does a job should have the same prestige as a mother who has brought up six children."

In a panel on "The Woman Who Works," three men gave their opinions on working women. Each said that his job permitted wide observation on the subject. All declared that women took their jobs too personally.

One said that women who felt that male resentment hindered their progress should get rid of their inferiority complexes. Another asserted that women would not meet issues head-on, but sought to win their business, battles by stratagems.

Three career women gave counter arguments.

March 11, 1955

STUDY OF SCHOOLS STRESSES LOW PAY

Comparison With 1904 Notes Discouraging Prospect for Qualified Educators

By LEONARD BUDER

The inadequate salaries paid to many persons in the teaching profession, especially to those in executive positions, are discouraging qualified young persons from entering the field.

This was brought out in a report made public yesterday by the Fund for the Advancement of Education, which was established four years ago by the Ford Foundation. The report presents a fifty-year comparison of school and college salaries with those in other occupations.

The study was made by Beardsley Ruml and Sidney G. Tickton. In addition to supervising the undertaking, Mr. Ruml also wrote a section on "Inferences and Impressions" based on the findings. In it, he declared:

"The ablest young men and women eligible for graduate and professional training are not turning to education as they once did and as the nation's needs require. The graduate schools do not have students in the numbers and the quality that are desirable; and in the academic subjects, scholarships and fellowships are required to lure them in. No such subsidy is required to fill professional schools of medicine and law, and in these schools there is the necessity of selective admission so that the quality of the professions is likely to be maintained."

50-Year Period Covered

The study, which dealt with the period from 1904 through 1953, found that, taking the teaching profession as a whole, there had been little or no "absolute deterioration" in salaries except at the top. In fact, it said, all public school teachers, other than those in big city high schools, have gained.

This conclusion was arrived at after considering 1953 salaries in the light of 1904 purchasing power. For example, the average big city elementary school teacher earned $873 in 1904 and $4,817 in 1953. When the latter figure is "deflated" to 1904 purchasing power, it amounts to $1,394. Other comparisons, which are less exceptional, are:

¶Big city high school teacher: 1904 salary, $1,597; 1953 salary, $5,526, and "deflated" salary, $1,577.

¶Big city high school principal: 1904 salary, $3,552; 1953 salary, $9,156, and "deflated" salary, $2,497.

¶University professor: 1904 salary, $2,000; 1953 salary, $7,000, and "deflated" salary, $1,956.

Teachers' Pay—'04 to '55

The 1904, 1953 and 1955 salaries of some city schools and college employes follow. The data showing 1953 salaries in terms of 1904 purchasing power were taken from the report of the Fund for the Advancement of Education or were based upon the formula used in the report.

New York City Schools

Position.	1904 Salary.	1953 Salary.	1953 income required to provide same purchasing power as 1904.	1955 Salary.
Elementary school teacher				
To start ....$	600 (women)	*$3,000	$1,893	†$3,750
Maximum	1,240 (women)	*6,100	4,203	†7,050
To start	900 (men)	*3,000	2,885	†3,750
Maximum	2,160 (men)	*6,100	7,810	†7,050
High school teacher				
To start	1,100 (women)	3,200	3,675	4,050
Maximum	1,900 (women)	6,300	6,780	7,350
To start	1,300 (men)	3,200	4,450	4,050
Maximum	2,400 (men)	6,300	8,770	7,350
High school principal				
To start	5,000	11,050	20,345	11,900
Maximum	5,000	13,000	20,345	13,850

City College

Position.	1904 Salary.	1953 Salary.	1953 income required to provide same purchasing power as 1904.	1955 Salary.
Instructor	‡	5,350	......	5,853
Assistant professor	3,250	6,365	12,284	6,994
Associate professor......	§	7,898	......	8,406
Full professor	4,750	9,472	19,110	10,193
President of college.....	8,250	20,000	39,858	25,000

*Teachers who hold master's degree or equivalent received $200 extra.

†Teachers who hold master's degree or equivalent receive $300 extra.

‡Salary figures not available.

§No such category in 1904.

NOTE: College salaries shown are averages.

¶University president: 1904 salary, $4,300; 1953 salary, $16,-500, and "deflated salary," $4,196.

The most serious losses have occurred in the compensation of educational executives. The report observed that the Superintendent of Schools of New York City would have had to receive $50,400, as against the $32,500 he earned, to restore his economic status to the 1908 level, when the position paid $10,000.

However, it is in the matter of "relative deterioration"—that is, how the group has fared in relation to other occupational groups—that many educators have suffered the most. Teachers in big city high schools would require an additional $9,400 to give them economic status comparable with 1904. Similarly, big city high school principals would require an additional $14,644; professors in large universities an additional $5,070, and the presidents of those universities an additional $14,000.

But there are some exceptions. Elementary school teachers in big cities have gained 60 per cent in purchasing power in fifty years, and university instructors, 38 per cent.

Cost Held 'Not Unmanageable'

The study did not estimate the amount of money needed to rectify the salary situation of those on the top rungs of the academic ladder, but it expressed the opinion that the sum "is not unmanageable." It added that the correction "should be made over a period of time and on a merit basis."

What all this means, Mr. Ruml said in his analysis, is that "the American society is deteriorating in the sector most critical for future progress and well-being."

The economic situation, Mr. Ruml asserted, has also created "disaffection" at the "most sensitive point in our society."

"Pervading pessimism, extending in extreme cases to subversion, fellow-traveling, and other educational sabotage, springs basically from a sense of unfair treatment by a non-conscious social drift, not from a blazing passion to reform," he said. "The pessimism and disaffection expresses itself in lecture, classroom, and community activity. And the teacher, being literate and articulate, attracts both the other disaffected and the uninformed who earnestly wish for a better world.

"Adequate compensation is not a bribe nor is it a cure; it is simply an assurance that intellectual leadership maintains a balanced economic status with its contemporaries. On that foundation we can still expect deviation and criticism, but it can be sincere and rational, not poisoned by the facts of injustice, neglect and humiliation."

There's Romance in the Air As Stewardesses Find Mates

By AGNES McCARTY

ALTHOUGH airline tickets are almost as ordinary as subway tokens, and stewardesses seldom marry pilots or wealthy passengers, there's still a lot of romance in flying.

A recent survey in the marriage rates of American Airlines stewardesses indicated that of the 238 who resigned jobs last year, 200 did so to get married.

Further arithmetic showed that 30 per cent married company employes, 26 per cent returned to keep house for the boy back home, 21 per cent became the wives of passengers, and 23 per cent wed men they met through "outside resources." Of the 1,100 marriages since 1938, only seven have ended in divorce.

When commercial flying was young, most stewardesses married pilots, but today the supply of eligibles is exhausted. The company husbands are found among the ground personnel. Catching a millionaire passenger is very unlikely since most of the passengers are now in the middle-income bracket.

In 1938 American employed seventy-five stewardesses. Now 1,100 are on the payroll. The average girl meets 17,000 people during her usual two-year stay with the company. Many of these are women, but occasionally, after a feminine passenger watches a stewardess warm baby bottles and serve a meal graciously, she attempts to arrange a date for the stewardess with her bachelor son.

Transfer Applications

Miss Millie Alford, supervisor of procedures and training for American Airlines, guides new stewardesses through their training and then arranges for their assignments after graduation.

"Most girls want to be based near home," she says, "and burst into tears when told they will be 1,000 miles away. Two weeks after they land at the new base, they call me to cancel their application for transfer.

"In another few months I get a letter of resignation because they're getting married, or I get a frantic request for a move to another base to help mend a broken heart. A transfer request usually means a transfer of affections."

Miss Alford tries to impress on stewardesses that they must pay as much attention to crochety old ladies on board a flight as they do to dashing young men.

"But I'm afraid it's against nature," she admits.

Walfrieda McAssey, who as stewardess supervisor for American at La Guardia Airport is sort of a "flight mother," reports that her alert charges can easily spot a "wolf" among the passengers. "Mac," as the lively supervisor is called, says that a man who is trying to get acquainted always heads for the last seat on the left-hand side in the ship. He piles belongings on the empty seat next to him to ward off other passengers. As soon as the flight taxis for take-off, he removes the packages and waits for the stewardess to take the seat.

Get-Acquainted Dodges

Other get-acquainted dodges include constant running to the back of the ship for a drink of water, asking after other hostesses known only by name plate, and then the final attempt when getting off—"You've been so nice to me, I'd like to repay you by taking you to dinner."

Typically feminine, the girls prefer men who are unassuming and make no attempt to strike up a friendship. "We like subtle operators." one hostess explains.

If a passenger calls the airline to request a stewardess' home address or phone number, he is told, politely but firmly, "We do not give out that information." If he persists, usually arguing that he is a friend of the family's and has a message from the girl's mother, he is asked to leave his name and phone number and the message is passed on.

Miss McAssey finds Dallas and Chicago to be the most popular bases. Why? "Dallas because of the tall men and Nieman-Marcus; Chicago because of central location and Marshall Field." New York's quota is always filled with girls who come from its vicinity, it turns out.

The Woman in the Gray Flannel Suit

The modern career girl plays the game by the men's rules, briefcase and all, but here's one vote for the 'executive wife,' whose place is still in the home.

By SLOAN WILSON

Wifely Executive—"A man needs a capable wife to screen engagements and run his house."

THIS whole thing started not long ago when I read a newspaper story headed "Career Women Warned of Occupational Ulcers." The story went on to say, "Stomach ulcers have increased more than 30 per cent in the last ten years among women who aspire to 'wear the pants in the family' * * *. Dr. John E. Cox of Memphis, Tenn., said that the so-called modern career woman was a special ulcer candidate as she moved into areas of business and other activities once dominated by men. 'If the women want such opportunities, they'll have to take

SLOAN WILSON is author of the best-selling novel, "The Man in the Gray Flannel Suit."

the consequences that go with them,' Dr. Cox said."

Another article entitled "Opportunities for Women in the Administrative Level," which appeared in The Harvard Business Review, came along to alarm me a short while later. A large majority of business executives interviewed, this article stated, "dwelt upon the 'increasing importance' of women in business. This comment from the president of a large international food manufacturing company was typical: 'There is no one phase of business or industry which does not have women in its employ. In the last fifty years women in business have increased tremendously. In the next twenty-five

years they will advance more rapidly than men ever did."

WELL, I don't doubt it. We men have been awfully slow. I can easily foresee a day when women will briskly dress themselves in gray flannel suits every morning and dash off to work carrying briefcases, while the men are left behind to loll around the house in kimonos, smoking cigars and cussing as they do the dishes. Or maybe both men and women will dash out to work and some great twelve-handed machine will stay home to mind the children. The only other solution I can think of is for men and women to take turns on careers. You have yours on Mondays, Wednesdays and Fridays, honey. I'll take the rest of the week.

I think this is going to be horrible. Unless the twelve-handed machine for the children can be developed soon, there is no choice but for men to become more motherly as women become more fatherly. The more I think about this, the more I wonder whether women should be in business at all. Maybe even in 1956 the place for women is in the home.

This is obviously an unpopular conclusion. It's not modern. I don't like to have these stuffy old thoughts—they just keep coming. The trouble is I keep getting into deeper and deeper waters. If it's impossible for a woman to have both a wholehearted marriage and a wholehearted career—if, in fact, marriage and careers don't mix very well for women—what about the whole feminist movement in business? More and more documentary evidence concerning this movement keeps coming my way. A booklet entitled "Women in Higher Level Positions," published by the United States Department of Labor, estimates that there are more than 17 million women with jobs in the United States. Forty-four per cent are listed in the category, "Married, husbands present," and only 4 per cent are in the category, "Married, husbands absent," so all men can't feel the way I do about this thing.

SOME 860 of the ladies covered by the survey were in "higher level positions"—vice presidents of corporations and that sort of thing. The female executives interviewed had some sterling comments to make on how girls get ahead. "It was apparent that women who held the responsible jobs had taken a marked interest in their work and had made unusual attempts to be successful at it," the booklet said. "The vast majority of the women interviewed believed that they owed their promotion to having done well at the job." Well, fancy that! This certainly goes to show that women are finding out all the secrets nowadays. If that weren't proof enough, the ladies who talked to the Labor Department gave some new and startling views on "what leads to advancement." "Be willing to work," they said. "Become well prepared for a job. Be ambitious." As far as I can see not one lady in the lot had anything to say about feminine wiles.

Obviously, the women are trying to play the game under the men's rules. Schools and universities are doing all they can to help them. As just one small example, Radcliffe College has a Management Training Program, "a one-year graduate course consisting of classroom instruction in administrative techniques, accounting, marketing, retailing and community relations, with two concentrated periods of field work providing actual job experience."

WHEN I read that list, I thought, For whom is this course designed? For ambitious spinsters, or women planning to make some guy a half-hearted wife? Then I felt ashamed of myself. It's no fun to find one doesn't like the idea of women executives. It's like finding oneself an enemy of air travel, jazz and vaccination. I've never thought of myself as unduly old-fashioned, but I began wondering if I didn't belong in some musty old gentlemen's club, where I could sit around with the other old codgers who still while away their time by criticizing the New Deal. I've got to be reasonable about this thing, I told myself, reasonable, modern and tolerant. One can't just say that women should stay home. What are the exceptions?

All kinds of qualifications immediately came to mind. How about married women who don't have any children? Well, I wasn't talking about them. How about women whose children have grown up? Neither was I talking about them. How about women who just plain don't want to get married, or who haven't been asked? May their careers prosper. How about the fact that people can't really plan their lives mathematically, and that in the process of doing the best they can, many women find they have to take jobs to keep a family together? Certainly no one can blame them.

HOW about the fact that some women find they are incapable of being happy without a career? How about women of extraordinary ability which should not be kept from the world? How about high-powered individuals who have something like twice the energy of most women? Couldn't they devise ways to have both a successful career and marriage?

Maybe a few, I thought, feeling very enlightened and reasonable. After all, no sane person would want to throw rocks at ladies, even those with careers. Life is a compromise for most of us and career women undoubtedly have their reasons. God knows, we all live in glass houses. I like women who have careers, I thought. I like them very much—many of them are fine people.

Then the real nature of my misgivings came to me. What I object to is not women who have careers, but the theory that women should have careers, must have them, and that something is wrong with them if they do not. I know that my wife feels vaguely defeated whenever she writes "housewife" as her occupation and that a lot of other women do, too. It's getting to the point where a woman who devotes herself wholeheartedly to helping a man and children is considered hopelessly old-fashioned—just as old-fashioned as a man who doesn't like career women.

YOUNG girls are steered into careers by schools and colleges. I know hardly any junior misses who want to grow up to be wives and these few are treated condescendingly by their teachers. It seems to me that "careers for women" are being glamorized out of all proportion and that the work of a good wife is being made to appear far more drab than it actually is.

Drawing by Carl Rose

Business Executive—"Careers for women are now being glamorized out of all proportion."

Young girls should be told that there is more to being a housewife than eternal scrubbing and vacuum-cleaning.

I know plenty of women who, as the wives of successful men, learn more about investments, accounting and upper-bracket public relations than 99 per cent of the women in offices. There's happiness and money in marriage, girls! The retirement benefits and opportunities for travel are often excellent—at least as good as in most offices. Be an executive wife! The hours are long but the rewards can be great.

I have two reasons for wanting to see this idea of the executive wife sold, as the saying goes, and sold hard. One reason is that male executives are obviously becoming more and more helpless in their personal lives nowadays and somebody has to take up the slack at home. I don't mean that men are mysteriously withering away, as Communist dictators were supposed to do. I mean that many jobs are becoming so incredibly complex and competitive that key executives have almost no time for anything but work.

A FRIEND of mine, who was serving as president of a small college, brooded about this a great deal. What with planning new programs of study, supervising the construction of several new buildings, raising funds and coping with the usual stream of urgent complaints from faculty, students and alumni, he had virtually no time to himself. Without a capable wife to screen his speaking and social engagements, keep track of his personal finances, run his house and take care of his children, he would have been lost. If his wife, who had great executive ability, had suddenly decided to have a career of her own, he would have succumbed from sheer confusion and bewilderment.

Being an academic man, he couldn't just accept this situation—he had to theorize about it. The theory he worked out scared me half to death. The leadership of any large organization requires so much energy nowadays, he said, that only compulsive workers—that is to say, neurotics—are capable of large-scale success. In effect, the human race has now evolved a system which automatically selects confirmed neurotics for the top jobs in all fields—industry, the arts, education and government.

THIS is one reason why we have so many wars, my friend thought — these compulsive workers are seething with all kinds of hatreds, and are much more likely to fight than the ordinary people they lead. A corollary of the theory, he said, is that the children of successful men are simply damned unless such men are fortunate enough to have unusually warm, dedicated and capable wives. Without such women, the children of most successful men would be sacrificed, and there would be no reproduction of the great.

I don't really believe this theory as a general truth, but it does apply to a lot of individuals. To state the case in blunter terms, modern man needs an old-fashioned woman around the house. In other societies, a man can have a large group of wives, and the more successful the man, the more wives he is entitled to. We men of the West have gracefully accepted the limitation of one wife, but if all this career talk is going to reduce

that one to a fraction, I don't know what we're going to do. Maybe it's time to rebel.

Another reason I have for promoting the advantages of executive wifehood is that I have two daughters and I'd hate to see them get into some of the offices where I've worked. When I was around New York, I saw all kinds of career girls—and many of them actually did wear gray flannel suits, and carry briefcases. They may have looked glamorous on the street but most of the unmarried ones lived in lonely little walk-up apartments, and their social life consisted largely of going to the movies with girls like themselves.

One girl I knew used to sneak into the office to work late at night, simply because she had nothing else to do. Many were attractive women but the city is a pitiless place for most unmarried girls once they get outside the family and social structure in which they have been brought up. The married career women I knew weren't much better off for long. While they didn't have children, life was gay, for two working people can afford to live far more expensively than one. The trouble usually came with the first pregnancy. Should the girl quit her job permanently or not?

IF the answer were yes, a painful reduction of the family's standard of living usually was necessary at a time of maximum expense and some of the girls had got so used to office clatter that they had pathetic difficulty in adjusting themselves to a quiet apartment. If they decided to

hang onto their jobs, the endless search for nursemaids commenced. As the couples grew older, the semi-fulfilled mother and the harried husband often showed signs of strain. Hard lines of discontent set in. I wouldn't want to see my daughters get into anything like that.

When one comes right down to it, the basic situation seems to be that two of the main streams of modern thought about women are directly opposed to each other and the resulting collision spells unhappiness for many people. On one hand, we have the whole feminist movement, outside of business as well as in it. Women should be independent, we are told—there's hardly anything a man can do that a woman can't do at least as well. On the other hand, we have many findings of psychiatrists which seem to indicate that women can find happiness only by accepting their role in life as women and that all kinds of conflicts arise when in their own minds they become competitive with men.

A PSYCHIATRIST friend of mine claims that one of the great troubles of the world is that men are becoming more and more feminine and that women are becoming more and more masculine. The feminization of men started when they began to shave off their beards, he claims, and is continuing to the point where mothers are becoming the actual heads of most families —the ones who do the managing, and make most of the important decisions.

The real trouble with Mom is that she's a man in most of

her reactions, he says, and the trouble with Dear Old Dad is that he's beginning to like it. What my psychiatrist friend would say about women who put on gray flannel suits and embark on careers of their own, I don't know, and I'm not very anxious to find out. One thing does appear clear to me: almost everything psychiatry has to say about children emphasizes the importance of a warm atmosphere in the home and a loving mother who has plenty of time to give her sons and daughters.

A LOT of the theories of psychiatrists seem to buck traditional thought but one thing they have done is to prove pretty conclusively that the hand that rocks the cradle really does rule the world. How this whole line of reasoning can be reconciled with the growing conviction that modern women should have careers outside the home and that being a housewife isn't quite admirable, I have no idea. I don't want to see either of my daughters get caught in the middle. I think they ought to leave the ulcers to the men.

Just to make sure that my views weren't too much influenced by male vanity, I reviewed all this with my wife. She agreed that married women with children shouldn't have careers but she said that men with young children should spend more time at home, too. She said that psychiatry has a good deal to say about that. There are too many witlessly ambitious people of both sexes, she added. Rather uneasily, I agreed. Maybe it's time for us all to relax.

January 15, 1955

Woman in the Gay Flannel Suit

A career woman says her sex can best achieve happiness with homes, children—and jobs.

By BERNICE FITZ-GIBBON

TWO weeks ago in these pages, Sloan Wilson came right out (almost) and said (almost) that

women's place is in the home. Some women's place. I'm here today to answer him. It's not easy. If he had come out fairly and squarely and swinging in all directions like a man fighting bees, it would be easier. But

he came out—or stayed in—not fighting, but ducking guiltily, and taking a swing at only one very small bee. Mr. Wilson admitted right off that it'd sound pretty silly to say women shouldn't have careers. In fact, for all of him, most women *could* have careers: women without children, women with grown children, spinsters, women whose families needed the money to stay together, women who had extraordinary abilities which should not be kept from the world. Indeed, Mr. Wil-

BERNICE FITZ-GIBBON is a career woman who heads her own advertising agency, was Woman of the Year in Business for 1955, and has two children and three grandchildren.

son (after all the modifying and mitigating and qualifying) decided that the only ones who should not have careers are the young women with small children.

Well, I say it's the young women with small children who definitely *should* have careers. First, for the sake of the men who, let's admit, are the kings of creation. Second, for the sake of the women themselves, whose happiness, let's admit, should lie in wifehood and motherhood and grandmotherhood, and whose main mission in life should be creating a warm, happy, safe home for a husband and children. And, third, for the sake of the children who will be far, far happier if mama is in town carving out a career for herself. I'll take these points up, one by one, but first let's stop and consider what all the commotion is about.

Now, let's get this clear. Women have always worked. And the men have always warmly approved. And the harder and grubbier and dirtier the work, and the longer the hours, and the lower the pay, and the grimier the environment—the more warmly and heartily have the men approved. It is only since some of the girls began to climb out of the Hoover aprons and into the Chanel and Dior suits and onto the five-figure payroll and into the corner office with the broadloomed floor that the boys have gone in for headshakings and mutterings and hues and cries and anguished plaints (like Sloan Wilson's) about woman's place being in the home.

AS a matter of fact, the men can relax. Only half of 1 per cent of women make $5,000 or over. And a full 12 per cent of men make $5,000 or over. Mr. Wilson approves of wholehearted marriages. He likes warm, capable, dedicated women. He approves of feminine women who make devoted wives and are loving mothers to their sons and daughters. Mr. Wilson plays the wholesome side of the street—and plays it hard. If you differ with him, it almost puts you on the side against wholesomeness. But he's not going to put me there. Dibs on wanting women wholesom*er* and warm*er* and loving*er* and dedicated*er* than you do, Mr. Wilson. I can want them that way, and do want them that way, and yet come out with exactly the opposite conclusions from yours.

I believe that young women with small children *should* have careers, because the careers will make them warmer, more loving, more understanding, more dedicated wives. They will make their husbands happier. Santayana once referred to American college professors as "mediocre, seedy, hungry, and henpecked." *Their* wives, goodness knows, were not career girls. And Wylie's Mom didn't have a stitch of career to her back. I agree with Mr. Wilson that men's jobs are becom-

ing incredibly complex and competitive. He could have gone further.

I SEE a lot of young men on their way up. It's a tough, lonely business. Woman was created to assuage man's loneliness, to be his helpmate and companion and confidante. Instead, he waves good-by to his home girl and the children at the Bedford Village station, and goes to town all alone to face the hard, cruel competition of the business jungle. The Lord told Adam and Eve "to fill the earth and subdue it." Well, filling Bedford Village isn't so hard, but *subduing* Madison Avenue is something else again. A husband needs help in *both* areas.

These days, it takes *two* to get the world by the tail. First, let's take the money situation. The average young couple (who do not have a millionaire aunt as Tom had in "The Man in the Gray Flannel Suit") desperately need that second income. Like the man said: "It's not that I love money so much. It's just that it calms my nerves." And, boy oh boy, how men need their nerves calmed!

I HAVE just come upon a manufacturer's brochure advertising offices designed especially for "executives working under pressure." The copy says: "There are real hazards connected with work involving important responsibilities. Business and the professions are losing far too many of their distinguished members. A technique of office planning has been developed which, it is hoped, will lessen, if not eliminate, emotional and physical crackups among top business and professional men." Then there are pictures of elegant offices with pale-gold rugs and soft restful green-leather chairs and soothing lighting devices. Too bad—but it just won't work. It isn't the *lack* of elegant décor that's responsible for breakdowns. Therefore, the *presence* of elegant décor won't cure them.

The man is carrying too big a burden and carrying it all alone. Male and female created He them—that they might be able to enrich one another. "It is not good for man to be alone. Let us make him a help like unto himself." Eve—*like* Adam and *different* from Adam. Sure, let's vive la différence. But also, let's vive la similarity. Let the woman, the keeper of the hearth, get in there and pitch by her man's side for a few years in order to be sure that there's a hearth to keep. It isn't merely the physical things that the career woman's income can swing. But electric dryers and dishwashers and a second vacuum cleaner upstairs, and three telephone extensions *do* cut down the drudgery of running a house.

WHAT'S bothering our young tycoon in the making? First, he has a fear of inadequacy. Second, he has a fear that his being inadequate will be found

"Men began to get warm about women at work when the ladies started to get good jobs."

out. He's saddled with a mortgage, he is trying to maintain a living standard higher than his income justifies, the competition in his particular suburb pushes him into Veblen's conspicuous consumption, and he feels that he must have a wife who looks as if she were expensive to maintain.

He may be trapped in work that he loathes. Maybe he's in insurance and would be happy only in a pewtering business of his own in Woodbury, Conn. Maybe he despises the public-relations business and wants to build boats. Maybe he didn't finish college and all the other men in the office have Mother Hubbards and four-cornered hats. Maybe all the others went to Harvard and he went to Colgate. Maybe he's shy and wants to be bold. Maybe he's worried about a thorny bit of office protocol.

Anyway, he's scared stiff. And he has no one to talk to. He can't talk to his never-had-a-career home wife. He can't reach her. She can't reach him. "My husband never tells me anything." He can't tell her things because she wouldn't understand. She'd make too much of it, or she'd make too little of it. Or she'd tell it to the girl two doors down who would promise not to breathe a word. This inability to reach one another is the basic reason why

the average marriage gets awfully tired along about the middle. He has no one to confide in. And he has no sounding board. And so our young career man's mind is an inky canal filled with the little unshared hurts and problems of the day. As Edwin Arlington Robinson says:

*"We die of what we eat and drink,
But most we die of what we think."*

He's alone and scared. Daily he chips little pieces off his integrity, makes weak little compromises and sells little bits of his soul, all because he's afraid to say boo to the boss. A wife should have a career if for no other reason than that she makes it possible for her husband to say boo to the boss. I owe any success I have had to the fact that my husband was a successful lawyer and I could always say boo to the boss.

IF a man has a working wife, a through-thick-and-thin working wife, he is able to relax, recover his sense of humor and his ability to think creatively and daringly; he gets back his what-the-hell abandon. He's no longer afraid that he will lose his job and so doesn't lose it. Instead of limping along, he soars. He has a *helpmate*.

And, of course, a career is good for the wife herself because she knows she is helping her husband and what's good for him is bound to be good for her. In one of my monthly pieces for another magazine, I answered a letter from a mother of two who loved her husband and children but still wanted to put her mind to work. I suggested in print that she might be content to be a "late bloomer" — that is, to rear her children and *then* think about going to work. Well, I've gotten letters of protest by the hundreds from young mothers who want to put their minds to work now! One woman said she wanted to give her mind *muscle*.

THERE isn't space to take up all of Mr. Wilson's worries, but I'd like to say a few words about women getting more masculine and men getting more feminine. That won't happen to the career mother's children. She's hep. She's on the ball. She has made an intelligent study of nutrition and she'll see to it that her daughters get plenty of vitamin E to make them curlier and curvier and that her sons get plenty of vitamin E to make them leaner and straighter and maler.

I was dismayed to discover that Mr. Wilson agrees with the feminist contention that the average woman feels that there is something demeaning about caring for a home and that she feels vaguely defeated when she has to write down her occupation as "housewife." That's feminist propaganda, Mr. Wilson. Don't you believe

one word of it. Equally absurd is the old feminist contention that it is not good for college-trained women to spend long, continuous hours with small children. Certainly no one has ever pointed out what evil is done teachers or librarians who spend long, continuous hours with small children.

In most cases having mama around all day is not good for the children (did you know that the most successful treatment for asthma in children is removing the child from its

"If a man has a wife who also works, he has a real helpmate."

mother as far as possible and as long as possible?), but it is certainly not debasing or degrading to the mother. Gilbert Keith Chesterton takes a poke at this view:

Mother is happy in turning a crank
  That increases the balance at somebody's bank;
And I feel satisfaction that mother is free
From the sinister task of attending to me.

Also the feminists have contended that home work is too routine. I cannot imagine a business career (stylist, copywriter, magazine editor, sportswear buyer or what have you) that isn't more routine. Of course, these jobs are packed with fun, too.

No, the young mother should get out of the house *because* the children will be better off that way. Many primitive tribes have been a lot more successful than we in rearing happy, well-adjusted children. Take the Bantu tribe in South Africa. They seem to be able to turn out well-behaved, merry children with no juvenile

delinquents and no embittered adolescents filled with neuroses and hostilities. Who takes care of the Bantu children? The grandmothers and the great-grandmothers.

Whom do I suggest to care for the children of Westchester and Nassau and Fairfield counties' career mothers? Their grandmothers and possibly youngish, healthy great-grandmothers. This is how it works among the Bantus who live in the shade of the Drakensburg Range in South Africa. The mother stays in her hut for three months after the birth of the baby, seeing the baby only for nursing purposes. Warm-hearted, well-adjusted grandmother takes care of the child. After the three-month isolation period, the mother goes right on with her career of stamping mealies in the fields.

THE toddlers go around in swarms, it apparently being more natural for children to be with other children than with their mothers. Three-year-olds swarm and mill around with 3-year-olds, 5-year-olds with 5-year-olds—possibly disciplining one another for everybody's good. They go back to grandmother for food and naps and bruise-kissing and cuddling —and then back with the children again. They see their mothers, of course, but not too much. And they love their mothers. Because it is the *quality* of the time a mother spends with her children—not the *quantity*—that counts.

La Rochefoucauld said, "Absence abates a moderate passion and intensifies a great one—as the wind blows out a candle but fans a fire into a flame." Apparently the person least equipped to take care of a first baby is its mother. She probably has scarcely looked at a baby before in her life. But the people best equipped are the older grandmothers and nurses who have had fifty years' experience with wave after wave of various people's babies.

Putting the grandmother age-bracket to work will solve a whole clutch of problems. It will solve the where-can-we-get-a-nurse problem. (Most parents can't get a nurse because they go after the wrong kind of nurse. They look for a woman practically as young as—and, therefore, just as inexperienced as — mama.) It will solve a little more of the

geriatrics problem. (What old people need more than anything—unless it's money—is a feeling of being needed and wanted.)

And it will solve an economic problem. (The proportion of people in this country over 65 is growing every day. Who's to support them if they aren't blessed with savings or prosperous progeny? Most of them want nothing more than to be able to support themselves.)

Psychologists and psychiatrists point out that mothers can often meet their children's emotional needs more satisfactorily if they work outside the home each day. The career mother's home will be merrier. By the time father and mother get home at night, the little frictions and problems of the day will have been resolved by that competent 72-year-old, who knows enough to shrug off details and adjust minor sibling battles, and who has learned through the decades that children are happier being with other children.

IF other children in the 2-to-6-year age group are not available, the career mother's salary can cover the tuition of play or nursery school. Of course, these 72-year-old jewels must have verve and vitality. (Many of them now have that and others will bounce into radiant health when they know they are needed and appreciated.)

Their mellowed, matured philosophy of child-raising will be, "Feed 'em and love 'em and lave 'em and let 'em alone." In the evenings, the children are tickled stiff to see their parents who are tickled stiff to see them. Father is not grim and abstracted. Mama isn't snappy after a vinous afternoon with the girls of the bridge club. The laughter of the children ripples through the house and everybody's ready for fun and foolishness and antic goings on in the precious time together.

You may say, "But won't there be mayhem in the A. M. with getting father and mother and the children off?" There's mayhem in the A. M. now. It can't be one whit worse with a tranquil grandmother in command. And think how very, very pleasant will be the powwows in the P. M.!

MOTHERS REPLACING THE CAREER WOMAN

The old-time career woman is disappearing and her place is being taken by the mother who goes to work when her children reach school age.

Dr. Henry David, executive director of the National Manpower Council, said yesterday that this was one of the most significant opinions brought forward in a two-day conference at the Gotham Hotel of twenty-one representatives of women's organizations.

The conference was called in connection with a study of womanpower in the nation, nearing completion after a year's work by the National Manpower Council. To date, the council has made three reports on the national manpower problem since the agency was created in 1951 by General Eisenhower under a Ford Foundation grant to Columbia University.

Early marriage and concentration of childbearing in the early years brings women permanently into the labor market at about the age of 35, Dr. David declared. Women live longer, he said, and can work longer.

Today, with 30 per cent of the total labor force women, conference figures showed, 60 per cent of employed women are married and half of them are over 40 years old. Of all wives in the country one-quarter are in the labor force.

January 18, 1955

The Vigilant Sex

Tests Show Women Are Better At Monotonous Work

Tests made by Dr. Paul Bakan of Michigan State University suggest that women generally are better than men in doing prolonged, monotonous work. But in 1½-hour tests given to twenty subjects, both sexes scored better in the first fifteen minutes than in the remaining hour and fifteen minutes.

Bakan carried out some of his researches for the United States Air Force, which wants to learn more about vigilance as it applies to radar and watching instruments for long periods. Obviously his findings have implications for workers in scores of industries where monotonous work still is done by hand. It looks to Bakan as if anyone engaged in a lengthy, monotonous task "gets into a state somewhere between wakefulness and sleep." Rest periods or the use of such drugs as benzedrine increase alertness.

In Dr. Bakan's first tests, ten men and ten women between the ages of 16 and 35 were asked to watch a light for 1½ hours and note changes in brightness.

"In the first fifteen minutes the light had to be about 16 per cent brighter to be noticed," he said. "But after 1½ hours it had to be stepped up about 45 per cent." "Poor" subjects did progressively worse, "good" subjects reached a certain low point and then did better.

TEMPORARY HELP FULL-TIME AFFAIR

Agencies Supply Stevedores, Clerks or Domestics at Drop of Phone Hook

By ALBERT L. KRAUS

A Chicago insurance company's accounting department was so swamped recently that a crew of twenty-five workers would have had to work a full shift overtime for two months to catch up.

A call went out to one of the nation's growing army of temporary help rental agencies. Working nights, the agency helped the insurance company solve its problem in weeks.

Supplying part-time and temporary help to banks, life insurance companies, brokerage houses, manufacturers, department stores and others who experience seasonal or irregular peak job needs is becoming a major business.

One concern, with seventy-eight offices in the United States and four in foreign countries, estimates it has 50,000 temporary and part-time workers on its payrolls. Perhaps fifty other large concerns and several hundred smaller ones may bring the national total to 250,000 or more.

40,000 in New York

The New York metropolitan area alone, according to one source, employs more than 40,000 temporary and part-time office workers.

Most of the demand has been for typists, stenographers, clerks, comptometer operators and punched-card machine operators — the day-in-day-out requirements of normal office operations.

On occasion, however, the temporary help rental agencies get some unusual requests.

A Philadelphia rope manufacturer called for "200 strong men" to hold one end of a length of his product while a passenger-carrying balloon tugged away at the other end.

Liberace asked for eight helpers to address 75,000 Christmas cards.

A Roman Catholic priest, just back from Red China, wanted someone to type the manuscript of his experiences.

Demand for part time and temporary workers has grown, the rental agencies say, because of a continuing shortage of experienced office workers. It has grown also, they add, because of the increasing reluctance of employers to undertake the myriad and costly tasks of hiring, firing and record keeping associated with putting a one-week or two-week employe on the payroll.

Workers Are Bonded

Reputable temporary help rental agencies screen, test, bond and insure workers before sending them out. Employes are paid a fixed hourly rate, the rental agencies billing customer companies for these services at a mark-up.

Employes are covered by social security and unemployment insurance, even when the customer company would not normally be required to provide such coverage. Withholding taxes and other deductions are made by the rental agency.

Banks, insurance companies and investment banking houses are among the oldest and most frequent users of temporary help rental agency services. Dividend distributions, large stock transfers and wholesale accounting system change-overs, special jobs that must be done without interfering with the regular operation of a business, are the meat of the agencies.

When General Motors split its stock last year and when Ford made its first public stock distribution last spring, temporary workers handled the bulk of the transactions.

When Textron merged with the American Woolen Company and Robbins Mills, sixteen girls worked in a bank vault to accomplish the transfer.

When Louis Wolfson attempted to win control of Montgomery Ward, both sides in the proxy fight hired temporary workers to round up votes.

Not all jobs are one-shot affairs. About thirty clerks at the New York Stock Exchange — students, teachers and would-be actors — work twenty hours a week or less sorting and pigeon-holing securities, their services supplied by temporary help rental agencies.

One of the city's largest banks employs another crew once each month clipping thousands of dollars of coupons from bonds.

Who is the temporary worker? Many are school teachers, students on vacation, office workers seeking extra income. The largest number, however, are housewives who welcome the opportunity to add to the family paycheck without tying themselves to a steady position.

A Washington state school teacher paid for her vacation in New York by working as a "temporary." A Johannesburg, South Africa, couple toured the country on earnings as "temporaries."

Recently, a number of temporary help rental agencies have begun broadening their services. Even such an old-line concern is the Graham Accounting and Statistical Corporation, oldest and largest in New York, has added a plan for putting household domestics on its payroll. Housewives do their own hiring, Graham handles all the payroll problems.

However, both Graham and Office Temporaries, another large local agency, hold chiefly to clerical and office positions. Workman's Service, Inc., with headquarters in Chicago, and Manpower, Inc., with headquarters in Milwaukee, have added

July 1, 1956

314

light stevedoring and other out-side-the-office men's services.

Manpower, which operates in part through a franchise system, has jumped to the lead in the temporary help field nationally in a little less than nine years largely because of its advertised willingness to tackle anything. One large field pioneered by Manpower is supplying product demonstrators in supermarket and variety chains.

Almost all the agencies now undertake to supply research and survey personnel for adver-tising and marketing organiza-tions. No one has said so yet, but without question temporary help rental agencies will supply

many of the thousands of straw vote takers for this fall's na-tional political campaign.

On occasion temporary help rental agencies find their serv-ices required in emergencies. Fifty men supplied by one con-cern helped dike the Mississippi below St. Louis when flood threatened several years ago. Another team was organized after Waterbury, Conn., was visited last year by Hurricane Diane. And a Providence, R. I., agency operator was forced to operate out of his kitchen after Hurricane Carol, supplying in-formation for the National Board of Fire Underwriters. All work stopped at sundown, though. There was no electricity.

August 5, 1956

Women and Jobs Studied by 2 Men

Girls tend to surpass boys in both high school and college, but the situation is reversed when they enter the working world.

According to a study by W. L. Slocum and LaMar T. Empey at the State College of Wash-ington, women are rarely found in the top posts of business and industry. However, in school they not only get better marks, but also are more advanced than their male schoolmates in plan-ning for a career. Unlike boys, who feel that education is a step to an occupation, girls be-

lieve that a broad general educa-tion is valuable in its own sake.

Other survey findings indicate some of the reasons that women, after their surpassing high school and college records do poorly in the career world:

The girls concentrate on oc-cupations that are traditionally regarded as women's. Only a few are interested in fields in which they would compete with men. Girls are less interested in money and security than boys, which, the study report states, reflects the fact that boys be-lieve that they must support a home and family, while girls, who generally prefer marriage to a career, feel that they can indulge in a job that is interest-ing rather than secure.

November 15, 1956

Job Call Out For Women In Libraries

"KNOWING where to find things is oftentimes better than knowing them originally." This is the sage appraisal of li-brary work, the subject of a re-cent issue of Pratt Institute's Career Briefs.

There is no lack of jobs for women in library work, accord-ing to the report, and opportuni-ties are expanding. The United States has at least 7,000 public libraries, with more than 3,000 branches; 1,800 junior and sen-ior college and university librar-ies and hundreds of others that specialize in law, medicine, gov-ernment, business and other subjects.

¶Types of Work: Library workers, who number 55,000 to 60,000, fill jobs as reference and circulation librarian, readers' ad-viser, curator of special collec-tions (music, pictures, films, re-cordings), cataloguer, classifier, bibliographer, researcher, li-brarian who orders books, ad-ministrator.

¶Salaries: In the New York area salaries start at $4,000 for professionally trained librarians, higher in specialized or school libraries.

¶Personal Qualifications: Pro-ficiency in academic work, a lik-ing for people and concern with their problems, a sense of humor and, for cataloguing work, cleri-cal aptitude and "passion" for detail.

¶Training: Few libraries will hire an applicant who has not had professional training for an executive job. Preparation can-not start too early. Pratt rec-ommends that a young person interested in library work start to prepare in high school. The teen-ager should consult library school catalogues before deter-mining on her undergraduate college to be sure that she will meet the entrance requirements of the school of her choice. Work in high school, college and pub-lic libraries, either paid or vol-unteer, gives practical experi-ence. This not only bears weight when she applies eventually to library school, but also helps her make sure that such work is really for her. Some municipal libraries require also that the applicant pass a civil service ex-amination, and she must have the appropriate degree to apply for such an examination.

August 14, 1956

WOMEN, 62, ELIGIBLE FOR BENEFITS TODAY

WASHINGTON, Oct. 31 (AP)—Women become eligible for social security retirement benefits at the age of 62, instead of 65, be-ginning tomorrow.

The Department of Health, Education and Welfare, which

administers the Social Security system, reported that 311,000 women had filed claims under the new law by Oct. 18. An esti-mated 850,000 women are eligible or the earlier retirement benefits.

The first Government checks to women retiring at ages 62, 63 or 64 will be in the mails early in December, the Department said.

November 1, 1956

15,000 Women Realty Brokers Add New Touch to Home Sales

Fifteen thousand women are putting a broad and profitable interpretation on the adage, "A woman's place is in the home." They are licensed real estate brokers, and in many parts of the country they have demon-strated the value of a woman's touch in selling and renting property.

In Chicago, for example, Miss Frances H. Mazurk and her 250 companions in the women's divi-sion of the local realty board have set up a "charm school" where they prepare to deal with the potential buyer through voice culture courses, dress advisory classes and patience-training lec-tures.

Convinced that goodwill is a long-range asset, the women fol-low through after a sale or rental with a series of small teas and luncheons at which a new resident is introduced to three or four neighbors. They arrange parties for children and make the services of an interior deco-rator available to housewives.

Miss Mazurk said the cost of these "asides" was negligible compared to the contribution made to good relations among neighbors. She said such ges-tures had helped make new resi-dents more conscious of the need for home maintenance.

The success of these innova-tions prompted the Chicago real estate women to set up courses in minor home repairs. As a result, many housewives are do-ing small jobs that used to be done by the electrician, the plumber and the carpenter.

Miss Mazurk has a linguistic advantage over many of her

colleagues. She speaks Polish, Spanish, Italian and Greek, in addition to English. But in all of them, she speaks a woman's language when it comes to buy-ing a home.

Another woman broker, Mrs. Grace Sebastian of Sacramento, Calif., who is president of the Women's Council of the National Association of Real Estate Boards, says that while hus-bands make out the checks, wives usually decide whether to buy a house.

"During my fifteen years in the profession, I have learned that the items usually overlooked by men are the decisive factors in the sale of a house," she ob-serves. These items include closet space, proximity of windows to the children's play area, shape of rooms, and distances to shop-ping sections, schools and churches.

Mrs. Sebastian and Mrs. Gladys Manion, who has had seventeen years of experience in and around St. Louis, support Miss Mazurk's observation that architects and builders are tend-ing with greater frequency to discuss designs and location be-fore picking up their T-squares and moving tractors across de-velopment sites.

Members of the National As-sociation of Real Estate Boards, particularly the men who head them, are recruiting women brokers at a national rate of twenty-five a week. From Jan-uary of this year through Oc-tober, more than 1,000 women have become members of the national association.

November 25, 1956

WORKING MOTHER WARNED ON ROLE

Emotional Stress to Husband and Wife Cited at Chicago by Columbia Economist

By EMMA HARRISON
Special to The New York Times.

CHICAGO, March 8 — The working mother and her husband may both be suffering psychological strains as a result of her dual role, an expert on human resources suggested today.

Dr. Eli Ginzberg, Columbia University economist explored the matter before the American Orthopsychiatric Association meeting here. He said the problems involved were "psychological corrolaries" to the National Manpower Council's study on womanpower, to be presented next Wednesday to President Eisenhower. He was its director of staff studies.

He said:

"Although the 28,000,000 women who worked out of the house last year—40 per cent of all women over 14 years of age —earned more than $40,000,000, no one yet knows how many women worked beyond their physical and emotional limits in coping with two jobs—in and out of the house."

Dr. Ginzberg added:

"The United States has need to consider carefully the full implications growing out of the fact that two out of five mothers with school-age children held down jobs out of the house last year."

Dr. Ginzberg said that young girls now encountered no clear image of a woman's role. They perhaps see, he said, a non-working mother, a career aunt and a teacher who is married. In 1900 they were not presented with such conflicting "multiple models," he added. This leads to confusion in choosing courses in school, the economist warned.

The woman of today is generally anxious to fulfill herself in both a career and in marriage and motherhood, Dr. Ginzberg said. He emphasized consideration of these two factors: The reality problem of time and energy and her physical capacities to fulfill both, and the role of her husband in this picture.

"To what extent," asks Dr. Ginzberg, "is the male to take a different attitude toward his role and modify his demands on the wife who is working?"

And even if a husband does modify his demands, Dr. Ginzberg added, who is to tell if he does not really resent the lessening of his wife's household attentions. The fact that the family may need and welcome the extra income does not always reduce his suffering, he warned.

Jobs That Women Don't Get

By BERNARD ROSHCO

THE time when hardly more than three jobs were open to a woman—cook, maid or seamstress —is long past. Today, women earn their livings in occupations in which the most ardent early feminists scarcely dreamed of demanding employment. The Census Bureau reports that at least some women now hold jobs in every one of the more than 400 occupations the bureau classifies.

Still, pointing out the enormous variety of jobs women have come to hold since the time "equal rights for women" was considered a daring battle cry tells only part of the story of how women are faring at present in the world of work. Although a woman may head a brokerage house, manage a department store or help to rewrite the laws of physics, the "career woman" can rarely hope to rise as high as a man of comparable ability. The fact is that one-fourth of all women employes are in occupations in which at least 90 per cent of the workers are women, and nearly half are in occupations in which at least 75 per cent are female.

A true description of the American woman's current role in this country's labor force must take note of the employment limitations women still face. But to what extent are the generally acknowledged prejudices against women in many fields of work justified or unfair? How can we determine in which cases we could better utilize the nation's human resources by giving women increased job opportunities?

Recently the National Manpower Council, a nonprofit organization operating under a grant from the Ford Foundation and located at Columbia University, sponsored a series of conferences among representatives from a wide variety of businesses and industries—of various sizes in different parts of the country—to learn firsthand about management's policies and practices regarding the employment of our women. On the whole, the reasons the conferees gave for why employers hire or do not hire women fell into three broad categories: traditions, special traits and abilities, costs.

Let us examine the most frequent explanations. In each case the problem is to determine whether the employer's preference for either male or female employe appears justified and, in some instances, what is the real, but unspoken, reason for such a preference.

BERNARD ROSHCO served with the National Manpower Council from 1954 to 1956, and is now with the New York Housing Authority.

TRADITION

(1) "I hired a man rather than a woman because a man has always done this job."

The fact that a job has been customarily performed by a man or a woman is usually the most important consideration in determining whether the next employe assigned to the same job will be a man or a woman—regardless of who might be most qualified. Sometimes an exceptional woman gains what is usually considered a man's job. But, when she moves on, the job will often be deliberately reassigned to a man. An insurance company that until recently had a woman as its specialist in yacht insurance—usually a man's job—chose a man as her successor, although a competent woman was available, because it did not want to establish the idea that the position was a "woman's job."

TRADITIONAL distinctions between "men's" and "women's" jobs are especially marked in certain fields of manufacturing. Even in the professional, service and sales fields, however, jobs are often closed to women simply because it is taken for granted they should be held by men. In one instance, a very capable woman agricultural student found that because of her sex no one would hire her as an agriculture teacher.

Thus, in many cases, tradition is an excuse for not changing because it is easier not to. But when altered conditions, such as wartime labor shortages, bring women into new jobs, traditions are often permanently changed.

(2) "I hired a man rather than a woman because I was afraid the supervisor, the other workers or our customers wouldn't like having a woman in that spot."

Traditions based on social relationships often restrict women's opportunities in the business world. Most men do prefer to work with—and for —other men. Many would be uncomfortable to find themselves entertained by women for business purposes or traveling in their company on business missions. Typically, an executive may find that if a saleswoman arrives when he is busy, or presses her case in spite of his lack of interest, he cannot bring himself to dismiss her as quickly as he would a man. He may therefore refuse to see her at all.

EMPLOYERS often fear that customers will doubt a woman's business judgment. Some banks, therefore, will not employ women in their trust departments or as loan interviewers. Some insurance companies do not employ women as accident and health underwriters because they believe customers will not accept women's decisions. Other banks and insurance companies, however, are employing women successfully in these positions.

Thus, traditional patterns of job assignment may be retained because employers are unaware that changing social attitudes have made them obsolete. However, in situations where deep-rooted social relationships are still important, only an exceptional woman can, at present, overcome tradition. She may pave the way for a more general acceptance of women in the same job area later on.

(3) *"I hired a woman for that job rather than a man because a man won't do that kind of work."*

Tradition sometimes turns the tables on men. When the pits closed down in one Southern mining town, the men stayed home

and kept house rather than accept factory jobs that would have required them to do what they considered women's work. In the small communities where many shirt factories are located men refuse to work as sewing-machine operators despite desirable pay rates. Even though a good deal of physical effort is required to handle the materials, the jobs have been traditionally associated with women.

TRADITIONAL job assignment patterns create other contradictions. On the West Coast, fish-packing is considered men's work. But a short distance away, in California's Salinas Valley, fruit-packing is women's work. In the Midwest, corn huskers are traditionally women, trimmers are almost always men. In the Far West, corn huskers are men and trimmers are women.

These are examples of how traditional patterns of job assignment continue through unthinking acceptance of historical accident. Here again, changing economic or social conditions can alter the patterns of job assignment.

TRAITS AND ABILITIES

(4) *"I hired a man rather than a woman because the work is too hard for a woman."*

Sometimes women simply cannot compete with men because of muscular differences. When it comes to felling trees, climbing telephone poles or

lifting chases of printing type, the average man is a better choice than the average woman. But chivalry often plays second fiddle to economics when men are able to secure better and easier jobs. Women do hard, dirty work in many factories while men do cleaner, lighter work that requires greater skill and offers higher pay.

Thus, while there are cases in which assigning certain jobs to men because of their superior muscular strength is obviously justified, in other cases women will be assigned strenuous jobs as long as they lack the training to compete for the easier ones.

(5) *"I hired a man rather than a woman because a woman isn't as interested in her job and can't handle people as well as men."*

Women employes are often criticized for shirking responsibility, not seeking promotion and not being able to supervise subordinates. These characteristics are probably not inherent feminine traits but rather most women's way of responding to prevailing employment conditions. Not many women will prepare themselves for advancement and actively seek it if they know they will probably be barred from promotion for reasons having nothing to do with their individual abilities. After all, most men do not want responsibility, either. It is part of management's job to find and encourage the exceptional employe who is willing to work harder in order to go farther.

NEVERTHELESS, it is true that job interest and the ability to supervise will probably remain higher among men *as a group* simply because fewer women will be intensely concerned with personal advancement and willing to spend the time and effort necessary to develop executive ability.

(6) *"I would rather hire a woman than a man for that job because a woman can do it better."*

Women probably do have greater finger dexterity than men and are generally able to out-perform men in repetitive tasks. But most women employes are allowed to utilize their digital superiority only in semi-skilled jobs.

The real reason women accept repetitive jobs more readily than men and do them better may be that they know they have less chance than men of finding interesting kinds of work. The high rate of turnover among female employes in lower-level jobs

may be, to a large extent, a result of their monotony.

It seems probable that, as women's job opportunities gradually broaden, they will increasingly gravitate into occupations for which they may truly have greater aptitude than men. On the whole, however, women will probably continue to predominate in certain occupations not because of any superior attitude, but because their generally less intense concern with advancement often makes them content to accept repetitive jobs, or because they lack the training and skills to compete successfully for more desirable positions.

COST

(7) *"I hired a man for this job because, in the long run, a woman employe would be more expensive."*

The greater cost of absenteeism and turnover among women workers as compared with men is a familiar complaint. However, comparisons are significant only when they can be made between men and women holding similar jobs, rather than between men and women employes in general.

Some employers have found that as women workers adjust to the standards of the business world their absenteeism declines. Employers also tend to exaggerate the failings of women workers, while they tolerate the failings of men because they are used to them. If a man turns up on the job with a hangover, nobody says, "That's just like a man." But if a woman claims she has a headache, that may

be taken to symptomatize certain failings of the whole sex.

However, there is another, more valid, aspect to the cost problem. Because most women's primary allegiance is to their homes and children, management is often reluctant to make the long-term, expensive investment necessary to train them as future skilled workers or executives. Even highly capable young women usually view their jobs as temporary.

AND even those willing—and given the chance—to go through the long preparation required to rise to high positions frequently create "hidden costs" because they cannot be utilized as flexibly as male executives. There may be jobs on the regular promotion ladder they cannot be assigned to. Many women are reluctant to travel in connection with their work. Nor can a company transfer a married woman

executive as readily as a man. Finally, because married women may leave paid employment for prolonged intervals, an older woman is likely to have less experience than a man of the same age and thus be less qualified.

Thus, where the preference for male employes is genuinely based on considerations of comparative cost, the employer's bias is frequently justified. The major injustice to women in these cases occurs when an individual woman's ambition and ability are ignored because she is automatically grouped with members of her sex who are less interested in personal advancement.

(8) *"I employed a woman for this job because I could hire her for less than an equally capable man would cost."*

Sometimes the fact that women can be hired for less than men gives them preference in certain fields. For example, women are increasingly employed as bank tellers because it is difficult to hire able young men at the prevailing salaries.

INCREASED mechanization may cause a job to be downgraded as it comes to require less skill. Comparatively unskilled women will then be employed at a lower wage than more highly skilled men received before. Women may also get preference in industry if they have superior qualifications and can be hired at the same pay scale as less skilled men.

Management is probably least willing to speak frankly of the role that costs play in determining women's employment opportunities. Separate pay scales frequently prevail for men and women doing the same job. Often a man may be preferred for a particular post. But if a suitable male is not available, an equally competent woman may get the job at a lower salary.

As the employment of women expands and their acceptance as employes grows, many of these wage differentials probably will disappear. But as long as women as a group devote less of their working lives to paid employment than men do, and therefore continue to be in a poorer position to compete for many of the more desirable jobs, most of them will probably continue to be employed at lower average pay than men.

* * *

THE stanchest advocate of increased employment opportunities for women must concede that certain criticisms of women as employes are justified. But it can also be pointed out that the growing labor needs of an expanding economy are constantly drawing more women into paid employment. Today, women constitute approximately 30 per cent of the labor force. In 1890 they made up only 15 per cent. At that time probably half the women in this country never worked for pay. Today more than one of every three women over 14 holds a job, and almost every young woman has some work experience before she starts raising a family. Furthermore, almost 60 per cent of all working women are married and almost half of all working women are past 40.

Women today not only are devoting a greater part of their lives to paid employment, but also are devoting more time to advanced education and to preparation for work. Almost 10 per cent of college-age girls now acquire baccalaureate degrees and about one-third of female college graduates go on to take advanced degrees.

FOR a variety of reasons many women are committed to paid employment for the rest of their working lives. These are the women who are unmarried, childless, divorced or who have completed childbearing and returned to work. Taken together, they constitute a sizable proportion of the female population.

Vast changes, therefore, have taken place in the composition of the female working population. The employer who depends on old stereotypes will find they no longer provide an accurate picture of many of the women working for him.

Employers would, therefore, benefit themselves if they distinguished more carefully between those problems presented by women employes that make a male preferable in specific cases, and those preferences that result from unexamined prejudice and unjustified bias.

In a period of high labor costs and shortages of skills, the basic womanpower policy that management should adopt for its own sake is to give each woman employe as much opportunity as she individually deserves.

EXPERTS ENDORSE JOBS FOR MOTHERS

Conference at Arden House Finds Employment Rising and Welcomes Effects

By ANNA PETERSEN
Special to The New York Times.

HARRIMAN, N. Y., Oct. 25—The social and economic effects of the widespread employment of married women are largely desirable, a conference called by the National Manpower Council asserted today. And the job trend will continue, the delegates said.

The conclusions were reached after five days of discussions at Columbia University's Arden House. Ninety men and women took part, representing a cross-section of views from business, industry, education, labor unions, child welfare and religion.

Dr. Henry David, the council's executive director, said that a new pattern in American life was emerging because of the number of jobs held by mothers. Most are in their thirties, forties and fifties, he added, and come from all groups of society.

Signs of such a "revolution in womanpower," he said, are found in statistics showing that three of every ten married women are working and two of every five mothers with children of school age are also in the labor force.

With their earnings they have raised the living standards of their families, improved the prospects for their children and expanded the American middle class, he said. While the effects, in general, are favorable, Dr. David went on, some of the consequences of this "revolution" are unknown because of a lack of reliable knowledge.

He took note of charges that the employment of mothers was related to the rise in juvenile delinquency. But he declared that delinquency was a broader question and that no problem rose from a single cause.

Dr. David said that, given a continuing high level of employment, the trend toward the increasing employment of married women would continue. Many will work out of economic necessity; others, he said, are being encouraged to return to work by social pressures.

October 26, 1957

Recession Hits Women Harder, State Reports

Women workers in New York State have been harder hit by the recession than men, according to The Industrial Bulletin, monthly publication of the New York State Labor Department.

Since September, 1957, women have been losing factory jobs at the rate of 14,000 a month. Between September and May of 1957 the total number of women factory workers dropped from a high of 670,000 to 556,000 in a decrease of 17 per cent. The total employment of men factory workers dropped 11 per cent.

A THIRD OF WOMEN JOIN LABOR FORCE

1960 Census Notes Change From U. S. Life in 1890

By WILL LISSNER

More than a third of the women of working age in the United States are employed or are actively seeking employment, compared with less than a fifth in 1890.

This is one of the most significant changes in American life and it is mirrored in census statistics, Prof. Philip M. Hauser of the University of Chicago reports.

Dr. Hauser, one of the nation's leading demographers, has completed an analysis of the results of the 1960 population census tabulated so far.

The increasing percentage of women entering the labor force more than offsets a decline in the percentage of the male population of working age in the labor force. Men of working age supplied 84 per cent of the labor force in 1890 but only 77 per cent in 1960.

The shifts are explained in major part by the increased enrollment in high school and college that nowadays postpones entrance into the labor force, Dr. Hauser writes in an article that will be published in The Scientific American next month.

Whereas half the young men from 14 to 19 years old were job-seekers or job-holders in 1890, only a third are today, Dr. Hauser points out. Today, as in 1890, about a fourth of the young women in this age group were at work or looking for jobs.

Fewer Older Men Work

About the same percentage of males between 20 and 64 are in the labor force as a half century ago. But the proportion of men 65 and older who consider themselves in the labor force shows a decline from more than two-thirds in 1890 to 41.4 per cent in 1950 and to 30.5 per cent in 1960. This is attributable to the availability of pensions and the increase in compulsory retirement at 65.

"The older men have been replaced—not in their jobs, but in entirely new functions in the constantly changing work force —by women," Dr. Hauser reports.

This is seen when one analyzes the composition of the labor force, he says. At the turn of the century nearly three-fourths of the labor force worked on physical goods. Less than a fourth provided services. In 1960, most of the labor force worked in service occupations

Prof. Philip M. Hauser

—42.2 per cent in white-collar service jobs and 12 per cent in household service.

The decline in production workers is entirely accounted for by the reduction in the number of farmers, farm laborers and nonfarm laborers, Dr. Hauser finds.

Since 1900, agricultural employment has fallen from 37.5 per cent to only 6.3 per cent of the labor force. The percentage of nonfarm laborers has dropped from 12.5 to 5.5 per cent. These declines more than offset the increases in other lines of production.

Three-fifths of the male work force is engaged in production work, compared with four-fifths in 1890.

However, clerical workers increased fivefold, sales workers almost twofold, professional and technical workers threefold and managerial and proprietorial occupations almost half.

Household workers declined 50 per cent, but other service workers — barbers, beauticians, cooks, policemen, firemen, janitors, waitresses — doubled, so that on balance service occupations increased by a third.

"In sum, the economic life of the country is now much less dependent on muscle power and more dependent on professional, technical and clerical skills," Dr. Hauser concludes. "This shift in emphasis from brawn to brain, dexterity and education, has opened the ranks of the labor force to women.

"The percentage of clerical workers in the female labor force has increased almost eightfold; the percentage of sales people has doubled; the percentage of managers and proprietors has more than doubled, and the percentage of professional and technical workers has increased by nearly 50 per cent."

CHAPTER 6

Women in the Arts

*Martha Graham, dancer
and choreographer, December 4, 1947.*
Courtesy Compix.

HARRIET BEECHER STOWE

DEATH OF THE AUTHORESS OF "UNCLE TOM'S CABIN."

She Was Attacked with Congestion of the Brain and Partial Paralysis Last Friday—Totally Unconscious Since Tuesday Afternoon—Her Death Bed Surrounded by Relatives and Friends—The Funeral Services This Afternoon.

HARTFORD, July 1.—Mrs. Harriet Beecher Stowe, the authoress of "Uncle Tom's Cabin," "Dred," and other works of world-wide reputation, died at her home, 73 Forest Street, at noon to-day without regaining consciousness. She passed peacefully away, as though into a deep sleep.

By her bedside at the time were her son, the Rev. Charles Edward Stowe of Simsbury, her two daughters, Eliza and Harriet; her sister, Mrs. Isabella Beecher Hooker, and her husband, the Hon. John Hooker; Dr. Edward B. Hooker, her nephew, who was also her medical attendant, and other relatives. Mrs. Stowe's malady of many years' continuance, a mental trouble, took an acute form on Friday, when congestion of the brain, with partial paralysis, appeared. During Friday, Saturday, and Sunday Mrs. Stowe was about the house, but suffering very much. Since Monday she had been confined to her bed, and yesterday afternoon became unconscious.

Mrs. Stowe, until about seven years ago, was in good health, although she was frail bodily. She was about the city and attended church regularly at the Winsor Avenue Congregational Church, of which her son, the Rev. Charles E. Stowe, was then the pastor. Her health for some time, however, had been precarious, and she had needed the constant attention of a nurse, who accompanied her about her walks in the vicinity of her home. She always had pleasant words for the children of the neighborhood, with whom she talked in her rambles, and seemed to be at her brightest when thinking of and talking with them.

Her condition has been such that her death at almost any time during the last three or four years could hardly have been unexpected. She first came to Hartford in 1824, as a schoolgirl, and had lived here permanently, with a Winter residence in Florida, since 1865.

Mrs. Stowe's funeral will be attended at her home at 5 o'clock to-morrow afternoon. Relatives, friends, and neighbors are invited. Her body will be taken to Andover, Mass., Friday, on the train leaving here at 2 A. M., on the New-England Road. The burial will be in the cemetery connected with the Andover Theological Seminary, where Mrs. Stowe's husband, Prof. Calvin E. Stowe, and her son Henry, are buried.

CAREER OF THE FAMOUS AUTHORESS

How the Story of "Uncle Tom's Cabin" Came to be Written.

The death of Harriet Beecher Stowe is more than the ending of a woman's life of whatever degree of fame. It marks the extinction of genius in a family, and is one of the closing leaves in an era of our century. The more famous children of a famous father leave worthy descendants, but none of their own mental gifts or rank. Rarely, indeed, is there so much in a single life so memorable or so interesting as in that of the writer of probably the most widely read work of fiction ever penned.

Mrs. Stowe in Her Parlor.
A Scene in the Old Lady's Daily Life at Home.

"Beecher on Intemperance" was a famous book in its day. Its author was the Rev. Lyman Beecher, father of Henry Ward and Harriet and the rest, who almost constitute a genus by themselves, so marked are they in their talents. The stern and eloquent old Calvinist parson was settled in Litchfield, Conn., and there the daughter, who was to surpass her father, marked man as he was in his time, was born on June 14, 1812. In those earliest days of hers perhaps nothing is more remarkable than that simplicity of training which is still characteristic of New-England life in regions not yet modernized. They were the affectionate children of loving parents, and became such masters of laughter and tears as men and women seldom are. Yet they grew up in a home atmosphere where feeling was repressed. Birthdays and family festivals and such little loving gifts and words as now pass between brothers and sisters were infrequent, if not actually discouraged in that family. Of her mental traits none was earlier or more fully developed than her memory. The bulk of the Bible and extended passages from most of the English classics were at her tongue's end and instantly upon demand. But it cannot be said that her literary gifts were precocious. Last year she herself recalled, in an article published for a charitable purpose, her first attempt at authorship. It was an epitaph composed at the age of eight apropos of the death of a kitten. It was decently buried beneath such an inscription as any bright little girl might write about a loved and dead Tabby:

> Here lies poor Kit,
> Who had a fit
> And acted queer.
> Killed with a gun,
> Her race is run,
> And she lies here.

Her fifteen years of childhood were uneventful, but spent in an exceptional environment of cultured society with lawyers, ministers, and professors, who were frequenters of her father's circle. Her mother died in her early youth, and she was still a slip of a girl when she went to help her sister Catharine, who was the head of

a successful girls' school at Hartford. Thus prosily her life passed until, in her twenty-first year, on Jan. 6, 1833, she married Calvin E. Stowe, Professor of Languages and Biblical Literature at Lane Seminary, Cincinnati. That was the turning point of her career. Nowhere were the "underground railway" and pathetic incidents under the fugitive slave law more familiar than on the border of Ohio. Nowhere was there a stronger anti-slavery agitation or more flourishing hotbed of abolition than at Lane Seminary. That this remark is not made at random appears from the record that a majority of the students left the seminary because the Trustees insisted upon their disbanding an anti-slavery debating society. Perhaps the seminary owed its escape from such scenes as attended the mobbing of the Colored Orphan Asylum in this city solely to the difficulty of reaching it from Cincinnati. In anticipation of violence, the Stowe residence was armed and equipped with a large bell to summon help. In her husband's house many a fugitive was sheltered and many a thrilling tale rehearsed. Thus, in a sense, "Uncle Tom's Cabin" was not a freak of fancy. Its inspiration and its incidents came from actual life. But the story of that book—a historical event and influence second only to some of the Bibles of the world—must be reserved while its author's life is followed hastily to its close.

After leaving Cincinnati the Stowes lived for a time in Brunswick, Me., her husband being a professor at Bowdoin College. In 1852 they settled in Andover, in the famous theological seminary of which village he also held a chair. Thus it is not left to inference that he was a man of character and parts, and in no danger of being submerged even in his wife's more famous personality. He was an ideal old-time New-Englander, about ten years older than his wife. His flowing white beard and silvery hair, falling from a fine head bald on top, suggested the reference to the "dear old rabbi" contained in a personal letter to his wife from George Eliot. His death preceded his wife's about ten years. Mrs. Stowe has left this picture of herself at the age when she wrote her most famous book: "A little bit of a woman, rather more than forty, as withered and dry as a pinch of snuff, never very well worth looking at in my best days, and now a decidedly used-up article." But she held her own very well, and in another personal letter, in firm and regular writing, she said of herself: "I was seventy-six on my last birthday, and have all my bodily powers perfect; can walk

Mrs. Stowe's Residence,
Where the Aged Authoress Died in Hartford, Conn.

from three to seven miles per day without fatigue; have a healthy appetite, and quiet sleep every night." She was one of the young friends of the professor's first wife. Accordingly their first children, twin daughters, were named Harriet Beecher and Eliza Stowe. A younger daughter is the wife of the Ritualistic pastor of the Church of the Messiah, Boston. A son, the Rev. Charles E. Stowe, was ordained in 1873 as the pastor of the Windsor Avenue Congregational Church, Hartford. Between that city in the Summer, and in the Winter at their orange plantation, at Mandarin, Fla., on the St. John's River, the family divided its later years. In Hartford they were members of a delightful coterie, including Charles Dudley Warner and Mark Twain as near neighbors. Their plain brick residence on Forest Street is remarkable chiefly for the portraits, souvenirs, and tributes which have come unsought from famous people all over the world, but the walls are also adorned with many paintings by Mrs. Stowe. She was an artist only in the second place, and if she had not become famous by her writings her transcripts of natural scenes in color would have won her credit enough to satisfy most women. In her library are 26 volumes of a somewhat unusual character. They are folios sumptuously bound in morocco, and all cased in rare old oak. On the first page is an address illuminated on vellum, and adopted at a meeting at Stafford House, London, Lord Shaftesbury presiding. Following the address come the signatures of 562,448 women, from her who ranks next to the Queen to the humblest mill operator in Manchester. But this is properly part of the history of a book more fully to be described.

Mrs. Stowe's literary life began shortly after marriage, and was long confined to fugitive tales and sketches, afterward assembled and printed under the title of "The Mayflower." She did nothing memorable until her maturity, and then leaped full-fledged into the company of the illustrious women of the century. Besides "Uncle Tom's Cabin," of which the narrative is given below, she did nothing better than "The Minister's Wooing," (1859,) which pleased the critics at least as well as it did the public. Possibly her least happy venture was "Lady Byron Vindicated." In 1853 she had visited England and formed the acquaintance of the un-

happy wife of the poet, and upon what she then learned was based an unmentionable charge against him. Upon this tour was based "Sunny Memories of Foreign Lands." In 1856 appeared her second anti-slavery novel, "Dred." It was a powerful work, but marred by the sentiment inspired by the attack upon Sumner in the Senate Chamber. It was thus that the bitter, avenging spirit was given to Dred at the expense of the art of the story. She has written other works creditable enough, but they will not live.

She wisely stayed her pen while still it commanded readers. She had made no sustained effort since the garden party in 1882, the third in the series given by her publishers to distinguished American authors who had attained threescore and ten. The galaxy assembled at Gov. Claflin's seat. The Old Elms, at Newtonville, goes far to answer the taunting query, "Who reads an American book?" Surely no history of the Nation and generation is complete without taking account of those then assembled in tribute to her genius. The half of them cannot be mentioned here, but there were Holmes and Whittier and Howells and a score of others, not to mention the Beechers, and the authoress of "Uncle Tom's Cabin," of which some tardy and insufficient account may now be given.

America's greatest orator has said that true eloquence is very rare, because there go to make it up three things almost never found together—the man, the subject, and the occasion. Never was there a riper occasion than when this country was writhing in its death grip with slavery. Never was there a subject appealing more deeply to the tenderest sentiments of every human being. And if it is added with appearance of extravagance that never was there an uninspired intellect better adapted to strike the glowing iron, the record is confidently appealed to for the prototype. In the English language the Bible and Shakespeare's works are its only rivals. Within five years a half million copies were sold in the United States alone, a degree of success phenomenal, but far inferior to that recorded in England. In 1855 The Edinburgh Review declared that no record was possible after 1852, but in that year a million copies were sold in England, probably ten times as many as of any other volume except the Bible and Prayer Book. In

each year of the generation since gone by the sale has steadily continued, and every year the book in its dramatic form is seen upon the stage by many audiences. There could not be a greater error than to limit the vogue of the book to the comparatively few millions who speak English. Here is a stanza by Holmes, read at the garden party above mentioned:

> Briton and Frenchman, Swede and Dane,
>   Turk, Spaniard, Tartar of Ukraine,
>   Hidalgo, Cossack, Cadi,
> High Dutchman and Low Dutchman, too,
> The Russian serf, the Polish Jew,
>   Arab, Armenian, and Mantchoo,
>   Would shout, " We know the lady."

Lest this should be thought poetic license it will be well to give what the lawyers call a " bill of particulars " in the shape of a few of the titles under which this lady has carried her fame to the ends of the earth. Here they are, selected incompletely and at random, from a compilation by one of her publishers: " Oncle Tom's Hütte," " Onkel Tomas," " De Negerut," " De Hut van Onkel Tom," " Tama's Bataya," " La Capanna dello Zio Tommaso," " Chata Wuja Tomasza," " A Cabana do Pai Thomaz," " La Cabaña del Tio Tomas," " Khizhina dyadi Tomaj," " Onkel Tom's Stuga," &c. Who reads an American book, indeed? In one of the above languages there were twelve versions, and no one knows how many editions.

It has already been hinted how the book came to be written. Escaping slaves were familiar to her. She heard their stories, she saw their wounds, she helped their flight. Uncle Tom was the husband of a domestic in her family, and his death was the chapter first written. Topsy was a pickaninny named Celeste who lived on Walnut Hills, Cincinnati. Eliza's escape across the ice floating in the Ohio was an incident recorded in the press of that period by a witness of it, and so the story came to her eyes. Thus she was brimming over with her topic when she was asked to write a story for The National Era. It was begun in the expectation that it would run through a month or so, but it was scarcely finished within a year. Week by week, the installments were produced and read aloud to the family before being dispatched to the narrow circle of readers who saw it first. To say that it was not appreciated in serial form is to state the case mildly. Her publisher was anxious for her to stop. Her brother, Henry Ward, warned her to cut it short, lest its length should prevent printing it as a book. She answered them never a word. Her genius was in travail, and, whatever others might think, she could not stop or turn.

The death of Uncle Tom was conceived at the communion table, and when her little sons heard it they declared slavery was the wickedest thing in the world. After the chapter of Eva's death, the author was prostrated three days in bed. In one sense, a wholly reverent one, it may be said that she was inspired. She was wholly beside herself and in the control of her idea. She did not consider the book hers. She belonged to the book. In her own phrase: " That wasn't mine; that was given to me." Possibly from this accustomed expression of hers came the preposterous story that the wonder-working volume was not hers, but her brother Henry's. In his jesting way he said that he wrote " Norwood," just to show what he really could do in the way of fiction, and the result " killed dead " the theory that he wrote " Uncle Tom's Cabin."

At length the book was finished, and the next thing was to find a publisher for it. Mrs. Stowe hoped it would at least bring her a silk gown, then the unfulfilled object of her womanly ambition. Accordingly, her sister Catharine offered it to the publishers of one of her own books. Mr. Lee replied—the book being, it will be remembered, then in print and not the proposal of an unread writer—that he could not sell a thousand copies, and, as it would ruin his trade with the South, he declined the project. John R. Jewett of Boston finally undertook to bring it out. He as little as any one else saw the end from the beginning. That within a few months he should hand to her $10,000 as her share of the profits was beyond his wildest conceptions. How far it fell short of the reality is in some degree set forth above.

"The Letters of Emily Dickinson," reviewed below, contain many hitherto unpublished letters. Here are excerpts from some of them.

We miss you very much indeed you cannot think how odd it seems without you there was always such a Hurrah wherever you was I miss My bedfellow very much for it is rare that I can get any now for Aunt Elisabeth is afraid to sleep alone and Vinnie has to sleep with her but I have the privilege of looking under the bed * * *.
To Austin Dickinson, 1842.

* * *

I have never lost but one friend near my own age & with whom my thoughts & her own were the same. It was before you came to Amherst. My friend was Sophia Holland. * * * There she lay mild & beautiful as in health & her pale features lit up with an unearthly—smile. I looked as long as friends would permit & when they told me I must no longer I let them lead me away. I shed no tear, for my heart was too full to weep, but after she was laid in the coffin & I felt I could not call her back again I gave way to a fixed melancholy.
To Abiah Root, 1846.

* * *

How I wish you were mine, as you once were, when I had you in the morning, and when the sun went down, and was sure I should never go to sleep without a moment from you. I try to prize it, Jennie, when the loved are here, try to love *more*, and *faster*, and *dearer*, but when all are gone, seems as had I tried *harder*, they would have stayed with me. Let us love with all our might, Jennie, for who knows where our hearts go, when this world is done?
To Jane Humphrey, 1855.

To have woven Wine so delightfully, one must almost have been a Drunkard one's-self—but that is the stealthy franchise of the demurest Lips. Drunkards of Summer are quite as frequent as Drunkards of Wine, and the Bee that comes home sober is the Butt of the Clover.
To Mrs. J. Howard Sweetser, 1883.

When Jesus tells us about his Father, we distrust him. When he shows us his Home, we turn away, but when he confides to us that he is "acquainted with Grief," we listen, for that also is an Acquaintance of our own.
To Mrs. Henry Hills, c. 1884.

On the Letter-Writer Was the Indelible Mark of the Poet

THE LETTERS OF EMILY DICKINSON. Edited by Thomas H. Johnson and Theodora Ward. 3 vols. Illustrated. 999 pp. Cambridge: Belknap Press of Harvard University Press. $25, the set.

By ROBERT HILLYER

WITH the publication of the letters of Emily Dickinson, Thomas H. Johnson (assisted by Theodora Ward as associate editor) has completed the monumental task he set himself when he edited the three volumes of Dickinson poems, published in 1955. The six volumes, considered as a unit, contain every word, including prose fragments, that Emily Dickinson is known to have written. In addition, the introductions and notes, together with Mr. Johnson's "Emily Dickinson, An Interpretive Biography," form a complete and balanced presentation of the poet's life. There is no greater achievement of editing and research in the field of American literature.

These thousand and forty-nine letters, addressed to some hundred odd recipients, are arranged chronologically. As with the poems, each letter is followed by notes fully explaining the source and present status of the manuscript, previous publication, the identity of persons and quotations, and the attendant events or emotional background. Appended are short biographical sketches of all the recipients and most of the people named. After 1850, when she was 20, Emily Dickinson seldom bothered with dates. Hence these important

Mr. Hillyer, who is a Pulitzer-prize poet and author of many books of verse, teaches at the University of Delaware.

items had to be supplied by recognizable changes in her penmanship and such internal information as her references afforded.

About one hundred letters are here published for the first time. Many others have been restored to their original form after being abridged or combined in previous editions. The partial collection of 1894, Mabel Loomis Todd's labor of love, preserved many, such as those to the Norcross sisters, that were subsequently destroyed.

Mr. Johnson divides his material into twelve sections according to the development of Emily Dickinson's life and art. They range from the chatty account of doings in the hen-yard and the town, written to her brother, Austin, when she was 11, to her deathbed message to her Norcross cousins—"Called Back," which is inscribed on her gravestone in Amherst. The chief correspondents of her girlhood were her brother and her friend, Abiah Root. The bonds between brother and sister were strong and intimate; the entire Dickinson family was unusually close-knit.

Emily's girlhood friend, Abiah Root, was her confidante and, to a degree, her exemplar. Abiah, typical of her place and time, underwent "conversion to Christ" in her late adolescence, an experience that filled Emily with awe and some envy: "I am not happy, and I regret that last term [at Mount Holyoke] when that golden opportunity was mine, that I did not give up and become a Christian." She never did, in the orthodox sense. In a letter to Thomas Wentworth Higginson she wrote, "They are all religious—except

Emily Dickinson, about 17.

me—and address an Eclipse—every morning—whom they call their 'Father.'"

HER first letter to Higginson, in 1862, marked a turning point in her life. For several years she had been writing verses, and she sent him some. They must have been astonishing to one who was the embodiment of the literary taste of the period, and the wonder is not that he found them faulty but that he was impressed by them at all. Until her death in 1886 she deemed herself his "scholar." Higginson, on his part, fluctuated between a lively, tender interest and a suspicion, fostered by his wife, that his scholar was "half-cracked." It may be, however, that he was right in urging her not to publish: the impact of publicity might well have been disastrously exciting.

Her letters to Susan Gilbert began in 1850, six years before Susan married Austin Dickinson, and continued until Emily's death. The early ones are lengthy and painfully effusive. After the marriage, Austin and his wife moved into a house next door to the Dickinson "mansion," and there was no further need for extensive correspondence. Short notes, almost daily, sufficed, and they provide a record of a human relationship trembling between love and doubt.

Her earliest letters give no hint of her future withdrawal from the world. One would say that she was an unusually high-spirited girl devoted to jokes, nonsensical valentines and parties. In the Eighteen Fifties her mood grew more serious, and her epistolary circle expanded. During this decade she inaugurated some of her most important correspondence, with Samuel Bowles, editor of The Springfield Daily Republican; with J. G. Holland, associated with Bowles for a time, who afterward became editor of Scribner's Monthly and with Louise and Frances Norcross, her Boston cousins. Her literary correspondence is shot through with emotion; her personal letters abound in literary allusions. Occasionally, she is exasperatingly coy.

As time went on, and death after death shook her to the roots, the letters steadily darkened. They became shorter and more epigrammatic. Frequently, as is shown by the existence of first drafts, she worked over her letters as though they were poems. They are, in fact, an extension of her poetry. She could summon the weather into a phrase, cut through melancholy with a burst of her old-time gaiety, share her delight in a circus parade—"the Procession from Algiers," or depict unforgettably a local event such as a conflagration at night. Her little notes to children captivate us still. Her satirical passages are full of wit. But her morbidity, which, even when she was a girl of sixteen, impelled her to witness the final coma of a dying playmate, is often shocking. Some of her recurrent notes of condolence must have added, as Mark Twain said of Mrs. Sigourney's elegies, a new terror to death.

The kinship of her verse and letters is apparent from 1858 on. We find passage after passage that scans metrically and sometimes even rhymes, thus: "Indeed it is God's house/and there are gates of Heaven/and to and fro the angels go/with their sweet postillions." Scores of such submerged stanzas could be cited, and the iambic rhythm pervades her prose. Her diction

became ever sharper, her style so elliptical that it often needs study. Mr. Johnson is mistaken in stating that she mentioned Sir Thomas Browne only once; she quoted him in a later note, and her use of place names, and legendary figures as a fluid symbolism, as well as her frequent capitalization, suggests, in my opinion, some influence from Sir Thomas Browne's metaphysical prose, with which she was familiar.

It is possible to give only a hint of the richness of these letters. Here are a few typical apothegms: on art, "Nature is a Haunted House—but Art—a House that tries to be haunted"; on her need of a mentor, "I had no Monarch in my life, and cannot rule myself"; on a religious revival, "I know of no choicer

ecstasy than to see Mrs. [Sweetser] roll out in crape every morning, I suppose to intimidate antichrist; at least it would have that effect on me"; to some children, "Please never 'improve'—you are perfect now"; on autumn, "How softly summer shuts, without the creaking of a door"; on skepticism, "Science will not trust us with another World."

AS Mr. Johnson points out in his introduction, Emily Dickinson was unmoved by world events. She thought of the Civil War as merely an "oblique place" until an Amherst boy was killed, when suddenly the tragedy became embodied. During the Franco-Prussian War

she wrote to Mrs. Holland, "What Miracles the News is! Not Bismarck but ourselves." She never scattered her attention; she directed every perception and feeling, like a burning-glass, to a single focus, something local, personal, and immediate. After his visit to her in 1870, Higginson wrote, "I never was with anyone who drained my nerve power so much * * * I am glad not to live near her."

To be the focus of a burning-glass is not comfortable. This concentration on the object in view has made her letters the most intense in literature. They exercise a fascination that draws one on, page after page, for they are, in truth, "the chariot that bears the human soul."

March 16, 1958

Old Stories for New Readers

Miss Willa Cather Selects Two Volumes From the Works of Sarah Orne Jewett

THE BEST STORIES OF SARAH ORNE JEWETT. Selected and arranged, with a preface, by Willa Cather. 2 Vols. Houghton Mifflin Company. $4.

By RICHARD LE GALLIENNE

WE may assume that the aim of Miss Cather in making these selections from the stories of Sarah Orne Jewett is to gain new readers for a writer who has for some time quietly taken her place as an American classic, and, therefore, like all classics in these days, stands in need of a friend. If the assumption be correct the present reviewer may be counted among the new readers thus gained, for, while, of course, Miss Jewett's name has been familiar to him as affiliated with the little group of Boston "immortals," her work was entirely unread by him till he opened these two charming volumes. It is to be hoped that this admission will not seem to disqualify him as their reviewer. At all events, he thus brings to them a fresh mind, uninfluenced by memories of previous reading or predispositions of any kind. To him the work is as new as if it were published for the first time, though, as a matter of fact, Miss Jewett has been dead for sixteen years. She was born in 1849 and died in 1909, and her most famous book, of which the first of these two volumes is composed, "The Country of the Pointed Firs," was published in 1896, nearly thirty years ago. The only matter on which his previous ignorance precludes him from offering an opinion is how representative a selection Miss Cather has made,

but, as his ignorance does not extend to Miss Cather's own writings, he feels confidence in accepting her as his guide without question. Miss Jewett published some twelve volumes in all, and "The Country of the Pointed Firs" being republished here entire, Miss Cather's second volume of selections is thus drawn from the eleven remaining volumes. There must, therefore, be much admirable writing left behind, to which Miss Cather's selections should, one would think, form a persuasive introduction. With a writer of Miss Jewett's calibre and even accomplishment, all her writing must have value, particularly such as is descriptive of the natural scenes which form the background of her stories, and are of the very life of her characters, as they were first of all of her own.

Born in South Berwick, Me., the daughter of a country doctor (one of her earliest novels, by the way, is entitled "A Country Doctor"), the seaboard of Maine and its sailor-farmer inhabitants were in her blood, the familiar material of her every-day life from childhood. As she was, too, the constant companion of her father, accompanying him on his professional visits, she had peculiar opportunities of becoming familiar with the character of the people to whom he ministered. Familiarity with such a "provincial" environment may influence a writer in two ways. It may generate the proverbial "contempt" and result in rebellious satire, as we have seen it doing recently in some portrayers of this or that provincial American milieu, or it may begin and continue

in affection and an ever-deepening humane understanding. The latter was Miss Jewett's experience. The better she knew her childhood's Maine and its people the more she loved them and the more she desired to express them just as they are, or as they seemed to her. Thus she possessed one of the most important qualifications for the creation of real literature, personal identification with and delighted absorption in her material. There was recently a schism which pooh-poohed the importance of material in art, but it was short-lived, and Pater himself, the idol of the mere "stylists," has pronounced "against the stupidity which is dead to the substance, and the vulgarity which is dead to form." He has also made a distinction between "great art and good art," which we may bear in mind in considering Miss Jewett, the distinction "depending immediately," he considered, "as regards literature, at all events, not on its form but on the matter."

Probably the deep difference between genius and talent in writing is that talent can write equally well on all subjects, but genius only on subject-matter predestined for its use by natural affiliations of taste and association. Thus a poet like Mistral was born to write only of Provence and its people, and his gifts would have been all at sea had he applied them, say, to Paris and the Parisians. Miss Cather rightly makes much of this point of view in her admirable preface. "If," she says, a writer "achieves anything noble, anything enduring, it must be by giving himself absolutely to his

Sarah Orne Jewett.

material. And this gift of sympathy is his great gift; is the fine thing in him that alone can make his work fine. He fades away into the land and people of his heart, he dies of love only to be born again." To employ a homely image, subject-matter is only available to the artist when it has lain long "in soak" in his mind and heart, and Miss Cather quotes an observation from one of Miss Jewett's letters to the same effect, and illustrative of her own artistic processes: "The thing that teases the mind over and over for years, and at last gets itself put down rightly on paper—whether little or great, it belongs to Literature." The final value of the product of this "teasing" process, the literary skill of the writer being assumed, will depend on two other values, the value of the subject-matter and the personal value of the individual using it. For the making of a great book three forms of greatness must combine, greatness in the material, greatness in the personality of the writer and greatness in the writing. But writing may be good, that is real, without being great, as we have seen Pater admonishing us, and if we cannot call Miss Jewett's writing great there is no doubt about its being superlatively good. This cannot be questioned, and, that being admitted, it really does not matter whether or not we agree with Miss Cather when she says: "If I were asked to name three American books which have the possibility of a long, long life, I would say at once, 'The Scarlet Letter,' 'Huckleberry Finn' and 'The Country of the Pointed Firs.' I can think of no others that confront time and change so serenely."

Granted the doubtful value of such categories the present reviewer ventures to think of one other at least—Miss Zona Gale's "Birth." But actually, such categories are misleading, and express what, of course, is all that Miss Cather means to do, a personal preference. To some it may seem, leaving "Huckleberry Finn" aside, that there is no parity of comparison between such a great tragic symbol of dramatic life as "The Scarlet Letter," and the quiet, interpretative observation and embodiment of lives, lived, so to say, in such "low relief" as those to which Miss Jewett brings her illuminating humanity. Of course, all human lives, however limited, or miniature, have the importance which the mere living of them gives, and in a sense there is nothing insignificant to the eye of the philosopher or the artist, yet these are lives and environments which illustrate our common humanity and its conditions, its tragedy, its pathos, its humor, its romance, more vividly, more significantly and more completely than others; but such lives and such environment were not the material which Miss Jewett found and so lovingly studied at Dunnet Landing, on the coast of Maine. Large or intense symbolic figures of passion and sorrow and tragic destinies one must find in other writers, but readers of Miss Jewett must be satisfied, as she was, with homely, "humble" country people, very small farmers and poor fishermen, lonely work-worn old women and old men, narrow, uneventful lives of pathetic little interests, country characters and oddities, now and again touched with a pale ray of romance, extremely insignificant, hum-drum, folk whom it needs the magnifying glass of sympathetic inti-

macy even to differentiate. Yet how wonderfully under Miss Jewett's magnifying glass their individual colors come out, and, as we listen with her to their quaint country gossip, how poignantly there comes to our ears "the shrill, sad music of humanity" with its immemorial burden.

———

It is one of the continual surprises of literature how it is able to interest us in people whom in real life we pass unnoticed, or who when we listen to them, even with sympathy, bore us to death with, irrevently to parody Gray's famous lines, the long and tedious annals of the poor. Once more Miss Jewett shows with remarkable success what a sympathetic writer can do with the most unpromising material, for without her art, and the deep imaginative understanding that animates it, these Maine people of hers would be interesting only to specialists in American local character and conditions. Whether or not even she has been able to universalize them into lasting-significance is questionable, but certainly while we read, sometimes even in spite of ourselves, we live with them as she does, and in the end even love them as she and are loath to part from them. How long out of all the vast and vividly populated world of literary creation they will have power to remain in our memories is not easy to say, but surely it would be hard to forget Miss Todd, and there are several lonely old women such as Mrs. Blackett, beautiful as old silver, whose brave smiles one would not willingly lose. Old women, indeed, would seem to be Miss Jewett's specialty. Miss Cather tells how Miss Jewett once laughingly told her "that her head was full of dear old houses and dear old women, and that when an old house and an old woman came together in her brain with a click, she knew that a story was under way."

———

To see what a perfect idyl Miss Jewett can make of an old house and an old woman, the reader will have to visit "Green Island" for himself, where Mrs. Todd's mother, Mrs. Blackett lived with her son William, a shy oldish fisherman, frightened to death of women, yet hidden in whose heart is a love romance, whose final consummation is one of the few touches of drama in "The Country of the Pointed Firs." Miss Jewett's writing only lends itself occasionally, in perfect bits of description, to quotation, and her characters as a rule come gradually out of her pages, in numerous small touches, or in the course of her remarkable life-like country conversations. Here, however, is a glimpse of Mrs. Blackett that may be detached from its context:

William did not talk much, but his sister Todd occupied the time and told all the news there was to tell of Dunnet Landing and its coasts, while the old mother listened with delight. Her hospitality was something exquisite; she had the gift which so many women lack, of being able to make themselves and their houses belong en-

tirely to a guest's pleasure—that charming surrender for the moment of themselves and whatever belongs to them so that they make a part of one's own life that can never be forgotten. Tact is after all a kind of mind reading, and my hostess held the golden gift. Sympathy is of the mind as well as the heart, and Mrs. Blackett's world and mine were one from the moment we met. Besides, she had that final, that highest gift of heaven, a perfect self-forgetfulness. Sometimes, as I watched her eager, sweet old face, I wondered why she has been set to shine on this lonely island of the Northern coast. It must have been to keep the balance true, and make up to all her scattered and depending neighbors for other things which they may have lacked.

But it is less by any description than by the way Miss Jewett makes us feel how all those "scattered and dependent neighbors" loved Mrs. Blackett that we come to love her for ourselves, and seem, as we read, to have kissed her sweet old face. Mrs. Blackett is the queen of all Miss Jewett's old women, but there are several others, quaint old lonely figures, all "with life's own colors on them," all with decided odd characters of their own, and all with a charming gift of courage, which would seem to be typical of Maine women, who sail their own boats, and have, some of them, brought up families aboard their husband's ships in the days of long voyages, thus coming to have their imaginations touched with the large horizons and far ports of the seven seas. "Provincial" in their environment, their minds have windows that surprise one sometimes with their long outlooks into the universal world. "The Flight of Betsy Lane," one of Miss Jewett's masterpieces, introduces us to three such old women, and the opening of that story may be quoted as a good example of Miss Jewett's method:

One windy morning in May three old women sat together near an open window in the shed chamber of Byfleet Poorhouse. The wind was from the northwest, but their window faced the southeast, and they were only visited by an occasional pleasant waft of fresh air. They were close together, knee to knee, picking over a bushel of beans, and commanding a view of the dandelion-starred, green yard below, and of the winding, sandy road that led to the village, two miles away. Some captive bees were scolding among the cobwebs of the rafters overhead or thumping against the upper panes of glass; two calves were bawling from the barnyard, where some of the men were at work loading a dumpcart and shouting as if every one were deaf. There was a cheerful feeling of activity, and even an air of comfort, about the Byfleet Poorhouse. Almost every one was possessed of an interesting past, though there was less to be said about the future. The inmates were by no means distressed or unhappy. * * *

I must leave the reader to discover for himself the romantic nature of poor Betsy Lane's "flight," promising him a most quaint and touching story; as likewise I must be content

with recommending to him the story Miss Jewett herself liked best, "The Hiltons' Holiday," just a simple story of how a Maine father took his two little girls for an outing in the neighboring town, the mother smiling humorously to herself, as she chose to stay behind and keep house, at her boy-hearted husband's evident desire to take a holiday too. The lovableness of the whole thing, the atmosphere of affection pervading it, leave a glow of happiness in the heart, and has the wistfulness too that breathes "from the full heart of happy things." And how tenderly the spirit of the whole day is gathered up in this twilight close:

It was evening again; the frogs were piping in the lower meadows, and in the woods, higher up the great hill, a little owl began to hoot. The sea air, salt and heavy, was blowing in over the country at the end of a hot, bright day. A lamp was lighted in the house, the happy children were talking together, and supper was waiting. The father and mother lingered for a moment outside and looked down over the shadowy fields; then they went in, without speaking. The great day was over, and they shut the door.

Miss Jewett is a master of atmosphere, another indispensable quality of real imaginative writing, in which she is one with the masters of her craft. With all her fine characterization and the verisimilitude of her dialogue, it is perhaps the power of creating atmosphere that chiefly makes her work so alive and real. Her brief and lovely descriptions of Maine scenery, so firm and unrhetorical, greatly contribute to this, and this scenery, too, is more than a mere background. "The Country of the Pointed Firs," in particular, makes one feel that it is not merely the stories of a certain human group she is telling, but that they are only a component part of the whole scene, not detached from it but springing from it, and but one vital expression of it, no more detachable, or in a sense more important, than the wild birds and animals that are their fellow inhabitants, or the herbs that grow there for Miss Todd's mysterious gathering. It is in the same way that Mr. Thomas Hardy makes us feel that Wessex and his Wessex folk are one. Then, although Miss Jewett so completely identifies herself with her characters as to seem one of them, she at the same time makes one feel the presence of a mind that sees them "in speculi aeternitatis," in relation to the whole sum of humanity through all its moving story. Here is, perhaps, the quality we miss most in contemporary writing, and it is for this reason, if for no other, that Miss Cather's revival of Miss Jewett's work is most timely. Nor must one forget Miss Jewett's all-pervasive, delightful humor. Whatever rank among masterpieces "The Country of the Pointed Firs" may hold, a masterpiece of flawless art it unquestionably is, and a model for all those who would depict some corner of the world so that we may forget its superficial provinciality and see in it, as Whitman wrote, "the developments and the eternal meanings."

April 19, 1925

EDITH WHARTON

Novelist Wrote 'Ethan Frome,' 'The Age of Innocence' and 36 Other Books

WON 1920 PULITZER PRIZE

Chronicler of Inner Circle of New York Society, in Which She Had Been Reared

Edith Wharton was the child as well as the author of the Age of Innocence. In her seventy-five years of life she published thirty-eight books, including that great love story, "Ethan Frome." But her reputation rested mostly upon her achievement as the chronicler of Fifth Avenue, when the brownstone front hid wealth and dignity at its ease upon the antimacassar-covered plush chairs of the Brown Decade.

As a child she lived within the inner circle of New York society that always thought of itself as spelled with a capital S. In her ancestry was a long succession of important names: The Schermerhorns, the Joneses, Pendletons, Stevenses, Ledyards, Rhinelanders and Gallatins, who had led the social life of New York before Mrs. Astor's horse was a symbol, before a Commodore from Staten Island, or men with strange new names from the West had descended on the town. Her own father, although not overly rich, was, nevertheless, able to live, as she said, "a life of leisure and amiable hospitality."

Besides Fifth Avenue, there was Newport. Beyond that was only Europe. When little Edith walked on the Avenue she passed nothing but brownstone and the cow pasture of the Misses Kennedy. When she went on Bailey's Beach she shielded her fair skin from the sun with a black veil. When she went to Europe it was an escape from the crudities of American society—even that with a capital S. Innocence was the life of her childhood and it was the stuff of her better books.

Much Abroad as Child

Edith Wharton was born Edith Newbold Jones on Jan. 24, 1862. Her father was George Frederick Jones; her mother was the former Lucretia Stevens Rhinelander, and back of each were Colonial and Revolutionary ancestors. When she was 4 the family went abroad in pursuit of culture, health and economy, for her father's inherited funds had not increased during the Civil War that was just ended.

Her early impressions were thus international—New York and Newport, Rome, Paris and Madrid. Added to this was a vivid imagination, which found outlet in story telling even before she could read. In keeping with the sheltered life of the time, she was never sent to school, but was taught at home. She began writing short stories in her early teens, but they were never about "real people." Little happened to the real people she knew; what did "happen" was generally not talked about.

It was from this background that Mrs. Wharton was to inherit the belief from which she never de-parted, that "any one gifted with the least creative faculty knows the absurdity of such a charge" as that of "putting flesh-and-blood people into books." Later critics were to say that in this was her greatest lack.

The young author wrote her first efforts on brown paper salvaged from parcels. She was not encouraged. "In the eyes of our provincial society," she was later to say, "authorship was still regarded as something between a black art and a form of manual labor." Each was equally despised in her social level. Her first acceptance was three poems which she sent to the editor with her calling card attached.

Wrote a Novel at 11

In her autobiography Mrs. Wharton gives a picture of her literary beginnings along with a picture of her life. Her first novel, written when she as 11, began: " 'Oh, how do you do, Mrs. Brown?' said Mrs. Tompkins. 'If only I had known you were going to call I should have tidied up the drawing room.' " The little girl showed it to her mother, whose icy comment was: "Drawing rooms are always tidy."

Her first published book was a collaboration called "The Decoration of Homes." How many short stories she wrote before 1899 is not known. But she was encouraged in her writing by such friends as Egerton Winthrop and Walter Berry and somehow, while abroad, met Paul Bourget, the "chronicler of the bourgeoisie." Other mentors were William Brownell and Edward Burlingame, for many years editor of Scribner's Magazine. In her autobiography she writes: "I do not think I have ever forgotten one word of the counsels they gave me." To which a well-known critic added, "One well believes it."

But it was Henry James who was her closest friend and most worthwhile advocate. She was always his respectful disciple and, although in their many meetings he disguised the severity of his judgments with his usual elaborate verbal courtesies, he managed to convey the meaning of his criticism. He remained her close friend until his death.

In 1899 Mrs. Wharton—she had been married to Edward Wharton, a Boston banker, in 1885—published her first book: "The Greater Inclination." In this may be found two of her best short stories, "The Pelican" and "Souls Belated." This volume did not make her a wide reputation overnight. In fact, it was not until 1905 that she gained a large public, although in the interim there had appeared these books: "The Touchstone," "Crucial Instances," "The Valley of Decision" and "The Descent of Man and Other Stories," and her flair for travel books had asserted itself in two volumes on Italy, its villas and gardens.

In 1905 she published her first of many best-sellers, "The House of Mirth." Most critics do not consider this her greatest book, but its popularity established her as a writer. This was in reality her first novel, although she had written long short stories in her other books. Its title came from the biblical assertion, "The heart of fools is in the House of Mirth," and it was a happy title for projecting, as Wilbur Cross once put it, "a group of pleasure-loving New Yorkers, mostly as dull as they are immoral, and letting them play out their drama unmolested by others."

Other novels came in rapid succession, but none attracted the attention in this country that was reserved for the book Elmer Davis once called "the last great American love story"—"Ethan Frome." Those which had gone between were "Madame de Treymes," in which certain French critics detected the influence of Flaubert and Maupassant; "The Fruit of the Tree," "The Hermit and the Wild Woman" and "Artemis to Actaeon."

"Ethan Frome," which was most successfully dramatized two seasons ago, was written in 1911. In it she most successfully blended the psychological refinements she had learned from Henry James with her own inimitable ability to tell a story with a beginning and an end. One critic has said it is comparable only to the work of Nathaniel Hawthorne as a tragedy of New England life. A novelette, it is considered a masterpiece of love and frustration, and is likely to stand, despite its comparative brevity, as her most accomplished work.

EDITH WHARTON

Until 1906 Mrs. Wharton had divided her time between New York and her Summer home at Lenox, Mass. In that year she went to live in France, in Summer at Saint Brice and in the Winter at Hyeres in Provence.

Did Relief Work in War

When the World War broke out she was in Paris and she plunged at once into relief work, opening a room for skilled women of the quarter where she lived who were thrown out of employment by the closing of workrooms. She also fed and housed 600 Belgian refugee orphans. In recognition France awarded her the Cross of the Legion of Honor and Belgium made her a Chevalier of the Order of Leopold. Meanwhile she wrote stories and articles on the war, including "Fighting France" and "The Marne." After the war she visited Africa with General Lyautey at the invitation of the French Government, and wrote as a result "In Morocco."

"The Age of Innocence" was her next book and in terms of sales her most successful. Here she used actually the materials she had hitherto used only for background— the social life of the New York into which she had been born and in which she was bred.

Published serially here and abroad, it was widely read, and was awarded the Pulitzer Prize for 1920. It showed Mrs. Wharton at her best, understanding the cramped society of her youth, unaware of the world beyond it. Four years later she followed it with four novelettes published under the title of "Old New York," a constricted panorama of society in the Forties, Fifties, Sixties and Seventies respectively.

Shortly after the publication of this volume she was made an officer of the Legion of Honor. Then she returned to America, to be awarded the Gold Medal of the National Institute of Arts and Letters, the first woman to be so honored. In 1924 she also became the first woman to be awarded an honorary Doctor of Letters degree by Yale University. In 1930 she was made a member of the National Institute of Arts and Letters. Four years later she was elected to membership in the American Academy of Arts and Letters.

Since that time she had written other books, including "Twilight Sleep," a story of fashionable life in modern New York; "The Children," a study of the children of expatriated divorcées; "Hudson River Bracketed," a study of a modern writer, and "Certain People," a collection of short stories.

But that was many years ago.

That generation which knew her best for "The Age of Innocence" flocked to see "Ethan Frome" when it was adapted for the stage by Owen Davis and his son, Donald. Presented on Broadway with Pauline Lord, Ruth Gordon and Raymond Massey in the leading roles, the grim tragedy proved to be as good theatre as it had previously been a great book.

"Ethan Frome" was not the only one of her books to have been translated into plays in recent years. "The Age of Innocence" helped add to the luster of Katharine Cornell eight years ago, and one of her shorter pieces became "The Old Maid" of the theatre, in which Judith Anderson and Helen Menken starred in 1935.

August 13, 1937

MRS. ATHERTON NOVELIST

In the novels that she wrote, Gertrude Atherton chose for her background all sorts of places from ancient Greece to modern California. She described the sufferings of early American pioneers in the Far West and the chatterings of society in London, Paris and Munich. While some of her novels remain highly popular, other products of her pen were long since doomed to oblivion. The quality of her writing was by no means uniform, for she could sit down and rattle off a piece of fiction, while at other times she would take great pains in the line of study and research work to produce such a book as "The Conqueror."

Mrs. Atherton looked back upon a fruitful past in her autobiographical "Adventures of a Novelist," which appeared in the spring of 1932. In this volume she revealed her independence of opinions and her disdain of the conventional. She described her childhood in San Francisco, where she was born on Oct. 30, 1857, the daughter of parents unhappily married and divorced while she was still a little girl. Her father, she wrote, was a drunkard who taught her "to stand on the table while he was giving a dinner party and * * * kick the plates into the laps of the guests."

Of herself at that tender age she wrote that she was "a little fiend," and that she generally finished playing with other children by "beating them up and throwing them downstairs."

She was equally direct when describing her married life. Her husband, George H. Bowen Atherton, "pestered" her into marriage, and she was not the least in love with him. "He talked a good deal," she wrote, "but he never said anything." When her husband died in 1920 and in the same year 1887 she devoted herself to a literary career.

Earlier Works Unpublished

Her earlier efforts went largely unpublished and almost entirely unrewarded. Her first novel, "The Doomswoman," appeared in 1892 and was frigidly received by the critics. It was a tale of California in 1840, the first of a series of novels depicting conditions in that state between 1800 and 1906, the year of the great earthquake and fire.

Mrs. Atherton packed her trunks and went to Europe with her young daughter. She wrote her books in longhand and never used a secretary to type her manuscripts. The English public took to her novels; a title like "American Wives and English Husbands" aroused curiosity, and as the years went by she was rewarded by heavy sales and a comfortable income from her royalties.

Her earlier works included "A Whirl Asunder," "Patience Sparhawk and Her Times," "His Fortunate Grace," "The Californians," "A Daughter of the Vine," "The Valiant Runaways," "Golden Peacock" and "Rezanov and Donaconcha."

With the turn of the century came "Senator North." The element of interest in this book was the problem of Negro blood and miscegenation, with the scene laid in Washington, D. C. Then, after "The Aristocrats," a romance of the Adirondacks, she wrote "The Conqueror" which, with "Black Oxen," was probably her most successful novel. "The Conqueror," semi-historical and semi-biographical, was an account of the life of Alexander Hamilton, and to gather material for it she went to the West Indies, discovering her hero's birthplace on the little island of Nevis.

Sketches of California

In turn came "The Splendid Idle Forties," sketches of California between 1800 and 1846; "Rulers of Kings," "The Bell in the Fog," a book of short stories; "The Traveling Thirds," impressions of Spain; "Rezanov," "Tower of Ivory," "Julia France and Her Times," "Perch of the Devil," "California: An Intimate History" and "Mrs. Belfame," the last being one of the more hastily written and inconsequential of her books, dealing with a murder mystery.

More Gertrude Atherton books appeared with consistent regularity, including "The White Morning," "The Avalanche," "The Sisters-in-Law," "Sleeping Fires," "Black Oxen," "The Crystal Cup," "The Immortal Marriage," "The Jealous Gods," "Dido, Queen of Hearts" and "The Sophisticates."

Non-fiction works by Mrs. Atherton included "A Few of Hamilton's Letters," "The Gorgeous Isle," an account of Nevis; "The Living Present," being war observations and studies of contemporary feminists, and her autobiography.

She found the material for her "Immortal Marriage," a story of Aspasia, Pericles and other great personages of Athens, in Greece. "Black Oxen," published in 1923, was inspired by accounts of the Steinach method of rejuvenation. It was barred from the public libraries of Rochester, N. Y., by the Mayor of that city—a ban which spurred the sales of the book. In 1935, when she was 78 years old, Mrs. Atherton said she had twice undergone operations for "rejuvenation" and never felt younger or better in her life.

Her prolific output of books continued through her ninth decade. She published successively "Can Women Be Gentlemen?" a book of essays, "The Horn of Life," a novel of San Francisco, "Golden Gate Country," a 100,000-word history, and "My San Francisco," a book of reminiscences.

During the first World War, Mrs. Atherton spent some time in France and was active in relief work. For this she later received the Legion of Honor. A lesser decoration was offered but declined, with characteristic outspokenness:

"There is only one way left in this world to be distinguished," she wrote to Ambassador Jusserand, "and that is not to be decorated by France."

The red rosette of the Legion of Honor was not forthcoming until 1925. In 1934 she was elected president of the National Academy of Literature.

On Oct. 30, 1947, on the occasion of her ninetieth birthday, a gold medal was presented to Mrs. Atherton by the City of San Francisco. At that time she said she was suffering from neuritis in her hand and further writing would have to wait until the hand improved for she "couldn't endure to have a secretary about when I'm writing."

Gave Collection to U. S.

In 1943, at the request of the Library of Congress, Mrs. Atherton presented a collection of her manuscripts and memorabilia to the library.

Mrs. Atherton, who in her declining years was called—much to her disgust — "the dowager of American letters," wrote many articles for daily newspapers. They were of no great merit, and a few of the titles are as follows: "There Is No Such Blight on Sanity as Jealousy, and Without Sanity No Marriage Can Be a Success"; "Married Out of a Schoolroom, She Pasted Back Her Baby's Outstanding Ears With Mucilage and Gave Him Green Apple to Help Cut His Teeth," and "Many a Woman Cherishes Delusion That by Marrying a Drunkard and Having Him Constantly Under Her Influence She Can Eradicate His Thirst and Make Him a Model Husband."

But those were incidental literary peccadillos. Some of her works revealed the personality of a brilliant and very unusual woman. When she wrote unhampered by some pet aversion, her narrative was fine and flowing.

June 15, 194

AMY LOWELL, POET

Amy Lowell won recognition as perhaps the chief practitioner and exponent of "the new verse." She published more than half a dozen volumes of poetry and several volumes of prose criticism. Her recently published biography of Keats in two volumes has been received among literary critics with marked respect.

She lectured frequently and had given public readings from her poetry. She delivered lecture courses at the Brooklyn Institute of Arts and Sciences in 1917 and 1918; was the Francis Bergen Foundation lecturer at Yale in 1921, and the Marshall Woods lecturer at Brown University in the same year.

Miss Lowell was born in Brookline in 1874 and was educated in private schools there. She received the degree of Doctor of Letters from Baylor University in 1920 and in the same year received the Phi Beta Kappa key of scholarship from Columbia University. She was Phi Beta Kappa poet at Tufts College in 1918 and at Columbia in 1920. She was a member of the Poetry Society of America and the New England Poetry Club. Her clubs are the Colony, the MacDowell, New York; the Chilton, Boston, and the Lyceum, London.

Her first published volume was "A Dome of Many-Colored Glass" in 1912. "Sword Blades and Poppy Seeds," published two years later, made some stir and won her wider recognition. Previous to the life of Keats, her last volume had been "A Critical Fable," published in 1922.

Miss Lowell thus defined the type of poetry with which her name is so closely associated: "Vers libre is based upon rhythm. Its definition is 'A verse form based upon cadence rather than upon exact meter.' It is a little difficult to define cadence when dealing with poetry. I might call it the sense of balance. The unit of vers libre is the strophe, not the line or the foot, as in regular meter."

Norreys J. O'Conor's Appreciation.

In an appreciation of Miss Lowell that appeared in The Landmark in January, 1922, Norreys Jephson O'Conor wrote of her:

"Miss Lowell was endowed by fortune for her career. Her forebears, successful New England merchants, amassed wealth, enabling her to have the advantages not only of the education given at school but of that more valuable training which comes from the opportunity to travel and of meeting men and women of achievement. Naturally a book-lover, she has been able to acquire one of the finest private libraries in America; her collection of Keats manuscripts is surpassed by only one other in the world, that of the Marquis of Crewe. These artificial advantages by which Miss Lowell helped to prepare herself for the profession of letters would, however, have counted for little had she not also possessed a nature remarkably sensitive to impressions, the true inheritance of a poet. Coupled with these gifts is another too rarely granted writers, one possibly inherited from her trading ancestors, tenacity of purpose.

"Contrary to the prevailing idea that poets publish early in life, Miss Lowell reached her thirties before she determined to devote herself to poetry. It is worthy of stress that her passion for Keats, leading to the study of his painstaking revisions, fixed her purpose. The format and type of Miss Lowell's first book, 'A Dome of Many-Colored Glass,' published in 1912, followed that of Keats's 'Poems,' and her subsequent volumes of poetry have been of similar appearance."

Noted for Her Independence.

Miss Lowell was always noted for her independence. Surrounded all her life by wealth and luxury, she was accustomed to do pretty much as she pleased.

Possessing the entrée to the most exclusive circles, she devoted very little time to social affairs. She was more interested in literature, art and her dogs, of which she had some of the finest at her kennels in Brookline. The dogs she called her "darlings," and was rarely seen about the place without a few of them tagging at her heels.

May 13, 1925

MARY CASSATT AMERICAN ARTIST

Noted Painter of Women and Children

In pursuing her art talents, Miss Cassatt's subjects were almost invariably women and children. Among her best known paintings are "The Bath," "Breakfast in Bed," "Mother's Caress," "Children Playing With a Cat," "In the Garden" and "Maternity."

She is represented in the Wilstach collection in Memorial Hall, Fairmount Park, Philadelphia, while other examples are owned by the Metropolitan Museum of New York. The Corcoran Art Gallery, Washington, Chicago, Detroit and Providence also possess works of her brush.

A distinction Miss Cassatt cherished was the purchase by the French Government of one of her pictures for the Luxembourg collection.

Miss Cassatt was born in Pittsburgh in 1845. In the last fifty years her visits to the United States were infrequent and of short duration.

Taken to Paris at Early Age.

Mary Cassatt was born in Pittsburgh. Her father's family is traced back to a Frenchman, Cossart, who emigrated from France to Holland in 1612, and whose grandson came to Pennsylvania. Her mother's ancestors were Scottish people who came to America about 1700. At the age of 5 or 6 years Mary Cassatt was taken to Paris, where she lived with her parents for five years. She then returned to Philadelphia, but upon deciding, toward 1868, to become a painter, she went again to Europe and set herself to study in the museums and galleries of Italy, Spain and Belgium, believing that an art education could thus be acquired more satisfactorily than by attending the conventional art schools. In 1874 she settled permanently at Paris.

Her first picture, painted in 1872, represented two young women at a carnival, throwing confetti. It was painted at Parma and showed the influence of Correggio. It was accepted at the Salon and so were her contributions of the following years until 1877, when the picture submitted was refused. She was then invited by Degas to join in the exhibitions of the Impressionists and accepted with enthusiasm, recognizing in that group her true masters. Although she has been called the disciple of Degas, she received no formal instruction from him.

Miss Cassatt made a special study of women and children and created a type of sturdy wholesomeness and naturalness now identified with her work.

In March, 1924, Miss Cassatt, threatened with total blindness, opened an exhibition in a Paris gallery of her works, which she had refused hitherto to sell.

June 16, 1926

ISADORA DUNCAN

Copyright, 1927, by The New York Times Company.
Special Cable to THE NEW YORK TIMES.

PARIS, Sept. 14.—Isadora Duncan, the American dancer, tonight met a tragic death at Nice on the Riviera. According to dispatches from Nice Miss Duncan was hurled in an extraordinary manner from an open automobile in which she was riding and instantly killed by the force of her fall to the stone pavement.

Affecting, as was her habit, an unusual costume, Miss Duncan was wearing an immense iridescent silk scarf wrapped about her neck and streaming in long folds, part of which was swathed about her body with part trailing behind. After an evening walk along the Promenade des Anglais about 10 o'clock, she entered an open rented car, directing the driver to take her to the hotel where she was staying.

As she took her seat in the car neither she nor the driver noticed that one of the loose ends fell outside over the side of the car and was caught in the rear wheel of the machine.

Dragged Bodily From the Car.

The automobile was going at full speed when the scarf of strong silk suddenly began winding around the wheel and with terrific force dragged Miss Duncan, around whom it was securely wrapped, bodily over the side of the car, precipitating her with violence against the cobblestone street. She was dragged for several yards before the chauffeur halted, attracted by her cries in the street.

Medical aid immediately was summoned, but it was stated that she had been strangled and killed instantly.

This end to a life full of many pathetic episodes was received as a great shock in France, where, despite her numerous eccentric traits, Miss Duncan was regarded as a great artist. Her great popularity in France was increased by the entire nation's sympathy when in 1913 her two young children also perished in an automobile tragedy. The car in which they had been left seated started, driverless, down a hill and plunged over a bridge into the Seine River.

During the war she acquired the further gratitude of the French by turning over her palatial home here for war relief headquarters.

Husband Committed Suicide.

Her love affair with the young poet laureate of Soviet Russia, Serge Essinin, terminated in divorce and Essinin's suicide two years ago. She herself was reported to have made an attempt at suicide in the Mediterranean.

Miss Duncan, reduced in her resources recently, succeeded through the aid of friends in completing plans for a school of aesthetics which she meant to start on the Riviera.

It was recently a current rumor among the friends of Miss Duncan that she would find happiness in a marriage with an American, which was to be celebrated at Nice Oct. 11.

In connection with her fatal accident it is recalled that Miss Duncan for years affected an unusual dress cult and, with her brother, Raymond, often appeared in the streets of Paris and elsewhere garbed in a Roman toga with bare legs and sandals. Roman purple in recent years was her preferred color and she often walked about Nice in flowing scarfs and robes.

Petit Parisien Pays a Tribute.

The Petit Parisien tomorrow will say, in commenting on the tragedy:

"Sad news which will spread consternation through the world of arts and artists arrived today from Nice: Isadora Duncan has been killed in a frightful manner.

"This woman who throughout her life tried to shed grace and beauty about her met with the most tragic end imaginable.

"She danced as rarely, if ever, has been danced before her, with a fervor which seemed to raise her, transport her. She created a style school in her art. In her time she knew the most complete success in interpreting by that sort of mystic fury which filled the scene and put to rout all theories.

"Had she been practical she could have amassed an immense fortune, but she dies poor. Poor, and doubtless disillusioned, for what sorrows had she not suffered?

"Who does not remember the death of her children in an auto which, suddenly starting by itself, rolled into the Seine? And Isadora 'danced' her grief at their funeral, her grief which was profound and sincere. Few could comprehend such a form of grief which, to those who understood, was nothing short of sublime."

Dancer Was Writing Her Memoirs.

NICE, France, Sept. 14 (P).—The medical examination after Miss Duncan's death here showed that her neck had been cleanly broken by the red silk scarf. No other marks were apparent.

Paris Singer of the sewing machine family, an old friend of Miss Duncan's, and Mrs. Mary Desto Parks, British journalist, who was helping Miss Duncan with her book, are making the arrangements for the funeral.

At the time of the accident Miss Duncan was accompanied by Mrs. Parks, who came to see her with reference to the publication of her memoirs.

The dancer's body was taken to St. Roch Hospital, and then to her studio. In a conversation with a correspondent of The Associated Press yesterday, Miss Duncan said:

"For the first time I am writing for money; now I am frightened that some quick accident might happen."

This premonition of her doom was only too true.

Many Accidents in Her Life.

Fate seemed to have caused automobiles to play no small part in the life of Isadora Duncan. On several occasions she was injured, sometimes seriously, in automobile accidents, and in 1913 her two children were drowned in the Seine River, near Paris, when their automobile crashed into the river.

Later in the same year she was seriously injured in an automobile accident, and in May, 1924, was knocked unconscious when her car was in collision with another in Leningrad. On other occasions she narrowly escaped death from drowning. One of these accidents occured at Nice, where she was killed.

Isadora Duncan was the first exponent of the modern version of classical dances and as such won fame and much criticism in this and many foreign countries. She was born in San Francisco in 1880 and made her first stage appearance at Daly's Theatre in this city when she was 15 years old. She appeared as a fairy in Augustin Daly's company giving "A Midsummer Night's Dream."

It was a year or two later that she conceived her idea of interpretative dancing, and so well did she place her offering before the theatre-going public that within a few years she had amassed a considerable fortune and her name was famous on two continents.

She introduced what was then the shocking novelty of dancing with her limbs bare and her body clothed only in wisps of the most translucent material. In Paris and London she soon became the vogue, and she opened a number of dancing schools in different large cities in Europe. Then came the first of the many tragedies that later swept through her life.

Though she had never married she had two children, Patrick, 5 years old, and Deidre, a year younger. She had often said that she despised the institution of marriage, and she would never reveal the name of the father of her children. The children were drowned in the River Seine in France, when the automobile in which they were riding ran over an embankment and plunged into the river.

In 1915 she returned to this country and organized a dancing school, training her pupils on the stage of the Century Theatre. She became ill and her venture here failed. She was about to return to France, but debts of $12,000 detained her. They were finally settled by some of her friends and she was allowed to leave.

After the war she became an ardent advocate of the Soviet Union of Russia, and Lenin invited her to Moscow, where he gave her the mansion of a former nobleman in which to establish one of her dancing schools. While in the Soviet capital she met and married Sergei Essenin, the so-called "poet laureate of the revolution." He was a youth in his early twenties and was subject to fits of epilepsy. The dancer and the poet soon ran out of funds, and they decided to come to this country and appear on the stage.

Forbidden to Appear in Boston.

They were detained at Ellis Island on their arrival in 1922 because Miss Duncan had lost her American citizenship by marrying a foreigner. After considerable controversy they were allowed to land, and Miss Duncan appeared at various theatres and halls in the East.

In Boston on Oct. 22, 1922, she created a sensation when she danced at the Symphony Hall in filmy attire and at the end of her dance advanced to the footlights and shouted a denunciation of her critics. The following day Mayor Curley issued an order prohibiting her from appearing again in the Massachusetts city.

She returned to Paris with her husband and soon afterward there were reports of friction between the couple. She obtained a divorce from him in Russia and last year he committed suicide, cutting his wrists and writing a poem in his own blood.

In 1924 she was in trouble in Berlin owing to her inability to raise funds to pay her debts, and last year her house in Paris was put up for auction in behalf of her creditors. Friends came to her aid by raising 50,000 francs but this only postponed the evil day. The date of Feb. 17 of this year was then set for the sale of the house, but once again her friends pledged themselves to raise sufficient money to save the place.

Her studio and fittings, however, were sold and she went to the Riviera, where a few months ago it was reported that she had attempted to commit suicide by walking into the sea. She was rescued from the water by an English Army officer.

A few days ago it was reported from Paris that she was engaged to marry Robert Chanler, the former husband of Lina Cavalieri, the opera singer. She was one of a large party of guests being entertained on board the Chanler yacht at Nice. Yesterday she was quoted as saying that the report of the engagement was the result of a joke.

September 15, 1927

Georgia O'Keeffe

By EDITH EVANS ASBURY
Special to The New York Times

ABIQUIU, N. M.—Georgia O'Keeffe, who decided when she was young to paint, dress and live as she chose, is still living happily ever after in that manner, as she approaches her 81st birthday on Nov. 15.

Near this village of 250, about 40 miles north of Santa Fe, she continues to seek new ways of expressing her vision on canvas while living comfortably on the proceeds of past successes. And for the people of Abiquiu, many of whose parents and grandparents have worked for her over the years, she is building a $50,000 gymnasium. It will rise between the small Roman Catholic church and the even smaller post office.

For more than a half-century Miss O'Keeffe has put freshness, intensity and discipline and cool and luminous colors into her paintings to create a singular, silent world of oversized flowers, bleached animal skulls, stylized cityscapes and stark, lonely desert scenes. Battling courageously and assiduously for acceptance in the "man's world" of painting, she has become one of the most distinguished pioneers of modern American art.

A Free Moment

The artist, interviewed during one of the rare times when she was not busy, dropped her affability when asked, "What is the meaning of your art?"

"The meaning is there on the canvas," she snapped. "If you don't get it, that's too bad. I have nothing more to say than what I painted."

She was somewhat mollified, however, by her visitor's comment that a great many people seemed to have got her message, judging by the continued demand for her paintings. But the temper flared again when she was asked what prices her paintings bring.

"You are not going to get that out of me!" she exclaimed.

The large, dark eyes in the weather-beaten, wrinkled face softened.

"I have gone with the market, I doubt there are many that get more. But the market," the voice rose angrily, "is ridiculous now, fantastic. When I think how hard we used to work, how little we used to get. . . ."

"We" would be John Marin, Marsden Hartley, Arthur Dove and Charles Demuth, protégés, as she was, of her husband, Alfred Stieglitz, in the nineteen-twenties in New York. Their paintings and his pioneering photography now hang in the leading museums and art galleries. Mr. Stieglitz died in 1946.

"But it was hard going then," the lone survivor of the circle recalled. "We kept trying new things and appreciated each other, but we were not the ones with the mony to buy the pictures."

Before moving to New York to paint in 1918, Miss O'Keeffe, who was born on a farm in Sun Prairie, Wis., had been a commercial artist in Chicago, and an art teacher in Texas and Virginia.

She had been in New York earlier, as a student. While

she was in Texas teaching, a classmate at Teachers College of Columbia University showed some of her watercolors to Mr. Stieglitz. He exclaimed, "At last, a woman on paper!" He exhibited the paintings in his New York gallery with startling effect, and the career of Georgia O'Keeffe, ruggedly individualistic painter was launched.

"It was a time of great change," Miss O'Keeffe said of the years after 1918, when she moved to New York to devote full time to painting, became part of the Stieglitz circle and shone within it.

"Everybody was still talking about the Armory Show, and trying to find out what it was all about, and about the French painters Alfred was introducing to America. I seemed to be the only artist I knew who didn't want to go to Paris.

"They would sit around and talk about the great American novel and the great American poetry, but they all would have stepped right across the ocean and stayed in Paris if they could have. Not me. I had things to do in my own country."

Outside the large glass window of her studio, the New Mexican desert spread toward abruptly rising, red mountains, named by the early Spanish settlers Sangre de Cristo, the blood of Christ.

Clumps of yellow-blooming chamiso bushes, wild purple asters and stunted, twisted, water-starved piñon trees thrust up here and there, and an electric wire stretched above the narrow, rutted road leading down to the highway.

When Miss O'Keeffe found the place in 1934, on a 50,000-acre expanse called Ghost Ranch, there was no highway and no electricity. There were few people and many rattlesnakes.

Visit to Paris

Miss O'Keeffe stayed in the United States until the early nineteen-fifties, when she finally visited Paris. She "enjoyed it very much, but I don't care to go back." In recent years, she has done a lot of traveling, making several trips around South America and Mexico. She returns to New York two or three times a year to take care of business, but leaves as soon as possible.

Todd Webb

Geargia O'Keeffe, who celebrates her 81st birthday Nov. 15

"I am afraid of the city," Miss O'Keeffe said. "The longer I stay there, the more I get tangled up in more and more things to do, and can't stop. The only thing to do is to go home.

"I'd get too odd if I stayed here all the time, I know that," she conceded. "If I stayed here and talked to no one but Dorothea and Stephen and Frank, I'd be very odd indeed."

Dorothea is her cook and housekeeper, Stephen her gardener and Frank her handyman. They take care of the rambling adobe pueblo house Miss O'Keeffe bought in 1946 and remodeled extensively.

In the summer, with Jerrie, a buxom, industrious woman who cooks, keeps house and drives Miss O'Keeffe's air-conditioned Lincoln, the artist stays during the week at the comfortable house at Ghost Ranch that she bought in 1940 while she was still living in New York.

Both houses have large studios and large picture windows that frame spectacular views of the mountains. Both have earth-colored adobe exteriors, white cotton curtains and American Indian rugs, usually in the natural colors of white, black or brown wool.

Brighter color is limited to an occasional red Indian rug, the tubes and cans of paint in the studios and the brilliant tones of O'Keeffe paintings that she constantly tries out in different locations, and puts away and replaces.

Along the numerous and long window sills are rocks, bones, skulls, driftwood and other objects found by the artist on her daily walks around the desert and expeditions into the canyons and mountains.

Nearly always, in both studios, there is a new canvas. At almost any time of the year, some friend from some part of the world is a house guest at one of the Abiquiu houses, and sometimes the guest rooms at both places are filled. But Miss O'Keeffe's studios are forbidden territory. A guest who intrudes there is never asked to be a guest again.

Forty-four years ago, the critic Paul Rosenfeld wrote: "A combination of Picasso-like power and crisp daintiness exists not alone in the color of O'Keeffe. It exists likewise in the textures of shapes born in her mind with her color schemes, and expressed through them."

Miss O'Keeffe was painting landscapes of Manhattan and Lake George, then, and striving for new ways of "filling space in a beautiful way."

She turned a microscopic eye on flowers, painted them giant size, and was accused of being pornographic. She painted a cow's skull with a calico flower stuck in an eye socket, and was said to be painting "life and death." She used the shapes of stones and bones and roads and mountains in other paintings that evoked a variety of interpretations.

"They read into my painting things about themselves that had nothing to do with me at all," Miss O'Keeffe said of the critics. "I don't think my subconscious is all that crazy!"

Today most critics agree that Miss O'Keeffe, unperturbedly pursuing her own ideas, often anticipated new movements in art.

"Others may catch up, but then she is off on a new tack," Daniel Catton Rich, a close observer of her work since the middle nineteen-twenties, commented recently.

Then she mellowed. At nearly 81, the resentment is not as sharp as it once was. But the questing urge is. She said:

"I am working on something I shouldn't be working on, something I saw in another city, another country, something everyone would say I shouldn't try. That's all I'll say about it now."

What are you now painting, Miss O'Keeffe was asked by her visitor.

"Nothing, because I am talking to you," she snapped, the innate resentment against interference with her work popping up.

GERTRUDE STEIN

Although Gertrude Stein could and did write intelligibly at times, her distinction rested on her use of words apart from their conventional meaning. Her emphasis on sound rather than sense is illustrated by her oft-quoted "A rose is a rose is a rose."

Devotees of her cult professed to find her restoring a pristine freshness and rhythm to language. Medical authorities compared her effusions to the rantings of the insane. The Hearst press inquired, "Is Gertrude Stein not Gertrude Stein but somebody else living and talking in the same body?" Sinclair Lewis concluded she was conducting a racket.

Born Feb. 3, 1874, in Allegheny, Pa., the daughter of Daniel Stein, who was vice president of a street railway, and Amelia Keyser Stein, she spent her infancy in Vienna and Paris, and her childhood in Oakland and San Francisco. She was, in her own words, "an omnivorous reader, going through whole libraries, reading everything."

From 1893 to 1897 she was a student at Radcliffe College, where "like almost everyone else I wanted to be a writer but nobody encouraged me much." Miss Stein was, however, a favorite pupil of William James and specialized in psychology. When she sat down to write her final examination for him, she was tired, having been to the opera the night before. "Dear Professor James," she wrote on her paper, "I am so sorry but I do not feel a bit like an examination paper in philosophy today."

William James replied by postcard: "Dear Miss Stein, I understand perfectly how you feel. I often feel like that myself." He gave her the highest mark in the course.

During this period she published in a psychological journal a paper recording her experiments in spontaneous automatic writing—the method, according to some critics, by which her books were produced.

She then studied medicine four years at Johns Hopkins University, specializing in brain anatomy, but took no degrees, explaining that she was interested only in her studies and that she was bored by tests.

After a year in London studying Elizabethan prose, she moved in 1903 to Paris with Alice B. Toklas, a San Francisco friend, who was to be her lifelong secretary-companion.

On her arrival in Paris, she met the artists, Picasso, Matisse and Bracque. Possessed of an independent income, she became a patron of these men, was influenced by them and handed along that influence to younger artists and writers, among them Ernest Hemingway and the late Sherwood Anderson.

Her hobby was collecting the works of painters before they were famous. She claimed to have dis-

GERTRUDE STEIN
Associated Press, 1944

covered Picasso, Juan Gris, Matisse and Bracque and introduced them to the French and American public. Her shrewd connoisseurship is indicated by the fact that her collection of paintings was worth more than ten times what she paid for it.

Her first book, "Three Lives," 1909, written in completely intelligible style, contained realistic tender portraits of two servant girls and a more difficult study of the unhappy love affair of a Negress. Carl Van Vechten, the critic, classed it with the greatest books of the age in his introduction to the Modern Library edition, which was a best seller.

Also written with more or less lucidity were her two biographies of herself, entitled, "The Autobiography of Alice B. Toklas" and "Everybody's Autobiography," containing chitchat about Paris artists and American writers in Paris, with discourses on celebrities, art, literature, history and life in general and the genius of Gertrude Stein in particular.

During the first World War, Miss Stein drove a Ford down the lines distributing supplies to soldiers and visiting hospitals.

Her publications included "Making of Americans," 1926, and "Prayers and Portraits," 1934, the latter described as "unadulterated Steinese" and compared by John Chamberlain in THE NEW YORK TIMES to "the Chinese water torture; it never stops and it is always the same."

Another critic once remarked that Miss Stein "elected to write in a manner which much of the time makes her concrete meaning inaccessible to the reader. . . . She pushed abstraction to its farthest limits." Clifton Fadiman dismissed Miss Stein as "the Mamma of Dada."

Perhaps the peak of her publicity was reached in 1934 when she came here on a lecture tour, and her opera "Four Saints in Three Acts," with music by Virgil Thompson, containing the famed

line "Pigeons on the grass alas," as significant as the rest of the libretto, was produced.

As a lecturer, Miss Stein demonstrated her genius for self-press agentry by at once limiting her audiences to 500 because she "didn't wish to be stared at as a marvel."

Her lectures went off well. Her audiences, if addled and bewildered by her pronouncements, were also entertained by this roughly dressed woman, with close-cropped hair that set off her strong features.

Among her most recent works were "Paris, France," "a love letter to France," and "Wars I Have Seen," her experiences in occupied France until the arrival of the Americans. For this last book, her publisher, Bennett Cerf, had to abandon his amiable custom of remarking on the blurb of a Stein book that he had no idea what it was about.

For in it she forgets herself and her genius in following life in a French village from day to day in defeat and after liberation. She wrote the book in Culoz beyond Grenoble, under the noses of the Nazis whom she lodged at their insistence.

She had to walk seven and a half miles to town for food during this period.

Writing of this book, Francis Hackett, TIMES reviewer, concluded, "Hers is a powerful personality, but it needed the American Army to liberate her."

Her Talks With U. S. Soldiers

In June, 1945, writing in THE NEW YORK TIMES magazine section, Miss Stein analyzed the moral and intellectual fate of the young men of this generation. She based her comments on the frequent talks she had had in Paris with American soldiers and concluded that they would not become dissolute in the manner of the generation that lived in the wake of the first World War.

Miss Stein's latest book was published only a week ago under the title "Brewsie and Willie," and was described by Charles Poore in last Sunday's TIMES Book Review as a book about what the GI's talked of when they gathered around her feet in Paris. "* * * or rather," Mr. Poore remarked, "what she would like to think they talked about, for Miss Stein is a very powerful character and things are apt to change dizzily when translated into Steinese."

A new Gertrude Stein play, "Yes Is for a Very Young Man," which the author has described, despite the title, as "a perfectly simple, straightforward play, completely understandable," is scheduled to be presented on Broadway this fall. Apparently based in some degree on her "Wars I Have Seen," the play will deal with the emotional conflicts which divided France and much of the world during the heyday of fascism.

Her other books included "Geography and Plays" (1922), "How to Write" (1931), "The World Is Round" (1939), and "Ida" (1941).

EDNA ST. V. MILLAY

Edna St. Vincent Millay was a terse and moving spokesman during the Twenties, the Thirties and the Forties. She was an idol of the younger generation during the glorious early days of Greenwich Village when she wrote what critics termed a frivolous but widely known poem which ended:
My candle burns at both ends,
It will not last the night;
But ah, my foes, and oh, my friends
It gives a lovely light!

All critics agreed, however, that Greenwich Village and Vassar, plus a gypsy childhood on the rocky coast of Maine, produced one of the greatest American poets of her time. In 1940 she published in THE NEW YORK TIMES Magazine a plea against isolationism which said, "There are no islands any more," and during the second World War she wrote of the Nazi massacre of the Czechoslovak city of Lidice:
The whole world holds in its arms today
The murdered village of Lidice,
Like the murdered body of a little child,
Innocent, happy, surprised at play.

Before this, when Miss Millay won the Pulitzer Prize for poetry in 1922, her work had become more profound and less personal as she grew out of the "flaming youth" era in the Village. The nation and the world had become her concern.

Was Raised in Maine

Miss Millay was born in Rockland, Me., on Feb. 22, 1892, in an old house "between the mountains and the sea" where baskets of apples and drying herbs on the porch mingled their scents with those of the neighboring pine woods.

She was the eldest of three sisters, brought up by their mother, the former Cora Buzelle. Of the younger sisters, Norma became an actress and Kathleen a writer, whose first novel, published in 1927, was succeeded by fairy stories, short stories, plays and verse.

Floyd Dell, novelist and unofficial historian of the Village in the early Twenties, has written how the mother worked to bring up her daughters in "gay and courageous poverty."

Edna, the tomboy of the family, was usually called "Vincent" by her mother and sisters. Her talent was recognized and encouraged and poetry was read and reread in the household. At 14 she won the St. Nicholas Gold Badge for poetry, the first of many honors. In the poem that gave its name to her volume, "The Harp-Weaver," some have discovered the inspiration of her poor youth and her mother's devotion.

Edna entered Vassar late. She was then 21 years old, but when she was 18 she had finished the first part of her first long poem, "Renascence," and at 20 had ended it. It was published in a prize contest, which incidentally, it did not win. Sonnets and lyrics followed while she still was in college. She was graduated in 1917 and came to live in the Village, remaining for years, something of a tradition in her college.

Miss Millay, says Floyd Dell, was in those days "a frivolous young woman, with a brand-new pair of dancing slippers and a mouth like a valentine," young, red-haired and unquestionably pretty. But the Village was the wartime Village, and Miss Millay took the radical stand.

John Reed, Communist and war correspondent, was among her friends. Inez Milholland, feminist leader, to whom the sonnet "The Pioneer" is a tribute, was one of her admirers. In a play, "Aria da Capo," written in 1921, she expressed her hatred of war, and it has been recorded that she haunted court rooms with her pacifist friends, reciting to them her poetry to comfort them while juries decided on their cases.

With Provincetown Players

At first poetry in Greenwich Village did not pay, and Miss Millay turned to the theatre, briefly. She acted without pay with the Provincetown Players in their converted stable on Macdougal Street and got a part in a Theatre Guild production. For some time she did hack writing for magazines under a pseudonym.

It was her second volume of verses, "A Few Figs From Thistles," that turned national attention to the nine-foot-wide house on Bedford Street where she lived. There followed "Second April" in 1921 and "The Lamp and the Bell" and a morality play, "Two Slatterns and a King," in the same year, and in 1922, with the Pulitzer Prize, her position as a poet was established.

"The Harp-Weaver" was published in 1923, and then the Metropolitan Opera House commissioned Miss Millay to write a book for the core of an opera composed by Deems Taylor. For her plot she went to the Anglo-Saxon Chronicle of Eadgar, King of Wessex, a story not unlike that of Tristan and Isolde, and the result was "The King's Henchman," called by one writer the most effectively and artistically wrought American opera ever to reach the stage.

It was produced at the Metropolitan Opera as the most important production of the 1927 season, with Lawrence Tibbett, Edward Johnson and Florence Easton, and later was taken on an extensive tour. Within twenty days of the publication of the poem in book form four editions were exhausted, and it was calculated that Miss Millay's royalties from her publishers ran to $100 a day.

In the summer of 1927 the time drew near for the execution of

EDNA ST. VINCENT MILLAY
The New York Times, 1944

Nicola Sacco and Bartolomeo Vanzetti, Boston Italians whose trial and conviction of murder became one of the most celebrated labor causes of the United States. Only recently recovered from a nervous breakdown, Miss Millay flung herself into the fight for their lives.

Contributed Poem to Fund

A poem which had wide circulation at the time, "Justice Denied in Massachusetts," was her contribution to the fund raised for the defense campaign. Miss Millay also made a personal appeal to Governor Fuller.

In August she was arrested as one of the "death watch" demonstrators before the Boston State House. With her were John Howard Lawson, the playwright; William Patterson of the American Negro Congress, Ella Reeve, "Mother" Bloor and others.

"I went to Boston fully expecting to be arrested—arrested by a polizia created by a government that my ancestors rebelled to establish," she said, when back in New York. "Some of us have been thinking and talking too long without doing anything. Poems are perfect; picketing, sometimes, is better."

Miss Millay was married to Mr. Boissevain in 1923. They spent most of their married life at Steepletop, their Columbia County home. They traveled to Florida, the Riviera and Spain and, in 1933, bought an eighty-five acre island in Casco Bay, Me.

THE DANCE: DE MILLE'S OKLAHOMA

By JOHN MARTIN

A COUPLE of lusty yippees are clearly in order for Agnes de Mille and the dancing she has staged for the Theatre Guild's utterly charming "Oklahoma!" It is frequently the case that when artists from the ballet and the concert stage turn to Broadway they unconsciously look down their noses even at their own work. Miss de Mille, on the contrary, has turned in as sensitive and finished a job here as any she has done for more lofty (and less well-paid) divisions of the theatre arts.

Indeed, it is quite possible that her long ballet, called "Laurey Makes Up Her Mind," at the end of the first act of "Oklahoma!" marks an actual advance over what she has done previously. Here for the first time she has created an altogether objective work; in everything that has preceded it she has built a central role so specifically in terms of herself and her highly personal idiom as a dancer that no other dancer undertaking it could hope to be much more than a little imitation de Mille. That is, to be sure, a wonderfully sound way to work, for it bases its entire psychology and the movement that stems from it on the true premises of actual experience; but to have grown through that method into a strength that is independent of it is to have attained the real freedom of the creative artist.

A Part of the Play

"Laurey Makes Up Her Mind" is a first-rate work of art on several counts. For one thing, it is so integrated with the production as a whole that it actually carries forward the plot and justifies the most tenuous psychological point in the play, namely, why Laurey, who is obviously in love with Curly, finds herself unable to resist going to the dance with the repugnant Jud. Many a somber problem play has been built on just such a question of emotional compulsions and has failed to illuminate it half so clearly after several hours of grim dialogue. Yet this is a "dance number" in a "musical show"!

For another thing, Miss de Mille has turned her back entirely on the established procedure of making "routines." She has selected some delightful young people to dance for her, and she has built her

dances directly and most unorthodoxly upon them. As a result they emerge as people and not as automata—warm and believable people made larger than life and more endearing by the formalized movement through which they project themselves. Katharine Sergava with her strangely remote quality of beauty becomes the ideal heroine of a rather terrifying dream in which great personal decisions must be made. Marc Platt, faced with the difficult assignment of sheer romantic maleness defeated by sinister forces, comes forth with an artistic performance that far surpasses anything he ever did as Marc Platoff of the Ballet Russe. George Church is made to embody those sinister forces quite frighteningly simply by making imaginative use of his bulk, his strength and his ability to move.

Western Choreography

Even in the smaller dance numbers throughout the evening, of which there are several topnotchers, Miss de Mille has employed the same method. The radiant Joan McCracken fairly bursts with minxishness whenever she puts foot to stage, and little pale-haired, wide-eyed Bambi Linn darts in and out of the action with a wonderful childish freshness.

As for the choreography itself, Miss de Mille is on sure ground. Not only has she a gift for dramatic invention in this field, but in particular the West is her own and has long been so. Way back in 1928 when she gave her first recital there was a lusty and touching number called "'49" which was in a sense the root of all the more elaborate Western things that have developed since. The first sketch of her "Rodeo" was a little number of the same title in an "American Suite" which she made nostalgically in London in 1938 and showed here a few months later.

Those Imagined Mounts

Here, incidentally, were born those remarkably convincing riders of invisible horses which were later to play so important a part in Eugene Loring's "Billy the Kid," Miss de Mille's own "Rodeo" for the Ballet Russe and now her "Oklahoma!" They are so pat a symbol of horsemen, in fact, that they have passed more or less into the public domain. Because the material is so much a part of her motor vocabulary, the movement itself and the composition throughout "Oklahoma!" are spontaneous in feeling, simple in form and altogether right. For other reasons far less tangible, the whole thing

Vandamm

Marc Platt and Katharine Sergava in the ballet in "Oklahoma!"

Marianne Moore

Shaper of Subtle Images
By ALDEN WHITMAN

A writer with the dazzling ability to describe things as if she were observing them for the first time and with a remarkable talent for subtle imagery, Marianne Craig Moore was one of the country's most laureled poets and among its most ingenuous talkers and public personalities.

Indeed, Miss Moore, the personality, was more extensively known than Miss Moore, the poet, for she was an inveterate frequenter of concerts, balls, parties, fashion shows, unveilings, public receptions, lecture platforms, grocery shops, department stores, subway trains, baseball parks, exhibitions of boxing and literary salons.

A slight (5 feet 3½ inches) woman with luminous, inquisitive blue-gray eyes, she was immediately recognizable for her invariable attire—a cape and a tricorn hat. "I like the tricorn shape," she explained, "because it conceals the defects of the head."

Her tricorn (she had dozens that shape) was, after middle age, perched on a braid of gray hair that she wrapped around her head and held in place with a celluloid hairpin. Her face, likened to that of an angelic Mary Poppins, was once round and soft, and although lines of age creased it over the years, it never lost its glow.

Her conversation, which tended to breakneck monologue, was notable for its diversity. Sometimes it seemed that she was as discursive and as superficial as a teen-ager; but this was deceptive, for her associative mode of thought had a way of coming to a profound (or at least important) point by the time she stopped talking. Her remarks, delivered in a Middle Western drawl, charmed and enthralled persons as disparate as Casey Stengel, E. E. Cummings and John Hay Whitney, about whose horse Tom Fool she wrote a poem. It read in part:

"You've the beat of a dancer to a measure or harmonious rush of a porpoise at the prow where the racers all win easily."

Saw Herself as 'Observer'

Although T. S. Eliot, expressing a generally held view, once remarked that "her poems form part of the small body of durable poetry written in our time," and although W. H. Auden confessed to pilfering from her, Miss Moore did not think of herself as a poet in the popular sense, one who wrote resonant sonnets, epics and odes. She was "an observer," she said, who put down what she saw.

"In fact, the only reason I know for calling my work poetry at all is that there is no other category in which to put it," she said on one occasion, adding:

"I'm a happy hack as a writer."

Few agreed with this self-disparagement, for Miss Moore was a painstaking craftsman whose verse, which she composed in a spidery hand, was notable for its rhythms and for its use of homely speech.

"I think the thing that attracted me to put things in verse was rhythm," she told an interviewer on her 75th birthday in 1962. "Someone said the accents should be set so it would be impossible for any reader to get them wrong. If you can read it in 10 different ways, it's no good. That's very important to me.

"There are patterns in verse, just as you have restatement after contrast in music—as you have in Bach particularly. Also, I admire the legerdemain of saying a lot in a few words."

Miss Moore's poems utilized rhythms to create moods as well as to convey her admiration of such no-nonsense virtues as patience, firmness, courage, loyalty, modesty and independence. Much of her writing in this vein was a wry but gentle criticism of human conduct, literature and art, sometimes presented in unusual or baffling typographical arrangements. She made her point obliquely, for animals and plants rather than people were usually the formal subjects of her verse.

Some thought her poetry cold and austere because it seemed so detached from human life, but Miss Moore insisted that she wrote with affection. "She is a naturalist without pedantry, and a moralist without harshness," was the verdict of Louise Bogan, the critic.

Miss Moore's compact verse was not always easy to read or to comprehend, even though she professed "a burning desire to be explicit"; but for those who might have preferred the obvious she had this answer:

"It ought to be work to read something that was work to write."

Miss Moore took pride in catching attention with the first lines of her poems. "I am very careful with my first lines," she advised a questioner. "I put it down. I scrutinize it. I test it. I evaluate it."

---

has texture and sheen and fine imagination.

The land of the cowpuncher, to be sure, is by no means the only country in the de Mille geography, and it is sincerely to be hoped that she can free herself from the success of two straight winners in a row in this métier and go on to other subjects. She has a genius for capturing human people of whatever locale or social level in their simplest and most honest phases, ridiculing them sometimes, fairly devastating them at other times, and at still others making them seem like members of a mighty likable race.

Certainly what she had done for "Oklahoma!" gives rise to a strong temptation to paraphrase one of Oscar Hammerstein's admirable lyrics and chant to Richard Rodgers's haunting tune, "Oh, What a Wonderful Evenin'."

One of her poems, "Values in Use," illustrates her concept of a catchy opening, as well as her economy of phrase and her use of aphorism to make an ironic and faintly pessimistic thrust. It reads:

I attended school and I liked the
place—
grass and little locust-leaf shadows
like lace.

Writing was discussed. They said,
"We create
values in the process of living,
daren't await

their historical progress." Be ab-
stract
and you'll wish you'd been specific;
it's a fact.

What was I studying? Values in use,
"judged on their own ground." Am
I still abstruse?

Walking along, a student said off-
hand,
" 'Relevant' and 'plausible' were
words I understand."

A pleasing statement, anonymous
friend.
Certainly the means must not de-
feat the end.

In some of her other verse the poet celebrated the weak as standing off a hostile natural environment, as she did in this fragment from "Nevertheless":

The weak overcomes its
menace, the strong over-
comes itself. What is there
like fortitude! What sap
went through the little thread
to make the cherry red?

As poets go, Miss Moore was unprolific. Only 120 poems, occupying 242 pages, were in "The Complete Poems of Marianne Moore," published by Viking Press and Macmillan for her 80th birthday in 1967. In addition to this fruit of more than 50 years, there were nine translations in verse from "The Fables of La Fontaine."

Miss Moore was not a writer-to-order. "I don't believe in substituting conscious expression for spontaneous devotion," she once said in response to a request from her church—the Lafayette Avenue Presbyterian in Brooklyn—for a special benediction for ceremonial occasions.

She labored to compose, "fiddling," she called it, going over and over each poem until she was satisfied of its perfection for her. This accounted for much of the intricate detail in the verse, its quality of seeming like an exquisite needle-point embroidery.

Miss Moore's gift for magical words was enlisted in 1955 by the Ford Motor Company in a quest for a name "for a rather important new series of cars." In the exchange of letters, subsequently published in The New Yorker magazine, she suggested The Ford Silver Sword, Hurricane Hirundo, The Impeccable, The Ford Fabergé, The Resilient Bullet, The Intel-

The New York Times
Marianne Moore

ligent Whale, The Arcenciel, Regna Racer, Varsity Stroke, Cresta Lark, Chaparral and The Turtletopper.

Final Letter

The final letter in the exchange, from Ford, said:

"We have chosen a name [that] fails somewhat of the resonance, gaiety and zest we were seeking. But it has a personal dignity and meaning to many of us here. Our name, dear Miss Moore, is—Edsel. I hope you will understand."

(Edsel was a son of Henry Ford, founder of the company. The car that bore his name failed for lack of sales.)

For 37 years, from 1929 to 1966, the poet lived in a snug fifth-floor apartment at 260 Cumberland Street, in the Fort Greene section of Brooklyn. It was crammed with books and bric-a-brac—porcelain and ivory animals, a walrus tusk, prints and paintings, shells and feathers, old coins.

The kitchen, though, was sparsely furnished ("I cook only the essentials—meat and potatoes. I've never baked a pie") but it contained a vegetable squeezer in which Miss Moore made her own carrot juice, a libation of which she was fond. "Carrot juice increases vigor," she explained.

As Miss Moore's renown increased, her apartment was seldom without visitors—poets, artists, critics, admirers. Reluctantly, when the neighborhood became unsafe, she moved to Ninth Street in Greenwich Village in June, 1966.

Miss Moore's rise to eminence was slow. She was the daughter of John Milton and Mary Warner Moore and was born in Kirkwood, Mo., a suburb of St. Louis, on Nov. 15, 1887. She never knew her father, a construction engineer, who was institutionalized before her birth. After a brief stay with relatives,

Mrs. Moore took Marianne and John, her elder brother, to Carlisle, Pa., where the mother taught in Metzger Institute, now a part of Dickinson College.

Marianne was sent to Bryn Mawr, where for lack of aptitude in English she studied biology and contributed some ephemeral verse to the literary monthly. Upon graduation in 1909 she took courses in typing and shorthand at the Carlisle Commercial College and then got a job teaching these subjects at the Carlisle Indian School. One of her pupils, before she resigned in 1916, was Jim Thorpe, the athlete.

Her Brother a Chaplain

Miss Moore moved to Chatham, N. J., to help keep house for her brother, a Presbyterian minister and later a Navy chaplain. In 1918, when he joined the Navy, she and her mother went to New York, where they lived for 11 years in an apartment on St. Luke's Place in Greenwich Village.

After a stint as secretary to a girls' school, Miss Moore became, in 1921, assistant librarian at the Hudson Park Branch of the New York Public Library, a post she filled until 1925.

Meanwhile, her first serious verse was published in The Egoist, a London magazine in which the Imagists were influential, and in Harriet Monroe's Poetry magazine in Chicago. The poems had a select, but impressed, readership, and in 1921 H. D. (Hilda Doolittle) and Bryher (Winifred Ellerman), the historical novelist, collected and published these works in a small volume called "Poems." It was issued in London without Miss Moore's knowledge.

The poems, with some later additions, were printed as "Observations" in the United States in 1925, winning for their author her first literary prize, the Dial Award, and enthusiastic critical notices. Edwin Seaver's review in The Nation, which was typical, said:

"In respect to her work Miss Moore hews to an ideology that is aristocratic and severe and pure. Against the commonplace and the easy her subtlety of sarcasm is devastating."

Now an established writer, Miss Moore left her library job to join the staff of The Dial, first as acting editor and then as editor. She remained with the magazine, one of the great literary periodicals of its day, until it expired in 1929.

After moving to Brooklyn that year with her mother, Miss Moore devoted herself to writing and published "Selected

Poems" in 1935, winning the Ernest Hartsock Memorial Prize. The verses, The New York Times said, were "positive and exhilarating."

More encomiums greeted "What Are Years" when it appeared in 1941. Malcolm Cowley, for example, described the title poem as "among the noblest lyrics of our time."

With each succeeding slim book, Miss Moore fattened the list of her awards—the Harriet Monroe Poetry Award in 1944, a Guggenheim Fellowship in 1945, a joint grant from the American Academy of Arts and Letters and the National Institute of Arts and Letters in 1946, the Bollingen Prize in Poetry in 1952, the National Book Award for Poetry and the Pulitzer Prize the same year, the M. Carey Thomas Memorial Award in 1953, the Gold Medal of the National Institutes of Arts and Letters in 1953, the MacDowell Medal in 1967.

Honored for Translation

In addition, France gave her the Croix de Chevalier des Arts et Lettres for her translation of "The Fables of La Fontaine." She also held honorary degrees from at least eight colleges.

Despite all these honors, Miss Moore remained unaffected, saying, "There's nothing very special about me." She played tennis with neighborhood children in Fort Greene Park, rode the subway to and from appointments and became a fiery rooter for the Brooklyn Dodgers baseball team, whose feats she extolled in verse. When the Dodgers deserted Brooklyn for Los Angeles she changed her allegiance to the Yankees.

Miss Moore had become hooked on the Dodgers (and on baseball) after a friend had taken her to Ebbets Field in 1949. "These men are natural artists," she recalled in 1962. "Why, I remember Don Zimmer playing at third base. He was moving toward the home plate when a fly came toward him. He had to get back to third and he backhanded it with his left hand."

Medal but No Poem

She also held a high regard for Floyd Patterson, the heavyweight pugilist, for whom she obtained a medal blessed by the Pope. But she did not write a poem about him.

Miss Moore delighted to entertain in moderation. Her guests received tea and cookies, a glimpse of her water-colors (insects, flowers and landscapes executed with minute care) and the offer of a subway token for the trip home. The token was

The New York Times/Ernest Sisto

Tossing out baseball to open 1968 season at Yankee Stadium, At left is Michael Burke, Yankees' president.

proffered because she worried about her friends' financial health just as she was concerned, in a mother-hen way, about their physical state.

Guests were also likely to experience one of her monologues. Winthrop Sargeant described one of them in an article for The New Yorker in 1957. The starting point was a label on a sherry bottle. Mr. Sargeant wrote:

"At an afternoon gathering in her apartment a couple of months ago, the label led her to a consideration of other labels (though she might just as easily have veered in the direction of rabbits or quail), and this, in turn, led her to comment on grocery-store stocks, specifically on the stocks of the S. S. Pierce store, in Boston.

" 'Very discriminating grocers,' she went on. 'Even if they do carry cigars and wine and cosmetics along with their cheese, jam, cakes, soups and all kinds of crackers. I can't abide dilutions or mixtures, but I like candy. If I drank whisky,

I would drink it straight. I have a lethal grudge against people who try to make me drink coffee.

" 'My friend Mrs. Church grinds her own coffee from French and American beans. Her husband's grandfather was a chemical inventor who invented a brand of bicarbonate of soda. His wife is a Bavarian. Mrs. Church, I mean. She had a house at Ville-d'Avray with a big cedar of Lebanon and a dog named Tiquot. They had a gardener who also drove the car. They wouldn't have begonias on the place. They did have a few geraniums, though.

Favorite Language

" 'Mr. Church was a close friend of Wallace Stevens, who wrote 'The Necessary Angel.' He reprinted an anecdote about Goethe wearing black woolen stockings on a packet boat. I like Goethe. My favorite language is German. I like the periodic structure of the sentences. 'And Shakespeare inspires me, too. He has so many

good quotations. And Dante. He has a few, too.' That's from Ruth Draper.

" 'At Monroe Wheeler's once, we played a game called 'Who would you rather be except Shakespeare?' I wouldn't mind being La Fontaine, or Voltaire. Or Montaigne? No. I wouldn't be Montaigne—too somber.

" 'I have always loved the vernacular. It spites me that I can't write fiction. And that book of essays I wrote ['Predilections']. I let myself loose to o my utmost, and now they make me uneasy. The critics didn't care a great deal for hem, but their reviews weren't really vipish.

" 'Those readings of my verse I made for the phonograph— well, they're here forever, like the wheat in the pyramids. I'm fond of Bach and Pachelbel and Stravinsky. I'm also fond of drums and trumpets—snare drums. If I find that a man plays the trumpet I am immediately interested. . .'

" . . . One of the guests finally reached the point of exhaustion, and exclaimed, 'Marianne, don't jump around so in your conversation!'

"Miss Moore paused, turned pityingly toward the heretic and replied with spirit, 'It isn't jumping around. It's all connected.' Then she was off again."

Miss Moore was as cryptic a lecturer as she was a conversationalist, and she appeared to enjoy herself immensely, whether she talked at Harvard or to a woman's club. At one woman's club meeting she read some of her verse that included a line dealing with "metaphysical newmown hay." Afterward, a listener demanded to know what sort of hay that was.

In a patient tone of voice, the poet replied:

"Oh, something like a sudden whiff of fragrance in contrast with the doggedly continuous opposition to spontaneous conversation that had gone before."

Miss Moore took her advanced age with equanimity. "I'm all bone," she told a visitor in 1967, "just solid, pure bone. I'm good-natured, but hideous as an old hop toad. I look like a scarecrow, like Lazarus awakening. I look permanently alarmed.

"I aspire to be neat. I try to do my hair with a lot of thought to avoid those explosive sunbursts, but when one hairpin goes in, another comes out.

"My physiognomy isn't classic at all, it's like a banananosed monkey. Well, I do seem at least to be awake, don't I?"

Ruth St. Denis and La Meri Join Forces

By JOHN MARTIN

RUTH ST. DENIS and La Meri have united in a project of more than usual interest in the establishment of a "School of Natya." In spite of its name and the fact that it will be, in fact, a school in which the Hindu dance is taught, it will be considerably more than that, if the intentions of its directors are carried out. It will be "a center for the study and diffusion of the dance, music, drama and allied arts of the Orient," and will present to the public short performances, both professional and amateur, as well as lecture demonstrations.

In writing of the organization Miss St. Denis says: "Need I tell you that I have long loved the Orient, its philosophies and arts, with a deep abiding love; but I have had neither the talent nor the time to study its techniques as they should be studied. In La Meri's fascinating performances and lecture demonstrations I found what seemed to be at last the right person to cooperate with me in a workable plan for a center for oriental dancing which would have as its base as authentic a substance of teaching as was possible here in the West.

"Heaven knows, neither of us claims that we know all there is to know about oriental dancing! Our students will be told when a technique, a costume or a dance is authentic, when it is adapted but still retaining a large measure of authenticity, and lastly when, as with the majority of my own things, it is purely a mood of reaction to some oriental subject.

"We do hope to make a center here in sympathetic relationship with all native artists who may be in New York from time to time. It is our intention to make all lovers of the Orient feel that here is a sympathetic place above politics and strife where at least some phases of Eastern cultures may find sanctuary."

The material dealt with will not be confined to the arts of India, but will also include those of Japan, Java and other countries.

For the present the center is housed in Miss St. Denis's studio, 66 Fifth Avenue, but that is a temporary arrangement.

WILLA CATHER

WILLA SIBERT CATHER
The New York Times Studio, 1926

One of the most distinguished of American novelists, Willa Sibert Cather wrote a dozen or more novels that will be long remembered for their exquisite economy and charm of manner. Her talent had its nourishment and inspiration in the American scene, the Middle West in particular, and her sensitive and patient understanding of that section of the country formed the basis of her work.

Much of her writing was conceived in something of an attitude of placid reminiscence. This was notably true of such early novels as "My Antonia" and "O Pioneers!" in which she told with minute detail of homestead life on the slowly conquered prairies.

Perhaps her most famous book was "A Lost Lady," published in 1923. In it Miss Cather's talents were said to have reached their full maturity. It is the story of the Middle West in the age of railway-building, of the charming wife of Captain Forrester, a retired contractor, and her hospitable and open-handed household as seen through the eyes of an adoring boy. The climax of the book, with the disintegration of the Forrester household and the slow coarsening of his wife, is considered a masterpiece of vivid, haunting prose.

Won Pulitzer Prize in 1922

Another of her famous books is "Death Comes for the Archbishop," 1927, in which she tells in the form of a chronicle a simple story of two saints of the Southwest. Her novel, "One of Ours," won the Pulitzer Prize in 1922.

In 1944, Miss Cather received the gold medal of the National Institute of Arts and Letters, the institute's highest award and designed not to honor a specific work but the sustained output of a writer or artist.

Although generally thought of as a Western writer, Miss Cather was born on a farm near Winchester, Va., on Dec. 7, 1876. Her ancestors, on both sides, had been Virginia farmers for three or four generations. They came originally from England, Ireland and Alsace.

When she was 8 years old, her father took his family to Nebraska and bought a ranch near Red Cloud. The little girl did not go to school at first but spent many hours reading the English classics with her two grandmothers. Later, when her family moved into Red Cloud proper, she attended high school and then the University of Nebraska, from which she was graduated in 1895.

She spent a few years in Pittsburgh teaching and doing newspaper work, choosing that city rather than New York because she had many friends there. Each summer she visited in Nebraska, Colorado and Wyoming. Meanwhile, she had started writing, and her first published book was a volume of verse, "April Twilights," reissued in 1923 as "April Twilights and Later Verse."

Editor on McClure's Magazine

Miss Cather's first volume of stories was "The Troll Garden," published in 1905 by McClure-Phillips. Two years later she became an associate editor in New York of McClure's Magazine. She then was managing editor of the publication or four years.

During this period she wrote very little but traveled a great deal in Europe and the American Southwest, Arizona and New Mexico. In 1912 she gave up editorial work to write her first novel, "Alexander's Bridge." This was followed by "O Pioneers!" "The Song of the Lark" and "My Antonia."

In "The Professor's House," 1925, she began experiments with new technique of story-telling, constructing her tale of an intellectual's soul development according to the familiar methods of music.

The next year she wrote "My Mortal Enemy," which was compared by many with "A Lost Lady" but, for the most part, suffered by the comparison. A reviewer in THE NEW YORK TIMES said of the book that while it was inferior to the former work it did impress as a "later" book.

In 1931 Miss Cather wrote "Shadows on the Rock," which was considered the most popular novel in America during that year in the annual Baker & Taylor survey, and won for her the Prix Femina Americaine.

Miss Cather, who in 1931 was ranked by J. B. Priestly, the English author, as this country's greatest novelist, received the honorary degree of Litt. D. in 1924 from the University of Michigan. Columbia University conferred the same distinction on her in 1928, Yale followed suit in 1929 and Princeton two years later.

Among her other novels were "Lucy Gayheart" and, her last, "Sapphira and the Slave Girl," published in 1940. She also wrote two books of short stories, "Obscure Destinies" and "Youth and the Bright Medusa," and a collection of essays under the title, "Not Under Forty." For many years her publishers have been Alfred A. Knopf.

April 25, 1947

Dorothy Parker

By ALDEN WHITMAN

In print and in person, Miss Parker sparkled with a word or a phrase, for she honed her humor to its most economical size. Her rapier wit, much of it spontaneous, gained its early renown from her membership in the Algonquin Round Table, an informal luncheon club at the Algonquin Hotel in the nineteen-twenties, where some of the city's most sedulous framers of bon mots gathered.

Franklin P. Adams, the somewhat informal elder statesman of the group, printed Miss Parker's remarks in his "Conning Tower" column, and fame was quickly rapping on her door.

Miss Parker was a little woman with a dollish face an basset-hound eyes, in whose mouth butter hardly ever melted. It was a case, as Alexander Woollcott once put it, of "so odd a blend of Little Nell and Lady Macbeth."

Many of Miss Parker's writings appeared in The New Yorker magazine, to which she was a contributor from its second issue, Feb. 28, 1925, until Dec. 14, 1957. In paying tribute to her last night, William Shawn, the magazine's editor, said:

"Miss Parker, along with Robert Benchley, E. B. White, James Thurber, Frank Sullivan, Ogden Nash and Peter Arno, was one of the original group of contributors to The New Yorker who, under Harold Ross's guidance, set the magazine's general tone and direction in its early years."

The humorist's personal and literary style, Mr. Shawn added, "were not only highly characteristic of the twenties, but also had an influence on the character of the twenties—at least that particular nonserious, unsolemn sophisticated literary circle she was an important part of in New York City."

Sentimentalist at Heart

Her lifelong reputation as a glittering, annihilating humorist in poetry, essays, short stories and in conversation was compiled and sustained brickbat by brickbat. One of her quips could make a fool a celebrity, and vice versa. She was, however, at bottom a disillusioned romantic, all the fiercer because the world spun against her sentimental nature. She truly loved flowers, dogs and a good cry; and it was this fundamental sadness and shyness that gave her humor its extraordinary bite and intensity.

When the mood was on her,

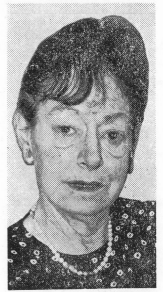

Associated Press
Dorothy Parker

Miss Parker's conversation was like a Fourth of July sparkler; but humor did not come easily to her pen. "I can't write five words but that I change seven," she once confessed.

The best of Miss Parker's humor was wry and dry, antic and offbeat, even that about herself. For her epitaph she suggested "Excuse My Dust," and of her poetry she said, "I was following in the exquisite footsteps of Miss Edna St. Vincent Millay, unhappily in my own horrible sneakers."

Barred Glasses in Public

She took seriously her couplet about women and glasses: Men seldom make passes/At girls who wear glasses. Although she was quite nearsighted, she refrained from wearing her horn-rimmed spectacles in public, or when men were present: She much preferred to blink her luminous hazel-green eyes.

"Deceptively sweet" was the phrase her friends most often applied to her. And indeed she looked it, for she was elfin, with a warm smile and perfect manners and a short-stepped, ladylike walk. She had a mass of dark hair that, toward middle age, she cut off and wore in bangs.

She was "the verray parfit, gentil knight" of the squelch, which she delivered deadpan in a clear, mellow, lamblike voice. Informed that Clare Boothe Luce was invariably kind to her inferiors, Miss Parker remarked, "And where does she find them?" Of a well-known author, "The only 'ism' she believes in is plagiarism." And of a cocky friend, "his body has gone to his head."

Miss Parker's background was not literary. She was born on Aug. 22, 1893, in West End, N. J. Her father, J. Henry Rothschild, was a New Yorker of means; her mother, the former Eliza Marston, was of Scottish descent. She attended Miss Dana's School at Morristown, N. J., and the Sacred Heart Convent in New York.

She was, she recalled, "a plain disagreeable child with stringy hair and a yen to write poetry."

After she had by chance sent some of her verses to Vogue magazine, she was hired at $10 a week to write picture captions. At the same time, Mr. Adams, who was generally known by his initials of F.P.A., published some of her poetry in his column, then appearing in The Daily Mail.

Miss Parker worked for Vogue for two years, 1916 and 1917; and in the latter year was married to Edwin Pond Parker 2d. The marriage was terminated by divorce in 1928, but she retained Parker as her professional name.

After her marriage, Miss Parker became drama critic for Vanity Fair from 1917 to 1920, when, during an office reorganization, she resigned. It was during the following five years that she attained her celebrity for sizzling, off-the-cuff wit from her repartee at the Algonquin Round Table.

Miss Parker, Mr. Benchley and Robert E. Sherwood were the founders of the group when they all worked at Vanity Fair, which had offices at 19 West 44th Street. The group got going because the Algonquin was nearby on 44th Street, and the three could not bear to suspend their office conversations.

The group rapidly expanded, and Frank Case, the hotel's proprietor, provided a round table for it. The group, usually about 10 a day, lunched together for about a decade. At one time or another it included George S. Kaufman, Harold Ross, Donald Ogden Stewart, Russel Crouse, Edna Ferber, Heywood Brown. Ruth Gordon, and, of course, F.P.A., and the three founders.

Miss Parker was one of the luminaries, but she later took a down view of the Round Table. "People romanticize it," she said. "This was no Mermaid Tavern. These were no giants. Think of who was writing in those days — Lardner, Fitzgerald, Faulkner and Hemingway. Those were the real giants. The Round Table was just a lot of people telling jokes and telling each other how good they were.

"At first I was in awe of them because they were being published. But then I came to realize I wasn't hearing anything very stimulating.

"I remember hearing Woollcott say, reading Proust is like lying in someone else's dirty bath water. And then he'd go into ecstasy about something called "Valiant Is the Word for

Carrie,' and I knew I had enough of the Round Table.

"The one man of real stature who ever went there was Heywood Broun. He and Robert Benchley were the only people who took any cognizance of the world around them. George Kaufman was a nuisance and rather disagreeable. Harold Ross, The New Yorker editor, was a complete lunatic; I suppose he was a good editor, but his ignorance was profound."

As one result of her poems and stories, Miss Parker was pointed out at parties and literary gatherings, not always to her amusement.

"Are you Dorothy Parker?" a woman at one party inquired. "Yes, do you mind?" the humorist retorted.

On another occasion, assured by a drunk who accosted her that he was really a nice person and a man of talent, Miss Parker replied:

"Look at him, a rhinestone in the rough."

"This reputation for homicidal humor," Miss Parker recalled in after years, "used to make me feel like a fool. At parties, fresh young gents would come up defiantly and demand I say something funny and nasty. I was prepared to do it with selected groups, but with others I'd slink away."

An Admirer Disappointed

At one party a man followed her around all evening waiting for a bright remark. He finally apologized, saying, "You're not at all the way I thought you'd be. I'm sorry."

"That's all right," Miss Parker rejoined. "But do me a favor. When you get home, throw your mother a bone."

Miss Parker herself understood the ephemerality of conversational humor. "Wit has truth in it," she said. "Wisecracking is simply calisthenics with words."

Nonetheless, it was the sort of gymnastics at which she could be very good indeed. At a party where she was seated with Somerset Maugham, the author asked if she would write a poem for him. "I will if you like," Miss Parker said, and scribbled out:

Higgledy Piggledy, my white hen;
She lays eggs for gentlemen.

"Yes, I've always liked those lines," Mr. Maugham commented.

Miss Parker bestowed a cool smile and without an instant's hesitation added:

You cannot persuade her with gun or lariat
To come across for the proletariat.

Miss Parker laced her wit with heady truth as a book reviewer, first for The New Yorker as Constant Reader and then for Esquire as book review editor for many years. Her notices were written with a chatty trenchancy, as though she were talking informally to the reader; but she could (and did)

impale authors who displeased her, either by synopsizing a pompous plot in all its ludicrousness or by pulverizing the book with a phrase.

Book Briefly Dismissed

She reduced A. A. Milne's sugary "The House at Pooh Corner" to water by remarking that "Tonstant Weader Fwowed up" after reading one too many of the word "tummy."

Her verdict on Edith Wharton's autobiography was equally to the point: "Edie was a lady." Edward W. Bok, the prestigious editor of The Saturday Evening Post, was left in tatters with Miss Parker's summary of him as "the Eddie Guest of prose."

"Inseparable my nose and thumb," she once wrote, "and she delighted in wiggling her fingers at folk gods. " 'In the Service of the King' has caused an upset in my long-established valuations," she wrote. "With the publication of this, her book, Aimee Semple McPherson has replaced Elsie Dinsmore as my favorite character in fiction."

Miss Parker was not entirely negative, however. She praised F. Scott Fitzgerald, the early Ernest Hemingway, some of Sinclair Lewis, James Baldwin and Edward Albee.

Miss Parker's reputation for light poetry was based on four books of verse: "Enough Rope" (1926), "Sunset Gun" (1928), "Death and Taxes" (1931) and "Not Deep as a Well" (1936). On the surface the poems were a blend of the cynical and the sentimental — just right for the sweet-winning generation of the late nineteen-twenties and early thirties.

If there was a touch of Miss Millay in them, there was also an overtone from Housman, as in "Pictures in the Smoke:"

Oh, gallant was the first love, and glittering and fine;
The second love was water, in a clear white cup;
The third love was his, and the fourth was mine;
And after that, I always get them all mixed up.

In Miss Parker's evocation of heartburn, there was, too, a bit of Donne and a hint of La Rochefoucauld, as in "Words of Comfort to Be Scratched on a Mirror:"

Helen of Troy has a wandering glance;
Sappho's restriction was only the sky;
Ninon was ever the chatter of France;
But oh, what a good girl am I!

Miss Parker wrote her last published poem in 1944, and then gave up the craft. "Let's face it, honey," she explained, "my verse is terribly dated."

But her final poem, "War Song," was her favorite. It is quintessentially Miss Parker, and it reads:

Soldier, in a curious land
All across a swaying sea,

Take her smile and lift her hand—
Have no guilt of me.
Soldier, when were soldiers true?
If she's kind and sweet and gay,
Use the wish I send to you—
Lie not alone until day.
Only, for the nights that were,
Soldier, and the dawns that came,
When in sleep you turn to her
Call her by my name.

As a short-story writer, Miss Parker produced several that were more than merely excellent: "Big Blonde," which won the O. Henry Memorial Award in 1929; "Telephone Call"; "Soldiers of the Republic" and "Arrangement in Black and White."

The latter is a particularly mordant satire of a woman explaining her own and her husband's attitude toward Negroes. Its most memorable passage reads:

"But I must say for Burton, he's heaps broader-minded than lots of these Southerners. He's really fond of colored people. Why, he says himself he wouldn't have white servants."

In 1933 Miss Parker was married to Alan Campbell, an actor. They were divorced in 1947 and remarried three years later. The Campbells went to Hollywood and collaborated on a number of motion picture scenarios; between times Miss Parker wrote short stories and book notices.

Writing Always Careful

Miss Parker, for all her mercury-quick mind, was a careful, even painful, craftsman.

"To say that Miss Parker writes well," Ogden Nash once remarked, "is as fatuous as proclaiming that Cellini was clever with his hands."

She had her own definition of humor, and it demanded lonely, perfectionist writing to make the truly funny seem casual and uncontrived.

"Humor to me, Heaven help me, takes in many things," she said. "There must be courage; there must be no awe. There must be criticism, for humor, to my mind, is encapsulated in criticism. There must be a disciplined eye and a wild mind. There must be a magnificent disregard of your reader, for if he cannot follow you, there is nothing you can do about it."

Toward the close of her life Miss Parker was convinced that humor had fallen on evil days.

"There just aren't any humorists today," she said on her 70th birthday in 1963. "I don't know why. I don't suppose there is much demand for humor. S. J. Perelman is about the only one working at it, and he's rewriting himself."

In 1953 she and Arnaud d'Usseau collaborated on "Ladies of the Corridor," a Broadway play of middling success about the pointless lives of middle-aged women without families. She also contributed some lyrics to Leonard Bernstein's musical "Candide." Mr. Campbell died in California in June, 1963, and Miss Parker, already ill, moved back to New York.

From the late nineteen-twenties, when Miss Parker was fined $5 for "sauntering" in a Boston demonstration against the execution of Nicola Sacco and Bartolomeo Vanzetti, she was active in liberal causes. In the Spanish Civil War and afterward, she was national chairman of the Joint Anti-Fascist Refugee Committee and active in its behalf.

Faced House Committee

This had repercussions in 1951 when she was cited, by the House Un-American Activities Committee, with 300 other writers, professors, actors and artists, for affiliation with what the committee designated as "Communist-front" organizations. One committee witness identified her as a member of the Communist party, an accusation she persistently denied.

In her final illness Miss Parker was melancholy about her life's accomplishments. She wanted to write again, especially short stories, but she lacked the strength.

The summing up came from Edmund Wilson, the critic, who wrote:

"She is not Emily Brontë or Jane Austen, but she has been at some pains to write well, and she has put into what she has written a voice, a state of mind, an era, a few moments of human experience that nobody else has conveyed."

Malvina Hoffman, Sculptor

Malvina Hoffman, one of the few women to reach first rank as a sculptor, died of a heart attack in her sleep yesterday morning in her studio at 157 East 35th Street. She was 81 years old.

As a girl, Miss Hoffman had to fight her way into Auguste Rodin's atelier to learn her craft. As a mature artist, she was often overwhelmed with commissions.

In 1929, she was given what probably was the largest commission ever granted any sculptor—110 bronze studies for the "Races of Mankind" exhibition at the Field Museum of Natural History in Chicago, 25 of them full figures, the rest busts. The commission sent Miss Hoffman ranging around the world on arduous voyages to sketch and sculpture primitive peoples in their living environments.

Though she lived through one of the most revolutionary eras in the history of art, when experimentation and innovation were the very breath of the work of most of her contemporaries, Miss Hoffman remained true to the classical and the realistic.

After a meeting with Brancusi, whose almost featureless and abstract brass sculpture "Bird in Flight" is one of the landmark creations of 20th-century art, she said:

"I wondered if it might not be a defect in me not to have experimented more. But I wasn't sufficiently impelled."

On another occasion, she said of the work of more modernist colleagues: "Some of it is stimulating and original. But the mass of abstract sculpture is not excellent."

Her own work, typically, was the accurate portrait bust—she did, among others, Ignace Paderewski, Wendell L. Willkie, Dean Virginia Gildersleeve of Barnard College, Anna Pavlova, Felix M. Warburg, Ivan Mestrovic and Katharine Cornell—or the dramatically monumental, like the "The Sacrifice," in which she cradled the head of an armored knight in the lap of a hooded grieving woman, a piece destined for the War Memorial Chapel at Harvard University.

A Dauntless Figure

But if she was not daring in her art, she was dauntless in the way she lived. When, in 1925, her heroic-sized figures of England and America were being mounted at Bush House in London's Aldwych, she thought they needed modification because of the way the light struck them.

Mounting a porch 90 feet above the ground with mallet and chisel, she did her modifying, behaving, in the words of her long-time friend, the poet Marianne Moore, "as if she had wings and carried a torch."

Her adventures with bushmen, head hunters, the Hairy Ainu of Japan and other primitive people made excellent copy in the tabloid journals of the nineteen-thirties. She seemed to know what would make a good story and told, in interviews, of the 6-foot 8-inch man she met in North Africa who had an inferiority complex because he lived among a tribe of 7-footers, or of bushwomen with buttocks so large that their babies could stand on them.

Those adventures were the product of her travels for the "Races of Mankind" commission. She refused to reveal who the model was for the figure of the Nordic man, and refused comment when The Brooklyn Eagle discovered it was an Italian-American body builder named Anthony Sansone.

For posed photos, she always seemed to have at hand a floppy velvet beret and a flowing duncolored smock, along with the standard mallet and chisel props expected of sculptors.

She gave many parties in her East 35th Street studio—it was her home for more than 45 years—and the parties were reported in the society columns. One, a costume ball with an Eastern theme, to which Miss Hoffman invited 150 guests, was called a "brilliant affair" by the breathless writer for The Evening Mail.

Entertained Notables

The guest of honor was the ballerina Pavlova, and among more than a score of French, Russian and Italian titles were such Americans as Ruth Draper, Mrs. Otto Kahn, Miss Helen C. Frick, Paul Draper and Mr. and Mrs. Marshall Field.

Another of her studio parties was for merchant seamen from 32 nations at war with Hitler's Germany. The Office of War Information recorded New Year's greetings from the men to their homelands at the party, then broadcast them overseas.

Miss Hoffman had by that time been working to aid refugees for more than 20 years. Her first mission was to investigate the need for United States aid in Yugoslavia after World War I for Herbert Hoover. She continued to aid Yugoslav causes, and for many years was chairman of the New York Chapter of the United Yugoslav Relief Fund.

Miss Hoffman was born June 15, 1885, in a brownstone house on West 43d Street, across the

Malvina Hoffman

Street from the site of Town Hall. Her father was Richard Hoffman, a pianist with an international reputation, who first came here from England as accompanist to Jenny Lind, the Swedish soprano.

The house was filled with art and artists and Miss Hoffman grew up with what one family friend called an inevitable interest in art. Miss Hoffman herself said of the origin of her interest in sculpture that, as a child, "I was always taking toys apart to see how they worked."

Knocking at Rodin's Door

She studied in this country with the painter John Alexander and Gutzon Borglum, the Mount Rushmore sculptor. Then, armed with a letter of introduction from Borglum, she went to France to become a pupil of Rodin. Five times she went to his studio-home in Meudon, north of Paris, and five times he refused to see her.

Finally, Miss Hoffman told a maid she was going to stand on the doorstep until she was admitted to see the master. She got in, and then immediately won his interest by quoting from memory a sonnet by Alfred de Musset that he was trying to recall for a roomful of friends.

She worked with Rodin for almost three years, and it was he who formed her as an artist. One of her earliest successes was "Bacchanale Russe," a representation of the dancers Pavlova and Mordkin. It was bought by the French Government and placed in the Luxembourg Gardens in Paris.

Miss Hoffman's works are in the permanent collections of the Metropolitan and Brooklyn Museums in New York, in the Frick Collection, and in museums in London, Rome, Chicago, Stockholm and Buffalo.

"Mongolian Archer," for which Malvina Hoffman won a Gold Medal of Honor from Allied Artists of America in '62.

Other works — anatomical models, chiefly—are on display anonymously in several medical schools, where they were commissioned as teaching aids. The work also taught her; Miss Hoffman had a professional's knowledge of anatomy, partly as the result of her study with Dr. George Huntington of the Columbia University College of Physicians and Surgeons.

Besides the Harvard memorial, Miss Hoffman did a 9 by 12 foot bronze plaque for the 71st Regiment of the New York National Guard, which is in the armory at Park Avenue and 34th Street, and the American Battle Monument at Epinal, France.

Five American colleges awarded honorary degrees to Miss Hoffman; she was made a member of the French Legion of Honor, and she was given the medal of the National Sculpture Society in 1964, among many other honors. Her figure, "Mongolian Archer," won a gold medal of honor in 1962 from Allied Artists of America.

She wrote two autobigraphical works, "Yesterday Is Tomorrow" and "Heads and Tales," and several books on sculpture.

Miss Hoffman was married to Samuel B. Grimson, an English inventor and musician, in 1924. They were divorced in 1936.

Graham's Divine Discontent

By CLIVE BARNES

ON TUESDAY a woman, small-boned and delicate, will curtsey gravely to a welcoming Broadway audience at the 54th Street Theater. It will be Martha Graham at the commencement of her longest ever New York season. It is Miss Graham's fortune to become a legend in her lifetime and indisputably the greatest figure ever to be developed within the modern-dance movement.

When Whitman had his vision of America dancing it is doubtful whether he envisaged quite this vital and intense woman who was born in Pittsburgh more than 70 years ago. Yet Graham has perhaps become the archetypal American choreographer, and whether her themes touch Greek myths, bible stories or world literature, they are never far away from the soil of her native land, and she has yet to create a character that was not American.

In "Phaedra," for instance, Graham creates a Greek queen wracked with incestuous passion for her stepson, but above and beyond the work's Hellenic feel and feeling, we glimpse a small-town American matron in sexual torment, as it is part of Graham's genius to relate myth and mystery to the contemporary world. Graham's genius is so many-sided that it has won her supremacy in her world as a dancer, choreographer, and teacher. But even more than this Graham has become a living symbol of the modern-dance movement to the outside world, while inside the movement the influence she wields and the inspiration she offers have been unrivalled since the death of Doris Humphrey.

Oddly enough, because of the opposition of her father, Graham did not start to dance until she was past her 21st birthday and she enrolled at the Denishawn to study with her first (and last) teachers, Ruth St. Denis and Ted Shawn. In 1919 Graham made her stage debut with the Denishawn company, dancing the title-role in "Xochitl," a Mexican ballet choreo-

graphed by Shawn especially for Graham. Graham stayed with the Denishawn dancers until 1923, when she left to join a Broadway revue, "The Greenwich Village Follies," where she performed a few Denishawn-like solos.

By now Graham was around 30, and she was a dancer like many other dancers only perhaps a little bit better than most. Her career seemed to be settled, and she could have continued for years performing her little cameo dances in revues and vaudeville. But Graham had a divine discontent.

She left Broadway and one day—a day that should be illuminated in the annals of our dance history—she took a job as a teacher at the Eastman School of Music in Rochester, N.Y. Here Graham first started to teach dancing and her first serious pupil was herself.

She had already, when she came to think about it, received one important lesson, and that from the father who stopped her from dancing as a child. Her father was a physician from stern New England stock. In a story Martha Graham still delights in telling, her father once said to her: "Martha never lie to me, for if you ever do lie I will know. Your body will tell me." In a very real sense this is the thinking behind all her work, which is motivated by the conviction that some feelings and even some thoughts are too deep for words and have to be seen to be believed.

In all her dances and ballets Graham has tried to explore what she calls "the interior landscape," and she has never been interested in either purely decorative dance or simple story-telling. Her aim has always been for a fusion of form and content, and to use this to unveil human psychology. Questions like "When?" and "How?," those two props of playwrights and choreographers for centuries, have little interest for her. Graham, in her work, wants to know "Why?"

While she was working in Rochester, Graham began to develop what has come to be known, rather inaccurately, as the "Graham technique," but which more properly speaking is a certain dance style combined with a specific teaching method. The aim of the style and teaching method is to join together the natural and the spectacular.

At Denishawn Graham would have come under the influence of the theories and techniques of gesture developed by the 19th-century French teacher, Francois Delsarte, in which both Shawn and St. Denis were interested. But what Graham needed was a dance style that could incorporate gesture into the very fabric of the dance. Her idea was, in effect, to base her choreography upon the most natural function known to man—breathing. This is the celebrated "contraction and release," and in addition to its validity as a heightened form of natural movement, it also lends itself on the physical level to a wide range of virtuosity and its

counterpoise of tension and relaxation has enormous adaptability in providing the emotional coloring of a dance.

Years of Struggle

After a year of work and rethinking Graham was ready, and in 1926 she made her New York concert debut. The years of struggle were still ahead, but her ultimate triumph was no longer in any doubt.

For years Miss Graham was regarded as primarily a dancer. She naturally, in the modern-dance tradition, arranged the choreography for her own solos, but with her the act of creation and the act of renewal in performance were so closely linked that it would have been difficult, one presumes, to have sorted them out. In time Graham formed first a small company, and then a larger company. Soon she was choreographing full-scale ballets, and much later still she even choreographed bal-

lets in which she herself no longer appeared.

Theatrical

Few people under 40 can have seen Graham at her best as a dancer, and today while she remains a significant theatrical personality her actual dancing is negligible. It is in recognition of this that she has this season handed over three of her most famous roles to younger dancers, which while common enough practice in the classic ballet, has been much rarer in the world of modern-dance. Graham the dancer will only live in photographs and words of a few writers, such as John Martin, who managed to capture for posterity something of her tempestuous spirit. But Graham as an inspiration is immortal, and with good fortune some of her works will survive to bear testimony to her greatness as a choreographer.

The versatility and unquenchable vitality of Graham finds a parallel to an-

other founder of the total American dance theater, George Balanchine, and in some respects their achievements have proved oddly similar. For both of them, with little creative as opposed to administrative assistance, have built up a repertory, and built up a company, translating their vision of America dancing into positive action.

The power and eloquence of Graham's choreography derives from her belief in expressive dance and its ability to expose the human heart and mind. It would however be doing her less than justice to neglect the pure dance aspect of her work. In Indian dancing, as the sublime Balasarasvati reminded us in her recital the other week, the two elements of dance, "nritta" (the pure dance) and "abhinaya" (the gestural or mimetic part) co-exist to their mutual enrichment. So it is in Graham's dance.

Even at a time when "theatrical" was a dirty word

The New York Times (by Sam Falk)

Martha Graham rehearses Ethel Winter and Bertram Ross in "The Witch of Endor," to be presented on Tuesday.
". . . a legend in her lifetime and indisputably the greatest figure in modern-dance"

in the modern-dance scene, Graham was gloriously theatrical. And also with her beautifully trained dancers, those very special "acrobats of God," she has never hesitated to use spectacular dance in a way and with a freedom that pre-Graham only classical ballet choreographers took for themselves.

Retrospective

What we are about to see at the 54th Street Theater is, despite Graham's two new creations, if you like, a retrospective of Graham. At the moment no one can tell whether the Martha Graham Dance Company is at the beginning of its end or, more hopefully, the end of its beginning. Americans appear to have a traditional reluctance to form permanent organizations except to make money. In the performing arts, however, permanent organizations are needed to make art. It would be a great thing for American dance if the Graham Company, in some amplified way, could become one of the permanent organizations we need. But more of this later.

Martha Graham, Dancer

Pearl Buck Wins Nobel Literature Prize; Third American to Get the Swedish Award

Wireless to THE NEW YORK TIMES.

STOCKHOLM, Sweden, Nov. 10.— The Swedish Academy today awarded the 1938 Nobel prize for literature to Pearl Buck, American, author of "The Good Earth" and other novels about China.

The Academy of Science awarded the Nobel prize for physics to Professor Enrico Fermi of Rome University "for his discovery of new elementary radioactive substances produced by irradiation of neutrons" and for other research on reactions created by neutrons.

Thanks to his discovery of the great explosive power of slow neutrons, Professor Fermi and his associates have been able to produce radio-activity in most elements, including the heaviest ones. Professor Fermi, who is 37 years old, is the discoverer of chemical element 93. Educated at Pisa, Goettingen and Leyden Universities, he was at one time Professor of Physics at the University of Florence.

A member of the Italian Academy since 1929, he is a corresponding member of the Turin and Leningrad academies of science.

The Nobel chemistry prize will probably be reserved until 1939.

———

Pearl Buck, in private life Mrs. Richard J. Walsh, said yesterday morning, one hour after learning of her triumph, that she was taken aback with the totally unexpected honor. Speaking in the office of her publisher, John Day Company, 40 East Forty-ninth Street, she recalled her first words as follows:

"I said, 'That's ridiculous,' and I suppose a great many others will say the same thing. Did Chinese expressions of gratitude come to mind? Certainly, I thought—though probably not aloud: 'O pu sing sin' (I don't believe it), but 'kung shi-kung shi' (congratulations)."

The author of "The Good Earth" and ten other books, numerous short stories and articles since 1930 was grateful that the Nobel Prize for literature was based on the sum of a writer's work rather than any single product. In a broadcast to Sweden yesterday at noon she defined one successful book as a sign of growth and was hopeful that her development would continue.

Theodore Dreiser merited the honor, the author said over the air, continuing:

"I don't know him and he doesn't know me, but I feel diffident in accepting the award just the same."

She told of having visited Stockholm on a pleasure trip in 1932 and said she would try to be there on Dec. 10 to accept the medal, scroll and check from the hands of King Gustaf. The money will amount to between $40,000 and $50,000, it was learned.

Mrs. Buck, as she prefers to be known publicly, was dressed in a brown and blue ensemble trimmed

Times Wide World

Pearl Buck as she was notified here of the award.

with fur. She replied to questions carefully, yet appeared to enjoy the ordeal of flashlight bulbs and swift changes of topic in the interview.

She implied the Nobel Prize was a shade less thrilling than her notification in Nanking seven years ago of the Pulitzer Prize. "It was the first intimation I had that my work interested my own people," she explained.

Third American to win the Swedish honor, Mrs. Buck follows Sinclair Lewis and Eugene O'Neill. She was the second woman in a decade to win this recognition for writing. The other was Sigrid Undset just ten years ago. Her name will now appear alongside those of such famous winners as Maurice Maeterlinck, Rudyard Kipling, Anatole France, William Butler Yeats, George Bernard Shaw, John Galsworthy, Luigi Pirandello and Thomas Mann.

Born In West Virginia

She was born in Hillsboro, W. Va., on June 26, 1892, the daughter of two missionaries on leave from China—Absalom and Caroline Sydenstricker. Her childhood was spent on the Yangtze River in the town of Chinkiang. She mastered Chinese before she had learned English.

Pieces written by the little girl were published by the Shanghai Mercury. But she really found her way into print in 1923 with magazine articles on China. "East Wind, West Wind," a novel, had evolved by 1930 and, close on its heels came the best seller, "The Good

Earth." Mrs. Buck declared yesterday that her favorite work was "Sons," 1932, which "Americans failed to understand because it marked strongly my Chinese phase."

She was educated at Randolph Macon Woman's College, Lynchburg, Va., did post-graduate work at Cornell and Yale, and taught in three Chinese universities. Her own activity as a missionary ended about six years ago. She has two children and has adopted four more. Following her divorce from John Lossing Buck she married Mr. Walsh.

An almost unbroken literary identification with the Far East was interrupted last year when Mrs. Buck, wrote "This Proud Heart," a novel set in America. Another with a New York locale has been finished, she disclosed. Publication will be deferred until "The Patriot" is on the market.

"The latter is a Chinese-Japanese story dealing with the conflict," the writer said. "I'm altogether on the Chinese side personally and politically, yet I'm very fond of the Japanese people. I will never live in China again. I hope to visit the country when it becomes certain what shape it will assume."

Discusses Method of Writing

She discussed her method in writing, thus:

"I don't wait for moods—you'd never get anything done if you did. I write about four hours a day in terms of episodes, never stopping in an emotional crisis nor, for example, going into one just before luncheon.

"I think in the Chinese idiom and translate. That may be why the result occasionally resembles scriptural English. The Chinese language, like King James's English, is simple and from the soil. My reading habits? Well, I keep something new and something old going all the time."

A telegram delivered to her at 11:40 o'clock in the course of the interview was the first official word she received. It read:

"The Swedish Academy has this day assigned to you the Literary Nobel Prize and would be grateful to receive by wire your acceptance to the secretary of the Swedish Academy. [Signed] Per Hallstroen."

Mrs. Buck laughingly denied that she would "go on a spree" with the prize money; nor had she any need for a yacht or jewelry. After reflecting a moment, she observed:

"Now I can devote myself to writing books I want to write. Fewer short stories will need to be written."

Lillian Hellman

Playwright.
By Richard Moody.
Illustrated. 361 pp. New York:
Pegasus. $6.95.

The Collected Plays

By Lillian Hellman.
815 pp. Boston:
Little, Brown & Co. $15.

By CHARLES THOMAS SAMUELS

Almost all the biographical data in this study of "Lillian Hellman: Playwright" comes straight from her memoir, "An Unfinished Woman." The interpretations of her plays are equally secondhand: run-throughs, eked out with quotations. In place of criticism, there are surveys of early drafts to show that later ones were improvements, and summaries of contemporary reviews with plaudits appropriated and strictures modified. When no other ground for praise exists, Richard Moody, professor of theater and drama at Indiana University, points to a successful box-office.

Such press-agentry also explains the author's opening assertion: "Among her contemporaries only Tennessee Williams and Arthur Miller have matched her record; they alone belong in her league." As his language suggests, Mr. Moody isn't concerned with excellence; enough to recall that each playwright enjoyed a comparable number of hits. That Miss Hellman is less frequently revived, that she comes nowhere near having inspired as much discussion (in quantity, to say nothing of quality), these facts Moody ignores. He admits that her plays raise "later retrospective questions," but he evades them by reminding us that she succeeds onstage.

Theatrical effectiveness didn't seem a sufficient argument to the playwright. In 1942 while introducing the Modern Library collection of her earliest plays, Miss Hellman was careful to defend herself against charges of melodrama and contrivance. Now that we have "The Collected Plays" and its implicit bid for a summing-up before us, we can see that her defense was insufficient.

Contrivance is formally essential to drama, Miss Hellman rightly contends: "the theater is a trick"; tricks are bad in it only "when they are used trickily and stop you short." By this test, however acceptable in the heat of performance, her tricks don't survive the glare of reading. That her first play, "The Children's Hour" (1934), reaches its crisis through an overheard conversation, we can put down to beginner's expediency; but she uses this device as late as "Toys in the Attic" (1960). In "The Autumn Garden," widely praised as a retreat from the machinations of her earlier dramas, characters regularly discover each other in compromising situations, recalling not so much Chekhov (as reviewers asserted) but French bedroom farce. Her plays hang skeletons in a number of closets and blow open the doors at dramatic intervals.

Sometimes, as in "The Little Foxes," she makes this strategy effective; at other times ("The Searching Wind" is the egregious instance) her work expires from its own efforts at flashing back. Retrospective confessions are so nearly the language of her drama that she is vulnerable to self-parody. Minutes after the curtain rises on "Toys in the Attic," one of the old maid Berniers says to the other, "Funny how you can live so close and long and not know things, isn't it?" But this anomaly is essential; if, before the curtain, any of Miss Hellman's characters had ever said anything important to the others, there could be no play. The very relentlessness of their need to disclose a predramatic life proves that it never existed.

Were the burden of the past her subject, retrospection would not seem the artificial contrivance of a playwright who thrives on disclosures, rifled safe-deposit boxes, clandestine contracts, the paraphernalia of intrigue. But Miss Hellman does not have an important subject; the gradual revelation of chicanery is her concern. This is naked in "The Children's Hour," her longest-running play, which, as Eric Bentley first asserted, is also thematically self-defeating. It can't be the critique of character assassination that it first seems, because Martha, who along with Karen, is accused of lesbianism, later accedes to the charge. Miss Hellman doesn't dramatically represent either the process whereby Mrs. Tilford destroys the heroine's reputation or the gradual recognition by Martha that she had denied her own perversity. Instead, we watch Mary procuring and conveying the damaging information to her grandmother. Despite its pretense of dealing with social and personal morality, "The Children's Hour" is really a thriller about a nasty little girl and a gullible old woman.

But even that is too much of a threat for Miss Hellman's world, where real evil — like dramatic inefficiency — is an unacceptable disorder. So the play ends with Mrs. Tilford's avowal of guilt, Karen's forgiveness and the implication that villains suffer more than their victims.

Like the dramaturgical clarity, the thrilling revelations and the misleading aura of issues at stake, this constant defanging of villainy is a device — however unconscious — to assure that the audience be left feeling both edified and safe. Hence "The Little Foxes" ends by suggesting that Regina may be weaker than her virtuous milksop of a daughter, "Days to Come" shows a capitalist who had hired murderous strike-breakers finally awash in contrition. And "Watch on the Rhine," a play apparently written to warn compatriots that they'd best not be complacent about Nazism, comforts them instead with both dramatic and rhetorical proof, to use the words of its hero, that "in every town and every village and every mud hut in the world, there is a man who might fight to make a good world."

No wonder that Miss Hellman's major revision in turning Anouilh's play into "The Lark" was the addition of a final scene in which Joan of Arc is resurrected and allowed to relive the happiest day of her life. (Moody's acumen is fairly indicated by his remark on this emendation: "Compared to the original, it may seem unduly loaded with cheerful sentimentality, but it rings true for a Joan who is to be declared a saint for all the world.")

Despite a reputation for seriousness and integrity, and her loudly proclaimed disdain for the commercial theater, Miss Hellman has worked wholly within its conventions. Her protagonists are always middle-class and, to the gratification of audience and actors, physically invulnerable to vicissitude or time. They live in single-set dwellings — which please producers — and are as tidily articulate as they are respectable. Should they indict manners dangerously close

to those of the audience, Miss Hellman is careful to provide sympathetic lesser characters with whom we can identify.

One has only to compare the Hubbards with Faulkner's Snopses—an analogy frequently cited by those admiring "The Little Foxes" for historical insight — to see that Miss Hellman's famous indignation always leaves a saving remnant. In Faulkner, the Snopses take over a small Southern town because its corrupt and racist establishment cooperates; in Miss Hellman, the aristocrats are too ineffectual for collusion, they are nice to Negroes and they have high-toned taste.

Her Modern Library apologia concedes that melodrama must be justified, but Miss Hellman wasn't able to avoid the form's addiction to luridness and simplification. In the play both she and Mr. Moody regard as her best, she made strenuous efforts to do so; but "The Autumn Garden," designedly Chekhovian, is nonetheless typical in its limitations. Whereas Chekhov avoids plot because it would contradict the purposelessness and debilitation of his characters, Miss Hellman falls back on blackmail, scandal, a network of dramatic disclosures. Chekhov unearths the roots of his blighted compatriots, who talk of native art, music, thinkers and events; but Miss Hellman's people refer only to stage conventions.

In a play like "The Three Sisters," which "The Autumn Garden" recalls, Chekhov knows that one can't fathom the deepest cause of human malaise, but Miss Hellman would never risk disturbing her audience with intimations of the inscrutable. Her characters show a psychoanalyst's skill at ferreting out motives and explaining mistakes. Indeed, they are so energetic and conclusive in their comprehension that their defeats seem arbitrarily imposed by the playwright.

Neither inscrutability nor any other true pain lives in Miss Hellman's dramas. For all their flirtation with suffering, it is kept at bay. Moreover, impersonality joins "well-made" craftsmanship as a hedge against sensibility; few of the plays reflect the author's life. "The Children's Hour" was written up from a criminal record; "Days to Come," "The Searching Wind" and "Watch on the Rhine" are forensic responses to contemporary problems; in "The Autumn Garden" Miss Hellman imitates Chekhov and in "Toys in the Attic," Tennessee Williams; three of her plays — as one would expect from a screen-writer, which she has been, rather than an important playwright—are adaptations of others' work.

Yet her best play, "The Little Foxes," is demonstrably her most personal. Both an "An Unfinished Woman" and Moody's book reveal how indebted she was in writing the first Hubbard chronicle (and the second, "Another Part of the Forest," as well as the dazzling first act of "Toys in the Attic") to family history. Giving vent to anger over greed and materialism that had swirled around her youthful head, "The Little Foxes" is no less melodramatic than her other plays; but it contains emotion powerful enough to keep the form from cropping the substance. The Hubbards may be too singular and simple to refer beyond themselves, but they promise to live through their flamboyance and energy. Here alone, Miss Hellman allowed her villains something like full force.

For all its faults, then, "The Little Foxes" remains stageworthy, whereas the other plays are already dated. "The Children's Hour" could be revived only because of Senator McCarthy; by now, even McCarthyism couldn't render it invulnerable to gay lib. The topical works expired with their "issues." Even "The Autumn Garden" has lost credibility because it depends for a climax on the scandal of a man waking up in the bed of an unmarried girl.

Contrived without compensating stylization; realistic

in style but lacking reality; mechanically tooled but noisily clanking; engaging evil only to reduce it melodramatically; Lillian Hellman's plays belong in the league not of Williams or Miller — the one personally, the other socially obsessed — but of a contemporary like Neil Simon. Like him, Miss Hellman is a thorough professional. Like him, she concocts plays that maintain interest, quicken the pulse, provide — as one says—"an evening in the theater." If she is more earnest, more apparently engaged with important matters, he is more entertaining. Both exemplify a narrow conception of drama; they hold a mirror up not so much to man as to the needs of the Broadway audience.

Since a need for literate entertainment does exist, Broadway will always have a place for writers like Lillian Hellman; but a show-shop isn't a theater, and dramaturgical savvy isn't the whole of the art. When audiences and reviewers fail to make these distinctions, one is saddened but unsurprised; when critics join them, one is — or ought to be — shocked. For this reason, Moody's study is deplorable as well as inept. Confronting, for example, Miss Hellman's reduction of Anouilh — himself the reductive imitator of masters of European drama — Moody has this to say:

"She reduced the discursive arguments, dramatized rather than reasoned her way through the sacred mystery, changed the ending, added a biting briskness, and energized the proceedings with an emotional charge that was absent in Anouilh and in Fry. She also maintained a constant reminder of the religious overtones, with incidental music composed by Leonard Bernstein and sung by seven men and women, without instruments and with solos by a countertenor."

"With the critics' enthusiastic send-off, *The Lark*," he tells us "was gloriously embarked on a run of 229 performances." Of such, on Broadway, is "glory" made. ∎

June 18, 1972

Grandma Moses Primitive Artist

HOOSICK FALLS, N. Y., Dec. 13—Grandma Moses, the spry, indomitable "genuine American primitive" who became one of the country's most famous painters in her late seventies, died here today at the age of 101.

She died at the Hoosick Falls Health Center, where she had been a patient since August, after a fall at her home in nearby Eagle Bridge. Her physician, Dr. Clayton E. Shaw, said she had died of hardening of the arteries, but the best way to describe the cause of death, he suggested, was to say "she just wore out."

The simple realism, nostalgic atmosphere and luminous color with which Grandma Moses portrayed homely farm life and rural countryside won her a wide following. She was able to capture the excitement of winter's first snow, Thanksgiving preparations and the new, young green of oncoming spring.

Gay color, action and humor enlivened her portrayals of such simple farm activities as maple sugaring, soap-making, candle-making, haying, berrying and the making of apple butter.

In person, Grandma Moses charmed wherever she went. A tiny, lively woman with mischievous gray eyes and a quick wit, she could be sharp-tongued with a sycophant and stern with an errant grandchild.

Cheerful, as a cricket, even in her last years, she continued to be keenly observant of all that went on around her. Until her last birthday, Sept. 7, she rarely failed to do a little painting every day.

Grandma Moses is survived by her daughter-in-law, Mrs. Dorothy Moses; nine grandchildren and more than thirty great-grandchildren.

A funeral service will be held Saturday at 2 P. M. from the painter's home. Burial will be in the Maple Grove Cemetery here.

Crippled by Arthritis

Grandma Moses, whose paintings hang in nine museums in the United States and in Vienna and Paris, turned out her first picture when she was 76 years old.

She took up painting because arthritis had crippled her hands so that she no longer could embroider. She could not hold a needle, but she could hold a brush, and she had been too

Associated Press

Grandma Moses shown working on one of her paintings

busy all her life to bear the thought of being idle.

Two years later a New York engineer and art collector, Louis J. Caldor, who was driving through Hoosick Falls saw some of her paintings displayed in a drug store. They were priced from $3 to $5, depending on size. He bought them all, drove to the artist's home at Eagle Bridge and bought ten others she had there.

The next year, 1939, Grandma Moses was represented in an exhibition of "contemporary unknown painters" at the Museum of Modern Art in New York. She did not remain unknown for long.

A one-man show of her paintings was held in New York in 1940, and other one-man shows abroad followed. Her paintings were soon reproduced on Christmas cards, tiles and fabrics here and abroad. She was the guest of President and Mrs. Harry S. Truman in 1949 at a tea at which the President played the piano for her.

Honored by Governor

Governor Rockefeller proclaimed the painter's 100th and 101st birthdays "Grandma Moses Days" throughout the state, declaring this year that "there is no more renowned artist in our entire country today."

Yesterday the Governor said, "she painted for the sheer love of painting, and throughout her 101 years she was endeared to all who had the privilege of knowing her."

But to say that she was an American painter was less than

the full portrait of Grandma Moses; European critics called her work "lovable," "fresh," "charming," "adorable" and "full of naive and childlike joy." A German fan offered his explanation for her wide popularity:

"There emanates from her paintings a light-hearted optimism; the world she shows us is beautiful and it is good. You feel at home in all these pictures, and you know their meaning. The unrest and the neurotic insecurity of the present day make us inclined to enjoy the simple and affirmative outlook of Grandma Moses."

As a self-taught "primitive," who in childhood began painting what she called "lambscapes" by squeezing out grape juice or lemon juice to get colors, Grandma Moses has been compared to the great self-taught French painter, Henri Rousseau, as well as to Breughel. Until the comparisons were made, she had never heard of either artist.

Grandma Moses did all of her painting from remembrance of things past. She liked to sit quietly and think, she once said, and remember and imagine. "Then I'll get an inspiration and start painting; then I'll forget everything, everything except how things used to be and how to paint it so people will know how we used to live."

She would sit on an old, battered swivel chair, perching on two large pillows. The Mason-

345

ite on which she painted would lie flat on an old kitchen table before her. There was no easel. Crowding her in her "studio" were an electric washer and dryer that had overflowed from the kitchen.

For subject matter, Grandma Moses drew on memories of a long life as farm child, hired girl and farmer's wife. Her first paintings had been sent to the county fair along with samples of her raspberry jam and strawberry preserves. Her jam had won a ribbon, but nobody noticed those first paintings.

She would paint for five or six hours, and preferred the first part of the session because, as she said, her hand was fresher and "stiddier." At night, after dinner, she liked to watch television Westerns, not for the drama but because she liked to see horses.

Grandma Moses, who was born before Abraham Lincoln had yet taken office, spent a lot of her time on what she called her "old-timey" New England landscapes. She painted from the top down: "First the sky, then the mountains, then the hills, then the trees, then the houses, then the cattle and then the people." Her tiny figures, disproportionately small, cast no shadows. They seem sharply arrested in action.

She learned as a child to observe nature when her father took the children out for walks. He was a Methodist, but never went to church, and he allowed his children to believe what they wanted. Instead of going to church, they went for long walks in the woods.

Grandma Moses had had a hard life most of her many years, but neither her fame nor her advanced years cut into her formidable production. During her lifetime she painted more than 1,000 pictures, twenty-five of them after she had passed her 100th birthday. Her oils have increased in value from those early $3 and $5 works to $8,000 or $10,000 for a large picture.

Otto Kallier, owner and director of the Galerie St. Etienne in New York and president of Grandma Moses' Properties, Inc., will not discuss her earnings, but they are reliably estimated to have reached nearly $500,000.

Two one-man shows of Grandma Moses' work toured Europe, each for two years, and a third tour abroad is scheduled in 1962-63.

"Grandma Moses Story Book," an anthology for children illustrated by forty-seven color reproductions of her paintings, was published this year by Random House, and 20,000 copies were sold before publication.

Grandma Moses, the former Anna Mary Robertson was born at Greenwich, N. Y., in 1860, one of five daughters and five sons of Russell King Robertson and the former Margaret Shannahan. What little formal education she had was obtained in a one-room country school.

At the age of 12 she left home to work as a hired girl. She worked in the same capacity until she was 27 years old, when she was married to Thomas Salmon Moses. He was the hired man on the farm where she was doing the housework.

Invested in Farm

The couple took a wedding trip to North Carolina. On the way back, they decided to invest their $600 savings in the rental of a farm near Staunton, Va.

They remained in Virginia for twenty years. Ten children, five of whom died in infancy, were born to them. In addition to caring for the children and running the house, Mrs. Moses made butter and potato chips, which she sold to neighbors.

The couple returned to New York State and began farming at Eagle Bridge. Mr. Moses died there in 1927. For several years his widow continued to operate the farm with the help of her son, Forrest. But she had to give up farm chores, and then embroidery, when arthritis attacked her hands.

She had been embroidering in wool pictures that were reminiscent of Currier and Ives prints of country scenes. Grandma Moses' first paintings were copied from the prints and post cards. Gradually, however, she began to compose original scenes, drawn from her memories of farm life in past generations.

For her work, the painter received honorary doctoral degrees from Russell Sage College in 1949 and from the Moore Institute of Art, Science and Industry, Philadelphia, in 1951.

Late in life she became a member of the Daughters of the American Revolution and the Society of Mayflower Descendants after the local chapters had traced her ancestry and invited her to join.

"My Life's History," her autobiography, was published in 1951 by Harper & Brothers. "Grandma Moses, American Primitive," a biography written by Mr. Kallir, was published in 1947 by Doubleday & Co.

It was in "My Life's History" that Grandma Moses expressed her basic philosophy:

"I look back on my life like a good day's work, it was done and I feel satisfied with it. I was happy and contented, I knew nothing better and made the best out of what life offered. And life is what we make it, always has been, always will be."

December 14, 196

THE DANCE: A NEGRO ART

Katherine Dunham's Notable Contribution —Programs of the Week and After

By JOHN MARTIN.

WITH the arrival of Katherine Dunham on the scene, the prospects for the development of a substantial Negro dance art begin to look definitely bright. Her performance with her group last Sunday at the Windsor Theatre may very well become a historic occasion, for certainly never before in all the efforts of recent years to establish the Negro dance as a serious medium has there been so convincing and authoritative an approach.

Miss Dunham has apparently based her theory on the obvious fact so often overlooked that if the Negro is to develop an art of his own he can begin only with the seeds of that art that lie within him. These seeds are abundant and unique. Indeed, it would be difficult to think of any people with a richer heritage of dance begging to be made use of. Yet in the past (and even in Miss Dunham's present company in certain instances) there have been those who have started out by denying this heritage and smoothing it over with the gloss of an alien racial culture that deceives no one. The potential greatness of the Negro dance lies in its discovery of its own roots and the careful nursing of them into growth and flower.

Certainly this seems to be exactly what Miss Dunham has done. Several years ago she went to Haiti and the neighboring islands on a Rosenwald Fellowship to study the native dances and rituals, and since then she has carried on the study of her subject under a grant from the Rockefeller Foundation. All of which has given her a basis for her work that is entirely solid and true. But manifestly if she were not possessed of creative gifts, no amount of research could possibly turn itself automatically into art. It is because she has showed herself to have both the objective quality of the student and the natural instinct of the artist that she has done such a truly important job.

* * *

PERHAPS one of the most notable aspects of her program is the absence of all sense of self-importance. Here is simply a performance about which no explanations or announcements need be made to any normal human being who likes theatrical entertainment. It is, in short, a good show. That it is basically something far more significant does not in any way interfere with its sprightly and vivacious surface values.

Ivan Busatt

Julia Levien, dancing with group at Labor Stage Theatre tonight.

This is quite in character with the essence of the Negro dance itself. There is nothing pretentious about it; it is not designed to delve into philosophy or psychology but to externalize the impulses of a high-spirited, rhythmic and gracious race. That Miss Dunham's dances accomplish this end so beautifully can mean only that she has actually isolated the element of a folk art upon which more consciously creative and sophisticate forms can be built as time goes on. This is cultural pioneering of a unique sort.

To sit before a program such as this is to be impressed both with the existence of a constant element in it that is different from all other types of dance and with the great range and variety with which that constant element manifests itself. Miss Dunham has composed a primitive ritual in a somewhat mythological vein and has gradu-ated her material from this point through rituals that are for the release of personal tensions in primitive and semi-primitive societies down to the jazz and swing variants of those same impulses that are current in sophisticated communities. This sounds tremendously anthropological and "important," and it is; but it is also debonair and delightful, not to say daring and erotic.

BECAUSE Miss Dunham's researches have been made in countries which have come under Latin and Gallic influences, she gives us rumbas and dances of coquetry that are almost Parisian in their chic. But in so doing she manages somehow to show them as fundamentally Negro underneath and links them up indefinably with the universal quality of the art she is working in. Her rumbas from Santiago de Cuba and Mexico, her "Island Songs" from Haiti and Martinique, her delicious little scene called "Tropics—Shore Excursion," are all as fine a genre as her truly wonderful little genre piece called "Florida Swamp Shimmy."

At present, if her version of "Br'er Rabbit and de Tah Baby" can be taken as typical, she has not got to the point where she can make a ballet (or dance drama or what you will) out of independent material, but at least she has sensed the form upon which such a type of work can be built and the ingredients that belong in it. This present work is a failure, to be sure, but it is the kind of failure on which a future success can be based, for it clears the ground to a considerable extent.

In her supporting company Miss Dunham has in Archie Savage a dancer eminently worthy of her efforts. He can not only dance like a house afire but he is a good actor and a genuine stage personality. The group as a whole is handsome and competent, though there is among certain of the male dancers, including Talley Beatty, a distressing tendency to introduce the technique of the academic ballet. What is there in the human mind that is so eager to reduce the rare and genuine to the standard and foreign!

Musically the program is excellent, from the drumming of Gaucho (and of Miss Dunham herself) to the piano arrangements of Paquita Anderson. John Pratt's costumes are beautifully effective and ingenious, and the whole show is well staged and colorful. Happily, a whole series of further performances is to be given, as the month's calendar elsewhere on this page indicates in detail.

P. S.—Better not take grandma.

February 25, 1940

Carson McCullers

The literary art in Mrs. McCullers's hands—which one interviewer likened to "elegant ivory carvings"—was a dreamlike, mysterious process that produced fragile, misty, oblique and sometimes almost morbidly sensitive cameos of the American South.

Much of the grotesque, gothic quality of her art was undoubtedly the legacy of her Southern upbringing; but, in recent years at least, it seemed to have flowed from her own tortured life. One critic found a "vocation of pain" running through both her writing and her life.

She knew pain—sometimes excruciating and in recent years crippling—most of her days. Much of her ill health could be traced to a childhood bout with rheumatic fever that doctors in her native Columbus, Ga., diagnosed as tuberculosis. Before she was 29, she suffered three strokes, which left her paralyzed on the left side.

Career Started By Lost Wallet

Her last years were spent in a wheelchair in her Victorian-gothic house ("the color of vanilla ice cream") across the street from a Methodist church in Nyack, N. Y. There, dressed in a long white nightgown and tennis shoes, she would receive a few selected guests while her Negro cook, housekeeper and companion hovered over her.

When she felt up to it, she pecked away on a typewriter with one finger of her good hand—but the process was so slow and painful that she had not turned out a book since "Clock Without Hands" in 1961.

The illness of her later years left her with only a small body of published work: "The Heart Is a Lonely Hunter" (1940); "Reflections in a Golden Eye" (1941); "The Member of the Wedding" (1946); "The Ballad of the Sad Cafe" (1951); "Clock Without Hands," (1961); two plays, "The Square Root of Wonderful" (1957) and the 1950 dramatization of "The Member of the Wedding," and contributions to Vogue, Harper's Bazaar, Mademoiselle and other magazines.

If she had not lost her wallet on a New York subway one day in 1934, Carson McCullers might never have written anything at all.

The money was intended to pay her tuition at the Juilliard School of Music, where she wanted to study to become a concert pianist.

With these plans shattered, she turned back to the writing she had begun several years before in Columbus.

She was born in Columbus on Feb. 17, 1917, the daughter of Lamar and Marguerite Smith. Her father's ancestors were French Huguenots who came to this country to escape persecution; her mother's family was from Scotland.

"I have been writing since I was 16 years old," she recalled some years ago. "My first effort was a play. At that time my idol was Eugene O'Neill, and this first masterpiece was thick with incest, lunacy and murder. The first scene was laid in a graveyard and the last was a catafalque. I tried to put it on in the family sitting room, but only my mother and my 11-year-old sister would cooperate.

"My father, who was startled and rather dubiously proud, bought me a typewriter. After that I dashed off a few more plays, a novel and some rather queer poetry that nobody could make out, including the author."

After the abortive Juilliard venture, she tried several jobs in rapid succession. She played the piano for dancing classes in a settlement house, worked in a real-estate office and for a short time was on the editorial staff of More Fun, a comic sheet.

At night she attended Sylvia Chatfield Bates's fiction workshop at New York University, and one summer she took Whit Burnett's writing course at Columbia University.

Married in 1937

"But the city and the snow (I had never seen snow before) so overwhelmed me that I did no studying at all. In the spring I spent a great deal of time hanging around the piers and making fine schemes for voyages," she said.

She kept writing, however, and in 1936 Mr. Burnett introduced her to the readers of Story magazine with her first published work, a short story called "Wunderkind."

The next year she was married to Reeves McCullers, a fellow Southerner. They went to live in North Carolina, where she started her first novel, "The Heart Is a Lonely Hunter."

The book was published in 1940 and made her the most widely discussed young author of the year. Not everyone was enthusiastic about the novel, but its eerie, nightmarish quality arrested the critics' attention.

Set in a small Southern mill town, it describes the relationships between an awkward adolescent tomboy, Mick Kelly, a mystical deaf-mute, John Singer, and another deaf-mute, fat, greedy Antonapoulos.

Mrs. McCullers proclaimed a larger intention. She said it was an ironic treatment of fascism. Few critics thought this political symbolism worked but, on the novel's literary merits, many pronounced her a stunning talent.

Sherry and Music in Brooklyn

With the profits from the book, she went north again and with George Davis, the late literary editor of Harper's Bazaar, she helped to establish an informal literary salon in an old Brooklyn brownstone called February House.

From time to time the boarders there included Christopher Isherwood, Richard Wright, Thomas Mann's son, Golo, Oliver Smith, Jane and Paul

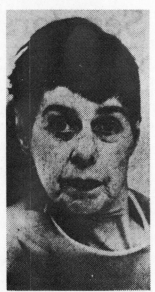
Steve Schapiro
Carson McCullers

Bowles and "such unclassifiable artists as Gypsy Rose Lee."

Miss Lee provided the cook, W. H. Auden kept house and all chipped in on the groceries.

In and out of the house at all hours were such people as Anaïs Nin, Leonard Bernstein, Salvador Dali, Marc Blitzstein and Aaron Copland.

Amid sherry bottles and symphonies, Mrs. McCullers managed to get on with her writing. In 1941 she published "Reflections in a Golden Eye," a brief, intense novel about sexual perversion and domestic tragedy in a Southern Army camp. At the time, many critics labeled it "neurotic"; but it has since been recognized as one of her most powerful and strangely moving works.

"The Member of the Wedding"

In the 1940's, the McCullerses lived in a New York City apartment lined with books that reflected her tastes: Dostoevski, D. H. Lawrence, Marcel Proust, James Joyce, Thomas Mann, Thorsten Veblen. For a respite from writing and reading—her two primary preoccupations—she listened to records.

The mid-40's were crowned by her best-known work, "The Member of the Wedding," the story of a lonely adolescent girl named Frankie Addams who believed that when her brother married, she would e married, too, and would go off with a husband and wife into the world.

But Mrs. McCullers gave this obsessive notion of Frankie's

that she was a "member of the wedding" a more universal meaning. As she put it, the novel was about "identity and the will to belong."

In 1950 she adapted the book to the stage, where—with fine performances by Julie Harris as Frankie, Ethel Waters as the housekeeper and Brandon De Wilde as the boy—it won the New York Drama Critics Circle Award as the best American play of the year.

Brooks Atkinson, then drama critic of The New York Times, called it "a vivid fragment of the living truth."

"The Member of the Wedding" was later filmed in Hollywood.

After a stroke in 1947, she had developed what she later called "a block about writing." Then she met Mary Mercer, who became her physician.

"Darling I've lost my soul," she told her.

Dr. Mercer replied, "No you haven't," and gradually persuaded her patient to begin writing again—one page a day on the large, marble-topped table in the dining room, overlooking the garden and the Hudson River.

The ever-present pain in her life became more intense in the 1950's. Her husband committed suicide in 1953, and gradually her illnesses turned her into a virtual cripple.

Normally reticent about her troubles, Mrs. McCullers talked about them unusually frankly in an interview in April, 1967.

"Sometimes I think God got me mixed up with Job," she said. "But Job never cursed God, and neither have I. I carry on."

"I've been a writer so long I have to—and want to—do it. There are awful days when the pain is so intense I can't write. Those are the dreadful times, and I drop out for a while, but I always snap back again."

After 1957, however, her publishers, Houghton-Mifflin, brought out only two more of her novels, "Clock Without Hands," and "The Ballad of the Sad Cafe," which Edward Albee later adapted for the Broadway stage.

She said during the April interview that she was working on a collection of stories about Negroes she had known in the South.

"The speech and feeling of one's childhood are always inherent to me as an author," she remarked, "and Negro speech is so beautiful."

OUT OF VASSAR AND ON THE TOWN

THE GROUP. By Mary McCarthy. 378 pp. New York: Harcourt, Brace & World. $5.95.

By ARTHUR MIZENER

"IT'S called 'The Group,' and it's about eight Vassar girls. It starts with the inauguration of Roosevelt, and . . . [ends] at the inauguration of Eisenhower. It was conceived as a kind of mock-chronicle novel. It's a novel about the idea of progress, really. The idea of progress seen in the feminine sphere. You know, home economics, architecture, domestic technology, contraception, child-bearing. . . . It's supposed to be the history of the loss of faith in progress, in the idea of progress, during that twenty-year period. . . ." So Mary McCarthy, several years ago, described "The Group" to a Paris Review interviewer. Apart from a few details (for example, the novel now ends in 1940 instead of 1952), this is an accurate description, and more revealing than anything a mere reviewer is likely to produce.

Miss McCarthy is herself a Vassar girl of the class of 1933, as are her eight heroines, and she too went from Vassar to New York, where she lived the earnest, intelligent, excited life of the independent left with the Partisan Review crowd of that time. There has already been a suggestion that some of the characters in "The Group" will be recognized by her generation at Vassar, and it is probably inevitable that the book will be widely read as a titillating insider's report on the life actual Vassar girls lived around New York in the late thirties.

To some extent, perhaps, Miss McCarthy has asked for this. She has written a good deal of the kind of autobiography that encourages readers to take her literally; her non-fiction, such as "Venice Observed" and "On the Contrary," has a personal intensity that makes the reader very aware of the author; above all, her previous fiction—"The Company She Keeps," "The Groves of Academe," "A Charmed Life"—seems to invite the reader to identify the originals of the characters and to treat these books as *romans à clef*. But if the earlier fiction fails to

Mr. Mizener, who teaches at Cornell, wrote "The Far Side of Paradise," a biography of F. Scott Fitzgerald.

achieve the effect Miss McCarthy presumably aimed at and fairly encourages the reader to take it as clever, malicious gossip, "The Group" does not.

There may well be disagreement about the final value of "The Group," about whether it is truly funny or only tasteless. But if there is, it will be because we are unaccustomed to the kind of fiction "The Group" is, rather than because it fails to achieve the effect it aims at.

The unusual thing about "The Group" is that it is wholly lacking in romantic solemnity and emotive rhetoric. Miss McCarthy's voice is cool and reasonable, and her eye is fixed, not on her own emotions, but on the revealing particulars of people's lives — on the grubby ostentation of their surroundings ("Norine and Put were surrounded by articles of belief, down to the last can of evaporated milk and the single, monastic pillow on the double bed"), on the heroic absurdity of their conduct. ("So I sent Harald out to get [a cucumber pickle] at a delicatessen, and he never came back.")

This precise, commonsense voice is perhaps most appealing in her autobiography, "Memories of a Catholic Girlhood." There Miss McCarthy runs no risk of sounding unfeeling rather than self-possessed. The pathos of the young Mary McCarthy's life is so self-evident that Miss McCarthy can tell us without risk how the girl, who was finally convinced her Protestant grandfather was in invincible ignorance rather than damned, hastened to give up the ostentatious piety with which she had been seeking to impress him, "lest the light of my example shine upon him too powerfully and burn him with sufficient knowledge to a crisp."

As Miss McCarthy's imagination moves away from autobiography to fiction, however, this dry, sensible voice gives her characters an air of caricature such that we may agree in a mistaken way with her own observation that "I'm not sure any of my books are novels. . . . Something happens in my writing—I don't mean it to—a sort of distortion. . . . The description takes on a sort of extravagance." It becomes, in fact, like some "Sense and Sensibility," entirely populated by 20th-century Marianne Dashwoods.

MISS McCARTHY'S passion for good sense creates this effect, and she is dead in earnest about it. But she is also amused, and sometimes perhaps fails to judge how tough-minded her jokes seem. The third chapter of "The Group," for example, shocked some readers when it first appeared in Partisan Review. It begins, "Get yourself a pessary." This is the "muttered *envoi*" of Dick Brown to Dottie Renfrew, the Vassar girl from Boston, who, in her inexperience, imagines Dick has said, " 'Get yourself a peccary,' and a vision

Mary McCarthy, Paris, 1963.

Photograph by Gisele Freund.

of a coarse piglike mammal they had studied in Zoology passed across her dazed consciousness." It is a little confusing. But presently light dawns, and she is delighted: "In a person like Dick, her feminine intuition caroled, this was surely the language of love. . . . Luckily, he could never imagine the thing she had been thinking about the peccary!"

She is then given by her classmate, Kay, an account of the courtly love code of the pessary. "A married woman," Kay explains, "pledged her devotion by committing her second pessary to her lover's care; only a married woman of very coarse fiber would use the same pessary for both husband and lover," etc. It is all hilariously funny, but it is so unsoftened by the sentimental haze or the symbolism usually used to make clinical details palatable

that it may, like much of Ben Jonson's comedy, appear brutal to 20th-century readers. We are never encouraged to identify ourselves with Miss McCarthy's characters and to see them in the all-forgiving way in which we see ourselves. What we are asked to feel is the rational self-awareness Miss McCarthy clearly believes human dignity requires.

This is the way we see "The Group," the eight Vassar girls of the class of '33 who had lived together during their upperclass

years in the South Tower of Main. We see them first at the wedding of Kay Strong to Harald Petersen a week after Commencement; here Miss McCarthy sketches them all and shows us the period attitudes they share: "they all adored brandy Alexanders," thought it

349

"terribly original" of Kay to have baked Alaska at her wedding breakfast, and "could see the good Roosevelt was doing." We see them last at Kay's funeral seven years later, much changed by time and circumstance, but still The Group. Between these neatly balanced framing chapters, Miss McCarthy follows one of them at a time, staying with each through a crucial period in her career.

BENEATH the appealingly earnest, provincial attitudes they have in common, these eight girls are very different. Libby MacAusland is a romantic snob who thinks of herself as "a gentlewoman"; she becomes a successful literary agent and marries a famous writer. Polly Andrews, after a love affair with a man helplessly—and needlessly—in the clutches of an analyst, marries a psychiatrist who is glad to have her divorced father live with them (The Group is horrified). Pris Hartshorn marries a pediatrician and struggles anxiously to raise her child according to his theories; she has a wildly funny encounter in the park with Norine Schmittlapp, who has her own theories about raising children. Together with Kay and Dottie, these are the prominent members of The Group. In the background are Pokey Prothero, the innocently insensitive rich girl, Helena Davison, the ugly intelligent one, and Elinor Eastlake, the cultivated Lesbian.

In her persistently reasonable, acutely amused way, Miss McCarthy knows everything about these girls. If they seem to some readers grotesque, it is because we are made to see them, with unsentimental clarity, as all too human. Perhaps, as Miss McCarthy has implied, "The Group" is not, in the conventional contemporary sense of the word, a novel. But whatever we may call it, it is, in its own way, something pretty good.

A POET OF THE STORY

THE COLLECTED STORIES OF KATHARINE ANNE PORTER. 495 pp. New York: Harcourt, Brace & World. $5.95.

By HOWARD MOSS

PRAISED so often as a "craftsman," a "stylist" and a "master of prose," Katherine Anne Porter must occasionally long to be admired for what she is—a writer. Through an inability to compromise and sheer endurance, Miss Porter, who is an artist, has come to represent Art, and though the role has never obscured the quality of her work, it has shifted attention away from the content of the work itself. The first concern of these stories is not esthetic. Extraordinarily well-formed, often brilliantly written, they are firmly grounded in life; and the accuracy and precision of their surfaces, so disarmingly easy to read, hold in tension the confused human tangles below. Experience is the reason for their having been written, yet experience does not exist in them for its own sake; it has been formulated, but not simplified.

These stories turn on crises, as stories should, but two special gifts are evident: depth of characterization, which is more usually the province of the novelist, and a style that encompasses the symbolic without sacrificing naturalness. Miss Porter is a "realist," but one who knows the connotations as well as the meaning of words. Understatement and inflation are equally foreign to her; she is never flat and she is never fancy. In the best of her work, the factual and the lyrical are kept in perfect balance.

She values the symbol, but she is not, strictly speaking, a symbolic writer. Observed life is the generating factor, and though it may connect with a larger metaphor, it is rooted in the everyday realities of people, situations and places. The names of the three books collected here supply us with a clue to their author's method: though the stories from which they are drawn have, of course, their singular characters and actions, the title of each suggests a wider

Mr. Moss is the author of "The Magic Lantern of Marcel Proust" and other books.

meaning. Betrayal in "Flowering Judas," death in "Pale Horse, Pale Rider," and precarious balance in "The Leaning Tower" are both specific and general. Their titles do not belie their particular natures. Yet, being themselves, they are more than themselves. They have subjects, but they also have themes.

The clarity of the prose in which these stories are written allows for subtle undercurrents. The qualities of poems—compression, spontaneity, the ability to make connections, the exploitation of all the resources of language—are present, but nothing could be more inimical to Miss Porter's way of doing things than the self-consciousness of "poetic prose." Incident and character are her means; syntax is her instrument; and revelation is her goal. Cocteau once made a distinction between poetry in the theater and the poetry of the theater. Miss Porter is a poet of the short story, and she never confuses the issue.

Because the ambiguity of good and evil is the major theme, betrayal is a frequent subject of these stories—betrayal of the self as well as of others. Certain preoccupations reoccur: the hollowness of faith, both religious and political; the mask of charitableness used by the uncommitted and the unloving to disguise their lack of involvement; the eroding effects of dependency; the power of delusion. Many of the characters have something in common: their actions being hopelessly at war with their motives, with the best of intentions, they are lured toward an ironic terror.

Representatives of one of Miss Porter's major notions—since we cannot leave each other alone, it is not always as easy as it looks to tell the victim from the victimizer — they struggle to escape the necessity of confronting themselves. Vaguely hopeful of doing the right thing, they are hurled into a maelstrom of conflict by forces as mercurial and cunning as those used by the Greek gods. Fate is not, however, an abstraction in these stories. It is more the consequence of character—of weakness, dependence, or the inability to let go of illusion—than it is the drawing out of cosmic plots. Only in "Pale Horse, Pale Rider" do forces outside the self, war and disease, become the adversaries.

Evil, to Miss Porter, is a form of moral hypocrisy. In the person of Homer T. Hatch, the malevolent, Lucifer-like catalyst of "Noon Wine," who roams the country collecting rewards on escaped prisoners and mental patients, it operates under the banner of social justice in the cause of profiteering. In Braggioni, the successful revolutionary of "Flowering Judas," it is seen as the degraded daydream of the ideal, which has not only been corrupted by power and sentimentality, but has transformed itself into a complacent form of intimidation. In the two Liberty Bond salesmen who menace Miranda in "Pale Horse Pale Rider," it takes on the totalitarian cloak of enforced "patriotism."

Moral hypocrisy can disguise itself as anything from a world-wide political movement to self-delusion but the self-deluded are not necessarily evil. They can evoke our sympathy, perhaps treacherously; they are distinguished from the evil-doer by two important facts. Evil is single-minded a rough definition of it, in the canon of Miss Porter's fiction, might simply be a view of life that cannot see that everything is at least two-sided. And it lies in a special way, by producing terror in the name of good. By having the power or worse, by being given it to impose its vision of the world on other people, it destroys.

The nature of how and why power is given, where the distinction between the victim and the victimizer gets blurred, is the subject of "Theft." More than a purse is stolen; identity and self-respect are lost by a middle-aged woman who allows herself to be victimized. The innocent can be made to feel guilty. But Miss Porter brings up an unpleasant question: By *allowing* themselves to be *made* to feel guilty, are they *not* guilty? The problem becomes more profound as the field widens or deepens. In "The Leaning Tower," the identity and self-respect of a whole nation *is* at stake. In "Noon Wine," the very nature of guilt, identity and self-respect is brought under scrutiny.

Miss Porter can reverse the binoculars either way; she is after the small despot as well as the large one. No one knows better than she that tyranny begins at home. The egotism, pride and self-pity of the Germans in "The Leaning Tower" have their domestic counterparts in an American family in "The Downward Path to Wisdom." It ends with a little boy singing a song to himself that goes "I hate Papa, I hate Mama, I hate Uncle David, I hate Old Janet, I hate Marjory, I hate Papa, I hate Mama." The little boy, unlike some of the characters in "The Leaning Tower," has not yet learned to hate whole races and nations. But since his song is an early composition, the chances that he will are good.

Katharine Anne Porter.

The closest thing to a spokes-man the author allows herself is a woman called Miranda, but the one truly innocent world that emerges from these stories can be found in the eight rem-.....ences of the South that were originally published in "The Leaning Tower." Officially "fiction," they seem to be creations of pure memory and are filled with the sights and sounds of childhood recollection. Beyond this limited nostalgia, innocent but often painful, only the natural and the primitive remain undamaged by the counter claims of the world.

That may be why Miss Porter's two favorite settings are Texas and Mexico. In both, a primitive view of life does not exclude what is morally decent and necessary. The Indian peasants in the Mexican stories, the farmers and Negroes in the Southern ones, are neither good nor bad in any conventional sense. They may be violent, but they act from an implicit set of values in which instinct and feeling have not yet been corroded. The heroine of "Maria Concepcion" kills her rival but is protected from the police by her friends—and even her enemies—in a pact as ancient as jealousy and murder. Morality is pragmatic and involves the living. The mere fact of being alive is more important than justice for the dead.

A different but analogous situation confronts Miranda in "Old Mortality." Nurtured on a romantic version of the past, she learns others; having come to doubt them all, she believes that in *her* life, at least, she will be able to separate legend from falsehood—"in her hope-fulness, her ignorance," Miss Porter adds. But the code of the Indian peasant is centered on the continuation of life; it is less concerned with truth as a specific fact, and least of all with truth as an abstract generalization. Maria Concepcion is separated from Miranda by a wide gulf. Maria has faith in life, whereas Miranda puts her trust in the truth. Over and over in these stories, they turn out not to be the same thing. Maria (like Mr. Thompson in "Noon Wine") commits an act of murder that is, paradoxically, an act of faith in life. Miranda (like Laura in "Flowering Judas" and Charles in "The Leaning Tower") has no faith in the name of which an act can be committed.

The author has added to this collection of her three books of stories a magnificent new long story, "Holiday," three shorter ones and a modest preface. Good as most of these stories are, they are overshadowed by one work. If it is the function of the artist to produce a masterpiece, Miss Porter may rest easy. In "Noon Wine" she has written a short novel whose largeness of theme, tragic inevitability, and steadiness of focus put it into that small category of superb short fiction that includes Joyce, Mann, Chekhov, James and Conrad. A study of the effects of evil, it is a story one can turn around in the palm of one's hand forever. So many meanings radiate from it that each reading gives it a new shade and a further dimension. Without once raising its voice, it asks questions that have alarmed the ages, including our own: When a good man kills an evil man, does he become evil himself? If the answer is yes, then how are we to protect ourselves against evil? If the answer is no, then how are we to define what evil is? It is one of the nicer ambiguities of "Noon Wine" that the two "good" men in it commit murder while the one character who is "evil" does not.

In the fateful meeting of the farmer, Mr. Thompson, the deranged Swedish harmonica player, Mr. Helton, and the Devil's salesman, Mr. Hatch, Miss Porter has constructed one of those dramas that seem not so much to have been written as discovered intact, like a form in nature. In the perfection of "Noon Wine," she has achieved what she has worked for—the artist in total command, totally invisible.

Louise Nevelson Puts Green Thumb to Good Use

Sculptures for Outdoors at the Pace Gallery

By JOHN CANADAY

WITH the foundations pouring as much money into art as they do these days, you would think that one of them would commission a team of biologists, physicians and phychologists to put Louise Nevelson under observation and determine how she keeps up such a head of steam. For several years now, from show to show, she has reached points where she could have rested on her laurels, but with each new show she has kicked the laurels aside like so many uprooted weeds and has gone on gardening the fertile soil of her creative inventiveness.

The major sculptures in Mrs. Nevelson's new show at the Pace Gallery, 9 West 57th Street, are like nothing she has done before, but at the same time they are pure Nevelson. Back when she was concocting her assemblages of anonymous architectural fragments — balusters, knobs and other odds and ends of wooden buildings — she was frequently asked to cast them in metal so that they could go out of doors. But they were conceived as wall pieces, and she saw no point in transplanting them into an unnatural habitat. Her new sculpture, planned for the out-of-doors, is composed not of odds and ends but of enameled aluminum elements (some tubular, some rectangular) manufactured according to her specifications and assembled according to her instructions after she had figured out their combinations in miniature scale models. She did not even see the completed sculptures until they were installed in the gallery.

●

But the impersonalism deliberately cultivated by a current school of sculptors who create on the drawing board and then turn the plans over to a manufacturer, does not mark Mrs. Nevelson's new work. Compared with her very personal compositions of old wood (you could always imagine her with a wheelbarrow going around to wrecking sites and collecting her raw material), these more chaste and more regular designs may be once removed from the artist's hand, but they still bear her stamp.

Sculpture by Louise Nevelson for setting outdoors is on exhibition at the Pace Gallery

These are see-through structures. The tubes and rectangular boxes are open at each end, so that when they stand in the out-of-doors you must see sky and trees and fields merged with the sculpture itself. The black surfaces, as glossy as mirrors, must also take on the reflections of clouds and landscape. This fine conception of a unity between sculpture and site is as simple and as direct as possible—too simple and too direct to have occurred to many sculptors. Mrs. Nevelson works with a kind of ebullience that hits straight through incidental considerations to the heart of whatever problem she takes on, and she has hit the target again in her present exhibition.

The gallery has been carpeted with artificial grass, and some large potted plants have been introduced, to help the visitor visualize the sculpture in a natural site. The announcement brochure is worth mentioning too: it shows not a Nevelson on its cover, but a vista of the gardens of Versailles, with some Nevelsonesque balusters in the foreground and a union of sculpture with nature that ties Mrs. Nevelson's art into that of André Le Nôtre, who worked at Versailles a little matter of three centuries ago. He would have understood perfectly what Mrs. Nevelson has done, although he might not understand, for a few minutes, how culverts could be as adaptable as balustrades to sculptural use.

Mrs. Nevelson may now rest on her laurels over the summer.

●

Tom Wesselmann (Janis, 15 East 57th Street): Summer has come in again, or almost, and Mr. Wesselmann celebrates its arrival with a set of variations on his theme of the Great American Nude. Already deeply sun tanned, she removes her bikini to reveal all, which is sometimes too much. The curious thing about these vehemently sexed females is that they seem to have been delineated by someone who has never seen a girl with her clothes off, but has listened in at great length to the snickering conversations of a bunch of 12-year-olds after lights-out at summer camp. This evaluation of Mr. Wesselmann's art is not meant to be quite derogatory. His Great American Nudes may be intended as comments on the sexual immaturity of the American psyche. In that case, the only criticism would be that Mr. Wesselmann is behind the times.

Daniel Newman (Grippi & Waddell, 15 East 57th Street): Since his painting owes debts to futurism and orphism, Mr Newman is virtually an academician, but he is a very thoughtful and selective one. These abstractions on nature themes range from sketches a few inches in dimensions to a wall-sized mural. In some of the tiny paintings Mr. Newman is a kind of cubist Constable. In some large ones (notably, the very fine mountainscape called "Rising Ranges") he is lyricist working in a complicated, tightly knit verse form. He is a very good painter.

Victor Colby (The Contemporaries, 992 Madison Avenue at 77th Street): With great good humor and the most engaging cleverness, Mr. Colby offers some really fetching adaptations of American folk sculpture without pretending less than high sophistication. His sculptor's feeling for wood — whether carved or picked up somewhere and assembled—is true. Beneath its tricky (and, here and there, even cute) surface this is a real sculptor's show.

Collectors Choice (Schweitzer, 958 Madison at 76th Street): This dealer's specialty is the 19th century without regard for current vogues, and this selection includes everything from a portrait of Ulysses S. Grant by Constant Mayer to a Renoir drawing. The juxtapositions are piquant in this offbeat show, which is well worth a visit.

May 14, 1966

MARISOL: THE ENIGMA OF THE SELF-IMAGE

By BRIAN O'DOHERTY

THE Marisol exhibition at the Stable Gallery, 33 East 74th Street, is full of Marisols — plaster Marisols, photographed Marisols, wooden Marisols—and it was being haunted by Marisol herself in person. She drifted around in a loose gray sweater, blue jeans tucked into high boots, touching up her new exhibition -- which runs from a huge John Wayne (looking like a male hormone in jackboots) to two monstrous children over 7 feet tall, each holding a doll with Marisol's face.

Her exhibition—which marks a giant step forward in her power, subtlety and seriousness as an artist—is a frozen "Marienbad" full of puzzled self-images at different ages and in different roles. Marisol finds it easier to make art out of herself than to talk about herself. She refuses to join you in contemplating her own mystery, but remains an island, sometimes distant, sometimes close, according to the conversational weather. But always separate. "Why is my own face one of my preoccupations? Because I can't find out what I look like."

A widely multiplied enigma, Marisol is also an enigma to herself. Sometimes she sees herself sharp-featured and high-fashion, sometimes blunted and round, the face set in an Egyptian tunnel of hair, occasionally as a woman out walking with four faces looking simultaneously in all directions. Her face is open and yet closed. She keeps her large dark eyes fixed on you. When puzzled she rubs her lower lip with the back of her little finger. Her dialogue is Pinteresque.

"Who do you like?"
"?????"
"Artists, I mean?"
"I like them all."
"Do you like Pop?"
"Bob?"
"Pop."
"Yes, I like Pop."
"What beautiful women do you identify with?"
"With nobody."
"Do you have a sense of humor?"
"Yes."
"Do you want your work interpreted as satire?"
"I don't care what they think." Pause. "I don't think much myself. When I don't

TETE-A-TETE—Marisol joins three images of herself at her show at Stable Gallery.

think all sort of things come to me."
"What sort of things?"
"Ideas. Like the big babies" (The huge 7-footers).
"Did you think of Goya's 'Saturn' when you did them?"
"No."
"Do you ever go mad, break things, use bad language?"
"Very rarely."
"You don't like to talk about your work?"
"I don't know what to say."
"Do you go to much theater?'
"No, I never go. It makes me nervous."
"Do you like movies?"
"Yes."
"'Marienbad'?"
"It is my favorite. I even copied some of the gestures in it, the hand of the man who played with the match boxes. And 'Mondo Cane.' That's where I got my dog from." She has constructed a small dog to accompany four Marisols (three adults, one child) out on a walk.

All this is much less cool than it sounds, for Marisol is far from dead-pan. The questions go inward with an almost physical impact through the extraordinary waiting face, with arched nostrils, slim Spanish nose, high cheekbones, all emerging from a streamlined inky wave of hair. It is a face uncovered by her concentration;

small subtle changes produce large effects. At times she is as dark and slicingly remote as a bullfighter, sometimes vulnerably female, and when she smiles it is like watching someone come out of a tunnel. Since words seem to be a form of direct experience that is painful to her, conversation with her is an extraordinarily bare experience. Like Jeanne Moreau, she frequently has one of the great properties of the legend-provoking female — the magnetic asexuality of an exceptionally beautiful woman who makes absolutely no concessions to her beauty.

Marisol's vital statistics are sparing. She was born in Paris 33 years ago and has been traveling since. Her childhood was spent in Europe and Venezuela. Her parents were business people; they had nothing to do with art. She has one brother, an economist. She doesn't like Venezuela or Europe, where she spent 18 months in Rome. She has never been to Spain because she thought it would be like Venezuela. She came to New York in 1950, went briefly to the Art Students League and then to Hans Hofmann.

"How did you paint then?"
"Like a Hans Hofmann student. The sculpture? I picked it up on my own."

Her virtuosity is astonishing. The show is a compendium of people (personal friends, including Andy Warohl), environments and events — people dancing, out for an automobile ride, at a restaurant with food painted on to the table, a wedding, with Marisol — the bride — marrying Marisol — the bridegroom. One can assemble a catalogue of real objects — lots of shoes, a couch, a handbag, a mandolin, saxophone and trumpet from a jazz group with a vague cousinship to Picasso's "Three Musicians."

Everything has been hauled into a sawed-up, hammered world where reality and abstraction, objects and their painted images, statement and suggestion all lock into a solid kaleidoscope in which her face appears and disappears like a mute obsession, never smiling, a mystery like Garbo.

Watching her going through her exhibition, constantly meeting her own image, I asked her if she had ever met her doppelgänger, that ghostly projection of oneself that one can meet face to face. At last she said, "I saw myself once, one evening when lying in bed, a shadow flying through the air, like a silhouette, a cut-out, front face."
"Were you terrified?"
"Yes."

March 1, 1964

Flannery O'Connor

In Miss O'Connor's writing were qualities that attract and annoy many critics: she was steeped in Southern tradition, she had an individual view of her Christian faith and her fiction was often peopled by introspective children.

But while other writers received critical scorn for turning these themes into clichés, Miss O'Connor's two novels and few dozen stories were highly praised.

In reviewing her second novel, "The Violent Bear It Away," for The New York Times in 1960, Orville Prescott described Miss O'Connor as a "literary white witch" whose "talent for fiction is so great as to be almost overwhelming."

"She writes with blazing skill about the most appalling horrors," he continued, "and sometimes makes them entirely real and perfectly natural."

In contrast Miss O'Connor saw herself as "a novelist with Christian concerns" who wrote her stories "in relation to the redemption of Christ." Many readers failed to see this relation, but they enjoyed her nevertheless.

Miss O'Connor was a Roman Catholic, but her main characters were Protestant Fundamentalists and fanatics. She suggested that the intensity of their faith was preferable to the tepid religion of a secularized churchman.

Miss O'Connor, who was born in Savannah, moved as a child to Milledgeville, a small town of mansions and farms. She lived in a two-story house set on a profitable farm. She did not take part in the business of the farm, except for raising the peafowl that strutted around the grounds, and, frequently, in her stories.

She wrote every day of the week when possible. "I write from 9 to 12," she once said, "and spend the rest of the day recuperating."

A self-portrait hanging in the family living room stressed Miss O'Connor's plain features. Sharing the painting is a peacock that, like Miss O'Connor, stares forward harshly.

In rating her among the most promising of the current generation of writers, critics frequently attempted to categorize her talent in terms of the South or her religious outlook. She did not object, but declared: "My characters are not sociological types. I write 'tales' in the sense Hawthorne wrote tales—though I hope with less reliance on allegory. I'm interested in the old Adam. He just talks Southern because I do."

Miss O'Connor was graduated from the Woman's College

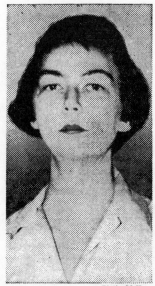

Blythe McKay
Flannery O'Connor

of Georgia, in Milledgeville, and in 1947 received a master's degree in Fine Arts from the University of Iowa. Her work at the Writer's Workshop there directed by Paul Engle resulted in publication. Stories appeared in such journals as the Sewannee Review, Harper's Bazaar, Partisan Review, and Kenyon Review, which last year published a special collection of appreciation and criticism of Miss O'Connor.

Her first novel, "Wise Blood," published by Harcourt, Brace in 1952, was generally praised by the critics. Ten of her stories were published by Harcourt, Brace in 1955 under the title, "A Good Man is Hard to Find."

Her awards included O. Henry citations in 1955 and 1957, and a Ford Foundation grant in 1959.

Miss O'Connor's first-floor workroom was crammed with books and journals ranging from Faulkner to weekly Catholic newspapers. She read and reread the Bible, and made frequent allegorical comments in her stories. "The Violent Bear It Away," for example, is from Matthew, 11:12.

A collection of stories to be published next February by Farrar, Straus & Co. is entitled "Everything That Rises Must Converge." This is a line from the writings of the late Jesuit anthropologist and philosopher, Pierre Teilhard de Chardin.

Miss O'Connor's full name was Mary Flannery O'Connor, but she dropped the first name by choice many years ago.

A Piano Prodigy at 3, Now the Conductor of 'Hair'

BY JOAN COOK

She has skin the color of molasses taffy, eyes as black as olives and a mop of black curls that give her a piquant look. She's Margaret Harris, a musical prodigy who grew up to become the first woman—let alone black woman—conductor of the hit Broadway musical, "Hair."

"There are eight of us, seven musicians, all men, and me," Miss Harris said over luncheon the other day. "They don't give me a bit of trouble personally or professionally. It's like having an unlimited charge account at Saks Fifth Avenue."

A child of Virgo in the Age of Aquarius, she managed to overcome potential astrological difficulties with the cast by saying "I'm Virgo, but the moon is in Aries and the rising sun is Aquarius."

She appears on stage through the performance and can wear almost anything she gets a kick out of.

"Tonight I'll wear what I have on," she said, with a gesture toward her black sweater and matching pants.

Miss Harris, who describes herself as "strong-willed but very quiet in a new situation, which sometimes fools people," recalled that her first two weeks with the cast were as a substitute conductor to see how she would work out.

"Once I became the conductor, one of the cast members promptly came up to me and said, 'Can't I sing?' and when I shook my head, persisted. I said 'No, nein, nyet, uhuh; I haven't auditioned you for the part.' He said, 'I still love you, but you're not like you were when you came in. You were so quiet.'"

An Early Debut

Chicago-born, Miss Harris, who is now 27, made her debut there at the age of 3 and with the Chicago Symphony at 10, the same year she received a scholarship to the Curtis Institute in Philadelphia, where she was the youngest of 125 students, one of two black pupils.

"In order to take advantage of the scholarship, my mother had to come with me

The New York Times
Margaret Harris

because I was so young," she said. "My father had to stay in Chicago where his work [as a railroad employe] was, and even though we went home for visits and vacations, it was a very real sacrifice they made to give me this opportunity."

Later Miss Harris went on to receive her bachelor and master of science degrees with honors from the Juilliard School of Music, and at 23, she toured 13 European countries as musical director, conductor and pianist of the "Black New World" production.

Two years later, she again toured Europe as musical director of the Negro Ensemble Company of New York. On Nov. 15th, she will make her New York debut as a concert pianist at Town Hall and on Jan. 22 in London.

Miss Harris, an only child, now lives in an apartment in Lincoln Towers, behind Lincoln Center with her widowed mother.

More Like Sister

"She's anything but a stage mother," Miss Harris said. "She's more like a sister. All the years I was growing up, she treated me like every other child. I fell off my tricycle with the rest of the kids. There was never any of this precious stuff about my hands."

Her mother did see to it, however, that she practiced her music, something she does from three to four hours a day except for matinee days.

"You have to practice; you have to have a goal. Discipline is very much needed," she said seriously. "Young people go off on tangents because they lack discipline."

Miss Harris said she feels fortunate that although the concert piano is her first love, she is equally at home with other musical forms.

"This enables me to earn my living doing what I love and still continue working on my career as a concert pianist," she explained.

When she isn't practicing or on stage, Miss Harris is likely to be composing, arranging music or knitting.

"My hours are such that I have to limit my social life to three or four people," she admitted. "I'd like to get married, I'm crazy about kids, but I would always have to have my music."

And there is no question but that music is her "thing." Politics bore her, and she dismisses women's lib with "It's nice, but they'd better make sure they're prepared to take over the jobs they're fighting for."

Her biggest annoyance is that people don't believe she is a conductor.

"Are you really a musical director? You're so pretty," she said, mimicking her detractors disdainfully. "Just because you play the piano, do they expect you to look like one?"

New Group to Offer Plays by Women

By MEL GUSSOW

One friendly male producer suggested that they call it the Clear and Present Danger Company. María Irene Fornés wanted to call it the Industrial Theater Bank. Rosalyn Drexler held out for Stone Soup. But six of America's leading, active women playwrights—Miss Fornés, Mrs. Drexler, Julie Bovasso, Adrienne Kennedy, Rochelle Owens and Megan Terry—decided to name their new cooperative theater the Women's Theater Council.

The group is as serious as its name indicates. The W.T.C. plans to present six "major" plays a year, beginning next season with one each by the founding playwrights, as well as "neglected" works by women writers of the past. It is the theater's intention to discover, and encourage, new women playwrights and also to provide opportunities for women in other areas of the theater—as directors, designers and actresses.

Not Closed to Men

The W.T.C. is not closed to men. In fact, there is at least one male playwright with whom all the women feel a kinship: Sam Shepard. And men will be hired—as directors, actors—when they are needed. This is not, by design, a feminist theater, but the accent is on women.

In common, the founding sisters all come from Off Off Broadway, are exceedingly prolific, have had their plays staged throughout the United States and in many foreign countries and feel neglected by the New York commercial theater.

Each has a distinctive voice, but their work is related in being largely non-realistic and experimental. The women feel unified as innovators and by their artistic consciousness.

They believe that their work can best be served by producing it themselves. The Playwrights Company is their model. They are in the process of raising the $400,-000 necessary for their first season. The object is to find a 300-seat theater and to produce the six plays in rotation, each running for six weeks—regardless of reviews or audience reception.

New Plays Listed

The women and their new plays:

Julie Bovasso: Playwright,

Julie Bovasso

Rosalyn Drexler

actress and director, often at the same time; she starred recently in Gênet's "The Screens." Her play for the W.T.C. will be either a revised version of "Down by the River Where Waterlilies Are Disfigured Every Day," which was recently staged at the Trinity Square Playhouse in Providence, or a new work entitled "El Rancho del Rey."

Rosalyn Drexler: Playwright ("Home Movies"), novelist ("To Smithereens"), painter and former professional wrestler, she has been commissioned to write a play for

Lincoln Center and is currently doing the screenplay for "Naked Came the Stranger." Her W.T.C. play is "Invitation."

María Irene Fornés: Playwright, director and designer, she wrote "Promenade" as well as "Molly's Dream," "The Successful Life of 3" and many other plays. Her new work is called "Fefu and Her Friends."

Adrienne Kennedy: The only black on the six-member board, she is the author of "Funnyhouse of a Negro," "The Owl Answers" and "A Rat's Mass." Her new play is untitled.

Rochelle Owens: Poet and playwright, author of "Futz," "Beclch," and "Istanboul." Her new play is "Kontraption."

Megan Terry: Playwright and director, author of "Viet Rock," "Approaching Simone" and many other plays including the forthcoming "Lady Rose's Brazil Hideout: or the Sado/Macho Blues."

Recently five of the founders—Miss Kennedy was out of town—gathered for an organizational meeting in Miss Bovasso's garden apartment in Greenwich Village. At times the session seemed like a cozy kaffeeklatsch, at other times like a caucus of revolutionaries.

The discussion began.

Bovasso: This is not a women's lib organization.

Fornés: Don't say that. It begins with the six of us, secondarily because we are women.

Bovasso: We're trying to find the feminine consciousness. We're concerned with psychic and unconscious feelings and fantasies.

'A Singular Viewpoint'

Terry: In the masculine-oriented theater, there are only three kinds of women—the bitch, the goddess and the whore with the heart of gold.

Owens: We want to investigate the multitudinous areas women are in. We have a shared esthetic viewpoint. We respect each other as artists.

Terry: We turn each other on.

Owens: It's a Gestalt corpuscle. Irene's a great designer. Julie's a great actress. Rosalyn's a . . . great mother. We draw upon Rosalyn for our sustenance.

Fornés: Men are writing out of their dreams. Ours are feminine dreams. Now we can say yes, we are women.

November 5, 1970

The New York Times

María Irene Fornés

Adrienne Kennedy

Owens: For years we felt glad when men called our plays male. Now for once, and because of the women's movement, we can say we have a singular viewpoint and it is female.

Terry: Jane Austen wrote under her embroidery. My grandmother wrote, and no one knew it until she died. The fact that we exist will give other women a chance to come out.

Drexler: We have to handle other subjects besides ones men usually handle.

Terry: I'm tired of being hit over the head by male obviousness.

Drexler: Would you say Beckett has a male obviousness?

Terry: No . . . We're going to rehabilitate great women writers of the past. Gertrude Stein was the greatest writer of American English.

'Very Volatile People'

Owens: We're all high-powered individuals. Any one of us can destroy. We're very volatile people. All of us encompass these energies. The Mighty Corpuscle!

Terry: Right on!

Fornés: We should call ourselves The Mighty Corpuscle.

Owens: All of us have a sense of humor, so it's not pathological.

Fornés: A joke: Megan writes a play. We all think it's too good and we burn it.

Owens: And if we can make her laugh after we burn it . . .

Fornés: I've already started writing a play about the group.

Terry: We've made horrible compromises just to get work produced.

Owens: "Istanbul" was given a terrible production. I was a vehicle for feminine violation.

Fornés: All my life I've been made to feel that my intelligence was distasteful.

Drexler: Total encouragement is very unhealthy. I'm glad I had a sort of unhappy childhood.

Terry: We'll have 600 plays on this table next year.

Owens: It's like an elixir.

Bovasso: We'll all leave here and go home and write plays.

Chorus: No, Julie, you stay here and write plays.

At 77, She's Made It to the Whitney

By DAVID L. SHIREY

"Who would have ever dreamed that somebody like me would make it to the Whitney in New York? I'm a 77-year-old Negro woman, after all, who was born in Columbus, Georgia." But Alma Thomas has made it to the Whitney Museum, where she is being honored with an exhibition of her lively and colorful abstract paintings, and she has made it to other places as well.

painters, which includes the late Morris Louis, Kenneth Noland and Gene Davis.

"When I was a little girl in Columbus, there were things we could do and things we couldn't," Miss Thomas recalled in a recent interview. "One of the things we couldn't do was go into museums, let alone think of hanging our pictures there. My, times have changed. Just look at me now."

Her abstractions, which

The New York Times/John Soto

Alma Thomas alongside one of her paintings

Rewards Come In

Within the last 10 years her talents have been rewarded with an abundance of art prizes and representation in more than 70 group and solo art shows all over the country. More recently, she has received favorable critical attention. A resident of Washington, Miss Thomas is considered as an artist working in the style of the Washington school of color

are rather large canvases composed of thumb-size irregular brush strokes placed in straight lines and in concentric circles, are, she said, "earth and space paintings inspired solely from nature." She explained that the earth canvases are her versions of cherry blossoms, holly leaves, circular flower beds and nurseries as "seen from planes that are airborne." Her space painting, she said, were inspired from the "heavens and stars and my idea of what it is like to be an astronaut, exploring space."

Miss Thomas feels most emphatically that color, however, is the most important element in her art. "A world without color would seem dead," she said. "Color for me is life."

Miss Thomas got her start in art," she said, from her mother, who "painted dainty pictures on velvet," and from the "artsy" household atmosphere of her childhood. She said that both her parents were teachers and always had "educated folks" such as Booker T. Washington in their home. Later, she went to Howard University where she was the only art student and the first graduate in 1924, of the University's art program.

After graduation, Miss Thomas was a teacher at Shaw Junior High School in Washington until her retirement in 1960. She said she attempted to teach her students that "art could be anything—it could be behavior—as long as it's beautiful." While teaching, she continued to paint in the kitchen of her home, in Washington's most densely populated ghetto. "I have been in this house most of my life. It has a tradition," she said. "I do not plan to leave it."

She "never married a man but my art," she said. "What man would have ever appreciated what I was up to?" She spends much of her free time entertaining Washington artist friends and seeing art shows.

Miss Thomas feels no bitterness about discrimination against women and blacks. "Everybody says I paint like a man anyway," she said. Refusing flatly to use the word "black," she said that "Negroes have now made their political statement about their problems in the art world." "It's time," she added, "that they get down to work and produce an art they can really be proud of."

She said she doesn't want to hold up her own life as an example to anybody. All she wants, she concluded, is "the chance to do some more paintings. As long as I can get a stroke to the canvas, I know I'm moving on."

Visual Arts Hears From Women's Lib

By DAVID L. SHIREY

Special to The New York Times

WASHINGTON, April 22—More than 350 professional women in the visual arts came here this week to discuss discrimination against their sex in the "male-dominated" art world and the possibility of structuring one in which men and women could function as equals.

In an impressive display of strong support at the first national conference for Women in the Visual Arts, female artists, art historians, critics and museum curators convened at the Corcoran Gallery of Art from Thursday through today. Through lectures, panel discussions and workshops they hoped to foster greater communication among themselves and eventually with their male colleagues.

Issues raised included male discrimination against the exhibition of women's art in musemus and galleries, discrimination against women in hiring, promotion and salaries, the education of women in art schools and the prejudices of the press and critics against women's art.

'Dainty and Unoriginal'

The artists claimed that they had not had fair representation in museum shows and that galleries preferred to display the work of men. They said that men in museums have usually dismissed women's art as "dainty and unoriginal" and that both male and female dealers have shied from work by women, explaining that it wouldn't sell.

The women said that male art critics also tend to ignore

and downgrade women's art and recalled that their male art-school teachers had discriminated against them by lack of attention and encouragement.

Most women teachers, museum officials and critics said that they were subject to fewer prejudices than women artists because their jobs were considered the "housekeeping chores of art," not so important as the "primary function of creating art."

These women said, however, that they rarely rose above assistant curator in museums and assistant professor in universities. They said they were paid "minimal" salaries, were not given adequate responsibility and were scorned by the male superiors as "unreliable and frivolous."

Feminine Art?

One of the principal disagreements centered on whether a "feminine" art exists.

Judy Chicago and Miriam Schapiro, artists who initiated a feminist art program at the California Institute of Arts, said it was based on a "state of emotional reality and a focus on the nature of female identity."

Other artists said that an imagery of "repeated circular forms" and preoccupation with "inner space" could be seen in works by women. Some advocated the establishment of a movement of "feminine" art.

But Agnes Denes, a conceptual artist, adamantly denied a "vaginal sensibility."

"The only inner space I recognize is where my brain is —and my soul," she said as many applauded. Pat Sloane, a

New York artist, philosophized that "art has no gender," and asked:

"When the women's movement is quite properly committed to the proposition that biology is not destiny, how can we as women artists be so stupid as to propose that biology might be the determinant of one's artistic destiny?"

Seminar Described

Other discussions were directed at the history of women in art, as both creator and subject. Linda Nochlin, an articulate art-history teacher at Vassar, described her seminars on women's art which attempt to "provide a total cultural conception of women in the society of their age."

Some artists such as Elaine de Kooning and Alice Neal gave personal reflections of their lives and their search for identity. Miss Neal also showed slides of pregnant women she had painted and said they "showed that woman was something more than menstruation." She was, however, booed when she suggested that "women should retreat during pregnancy."

Leila Katzen shot back: "I have done my best work during pregnancies."

Before adjourning the conference the women vowed to "continue to raise the consciousness of women's problems in the visual arts" through demonstrations, publications, documentation of their work and more conferences, projects which they hoped would interest men as well.

"We're a new breed of women," says Judy Chicago. "We are asking for a new world."

Women Filmmakers: Doors Opening

Mrs. Perry Miller Adato
Believes women's movement has opened many doors for her sex.

Barbara Loden
Believes the women's drive will ease problems of older artists.

Kate Millett
Feminist movement "has begun to break through stereotypes."

By GEORGE GENT

"Working with men in an authority situation is very difficult for a woman like me. I find it very, very hard to assert myself."

The speaker is Perry Miller Adato, the award-winning producer and director of cultural documentary films for the national production arm of Channel 13 here. Her views, while reflecting her special situation as a woman in television's male-dominated hierarchy, were echoed in varying degrees by several American women whose films are now being exhibited at the First International Festival of Women's Films at the Fifth Avenue Cinema here through June 21.

An outgrowth of the new female self-consciousness fostered by the women's liberation movement, the festival has brought together under one cinematic roof many of the world's leading women film directors and producers for the exhibition and discussion of women's role in film history, both as subject and creative artist.

Varied Works Shown

The festival, a program of 13 narrative feature-length films, 4 feature-length documentaries and 15 programs devoted entirely to short films — experimental, animated, documentary and narrative — is presenting works by comparative newcomers and such prominent

names as Mai Zetterling ("The Girls"), Liliana Cavani ("The Year of the Cannibals"), Leontine Sagan ("Maedchen in Uniform"), Ida Lupino ("The Bigamist"), Agnès Varda ("Cleo From 5 to 7") and many others.

Interviews with a number of American participants disclosed that not even the oldest of them has been completely untouched by today's women's movement, yet that a definite "generation gap" exists among them on the significance of their sex to their careers.

In general, they agreed that women today are far more likely to enter the creative side of filmmaking than in the past, largely because the movement was breaking down the cultural and frequently self-imposed psychological barriers to certain types of endeavor. But the younger women tended to be more militant in their attitudes, while the older ones generally favored the view that, in the world of creative cinema, talent will usually tell.

Holding somewhat the middle ground was Mrs. Adato, a veteran filmmaker for television, who believes that the women's movement has opened many new doors for her sex but who still wrestles with the guilts accumulated in trying to mix motherhood with a career.

Mrs. Adato is represented at the festival by her fea-

ture-length N.E.T. documentary, "Gertrude Stein: When This You See, Remember Me." Before moving to N.E.T. in 1968, she had spent 10 years at the Columbia Broadcasting System as "one of the two best film consultants in the country," she said proudly.

"I really knew film," she said. "I had studied it for an entire year in Europe but, because I had a family, I remained a film consultant for 10 years. If I had been a man, I would have pushed harder or left. But I loved my work and besides, I couldn't spend the long hours in the cutting room required of a director without neglecting my family.

"Sure, I feel guilt, even now. I can never know whether my family might have been different, better or worse, if I had been home more. Maybe the younger women coming up now won't feel the same guilt, or maybe their home situations will be arranged differently. Our culture demands that women play many different roles and it takes a lot out of us trying to measure up."

The women's movement is credited by Mrs. Adato with opening the professional and psychological gates to women filmakers and greatly expanding the cinematic subject matter available to them.

Younger women, such as Kate Millett and Barbara Loden, whose first cinematic efforts are being shown at the festival, believe the growing women's movement will ultimately obviate many of the problems faced by older artists.

Miss Millett, author of "Sexual Politics" and producer of a feature-length documentary, "Three Lives," said that the feminist movement had "begun to break through the stereotypes of women as wife, mother, et cetera, and women are now beginning to be portrayed as human beings."

Expanded Opportunities

This thrust, she said by telephone from San Francisco, has expanded the opportunities open to women in the film industry,

Not all the women, however, felt that their sex had been a handicap in their careers. Those who did not included Dorothy Arzner, who entered the film industry in 1920 and became Paramount's first woman director in 1926 and later a producer; Mary Ellen Butte, who directed the highly regarded "Passages From Finnegan's Wake"; Storm De Hirsch, poet and director of "The Color of Ritual and the Color of Though," and Faith Hubley, producer of animated films.

Miss Arzner, who is represented at the festival by Paramount's first "talkie," the 1929 feature "The Wild Party," starring Clara Bow, which she directed, said she had not encountered male hostility "perhaps because I broke into the industry when it was all so new."

"I can't say I had any difficulties," said Mis Arzner, who produced her last film in 1944 and now lives in retirement in La Quinta, Calif., "certainly no more difficulties than the men had. It is my theory that if you have authority, know your business and know you havet authority, you have the authority."

Mrs. Butte, who is the mother of two grown sons, even found that there were certain advantages to being a woman. "At one point," she said, "I located a scientist who had developed a production technique I was interested in and he devoted considerable time instructing me in the principles. I think he thought of me like a wife or sister," she added with a laugh.

Had she had any problems directing men, as several of her colleagues had experienced?

"Not at all. As you know, I'm now working on Thornton Wilder's 'The Skin of Our Teeth,' and one performer I wanted has since dropped out because we couldn't get along. Unfortunately for the ladies," she said with a giggle, "it was an actress."

Sexual Emancipation

URGES FAIR TEST OF 'TWILIGHT SLEEP'

Results in Banishing Pain, Says Dr. Rongy, Compel Wide Attention.

REPORTS ON 125 CASES

More Than 80 Per Cent. of Patients Remembered Nothing—Some Difficulties in Early Experiments.

Special to The New York Times.

BUFFALO, Sept. 17.—Dr. A. J. Rongy of New York read a paper here today before the American Congress of Obstetricians and Gynecologists on "Twilight Sleep," the scopolamine-morphine method of abolishing pain and memory in labor cases, which is being tried out in various hospitals in the United States, but whose chief advocates are Prof. Krönig and Prof. Gauss of the Frauenklinik at Freiburg, Germany. He related the history of the treatment for the last twelve years, and gave a detailed report of some 125 cases observed in the Jewish Maternity and Lebanon Hospitals in New York City.

The physician also revealed for the first time the name of the disciple of Krönig and Gauss under whose direction the patients at the two hospitals have been treated. He is Dr. K. Schlossingk, and for two years he was a pupil and assistant at the Freiburg clinic.

This is the first time an authoritative statement has been made on the subject before a body of American physicians since the scopolamine treatment received its present impetus in this country, and, therefore, some of Dr. Rongy's statements are extremely interesting. He asserted that Dr. Schlossingk followed the technique of Krönig and Gauss without deviation. He also said that patients were not admitted to the Jewish Maternity Hospital until they were in active labor, so that the physicians had no means of judging accurately when it started. These extracts are from Dr. Rongy's paper:

"When this treatment was first instituted many difficulties were encountered. Being an experiment, with final results uncertain, we hesitated to inform our patients, and therefore lacked their co-operation. Dr. Schlossingk was not quite familiar with our type of women and consequently could not accurately gauge the dosage and intervals. For our solutions we had to depend upon a local chemist, who at best sent us preparations which quickly deteriorated. Our accommodations at that time were such that it was impossible to devote a special room to this work.

"Our experience with this form of treatment consists of a series of 125 consecutive cases in the obstetric services of the Jewish Maternity and Lebanon Hospitals. Our cases were subdivided into three groups, with the following results: (A) 104 cases, or 83.2 per cent., in which there was complete amnesia, (loss of memory,) with analgesia, (loss of sensibility to pain); (b) nine cases, or 7.2 per cent., in which there was analgesia without amnesia; (c) twelve cases, or 9.6 per cent., in which the treatment failed to produce the desired effects.

"The average time that the patients were under the influence of scopolamine was about six and one-half hours. The longest period that a patient was kept under was nineteen hours. The shortest period was one and one-half hours. The average number of inspections was five, the highest number was twelve, and the lowest one.

"In our series 102 babies, or 81.6 per cent., cried spontaneously. There were four cases, or 3.2 per cent. of asphyxiated children. The total infant mortality was three deaths, or 2.4 per cent. One was a premature infant with spina bifida. The second died from melena neonatorum, and the third from subdural (brain) hemorrhage.

"It has been found that in order to carry out this form of treatment successfully, the patient must be constantly kept under the influence of the drug. Narkophen, a synthetic preparation of opium, was used in these cases instead of morphine."

These are among the conclusions reached by Dr. Rongy:

"Standard solutions are absolutely essential for the success of this treatment.

"No routine method of treatment should be adopted. Each patient should be individualized.

"Facilities should be such that the patient is not unduly disturbed.

"A nurse or physician must be in constant attendance.

"This form of treatment is carried out in hospitals, although there is no reason why it cannot be accomplished in all well-regulated private houses.

"It does not affect the first stage of labor, but the second stage is somewhat prolonged.

"Pain is markedly diminished in all cases, while amnesia (loss of memory) is present in the greatest number of patients.

"This treatment does not in any way interfere with any other therapeutic measures which may be deemed necessary for the termination of labor.

"To condemn or advocate a given therapeutic measure without a thorough personal investigation is truly unscientific and not in accordance with the tenets of progressive American medicine."

September 18, 1914

EMMA GOLDMAN ARRESTED.

Police Say She Violated Law in Lecture on a Medical Topic.

Emma Goldman, anarchist and lecturer, was arrested last night as she was about to enter Vorwart Hall, 153 East Broadway, where she was to have lectured on the Philosophy of Atheism. The warrant, which was served by two detectives of the Fifth Inspection District, charged Miss Goldman with having lectured on a medical question in defiance of Section 1,142 of the Penal Code.

In a number of lectures in this city Miss Goldman has touched upon the subject which led to her arrest, but, according to Policeman Caspers of Inspector Bolan's staff, she went beyond the bounds set by law at a lecture on Tuesday in the New Star Casino. The warrant upon which she was arrested was issued by Magistrate Breen on Feb. 8 in the Harlem Court.

Dr. Ben Reitman, her manager, said that, though Miss Goldman could have been arrested at her home, the police waited until nearly a thousand persons were inside the hall. When she appeared they refused to allow her to enter the hall for a moment. Some 500 followed, cheered Miss Goldman, and scoffed at the police.

February 12, 1916

DROPS MRS. SANGER'S CASE.

Federal Action Followed by Plans for a Celebration.

The Government entered yesterday before Judge Dayton in the Federal District Court a nolle prosequi against Mrs. Margaret H. Sanger, who was under indictment for sending improper matter through the mails. This consisted of copies of a publication, "The Woman Rebel," in which was an article on birth control. The case was set for next Monday, and its dropping caused jubilation among Mrs. Sanger's supporters.

Assistant District Attorney Content explained the Government had decided not to continue the case because there had been many assertions that the defendant was the victim of persecution, and that never had been the intention of the Federal authorities. The case was laid before the jurors as impartially as possible, and since they had voted an indictment there was nothing that the District Attorney could do but prosecute. Now, however, as it was realized that the indictment was two years old, and that Mrs. Sanger was not a disorderly person and did not make a practice of publishing such articles, the Government had considered there was room for reasonable doubt.

A hurried meeting of the Sanger Defense Committee was held, and the Bandbox Theatre at 205 West Fifty-seventh Street was engaged for tomorrow night for a celebration. Mrs. Sanger and some of her sympathizers will speak. Sada Cowan will read her play, "The State Forbids." On the committee are Mrs. Heaton Force O'Brien, Mrs. Elise Clews Parsons, Miss Jessie Ashley, Mrs. Rose Pastor Stokes, Dr. Gertrude Slight, Miss Henrietta Rodman, Mrs. William Colt, Miss Helen Todd, Mrs. J. Sergeant Cram, Mrs. Allan Dawson, Mrs. Frank Cothren, Mrs. Florence Woolston, and Mrs. Albert De Silver.

February 19, 1916

MOTHERHOOD DEATHS GROW

Bill for Health Safeguards Is Expected to Pass the House.

WASHINGTON, Jan. 28.—Motherhood is safer in any of seventeen foreign countries than in the United States and babies in ten other countries have a better chance of living through their first year, according to the House Commerce Committee's report today on the Sheppard-Towner bill to appropriate $1,480,000 for safeguarding the health of mothers and babies.

The report classed the bill as emergency legislation and said that there was practically no opposition to it.

The committee found, it said, that maternal and infant mortality in the United States was not decreasing, statistics before it showing a 15 per cent. increase in deaths from childbirth between 1919 and 1920.

Infants under one year old are dying from preventable ailments at the rate of 250,000 a year, the report said.

"In rural sections studied, it was ascertained," the report added, "that 80 per cent. of mothers received no advice or trained care preceding the birth of children."

January 27, 1921

SIX STATES ACCEPT NEW MATERNITY LAW

Six States have passed laws accepting the maternity bill, providing for Federal co-operation with the States in promoting the welfare of maternity and infancy, recently signed by President Harding, the Children's Bureau of the United States Department of Labor announced yesterday. These States, the Legislatures of which authorized co-operation before the bill became law, were Delaware, Minnesota, New Hampshire, New Mexico, Pennsylvania and South Dakota.

The rest of the States will not have to wait for the next regular sessions of their Legislatures, it was explained, for the law provides that, if the State has not acted, the Governor may, in so far as the laws of his State permit, accept the provisions of the act and authorize a State agency to co-operate with the Children's Bureau until the Legislature has had an opportunity to act. More than thirty States have child welfare or child hygiene divisions in their State Boards of Health. Any State desiring to benefit from the act must submit to the Children's Bureau detailed plans for its administration, and these plans are subject to approval of the Federal Board of Maternity and Infant Hygiene.

States co-operating will receive $10,000 the first year and $5,000 a year thereafter. An additional $5,000 will be paid, if the State appropriates a like amount. In addition, $710,000 a year is provided by the law to be distributed among the States on the basis of population, providing the amounts thus apportioned are matched by State appropriations. The law authorizes a total appropriation of $1,480,000 for the current fiscal year and an appropriation of $1,240,000 for each of the five years thereafter.

December 4, 1921

FIRST BIRTH CONTROL CLINIC TO OPEN HERE

Staff of 40 Physicians, Says Mrs. Margaret Sanger, Selected for Institution.

A birth control clinic, the first in the United States, will be opened in this city next Wednesday, according to an announcement made last night by Mrs. Margaret Sanger at a dinner at the Hotel Plaza in connection with the first American Birth Control Conference, of which Mrs. Sanger is Chairman. The guest of honor was Harold Cox of London, former Member of Parliament an editor of The Edinburgh Review.

The clinic is at 317 East Tenth Street, where four rooms on the ground floor have been leased for a year. A staff of forty physicians has been selected, of whom thirty will be in regular attendance and ten who will act in an ad

visory capacity. "The little clinic is practically ready to open within the next few days," said Mrs. Sanger.

"The next question will be that of establishing similar clinics in the cities of the various other States of the nation."

After Mrs. Sanger had given a brief outline of the clinic, a collection was taken up, and in a few minutes more than $1,200 was donated. Mrs. Sanger did not give further details in regard to the new clinic, but from Mrs. Anne Kennedy, a member of the committtee that arranged the conference, it was learned that the backers of the institution have no fear of the police. "Under a decision of the Court of Appeals," explained Mrs. Kennedy, "Mrs. Sanger was found to have been entirely within the law. The clinic will afford an opportunity to women suffering from a disease, such as tuberculosis, to inform themselves." Mrs. Kennedy further explained that a large staff of doctors was necessary because the plan of those backing the project is to make the clinic immediately a first-class institution for research.

This evening's session of the conference will be held at the Town Hall in West Forty-third Street.

November 13, 1921

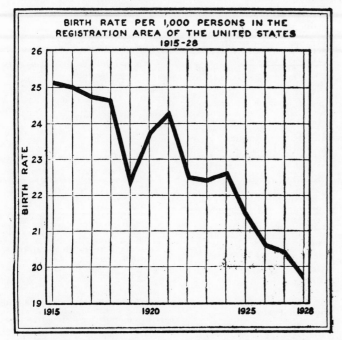

OUR FALLING BIRTH RATE

BIRTH RATE PER 1,000 PERSONS IN THE REGISTRATION AREA OF THE UNITED STATES 1915-28

The Chart Indicates a Decline of More Than Five Births per Thousand of Population in the United States Since 1915. The Diagram is Based on One Published in "A Graphic View of Recent Trends in Our Schools," by Frank M. Phillips, Statistician of the United States Office of Education.

March 2, 1930

FINDS BIRTH CONTROL WRECKING HOME LIFE

Justice Lewis Deplores Childless Marriages as Cause of Unrest and Divorce.

Supreme Court Justice Harry F. Lewis said in a statement issued yesterday in his chambers that he deplored the apparent inroads of birth control propaganda in Brooklyn.

He also asserted that there was an "almost complete absence of real home life today in Brooklyn," ascribing this condition to "childless homes." "Birth control information," he said, "may have its good points but can truly be indicted on many counts, the least of which will be responsibility for unhappy marriages and a falling off in the census."

In sixty-four undefended divorce cases tried before him in one day he found that there was only one child for every two families and that the duration of each marriage averaged less than three years.

"Not long ago a home meant something," Justice Lewis said. "It was the location of our birth. It was the place where we entertained our friends and where we held all our family functions. Today we are born in hospitals, we entertain in our clubs, we eat in restaurants, we entertain our visiting friends in cabarets or entertain our visiting friends in cab-parlors. I cannot help but reach the conclusion that if our Brooklyn women had children there would be more happiness and fewer divorces.

"Presence of children attracts the husband to his home and keeps the mothers from the gossiping neighbors and bridge parties. Absence of children promotes discord. Their presence makes for harmony."

June 10, 1930

Amity Between Sexes.

Should sex education, even in the high school, concern itself less with physiological knowledge and more with the emotional problems of courtship and marriage? The White House Conference on Child Health and Protection, in a new bulletin on education for home and family life, expresses the opinion that it should. The existing school program, consisting mainly of biological informa-tion and a little instruction in personal health habits, in the conference's view, completely ignores "the vastly more important matter of the emotional aspects of mating and the psychological reactions of the sexes."

Girls and boys, it holds, need to be taught how to develop attractive personalities, and to be fortified with some understanding of "masculine and feminine psychology in regard to the potential mate." In addition, it believes, the school should try to offset "the sex antagonism apparent in American life today" as a result of woman's changing economic and social status.

"Until educators have the courage to face these problems," the report declares, "it is useless to talk of education for family life, when the family, whether one wishes to be reminded of the fact or not, has its origin in sex."

August 8, 1932

SEX FACTS TAUGHT TO YOUNGER PUPILS

Bronxville Seventh Graders Study Subject From the Viewpoint of Biology.

A PROGRESSIVE SURVEY

Simple Organisms Studied First, Then Human Beings—Parents Cooperate With Teachers.

By WILLARD W. BEATTY,
Superintendent of Schools, Bronxville, N. Y.

In the last thirty years, the work of the American Social Hygiene Association and similar organizations has brought the topic of sex out of the dark corners of basement and attic into the realm of honest, frank and sincere discussion. Parents and educators are forced to recognize that children can no longer be kept in ignorance of the facts regarding reproduction. As a result, many attempts are being made today to include in the school curriculum courses designed to teach the facts of human reproduction.

The earliest attempts were in the colleges and in the high schools. Sex hygiene lectures, as a part of the health courses, were given with varying success. Facts gleaned from classes of this type convinced many educators of the need of sex instruction for younger students. Investigations, as that of Exner and others, showed that an average group of college men recalled their first conscious recognition of sex phenomena at six years of age. A great majority of them received misinformation from other children or vicious adults concerning the facts of human reproduction while their own parents were ignoring their honest questions.

Courses to meet this need in young children have been designed in many localities. During the past five years, a successful course has been developed in connection with the work of the Bronxville Public Schools.

A Seventh-Grade Course.

At the present time the Bronxville course is given in the seventh grade and is called elementary biology. For this instruction the boys and girls are segregated; administratively the course alternates with physical education, where girls and boys are normally segregated. The classes last from eighteen to thirty-six weeks and meet five times a week for forty-five minute periods. As the title of the course indicates, the material studied covers a survey of living things from the simplest to the more complex organisms, including man, and involving all the essential life functions such as growing, eating, breathing, reproducing, etc.

The course opens with discussions concerning the meaning of the term biology. Then the earth as the home of living things is discussed in its relationship to the solar system and the universe. The changes through which the earth has passed since its origin bring in interesting research problems in geology, formation of fossils, rocks, valleys, mountain ranges, glaciers, &c. Supplementary reading is done and many interesting facts are collected. As a result of the study of fossils from simple forms in lower strata to more complicated forms in higher strata the geological principle of evolution is explained.

All through the course an attempt is made to understand the scientific approach to biological principles. Living things are organized into plants and animals and their differences discussed. The plant kingdom is studied first.

Study of Protozoa.

Next the animal kingdom is classified into vertebrates and invertebrates. The simpler animals—protozoa—are studied first. Reproduction is again seen as only one of the life functions. Its study advances from asexual reproduction, where no sperms or eggs are present, through the presence of sperms and eggs in the same animal, and hence no male or female, to the separation of sperms and eggs and the appearance of males and females as separate sexes.

This, it is shown, logically calls for pairing in fertilization. Some animals are found to have external fertilization, some internal; some are oviparous and some are viviparous. The higher animals (mammals), it is pointed out, are viviparous, and among them may be classified man.

It will be noted that, prior to the discussion of man, reproductive functions and the terms connected with them are freely discussed by their scientific names and carry no emotional significance. Now man and his complicated body machinery is discussed as that of the highest of the vertebrates.

Because of the approach during the course from simple to more complicated forms, it is easily explained that man, standing at the top of the animal kingdom, is the sole animal with reasoning ability. This gives him the power to study his own reactions and develop methods of conduct that will be beneficial to him and his children. The social significance of the family and the ethical values of self-control in sexual matters develop naturally out of these discussions.

Cooperation of Parents.

At the beginning of the course a conference is held to which all parents of seventh-grade children are invited. The high school principal or the instructor in elementary biology discusses the coming course in detail so that each parent may be fully informed as to what is coming. Throughout the course every effort is made to establish full and frank understanding between children and parents. Children are urged to carry home the classroom discussions.

The faculty of the school is unanimous in testifying that the ultimate effect upon the students, judged by their behavior and ethical ideals, has been most constructive. There is growing among parents and teachers, however, a feeling that facts of reproduction might better be taught to children even earlier, so as to forestall ever-present sources of misinformation. Perhaps the fifth or sixth grades will prove to be the most efficient teaching periods.

October 18, 1931

PATH HELD CLEARED FOR BIRTH CONTROL

Ernst Says Court Decision Has Removed Last Barrier to Program of League

NEW RESPONSIBILITY SEEN

The recent Federal court decision upholding the right of physicians to give contraceptive advice for the well-being of patients has removed the last restriction on birth control, according to speakers yesterday at the sixteenth annual luncheon of the American Birth Control League at the Hotel Roosevelt.

The speakers referred to the ruling of the United States Circuit Court of Appeals, which upheld Federal Judge Grover M. Moscowitz in dismissing a customs libel suit filed against a package of contraceptives sent by a Japanese physician to Dr. Hannah M. Stone, gynecologist and birth control advocate.

Morris L. Ernst, attorney for Dr. Stone in the case, told the gathering he had been advised only yesterday that Attorney General Cummings had decided not to appeal the case to the Supreme Court.

"This means in effect," Mr. Ernst said, "that the decision is accepted as the law of the land."

Dr. Eric M. Matsner, secretary of the National Medical Council on Birth Control and chairman of the meeting, said:

"With the last legal restrictions removed by the recent court decision, contraceptives must be added to those medical services which are available to all of our people. Only in this manner can birth control become a eugenic movement and reach its final objective—complete democratization."

Dr. C. C. Little, president of the American Birth Control League, saw the Ohio River flood as "appalling" but as "nothing compared to the flood of unwanted humanity all around us." He added that "the 8,000,000 unemployed who have risen over the banks of industry make the flood in the Midwest look like a rain spout."

Mrs. Margaret Sanger, founder and president of the league and now president of the National Committee on Federal Legislation for Birth Control, told the group that "we not only have work to do in this country, but people throughout the world are looking to us to do something for them."

Mrs. Louis deB. Moore, chairman of the board of directors of the league, reported that the past year brought the establishment of three new State birth control leagues in New Hampshire, Texas and North Dakota, making a total of twenty-three State member organizations.

Dr. Little was re-elected president of the league and Mrs. Moore chairman of the board. Newly elected officers included Gilbert Colgate, treasurer.

January 29, 1937

Sex Education in Schools Again Provokes a Debate

The Attitude of Many Is Shown to Depend on the Range of the Program and the Manner in Which Subject Is Approached

By MAUDE DUNLOP

Shall we have sex education in the public schools?

In some opinions the answer is "Yes," in others "No." Much of the attitude toward the subject is less clearly defined, depending on the range of the program, how it is approached and to what age groups it is presented. Every one agrees that a final decision is one for parents.

The question was raised again last week when the case for sex education in New York's schools was presented to the Board of Education by its vice president, Ellsworth B. Buck. Mr. Buck offers evidence that sex instruction is needed, that young people want it and that homes do not provide it. He quotes supporting opinions of educators, leaders of youth and experts in the field of social hygiene. None of them is more impressive, Mr. Buck thinks, than the views expressed by young people themselves.

"Yes, knowledge is so much better than mystery," is a sample reply to the question "Should sex education be taught in the schools?" according to a study made by the American Youth Commission of the American Council of Education. Eighty per cent of the 13,528 young people interviewed, aged 16 to 24, thought in general that the subject "should be taught just like biology." The commission regards this cross-section survey as representative of young American opinion.

Opinion of the Young

Some of the young folks had these enlightening remarks to make:

"Sex education should start being taught in the elementary schools, because so many parents are ignorant on this subject and others are so old-fashioned that they feel that such things shouldn't be talked about."

"I heard all about it before I went to high school. I learned it the wrong way."

"It should be begun very quietly, early, so it isn't such a shock to the kids."

"School never taught me anything about my body. I can tell you

how to cut up an ant or a caterpillar but I can't tell you anything about myself."

Mr. Buck presents his case in a voluminous report compiled from many sources by his secretary, Eugene R. Canudo. It rehearses the views of many experts to the effect that, while sex education may be properly a task for the home, "for reasons beyond their control the vast majority of homes do not meet the child's needs in this respect," and the school must assume some responsibility. "Assuming adequate knowledge and understanding on their part," Mr. Buck says, "it seems that few parents are able to remain impersonal, unembarrassed and unemotional in talks with their children on 'the facts of life.'"

Experts contend, he adds, that most of the parents are grateful for being relieved of "this trying task."

An Increasing Role

Mr. Buck points to the school's role in assuming many functions once belonging to the home—teaching girls to cook and to sew, boys to handle tools; instructing in habits of health and diet and social behavior. The school, he says, is the only agency which reaches all the children, regardless of color, creed or background. And still, he says, "the school system does nothing to help thousands of young people who, suddenly aware of sex urges and sex curiosities, have neither the education nor the understanding to adjust themselves properly."

How shall it be done? The suggestion is made that parents, parent-teacher associations, the church, the Y.W.C.A. and other educational and social agencies should correlate their efforts in working out a program.

A third of the forty-two-page report is devoted to procedure outlined in the handbook "High Schools and Sex Education" of the United States Public Health Service and the United States Office of Education. The recent revision of this manual by its editor, Dr. Benjamin C. Gruenberg, has been available to Mr. Buck in manuscript, and from it he presents the theme that sex

A science class in a New York City high school. Whether sex should be a topic for scientific teaching is now being debated.

Ewing Galloway

education should not be taught as a subject in itself, but as an integral part of the curriculm. For example, the subject relates to botany, zoology, biology, agriculture, psychology and home nursing, and interpretation is possible in courses as widely distributed as literature and history, athletics and home making.

Opposition to sex education in the schools is expressed in various terms. It is said that children in junior high schools are too young for such instruction; that, at any age, it should come from parents, not from teachers. Young people among the 20 per cent who, according to the American Youth Commission study, were opposed to sex education, remarked:

"School teachers haven't any children and they don't get married. Their [the young people's] parents should be made to tell them."

"Should have reading matter on sex available at schools so that young people could get it if they wanted."

"Mother knows the child and every child is different. Teacher can only talk to group. This way would be bad."

"That's a home problem," one young person thought; another said, "They get it quick enough anyway."

Opposition in other quarters relates more to the approach than to the subject itself. Francis S. Moseley, president of the Teachers Alliance, thinks that the subject belongs to the field of the professional educator rather than to a layman's group such as the Board of Education, and that "there is no such thing as sex education," except as it is linked with the cultural and emotional problems of youth, and with the teaching of ideals and self-control.

"The mere giving of information is not enough," he says, "but there is a place for a combination of sex-character education in the schools," if worked out in proper cooperation of home and church and other forces in the community. The alliance does not approve of the current trend toward "usurpation of parental rights" which, Mr. Moseley says, "we consider a dangerous form of educational totalitarianism." He adds that the alliance favors a thorough investigation of the whole subject of sex-character education, bearing in mind its relation to a larger program of adult education from which it cannot be divorced.

How About Parents?

Mr. Buck's "Case for Rational Sex Education in New York Schools" will be referred to the Board of Superintendents in due course. Frederick Ernst, associate superintendent in charge of the junior and senior high schools, in which sex education would be given, has this to say:

"The term 'sex education' is quite meaningless. It may cover intensively a very limited field, or, in a general way, a very broad field. In my opinion the subject should be taught in the very best possible way—by people in whose special qualifications we have confidence—or not at all. Furthermore, sex education should not be introduced into the schools until those responsible for the school system have full parent support for the approach.

"In my opinion, the chief objection to a program of sex education has been this: Parents do not know what it is about; they fear the subject in general without any clear idea of its purpose. In my opinion, a program of parental education in the subject is the first step."

Mr. Ernst's point of view was expressed in another way by a member of the younger generation, quoted by Mr. Buck: "There ought to be classes for parents. They are the ones that need it."

February 5, 1939

The Complex Kinsey Study and What It Attempts to Do

SEXUAL BEHAVIOR IN THE HUMAN FEMALE. By the staff of the Institute for Sex Research, Indiana University: Alfred C. Kinsey, Wardell B. Pomeroy, Clyde E. Martin, Paul H. Gebhard. 842 pp. Philadelphia: W. B. Saunders Company. $8.

By CLYDE KLUCKHOHN

AMERICANS who read almost any newspaper or magazine hardly need to be reminded at this date of most of the conclusions of this volume which have any popular interest. Many readers are doubtless tired of seeing them printed so often. Actually, except for the "justification by numbers," a majority of the findings of broad general interest were hinted at or stated in tentative

Mr. Kluckhohn is Professor of Anthropology at Harvard.

form in "Sexual Behavior in the Human Male."

Any selection from a book so crammed with fact and interpretation as "Sexual Behavior in the Human Female" is invidious, but some of the salient points in this whole volume appeared to be these:

The more general information and thinking on female sexual behavior are based on a larger body of material (interviews with 7,789 women and 8,603 men, plus various kinds of supplementary material), but the statistical analyses have been restricted to 5,940 women with an age range of 2 to 90 years; 456 cases were born before 1900 and 784 in the first decade after 1900; 147 were pre-adolescent; 3,313 had never married at the time of the interview; 785 cases had been widowed, separated, or divorced; 56 per cent had some college background and 19 per cent had gone beyond college into graduate work; 69 per cent came from ten states which include some 47 per cent of the total population of this country.

THE author states that generalizations arrived at are least likely to be applicable to the following groups: Over 50 years; those with only grade school education; those with high school education who are over 40 years of age; previously married females, now widowed, separated, or divorced; all Catholic groups, especially among older females; devoutly Jewish groups; some laboring groups, especially among older females; all rural groups, groups originating in the Southeastern quarter of the country, from the Pacific Northwest and from the high plains and Rocky Mountain areas.

"Calculations on the marital history indicate that those females who had not responded to the point of orgasm prior to marriage failed to respond after marriage three times as often as the females who had a fair amount of orgasmic experience before marriage * * * the type of pre-marital activity in which the female has acquired her experience did not appear to have been as important as the fact that she had or had not experienced orgasm * * * it is sometimes said that pre-marital petting may make it difficult for the female to be satisfied with coitus in marriage. The statement has never been supported by any accumulation of specific data, and we have not seen

Dr. Kinsey (left) with his co-authors, Dr. Gebhard, Dr. Martin and Dr. Pomeroy, at Bloomington, Ind.

more than three or four such cases. On the other hand, we have the histories of nearly a thousand females who had done pre-marital petting and who had then responded excellently in their marital coitus."

"Nearly 50 per cent of the females in our sample had had coitus before they were married."

"Among the married females in the sample, about one-quarter had had extra-marital coitus by age 40. Between the ages of 26 and 50, something between one in six and one in ten was having extra-marital coitus."

"The range of variation in the female far exceeds the range of variation in the male."

"We may predict that the persons who will be most often incapable of accepting our description of American females will be some of the promiscuous males who have had the largest amount of sexual contact with females. Most of these males do not realize that it is only a select group of females and usually the more responsive females who will accept pre-marital or extra-marital relationships."

"THE sexual history of each individual represents a unique combination * * * there is little chance that such a combination has ever existed before or ever will exist again. We have never found any individual who was a composite of all the averages on all of the aspects of sexual response and overt activities which we have analyzed in the present volume. This is the most important fact which we can report on the sexual behavior of the females who have contributed to the present study."

"In spite of the widespread and oft-repeated emphasis on the supposed differences between female and male sexual

ity, we fail to find any anatomic or physiologic basis for such difference." (However, female sexual behavior appears to be appreciably less affected than male by psychological factors.)

"Within limits, the levels of sexual response may be modified by reducing or increasing the amount of available hormone, but there seems to be no reason for believing that the patterns of sexual behavior may be modified by hormonal therapy."

Perhaps the most startling new finding is that females are not conditioned as much as males by the attitudes of the social groups in which they live and by the sexual experiences which they have had. In addition, there are rich masses of information the full significance of which will become apparent only after many years of critical evaluation and comparative analysis. Particularly noteworthy are the concluding chapters on anatomy, physiology, psychologic factors, neural mechanisms and hormonal factors. These represent a genuine advance beyond the point reached in "Sexual Behavior in the Human Male."

TO understand this book—even superficially—one cannot simply read it; it must be studied. Study, ideally, should take place against the background of some knowledge of at least a few of the specialized fields involved and some appreciation of scientifically unsolved problems.

Few readers have the time and not too many the sophistication to make such a study. What all readers can do is to cultivate an attitude of cautious reserve against drawing too sweeping inferences on the basis of pioneer work. They would

also do well, even as far as the conclusions of Dr. Kinsey and his associates are concerned, to remember the wise words of Santayana: "Skepticism is the chastity of the intellect—not to be surrendered too easily to the first comer."

Americans still have an alarming predilection for "either-or" answers. Something is true or it isn't. "Kinsey is nonsense" (rather nasty nonsense). "This is the 'scientific' answer to problems of sex." Both extremes are equally absurd, and all sensible people, if pressed, would admit this verbally. Yet most reviews of the first volume in serious or semi-serious periodicals tended, at least in tone, toward extravagant praise or extravagant damnation.

THERE were honorable exceptions, but they were few. Usually, Kinsey was the moral crusader or the giant scientific revolutionary of the Darwin-Freud sort—or both. To others he was hopelessly naive and misguided or a mere headline hunter—and there were thinly disguised overtones suggesting that in either case he should somehow be suppressed.

This review will attempt a wary but safe landing in the small space between the sea and the cliff. Obviously, this book isn't "nonsense." There are undoubtedly statements in it which are just plain wrong and many more which need correction to greater or lesser degree. Nevertheless the data were gathered with great care and honesty and with, to make a minimum statement, considerable skill.

A large number of Americans made certain statements about their sexual experiences and attitudes—and these statements are of far-reaching scientific importance. On the other hand, this volume must be clearly recognized as being what it is—the second venture of this magnitude in a field of frightening complexity, in territory previously entered only by a few hardy explorers who usefully reconnoitered some delimited fringes.

FIRST, lest silence be misunderstood, let me make my positive convictions explicit. I admire courage, persistence, the ambitious sweep of the total plan. Of course I agree that "the happiness of individual men, and the good of the total social organization, are never furthered by the perpetuation of ignorance." I have no patience with the prudery ("hush, hush, child") and the anti-scientific, anti-rational attitudes expressed in the August, 1948, symposium

of the Reader's Digest—even by the president of a distinguished university (Princeton). Such expressions in the mid-twentieth century by individuals who ought to know better are indeed disheartening and substantiate the view of A. J. Carlson and others that, sadly, it takes a long time for science to penetrate beneath the surface of many trained and educated minds.

At the same time the freedom of the scientist to investigate and to publish his results (which is a crucial part of the academic freedom cherished in the United States) means also that other scientists, scholars and laymen have the right and the duty to challenge—so long as this is on intellectual grounds. It would be a monstrous reversal of the scientific attitude to insist, however obliquely, that because something is written in the name of "science" everything in it is therefore to be accepted as "true."

THIS book makes an enormous contribution of fact not only to our knowledge of sexual behavior and sexual biology but also to our information on the social organization and cultural patterns of certain large sectors of our population. These latter materials constitute a vast storehouse which social scientists ought to exploit for a generation. The sections on comparative psychology, anthropology and art also represent supplements which are valuable in themselves. Dr. Kinsey and his colleagues are prodigiously industrious in accumulating facts and at least partly successful in integrating them.

The Kinsey group learned a good deal from criticisms of the first volume, although not quite as much as some of us had hoped. They do recognize more adequately the unsatisfactory and limited nature of their samples. They state (but do not always follow this judicious principle to the letter) that generalizations have "been restricted to the particular samples that we have had available."

In general, I think, professional statisticians will have fewer quarrels with the procedures followed. Statistically, this is a better book than any previous study of sexual behavior in wide scope.

I AM afraid the psychoanalysts and psychiatrists will howl almost as loudly as they did five years ago—though this time much more space is given to psychological factors and the treatment seems to me appre-

Brownstone sculpture by Henry Kreis. Collection Metropolitan Museum of Art.

social characteristics of those who were approached but refused; we are told only the number of those who began but failed to complete the interviews). Finally, in some instances, assertions do not stay within the data.

Presentation is clear enough for the most part, albeit a little turgid and needlessly repetitious. The general tone is more confident, less defensive, more relaxed than in the first volume. In places this leads to essentially undisguised preaching. Most of the text remains, however, almost painfully objective—without even the slightest trace of restrained, implicit, or ironic humor. This is not only a book about Americans. It is, equally, an intensely American book—almost a parody on the humorless kind of American science which worships the quantitative and scrupulously observes the ritual pedantries.

Nevertheless this book is science, serious science, and science in the grand style. I defy trivial readers to be amused by it or diverted more than a very little here and there. Only the really corrupted can find the slightest pornographic titillation.

THE unequivocal criticism one can level at this book is the pretentiousness of the title. I am aware that the authors have given a reasoned justification. Yet, if I too may parody the academic, the honest title would have been: "Some Aspects of Sexual Behavior in American Females (Primarily Educated, Protestant, Regionally Localized, Adolescent through Middle-Aged)."

There are not only the quantitative and qualitative sampling problems. The book does not treat many time-honored questions in this area, such as the time of night or day when coitus takes place, frequency of rectal heterosexual coitus, the experience of defloration and reactions to it.

These latter are not genuine criticisms; they merely document that the book is not all-inclusive. Kinsey & Co. would surely agree to this—after all, they still have some 84,000 subjects and goodness knows how many books to go. They have made a brilliant and arguable contribution for which we are all in their debt. But this is a contribution—not a definitive treatise. Let the buyer profit but beware.

ciably more sensitive. The subjects no longer appear quite so starkly as animals who have orgasms at varying intervals and in varying ways. In the long run, both the psychoanalysts and the behaviorists of the Kinsey persuasion will, I believe, have to give some ground.

This is not an appropriate place for a technical review of the methodology. Briefly, there are grounds for praise and for disagreement or argument. There is much evidence of excellent workmanship and of respect for the minutiae of science. These authors pack a great deal into tables, and their text ordinarily draws attention to the meat of a table—incisively and compactly.

There are internal signs that they have had more wide-ranging and skillful statistical advice for this volume. Any statistician will say that for these problems the Indiana group needed the help of the best statisticians in the world. Perhaps in this instance the *expertise* came too late for some important purposes—namely, after the collection of most of the data. The authors still do not give some of the information the scientist has a right to require (e. g. the numbers and demographic and

September 13, 1953

DOCTORS ENDORSE TEST-TUBE BIRTHS

Artificial Insemination Gets Approval in Sterility Study as 'Ethical and Moral'

Special to The New York Times.

ATLANTIC CITY, N. J., June 4—The American Society for the Study of Sterility today approved artificial insemination as a "completely ethical, moral and desirable form of medical therapy."

The surprise resolution was adopted by the organization, which represents 500 medical doctors specializing in the problems of sterility, by a vote of 79 to 8. It was said to be the first formal statement by a medical society approving the practice of artificial insemination.

The resolution set forth three conditions that it said must exist to make artificial insemination acceptable. They were:

1. Urgent desire of the couple to have such therapy applied to the solution of their infertility problem.
2. Careful selection by the physician of a biologically and genetically satisfactory donor.
3. The opinion of the physician, after thorough study, that the couple will make desirable parents.

Preferred to Adoption

The resolution went on to say: "Those physicians who have carried out donor inseminations for several decades can attest that in many cases it is a more desirable procedure for acquiring a family than adoption. One great advantage of donor insemination is that it provides the opportunity for the husband to share the months of his wife's pregnancy and her childbirth.

"From observation over many years, the membership is impressed by the almost universal good results achieved in respect to children and the entire family unit. The fact that, in some instances, parents have returned for as many as four children by donor insemination, is further proof of the happiness it bestows."

Dr. John O. Haman of San Francisco, retiring president of the society, explained why the action had been taken.

"This group for years never took any formal stand on the issue," he said, "but in view of recent publicity in the lay press and requests for legal opinions, we feel that we should make our opinion known, since included in the membership of this society is the overwhelming majority of those who practice this type of medicine."

Long a Controversial Issue

Artificial insemination has long been opposed by some churches. Recently a Superior Court judge in Illinois held that it could be grounds for divorce.

Judge Gibson E. Gorman of Cook County ruled that "donor insemination, with or without the consent of the husband, is contrary to public policy and good morals and constitutes adultery on the part of the mother." He added: "A child so conceived is not a child born in wedlock and is therefore illegitimate."

In the debate before the resolution was approved Dr. S. Leon Israel of Philadelphia contended that "unless we take the lead in supporting therapeutic insemination the courts of the nation will never pass the necessary laws."

But Dr. Haman, in his explanation, emphasized that nowhere in the United States was the practice of artificial insemination illegal. Dr. Haman was succeeded as president of the society by Dr. Summers H. Sturgis of Boston.

June 5, 1955

EDUCATION URGED IN BIRTH CONTROL

Mrs. Meyer Sees Hypocrisy —Illegal Abortions Put at 750,000 a Year

Mrs. Eugene Meyer called yesterday for an end to hypocrisy about birth control. She said it had been conservatively estimated that at least 750,000 criminal abortions were performed annually in this country. Most of them, she said, are obtained by married women with three or more children.

"How many of these mothers are so beset with socio-economic problems that they are forced to this drastic expedient because they are ignorant of other means for controlling the size of their families?" she asked.

Mrs. Meyer blamed public prudishness and physicians' timidity for the failure to teach American women about birth control. She said that birth control should be taught here as a public health measure.

Mrs. Meyer, the wife of the chairman of the board of The Washington Post and Times Herald, addressed the annual luncheon of the Planned Parenthood Committee of Mothers' Health Centers. Four hundred and fifty persons attended.

She described the poverties caused by over-population and under-production in Asia and said the same problems existed in some circumstances here. And many American women are ignorant of birth control methods, she said.

Mrs. Meyer declared that individuals would never solve the problem of teaching birth control here until public health had incorporated contraception into the material welfare program.

She said she thought it was "escapism" to blame the Roman Catholic Church for "the taboo which surrounds the subject of birth control." She held that the Catholic Church had a right to promulgate its ideas as did other groups. If non-Catholics were "as honest and forthright in advancing their theories, the influence of the Catholic Church would be confined to its own members, and the fog of obscurity, vacillation and cowardice which surround the need for a nation-wide contraceptive program would be dissolved," she said.

Mrs. Meyer declared that married women had a right to a sex life without the burden of unwanted children. She urged that children from the fifth grade up should receive sex education in accordance with their age.

Samuel W. Anderson, chairman of the fund-raising committee of the Planned Parenthood Federation of America, declared that the United States was not free from the dangers of a large growth of population. Ability to provide for as many as 61,000,000 more people in twenty years may be the "key to a successful future for the nation," he said.

January 20, 1955

POPE SANCTIONS PAINLESS BIRTHS

Sees No Moral Bar to Use of Method Backed in Russia to Ease Mothers' Rigors

By ARNALDO CORTESI

Special to The New York Times.

ROME, Jan. 8—Pope Pius XII said today that all women were at liberty, from both an ethical and a theological standpoint, to use a method of painless childbirth developed by Russian scientists. The method is widely applied in the Soviet Union and Communist China.

Whether the Russian method is adopted or rejected, the Pope indicated, women may employ any of the legitimate methods for eliminating or reducing the pain of childbirth. He made some scattered references to the use of hypnosis, anesthetics and analgesics, or pain killers, without any specific word of condemnation.

"In sorrow shalt thou bring forth children" [Genesis, sixteenth verse of third chapter] should in no case be interpreted to mean that mothers are forbidden to make use of means to make childbirth easier and less painful, the Pope declared.

The Pope neither endorsed nor recommended use of the Soviet method for painless childbirth. He did, however, say in its favor that if pain and fear were successfully eliminated from childbirth there would be a decrease of inducement to "commit immoral acts in the use of marriage rights."

The fact that the psycho-prophylactic method was applied in Russia, which is dominated by a materialistic ideology, cannot, according to the Pope, be held against it. Nevertheless the Pope uttered a word of warning against adopting it unquestioningly because he said "when faced by the scientific discovery of painless childbirth the Christian is careful not to admire it unreservedly and not to use it with exaggerated haste."

The Pope was speaking to 700 gynecologists and other physicians who met in Rome from many countries, including the United States, for a gynecological symposium. The audience was held in the Royal Hall at the Vatican, where the Pope's throne had been erected.

Pope Speaks in French

The Pope addressed the physicians in reply to a specific query as to what the Church's opinion was of the Russian method of painless childbirth. The Pope spoke in French for forty minutes.

The Pope said that many researchers believed that the functions of the organism when normal and properly carried out should not be accompanied by pain. Pain, according to these experts, denotes the presence of some complication. It is their opinion that pain experienced at childbirth results from "contrary conditioned reflexes set in motion by erroneous ideological and emotional reflexes."

Followers of Pavlov, who was awarded the Nobel Prize for Medicine in 1904, believe that childbirth was not always painful but was made so by conditioned reflexes. They believe, the Pope said, that when muscular contractions are felt at the beginning of labor "the defense reaction against pain sets in; this pain provokes a muscular cramp which in its turn causes increased suffering. Labor pains are therefore real pains but result from falsely interpreted causes."

The psycho-prophylactic method, the Pope said, "consists in giving mothers long before the period of childbirth intensive instruction—adapted to their intellectual capacities—concerning natural processes which take place in them during pregnancy and in particular during childbirth."

At the same time, the Pope added, "a repeated appeal is made to the mothers' will and emotions not to permit feelings of fear to arise which are and have been proved to be without foundation."

Detailed technical explanations are given to prospective mothers about what they must do to insure normal labor and delivery and during labor the mothers receive constant supervision and the assistance of a personnel trained in the techniques.

The method, the Pope said, was developed by Russian researchers. A Briton, Dr. Grantly Dick Read, perfected its theory and technique. It is reported, the Pope said, that the new method has been used in hundreds of thousands of cases in the Soviet Union and Communist China. It is further reported that 85 to 90 per cent of the births that took place in this manner were "really painless." In the west there are few maternity hospitals organized exclusively according to these principles. The Pope mentioned a Communist hospital in Paris and two Catholic hospitals in Jallieu and Cambrai, France.

The Pope said the method "considered in itself contains nothing that can be criticized from the moral point of view."

Pius Says Artificial Insemination Contravenes Ethics and Nature

Pope Also Tells Gynecologists' Session 'Test Tube Baby' Experiments Must Be Rejected as Immoral and Illicit

Special to The New York Times.

ROME, May 19—Pope Pius XII again condemned artificial insemination today as a means of helping childless couples to have offspring.

Acknowledging that "the use of artificial fecundation is spreading more and more" the Pontiff declared these practices violated natural law and were "contrary to right and morals." He was reiterating a view first voiced in 1949.

Of experiments to create "test tube babies" in a literal sense of this expression, the Pontiff said "they must be rejected as immoral and absolutely illicit." He did not elaborate on the nature of such experiments.

The Pontiff was addressing 150 gynecologists and others taking part in the second world congress on fertility and sterility in Naples. The first congress took place in New York in May, 1953.

Pointing to the church doctrine that the production of progeny is the principal purpose of matrimony, Pope Pius said "sterility in marriage may become a serious danger to the union and stability of the family."

However, he continued, the Church rejects any attempt at separating "the biological activity [of procreation] from the personal relations" of the couple. Conjugal union, according to the Pope, is complete and lawful only when consisting of "organic functions, the emotions linked with them and the spiritual and disinterested love that animates it."

"It is never permitted to separate these divers aspects to such degree as to exclude positively either the intention to procreate or the conjugal act," the Pope stated.

Quoting from his 1949 pronouncement on artificial insemination, the Pope said the church did not necessarily disapprove of "the use of certain artificial means uniquely aimed at either facilitating the natural act or helping the normally performed natural act to attain its purpose."

Artificial insemination, the Pope said, goes beyond the limits of the rights that spouses have obtained through the matrimonial contract, namely, to exercise their natural sexual capacity fully by naturally performing the matrimonial act."

At this point the Pope switched from French to Latin because he said this language was more appropriate for discussing some delicate and highly technical questions arising from the theme he was treating.

He explained that the church considered any method of obtaining semen from men outside the natural conjugal act as sinful. This condemnation, the Pope said, applied whether the purpose was artificial fecundation or the use of semen for clinical examinations and scientific research.

Vatican experts said tonight the Pope had restated his condemnation in unequivocal terms because he realized that the practice of artificial insemination was gaining ground.

These experts could not recall any previous statement by this Pope or by any of his predecessors considering the possibility of laboratory "test tube" creation of new life. After sternly rejecting such experiments in one sweeping sentence Pius devoted the main part of his pronouncement to 'what he termed "artificial fecundation in the ordinary sense of this word or 'artificial insemination.' "

Widely Practiced Here

Artificial insemination is "widely practiced" in the United States, according to Dr. Alan F. Guttmacher, chief of obstetrics and gynecology at Mt. Sinai Hospital here. He said it was impossible, however, to estimate the total number of cases.

The physician noted that last June the American Society for the Study of Sterility, after making a poll of its members, voted at Atlantic City to approve artificial insemination as a "completely ethical, moral and desirable form of medical therapy."

The resolution was adopted by a vote of 79 to 8. The organization represents 500 medical doctors specializing in the problems of sterility.

In 1954 a Chicago judge ruled that a child born of artificial insemination was illegitimate when the donor was not the woman's husband. The New York State Supreme Court ruled in 1947 that such a child was not illegitimate because the husband, while not contributing to conception, assumed the role of foster or adoptive father.

PILL HELD SUCCESS

SAN FRANCISCO, Sept. 18 (AP)—A gynecologist said yesterday that a 50-cent pill to prevent pregnancy had proved 100 per cent effective in a two-and-one-half-year test.

Dr. John Rock, Clinical Professor Emeritus of Gynecology at the Harvard Medical School, told a news conference called by the Planned Parenthood Association of San Francisco Inc. that results had been decisive in experiments with 285 women in Puerto Rico and also in Los Angeles. He said there had been no lasting side-effects.

The pills, which cost 50 cents each, are taken on a one-a-day basis. They are available on physician's prescription. Dr. Rock said the drug had no effect on ova already fertilized.

Dr. Rock's views differed markedly from those of two physicians who tested the pills and reported results at the American Medical Association convention here last June.

Dr. Edward T. Tyler and Dr. Henry J. Olson of the Medical School of the University of California at Los Angeles told the A. M. A. that in tests covering 3,082 woman-months there had been twenty-two pregnancies. This was a 9.3 per cent rate, about the same rate as for standard contraceptive methods.

The drug is a synthetic compound, chemically related to sex hormones, that halts production of eggs in the female ovary, Dr. Rock said. Egg production resumes when the pill-taking stops, he declared.

Dr. Rock and his associates in the Puerto Rico tests told of earlier results last Oct. 8 at a conference here sponsored by the New York Academy of Sciences.

As of Aug. 31, 1957, they reported, there were no pregnancies among women who took the tablets as suggested between the fifth and twenty-fifth days of their menstrual cycle. The women were also asked to note when they forgot to take the tablets. In cases in which one to five of the daily tablets were missed, two pregnancies occurred, and where six or more tablets were missed, three pregnancies occurred, the researchers reported at the time.

Dr. Alan F. Guttmacher, director of obstetrics and gynecology at Mount Sinai Hospital and chairman of the medical committee of the Planned Parenthood Federation of America, said yesterday that "much more extended research is needed" in the field before any conclusion could be reached.

The inconsistency between Dr. Rock's findings and those of the Tyler-Olson study, he suggested, might be explained in part by differences in population, with perhaps better facilities for more accurate follow-up in the California study than in Puerto Rico.

January 9, 1956

May 20, 1956

September 19, 1958

Birth Control Ban Ended By City's Hospital Board

By EDITH EVANS ASBURY

The ban on birth control therapy in city hospitals was lifted yesterday by an 8-to-2 vote of the Board of Hospitals. The decision was announced by Commissioner Morris A.

Jacobs, who had set forth the ban in July. The prohibition has always been unwritten.

Dr. Jacobs said he would implement the board's ruling "as soon as possible, certainly within a week."

He is chairman of the board and a member, but did not vote.

The board's resolution directs municipal hospitals to provide "medical advice, preventive measures and devices for female patients under their care whose life and health in the opinion of the medical staff may be jeopardized by pregnancy and who wish to avail themselves of such health services."

Without naming Roman Catholics, whose church opposes all artificial birth control as immoral, the board's resolution stated:

"Physicians, nurses and other hospital personnel who have religious or moral objections should be excused from participation in contraceptive procedures."

The board's resolution said: "When there are clearly defined medical conditions in which the life or health of a woman may be jeopardized by pregnancy, it is generally recognized by the medical profession that contraceptive measures are proper medical practice."

This has been the contention of the numerous religious, medical and civic groups who loosed a storm of protest on Dr. Jacobs and the board in the last two months. Many of the groups hailed the board's action last night.

On the other hand, the Roman Catholic Archdiocese of New York, in a joint statement with the Diocese of Brooklyn, declared that the board's decision "introduces an immoral practice in our hospitals that perverts the nature and the dignity of man."

Catholics Warned

The statement said, "Such a practice and policy can in no way be sanctioned by the church. All Catholic personnel of our hospitals are reminded of their grave obligation in conscience to, in no way, cooperate with such a procedure."

The Protestant Council of New York, which had demanded that Dr. Jacobs' policy be reversed, will meet at noon today "to consider the implications" of the section of the board's resolution excusing Roman Catholic personnel from participation in contraceptive procedures.

Dr. Jacobs said that the board's decision had been reached after an hour of discussion at its closed meeting in his office at 125 Worth Street.

All members of the board, which consists of five physicians and five laymen, plus Dr. Jacobs, attended. Nine members left the meeting without commenting to the press. Judge Louis Goldstein distributed statements defending Commissioner Jacobs' policy.

Dr. Jacobs, at a press conference following the meeting, said he considered the board's resolution merely "a clarification and elaboration" of his letter to the Academy of Medicine.

That letter, a reply to an inquiry from the academy, phrased the board's policy as follows:

"There shall be no interference in proper and accepted therapeutic practices nor intervention in ethical relationships between patient and physician."

It did not specifically mention contraception.

Following publication of the letter, which was dated April 11, Dr. Jacobs refused to clarify it.

The controversy was precipitated July 16 when Dr. Louis Hellman informed the Commissioner that he intended to fit a patient for a contraceptive device at Kings County Hospital. Dr. Jacobs forbade him to proceed.

The patient was a Protestant. The Protestant Council of New York and various Protestant denominations and Jewish organizations protested.

Dr. Jacobs said yesterday that he had not voted on the resolution, and he refused to identify those who voted against it.

There are two Roman Catholic members, John J. Lynch, prominent in Brooklyn religious and civic affairs, and Dr.

Charles A. Gordon, also of Brooklyn.

Asked his opinion of the decision, Dr. Jacobs said:

"I feel that the Board of Hospitals is composed of outstanding physicians and eminent lay members and therefore I have decided to be guided by their opinion."

He denied that the board's action was a reversal of his ruling. He described it as "a recommendation to me which I am following."

He added, "There has been considerable airing of the subject since July and considerable events which resulted in this present recommendation."

Notes His Concern

Dr. Jacobs said that his main concern about the introduction of a contraceptive program in the hospitals was that administrative disruption would result because of objections of Roman Catholic personnel and patients.

He said that he believed the board's resolution contained "necessary safeguards" to prevent administrative difficulties on that score.

He also explained that the decision that contraception was medically indicated would be made by a group of physicians, not just one, who might be a Roman Catholic.

"A patient in a city hospital is assigned to a service, not to a doctor," he said. "Several physicians and conferences are involved in decisions."

The American Jewish Congress, one of several Jewish groups that had protested Dr. Jacobs' ban, praised the new policy last night as "a solution based on medical considerations, leaving the question of religious principle to the individuals directly involved."

The Planned Parenthood Federation of America also praised the board's action as a "great victory" for the people of New York "which has nationwide significance and consequences."

Lay members of the board, in addition to Mr. Lynch and Judge Goldstein, are: Mrs. Mary Lasker, head of the Albert and Mary Lasker Foundation and honorary vice president of Planned Parenthood Federation; David M. Heyman, financier and philanthropist, and Mrs. Anna M. Rosenberg, former Assistant Secretary of Defense.

Physician members, in addition to Dr. Gordon, are Dr. Willard C. Rappleye, Dr. Howard A. Rusk, Dr. Peter Marshall Murray and Dr. George Baehr.

Dr. Jacobs' two deputies, Dr. Henry I. Fineberg and Robert J. Mangum, and the department counsel, Herbert Lefkowitz, met with the board.

Kennedy Is Praised For 1963 Warning Of Population Peril

By JACK LANGGUTH
Special to The New York Times

DALLAS, April 30—President Kennedy, a Roman Catholic, did more than any of his predecessors for the cause of population control, the national president of Planned Parenthood—World Population said today.

Dr. Alan F. Guttmacher of New York told 380 delegates to a four-day conference of his organization that Mr. Kennedy's warning at a 1963 press conference about the severity of population growth was the first issued by an American President.

The conference, which began yesterday, will mark the first occasion that a Roman Catholic priest has joined in a national planned parenthood program.

The Rev. John L. Thomas, S.J., of St. Louis University, will speak tomorrow on "How Can All Churches Work Together for Family Planning?"

Dr. Guttmacher said Roman Catholic clergymen had in the past declined invitations to attend national conferences. "This is a step of great significance," he said.

A new kind of contraceptive, considered by many experts preferable to birth control pills, has also been a major topic among the delegates.

The intra-uterine devices, now being tested in four patterns, have not yet been approved by the Food and Drug Administration.

Dr. Guttmacher said the devices, made of plastic or stainless steel, would be "damned cheap, probably only a few pennies," and would last for several years.

They must be fitted and removed by a doctor, however, and that would add to their cost.

The Pill: Revolution in Birth Control

By JANE E. BRODY

Six years ago this month a drug appeared on the American scene that was destined to exert a profound effect on the emotional and social life of the nation.

It was The Pill—the first contraceptive both 100 per cent effective and completely independent of the sex act.

The pill was hailed as a scientific dream-come-true, the emancipator of women, the answer to birth control.

While it was none of these entirely, it was all of them in part. Many women were cautious at first, but soon thousands were asking their physicians to prescribe it. As one of them, a mother of three, explained:

"With the pill, we don't have to worry any more."

Today almost six million American women—nearly one-fifth of those of childbearing age—are believed to be using oral contraceptives. And the number grows steadily.

The pill would seem to be here to stay.

For most of its users, it has revolutionized family planning and relieved a traditional source of family tension: the fear of having unwanted children.

With the pill, newlyweds are confident that their first child will not catch them emotionally and financially unprepared. Middle-aged couples are protected against late-in-life accidents. Others have children precisely when they want them.

The pill also is having an impact on birth control among those women who, because of ignorance or poverty, cannot successfully use older contraceptive techniques. There are definite indications that women in poverty-stricken areas can and will use the pill faithfully.

Many sociologists believe that, because the pill can be talked about on a general, impersonal basis, it has helped remove the fetters from discussion of sex and that this freedom will lead to healthier and better informed attitudes toward all aspects of sex.

But it is precisely this free talk that has caused some to fear that Americans are losing too many personal inhibitions and are headed for a general decline of moral standards. Such fears are difficult to substantiate. The limited research done on attitudes and actions of single women indicates that most using the pill have previously used some less effective contraceptive techniques. Others who sarted with the pills were waiting for the right man rather than the right devices.

There is also some concern about the medical implications of the contraceptive pill. For the first time millions of young, healthy women are taking a powerful drug regularly for long periods primarily for a nonmedical reason. Some doctors fear prolonged use could have serious consequences because oral contraceptives disrupt normal hormone balance.

To better define the risks of prolonged pill use, the Food and Drug Administration's advisory committee on oral contraceptives is expected to recommend in a report next month a study of 30,000 women over a ten-year period.

Basically, the pills now in general use contain man-made versions of two natural female hormones, progesterone and estrogen. These work to prevent ovulation—the release of an egg from the ovaries — normally occurring once a month, about midway between menstrual periods.

Oral contraceptives are available only by prescription, usually limited to a six-month supply. This is to assure that the woman will return to her doctor every half year for the recommended checkup to detect any possible complications.

The cost of a month's supply ranges from nothing for indigent patients at Planned Parenthood clinics to about $2.50 for private patients.

The woman is instructed to take one pill at about the same time each day for 20 days. Then the pills are stopped, and within three to five days the woman begins to menstruate. On the fifth day of menstruation, the next 20-day pill cycle is begun.

8 Brands on Market

There are eight brands of oral contraceptives now on the American market. They vary in the combination and amounts of active ingredients.

Six brands combine synthetic progesterone and estrogen in each pill. In the two other brands, called "sequentials," the first 15 pills taken in the 20-pill cycle contain only estrogen. The last five are a combination of progesterone and estrogen.

Manufacturers of the sequentials maintain that this sequence is more representative of the woman's natural hormone balance. But it has not been proved that the sequentials affect women any differently than the combination pills.

Although both the combination and the sequential pills offer complete protection against pregnancy when taken as prescribed, reports from a World Health Organization committee and others say the sequentials are more likely to fail if one pill is missed.

Remembering to take the pills is sometimes the woman's greatest problem.

One user remarked: "I often find myself taking two or three pills a day because I forget I've already taken one."

To help women remember, manufacturers have produced such ingenious devices as a pill calendar with punch-out pills. With one calendar, the woman dials a wheel to select a pill for the day of the week. In another device, a pill card refill fits into a slim compact; markers on the card correspond to the day she began menstruating and the day she is to start the pills.

Despite the problem of remembering, personal histories attest to the fact that oral contraceptives offer the desired protection for millions.

For Mrs. Helen B., the pill has restored the sexual happiness and spontaniety she and her husband knew during their first years of marriage.

"We have three children," she said, "and we can't afford any more. I have a job now to help put the children through college, and another pregnancy would ruin our plans. A diaphragm didn't work for us, as the birth of our third child showed.

"After that, I felt we had to limit sexual relations to times of the month when I'm almost certain I won't get pregnant. That's not too often, you know.

"But now with the pills, we don't have to worry any more. It's just great—like a second honeymoon."

For Susan and Marty W., who married while both were students, the pills meant three worry-free years. Now, with degrees in hand and savings in the bank, they are awaiting the birth of their first child.

Disturbing Questions

Jean L., a college-educated career girl, used the pills for several years before she married.

"The possibility of pregnancy was the only reason I could see for not sleeping with a man I loved and was thinking of marrying," she said. "With the pills, this possibility was removed."

Attitudes like Miss L.'s raise disturbing questions in the minds of many:

Will the ready availability of a completely effective contraceptive create a moral as well as a birth-control revolution? Will more youngsters, free from the fear of pregnancy, engage in premarital sexual relations? Will more adults, married or single, become promiscuous?

"There is no virtue in morality if we are pure only because we fear being caught," according to Dr. Roger Shinn, dean of instruction at Union Theological Seminary.

Others, who also note that a morality based on fear is no morality at all, believe the existence of the pill will force many persons to search for a higher standard of sexual morality.

'A Lot of Nonsense'

To charges that the pill is contributing to a decline in moral standards, Lewis Frank, executive director of the Information Center on Population Problems, says:

"A lot of nonsense. Promiscuity and the fruits of promiscuity have always been with us. There are 125,000 to 300,000 illegitimate children born each year. Many youngsters, using Saran wrap and Seven-Up douches, are practicing contraception on the level of the ancients. We get the results of that in foundling homes and shotgun marriages."

However, Dr. Shinn believes the pill will make a difference for a few teen-agers, who really want to have premarital sexual relations but have been deterred by fear of pregnancy.

A situation described by a Long Island mother emphasizes that many parents now have to find a more meaningful admonition than "Don't get involved or you'll get into trouble."

"My pills," the mother told a neighbor, "seem to be disappearing twice as fast as they used to. I wonder if Joanie [her teen-age daughter] is snitching a few. I hope she's at least taking them according to schedule."

Although the pills are legally available only through a prescription, there is no way to stop a single woman from taking pills prescribed for a married friend. Also, many doctors will prescribe them for any woman who requests them, married or not.

Some doctors balk when faced with an unwed teen-ager not accompanied by a parent. But others are inclined to give her the pills because they fear she will turn to a less effective form of contraception, if any at all, and risk an illegitimate pregnancy.

Education Affects Use

It is anyone's guess exactly how many single women use the pill. But it is thought the percentage rises with age and education.

A similar relationship of education and pill use exists among married women. But here, the younger the wife the more likely she is to use the pill, a recent nationwide survey of 5,600 women showed.

The survey, by Dr. Charles F. Westoff of Princeton University and Dr. Norman E. Ryder of the University of Wisconsin, indicated that 56 per cent of married women under 20 were using or had used the pill. Among non-Catholic college graduates under 25, 81 per cent of those married were pill users.

The Roman Catholic Church officially views the pill as another of the artificial contraceptive techniques forbidden because they interfere with nature's way. However, a growing number of Catholic priests are advising parishioners to follow their own consciences regarding pill use.

Dr. Ryder and Dr. Westoff found that 21 per cent of Catholic wives under 45 were pill users. This compares with 29 per cent of non-Catholic wives.

Effect on Birth Rate

In matching use of the pill with family size, they concluded that Catholics were more likely to use oral contraceptives to terminate childbearing, whereas non-Catholics used them to space their families.

Dr. Ryder, Dr. Westoff and other population experts do not believe the pill has had much effect on the nation's birth rate.

The rate climbed steadily in the early 1950's to a peak of 25 for each 1,000 of population in 1957. Since then it has declined to the current 19.1 for each 1,000.

Dr. Westoff and Dr. Ryder have noted that the decline began in 1958, before arrival of the pill, and that the decrease in childbearing had not been concentrated only among the young, where the pill is most widely used. They also observed that "other highly effective means of contraception have been available for years and their existence did not prevent fertility rates from soaring during the fifties."

Robert C. Cook, president of the Population Reference Bureau, Inc., pointed out that in 1933, "long before fancy contraceptive techniques, the birth rate went down to 18 per 1,000 —an all-time low."

Mr. Cook believes the rising cost of living is a major influence in decline of the birth rate.

"Youngsters now starting families have taken a hard look at the difficulties and cost of having more children," he said.

But he noted that "unwanted births are continuing."

"About one-fifth of United States families are having more than four children," he says.

Preventing unwanted births may not greatly affect the birth rate, but it should have a significant impact in the na-tion's "poverty pockets," the experts believe.

"Birth control is no solution to poverty, but without it no solution to poverty will be effective," Dr. Steven Polgar, research director of Planned Parenthood, said.

Federal antipoverty forces are starting birth-control programs throughout the country in which the contraceptive pill is expected to play a major role.

Studies show that when indigent women are told birth control materials are available at little or no cost, most ask for the pill. At Planned Parenthood centers in Chicago, the patient load increased 47 per cent last year, with a large majority asking for the pill.

Throughout the country last year, 150,000 of the 320,000 Planned Parenthood clients were using the pill.

Impact in Poverty Areas

Whereas clinic patients often give up diaphragms and other devices after brief trials, a recent study at the Chicago centers showed that 70 to 83 per cent of pill users were taking them after two and one-half years.

The pill has already had an impact in some areas where soaring birth rates made escape from poverty virtually impossible.

In Wolfe County, Kentucky, where $8 of every $9 of income is Federal money, the birth rate dropped from 50 per cent above the national average to about the national average just three years because of oral contraceptives. Dr. Paul Maddox, the county's only doctor, had turned to the pill after all else had failed.

Corpus Christi, Tex., the first city to receive Federal antipoverty funds to take birth control to the poor, measured the contribution of the pill partly in terms of a falling abortion rate.

In 1960 alone 1,000 abortions were performed there. A physician at Memorial Hospital, where much of the city's postabortion "repair work" is done, recently said: "We were getting three or four such cases every day, but I doubt we saw a half-dozen all last month."

Intrauterine Devices

These and similar successes notwithstanding, few family planning experts expect the contraceptive pill to bear the full burden of controlling world population. Intrauterine devices, or I. U. D.'s, are expected to play a significant part—especially in underdeveloped lands, where the pills might be too costly and the pill regimen too complicated for uneducated women.

An I. U. D. is a small piece of plastic, nylon or metal that may come in any of a number of shapes—like a loop, coil, ring or bow. A physician must insert it in the uterus.

Totally effective population control through I.U.D.'s is limited by the fact that the devices fail from 2 to 11 per cent of the time, depending on the type of device; and they are sometimes expelled from the uterus without the woman's knowing it.

In this country, the failure rate of I.U.D.'s could make birth control among the poor more costly than it would be with the pills, according to the Information Center on Population Problems, which is supported by G. D. Searle & Co., Chicago drug concern. It notes that although an I.U.D. costs less than the pills (at clinics, about $25 for the method's failure rate would mean at least 20 unwanted births among every 1,000 users.

"To have prevented [these births] we would have had to spend $13,000 on pills for all 1,000 women" for the year, it says in a memorandum. But the 20 babies, born to women on welfare, would cost taxpayers from $140,000 to $200,000 to clothe, feed and educate, it adds.

It was on May 20, 1960, that the first oral contraceptive—Enovid, made by G. D. Searle—was approved for marketing in the United States. This month, Searle introduced the newest contraceptive pill in this country, Ovulen.

The six other oral contraceptives sold in the United States and their manufacturers are as follows: Ortho-Novum, the Ortho Pharmaceutical Corporation; Norinyl, Syntex Laboratories, Inc.; Norlestrin, Parke, Davis & Co.; Provest, the Upjohn Co.; Oracon, Mead Johnson & Co., and C-Quens, Eli Lilly & Co.

A $90-Million Market

The pill has already had a substantial financial impact on the seven manufacturers. These companies are looking for a $90-million pill market this year, up from $67-million last year and only $16-million in 1962.

The companies foresee continued growth in this market, especially if cheaper pills with fewer side effects are developed.

Minor side effects now attributable to the pill include symptoms of early pregnancy: nausea, small weight gain, breast soreness. In addition, there are infrequent incidents of minor bleeding between menstrual periods. In nearly all patients, these side effects disappear after the first few pill cycles.

Various manufacturers claim the "lowest" incidence of side effects for their pill. But experience indicates that the pills with the smallest amount of hormone have the smallest incidence and that different brands may have different side effects in the same woman.

More troublesome than minor side effects are occasional reports—which frighten pill users and scare off potential ones—that oral contraceptives may have hidden and possibly life-threatening dangers. There have been reports of blood clots, cancer, eye damage and sterility occurring in women or animals taking oral contraceptives.

Several expert committees studied all available statistics and could find no cause-effect relationship between these ailments and pill use. And no increase in such ill effects has occurred among the thousands of women who have been tested for more than 10 years.

But as an added precaution, the Food and Drug Administration recommends that women with a history of breast or genital cancer, blood clots, stroke or liver disease should not take the pills, and that great care should be exercised in giving oral contraceptives to women with certain other serious ailments.

An international committee of experts, meeting last winter under auspices of the World Health Organization, reviewed all available information about oral contraceptives and concluded they were safe. However, the committee listed several "areas of uncertainty" that warranted further research.

According to the chairman of the F.D.A.'s advisory committee on the pill, Dr. Louis Hellman of Downstate Medical Center, the greatest difficulty in removing these uncertainties will be in determining how often rare diseases, such as blood clots, occur in women not taking the pill.

Such "controlled" studies—in which the incidence of illness in people taking a drug is compared with that in people not taking it—have been lacking in reports to date that associate hazards with pill use.

Cancer Studies Due

The cancer question is expected to receive a great deal of attention in future controlled studies. Cancer, especially of the reproductive tract, may develop over as long as 20 or 30 years, and the pill has been tested for little more than 10 years.

Thus far, doctors have found no increase in the incidence of cancer in women using pills. In fact, some have found a decrease.

Dr. Gregory Pincus, a pioneer in the pill's development, concluded from his studies of Puerto Rican and Haitian women using it for at least 10 years: "There is clear evidence that potential precancerous conditions in the uterine [lining], the cervix and the breasts are markedly reduced in incidence in oral contraceptive users."

Dr. Pincus is director of the Worcester Foundation for Experimental Biology, at Shrewsbury, Mass.

Despite such reassurances, several leading physicians and medical organizations have urged discriminating use of the pill and careful weighing of known benefits against possible risks.

The Medical Letter, an independent, nonprofit newsletter

prepared by physicians and published by Drug and Therapeutic Information, Inc., advised in a recent issue that "women who can satisfactorily and successfully use [other] contraceptive measures should not use oral contraceptives."

The Food and Drug Administration and manufacturers are being extremely cautious in testing and marketing new oral contraceptives.

Last March Mead Johnson & Co. stopped tests on humans of a pill similar to one on the British market. Tests by the British manufacturer showed that blood clots developed in three of ten dogs given continuous massive doses.

No similar effects have been noted in the hundreds of thousands of women using the British drug, and the company is not considering taking its pill off the market. But to the F.D.A. and Mead Johnson, this "inconclusive" evidence of danger was cause enough to discontinue tests.

Injectable Drugs

The development of new anti-ovulatory contraceptives, such as the Mead Johnson drug, is likely to continue for a number

But far more exciting to scientists and sociologists alike are studies of new drugs that introduce entirely new principles of contraception.

Several companies are studying low-dosage, single-hormone compounds that apparently do not upset the hormone system. They seem to prevent pregnancy by creating a "hostile climate" to sperm in the cervix.

Perhaps even more promising, particularly for under-developed countries, are studies of injectable contraceptives that protect against pregnancy for up to three months.

Dr. Edwin R. Zartman, medical director of Planned Parenthood in Columbus, Ohio, reported last month that one such compound has proved 100 per cent effective during a one-year test among 274 women.

But the experimental drug that has stimulated the most curiosity and controversy is a pill that works retroactively. It can be taken up to six days after sexual intercourse.

Dr. John McLean Morris and Dr. Gertrude Van Wagenen of Yale University, who reported recently on successful tests of such a pill in monkeys, said it apparently prevented preg-

nancy by preventing the fertilized egg from attaching itself to the uterus.

Dr. Morris, Dr. Pincus and several drug concerns are working on estrogen compounds effective "after the fact" in animals. Such a drug would be taken only after a woman had intercourse when she was likely to be fertile, perhaps only once a month.

Although a once-a-month pill might reduce the fear of medical hazards now associated with oral contraceptives, a retroactive contraceptive would likely create social and religious dilemmas far exceeding those associated with the current pill.

Abortion View

To Roman Catholics, who maintain that life begins with the fertilized egg, such a pill would be considered an abortive agent.

Controversy could result from the fact that any woman who had sexual relations without taking precautions, and who feared a consequent pregnancy, could take a pill and perhaps perform—as some would view it—a preventive abortion.

On the other hand, for the girl or woman who is raped and faces a possible pregnancy, a retroactive pill could save her psychological and physical trauma. And among uneducated women, who are more likely to think of preventing pregnancy after the possibility exists, such a pill could be the answer to population control.

It may be years before a retroactive contraceptive reaches the American market. When it does, it will doubtless be a strong competitor for the currently used pill.

So might other oral contraceptives whose hypothetical mechanisms now sound like science fiction. Perhaps one day, for instance, a woman will be able to take one pill at puberty that will prevent pregnancy until she takes a counteracting pill.

Meanwhile, increased use of the present pill seems assured, unless long-term studies uncover hazards associated with prolonged use. Most manufacturers are confident that the risks are minimal.

They agree with the prediction of Dr. Westoff and Dr. Ryder that "in the near future the pill may well become the method used by most American women."

UNWED TO RECEIVE BIRTH CONTROL AID

Services Will Be Available to All American Women Who Need and Request Them

By NAN ROBERTSON
Special to The New York Times

WASHINGTON, April 1—Birth control instruction and contraceptives will now be supplied to all American women who need and request them under a significant new policy laid down by John W. Gardner, Secretary of Health, Education and Welfare.

That policy, which goes farther than any previously enunciated by a Government agency, came to light last night in a speech by Mrs. Katherine Oettinger, head of the Children's Bureau.

Mrs. Oettinger told a Planned Parenthood audience in Boston that the Department of Health, Education and Welfare, of which the bureau is a part, was carrying out the "clear mandate" of President Johnson to support birth control programs.

In the family planning section of his Health Message to Congress March 1, the President said:

"It is essential that all families have access to information and services that will allow freedom to choose the number and spacing of their children within the dictates of individual conscience."

"Let me emphasize," Mrs. Oettinger said last night, "that if the true meaning of President Johnson's insistence on freedom of choice is to be carried out, it will not be the role of the Federal Government to dictate which women shall or shall not have family planning services if they desire them."

This would mean that such services would be available to unwed mothers as well as married women living with their husbands. It lifts what one department spokesman called "judgmental restrictions" on

giving birth control advice, pills or contraceptive devices to applicants for public health services.

Mrs. Oettinger's speech was based on a hitherto totally unpublicized policy directive that Secretary Gardner sent Jan. 24 to his agencies across the country. The language in the crucial sections of the directive was virtually duplicated by President Johnson in his subsequent message.

It was reinforced by another unpublicized memorandum dispatched March 4 by Mrs. Oettinger and Fred H. Steininger, director of the Bureau of Family Services.

The guidelines stipulated that "the department will make known to state and local agencies that funds are available" for such programs, "but it will bring no pressure upon them to participate."

Family planning projects conducted or supported by the department's agencies "shall guarantee freedom from coercion or pressure of mind or conscience," the directives stated.

"If you have not already adopted policy in this area, we ask that you consider the steps appropriate for your state in line with the position stated above," the department said.

The Government has greatly accelerated its movement toward liberalizing birth control projects since the White House Conference on Health last November. That conference called on the President to make instruction and devices available to all Americans, particularly the poor.

In her speech last night, Mrs. Oettinger said that surveys among the poor had shown that "eagerness for family planning information was coupled with a simple frightening ignorance about causes of pregnancy" and effective means of contraception.

The Children's Bureau is the most important single source of Federal funds for family planning. This year it is spending $3-million in 32 states for such projects. Next year it expects to spend $5-million.

The other important source is the Office of Economic Opportunity, which has spent $1.25-million on family planning in the last 15 months. However, that agency prohibits giving birth control devices to needy unwed mothers.

It will allow physicians to give information to all who seek it. This information clause is sometimes interpreted to include giving prescriptions for devices, which the women then purchase with their own money.

May 31, 1966

April 2, 1966

Major Progress in Sex Therapy Is Reported by Research Team

By NATALIE JAFFE
Special to The New York Times

ATLANTIC CITY, May 7— The directors of the controversial St. Louis sex research project reported major gains in the treatment of sexual inadequacy to a major convention of psychoanalysts here this weekend.

Dr. William H. Masters and Mrs. Virginia E. Johnson—authors of the recently published book "Human Sexual Response" —said more than 80 per cent of the 263 carefully selected couples who had gone through a three-to-six-week training program at the Reproductive Biology Research Foundation had reached a satisfactory sexual adjustment.

Dr. Masters's statistical review was met by an audible gasp of astonishment from an audience of about 400 doctors attending a closed session at the 10th annual meeting of the American Academy of Psychoanalysis last night at the Traymore Hotel, it was reported later.

In a continuing discussion of the project today, most of the analysts call the rate of success far greater than any reported before. But they and Dr. Masters agreed that the results should be viewed with three major qualifications in mind:

First, the couples involved were highly motivated to improve the conjugal relationship and were persons who were willing to expose their sexual lives to close scrutiny.

Data for Future

Second, the concentrated, technical approach to sexual problems may create its own artificial excitement. And third, sexual maladjustment must be viewed as just one symptom of more general difficulties.

Dr. Masters said repeatedly that his main interest was to provide data on which therapists could build.

The material presented here, which he described in an interview, will be published in 1968 in a book entitled "Human Sexual Inadequacy." By July, 1967, the foundation hopes to set up a post-graduate training program, to instruct professional therapists in the procedures developed in St. Louis.

Dr. Masters said that of the more than 1,000 letters he had received since word of the 10-year-old project was disclosed last spring, 70 per cent were pleas for advice. The remainder, he said, were divided between "hate letters," conscientious objections to the scientific study of sexual behavior and notes of congratulation.

Although the psychoanalysts expressed many reservations about the unrepresentative population under study and about a technical approach to sexual problems, there was general agreement that scientific discussion of sex is long overdue.

Dr. Harold Kelman, dean of the American Institute for Psychoanalysis in New York, reflected the general view when he said today that removing the discussion of sexual behavior from a "overcharged psychological atmosphere to a medical one can undercut some of our deeply imbedded puritanical attitudes and vicious moral inhibitions."

However, in an address to a conference session on feminine psychology, Dr. Kelman suggested that a true perception of natural sexual behavior could only be obtained from female therapists working for long periods with women who become able to discuss their own and their children's experience freely and openly.

May 8, 1966

Study Finds Birth Control Used By Most Catholic Wives 18-39

By DONALD JANSON
Special to The New York Times

SOUTH BEND, Ind., Dec. 2 —A nationwide study based on interviews with 5,600 married women of all faiths indicated that a majority of Roman Catholic wives between the ages of 18 and 39 no longer conform to church doctrine on birth control.

About 25 per cent of the women in the samples were Catholic, approximately the proportion of Catholics in the population

The survey was conducted by National Analysts, Ind., of Philadelphia. Comparable surveys for noting trends were conducted by the University of Michigan's Social Research Center in 1955 and 1960.

The results of the survey were presented tonight to the fifth annual Notre Dame Conference on Population by Prof. Charles W. Westoff of Princeton University and Prof. Norman B. Ryder of the University of Wisconsin.

The two sociologists reported that the proportion of Catholic wives complying with the church's ban on contraceptives had declined from 70 per cent in 1955 to 62 per cent in 1960 and 47 per cent last year. The 1965 study, directed by Dr. Westoff and Dr. Ryder, was sponsored by the National Institute of Child Health and Human Development.

Dr. Westoff, chairman of Princeton's department of sociology, told a dinner meeting of the conference that the proportion of married couples using contraceptives was up substantially since 1960 among Catholics and non-Catholics alike.

He said that the appearance of the birth control pill in 1960 had contributed significantly to this rise, with proportionately greater use by non-Catholics than Catholics. He said the study showed that the pill had replaced the rhythm method for avoiding conception for many Catholics and had also attracted couples of all three major faiths who had previously used other contraceptives.

Dr. Ryder, director of the University of Wisconsin's Population Research Center, said that the increased use of contraception had been accompanied by a parallel decline in fertility, with the American birth rate falling 22 per cent since 1957.

Orren Jack Turner

Prof. Charles W. Westoff of Princeton, who presented results of the survey.

The decline has accelerated in the last two years, he said, "and the simultaneous acceleration in the adoption of oral contraception is unlikely to be merely a coincidence."

But, he said, the decline in the birth rate also reflected a reversal in the nineteen-sixties of a post-World War II trend toward bearing children at earlier ages. In recent years, he said, women are getting married a little later, waiting longer to begin having children, and adding to their families at longer intervals.

Dr. Westoff said that defiance of church doctrine by Catholic wives included a large proportion of women who report regular church attendance.

For those who go to mass every week, he said, conformity with doctrine has plummeted from 78 per cent in 1955 to 69 per cent in 1960 to 56 per cent last year, a pattern matching the rate of decline for Catholic women as a whole.

The most recent statement by Pope Paul VI on birth control was on Oct. 29. He said that he needed more time to decide on the question and, in the meantime, Catholics must abide by church rules against artificial contraception.

The sociologists said that the deliberations of church officials may partly account for the decline in conformity since 1960 because it has created expectations of a more lenient stand.

But they noted that the trend to nonconformity had begun long before the deliberations began.

The three-day conference is being held on the Notre Dame campus under the auspices of the university's new Institute for the Study of Population and Social Change.

Prof. William T. Liu, director of the Institute, said in an interview that the first two of the five conferences held here were closed, unpublicized meetings. The meeting this weekend is being attended by 50 specialists in sociology, theology, law, medicine, biology and other disciplines, many of them from the Notre Dame faculty. The meetings are also open to interested students and others.

A spokesman for the university said that research in sociological subjects and the humanities had markedly increased at Notre Dame since George N. Shuster, former president of Hunter College in New York, came to Notre Dame in 1960.

Dr. Shuster is assistant to the president at Notre Dame and director of the university's Center for the Study of Man in Contemporary Society, of which the Institute for the Study of Population and Social Change is a part.

Dr. Westoff reported tonight that the birth control pill seemed to have been adopted "primarily" by couples who would otherwise have used other methods of preventing conception.

'Increasing Rate'

He said the use of the pill had "increased at an increasing rate" since 1960 till "by the time of our interviews in late 1965, 33 per cent of white women and 29 per cent of nonwhite women reported having never used the pill."

Among those who practiced birth control, 36 per cent of the Protestants and 25 per cent of Catholics and Jews favor the pill. Its use increases as the level of education rises, the survey shows.

Dr. Westoff said that the proportion of Catholic women who sought to regulate fertility exclusively by the use of rhythm had decreased from 27 per cent in 1955 to 25 per cent last year.

A Statistic Named Mary

By GERTRUDE SAMUELS

Harlem Youth Unlimited— Training & Rehabilitation Center For Young & Unwed Mothers

THE sign on the door, which was illustrated with a mother-and-baby drawing, listed a number of study projects offered to the new registrants at the Drew Hamilton Community Center in Central Harlem: homemaking, counseling, prenatal care, postnatal care, heritage-appreciation. I entered a large room, where Mary and a dozen other girls were waiting for me.

A tall, attractive teen-ager with smooth, shining black hair, Mary looked like any schoolgirl in her sweater and skirt, knee - high white stockings and brown loafers—except for her obvious pregnancy. Aside from the four Youth Leaders, all of the girls sitting around the long table, or registering for the first time like Mary, were in early or advanced stages of pregnancy. The Youth Leaders themselves had gone through Haryou's program for unwed mothers last year, and had already given birth; they were now helping with the orientation of "new girls." All were in their teens—Mary being 15.

Mary had filled out a registration form which gave some essential details: she was living with her mother, had dropped out of high school four months before "because of morning sickness"; didn't know what "career" she was interested in, but she liked to type; the family wasn't on welfare —her father was in construction work overseas; no, she wasn't married; her "fiancé" was in the South with his family.

Another girl registering was having a second baby out of wedlock. Yes, she said to a Youth Leader, it was the same 20-year-old father. Yes, she expected to marry him . . . maybe . . . in 1968 "when he was furloughed." She loves him, but he had told her that he felt that he wasn't ready for marriage.

"He's ready to produce babies, but not ready to marry?" the Youth Leader asked.

The girl nodded dumbly.

The Youth Leader scribbled furiously, head down, mumbling, "Lots of them like that."

GERTRUDE SAMUELS is a staff writer on this magazine and author of a forthcoming documentary novel about delinquency, "The People Vs. Baby."

THIS was Mary's first day at Haryou Unlimited, and my first meeting with her. But in a way I had met Mary before—as a statistic.

A constantly startling fact of modern American life is that girls under 17 years of age account for about 50,000 annual out-of-wedlock births. Illegitimacy in the U.S. has been increasing steadily, from 3.8 per cent of all live births in 1940 to 6.9 per cent in 1961—from an estimated 89,500 to 240,000. Despite more interest in birth-control information in the last few years, the figures keep going up: some 275,700 illicit births in 1964. Among nonwhites, illicit births are highest: 25 per cent of all nonwhite babies, compared with 3.4 per cent of white babies.

In New York City in 1965, of a total of 158,815 live births, 20,980 were out of wedlock. More than 3,000 of these so-called O.W.'s were to girls 17 years of age and younger. Most depressing was the Department of Health report that in 1965, 46.5 per cent of all births in Central Harlem, where Mary lives, were out of wedlock, in contrast with 13.2 per cent for the whole city.

Thus when the statistic that is Mary comes to life at Haryou Unlimited — a social work group that is struggling to teach and train some of these young unwed mothers-to-be— the visitor tries to learn why the tragedy occurred, especially so early in life.

AS soon as one steps from subway to street in Central Harlem, one "sees" Mary in the context of her surroundings. For I clearly wasn't about to interview a girl from a sheltered white culture with its middle - class morality and code of behavior. Going into Central Harlem is like going into another country. To be sure, the main streets are modern enough, with their generally attractive shops. But many of the side streets on which the people live, in deteriorated brownstones and apartment buildings, are dreary and sinister-looking, some of them haunts of policy runners and drug addicts; here a white face draws more curiosity than hostility.

Many sidewalks were heaped with rubbish. Basement alleyways overflowed with trash. One long fence, shutting off a filthy lot between buildings, was decorated, mockingly it seemed, with ashcan covers hung as if they were gladiators' shields on display.

The community center stood like a beacon—bright, inviting.

I met Mary and the other girls through Mrs. Charlotte Jefferson, a social worker who created the Haryou program two years ago. A graduate of Stillman College in Alabama, Mrs. Jefferson is a young mother, married to a brokerage assistant. She carefully explained the purpose of my visit to the girls, assuring them that none needed to talk except voluntarily; but that I sought one girl who would articulate her feelings and would be candid and honest—to help me and others understand her story. Mary volunteered.

* * *

She was four months pregnant when we began the interviews. Besides Haryou, she was occasionally attending a prenatal clinic at Harlem Hospital, which admits many girls having O.W. babies from the area. Their babies are eventually born there.

What follows is the substance of several interviews I had with Mary:

How do you feel about motherhood, Mary?

It's all right. I don't hate the idea.

Well, do you think it's going to hurt your child not to have a father?

No. Because we could get married when I finish school, which may be two years from now.

Mary, the law says that people should be married to protect the babies and give them a good start in life. How do you feel about that?

It is a sin, I feel, to have babies before you're married. But (defensively) it's not no crime. Because it's nature.

What do you mean—nature?

Having babies is nature.

Who told you that?

A lot of people told me that having babies is nature, ain't no sin.

But, Mary, you said that it is a sin.

Well, it is a sin by the Bible and by law. But I don't feel that it's a sin to myself. I'm kinda happy that I'm pregnant 'cause this is my first child.

What did your boy friend say when you told him you were pregnant?

I wrote him. He's down South. He said he would get a job and take care of the baby.

Well, did he seem happy with the news?

He was happy.

How old is he?

He's 17.

How long has he been down South?

For several months. He's with his family.

Has your boy friend finished school?

No. He wants to get a job.

Mary, would you say what you and your boy friend decided, about the baby?

Well, I was supposed to go South and get married.

Why didn't you go?

Because . . . I didn't want to get married. I . . . wouldn't have been able to finish school.

But you left school. Is that the only reason, Mary? Was his family against it?

No. His mother called my mother long-distance.

Why did you think you couldn't finish school if you got married?

(Hesitant, confused) Because I . . . guess I didn't think about that.

In other words, you haven't really thought the situation through?

No . . . that's true.

Are you telling me, Mary, that you're uncertain about what you really feel for your boy friend?

Yes. Because I really don't know if I'm . . . in love.

Well, how long were you and Robert dating?

About 10 months.

Where did you go on dates?

We didn't go no place. We went to the movies sometimes. We went to his house.

Is that where you had sex relations?

Yes.

Mary, were you a virgin before you met Robert?

Yes, no relations before him.

Well, how did you learn about sexual intercourse?

My mother told me, a long time ago. She said I could get pregnant by having intercourse with a boy. And she said that she hoped that I wouldn't get pregnant and let her down. She didn't tell me not to do it, and she didn't tell me to do it. She just said not to let her down.

Why did you have sex relations?

I don't exactly know why. He didn't force himself on me. I wanted it . . . because if it would please him, then I wanted to have the relationship with him.

Was it love then, Mary?

Yes, I think so. That's what I thought it was . . . then.

Did you tell your mother?

No.

Why not?

Because I thought she would get mad at me.

When did your mother learn about your pregnancy?

Well, she found a letter from my boy friend that he'd written in reply to mine, saying he was going to 'take care of the baby' and get a job.

What did your mother do, Mary, when you said you were pregnant?

She cried and fussed, and said what was I going to do. But then she said there's a first mistake for everybody. She said she was proud of being a grandmother.

What did your father say?

My father was overseas when my mother wrote that I was pregnant. And at first he was so angry he wrote back that he wanted to put me away—in an unwed mother's home or something. He told my mother that either she puts me away or he wasn't going to come home. But then my mother wrote letters to him, begging, and he sent a telegram saying he changed his mind and I could stay home.

Who's going to pay for your medical care, Mary, and for the baby's clothes and food and all the other things that babies need?

Well, my mother and my father and the baby's father.

Do you have sisters?

Yes, an older sister. She asked me, did I want to get rid of the baby, so I said no. So she said, I'd better tell my mother. Then about a week after I told my sister, my mother found the letter.

Is your sister ashamed of you?

No, she's not ashamed. She keeps telling me that she's proud to be an aunt.

And how do you feel? Are you ashamed, Mary?

(Surprised) No. Because I'm not the first one in my block that had a baby that's my age. 'Cause one of my friends had a baby when she was 14. Her mother sent her away to a home for unwed mothers in Queens. There's a lot of girls on my block who had babies when they were young.

* * *

AS an inducement to attend the Haryou program, the girls are paid $1.50 an hour for a six-hour day. The program is basically an attempt to reorient the girls in their behavior and thinking, and also to train them for the responsibilities of motherhood. One "must" is that they go on with some regular schooling—despite the fact that the Board of Education has not established a full-time program for these dropouts. Harlem Hospital has instituted a two-hour-a-day academic program in a nearby center, to which the school board has assigned an accredited teacher. One morning soon after Mary had entered the Haryou program I went with her to her first "day" at the "school."

In a well-lighted room with a small library, a spinet piano and a bulletin board hung with art and music notices, half a dozen pregnant girls sat at two tables which had been pushed together, facing the blackboard. The white teacher, very blonde and earnest, was attempting to teach several subjects practically at the same time.

Mary and one or two other girls pored over books on biology and science, in particular a chapter headed "Your Cells and Their Needs," which seemed not untimely. The teacher moved first to this group, then to that, working with girls at various stages of stenography, math, Spanish, science. (On the blackboard the "Words to Learn" included "foe, oath, showed.")

"What do the chromosomes contain, Mary?" she asked.

Mary hesitated, made a stab at it, guided by her book. "Genes?"

"Genes, good."

The teacher briskly described the place of the "nucleus" in the scheme of life, the "genes that we inherit from our ancestors," and how everything "starts from the cell."

Mary yawned and looked tired. She read quietly to herself, her lips moving.

"Mary, that's slowing up comprehension," the teacher called. "Lips closed, please." Mary nodded and closed her lips.

After the two hours the girls put their books away and said good-by. Mary and I then walked together to Harlem Hospital, where she wanted to make an appointment with a social worker connected with the prenatal clinic. She greeted a girl—pregnant like herself.

"She's coming to Haryou this afternoon," Mary confided. "I told her about the program, and she wants to be in it. I like it better than just seeing a social worker [at the hospital] a couple of times a month."

Why was she so tired, yawning in class?

"Yeah, well, I'm not used to getting up so early. I been sleeping late since I dropped out of school, and I still have morning sickness. The hospital give me some yellow pills to take."

What I learned later was that Mary was going out with her fr'ends several nights a week to a neighborhood candy store and staying there until 1 or 2 o'clock in the morning, dancing to the jukebox. That information came from her worried mother, who sought Mrs. Jefferson's help in getting Mary to stay home evenings.

Now at Harlem Hospital, Mary guided me expertly through a labyrinth of corridors to the elevators. On the crowded third floor, she made an appointment with her social worker. Mary had been born here, and her baby would be born here.

We went out to lunch, and I pointed to a luncheonette that seemed satisfactory from the outside, but Mary shuddered.

"Oh, no, not that one. It's full of dope addicts and number men. I stay far away from them," she said.

* * *

BACK at the Drew Hamilton Center where the Haryou girls were waiting for an afternoon session, other activities were in full swing: preschool children were playing in the nursery; older children

were coming in for their after-school games; old people had gathered to play bingo.

Mary and a score of new registrants sat together in their own room for orientation from the Youth Leaders. (More formal counseling from adults, like Charlotte Jefferson, has since begun.) The 1966 program from which these Youth Leaders had emerged had been made up of 40 girls aged 16 to 21 years. Most were high-school dropouts; some were motivated by Haryou to get jobs, as telephone operators, waitresses, clerks, nurse's aides. Three of the 40 had had a previous pregnancy out of wedlock. Seven of the 40 were now married, and a number were "engaged."

Now Helen, the most vocal of the Youth Leaders, who married her boy friend, told the others earnestly: "We feel that you shouldn't be here just for the money, but for the training that you're going to get—on home life and family planning and education. The experts are trying to make sure that we're getting off on the right foot—even after we've made a mistake."

Mary leaned into the table. "Do you have mother's care?"

Helen started to describe the prenatal instruction that would be provided, and suddenly the girls were talking all at once, eager to unload their feelings:

"I didn't even know what was happenin' inside . . ."

"My baby bothers me so much, it stops me from sleepin' . . . "

"My baby kicks me at my back . . ."

"You have to have that suitcase ready, you know, two weeks ahead of time, with your hair rollers an' robe an' slippers . . ."

Nina, the prettiest and most volatile girl at the meeting - she had just had her baby -- turned the discussion to love and marriage, and now said contemptuously: "There's nothing wrong in not getting married just because you're pregnant. I feel that if my fiancé don't want me, I can live without marriage . . . unless I can find another fella."

"Well, I don't agree," Helen argued. "It's not really all right. You're not supposed to go out on the street and have a baby with someone you think you happen to love."

"That's like saying, get married with someone you don't even love no more," Nina scoffed, "just because you're having his baby." She added that the father of her child was in Vietnam, and she could

have married him when he came home on furlough, but she found that he had been writing to her girl friend.

"But I wasn't positive I wanted to marry him anyway," she added, tossing her head. "Be sure, I say!" she told the girls. "Be positive! I have a feeling I want to be free. Now I'm loco. I don't know if I want to get married or if I want to stay single."

Some of the girls nodded with understanding. Helen looked glum.

Did they feel they should give up their babies, for adoption or foste.-ho..ie care?

Mary spoke up sharply. "I don't want to give my baby up for no adoption. It's mine, my child, I'll bear the pain to have it. I don't think it's fair to give your child away."

"Why?"

"Because it's not their right mother and father, and that's cruel."*

Helen added fervently: "He didn't ask to come in the world in the first place. I don't think I should give him to anyone else. I would be afraid I mightn't ever see him again and that would bother me most of all. With me, if I had it to do all over again," she told the girls sadly, "I would have waited and not got pregnant. I would have taken pills or something. But I saw other girls were worse off than me. Some girls, their mothers threw them out. Some girls went to homes. But my

mother stood by me. She helped me."

All the girls listened quietly to Helen. Mary nodded. She, too, was being helped by her mother. Her mother had come to talk to the social worker, Charlotte Jefferson. She was a tall, neatly dressed woman with easy, weary smiles who worked, she said, as a clean-up woman, earning about $44 a week.

"Who's going to take care of the baby when Mary goes back to school?"

"Me. I'm going to give up my job and stay home when the baby comes," the mother said. She wanted Mary to go back to school. She was "thankful" that Mary was in the Haryou program—"better than her laying around at home, in bed all the time."

────────

*Studies show that few white unmarried mothers keep their O.W.'s; that more than two-thirds of the girls and women bearing O.W.'s and keeping them are nonwhite.

—Harlem Youth Unlimited——
Training & Rehabilitation Center~
——FOR YOUNG & UNWED MOTHERS

REGISTRATION
—AND—
PROGRAM
BEGINS
JAN. 3RD 1PM-
7PM

HOMEMAKING
EDUCATION
COUNSELING
CONSUMER EDUCATION
PRE-NATAL CARE
POST-NATAL CARE
CAREER DEVELOPMENT
HERITAGE
POLITICAL SCIENCE

LOCATION:
Drew Hamilton Community Center
143 RD ST. & 7TH AVE.

Did she think that Mary should get married?

The mother smiled her tired smile. "No, no, no. He's too young, only 17. They'll only have more children for me to take care of."

What would the new baby do to the income of the home if she quit her job and took on the whole responsibility? Her husband would send enough, they would manage. But, she told Mrs. Jefferson heavily, she had a real problem — and she spoke of Mary's going to the candy store and dancing half the night. When Mary got home, the mother said, and she was warned that she was ruining her health and the baby's, Mary replied: "I've gotta have fun."

Would Mrs. Jefferson talk to Mary and tell her that it was hurting her health?

Mrs. Jefferson would.

"I did my best," the mother said, her eyes filling.

"This isn't something that happened just to you," Mrs. Jefferson told her firmly. "Keep your chin up. It happens to rich and poor. Mary is lucky to have a mother who is taking on her problem and has chosen to let her have her baby and stay in the home. That's an awful lot."

After the mother had gone, Mrs. Jefferson talked to Mary in a no-nonsense tone: "Don't you feel you're being unfair to your mother? You've got to stop thinking of yourself and more about the baby. Now you will be getting assignments to work on at home when you leave here each day, and you must go home to rest. Are any of you: friends that you go dancing with pregnant?"

Mary hesitated.

"Yeah, one of them is."

"Okay, she's not in the program, so try to interest her in coming in, too," Mrs. Jefferson said briskly.

THE scope of the O.W. problem has so alarmed New York officials that the State Board of Social Welfare has revised its regulations to allow local welfare boards to give birth-control information to its clients— even when the clients do not ask for it. And now the 1967 Yellow Pages of the New York City telephone directory contain a new addition—a complete listing of "Birth Control Information Centers."

At a home-making session at the Drew Hamilton Center (the girls had prepared a sample breakfast of waffles and syrup), I asked Mary if she knew about birth control and contraceptives.

"Yeah, I knew about them. I heard that if you had sex you could take quinine pills and a bottle of gin— you have to boil the gin—to bring on your period."

"Did you do that, Mary?"

"No. One of my girl friends did it but it didn't help her. She got pregnant just the same. That's why I didn't trust it."

"But didn't you know about birth-control pills or other ways to protect yourself?"

"Yeah, I heard about them, but I didn't use them because every time after I had sex, I had my period. So I felt lucky, until I got caught." She grimaced. "Now I'm getting a coil at the hospital, after I have my baby." (She referred to the Margolies coil, named for its developer, one of a number of I.U.C.D.'s, or intrauterine contraceptive devices, that must be installed by physicians.)

"Who suggested that to you, Mary?"

"My girl friend who had her baby. You can't get pregnant with that. It stays in you until you want to have another baby. Then you take it out."

A FEW days later Mary went with the girls of her group to the Y on West 135th Street, where Haryou had arranged for a lecture on family planning. Seated on chairs before a blackboard, the girls — who were joined by a second Haryou group, over half of whom had had their babies—were told by Mrs. Jefferson: "This is Mrs. Relva Harris, a registered nurse in the field of education who has taught at Tuskegee Institute School of Nursing and at Montefiore Hospital, and she is going to talk to you about the reproductive system of the female—how you get pregnant and how not to get pregnant."

Mrs. Harris, a vibrant, informal young woman in a red knit suit, established a quick rapport with the girls. "Now this is the uterus and the womb," she said briskly, making sketches on the board under the heading, "Human Reproduction." Briefly she lectured them on the menstrual cycle. Then: "How does pregnancy take place?"

Dead silence. Mary leaned forward intensely, but remained as silent as the others. At last one girl ventured: "Don't the ovaries move?"

"No, the ovaries don't move. Mary?"

"No, I don't know."

A show of hands revealed that none of the pregnant girls knew how pregnancy actually happens.

"If intercourse takes place, how many sperms are ejaculated?" asked Mrs. Harris.

"One . . . ?"

"About a . . . million?"

"About 250 million," Mrs. Harris said slowly and firmly, "at one time, in just a little bit of male semen, and they are deposited in the vaginal canal. Most of those, of course, don't go up here," pointing to her drawing, as she explained, in technical and nontechnical terms, how human life is created.

The lecture turned to birth control—the pill and other contraceptives. "The most common and easiest to use is the pill," Mrs. Harris said. "I don't care if you get those sperms by the hour"—self-conscious laughter from the girls — "the pill, if taken regularly, will stop the ovulation."

"So what happens to the sperms?"

"They die."

Mrs. Harris described the alternative contraceptives: the diaphragm ("Don't borrow anyone else's, because it won't work; it must be measured for you alone and fitted by a doctor —you have to wear it like your underwear"), and the coil, sometimes called the loop. "So you have a choice, the pill, the diaphragm and the coil —and if you use one or the other, you will not get pregnant."

Earlier Mrs. Jefferson had asked the girls: "What about your boy friends? All they have to do is go to the drugstore and buy what they need to protect you." Several girls had laughed derisively: "They wouldn't!"

After this meeting, Mrs. Jefferson asked Mary, "Do you think it would have helped you if you had been given this sort of lesson in school before you got pregnant, Mary?"

The girl nodded.

"I'm interested now in . . . birth control," she said.

ONE evening Mary took me to visit her mother at home. Home was a railroad flat in a rundown apart-ment house. Sparsely furnished, with peeling walls and torn linoleum, it was nevertheless clean. In the kitch-en, the mother, wearing a bright yellow, starched apron, was cooking a chicken-giblet stew for herself and her four children.

One bedroom contained, besides a large bed, a dozen family pictures and a portable TV. A nondescript dog and a cage of canaries were part of the scene in the small living room.

With Mary listening, her mother said with her sad smile: "Yes, I felt hurt when she told me she was preg-nant. But after I got over it, and my husband got over it . . ." She shrugged, as though listening to her thoughts. Mary nodded.

"Now you're going to have work from that Mrs. Jefferson," the mother told Mary, "so you'll stay in, darling, and have your rest. A pregnant girl needs her rest."

Mary nodded again.

"Everyone in my family—everyone —had kids before they was married," the mother said suddenly. "So it's sort of in the family—what can you do?" She seemed to be struggling with her feelings. "I made a mistake myself before I got married, with my first one. So who am I to put my daugh-ter away?"

There was a silence. Mary, sunk deep in the overstuffed chair, stroked the dog and looked at her mother.

"We'll work it out," the mother said calmly. ∎

March 5, 1967

'We Don't Call It Natural Childbirth, but Educated Childbirth'

By MARYLIN BENDER

NATURAL childbirth has moved from the status of controversial cult to ecumenical movement.

During the last decade, it has shed its mystical fervor, liberalized its strict tenets, won new adherents and forced hospital administrators to revise their rules.

"The fad element has been weeded out," said Barbara Williams, a nurse who conducts a free course in prepara-tion for childbirth at the Maternity Center, 48 East 92d Street. "Now it's in the middle of the road, accommo-dating a wide variety of needs." Mrs. Williams is expecting her first child in August and her husband, an interne, has no intention of being present in the delivery room.

Matter-of-Fact Attitude

The trend is away from idyllic rhapsody toward matter-of-fact dis-semination of information and prepa-ration for labor.

The apostle of the movement was Dr. Grantly Dick Read, a British ob-stetrician who reasoned that fear pro-voked a state of tension that inhibited the natural process of childbirth. If women were educated to overcome fear and tension, he contended, they could give birth without pain. Education consisted of exercises and controlled breathing.

Dr. Read's book, "Childbirth Without Fear," published in 1942, was trans-lated into 10 languages. In 1956, Pope Pius XII endorsed his concepts. Never-theless, natural childbirth encountered the hostility of obstetricians, a hostil-ity that survived Dr. Read's death in 1959.

In 1951, a French obstetrician named Fernand Lamaze introduced a method, called the psycho-prophylactic tech-nique, based on Pavlovian conditioned-reflex theories that he had observed being applied in the Soviet Union.

Although the goal was the same— childbirth with minimal discomfort and without medication, enabling the mother to see her child coming into the world—the Lamaze method dif-fered from the Read method chiefly in advocating that the mother be very active during a contraction instead of concentrating on relaxing.

The Lamaze method was introduced to the United States in 1959 with the publication of "Thank You, Dr. La-maze," a book written by Marjorie Karmel, an American whose first child had been delivered by the French physician in Paris.

The following year, Mrs. Karmel and Elisabeth Bing, a Berlin-born physical therapist, founded the American So-ciety for Psychoprophylaxis in Obstet-rics, a nonprofit teaching organization of doctors, teachers and parents.

"We don't call it natural childbirth, but educated childbirth," said Mrs. Bing, who is vice president of the so-ciety. "Read says it's a normal physio-logical process, which shouldn't hurt if you think right. He's very mystical. We say labor is a situation of stress and we try to cope with that situa-tion."

Since the founding of the society, the Lamaze method has spread steadily.

It has acquired six chapters and five affiliates throughout the country.

Mrs. Bing estimates that 150 teach-ers have been trained in the method since 1962. She gives classes in her apartment at 164 West 79th Street to about 350 expectant mothers a year. The six-session training course starts at the end of the student's seventh month of pregnancy. The fee is $40.

Mrs. Bing also teaches at Flower-Fifth Avenue Hospital, the first of several hospitals in the metropolitan area to offer courses in prenatal edu-cation and the Lamaze method. Fees for such hospital courses range from $15 to $25.

Flower-Fifth Avenue Hospital is one of eight hospitals in Manhattan that permit husbands in the delivery room with the consent of the attending physician. Six years ago there was only one, New York Hospital. Eleven hospitals permit husbands in the labor room.

Natural childbirth is a family-cen-tered movement. It advocates a work-ing team consisting of the wife, her husband, the physician and, in some cases, a monitor or instructor. The husband helps his wife during preg-nancy by drilling her in her exercises. During labor, he acts as a coach, see-ing to it that she responds to her contractions with proper breathing and assisting her with back massage. He is present when the child is delivered.

Controversy About Husbands

The husband's presence in the de-livery room is the constant-crusade of all factions of the natural childbirth movement. It is also one of the most hotly disputed not only among physicians but also among cocktail party conversationalists.

Dr. Martin L. Stone, chairman of the department of obstetrics and gynecology of the New York Medical College, under whose auspices the Lamaze method is taught at Flower-Fifth Avenue Hospital, has this to say:

"I personally don't believe fathers belong in the delivery room any more than they belong in the operating room, but I'm allowing it on a trial basis because of some patients' and some doctors' needs. Some husbands are very gung-ho on all this and other husbands are tickled silly to be relieved of the obligation."

The gung-ho husband usually attends the training courses given in the evening with his wife. Women who go it alone usually take the daytime courses. He also sees the educational films shown in hospital auditoriums that illustrate actual childbirth by Lamaze-trained mothers.

A relaxation of other natural childbirth doctrines has won a wider following for the movement, although its critics seem unaware of the changes. Many doctors say that the woman who commits herself to natural childbirth and then fails to go the whole way without an analgesic (pain-killer) or anesthetic feels guilty and thereby acquires a psychological burden.

In her book, "Six Practical Lessons for An Easier Childbirth," just published by Grosset & Dunlap, Mrs. Bing writes:

"There is no absolute goal, no threshold that all or any of us must reach. You certainly must not feel any guilt or sense of failure if you require some medication, or if you experience discomfort."

Episiotomy, or a small incision made in the mouth of the vagina just before the baby's head is delivered (often done with a local anesthetic), is also now regarded by the American Lamaze forces as a proper surgical procedure consistent with the psychoprophylactic method.

The preparation-for-labor training at the Maternity Center Association contains elements of both Read and Lamaze methods. Emphasis is placed on controlled relaxation à la Read in the first stage of labor. Exercises are integrated in the discussion and showing of films.

"People come thinking the goal is to be awake or to be asleep," said Mrs. Albert H. Wiggins, one of the association's parent educators. "We stress the health of the mother and baby and say that if you can also have this other experience, fine. But nobody can commit herself during pregnancy."

In Europe, natural childbirth has working-class overtones. Dr. Lamaze introduced his method in the Paris metalworkers' union clinic. In the United States, it started with a middle-class, intellectually oriented following. One physician described the typical Lamaze patient as "a Sarah Lawrence graduate with Ramparts under her arm, a college beatnik type."

But the movement has broadened. A natural childbirth film audience includes late adolescent bearded boys and miniskirted brides, a sprinkling of interracial marriages, corporate junior executive couples and a few blue collar representatives.

In the preparation for childbirth courses, they discuss their fears, are disabused of their old wives' tale notions and are supplied with factual information about what is in store for them—from officious hospital clerks to nausea and hiccups. The courses are a kind of group therapy in which some members arrive as fanatics and depart with a tolerant, wait-and-see attitude.

Women who have seen their children born, through whatever method of natural childbirth, tend to wax enthusiastic about their accomplishment.

"It wasn't all that ecstatic as I thought from reading Marjorie Karmel's book," said Mrs. John Friedler of Summit, N. J., who had a partial indoctrination in Argentina before the birth of her first child and then exercised and read by herself before the birth of her second child last February.

"I think the breathing helps because it gives you something to do," she added. Her daughter was born less than three hours after she entered the hospital. "If it had been a long session, I don't know how great I would have been."

Mrs. Christos Lefkarites of Kew Gardens, Queens, is a self-taught Lamaze graduate. Her second child was born at Lenox Hill Hospital.

"I remembered such pain from the birth of my first child," she said. "Reading the Karmel book was such a comfort because it taught me what to anticipate. I felt I could control things. I learned that there was a time when I could relax, and that the pain does diminish."

Dr. Stone pronounced the preparation-for-childbirth courses "whether Read or Lamaze" to be of definite value, "in being able to have an educated, prepared, understanding patient who can go through labor with less need for analgesic or anesthesia." Anesthesia is still one of the biggest problems in obstetrics, he said, because of shortages of trained personnel in hospitals and because "at any time it has inherent risks."

He said that he did not impose natural childbirth methods on his patients. "It can't work unless they want it to," he explained. "It can also work to degrees. It's not an all-or-nothing proposition."

Wives in Quest of 'the Colored Lights'

By DONALD JANSON

ATLANTIC CITY—The subject of sex played a larger role in the program of the American Medical Association convention here last week than in past years. One thing doctors were apprised of was a growing frustration among wives.

Robert R. Bell, a Temple University sociologist, reported to the 12,000 doctors assembled here that a fourth of 196 wives surveyed complained that sexual intercourse came too infrequently in their marriages.

Dr. Bell drew some far-reaching conclusions.

"The social and psychological sexual liberation of the modern woman has led some to shed many past restrictions and inhibitions," he said, "and emerge in their marriages with greater sexual interest than their husbands."

What this may mean for "the near future," he felt, is that marriages will be wracked by more and more problems centering on wifely dissatisfaction.

He conceded that this was "an ironic switch from the patriarchal past." when the wife was relegated to a passive, compliant role intended to serve the desires of a dominant mate.

19th-Century Attitude

Past professional attitudes were offered to illustrate the contrast. Throughout the 19th century moral and "scientific" views frowned upon the thought that women might find sex pleasurable.

William Acton, in a standard text on the reproductive system, wrote that "the belief that women had a sexual appetite was a vile aspersion." William Hammond, a surgeon-general of the United States, recorded the official view that "nine-tenths of the time decent women felt not the slightest pleasure in intercourse." Many published poets, physicians and moralists shared the contention that female sexual satisfaction was achieved only by the "depraved" prostitute.

Today it is next to impossible to find any reputable writers voicing the old double-standard values. Now the pendulum has swung so far the other way, Dr. Bell noted, that writers not only take female sex "rights" for granted, but frequently romanticize sexual intercourse sufficiently to guarantee disappointment.

"If a woman has been assured that she will . . . see colored lights, feel like a breaking wave, or helplessly utter inarticulate cries," writes Morton M. Hunt, "she is apt to consider herself or her husband at fault when these promised wonders do not appear."

The better educated wife, Dr. Bell finds, is the one who is finding fault with the sexual capacity of her husband. The problems for husbands will increase because more and more wives are gaining an education and coveting their right to sexual joy in marriage.

The male is taxed, Dr. Bell noted, because, as Kinsey found, men reach their sexual peak in their late teens, many years before women do.

The difficulty is compounded, the sociologist adds, because in addition to declining male desire during the years of marriage there is the problem of biological restriction on frequency that applies only to the man.

The Bell survey on the emancipated woman was conducted among college graduates, all married and living with their husbands. The 196 averaged 26 years of age and four years of marriage.

Dr. Bell contrasted the results with those of similar studies a quarter century and a half century ago. Female desire for greater sexual satisfaction in the 1940's was increasing but in the 1920's "very few gave any indication of a desire for sex that was greater than that of the husband."

Dr. James L. Mathis, a psychiatrist at the University of Oklahoma Medical Center, held a news conference on the matter with Dr. Bell.

"A marriage is no longer seen as a union for the pleasure of the male in exchange for the support of the female," Dr. Mathis said. Many men are reluctant to accept the new order, he said, creating a troublesome conflict that should "make it mandatory that the practicing physician concern himself with marital problems far more than in the past." He suggested that medical schools act to meet the crisis by providing courses on the subject.

Sex and the College Girl

By JANE E. BRODY

Many coeds of decades past avowed that if there were a perfect contraceptive they would not hesitate to indulge in premarital sexual intercourse.

Today's coeds have that foolproof contraceptive — The Pill — which has led many parents to worry that with the deterring fear of pregnancy gone their daughters would have a sexual free-for-all.

Authorities on the subject asserted recently that this has not occurred, that the coed of today is no more likely to express herself sexually than was the coed of 10 or 20 years ago. Their studies indicate that the pattern of premarital intercourse has changed relatively little in the past 30 years.

What has changed, the authorities said, is the emotional context of these sexual relationships.

Annual Meeting

The authorities participated in a symposium on changing sex behavior held at the annual meeting of the American Association for the Advancement of Science.

Dr. Paul Gebhard, director of the Institute for Sex Research at Indiana University, said that, for the coed of this decade, the premarital sexual relationship is surrounded by more pleasure and less guilt.

As in the past, he said, college girls almost invariable limit their sexual encounters to men they love. But, he added, girls seem more willing today to enter love relationships that they do not expect will lead to marriage.

College males, on the other hand, are more likely than in the past to be emotionally involved with their sexual partners, Dr. Gebhard said.

Dr. Gebhard based his statements on the early findings of a survey conducted last summer among 1,200 college students throughout the country. The results of this survey were compared with a similar one made 20 years ago by the late Dr. Alfred C. Kinsey.

Dr. Gebhard's data on the extent of premarital sex among today's college students is still to be processed, but other symposium participants said that the arrival of the Pill has not contributed significantly to its rise.

"Contraceptives are not changing sexual behavior. They are simply making safer sexual behavior that would have occurred anyway," said Dr. Mary Calderone, executive director of the Sex Information and Education Council of the United States. "People are going to behave sexually regardless of the availability and type of contraception."

Ira L. Reiss, sociologist at the University of Iowa, agreed that the effect of contraception on rates of premarital intercourse was small indeed. But, he observed, there is today "a new social context of premarital sexual permissiveness" evolving in America.

"In the old days," he said, "the highest degree of sexual permissiveness was found among the lower classes. Now it is highly rooted in the college-educated community. There is a more intellectualized attitude toward sex as acceptable, particularly when a love relationship is involved."

Dr. Reiss said that no change has occurred in the percentages of people performing sexually, but a change has occurred in male behavior — "from the prostitute to the girl next door."

He concluded that "males today are much tamer than their fathers or grandfathers."

Sterilization:

Simple New Surgery

Willie, 32, and Carol, 30, are the parents of two bright, healthy children—all the family they intend to have. Faced with the fact of perhaps 20 more fertile years together, they ask: "What can we do to prevent an 'accident?'" It is a familiar question for millions of American couples and countless millions more around the world. The possible answers include:

● The Pill. But some women, because of pre-existing medical problems, cannot use the Pill safely, and others dislike the prospect of having to pop a pill in their mouths every day for the next two decades.

● The intrauterine device, or IUD. But the bodies of some women cannot adjust to an IUD. Other women fear the unknown hazard of a foreign object residing in them for many years.

● Vasectomy, the male sterilization procedure. But many men balk at an operation they fear will affect their masculinity and virility.

● Female sterilization. But to many women, this means a costly operation with up to a week in the hospital and another week or two recovering.

Last week, however, a Johns Hopkins gynecologist reported major advances which he believes will make female sterilization a far more popular solution to the contraceptive dilemma both here and abroad. Thanks to new surgical techniques and equipment, Dr. Clifford R. Wheeless told a meeting of Planned Parenthood physicians in Detroit, a woman can now be sterilized in a 15-minute operation and leave the hospital a few hours later. Most women are able to resume their regular activities within a day.

What may be the answer to a matron's prayer, a 15-minute sterilization procedure, was announced last week. Above, the female version of pins provided by the Association for Voluntary Sterilization for those who have.

Dr. Wheeless is one of several score of doctors in hospitals and surgical centers around the country who are performing female sterilization operations on an outpatient basis—without even one night spent in the hospital. Many other hospitals require only overnight hospitalization the night before the operation. And at least one Planned Parenthood clinic —in Syracuse, N. Y.—is planning to start doing the procedure in a nonhospital facility.

The heroine of the procedure is an instrument called the laparoscope—a lighted tubular device about as wide as a fountain pen with operating tools built into it. Using the operating laparoscope, Dr. Wheeless said, the Fallopian tubes, where conception takes place, can be electrically sealed and severed through a tiny incision made just below the navel.

The procedure, nicknamed "belly button surgery," can be done under local anesthesia, Dr. Wheeless said, though some patients prefer a general anesthetic. The patient leaves the hospital with a Band-aid on her incision, which heals to leave no visible scar.

A slightly different procedure preferred by some doctors uses an instrument called a culdoscope, which is introduced through the vagina and involves no visible incision. Neither operation, however, is reversible.

As a result of the simplified techniques, cost of the operation has been greatly reduced—from a typical hospital bill of more than $1,000 to about $150. The surgeon's fee usually ranges from $150 to $300. In most states, the cost is covered by Blue Cross and Blue Shield.

Dr. Wheeless says his technique is applicable to poor populations in underdeveloped countries. He is now working on developing miniaturized equipment that can run on any type of current and can be packed in a suitcase.

In the United States, where an estimated 300,000 female sterilization operations were performed last year (compared to 800,000 vasectomies), Dr. Wheeless predicts that the tubal surgery will become increasingly popular among women who have decided that their child-bearing days should end—not to mention those younger women who don't want to have any children at all. A number of doctors are also trying to perfect reversible female sterilization techniques, which, if successful, are expected to result in a second contraceptive revolution.

—JANE BRODY

April 9, 1972

Sex Revolution:

Vanishing Virginity

It turns out to be something less than a virgin spring. Last week many a parent's head was spinning over new evidence of the sexual revolution: a Federal study indicating that nearly half of America's unwed daughters have had sexual intercourse by age 19—and most of them haven't bothered with contraceptives.

The study, prepared for the Presidential Commission on Population Growth and the American Future, is based on a survey of 4,611 unmarried girls said to be a representative cross-section of the nation. Some of the results:

● More than 32 per cent of the black girls had sexual intercourse by the age of 15, three times the figure for white girls; by age 19, the black-white ratio was 2-to-1. But while 16 per cent of the white girls had intercourse with four or more partners, the figure for blacks was less than 11 per cent. The study's conclusion: ". . . it is the white nonvirgins who have sex more frequently and are the more promiscuous." In general, regardless of race,

the majority of the girls said that intercourse had been limited to one partner, whom they said they intended to marry.

● More than three-fourths of the nonvirgins never used contraceptives, or used them only occasionally. There is, the report said, "a good bit of pregnancy, most of which appears to have been unwanted." Such facts lay behind a recent report by the Presidential commission recommending that contraceptive services and information be provided to teen-agers. But that recommendation met a cold shoulder from President Nixon last weekend. "Such measures," he said, "would do nothing to preserve and strengthen close family relations."

May 14, 1972

CHAPTER 8

Radical Feminism

*Betty Friedan, feminist author
and leader, calls on women to boycott
products advertized in terms insulting
to women, August 26, 1970.*
Courtesy Compix.

The Female of Our Species

THE SECOND SEX. By Simone de Beauvoir. Translated from the French and edited by H. M. Parshley. 732 pp. New York: Alfred A. Knopf. $10.

By CLYDE KLUCKHOHN

"ONE wonders if women still exist, if they will always exist, whether or not it is desirable that they should, what place they occupy in this world, what their place should be." The questions are radical enough, comprehensive enough, searching enough. And Simone de Beauvoir's answers are subtle and profound. This is no piece of flamboyant journalism and certainly not a petulant defense of her sex. Nor is it merely an extended essay, although it is indeed literature in the grand sense.

Essentially this is a treatise which integrates the most variegated strands of history, philosophy, economics, biology, belles-lettres, sociology and anthropology. I cannot think of a single American scholar, man or woman, who controls such a vast body of knowledge as this French writer. But it is a very lively treatise. In part this is because the style is never tiresome. In part it is because of the intrinsic interest to all of us of most of her material. Then there is a seasoning of bits of malice (e. g., against Claudel and Mauriac) and of sheer curiosa such as some startling details on the psychopathic aberrations of some Roman Catholic saints.

NO, this is never a dull book in spite of its immense learning, though occasionally it is an infuriating one because of unfamiliar existentialist terminology and because of the tortuous intricacy of the argument.

The main themes are introduced at once. Women throughout history have been a disadvantaged group like the proletariat. The concept of "the eternal feminine" has as much validity as those of "the Black soul" and "the Jewish character," and the situational and psychological factors that have led to the development and perpetuation of such stereotypes are revealingly analogous. On the other hand, women are on the whole inferior to men today because their *situation* affords them fewer possibilities.

Book One develops these

Professor of Anthropology at Harvard, Mr. Kluckhohn is the author of "Mirror for Man: The Relation of Anthropology to Modern Life."

themes with material from the facts of biology and history and from popular and literary myths. The sketch of the biological "givens" is an excellent example of Mlle. de Beauvoir's workmanship. This chapter is not just a tight and skillful digest based upon data from several good secondary works and carried through with severe accuracy in particulars. The recent technical literature in monographs and journals is drawn upon and fused amazingly with philosophical, psychological and even theological discussion. There are at least a few reflections of the author which appear to be quite independent and original, worth the serious attention of biologists. Her ending point is one which the anthropologist can applaud (with a slight caveat upon the one word "conscious"):

"The enslavement of the female to the species and the limitations of her various powers are extremely important facts; the body of woman is one of the essential elements in her situation in the world. But that body is not enough to define her as woman; there is no true living reality except as manifested by the conscious individual through activities and in the bosom of a society."

The historical chapters are rich in piquant detail, pointed but objective in their selectivity, marred in validity only, so far as the reviewer's competence goes, by a partial adherence to the Morgan - Engels - Marx scheme of "stages" in cultural evolution and by a few minor ethnographical slips. "The Myth of Woman in Five Authors" is so well done that one gets the same kind of almost physical pleasure that one does from the superb performance of music that matters.

IT must not be thought, however, that the book depends for its power entirely upon beautiful language and imagery. There is a carefully constructed theoretical scheme for the analysis, coming largely from three sources: Existentialist philosophy (especially Sartre, of course, but with fairly numerous references to Kierkegaard and Heidegger), psychoanalysis and historical materialism. Some knowledge of the first of these on the part of the reader is apparently assumed, for there is no systematic presentation of this philosophy. The uninitiated reader can piece together a picture from the contexts in which key terms such as "alienation" and "immanence" are used and from passages such as: "I shall place woman in a

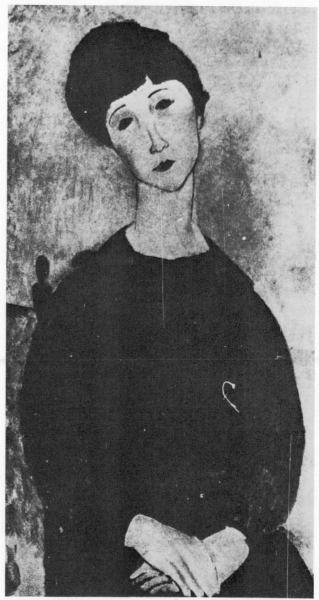

From a painting by Amadeo Modigliani.
"Seated Woman."

world of values and give her behavior a dimension of liberty."

Psychoanalysis and historical materialism are discussed in Book One—and both critically.

The fact that Mlle. de Beauvoir approaches historical materialism with great discrimination — and also differentiates skeptically between Soviet propaganda and Soviet reality—is of topical interest in view of the current Camus-Sartre controversy. She recognizes that it is indispensable to know the economic and social structure of the world, but historical materialism has no exclusive copyright on this premise. She quotes Marx, Engels, Bebel approvingly on some points which one may well do. Yet she challenges Communist orthodoxy as

sharply as psychoanalytic:

"Historical materialism takes for granted facts that call for explanation * * * we reject for the same reasons both the sexual monism of Freud and the economic monism of Engels."

IF Book One is largely analytical and historical, Book Two is primarily clinical. And Simone de Beauvoir strikes me as a far better clinician than are most intellectuals who have her analytic and verbal gifts. I suspect she understands herself very well indeed. She appears to have a sure feel for the significant in the case histories of others, even non-intellectuals—and this, I confess, surprised me a good deal. At any rate, her interpretations rang true to me.

It is a truly magnificent book, even if sometimes irritating to a mere male. It should be a required companion volume to all who read the forthcoming report of Kinsey and his associates. For Mlle. de Beauvoir says much about sexuality that is important which we are not likely to get from the Indiana group. Statistical tables of the incidence of various types of sexual acts need to be balanced by the historical depth, philosophical sophistication and exquisite psychological sensibilities of a Simone de Beauvoir.

My reservations are on a host of specific matters and two general issues. Of the former category I can mention only a few by way of example. I think Mlle. de Beauvoir, as an intellectual, underestimates the extent to which women can be creative and "free" through the exercise of household responsibilities which need not be nearly as demeaning or "enslaving" as filing the same kinds of papers day by day or repeating endlessly the same routines in a factory. If one presses some of the author's statements to their logical extremes, it would seem that she wanted and thought it possible that *all* women should become artists or intellectuals. We know that neither all men nor all women have such potentialities. Nor do they want to have them—granted fully that women's artistic and intellectual potentialities have, thus far in history, been more blocked by blind custom than those of men.

This should (I am not afraid of this word) be changed as Mlle. de Beauvoir so eloquently argues. My second specific reservation is intimately related to the first. The book is too intellectualistic. Even where rationality is recognized as not present, there is a strong hint that it ought to be.

Third, I think that perhaps there is too much about sexuality in "The Second Sex" and relatively little said (though well) about economic, political and social factors. Her discussion of sexuality is also exceedingly illuminating, though the continued stress on homosexuality and its importance in the life of women generally may be overdone. In any case my query is that of balance between sexuality and other determinants in the life of woman as a whole. In this respect I think that Margaret Mead's "Male and Female" may be a wiser book.

THE two general points on which I would take issue are related and may appear paradoxically so. On the one hand, I find that she has overemphasized cultural forces; on the other hand, that she has neglected them. In spite of her careful and precise attention to the facts of biology she seems at times to be saying, "Oh, but women can transcend all this." One is reminded occasionally of the one-line book review of another famous book by a woman, "Does she really know any culture in which the men have the babies?" It is true that Mlle. de Beauvoir speaks of maternity as one function of woman which inevitably imposes restraints upon her full liberty. Likewise she sees that woman's eroticism will always have its special form. It is also true that elsewhere she explicitly restricts the artificial shaping by "custom and fashion" (which can be altered because "imposed upon each woman from without") to those "canons of propriety" which can be gradually transformed so that they "approach those adopted by males."

NEVERTHELESS this reviewer was left with the conviction that Mlle. de Beauvoir was most reluctant to accept any genuine determination of woman's psyche by her biological nature. "Complete economic and social equality will bring about an inner metamorphosis." It is not a question of there being, except at the most abstract level, "a feminine psychology." It is a question of there being *some* modalities more characteristic of women than of men, quite apart from the various distinct cultural traditions.

On the other hand, this book appears to me to be culture-bound in some important respects. At the beginning Mlle. de Beauvoir utters something like the precautionary phrase "In Our Culture" which has become a compulsive ritual among American social scientists. And she repeatedly talks of "social context" and the like. Yet she does make many broad generalizations which, it seems clear, are not to be restricted to Western Europeans, the French, or, indeed, French intellectuals. I also want to say "culture-bound" with respect to some of her observations on the American scene. Mlle. de Beauvoir does say some perceptive things which no American has had the wit to say. Nevertheless, French culture is always palpably her standard of reference, and it is equally evident that she has had a limited acquaintance with American life. Take the following statement:

"Many American women particularly are prepared to think that there is no longer any place for woman as such; if a backward individual still takes herself for a woman, her friends advise her to be psychoanalyzed and thus get rid of this obsession."

"MANY?" "Many?" — in respect to our total population? Perhaps in certain small circles in New York City and elsewhere. Conversely, while she is aware of the "Momism" concept, she has failed to use for her own argument some of the theses advanced by acute American observers on certain trends toward hostility between the adults of the two sexes and the claimed relation of this to the frequent, perhaps modal, role of the American middle-class mother.

Enough of this cavilling. "The Second Sex" has what Plutarch said of the buildings on the Acropolis: "There is such a certain flourishing freshness in it." It is a threadbare cliché to speak of not doing justice to a book, but in this case I must resort to the cliché, for I have never been so acutely conscious of incomplete justice.

The translation is generally good except for an occasional stilted phrase such as "would fain." I spot-checked the translation against the first volume of the French edition and could detect no distortion and only one significant omission (which I later discovered the editor put out in the Translator's Preface). The notes added to the pages of the text by the editor-translator are often interesting and helpful, sometimes a bit academic and forced. Alfred Knopf has produced an unusually handsome volume.

February 22, 1953

They Meet in Victorian Parlor to Demand 'True Equality'—NOW

By LISA HAMMEL

ALTHOUGH no one in the dim ruby and sapphire Victorian parlor actually got up and cried: "Women of the world, unite! You have nothing to lose but your chains," that was the prevailing sentiment yesterday morning at the crowded press conference held by the newly formed National Organization for Women.

NOW, which is the organization's urgent acronym, was formed three weeks ago in Washington to press for "true equality for all women in America . . . as part of the world-wide revolution of human rights now taking place."

The organization has been informally styled by several of its directors the "N.A.A.-C.P. of women's rights."

The board of directors asked President Johnson, in the text of a letter released yesterday, to give "top priority among legislative proposals for the next Congress to legislation which would give effective enforcement powers to the Equal Employment Opportunity Commission," which, the letter stated, "is hampered . . . by a reluctance among some of its male members to combat sex discrimination as vigorously as they seek to combat racial discrimination."

Separate letters were also sent to Acting Attorney General Ramsey Clark and the three current commissioners of the Equal Employment Opportunity Commission.

"As part of the Great Society program," the letter to the President read, "your administration is currently engaged in a massive effort to bring underprivileged groups — victims of discrimination because of poverty, race or lack of education — into the mainstream of American life. However, no comprehensive effort has yet been made to include women in your Great Society program for the underprivileged and excluded."

The press conference was held amid the dark Victorian curlicues and oriental carpeting in the apartment of the organization's president, Betty Friedan.

Mrs. Friedan, who became a household word when she gave "the problem that has no name" the name of "The Feminine Mystique" in a best-seller published three years ago, explained in her book to disgruntled housewives across the country that they had been sold a bill of goods by society.

Creative dishwashing and a life unremittingly devoted to the care and feeding of a husband and children is not the alpha and omega of a woman's existence, Mrs. Friedan maintained, nor is a woman likely to find complete fulfillment as an adult human being either among the diapers and soapsuds or in the boudoir.

"Our culture," Mrs. Friedan wrote, "does not permit women to accept or gratify their basic need to grow and fulfill their potentialities as human beings, a need which is not solely defined by their sexual role."

Mrs. Friedan said last week in an interview in her apartment that NOW had "just begun to think about methods" to implement its goals of enabling women to "enjoy the equality of opportunity and freedom of choice which is their right . . . in truly equal partnership with men."

Speaking in a gravelly alto from the depths of the large fur collar that trimmed her neat black suit, the ebullient author suggested that women today were "in relatively little position to influence or control major decisions."

"But," she added, leaning forward in the lilac velvet Victorian chair and punching the air as if it were something palpable, "what women do have is the vote.

"We will take strong steps in the next election," Mrs. Friedan continued, "to see that candidates who do not take seriously the question of equal rights for women are defeated."

The position paper issued by NOW at its formation on Oct. 29 stated that: "We will strive to ensure that no party, candidate, president, senator, governor, congressman, or any public official who betrays or ignores the principle of full equality between the sexes is elected or appointed to office" and that to this end the organization would "mobilize the votes of men and women who believe in our cause."

"Politics?" the Rev. Dean Lewis repeated yesterday in answer to a question. "What do you have for women in that field? Women's political auxiliaries. They are put aside in nice separate structures without policy-making powers."

Reason for Joining

Mr. Lewis, a slender man with a neat pointed beard, is the secretary of the Office of Social Education and Evangelism of the United Presbyterian Church in the United States.

"Why did I join NOW?" he said. "It's like asking somebody why they joined the N.A.A.C.P. I'm interested in equal rights for anybody who desires them. The structure of both law and custom in our society deprives women of their rights."

Mr. Lewis is one of the 5 men on NOW's 28-member board of directors. The vice president of the organization is Richard Graham, director of the National Teacher Corps and a former Equal Employment Opportunity Commissioner.

NOW states in its position paper that it is concerned with discrimination where it exists against men as well as against women.

Mrs. Friedan explained that the organization believed that most alimony laws were discriminatory against men and that NOW intended to re-examine current laws.

The 500 members of NOW have been drawn from many fields, including education, labor, government, the social sciences, mass communications and religion. Two Roman Catholic nuns are members of the board of directors.

"There is religious discrimination in the church, but that is not my main reason for joining the organization," said Sister Mary Joel Read, chairman of the department of history at Alverno College, a Roman Catholic college for women in Milwaukee.

"This is not a feminist movement," the nun continued. "It is not a question of getting male privileges. In the past the possibility of realizing one's humanity was limited to an élite group at the top. Women are not equal in our society. This movement centers around the possibility of being human."

Meet the Women Of the Revolution, 1969

By PETER BABCOX

ON a serene afternoon in early September, the boardwalk at Atlantic City is thronged with determined celebrants, gathering to bear witness to a still-unspoiled national ritual. For on this night Miss America will be crowned, the popular grail refurbished. Disported beside a sun-spangled late summer sea, the city has about it all the calculated euphoria of a Busby Berkeley fantasy. Chicago's reeking littorals are only two weeks removed, yet the distance seems one of decades.

Now, in front of the convention hall where shortly the assembled beauty queens are to be judged, the contrived consensus of the afternoon is tumbling into a riptide of political obloquy. "Miss America Sells It!" declares the rude placard carried by a demure woman graduate student. About 150 other women in slacks and shifts and miniskirts form a circle of dissent. Most are young, some visibly nervous. They are members of a newly assertive radical left group called Women's Liberation and they are gathered to protest "the degrading, mindless boob-girlie symbol" that is Miss America.

Quarantined by a double line of sawhorses and a squad of city police, the women hold their ground from midafternoon until the early morning hours. The line of march bristles with unsettling placards: "No More Beauty Standards—Everyone Is Beautiful!" "The Living Bra—The Dead Soldier!" "Girls Crowned—Boys Killed!" "Miss America Is Alive and Angry—in Harlem!" "I Am a Woman—Not a Toy, a Pet or Mascot!"

The protesters stage intermittent guerrilla theater—a raucus auction of a star-spangled, great-bosomed dummy to which four of the demonstrators have chained themselves; a solemn, ceremonious crowning of a live sheep as Miss America; the ritual discard into a "freedom trashcan" of assorted items of female oppression—padded bras, false eye-

PETER BABCOX reports on education for Time Magazine.

lashes, Playboy, women's magazines, steno pads. And there are songs of derision. To the tune of "Ain't She Sweet" for example:

Ain't she sweet?
Makin' profit off her meat.
Beauty sells, she's told,
So she's out pluggin' it.
Ain't she sweet? ...

"The soft white underbelly of the American beast was being socked in Atlantic City," explains Robin Morgan, a young radical poet and an organizer of the demonstration. "The Miss America Pageant was chosen as a target for a number of reasons. It has always been a lily-white racist contest; the winner tours Vietnam entertaining the troops as a murder mascot. The whole gimmick is one commercial shell game to sell the sponsors' products. Where else could one find such a perfect combination of American values? Racism, militarism and capitalism—all packaged in one 'ideal' symbol: a *woman!*"

Predictably, this political reasoning is lost on the boardwalk crowd, whose reactions to the radical women's protest range from perplexity to bemusement to uncontained fury. Throughout the afternoon and evening, the demonstrators draw shouted aspersions on their patriotism, moral quality and personal hygiene. One demonstrator, wandering from the cordoned area, narrowly misses being run down by a glowering, florid Texan behind the controls of an electric roll chair.

The columnist Harriet Van Horne angrily dismissed the demonstration's political intent. She imagined a band of ferocious feminists afflicted with a virulent case of neurotic frustration. "Those sturdy lasses in their sensible shoes . . . have been scarred and wounded by consorting with the wrong men [of dubious masculinity who wear frilly Edwardian clothes] . . . men who do not understand the way to a woman's heart—i.e., to make her feel utterly feminine, desirable and almost too delicate for this hard world." As for the "mindless boob-girlie symbolism," there may be a germ of truth in that, said Miss Van Horne, "but most of us would rather be some dear man's boob girl than nobody's *cum laude* scholar."

UNWITTINGLY, perhaps, Miss Van Horne illuminates the unnatural dichotomy over which increasing numbers of young women are forced to agonize. Says Bernadine Dohrn, the attractive and scholarly interorganizational secretary of Students for a Democratic Society: "In almost any woman you can unearth an incredible fury. It is often not even conscious, a threshold thing. But it's

there, and it's an anger that can be a powerful radicalizing force. To date, our movement has not really made room for the enormous political potential of women's repression."

In Miss Dohrn's view, woman's situation is uniquely revealing of a larger structure of human exploitation than the inequities of male-female roles that have preoccupied feminists from Emmeline Pankhurst to Betty Friedan. In a position paper on the matter, Miss Dohrn and Naomi Jaffe, a former student of Herbert Marcuse's at Brandeis, and currently a graduate student in sociology at The New School, admonish women to "come together, not in a defensive posture to rage against our exploited status vis-à-vis men, but rather in the process of developing our autonomy to expose the nature of American society in which all people are reified (manipulated as objects)."

THE crucial need, argue Dohrn and Jaffe, is to "demystify the myth of women," specifically by recognizing "the domestic imperialism of consumption which defines persons as consumers and cripples their development as free human beings. Women are the consummate products of this process, both the beneficiaries and the victims of the productivity made possible by advanced technology. The very innovations that offer us immediate freedom also force us into the service of an overall system of domination and repression. The more we realize ourselves through consumption, the greater the power of commodities to define and delimit us.

"The real needs of people are translated into a currency of possession, exclusivity and investment, a language of commodities where people are the goods. Both men and women are manipulated into functioning within these categories. But it is the uniquely visible conditions of women as primarily sexual creatures, as decorative, tempting, passive, pleasure-giving objects, that exposes the broader framework of social coercion.

"A strategy for the liberation of women, then, does not demand equal jobs, but meaningful, creative activity for all; not a larger share of power, but the abolition of commodity tyranny; not equal, reified sexual roles, but an end to sexual objectification and exploitation."

There is a quickening disposition among the young—as much a response to the works of Madison Avenue as to the works of the Pentagon—that the salvation of our culture is revolution. It is an amorphous, tumultous phenomenon, both a state of mind and an organized political force, called The Movement.

As it repudiates conventional political process and becomes ever more avowedly revolutionary, to cast one's fortunes with it requires an ever more complete and opprobrious break with the majority culture. Especially for women. Liberal analysts who may indulge some sneaking sympathy for the young male who invests his "misguided but laudable" moral energies in S.D.S., nevertheless tend to see similarly inclined women as incomprehensible freaks. The view is perhaps no more baldly stated than by the editor of the alumni magazine of one Ivy League college, an unremitting defender of his beleaguered institution. With mordant glee he recalls an anecdote about a student leader who is caught in a taut confrontation with his university administration and is frantically trying to compose a crucial manifesto. These urgent efforts are repeatedly confused, in spite of his earnest rebuffs, by a passionate coed who persists in stroking his thigh. "Many of these girls," declares the editor, "are attracted to The Movement because they think it's where the over-sexed guys are." This view—it might be classified as the Houri Theory of Political Behavior—is a splendid example of that durable cultural fantasy that feminine assertiveness — political, professional or sexual—is but a symptom of raging nymphomania or other grave psychic disorder.

In spite of this sort of onslaught—or perhaps because of it—greater and greater numbers of young women have found themselves drawn into the purposes and fortunes of The Movement. More than 30 per cent of those arrested in Columbia's occupied buildings last spring were women. Similarly, women were a highly visible element in the contention in Chicago's streets, accounting for one out of eight arrests.

Three who would make a revolution:

ROBIN MORGAN

THE letter is anonymous, typewritten. "Dear Ugly"

Says Robin Morgan, former child actress: "We will have a revolution in this society."

Josephine Duke, of THE Dukes. During the Columbia riots, she "reached the point of no return."

Susan Adelman, a cheerleader turned radical: "You can't be a political person part-time."

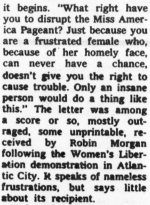

it begins. "What right have you to disrupt the Miss America Pageant? Just because you are a frustrated female who, because of her homely face, can never have a chance, doesn't give you the right to cause trouble. Only an insane person would do a thing like this." The letter was among a score or so, mostly outraged, some unprintable, received by Robin Morgan following the Women's Liberation demonstration in Atlantic City. It speaks of nameless frustrations, but says little about its recipient.

Ugly, Miss Morgan is not, and she is nothing if not self-possessed. She is also quite accustomed to public scrutiny. At 4, she was "Little Robin Morgan," hosting a weekly radio show on which she offered listeners precocious advice on life's everyday perplexities. There followed a stint on TV's "Juvenile Jury." At 7, Miss Morgan achieved minor stardom as the character Dagmar in the C.B.S. network program "I Remember Mama"—she played the role for seven years.

Now 27, Miss Morgan publishes poems of revolution. She writes:

I am pregnant with murder.
The pains are coming faster now.
And not all your anesthetics
Nor even my own screams can stop them.
My time has come.

As it happens, Miss Morgan is also pregnant with child. Her husband, Kenneth Pitchford, is a poet and leftist

writer; together they form a "two-member commune." Says Miss Morgan: "You have to keep the revolution going in your own life. Having children in The Movement is a tremendous act of affirmation. If you really believe in what you believe, having a child becomes all the more radicalizing, all the more reason to fight.

"It's a tactic of confrontation with your own honesty or hypocrisy. You see the kids trotting around at almost any Movement meeting now. You see them on picket lines, in the demonstrations. They're growing up in the middle of it. It's scary and it's very beautiful at the same time. Children are extremely sensitive to repression, and they're sensitive to freedom. They know. These kids growing up in The Movement face the greatest conflagration, but also the greatest possible hope. They may see the society that humankind has been dreaming about since the beginning."

Miss Morgan's vision of terrible beauty was arrived at through a familiar cycle of commitment and disillusionment with earlier and other causes. "My first approach to politics had been that of the artistic community. Most of the actors and artists I knew were fifties artists who had just barely survived the McCarthy years. They were either apolitical ivory-tower types or superficially political in the best liberal tradition. During the Death Valley days of the Eisenhower years when nothing was possible, nothing

imagined, about the most political act you could commit was participating in a benefit for the U.J.A."

A brief but embittering experience with the Democratic Reform movement was followed by involvement in civil rights. "I was a volunteer worker in the CORE office when Goodman, Chaney and Schwerner were murdered," recalls Miss Morgan. "The whites, who kind of dominated the organization then, were in a state of stunned disbelief, while the blacks almost seemed to shrug, as if to say: 'What did you expect?' You could see that a lot of whites were projecting a sense of guilt into the situation and were almost relieved that their black cause now had white martyrs. It was awful. I really think that that whole episode marked the beginning of the end for non-violence and the beginning of the blacks' rejection of whites in the civil-rights movement. It was a subtle change, but I pretty soon began to feel like a fifth wheel around the CORE office."

The Vietnam war gradually began to encompass moral consciousness, and to help define a new political consciousness. Late in 1966, Miss Morgan participated in Angry Arts Week, reading National Liberation Front poetry on flat-bed trucks around the city. Then she joined the mammoth April, 1967, peace march to the United Nations; in October, the march on the Pentagon; in November, the demonstration against Dean

Rusk at the New York Hilton; then the demonstration at the Whitehall induction center. Last April, she helped to swell the ranks at Columbia.

G RADUALLY dissent turned to opposition, opposition to insurgency. "On the U.N. march," says Miss Morgan, "I wore a conservative skirt to show that I was a member of the law-abiding but morally outraged middle class. And I remember I was uneasy about a group that carried an N.L.F. flag. Since the Pentagon, I never go into the streets without jeans and boots."

And she adds: "It used to be that you would build up to a demonstration for months. Then it was weeks, and now it's just another day in the life. Once, I was a pacifist. I had such a strong, self-righteous feeling then. Now, as each day goes by I get more scared. It's the kind of terror that comes of the realization that with each passing day I am a little more willing to fight and to die."

Miss Morgan and her husband had joined a Lower East Side artists' and writers' chapter of M.D.S.—the Movement for a Democratic Society. "The Pentagon was over, so where did we go now? We all sat around and talked and thought there must be something we could do as artists and writers. But there wasn't, and we were beginning to get a little disillusioned by what seemed to be a joylessness in The Movement, an overritualized ideological seriousness."

Then, early last year, Miss Morgan discovered the newly organized Yippie. "It blew our minds! I just walked into the Yippie office one day. There was this hysterical loft with the groovy posters and people sitting around rapping and coffee spilled on the floor, and whenever the phone would ring whoever picked it up would yell: 'Yippie!' It seemed life-affirming, myth-making, just beautiful! It was like the last gasp of the love generation, a real feeling of *communitas*."

It was as Yippies that Miss Morgan and her husband joined the fray at Columbia— the first action in which they had not marched as independents.

L AST summer, Miss Morgan's authentic inventive genius found roots in the Women's Liberation. "From the beginning," she says, "it was clear to me that The Movement didn't really make room for women. A lot of women came in expecting a radically new scene. Like, here was a group of young people with a new politics, a new life style, a new sexual honesty and freedom. And still, the notion of liberated woman was someone who is indiscriminate about whom she sleeps with, not a realization that women don't want to be objects. A lot of Movement women might just as well have gone to Scarsdale."

While most of the Yippies were engrossed in plans for Chicago, Miss Morgan was planning for Atlantic City. "The Miss America action hit the entertainment industry squarely. It ought to be clear by now that no American institution, whether political or cultural is safe from challenge by the radical left. The crazy kooks are everywhere. This may be the only political tactic short of sabotage and terrorism that is left to us now that the day of the mass march has passed. But humor is an extremely potent political tactic because it gives people a sudden and transforming insight into where they're at and where their society is at.

"We will have a revolution in this society," Miss Morgan continues. "It will be a very American revolution. Ours is a very American kind of movement — the tremendous ingenuity and energy, the peculiar kind of naiveté and idealism, the peculiar kind of conviction that our cause is just. Ours is the oldest kind of truly American patriotism."

Miss Morgan's child is due on July 4.

JOSEPHINE DUKE

AFTER Mark Rudd, who became something of a journalistic fetish during last spring's travail at Columbia, few young radicals have intrigued city desks more than Josephine Biddle Duke, 19, child of a celebrated family of old and immense fortune. Although Miss Duke has enjoyed the most correct, even cordial, relations with the press—she was briefly press secretary for Columbia S.D.S. last fall —she has steadfastly refused to let herself be written up on, as she put it, taken on "a personality trip that would transform me from a political person into some cardboard atrocity straight out of Hollywood."

Miss Duke's reluctance to discuss her family and her background is put in political terms, but personal reticence is hardly ill-founded. The Duke family has provided more than its share of titillating copy, and all the makings of an extravagant fable surround Josephine Duke's background— the horsy ambience of Long Island's North Shore, a lush winter enclave in southern Florida, exaggerated social rituals, famous company, the power and self-indulgence and cynicism of the hereditary rich.

WHATEVER the material sophistication of Josephine Duke's childhood, her exposure to political issues was negligible. Once, she recalls, she accompanied classmates on an uninteresting ritual peace march. Miss Duke's first exposure to any political issue that transcended the security of wealth and position was the Cuban missile crisis of 1962. The Everglades School, near Miami, where she was enrolled, was boarded up for the duration. "That was the first time politics was really presented to me," she says, "the politics of doom, the politics of making your peace."

Miss Duke entered Barnard College in the fall of 1967, never having heard of S.D.S. "But I was already very much into the social alienation of the New Left," she says. "I just didn't know where to send it." Inevitably, Columbia's radical movement attracted her.

S.D.S. meetings, during the early months of Miss Duke's freshman year at Barnard, were more concerned with the intricacies of dialectical analysis than with the logistics of confrontation. They seemed interminable, and at first Miss Duke found them incomprehensible. But S.D.S. had about it an aura of mission and a strong internal sense of community. She continued to attend meetings, trying to articulate a politics that would inform her deepening alienation.

That November she took part in a concrete political action—the mass turnout of New York radicals outside the New York Hilton to greet Secretary of State Rusk as he addressed the Foreign Policy Association on the irreversible logic of the Vietnam war. A few demonstrators brandishing spray cans of Day-glo

paint broke through police lines to inscribe mixed obscenities and gentle epithets on the limousines of arriving dignitaries. Other demonstrators, including Miss Duke, hurled bags of blood. Among the targets: the limousine of the State Department's former chief of protocol, Angier Biddle Duke, her uncle.

Miss Duke was among the demonstrators who were chased and clubbed by the police. "That evening was the first time I felt like an urban guerrilla," she says. "It was a sense of fear and excitement. I came into this movement through human action rather than as an intellectual leftist. It was definitely not the doctrines of Marx, Engels or Lenin that made me a radical."

THE Hilton demonstration contributed to Miss Duke's radical consciousness and galvanized her militancy. But it was not until the Columbia insurrection later in the spring that "I reached the point of no return." That was the experience that fully engaged her in the fortunes and perils of revolution.

Josephine Duke was among the original group of S.D.S.-led insurgents who occupied Hamilton Hall and later seized President Grayson Kirk's offices in Low Library, establishing there a commune. She regards the experience of the commune as a still-living presence in her life, an intimation of the concrete potential of revolution. "In many ways I still feel as if I were in Low," she says. "People who talk about it as if it were something past have dropped back. It was a high level of politics, a high level of crisis and a high level of community. I found I was able to articulate all the things I had been feeling and trying to think about before then." Miss Duke was among the 697 students arrested when the police cleared the occupied buildings.

By the time Columbia classes adjourned last spring, Miss Duke had been elected to the radicals' Strike Coordinating Committee. Over the summer, she joined a radical action project on the New York courts organized by the S.D.S.-run Summer Liberation School. In August, she took over press relations. Reporters who covered the reopening of Columbia last fall recall her self-possession and organization with professional respect. One

evening, S.D.S. staged a student march around the campus. As a television crew prepared to film the scene, students in the front ranks raised their hands in the familiar V that had been the emblem of student defiance only three months before. "Not V's!" barked Miss Duke, several ranks back, "Fists!" During the summer, national S.D.S. had adopted the clenched fist as the symbol of revolutionary militancy.

WITH the resumption of classes at Columbia, the radical movement at the university dropped into a continuing period of introspection. Miss Duke withdrew from Barnard "to give full time to the revolution," and invested her galvanic activism in yeoman service with the New York regional office of S.D.S. "Dropping out of Barnard was important, as perhaps a final break with what I was supposed to be," says Miss Duke. "In the classroom I was supposed to compete with other people for grades, just as in business people compete with one another for profits. This is a society that isolates people and makes them enemies. But The Movement is a liberating experience. We are people who understand our oppression together and become freer because we understand it."

Leaving Barnard was additionally significant in that it marked a personal commitment to the practical business of building for revolution. "Politics develops only when you get down to solid organizing," says Miss Duke. "I didn't really develop new organizing skills during the Columbia crisis. I had to find a new constituency; I could have gotten lost at Columbia."

The work of the regional office is almost wholly organizing. With the dozen or so radicals—mostly women—who run the operation, Miss Duke is involved in the continuing and often exhausting routine of liaison with the several college chapters in the area, organizing and staffing a coffeehouse for G.I.'s near Fort Dix, distributing leaflets and talking with G.I.'s at the Port Authority bus terminal on weekends, organizing radical groups in high schools. Shortly, Miss Duke will become a revolutionary traveler, visiting women's colleges in the Northeast.

IT is the confrontation, the

action, that turns Josephine Duke's radical stamina into revolutionary fervor. Since the Columbia bust, she has taken an aggressive and visible part in almost every major radical action. When New York police made a second violent sweep of the Columbia campus last spring, 10 days after the first, it was Miss Duke who led a counForge across the college quadrangle against a group of T.P.F. who had pursued students into a dormitory. Felled from behind by a hurtling fragment of paving tile, she picked herself up and continued the charge. The T.P.F. retreated.

When a superior force of police was dividing and driving a radical demonstration out of Rockefeller Plaza on election night, it was Miss Duke who marshalled their confused movements. When a combined force of New York area radicals invaded a polite evening discussion between N.Y.U. students and South Vietnam's Ambassador to the United Nations, enshrouding the man in a Nazi flag and dousing him with water, it was Miss Duke who planted herself squarely before his dripping excellency, wagged an admonitory finger at him and demanded: "Why don't you give up, little man? The F.L.N. is going to win!"

Inevitably, members of Josephine Duke's family view her unremitting radicalism with uneasiness. "What happens," she is asked, "when you have to start being responsible?" Says Miss Duke: "I guess responsible means going back to school or coming home or getting married. But to me, responsibility means enlarging my own education, to read and act and develop my political consciousness. That is the only way to become free. But everybody has to discover that in his own life. I know that as long as I fight, things are getting better, anyway. I don't know when revolution will come, maybe not in my lifetime. I only know there is no time for fence-sitting. I think about tomorrow and the next day, but I don't think about the future the way the man on the street or the girls in my class at Barnard think about it. I think of the future only in terms of my being with The Movement. I change as The Movement changes."

SUSAN ADELMAN

"THIS radicalism is a passing fancy for most of these girls," asserts one Barnard College instructor. "In 10 years they'll have fond memories of life on the barricades as they tuck in their kids up in Scarsdale or someplace like that, and get ready to go down and meet their guests."

Replies Susan Adelman, 23, a member of Liberation News Service, the collectively run radical media project: "Movement people have always been able to reject that kind of life and all it stands for. But until recently there were no concrete alternative lives in which people could be comfortable."

Liberation News Service is one of the few functional life alternatives, or counter institutions, that The Movement has produced. The two, well-produced, weekly packets of political news and radical analysis that L.N.S. mails to nearly 300 subscribers are a principal pillar of the U.S. underground press. For the collective's 15 members it is an alternately exuberant and exhausting act of insurgency. Says Miss Adelman: "The act of collective decision-making, critique of our work, nightly communal dinner, the sharing of all the crud work —typing and purchasing and mailing and billing and stuffing the packets in the envelopes at 3 A.M.—all of it is important.

"I had felt confused about my place in The Movement. But I don't feel that way now. I've come to feel competent for the first time — even though I have never thought of myself as incompetent. It's just that now I have a sense of ease in what I'm doing and feel so much a part of it. It's a competence that comes out of political consciousness."

Miss Adelman's radical odyssey began at Berkeley, where she arrived as a freshman in 1964 just as the Free Speech movement was in full cry. The only child of a successful, self-made entrepreneur, she had grown up in the tense and cloying atmosphere of Beverly Hills. "It was a strange place," she recalls. "There are either people who like what they are and want more of what they already have, or people who really dislike what they are—a place with a lot of anti-Semitic Jews. Among the kids you weren't accepted unless you were pretty and thin and rich." Miss Adelman was a high-school cheerleader and editor of the school yearbook. But she had already developed an incipient political consciousness as a dedicated peace marcher. "I thought peace marches were groovy," she says, "but by the time I left for Berkeley it was pretty clear that peace wasn't coming by itself."

Initially, she found the ferocity of Berkeley's Free Speech movement overwhelming. "It was exploding all over the place and I was really terrified! There were all these radicals running around screaming about free speech. I really didn't know what to do. I sort of wanted to join the sit-in because I thought they were probably right. But I had never done anything like that and I just couldn't bring myself to do it. I did go on strike along with about 85 per cent of the student body, so I didn't even go to classes for the first six weeks of my college career."

Miss Adelman continued to regard Berkeley's fractionated radical movement with some circumspection during her first two years, finding it somewhat exclusivist and condescending. In her sophomore year, her principal political activity was a group called Americans for Reappraisal of Far Eastern Policy. "It must have been a C.I.A. front, with a name like that. I crack up everytime I think of it," she says. "We used to do things like put ads in the paper demanding a review of U.S. China policy."

AFTER Miss Adelman's second year at Berkeley she spent a year in France. "Supposedly, I was there to study. It was like a junior year abroad. I had a room with a French family, and they were awful, disgusting, horrible! They were a dreadful caricature of the U.S. middle-class family and subtly anti-Semitic as well. I did learn to speak French fluently, though."

She also came to see American involvement in Vietnam through unsympathetic French eyes, and returned home in the summer of 1967 "really on fire."

"I guess I felt sort of guilty for having spent a year sitting around in Left Bank cafés when I should have been here doing things." She immediately joined a Vietnam summer project in Los Angeles and spent the remainder of the summer handing out draft-resistance leaflets to inductees.

RETURNING to Berkeley in September, 1967, for her junior year, Miss Adelman was shorty embroiled in political contention. She helped to organize the spectacular Stop the Draft movement. "We demonstrated around the Oakland induction center. For three days up to 10,000 demonstrators milled through city streets confounding police efforts to contain them." Miss Adelman remembers the experience as a crucial one in her own radicalization.

"The Oakland demonstrations were important to me," she says, "mostly because of the way people were relating to each other in the streets. I had been in demonstrations before, and I had seen people get their heads wacked before. But I had never seen all kinds of people doing something in a spontaneous, yet effective, way, just because it was meaningful and necessary."

It wasn't like a Pauline conversion to radicalism, "but a cumulative awareness that I wasn't going anywhere politically or academically—that you just couldn't be a political person on a part-time basis."

A little more than a semester short of her degree, Miss Adelman withdrew from the University of California. For the next six months, she scuttled back and forth across the continent, attending radical retreats and S.D.S. conventions. After a short, distressing stint as an S.D.S. traveling organizer in the State of Washington, she was contemplating a return to college. Last June she arrived in New York to enroll in The New School. She found herself instead involved in an intricate schism within the Liberation News Service. She was among the truckload of L.N.S. insurgents who participated in a predawn raid on the Massachusetts farm of L.N.S. founder Marshall Bloom in an effort to retrieve a printing press and several thousand dollars expropriated from the New York offices.

Miss Adelman went to Atlantic City in August both to participate in the Women's Liberation demonstration and to cover it for L.N.S. An inactive member of Women's Liberation, she remains uneasy lest a radical feminist movement should become preoccupied with the discomforts of male chauvinism and neglect the larger imperatives of revolutionary politics.

392

Bernardine Dohrn, interorganizational secretary of S.D.S., says: "In almost any woman you can unearth an incredible fury."

"There is no women's liberation without men's liberation," she says. But Miss Adelman does concede that "women are more sensitive to repression than men because for them it's a 24-hour-a-day thing. Women have become an important force for the survival of The Movement, because the more women make men aware of their own repression the stronger they'll be together. Radical politics is getting to be less and less a male thing anyway. In confrontations, cops don't pick out only guys anymore. Chicago demonstrated that. The policeman's club can be a remarkably equalizing instrument."

DESPITE the explicit concern of Marx and Lenin and subsequent analysts of the left with women as an op-

pressed class, and the emergence of extraordinary women like Rosa Luxemburg, large segments of The Movement have been afflicted with a curious ambivalence toward woman's role. Until recently a woman who attempted to assert herself politically or personally within The Movement was likely to run head-on into a virulent male chauvinism. Typical was the experience of Naomi Jaffe and three other Movement women of acknowledged analytical gifts who, on the eve of the police action at Columbia last spring, were struggling to complete a theoretical statement affirming the insurgents' position. Into their deliberation marched a male member of the Strike Coordinating Committee demanding "a chick to do some typing."

The most obtrusive example of woman's travail within The Movement itself has been the underground press's treatment of her—it could be characterized as unglazed Hugh Hefner. So crude has this morbid journalistic voyeurism become that Tom Hayden, the young doyen of the radical left, recently filed an angry protest with The Berkeley Barb, a prime offender. The Movement press, said Hayden, "seems to suppose that whatever is taboo in America should be celebrated by radicals. But there is such a thing as sexual decadence which should be uninteresting while not being taboo to radicals. The Barb represents a hip version of the morality of the dirty old man, rather than exploring real alternatives to America's sexual neurosis. . . .The question cannot be postponed until 'after the revolution,' because revolution is not possible without sharp personal breaks with

bourgeois patterns of life, especially with America's repressive and property-oriented male-female relationships."

Against the wantonness of The Movement's male chauvinism—greatly enhanced by the *machismo* mystique that inevitably flowed from the Columbia and Chicago confrontations, it was surely a revolutionary commitment that S.D.S. undertook at its recent national council meeting in Ann Arbor. There, less than two years after another national council had laughed a proposal on woman's role out of the convention, the assembled delegates proceeded to acknowledge both the existence of male supremacy within The Movement and the possibility that a socialist revolution could take place that might still leave woman relegated to a secondary position. In a major resolution, handily passed, the delegates affirmed that "the liberation of women must become a conscious part of our struggle for all peoples' liberation." Although the exploitation of the working class was still the fundamental contradiction of capitalist society, noted S.D.S., women's repression might well be the most sharply delineated, most immediate struggle, "the concretization of the struggle for the liberation of all people from oppression."

Thus, resolved S.D.S., The Movement must now begin a major drive toward the radicalization and liberation of women. Concrete action may include campus campaigns to force equal pay scales for male and female university employes, organized demonstrations against such institutions as beauty schools and secretarial schools which feed

women into routinized service roles, and a challenge to college counseling programs for women.

"WOMEN bring to The Movement the ultimate revolutionary test," maintains Robin Morgan. "Sooner or later we are going to have a revolution because we must. But it has got to take place in a way that has never happened before—not just politically and economically, but in a cultural and even biological sense as well. The role of women is absolutely crucial to these new dimensions of revolution and liberation. In a male-dominated society like ours, women are exploited principally through their sex roles. Yet sex roles are the most basic, concrete roles through which human beings relate to one another, as well as perpetuate the race. These roles have now got to be freed from oppression and gotten straight, because if we don't make peace with one another as human beings pretty soon — well, that's the end of life on this planet."

What might then be called the politicization of libido, to which Miss Morgan refers, has been assigned a concrete function by A. S. Braverman, a physician at Columbia's College of Physicians and Surgeons. "If the political and sexual revolutions do come to be inextricably bound," he suggests, "then we may hope that the political revolution will save the sexual revolution from becoming frivolous, decadent and useless to the concrete advancement of human needs. On the other hand, it is the sexual revolution that can save the political revolution from becoming centralized, despotic, repressive communism." ■

WOMEN'S GROUPS PRESSING REFORMS

Approve Proposals in Drive to Improve Status

By LINDA GREENHOUSE

The Congress to Unite Women, a new national coalition of women's rights groups, called yesterday for a wide-ranging series of reforms that included free 24-hour child care centers, women's study programs in colleges, employment equality for women, repeal of abortion laws and an equal-rights amendment to the Constitution.

The proposals were presented at a news conference called to discuss the congress's first Northeastern regional meeting, which was held here last weekend and which was closed to the press.

Five hundred women, including representatives of 25 chapters of 15 different organizations from Massachusetts to Maryland, attended the three-day convention at Intermediate School 70, at 333 West 17th Street.

The organizations included the National Organization for Women and the Women's Liberation Movement; two of the best known women's rights groups, as well as professional and political groups and Witch (Women's International Terrorist Conspiracy from Hell).

Regional meetings of the Congress were held earlier this fall in San Francisco and Chicago.

The proposals grew out of 12 discussion workshops, which formed one day's program at the convention. There were workshops on education, employment, the "feminine image," the sex-role system, "how women are divided," and political power.

Among the proposals, which were adopted on Sunday by the convention, were: deduction of child-care expenses from taxable income until free child-care centers are established; legal steps to open trade schools and unions to women; and withholding of support from politicians who oppose women's rights.

The convention set up a continuing committee to make specific recommendations for implimenting the proposals. It will have its first meeting Dec. 14.

By vote of the convention, the spokeswoman at yesterday's news conference, a young woman in her mid 20's who was wearing a purple knit dress, remained anonymous.

She read a prepared statement, which said, "The Congress to Unite Women is committed to the liberation of all women now. We know that only with power can we end the oppression of women. Together, in a united congress, we will ight or what is good for women."

The news conerence was held in the apartment of one of the participants in the Congress.

November 25, 1969

Women March Down Fifth in Equality Drive

The New York Times (by William E. Sauro)

Demonstrators fill Fifth Avenue from curb to curb. The view is to the north from between 50th and 51st Streets.

By LINDA CHARLTON

Celebrating the 50th anniversary of the day women won the right to vote—and the start of a new crusade for equality — a crowd of more than 10,000 people, mostly women of all ages, occupations and viewpoints, marched down Fifth Avenue last night to a rally in Bryant Park.

The march got under way at 6:05 P.M. from the designated rallying point at 59th Street and Fifth Avenue, but it was 7 P.M. before the last of them set off for the rally, scheduled to start at 7:30 P.M.

Although the police department had officially given the marchers the use of only one lane of the avenue, they overflowed the barricades almost immediately, causing a continuing traffic tie-up in the blocked cross-streets that filled the air with blaring horns.

The march was augmented as it moved, slowly because of the traffic ahead, and the marchers called, "Come join us, sisters," to women on the sidewalks.

Because of the disorganization, the first group in the march carried a banner that read, "Free Abortion on Demand — Women's Liberation Supporters of the Socialist Workers Party Candidates." But the marchers included both suffragettes who are veterans of the movement to win the right to vote and leaders of the new movement, such as Mrs. Betty Friedan, founder of the National Organization for Women.

One group, the New York Feminists got started after one of them called: "Are we as together as we're going to be?" Others included the Emma Goldman Brigade, lesbian groups and some whose placards gave no immediate clue to any ideology, such as those reading: "I Love You, Susan B. Anthony," and "Liberte, Egalite, Sororite."

One of the marchers was Mrs. Elsie K. Belmont, 79 years old, who said: "I marched when I was 16. They used to call us suffrage-cats. It always does my heart good to see a few people thinking—thinking."

The women ranged in age from a group that called themselves "H.S. Woman Unite" and seemed of high-school age to Older Women's Liberation, and their occupations included secretaries, housewives, lawyers and typists. Three who marched together, were a grandmother, a daughter and her daughter, Mrs. Ionella Church, 70, her daughter, Mrs. Veronica Bock, 48, and her daughter, Mrs. Veronica Caruso, 23.

There were indications of hostility from the spectators, who were predominantly male. At 45th Street one man appeared wearing a brassiere; opposite St. Patrick's Cathedral, at 50th Street, there were jeers of "Bra-less traitors!"

The day, conceived as Women's Strike for Equality, was given official recognition at the local, state and national level, with Mayor Lindsay, Governor Rockefeller and President Nixon all issuing proclamations endorsing its significance.

In New York, as elsewhere in the country, the impact of the day of demonstrations beyond those already involved or interested in the women's liberation movement appeared to be minimal. Mrs. Friedan said repeatedly that she was not disheartened:

"The whole thing to me is just so tremendously moving that it isn't simply a numbers game," she said at the City Hall rally. "I palpably feel that women's consciousness is changing and it's irrelevant to me whether 500 or 5,000 women turn out. This is already a

huge success because the women's movement is going to be the biggest movement for social and political change in the nineteen-seventies."

The city's businesses reported no unusual absenteeism, and the retail stores also noted no adverse effect on business. The president of Bonwit Teller said that there had been no great absenteeism among employes, and reported "our best [shopping] traffic" in 10 days.

In other large cities, the business communities indicated the same lack of absenteeism. But most large cities, and several smaller ones, did have a demonstration.

About 5,000 women gathered on Boston Common for a rally and 1,000 went on to march through downtown Boston. The groups represented included a contingent dressed in academic gowns carried a banner pointing out that "Veritas is a Feminine Noun." "Veritas," the Latin word for truth, is the motto of Harvard University.

Karate in Philadelphia

A noon rally drew 2,000 people in San Francisco's Union Square. In Miami, women staged a "mock coffee-cup-breaking garden party." About 125 women marched on City Hall in Syracuse, N. Y., and in Manhasset, L. I., women gathered signatures on a petition urging Senate passage of the Equal Rights Amendment.

Leaflets were distributed in Denver, and Philadelphia's Rittenhouse Square was the site of a demonstration that included karate exhibitions. In Seattle about 150 women participated in an open house in the Mayor's office.

Los Angeles marked the day with several demonstrations—including two by women's groups opposing the women's liberation movement—a motorcade, and an evening rally. About 1,000 people, most of them men, gathered for a noon rally in Center Square in Baltimore, and a 13-hour conference on women's rights was held under the sponsorship of a coalition of women's groups in Pittsburgh.

Although the march and rally were, as planned, the climactic events of the day in New York, there were activities scattered around the city included:

10 A.M.—A dozen women showed up for a ceremony to "consecrate" a site at Duffy Square on Broadway from 46th to 47th Street, for a statue of Susan B. Anthony, the "mother of the movement."

The ceremony was presided over by Ms. Mary Orovan, dressed in cassock and surplice as a "symbolic priest." As she made the sign of the cross, she

intoned: "In the name of the Mother, the Daughter and the Holy Granddaughter. Ah-women. Ah-women."

"Ms." is used by women who object to the distinction between "Miss" and "Mrs." to denote marital status."

10:45 A.M.—In the strike-coalition headquarters, a dusty second floor at 229 Lexington Avenue, formerly the Murray Hill Democratic Club, a half dozen women answered telephones, coaxed a reluctant mimeograph machine and answered questions. Outside, two women pasted handbills onto a white station wagon-sound-truck.

NOON—In City Hall Park, about 35 children played, napped and ate on the grass under the care of their mothers in an area designated as a "demonstration day-care center," the need for which was the central issue of the rally planned for the park. The number of police—male and female—around City Hall indicated that a large, and aggressive, turnout was expected.

One woman, Lucy Komisar, a vice president of NOW, attempted to enter the day-care area without the necessary special identification. Miss Komisar, dressed in a white-and-purple flowered pants suit, was stopped by a policewoman and escorted away, under protest. The matter was adjudicated by Barry H. Gotteherer, an assistant to the Mayor, and Miss Komisar was released.

"She's a lady, let her go," said the policeman who was with Miss Komisar.

"I'm sure you're not a gentleman," said Miss Komisar to the policeman. She said later that the incident was "the most outrageous way I've ever been treated." Miss Komisar was ejected from McSorley's Old Ale House on Aug. 10 when she became involved in a dispute there shortly after all places of public accomodation were ordered by the city to serve women.

By 12:30, a crowd of 1,500 people — as many, if not more, men than women, and an apparent mixture of the already converted and the lunch-hour curious — had gathered to hear the speakers who battled with erratic sound equipment. Some of the crowd carried placards, such as one reading: "Repent, Male Chauvinists, Your World is Coming to an End" and "Don't Cook Dinner Tonight—Starve a Rat Today."

The speakers included Gloria Steinem, the writer and feminist; Mrs. Bess Myerson Grant, the city's Commissioner of Consumer Affairs; Mrs. Eleanor Holmes Norton, chairman of the city Commission on Human

The New York Times (by Neal Boenzi)

Rights; Mrs. Bella Abzug, the Democratic Congressional candidate, and Mrs. Friedan. Deputy Mayor Richard R. Aurelio read the Mayor's proclamation of Equality for Women Day.

Mrs. Abzug, whose vigorous tones overcome the lapses in the sound system, drew the most enthusiastic response from the crowd with her finger-jabbing calls for the implementation of the strike's three principal demands—free abortion on demand, the establishment of community-controlled, 24-hour day-care centers for the children of working mothers, and equality of educational and employment opportunity—". . . and we mean to have it now!"

Mrs. Norton stressed that her mandate to prevent job discrimination "is an empty mandate unless the women have a place to leave their children."

Until after 2 P.M., small groups of spectators, almost all men, lingered to engage in "dialogues" with women of the movement.

"Women seeking this kind of equality are really seeking to free men," said a woman who refused to give her name but said she was "almost 50" and had grown children. "To enslave men," murmured one of her male listeners.

"Are you against alimony?" called another man to a young woman wearing a woman's equality button. "Abolish alimony and I'm with you."

Harry Nischanim, 71, tried to explain that he was against women working because when both husband and wife work, "they're both tired and there's no love in the house."

"If I were your wife, I'd want to work so you wouldn't be so tired," said his young debating opponent, but Mr. Nischanim just shook his head.

At the Interchurch Center, 475 Riverside Drive, an "ad hoc women's group" sponsored a noon meeting attended by about 150 persons, mostly women. Miss Theressa Hoover, associate general secretary of the board of missions of the United Methodist Church, said that the winning of equal rights for women would be a "bulldozing process that will have to go on for the rest of our lives."

2 P.M.—The second-floor office of Thomas Lenane, the Acting City Clerk, was invaded by about 20 women, who presented Mr. Lenane with a pamphlet, "You and Your Marriage," that they suggested he distribute with marriage licenses.

The pamplet, prepared in paste-up form by the Marriage and Family Committee of the National Organization for Women, was a 19-page series of explanations of the law as it applies to marriage.

One of the group, Mrs. Mavra DeRise, 28, of the Canarsie section in Brooklyn, said she was not against marriage. The purpose of the pamphlet, she said, was to "warn people about what they're getting into."

Feminist Philosopher

Katharine Murray Millett

By FRANK J. PRIAL

The principal theoretician of the women's liberation movement is a 35-year-old former Barnard instructor who lives in a Bowery loft. She swears, one friend says, "like a gunnery sergeant," and stands to make $100,000 from a book on how tough it is to be a woman.

Woman in the News

Kate Millett's first book, "Sexual Politics," was conceived as a doctoral thesis and did, in fact, earn her Ph.D., with distinction, from Columbia University. It also made her a current heroine of the world of instant culture, with the attendant book-introduction parties, television and radio interviews and meetings with foreign journalists.

It has also turned her into something of a high priestess of the current feminist wave, a movement long on gimmicry but short on philosophy until Miss Millett appeared on the scene.

Briefly, Miss Millett's thesis is this: The relationship between men and women is political, much the same as the relationship between blacks and whites, has been found to be political, with the dominant group, men, dominating the subordinate women, and denying to them any means of redress.

Developed Traits

While male-female (or sex) differences are evident at birth, Miss Millett argues, masculine-feminine (or gender) differences come later and are, in fact, imposed by society—a male-dominated society.

"Psychosexually," she writes, "there is no differentiation between the sexes at birth. Psychosexual personality is therefore postnatal and learned."

Psychosexual personality means aggressiveness for men and passivity for women, Miss Millett believes.

She, herself, is hardly passive. Starting her book in February, 1969, she wrote and researched for eight months, often working 18 hours a day. "It usually takes

A new high priestess of feminist wave.

five years to bring out a book that started as an academic thesis," said Mrs. Betty Prashker, Miss Millett's editor at Doubleday & Co.

Katherine Murray Millett was born on Sept. 14, 1934, into an unhappy, middle-class Irish family in St. Paul, Minn. Her parents separated when she was 14 and her mother, a college graduate, went to work selling insurance to support herself and her three daughters.

After a series of clashes in the local parochial schools over her rapidly dwindling belief in Roman Catholic doctrine, Miss Millett entered the nearby University of Minnesota and graduated as a member of Phi Beta Kappa in 1956. Moving to Oxford University, she took high honors in English literature, specializing in the Victorian period.

Back home, she taught English and took up sculpting. In 1961, she moved to Japan. There she met her husband, sculptor Fumio Yoshimura. No advocate of the family unit—she calls it "patriarchy's chief institution"—Miss Millett notes that her marriage was a matter of expedience, not choice. It enabled Mr. Yoshi-

mura, whom she prefers to call a "friend" rather than a husband, to remain in this country.

As a serious woman radical, Miss Millett eschews not only her husband's name, but the titles Miss and Mrs., both terms of subjugation to feminists. Nor does she bother with the Dr. to which her Ph.D. entitles her.

Miss Millett (her name rhymes with "will it," not with Villette), actually came late to the feminist movement. She attended a series of lectures on the movement in 1965 and then became an officer in a chapter of NOW, the National Organization for Women, founded by Betty Freidan.

But, said Mrs. Prashker at Doubleday, "Kate was not nearly as much into the women's lib thing when she started the book." Now she is a member of or gives support to a wide range of radical women's groups, working almost as hard as an activist as she did last year behind the typewriter.

"In a sense," said one associate, "'Sexual Politics' has had as much influence on its author as it appears to be having on its readers."

Second Book Planned

And those readers are growing in number. Some 22,000 copies have been sold, so far, 10,000 of them in the last two weeks. The paperback rights were sold, according to one report, for around $75,000.

There is another book in the offing. "We're talking about an autobiography," said Mrs. Prashker, "but it's only in the talking stage. One thing, though, it won't be anything academic like the first book."

One of Miss Millett's best fans is her mother, Mrs. Helen Millett, who still lives in St. Paul. She found no time to participate in the Women's Strike for Equality yesterday. "I was too busy watching Kate on television and answering the telephone," she said happily.

Mrs. Millett said she was pleased to see her daughter explaining the feminist movement on television "because so many weird people have been coming on representing the movement."

The Best Feminist Book So Far

By CHRISTOPHER LEHMANN-HAUPT

THE FEMALE EUNUCH. By Germaine Greer. 349 pages. McGraw-Hill. $6.95.

Yes, another woman's-liberation book—this time from a 31-year-old Australian who seems to have grabbed up all the academic honors as she breezed through Melbourne University, Sydney University and Newnham College, Cambridge; who now lives in England, where she teaches, writes and appears on television; and who can't exactly be accommodated to the argument that feminists are dogs, Marty (in case you ever have the urge to argue that). And judging from her table of contents (BODY: Gender, Bones, Curves, Hair, Sex, The Wicked Womb, etc.) and the footnotes at the back of the book (S. Freud, N. Mailer, L. Tiger, etc.), we are in for the now-familiar litany. Male chauvinist

Paul Sanders
Germaine Greer

vampires! Charles Revson oppresses women! Freedom to die in Vietnam Now!

Well, the litany of woman's degradation is here all right, but what's this? Hardly has Miss Greer gotten under way when she starts chipping at a cornerstone of the movement: Masters and Johnson and the clitoral orgasm.

"Many women who greeted the conclusions of Masters and Johnson with cries of 'I told you so!' and 'I am normal!' will feel that this criticism is a betrayal. They have discovered sexual pleasure after being denied it but the fact that they have only ever experienced gratification from clitoral stimulation is evidence for my case, because it is the index of the desexualization of the whole body, the substitution of genitality for sexuality. The ideal marriage as measured by the electronic equipment in the Reproduction Biology Research Foundation laboratories is enfeebled—dull sex for dull people. The sexual personality is basically antiauthoritarian. If the system wishes to enforce complete suggestibility in its subjects, it will have to tame sex. Masters and Johnson supplied the blueprint for standard, low-agitation, cool-out monogamy. If women are to avoid this last reduction of their humanity, they must hold out not just for orgasm but for ecstasy."

And here is Miss Greer on some of the sister movements: Betty Friedan "represents the cream of American middle-class womanhood, and what she wants for them is equality of opportunity within the status quo, free admission to the world of the ulcer and the coronary." Evelyn Reed's pamphlet "Problems of Women's Liberation: A Marxist Approach" (1969) contains arguments "couched in typical Marxist

doctrinaire terminology, buttressed by phony anthropology and poor scholarship. The cover features a reproduction of a figure on an Attic vase, misidentified as a 'goddess symbol of the matriarchy' when it is actually a graceful Bacchante with thyrsus and dead wildcat . . . the symbol of hippiedom and drug culture."

On violence: ". . . learning to protect oneself is not such a difficult matter, for weapons are easy enough to acquire and karate lessons are included in the syllabus of debutantes' finishing schools: the difficulty is to render physical violence irrelevant, which is the only hope of any human being, but none of the feminist groups has so far emerged with a strategy."

One could go on, if space permitted.

One can argue with certain points too. In throwing out all psychoanalytic theory because of Freud's misunderstanding of women, hasn't Miss Greer deprived herself and the movement of a tool for understanding masculine hatred and fear of the vagina? Of a device for raising male consciousness? And how is one to reconcile her attack on the various forms of contraception with the statement she makes elsewhere while arguing against marriage that "contraception is very possible"?

And while I sympathize with her apparent longing for the feudal "stem family" (in which "the head was the oldest male parent, who ruled a number of sons and their wives and children) as opposed to the modern "nuclear family," I am not convinced that communal child-rearing produces the same results or better ones. And finally, the argument that Miss Greer anticipates from her sisters on the left: can a revolution of consciousness—to be brought about by women ceasing to marry and ceasing to be the major consumers of capitalist products—really change the system? Might this not be the same chimera as Charles Reich's Consciousness III?

But never mind: most of these points seem like chips on the mainstream of Miss Greer's argument, which is that it is history and civilization, not a conspiracy of male egos, that have created the nightmare from which women are trying to awake. "The first significant discovery we shall make as we rocket along our female road to freedom is that men are not free, and they will seek to make this an argument why nobody should be free. We can only reply that slaves enslave their masters, and by securing our own manumission we may show men the way that they could follow. . . ."

I only wish that the timing of the publication of this book had been such that it could have caught the lightning that struck "Sexual Politics," for it is everything that Kate Millett's book is not—lively, spontaneous, witty, well-organized without being rigid, comfortable with scholarship, personal when biases need explaining, assertive when the evidence is clear—a book with personality, a book that knows the distinction between the self and the other, a book that combines the best of masculinity and femininity.

April 20, 1971.

Goals Set by Women's Political Caucus

Special to The New York Times

WASHINGTON, July 12—The Women's National Political Caucus, a new organization dedicated to increasing the political power of women, announced today the guidelines it will use in deciding what candidates it will support for public office.

The guidelines emphasize "the elimination of sexism, racism, violence and poverty." They also call for an immediate withdrawal from Vietnam.

The multipartisan organization, formed here this weekend, also announced the election of a 21-member policy council, which will direct the group until a permanent structure is worked out.

Well-Known Names

The council contains some of the best-known names in the feminist movement, including Representative Bella S. Abzug of Manhattan and Representative Shirley Chisholm of Brooklyn, both Democrats; Betty Friedan, the founder of the National Organization for Women, and Gloria Steinem, the writer.

Of the 21-member council, seven members are black and one is Indian. Eleven are Democrats, two are Republicans, and the rest either have no political affiliation or do not state it.

Only one of the members is under 30 years of age. Four new members will be named to the council later to expand the representation of young women and of a group that is not represented at all among the 21—women of Hispanic extraction.

The decision to add more young women to the policy council was made yesterday after a group of radical young women protested the age distribution on the council.

Radicals Doubtful

Paula Page, a representative of the National Student Association, who is the only under-30 member of the council, said today that she did not yet know whether the radical young women that she represents would decide to remain a part of the caucus. The group is skeptical about the basic aim of the caucus, which is to increase the representation and influence of women

WOMEN'S POLITICAL GOALS DECLARED: National caucus group at news conference in Washington yesterday. Seated, from left: Gloria Steinem, author, Representative Shirley Chisholm, Brooklyn Democrat, and Betty Friedan, National Organization for Women founder. Standing is Representative Bella S. Abzug, Manhattan Democrat.

in existing political institutions.

Mrs. Abzug declared at a news conference that "a new political force was born."

Mrs. Chisholm said that the members of the caucus realized that "no one gives away political power."

"It must be taken," she said, "and we will take it."

Mrs. Chisholm, who is black, said that she had long believed that "if women and minorities ever got together on issues and on their own tragic underrepresentation in the places of power that this country would never be the same. I believe we have taken a step in that direction."

'Now We Are United'

She continued: "We understand the problem of overcoming the false standards that have been used to divide us for so long—race, age, political party, economic class and even physical duty. But we are all second class, and now we are united."

The caucus, which intends to organize groups in every state, will aim at the election of women and also of men "who declare themselves ready to fight for the needs and rights of women and all under-represented groups."

The group decided that, in general, it did not wish to impose rigid requirements that candidates commit themselves to specific issues to receive the support of the caucus. There was one exception to this general rule: an absolute prohibition of support for any candidate, male or female, who held or advocated racist views.

On other issues, the caucus merely adopted "guidelines" while "recognizing that candidates must shape their platforms to meet the needs of their constituencies."

A number of the guidelines involved issues with immediate and direct impact on women. Among these were the passage of the proposed equal rights amendment of the Constitution.

which would wipe out legal discrimination on the basis of sex; repeal of laws "that affect a woman's right to decide her own reproductive and sexual life", elimination of tax inequities that affect women, mainly the higher rates for single persons, and expansion of the Federal antidiscrimination laws and the powers of the Equal Employment Opportunity Commission.

Other guidelines involved advocacy of "an immediate withdrawal from the war in Indochina, but, more than that, an end to the use of physical violence as an acceptable way of resolving conflict"; advocacy of adequate housing and medical care for all Americans, and an end to the use of repressive measures against individuals advocating social change.

Members of the policy council, in addition to those mentioned, are the following:

Shana Alexander, editor in chief, McCall's magazine.

Virginia Allen, chairwoman, President Nixon's Task Force on Women's Rights and Responsibilities.

Nikki Beare, president, Dade County (Fla.) National Organization for Women.

Joan Cashin, National Democratic party of Alabama.

Mary Clarke, California Women's Strike for Peace.

Myrlie Evers, California civil rights leader.

JoAnne Evans Gardner, Republican nominee for the Pittsburgh City Council.

Elinor Guggenheimer, chairwoman, New York City Democratic Advisory Council.

Fannie Lou Hamer, candidate for Mississippi State Senate.

La Donna Harris, Indian rights leader.

Wilma Scott Heide, chairman, board of directors, National Organization for Women.

Dorothy Height, president, National Council of Negro Women.

Olga Madar, vice president, United Automobile Workers.

Vivian Carter Mason, second national president, National Council of Negro Women.

Midge Miller, Wisconsin State Representative.

Beulah Sanders, vice president, National Welfare Rights Organization.

July 13, 1971

Man's World, Woman's Place

A Study in Social Mythology.
By Elizabeth Janeway.
319 pp. New York:
William Morrow & Co. $8.95.

By MARGARET MEAD

This is a lucid and fascinating book, a book that draws so skillfully on the best of our fragmented social science, that, as a social scientist, it gives me renewed faith that we may in time, produce an integrated understanding of the world. With her disciplined and perceptive mind, and high standards of craftsmanship, the novelist and critic, Elizabeth Janeway, set out—in those long lost days of the early 1960's—to explore the problem of why we were continuing to live with the myth that woman's place is in the home. The myth, though patently untrue in many ways, forms the basis of most private attitudes and public discussions.

Mrs. Janeway went back into medieval history, to the bustling life of the big manors and the terrible conditions of the poor, and came out with the belief that the particular form that the myth of male and female differences takes today, although it is as old as the Chinese concepts of yang and yin, is a product of the rise of the Victorian middle class. Before that time, women were part of the world in many ways. Only Victorianism and modern suburbia have been able to put women in homes, with only one other adult and small children, completely cut off from the rest of the world.

With an unerring instinct she has drawn on the best of modern social science—some of it rather hard for the layman to find, some part of the whole climate of opinion of the 1960's: Erik Erikson, Robert Jay Lifton, Talcott Parsons, Kenneth Keniston, David Reisman, David McClelland, Bruno Bettelheim, Philippe Aries and the rarer and less known work of Margaret Field on witchcraft and depressions, of Mircea Eliade on myth, of Masters as well as Kinsey. Without partisanship, without jargon, in a pleasant, slightly ironic, lively way, she has woven their theories together, stopping now and then to find the myth of inalienable female difference surfacing at the very heart of social science itself.

As I read, I was not only delighted, but also reminded of a book that made a great deal of sense 50 years ago, James Harvey Robinson's "Mind in the Making," which gave to the literate world some understanding of the whole process of rationalization, and has been a part of our thinking ever since. Mrs. Janeway's discussion of myth-making, its social function as described by Bronislaw Malinowski, its recurrent characteristics, its imperviousness to "facts" and what happens to those who challenge it, might well do the same thing for contemporary readers.

She weaves together descriptions of what the real world was like before the rise of the Victorian affluent middle class, and makes occasional forays into the art of the cave men and their respect for female sexuality. But these discussions hardly ascribe tremendous power to women before a patriarchal revolution. Nor is the transmutation of the female Goddess into a figure of the Mother of God, which seems to her a more vicarious role, overdone though I, who am used to the way in which primitive men treat women's maternal capacities, can't quite see this.

There is a good discussion of the residue of early childhood which we carry around with us. The male child —and when she speaks of children they are almost always male!—both loves and fears the all powerful mother, whose shadow is the witch. (Men also are shadowed and turn into ogres but less is made of this— just a few side remarks about Lyndon Johnson.) She stresses the way men are permitted—in marriage, in the privacy of the home— to act out their childish emotions and in so doing find women overconcerned with emotion. The witch mother may fade, but the bitch, the shadow behind the loving, giving wife lasts longer, becoming greedy and destructive: the shrew is another direct reversal, the negative of the pleasure-giving woman, who dominates and fails to please.

There is an excellent discussion of the three roles women are asked to play—wife, mother and housekeeper —and how they overlap and conflict simultaneously, all in one place, while men are permitted to be one thing at a time. We have, in fact, with our recent invention of a new kind of home, given women's "place" a new meaning, narrower, less rewarding, more likely to produce children who fear the witch and take to drugs because they know only the world of the emotions in the modern suburban home where there is little contact with the real world.

But in every instance these discussions of mythic roles, assigned and reassigned to women throughout history, and given a special flavor in today's affluent suburban world, are tempered by a recognition of the plight of working-class women, of black women, of women divorced, widowed and separated who have to work, for whom work is not just a way of rejoining the rest of the world, but a desperate addition to the responsibilities of home and children.

In reading the book it is important to keep in mind that it comes from the other side of the generation gap, before women's liberation, before the era of communes and experimentation with genuinely new roles for men and women.

She had no comparable time to deal with the deeper issues that have become apparent since she began her quest. These issues include the extent to which the population explosion by encouraging birth control is freeing women — and men—from the demand that almost all women (and a large number of men) devote their entire lives to parenthood; the demand for a totally new kind of living—in community again where children will be cared for by groups of people (who also provide new role models); and perhaps most important (something which Mrs. Janeway never even hints at) men will play an equal part with women in the care of children. The age-old reasons why women's place has always been, if not *in* the home, at least *with the children,* on foot or horseback or camel back, may well disappear, and with it the inevitable antagonisms and fears of both men and women who have been members of a sex first and the human race second. ∎

'Sisterhood Is Powerful'

A member of the Women's Liberation Movement explains what it's all about

By SUSAN BROWNMILLER

"Women are an oppressed class. Our oppression is total, affecting every facet of our lives. We are exploited as sex objects, breeders, domestic servants and cheap labor. We are considered inferior beings whose only purpose is to enhance men's lives. . . ."

—REDSTOCKINGS MANIFESTO.

"While we realize that the liberation of women will ultimately mean the liberation of men from the destructive role as oppressor, we have no illusion that men will welcome this liberation without a struggle. . . ."

—MANIFESTO OF THE NEW YORK RADICAL FEMINISTS.

THERE is a small group of women that gathers at my house or at the home of one or another of our 15 members each Sunday evening. Our ages range from the early twenties to the late forties. As it happens, all of us work for a living, some at jobs we truly like. Some of us are married, with families, and some are not. Some of us knew each other before we joined the group and some did not. Once we are settled on the sofa and the hard-backed chairs brought in from the kitchen, and the late-comers have poured their own coffee and arranged themselves as best they can on the floor, we begin our meeting. Each week we explore another aspect of what we consider to be our fundamental oppression in a male-controlled society. Our conversation is always animated, often emotional. We rarely adjourn before midnight.

Although we are pleased with ourselves and our insights, we like to remind each other now and then that our small group is not unique. It is merely one of many such groups that have sprung up around the city in the last two years under the umbrella of that collective term, the women's liberation movement. In fact, we had been meeting as a group for exactly four Sundays when one of us got a call from a representative of C.B.S. asking if we would care to be filmed in our natural habitat for a segment on the evening news with Walter Cronkite. We discussed the invitation thoroughly, and then said no.

SUSAN BROWNMILLER, who regularly writes on politics and social problems, is a member of the New York Radical Feminists.

Women's liberation is hot stuff this season, in media terms, and no wonder. In the short space of two years, the new feminism has taken hold and rooted in territory that at first glance appears an unlikely breeding ground for revolutionary ideas: among urban, white, college-educated, middle-class women generally considered to be a rather "privileged" lot by those who thought they knew their politics, or knew their women. From the radical left to the Establishment middle, the women's movement has become a fact of life. The National Organization for Women (NOW), founded by Betty Friedan in 1966, has 35 chapters across the country. Radical feminist groups—creators of the concept of women's liberation, as opposed to women's rights—exist in all major cities side by side with their more conservative counterparts.

Without doubt, certain fringe aspects of the movement make "good copy," to use the kindest term available for how my brethren in the business approach the subject matter. ("Get the bra burning and the karate up front," an editor I know told a writer I know when preparing one news magazine's women's liberation story.)

But the irony of all this media attention is that while the minions of C.B.S. News can locate a genuine women's liberation group with relative ease (they ferreted out our little group before we had memorized each other's last names), hundreds of women in New York City have failed in their attempts to make contact with the movement. I have spoken to women who have spent as much as three months looking for a group that was open to new members. Unclaimed letters have piled up at certain post office box numbers hastily set up and thoughtlessly abandoned by here-today-and-gone-tomorrow "organizations" that disappeared as abruptly as they materialized. The elusive qualities of "women's lib" once prompted the writer Sally Kempton to remark, "It's not a movement, it's a state of mind." The surest way to affiliate with the movement these days is to form your own small group. That's the way it's happening.

TWO years ago the 50 or so women in New York City who had taken to calling themselves the women's liberation movement met on Thursday evenings at a borrowed office on East 11th Street. The official title of the group was the New York Radical Women. There was some justification at the time for thinking grandly in national terms, for similar groups of women were beginning to form in Chicago, Boston, San Francisco and Washington. New York Radical Women came by its name quite simply: the women were young radicals, mostly under the age of 25, and they come out of the civil rights and/or peace movements, for which many of them had been full-time workers. A few years earlier, many of them might have been found on the campuses of Vassar, Radcliffe, Wellesley and the larger coed universities, a past they worked hard to deny. What brought them together to a women-only discussion and action group was a sense of abuse suffered at the hands of the very protest movements that had spawned them. As "movement women," they were tired of doing the typing and fixing the food while "movement men" did the writing and leading. Most were living with or married to movement men who, they believed, were treating them as convenient sex objects or as somewhat lesser beings.

Widely repeated quotations, such as Stokeley Carmichael's wisecrack dictum to S.N.C.C., "The position of women in our movement should be prone," and, three years later, a similar observation by Black Panther Eldridge Cleaver had reinforced their uncomfortable suspicion that the social vision of radical men did not include equality for women. Black power, as practiced by black male leaders, appeared to mean that black women would step back while black men stepped forward. The white male radical's eager embrace of *machismo* appeared to include those backward aspects of male supremacy in the Latin culture from which the word *machismo* is derived. Within their one-to-one relationships with their men, the women felt, the highly touted "alternate life style" of the radical movement was working out no better than the "bourgeois" life style they had rejected. If

man and wife in a suburban split-level was a symbol of all that was wrong with plastic, bourgeois America, "man and chick" in a Lower East Side tenement flat was hardly the new order they had dreamed of.

In short, "the movement" was reinforcing, not eliminating, their deepest insecurities and feelings of worthlessness as women—feelings which quite possibly had brought them into radical protest politics to begin with. So, in a small way, they had begun to rebel. They had decided to meet regularly—without their men—to talk about their common experience. "Our feminism was very underdeveloped in those days," says Anne Koedt, an early member of the group. "We didn't have any idea of what kind of action we could take. We couldn't stop talking about the blacks and Vietnam."

IN Marxist canons, "the woman question" is one of many manifestations of a sick, capitalist society which "the revolution" is supposed to finish off smartly. Some of the women who devoted their Thursday evening meeting time to New York Radical Women believed they were merely dusting off and streamlining an orthodox, ideological issue. Feminism was bad politics and a dirty word since it excluded the larger picture.

But others in the group, like Anne Koedt and Shuli Firestone, an intense and talkative young activist, had begun to see things from a different, heretical perspective. Woman's oppressor was Man, they argued, and not a specific economic system. After all, they pointed out, male supremacy was still flourishing in the Soviet Union, Cuba and China, where power was still lodged in a male bureaucracy. Even the beloved Che wrote a guidebook for revolutionaries in which he waxed ecstatic over the advantages to a guerrilla movement of having women along in the mountains—to prepare and cook the food. The heretics tentatively put forward the idea that feminism must be a separate movement of its own.

New York Radical Women's split in perspective—was the ultimate oppressor Man or Capitalism?—occupied endless hours of debate at the Thursday evening meetings. Two warring factions emerged, dubbing each other "the feminists" and "the politicos."

But other things were happening as well. For one thing, new women were coming in droves to the Thursday evening talk fest, and a growing feeling of sisterhood was permeating the room. Meetings began awkwardly and shyly, with no recognized chairman and no discernible agenda. Often the suggestion, "Let's sit closer together, sisters," helped break the ice. But once the evening's initial awkwardness had passed, volubility was never a problem. "We had so much to say," an early member relates, "and most of us had never said it to another woman before."

Soon *how* to say it became an important question. Young women like Carol Hanisch, a titian-haired recruit to the civil rights movement from a farm in Iowa, and her friend Kathie Amatniek, a Radcliffe graduate and a working film editor, had spent over a year in Mississippi working with S.N.C.C. There they had been impressed with the Southern-revival-style mass meeting at which blacks got up and "testified" about their own experience with "the Man." Might the technique also work for women? And wasn't it the same sort of thing that Mao Tse-tung had advocated to raise political consciousness in Chinese villages? As Carol Hanisch reminded the group, Mao's slogan had been "Speak pain to recall pain"—precisely what New York Radical Women was doing!

The personal-testimony method encouraged *all* women who came to the meeting to speak their thoughts. The technique of "going around the room" in turn brought responses from many who had never opened their mouths at male-dominated meetings and were experiencing the same difficulty in a room full of articulate members of their own sex. Specific questions such as, "If you've thought of having a baby, do you want a girl or a boy?" touched off accounts of what it meant to be a girl-child—the second choice in a society that prizes boys. An examination of "What happens to your relationship when your man earns more money than you, and what happens when *you* earn more money than him?" brought a flood of anecdotes about the male ego and money. "We all told similar stories," relates a member of the group. "We discovered that, to a man, they all felt challenged if we were the breadwinners. It meant that

we were no longer dependent. We had somehow robbed them of their 'rightful' role."

"We began to see our 'feminization' as a two-level process," says Anne Koedt. "On one level, a woman is brought up to believe that she is a girl and that is her biological destiny. She isn't suppposed to want to achieve anything. If, by some chance, she manages to escape the psychological damage, she finds that the structure is prohibitive. Even though she wants to achieve, she finds she is discouraged at every turn and she still can't become President."

FEW topics, the women found, were unfruitful. Humiliations that each of them had suffered privately—from being turned down for a job with the comment, "We were looking for a man," to catcalls and wolf whistles on the street—turned out to be universal agonies. "I had always felt degraded, actually turned into an object," said one woman. "I was no longer a human being when a guy on the street would start to make those incredible animal noises at me. I never was flattered by it, I always understood that behind that whistle was a masked hostility. When we started to talk about it in the group, I discovered that every woman in the room had similar feelings. None of us knew how to cope with this street hostility. We had always had to grin and bear it. We had always been told to dress as women, to be very sexy and alluring to men, and what did it get us? Comments like 'Look at the legs on that babe' and 'would I like to — her.' "*

"Consciousness - raising," in which a woman's personal experience at the hands of men was analyzed as a *political* phenomenon, soon became a keystone of the women's liberation movement.

IN 1963, *before* there was a women's movement, Betty Friedan published what eventually became an American classic, "The Feminine Mystique." The book was a brilliant, factual examination of the post-World War II "back

---

*My small group has discussed holding a street action of our own on the first warm day of spring. We intend to take up stations on the corner of Broadway and 45th Street and whistle at the male passers-by. The confrontation, we feel, will be educational for all concerned.

to the home" movement that tore apart the myth of the fulfilled and happy American housewife. Though "The Feminine Mystique" held an unquestioned place as *the* intellectual mind-opener for most of the young feminists—de Beauvoir's "The Second Sex," a broad, philosophical analysis of the cultural restraints on women, was runner-up in popularity—few members of New York Radical Women had ever felt motivated to attend a meeting of Friedan's National Organization for Women, the parliamentary-style organization of professional women and housewives that she founded in 1966. Friedan, the mother of the movement, and the organization that recruited in her image were considered hopelessly bourgeois. NOW's emphasis on legislative change left the radicals cold. The generation gap created real barriers to communication.

"Actually, we had a lot in common with the NOW women," reflects Anne Koedt. "The women who started NOW were achievement-oriented in their professions. They began with the employment issue because that's what they were up against. The ones who started New York Radical Women were achievement-oriented in the radical movement. From both ends we were fighting a male structure that prevented us from achieving."

Friedan's book had not envisioned a movement of young feminists emerging from the college campus and radical politics. "If I had it to do all over again," she says, "I would rewrite my last chapter." She came to an early meeting of New York Radical Women to listen, ask questions and take notes, and went away convinced that her approach—and NOW's—was more valid. "As far as I'm concerned, we're *still* the radicals," she says emphatically. "We raised our consciousness a long time ago. I get along with the women's lib people because they're the way the troops we need come up. But the name of the game is confrontation and action, and equal employment *is* the gut issue. The legal fight is enormously important. Desegregating The New York Times help-wanted ads was an important step, don't you think? And NOW did it. The women's movement *needs* its Browns versus Boards of Education."

Other older women, writers and lifetime feminists, also

came around to observe, and stayed to develop a kinship with girls young enough to be their daughters. "I almost wept after my first meeting. I went home and filled my diary," says Ruth Herschberger, poet and author · of "Adam's Rib," a witty and unheeded expostulation of women's rights published in 1948. "When I wrote 'Adam's Rib,' I was writing for readers who wouldn't accept the first premise. Now there was a whole roomful of people and a whole new vocabulary. I could go a whole month on the ammunition I'd get at one meeting."

IN June of 1968, New York Radical Women produced a mimeographed booklet of some 20 pages entitled "Notes from the First Year." It sold for 50 cents to women and $1.00 to men. "Notes" was a compendium of speeches, essays and transcriptions of tape-recorded "rap sessions" of the Thursday evening group on such subjects as sex, abortion and orgasm. Several mimeographed editions later, it remains the most widely circulated source material on the New York women's liberation movement.

The contribution to "Notes" that attracted the most attention from both male and female readers was a one-page essay by Anne Koedt entitled, "The Myth of Vaginal Orgasm." In it she wrote:

"Frigidity has generally been defined by men as the failure of women to have vaginal orgasms. Actually, the vagina is not a highly sensitive area and is not physiologically constructed to achieve orgasm. The clitoris is the sensitive area and is the female equivalent of the penis. All orgasms [in women] are extensions of sensations from this area. This leads to some interesting questions about conventional sex and our role in it. Men have orgasms essentially by friction with the vagina, not with the clitoris. Women have thus been defined sexually in terms of what pleases men; our own biology has not been properly analyzed. Instead we have been fed a myth of the liberated woman and her vaginal orgasm, an orgasm which in fact does not exist. What we must do is redefine our sexuality. We must discard the 'normal' concepts of sex and create new guidelines which take into account mutual sexual enjoyment. We must begin to demand that if a certain sexual position or technique now defined as 'standard' is not mutually conducive to orgasm, then it should no longer be defined as standard."

Anne Koedt's essay went further than many other women in the movement would have preferred to go, but she was dealing with a subject that every woman understood. "For years I suffered under a male-imposed definition of my sexual responses," one woman says. "From Freud on down, it was *men* who set the standard of my sexual enjoyment. *Their* way was the way I should achieve nirvana, because their way was the way it worked for them. Me? Oh, I was simply an 'inadequate woman.'"

BY September, 1968, New York Radical Women felt strong enough to attempt a major action. Sixty women went to Atlantic City in chartered buses to picket the Miss America pageant. The beauty contest was chosen as a target because of the ideal of American womanhood it extolled—vacuous, coiffed, cosmeticized and with a smidgin of talent.

But New York Radical Women did not survive its second year. For one thing, the number of new women who flocked to the Thursday evening meetings made consciousness-raising and "going around the room" an impossibility. The politico-feminist split and other internal conflicts—charges of "domination" by one or another of the stronger women were thrown back and forth—put a damper on the sisterly euphoria. An attempt to break up the one large group into three smaller ones—by lot— proved disastrous.

Several women felt the need for a new group. They had become intrigued with the role of the witch in world history as representing society's persecution of women who dared to be different. From Joan of Arc, who dared to wear men's clothes and lead a men's army, to the women of Salem who dared to defy accepted political, religious mores, the "witch" was punished for deviations. Out of this thinking grew WITCH, a handy acronym that the organizers announced, half tongue-in-cheek, stood for Women's International Terrorist Conspiracy from Hell.

Much of WITCH was always tongue-in-cheek, and from its inception its members were at great pains to deny that they were feminists. The Yippie movement had made outrageous disruption a respectable political tactic of the left, and the women of WITCH decided it was more compatible with their thinking to be labeled "kooks" by outsiders than to be labeled man-haters by movement men.

In the WITCH philosophy, the patriarchy of the nuclear family was synonymous with the patriarchy of the American business corporation. Thus, four women took jobs at a branch of the Travelers Insurance Company, where a fifth member was working, and attempted to establish a secret coven of clerical workers on the premises. (For the Travelers' project, WITCH became "Women Incensed at Travelers' Corporate Hell.") In short order, the infiltrators were fired for such infractions of office rules as wearing slacks to work. Undaunted, a new quintet of operatives gained employment in the vast typing pools at A.T. & T. "Women Into Telephone Company Harassment" gained three sympathizers to the cause before Ma Bell got wise and exorcised the coven from her midst. Two WITCHes were fired for insubordination; the rest were smoked out and dismissed for being "overqualified" for the typing pool.

WITCH's spell over the women's movement did not hold. "At this point," says Judith Duffet, an original member, "you could say that WITCH is just another small group in women's liberation. We're concerned with consciousness-raising and developing an ideology through collective thinking. We don't do the freaky, hippie stuff any more."

WHILE WITCH was brewing its unusual recipe for liberation, another offshoot of New York Radical Women emerged. The new group was called Redstockings, a play on *bluestockings*, with the blue replaced by the color of revolution. Organized by Shuli Firestone and Ellen Willis, an articulate rock-music columnist for the New Yorker and a serious student of Engels's "Origins of the Family," Redstockings made no bones about where it stood. It was firmly committed to feminism and action.

Redstockings made its first public appearance at a New York legislative hearing on abortion law reform in February, 1969, when several women sought to gain the microphone to testify about their own abortions. The hearing, set up to take testimony from 15 medical and psychiatric "experts" — 14 were men—was hastily adjourned. The following month, Redstockings held its own abortion hearing at the Washington Square Methodist Church. Using the consciousness-raising technique, 12 women "testified" about abortion, from their own personal experience, before an audience of 300 men and women. The political message of the emotion-charged evening was that *women* were the only true experts on unwanted pregnancy and abortion, and that every woman has an inalienable right to decide whether or not she wishes to bear a child.

Redstockings' membership counts are a closely held secret, but I would estimate that the number does not exceed 100. Within the movement, Redstockings push what they call "the pro-woman line." "What it means," says a member, "is that we take the woman's side in *everything*. A woman is never to blame for her own submission. None of us need to change ourselves, we need to change men." Redstockings are also devout about consciousness-raising. "Whatever else we may do, consciousness-raising is the ongoing political work," says Kathie Amatniek. For the last few months, the various Redstocking groups have been raising their consciousness on what they call "the divisions between women that keep us apart"—married women *vs.* single, black women *vs.* white, middle class *vs.* working class, etc.

While Redstockings organized its abortion speak-out, the New York chapter of NOW formed a committee to lobby for repeal of restrictive abortion legislation. These dissimilar approaches to the same problem illustrate the difference in style between the two wings of the women's movement.

BUT within New York NOW itself, a newer, wilder brand of feminism made an appearance. Ti-Grace Atkinson, a Friedan protégée and the president of New York NOW, found herself in increasing conflict with her own local chapter and Friedan over NOW's hierarchical structure, a typical organization plan with an executive board on top. Ti-Grace, a tall blonde who has been described in print as "aristocratic looking," had come to view the power relationship between NOW's executive board and the general membership as a copycat extension of the standard forms of male domination over women in the society at large. She proposed to NOW that all executive offices be abolished in favor of rotating chairmen chosen by lot from the general membership. When Atkinson's proposal came up for a vote by the general membership of the New York chapter in October, 1968, and was defeated, Ti-Grace resigned her presidency on the spot and went out and formed her own organization. Named the October 17th Movement — the date of Ti-Grace's walkout from NOW— it made a second debut this summer as The Feminists, and took its place as the most radical of the women's liberation groups. (New York NOW suffered no apparent effects from its first organizational split. Over the last year it has *gained* in membership as feminism has gained acceptabilty among wider circles of women.)

The Feminists made anti-élitism and rigorous discipline cardinal principles of their organization. As the only radical feminist group to take a stand against the institution of marriage they held a sit-in at the city marriage license bureau last year, raising the slogan that "Marriage Is Slavery." Married women or women living with men may not exceed one-third of the total membership.

Differences over such matters as internal democracy, and the usual personality conflicts that plague all political movements, caused yet another feminist group and another manifesto to make their appearance this fall. In November, Shuli Firestone and Anne Koedt set up a plan for organizing small groups— or "brigades," as they prefer

AUTHOR
Susan Brownmiller

to call them—on a neighborhood basis, and named their over-all structure the New York Radical Feminists. Eleven decentralized neighborhood units (three are in the West Village) meet jointly once a month.

The Radical Feminists coexist with the Feminists and the Redstockings without much rivalry, although when pressed, partisans of the various groups will tell you, for instance, that Redstockings do too much consciousness-raising and not enough action, or that the Feminists are "fascistic," or that the Radical Feminists are publicity hungry. But in general, since interest in the women's liberation movement has always exceeded organizational capacity, the various groups take the attitude of "the more the merrier."

DESPITE the existence of three formal "pure radical feminist" organizations, hundreds of women who consider themselves women's liberationists have not yet felt the need to affiliate with any body larger than their own small group. The small group, averaging 8 to 15 members and organized spontaneously by friends calling friends has become *the* organizational form of the amorphous movement. Its intimacy seems to suit women. Fear of expressing new or half-formed thoughts vanishes in a friendly living-room atmosphere.

"After years of psycho-analysis in which my doctor kept telling me my problem was that I wouldn't accept—quote—*my female role*," says a married woman with two children who holds a master's degree in philosophy, "the small group was a revelation to me. Suddenly, for the first time in my life, it was O.K. to express feelings of hostility to men." Says another woman: "In the small group I have the courage to think things and feel feelings, that I would never have dared to think and feel as an individual."

THE meetings have often been compared to group therapy, a description that most of the women find irritating. "Group therapy isn't political and what we're doing is highly political," is the general response. In an early paper on the nature and function of the small group, Carol Hanisch once wrote, "Group therapy implies that we are sick and messed up, but the first function of the small group is to get rid of self-blame. We start with the assumption that women are really 'neat' people. Therapy means adjusting. We desire to change the objective conditions."

The groups are usually leaderless and structureless, and the subjects discussed at the weekly meetings run the gamut of female experience. The Radical Feminists offer to new groups they organize a list of consciousness-raising topics that includes:

● Discuss your relationships with men. Have you noticed any recurring patterns?

● Have you ever felt that men have pressured you into sexual relationships? Have you ever lied about orgasm?

● Discuss your relationships with other women. Do you compete with women for men?

● Growing up as a girl, were you treated differently from your brother?

● What would you most like to do in life? What has stopped you?

"Three months of this sort of thing," says Shuli Fire-

stone, "is enough to make a feminist out of any woman."

THE kind of collective thinking that has come out of the women's liberation movement is qualitatively different from the kinds of theorems and analyses that other political movements have generated. "Women are different from all other oppressed classes," says Anne Koedt. "We live in isolation, not in ghettos, and we are in the totally unique position of having a master in our own houses." It is not surprising, therefore, that marriage and child care are two subjects that receive intensive scrutiny in the small group.

If few in the women's movement are willing to go as far as the Feminists and say that marriage is slavery, it is hard to find a women's liberationist who is not in some way disaffected by the sound of wedding bells. Loss of personal identity and the division of labor within the standard marriage (the husband's role as provider, the wife's role as home maintenance and child care) are the basic points at issue. "I have come to view marriage as a built-in self-destruct for women," says one divorcée after 12 years of marriage. "I married early, right after college, because it was expected of me. I never had a chance to discover who I was. I was programed into the housewife pattern." Many married women's liberationists will no longer use their husbands' last names; some have gone back to their maiden names, and some even to their mothers' maiden names.

One paper that has been widely circulated within the movement is entitled "The Politics of Housework," by Pat Mainardi, a Redstocking who is a teacher and painter. "Men recognize the essential fact of housework right from the beginning," she wrote. "Which is that it stinks. You both work, you both have careers, but *you* are expected to do the housework. Your husband tells you, 'Don't talk to me about housework. It's too trivial to discuss.' MEANING: *His* purpose is to deal with matters of significance. *Your* purpose is to deal with matters of insignificance. So *you* do the housework. Housework trivial? Just try getting him to share the burden. The measure of his resistance is the measure of your oppression."

Not only the oppression of housework, but the oppression of child care has become a focus of the women's movement. Much of the energy of young mothers in the movement has gone into setting up day-care collectives that are staffed on an equal basis by mothers and fathers. (Thus far they have proved difficult to sustain.) "Some of the men have actually come to understand that sharing equally in child care is a political responsibility," says Rosalyn Baxandall, a social worker and an early women's liberationist. Rosalyn and her husband, Lee, a playwright, put in a morning a week at an informal cooperative day nursery on the Lower East Side where their 2-year-old, Finn, is a charter member.

In November, at the Congress to Unite Women, a conference that drew over 500 women's liberationists of various persuasions from the New York area, a resolution demanding 24-hour-a-day child care centers was overwhelmingly endorsed. Women in the movement have also suggested plans for a new kind of life style in which a husband and wife would each work half-day and devote the other half of the day to caring for their children. Another possibility would be for the man to work for six months of the year while the woman takes care of the child-rearing responsibilities—with the roles reversed for the next six months.

THE "movement women" who did not endorse the separatism of an independent radical feminist movement last year and chose to remain in what the feminists now call "the male left" have this year made women's liberation a major issue in their own political groups. Even the weatherwomen of Weatherman meet separately to discuss how to combat male chauvinism among their fellow revolutionaries. The women of Rat, the farthest out of the underground radical newspapers, formed a collective and took over editorial management of their paper last month, charging that their men had put out a product filled with sexist, women-as-degraded-object pornography. Twenty-two-year-old Jane Alpert, free on bail and facing conspiracy charges for a series of terrorist bombings, was spokesman for the Rat women's *putsch*. A black women's liberation committee functions within S.N.C.C., and

A MEETING OF THE RADICAL FEMINISTS
One response to the white male radical's eager embrace of machismo

its leader, Frances M. Beal, has said publicly, "To be black and female is double jeopardy, the slave of a slave."

The new feminism has moved into some surprisingly Establishment quarters. A spirited women's caucus at New York University Law School forced the university to open its select national scholarship program to women students. Women's caucuses exist among the editorial employes at McGraw Hill and Newsweek. Last month, 59 women in city government, sent a petition to Mayor Lindsay demanding that he actively seek qualified women for policy-making posts.

THE movement is a story without an end, because it has just begun. The goals of liberation go beyond a simple concept of equality. Looking through my notebook, I see them expressed simply and directly. *Betty Friedan: "We're going to redefine the sex roles." Anne Koedt: "We're going to be redefining politics."* Brave words for a new movement, and braver still for a movement that has been met with laughter and hos-

tility. Each time a man sloughs off the women's movement with the comment, "They're nothing but a bunch of lesbians and frustrated bitches," we quiver with collective rage. How can such a charge be answered in rational terms? It cannot be. (The supersensitivity of the movement to the lesbian issue, and the existence of a few militant lesbians within the movement once prompted Friedan herself to grouse about "the lavender menace" that was threatening to warp the image of women's rights. A lavender *herring*, perhaps, but surely no clear and present danger.)

The small skirmishes and tugs of war that used to be called "the battle of the sexes" have now assumed ideological proportions. It is the aim of the movement to *turn men around*, and the implications in that aim are staggering. "Men have used us all their lives as ego fodder," says Anne Koedt. "They not only control economics and the government, they control us. There are the women's pages and the rest of the world." It is that rest of the world, of course, that we are concerned with. There is a women's rights button that I sometimes wear and the slo-

gan on it reads, "Sisterhood is Powerful." If sisterhood were powerful, what a different world it would be.

Women as a class have never subjugated another group; we have never marched off to wars of conquest in the name of the fatherland. We have never been involved in a decision to annex the territory of a neighboring country, or to fight for foreign markets on distant shores. Those are the games men play, not us. We see it differently. We want to be neither oppressor nor oppressed. The women's revolution is the final revolution of them all.

How does a sympathetic man relate to a feminist woman? Thus far, it has not been easy for those who are trying. The existence of a couple of *men's* consciousness-raising groups—the participants are mostly husbands of activist women—is too new to be labeled a trend. "When our movement gets strong, when men are forced to see us as a conscious issue, *what are they going to do?*" asks Anne Koedt. And then she answers: "I don't know, but I think there's a part of men that really wants a human relationship, and that's going to be the saving grace for all of us." ∎

Feminists Shifting Emphasis From Persons to Politics

By DEIRDRE CARMODY

The women's liberation movement — a massive behavioral revolution aimed at overturning the very structures of a male-dominated society—has entered a new stage of development. It is now concentrating its energies on legislative lobbying and politics.

Many women have passed through the movement's consciousness-raising phase. However, there are still thousands of women meeting in groups after breakfast in suburban kitchens and after work in offices, sipping sherry in living rooms with chintz curtains and smoking pot in lofts without curtains, to discuss the measure of their personal oppression in a patriarchal society.

Women have held these sessions to help purge themselves of the belief that they are inferior to men and that the roles decreed for them are inevitable. As consciousness was, in fact, raised, the emphasis shifted to specific issues such as equal pay for equal work, day-care centers and the repeal of abortion laws. For many women, the next logical step was to move into politics.

"Once women step out of that troubled silence, they can't step back," said the author of "Memoirs of an Ex-Prom Queen," Alix Kates Shulman. "Once women become politicized over something like the abortion issue, they remain politicized."

Today, with women making up 51.3 per cent of the country's population, thousands of women across the country are organizing to celebrate the third annual Women's Strike for Justice and Equality this Friday and Saturday. Saturday, which is the Bastille Day of the feminist movement, is the 52d anniversary of the 19th Amendment, which gave women the right to vote.

The women's movement is now so large and so fragmented that it can no longer properly be referred to as a single movement. It has become multilayered, multifaceted, multipurposed.

Its membership now ranges from women who are getting their husbands to help with the housework to women espousing gynocracy, where women would hold the power and would have such choices as whether to bear children in utero or in test tubes—a world, in the words of radical feminist Robin Morgan, "which would make 1984 look like Mary Poppins."

The largest of the groups, the National Organization for Women (NOW), has about 20,000 members, and there are so many feminist groups —ranging from Older Women's Liberation (OWL) to Radicalesbians—that it is impossible to count them all. Many of these groups do not fall into neat pigeonholes of radical or reformist.

"NOW started out as a reformist organization, although many of the first women were masking as reformists, whereas they were really revolutionaries," says Jacqueline Ceballos, its eastern regional director. "Then, as radical women became louder, NOW became more acceptable."

Feminist accomplishments have ranged from a vast lobbying effort that culminated in passage of the Equal Rights Amendment this year to establishment of day-care centers and commitments from companies throughout the country to hire and promote more women.

Perhaps most important, however, in the opinion of most feminists, is a new awareness, demonstrated in part by a flood of books and television programs that presented the movement's case.

Convention a Milestone

A recent milestone of the movement was the Democratic National Convention last month, where women made up almost 40 per cent of the delegates as opposed to 13 per cent in 1968.

It was a heady experience for them: Representative Shirley Chisholm received 151 votes for President; Frances Farenthold of Corpus Christi, Tex., who had been defeated in her bid to become Governor, received 408 votes from delegates in 42 states and territories to make her runner-up for the nomination for Vice President; Mrs. Jean Westwood was unanimously selected by the 303 members of the Democratic National Committee as its chairwoman

(the first time either the Democratic or Republican party had given the job to a woman), and the convention passed a rules change that calls for a woman to chair the 1976 convention and every alternate convention thereafter.

"Women were the most together group at the convention," Representative Bella Abzug, New York Democrat, said the other day in a telephone interview from the Ladies Retirement Room ("I must do something about that name," she said) in the House of Representatives.

"We showed we could put something together politically," said Mrs. Abzug, who was defeated in the Democratic primary by Representative William F. Ryan. "I think that it's fair to say that what has happened in the last year or so is the first real political movement by women of any national scope since the suffrage movement."

There were some defeats for feminists at the convention, however, when their intensive backstage maneuvering failed to pass either the South Carolina challenge, which would have put more women in that state's delegation, or a pro-abortion minority plank. However, the fact that the emotional issue of abortion even reached the floor, despite the tough lobbying against it, indicated the power of women at the convention.

"You can't count success by either winning or losing the abortion votes," said Brenda Feigen Fasteau, coordinator of the women's rights project of the American Civil Liberties Union and a member of the policy council of the National Women's Political Caucus.

"That whole convention was an enormous victory— just to have 40 per cent of the delegates be women, not just sitting there, but actively participating."

Much of the success was attributable to a mammoth drive launched by the National Women's Political Caucus, which was formed last summer by Mrs. Abzug, Mrs. Chisholm, Gloria Stein-

The New York Times

A coalition of women's liberation groups demonstrated at the Statue of Liberty two years ago.

em and Betty Friedan to "awaken, organize and assert the vast political power represented by women."

Through its tax-exempt arm, Women's Education for Delegate Selection, the caucus held seminars around the country to teach women how to become convention delegates.

At the Republican National Convention which opened in Miami Beach yesterday, 35 per cent of the delegates are women (469 of a total of 1,348). Many of the women have been active in politics, participating on county and state levels as vice chairwomen.

Mrs. Anne Armstrong, co-chairwoman of the Republican party, is the convention's secretary and five women (and nine men) hold positions as chairpersons or co-chairpersons of the seven subcommittees of the platform committee.

It is six years now since the birth of the movement. "The Feminine Mystique" by Betty Friedan had been published that year, and it made millions of women realize that they were not alone in the frustration of trying to reconcile their potential as educated women with the demands of housewifery.

At the same time, young women from the New Left who had joined the civil rights movement and flocked to the South to combat injustice were beginning to pour out their wrath to one another over the fact that their male colleagues had banned them from the front lines and relegated them to the kitchen, the mimeograph machine and the bed. America was in the throes of a sexual revolution at the time, spurred by the advent of the pill, and the old morality was challenged as never before.

A Rapid Spread

The movement has grown enormously since those days, when small numbers of young women met to discuss radical feminist concepts and a handful of women formed NOW "to take action to bring women into full participation in the mainstream of American Society...in truly equal partnership with men."

The movement has spread abroad, and although no one knows how extensive the impact is, groups of women are getting together in a number of countries, and a NOW chapter was recently opened in Paris.

At first, the movement appealed predominantly to white, upper-middle-class women and, in a lesser way, to black middle-class women. But there are signs now that white, ethnic, working-class women and poor blacks, Chicanos and American Indians are being drawn into it by its emphasis on rights for welfare women, day-care centers and equal pay. The small radical groups have split and split again because of ideological differences and the names of groups that gave such flavor to the early part of the movement — Red Stockings, WITCH, Bread and Roses— are no longer bandied about.

In some cases, they have simply dissolved because they tried to stick to one of the original tenets of the movement, which was that there would be no leaders,

Some Legislative Breakthroughs

Among the legislative breakthroughs cited by feminists that have changed or will change the status of women are:

Passage of the Equal Rights Amendment by Congress in March. The amendment, which must be ratified by 38 states, would prohibit discrimination based on sex by any law or action of Federal, state or local government.

Title VII of the Civil Rights Act of 1964, which added sex discrimination to the ban against race bias.

Strengthening powers of Equal Employment Opportunity Commission to enforce nondiscrimination in employment.

Revised Order 4, issued last December by the Department of Labor, which applies to companies having at least 50 employes and doing at least $50,000 in Federal Government business a year. The order requires companies to submit affirmative action plans to move women into job categories where they are under-represented. The goals and timetables must relate to the number of women potentially available for these jobs.

Extension of the Equal Pay Act of the Department of Labor. The extension provides additional economic benefits to an estimated 15 million executive, administrative and professional employes. This will benefit women because the new law requires the same pay for men and women doing substantially the same work.

New rules of the Equal Employment Opportunity Commission giving more rights to pregnant women employes. The new rules say that to deny a woman a job because she is pregnant is a violation of the Civil Rights Act of 1964. They also say that pregnancy must be regarded as an illness and therefore women who leave to give birth must be eligible for sick pay.

and it did not work. As the extremists in the movement became more radicalized, NOW appeared more moderate until it was dubbed by many the N.A.A.C.P. of the women's liberation movement.

"The big difference within the movement is that the reform movement is after equality within the system and the radical movement is after changing the system— and by the system, I don't just mean capitalism, but patriarchy," said Robin Morgan, author of "Sisterhood Is Powerful," a women's liberation anthology.

The visible victories and breakthroughs, those that can be enumerated, are mainly the result of the new thrust toward politics and legislation, although some of the specific efforts date back years.

The passage of the Equal Rights Amendment by Congress last March was, perhaps, the most significant signpost of women's gains. The amendment, for which feminists have struggled for 49 years, would prohibit discrimination based on sex by any law or action of Federal, state or local government. An intensive and organized lobbying effort is now being directed at ratification into law by the states. So far, 20 states have ratified the amendment out of the 38

necessary to amend the Constitution.

"We got this far only because of our nuisance value," says Gloria Steinem, one of the organizers of the National Women's Political Caucus. "You've got to get to the state where your legislators say, 'Call your people off!' "

The more radical elements of the movement, who say they refuse to work within the political system, are, however, holding conferences on rape and prostitutions; establishing self-help clinics where women can get free or low-cost medical care from women doctors and nurses; starting law clinics to deal with legal questions of particular interest to women and forming women's centers and action alliances to give information on child-care projects, welfare rights and abortion.

Probably the most important and most emotional issue that unites the reformers with the radicals is the proposed repeal of all abortion laws. A vital tenet of women's liberation is that a woman has the right to control her own body, and many feminists feel that there should be repeal of all governmental interference in reproductive and sexual matters.

Feminists are also turning their energies toward reforming marriage and divorce laws.

The more revolutionary denigrate efforts to achieve change through the legislative process because they believe that to attempt to reform society is to perpetuate an oppressive patriarchy.

To give women full participation in society, they say, it is necessary to overthrow the structures on which the system is based. The first things to go would be the political institutions that perpetuate the system, such as institutional marriage, which, they assert, enslaves women for economic reasons.

A Divided View

Many women who are still trying to define their own feminist consciousness are struggling with the questions of marriage and children and their feelings toward men in general. These women find it difficult to reconcile their intellectual view of man as the oppressor to their individual relationships with the men in their lives.

"It's quite rational for me to say that I am a man-hater— intellectually I am quite committed to being a man-hater —even though I like individual men," says Susan Brownmiller, an author and one of the early radical feminists who is researching a book on rape.

"There may come a time when you are able to say you know you never want to get married—you say it for the first time, and thunder doesn't strike—and then later you may say the hardest thing to articulate, which is that you don't want to have children."

Recently, Betty Friedan wrote an article for McCall's saying there were anti-male overtones in the movement and that they were alienating many women. The article was widely deplored by many feminist spokeswomen, and it was said that Mrs. Friedan had taken the occasion to fire some personal shots at Gloria Steinem and Bella Abzug, both prominent leaders in the movement.

Mrs. Friedan, however, insists that the extremists who are against marriage have given the movement a bad image and that many women around the country have been alienated because they believe this is the view all feminists espouse.

A major topic of conversation among all parts of the movement is female sexuality. A revolutionary essay, which is still being discussed, was written early in the movement by Anne Koedt, a founder of the radical feminist movement in New York.

Drawing by Ed Fisher © 1971, The New Yorker Magazine, Inc.

Entitled "The Myth of the Vaginal Orgasm," it challenged the commonly held concepts that women experience their most mature orgasm in the vagina and that, as Freud contended, the clitoral orgasm is adolescent.

Her thesis, in effect, says that the vaginal orgasm is a myth perpetuated by men because it enables them to be in control in the sexual act. In actuality, Miss Koedt says, women prefer clitoral stimulus more than any other form of sexual activity.

"Women have thus been defined sexually in terms of what pleases men," she says, and urges women to "redefine" their sexuality and "discard" the normal concepts of sex.

Lesbianism has been a difficult issue in the movement. Many feminists believe that lesbians should have the same status as all other feminists, but other women have been wary of lesbianism becoming too closely identified with the movement in the public consciousness.

NOW evaded the subject for a long time, but it passed a resolution at the 1971 conference, which read: "A woman's right to her own person includes the right to define and express her own sexuality and to choose her own life-style and, be it further resolved, that NOW acknowledge the oppression of lesbians as a legitimate concern of feminism."

As the movement — and

the controversies surrounding it — have grown, it has received widespread publicity. A number of national magazines have devoted entire issues to it and a new feminist magazine, MS, says it sold out its first three issues with sales ranging from 300,000 to almost 500,000.

A number of celebrities, such as Germaine Greer and Kate Millett, surfaced suddenly when they wrote feminist books. One of the major voices in the movement is still Simone de Beauvoir's, whose "The Second Sex," published in the nineteen-fifties, was a precursor of the movement.

A new vocabulary has also erupted with such words as chairperson, instead of chairman, and the designation Ms. (pronounced Miz or spelled out loud), which many feminists prefer to Miss or Mrs. because, they say, a woman should not be identified by her marital status.

There have been many tangible victories, but feminists say that the biggest victory is the over-all impact that the movement has had. "Women's lib" — a phrase known only to the élite in the feminist movement two years ago — has become a household word, although it no longer seems to be used by women in the movement. By the very force of its existence, the movement gives moral support and credibility to every woman who sets out on her own to amend inequities in her marriage or in her job.

"No woman, no man, no child who is aware of the issues of this movement can ever be the same again," said Wilma Scott Heide, president of NOW.

WOMEN SURVEYED ON EQUALITY VIEW

Most Feel They're Treated as Fairly as Men Are

Special to The New York Times

PRINCETON, N. J., Aug. 22 —According to a recent Gallup Poll, most American women believe that they are treated as fairly as men. The survey, which focused on the attitudes of American women toward their role in life, interest in working and job discrimination, indicated that two-thirds of American women believe that they get as good a break in the world today as men do.

However, among those women who have attended college, from whose ranks the women's liberation movement has drawn much of its support, far fewer (53 per cent) believe that they get as good a break as men.

Moreover, the survey finds that a majority of women believe that members of their sex have it somewhat more difficult when it comes to reaching the upper echelons in business.

Women are now organizing in city after city — publishing handbills, taking out full-page newspaper ads, picketing and threatening court suits. On Wednesday, the National Organization for Women will lead a nationwide strike for equality with men.

The feminists are protesting what they regard as "intolerable discrimination" against them in industry, government and the professions. They say they are hired last, dismissed first, paid less, passed over for promotion and are held to the drudgery of routine jobs.

Some of the other highlights of this just-completed survey include the following:

¶Among the two-thirds of American women (67 per cent) who are not working in jobs outside the home, the weight of preference is not to work. Among those women who do crave outside employment (27 per cent), most would choose a part-time job over a full-time position.

¶Reasons cited by women not now working who want outside employment, divide mainly between those who "need the money" and those who admit to being bored at home.

¶Although 65 per cent of American women believe they get as good a break in life as men, a majority believe women do not have the same chance as men to become corporate executives.

¶Those women who believe that men have an advantage as far as breaks in life are concerned say that "women do the same work for less money" (38 per cent) or that "they are given lesser jobs" (37 per cent).

¶A majority of 55 per cent of women believe that women can run businesses as well as men.

¶The weight of opinion among women is that they have an easier life than men do. This view is held by 46 per cent of women compared to 30 per cent who believe men have it easier.

The survey was conducted in more than 300 scientifically selected sampling points July 10-12. Following are the questions asked of the 778 women interviewed. The results are shown by all women, women who have children under 21 and by the respondent's educational level.

In your opinion, do women in the U.S. get as good a break as men?

	Yes %	No %
All women	65	35
Women/children under 21	66	34
Women/attended college	53	47
High school	68	32
Grade school	69	31

Do you wish you had a part-time or full-time job outside your home, or not?

	Yes, Part %	Yes, Full %	No %	Have No Job %	Opin. %
All women	19	8	40	32	1
Women/children under 21	20	9	37	32	2
Women/attended college	11	9	34	43	3
High school	21	8	39	31	1
Grade school	20	8	50	22	—

If a woman has the same ability as a man, does she have as good a chance to become the executive of a company, or not?

	As Good %	Not As Good %	No Opin. %
All women	39	54	7
Women/children under 21	33	60	7
Women/attended college	22	75	3
High school	39	54	7
Grade school	54	36	10

Do you think women could run must businesses as well as men, or not?

	Yes %	No %	No Opin. %
All women	55	40	5
Women/children under 21	53	43	4
Women/attended college	53	42	g
High school	56	40	4
Grade school	55	38	7

Which do you think has the easier life in the U.S. today—men or women?

	Men %	Women %	No Opin. %
All women	30	46	24
Women/children under 21	31	49	20
Women/attended college	28	44	28
High school	30	50	20
Grade school	34	39	27

August 23, 1970

The Woman Homosexual

By ENID NEMY

THE young homosexual woman, to an increasing degree, is refusing to live with the limitations and restrictions imposed by society and is showing a sense of active resentment and rebellion at a condemnation she considers unwarranted and unjust.

She considers herself part of what many refer to as the "current sexual revolution." When the necessity arises, she is now more frequently willing to risk open discrimination and prejudice —in jobs and with friends and acquaintances ("some people won't talk to us; they think it's catching.")

The new assertiveness and increasing visibility has resulted in:

¶A rise in attendance at the weekly meetings of the New York chapter of the Daughters of Bilitis, a national Lesbian organization. Several years ago, 20 to 40 was considered average; today the figure ranges between 60 and 125, a threefold increase.

¶Active participation in some of the newer homosexual organizations, including the Student Homophile League and the Gay Liberation Front. Although these groups are supported primarily by homosexual males, a woman is chairman of the New York University Student Homophile League and there are women executive members at Cornell University and at Columbia, where the organization was founded three years ago.

¶A marked increase in the number of women picked up by New York City Police for "loitering," a charge applied "for soliciting another for the purpose of engaging in deviate sexual intercourse." Ten women were picked up under this charge in 1968 and a police spokesman estimated that the ratio of men to women was, at the time, 12 to 1. A total of 49 women and 69 men have been apprehended on the same charge in the first nine months of 1969.

Homosexual League Has Been Expanding

One of the aims of the Daughters of Bilitis, founded in 1955 and named after 19th century song lyrics glorifying Lesbian love, is to explore the possibility of changing present laws. The organization, with headquarters in San Francisco, now has four official and five probationary chapters; until last year the only chapters were in San Francisco, Los Angeles and New York.

In addition to social activities, self-discussion and providing a forum for professional advice (legal and psychological), the organization is prepared to assist in what it terms "responsible" studies and research.

"We are a civil liberties organization," said Joan Kent (a pseudonym), national vice-president, Eastern division.

It is not illegal to be a Lesbian in

New York State but it is illegal to perform a Lesbian act. A Temporary State Commission on Revision of the Penal Law recommended, in November, 1964, that "deviate sexual acts privately and discreetly engaged in between competent and consenting adults should no longer constitute a crime."

Decisive votes in both houses of the State Legislature rejected the proposal. Subsequent bills have gotten no further than committee, although John V. P. Lassoe Jr., one of the men who testified before the commission, said that he intended to see another bill introduced at the next session in January.

"But I don't expect it to move," he conceded. "I expect it will wither and die, but I will work for it."

Religious Groups Gave No Support

Mr. Lassoe, who was director of Christian social relations of the Episcopal Diocese of New York at the time of his testimony, and is now an assistant to the Diocesan Bishop, the Right Rev. Horace W. B. Donegan, thought that the most significant reason for the defeat was "the absence of support from religious bodies in New York State."

"To the best of my knowledge," he said, "my department and the Department of Christian Social Relations of the Protestant Council of the City of New York endorsed the proposed change . . . other religious groups either opposed it, or, more commonly, remained silent."

Many Lesbians have rejected the church but almost all are encouraged by the increasing dialogue between religious leaders and homosexuals. Many theologians are inclined to agree with a statement made by Rabbi Norman Lamm, the spiritual leader of the Jewish Center in New York and professor of Jewish philosophy at Yeshiva University.

"Homosexuality between consenting adults should not be treated as a criminal offense," Rabbi Lamm said, "but to declare homosexual acts as morally neutral and at times as a good thing is scandalous." The statement, made last year and repeated recently, has been both supported and attacked by other rabbis.

Whatever the general feeling on the morals and ethics of homosexuality (a recent Louis Harris poll reported that 63 per cent of the nation believes that homosexuals are "harmful to American life"), there is apparently increasing support from public bodies for a change in the laws.

A task force of 14 experts, appointed by the National Institutes of Mental Health, last month issued a majority report (three members expressed reservations on some of the recommendations) urging states to abolish laws that make homosexual intercourse a crime for consenting adults in private. Two states have such laws. The Illinois measure was passed in 1961 and Connecticut approved one last summer, to take effect in 1971.

A recent poll conducted by Modern Medicine, a publication, reported that 67.7 per cent of the 27,741 doctors polled were in favor of allowing homosexual acts.

There is, on the other hand, some be-lief that the proliferating number of articles and reports and increased public awareness of homosexuality has produced a "sexual backlash."

"The general public assumes that to remove an inappropriate law is to vote for lawlessness," said Robert Veit Sherwin, a lawyer who specializes in domestic relations and is the author of "Sex and the Statutory Law."

Despite the increasing activities of the homosexual female, many experts in the field define her relationships as "generally more discreet" than those of the homosexual male.

"With many women, a homosexual relationship evolves or devolves into a kind of companionate pair," according to Dr. Charles W. Socarides, a medical psychoanalyst and author of "The Overt Homosexual." "They protect each other and depend on each other; there is often very little actual sexual contact."

Dr. Socarides, who has treated many homosexuals, believes that "women are much more emotionally committed; they can't have one-night stands and leave."

At the Daughters of Bilitis, the relationship between Doris and Terry, two women in their 50's who have shared a home in the suburbs for 20 years, is held up as an example of Lesbian stability. Both women are scientists by profession, but Terry now stays home and keeps house.

"We don't run around and do wild things," commented Terry, who thinks there is no doubt that the neighbors know of their relationship. "If you behave yourself, pay your bills and don't offend, the community accepts you."

There are others like Doris and Terry but, according to many Lesbians, "the male-female aping of marriage is changing."

"The majority of the young Lesbians interchange responsibilities," said Miss Kent. "Alice [her friend] and I consider ourselves involved in a commitment, not husband and wife but partners."

Not Having Children Is Difficult to Accept

Miss Kent, who had a heterosexual relationship (her engagement was broken because "our religious backgrounds were different and the families disapproved") before she became a Lesbian, said it took her "three or four years to adjust to the idea of not having children."

Other Lesbians went through similar periods of adjustment but some said they had no desire for children ("I like them but I wouldn't want to be a mother; I might want to be a father," said one).

A few Lesbian couples adopt children. "Of course, they don't announce what they are," Miss Kent explained.

(There is no law against the placement of a child with Lesbians but, in divorce cases, there are generalities about the moral atmosphere in the home. Most judges would not place a child in a home shared by Lesbians, according to Carl Zuckerman, lawyer for the Community Service Society, "but if there were no better alternative, the child would be placed with a homosexual parent.")

Women with children, who enter into a homosexual relationship, rarely live with their partners.

"We have our own apartments," said Justine, a tall, 28-year-old black Lesbian with a master's degree, who is having an affair with the mother of a 5-year-old child.

Although "an act of deviate sexual intercourse" was added in 1966 to New York State's divorce law, it is still rarely used as a basis for action, according to Geraldine Eiber, a lawyer who has handled several such cases. Most parties prefer to use other grounds.

Jean and Ruth, Long Island matrons, each maintain a residence, one with three children (aged 8 to 20) and the other with two (aged 10 and 12). Both women are divorced. Neither divorce was granted under the deviate law despite the fact that the homosexual propensities of one of the women was known to her husband throughout their 14-year marriage.

"I had had an affair with a girl while my fiancé was in the service," said Ruth, a pleasant-looking woman with intense brown eyes and cropped brown hair. "I married him when he returned because of pressure from my family—I loved my mother very much—and I felt, too, that with marriage would come respectability."

Ruth continued her relationship with the other woman for a year after marriage. When she broke it up, "the girl told my husband." He was "shocked and angry," but the marriage continued and she immediately began a relationship with another woman that continued for 13 years.

Both Left Their Jobs And Stayed at Home

"We both had jobs," she recalled. "When I had a baby, I persuaded her to have children so she could stay home too. We lived within walking distance of one another."

She ended her long-time affair after meeting Jean, an encounter she described as "like the old cliché—bells started ringing."

"I felt that any time I had, I wanted to spend with her. My husband thought he would frighten me by leaving. It didn't work out that way."

Ruth is comfortable in her role; Jean is not. She is in her 40's and had been married for more than 20 years, but was separated from her husband when she met Ruth. She had never had, or thought of having, a homosexual relationship.

"When I met Ruth, she was just another woman, another mother," she said. "We had lunch together occasionally and I found that I had extremely warm feelings toward her which I had never experienced before. It evolved from there."

The carefully made-up face beneath the bouffant hair looked troubled.

"I have a guilt complex because I'm living a lie," she said. "I lived for a long time in an unfeeling existence and I felt there must be something more. I had affairs with men while I was married, all of them satisfactory sexually, but I was always looking for someone to care for. This came to me late in life. When I see young girls who know they are Lesbians, I'm very glad for them because they have found out in time to avoid a series of traps."

Jean is an example of what Dr. Socarides terms "the consciously motivated homosexual"—people who become homosexuals or engage in homosexual acts for many reasons—power, extra thrills and kicks and, in women, often at times, "despair, disappointment or fright."

"Women can easily regress to a mother-child relationship with another woman who will take care of them at times like first menstruation, first intercourse, a disappointing love affair or a divorce," he explained.

Dr. Socarides characterizes as "ill" the true "obligatory" homosexual who is "obliged" to carry out the homosexual act and afterwards "feels restored, the way a narcotics addict takes a shot."

"It is quite a severe illness but amenable to therapy in a great majority of cases," he said. His own estimate of the number of homosexuals in New York City is about 200,000 and "in my opinion, the percentage of females is the same as males." (To Miss Kent, the number of known or suspected Lesbians "is like the tip of the iceberg.")

Dr. Socarides, who rates the incidence of suicide and alcoholism as "high" among Lesbians, insists that "a vocal minority of society is trying to sell a bill of goods that the homosexual is normal."

"The homosexuals themselves know it is not normal," he asserted.

An opposing view is taken by Dr. Lawrence Le Shan, a research psychologist with a doctorate from the University of Chicago. He believes "it is not a disease; it is a choice and everybody should be allowed to choose."

Dr. Le Shan and his wife, Eda, also a psychologist, said that the homosexual "arouses terrible anguish and enormous psychological fear in society" but that "the goal, the hope, the dream of society is the sense of the miracle of individuality."

Mrs. Le Shan thought that the change would come through the younger generation.

"Young people make no value judgments about homosexuality," she said. "They have the attitude that there are many different ways of loving and that it's no one's business. They are a tremendously moral generation. They care only about how people feel about each other."

One area where the homosexual woman appears to have made little headway is with her parents. The umbrella of parental understanding shelters few Lesbians.

"Nothing frightens parents more than the possibility that their children might become homosexuals," one psychologist said.

"I told my two brothers that I was a Lesbian," said Audrey, a diminutive, 28-year-old brunette. "The 21-year-old asked, 'Are you happy?' and the 18-year-old shrugged his shoulders and said, 'It's your bag.' But most parents won't believe it, won't discuss it and think it will go away."

Organization Purports Dual Educational Aim

The dual purpose of the Student Homophile League is, according to Helen, one of its executives, "to educate homosexuals that they have nothing to hide and to educate heterosexuals what it

N. Tuck

Homosexuals, male and female, picketing in Washington last July 4

means to be discriminated against for something so minor as sexual orientation."

Last May, the league held "New York's first gay mixer" dance at the Church of the Holy Apostle. Six hundred students, instructors and friends ("some of them were straight, we don't discriminate") attended.

"I knew the mixer was to be a gay dance—for homosexuals," said Rev. Robert O. Weeks, the rector, who was "very proud" of the event. "It was a real revelation to me, a very pleasant scene. There was no rowdy behavior, no bad vibrations."

Father Weeks, an Episcopalian, had three students from the General Theological Seminary attend, wearing clerical collars.

"Homosexuals should be free to have social gatherings in places other than gay bars and the church's attitude should be one of compassion in accordance with the strictures of Jesus Christ," Father Weeks said.

Father Weeks admitted that there had been some negative reactions on the part of his parishioners but he chose to make the facilities available "to show that the church cares about homosexuals as people and that it is an un-Christian idea that they be shunned."

The Daughters of Bilitis (who answer their telephone on meeting nights with "D.O.B. Can we help you?") holds meetings in unprepossessing quarters on an unprepossessing street in midtown Manhattan.

Women under 21 are not allowed to join the organization, a proviso that prompts some of the younger Lesbians to inquire "do they think you have to be 21 to be a Lesbian?"

The national membership is now about 500 but, according to Rita Laporte, the national president (who uses her real name), there are many more who are interested and come to meetings but are "afraid to get on our mailing list."

The homosexual woman can, if alone, find friends in the long, narrow red-walled room, illuminated with globe-shaped bulbs. She can also, if she is with a woman friend, reach out to touch her arm or hold her hand without exciting comment. The physical demonstrations are generally mild and infrequent.

Not Many in 'Drag' At One Popular Bar

There is notable absence of the "drag dykes," the women who imitate men in their dress and manner, at both D.O.B.

and at one of the most popular Lesbian bars, a retreat of pleated red velvet walls and crystal chandeliers.

There, its portals guarded by two men who extract a minimum $3 for two drink tickets, and who are said to look unkindly on any male patronage (male homosexuals are passively, and straight males more actively, discouraged), the girls gather, young and middle-aged, white and black, miniskirted and pantssuited.

The "femmes" (the more feminine Lesbians), and the "butches" (the more aggressive and domineering Lesbians, with both masculine and feminine characteristics), talk, drink and dance to juke box records, usually with arms around each other's waist or neck.

There are also a few "dykes," the women with masculine clothing and mannerisms, who are more easily identifiable as homosexuals but do not imitate men to the same degree as "drag dykes."

Most of the Lesbians count male homosexuals among their friends "because you can feel relaxed with them—there are no sexual tensions." A number of them said that although they preferred women, they also like men and had had heterosexual relationships. A small minority were leading a bisexual life.

Almost all of them thought that straight men were generally intrigued by Lesbians. "Straight men feel challenged by us," said one Lesbian.

Many Lesbians undergo therapy; some because they have a genuine desire to belong to a heterosexual community and others because of the pressures of society. But many resent being called "sick."

"I don't think homosexuality is an illness," said one. "If I am capable of loving someone, a woman, and I feel good, why am I sick?"

"I don't think there is anything unnatural about it," Audrey said. "I wish that some day people would consider it another form of normality. I just feel dirty when I hide.

"We all wonder why we are the way we are. Other people have the same experiences and it doesn't add up to the same total. But I can't imagine being what I'm not."

Traditional Groups Prefer to Ignore Women's Lib

By LACEY FOSBURGH

The traditional organizations that for decades have championed women's rights to vote to work, to be educated and to serve their communities are facing a challenge from a movement that many consider bizarre, alien and totally unacceptable.

The problem for such groups as the Daughters of the American Revolution, the Women's Christian Temperance Union, the League of Women Voters, the Junior League and the Young Women's Christian Association is what attitude to take toward the militant women's liberation movement.

At stake in this question, leaders of some of the groups believe, is whether they will deteriorate into worthless anachronisms operated by tired, vacuous women and, one day, simply die out altogether.

Most of the officials say, however, that their traditional programs will easily outlast the women's liberation movement.

Militancy Called Necessary

Dr. Shirley D. McCune, a sociologist, teacher, wife and associate director of the 170,000-member American Association of University Women takes a different view. She believes the traditional groups must adopt a spirit of activism and militancy if they wish to remain timely and viable.

"There's no doubt about it," she said, "the old established women's organizations are under the gun today. And it's a question if they'll survive, unless they become more militant, really militant, and change their whole stance."

"The question facing us is whether we admit the women's revolution is here, or go on trying to deny that it's taking place," she continued during an interview in the organization's national headquarters in Washington.

"Young women just aren't being turned on any more by big groups like ours," she went on. "They want to belong to something small and effective. They're militant, free and strong and the whole concept of ladies' luncheons, teas, charities and good works to fill their leisure time turns them off."

Dr. McCune's ideas on women's liberation, however, are not widely shared by women with similar positions. Recent interviews with dozens of other officials and members of traditional organizations about the impact the women's liberation movement is having—or, more often, not having—on their activities revealed a broad pattern of hostility, indifference or ignorance.

Some thoughtfully gave the opinion the movement was contributing to a general awakening among women. Most, however, maligned it, and considered the feminists "ridiculous exhibitionists," "a band of wild lesbians" or "Communists."

"I just don't think this movement even has a legitimate purpose," said Mrs. Saul Schary, executive secretary and forthcoming president of the 23-million-member National Council of Women.

Women Called 'Self-Limiting'

"There's no discrimination against women like they say there is," Mrs. Schary said. "Women themselves are just self-limiting. It's in their nature and they shouldn't blame it on society or men."

"I simply don't think these so-called liberationists really want all the things they say they do," she continued during an interview in her office at 345 East 45th Street.

"They're doing it 'pour le sport.' I think their noses are out of joint. There's been too much emphasis everywhere on youth and drugs and Black Panthers and these women just said to themselves, "What can we do to get in the act?" "

"And so many of them are just so unattractive," she added, "I wonder if they're completely well."

Today, at a time when the membership of the traditional women's groups is decreasing, their age level getting older and fewer and fewer young women joining, their general position regarding the current feminist movement seems clear.

Virtually none of the organizations has officially endorsed the Women's Strike for Equality the movement has planned for today because, as Mrs. Lucille Shriver, director of the 177,500-member National Federation of Business and Professional Women's Clubs, said:

"We're going to be dignified and ladylike. We're going to stay on the job and continue working in our established way to improve women's status.

411

ENDORSES WOMEN'S ACTIONS: Senator Charles E. Goodell, New York Republican, at news conference in his office on East 45th Street with group from Women's Strike for Equality. At center is Betty Friedan, a strike leader. Mr. Goodell said he would introduce legislation for free child-care centers and legalized abortion throughout U.S.

We're not exhibitionists, and we don't carry signs."

The common bond between the traditional women's organizations is their dedication to work.

The Daughters of the American Revolution supports schools for poor whites in the south and the Women's Christian Temperance Union sponsors education programs for youngsters in the Midwest on "the evils of alcohol." The Country Women's Council, centered in Keota, Iowa, collects "pennies for friendship" from housewives. The Young Women's Christian Association seems to do everything.

They all send letters to Congressmen supporting equal-rights legislation to improve the status of women. They belong to garden clubs and educational societies. They beautify gas stations and operate day-care centers.

"We're conservative and constructive," said Mrs. Wilson Christian, executive secretary of the General Federation of Women's Clubs, which has 11 million members here and overseas. "I'd like to know what women's lib can do to match that."

The vast majority of women interviewed strongly endorsed the traditional concept of woman as a mother and a homemaker who can, and sometimes even should, supplement these activities with a career or with volunteer work.

"I just don't think any of us can agree with what women's lib seems to be saying," argued Mrs. Joe Chittenden, director of research and legislation for the General Federation of Women's Clubs. "I mean, do they really think the American woman is oppressed? And chained to the home? The idea frankly embarasses me."

"I'm a product of my upbringing and I'm a traditionalist," she said, "and I don't have any complaints about the way things are."

Like most of the other spokesmen, Mrs. Chittenden is confident that the women of today and tomorrow will have the same amount of leisure time to devote to traditional volunteer programs as the women of yesterday had.

"The busiest women in the world are clubwomen," she said, "and there'll always be mothers and housewives not just looking for something to do to fill time, but seeing something that needs to be done and doing it."

This attitude of confidence that currently seems to pervade the traditional organizations is dangerous, some officials believe, because, in the words of one who asked to remain anonymous. "It's allowing us to proceed blindly into obsolescence."

"If we go on operating as usual, pretending that change won't ever affect us, we're obviously in trouble," said Dr. McCune, who frankly admits that her radical views about the role of women in American society are far more progressive than those of the Association of University Women's membership in general.

To Dr. McCune, who predicts that within a year the traditional organizations generally will rise out of their current period of stagnation and try to adapt to the growing activism, older women's resistance to the liberation movement is understandable.

"For the 30-to-60-year-old woman the idea of liberation is very threatening," she said. "She's been in shackles all her life and now girls 20 years younger than her and much prettier are telling her to run.

"Her whole sense of identity is deeply threatened by the freedom the new woman enjoys because it's a rejection of everything she stands for. No matter how bright or educated she may be, she's been conditioned in such a way she's never had the chance to find out who she really is or what she could become."

"And the point is," Dr. McCune added, "she doesn't want to find out."

She Takes a Stand Against Liberation

By JOAN COOK

Helen B. Andelin, a 50-year-old housewife from Santa Barbara, who looks considerably younger than her years, is a self-appointed spokesman for the "silent majority" of American women who believe that women's place is in the home.

Married for 27 years, with eight children ranging in age from 8 to 23, she has spelled out her message in a book, "Fascinating Womanhood," which her husband published privately (Pacific Press, $5.95).

"I'm touring Dallas, Atlanta, Washington, D. C., Detroit and here to talk about 'Fascinating Womanhood' and why I am opposed to women's lib," Mrs. Andelin said, crossing her shapely legs. She was wearing pink pumps to match her pink jersey dress.

Against Day Care

"Women's lib has degraded women's importance in the home, making pots, pans and children menial tasks and urging women to find fulfillment in contributions outside the home," Mrs. Andelin said, settling back in her chair.

Women's lib has particularly gained her ire with its proposals for more day care centers.

"Day care centers will encourage women to leave home," she said. "They will make it easier for those who are tired and bored to take jobs away from their homes."

Through her book, Mrs. Andelin dangles the prospect of achieving "celestial love," a state that turns a garden variety housewife into a "domestic goddess." To do this requires that a woman combine her angelic and human sides, she says, and her ideal woman is called "Angela Human."

"Fascinating Womanhood," which gives step-by-step instructions on her method for captivating a husband, was

published in 1963 as the result of some booklets Mrs. Andelin stumbled on and decided to revise called "Secrets of A Fascinating Woman" written in the twenties.

"I came to New York three times hoping Doubleday would publish it, but they decided it went against the mainstream," she said.

With the onslaught of women's lib, however, "Fascinating Womanhood" as a philosophy was never more needed, she feels.

On role-playing within a marriage, she describes the man's role as threefold: guide (he rules the household), protector (he performs tasks requiring superior strength), and provider (as enunciated in the Bible).

A woman, by the same token must be feminine, mature, childlike and beruffled. The feminine woman, according to Mrs. Andelin eschews tweeds or tailored clothes, anything that is masculine in dress.

Superior Character

"A man wants a woman he can put on a pedestal and worship from below, someone whose character is superior to his," Mrs. Andelin said.

She met her husband, Dr. Henry B. Andelin, a former dentist turned businessman, when they were both students at Brigham Young University (they are Mormons) where she was majoring in home economics. After two years, she dropped out in favor of marriage.

Dr. Andelin promotes cattle ranches in this country and Australia where Mrs.

The New York Times (by William E. Sauro)

Mrs. Helen B. Andelin is organizing a womanhood day on behalf of antiliberation forces.

Andelin said he owned a million-acre ranch.

Her concern with womanhood stems from the state of American marriage, she said.

"I began to observe all the troubles marriages around me were having . . . and I felt that my own marriage had drifted to a state of mediocrity," she said. "I thought that marriage should be like a fairy tale. I knew something was wrong."

Since "Fascinating Womanhood" transformed her own life, Mrs. Andelin has tried to bring the word to others through classes, a newsletter and another book aimed at single women called "The Fascinating Girl" (also privately published).

Further, she is organizing a nationwide "Celebration of Womanhood" for Sept. 30, when women are urged to wear their most feminine dresses, sing before breakfast, serve their husbands breakfast in bed with a smile, tell them how great they are and how much their wives love being homemakers and mothers.

It goes without saying that Mrs. Andelin takes a dim view of the equal rights legislation, save for the equal pay part.

"Women shouldn't try to take over men's jobs," she said. "To do it a woman would have to take on masculine traits. Women are not meant to have top jobs."

NORMAN MAILER VS. WOMEN'S LIB

By ISRAEL SHENKER

For a while last night it seemed like Norman Mailer against the world—in "A Dialogue on Women's Liberation" at Town Hall.

In a sellout benefit sponsored for itself by the Theater for Ideas, the hall was filled with the élite of a thousand intellectual battles. In France they would have made a brilliant salon, but here they had simply made it—and were on hand to hear Norman Mailer finally confront the critics of his study of women's liberation.

Gregory Corso, the poet, was there, trying to find an usher. When he found his seat he got right up again and objected to the first speaker's defense of the womanly half of humanity. Mr. Corso shouted for the rights of "all humanity."

"Hey, Gregory," Mr. Mailer called, "you'll get bounced. Keep it up." But Mr. Corso was already en route to the exit—and into the night.

"There's a woman outside who can't afford to get in," shouted a voice from the balcony

Mr. Mailer allowed as how "It'll always be true until it's not true."

When the audience kept interrupting the first speaker—Jacqueline Ceballos, head of the New York chapter of the National Organization of Women (NOW), Mr. Mailer predicted that the perspective of the future was universal, asanine dialogue.

Miss Ceballos argued in favor of women's rights to equality with men. "Is there anything in your program," Mr. Mailer asked, "that would give men the notion that life would not be as boring as it is today?"

The second scheduled speaker was Germaine Greer, author of "The Female Eunuch," who attacked the male artistic ego. It was impossible to be goddess of love and menial drudge at the same time, she complained, adding: "We broke our hearts trying to keep our aprons clean."

Miss Greer concluded with an appeal for artists such as those who produced the cathedral of Chartres and the mosaics of Byzantium — "who had no ego and no name."

Mr. Mailer assailed the speech — indeed much of the rhetoric of women's liberation— for failing to provide the means to the end. "Diaper Marxism," he called it, and suggested that a woman can be a goddess and a slob at different moments."

Third of the scheduled speakers was Jill Johnston, dance columnist for The Village Voice. Her prepared speech was a free verse, free association, pun-infested, Bible-belting cry for the rites of lesbians.

When she had finished, another young woman jumped onto the stage and embraced her ardently. A third young woman joined the other two—and soon the three were groveling on the stage in close concert.

"You know, it's great that you pay $25 to see three dirty overalls on the floor," said Mr. Mailer, referring to the $10 to $25 admission charge. He pleaded with Miss Johnson and her cohorts to cede and desist.

"Come on, Jill," he said "be a lady."

Finally he took a vote by arms' raised, then a roaring voice vote ruled that Miss Johnson et al would have to clear off.

Diana Trilling, the critic of the arts, was easily the most learned of the four scheduled speakers, and she took Mr. Mailer to task for the way he had dealt with women in his article on "The Prisoner of Sex."

Mr. Mailer had extended the "passivity" of women beyond its strict biological application, she complained. He had already told the audience that the Harper's piece was "probably the most important single intellectual event of the last four years," a judgment that was greeted with good-natured laughter from his friends.

The article coincided with a shift of editors at Harper's which had not earlier run such an abundance of frank language. A good deal of that same language resounded from the Town Hall stage—and floor.

The audience included such luminaries as Norman Podhoretz, editor of Commentary, and his wife, Midge Decter, formerly of Harper's. Arthur Schlesinger was there with the Smiths, Stephen and Jean. Jules Feiffer was on the aisle. Betty Friedan made a statement and Susan Sontag objected to Mailer's use of the word "lady."

The verbal battles spilled over into the lobby and the ladies lounge, where two women commented acidly on a third, who finally flounced out, calling over her shoulder: "You're getting as bad as the brothers, sisters."

May 1, 1971

What the Black Woman Thinks About Women's Lib

By TONI MORRISON

THEY were always there. Whenever you wanted to do something simple, natural and inoffensive. Like drink some water, sit down, go to the bathroom or buy a bus ticket to Charlotte, N. C. Those classifying signs that told you who you were, what to do. More than those abrupt and discourteous signs one gets used to in this country—the door that says "Push," the towel dispenser that says "Press," the traffic light that says "No"—these signs were not just arrogant, they were malevolent: "White Only," "Colored Only," or perhaps just "Colored," permanently carved into the granite over a drinking fountain. But there was one set of signs that was not malevolent; it was, in fact, rather reassuring in its accuracy and fine distinctions: the pair that said "White Ladies" and "Colored Women."

The difference between white and black females seemed to me an eminently satisfactory one. White females were *ladies*, said the sign maker, worthy of respect. And the quality that made ladyhood worthy? Softness, helplessness and modesty—which I interpreted as a willingness to let others do their labor and their thinking. Colored females, on the other hand, were *women*—unworthy of respect because they were tough, capable, independent and immodest. Now, it appears, there is a consensus that those anonymous sign makers were right all along, for there is no such thing as Ladies' Liberation. Even the word "lady" is anathema to feminists. They insist upon the "woman" label as a declaration of their rejection of all that softness, helplessness and modesty, for they see them as characteristics which

TONI MORRISON, an editor at Random House and author of "The Bluest Eye," is at work on her second novel.

414

Nefertiti.
The black queen of ancient Egypt, she of the enviable neck, is a romantic archetype whom many young black women have appropriated for themselves. But romanticism, says the author, though it may appear to make life livable, separates one from reality.

served only to secure their bondage to men.

SIGNIFICANT as that shift in semantics is, obvious as its relationship to the black-woman concept is, it has not been followed by any immediate comradery between black and white women, nor has it precipitated any rush of black women into the various chapters of NOW. It is the *Weltanschauung* of black women that is responsible for their apparent indifference to Women's Lib, and in order to discover the nature of this view of oneself in the world, one must look very closely at the black woman herself—a difficult, inevitably doomed proposition, for if anything is true of black women, it is how consistently they have (deliberately, I suspect) defied classification.

It may not even be possible to look at those militant young girls with lids lowered in dreams of guns, those middle-class socialites with 150 pairs of shoes, those wispy girl junkies who have always been older than water, those beautiful Muslim women with their bound hair and flawless skin, those television personalities who think chic is virtue and happiness a good coiffure, those sly old women in the country with their ancient love of Jesus—and still talk about The Black Woman. It is a dangerous misconception, for it encourages lump thinking. And we are so accustomed to that in our laboratories that it seems only natural to confront all human situations, direct all human discourse, in the same way. Those who adhere to the scientific method and draw general conclusions from "representative" sampling are chagrined by the suggestion that there is any other way to arrive at truth, for they like their truth in tidy sentences that begin with "all."

In the initial confrontation with a stranger, it is never "Who are you?" but "Take me to your leader." And it is this mode of thought which has made black-white relationships in this country so hopeless. There is a horror of dealing with people one by one, each as he appears. There is safety and manageability in dealing with the leader—no matter how large or diverse the leader's constituency may be. Such generalizing may be all right for plant analysis, superb for locating carcinogens in mice, and it used to be all right as a method for dealing with schools and politics. But no one would deny that it is rapidly losing effectiveness in both those areas—precisely because it involves classifying human beings and anticipating their behavior. So it is with some trepidation that anyone should undertake to generalize about still another group. Yet something in that order is legitimate, not only because unity among minorities is a political necessity, but because, at some point, one wants to get on with the differences.

WHAT do black women feel about Women's Lib? Distrust. It is white, therefore suspect. In spite of the fact that liberating movements in the black world have been catalysts for white feminism, too many movements and organizations have made deliberate overtures to enroll blacks and have ended up by rolling them. They don't want to be used again to help somebody gain power—a power that is carefully kept out of their hands. They look at white women and see them as the enemy—for they know that racism is not confined to white men, and that there are more white women than men in this country, and that 53 per cent of the population sustained an eloquent silence during times of greatest stress. The faces of those white women hovering behind that black girl at the Little Rock school in 1957 do not soon leave the retina of the mind.

When she was interviewed by Nikki Giovanni last May in Essence magazine, Ida Lewis, the former editor-in-chief of Essence, was asked why black women were not more involved in Women's Lib, and she replied: "The Women's Liberation Movement is basically a family quarrel between white women and white men. And on general principles, it's not good to get involved in family disputes. Outsiders always get shafted when the dust settles. On the other hand, I must support some of the goals [equal pay, child-care centers, etc.].... But if we speak of a liberation movement, as a black woman I view my role from a black perspective—the role of black women is to continue the struggle in concert with black men for the liberation and self-determination of blacks. White power was not created to protect and preserve us as women. Nor can we view ourselves as simply American women. We are black women, and as such we must deal effectively in the black community."

To which Miss Giovanni sighed: "Well, I'm glad you didn't come out of that Women's Lib or black-man bag as if they were the alternatives...."

Miss Lewis: "Suppose the Lib movement succeeds. It will follow, since white power is the order of the day, that white women will be the first hired, which will still leave black men and women outside...."

It is an interesting exchange, Miss Lewis expressing suspicion and identifying closely with black men, Miss Giovanni suggesting that the two are not necessarily mutually exclusive.

BUT there is not only the question of color, there is the question of the color of experience. Black women are not convinced that Women's Lib serves their best interest or that it can cope with the uniqueness of their experience, which is itself an alienating factor. The early image of Women's Lib was of an élitist organization made up of upper-middle-class women with the concerns of that class (the percentage of women in professional fields, etc.) and not paying much attention to the problems of most black women, which are not in getting into the labor force but in being upgraded in it, not in getting into medical school but in getting adult education, not in how to exercise freedom from the "head of the house" but in how to be head of the household.

Black women are different from white women because they view themselves differently, are viewed differently and lead a different kind of life. Describing this difference is the objective of several black women writers and scholars. But even without this newly surfacing analysis, we can gain some understanding of the black women's world by examining archetypes. The archetypes created by women about themselves are rare, and even those few that do exist may be the result of a female mind completely controlled by male-type thinking. No matter. The most unflattering stereotypes that male minds have concocted about black women contain, under the stupidity and the hostility, the sweet smell of truth.

Look, for example, at Geraldine and Sapphire—Geraldine, that campy character in Flip Wilson's comic repertory, and Sapphire, the wife of Kingfish in the Amos and Andy radio and TV series. Unlike Nefertiti, an archetype that black women have appropriated for themselves, Geraldine and Sapphire are the comic creations of men. Nefertiti, the romantic black queen with the enviable neck, is particularly appealing to young black women, mainly because she existed (and there are few admirable heroines in our culture), was a great beauty and is remote enough to be worshiped. There is a lot of talk about Sojourner Truth, the freed slave who preached emancipation and women's rights, but there is a desperate love for Nefertiti, simply because she was so pretty.

I suppose at bottom we are all beautiful queens, but for the moment it is perhaps just as well to remain useful women. One wonders if Nefertiti could have lasted 10 minutes in a welfare office, in a Mississippi gas station, at a Parent Association meeting or on the church congregation's Stewardess Board No. 2. And since black women have to endure, that romanticism seems a needless *cul de sac*, an opiate that appears to make life livable if not serene but eventually must separate us from reality. I maintain that black women are already O.K. O.K. with our short necks. O.K. with our callused hands. O.K. with our tired feet and paper bags on the Long Island Rail Road. O.K. O.K. O.K.

AS for Geraldine, her particular horror lies in her essential accuracy. Like any stereotype she is a gross distortion of reality and as such highly offensive to many black women and endearing to many whites. A single set of characteristics provokes both hatred and affection. Geraldine is defensive, cunning, sexy, egocentric and transvestite. But that's not all she is. A shift in semantics and we find the accuracy: for defensive read survivalist; for cunning read clever; for sexy read a natural unembarrassed acceptance of her sexuality; for egocentric read keen awareness of individuality; for transvestite (man in woman's dress) read a masculine strength beneath the accouterments of glamour.

Geraldine is offensive to many blacks precisely because the virtues of black women are construed in her portrait as vices. The strengths are portrayed as weaknesses—hilarious weaknesses. Yet one senses even in the laughter some awe and respect. Interestingly enough, Geraldine is absolutely faithful to one man, Killer, whom one day we may also see as caricature.

Sapphire, a name of opprobrium black men use for the nagging black wife, is also important, for in that marriage, disastrous as it was, Sapphire worked, fussed, worked and fussed, but (and

this is crucial) Kingfish did whatever he pleased. Whatever. Whether he was free or irresponsible, anarchist or victim depends on your point of view. Contrary to the black-woman-as-emasculator theory, we see, even in these unflattering caricatures, the very opposite of a henpecked husband and emasculating wife—a wife who never did, and never could, manipulate her man. Which brings us to the third reason for the suspicion black women have of Women's Lib: the serious one of the relationship between black women and black men.

THERE are strong similarities in the way black and white men treat women, and strong similarities in the way women of both races react. But the relationship is different in a very special way.

For years in this country there was no one for black men to vent their rage on except black women. And for years black women accepted that rage—even regarded that acceptance as their unpleasant duty. But in doing so, they frequently kicked back, and they seem never to have become the "true slave" that white women see in their own history. True, the black woman did the housework, the drudgery; true, she reared the children, often alone, but she did all of that while occupying a place on the job market, a place her mate could not get or which his pride would not let him accept. And she had nothing to fall back on: not maleness, not whiteness, not ladyhood, not anything. And out of the profound desolation of her reality she may very well have invented herself.

If she was a sexual object in the eyes of men, that was their doing. Sex was *one* of her dimensions. It had to be just one, for life required many other things of her, and it is difficult to be regarded solely as a sex object when the burden of field and fire is on your shoulders. She could cultivate her sexuality but dared not be obsessed by it. Other people may have been obsessed by it, but the circumstances of her life did not permit her to dwell on it or survive by means of its exploitation.

So she combined being a responsible person with being a female—and as a person she felt free to confront not only the world at large (the rent man, the doctor and the rest of the marketplace) but her man as well. She fought him and nagged him—but knew that you don't fight what you don't respect. (If you don't respect your man, you manipulate him, the way some parents treat children and the way white women treat their men—if they can get away with it or if they do not acquiesce entirely). And even so, the black man was calling most of the shots—in the home or out of it. The black woman's "bad" relationships with him were often the result of his inability to deal with a competent and complete personality and her refusal to be anything less than that. The saving of the relationship lay in her unwillingness to feel free when her man was not free.

In a way black women have known something of the freedom white women are now beginning to crave. But oddly, freedom is only sweet when it is won. When it is forced, it is called responsibility. The black woman's needs shrank to the level of her responsibility; her man's expanded in proportion to the obstacles that prevented him from assuming his. White women, on the other hand, have had too little responsibility, white men too much. It's a wonder the sexes of either race even speak to each other.

AS if that were not enough, there is also the growing rage of black women over unions of black men and white women. At one time, such unions were rare enough to be amusing or tolerated. The white woman moved with the black man into a black neighborhood, and everybody tried to deal with it. Chances are the white woman who married a black man liked it that way, for she had already made some statement about her relationship with her own race by marrying him. So there were no frictions. If a white woman had a child out of wedlock by a black man, the child was deposited with the black community, or grouped with the black orphans, which is certainly one of the reasons why lists of black foundling children are so long. (Another reason is the willingness of black women to have their children instead of aborting—and to keep them, whatever the inconvenience.)

But now, with all the declarations of independence, one of the black man's ways of defining it is to broaden his spectrum of female choices, and one consequence of his new pride is the increased attraction white women feel for him. Clearly there are more and more of these unions, for there is clearly more anger about it (talking black and sleeping white is a cliché) among black women. The explanations for this anger are frequently the easy ones: there are too few eligible men, for wars continue to shoot them up; the black woman who complains is one who would be eliminated from a contest with any good-looking woman — the complaint simply reveals her inadequacy to get a man; it is a simple case of tribal sour grapes with a dash of politics thrown in.

But no one seems to have examined this anger in the light of what black women understand about themselves. These easy explanations are obviously male. They overlook the fact that the hostility comes from both popular beauties and happily married black women. There is something else in this anger, and I think it lies in the fact that black women have always considered themselves superior to white women. Not racially superior, just superior in terms of their ability to function healthily in the world.

Black women have been able to envy white women (their looks, their easy life, the attention they seem to get from their men); they could fear them (for the economic control they have had over black women's lives) and even love them (as mammies and domestic workers can); but black women have found it impossible to respect white women. I mean they never had what black men have had for white men—a feeling of awe at their accomplishments. Black women have no abiding admiration of white women as competent, complete people. Whether vying with them for the few professional slots available to women in general, or moving their dirt from one place to another, they regarded them as willful children, pretty children, mean children, ugly children, but never as real adults capable of handling the real problems of the world.

White women were ignorant of the facts of life—perhaps by choice, perhaps with the assistance of men, but ignorant anyway. They were totally dependent on marriage or male support (emotionally or economically). They confronted their sexuality with furtiveness, complete abandon or repression. Those who could afford it, gave over the management of the house and the rearing of children to others. (It is a source of amusement even now to black women to listen to feminists talk of liberation while somebody's nice black grandmother shoulders the daily responsibility of child rearing and floor mopping and the liberated one comes home to examine the housekeeping, correct it, and be entertained by the children. If Women's Lib needs those grandmothers to thrive, it has a serious flaw.) The one great disservice black women are guilty of (albeit not by choice) is that they are the means by which white women can escape the responsibilities of womanhood and remain children all the way to the grave.

It is this view of themselves and of white women that makes the preference of a black man for a white woman quite a crawful. The black women regard his choice as an inferior one. Over and over again one hears one question from them: "But why, when they marry white women, do they pick the raggletail ones, the silly, the giddy, the stupid, the flat nobodies of the race? Why no real women?" The answer, of course, is obvious. What would such a man who preferred white women do with a real woman? And would a white woman who is looking for black exotica ever be a complete woman?

Obviously there are black and white couples who love each other as people, and marry each other that way. (I can think of two such.) But there is so often a note of apology (if the woman is black) or bravado (if the man is) in such unions, which would hardly be necessary if the union was something other than a political effort to integrate one's emotions and therefore, symbolically, the world. And if all the black partner has to be is black and exotic, why not?

This feeling of superiority contributes to the reluctance of black women to embrace Women's Lib. That and the very important fact that black men are formidably opposed to their involvement in it— and for the most part the women understand their fears.

In The Amsterdam News, an editor, while deploring the conditions of black political organizations, warns his readers of the consequences: "White politicians have already organized. And their organizers are even attempting to co-opt Black women into their organizational structure, which may well place Black women against Black men, that is, if the struggle for women's liberation is viewed by Black women as being above the struggle for Black liberation."

The consensus among blacks is that their first liberation has not been realized; unspoken is the conviction of black men that any more aggressiveness and "freedom" for black women would be intolerable, not to say counterrevolutionary.

There is also a contention among some black women that Women's Lib is nothing more than an attempt on the part of whites to become black without the responsibilities of being black. Certainly some of the demands of liberationists seem to rack up as our thing: common-law marriage (shacking); children out of wedlock, which is even fashionable now if you are a member of the Jet Set (if you are poor and black it is still a crime); fami-

lies without men; right to work; sexual freedom, and an assumption that a woman is equal to a man.

Now we have come full circle: the morality of the welfare mother has become the avant-garde morality of the land. There is a good deal of irony in all of this. About a year ago in The Village Voice there was a very interesting exchange of letters. Cecil Brown was explaining to a young black woman the "reasons" for the black man's interest in white girls: a good deal about image, psychic needs and what not. The young girl answered in a rather poignant way to this effect: Yes, she said, I suppose, again, we black women have to wait, wait for the brother to get himself together—be enduring, understanding, and, yes, she thought they could do it again . . . but, in the meantime, what do we tell the children?

This woman who spoke so gently in those letters of the fate of the children may soon discover that the waiting period is over. The softness, the "she knows how to treat me" (meaning she knows how to be a cooperative slave) that black men may be looking for in white women is fading from view. If Women's Lib is about breaking the habit of

genuflection, if it is about controlling one's own destiny, is about female independence in economic, personal and political ways, if it is indeed about working hard to become a person, knowing that one has to work hard at becoming anything, Man or Woman—and if it succeeds, then we may have a nation of white Geraldines and white Sapphires, and what on earth is Kingfish gonna do then?

The winds are changing, and when they blow, new things move. The liberation movement has moved from shrieks to shape. It is focusing itself, becoming a hard-headed power base, as the National Women's Political Caucus in Washington attested last month. Representative Shirley Chisholm was radiant: "Collectively we've come together, not as a Women's Lib group, but as a women's political movement." Fannie Lou Hamer, the Mississippi civil-rights leader, was there. Beulah Sanders, chairman of New York's Citywide Coordinating Committee of Welfare Groups, was there. They see, perhaps, something real: women talking about human rights rather than sexual rights — something other than a family quarrel, and the air is shivery with possibilities. ■

August 22, 1971

In Small Town, U.S.A., Women's Liberation Is Either a Joke or a Bore

By JUDY KLEMESRUD
Special to The New York Times

HOPE, Ind.—Hardly anyone in this central Indiana farming town of 1,500 has heard of Betty Friedan. Gloria Steinem is as foreign to the white Protestant natives as a breakfast of bagels and lox. The term "consciousness-raising" is likely to elicit a furrowed brow and a "Huh?" while a male chauvinist pig would probably be identified as just another breed to haul to next summer's Bartholomew County Fair.

No, women's liberation has not reached Small Town, U.S.A.

At least it hasn't reached Hope, which seems fairly typical of the thousands of small towns scattered throughout the

country, towns where traffic lights are nonexistent because traffic is almost nonexistent. And the first (and last) picture show has closed down because of lack of business. And strangers are greeted with smiles and "Hi's" on the town square. And hardly anyone has been to college. And bored teen-agers guzzle Cokes at a hang-out on the outskirts called Judy's Drive-In.

It has been called a major weakness of the women's movement, this failure to reach the boondocks. It is not that the people haven't heard of women's lib. They hear about it regularly from their beloved Johnny Carson and read about it in their favorite magazines, Life, Redbook and Good Housekeeping. It's just that they don't care enough about it, or don't understand it, to want to know more of the specifics.

"What you have here are a lot of happy women," explained Mrs. Katherine Stafford, the 56-year-old college-educated Hope librarian, who so far has not added any of the various women's lib books to the town stacks. "Maybe if they weren't so happy, there might be more interest in women's liberation. As it is, we talk about it only very jokingly—if at all."

So far, none of the town's major women's organizations — the Royal Neighbors of America, Eastern Star, Kappa Kappa Sigma and the Woman's Christian Temperance Union—have discussed the women's movement at their meetings. But last summer, a woman described as "a radical school teacher" from nearby Columbus, Ind., came to speak about women's liberation to members of the all-male Lions Club.

"The men were fighting-mad afterwards," recalled Mrs. Betty Taylor, 39, who runs the town's only hardware store while her husband works at the Cummins Engine Company in Columbus, employer of many Hope men. "She told them that people shouldn't be judged by what's between their legs, and ever since, people around here just haven's been too serious about women's lib."

The gray-haired Mrs. Taylor is probably one of the more liberated women of Hope, but she doesn't think of herself that way. She does all of the things in her work that a man would do, including cutting pipe. Her back room doubles as a day-care center for female employes who want to bring their babies with them to work. She believes she started the fad among Hope women of wearing pants to work. Her husband, Kenneth, helps with the housework.

Like most Hope women, she is vociferously in favor of equal pay for equal work. But the first words that come out of her mouth when asked about women's lib are: "What does burning bras have to do with making things equal?"

And the so-called "radicals" in the movement bother her. "Some of them are just like the radicals of the colored race," she said. "They do more harm than good."

Still, change has come creeping into Hope, not all of it the kind Hope residents like. People are still talking about the woman who ran out on her husband and children a few years ago and hasn't been seen since. She is referred to as "that runaway mother."

Four housefuls of alleged drug peddlers were recently run out of town after irate residents held a "town meeting" at Hauser High School, named after the town's Moravian founder, Martin Hauser. The high school pregnancy rate is up, and so is the town's divorce rate. In fact, some squabbling couples have taken the somewhat radical step of bypassing their local clergymen and taking their troubles to a family counseling service in Columbus.

"Are those city women really feeling oppressed?" asked Mrs. Judy Douglas, 26, with a grin. "Why do they get married then? Why make innocent kids stay home with a baby sitter?"

Mrs. Douglas has two sons, age 8 and 7, and after school lets out, they come to the jewelry store she runs on the town square, and they sit in a back room and watch television until closing time. Someday, when Mrs. Douglas's husband takes over the store (he is now attending a watchmaker's school in Seymour, Ind.) Mrs. Douglas and her sons will both be at home after school.

"I for one don't want equal rights with men," she said vigorously. "I just want to be a woman. I believe a man should be the head of the house. I want to can, freeze, baby-sit, all those things that bore most women."

Bridge, Bowling, the Movies

Several women said they thought that the lack of interest in the women's movement was because so many Hope women were born and raised on farms.

"The women on the farm have always been working hand-in-hand with their men," said Mrs. Marie Harker, 59, whose husband farms 80 acres northeast of Hope. "I don't think we feel this pressure [for equality] that some women do. But then I'm not so sure that women are held down as much as they pretend to be, either."

What do Hope women do for entertainment? Almost every woman seems to belong to a bridge club, where she exchanges town gossip with friends and talks about how she plans to vote for President Nixon again. Sometimes couples go bowling or to the movies in Columbus, or for a big night out, they might drive the 50 miles northwest to "Indy." And almost everybody is an avid fan of the athletic teams at Hauser High School.

Most of the women who were interviewed seemed strongly opposed to legalized abortion and felt that they could never bring themselves to mark an X beside the name of a woman Presidential candidate.

"I think if someone has an abortion, they ought to take 'em out and hang 'em," said Mrs. Wavelene Embs, 32, a self-styled "grease monkey" at her husband Herbie's Sunoco service station. "If it wasn't God's will, they wouldn't have gotten pregnant in the first place."

Mrs. Embs, a Baptist who was married at the age of 14 and now has four children, slapped her hand against a stack of tires and howled when asked if she would vote for a woman for President.

"Hell, no!" she replied. "They're so weak, they'd have headaches and wouldn't be able to run the country. They'd be sick in bed all the time."

Mrs. Shirley Mills, whose pharmacist husband pays her $75 every Friday for doing the bookkeeping at their drugstore, was one of the few women who could identify a women's liberation leader.

"I read Germaine Greer's article in Playboy," said Mrs. Mills, who like many of her friends has a puffy bouffant hairdo and rhinestone-trimmed eyeglasses, "and I saw her on Johnny Carson. I think she's very gross. Being in the drugstore, I hear a lot of off-color talk, but Germaine Greer's talk is just outlandish!"

One of the few—and perhaps the only—women in Hope who is openly sympathetic to the women's movement is Mrs.

Kathie Johnson, 23, a former Purdue coed who has returned home "to get my ship together" while going through a divorce. She has a 4-year-old son, Scott.

"I especially like this Ms. thing they talk about," she said, while sitting on a bicycle stand in front of her father's Clouse's Regal Market ("Super Foods"), the town's largest business. "It's been pointed out to me now that I'm going to be divorced that I'll still be called Mrs. I don't like that. I'm nobody's wife now."

Out at the modernistic $1.5-million Hauser High School, on the south edge of town, women's lib has seemed to have made a slight dent. Mrs. Betty Burney, who has been the home economics teacher for 16 years, tells her girl students as well as the boys in her health class that "there is no such thing as women's work" and that a married couple should share the housework if the wife has a job.

'A Bit of Static'

"I get quite a bit of static from the boys," the soft-spoken teacher said, "and some of the girls think it's degrading for a man to do housework or the dishes. But the fact is that it's impossible for a woman who works to take care of the children and the housework and her job, too. That really takes a superwoman."

Otherwise, things at Hauser High seem pretty much the way they always were. Cheerleading is still the most prestigious activity for girls. One of the smartest students in the senior class, Susan Boyle, 18, yearns for the day when she will walk down the aisle in a long white wedding gown and then go on to have five children. Debbie Smith, 16, a former homecoming queen and a majorette, said she had heard of the term, "sex object," but didn't think there was anything wrong with a girl trying to look as pretty as she could for the opposite sex. She would never, she said, think of going without make-up—or a bra.

Back in Hope, Mrs. Patsy Harris, 30, who described herself as "a wife [of a school teacher], mother and homemaker, in that order," sat watching color television with her hair still in rollers. A colored picture of Jesus Christ hung over the set.

"I just don't want a job," she insisted, as two of her four children, Tracy, 6, and Jennifer, 4, squirmed on her lap. "I love staying home. I cannot imagine in my wildest dreams getting up in the morning, dragging the kids to a baby sitter and going to work. I like to be able to sit down and read a book. I feel like my time is my own. I mean, how could a woman be any happier than that?"

Is Women's Lib A Passing Fad?

By JOSEPH ADELSON

IT is curious that, in an age and nation so given over to information, we never seem to know what we want to know; in fact, the more we are told and the more we think we know, the less we really know. As a case in point, I suggest the Women's Liberation Movement. We will all accept, I am sure, that it exists, but beyond that, our certain knowledge ceases. The glare of publicity blinds us. One would like to know, for example, whether the movement, having so successfully captured our common attention, has, in fact, captured the sympathy of women, and if so, which women, and how deeply, and for how long. Are we dealing with something which matters, or which only seems to matter? Do we have here one more of those items of sociological entertainment which the educated classes invent and consume so relentlessly? Will Kate Millet and Germaine Greer go the way of Charles Reich and Timothy Leary, whom you may or may not remember; or do we indeed see the beginnings of something which will change our lives profoundly? The fact is that we do not know; not only do we not know what the future holds, which is understandable, we do not even know much about the shape of the present.

We can begin by making a cautious appraisal of where the movement now stands. For these purposes we should first distinguish between the banal and the extravagant aims of the recent outcry for a change in the status of women. I use neither of these terms pejoratively. I call certain aims banal simply because everyone seems to agree with them, men and women alike; they are now nonissues. Everyone believes in equal pay for equal work; most everyone believes that women should not be sharply limited in the economic roles available to them; and so on. The one public-opinion poll I have been able to find tells us plainly enough that these goals have won nearly

JOSEPH ADELSON is a professor of psychology at the University of Michigan and co-director of its Psychological Clinic.

universal concurrence. The aims I call extravagant are those which involve radical changes in sexual socialization and identity, radical changes in the nature of the family, or its dissolution altogether, and so on. These goals are, at this time, decisively rejected by the population at large, and somewhat more so by women than by men. Finally, I will define the movement as composing those who share a firm commitment to these latter aims, and who extend some personal effort to achieve them.

So much for definitions; now, how wide is the current appeal of the movement? To begin with, it is fairly clear that it is decisively class-linked. Occasional brave words to the contrary, it has had almost no impact outside the educated classes. For the average citizen the movement and its issues are as remote as happenings on the moon, and this despite the enthusiasm of the media. The average he and she may sometimes find the movement's ideas to be offensive, or a bit *outré*, but above all, they find the ideas to be exotic, not vitally connected with one's immediate experience. Not too surprising; radical movements usually begin among élites, and only later ramify. What is more surprising is the generally feeble impression it has so far made on the educated class itself.

One of my graduate students is now doing a doctoral dissertation on the achievement of identity in late adolescent women. Her work is not yet completed, but it is near enough done so that we can be fairly confident of its ultimate findings. She has been interviewing college seniors in the Boston-Cambridge area, women who are largely urban, cosmopolitan, and now engaged in making significant life choices—whether to pursue work, or graduate study, or marriage, or some combination thereof. One would think this group, in view of its age, its education and its current circumstances, would represent an obvious, natural constituency of the movement. The student doing these interviews is herself a most

ardent feminist, and so she was astonished and discouraged to find that of the 34 young women she has spoken to, at length and in depth, only one has had any connection with, or interest in, the movement. One out of 34; 3 per cent. The figure seems to me to be far too low, but I have been intrigued enough to undertake my own impressionistic survey, impressionistic being the polite word for random and chaotic. To put it plainly, I have been pestering every woman who crosses my path—undergraduates, graduates, neighbors, colleagues and wives of colleagues—on the streets, in supermarkets, at dinner parties, cocktail parties, seminars and staff meetings. My sample is suburban, cosmopolitan and formidably well-educated. And I find in this sample that the 3 per cent figure, though probably too low, is not altogether unrepresentative.

WHAT I find, and what a more formal opinion poll might not, is something of the *quality* of thought and feeling about the movement. By and large, women do not care for it; many of them are, of course, glad that the issues are being raised, but are alienated by the terms in which these are addressed. Some are bitterly affronted by the moral blackmail they feel to be implicit or actual in movement literature; they see themselves as free women, who have chosen their situations freely, and not out of fear or passivity or prior indoctrination. By far the largest group of women feels toward the movement an attitude somewhere between irritation and indifference. It does not speak to them, much less for them. For some, the problems they face seem to lie outside their lives as women. But others are facing directly "feminine" issues—the joining of career and motherhood, for example—and do not believe that the rhetoric of the movement, or its fundamental attitudes, or the solutions it proposes to them, connect to the subtle and complex particularities of their lives.

A talk I had with one woman is a characteristic example: She is a freshly minted Ph.D., as is her husband, and they find that she is, for the moment, somewhat more marketable than he, since his field is glutted with new doctorate-holders. This is a problem, a difficult problem, that they will have to work on and work out—as they will have to work out her wish to raise a family and sustain a promising career. She speaks of these problems articulately, even eloquently; yet, she speaks not of

CYCLES. *In the ever-changing round of ideological faddism, Timothy Leary and Charles Reich have had their recent day. Is it possible that Germaine Greer and Kate Millet will follow them?*

ideas, but of who she is and who he is and who they are together, what they have become together, and what they hope to become singly and together. As for the movement, she dismisses it with an impatient shrug; it is simply not germane to her actualities.

Conversations such as this were more the rule than the exception, and I found them inspiriting—not as you might imagine, for the attitudes expressed, which were in fact various, but because they were so blessedly nonideological. These women were of the party of experience, in tou... with and responding to the concrete-

nesses of their lives, however complex and delicately nuanced these might be. I had not expected it, because the men and women of the educated class are so often of the party of ideology. We do not take ourselves for granted; as Simone de Beauvoir says, we have an idea of ourselves. We live by and for and off ideas and ideologies in general,

ideologies which we take to be liberating, since they free us from conventional perceptions. In doing so, they generate and demand other perceptions, which in turn become conventional. Thus, we

merely exchange one set of chains for another. At their worst, ideologies intoxicate; we are so possessed by some metaphor of ourselves and others that we are totally cut off from any accurate recognition of the mundane. And then we are at the mercy of our fantasies.

CONSIDER two of the common ways the movement portrays sexuality. It will sometimes equate male sexuality with rape. Sometimes this is conceived symbolically, that

421

is, rape is seen as the distillation of the normal male sexual attitude; at other times the notion is taken quite literally, along with the organization of karate classes and the like. But, as any clinician knows, these days the problem of male sexuality lies in the opposite direction, not in phallic megalomania, but rather in sexual diffidence and self-doubt. At Ivy League universities, for example, the most common medical complaint among men, after colds and influenza, is sexual impotence.

A second idea is one which characterizes the married woman's sexual life as prostitution. It is an idea I find so quaint that I would not have believed it to be a point of feminist doctrine, had I not heard Gloria Steinem herself announce it. It is an idea that denies, tacitly, our contemporary conception of female sexuality, one which sees it as mutual, in that the woman seeks as much as she gives. In these two ideas, the man as rapist, the woman as whore, we abandon today's actualities; we in fact abandon the 20th century altogether, and return to an earlier world, the dark world of Victorian pornography.

But such is the power of ideology in a class ready to be possessed by it. I take as my text some lines from Midge Decter's brilliant book "The Liberated Woman and Other Americans." She tells us that her writing has tried "to account for the distance between what is, or must be, the experience of something and the way that experience has come to be talked about." She remarks that our failure to see ourselves as simply human "leaves us as a people gasping every five years for an understanding of what has happened since the last set of formulas captured our collective mind, and, in our breathlessness, empty and waiting for the next set to replace it." I want to explore some of these formulas as they bear on the lives of women, and to see whether some larger formula may lie behind them, and beyond that, to inquire who we are and what we are, as a people, as a class, that leads us to be so ruled by ideology.

MY first recognition of the power of ideas to constrain and distort the lives of women came 20 years ago. My first professional job was as a teacher in an expensive, progressive women's college. I soon discovered that the talented and vibrant young women who studied with me could not be persuaded to undertake graduate education, or even to seek jobs which might bespeak too serious a commitment to work. I found this attitude simply incomprehensible; for reasons rooted in my personal history, I took it for granted that women worked, in some cases because they had to, or if their life circumstances were fortunate, because they wanted to. No doubt my vanity was also involved, for I thought I needed intellectual heirs. At any rate, I soon found myself in initially avuncular but increasingly irritated conversations with my more promising students, in which my part of the dialogue ran something like this: "Listen, you are simply too gifted, too energetic, to waste yourself so totally on home and children. You are denying a part of your humanity, what you are, and what you have become, your native intelligence and the careful cultivation it has received. I tell you, you will live to regret it." Such was my melodramatic manner in those days, but all to no avail. My students, in the gentle and self-contained way that characterized feminine manners at that time, might say that they were flattered and would think about it, or might become a bit anxious, a bit distracted, and change the subject. They were too polite to tell me that it was none of my business, as some of my colleagues did. In five years of effort I convinced only one young woman to go as far as taking a master's degree. It was the blight of my life, and finally, in a state of high indignation, I advanced, or perhaps retreated, to a proper university. Such was the fate of a premature male feminist.

Looking back to that period, I think I can now understand what then escaped me. We had as a nation emerged from a great war, itself following upon a long and protracted Depression. We thought, all of us, men and women alike, to replenish ourselves in goods and spirit, to undo, by an exercise of collective will, the psychic disruptions of the immediate past. We would achieve the serenity that had eluded the lives of our parents; the men would be secure in stable careers, the women in comfortable homes, and together they would raise perfect children. Time would come to a stop. Call it what you will—a mystique, an illusion, a myth—it was an ideology of sorts, often unspoken but, perhaps for that very reason, most deeply felt. It was the *Zeitgeist*, the spirit of the times.

The spirit of that time, its ambience, its particular assumptions and perceptions and dogmas, are now difficult to recall, even for those of us who experienced them, and even more difficult to communicate to the young. For the ideologists, young and old, there is no problem at all. As far as women are concerned, they say, it was a sexist period; women were oppressed, had no control of their lives, had few decent job opportunities, had no models to emulate in the professions, and so forth. Much of this is simply wrong in fact; there were, for example, models aplenty, in the independent women of an earlier generation, but the women of the nineteen-fifties turned away from them. But it is even more wrong in spirit, for the ideological mind cannot entertain assumptions other than its own, cannot and indeed dare not penetrate the conditions of other experiences, other times, other places, other ideologies.

ONE more example: a television program devoted to the topic of women in history. The moderator, an intense young woman professor, is interviewing her guest, an expert on the medieval period. As the program goes along, an Alice in Wonderland quality seems to overcome it. Like Alice and the Red Queen, the interviewer and her guest talk at each other, brightly, but not to each other. One wants to know about such things as legal rights, and equal employment opportunities; the other reminds her, gently, that women then rarely lived beyond the age of 30, that they were subject to death in childbirth, pestilence and occasional starvation, that life was short and often brutal, and hints that the medieval woman might have all this on her mind, as well as the fate of her immortal soul. The interviewer does not quite hear this, and goes on about freedom and equality and opportunity. She is suffocated by her categories. Worse still, she cannot achieve distance from them; she cannot recognize how 20th-century she herself is, how American, how liberal, how bourgeois; and thus, how unafraid and unaware of death in childbirth, pestilence, starvation and the fate of her immortal soul. And so she scrutinizes history for its failings, examining, cross-examining, indicting and convicting.

I HAVE so far been concerned with the general tendencies of the ideological spirit: its insularity—that is, its incapacity to enter experiences of worlds alien to itself —and its ambition, its grandiosity, that is, its refusal to set limits on itself, its need to encompass and to reconstruct in its own terms other modes of experience. Let me turn now to the specific tendencies in the ideology of the movement. I begin with three rather strange statements. The first is from one of my graduate students, a highly intelligent young woman and an impassioned feminist, who burst out to say, during a discussion of sexuality, that "human beings no longer need to reproduce." The second is from a well-known polemic on female sexuality, which argues that since sexual pleasure can be achieved by women in a nongenital fashion, the penis is outmoded, a vestigial organ like the appendix. Finally, David Cooper, in his, well, let us say, curious book, "The Death of the Family": "Revolution . . . will only become a total enough reality when white men can assume all the colors of blackness and then have babies too."

Our first impulse surely must be to dismiss these statements as sheer frenzy, the issue of minds so inflamed as to have departed from reason. But now look at them more closely, more calmly.

422

They deal with certain human givens—anatomy, parturition, gender—and they wish them away in a spasm of the distended will as though the will, in pursuit of total human possibility, can amplify itself to overcome the given.

These are, I believe, merely overwrought expressions of familiar and, in fact, time-worn ideas, ideas which are so habitual for us that they remain unexamined. In the modern era, they have their origin in the thought of John Locke: specifically the idea of the empty organism, the conviction that human beings are born free of disposition; the idea of infinite human plasticity; and the idea of human perfectibility through social action. These are so much a part of the modern consciousness and, in particular, so deeply tied to the American tradition, to our ingrained belief in human equality, to our optimism, to our prevailing political liberalism, that it may require a considered act of hesitation before we can think otherwise. We are, as Americans, accustomed to the more muted, the more generous expressions of the Lockean spirit, in which we aim to reduce inequality whenever we can, in which we hope modestly for the best, and bend our efforts modestly to approach it. In this amiable form, we are sometimes led to fatuousness and sentimentality, to a certain good-hearted muddleheadedness, but rarely worse than that.

But there is a darker version of the Lockean spirit, in which it becomes intense, visionary, messianic. The dis pleasure with inequality is transformed into an assault upon difference itself, so that the pluralisms of the social order, even those pluralisms based on choice, are held to be too unbearable to endure. The belief in human plasticity, joined to a belief in technique, joined further to the Utopian impulse, ends in a fierce determination to manage habit, thought and personality so as to achieve human and social perfection. If we sustain that determination, we move towards totalitarianism—in America, that bland, cheery, optimistic liberal brand of totalitarianism we find so perfectly expressed in the utopian writings of B. F. Skinner

FROM this perspective we may view gender as the last frontier of the Lockean vision. In the past, however we may have defined masculinity and femininity, we understood there to be ultimate, irreducible differences between men and women, differences rooted in our evolutionary history. Now there is nothing new in our knowledge to force us to think otherwise; to the contrary, some of our most recent knowledge points to the importance of the intrinsic, not only as regards sexuality but in other domains as well. To mention only a few examples: Chomsky on language, Piaget on child development, Lévi-Strauss on culture, all indicate the presence of intrinsic, transcultural cognitive structures; experimental primate ethology, as in the work of Harlow, increasingly suggests inborn drive and other structures, supported by the careful infant observation of such writers as Spitz, Bowlby, Fraiberg and many more. In the domain of sex differences *per se*, we now know that infant boys and girls do differ in the first weeks and months of life, before the full impact of socialization is felt—the boys more aggressive and usually more active; the girls more social, so to speak, more responsive to touch and voice and to facial stimuli. And there is, finally, that line of thought in anthropology which stresses transcultural regularities — in particular, uniformities in sexual patterns which seem to be found in nearly all human societies.

But given today's intellectual climate on the topic of gender, none of this is easily taught. The women of the movement would rather not hear about differences between infant boys and girls, or about the commonalities of sexual differentiation across culture. They would rather hear anecdotes about fierce women and intimidated men in the jungles of Bongo Bongo. "You don't mean to tell me," a young woman told me, "that sex differences are anything but socially determined." Well, I did not mean to tell her, only to propose it as a possibility, but to no effect, as it turned out, for she believes that everything human is socially determined —everything, that is, save her own dogmas, which are as immutable as natural law.

If we believe that the organism is entirely empty, containing nothing but what we choose to place there, if we resist any notion of inwardness of spirit, of human complexity, of subterranean tendency, of the entangled and the demonic, then we are led inevitably to a belief in social and psychological engineering. The organism bereft of tendency, of need, of negative will, is an organism ripe for social technology. We will do to it what we choose to do to it, for its own good, for the general good, and who is there to argue against the general good? If it can be done, ergo it should be done, ergo it will be done.

Thus the Lockean spirit **produces its ultimate flower, the technician of human desire. In the early years of the movement, the voices most commonly heard were strident, aggrieved and at times charismatic. But now that our attention has been captured, now that we examine ourselves guiltily for the sin of sexism, now that the time for rhetoric is past—now we begin to hear a different voice, the voice of the technocratic intelligence, the voice of sweet reason, offering us plans and programs and proposals, telling us precisely what to do and precisely how to do it.**

It is the kind of intelligence which, pondering the problem of marriage, seizes upon the idea of the marriage contract. Here is Prof. William Goode, president of the American Sociological Association, expert on love and marriage, looking with us toward the future: "There may be a movement toward more marriages based upon explicit contract . . . formal contractual relations that spell out what their obligations are to each other, how they shall operate a joint household and under what conditions and penalties they will be permitted to leave it." "Explicit," "formal," "obligations," "operate," "conditions," "penalties"—the words of the objectifying mind, which thinks it can extinguish by such incantations contingency, chance, error, the un-expected, the unknown, the spontaneous, the unconscious —all that which is truly quotidian in human relationships as we know them.

And here is Prof. Alice Rossi, another distinguished sociologist, determining how the professional woman might be free to pursue her career: "If a reserve of trained practical mothers were available, a professional woman could return to her field a few months after the birth of a child, leaving the infant under the care of a practical mother until he or she reached the age of 2 years, at about which age the child would enter a day-care center for daytime care. Assuming a two-child family, this could mean not more than one year of withdrawal from her professional field for the working mother."

About this passage one might be led to wonder why the woman she describes feels she needs a child at all, let alone two; and one might also note, mordantly, that a movement devoted to feminine equality rather casually assumes the existence of a class of female servants. But let me point instead to what may not be quite so obvious—the tacit image of the child in writings such as these. He (or she) is transformed, ever so silently, from a creature to be nurtured and protected, to a perplexing problem that a good managerial intelligence will solve.

HERE we reach a most intriguing matter—the place of the child and child-rearing in the mind of the movement. Much of the time it seems to have no place at all—it is something like sex in the Victorian novel, invisible, unmentionable, taboo. One can read a vast anthology of fiery movement documents and find that children are conceived of only as things not to be conceived or, if conceived, to be aborted. Some of the time, girl children are mentioned, the issue being how to stamp out many nurturant impulses they might be impelled to show. But much of the time, silence, and when not silence, then lordly abstractions, or insouciant simplifications. One senses that minds which have been busy hammering out the clauses of marriage contracts, and indeed inventing ever-new forms of marriage, have not yet found the energy to treat what Freud considered one of the impossible tasks — the raising of children.

But perhaps it is not so impossible. Here once again is Professor Goode, whom I quoted earlier on the marriage contract. That quotation was from a remarkable interview in The Times, in which he discussed how we might produce more women business executives. The interview is remarkable both for the utter abstractness of its language and for the facility with which it imagines extravagant new domestic arrangements—one of these, interestingly, modeled after the large corporation. But it is, for all that, a utopian document, and, in the nature of such, it foresees a wonderful if somewhat hazy future for one and all: Women will rise to the top in large corporations, and thus enhance their sexual appeal; men will gladly lay these burdens down. As we read on, a nagging feeling develops— something has been left out— and, of course, it is the fate of the children. The interviewer seems to sense this too, and at last puts the question: What effect on the children? Professor Goode replies that it will be good for them, for they will thrive in being somewhat more neglected than they are now—especially, he says, in the upper-middle strata. Something for everyone: for the women, success and sexiness too; for the men, relief from the burden of achievement, and for the children, a greater degree of neglect.

At which point one must ask whether the children of the upper-middle class can really endure more neglect than they now do. Professor Goode mistakes indulgence for concern, not surprisingly, for the Lockean mind, attuned to surfaces, to acts and transactions and arrangements, cannot observe absences. So it observes the piano lessons and the orthodontia and the trips to Europe, and it further observes how often their recipients are simply miserable — depressed or addicted or enraged—and so it assumes that the one has caused the other, and thus proceeds to prescribe a benign neglect.

Yet our offices and clinics are filled to overflowing with just such casualties of neglect, the upper-middle-class young. What they tell us is by now drearily familiar: that my parents gave me everything I needed but nothing I wanted; that they cared nothing for me, only for themselves. A girl whose mother is a successful lawyer complains bitterly that to this very day her mother's clients can see her more easily than she can. But I would not want to imply that it is only the mothers who are so blamed, for fathers are too; nor is it the mother's working which is the issue, for the same refrain is heard about mothers who seem to do little all day but look in the mirror. What appears to matter is the extraordinary self-absorption of the parents, whatever its sources might be. This narcissism, whatever else it may produce—boredom or drug use or some form of fanaticism—will also produce a reactive narcissism in the child, partly because he models his parental modes, partly because his self-absorption is the best defense he can find to use against theirs. So he ends as one of the insulted and injured, and he cries out, in one language or another: "Me! Me! Look at me, pay attention to me, love me, admire me, tell me that I exist."

What is most troublesome in movement writings, as in much of the public discourse of the day, is the frequent presence of just such tonalities. They so often seem to be suffused by an overweening sense of self. Behind the rhetoric, behind the talk of freedom and equality and oppression, one senses an injured narcissism, the feeling of having been deprived and cheated. There is so much talk of self—of self-fulfillment, self-realization, self-determination—and so little of one's devotion and responsibility to particular others— I don't mean mankind; I mean particular others. Perhaps this accounts for the strange absence of the child in so much of the literature of the movement. With so little felt to be available to and for the self, what can be left to offer another?

Let me stress that I do not mean to single out the Women's Liberation Movement in anything I have written. It is not them against us, it is us, it reflects what we have become as a class and to some lesser degree as a nation—self-absorbed, but lacking inner confidence; unable to endure discomfort, let alone adversity; petulant; aggrieved; to tell the truth, a bit hysterical. And the problem is not psychological; it is at bottom sociological, a problem of class. The upper-middle class in America, what David Bazelon has called the New Class, is achieved not through property or heritage, but through the cultivation of self, through education, drive, nerve, talent, personality, ideas. Above all, ideas. So it is no surprise that in crisis we revert to what is most truly our self, to our ideas, to ideologies. Saul Bellow, in the voice of Moses Herzog, put it this way: Speaking of "civilized people," he has Herzog say, "What they love is an imaginary human situation invented by their own genius and which they believe is the only true and the only human reality."

Twenty years ago or so, my generation, in our genius, in our intoxication with perfectibility, invented just such an imaginary reality, the idyll of suburban domesticity, which would redress the grievances of the past and ensure a perfect future. Now the offspring of that generation and that ideology, having seen its imperfections, turn against it, turn it on its head, and in their genius and their intoxication, invent one more perfect and imaginary reality. ■

PRACTICING BELIEFS

To the Editor:

It may comfort Professor Adelson to note that "everyone believes in equal pay for equal work and that women should not be sharply limited in the economic roles available to them," but it is not much comfort to countless women. We in the women's movement are working to translate such egalitarian *beliefs* into egalitarian *practice*. As a social scientist, Professor Adelson must be perfectly well aware that the facts of the economic world are a far cry from societal consensus on goals. It is no comfort to a woman to be told job equality as a goal has won "nearly universal concurrence." She wants to see it reflected in her paycheck. It is the implementation of such goals that absorbs the energies of the women's movement today.

That the spearhead of the feminist movement has been middle-class in origin no one will deny. That its impact and concerns are exclusively middle-class is increasingly less true. Professor Adelson is clearly reading only what the media tell him about women's liberation, or he could not claim that as far as the average citizen is concerned, our issues are "as remote as happenings on the moon." A great deal of the real work of the women's movement is focused on bread-and-butter issues of state protective law repeal, *amicus curiae* briefs to defend the rights of employed factory women, the passage of the Equal Rights Amendment and the organization of countless thousands of women to assure their presence among the delegates to the national conventions this summer. And who does Professor Adelson think played a major role in the change in state abortion laws across the country during the past five years? The efforts of thousands of women have gone into these campaigns, seeking a right to control their reproductive lives that is the very opposite of "remote as the moon."

Professor Adelson questions whether educated women as a group are really interested in the movement, and cites as evidence that only one out of 34 women surveyed in a student dissertation "had any connection with, or interest in, the movement." So small a sample and so vague an indicator can mean almost anything. There are, in fact, impressive indices of the extent to which interest is being expressed by educated women with the concerns of the women's movement. In December, 1970, there were 110 women's studies courses and two women's studies programs on college campuses across the country. One year later, there were 610 such courses and some 15 women's studies programs. In just the past two months, Florence Rowe and Carol Ahlum who have been tracing this new trend in higher education, have added 60 new courses to their list, know of 17 additional institutions now considering a full women's studies program, and predict a sharp increase in such courses in secondary schools by this fall. Students who have taken these courses now number in the thousands. I suspect very few of them have as limited a knowledge of what the women's movement is concerned with as Professor Adelson shows.

In his desire to see the movement die, Professor Adelson does not tell his readers that membership in the National Organization for Women has doubled this past year, that there are now several dozen feminist journals and newspapers in the country, and that feminist presses have a backlog of manuscripts submitted for publication.

As for his supermarket/cocktail-party interviewing, if the attitude projected in his article was communicated to his interviewees, it does not surprise me that he got the responses he did. That many women are "irritated" by some of the ideas circulated by the liberation movement is undoubtedly the case. Depending on where you are at, they can be very irritating indeed. For some women, that irritation will be followed by anger and then by action, as they come up against experiences in life that give direct evidence of discrimination and ridicule against women.

This is not to deny that some silly and irritating things are being said by women in the movement. Since we are very diverse, and articulately reject any superorganization that funnels one "line" to the media, this is inevitably the case. But if Professor Adelson had an opportunity to hear a discussion within a women's group (which he wouldn't be able to do in any event since such a group would freeze upon his approach), he would learn that the specifics of family roles, of management of dual careers, of concern for a child's development, of meshing the desires and needs of a husband and a wife, are constant themes of dialogue and exploration. The movement cannot be gauged from reading a few extremist books and watching a TV interview.

And as a social scientist, I would also expect Professor Adelson to be sensitive to the phases of a social movement. In its early stages, one must expect a strong component of rhetoric. I suspect the rhetoric will be as strong in one direction as the culture has been in the other, but that with time, the dialectic of ideas in interaction will produce a more moderate, tested residue. It is the very extremity of the pressure toward pot-stirring and baby-rocking of the domestic ethos of the post-World War II period that is being reacted against, and in due course, current ideas will be shaken down and distilled.

Later in his article, Professor Adelson tells us that in the early days of the movement one heard strident but sometimes charismatic voices, while today we hear a different voice, that of the technocratic intelligence. He is too nonspecific to offer us "dates," but since the movement he is discussing has a very short history of at most five or six years, one might assume that by "new" voice he is referring to things said in the past two years or so. The passage he saw fit to quote from my work argued that with institutional arrangements for child care a professional woman could envisage a continuous career with only a year of withdrawal for childbearing. What he does *not* tell the readers is that this quote comes from my earliest essay on sex equality, written in 1963 and published in 1964. It was to combat the message his own field of psychology had been espousing for years, that women with children belong at home or their children would suffer emotional damage, that I undertook to review the empirical evidence of the effect of employment on children, and to suggest the problem might lie in institutional change. That analysis is no longer necessary in 1972 precisely because of the impact of the women's movement on educated women's planning for their futures.

Had Professor Adelson read what I have published most recently, he would have heard a rather different note, but then, it would not fit his desire to discredit the women's movement: "I suspect the technological futurists in our midst draw an erroneous conclusion from consumer-goods gullibility. The woman easily tempted to purchase a dress she does not need would surprise many futurists by her sales resistance to having a test-tube pregnancy. . . . Studies of maternal adaptation suggest that difficulty of adjustment is greater with multipara than primipara births. . . . A woman's need for help goes up with each additional child, but the help and emotional support available to her goes down. . . . Solutions involve not only more community help to adult mothers, but perhaps equally important, more challenging training in girlhood in carrying multiple responsibilities. . . . Child-care centers are only one, and not necessarily the best, of many possible institutional devices to assist young mothers—stay-at-home as well as career women" (American Journal of Psychiatry, March, 1972).

ALICE S. ROSSI,
President, Sociologists for
Women in Society,
Professor of Sociology,
Goucher College.
Baltimore, Md.

April 19, 1972

Older Women— Their Own Cry For Liberation

By JUDY KLEMESRUD

More than 500 "older women" (definition: females over the age of 30) met here over the weekend to reassure each other that wrinkles, gray hair and the menopause do not automatically relegate a woman to the scrap heap.

It was a conference born of rejection: Rejection the older women said they felt from younger members of the women's movement, and from America's youth-worshiping society in general.

And so they came, from as far away as Canada and Pennsylvania, but mostly from the metropolitan area, to "Speak Out for Change," as the gathering was called. It was sponsored by Older Women's Liberation (OWL), a Manhattan group, at Marymount Manhattan College, 221 East 71st Street.

It was an emotional weekend. Male newsmen were ejected during the keynote speeches after women in the audience became incensed by their presence, tears were shed in the various consciousness-raising sessions, and the mother of the women's movement, Betty Friedan, was booed following a speech.

Perhaps the atmosphere of the conference was best summed up by Barbara Seaman, author of "Free and Female" and one of the keynote speakers, when she said:

'On the Shelf'

"Men in middle age are regarded as at the height of their life and careers, while the middle-aged female is retired and put on the shelf —both as sex object and person."

Ti-Grace Atkinson, who was introduced as "our first radical feminist," put it more bluntly and, some thought, more honestly, when she said in a speech: "Older women are the garbage of society. Why haven't people wanted to deal with that issue in the women's movement?"

The average age of the women appeared to hover around the young side of 50. There were a few 70-year-olds and even fewer 20-year-olds, and only a handful of black or Spanish-speaking women. Almost everyone seemed to be wearing a political or protest button.

One of those sporting a "Bella [Abzug] for Congress" button was Mrs. Paula Landesman, 49, of Manhattan, a well-dressed blond wife of an artist and the mother of four, who kept shouting "Right On!" during a keynote speech by Representative Abzug.

"I'm a happily married housewife," Mrs. Landesman said in between speeches, "and the reason I'm here is because my role in life has been pretty much confined to motherhood. But now my children are grown and I'm no longer a mother, and I'm worried because I'm not trained to do anything else."

Three-Man Entourage

Mrs. Abzug caused something of a stir when she arrived at the Saturday morning session with a three-man entourage, including her husband, Martin. There were also four newsmen in the auditorium.

"Is this conference open to men?" a woman yelled irately from the audience, implying that it wasn't. "I feel the same way!" another one chimed in.

Jo Hazelton, a member of OWL's steering committee ("We have no leaders"), explained that the committee had decided to allow men in the keynote session "to help publicize women who are running for office."

'Male Power Structure'

The crowd hissed, but allowed Mrs. Abzug to speak, and then gave her a standing ovation after she urged women to "reverse the male power structure." But soon after she and her entourage had departed, the disgruntled audience made such a fuss over the presence of the newsmen that Miss Hazelton asked them to leave, which they did.

At the heart of the conference were workshops that were conducted in the consciousness-raising method of allowing each woman to speak from her own experience. The topics included "Menopause and Sexuality," "Divorce," "Alternate Life Styles," "Economic Survival," "Changing Legal Rights for Older Women," and "Re-Examining Marriage and the Family."

At one of the workshops on menopause, most of the women present seemed to agree that they didn't know very much about the subject —and, they said, neither did their doctors.

"Just what is a hot flash, anyway?" one woman wondered. "I've been through the menopause, and never had any."

"It's like you're a little pot sitting on the stove," another woman replied, "and you feel something snap inside you, and you get very hot. When it's over you break into a tiny sweat."

Several women said they disagreed with the much-touted hormone replacement therapy and suggested several "alternative methods" of staying young: Yoga, Vitamin E and biofeedback therapy.

"We really have it all over men at this age," said one blond post-menopausal woman. "We can speed up our libido with testosterone and we don't have to worry about getting pregnant."

At a divorce seminar, the consensus was that the fear of being alone was the biggest problem facing a formerly married woman. Some women suggested that women should not be hesitant about going out with each other socially. Another said that women should go places alone.

"Fascinating things happen when you go out without an escort," said a dark-haired, 58-year-old mother of three from Westchester County, who is "emotionally separated" from her husband. "I went to Roseland alone at a Labor Day matinee, and I danced with 16 men for nine and three-quarters hours."

Unhappy Relationship

One conclusion of the "Alternate Life Styles" workshop was that "a good man is hard to find." Suggested as alternatives to a relationship with one man were group sex, lesbianism, younger men, masturbation and consciousness-raising sessions.

Several women at the 'Re-Examining Marriage and the Family' workshops had never been married, including a slender 38-year-old Manhattan secretary who said she came to the conference because she was miserable in her relationship with a man.

"I've been living with him for four years now," she said, "but it hasn't worked out. He never asks me what I think or how I feel about anything. His work and his interests always come first. Finally, I began to feel resentful about this subservient role of serving man, and my sex drive was smothered."

'An Angry Feminist'

Between speeches and workshops, the women clustered around the National Organization for Women's "New York Boutique," to buy even more protest buttons, books, necklaces, T-shirts, ink stamps depicting clenched fists, and stationery that said, "From the desk of an angry feminist."

One of the oldest women at the conference was Clara de Miha, 73, Manhattan coordinator of the Jeannette Rankin Brigade, who said she came to "assert that age does not mean anything in spite of the fact that we call ourselves older women."

But age does matter, the white-haired woman conceded, and then went on to say that whenever she goes into a restaurant alone, she gets a bad table. "And the waiters always make you wait longer than a younger person," she said.

"You know, all these young people look alike to me," she added, smiling. "They all have long hair, and the same way of dressing"

As the conference came to a close on Sunday afternoon, several recommendations were made to the audience as a result of what had been said in the workshops: Women who were thinking about divorce should hire feminist divorce lawyers; a proabortion lobbyist should be sent to Albany next year; a women's medical referral service should be established to recommend women to "sympa-

thetic doctors who aren't going to give you a hysterectomy when you don't need one."

For Political Change

The last celebrity speaker was Betty Friedan, who was cheered and jeered after she told the women they should "avoid unproductive measures and stay reality oriented" by concentrating on organizing women for political change.

"I know it's not as sexy as debating clitoral versus vaginal orgasms," she said, "but who cares about that?"

"We do!" yelled a woman from the audience, amid a chorus of boos.

She did not, however, have the last word. That honor went to a woman in her 50's from Huntington, L.I., who walked to the microphone during a free-for-all session and concluded the conference by saying:

"The young women don't ever think it [aging] is going to happen to them. But it will. It will."

June 6, 1972

Consciousness ♀

By VIVIAN GORNICK

IN a lower Manhattan office a legal secretary returns from her lunch hour, sinks into her seat and says miserably to a secretary at the next desk: "I don't know what's happening to me. A perfectly nice construction worker whistled and said, 'My, isn't *that* nice,' as I passed him and suddenly I felt this terrific anger pushing up in me. . . . I swear I wanted to *hit* him!"

At the same time, a thoughtful 40-year-old mother in a Maryland suburb is saying to a visiting relative over early afternoon coffee: "You know, I've been thinking lately, I'm every bit as smart as Harry, and yet he got the Ph.D. and I raised the girls. Mind you, I *wanted* to stay home. And yet, the thought of my two girls growing up and doing the same thing doesn't sit well with me at all. Not at all."

And in Toledo, Ohio, a factory worker turns to the next woman on the inspection belt and confides: "Last night I told Jim: 'I been working in the same factory as you 10 years now. We go in at the same time, come out the same time. But I do all the shopping, get the dinner, wash the dishes and on Sunday break my back down on the kitchen floor. I'm real tired of doin' all that. I want some help from you.' Well, he just laughed at me, see? Like he done every time I mentioned this before. But last night I wouldn't let up. I mean, I really *meant* it this time. And you know? I thought he was gonna let me have it. Looked mighty like he was gettin' ready to belt me one. But you know? I just didn't care! I wasn't gonna back down, come hell or high water. You'll just never believe it, he'd kill me if he knew I was tellin' you, he washed the dishes. First time in his entire life."

None of these women are feminists. None of them are members of the Women's Liberation Movement. None of them ever heard of consciousness-raising. And yet, each of them exhibits the symptomatic influence of this, the movement's most esoteric practice. Each of them, without specific awareness, is beginning to feel the effects of the consideration of woman's personal experience in a new light—a political light. Each of them is undergoing the mysterious behavioral twitches that indicate psychological alteration. Each of them is drawing on a linking network of feminist analysis and emotional upchucking that is beginning to suffuse the polit-

VIVIAN GORNICK is a staff writer for The Village Voice.

Drawing by ALLAN MARDON

ical-social air of American life today. Each of them, without ever having attended a consciousness-raising session, has had her consciousness raised.

Consciousness-raising is the name given to the feminist practice of examining one's personal experience in the light of sexism; i. e., that theory which explains woman's subordinate position in society as a result of a cultural decision to confer direct power on men and only indirect power on women. The term of description and the practice to which it alludes are derived from a number of sources—psychoanalysis, Marxist theory and American revivalism, mainly—and was born out of the earliest stages of feminist formulation begun about three years ago in such predictable liberationist nesting places as Cambridge, New York, Chicago and Berkeley. (The organization most prominently associated with the growth of consciousness-raising is the New York Redstockings.)

Perceiving that woman's position in our society does indeed constitute that of a political class, and, secondly, that woman's "natural" domain is her feelings, and, thirdly, that testifying in a friendly and supportive atmosphere enables people to see that their experiences are often duplicated (thereby reducing their sense of isolation and increasing the desire to theorize as well as to confess), the radical feminists sensed quickly that a group of women sitting in a circle discussing their emotional experiences as though they were material for cultural analysis was political dynamite. Hence, through personal testimony and emotional analysis could the class consciousness of *women* be raised. And thus the idea of the small "woman's group" — or consciousness-raising group—was delivered into a cruel but exciting world.

●

CONSCIOUSNESS-RAISING is, at one and the same time, both the most celebrated and accessible introduction to the woman's movement as well as the most powerful technique for feminist conversion known to the liberationists. Women are *drawn*, out of a variety of discontents, by the idea of talking about themselves, but under the spell of a wholly new interpretation of their experience, they *remain*.

Coming together, as they do, week after week for many months, the women who are "in a group" begin to exchange an extraordinary sense of multiple identification that is encouraged by the technique's instruction to look for explanations for each part of one's history in terms of the social or cultural dynamic created by sexism —rather than in terms of the personal dynamic, as one would do in a psychotherapist's group session. (Although there are many differences between consciousness-raising and group therapy — e.g., the former involves no professional leader, no exchange of money — the fundamental difference lies in this fact: in consciousness-raising one looks not to one's personal emotional

history for an explanation of behavioral problems but rather to the cultural fact of the patriarchy.)

Thus looking at one's history and experience in consciousness-raising sessions is rather like shaking a kaleidoscope and watching all the same pieces rearrange themselves into an altogether *other* picture, one that suddenly makes the color and shape of each piece appear startlingly new and alive, and full of unexpected meaning. (This is mainly why feminists often say that women are the most interesting people around these days, because they are experiencing a psychic invigoration of rediscovery.)

What *does* take place in a consciousness - raising group? How *do* the women see themselves? What *is* the thrust of the conversation at a typical session? Is it simply the manhating, spleen-venting that is caricatured by the unsympathetic press? Or the unfocused and wrong-headed abstracting insisted upon by the insulated intellectuals? Or yet again, the self - indulgent contemplation of the navel that many tightlipped radical activists see it as?

"IN this room," says Roberta H., a Long Island housewife speaking euphemistically of her group's meetings, "we do not generalize. We do not speak of any experience except that of the women here. We follow the rules for consciousness-raising as set out by the New York Radical Feminists and we do not apply them to 'woman's experience'—whatever on earth that is—we apply them to ourselves. But, oh God! The samenesses we have found, and the way in which these meetings have changed our lives!"

The rules that Roberta H. is referring to are to be found in a mimeographed pamphlet, an introduction to the New York Radical Feminists organization, which explains the purpose and procedures of consciousness-raising. The sessions consist mainly of women gathering once a week, sitting in a circle and speaking in turn, addressing themselves

—almost entirely out of personal experience—to a topic that has been preselected. The pamphlet sets forth the natural limitations of a group (10 to 15 women), advises women to start a group from among their friends and on a word-of-mouth basis, and suggests a list of useful topics for discussion. These topics include Love, Marriage, Sex, Work, Femininity, How I Came to Women's Liberation, Motherhood, Aging and Competition With Other Women. Additional subjects are developed as a particular group's specific interests and circumstances begin to surface.

When a group's discussions start to revolve more and more about apparently very individual circumstances, they often lead to startling similarities. For instance, a Westchester County group composed solely of housewives, who felt that each marriage represented a unique meaning in each of their lives, used the question, "Why did you marry the man you married?" as the subject for discussion one night. "We went around the room," says Joan S., one of the women present, "and while some of us seemed unable to answer that question without going back practically to the cradle, do you know?, the word love was never mentioned *once*."

On the Upper West Side of Manhattan, in the vicinity of Columbia University, a group of women between the ages of 35 and 45 have been meeting regularly for six months. Emily R., an attractive 40-year-old divorcée in this group, says: "When I walked into the first meeting, and saw the *types* there, I said to myself: 'None of these broads have been through what I've been through. They couldn't possibly feel the way I feel.' Well, I'll tell you. None of them *have* been through what I've been through if you look at our experience superficially. But when you look a little *deeper*—the way we've been doing at these meetings —you see they've *all* been through what I've been through, and they all feel pretty much the way I feel. God, when I saw *that!* When

I saw that what I always felt was my own personal hangup was as true for every other woman in that room as it was for me! Well, that's when *my* consciousness was raised."

WHAT Emily R. speaks of is the phenomenon most often referred to in the movement, the flash of insight most directly responsible for the feminist leap in faith being made by hundreds of women everywhere—i.e., the intensely felt realization that what had always been taken for symptoms of personal unhappiness or dissatisfaction or frustration was so powerfully and so consistently duplicated among women that perhaps these symptoms could just as well be ascribed to *cultural* causes as to psychological ones.

In the feminist movement this kind of "breakthrough" can occur no place else than in a consciousness-raising group. It is only here, during many months of meetings, that a woman is able finally —if ever—to bring to the surface those tangled feelings of anger, bafflement and frustrated justice that have drawn her to the movement in the first place. It is only here that the dynamic of sexism will finally strike home, finally make itself felt in the living detail of her own life.

Claire K., a feminist activist in Cambridge, says of women's groups: "I've been working with women's groups for over two years now The average life of a group is a year to 18 months, and believe me, I've watched a lot of them fold before they ever got off the ground. But, when they *work!* There is a rhythm to some of them that's like life itself. You watch a group expand and contract, and each time it does one or the other it never comes back together quite the same as when the action started. Something happens to each woman, and to the group itself . . . But each time, if they survive, they have *grown.* You can see it, almost smell it and taste it."

I AM one of those feminists who are always mourning after the coherent and high-

minded leadership of the 19th century. Often, when I observe the fragmented, intellectually uneven, politically separated components of the woman's movement I experience dismay, and I find myself enviously imagining Elizabeth Cady Stanton and Lucretia Mott and Susan B. Anthony sitting and holding hands for 40 years, sustaining and offering succor to one another in religious and literary accents that make of their feminism a heroic act, an act that gave interwoven shape to their lives and their cause. And I think in a panic: "Where would we all be without them? Where would we be? They thought it all out for us, and we've got not one inch beyond them." Lately, however, I have changed my mind about all that . . .

I was on my way to a meeting one night not too long ago, a meeting meant to fashion a coalition group out of the movement's many organizations. I knew exactly what was ahead of me. I knew that a woman from NOW would rise and speak about our "image"; that a Third Worlder would announce loudly she didn't give a good goddamn about anybody's orgasms, her women were starving, for chrissake; that a Radicalesbian would insist that the woman's movement must face the problem of sexism from within *right now;* and 10 women from the Socialist party would walk out in protest against middle-class "élitist" control in the movement. I knew there would be a great deal of emotional opinion delivered, a comparatively small amount of valuable observation made, and some action taken. Suddenly, as the bus I was on swung westward through Central Park, I realized that it didn't matter, that none of it mattered. I realized it was stupid and self-pitying to be wishing that the meeting was going to be chaired by Elizabeth Cady Stanton; what she had done and said had been profoundly in the idiom of her time, and in the idiom of *my* time no woman in the movement was her equal, but something else was: the consciousness-raising group.

I saw then that the small, anonymous consciousness-raising group was the heart and soul of the woman's movement, that it is not what happens at movement meetings in New York or Boston or Berkeley that counts, but the fact that hundreds of these groups are springing up daily —at universities in Kansas, in small towns in Oregon, in the suburbs of Detroit—out of a responsive need that has indeed been urged to the surface by modern radical feminism. It was here that the soul of a woman is genuinely searched and a new psychology of the self is forged. I saw then that the consciousness-raising group of today is the true Second Front of feminism; and as I thought all this I felt the ghost of Susan B. Anthony hovering over me, nodding vigorously, patting me on the shoulder and saying: "Well done, my dear, well done."

That ghost has accompanied me to every movement meeting I have attended since that night, but when I am at a consciousness-raising session that ghost disappears and I am on my own. Then, for better or worse, I am the full occupant of my feminist skin, engaged in the true business of modern feminism, reaching hard for self-possession.

And now let's go to a consciousness-raising session.

EARLY in the evening, on a crisp autumn night, a young woman in an apartment in the Gramercy Park section of Manhattan signed a letter, put it in an envelope, turned out the light over her desk, got her coat out of the hall closet, ran down two flights of stairs, hailed a taxi and headed west directly across the city. At the same time, on the Upper West Side, another woman, slightly older than the first, bent over a sleeping child, kissed his forehead, said goodnight to the babysitter, rode down 12 flights in an elevator, walked up to Broadway and disappeared into the downtown subway. Across town, on the Upper East Side, another woman tossed back a head of stylishly fixed hair,

pulled on a beautiful pair of suede boots and left her tiny apartment, also heading down and across town. On the Lower East Side, in a fourth-floor tenement apartment, a woman five or six years younger than all the others combed out a tangled mop of black hair, clomped down the stairs in her Swedish clogs and started trudging west on St. Marks Place. In a number of other places all over Manhattan other women were also leaving their houses. When the last one finally walked into the Greenwich Village living room they were all headed for, there were 10 women in the room.

These women ranged in age from the late 20's to the middle 30's; in appearance, from attractive to very beautiful; in education, from bachelor's degrees to master's degrees; in marital status, from single to married to divorced to imminently separated; two were mothers. Their names were Veronica, Lucie, Diana, Marie, Laura, Jen, Sheila, Dolores, Marilyn and Claire. Their occupations, respectively, were assistant television producer, graduate student, housewife, copywriter, journalist, unemployed actress, legal secretary, unemployed college dropout, schoolteacher and computer programer.

They were not movement women; neither were they committed feminists; nor were they marked by an especial sense of social development or by personal neurosis. They were simply a rather ordinary group of women who were drawn out of some unresolved, barely articulated need to form a "woman's group." They were in their third month of meetings; they were now at Marie's house (next week they would meet at Laura's, and after that at Jen's, and so on down the line); the subject for discussion tonight was "Work."

The room was large, softly lit, comfortably furnished. After 10 or 15 minutes of laughing, chatting, note and book exchanging, the women arranged themselves in a circle, some on chairs, some on the couch, others on the floor. In the center of the circle was a low coffee table covered with a coffeepot, cups, sugar, milk, plates of cheese and bread, cookies and fruit. Marie suggested they begin, and turning to the woman on her right, who happened to be Dolores, asked if she would be the first.

Dolores (the unemployed college dropout): I guess that's okay. . . . I'd just as soon be the first . . . mainly because I hate to be the last. When I'm last, all I think about is, soon it will be *my* turn. (She looked up nervously.) You've no idea how I *hate* talking in public. (There was a long pause; silence in the circle.) . . . Work! God, what can I say? The whole question has always been absolute hell for me. . . . A lot of you have said your fathers ignored you when you were growing up and paid attention only to your brothers. Well, in my house it was just the opposite. I have two sisters, and my father always told me I was the smartest of all, that I was smarter than he was, and that I could do anything I wanted to do . . . but somehow, I don't really know *why*, everything I turned to came to nothing. After six years in analysis I still don't know *why*. (She looked off into space for a moment and her eyes seemed to lose the train of her thought. Then she shook herself and went on.) I've always drifted . . . just drifted. My parents never forced me to work. I needn't work even now. I had every opportunity to find out what I really wanted to do. But . . . nothing I did satisfied me, and I would just stop. . . . Or turn away. . . . Or go on a trip. I worked for a big company for a while. . . . Then my parents went to Paris and I just went with them. . . . I came back . . . went to school . . . was a researcher at Time-Life . . . drifted . . . got married . . . divorced . . . drifted. (Her voice grew more halting.) I feel my life is such *waste*. I'd like to write, I really would; I feel I'd be a good writer, but I don't know. I just can't get going. . . . My father is so disappointed in me. He keeps hoping I'll really do something. *Soon.* (She shrugged her shoulders but her face was very quiet and pale, and her pain expressive. She happened to be one of the most beautiful women in the room.)

Diana (the housewife): What do you think you *will* do?

Dolores (in a defiant burst): Try to get married!

Jen (the unemployed actress) and **Marie** (the copywriter): Oh, no!

Claire (the computer programer): After all that! Haven't you learned yet? What on earth is marriage going to do for you? Who on earth could you marry? *Feeling about yourself as you do?* Who could save you from yourself? Because that's what you *want*.

Marilyn (the school teacher): That's right. It sounds like "It's just all too much to think out so I might as well get married."

Lucie (the graduate student): Getting married like that is *bound* to be a disaster.

Jen: And when you get married like that it's always to some creep you've convinced yourself is wonderful. So understanding. (Dolores grew very red and very quiet through all this.)

Sheila (the legal secretary): Stop jumping on her like that! I know *just* how she feels. . . . I was *really* raised to be a wife and a mother, and yet my father wanted me to do something with my education after he sent me to one of the best girls' schools in the East. Well, I didn't get married when I got out of school like half the girls I graduated with, and now seven years later I'm *still* not married. (She stopped talking abruptly and looked off into the space in the center of the circle, her attention wandering as though she'd suddenly lost her way.) I don't know how to describe it exactly, but I know just how Dolores feels about drifting. I've always worked, and yet something was always sort of confused inside me. I never really knew which way I wanted to go on a job: up, down, sideways. . . . I always thought it would be the most marvelous thing in the world to work for a really brilliant and important man. I never have. But I've worked for some good men and I've learned a lot from them. But (her dark head came up two or three inches and she looked hesitantly around) I don't know about the rest of you, but I've always wound up being propositioned by my bosses. It's a funny thing. As soon as I'd being doing really well, learning fast and taking on some genuine responsibility, like it would begin to excite them, and they'd make their move. When I refused, almost invariably they'd begin to *browbeat* me. I mean, they'd make my life miserable! And, of course, I'd retreat. . . . I'd get small and scared and take everything they were dishing out . . . and then I'd move on. I don't know, maybe something in my behavior was really asking for it, I honestly don't know anymore. . . .

Marie: There's a good chance you *were* asking for it. I work with a lot of men and I don't get propositioned every other day. I am so absolutely straight no one *dares*. . . . They all think I am a dike.

Sheila (plaintively): Why is it like that, though? Why are men like that? Is it something they have more of, this sexual need for ego gratification? Are they made differently from us?

Jen (placing her coffee cup on the floor beside her): No! You've just never learned to stand up for yourself! And goddammit, they *know* it, and they play on it. Look, you all know I've been an actress for years. Well, once, when I was pretty new in the business, I was playing opposite this guy. He used to feel me up on the stage. All the *time*. I was scared. I didn't know what to do. I'd say to the stage manager: That guy is feeling me up. The stage manager would look at me like I was crazy, and shrug his shoulders. Like: What can *I* do? Well, once I finally thought: I can't stand this. And I bit him. Yes, I bit the bastard, I bit his tongue while he was kissing me.

A Chorus of Voices: You *bit* him????

Jen (with great dignity): Yes, dammit, I bit him. And afterward he said to me, "Why the hell did you do that?" And I said, "You know goddam well why I did that." And do you know? He respected me after that. (She laughed.) Didn't *like* me very much. But he respected me. (She looked distracted for a moment.) . . . I guess that *is* pretty funny. I mean, biting someone's tongue during a love scene.

Veronica (the assistant TV producer): Yeah. Very funny.

Laura (the journalist): Listen, I've been thinking about something Sheila said. That as soon as she began to get really good at her job her boss would make a pass—and that would pretty much signal the end, right? She'd refuse, he'd become an S.O.B., and she'd eventually leave. It's almost as if sex were being used to cut her down, or back, or in some way stop her from rising. An *instinct* he, the boss, has—to sleep with her when he feels her becoming really independent.

Lucie (excitedly): I'll buy that! Look, it's like Samson and Delilah in reverse. *She* knew that sex would give her the opportunity to destroy his strength. Women are famous for wanting to sleep with men in order to enslave them, right? That's the great myth, right? He's all spirit and mind, she's all emotion and biological instinct. She uses this instinct with *cunning* to even out the score, to get some power, to bring him down—through sex. But, look at it another way. What are these guys always saying to us? What are they always saying about women's liberation?—"All she needs is a good ——." They say that *hopefully. Prayerfully.* They know. We *all* know what all that "All she needs is a good ——" stuff is all about.

Claire: This is ridiculous. Use your heads. Isn't a guy kind of super if he wants to sleep with a woman who's becoming independent?

Marie: Yes, but not in business. There's something wrong every time, whenever sex is operating in business. It's always like a secret weapon, something you hit your opponent below the belt with.

Diana: God, you're all crazy! Sex is *fun*. Wherever it exists. It's warm and nice and it makes people feel good.

Dolores: That's a favorite pipe dream of yours, isn't it?

Sheila: It certainly doesn't seem like very much fun to me when I watch some secretary coming on to one of the lawyers when she wants a raise, then I see the expression on her face as she turns away.

Marie: God, that sounds like my mother when she wants something from my father!

Veronica (feebly): You people are beginning to make me feel *awful*! (Everyone's head snapped in her direction.)

Marie: Why?

Veronica: The way you're talking about using sex at work. As if it were so horrible. Well, I've *always* used a kind of sexy funniness to get what I want at work. What's wrong with that?

Lucie: What do you do?

Veronica: Well, if someone is being very stuffy and serious about business, I'll say something funny—I guess in a sexy way—to break up the atmosphere which sometimes gets so heavy. You know what I mean? Men can be so pretentious in business! And then, usually, I get what I want — while I'm being funny and cute, and they're laughing.

Diana (heatedly): Look, don't you see what you're doing?

Veronica (testily): No, I don't. What am I *doing*?

Diana (her hands moving agitatedly through the air before her): If there's some serious business going on you come in and say: Nothing to be afraid of, folks. Just frivolous, feminine little me. I'll tell a joke, wink my eye, do a little dance, and we'll all pretend nothing's really happening here.

Veronica: My God, I never thought of it like that.

Laura: It's like those apes. They did a study of apes in which they discovered that apes chatter and laugh and smile a lot to ward off aggression.

Marilyn: Just like women! Christ, aren't they always saying to us: *Smile!* Who tells a man to smile? And how often do you smile for no damned reason, right? It's so *natural* to start smiling as soon as you start talking to a man, isn't it?

Lucie: That's right! You're right! You know—God, it's amazing!—I began to think about this just the other day. I was walking down Fifth Avenue and a man in the doorway of a store said to me, "Whatsamatta, honey? Things can't be *that* bad." And I was startled because I wasn't feeling depressed or anything, and I couldn't figure out why he was saying that. So I looked, real fast, in the glass to see what my face looked like. And it didn't look like anything. It was just a face at rest. I had just an ordinary, sort of thoughtful expression on my face. And he thought I was *depressed*. And, I couldn't help it, I said to myself: "Would he have said that to you if you were a man?" And I answered myself immediately: "No!"

Diana: That's it. That's really what they want. To keep us barefoot, pregnant, and *smiling*. Always sort of *begging*, you know? Just a little supplicating—at all times. And they get anxious if you stop smiling. Not because you're depressed. Because you're *thinking*!

Dolores: Oh, come on now. Surely, there are lots of men who have very similar kinds of manners? What about all the life-of-the-party types? All those clowns and regular guys?

Claire: Yes, what about them? You *never* take those guys seriously. You never think of the men of real power, the guys with serious intentions and real strength, acting that way, do you? And those are the ones with real responsibility. The others are the ones women laugh about in private, the ones who become our confidantes, not our lovers, the ones who are *just like ourselves*.

Sheila (quietly): You're right.

Lucie: And it's true, it really does undercut your seriousness, all that smiling.

Sheila (looking suddenly sad and very intent): And underscore your weakness.

Dolores: Yes, exactly. We smile because we feel at a loss, because we feel vulnerable. We don't quite know how to accomplish what we want to accomplish or how to navigate through life, so we act *feminine*. That's really what this is all about, isn't it? To be masculine is to take action, to be feminine is to smile. Be coy and cute and sexy—and maybe you'll become the big man's assistant. God, it's all so sad. . . .

Veronica (looking a bit dazed): I never thought of any of it like this. But it's true, I guess, all of it. You know (and now her words came in a rush and her voice grew stronger), I've always been afraid of my job, I've always felt I was there by *accident*, and that any minute they were gonna find me out. Any minute, they'd know I was a fraud. I had the chance to become a producer recently, and I fudged it. I didn't realize for two weeks afterward that I'd done it deliberately, that I don't *want* to move up, that I'm afraid of the responsibility, that I'd rather stay where I am, making my little jokes and not drawing attention to myself . . . (Veronica's voice faded away, but her face seemed full of struggle, and for a long moment no one spoke.)

Marilyn (her legs pulled up under her on the couch, running her hand distractedly through her short blond hair): Lord, does *that* sound familiar. Do I know that feeling of being there by accident, any minute here comes the ax. I've never felt that anything I got—any honor, any prize, any decent job—was really legitimately mine. I always felt it was luck, that I happened to be in the right place at the right time and that I was able to put up a good front and people just didn't *know* . . . but if I stuck around long enough they would. . . . So, I guess I've drifted a lot, too. Being married, I took advantage of it. I remember when my husband was urging me to work, telling me I was a talented girl and that I shouldn't just be sitting around the house taking care of the baby. I wanted so to be persuaded by him, but I just couldn't do it. Every night I'd say: Tomorrow's the day and every morning I'd get up feeling like my head was full of molasses, so sluggish I couldn't *move*. By the time I'd finally get out of that damn bed it was too late to get a baby-sitter or too late to get to a job interview or too late to do anything, really. (She turned toward Diana). You're a housewife, Diana. You must know what I mean. (Diana nodded ruefully.) I began concentrating on my sex life with my husband, which had never been any too good, and was now getting really bad. It's hard to explain. We'd always been very affectionate with one another, and we still were. But I began to *crave* . . . passion. (She smiled, almost apologetically.) What else can I call it? There was no passion between us, practically no intercourse. I began to *demand* it. My husband reacted very badly, accused me of — oh God, the most awful things! Then I had an affair. The sex was great, the man was very tender with me for a long while. I felt *revived*. But then, a funny thing happened. I became almost hypnotized by the sex. I couldn't get enough, I couldn't stop thinking about it, it seemed to consume me; and yet, I became as sluggish now with sexual desire as I had been when I couldn't get up to go look for a job. Sometimes, I felt so sluggish I could hardly prepare myself to go meet my lover. And then . . . (She stopped talking and looked down at the floor. Her forehead creased, her brows drew together, she seemed pierced suddenly by memory. Everyone remained quiet for a long moment.)

Diana (very gently): And then?

Marilyn (almost shaking herself awake): And then the man told my husband of our affair.

Jen: Oh, Christ!

Marilyn: My husband went wild . . . *(her voice trailed off and again everyone remained silent, this time until she spoke again.)* He left me. We've been separated a year and a half now. So then I *had* to go to work. And I have, I have. But it remains a difficult, difficult thing. I do the most ordinary kind of work, afraid to strike out, afraid to try anything that involves real risk. It's almost as if there's some *training* necessary for taking risks, and I just don't have it . . . and my husband leaving me, and forcing me out to work, somehow didn't magically give me whatever it takes to get that training.

Laura (harshly): Maybe it's too late.

Diana: Well, that's a helluva thought. *(She crossed her legs and stared at the floor. Everyone looked toward her, but she said no more. Jen stretched, Claire bit into a cookie, Lucie poured coffee and everyone rearranged themselves in their seats.)*

Marie (after a long pause): It's your turn, Diana.

Diana (turning in her chair and running thin hands nervously through her curly red hair): It's been hard for me to concentrate on the subject. I went to see my mother in the hospital this afternoon, and I haven't been able to stop thinking about her all day long.

Jen: Is she very sick?

Diana: Well, yes, I think so. She underwent a serious operation yesterday—three hours on the operating table. For a while there it was touch and go. But today she seemed much better and I spoke to her. I stood by her bed and she took my hand and she said to me: "You need an enormous strength of will to live through this. Most people need only one reason to do it. I have three: you, your father and your grandmother. And suddenly I felt furious. I felt *furious* with her. God, she's always been so strong, the strongest person I know,

and I've loved her for it. All of a sudden I felt tricked. I felt like saying to her: "Why don't you live for yourself?" I felt like saying: "I can't take this burden on me! What are you doing to me?" And now suddenly, I'm here, being asked to talk about work, and I have nothing to say. I haven't a goddamn thing to say! What do I do? After all, what do I *do*? Half my life is passed in a fantasy of desire that's focused on leaving my husband and finding some marvelous job. . . . At least, my mother worked *hard* all her life. She raised me when my real father walked out on her, she put me through school, she staked me to my first apartment, she never said no to me for anything. And when I got married she felt she'd accomplished *everything*. That was the end of the rainbow. . . .

Dolores (timidly): What's so terrible, really, your mother saying she lived for all of you? God, that used to be considered a moral virtue. I'm sure lots of men feel the same way, that they live for their families. Most men *hate* their work. . . .

Marilyn: My husband used to say that all the time, that he lived only for me and the baby, that that was everything to him.

Lucie: How did you feel about that? What did you think of him when he said it?

Marilyn (flushing): It used to make me feel peculiar. As though something wasn't quite right with him.

Lucie (to Diana): Did you think something wasn't *quite right*, when your mother said what she said?

Diana (thinking back): No. It wasn't that something wasn't quite right. It seemed "right," if you know what I mean, for her to be saying that, but terribly wrong suddenly.

Lucie: That's odd, isn't it? When a man says he lives for his family it sounds positively unnatural to me. When a woman says it, it sounds so "right." So expected.

Laura: Exactly. What's pathology in a man seems normal in a woman.

Claire: It comes back, in a sense, to a woman always looking for her identity in her family and a man never, or rarely, really doing that.

Marie: God, this business of identity! Of wanting it from my work, and not looking for it in what my husband does. . . .

Jen: Tell me, do men ever look for their identities in their wives' work?

Veronica: Yes, and then we call them Mr. Streisand. *(Everybody breaks up, and suddenly cookies and fruit are being devoured. Everyone stretches and one or two women walk around the room. After 15 minutes . . .)*

Marie (peeling an orange, sitting yogi-fashion on the floor): I first went to work for a small publicity firm. They taught me to be a copywriter, and I loved it from the start. I never had any trouble with the people in that firm. It was like one big happy family there. We all worked well with each other and everyone knew a bit about everybody else's work. When the place folded and they let me go I was so depressed, and so *lost*. For the longest time I couldn't even go out looking for a job. I had no sense of how to go about it. I had no real sense of myself as having a transferable skill, somehow. I didn't seem to know how to deal with Madison Avenue. I realized then that I'd somehow never taken that job as a period of preparation for independence in the world. It was like a continuation of my family. As long as I was being taken care of I functioned, but when I was really on my own I folded up. I just didn't know how to operate. . . . And I still don't, really. It's never been the same. I've never had a job in which I felt I was really operating responsibly since that time.

Sheila: Do you think maybe you're just waiting around to get married?

Marie: No, I don't. I know I really want to work, no matter what. I know that I want some sense of myself that's not related to a husband, or to anyone but myself, for that matter. . . . But I feel so lost, I just don't

know where it's all at, really. *(Five or six heads nodded sympathetically.)*

Claire: I don't feel like *any* of you. Not a single one.

Dolores: What do you mean?

Claire: Let me tell you something. I have two sisters and a brother. My father was a passionately competitive man. He loved sports and he taught us all how to play, and he treated us all exactly as though we were his equals at it. I mean, he competed with us exactly as though we were 25 when we were 8. Everything: sailing, checkers, baseball, there was nothing he wouldn't compete in. When I was a kid I saw him send a line drive ball right into my sister's stomach, for God's sake. Sounds terrible, right? We loved it. All of us. And we thrived on it. For me, work is like everything else. *Competitive.* I get in there, do the best I can, compete ferociously against man, woman or machine. And I use whatever I have in the way of equipment: sex, brains, endurance. You name it, I use it. And if I lose I lose, and if I win I win. It's just doing it as well as I can that counts. And if I come up against discrimination as a woman, I just reinforce my attack. But the name of the game is competition.

(Everyone stared at her, openmouthed, and suddenly everyone was talking at once; over each other's voices; at each other; to themselves; laughing; interrupting; generally exploding.)

Laura (dryly): The American dream. Right before our eyes.

Diana (tearfully): Good God, Claire, that sounds awful!

Lucie (amazed): That's the kind of thing that's killing our men. In a sense, it's really why we're here.

Sheila (mad): Oh, that love of competition!

Marie (astonished): The whole idea of just *being* is completely lost in all this.

Jen (outraged): And to act sexy in order to compete! You degrade every woman alive!

Veronica (interested): In other words, Claire, you imply that if they give you what you want they get *you*?

Diana (wistfully): That notion of competition is everything we hate most in men, isn't it? It's responsible for the most brutalizing version of masculinity. We're in here trying to be men, right? Do we want to be men at their worst?

Lucie (angrily): For God's sake! We're in here trying to be *ourselves*. Whatever that turns out to be.

Marilyn (with sudden authority): I think you're wrong, all of you. You don't understand what Claire's really saying. (Everyone stopped talking and looked at Marilyn.) What Claire is really telling you is that her father taught her not how to win but how to lose. He didn't teach her to ride roughshod over other people. He taught her how to get up and walk away intact when other people rode roughshod over *her*. And he so loved the idea of teaching *that* to his children that he ignored the fact that she and her sisters were girls, and he taught it to them, anyway. (Everyone took a moment to digest this.)

Laura: I think Marilyn has a very good point there. That's exactly what Claire has inside her. She's the strongest person in this room, and we've all known it for a long time. She has the most integrated and most *separate* sense of herself of anyone I know. And I can see now that that probably has developed from her competitiveness. It's almost as though it provided the *proper* relation to other people, rather than no relation.

Sheila: Well, if that's true then her father performed a minor miracle.

Jen: You're not kidding. Knowing where *you* stand in relation to other people, what you're supposed to be doing, not because of what other people want of you but because of what you want for yourself . . . *knowing* what you want for yourself . . . that's everything, isn't it?

Laura: I think so. When I think of work, that's really

what I think of most. And when I think of *me* and work, I swear I feel like Ulysses after 10 years at sea. I, unlike the rest of you, do not feel I am where I am because of luck or accident or through the natural striving caused by a healthy competitiveness. I feel I am like a half-maddened bull who keeps turning and turning and turning, trying to get the hell out of this maze he finds himself in. . . . I spent 10 years not knowing what the hell I wanted to do with myself. So I kept getting married and having children. I've had three children and as many husbands. All nice men, all good to me, all meaningless to me. (She stopped short, and seemed to be groping for words . . .) I wanted to *do* something. Something that was real, and serious, and would involve me in a struggle with myself. Every time I got married it was like applying Mercurochrome to a festering wound. I swear sometimes I think the thing I resent most is that women have always gotten married as a way out of the struggle. It's the thing we're encouraged to do, it's the thing we rush into with such *relief*, it's the thing we come absolutely to *hate*. Because marriage itself, for most women, is so full of self-hatred. A continual unconscious reminder of all our weakness, of the heavy price to be paid for taking the easy way out. Men talk about the power of a woman in the home. . . . That power has come to seem such a lopsided and malevolent thing to me. What kind of nonsense is that, anyway, to divide up the *influences* on children's lives in that bizarre way? The mother takes care of the *emotional* life of a child? The vital requirement for nourishment? Out of what special resources does *she* do that? What the hell principle of growth is operating in *her*? What gives a woman who never tests herself against structured work the wisdom or the self-discipline to oversee a child's emotional development? The whole thing

is crazy. Just crazy. And it nearly drove me crazy. . . . What can I say? For 10 years I felt as though I were continually vomiting up my life. . . . And now I work. I work hard and I work with great relish. I want to have a family, *too*. Love. Home. Husband. Fathe· for the children. Of course, I do. God, the loneliness! The longing for connection! But work first. And family second. (Her face split wide open in a big grin.) Just like a man.

Lucie: I guess I sort of feel like Laura. Only I'm not sure. I'm not sure of anything. I'm in school now. Or rather "again." Thirty years old and I'm a graduate student again, starting out almost from scratch. . . . The thing is I could never take what I was doing seriously. That is, not as seriously as my brother, or any of the boys I went to school with, did. Everything seemed too long, or too hard, or too something. Underneath it all, I felt sort of *embarrassed* to study seriously. It was as if I was really feeling: "That's something the *grownups* do. It's not something for *me* to do." I asked my brother about this feeling once, and he said most men felt the same way about themselves, only they fake it better than women do. I thought about that one a long time, and I kept trying to say myself: What the hell, it's the same for them as it is for us. But . . . (she looked swiftly around the circle) it's not! Dammit, it's *not*. After all, style is content, right? And ours are worlds away . . .

Veronica: Literally.

Lucie: I don't know. . . . I still don't know. It's a problem that nags and nags and nags at me. So often I wish some guy would just come along and I'd disappear into marriage. It's like this secret wish that I can just withdraw from it all, and then from my safe position look on and comment and laugh and say yes and no and encourage and generally play at being the judging mother, the "wise" lady of the household. . . .

But then I know within six months I'd be miserable! I'd be climbing the walls and feeling guilty. . . .

Marilyn: Guilty! Guilty, guilty. Will we *ever* have a session in which the word guilty is not mentioned once? (Outside, the bells in a nearby church tower struck midnight.)

Diana: Let's wrap it up, okay?

Veronica (reaching for her bag): Where shall we meet next week?

Marie: Wait a minute! Aren't we going to sum up? (Everyone stopped in mid-leaving, and sank wearily back into her seat.)

Lucie: Well, one thing became very clear to me. Every one of us in some way has struggled with the idea of getting married in order to be relieved of the battle of finding and staying with good work.

Diana: And every one of us who's actually done it has made a mess of it!

Jen: And everyone who hasn't has made a mess of it!

Veronica: But, look. The only one of us who's really worked well— with direction and purpose—is Claire. And we all jumped on her! (Everyone was startled by this observation and no one spoke for a long moment.)

Marilyn (bitterly): We can't do it, we can't admire anyone who *does* do it, and we can't let it alone. . . .

Jen (softly): That's not quite true. After all, we *were* able to see finally that there was virtue in Claire's position. And we *are* here, aren't we?

Marie: That's right. Don't be so down. We're not 102 years old, are we? We're caught in a mess, damned if we do and damned if we don't. All right. That's exactly why we're here. To break the bind. (On this note everyone took heart, brightened up and trooped out into the darkened Manhattan streets. Proof enough of being ready to do battle.) ∎

11 Picket Times Classified Office

Eight women and three men picketed The New York Times' midtown classified advertisement office yesterday, charging that the newspaper discriminates against women by labeling help wanted ad columns female and male.

The pickets were members of an organization called National Organization for Women, which was formed last November to fight what it considers discrimination against women in jobs and legislation. There are about 300 members, mostly women, in the New York State chapter, Mrs. Jean Faust, chapter president, said.

The pickets yesterday carried signs saying, "Women can think as well as type" and "I didn't get a job through The New York Times."

The pickets also passed out leaflets to persons walking past The Times office on Broadway, between 41st and 42d Streets.

The group also has campaigned for such things as Constitutional amendments that would outlaw sex discrimination and for the right of women to terminate unwanted pregnancies. Betty Friedan, author of "The Feminine Mystique," is national president of the organization.

In a statement, Monroe Green, vice president of The Times said:

"It is my belief that the best interests of job applicant, employer, city, state and Federal antidiscrimination laws are being served by our present practice, which is to require the following legend on each page which includes Classified Help Wanted Advertising:

" 'The New York State and City Laws Against Discrimination and the Federal Civil Rights Act of 1964 prohibit discrimination in employment because of sex unless based on a bona fide occupational qualification. Help Wanted and Situation Wanted advertisements are arranged in columns captioned 'Male' and 'Female' for the convenience of readers and are not intended as an unlawful limitation or discrimination based on sex.'

"I believe too that the use of headings on our employment pages helps achieve full employment. The best evidence available that job seekers and others are satisfied with our present practice is the fact that since the Civil Rights Laws went into effect not a single complaint from a job seeker has ever been received by The New York Times. And during a nine-months period, we have published approximately 850,-000 commercial help wanted advertisements."

August 31, 1967

Women's Liberation Taking to the Stage

By MARYLIN BENDER

ONE is a suburban housewife, on the brink of middle age and ablaze with a rage from within. The other is a young law student's wife, recently pregnant and outwardly serene. They have written and composed the first women's liberation musical, the first to be produced above ground at least, "The Mod Donna," which opens May 1 at The New York Shakespeare Festival Public Theater, is being directed and produced by Joseph Papp, the zealous prophet of free Shakespeare in Central Park and the original impresario of "Hair," the rock musical that became a hippie manifesto as well as a commercial success on Broadway.

"There's been a little animosity from some women in the movement because I took a male director," said Myrna Lamb, the writing member of the team, during a break in rehearsals. There was both joy and anguish in her almond-shaped brown eyes, and the toss of her mahogany-colored mane. Her earth-mother form was loosely upholstered in a brown knit pants suit and her strong, gesticulating hands were bare of a wedding ring.

"I'm a feminist but I can't be a female chauvinist. I'm very alienated. I always try to belong and I never can. It's never comfortable for me. I don't like anyone telling me what to do even if it's women's liberation," she said in a lyrical voice that carried the menace of a volcano that has been erupting intermittently for 39 years going on 40. All but the first 17 of those years have been circumscribed by marriage and motherhood, two institutions that the women's liberation movement has every intention of altering by reform or revolution.

"The Mod Donna" blends two marriages one representing power, the other subservience, into "a macabre ménage à trois" in which the serving girl agrees to bear children for the other couple, explained Myrna Lamb.

She has two daughters, 14 and 20, by Marvin Epstein of Nutley, N. J., a food salesman who is her first and only husband although, as a feminist, she refuses to use his name.

"I want to be just me, Myrna. And I'm not Miss Lamb either.

Her collaborator nodded vigorously. "I would never introduce myself as Mrs. Timothy Bingham. I'm Susan Bingham or Susan Hulsman Bingham," said the 25-year-old concert pianist who composed the music for "The Mod Donna" in an apartment in New Haven, Conn., where she lives with her husband of a year and a half. A Yale law student, he is the son of Rep. Jonathan Bingham, the Democratic Bronx Congressman.

"I'm not militant because my experience has been so good. I feel my marriage is as free as it can be," said Susan Bingham, looking half her age and not the least rebellious in a beige tweed A-line dress and beige suède boots. A thin platinum wedding band was matched to a modest diamond solitaire on the third finger of her left hand.

The writer and the composer met last summer at Mr. Papp's Experimental Theater. Susan Bingham, a Boston banker's daughter, had written the music for a review put on by a group of Yale drama students. Myrna Lamb, whose father was a motor vehicle inspector in Newark, was involved with The New Feminist Theatre through her abortion play, "But What Have You Done For Me Lately," in which a man was impregnated and had to submit his frantic plea for an abortion to a board of women.

"It was no play," Myrna Lamb said. "It was mother's rage. I wrote it because my daughter suspected she was pregnant. She wasn't. But it put me in a rage."

"I understand what Myrna feels even though I don't have the venom. I don't disagree with her," Susan Bingham said. She is expecting her first child next September. Meanwhile she and her husband are discussing the division of child care. So far it is certain that he will help out at bedtime and that his mother will be tapped as a babysitter.

"You've got what I would have settled for," Myrna said to Susan. "Your marriage is rather sensible, an intelligent rapport between like human beings."

"I'm the older generation," she went on. "My husband is 48, a World War II veteran. It was a different culture. I wasn't allowed to do anything but be a housewife."

But she tried, as an actress, a suburban newspaper writer, a proofreader.

"The Mod Donna," Joseph Papp said, "is an oratorio, one woman's cry, the personal pain she feels."

"But as ideology, I feel it's an important statement to make today about the relations between men and women and about the state of women," he asserted.

The Donna in the title is a servant girl married to a war veteran named Charlie who doesn't think he can make it in the system except by living through his boss. "If his wife does a little something for the boss, he'll look away." Myrna Lamb said.

The boss is rich and powerful and married to a lady. "He like to play a game where he gives his power to her but only in a well-controlled situation," she said.

The play contains a female symbolically crucified but no nudity, Mr. Papp said, "because I feel it would be wrong here. There is the nakedness of the idea instead, a stripping away of things that are usually left unsaid."

March 26, 1970

Women in Pants

By BERNADINE MORRIS

Without any confrontation, demonstration or even artful campaigning, women are securing for themselves another human right: the right to wear pants to work. The privilege is being granted by men in industry, government, and financial institutions who have long since given up the struggle to keep women from wearing pants at home.

These male executives are doing it with the same grace that their forebears in Congress showed 50 years ago when they granted women the vote. Men today see it as inevitable. It will make life easier around the office, and besides, there's a larger bogey—the midiskirt.

While men don't equate the freedom to wear pants with equal pay, day care centers or abortion reform, women see it as a step in the right direction.

At any rate, they're taking advantage of it.

"Our office just changed its tradition yesterday," said Dorothy Nichols, who was sauntering along Fifth Avenue on her lunch hour Wednesday in a rust pants suit and plaid poncho. "Today, everybody's in pants."

Miss Nichols, a secretary at Vanity Fair, thought her company took so long about changing the rules "because we make petticoats and slips, and they were afraid women wouldn't wear any if they wore pants."

Everyone's Happy at Bank

Last week, the Irving Trust Company decided to permit pants. It made no official announcement, but the word got around.

"The first day, I saw two or three girls in pants; the next, there were 60," commented Don Phelps, an assistant secretary of the bank. "Everybody's happy about it—the tellers, the computer room girls, the customers and even the bank's officers."

The reasons for the change were threefold, according to Mr. Phelps.

First, there was the feeling that women should dress as they choose, a byproduct of the women's liberation movement; second, many women had difficulty in buying clothes this fall because of the prevalence of midiskirts, and third, "banks really aren't as stuffy as most people think they are."

Dominick & Dominick, a 100-year-old brokerage house on Wall Street, decided to permit pants suits this week.

"Most of the girls were asking about it, so I talked to Mr. Rockefeller, and he hashed it around for a while with the other executives," said Mrs. Connie Puma, executive secretary to Avery Rockefeller Jr., president of the company. "He said he'd just as soon see girls in pants as he would in midiskirts, so I guess that's why they gave in."

Accepting pants seems to be an easy way to indicate a financial institution's liberality these days. At any rate, the National Bank of North America has decided to include a pants suit in its tellers' wardrobes, and the American Stock Exchange adopted pants suit uniforms for its Gallery Guides.

The barriers are falling everywhere. Pan American World Airways included a pants suit in its winter uniform for its ground service force, and Gretchen Healy, a non-uniformed secretary, wrote a letter to a vice president asking whether she could wear pants, too. The letter went through channels to Najeeb Halaby, Pan Am president, who sent around an approving memorandum that described the move as "symbolic of being responsive to new ideas from employes."

Numbers Tell the Story

Pfizer, the pharmaceutical concern, decided to permit pants after a poll of employes disclosed that the staff was overwhelmingly anti-midi. (Of 353 female employes responding, 307 preferred the mini, 20 preferred the midi, the rest were undecided; of 286 men, 275 preferred the mini, six chose the midi.) Even though pants weren't mentioned in the poll, the company put out a policy statement accepting them as suitable business attire.

Pants have been infiltrating Government offices in Washington, too. Last week, five secretaries in the Department of Commerce, after checking with their bosses, turned up in pants.

The staff of Representative Edward I. Koch, Democrat of New York, has been wearing pants because he believes in letting them keep up with fashion. Because he doesn't believe in the fashion for midiskirts, Senator Jacob K. Javits is encouraging his staff to wear pants.

But the word at the White House is that Mrs. Nixon doesn't wear pants on official business and that her staff shouldn't either—at least not this year.

Mayor Lindsay pondered the question for a day and a half and then decided pants were acceptable in his office, according to his secretary, Kathy St. John.

Possibly the final arbiters of the social acceptability of pants, New York's fashionable restaurants, are no longer trying to stem the tide. Only two are saying no today, La Côte Basque and Lafayette. Other restaurateurs, such as Laurent Losa of Laurent, have given in.

"One night I turned away eight parties, some of my best customers, and some of those women in pants looked beautiful," he said. "I went home that night and I said, 'What am I doing?' and the next day I changed the policy."

But there still has to be some decorum. "Those mechanics' pants with zippers," said Mr. Losa, "we won't allow those." He was referring to jumpsuits.

The prevalence of pants is the one bright hope in the sticky-wicket fashion picture. Seventh Avenue, which in its upper, prestigious regions made no great effort to push pants for fall, is enjoying an unexpected increment as pants sales flower.

"The reorders are great, all over the country," said Bill Thomas, the head of Susan Thomas.

Mr. Thomas is one of the few manufacturers who saw the handwriting on the wall. He switched his production to 90 per cent pants.

"Last year, we did 50 per cent of our

"My husband hates long skirts," Mrs. Bruce Morrow explained.

business in pants, the year before maybe 10 per cent, but this time, there's no stopping it," said the manufacturer, whose styles sell for $50 to $120.

"There's no sign of its letting up," he added, "and the orders are coming from all over the country and for sizes we never made before—large sizes. While everybody's talking about skirt lengths, pants are selling."

Norman Norell, whose pants sell for $1,900, but include a sweater and coat, has noticed the boom, too.

"One of the things the midi length has accomplished is that it's made pants business better," the designer said. "We've always shown pants, but we've never sold so many."

In California, where anti-midi fever has turned into a mania, and where long skirts are languishing on the racks, pants sales are zooming.

They Saved the Day

In New York, where last week's hot weather and confusion about lengths slowed down business, pants were saving the day in stores as disparate in

United Press International

Senator Jacob K. Javits objects to the midi and encourages his staff to wear pants. Paula Schmidt, at left, and Kim Durney, oblige

"Frankly, I'm getting tired of pants," said Mrs. Allan Bennett.

their appeal as Abraham & Straus and Macy's, on the one hand, and Bonwit Teller and Lord & Taylor on the other.

Every store has its success story. Bonwit's, which was talking about setting up a separate room for pants in its junior area, found it was selling eight pairs of pants for each skirt in sportswear. Lord & Taylor reported $6,000 worth of mail orders in response to a small ad for a pants suit at $24, and sold more than 4,000 pieces of that style alone. Pants sales were up 40 per cent over last year in its suit shop.

"I can't get over seeing so many old ladies buying pants," an employe said.

On Fifth Avenue and in the stores, some women shopping for fall clothes or just thinking about them are busily denying they are copping out by wearing pants.

"I just think they're comfortable," said Mrs. William Rosen, whose husband owns Gatsby's restaurant.

"I think pants suits with turtle-neck sweaters and midicoats are the smartest thing going."

"If I weren't sure about myself, I'd wear pants," said Mrs. Bruce Morrow, whose husband is the radio performer known as Cousin Brucie. "I've bought a midi and some gaucho pants, but I think I have more pants in my wardrobe than anything else, and I wear them because I like them."

Some admit that pants are a protest. "I wear them all the time because I hate the midi, and I will not buy the midi," said Mrs. Martin Sherman of Ridgewood, N. J., whose husband is an architect. "I can't think of any place I wouldn't wear pants, except to temple on Yom Kippur—I've already worn them to bar mitzvahs and weddings." Her 17-year-old daughter likes the midi, Mrs. Sherman admitted, but she also likes pants.

For some women, pants are a liberation. "This is the first time I've worn them in the city," said Mrs. Stanley Sokoloff of Fort Lee, N. J., whose husband is an insurance broker.

She wore a green pants suit to a fur showing at Bergdorf Goodman and was cheered by seeing other women in pants.

One of them was Mrs. Henry Reichman, who had her white wool pants suit made to order by Cosmo Sirchio because "It's hard to find something in my size." Mrs. Reichman described herself as "full blown" and admitted to measurements of "45-35-45."

Evening pants have been more acceptable than formal daytime pants, but that trend is accelerating too, especially outside of New York, according to manufacturers. At the Restore Ball here, the season's first big charity event, sponsored by the Kennedy family, party pants had a considerable representation. And when Patricia Lynn Cummings is married to Eugene J. Gillespie, a lawyer, at Saint Patrick's Cathedral tomorrow, the bridesmaids will be wearing champagne-colored pants dresses.

Which may be the final indication that the most revolutionary fashion change of the year was not the hemline, but the power of women to wear pants whenever they please.

October 2, 1970

Ms Isn't Sweeping the Nation The Foes of Miss/Mrs. Find

By ENID NEMY

Representative Jonathan B. Bingham, Democrat of New York, says that "a profound question involving the status of women" is involved.

Representative Bella Abzug, Democrat of New York, says that "there is absolutely no justification for such idle curiosity about women."

Bess Myerson, Eleanor Holmes Norton and Helen Gurley Brown agree; Mrs. Richard M. Nixon, Mrs. John V. Lindsay and Mrs. Jacob K. Javits don't.

Subject of Controversy

The controversy revolves around the designations of Miss and Mrs. and the feminists' proposal to do away with any prefix that would indicate marital status.

The suggested substitution is Ms, a prefix thought to have originated with computers, which often use Ms when there isn't sufficient information to categorize a woman's status.

Now in use on a limited scale, Ms is pronounced Miz by some and Miss by others but whatever the pronunciation, it is considered by many an apt contraction of "Mistress," the word from which both Mrs. and Miss derive.

"There are an increasing number of American women who do not want to be identified as Miss or Mrs.," said Mr. Bingham in a statement read into the Congressional Record in April.

"I sympathize with the way they feel...I know from many conversations with women, including my wife and my daughter-in-law, that they resent being asked by strangers whether they are Miss or Mrs. They point out that men are called Mr. whether or not they are married."

Representative Bingham has introduced a bill requiring that states not have women disclose their marital status when registering to vote, unless the same disclosure is required of men. Mrs. Abzug more recently introduced another bill to prohibit the Federal Government from designating in any records, correspondence or documents, the marital status of an individual.

"It is not too much to ask that women be treated and considered as individuals and not as wives of individuals," she said.

Neither of the bills specifically mention the use of the prefix Ms, and many women activists think the bills do not go far enough.

"Why should I be asked if I am Miss or Mrs. in almost every application when a man, married or single, simply designates himself Mr.?" asked one young woman. "When you circle "Miss" on an application form, it's an automatic strike against you."

Although some business concerns do use application forms that require circling either Miss or Mrs., a great number of others are concerned only with stability of income. H. E. Menzer, assistant executive manager of the Credit Bureau of Greater New York Inc., pointed out that most department store credit applications require the same information from men and women. In all cases, the name, job and position of the "spouse" is asked, as is the length of employment. The Metropolitan Life Insurance Company reported it didn't require any prefix, merely a name.

A spokesman for the New York Telephone Company said customers would be addressed and billed "any way they wish," and a representative of Chemical Bank of New York said the bank had no objection to opening accounts with an Ms preceding the name. So far there have been no requests.

The New York State Bureau of Motor Vehicles offers no obstacles to women who wish to use their maiden names on their drivers' licenses.

"We'll accept any given name as long as we can establish the identity of a person through a birth certificate or other document," said Victor Carbonaro, assistant counsel to the Commissioner of Motor Vehicles. "If a woman is married and wants the license in her maiden name, there is no problem."

However, a three-judge Federal Court ruled in Montgomery, Ala., last month that a married woman does not have a constitutional right to have her driver's license issued in her maiden name.

The suit was brought by Mrs. Ronald P. Carver who filed under her maiden name of Wendy Forbush.

In denying the requested injunction, the court said: "The existing law in Alabama which requires a woman to assume her husband's surname upon marriage has a rational basis and seeks to control an area where the state has a legitimate interest."

An increasing number of businesses, particularly in larger cities where women's liberation groups are active, are receiving letters signed with Ms, rather than the traditional forms. Many of the same companies use the same designation when replying. There is usually, however, no set policy for the company as a whole.

"Some bank personnel will address people as they have signed themselves," a Chase Manhattan Bank spokeswoman said. "I've personally been using Ms for some time."

"It's very handy when you don't know if a woman is married or single," said a spokeswoman for Macy's. "It's not our policy but it's expedient."

Several airlines have received reservations requests from women who refuse to be designated by their marital status and insist on either Ms or the use of their name without any designation.

"We list them the way they prefer," said representatives of both American Airlines and United Air Lines.

The situation with international airlines is slightly more complicated.

"The question of Miss or Mrs. doesn't arise unless the woman is listed on her husband's passport," said a Pan American World Airways spokesman, who was seconded by Scandinavian Airlines System. "We list them any way they prefer but the name itself must be that used on the passport."

Whether the usual prefixes are required or are merely custom is irrelevant to many advocates of the new form.

"Prefixes now have implications of discrimination," said Mrs. Eleanor Holmes Norton, chairman of the City of New York Commission on Human Rights. "I prefer Ms for very practical reasons. A person's performance, character and personality should not be judged on whether she is married or not."

Helen Gurley Brown, editor of Cosmopolitan magazine, said she thought the idea was "swell."

"My vote is yes. Miss and Mrs. are quite artificial, what with divorce, separation, loose ties and long-term affairs."

For Jacqueline Ceballos, head of the New York division of the National Organization for Women, the new designation was "a matter of raising consciousness."

Bess Myerson, the City's Commissioner of Consumer Affairs, said, "We're supposed to be a country that doesn't believe in titles anyway."

"I really don't understand anyone who would oppose this," she added.

However, some of the principal objection to the use of Ms is coming not from men, but from women.

Mrs. Nixon, according to her press office, is for the status quo.

"Knowing Mrs. Nixon, I know she likes the Mrs.," said a spokeswoman for the First Lady. "Mrs. Nixon still uses Mrs. and Miss. She likes it, and that's the way it will be."

Mrs. Lindsay, who supports some of the aims of women's liberation groups, was less than lukewarm about the suggested prefix change.

"I like Mrs.," she said. "It took me long enough to get it."

Mrs. Javits, whose husband is the senior Republican Senator for New York, thought Ms might be fine for young people, but, she said, "I've been married 23 years, and I'm not giving up my Mrs. Besides, Ms sounds charmless."

Preferences Stated

Mrs. John L. Loeb, the City Commissioner to the United Nations, said that "everything you do should make things clearer and being Mrs. clarifies a situation.

"I prefer to be attached to the man to whom I am married," she said. "I like bearing his name. I find it more dignified to be Mrs. John L. Loeb."

Perhaps one of the cruelest blows to feminists was Mrs. Harding Lawrence's reaction.

"I'm much prouder of being Mrs. Harding Lawrence than I was of being Miss Mary Wells," said the woman considered to be one of the leading advertising executives in the country. "I wouldn't change it for the world."

For some women, even Ms is not the ultimate solution. They would prefer an asexual designation that would include not only women but men and children.

Mrs. Varda Murrell, a Los Angeles feminist, has suggested Person, which could be contracted to Pn.

Miss Ceballos thinks that Myself or Msf would be rather nice.

And Miss Myerson has come up with Citizen.

The FemLib Case Against Sigmund Freud

By RICHARD GILMAN

NOT long ago a man in his early 40's sat listening to the discussion at a women's liberation meeting. That he and other men were there meant the organization was among the more moderate of its kind; yet he became increasingly agitated as the evening went on. Finally rising to his feet, he proceeded to tell the women, his voice husky with sincerity, that he understood and sympathized with their complaints but was certain they were on the wrong track. The answer to their problems, as it was the answer to those of men as well, was psychoanalysis. The word was scarcely out when he was assailed by hoots, catcalls and epithets from everywhere in the room. Bewildered, he sat down, while the people around him marveled at the innocence that had led him to press so wrong a button.

That feminists of almost every degree of militancy respond with such resentment to the word "psychoanalysis" and, even more violently, to the name Sigmund Freud, comes as a great shock to the average cultivated man. To the liberal intellectual it is a kind of blasphemy. For Freud and Freudianism are among the constituents of modern cultivation and liberal thinking; whatever one's strictures on psychoanalysis, Freud's place as a culture hero has long been secure. The man of ideas is certain that from Freud's work we derive a central element of our sense of what being human entails. To which feminists reply: *your* sense of what being human *and male* entails. As a theory of culture and psychosexuality, Freudianism is to these women an egregious product of male chauvinism, and Freud, in the words of Kate Millett, is "beyond question the strongest individual counterrevolutionary force"

RICHARD GILMAN is a well-known critic. His latest book is a collection of essays and reviews, "Common and Uncommon Masks: Writings on the Theater, 1961-1970."

against the movement for female liberation.

Now, to think of Freud as any sort of counterrevolutionary requires a difficult mental adjustment for a man who, like myself, has been accustomed to thinking of him as a great insurrectionary. True, I understood that his insurrection was fundamentally a conservative act, that he wished to preserve the achievements of human nature against its own destructive tendencies. Still, the act was on the side of freedom, a Promethean blow against obscurantism and cultural darkness. That Freud was one of our true redeemers I accepted as an axiom of my liberal thinking, and in this spirit of reverence, when I was in Vienna some years ago I visited the house on Bergasse where, a modest plaque announced, he had lived and worked.

For a while during the early stages of my investigation for this article, the virulence of the feminist attack against Freud threatened to turn my original sympathy for the movement into impatience and even hostility. But about half-way through, I realized that nothing required me to defend Freud at every point, that his great achievements were unassailable, and that, despite them, he might very well have been a misogynist and had ideas that were, in certain respects, inimical to women. And, as I read on through the feminist critique (which for all the varied voices is, in effect, a single position paper) and, more decisive than that, went back to Freud's own writings, the evidence of his radical bias against women and the existence of that bias in the very texture of psychoanalysis came to seem indisputable.

As I said, most feminist writers tended to put me off. Besides their implacability and fierceness (a magnificent exception is the cool and sober Simone de Beauvoir), their intellectual delinquencies — overstatement, tendentious reasoning, lack of humor and subtlety, arguments that frequently throw out the baby with the bath water—provide enough ammunition for any scholarly critic to bring them down. But the least I could do, I thought, was to realize that their rhetoric was that of embattled dissidents, and ought not to discredit their case. When Shulamith Firestone called for the abolition of the family, or when the splendidly pseudonymed Betsy Warrior extended the proscription to the entire male sex, I winced but managed to keep in sight what had provoked them.

"ANATOMY is destiny" is a famous, ill-used phrase. Every element of Freud's taxonomy of women and its elaboration by most of his successors has its basis in the differences between male and female physiology, with the consequent division of biological function. The core of the feminist complaint is that these anatomical and biological differences, which have hardly escaped human attention, have been built by psychoanalysis (which is simply the newest and most powerful "scientific" reinforcement of perennial attitudes) into a system of psychological, moral, intellectual and societal values that mere physiology doesn't inexorably ordain. That men have penises and women do not, that women alone give birth and that men's role in procreation is comparatively remote, that men are on the average larger and stronger than women—none of this means that existing feminine and masculine roles are inevitable.

Above all, the differences don't in themselves validate the hierarchical male notion of a basic superiority, of an almost ontological pre-eminence, which men have felt and articulated in religion, art, political organization, jurisprudence and the very structure of language, which forces us to speak of "man" and "mankind" as of the whole human race. This male conviction of superiority is continually menaced by a number of female incarnations—the siren, the "castrating" wife, the Holy Mother, the Amazon—but it always manages to reassert itself as the prevailing masculine morale, although not of course in every individual male. And, as feminists are well aware, the majority of women have concurred with the men.

What struck me most when I went back to read Freud was not so much the hundreds of disparaging references to women scattered throughout his works (they are, he says, secre-

"In all his bold explorations of the inner life, women remained dark and unfathomable to him, like planets beyond the range of his instruments."

tive and insincere, they are envious and lack a sense of justice and honor, they are masochistic and deprived and, by continual implication, mutilated), nor the arbitrary assumptions behind the complex theories that are supposed to establish their inferiority. The astonishing thing, which had only rarely been pointed out until the feminists began waving their arms at it, is that Freud's entire theory of sexuality is built from a masculine model. In psychoanalysis, maleness is the norm and femaleness an incomplete or, even worse, deficient aspect of it.

WHAT psychoanalysis has done, in an act invisible to the ordinary male eye, is to move through its intellectual adventure in the spirit of *man's* conquest of knowledge. Nothing better illustrates this than Freud's remark in the "New Introductory Lectures on Psychoanalysis" that "throughout the ages the problem of women has puzzled people of every kind." Man is not problematic, woman is. And those to whom she is a problem are the "people," humanity defined as male. The people are the ones whose task it is to "solve" woman, although it is not hers to solve them, nor even to offer any advice about herself.

Once he had laid out the components of his interpretation of sexual difference in the extremely important "Three Essays on the Theory of Sexuality" in 1905, Freud would add to them and make slight adjustments, but never radically revise or repudiate his view of women as the abnormal, the questionable sex. His starting point is the penis, and

the discovery sooner or later by every child that this is an exclusively male attribute. Before that, he writes, "the assumption that all human beings have the same [male] form of genital," has been "the first of the many remarkable and momentous sexual theories of children." And he adds, in a pronouncement that profoundly shaped his future thought, that "the science of biology justifies the child's prejudice and has been obliged to recognize the clitoris as a true substitute for the penis."

Both boys and girls discover their difference. For boys this is a source of pride and the beginning of contempt for the "deprived" female. For girls, to whom the "penis of a brother or a playmate [is] strikingly visible and of large proportions," it is accompanied by recognition of the phallus as "the superior counterpart of their own small and inconspicuous organ. They are then overcome by envy culminating in the wish . . . to be boys themselves." In "Some Psychological Consequences of the Anatomical Distinctions Between the Sexes," Freud further develops this famous notion: "After a woman has become aware of the wound to her narcissism, she develops, like a scar, a sense of inferiority. When she has passed beyond her first attempt at explaining her lack of a penis as being a punishment personal to herself and has realized that the sexual character is a universal one, she begins to share the contempt felt by men for a sex which is the lesser in so important a respect."

The critique of this strange psychosexual melodrama isn't difficult to compose. To begin with, the power

440

and superiority of the penis is scarcely self-evident, especially when we consider that the organ of the little boy is much more likely to be tiny and shriveled, ridiculous from some perspectives, than large and imposing. It seems clear that as feminists and other critics of Freud agree, its dominance is conferred on it not by biology but by society.

"The little girl's covetousness," Simone de Beauvoir writes, "results from a previous evaluation of virility. Freud takes this for granted, whereas it should be accounted for." And she goes on to account for it by arguing that "the phallus assumes such worth as it does because it symbolizes a dominance that is exercised in other domains." Extending this idea, the feminist Susan Lydon asserts that as one effect of Freudian thought, "the penis functioned as the unalterable determinant of maleness which women could symbolically envy instead of the power and prestige given men by society."

Something more subtle and far-reaching is also suggested by Freud's theory of penis-envy. In his important and highly respectful study, "Freud: the Mind of the Moralist," Philip Rieff points out that Freud "assigned sexual meanings to the most elementary attributes of 'thing' —extension, solidity, protrusion—and those of 'void,'" attaching the former to maleness and the latter to femaleness and making no secret of which was superior. By doing this, it seems to me, he confirmed a Victorian, indeed a perennial Western and materialist bias in favor of the palpable. The Russian philosopher Berdyaev once wrote that the bourgeois is precisely the person who invariably "prefers the visible to the invisible." We might add that he prefers the larger to the smaller, too. It is one of the great ironies of cultural history that Freud, in so many respects the destroyer of bourgeois complacency, should also have been, on this deepest of existential levels, one of its secret confirmers.

NOTHING is allowed from now on to escape the primal influence of this apotheosis of the male protuberance. Whatever else it may be, the Oedipus complex, for example, is a drama with a hero but no heroine. Whereas both sexes are originally more attached to the mother, Freud says, it is the *task* of the girl to transfer this attachment to the father. For the boy there is no such assignment; there are only the majestic theatrics of his desire for the mother and rivalry with the father, with the ensuing threat of castration at the latter's hands.

But such a threat is itself a product of male pride and supremacy. For, says Freud, "in the boy the castration complex is formed after he has learned that the sexual organ which he prizes so highly is not a necessary part of the human being"; in other words, he fears that he may be reduced to the penisless condition of the girl, who, already disqualified from any eminence, has acknowledged the "fact of her castration." This prior acceptance of a mutilated condition will have overwhelming consequences for the entire female character.

Once more Freud has confused biological and social causation. His presumption of a universality for the Oedipus complex, a sort of fate within nature, is not borne out by evidence from anthropology, among other disciplines. Bronislaw Malinowski has written that "the Oedipus complex corresponds essentially to our patrilineal Aryan family with the developed *patria potestas*, buttressed by Roman law and Christian morals and accentuated by the modern economic conditions of the well-to-do *bourgeoisie*." Like certain other Freudian ideas—his theory that hysteria is peculiarly female, for instance—the Oedipus complex would seem to have emerged by a process of extrapolation from the nature of the society Freud knew.

Kate Millett may be oversimplifying when she writes that the Oedipus complex "is rather less a matter of the son's passion for the mother than his passion for attaining the level of power to which adult male status is supposed

to entitle him," but it is clear that Freud's acceptance of male superiority shapes his thinking about this central matter.

As the ordeal of puberty goes forward, its unfolding for males, Freud argues, "is more straightforward and more understandable, while that of the female actually enters upon a kind of involution." Before puberty, which is to say in the auto-erotic phase, "the sexuality of little girls is of a wholly masculine character." But now they are faced with the need to abandon their wish for the actual penis and to repudiate the clitoris, that "inferior" substitute. "With the change from girlhood to femininity, the clitoris must give up to the vagina its sensitivity and, with it, its importance . . . ."

This requirement is brought into being—if the woman has not remained "immature" or "arrested," or become actually "regressive"—by the present possibility and impending actuality of motherhood. But even motherhood, which we understandably think of as a uniquely female capacity and accomplishment, is indissolubly linked in Freudian thought with woman's inferiority to man. For the woman has never really given up her longing to have a penis, and this "unsatisfied wish," says Freud, "should be converted into a wish to have a child." In fact, "the girl's libido slips into place by means—there is really no other way to put it—of the equation 'penis = child.'"

WHAT Freud is saying is that the sexual energy of females, which has existed up to now largely as an imitative form of male libido, can only be released by the actuality or felt potentiality of giving birth, an act by which the penis is symbolically obtained. To give birth to a son is the most complete symbolical appropriation. The new mother's happiness "is great indeed when the desire for a child one day finds a real fulfillment; but especially is this so if the child is a little boy, who brings the longed-for penis with him."

Nowhere is Freud's male bias so flagrantly displayed or so destructive of the equality of women and men. This is why the question of the putative "hierarchy" of the sexual organs has feminists so strenuously exercised. In one of their key documents on the subject, Dr. Mary Jane Sherfey has argued that the clitoris, far from being a lesser or rudimentary penis, is actually only the visible tip of an underlying system of sexual tissue which is at least as large and responsive as that of the male. Again, some feminist theoreticians claim there is nothing like the big distinction between clitoral and vaginal responses which Freud said there was, and they have received significant support from the work of Masters and Johnson, whose research has convinced them that, contrary to Freud's presumption, clitoral and vaginal orgasms are anything but "separate physiological entities."

The controversy involves the largest questions of female sexual being and of woman's destiny in general. If the vagina is regarded as the exclusive or even the only proper organ of mature feminine sexuality, then, feminists maintain, women are once more confined to the function of child-bearing ("That the child is the supreme aim of woman is a statement having the precise value of an advertising slogan," says de Beauvoir) and to a passive acceptance of sexuality as male intrusion. Against this, some feminists, including, understandably, many Lesbians, argue that the clitoris is in fact the specific organ of female sexual response. And this swing of the pendulum has brought its own rebuttal from within feminist ranks. In her brilliant book, "The Female Eunuch," Germaine Greer writes that "unhappily, we have accepted, along with the reinstatement of the clitoris after its proscription by the Freudians, a notion of the utter passivity and even irrelevance of the vagina," and warns against the "stunting" of sexual experience this entails.

EVEN though Freud's data

were obtained, as has frequently been pointed out, from a highly suspect group of upper middle-class patients, Freud felt he knew enough to draw universal conclusions. Besides her much greater difficulty in attaining sexual maturity, the female is faced in Freudian thought with certain other permanent effects of being the derivative sex. She is much more prone to neurosis than is man, and this is due to her having had to "change her leading erotogenic zone" after having put aside her "childish masculinity." She is far more likely to be masochistic, because of the "repressions of [her] aggressiveness" by her "constitution" and, Freud adds in one of his rare concessions to other possibilities, by society. Masochism is, in fact, Freud asserts, "truly feminine," a notion which, as a feminist writer remarks, has the effect of justifying male abuse of women as "more food for her nature."

Beyond this constitutional handicap, women are described throughout Freud's writings as suffering from many other psychic disabilities, moral afflictions and existential disqualifications. They are more envious than men, which results from the primal anatomical envy; they are more subject to feelings of shame, because of their "wounded" condition. (Freud is never more far-fetched on the subject than when he speculates that women created weaving in order to hide their own privates: men, presumably, remained "strikingly visible.") They are less reliable, less self-sufficient, less admirable altogether. Most disastrous of all, they are barred in all but exceptional cases (and these to be regarded as examples of "masculinization") from contributing to the great intellectual, artistic and spiritual accomplishments of humanity.

The reason for this is that the male, through having overcome the castration-fear, is able to create a strong superego, the source of the "sublimations" by which sexual energy is converted into culture, while for the female the superego remains weak and undeveloped. "Feminists," Freud writes, "are not pleased if one points to the way in which this factor affects the development of the average feminine character."

No, they aren't pleased. Nor are they enchanted by Freud's continual talk of their "subjugation" by males, by his finding that passivity is a natural female condition, by his observation that women are like the masses in wanting to be mastered and ruled, by his frequent comparisons of them to children and, in short, by his fixing their role in history as *Kinder, Küche* and *Kirche*. Finally, they are less than enthralled by the magisterial unanswerability of his ultimate appeal against them to biology. "Nature," said Freud, "has paid less careful attention to the demands of the female function than to those of masculinity" and has built a "repudiation of femininity" into the very nature of things.

FREUD'S disciples and successors, as well as the psychoanalytic heretics, have for the most part left his basic views on women unchallenged. Otto Rank held the birth trauma to be more crucial for both sexes than the Oedipus complex, but retained the broad outlines of Freud's ideas. Jung, to whom feminists seem to be turning, placed much more emphasis on spiritual and mythical factors than on purely sexual ones, but offered no coherent opposition to Freud on women. Karen Horney timidly advanced a counter-notion of "womb-envy." Ernest Jones, Freud's biographer, suspected that the master's ideas were a bit "phallocentric." More recently, Erik Erikson has elaborated a theory of woman's "inner space" as the counterpart of male externality, an idea which most feminists despise for its subtle, deceptively generous restatement of Freud's position. Only Alfred Adler, the least influential of the great Freudians, flatly opposed him by declaring that women's "inferiority" is in no sense biological but wholly social in origin.

Yet the recognition is growing among psychoanalytic thinkers that the feminists have a strong position vis-à-vis Freud. Rollo May told me, after remarking that he was disturbed by the excesses of feminist polemic, that it was foolish to ignore Freud's "unsatisfactory" relations with women and that his "condescending and patronizing attitude toward them undoubtedly warped his scientific theorizing." Robert Jay Lifton put it simply: "Every great thinker has at least one blind spot; Freud's was women."

Still, many humanist intellectuals defend Freud, claiming that he has been misunderstood and that any thinker of his scope and brilliance could not possibly have been deficient in so important a respect. If he was wrong on women, how could he have been right on men? The reply to this might begin with Socrates' dictum that "none of us can know the whole truth, but each of us can say something true about the way things are." Freud enunciated the most liberating truths about the psyche; his discoveries of the nature of unconsciousness, the mechanisms of repression, the strategies of neurosis, the significance of dreams, are at work now in all our self-consideration. Nonetheless, in all his bold explorations of the inner life, women remained dark and unfathomable to him, like planets beyond the range of his instruments.

HE would admit this at times. Near the beginning of his "Three Essays on the Theory of Sexuality," he wrote that "the part of the theory which lies on the frontiers of biology . . . is still faced with undiminished contradiction" and that "we are ignorant of what constitutes a feminine brain." He spoke of how "the erotic life of [men] alone has become accessible to research," while that of women "is still veiled in an impenetrable obscurity." And in the late stages of his investigation he acknowledged that "it is not always easy to distinguish between what is due to the influence of sexual function and what to social training." To the reader (understood to be a man) who wished to know more about women, he offered the rather poignant advice "to interrogate your own experience, or turn to the poets, or else wait until science can give you more profound and coherent information."

But though he did occasionally preface his observations about women with such characteristic qualifications, he nevertheless went on to construct his portrait of them with an equally characteristic authoritativeness and lack of humility. The man who plunged alone and unarmed into the terra incognita of his own dreams was unable to detect his bias and untruthfulness in regard to women or to perceive how profoundly his theories demeaned them. The greatest irony is that his defenders so often betray his own ideal method and morale —to face up to whatever is true—in the interests of protecting him and their investment in his thought.

Not all defenses of Freud issue from passionate commitment to him or his ideas, however. As feminism threatens male convictions, Freudianism becomes more useful as a line of defense, in the same way as purported evidence from animal behavior does. There is a pretense of lofty, dispassionate inquiry. A nod is given in the direction of feminist claims for social and economic equality, while Freud and the primates are employed to throw doubt on the possibility of the kind of nonexploitative sexual arrangements the feminists want even more. One tactic is to accuse them of seeking not equality but the obliteration of difference; another is to suggest that both Freud and nature establish that however rights and privileges are apportioned we all really share the same fate, we all have our duties and challenges.

In this way, a recent savage *feuilleton* against Kate Millett by Irving Howe argues that in Freudianism "nature lets no one off easily." But this is to be at best disingenuous and at worst obtuse. Freud's image of existence is indeed basically tragic, but he saw men playing the leading roles in the drama and women as defective performers. Freudianism offers men the chance to be heroic, to rise above nature by conquering her in the external world and in themselves, while women remain in nature as the only partially redeemed. To ignore this is to commit the same humanist fallacy and outrage that are present when whites tell blacks that from the largest perspective we are all God's children.

Penis-envy is not "balanced" by castration-fear, as Howe asserts. For castration-fear, as I remarked earlier, is itself a sign of male supremacy; the fear is not simply that of losing the penis but of being reduced to the condition of a girl. Besides this, Freud's sketch of sexual development offers the male a "normal" way of overcoming his fear and so moving on to full human existence, while for females all that is possible is to become "reconciled" (Freud uses the word several times) to a less than complete, a compensatory life.

ANOTHER tactic is to exonerate Freud on the ground that he was only a "man of his time." Apart from the fact that it is Freudianism that matters, not Freud, and that psychoanalysis has extended his prejudice into our own era, this line may help explain but it doesn't exculpate. And Freudians ought to be wary of pursuing it, for the full portrait of Freud as a 19th-century paterfamilias wonderfully strengthens feminist arguments. That he was a misogynist is more proved than refuted by his own relationships with women.

He was extraordinarily attached to his mother, who died at 95 when he was 73, and of whom he once said that she had given him, by her devotion, "the feeling of a conqueror." His letters to his future wife are filled with a pompous banality and the condescension he was later to show all his female patients. "Am I to think of my delicate sweet girl as a competitor?" he writes after she has expressed interest in a career.

"After all, the encounter could only end by me telling her . . . that I love her and that I will make every effort to get her out of the competitive role and into the quiet, undisturbed activity of my home." Elsewhere, he writes that "nature has determined women's destiny through beauty, charm and sweetness," and that "the most delightful thing the world can offer us [is] our ideal of womanhood."

This kind of rhetoric, and especially the invocation of a feminine ideality, is quintessentially Victorian and, as we have ample reason to know, expresses the obverse of the Victorian male's contempt for women. Once more the parallel with blacks thrusts itself forward: to cover hatred, contempt and fear, we created the figure of the simple, childlike and innocently "natural" Negro. Negative virtues in both cases, or at least static virtues which in being assigned to one race or sex leave the way clear for the other to exercise the *really* important, ego-gratifying and world-mastering human faculties.

But Freud was much more than a conventional 19th-century male in relation to women. Philip Rieff has pointed out something of great and little noticed importance: that Freud's misogyny was "a vital intellectual link in his system." Rieff goes on to align Freud with 19th-century thinkers like Schopenhauer and Nietzsche, irrationalist philosophers who were also pronounced misogynists. This connection between a deep interest in the irrational—which was, after all, Freud's clinical and philosophical arena—and antifemale impulses is understandable in the light of the age-old male idea of women as incarnating the dark forces of the self, nature without consciousness, the "archaic heritage" which Freud thought women lived "dangerously close to."

"True," Rieff writes, "Freud would take women down from the Victorian pedestal of chastity and pure feeling; thereby he dispels one respectable form of masculine condescension. But what he substitutes

for it is an even less disguised hostility." This animus arose from Freud's whole effort to make consciousness replace unconsciousness, and his view of women as the ally of raw nature in resisting consciousness. "To the same degree as he respected intellect," Rieff writes, "he made the ordinary *Hausfrau*, whom he had elevated into a mystery, a 'problem,' the scapegoat of his rationalism."

INTENT on establishing that women's inferior status is socially caused, recent feminist writers have tended to see Freud much more as a conscious misogynist than as a perpetuator of myth and mystical bias. Yet male supremacy is hardly to be explained, in Freudianism or elsewhere, as the product of a deliberate scheme of exploitation. The woman who has seen this most clearly is Simone de Beauvoir, who pointed out that while men's superior status may have suited their economic aims, it also satisfied their moral and ontological ones, and that their exploitation of women is in large part a rationalization for largely unacknowledged feelings of resentment and fear.

Women exist for men, she writes, as the existential "other," the being in whom is "summed up the whole of alien nature." Men are unsettled by the reminder women give them of their own "carnal contingency," against which they are forever struggling. Men, who lack the same dense, complex bodily task as women, feel themselves the agency of a triumph over animality, a victory to which all their scientific, intellectual and artistic achievements contribute. "The female," de Beauvoir writes, "to a greater extent than the male is the prey of the species, and the human race has always sought to escape its specific destiny," that is, to supplant the Creation and the blueprints of nature with its own invented and ennobling fate. Dispensed from the bodily "handicaps" inflicted by the processes of maternity, men have seized the opportunity to raise themselves "above" nature.

Still, men are also sexual beings, as "animal" in their desires as women, and are therefore caught in an unending ambivalence. "What man cherishes and despises . . . in women," de Beauvoir writes, "is the fixed image of his animal destiny." To escape the conflict, men have created a vision of women as nature "transfigured," from which comes the masculine ideal of femininity, the woman as Beatrice, the sacrificing mother, the "conscience" of the race. But at the same time she is the object of male carnal desire. In either case, she remains the "other," the human whose identity and possibilities derive not from herself but from the "destiny" imposed on her by men.

This destiny is rapidly losing such coherence as it once had with the actual world. It might once have been true that man's superior strength provided the basis for his social power, as it was certainly true that pregnancy and maternity were limiting conditions for women. But sheer physical strength is increasingly meaningless in the age of automation and atomic power, while medical advances—in birth control, for instance — have lifted much of the biological burden from women. "Feminism," Shulamith Firestone writes, "is the inevitable female response to the development of a technology capable of freeing women from the tyranny of their sexual-reproductive roles."

At bottom, feminist anger against Freud stems from the fact that he reinforced the idea of biological determinism at the very moment when technology was becoming capable of eliminating or radically curtailing such coercion. The point is that even if biology had ordained an inferior condition for women—or, for that matter, for men—human beings are never at the mercy of their physical natures. We are perhaps best defined as the species capable of altering its destiny, the living beings who are both within nature and outside it. And this means that we do not have the right to fall back on nature in order to explain why we have failed to be fully human.

Mankind affects and changes the physical world, and it is a truism to say that moral and psychic reality lag behind. Mary Ellmann has written that "when nature ceases to enforce conditions to which the majority are accustomed or even devoted, these conditions are artificially prolonged by both sentiment and argument." This is what has happened to women in their relation to men. Yet even this presupposes that we have interpreted nature correctly. A possible way of looking at the past is that nature once merely made matters more difficult for women and that men, in a kind of weakness of pride, left them to face the consequences. To see this is the first step in healing the rift. Beyond that, men will have to face the truth of John Stuart Mill's assertion that "the knowledge men can acquire of women, even as they have been and are, without reference to what they might be, is wretchedly imperfect and superficial, and will always be so until women themselves have told us all they have to tell."

Feminists have begun to speak, and whatever forensic weaknesses their beleaguered status gives rise to, I, for one, am going to listen. A few weeks ago I sat talking to a young member of women's liberation. I spoke of how much there was still to learn about what we call "nature" and remarked, playing devil's advocate, that there was no way to disprove Freud's theory that women had been biologically shortchanged. She nodded, then said: "Well, if it were true that we were *created* inferior, then we'd have a right to cry out against nature, or God, or whatever. As it is, Freud set himself up as nature's interpreter, so we've got every right to cry out against him." ∎

The New York Times/Frank Lodge

As this sign at a recent conference of Roman Catholic bishops in Detroit indicates, the Christian church is under attack from a new quarter—women's lib.

Women's Lib:
Was It Really Eve's Fault?

Theologians may do a lot of talking about the next world, but over the centuries their discipline has been strongly influenced by what happens in this one. Kings in the Middle Ages justified their authority by religious sanctions. Max Weber and other sociologists found a causal connection between the Calvinist ethic of frugality and the rise of capitalism. Some historians have even asserted that the imperative in Genesis to assert "dominion" over the natural world has helped cause the current environmental crisis.

Now Christian theology's ties to sociology and economics are under attack from a new quarter — the women's liberation movement. In recent months, a small number of women theologians has begun to argue that Christianity, with its concept of God the Father, has helped create and perpetuate social practices that discriminate against women.

"The church has served to legitimize a patriarchal culture," said Dr. Mary Daly, a theologian at Jesuit-run Boston College, last week. "It's time to rework the basic myths and symbols of theology in light of the new awareness of how women have been exploited."

The feminist attack on Christian orthodoxy focuses on three areas:

The Masculine Godhead: Genesis says that God created man in His own image and as "male and female." Nevertheless, God has usually been portrayed as a man, referred to with masculine pronouns and thought of as possessing masculine qualities like sternness. Christians furthered the process by asserting that God became human in the person of a male.

Ethical Hypocrisy: According to the feminist theologians, Christian leaders developed an ethics based on passive virtues like humility and obedience, but then used them as a means of subduing the other sex. "While exhorting others, chiefly women, to practice Christian virtues, they have themselves pursued power, creativity and self-fulfillment on levels far removed from obedience, self-abnegation or, for that matter, chastity," wrote Barbara Sykes in a recent issue of The Episcopal New Yorker, the diocesan newspaper.

Religious Symbols: Feminists maintain that the fundamental symbols of Christianity are permeated with male chauvinism. For instance, the story of Adam and Eve blames women for the presence of sin in the world. Catholics complain that the figure of Mary has been idealized into a "sexless" projection of male vanities, and that the usual picture of her kneeling before her Son is an affront to the role God intended for women.

There are still probably only a few dozen woman theologians and graduate students in theology in the United States, but they have already begun the task of de-masculinizing their discipline. The obvious starting point has been to introduce female qualities to the concept of God in the manner that Christian Scientists have done for decades with their belief in a "Father-Mother God."

In a recent article in America magazine, Esther Woo, a doctoral student at Fordham University, speculated on the possibility of feminizing the Godhead—including the essential nature of the male Jesus—and creating a new Trinity of Mother, Daughter and Holy Spirit. She argued, "To pray to a Mother-God would be different from praying to a Father-God. There would be more trust in the efficacy of prayer if God is our Mother rather than our Father."

At a recent Episcopalian-sponsored conference here, Penelope Chen, a British graduate student, took a similar approach. "How much better to conceive of God the creator as pregnant with the world, giving birth to it and nourishing it, rather than as the divine watchmaker who never has to intervene in the machinery," she said.

Female theologians are consciously seeking to play down the masculinity of Jesus and emphasize his universal qualities. "It's not the maleness of Christ that was important, it was his humanity," said Dr. Elizabeth Farians, whose Ph.D. is from Notre Dame.

In accordance with this, women theologians generally back the current trend toward thinking of Holy Communion primarily as a communal meal, rather than as a re-enactment of the sacrifice of Christ for the sins of mankind. The latter interpretation, they charge, gives too much symbolic significance to a male figure.

Finally, feminist theologians are attempting to bring the women's point of view to bear on ethical thinking. For example, on the issue of abortion, Dr. Daly complained that Roman Catholic bishops and male theologians begin with "masculine" questions like the rights of the fetus.

"Women start with different questions," she said, "like 'How do you justify unwanted, repeated and harmful pregnancies,' or 'What are the rights of other children?'"

Likewise, Dr. Daly added, church tolerance of war is rooted in masculine values like fighting and valor. "Only a male orientation would keep us in Vietnam because we don't want to look like we're running away," she said.

Although women's-lib theology is still in the early stage of development, it has already begun to draw some fire from male scholars. James Hitchcock, a specialist in Reformation history at St. Louis University, has charged that, like black theology, it is essentially an attempt to "redefine theological terms and categories to serve political ends."

—EDWARD B. FISKE

May 9, 1971

Law of Rape:

'Because Ladies Lie'

For the crimes of robbery and assault and fraud and countless more, the victim's word is enough—enough for the prosecutor to make out a prima facie case, enough to take to a jury. But with the crime of rape, it is not enough at all.

Why? "Because," says lawyer and legal scholar Morris Ploscowe, "ladies lie."

Or because legislators believe women lie. Last week the Albany legislators modified New York's rape law—the toughest in the country—but true to their past, they left in the presumption that women who complain of rape are not always to be trusted.

The old law had required an almost insurmountable amount of corroboration of the purported victim's testimony. The new law requires less, but not that much less —especially in view of the fact that most crimes require none.

The old law (which remains in effect until Governor Rockefeller signs the new legislation as he is expected to do) requires that the purported rape victim's testimony be corroborated in three major aspects: force and lack of consent, penetration and identity of the rapist. The corroboration need not be the testimony of an eye witness. Physical evidence is allowed too—lack of consent, for example, can be corroborated by severe bruises and torn clothes. But the identify of the alleged rapist can be corroborated only by third-party testimony.

In most other crimes the victim's testimony need not be corroborated at all and is simply given to the jury to believe or not. Under the old rape law, testimony can not even be given to the jury unless there is corroboration on all major aspects.

One of the most glaring elements of the old law, in fact, was that it extended the corroboration requirement to any crimes considered "incidental" to the rape.

Thus, if a man assaulted a woman, a prima facie case of assault would consist of her testimony of the assault and her identification of the defendant. But if he assaulted her, then raped her, the case could not go to the jury on assault, much less rape, without corroboration of the three major elements of rape.

The new law requires only that the witness' testimony of the forcible, non-consensual nature of the rape be corroborated. There need be no corroboration of her testimony of penetration, or of the rapist's identity.

Further, it does away with the extension of the corroboration requirement to "incidental" crimes, such as assault. They can now be tried the way all other crimes are tried, with the outcome depending on the credibility of the witness.

Under the old law, prosecutors say and figures indicate, convictions have rarely been possible. In 1969, for example, there were 1,085 arrests for rape in New York City, and 18 convictions.

Clearly, the new law makes convictions a lot easier, and that is why the State District Attorney's Association sponsored it, and, presumably, the Legislature passed it.

Yet to feminists, and some lawyers, too, the new law has major defects. For one thing it still will be difficult to convict in a lot of rape cases—corroboration, even of the lessened degree, is not always available. The prosecution will thus often have to settle for an assault conviction.

So, why not do away with the corroboration requirement altogether?

Those who favor the requirement—and there are many, from lawyers to psychiatrists—justify it on the ground that it is necessary to protect innocent men. Women accuse men of rape for any number of reasons, they say, ranging from wishful thinking to injured pride; from getting pregnant and needing an excuse for one's parents, to feeling guilty about love making and needing an excuse to rationalize it.

Yet as for empirical evidence that people lie about rape more than about robbery, for instance, there appears to be a lot of opinion-filled literature, but little statistical fact.

Mr. Ploscowe, who favors some type of corroboration, says that the "experience" is that "too many innocent men have been charged." Professor Anna May Shepard of Rutgers Law School, on the other hand, says that this idea is "unsubstantiated." And even Bronx District Attorney Burton B. Roberts, one of the new law's chief backers, says that "it's very hard philosophically" to justify.

And so, because of the disparity in the requirement of proof between rape and other crimes, Professor Shepard and some others believe the New York law—the new one as much as the old—is subject to constitutional attack, as a denial to women of equal protection of the law. It could be done via a civil suit, she adds, stressing the argument that women are not getting the same deterrent value from the law as men.

Failing that? A little bit more compassion, perhaps. For as many rape victims attest, it is the persons who administer the law as much as the law itself that angers and shames them.

Countless women complain of calling a precinct to say they have been raped, only to be told it is no big deal; of having a policeman leer, or ask: "Did you enjoy it?" Black women in particular tell of indifference from the police. And that, to such as William Hellerstein of the Legal Aid Society, which opposed lessening the corroboration requirement, is the "real atrocity," as he puts it, of "the administration of rape complaints"—not the law.

—LESLEY OELSNER

May 14, 1972

NOW Says: TV Commercials Insult Women

By JUDITH ADLER HENNESSEE and JOAN NICHOLSON

The bride and groom have run directly from their wedding without bothering to change their clothes or go on their honeymoon, to the appliance store. The salesman is telling the groom (not the bride) how terrific the G.E. Toaster-Oven is. The bride is standing around in a daze, having just achieved the greatest ambition of her life—a husband. The two men decide that the groom should buy the product and then, as a polite afterthought, they turn to the bride and ask her what she thinks. Oblivious to everything she replies, "I do."

THE New York Chapter of the National Organization for Women (N.Y.-NOW) has just filed a petition with the Federal Communications Commission in Washington, asking that it take the American Broadcasting Company's flagship station, WABC-TV of New York, off the air. The legal action is based on three grounds: discrimination against women in employment; failure to ascertain women's needs and interests in programing and violation of the F.C.C. Fairness Doctrine, which requires that both sides be presented in "an issue of controversial public importance." The petition asks formally for F.C.C. denial of WABC-TV's application for the renewal of the station's three-year license to broadcast. WABC-TV is currently preparing an answer. NOW believes the ABC network is equally guilty but the only legal way to get at it is through the local affiliate. The Government may decide the case upon receipt of the answer, or it may order hearings. In the interim, the station has requested a meeting to negotiate with N.Y.-NOW and NOW lawyers at the Center for Constitutional Rights, a nonprofit group of attorneys who have volunteered their services. Meanwhile the TV company declines public comment except to say that it believes it does not discriminate against women.

JUDITH ADLER HENNESSEE is a liaison vice president of N.Y.-NOW; **JOAN NICHOLSON** is a member of the board. Both are freelance writers.

THE legal action results in part from NOW's monitoring of television programs during the course of a year and half. At first, the monitoring seemed to show that all TV programs portray women equally—that is, in an equally bad light. But in the over-all studies conducted by more than 100 monitors, WABC-TV came out considerably worse than other stations. In news programs, women in the movement are made to seem ridiculous, snide remarks trailing after them like broken arrows. In sports coverage of the Olympics, when women won seven out of eight U.S. medals, reporter Doug Johnson led off his 40-second story with "Thank heaven for little girls." The "little girls" remained anonymous—although, rest assured, the women in Clifford Irving's life were covered in loving and lengthy detail. In public affairs programs women's needs and issues—divorce and alimony, the Equal Rights Amendment, child-care centers, the earnings gap, abortion—are for the most part ignored.

Compared with its rival, the printed word, television is an ostrich. A generalized contempt for women is implicit in the entire pattern of programing. From "The Courtship of Eddie's Father" to "The Young Lawyers," women are domestic drudges and office ancillaries, dependent on men emotionally and economically, their extraordinary incompetence exceeded only by their monumental stupidity. Decision-making positions of power and leadership, authority and status in the community—these are the province of men only.

Nowhere is this more evident than in commercials. As part of its challenge, N.Y.-NOW did a study of 1,241 commercials. Almost all of them showed woman inside the home. In 42.6 per cent they were involved in household tasks; in 37.5 per cent they were domestic adjuncts to men, and in 16.7 per cent they were sex objects. That doesn't leave very many, and a lot of commercials don't even have people in them. Only 0.3 per cent showed women as autonomous people, leading independent lives of their own.

The majority of commercials sell either domestic or cosmetic products, and in these, of course, women are the stars. Above and beyond their consumer function (to keep the economy breathing), they play two stock roles—the housewife-mother or the sex object. In both, they are viewed solely in their relation to men. Biologically, the wife-mother is there to serve the species, socially, her purpose is to serve men, children and animals. Psychologically, she's an obsessive-compulsive. Her life alternates between the kitchen and the bedroom, persecuting the germs, guarding the wax on "her" floor, scrubbing dirt off collars, manufacturing delicious little miracles on the stove and coloring her hair to make it look more natural. The Downey Fabric Softener commercial offers an explicit definition of a wife. "Honey, here's your laundry," the new bride says brightly. "Did I wash it right?" Her husband registers his approval and she is fulfilled. "He noticed," she says euphorically. "I'm a wife!"

THIS sort of thing may seem absurdly funny to those of us who fancy ourselves above it, but when it goes on day after day and well into the night, endlessly repeating the same unnerving message to 40 million viewers, it's not so funny anymore. Last year, a Good Housekeeping Survey reported more than a third "of all respondents have, on occasion, been so offended by a commercial that they've turned it off." Our own monitors, most of whom were not feminists, found 40 per cent of the commercials objectionable. Watching commercials is like being blasted by some casually malevolent propaganda machine dedicated to the humiliation of women.

The woman in the Anacin commercial doesn't even have a headache to call her own. She takes Anacin to stay on her feet longer in order to serve her family. "No headache is going to make me explode at my husband," she says, gritting her teeth and vibrating with pain. The point isn't that Anacin will make her feel better but that it will spare her husband. No wonder the man in the Geritol ad is complacent. The product has given his wife the energy to take care of the baby, go to a school meeting, shop for groceries and cook dinner. Through it all she has still managed to stay attractive for him. "My wife, I think I'll keep her," he says. Who wouldn't?

In most ads women's lives are dreary. It's the men, children and even the family dog who have the fun while women do the work. In 54.4 per cent of the food commercials and 81.2 per cent of the cleaning commercials men are the beneficiaries. Maxim Freeze Dried Coffee shows a woman in a galley making coffee while her husband and son (not daughter—a daughter would be helping) are on deck enjoying themselves sailing. Fleischman's Margarine uses the same theme. This time, the husband and son are out playing ball while Mom is in the kitchen worrying about their eating habits. She doesn't get a vacation, either. She unpacks in the hotel room while her husband complains about how he can't sleep — and she stops unpacking to get him some Nytol. There's something inherently illogical in all this. A woman's main goal is supposed to be to catch a man, but once she's got him she spends her life slaving away in the kitchen. Maybe she ought to rethink her goals?

The television industry perhaps feels it has a vested interest in encouraging a conventional role for women. Keep women in the kitchen and you won't have to hire them, or worry about raising their pay. According to a Time magazine article: "If women workers got as much as men, wage costs would rise by some $109-billion — more than all pretax corporate profits last year." Women who are seen engaging in mad dusting contests with Endust provide their own justification for not being hired, much less being paid decent wages — incompetence and lack of intelligence. Even in their traditional roles as housewives women are put down.

In a Head and Shoulders Shampoo commercial a touching blind devotion is exhibited by Michael's wife, whose thinking apparatus seems to have dried up and flaked away since her marriage. Her delivery is naively sincere. "When I met Michael," she confides, "he was us-

ing Head and Shoulders. . . . When we don't have three tubes, I have to run out to the store to get that third tube." She laughs. "It works," she says, staring out with big brown, blank eyes. "Michael says it works."

But Michael's wife has no credibility. Females rarely do. Her small voice is followed by a male voice-over, the voice of authority, which confers the stamp of approval on the product. Male authority is a built-in assumption, and it teaches women to look up to men as experts; 89.3 per cent of the voice-overs are male. The consumers, who might normally be expected to know something about the products they use, are not granted even that slight margin of knowledge. Women *never* tell men what to do, but men are forever telling women what to do. And how to do it. Even in their own private beauty realm, women aren't quite with it. "I'm all thumbs," the helpless woman in the Revlon Fabuliner ad says. "It won't skip? It won't run?" The male voice-over keeps telling her, with decreasing patience, that no matter how clumsy and inept she is, she just can't mess herself up because "it draws a perfect line every time." She finally learns the lesson and repeats, with slow, dawning comprehension: "It draws a perfect line every time."

She really ought to haul off and sock him, but the need for male approval, implicit in 33.9 per cent of these commercials, stops her. Women, who have been traditionally dependent on the approval of men in order to survive, are frequently made to play the fool as the price.

Submissiveness is one way. It shows up in 24.3 per cent of commercials. Take the Maxwell House Coffee ad with Danny and Doubting Thomas. The one thing she doesn't doubt is male superiority. As she rattles away with her spiel, she says something he doesn't like—"Test my Instant Maxwell House Coffee" — and he pounces. "Hold it, young lady," he says, in mock sternness, having supervised her performance from the sidelines. It's her commercial, but he just can't resist taking over. And

she lets him. "Our coffee?" she asks meekly, divining his purpose on the spot. And smiles. And smiles. Women smile a lot. It goes with the shuffle.

Even more devastating is the new-Mr.-Clean-with-lemon commercial which features a marionettelike woman whose strings are pulled by an avuncular voice-over. "Nice nose," he says, touching it presumptuously. As if he had clicked a switch, her face lights up with a huge grin. "Thanks," she says gratefully. "Let's test it," he says—an order, not a question — and she acquiesces cheerfully and obediently, like a child. Even with all of her previous odor-sniffing experience she guesses wrong. But he is there to tell her the right answer while she listens, wide-eyed and respectful.

CAN'T these pursuits be presented with dignity? Taken by itself, there needn't be anything degrading about housework or caring for a family. Advertising agencies claim that they are in business to sell products and that their primary responsibility is to the client. In other words, if the manufacturers who advertise on television decide they won't approve any ads showing women driving station wagons, then the agency won't create any such ads. Last year, we met with the market-research people at B.B.D.&O. to convince them that they had some social responsibility toward the public in the area of image-making. They disagreed. At any rate, in most commercials the image of woman is an inferior one, and image makers have made housework a pejorative word. When men do the same work as women, the work is upgraded because they earn money at it. In two separate scenes, Campbell's Vegetable Soup shows a male chef and a housewife. She is the family cook, but cooking is his profession. The implication is that even a lowly housewife can make as good a bowl of soup as a professional cook can.

Yet not even the few professional women whose lives definitely do not revolve around the stove escape. In a

Dove commercial, a professional actress is shown hand-washing the dirty dinner dishes of 150 people. The important thing is not that she is an actress but that she is a female, and females wash dishes. Her career, her real work, is valueless. Eve Arden is actually in the kitchen demonstrating Roast 'n Boast, but you don't see Durward Kirby, who represents Ivory Liquid, washing the dishes with it. As a man, all he has to do is hand down the word. His identity and status are conferred on the product. A woman, who has none, derives hers from the product.

People tend to imitate the roles they see, to become what is expected of them. When they are given only one socially acceptable "choice," it inhibits them from choosing freely what they want to be. For the millions of women painfully breaking out of their traditional roles, the persistent television stereotypes are like a knock on the head telling them to stay in line. The psychological damage is immeasurable.

"Feedback," a WBAI series about television, discussed the problem: "Societies develop images about themselves, their purposes and their objectives. The system of such images forms a society's mythology and governs its actions, thoughts, and attitudes. . . . The passive viewer lets the TV image subvert his own . . . and the viewer is removed from the possibility of alternatives." The big concern of ad agencies is something they call "the reality of the market place." Bill Ballard, a Madison Avenue copywriter, says, "Ads are a reflection of society as the people who are responsible for advertising see it." But most ads reflect only one aspect of the life of the middle-class housewife. There are other realities. The life-style and problems of working women—43 per cent of adult women—are virtually ignored on commercials. They are still perceived primarily in their relationship to men, as wives who happen to be working. The working woman crops up occasionally, still close to the hearth, as in the Reynolds Aluminum ad, wrapping a quick gourmet dinner that cooks itself while she dresses for the dinner party she and her husband are giving. Reynolds hasn't yet got to the point where the husband, who also works, shares or—perish the thought —takes full responsibility for the dinner. In fact, television takes a positively reactionary moral stance toward women. On the rare occasions when they are let out of the house, they are generally chaperoned, as if all were Victorian virgins. They don't do anything alone. In commercials, they never buy airplane tickets or travel by themselves. If they use a camera, there is always a man taking pictures alongside them. If they go to a restaurant, they are accompanied by their family. If they smoke, the tobacco is offered to them by a man.

LOOKING at these capsule dramatizations of male fantasies, you would never know that 42 per cent of the first million Mustangs sold were bought by women. Ads for cars, banks and insurance were only 3.2 per cent of daytime commercials, as opposed to 19.1 per cent in prime time, when the men are home. These sex-segregated ads are saying in effect that women are incapable of making important decisions alone. Important decisions are decisions that cost a lot of money. In the bank ads, women who do use banks do so for frivolous reasons—the checks are pretty, or you don't have to bother about your balance because the bank will cover your overdraft anyway. As for cars, a woman by herself neither buys them nor has them serviced, and she is rarely shown behind the wheel. If she is with her husband, he is driving. Goodyear Tires has a stacked commercial showing a man driving along happily on a sunny day and a woman driving in the pouring rain at night, worried and nervous. Despite the fact that insurance tables show that women have fewer accidents than men, the woman is still imagined as the mechanically inept hairbrain who manages to run over a suitcase twice in the middle of her own driveway.

HOW WOMEN ARE PORTRAYED IN 1,200 TV COMMERCIALS

In 37.5% women were men's **DOMESTIC ADJUNCTS**

In 33.9%— **DEPENDENT ON MEN**

In 16.7%— **SEX OBJECTS**

In 22.7%—
DEMEANED HOUSEKEEPERS

In 24.3%—
SUBMISSIVE

In 17.1%—
UNINTELLIGENT

Just as women are barred from the world of money and power, so men are revealed as incompetent on the domestic scene. Since the things men do are socially and economically more valuable than the things women do, a man is not supposed to know his way around the house. There's something wrong with him if he *can* cope. If he is in the kitchen, he is usually filling in sloppily while his wife is out performing another of her sex functions—having a baby. Comet, which features Jane Withers as Josephine the Plumber, has a sink piled high with a week's worth of filthy pots, which the man asks her to clean for him. He wouldn't dare ask a male plumber to scrub those pots. Josephine, who looks more like a nurse than a plumber, is a fraud. All she ever does is clean sinks; you never see her actually take on a leaking faucet.

With all the work she has to do and with the small amount of intelligence allotted to her, the woman who will "always be a Maxwell housewife" certainly doesn't need an education. Education anyway is for the purpose of getting a job, to earn more money; and money, along with mental activity, is male territory. All of the ads for educational opportunities and careers invite only men to participate—except for one, the U.S. Auto Club Driving School. "There is a special division for women students," the male voice-over says patronizingly. Women are some strange subspecies whose coordination is questionable at best.

FOR women, self-betterment has nothing to do with

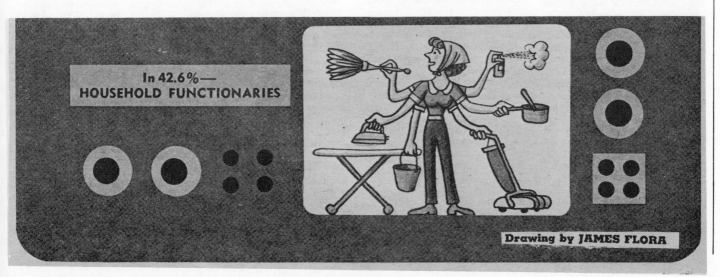

In 42.6%—
HOUSEHOLD FUNCTIONARIES

Drawing by JAMES FLORA

education or training. Rather, it is generally synonymous with sex appeal, and the pitch is to fear, a veiled threat that women won't be acceptable to men. Skinny Dip Cologne has a woman rejected by a group of men until she splashes on the scent. Then they welcome her. It is assumed that men are naturally acceptable to women because they are men. They may occasionally have to rinse their mouths with Listerine or spray their unruly locks with Command, but the object is polygamous fun, not the serious business of monogamy. For a woman, anything goes. As a physical entity, she commands no more respect than she do as an economic entity. Maybe less. Consider the Playtex bra ad, in which a woman wearing the bra, runs into a male friend who had ignored her charms in the past. The man, his popping eyes fastened on her chest, says in disbelief: "Is it really you?"

We all know what "Fly Me" really means, and why all the men in the office cluster around the Olivetti Girl. She is a plaything, a sex object. With the typewriter fixing up all the errors, she will have more time to entertain her bosses. "Two brains are better than one," says Olivetti, but she doesn't really need a brain at all. In the marketplace of television, women are just another commodity, peddling their wares like the model in the Shop-Rite pantyhose commercial who becomes the product. She sits there in the grocery cart like a big doll, smiling, her legs in one of the classic cheesecake positions, waiting to be picked up and bought.

There's no denying that sex sells, but it's safe to say that the male broadcasting oligarchy would be revolted at the sight of men perpetually displaying their bodies. It would strike them as obscene. But it hasn't occurred to them to consider whether a female sex symbol, selling not only a product but herself, strikes women as obscene. Maybe the best con-

sciousness-raiser would be to turn the ads around in a kind of reverse degradation, and show men slinking around in tight bikinis being ogled by appraising female eyes, or eating spoonfuls of Light 'n Lively in the reducing salon while the camera panned slowly up their legs. "Minute by minute, you become a man again," a condescending female voice-over would tell him as he soaked in the tub with his Softique.

Only 2.2 per cent of all commercials are for male personal-care products. And the image of the male is quite different from that of the female. He is rarely seen inside the home. In more than 70 per cent of the ads, men are engaged in a wide range of activities from politics to fishing, and the advertisers' approach to them is both serious and informative—in a word: adult. Provocative poses are out. The man in the Proteen 29 commercial barely glances in the mirror as he talks, merely a quick check for neatness and grooming. There isn't a hint that he is prettying up for a woman or that he is in love with his own image. There's a brisk, snappy efficiency about him, in contrast to the helpless woman in the Twice As Nice Shampoo commercial who turns down her date because she can't do a thing with her hair. A magic man materializes to tell her what to do, but the Proteen 29 man already knows, and he's telling us.

Women are forever put under the microscope, singled out for male scrutiny. Virginia Woolf noticed it, looking through the titles in the British Museum and seeing all the books about women written by men. Things haven't changed that much since 1928. A woman's anatomy is fair game. A man's sex is unmentionable. Even in the health ads, Blue Cross/Blue Shield talks about the pap test, never about prostate trouble. But if biology is destiny for one sex, then it has to be destiny for the other, too.

It is taken for granted that men perspire, but women are victims of their own bodies. "Emotions make a woman different from a man," the male voice-over insinuates, but he's got it all backward. If the female body were the norm for the whole human race—and the fact that the fetus starts out as a female strongly suggests that it is— the reasoning would be quite the opposite. Men, who are frequently shown engaging in strenuous sweaty activities, are the ones who need a "special" deodorant. It depends on whether you consider excessive perspiration to be normal. But women's needs are measured against the "normal" standard of male needs, and where those needs diverge, it is the woman, not the man, who is judged to be lacking, or peculiar, or delicate, or inferior. Her own standards don't apply. Indeed, it isn't recognized that she has any.

This subhuman creature, defective mentally and physically, has been endowed by men with a hypothetical need for extra iron, a gentler laxative, a thinner cigarette, a smaller car (presumably so she can park it alongside a man's without denting his fender). But now the final blow. She is the victim of an ancient taboo, a primal flaw in her sex. "It makes you feel fresh and it lasts all day," one woman tells another in one commercial. Women, obsessed with cleanliness, are unclean themselves. There are similar genital products for men, but they're not advertised on television. In fact, in ad-agency product categories, male deodorants are listed under "cosmetics" and female deodorants under "hygiene." This idea goes all the way back to the prejudices of the men who wrote Leviticus, a book of the Bible which reflects primitive beliefs that women, during their menstrual periods, are unclean, and must be isolated from other members of the group. Leviticus took it one step further—women were also unclean after they had borne a

child, and anyone who went near them risked defilement. This is tantamount to telling black people that their skin color is naturally dirty. No advertiser in his right mind would think of doing that, but it's all right to say it to women. The message is sadistic. And some of the products may be dangerous. They contain talc, which is under Government investigation as a possible cancer-producing agent.

I T is naive to expect spontaneous changes. The National Association of Broadcasters' code, the Ten Commandments of the industry, says, thou shalt not violate "the sanctity of marriage and the value of the home." No other life-style is valid. Marriage, home and children are television's hottest-selling items. In today's overpopulated, polluted world, this value is open to question. Ellen Peck, author of "The Baby Trap," accuses broadcasters of a "pronatalist" bias in their programing, which, she feels, discourages women's career aspirations. She suggests that television is the only medium that has access on a scale large enough to educate the public about these social issues. But discussion of this, and other socially pressing problems, according to the industry's own guidelines, is in bad taste. It is precisely this lack of information and lack of choices that motivated the N.Y.-NOW challenge.

The sad thing is that products can be sold without insulting people. Last year, Clairol received an "old-hat" award from NOW for its sexist advertising. Its new ad demonstrates what new habits of thought can do. One woman is shown as a jockey, another is congratulated by her husband and child on receiving her college diploma, a third is working competently and with aplomb in a professional capacity. All of them are away from home. If the corporate mind of Clairol, a bastion of genteel sexism, can do it, so can everyone else. ∎

On Becoming A Woman

By DOROTHY BARCLAY

IN a recent children's essay and art contest on the joys of reading, a 2-year-old girl expressed her strong preference for a work titled "Side Saddle for Dandy." She supported her opinion with a drawing of "Dandy," dressed in a fluffy ball gown, "standing at the head of the steps reconising her womanhood."

If we are to accept as general the findings of at least one extensive study, many adolescent and pre-adolescent girls today are having a difficult time doing just that—"reconising" their womanhood. Furthermore, many a woman mature in years is still as confused as a teen-ager on what The Woman's Role is or should be.

Controversy over women in gray flannel and gay flannel —the "career woman" vs. the "career" housewife—enlivened this magazine recently. The questions raised about the life of today's wife and mother need consideration not only in the light of her own needs but also in terms of her daughter's growing up.

REAMS of rhetoric have been spilled on the mental, emotional and temperamental differences between men and women. Are they innate or culturally conditioned? From the practicing parents' point of view it makes little difference. Without any thought at all, most adults treat boys and girls differently from the day they can toddle, if not before. Higher education, a constantly changing environment (woe to the mechanically inept woman in today's electrified home) and changed expectations by the community would appear to be the influences that have confused the old idea of what women should be.

"A woman should be," a bewildered member of that sex once told us, "whatever the speaker of the moment says she should." The goals, standards and demands set for her by others vary in direct relation to their principal interests in life. Yet, obviously, it is for each woman herself to determine what her goals and standards will be.

That very citadel of femininity, the Young Women's Christian Association, has found so much concern about the question among its college-age members that it has prepared a study booklet titled "Being a Woman," and is planning for its use in discussion groups by both men and women through the National Student Council of the Y. M. C. A. and Y. W. C. A. (The boys have been brought in on this for a clearly expressed reason. "The way a woman regards her being and calling as a woman," holds Fern Babcock, author of the booklet, "inevitably affects the way a man regards himself as a man.")

Fern Babcock worked with college students through the Y. W. C. A. until she resigned last fall, after twenty years with that organization, to take a new post with the Council for Social Action of the Congregational Christian Churches. Hers is no single back-to-the-kitchen or on-to-the-typewriter solution for woman's dilemma. "Both the home and public life are impoverished," she holds, "when the one is deprived of man's gifts and the other of woman's contribution." What's more, the marriage versus career question is only one aspect of the problem.

HOWEVER she manages the details of her life, woman's basic role, as Miss Babcock sees it, is to bring strength, security and serenity to those about her and to do her share to help develop these same qualities in the life of the community.

With so many needs to be met, society looks to college-trained women, she holds, in four major areas of life—employed work, primarily in the professions and managerial posts in business; family life, including child-bearing and rearing; community life, including responsible participation in government and work in such centers as the church, the school and community agencies; and cultural life, including support of art, music, drama and sports.

ALMOST never will a woman's interests become as specialized as a man's. As she goes through life, first one and then another of these responsibilities will be dominant. (Parents of adolescent daughters who complain of the youngsters' fluctuating interests may comfort themselves with the thought that the girls are practicing the much-needed feminine quality of flexibility!)

Helping a girl grow up in a warm and happy home is the surest way yet devised to insure her developing the warm human qualities which will stand her in good stead in her own home later on. This human warmth and a feeling for cooperation will also insure her functioning at her best as a woman in any business or profession she may enter and in her community work and dealings as well.

The kind of a girl parents raise, then—loved, loving, accepted and accepting—will largely determine the kind of woman she becomes. There's lots more to being a "successful" woman, though, than having a pleasant disposition.

First, it may have become rather "old-fashioned" in certain circles to think in such terms, but women need—and growing girls should be helped to acquire—a knowledge of meal planning and preparation of food; some facility with needle and thread; a feeling for decorating a room or a house attractively and expressively along with an ability to maintain its beauty by caring for it well.

Then comes the ability to manage a household in such a way that the mechanics of living are pleasant and easy; the spirit and skills to entertain gracefully; a practical knowledge of first aid and nursing; an understanding of budgeting; an expanding knowledge of the community and the individual's place in it, including an ability to judge where services and contributions are most effective.

FINALLY, she will need an appreciation of the arts, and— matters she will quite possibly work on all her life—spiritual understanding, an appreciation of all human values, and an understanding of herself and of those closest to her.

Although there will be differences of opinion on the relative importance of such skills, few thoughtful wives and mothers today, we'll wager, would cast any of them completely out. In pondering her role as a woman, today's mother would do well to consider how she may help her daughters grow in understanding of the many similar responsibilities they will face and in the ability to meet them.

The Growing Girl

By DOROTHY BARCLAY

WHEN we were young and some issues were more clear-cut than they seem to be today, parents of a baby girl adorned their child in pink and those with an infant son to dress chose shades of blue. Today in many circles a cheerful yellow serves for both. Toddlers of both sexes wear bright overalls. The pre-school boy is as likely to play with a doll as his little sister is to manipulate toy trucks.

Junior high school girls in many communities study household mechanics; boys don aprons and caps and cook. With early marriage popular, many women support families while their husbands do advanced professional study.

Since many of the differences in the roles of men and women are lessening all the time, one might think the problems of rearing daughters would vary little from those involved in rearing sons. Yet they do. Even parents who think they treat youngsters of both sexes "just alike" actually behave quite differently toward them.

They do so spontaneously for, deep inside, most adults today do expect different behavior from men and from women and from the children who will grow up to be men and women. Many who talk a great deal about their belief in "equality of sexes" (meaning, in this case, "sameness" in responsibilities and freedoms) will, when discussion switches to another topic, reveal how traditional their expectations really are.

THOSE who have made special studies of girls have found that, especially during the pre-adolescent and adolescent periods, young women-to-be show the effects of the extra rigidity and anxiety that our culture imposes upon them. Behind the facade, so well known to cartoon artists, of sloppy sports clothes or over-done glamour, behind the protection of giggles and endless phone calls, the research specialists see a bewildered, frightened, unsure little girl trying valiantly to grow.

Confused, and sometimes exasperated, parents of the growing girl may find her at times a puzzle too complex—or irritating—to try to fathom. Actually, her behavior, viewed in context of what has gone before and what is still to come, is as logical as the stages through which a baby passes as he learns to walk. Each stage of physical, social and emotional growth brings its own challenges, challenges that must be met successfully if a child is to pass smoothly to the next stage.

Specialists call these challenges "developmental tasks." Parents who find

their daughters both delightful and disturbing (and especially fathers who don't like to read lengthy books) should welcome a new series of leaflets, "Toward Understanding Girls," which describes these stages clearly and simply. Published just this week, they comprise a simple but comprehensive picture of the steps a little girl takes on her road to growing up.

The four six-page folders were written, of all things, by a man of many years experience in work with boys—Clarence G. Moser, an associate on the staff of

the Central Atlantic Area Council of the Young Men's Christian Association. Those who may recall his earlier series, "Toward Understanding Boys," will realize his latest effort is a natural sequel.

Each folder considers a period of roughly three years, the whole series covering the span from 6 through 17, first grade through high school. Emphasis throughout is on helping the girl feel secure in her parents' love, confident of her own abilities, happy and accepted with her friends. When these needs are satisfied in ways appropriate to the girl's stage of growth, she can go forward toward independence and consideration for others beyond herself.

THE mother who dislikes being a woman, the father who disparages "females" or is too possessive of "his little girl," the brothers who lord it over their sister or constantly challenge her abilities; can make a girl's growing up a lot more difficult than it need be.

Parents, at the other extreme, so determined to rear "a perfect little lady" that they continually overemphasize sweetness, neatness and femininity might produce a girl who is so weary of the whole pattern by the time she reaches adolescence that she rebels against it completely. Noise, dirt, scraped knees and broken bones are as logical accompaniments of little-girlhood as are doll play and tea parties, experi-

ments with make-up and efforts at cookie-making.

Folk-wisdom alone has so much to

offer parents guiding girls in their early years that it's often not till a daughter reaches junior high school age that parents begin to feel baffled. Trying to keep up with the early adolescent may seem well nigh impossible, Mr. Moser admits, even for the girl herself.

Her body is growing and changing. Parents and teachers expect from her more self-discipline and competence. She has a new role in the family and among her friends. Looking at her parents with new eyes she frequently finds much to criticize—and does.

At times, Mr. Moser admitted, this youngster seems to specialize in getting on everyone's nerves, including her own. She accepts responsibility but finds other activities (including doing nothing) so interesting she quickly forgets to follow through. (Constant reminding and help in scheduling time are indicated.) She eats ravenously yet will tell you, at length, of her struggles to lose weight. A scuffling proximity to boys is clearly a delight but these same boys she will complain of as "so childish." Great schisms rock her group of friends. She gushes superlatives, giggles at nothing, experiments at being adult.

MOVING ahead to the senior high school stage seems only to complicate the situation. The younger girl who criticized her family may now appear to find them just about impossible. When they don't change their ways to suit her standards she feels misunderstood. Their perverseness "proves," she feels, their lack of concern for her. How can a girl discuss vital matters with people like them! Boys and the whole exciting, frightening matter of Love absorb her interest. She must be attractive; she must do the things her friends do. All that sustains her through the storms of her first loves is the fact that her friends for the most part are suffering the same way.

Parents must keep their heads, their sense of humor and a steady hand throughout the girl's growing up. Making an effort to understand the why's of her behavior will make it easier to take and to control.

Mothers Carry Women's Lib Message to Grade School

By LISA HAMMEL

Women's lib has begun to show up in the elementary grades.

A group of mothers whose children go to the Woodward School, in the Clinton Hill section of Brooklyn, have organized themselves into a group called the Sex Roles Committee. The private, co-educational school is described by its director as "a little left of center" in the spectrum of orthodox to experimental.

The committee, whose 15 to 20 active members are mothers of children up through the middle grades, may be the only one of its kind around at the moment. Since it began in September, 1970, it has been bringing to the attention of the teachers the ways in which children, but mostly girls, are limited through social and traditional attitudes that are passed on, or reinforced, by the school.

The mothers say that almost every phase of schooling contributes to this in some way: the curriculum, the reading material, the ways in which children are encouraged—or not encouraged—to relate, to play, to work and to express themselves. The mothers also believe that sex-typing is further influenced by the unconscious attitudes of teachers.

On a recent evening, nine members of the committee—most of them women's lib members — met for one of their monthly meetings, and they made it clear at the outset that they did not identify themselves either by their husbands' first names or by their husband's professions. And almost all preferred the honoric, Ms.

Also at the meeting were Margaret (Meg) Bluhm, a teacher at the school who acts as liaison between the group and the school staff, and Ruth Fishman, the assistant director. The meeting took place at the home of the school's director, Gertrude Goldstein, in whom the group has found a sympathetic, but cautious, ear.

Opening the Floodgates?

"At first, we were worried," said the director, "about how much the parents would want to take over the running of the school if they were invited in."

"But we realized," said Vivian Ubell, mother of a girl of 8 and another, 2, "that ultimately decisions about the school were up to the staff. When dealing with them, we always put on those kid gloves . . ."

Notable by their absence, however, were the fathers of the children at the Woodward School. Once, when fathers were invited to a meeting, they took over. They were not invited again.

What are some of the problems that little girls, like their mothers before them, are likely to encounter?

The mothers discovered, first of all, that their small children had already formed a strong sense of sex role differentiation at home, and brought this with them when they started kindergarten.

"In the kindergarten," said Andrea Ostrum, the mother of two small boys and a 7-year-old girl, "there were two rooms. The blocks, trucks and all the doing toys were in one room; the dolls and ornamental things were in another room. I said to my daughter one day, 'Do you have a girls' room and a boys' room?' And Eva said, 'Oh, no, the girls are allowed to go into the boys' room, too!'"

When the girls did manage, generally with teacher intervention, to get near the blocks, the mothers reported, they built simple, low structures, which more often than not turned out to be a kind of container for their dolls, while the boys built more complex structures that were immediately praised by the teachers for size and ingenuity of design.

"But this year," said Vivian Ubell, "Jennifer came home and announced she had built a city!"

Conversely, a little boy who wanted to play with dolls would have just as hard a time of it.

"My son," said one mother, who declined to be identified, "had a doll that he loved a lot and wanted to take to school when he was in kindergarten last year. But he was afraid the girls would tease him. The first day in school this year, he took the doll with him and openly hugged it and kissed it."

What are some of the other ways in which sex-typing shows up?

Girls will read books about boys and take male parts in plays, but boys are very reluctant to change roles. A girl who is a natural leader many have particular difficulty.

In a lower grade class, one of the mothers reported, the children were putting on a play about astronauts. One girl did all the scenery and costumes, but when she wanted to play an astronaut, the boys demurred. The teacher intervened, and she played the part.

Downgrading of Expectations

Performance expectations are sometimes downgraded for girls, the mothers said. The girls at Woodward are taught woodworking (and the boys have cooking), but a girl is just not expected to "hammer the nail straight," said Mimi Meyers, mother of a 6-year-old girl and 3-year-old boy.

"The teacher seemed to feel it was enough that the girls came to the woodworking class," said Brett Vuolo, who has a boy, 11, and a girl, 8.

In mathematics and science, the girls generally do better at first, Gertrude Goldstein reported, but then "start dropping out" intellectually as they approach adolescence.

"According to a report we read," said Leah Matalon, mother of two small boys, "as the children get older, there is a change in aspiration and interests. The boys' worlds widen, and the girls' get narrower."

When the mothers first approached the school, Gertude Goldstein said, "Our reaction was 'who, me?' But now I think even the most resistant staff member has moved. I think even if people are not ready to be different, they're ready to act differently. I think they now see many instances of sexism where they didn't see it before."

Among things under consideration for the future at school are a women's studies course (a kind of feminist equivalent of black studies); a special section on women in the school library; a feminist newsletter for the school, and consciousness-raising with the girls.

Both the mothers and the staff representatives said that their work had produced changes, although it was hard to tell whether it came from school or the parents' home influence.

Mimi Meyers reported that now when her 6-year-old daughter plays house, "she goes out to work, and instructs the daddy to cook dinner."

The youngsters themselves, however, do not consider all of this concern an unalloyed blessing.

"That's the seventh time you've talked about women's lib this year," a little girl said testily to Meg Bluhm one day.

January 8, 1972

Should girls play football? And boys change diapers?

By SALLY WENDKOS OLDS

ARE parents encouraging stereotyping of sex roles in children's play? Few child-study experts have yet turned their thoughts to this question—or to whether or not it is helpful for a child's emotional development to have sex roles reinforced by play activities. This important area has been the almost exclusive concern of the Women's Liberation Movement.

Anne Grant West, an English teacher at Brooklyn College and coordinator of the education committee of the New York City chapter of the National Organization for Women, charges, "Boys are urged to play in a dynamic and creative way. In their play, they see how high they can build a tower of blocks or how many marbles they can shoot. Girls are encouraged to play in a much more static way, to follow directions for uncreative 'craft' kits, to dress and undress teen-age dolls. Too many toys on the market today exploit negative human qualities in a sex-linked way—competitiveness and violence in boys and narcissism in girls."

It would be difficult to find a thoughtful child-study expert who would not agree with Dr. Mark A. Stewart, professor of psychiatry and associate professor of pediatrics at Washington University Medical School in St. Louis, when he says, "These women are raising some important questions—questions that go to the core of individual development. Both men and women could have much healthier relationships if they were not so threatened about their masculinity or femininity."

THROUGH their play from earliest childhood, youngsters prepare to be adults. Play is real work for children. Jean Piaget, in his pioneering works on how children's minds develop, uses examples from the world of play to show how the child assimilates information and learns how to use it.

Most parents and teachers see pronounced differences between the play of boys and girls starting at a very early age: Boys are more vigorous and aggressive; girls engage in fantasy play revolving around people and relationships.

Why is their play so different? As Piaget asks, when you watch a little girl playing with her doll, "How much is instinct . . . and how much imitation of what the child appreciates in its own mother?"

"There is no way you can avoid the perfectly natural phenomenon of girls imitating females in their play and boys imitating males," says Dr. Stephen L. Zaslow, a child psychiatrist. "And you wouldn't want to discourage this. This is the way children identify with adults and develop a sense of their own sex.

"I can see this happening with my own children," says Dr. Zaslow. "After a repairman comes to the house, my 3-year-old son, Eric, picks up my tools and goes around trying to fix the stove and the dishwasher. My daughters have watched the same repairman, but they have never imitated him. They often assume the role of the teen-age girls who baby-sit for us, a part that has never interested Eric."

Recognizing that in their play children tend to emulate the parent of the same sex, parents who present "liberated" models to their children will see their sons washing dishes or "taking out the baby" and their daughters "fixing a flat tire" or "going out to work" —all without sacrificing a sense of their own maleness or femaleness. Parents can and should encourage their children to play in ways completely freed from stereotypes, without worrying about gender confusion. A girl can run and jump and play just as hard as any boy, and a boy can play quiet games with girls without either one's sexuality being in doubt. But there is a certain biological point from which there is no digression, and parents who try to raise their little girls to be boys or who don't respect the maleness of their sons are doing them a grave disservice.

Child-care professionals urge parents to be sensitive to their children's individuality, without worrying whether a youngster fits the picture of the "typical" boy or girl. Dr. Natalie Shainess, a New York psychiatrist, recalls her own childhood to make this point. As a little girl, she never

played with dolls. She much preferred mechanical toys and Erector sets. Yet Dr. Shainess developed a strong yearning to be a mother, took time out from her medical studies to raise two children and is now deeply interested in feminine psychology.

"A child's masculine or feminine identity is related more to family values and the feelings a youngster has about people than it is to his or her play activities," says Ronnie Gordon, director of the preschool developmental programs at the Institute of Rehabilitation Medicine at the New York University Medical Center. "We try to expose children to a variety of experiences. We recognize, for example, that it is appropriate for a little boy to wash a doll and for a little girl to be fascinated with woodworking. And we recognize that a child's self-esteem will go up when that youngster becomes competent in a specific area— whether that area is athletics or cooking and whether it is an activity traditional to one sex or the other."

"The young child has to find out who he is and how he fits into the world around him. The adults in his life need to help in this essential task by supporting the child's sex role as a part of his or her identity," says Hanna McElheny, curriculum coordinator at the Bank Street School for Children.

But this doesn't mean pushing a child into stereotyped sex-role play. One father teaching his 4-year-old daughter how to throw a ball said, "Nancy, you're going to be a great baseball player!" When Nancy said, "Oh, Daddy, I'm going to be a ballerina!" her father said cheerfully, "Well, whatever you're going to be, you're going to be good." And that, of course, was the important message — that she could determine her own future.

Dr. Richard A. Gardner, a child psychiatrist, urges parents to show respect for both the male and the female role. "While we want to encourage our children to be individuals within the society, we have to adapt somewhat to the standards of our own culture. Before a child can question societal norms, he or she has to know what those norms are

"Most women's primary instinctive orientation is toward child rearing and most men's is toward activities leading to the acquisition of food, clothing and shelter," Dr. Gardner says. "Each, however, has the innate potential for significant gratification in the other's primary area and should be given every opportunity and encouragement to derive such.

"In the ideal game of house, for instance, a boy would not play mommy, pretending to have breasts to nurse a baby. He would work instead with toy tools and sometimes care for a doll in the way his own father might care for his baby sister — by giving a bath or changing a diaper."

Children should be encouraged to value the prerogatives of their own sex. Boys don't seem to have much trouble in this area, since masculinity is so highly respected in our society. It is admired to such

a degree that Robert R. Sears, professor of psychology at Stanford University, recently reported a study in which he found that self-esteem in both boy and girl sixth-graders was positively correlated with masculinity. Another study a few years ago showed that American girls now play baseball and basketball and climb much more than they used to. This change toward more "masculine" pastimes is undoubtedly a response to changes in societal expectations—and also to the esteem in which these activities are held. Girls often say proudly, "I'm a tomboy"; boys don't say happily, "I'm a sissy."

The answer is not to bring up girls as if they were boys, but to place greater emphasis on female values. Child-rearing, for example, which is a woman's job in most cultures around the world, is held in low esteem in this country. Young women elsewhere are proud of their skills in caring for children, but our girls learn from an early age to devalue these tasks—and yet to associate them with femininity.

Dr. Shainess points to 5-year-old Karen. When asked what she wanted to be when she grew up, Karen replied, "A mommy." Her mother demanded impatiently, "That's not enough! What *else* do you want to be?" "This mother is robbing her daughter of the expectation of the joys of motherhood," says Dr. Shainess. "It would be far better to show approval for the little girl's desire to imitate her mother and then to ask in an open way, 'Is there anything else you want to do, too?'"

CHILD rearing is, of course, far from the only female attribute. In a recent report on the significance of the father-daughter relationship in the general personality development of the female, Henry B. Biller and Stephan D. Weiss emphasize the importance of defining femininity positively — stressing such traits as competence, confidence, warmth and affection, and

understanding. We can encourage girls in their play to act out such nurturing roles as doctors and such communicative roles as newspaper reporters.

Many parents are amazed to discover the stereotyped thinking displayed by very young children. One mother walked into her 4-year-old son's room as he was playing house with four little friends —two boys and two girls— just in time to hear one of the girls protest, "Boys don't set tables."

The mother asked, "Betsy, does your daddy or your big brother ever do any work in the kitchen?" "Oh, yes," she said. "My daddy makes pancakes and my brother takes the dishes out of the dishwasher."

It was perfectly natural for the mother to carry the conversation a step further and make the point that boys could set tables, sweep floors and make beds with no loss of masculinity. (This point is, of course, easier to make in homes where parents share household tasks.) "I think it would be healthier," says psychiatrist Mark Stewart, "if men felt freer to do the dishes and other household chores and if both husband and wife felt greater freedom from cultural pressure over who did what about the household and the children."

Parents are changing their own patterns of thought toward their children's play. More of them are walking into toy stores and buying doctor sets for their daughters and baking sets for their sons. If more manufacturers desexed their toys by showing children of both sexes in ads and on packages, parents might be encouraged even more in this direction.

One mother tells of how, when her little girl picked up a wooden barge, the boy next to her grabbed it away, saying, "That's for boys!" He lost his case when the girl triumphantly pointed to the box the toy had come in, picturing both a boy and a girl playing with the barge.

"'Together' is the most underused word in parenting," says Dr. Shainess, who believes parents should do more things with their children. The father who teaches his son and his daughter simple carpentry, who cooks with them, who plays "office" with them is showing his interest in them as individuals and is demonstrating the pleasures fathers derive from child-rearing. Similarly, a mother who takes advantage of the fact that with young children the line between work and play is a shadowy one can encourage both her son and her daughter to iron, cook and garden with her. She can also enter into games of "let's pretend" by encouraging her children to assume various nonhousekeeping roles.

Parents present models of womanliness and manliness to their children, not only in their own life-style but also in that of the other adults in their children's lives. Dr. Shainess, for example, knew from early childhood that her own mother took great pride in the fact that a woman doctor had delivered her babies. Another woman's sons admire their uncle who is a superb cook. A mother points out to her children that one of her women friends is a lawyer and that their favorite

uncle is a kindergarten teacher.

CHILDREN are sensitive to their parents' feelings. The woman who screams her discontent at "woman's lot" in front of her children or the man who tells his wife enviously, "Boy, are you lucky you don't have to be out there in that rat race!" is communicating to a child a distaste for womanhood or manhood. But a child who sees that a mother is capable, assertive, active, achieving and fulfilled will associate these qualities with womanhood. And if he or she sees a father who is devoted, affectionate and nurturing, these will be considered masculine attributes.

"There shouldn't be a difference between males and females in their professional roles, in the way they care about children and in being human beings. But there *is* a difference," says Rebecca Straus, director of the Bank Street School for Children. "Men are not women biologically and vice versa. But being equal doesn't mean being the same. Women have some delightful things to do that make life great for them and so do men, and I think we must respect our differences and rejoice in them." ∎

March 26, 1972

Male Chauvinist Piglets

"Johnny says girls aren't fun. . . . Janey says she wants to be a doctor when she grows up, but she knows girls cannot be doctors, so she will be a nurse instead. . . . Janey says she might be only a girl, but she isn't stupid."

Those are themes and quotations culled from 134 elementary-school readers by a group of 25 women in Princeton, N. J., who call themselves Women on Words and Images and are affiliated with the National Organization for Women (N.O.W.) Their study resulted in the just-published pamphlet, "Dick and Jane as Victims: Sex Stereotyping in Children's Readers" ($1.50; Box 2163, Princeton, N. J., 08540).

According to the pamphlet, the selected books from 14 leading publishing companies are sexist — "overwhelmingly male-oriented." The group's thesis comes through loud and clear: male chauvinist conditioning starts in kindergarten.

Some of the books studied were published some years ago, before Women's Lib became so popular, and many are being brought up to date or phased out.

The women say they found that stories about boys outnumbered stories about girls by 5 to 2. Boys outnumbered girls 4 to 1 in stories showing ingenuity, creativity, perseverance, strength, bravery, apprenticeship, earning money, competitiveness and exploration. On the other hand, girls exhibit such traits as passivity, docility and dependency six times as often as boys, the group contends.

The boys in most of the stories were found to lead adventurous lives, involving much travel and excitement; the girls rarely venture far from home and hearth.

The pamphlet makes a persuasive case, although it is difficult to believe that the study was undertaken, as it claims in its introduction, "without preconceived or doctrinaire objectives."

Questions may be asked about some of the yardsticks applied. For example, a listing of "sexist quotations" includes: "He remembered his mother's advice, 'always wait until your father has finished his food before asking him for anything.'" Or: "Mary is a good girl. She likes to help." To many observers these statements would seem normal, with no sexist overtones.

Another question is whether books for young children should be expected to go beyond reflecting the world as the children know it. When dealing with the realm of work, for example, it seems natural to the present scene to describe more male than female occupations, or to picture homes in which mothers do more of the household work than fathers.

But the pamphlet argues: "The society into which our children will be expected to fit is very different from that presented by the readers. . . . Whether or not we like these trends, we must prepare our daughters and sons to deal with them."

—FRED M. HECHINGER

Sally said, "Oh, Mother!

Look at Puff.

Look at me.

Puff and I can help you."

©Scott Foresman & Co., 1965

This picture is cited by a group of women as an example of "sex stereotyping" in selected grade-school reading texts which they studied. The group contends that the books are "overwhelmingly male-oriented." This book and some others are being replaced by their publishers.

CHAPTER 9

Challenge and Change

Women liberationists demonstrate
on the 51st anniversary of women's
right to vote, August 30, 1971.
Courtesy Compix.

CHILD CARE TERMED NO WAR PLANT TASK

Experts Tell Industry to Keep 'Hands Off'—Centers Called Only 'Lures' for Mothers

By DOROTHY BARCLAY

The day care committee of the Child Welfare League of America asked the country's industrial leaders yesterday to keep "hands off" the operation of child care centers and take part instead in community planning to meet emergency needs.

Day care specialists from all parts of the country, concluding a two-day meeting at league headquarters, 24 West Fortieth Street, reported that defense industries in several states already were planning to operate child care centers as a "lure" in recruiting mothers for their work forces. Among states named were California, Florida, Wisconsin and Virginia.

One national corporation with plants in all parts of the country is considering opening 100 centers to accommodate the children of 20,000 mothers they hope to employ, committee members said.

Opposition to such programs on the part of child development specialists is based on experience with industry-run centers during World War II. At that time, the experts hold, such centers were used to recruit mothers rather than to safeguard children, their schedules and activities being geared to mothers' working shifts rather than to children's needs.

They were usually located near plants, depriving youngsters of the relationships and experiences of neighborhood life, and parents, without access to other community services, were entirely dependent upon the industry's facilities, which lasted only as long as that particular industry needed the mothers' work.

Virtually every sizable city, a spokesman for the committee said, has a council of social agencies ready and willing to meet with industry representatives to work out a coordinating program to expand existing facilities to meet current needs. Instead of setting up new centers, it was held, those now in operation should be expanded, and present resources used as much as possible.

According to the committee, a properly operated defense day care program requires joint planning by health, education and welfare authorities as well as industry, labor and other community groups. The well-being of the child should be the prime concern, they held. Such a program is now getting under way in Wisconsin, it was said, with one of the state's largest industries taking leadership.

Mrs. J. Horton Ijams, chairman of the league's day care committee, presided at the two-day sessions, attended by delegates from twelve states. The Child Welfare League is a national federation of child care agencies, both public and private, sectarian and non-sectarian, with members in 146 cities in forty states, Canada and Hawaii.

March 7, 1951

Someone to mind the baby

By MAYA PINES

"I KNOW a lot of people say that mothers shouldn't work," Vice President Humphrey stated recently. "But I have been brought up to believe that what is, is." He called the lack of adequate day-care facilities for young children one of the greatest problems of tomorrow's America.

The trend is clear: more and more women are going to work. One out of every four mothers of children under the age of 6 is in the labor force; the number of such mothers has doubled since 1950. More than 4 million preschoolers have mothers who work, including 1,600,000 children under the age of 3.

Yet the nation has resolutely ignored the problem. American women remain almost totally deprived of opportunities to make satisfactory arrangements for the care of their children while they are working. As a result, millions of youngsters are being damaged emotionally, intellectually and sometimes physically during their most formative years.

Behind the paucity of services for young children lies the fear that providing good day-care facilities might encourage even more women to go to work—a fear entertained by male workers who wish to avoid competition and by moralists of both sexes who believe woman's place is in the home.

THERE are a few signs that this atmosphere may be changing. In Cambridge, Mass., for example, a manufacture of hi-fi equipment has just set up a demonstration day-care center for the children of its employes in cooperation with the U.S. Children's Bureau and the employes themselves.

The KLH Child Development Center, Inc., will be owned and operated by the children's parents. When it opens on Feb. 1 it will run from 7 A.M. to 3:30 P.M. to coincide with the parents' work day. It will take children between the ages of 2 and 6. Mothers will be free to come eat with their children during their own lunch hours. The center plans to offer all the educational advantages of a good nursery school, at a price the parents can pay, since the company will provide about 15 per cent of the cost and the Children's Bureau two thirds. It is meant as a replicable project—one that could be copied in many different kinds of industries.

"This is the beginning, we hope of a trend," declares Mrs. Richard Lansburgh, president of the National Committee for the Day Care of Children. "A tremendous acceleration will take place in the coming years. We'll need money for training, for personnel, so that these programs are constructive for children — not just baby-sitting!"

WHILE management started the KLH center, in Baltimore a union is taking the lead. Not surprisingly, it is a union largely dominated by women—the Amalgamated Clothing Workers' Union, makers of men's clothing, which plans to open centers for some 2,000 children in 15 areas of Virginia, Maryland, Pennsylvania, Delaware and North Carolina.

Maya Pines is the author of "Revolution in Learning — The Years from Birth to Six" (Harper & Row).

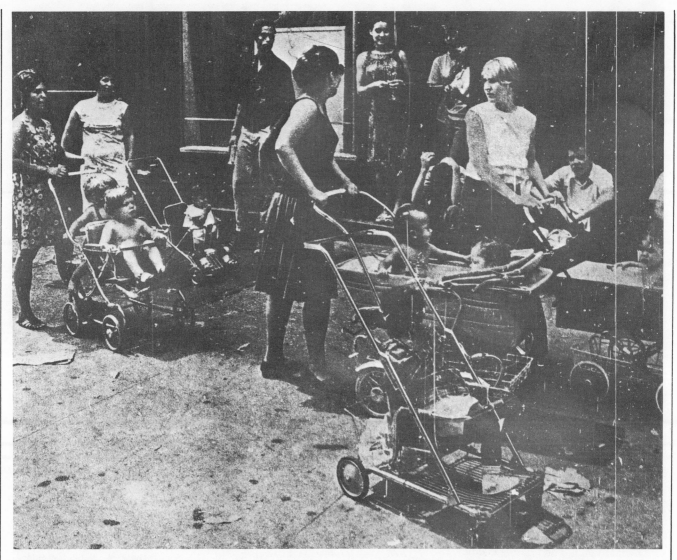

PRIVATE ENTERPRISE—These young women, setting off for Tompkins Square, take care of about 40 preschoolers whose mothers work. They receive no public funds, charge whatever a family can afford.

"We're the originators of this plan, because we operate in small towns where the membership is 100 per cent female," explains Samuel Nocella, vice-president of the ACWU and manager of its Baltimore region. "We've experienced some acute problems — absenteeism on the part of women, and nervous breakdowns, which are very frequent among them. And we've found that at the bottom of it there is always a child. The mother becomes anxious, worried about her child, she calls home or stays away from work, and unless she has parents or somebody close to her to take care of her child, the child may really be in bad condition. So why not do what people have been doing for a long time in Europe, for example in Sweden, and provide child-care centers?"

The Amalgamated is now supporting a bill in Congress to include child care among the benefits that can be negotiated for in union agreements, and day-care centers may become a standard item in collective bargaining next year.

In the long run, however, this is a problem that can only be met by the government on a nation-wide scale, declares Jacob Potofsky, president of the ACWU. "This step, creating day-care centers for working mothers, is the first taken by any union—and it is long overdue," he says. Just as his union pioneered in unemployment insurance in the twenties, and saw it included in the first Social Security Act 12 years later, "today we have the same hope that government will assume the responsibility throughout the land of

creating proper facilities for the young children of working mothers, for they are the future of our country."

The government's role in day care was prominent only during World War II when it became not merely acceptable, but positively patriotic for mothers to work. Suddenly enough nurseries and day-care centers blossomed, with government aid, to care for about 1,600,000 children. But nearly all these centers were closed at the end of the war. Today, when the number of working women exceeds the World War II total by 6 million, licensed public and voluntary day-care centers have shrunk to one-sixth their wartime capacity. They have also changed their orientation. Instead of opening their doors to all, they tend to concentrate on families with serious emotional or social problems. Their waiting lists are staggering.

STATE and Federal authorities will soon be forced to enter the day-care field on a large scale for the first time since World War II. A new amendment to the Social Security Act will compel thousands of mothers on welfare to enter work training or take jobs, and some facilities will have to be set up for their children while they work. However, since its goal is not to provide services to children but to cut welfare costs, the new law may lead to cheap custodial arrangements in many states. The law makes no provision for the children's education. As the National Committee for the Day Care of Children puts it, "Our country will then be in the anomalous position of giving some children a headstart, while giving others a push backward."

Day care must be recognized as a public utility for all children, some experts believe. "The new law again puts the emphasis on the underprivileged, on the welfare population, on troubled families," worries Professor Florence Ruderman, a Brooklyn College sociologist who recently completed a large-scale survey of day care for the Child Welfare League of America.

"Day care is needed on all levels of society — by the most normal families and by the middle class, as well as by others," she declares. "It should be available to the entire society, just like our public schools, parks, playgrounds and libraries."

According to Mrs. Lansburgh of the National Committee for the Day Care of Children, there is still tremendous resistance to the idea of day care. "Did Planned Parenthood have a more difficult selling job? We think not," she says. "Their resistances are verbalized and conscious; ours are not. Day care is threatening to many people—it says mother isn't in the home and there's nobody to make life nice and secure. Therefore, forget it, ignore it, pretend there's no need for it. Also, few people know the massive size of the problem or the serious consequences of neglect.

"I don't believe that all women should go to work," she adds. "But I do feel that in 1968 women

SO THAT'S A TURTLE . . .—Day-care centers should give children the same opportunities for learning and doing that nursery schools offer.

should have the choice, the freedom to choose whether they wish to use their intelligence, ability, training and education without penalizing their families." She points out that in Maryland alone, 400 nurses would be working today if they could find day-care services that they would trust for their children. Meanwhile hospital patients suffer from the critical shortage of nurses.

Just as professional women who want to work should be made to stay home, women who are on welfare should not be made to go to work, Mrs. Lansburgh declares. "There should be a free choice for both," she says. "This choice does not exist in this country today."

Altogether the nation's public and private licensed day-care facilities—many of them beyond the means of poor people — can accommodate only 450,000 children. Mothers, thus, are forced into all kinds of informal or "black market" arrangements.

Millions of "latchkey" children, for instance, find nobody at home when they get home from school in the afternoon. Carrying their house keys around their neck or in their pockets, they wander about or play without supervision, until their parents come back from work. Sometimes a neighbor

or an aunt is supposed to look in on them.

Few families can afford to hire a private nursemaid. In New York City, the going rate for a competent nanny is anywhere from $60 to $90 a week, if she can be found. Even middle-class parents often leave their children with untrained and irresponsible household help who may do the child great harm.

An estimated 38,000 children under the age of 6 are left without any care at all while their mothers work, according to Katherine Oettinger, former chief of the U.S. Children's Bureau; many of them are just locked up in their own homes. Twice as many preschoolers are looked after by a brother or sister not much older than they are.

CHILDREN under 3 are generally not admitted into the licensed day-care centers because they are considered too young. For many working mothers, the only alternative that remains is "family day care." In theory this does not sound too bad: The mother leaves her child with a woman who takes in several other children at the same time, for a small fee.

But a recent study in New York City showed what family day care

NANNY AT WORK—Since few families can afford a nursemaid like the young woman above, day-care centers would benefit working mothers of all economic levels.

is really like. Though the city has an established licensing procedure for family day-care homes, only 25 such homes have been licensed in the entire city. By contrast, 25,000 children—more than half of them under the age of 6—are parked in a variety of unlicensed homes.

One of the interviewers for the Medical and Health Research Association of N.Y.C., which did this study, still has nightmares about some of the places she visited. Many of the day-care "mothers" were physically ill, she reports—and their illness was the very reason for their doing this kind of work. Several were drunkards.

She recalls a harassed 20-year-old girl who had previously worked as a salesgirl but had lost her job because of a severe anemia which left her always tired. The girl lived in a crowded home with many relatives, including three small children, and took in three other children for day care. She hated what she was doing. She had lost control over the six children to the extent that she did not even bother to find out what part of the house they were in. One youngster, aged 4, did nothing but cry all day long, sitting alone on the top step of the porch. The girl said he was "spoiled."

In most of the family day-care homes the children's routine was breakfast, TV, lunch, nap, and TV. One third of the homes had no play materials of any kind. In 25 per cent of the homes the children were never taken out-of-doors. As many as 84 per cent of the homes were rated inadequate because they violated the Health Code, or because the children were severely neglected.

Throughout their study, the interviewers were assailed by desperate women who begged them to help find good day-care services for their children. They would try any trick to attract the inter-

viewers' attention, hoping it might somehow lead them to space in a day-care center. The study's associate director, Milton Willner, a social worker with long experience in day care, concluded that two kind of programs were urgently needed: a training program for women who would run licensed family day care for up to five children in their homes, bolstered by periodic inspections to make sure they provided enough play materials, nap facilities and fresh air; and many, many more day-care centers, including some for children under the age of 3.

THE years from birth to 6 offer a unique opportunity to break the cycle of failure that awaits America's poor children. The first four years of life are the most important time of all—the crucial years that determine a child's later personality and intelligence, according to modern psychologists. During these years, a child's environment plays a decisive role.

Now that private companies, unions and the Government are becoming more aware of the urgent need for day care, they have a chance to set a new pattern for such services. Until now, education has never been day-care's forte. "If there are qualified teachers, it's a nursery school; if it's custodial, it's day-care," has all too often been the working definition of the difference between the two. Unless the new day-care centers offer a truly effective educational program, they will waste their opportunity to make a major improvement in the lives of millions of children. ■

Day Care: Demand Outrunning Growth

By NANCY HICKS

Universally available day care for American children is inevitable, experts in the field say. They note that women, who make up 38 per cent of the work force, want and need it, and that many politicians back it.

But widespread disagreement over goals and over methods of implementation is hindering planning. This, in turn, means that day care is not becoming available at nearly the rate needed.

There are more than 11.6 million working mothers in the country today, more than 4 million of these with children under 6 years old. However, only 640,000 licensed day care spaces are available. More than one-third of these are privately run.

"Some mothers have always worked and arranged to have their children cared for," said Jule M. Sugarman, chief of New York City's Human Resources Administration, which supervises the city's day care programs.

"But people often live with whatever setups they can arrange. As soon as something else comes along, they take it. This is what is happening with day care," said Mr. Sugarman, the former acting head of the Office of Child Development of the Department of Health, Education and Welfare.

But it is becoming obvious to educators, psychologists and social scientists that before any major expansion comes about, serious problems must be overcome. The most basic decision ahead is whether day care will be custodial care or a form of early education.

Ideological leaders in the field have decided that day care is to be more than adult supervision geared, for example, to merely making certain that children do not stick their fingers in electric sockets while Mother is working. If these leaders' goals are realized, then expansion will have to be slow and expensive.

It will require the training of a cadre of personnel to teach children and to work with their parents. Centers would have to be built or renovated. A "quality program" also would have to provide meals, medical services and research units that would study the effects of group education on very young children.

Using the current average Federal expenditure for early childhood programs, it is estimated that this combination of services would cost $1,600 a year a child. This compares with an annual school cost of $870 a year a child, according to the latest figures of the National Education Association.

Even with supportive services and sound educational programs, some psychologists fear, day care for the very young might become impersonal and institutionalized.

Some earlier studies of child-rearing environments — including those conducted by Dr. Eleanor Pavenstedt, a Tufts University psychoanalyst, on failure-to-thrive infants — have shown that these characteristics retard development.

But against these financial and ideological concerns is a pressing need.

A Department of Labor study in 1964 showed the arrangements that 6.3 million working mothers made for their 12.3 million children under age 14.

Half of the children were cared for in their own homes, usually by another relative. One third were cared for in someone else's home. Thirteen per cent were watched by their own mothers during work, as might happen with a proprietor of a small store. Close to one million children, or 8 per cent, cared for themselves. These are the so-called "latch-key kids" who wear their house keys around their necks. Only 2 per cent of the mothers were able to find group day care centers.

The disparity between supply and demand has brought together traditionally warring factions in politics and education and set in motion a day care movement. Workers for women's rights are petitioning employers to begin on-premise centers for their children. Community groups are meeting at night to plan all-day and after-school centers in their neighborhoods. Mothers are setting up cooperative babysitting arrangements aimed at teaching the child as well as providing custodial care.

More organized efforts are being waged by groups like The Day Care and Child Development Council and the National Council of Negro Women, both in Washington.

Legislators have introduced a variety of bills into Congress to fund expanding services.

Economists and social scientists offer some specific reasons why day care has become such a popular issue. They include the following:

¶The dramatic increase in the number of working mothers, which has created a day care need that has outpaced the ability of society to handle it through informal arrangements. Forty per cent of mothers work today, compared with 1 per cent in 1940, according to Department of Labor figures. These figures are expected to increase by 30 per cent more by 1985.

¶The recent acceptance by industry and husbands of the movement of women out of the home and into the labor force.

¶Changes in the American family which used to be large and centrally located but which today is so widely spread around the country that the mother often needs day care, sometimes for illness or family crisis, aside from the workday applications.

Head Start as Model

Estimates that in the next few years, one child in 12 will grow up in a family with only one parent, because of divorce and other factors.

Acceptance by mothers of reports alleging the importance of very early education. This has particularly created support by centers that stress teaching.

Within this educational framework, there are several existing programs that could provide models for larger programs.

Head Start, the Federal preschool program for poor children, provides many all-day educational settings that would equal day care for a working mother. Boards of education in localities have pre-school programs that serve the same purpose.

Departments of social services offer day care for working mothers under Title IV of the Social Security Act of 1962, which provided funds for these centers.

More than 120,000 children are being cared for in what are called Family Day Care Homes, which are sponsored jointly by local social services agencies with money from the Federal Government. Under this arrangement, poor mothers are taught to care for children by educational specialists who provide them with equipment in their homes and "lessons" to teach the children. In this way, that mother becomes a skilled worker in addition to providing a service.

While the above are all public programs, voluntary and private groups provide variations on the same themes.

The Office of Child Development has assumed the job of looking at the various programs and setting the standards for what day care in America should be.

Zigler Favors Choice

Its director, Dr. Edward Zigler, one of the original Head Start planners, likes the varied approach now being used because it gives mothers a choice of settings. As a back-up, however, the Office of Child Development is testing some of these approaches in 32 parent-child centers developed by several universities.

"We really can't set up more day care centers overnight," Dr. Zigler said. "We have neither the staff nor the facilities to do so. We must expand existing frameworks. The Head Start orientation is good. A giant step would be the passing of the family assistance plan."

This embattled legislation is the President's plan to reform the nation's welfare system. It includes day care expansion. While many educators oppose the compulsory work provision of the plan, they see administrative commitment to 450,000 new day care spaces as a first step in expanding services.

"It is absolutely mandatory to develop a new cadre of people whose training is directed at raising children," said Dr. Zigler. "The Russians have them. They call such people 'upbringers.'"

The Russians, Israelis and Swedes have for years had mass day care programs for working mothers. While cultural differences have made it impossible to transfer their programs directly to American situations, they have shown that such widespread programs are possible to operate.

There is a consensus among the educators and economists studying the situation that if day care is going to work on a universal basis, the Government is going to have to pay for the majority of it simply because the size of the problem is larger than the private sector's ability to solve it.

A number of Congressmen have introduced bills that would create day care in addition to the family assistance plan.

Representatives John A. Brademas, Democrat of Indiana, and John R. Dellenback, Republican of Oregon, have introduced a bill that would repeal

Head Start and hand control of operations over to a state agency that would receive most of its money from the Federal Government.

A bill proposed by Senator Walter F. Mondale of Minnesota calls for the expansion of Head Start over the next five years from a $320-million a year program to a $5-billion a year program.

A third bill, proposed by Senator Russell B. Long of Louisiana, would set up a Federal Child Care Corporation that would create, but not pay for, services.

Private efforts to solve the problem have been met with some skepticism. Several years ago, entreprenuers, including several football stars, talked about setting up franchises. But because of the expense of running quality programs, most have left the field.

One private effort has received some praise from educators, however. This is the Educare project of the Universal Education Corporation of New York. It has signed a contract with the Pennsylvania State Department of Education to set up centers in four cities and hopes to expand from there.

Private industry has provided facilities for the children of employes on a very limited basis. A 1968 survey by the Department of Labor showed that fewer than 150 industry-sponsored centers were available and more than 100 of these were in hospitals.

Amalgamated Clothing Workers Union in Baltimore and Chicago has extensive programs, however. So do KLH Research and Development Corporation of Cambridge, the Whirlpool division of RCA, and the Department of Labor itself.

November 30, 1970

Senate, 40-37, Votes Rise In Tax Exemption to $800

Measure Would Cut Revenue $1.9-Billion —Democrats Planning Proposal for Public Financing of Campaigns

By EILEEN SHANAHAN
Special to The New York Times

WASHINGTON, Nov. 12— The Senate voted 40 to 37 today for a further tax cut of $1.9-billion for individuals. The reduction, effective next year, would come in the form of an increase to $800 in the personal exemption.

A number of other major actions were taken on the tax bill as the Senate went through the first full day of what is expected to be about a week of debate and votes on the measure.

In addition, it was learned that an attempt will probably be made next week by Senate Democrats to attach to the bill a provision for funding Presidential election campaigns out of tax money.

Among the major amendments adopted by the Senate were the following:

¶A proposal by Senator John V. Tunney, Democrat of California, that would increase from 39 weeks to 65 the maximum period over which an individual could collect unemployment insurance. The 26 additional weeks of benefits would be available only in states where the unemployment rate has averaged 6 per cent or more for 13 weeks. At present, this covers 13 states, plus Puerto Rico, and includes New York, New Jersey and Connecticut.

¶An amendment by Senator Hubert H. Humphrey, Democrat of Minnesota, that would give farmers the 7 per cent investment credit on farm machinery ordered on or after last Jan. 1. For all individuals and businesses, only equipment ordered after April 1 would eligible.

¶Another proposal by Senator Tunney that would make the deductions of money paid for child care or invalid care and for household help a business expense instead of a personal

deduction. This would mean that persons who did not itemize deductions would nevertheless get the benefit of this new deduction.

Several important proposed amendments were defeated. One of the most important was a proposal by Senator Birch Bayh, Democrat of Indiana, that would have repealed legislatively the action taken by the Treasury earlier this year liberalizing the rules under which businesses calculate their deduction for depreciation.

The depreciation liberalization was considered a major element of the Administration's over-all plan to stimulate the economy by stimulating business investment. The defeat of the Bayh amendment, by 35 to 37, was thus a significant victory for the Administration.

Also defeated, by the wide margin of 22 to 41, was an amendment sponsored by Senator Jacob K. Javits, Republican of New York, that would have created a wholly new type of investment credit that would have gone only to businesses that increased their number of employes. The traditional investment credit is given against the cost of equipment, whether or not the purchase creates new jobs.

The amendment increasing the personal exemption to $800, effective next Jan. 1, was offered by Senator Vance Hart, Democrat of Indiana.

The increase in the personal exemption would be $50 per person more than was already contained in the bill and the revenue loss would amount to an estimated total of $1.9-billion a year.

Under the tax bill as it passed the House, and as it was approved by the Senate Finance Committee, the present personal exemption of $650 was increased to $675 for this year and to $750 for 1971.

The plans of Senate Democrats to offer campaign financing amendments to the tax bill appeared likely to bog the bill in controversy for some days. The proposal would split the Senate on essentially party

lines; it is the Democratic party that urgently needs money for the 1972 campaign.

If the campaign financing amendment were adopted, however, as part of the tax bill, it would be extremely difficult for President Nixon to veto the entire measure just to get rid of the amendment.

It appeared probable that the joint Senate-House conference committee would approve a campaign financing provision if the Senate passed it. That is because the leader of the House conferees would be Representative Wilbur D. Mills of Arkansas, himself a Democratic Presidential hopeful.

The precise form that the campaign financing provision would take has not yet been worked out by the Senate leaders who were conferring on the matter with the chairman of the Senate Finance Committee, Russell B. Long of Louisiana.

It seemed likely that the proposal would have two parts. The first would provide that any individual who wished to do so could assign $1 of his annual tax payments for use in financing Presidential campaigns, with the money to be divided equally between the two major political parties. Provision would be made to divert some of the money to third or fourth parties providing they were large enough.

A second section of the proposal would provide for a tax deduction or a credit for contributions made to political parties.

The Senate's decision to increase the personal exemption to $800 came after several attempts at a different approach to individual tax deduction had failed.

The different approach was a tax credit of $25 or $50 per individual and $50 or $100 per couple.

Advocates of this approach, who included Mr. Bayh of Indiana and Senator Gaylord Nelson of Wisconsin, both Democrats, and Jack Miller of Iowa, a Republican, all argued that the tax credit was a fairer method of cutting personal taxes.

Their point was that a $50 credit brings a tax saving of $50 to every taxpayer, regardless of income level.

A $100 increase in the personal exemption, on the other hand, brings a tax saving of only $14 to those in the bottom taxable bracket but $70 to those in the top tax bracket.

Victory for Feminists

The amendment provision that deduction for day-care cost for children and invalids be treated as business deductions marked a departure in the law and a victory for the feminist movement.

Feminists have been arguing that it is unfair to permit business executives to charge off drinks, meals and entertainment as business expenses, necessary to their work, when working mothers cannot so charge the costs of child care.

At present, there is a child-care deduction in the tax law, but it is limited to very low-income families. The provisions adopted by the Senate today would permit deductions to up to $400 a month for child care or invalid care in the home, and for other household help, without any income limitations, if there were only one employable adult in the home.

For a working couple, the same deduction would be taken if their income did not exceed $12,000.

SENATE MODIFIES A CHILD-CARE BILL TO BAR NEW VETO

Gives States Equal Footing With Cities on Sponsors— House Fight Seen Likely

By MARJORIE HUNTER
Special to The New York Times

WASHINGTON, June 20—The Nixon Administration won major concessions today as the Senate passed a modified bill creating a vast network of day-care centers and child-development services. The vote was 73 to 12.

President Nixon had vetoed a broader bill last year, protesting that it was characterized by "fiscal irresponsibility, administrative unworkability and family-weakening implications."

As modified by the Senate, the new bill seeks to overcome the President's key objections. However, the Administration has not yet said whether the new version would be approved by the President.

Conflict Looms

Some of the modifications tailored to avoid a second Presidential veto may have made the bill unacceptable to key backers of pending child-care legislation in the House and a major conflict between the two houses is likely to develop.

In its major concession to the Administration, the Senate agreed, 45 to 38, to sharply limit the number of potential prime sponsors of child-care centers by giving states equal footing with local communities in competing to run such programs.

Under the bill vetoed last December, the Secretary of Health, Education and Welfare would have been required to give priority to local community applicants submitting satisfactory plans.

The effect of the Senate action today would be to rule out most small or even medium-sized communities as sponsors, for the present Secretary of Health, Education and Welfare, Elliot L. Richardson, has said, he felt that no community with a population of less than 500,000 should operate a program on its own.

Those units of government chosen as prime sponsors would set up and administer the child care centers and programs, either on their own behalf or by contracting out the job to nonprofit agencies or groups.

This issue of local vs. state prime sponsorship is certain to be the major point of dispute in the House. Representative Carl D. Perkins of Kentucky, chairman of the House Education and Labor Committee, insisted last year that the bill, later vetoed by the President, permit communities of at least 5,000 to become prime sponsors.

In still another concession to the President, the revised bill would provide a much slower start in setting up child-care centers by delaying until July of 1973 the authorization of actual operating funds.

The bill vetoed by the President called for $2-billion in the fiscal year starting next July 1. The revised measure would authorize $150-million for planning and training in the coming fiscal year; $1.2-billion a year later and $1.25-billion the following year.

In other major concessions to the Administration, the revised bill would earmark 5 per cent of the funds for innovative child-care programs with the public school systems and earmark 10 per cent of the funds for model programs created through the Secretary of Health, Education and Welfare.

While agreeing to these modifications, the Senate turned back efforts by several conservative Republicans to limit the scope of the bill still further.

By a vote of 60 to 25, the Senate rejected a move by Senator Peter H. Dominick, Republican of Colorado, to cut back the authorization by $600 million.

As approved by the Senate, the bill would create comprehensive child development services, including day care centers, family counseling and a vast array of other health and social services for pre-schools, older children of up to 14, and their families.

The services would be free to poor children with family incomes of under $4,320 a year. There would be modest fees for families with incomes of up to $7,000 annually. And even more affluent families could enroll their children at fees set by the Secretary of Health, Education and Welfare.

As modified by the Senate, prime sponsorship of such programs would be limited to states and to communities of at least 25,000 population. In a series of votes, the Senate rejected efforts to set the minimum community size at 100,000 or 50,000.

The prime sponsors, in turn, could enter into agreements with nonprofit agencies or groups to actually run the centers. The curriculum, policy and funding for the program would be set by councils on which at least 50 per cent of the members would be parents of enrolled children.

While the bill emphasizes that enrollment is voluntary, Senator James L. Buckley, Conservative-Republican of New York, protested that the availability of free day care "might tempt mothers to take jobs at the expense of a child's well-being." He added, "It will have the insidious effect of subsidizing parental neglect."

The modified bill represented months of negotiations — seeking to overcome Mr. Nixon's objections—among the four major sponsors, Senators Walter F. Mondale of Minnesota and Gaylord Nelson of Wisconsin, both Democrats and Jacob K. Javits of New York and Robert Taft Jr. of Ohio, both Republicans.

THEIR BAIL WAS MADE HEAVY.

Physicians and Women Who May Be Sentenced to Long Imprisonment.

Five physicians and ten midwives were arraigned in the Yorkville Police Court yesterday to answer to the charge of illegal practice. They were all held for examination next week. The prisoners were:

Lee Randall, 154 East Thirtieth Street; William Krausi, 216 East Seventeenth Street; Newton Whitehead, 218 East Forty-eighth Street; Selden W. Crowe, 217 West Forty-ninth Street; Benjamin Hawker, 116 West Sixteenth Street; Caroline Becker, 237 East Thirty-fourth Street; Louise Schott, 244 East Thirty-ninth Street; Mrs. Landau, 318 East Fifty-sixth Street; Bertha Schwab, 215 East Seventy-seventh Street; Amelia Winkleman, 334 East Eighty-first Street; Elena Landgraf, 249 East Sixty-second Street; Ella Laughlin, 300 West Fifty-third Street; Mrs. Karch, 308 East Seventy-eighth Street; Christina Rathkraws, 169 East Eighty-first Street, and Walley Fromberg, 983 Second Avenue.

Ten of the prisoners were released on $1,500 bail each. Dr. Crowe's bail was fixed at $2,500, and his case set for hearing Friday next at 2 o'clock. Dr. Whitehead was held on $2,000 bail. Mrs. Landau was charged with manslaughter and held in $10,000 bail, in default of which she was locked up. All the prisoners except Mrs. Landau were charged with a violation of Section 294 of the Penal Code. The crime is a felony and the extreme penalty four years in the penitentiary.

March 25, 1894

COLORADO EASING CURB ON ABORTION

Governor Signs Measure to Liberalize Old Statutes— Panel of Doctors Set

MENTAL PROVISO ADDED

Health of Mother and Child a Major Factor—Incest and Rape Are Covered

Special to The New York Times

DENVER, April 25—Gov. John A. Love signed today a bill designed to liberalize the state's existing statutes on abortion.

The Republican Governor said he had received thousands of letters urging him to veto the bill after it passed both houses of the Colorado Legislature by substantial margins.

But he said he also received thousands of letters and telegrams urging him to sign the bill. Out of more than 5,000 letters, the ratio was about three-to-one against the bill, he said.

Early in the legislative session, Governor Love said the bill "sounds like something I can support."

But after heated public and floor debate on the measure he promised to give the bill careful scrutiny and read as much of his mail as possible before acting on the bill. He received the bill April 17, and had until Thursday to sign it or veto it. If he had done nothing, it would have automatically become law.

Panel of 3 Physicians

The bill permits therapeutic abortion, with the approval of a hospital panel of three physicians, when a child is "likely" to be born with a "grave and permanent" physical or mental handicap, the pregnancy results from rape or incest and provided gestation is no more than 16 weeks, a girl under 16 is pregnant from statutory rape or incest and when the pregnant woman would suffer permanent physical or mental harm by bearing the child.

Opponents said the bill deprived the unborn child of his right to life and that it would make Colorado the "abortion mecca of the nation."

Supporters said it would save lives, prevent unnecessary suffering and cut down on illegal "abortion mills."

The abortion law is believed to be the most liberal in the United States, but whether it will attract women from other states to come to Colorado for abortions is not yet known.

Colorado Residency

To be eligible for an abortion under the new law, a woman need not be a Colorado resident, but Governor Love said he had no fear this would turn the state into an "abortion mecca."

Cases involving pregnancy as the result of rape or incest probably would, by their nature, involve Colorado residents, the Governor noted. And "I am certain that the operations provided for will occur only in hospitals, subject to a severe test of accreditation, which will successfully prevent anything approaching abortion clinics," he added.

Even so, the Governor said he intended to keep a sharp watch on how the law is followed. "If we detect omissions or if abuses do, indeed, occur, we shall be the first to seek changes," he said.

The measure was probably the most controversial of the legislative session. It passed the House by a 40-to-21 vote, and the Senate by 20 to 13.

In approving the bill, the Governor said:

"The action of the Legislature in passing a bill which seeks to amend Colorado law in regard to the legal termination of certain pregnancies has presented to me one of the more important and difficult decisions of my experience in office.

"I have first looked at the present law which the new law seeks to amend. The present law in regard to the legal termination of a pregnancy has been on the statute books of Colorado for over 100 years. It provides that a termination is legal when procured or attempted by or under the advice of a physician or surgeon with intent to save the life of the woman or to prevent serious and permanent bodily injury.

"This law obviously leaves something to be desired insofar as safeguards and proper controls are concerned. It also seems to me to argue strongly that it has long since been decided that certain pregnancies may be terminated under the law and that therefore it is the extension proposed in the amendment that is now an issue.

"The new law does several things. First it extends beyond the possible death of the woman or her serious physical injury to include mental impairment of a serious and permanent nature when verified by a psychiatrist. It also extends to cases in which it is likely that the child would have a grave and permanent physical deformity or mental retardation. Finally it extends to certain cases of rape and incest."

Governor Love also said that under the new law, the termination of the pregnancy could be performed only in hospitals licensed by the Colorado State Department of Health that are accredited by the state's Joint Commission on Accreditation of Hospitals.

Gynecologist Is Opposed

DENVER, April 25 (UPI)—One opponent of Colorado's new abortion law said it would "signal a flood of calls from all over the United States begging physicians in Colorado to solve pregnancy problems."

"The whole world now finds Colorado available," said Dr. Robert Stewart, a Denver gynecologist and former president of the Catholic Physicians Guild and now a member of its board of trustees. "It is a loose law and it needs tightening up badly."

Dr. Stewart said the board could include "three neurosurgeons, three chiropractors, three dandruff specialists or three specialists in itchy navels." He said he knew two Denver doctors who already had received telephone calls from women in New York City requesting abortions.

April 26, 1967

A GENETIC THREAT SEEN IN ABORTION

Mrs. Shriver Says Science Could Decide Who Lives

By FRED P. GRAHAM
Special to The New York Times

WASHINGTON, Sept. 8 — Mrs. Sargent Shriver said today that the use of legalized abortion to prevent mental retardation could lead to a society in which scientists would decide who should have children and when people should die.

Mrs. Shriver, sister of President Kennedy, said the Kennedy family foundation had joined in sponsoring the abortion conference at which she spoke today so that persons other than scientists would be brought into the decision making process on abortion.

The three-day conference at the Washington Hilton Hotel ended today. It was sponsored jointly by the Harvard Divinity School and the Joseph P. Kennedy Jr. Foundation for research in mental retardation.

Mrs. Shriver, who is married to the director of the Office of Economic Opportunity, said that serious moral questions had been raised by medical advances that made it scientifically feasible for some scientists to advocate the use of abortion as a remedy for mongolism or other birth defects.

If scientists are permitted to manipulate life in this manner, she argued, "someone lacking in moral judgment will surely advocate euthanasia as part of the solution to the population explosion."

She said a decision might be made to "do away with the people over 65 who are ill and tired of living," and that a board of scientists might select which couples could have children on the basis of a genetic prognosis.

The idea of the international abortion conference was to bring together theologians, social workers and lawyers, as well as scientists, to discuss the implications of legalized abortion, Mrs. Shriver said.

However, Miss T. Grace Atkinson, a delegate representing the New York chapter of the National Organization for Women, complained to conference officials that the discussion panels were dominated by academicians and by Roman Catholics. Most Catholics condemn abortion as a matter of religious faith.

In a press statement, Miss Atkinson termed it "outrageous" that only three women were included among 48 panelists The National Organization for Women advocates full legal access to abortions as a civil right of women.

At the final session this afternoon, Arthur J. Goldberg, chief United States representative to the United Nations, mentioned abortion only in passing and focused his remarks on the need to encourage peaceful qualities among men.

The abortion conference adopted no resolutions and announced no consensus. There were few demands for repeal of all laws against abortion and several speakers, including Protestant clergymen, suggested caution in liberalizing the abortion laws.

Dean Bayless Manning of Stanford University Law School said the state legislatures must balance "the reverence for the life of the unborn child with the well-being of the mother, other children and the prospective home environment of the unborn child."

He criticized the present laws, which he said were unenforced and tended to generate disrespect for law.

September 9, 1967

Abortion: Once a Whispered Problem, Now a Public Debate

By JANE E. BRODY

IN 1962, the local veterans' organizations in Rapid City, S. D., named LaVange Michael, a widow then 68 years old, as its "Gold Star Mother of the Year."

Three weeks after receiving this honor, Mrs. Michael was arrested for performing an abortion on a Minneapolis secretary who nearly died as a result of the septic operation.

By her own admission to this reporter, the elderly widow—a one-time nurses' aide—had been doing abortions since 1932 at prices ranging from $25 to whatever the traffic would bear. Her clients—eight or nine a week—came from all over the country. She assured herself of future business by giving each customer a small, white calling card.

When Mrs. Michael pleaded guilty to the abortion charge, the county attorney breathed a sigh of relief. He had wondered how he would be able to select a jury that he could be sure had in no way been helped by the defendant.

Mrs. Michael counts among her friends some of Rapid City's most prestigious citizens. Her son is a highly respected optometrist in the city of 43,000 and her daughter is married to a city councilman.

In a recent conversation, Sheriff Glenn Best asserted that until the Minneapolis girl had signed a complaint, he was unable to build a good case against Mrs. Michael, although virtually the entire town knew what went on in her attractive bungalow just a few blocks from the county courthouse.

Even the local medical society was not particularly anxious to put an end to Mrs. Michael's career, Sheriff Best said.

The widow finished serving her sentence — three years' probation —last June.

Her Case Typifies Problem

The case of the Rapid City Gold Star Mother typifies the abortion scene that has existed in cities and towns throughout the country for many years. Although abortion as a word was whispered behind closed doors, abortion as a practice has long been tolerated more or less as a necessary evil, something—as one Rapid City woman put it—"we swept under the rug."

In the last few years, however, interested men and women in many states have been peeking under the edge of the rug to see what is there and what might be done about it.

A four-week study of the current abortion picture indicates that their curiosity already has spurred several major changes:

¶It has brought abortion into public debate and cocktail party conversation thereby helping to dispel many myths long associated with both legal and illegal abortions.

¶It has compelled many persons who are seeking a liberalization of abortion laws—clergymen, doctors and others—to risk their reputations and often their jobs by helping women with unwanted pregnancies.

¶It has spurred many persons previously opposed to abortion law reform—including a number of prominent Roman Catholics—to restudy the matter and come out in favor of a change in the laws.

¶And it has succeeded in liberalizing the abortion laws in three states —Colorado, California and North Carolina—with many more states expected soon to follow suit.

"It is really remarkable how much the climate of public opinion has changed in just a few years," observed Robert W. McCoy, coordinator of the Minnesota Council for the Legal Termination of Pregnancy.

"I wouldn't be surprised if several states including Minnesota soon repealed their abortion laws and left the matter to physicians and their patients."

Until Colorado changed its law last April, abortion was a crime in all 50 states except to save the life of the mother. The District of Columbia and five of the states, including Colorado, permitted abortion when the mother's health was endangered by the pregnancy. The other states were Alabama, Maryland, Oregon and New Mexico.

Doctors Stretch the Law

In actual practice, however, many doctors throughout the nation have been stretching, twisting and torturing the law to fit what they regard as real medical needs—such as abortion when the mental as well as the physical health of the mother was threatened, or when her child was likely to be born seriously malformed.

These "extralegal" abortions have usually been justified on the grounds that carrying the pregnancy to term would so damage the woman's mental health that she might attempt suicide.

But extralegal hospital abortions have been an almost exclusive privilege of well-to-do women—particularly those who know about and can afford the psychiatric consultation recommending abortion to avert a possible suicide.

To Dr. Robert Hall, an obstetrician at Columbia-Presbyterian Medical Center and associate professor of obstetrics at Columbia University's College

The New York Times (by Ernest Sisto)

The Rev. Howard R. Moody
Outspoken advocate of reform

of Physicians and Surgeons, stringent abortion laws have forced both women and their doctors into a highly hypocritical situation. In a typical year, he said, 80 per cent of an estimated 800 hospital abortions in New York City are performed for "psychiatric reasons" to avert suicide.

"Yet, we know that all these women are not suicidal," the doctor said. "The abortions are done to preserve maternal health, not life."

"Abortion reform would permit us legally to do the hospital abortions that the more courageous obstetricians are now doing," Dr. Hall explained. "About 90 per cent of obstetricians simply tell their patients, 'I cannot help you,' period."

Even the woman of means must go through a tricky and elaborate procedure to obtain a hospital abortion. She must find the right doctor, the right psychiatrist, the right hospital with the right abortion committee.

The head of the abortion committee at one Middle Western hospital said that the decisions of these committees were often arbitrary. Some committee members may be swayed by animosity toward certain referring physicians or by the decisions of other members of the committee. In any case, he said, it is the patient who gets short-changed.

The woman without means or appropriate connections often finds herself seeking an end to her unwanted pregnancy in a bleak, dirty underworld where the Mrs. Michaels and many less savory characters thrive.

Estimates May Be Exaggerated

There are no reliable statistics on what goes on in this underworld. Estimates place the number of criminal abortions in this country each year at from 200,000 to one million. But the often quoted estimate that these

clandestine dealings result in the death of 8,000 to 10,000 women each year has been called highly exaggerated. Dr. Christopher Tietze of the Population Council says the number of deaths is more likely 500 or, at most, 1,000.

However, the victims of criminal abortions pay a heavy toll in terms of permanent injury and sterility.

For example, at Lincoln Hospital, in a socioeconomically deprived area of the Bronx, doctors finish about 400 abortions a year that have been botched up by amateurs. Dr. J. J. Smith, head of the hospital's obstetrics department, said that "at least 20 per cent of these women are admitted to the hospital seriously ill."

"Many suffer permanent kidney damage and sterility," he said. "Last year one girl died of a tetanus infection."

Most of the hospital's abortion victims are women with several children at home who felt that they simply could not house or feed another child.

Similar problems arise for the middle-class young woman who finds herself pregnant out of wedlock. Joan R., a 21-year-old New York girl who has been struggling along as a theatrical technician, said that in her job, "I could not even afford to be pregnant, much less have a baby."

Joan was unable to turn to her parents for help, and the abortion she obtained from a careless Pennsylvania doctor left her sterile for life.

The Rev. Howard R. Moody, pastor of Judson Memorial Church in Greenwich Village, is one of 31 New York City clergymen who are trying to help women like Joan take care of their problem pregnancies with a minimum of risk to their life and health.

The clergymen, Protestant and Jewish, formed a consultation service last June "to offer advice and counsel" to those women who are being "driven into the underworld of criminality or the dangerous practice of self-induced abortion."

Clergymen Counseled 800 Women

A woman seeking the service's aid first calls 477-0034 and obtains through a recording the names and numbers of participating clergymen in various parts of the city. Then she must make an appointment with the clergyman of her choice.

In the service's first five months, the clergymen counseled well over 800 women—half of them married, 20 per cent of them Negro and more than half of them between the ages of 18 and 25.

In all cases, the service provided "the best medical advice to take care of the problem pregnancy," Mr. Moody said. He added that about 90 per cent of the women chose to go through with an abortion.

Mr. Moody expects that clergymen in other cities will soon be offering similar services to women with problem pregnancies.

Such help also is being offered by a number of persons active in efforts to liberalize abortion laws. One of them, Lawrence Lader, has told college forums at Cornell University, Harvard Medical School and Michigan

State University that he will get "the best medical services" for "any woman in need."

Mr. Lader said that since his book, "Abortion," was published in April, 1966, by Bobbs-Merrill ($5.95), he has helped 400 women who have called or written to him.

Mr. Lader and others like him who are openly defying abortion laws believe they are acting in good faith to meet a "human need" that is not being answered by "cruel, inhuman laws."

Publicity Caused a Change

Efforts to reform these laws received their initial impetus in 1962 when Mrs. Robert (Sherri) Finkbine, a Phoenix, Ariz., mother of four, inadvertently took the birth-deforming drug thalidomide during the early weeks of her fifth pregnancy.

The fate of Mrs. Finkbine showed that stretching of abortion laws was not enough. Doctors saw just how restricted they could be in trying to exercise their best medical judgment. Mrs. Finkbine's abortion, which at first had been approved, was denied when news accounts of her case brought it to the attention of the county attorney. He said that he would be forced to prosecute if a complaint was filed about the operation.

After much delay, Mrs. Finkbine had an abortion performed in Sweden, where doctors confirmed that her child would have been severely deformed.

The Finkbine case coincided with another development that inspired extensive discussion of the nation's abortion laws. The American Law Institute, one of the most prestigious of legal bodies, formulated a Model Penal Code to serve as a blueprint for reform of outdated criminal laws.

The code suggests a law that would permit abortions to be performed in hospitals when the patient's physician and a hospital abortion committee agree that the pregnancy is endangering the mental or physical health of the mother, or when the pregnancy resulted from rape or incest, or was likely to result in the birth of a child with serious mental or physical defects.

As rational and conservative an approach as this bill seemed to many to be, it was soon discovered that it would be anything but easy to get state legislatures to adopt it.

Even the nationwide epidemic of German measles in 1963-64—which left in its wake 20,000 stillborn and 30,000 defective babies because their mothers had contracted the disease early in pregnancy—moved only a few legislators.

Bill Lacked Doctors' Support

Oddly enough, in many states it was lack of support by the doctors themselves that led to the bill's demise. In others, strong opposition from some church groups—primarily the Roman Catholic Church—made legislators fear that a vote for abortion reform would be political suicide.

The Roman Catholic Church officially takes the position that human life and the human soul begin at the moment of conception, and strictly forbids destruction of the resulting embryo. Several studies have shown, however, that Catholic women obtain abortions nearly as often as women of other faiths.

Cries of "Murder" and "Infanticide," warnings of "Fetuses first, blue-eyed Irishmen next," and displays of preserved and bottled human fetuses characterized much of the opposition that helped to kill abortion bills the first and sometimes the second time they were introduced.

But those who have been studying the situation closely are confident that at their next introduction, abortion bills will pass in many states.

Assemblyman Albert H. Blumenthal, a Manhattan Democrat who recently reintroduced his abortion reform bill into the New York State Legislature, said, "Its prospects are much improved."

He noted that, among other encouraging signs, many legislators had polled their constituents and found that the majority of voters—regardless of religion—were in favor of reforming the state's law, which permits abortion only to save the mother's life.

The legislators' findings are consistent with those of a national survey

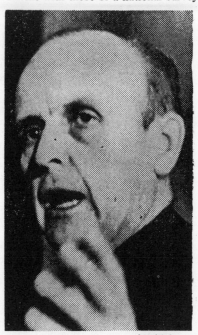

Associated

The Rev. Robert F. Drinan
Considers no law preferable

taken by the National Opinion Research Center in 1965.

Questions asked of a representative sample of 1,484 adult Americans revealed that 71 per cent would favor abortion if the woman's health was seriously endangered by the pregnancy, 56 per cent if she became pregnant as a result of rape, and 55 per cent if her child was likely to be born defective.

But when it came to social indications for abortion, 77 per cent said no to abortion if the family could not afford more children, 80 per cent said no if the woman was unmarried and did not want to marry the child's father, and 83 per cent said no if the woman was married but did not want any more children.

In Favor of Liberalization

"One of the most striking findings of the analysis," according to Alice S. Rossi, a research associate in human development at the University of Chicago, "is the relatively slight difference between Protestants and Catholics in their views on abortions."

Seventy-three per cent of the Protestants and 64 per cent of the Catholics said that they were in favor of abortion to preserve the mother's health. For rape, the figures were 57 per cent and 47 per cent respectively, and for a deformed fetus, 57 per cent and 48 per cent respectively.

While this survey is comparatively recent, many observers believe that the climate of public opinion is changing so fast that a survey today would show considerably higher percentages favoring the provisions of the model abortion law.

Some observers, among them Mr. McCoy of the Minnesota reform movement, think that a majority of adults would now sanction social indications for abortion as well. This would make abortion essentially a matter of personal choice.

Despite a history of inaction in this area, doctors also favor abortion reform, according to the results of a poll of the nation's practicing physicians taken early last year by the journal Modern Medicine.

Of 40,089 doctors who returned the questionnaire, 86.9 per cent said they were in favor of liberalizing abortion laws. Obstetricians and gynecologists were least in favor of liberalization with only 83.7 per cent voting for change as compared with 94.6 per cent of psychiatrists.

Slightly less than half the doctors who identified themselves as Roman Catholics were in favor of more liberal laws.

Well over half the physicians who answered the questionnaire said that abortion should be legally indicated in cases of risk to the mother's physical and mental health, chance of fetal deformity and pregnancy through rape or incest.

Two months after the results of the Modern Medicine poll were made public, the American Medical Association loosened its 94-year-old policy on abortion to favor the model abortion law. The association said the policy change was "in keeping with modern scientific safeguards, and permits the physician to exercise his personal conscience and medical judgment in the best interest of his patient."

This action by the largest and most powerful medical organization in the country—an organization noted for its conservatism—is expected to speed the trend toward more liberal abortion laws.

Even without a change in the laws, the new A.M.A. policy may allow doctors in at least one state to follow its recommendations. New Jersey law forbids abortions performed "without lawful justification."

In a recent statement, the state's county prosecutors interpreted this to mean that abortions could be performed in accordance with "accepted medical standards." This, in turn, could be interpreted as in accordance with A.M.A. policy

Bills to liberalize statutes on abortion were introduced during the last legislative sessions of more than 20 states. Legislators in those states where the measures were defeated are keeping a close watch on what is happening in Colorado, California and North Carolina, the three states that have enacted abortion reform legislation.

When Colorado passed its reform bill, which follows the guidelines of the Model Penal Code, opponents of reform predicted sourly that the state would become the "abortion mecca" of the nation.

This, in fact, has not happened. As Dr. David Cowen, manager of health and hospitals for the city and county of Denver, pointed out in a recent interview:

"In the first seven months under the new law, 115 abortions were performed in Colorado hospitals, 29 of them on women from out of state. That's hardly what I'd call an 'abortion mecca'."

Dr. Cowen explained, however, that only two hospitals in the state were accepting nonresidents for therapeutic abortions. He noted that before the law was two months old, the Colorado Medical Society strongly recommended that the statute should be limited to state residents.

"However, illness, including illness in pregnancy, does not respect state lines," Dr. Cowen commented. "If a heart patient who happens to live in Nevada can best be treated in Denver, we accept him. Why should we turn our backs on a nonresident who has a legitimate need for an abortion that can best be handled here?"

Most of the abortions done under the new Colorado law have been to preserve the mental health of the mother. This is the provision of abortion reform laws that has most frightened their opponents, who predict that it will lead to abortion on demand.

Dr. Abraham Heller, a Denver psychiatrist who has counseled many of the women treated under the new law, said:

"We are being very, very careful and discriminating. After all, there are few guidelines on what may be the proper psychiatric indications for abortion.

"Some women who have come to us for abortions have gotten pregnant for important emotional reasons

they're not even aware of. To grant them the abortion might do more harm than good."

In at least one Colorado hospital—Denver General—abortions that are medically indicated are done without regard to the patients' marital status. As Dr. Cowen said, "If a woman will suffer damage to her mental or physical health, it is just as real whether she is married or not."

More Restrictive Laws

California and North Carolina enacted somewhat less liberal abortion laws than Colorado. The California statute does not allow abortion when the child is likely to be deformed, and North Carolina excludes nonresidents from the benefits of its law.

Many reformers are now willing to admit that the model abortion law would barely touch the huge iceberg of criminal abortion. Mr. Moody noted that 99 per cent of the women his service has helped would not qualify for a hospital abortion even under the reform bill.

"The main reasons these women sought an abortion were emotional or economic," be said.

The Illinois Citizens for the Medical Control of Abortion advocates repeal of all laws governing abortions performed by licensed physicians. The reform group in Minnesota expects that a repeal bill will be introduced in the next legislative session, and that it may even have the backing of the state medical society.

Perhaps the most surprising move in the direction of repeal was made this fall by the Rev. Robert F. Drinan, a Roman Catholic priest and dean of the Boston College Law School. At an international abortion conference sponsored by the Kennedy Foundation and the Harvard Divinity School, Father Drinan described repeal as a more legally acceptable position than reform.

Priest States Position

He said that he was strongly opposed to putting the state in the position of "deciding who shall live and who shall die," as he said would be the case under the reform bill.

"It's a terrible thing to say in the law that we don't want any deformed or retarded children around," he said in an interview. "Furthermore, I think that the 'mental and physical health of the mother' is as phony as a $3 bill."

Father Drinan added that the model abortion law "won't reach the real problem, namely that 80 to 85 per cent of the abortions are for married women who just don't want this third, fourth or fifth child."

Associated Press

Mrs. Robert Finkbine
Her case spotlighted problem

"This is a social problem, not a medical one," he asserted.

His conclusion:

"If you say a problem exists, and that women will get an abortion and the law can't prevent this, all right then, withdraw the law. If we're going to have to change, I say the nonlaw has greater potential for solving the problem than the Model Penal Code."

Father Drinan and others pointed out that in a few years medical science will have made all abortion laws obsolete. Already under study are two kinds of drugs that can abort a woman in the very early stages of pregnancy.

One drug, referred to as the "morning-after" pill, can be taken up to six days after a woman has sexual intercourse, at a time when she is likely to be fertile. If she has conceived, the drug blocks implantation of the fertilized egg.

The other drug, called the Swedish "M-pill," initiates menstrual flow when taken once a month at the end of the menstrual cycle—regardless of whether or not the woman has conceived.

In both cases, the woman never knows if she really was pregnant. If not, well and good. If so, she has an instant, safe and sure abortion in the privacy of her personal life.

Advisers to Johnson Ask Repeal of Laws That Ban Abortion

WASHINGTON, July 12 (AP) —A Presidential advisory council recommended today repealing laws making abortion a crime and recognizing full legal rights of illegitimate children.

The council, headed by former Senator Maurine Neuberger, Democrat of Oregon, was appointed by President Johnson to suggest ways of improving the status of women. Its recommendations were proposed by various citizen study groups.

Mrs. Neuberger said the recommendations did not reflect Government policy but were made public to "stimulate constructive discussion on controversial topics and point the way to needed programs."

The council proposed drafting a model law that would give greater recognition to the property rights of married women, include voluntary separation as grounds for divorce and allow women to establish their own domicile for all purposes. Six states now give women that right.

Also proposed were laws to permit divorced mothers to receive public assistance without bringing criminal nonsupport charges against the fathers.

The panel called for a Federal-state system of temporary disability insurance tied to the unemployment insurance system that would include maternity benefits.

The council also recommended an earned income tax allowance for all employed people that would give a tax break to men and women, married or single, whose support came solely or largely from wages and salaries rather than from interest or earnings on investments.

July 13, 1968

Legal Abortion in Early Months Supported by 40% in Gallup Poll

PRINCETON, N. J., Nov. 29 — Forty per cent of the nation's adults favor legislation to permit a woman to terminate a pregnancy during the first three months, according to the Gallup Poll.

Among college-trained persons, the percentage in favor — according to a recent survey — is 58, the Gallup organization says.

Earlier Gallup surveys found a large majority of the public in favor of abortions where the health of the mother is in danger or when a child might be born deformed.

Moves are currently under way in many states to relax the legal restrictions on abortion. In most states abortion is illegal except when the life of the mother is threatened.

Ten states permit therapeutic abortions to protect the mental health of women, to prevent the birth of a deformed child and in cases of rape or incest.

Many Illegal Abortions

It is estimated that 8,000 legal abortions are performed in the United States each year, compared with 800,000 to a million illegal abortions.

Adults in their twenties are more likely to favor a law to permit abortion for any reason

than are persons over the age of 30 Gallup found. No difference was found between the views of men and women.

Three Roman Catholics in 10 expressed support for such a law, despite their church's official ban on the practice of abortion. About eight in 10 Jews indicated support for such a law.

The following question was asked of a national sample of 1,511 persons at least 21 years old who were interviewed between Nov. 14 and 17:

"Would you favor or oppose a law which would permit a woman to go to a doctor to end pregnancy at any time during the first three monts?"

Here are the results nationwide and by key population groups:

	Favor	Oppose	No Opin.
	%	%	%
National	40	50	10
College	58	34	8
High shool	37	53	10
Grade school	31	57	12
21-29 years	46	50	4
30-49 years	39	50	11
50 & over	38	50	12
Protestants	40	50	10
Catholics	31	58	11
Men	40	46	14
Women	40	53	7

January 28, 1970

ABORTION REFORM BY THE ASSEMBLY
DRAMA RUNS HIGH

Last-Minute Change Rescues Bill After Bitter Debate

By BILL KOVACH
Special to The New York Times

ALBANY, April 9—The dramatic last-minute switching of a single vote in the Assembly today moved New York State a step closer to the reform of its 140-year-old abortion law.

By a tally of 76 to 73, the Assembly voted to send the Senate bill, which would remove all but one restriction on abortions in the state. Since the Senate passed last month by a 31-to-26 vote an even more liberal version of the bill — one with no restrictions — sponsors in that house are optimistic they will accept the Assembly bill when it is considered tomorrow.

Governor Rockefeller has urged abortion reform this year and is expected to sign the bill if it reaches his desk.

An upstate Democrat, his voice choked with emotion, interrupted the roll-call at the last minute to switch his vote in a reversal that provided the key vote to pass the bill.

Stopped Roll-Call

Assemblyman George M. Michaels, of Auburn, his hands trembling and tears welling in his eyes, stopped the roll-call only seconds before the clerk was to announce that the reform bill had been defeated for lack of a single vote.

Seventy-six votes are required to pass an Assembly bill and without Assemblyman Michael's vote the bill would have been defeated.

"I realize, Mr. Speaker," Mr. Michaels said, "that I am terminating my political career, but I cannot in good conscience sit here and allow my vote to be the one that defeats this bill— I ask that my vote be changed from 'no' to 'yes.'"

In the confusion that followed —as secretaries applauded the move with tears streaming down their cheeks—few people saw Mr. Michaels slump in his chair holding his head in his hands, or heard Speaker Perry Dupyea ask that his name be called so that he, as Speaker could provide the final vote for passage.

After four years of concentrated effort and two long, emotional debates this year, the Assembly removed one of the remaining barriers to reform of the present law that allows an abortion only to save a woman's life.

The bill passed today would allow an abortion for any reason up to the 24th week of pregnancy and after that only to save the woman's life. The Senate version of the bill would leave an abortion up to a woman and her physician, with no restrictons.

Mr. Michaels's dramatic move came after four hours of debate during which five other Assembly members changed positions that they had recorded last week when the bill was defeated, but kept alive for the final vote today. Three of those changes were from "yes" to "no" and as today's roll-call moved toward an end, it appeared that the bill would be defeated.

Assemblyman Constance E. Cook, Republican of Ithaca and chief sponsor of the reform bill, was keeping her own tally and had given the bill up for lost when Mr. Michaels rose to save it from defeat.

Changes of votes from those cast last week reflected the intense lobby mounted over the weekend by the Roman Catholic Church, a sentiment expressed by Assemblyman Anthony J. Stella, Bronx Democrat, who switched from a "yes" to a "no" vote.

"Last week I thought I cast a vote representing the people who live in my area—it is overwhelmingly Catholic—and I did so because I thought it was not my job to legislate my own morality," said Mr. Stella, a Catholic. "But I was wrong. My fellow parishioners expressed their surprise that I voted the

472

way I did and made clear their feelings to me."

Other Catholic members, including some who did not switch their votes, reported intensive church pressure, including denunciations from the pulpit last Sunday.

One member reported that in his Catholic church in Brooklyn on Sunday, a young daughter sat by his side as he and others who supported the bill last week were described by the parish priest as "murderers."

"It was very tough pressure," this member said, "but I think the lay Catholic is far ahead of the church on this issue."

Another Catholic, Assemblyman Charles Rangel—a Manhattan Democrat and a Negro—denounced church pressure on the bill.

"My church," Mr. Rangel said, "saw fit to have my name called as one who acted improperly. And had it printed in the parish newspaper. But, I am hurt and disappointed that the clergy did not so act when we tried to stop the welfare cutbacks, or get decent housing, or get basic health care and hot water for our people."

"They did see fit to urge the parishioners to write me on the question of financial help for parochial schools and to protect the vested interest of their schools. But, I am amazed because I didn't receive one letter from a member about my vote."

The religious argument over the bill grew in intensity as the debate neared an end.

Other Catholics on both sides of the issue argued that their religious convictions did not form the basis of their votes. Instead, they argued, it was a moral issue and one dealing with individual concepts of life and death.

One Assemblyman opposed to the law, Neil S. Kelleher, a Republican of Troy, said the issue simply was one of "murder."

"It's our baby, so to speak," Mr. Kelleher said, his face red with anger. "I say, look at your own hands before you vote on this bill."

Picking up this theme, another opponent, Assemblyman John T. Gallagher, Queens Republican, warned his colleagues:

"I point the finger at every member who votes for this bill and say, 'You, sir, killed these innocent children.'"

At one point during the height of the debate, an elderly woman in the galleries had to be stilled by the capitol police.

"Murderer," she called out, her thin voice quivering in the still chamber. "You are murderers, that's what you are. God will punish you. You are murderers."

Similar emotional strains were woven through the debate in an ever recurrent thread that dominated all other arguments.

Mrs. Cook had attempted to guide debate with her opening statement along more pragmatic lines.

"This entire effort," Mrs. Cook said, "has been educational. It's just a matter of deciding that you can't sit here and decide who and when and how an abortion is to be performed — they are being performed now. My object is to get this whole question into the hands of a doctor and into the hospitals."

Much of the debate was a repetition of the hours already devoted to the measure this year and as the roll was called, it seemed clear that the vote would be a repeat of last week's narrow defeat.

When Mr. Michaels, who is convinced most of his constituents oppose reform, rose to offer the key vote, the battery of television cameramen were caught unaware, with their lens trained on the Speaker's chair to record the announcement that the bill was defeated. Mr. Michaels's first words were lost in the noise and confusion as cameramen jostled for position.

His face drained of color and his hands barely grasping the microphone, Mr. Michaels told of the fierce feelings within his own family over his opposition to the bill.

"My own son," Mr. Michaels said, sobbing, "my own son called me a whore for voting against this bill. And my other son begged me not to let my vote be the one that defeated the bill."

The other son Mr. Michaels referred to is a student at the Hebrew Theological Seminary in Cincinnati, and he served as Assembly chaplain for one day earlier in the session.

"I must," Mr. Michaels said, "keep peace in my family."

April 10, 1970

Sociologists Differ

Making abortion legal in New York solves a legal problem but raises substantial other questions: will it improve the lot of women, the sanctity of marriage, the morality of citizens?

The New York Times asked professors of sociology for their opinions, and got these divergent views:

DOROTHY SWAINE THOMAS, University of Pennsylvania —"From any viewpoint it's a good thing to relax the law and that's that. It's a good thing because the law is discriminatory against women. And I can see no way in which repeal of a law barring abortion could destroy the family or morality or religion. I see no harm at all, and I just do not agree that abortion means murder.

"Abortion has been an effective means of controlling population growth in Japan, Hungary, and Eastern European countries generally. It's likely to decrease the rate of growth of population here as well."

ROBERT NISBET, University of California, Riverside—"I am in favor of the utmost rational liberalization of our abortion laws, and that springs from my sociological mind as well as my human heart.

"It seems to me to be the right of any rational woman to make the decision to terminate pregnancy so long as it can be done within medically sanctioned circumstances."

THE REV. JOSEPH P. FITZPATRICK, Fordham University —"Abortion is primarily a moral problem that centers around the issue of human life, namely at what moment is a human life present in the womb and, if a human life is present, does anyone have a right to destroy it.

"The problem in the sociology of law arises when citizens no longer agree on the moral issue. If a majority of citizens no longer accepts a moral code, is it wise policy to attempt to enforce that moral code by law?"

"This is not a problem of morality: might does not make right; neither does a majority vote. Rather it is a problem of political wisdom: should a state seek to use the law to support a form of behavior which a majority does not consider morally binding:

"The decision of the New York State Legislature indicates that the consensus of opinion necessary to support a law is no longer present in the case of abortion legislation.

"Widespread violation of law is not in itself a reasonable ground for doing away with the law. But evidence of a loss of consensus does raise the question whether the law can reasonably be continued.

"Certainly the number of recorded abortions will rise sharply when the law is relaxed. Does this mean there are more abortions in fact than there were when abortions were illegal and clandestine? It is hard to say, but I rather think there will be.

"The social effects of legalizing abortion will be judged to be good or bad largely in terms of the way one judges social developments in a framework of one's moral values. In the framework of my own values, the legalizing of abortion is another indication of a loss of sensitivity around the basic issue of human life about which I cannot be optimistic."

MELVIN M. TUMIN, Princeton University—"Abortion is one of those cases in which we vote one set of morals against another.

"Judging by what's happened in the past with contraception, I suspect there will be significant use of the new liberty by all religious groups—including Catholics.

"Hopefully the new freedom will cut out the black market in dangerous abortions. It will save untold numbers of young men and women months of fear while they try to arrange an abortion. It will create a much healthier atmosphere for the bearing of children as an act of will, and will eliminate that horror called the accidental child."

MORRIS JANOWITZ, University of Chicago—"Abortion is indispensable for any rational and humane form of population control.

"What is striking is that the United States is so late in coming to abortion. Population experts here misled the country. They believed population growth could be controlled without abortion, and specialists in social sciences and policy made a decision to avoid pressing for abortion. The clamor in favor of abortion did not come from technical experts: it came from a popular movement."

JOHN E. HUGHES, Villanova University—"I don't think the legalization of abortion will make a lot of difference in family life. Abortion is not a step taken lightly—legally or illegally.

"For unmarried mothers it might be the lesser of two evils, and I don't think it's a catastrophe to legalize abortion. Certainly there are situations in which it's medically or psychologically indicated."

April 12, 1970

A.M.A. Eases Abortion Rules; City Health Unit Expands Plan

By RICHARD D. LYONS
Special to The New York Times

CHICAGO, June 25 — The American Medical Association voted for the first time today in its 123-year history to allow doctors to perform abortions for social and economic reasons, as well as medical.

After a bitter controversy that raged for a week at the association's annual convention, the A.M.A.'s House of Delegates, which sets policy for the group, voted 103 to 73 to consider the performing of abortions ethical if the following conditions are met:

¶That the doctor be properly licensed to practice medicine.

¶That the operation be performed in a hospital accredited by various public health organizations.

That two other physicians be called in for consultation.

Today's stand, which was regarded as a surprising turnabout by many physicians here, is not quite so liberal as the newly enacted abortion laws in New York, Hawaii, and Alaska, which do not require the last two conditions.

But the new position has far fewer legal qualifications than laws in the 47 other states and it is bound to affect abortion reform campaigns in them.

After the vote, Dr. Gino Papola of Upper Darby, Pa., the president of the 6,000-member National Federation of Catholic Physicians Guild, said he intended to resign from the A.M.A. and he urged the nation's other 35,000 Catholic doctors to do the same.

"In effect, the A.M.A. has made it ethical for doctors to become paid executioners," Dr. Papola said in a telephone interview. "I certainly don't want to be a doctor in the A.M.A. under these circumstances."

However, the resolution adopted by the House of Delegates specifically states that a doctor cannot be compelled to perform an abortion if it "violated his good medical judgment" or is "violative of personally held moral principles."

Today's action is not expected to affect Roman Catholic hospitals, which contain nearly one-third of the nation's general hospital beds, since the resolution also states that hospitals do not have to perform abortions if their directors do not want them to. Few abortions, if any, are performed in Catholic institutions.

For 120 years the A.M.A. considered abortions unethical, stating in 1871, for example, "that it to be the duty of every physician in the United States to resort to every honorable and legal means in his power to rid society of this practice."

Over the years, however, some respected physicians would perform abortions if they believed that the pregnancy was a threat to the health of the mother.

Three years ago the House of Delegates voted to consider the performing of an abortion ethical if there were a threat to the mother's physical or mental health, a threat that the child might be born deformed, or if conception had taken place under criminal conditions such as rape or incest.

A dozen states and the District of Columbia subsequently altered their abortion laws. This fall the Supreme Court is to take under consideration the issue of whether a law that restricts abortion is a violation of a woman's constitutional rights.

The A.M.A.'s shift on abortion was prompted by a report issued last month by the association's 15-man Board of Trustees that "recommends that the House of Delegates establish a policy on abortion that would permit the decision to interrupt pregnancy to be made by the woman and her physician."

The trustees said they were worried that the new state laws might force doctors practicing in those states that have liberalized their abortion laws into what might be construed as an unethical position.

A special A.M.A. committee on Monday heard 52 witnesses testify on the Board of Trustees' recommendation with many Catholic physicians urging that it not be adopted. The Catholic policy on abortion is that the practice is immoral except when medical treatment, such as radiation for cancer, might kill the fetus.

Dr. Wesley W. Hall of Reno was voted president-elect of the A.M.A. Dr. Hall, a member of the Board of Trustees, will succeed Dr. Walter C. Bornmeier when his term expires at the 1971 convention.

Dr. H. Thomas McGuire of New Castle, Del., was elected vice president.

At 17, the Road to Abortion Is Lonely

By JANE E. BRODY

At 2:30 on a Thursday afternoon Carol, a solemn 17-year-old girl from a small Midwestern tourist town, stepped out of the first airplane she had ever been on and walked into the passenger terminal at La Guardia Airport.

She carried a fringed shoulder bag and an overnight case stuffed with a nightgown, several popular romance magazines, toiletries and $440 in traveler's checks. She expected to stay just two days.

Carol, an unmarried, pregnant high school senior, had come to New York to take advantage of the state's liberalized abortion law. She is among thousands of out-of-state women—from their teens to their 40's—who have come here since July 1 in hope of obtaining a legal abortion unavailable in their home states.

Many have come with definite appointments, others on the basis of tips, still others with little more than the hope that if they are in New York they will be able to find some doctor to help them.

Many of these women, faced with seeming endless delays, insufficient funds or lack of connections, have returned home the same way they came—pregnant, but minus the money they spent on transportation and living expenses.

Beginning tomorrow morning, they will face new problems. New city regulations take effect then that will prohibit physicians from performing abortions in their offices.

Carol (not her real name) was met at the airport by this reporter through an arrangement with a mutual acquaintance.

"It's exciting coming to New York," Carol remarked as the taxi from the airport crossed the Triborough Bridge into Manhattan. "It's too bad I can't tell my friends back home about it." It was one of the few comments she made about her dilemma during her stay here.

Carol had found her way to New York through an abortion referral service in her home state, which had made an appointment for her with an obstetrician-gynecologist on Manhattan's Upper West Side. The doctor had already reserved a bed for her at a nearby voluntary hospital where he expected to perform a dilation and curettage on her the following day. The total cost was to be $400.

A pale, pretty girl with shoulder-length blond hair, green eyes and a nervous, throaty giggle, Carol was shy and scared. In a voice barely audible across the doctor's desk she told him that she had had intercourse on two occasions. She remembers little about either of them. Both times, she was drunk. No, she had not used a contraceptive.

Marriage Out of Question

A doctor near her hometown had examined her a week earlier and told her she was eight weeks pregnant. Marriage, she explained later, was out of the question. The boy responsible for her pregnancy was still in school and, besides, she didn't love him.

At first she considered having the baby. "But I couldn't have given it away," she said. "I would have kept it and given it all I could. But I realized that wouldn't be much. It wouldn't have been fair to the baby."

Carol's parents are divorced. She had been living with her mother, two small brothers and her stepfather, who she said has beaten her on more than one occasion. Recently she had moved out and rented a room, but the prospect of bearing and caring for a child was more than she could face on her own.

In New York, the gynecologist took Carol's medical history and explained what the abortion would be like. Then he examined her. He discovered that she was about 16 weeks pregnant, not nine weeks as she had thought.

"I'm sorry, Carol," the doctor said, "but you're too late. I can't help you."

'Salting Out' Suggested

He explained that at her stage of pregnancy, a D and C

—surgical removal of the womb's contents either by scraping or suction—was not safe; she would have to have what is commonly called a "salting-out"—an injection of a salt solution into the uterus that triggers a miscarriage some 12 to 48 hours later. The doctor cautioned her that a salting-out was a basically simple but potentially dangerous technique that required considerable medical skill.

The doctor further explained that one of the hospitals where he practiced would not allow him to do this procedure on its premises, and that the other hospital allowed only three salting - out procedures each day. At the latter hospital there was already a waiting list six weeks long.

Until early September, the doctor said, he had been doing salting - out procedures in his office. "Then I learned that the Board of Health was going to make office abortions illegal in the city, so I broke up the equipment."

As the doctor spoke, Carol's eyes welled with tears. She was told that most hospitals in the city where late-in-pregnancy abortions were performed had long waiting lists. Moreover, in a hospital a salting-out procedure was likely to cost considerably more than the $400 Carol's real father had managed to give her.

Difficult to Wait

Because of her limited financial and psychological resources and because Carol had neither friends nor relatives in the city, it was clearly out of the question to ask her to wait around for weeks until a hospital abortion could be arranged.

The doctor suggested she try to find someone outside the city who would do the injection as an outpatient procedure, either in his office or in a hospital clinic. She could fly home immediately afterward or else wait in a motel until labor began and then check into a hospital emergency room to have the miscarriage.

Finally, the Manhattan doctor gave Carol the name of a physician in Syracuse who might help her, and his nurse gave her a copy of New York magazine that contained a list of several sources of abortion referral.

Then began a telephone marathon: 37 completed calls, and countless others that did not go through, all over the state. Throughout the two-day phoning session Carol was sullen, almost as if she expected each call to prove "no go."

These were the results of the calls, referrals, tips, rumors and false leads:

¶The Syracuse doctor said

The New York Times (by Barton Silverman)

Carol, unmarried and pregnant, waits for admission to a hospital here, seeking abortion

that no one in his city was doing salting-outs. He himself no longer did abortions in his office, but he named two other doctors who might help.

¶A nurse in the office of an Ithaca doctor said that he did salting-outs as outpatient procedures, but that the doctor would not schedule her until he examined her. With Ithaca a five-hour drive from New York City, this sounded too vague to Carol to warrant a long trip.

¶A doctor in Norwich would do the injection in his office for $375, but his nurse said he usually liked to wait until the 18th week of pregnancy. Again faced with a possible wasted trip, the girl demurred.

¶The Woman's Abortion Project suggested a doctor on Long Island who charged about $300. The physician, it turned out, was on vacation, but his answering service said that a "covering" doctor would call

¶A call to the Clergy and Lay Advocates for Hospital Abortion Performance brought the response that they "usually didn't do referrals." Nevertheless, they gave Carol the name of a doctor in Westchester.

A Shock to Carol

That doctor was "completely booked and terribly overworked," according to his nurse. He was doing about 30 salting-out procedures a week

in his office in addition to all his regular obstetrical work. This was a blow to Carol, for this doctor's fee was only $150.

¶Several doctors, whose names were supplied by the helpful Westchester nurse, offered some hope. One would do the procedure in his office for $300. Another would do it in a hospital clinic: his fee was $200 if Carol went home after receiving the injection; $300 if she returned to the hospital for the miscarriage. Hospital charges would run about $150 in the latter case.

Faced With Dilemma

Carol was frightened and confused. Having an injection and then getting on a plane for the Middle West without knowing when labor might start was risky. On the other hand, going to a hospital was more than she could afford.

Back to the telephone. The Family Planning Information Service, operated by Planned Parenthood of New York City, advised against an outpatient procedure in Carol's case. They offered to help find someone who would do an in-hospital abortion without much delay and within Carol's financial means.

At noon on Saturday Carol was in the office of a Brooklyn obstetrician recommended by the family planning service. For two and a half hours she sat

in the waiting room listening to other patients—women happily chatting about their wanted pregnancies. Carol shut her eyes, put her hand over her face and sank lower and lower into her chair. She didn't say a word.

Finally, after all the other patients had left, the doctor called Carol in. Again, an examination, medical history and Carol's story.

The doctor told her that the hospital required an advance cash payment of $325 that would cover her regardless of how long she stayed. His fee, he said, was $350, but he was willing to do the procedure for the $75 Carol could give him if she promised to pay the rest in installments afterward.

"However," he added, "the hospital is heavily booked and I can't give you a definite appointment. You'll just have to wait for my call."

Thoroughly depressed, Carol slept for most of the next 36 hours. Late Monday morning, the doctor called and said she could enter the hospital the next morning. She called her father with the good news. "I can't wait to see you again," she told him.

Letter of Consent

At 9 A.M. Tuesday, Carol was admitted to the maternity floor of a small, old hospital in Brooklyn's East New York section. She was already in her nightgown in her hospital bed, two doors from a nursery full of newborn babies, when the administration decided that Carol's telegram of consent from her father was insufficient. Carol could stay in the hospital, but the procedure could not be done until they received a letter with her father's notarized signature.

Another call to her father. "I just want to get it over with and go home," she said over and over again.

At 10 A.M. Wednesday, the special delivery letter arrived and a few minutes later the doctor injected the salt solution. Then there was nothing to do but wait until labor started. Finally, at 10 P.M. Thursday the cramps began. All night Carol paced the floor, did situps and jumped up and down with her labor. At 8 A.M. the next morning she expelled the fetus. Two and a half hours later, the doctor assisted in removing the placenta, which she had retained.

When it was over, Carol was exhausted and running a high fever. In her almost delirious state, she muttered that she never wanted "anything like it to happen again."

The doctor spoke to her about birth control. He gave her a prescription for oral contraceptives and told her about contraceptive foam. He cautioned her that regardless of her intentions, sometimes things happen, and most men expect the woman to take care of contraception.

Carol was discharged from the hospital on Saturday morning with a prescription for antibiotics to control the low-grade fever she was still running. Seven hours later she was headed home by plane.

Throughout her experience Carol had said little of how she felt except for her periodic lament about getting it over with and going home. But her face spoke what her lips failed to utter. She left New York nine days after she had arrived and her once-babyish face seemed to have aged a year for every day she had been here.

Abortion Laws Gaining Favor As New Statutes Spur Debate

By JANE E. BRODY

A dramatic liberalization of public attitudes and practices regarding abortions appears to be sweeping the country, even in a number of states that still have restrictive abortion laws.

The change in the way Americans view abortions can be seen in the tremendous increase in legal abortions in this country, the growing participation of clergymen as prime movers in abortion reform and referral and the increasingly liberal interpretation of existing state laws by the medical profession.

Earlier this month, in the first instance in which a liberal abortion law was put to a public referendum, 55.5 per cent of voters in the State of Washington favored an eased law that leaves the decision to have an abortion up to the woman and her physician.

As abortion laws and attitudes relax, more and more doctors and hospitals are doing abortions. Dr. Christopher Tietze of the Population Council estimates that as many as 200,000 legal abortions will be performed in the United States this year, compared with about 18,000 just two years ago.

The new view of abortions reflects the combined action of many social forces, among them a growing concern with overpopulation, increasing demands for women's rights and roles outside the home, rising welfare rolls and illegitimacy rates, growing numbers of child abuse and child neglect cases and a general easing of sexual proscriptions.

Perhaps the most important liberalizing force has been the recent relaxation of restrictive abortion laws in 16 states and the publicity that surround these legal changes.

As one observer of the abortion scene remarked recently, "People tend to equate illegality with immorality; when abortion is no longer illegal, the stigma of immorality tends to fall away."

Reports from around the country this month revealed that fewer and fewer people tend to regard abortion as starting with a red letter "A." In some cases, in fact, the traditional hard-line opposition to abortion appears to be declining among Roman Catholics, laymen and clergy alike.

"A liberal abortion law shows a mature attitude of society," said Mrs. Myrtle Carr, a Portland, Ore., mother of one. "I used to feel that it was morally wrong to have an abortion —sinful, but I have read more on it, thought more about it."

Mrs. Q. Kenneth Bogaard, a middle-aged mother of two grown sons in Cedar Rapids, Iowa, remarked: "My attitude has changed over the last three years because of increasing published material presenting new information and the other side of the argument. I have misgivings about making abortions too easy for unwed mothers but I prefer this to the clandestine 'coat hanger' operation in back rooms by unskilled, unscrupulous operators."

Opponents Shift Views

Even among people who disapprove of abortions, many are broadening their views. As a West Coast father of two said, "Morally, I've thought abortion is wrong and I still do, but there are too many people for the bread that is available."

In Madison, Wis., several women made comments similar to this housewife: "I wouldn't have one myself, but if someone else wants to, why shouldn't they be able to?"

Although the Roman Catholic Church remains firmly opposed to abortions, the comments of the Rev. Carl Lezak, associate pastor of St. Sebastian's Roman Catholic Church in Chicago, were typical of a small but growing number of Catholic clergymen:

"I'm not taking any public position on the morality of abortion. I'm saying we ought to get out of legislating public morality in private matters. I'm certain there has been a great swing among Catholics toward favoring abortion reform."

One of those Catholics is Mrs. Arnold Geiger, a 26-year-old mother from Anchorage, Alaska. She said she had opposed abortions "as a matter of religious philosophy," but that recently her view has changed.

"I find there's more to a baby than having it—like supporting it, caring for it," she remarked. "I don't think adoption agencies are solving the problem of unwanted children. There's still too many kids around that aren't wanted."

Exceptions Are Asked

In Pittsburgh, where several Catholic physicians were reported doing abortions, Dr. Rose Middleman, medical coordinator of the Planned Parenthood center, said, "Quite often patients will say 'I'm Catholic but I feel I have to have this abortion,' or 'I'm Catholic but I don't agree with my church on abortion.'"

In the meantime, non-Catholic clergymen throughout the country are becoming increasingly active in the movement toward liberal abortion laws. There are now 28 Clergy Consultation Services on Abortion in 22 states, compared with just 11 eight months ago.

City's Year-Old Abortion Record Hailed

By JANE E. BRODY

In the first year under the nation's most liberal abortion law, New York City doctors have performed more abortions—165,000—than anyone thought possible a year ago, maintaining what health officials regard as an excellent safety record.

Despite a host of institutional difficulties, public confusion and professional footdragging when the law took effect last July 1, today there are almost as many abortions being done as there are babies born in the city —950 abortions for every 1,000 births. And the number of abortions continues to grow rapidly.

At the same time, the rate of medical complications has been lower than expected and compares favorably with that in other countries with liberal abortion laws.

'A Good Example'

Basically, the New York law leaves the decision to have an abortion up to the woman and her doctor within the first 24 weeks of pregnancy. It contains no residency requirement, and 64 per cent of the abortions in the city have been performed on women from other states and other countries.

"We have set a good example for other states to follow," said Dr. Jean Pakter, head of maternal services for the city. "New York would be happy to relinquish its role as abortion center for the country."

At a news conference yesterday, Gordon Chase, the city's Health Services Administrator, said that "the catastrophe many foresaw a year ago failed to materialize."

"We have been able to serve our residents as well as substantial numbers of out-of-state women, and, most important, we are serving women safely," he said.

Abortion capabilities outside of the city have evolved much more slowly. The abortions performed in other parts of the state will account for only about 20 per cent of the projected total of 207,000 abortions in the first year,

and most of those were done in only five counties — Nassau, Suffolk, Westchester, Erie and Monroe.

Some of the counties have reported only a handful of abortions, and a few have reported none at all. But a check of several major cities indicated that the needs there

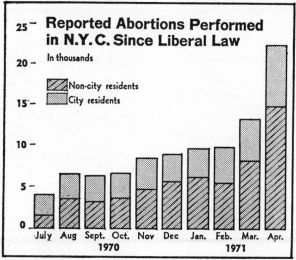

Reported Abortions Performed in N.Y.C. Since Liberal Law

In thousands

- Non-city residents
- City residents

July Aug Sept. Oct. Nov Dec Jan. Feb. Mar. Apr.
1970 — 1971

The New York Times   June 30, 1971

were being met. Only about 3 per cent of the city's abortion patients are from upstate.

Trends throughout the year continued to move in directions that buoyed the hearts of city health officials. At yesterday's news conference, officials cited the following statistics:

¶More women today are seeking their abortions early in pregnancy when the procedure is safest, easiest and least costly. In July and August, 68.6 per cent of the abortions were done before the 13th week of pregnancy. This percentage is now over 80.

¶Medical complications associated with legal abortions have declined from a rate of 12.4 for each 1,000 abortions at the outset to 8.7 for each 1,000 by mid-June.

¶The mortality rate s also dropping. As of February, there had been 15 abortion-associated deaths, eight of which followed abortions performed under legal auspices. There have been no deaths

reported in the last four months.

¶Nonwhite and poor women, who had little access to legal abortions prior to last July, apparently are getting abortions without much difficulty under the new law. In the first six months, nonwhites

and Puerto Ricans received half the abortions done on women in the city, and in the first nine months 31 per cent of New York City abortions done on state residents were reimbursable under Medicaid.

Illegal Operations Down

Health officials also cited, with gratification, statistics indicating that the number of illegal abortions had indeed dropped since legal abortions became readily available.

Hospitals in the city report that they are treating far fewer victims of botched abortions than they did in years past. The maternal mortality rate — to which criminal abortions have always contributed a major portion—is now at a record low of 2.3 for each 10,000 live births, compared with 5.2 for each 10,000 at this time last year.

Illegitimate births have also decreased for the first time in more than a decade, and the rate of live births

has begun to fall off in the municipal hospitals after years of steady increase.

All efforts in the Legislature to curtail the law with crippling amendments or repeal it entirely have thus far failed. None of the proposals to amend the law even came to a vote during the last session.

The only action the Legislature took concerning abortions was to ban profit-making referral services and fee-splitting between hospitals and referral services and to assure the confidentiality of abortion records.

Largely through the pressure of nonprofit groups and the proliferation of low-cost abortion clinics, the cost of an abortion has come down dramatically. Whereas in July, an early abortion was likely to cost $300 to $600, today no woman should have to pay more than $250. The cost of a late abortion has dropped from about $800 to about $400.

Procedures Change

Implementation of the abortion law has ushered in an entirely new approach to the delivery of health care. More than half the abortions in the city have been performed without costly overnight hospitalization —either as outpatient procedures in hospitals or in free-standing clinics.

Abortion clinics have sprung up throughout the city, with current estimates of the number ranging well into the twenties, and new ones are opening every week. However, only a few — the medically sound ones that handle large numbers of patients at low cost — are expected to survive.

Some communities, however, have moved to prevent abortions in clinics and restrict them to hospitals.

Dr. Nathanson, who had been highly skeptical of the city's ability to handle the abortion program, remarked the other day:

"I look around one year later and I'm astonished to find how smoothly, efficiently, safely and inexpensively it's all worked out despite the prophets of gloom and disaster."

Nationwide Drive for Abortion Planned in 3-Day Session Here

By LAURIE JOHNSTON

Leaders of a national conference on abortion pledged yesterday to pursue a coordinated campaign for the nationwide repeal of all laws against abortion, despite the walkout at their final session, on Sunday, of a caucus that sought to tie "the Lesbian issue" to the campaign.

The three-day conference, called by the Women's National Abortion Coalition, drew a registration of 1,025 women from 25 states to MacMillan Auditorium of Columbia University. It ended in some disorder when representatives claiming to speak for nearly a fourth of those attending took over the microphones to announce their withdrawal after a demand for laws guaranteeing "freedom of sexual expression" had been voted down.

A majority of the conference voted to campaign for legislation and litigation, on state and Federal levels, based on three issues: repeal of all laws against abortion, no forced sterilization and no restrictions on contraception.

Caucus members, calling themselves WISE — "Women for the Inclusion of Sexual Expression" — had demanded that the national campaign also should include efforts toward "free, quality abortions on demand," rather than mere repeal of laws against abortion.

The "WISE women" were joined at the opening and final sessions by Kate Millet, feminist author of "Sexual Politics."

The conference staff canceled a news conference scheduled for yesterday, but Deborah Notkin, a member of the staff, said that both demands by the caucus were "pretty far-out for a broad coalition," depending for its support on women from all over the country. She said "nearly all" of those involved in the walkout were from New York.

Joanne Steele, a leader of the caucus, issued an opposition statement on the sidewalk outside the conference's headquarters, at 137A West 14th Street.

Outside Influence Charged

She said the conference goal that "every woman should have control over her own body" was impossible without inclusion of the two caucus demands.

She also charged the conference had been unduly under the influence of the Socialist Workers party, of which Miss Notkin said she was a member.

Emily Campbell Moore, a staff member of the Population Council and former chairman of New Yorkers for Abortion Law Repeal, said she went to the conference "not expecting the Lesbian issue to come up."

She called it "counterproductive," and said, "I recognize that the issues of feminism and women's control of their own bodies involve both abortion and Lesbianism, but this was purely an abortion meeting, not a feminist meeting."

"We need to be single-minded," she added. "We have to go before gray-haired legislators all over the country, and there will be no 'free abortions on demand' where abortions are still illegal. Kate Millet may be right in principle but politically she's a fool."

Nancy Stearns, a lawyer for the Center for Constitutional Rights, said she talked to delegates from many states "who saw the conference as a turning point in abortion reform and wanted to unite around that one issue."

She said there were "gay women and straight women," as well as black women and white women, for and against the caucus positions and she did not "think they were being used by any political group."

Bar Group Supports Eased Abortions

By FRED P. GRAHAM
Special to The New York Times

NEW ORLEANS, Feb. 7—The American Bar Association endorsed today a uniform statute to permit women to obtain abortions "upon demand." The association, however, rejected a uniform no-fault divorce law.

Both proposals had been drafted by the National Conference of Commissioners on Uniform State Laws, a group of 250 judges, lawyers and law professors from the 50 states that tries to reduce disparities among state laws.

The A.B.A.'s 307-member House of Delegates, a traditionally conservative body heavily weighted with elderly corporate attorneys, approved the abortion proposal without debate and with only 30 dissenting votes.

The measure is more liberal than the laws now on the books in all states except New York and Hawaii, where abortion upon demand is now in effect. The proposed law would be slightly less liberal than these statutes, because abortions could be performed by physicians upon demand only within 20 weeks of the onset of pregnancy.

After that period, they would be allowed only to preserve the physical or mental health of the mother, if the fetus were gravely deformed or in case of rape or incest.

'After' Pill Backed

The uniform law would legalize a new development in birth control—the "morning after" pill that will eliminate any pregnancy if taken by a woman within 24 hours of intercourse. Pills of this type have worked in tests but have not yet been cleared for general use by the Food and Drug Administration. If they are cleared, the uniform law would make their use legal—even if technically this constitutes a self-induced abortion—as long as a doctor prescribes the pill.

The no-fault divorce proposal would have established "irretrievable breakdown" of a marriage as the sole grounds for divorce. California, Colorado, Michigan and North Dakota have recently passed laws adopting this concept, but in most other states divorces are granted only if one party is found guilty of such grounds as adultery, cruelty or abandonment.

On the issue of no-fault divorce, the association's section on domestic relations law objected. Some lawyers believe that the measure would drastically reduce domestic relations law practices.

Ralph J. Podell of Milwaukee, acting chairman of the section on family law, posed the issue as "whether the family itself in this country will go down the drain" because divorce would become too quick and easy.

The proposed law sets up a minimum 30-day cooling-off period after the filing of a divorce action and requires a divorce hearing within 30 days.

Speedy Divorces Scored

Frederick G. Buesser Jr. of Detroit, president of the Michigan Bar Association, assailed the "unseemly speed" of divorce under the new no-fault law in Michigan. He said the common experience of divorce lawyers was that reconciliations often occurred during the year or more required to obtain divorces in most states.

The statute would also reduce the legal age to marry to 18 years without parental consent and 16 with it. In many states the age is 21 without consent. It would also divide each couple's property evenly, rather than require judges to decide the amount of alimony on a case-by-case basis.

The National Association of Women Lawyers and the A.B.A.'s young lawyers section also opposed the uniform divorce act. It was rejected by a 170-to-72 vote.

The House of Delegates also rejected today, by a vote of 144 to 100, the District of Columbia Bar Association's request for endorsement of the concept of home rule and representation in Congress for the District of Columbia.

The Philadelphia Bar Association had asked the national organization to rescind the endorsement it voted last year of wiretapping by policemen with judicial approval. The House of Delegates declined to vote on the question, after the Philadelphia group agreed to discuss it further with other interested groups within the bar association.

The A.B.A. midyear meeting is being held at the Roosevelt Hotel here. The meeting will adjourn tomorrow.

Women Protesting Easier Abortions Storm Assembly

By WILLIAM E. FARRELL
Special to The New York Times

ALBANY, April 18—A dozen women stormed onto the floor of the Assembly today, swept past startled legislators and disrupted the proceedings by demanding repeal of the state's liberalized abortion law.

While attendants scurried after them and herded them to the back of the chamber, some of them yelled, "Stop abortion!" A few had to be carried out of the Assembly well into an antechamber.

One of the women, Mrs. Carol Joyce of Stony Brook, L. I., said: "We're not going to move until the Donovan-Crawford bill is let out of committee."

She was referring to bills sponsored by Senator James H. Donovan, Republican of Chadwicks, and Assemblyman Edward F. Crawford, Republican of Oswego, that would replace the abortion law with the one repealed in 1970, which permitted abortions only when the mother's life was imperiled.

The current abortion law allows a woman to have an abortion on demand up until the 24th week of pregnancy.

Today's incident, which irritated some legislators who favor the women's stand because they felt it hurt their efforts to bring a repeal bill to the floor, was another indication of the increased momentum here for repeal of the liberalized law. Yesterday 600 opponents of the new law rallied on the Capitol steps.

Amid reports that the Assembly Codes Committee might let a repeal bill out on the floor, Assemblyman Albert H. Blumenthal, a Manhattan Democrat who worked for years to effect the presnt abortion law, urged women throughout the state to "converge immediately on Albany to make known their support for the present law."

"Although the bill to repeal our present abortion law has not yet been reported out of the Assembly Codes Committee," Mr. Blumenthal said, "a strong possibility exists that this may happen within the next few days.

"It is urgent, therefore, that women immediately wire and call their local legislators, as well as descend en masse in Albany, to make known their determination that the present law not be changed."

The liberalized law passed in 1970 in the Assembly by a single vote, cast by Assemblyman George M. Michaels, Democrat of Auburn, when he switched from "no" to "yes." His vote was considered to have led to his defeat for re-election.

Opposition to the liberalized law has been well-organized and intense. Proponents of the new law fear that a repeal bill might carry in this election year. Many lawmakers who voted for the liberalization have been challenged in their home districts by its opponents.

President Supports Repeal Of State Law on Abortion

By ROBERT D. McFADDEN

President Nixon, taking an unusual step into a state legislative fight, enunciated his support yesterday for a campaign to repeal New York's liberalized abortion law.

In a letter to Cardinal Cooke, who has led a repeal campaign by the Archdiocese of New York, the President acknowledged that "this is a matter for state decision outside Federal jurisdiction," but he added:

"I would personally like to associate myself with the convictions you deeply feel and eloquently express."

With the Legislature slated to take up early this week bills to repeal or modify the 1970 law that permits a woman to have an abortion on demand until the 24th week of pregnancy, the President's support for repeal came amid intense debate on the emotionally and politically charged question.

The President's intercession drew prompt denunciations from two members of the Assembly, Albert H. Blumenthal, Democrat of Manhattan, and Mrs. Constance E. Cooke, Republican of Ithaca, who drafted and sponsored the current law,

More than 1,500 demonstrators opposed to any change in the law marched on Manhattan's East Side yesterday, spearheaded by a banner that read, "Abortion: A Woman's Right to Choose." Some counterdemonstrators engaged the marchers in shouted argument and carried placards of their own, including one that read, "Abortion Is Murder."

Commission's Plans Rebuffed

The President's letter to Cardinal Cooke, which was made public by the archdiocese, followed by a day Mr. Nixon's rejection of two major recommendations by his Commission on Population Growth. These called for greatly liberalized abortion laws in all states and a policy of making contraceptive devices and other family planning services widely available to teen-agers.

A spokesman for Governor Rockefeller, when asked for comment on the President's letter, reiterated the Governor's opposition to the repeal of the present law and said Mr. Rockefeller intended to support only his own measure to modify the statute.

On Friday, the Governor—who is Mr. Nixon's re-election campaign chairman in the state—sent the Legislature a bill that would permit elective abortions only until the 18th week of pregnancy. Mr. Rockefeller also reaffirmed that he would veto any total repeal of the present law.

A repeal bill, which would restore the 19th-century statute permitting abortions only when a mother's life is imperiled, is expected to spark a repetition this week of the fierce and impassioned debate that preceded the passage of the liberalized 1970 law. The repeal bill is sponsored by Assemblyman Edward F. Crawford, Republican of Oswego.

An Unusual Step

Mr. Nixon's letter in support of repeal was viewed by political observers in the state and in Washington as highly unusual in that it appeared to be a step into a pending state legislative fight.

While the President has commented publicly after state and Federal court decisions relating to school busing and integration, observers could recall nothing parallel to his taking a public posture on the abortion repeal campaign here.

The President first declared his opposition to abortion on April 3, 1971, in a directive to all military hospitals to conform to the abortion laws of the states in which they are situated. In thus reversing earlier regulations that had liberalized abortion policies in the hospitals, Mr. Nixon declared:

"Historically, laws regulating abortion in the United States have been the province of states, not the Federal Government. That remains the situation today, as one state after another takes up this question, debates it and decides it. That is where the decisions should be made."

In his letter to Cardinal Cooke, the President wrote:

"Recently, I read in The Daily News that the Archdiocese of New York, under your leadership, had initiated a campaign to bring about repeal of the state's liberalized abortion laws. Though this is

The New York Times/John Soto

ABORTION, PRO AND CON: Demonstrators marching up First Avenue carried signs defending abortion. A man, at right, held a sign calling abortion "a license to kill."

By WILLIAM E. FARRELL
Special to The New York Times

ALBANY, May 13 — In a strong denunciation of the "personal vilification and political coercion" that surrounded the issue, Governor Rockefeller fulfilled a pledge today and vetoed the Legislature's repeal of the state's liberalized abortion law.

The Governor's action meant that the current abortion law, passed in 1970, which permits a woman to have an abortion on demand until the 24th week of pregnancy, remains intact at least until next year.

In dooming the bill that would have abolished the current law and restored the state's previous abortion statute, which allowed an abortion only when a mother's life was jeopardized, Mr. Rockefeller said:

"I can see no justification now for repealing this reform and thus condemning hundreds of thousands of women to the dark age once again."

The Legislature, which adjourned last night, was under heavy election-year pressure in recent weeks from the Roman Catholic Church and "right to life" groups around the state to abolish the present law.

As the momentum to let a repeal bill be debated built up, Mr. Rockefeller attempted to head off the effort by announcing that he would veto a repealer, but would sign a bill that modified the present law and permitted elective abortions until the 18th week of pregnancy.

Governor Is Disturbed

But the antiabortion groups were not assuaged by this

---

a matter for state decision outside Federal jurisdiction, I would personally like to associate myself with the convictions you deeply feel and eloquently express.

"The unrestricted abortion policies now recommended by some Americans, and the liberalized abortion policies in effect in some sections of this country seem to me impossible to reconcile with either our religious traditions or our Western heritage. One of the foundation stones of our society and civilization is the profound belief that human life, all human life, is a precious commodity—not to be taken without the gravest of causes.

"Yet, in this great and good country of ours in recent years, the right to life of literally hundreds of thousands of unborn children has been destroyed — legally — but in my judgment without anything approaching adequate justifica-

tion. Surely, in the on-going national debate about the particulars of the "quality of life," the preservation of life should be moved to the top of the agenda.

"Your decision, and that of tens of thousands of Catholics, Protestants, Jews, and men and women of no particular faith, to act in the public forum as defenders of the right to life of the unborn, is truly a noble endeavor. In this calling, you and they have my admiration, sympathy and support."

Blumenthal 'Shocked'

Assemblyman Blumenthal, saying he was "shocked" at the President's letter, declared: "It's just inappropriate for the President to be doing this. It's a state issue, with strong religious overtones. We've been trying to avoid a religious blood bath, and no whe's come in and aggravated an already difficult situation only for political purposes. There's just no justification for it."

Mrs. Cook described the President's letter as a "patent pitch for the Catholic vote" and "obviously a political move." She asserted: "He hasn't had enough exposure to the pros and cons of the issue. I also think he greatly underestimates the support for the liberalized abortion law."

"The issue," Mrs. Cook added "is not whether we do or don't have abortions. The issue is where—in some dirty hotel room or some dingy back room of a doctor's office, or in a hospital under proper medical care."

The majority of marchers in the pro-abortion demonstration here yesterday were women. After parading from Bellevue Hospital to Herald Square and down Broadway to Union Square, the marchers attended a rally at which Mrs. John V. Lindsay was a principal speaker. She said she was "shocked" at Mr. Nixon's position on abortion.

May 7, 1972

480

move and said that it was "a numbers game" and that the only measure they endorsed was legislation restoring the old statute.

Those who favored revocation of the current law received support last week when the Archdiocese of New York released the text of a letter President Nixon had sent Cardinal Cooke. In the letter the President allied himself with opponents of the liberalized state law.

Mr. Nixon said in the letter to the Cardinal that "I would personally like to associate myself with the convictions you deeply feel and eloquently express."

Mr. Rockefeller, who is the President's re-election campaign chairman in the state, was reported to have been disturbed by the release of the President's letter in light of his vow to veto a bill repealing the 1970 abortion law.

In midweek, John D. Ehrlichman, the President's top adviser on domestic affairs, attempted to smooth over the issue by saying that the letter was intended as private correspondence and that granting permission to the archdiocese to publicize the letter was a result of "sloppy staff work."

Cardinal Cooke expressed his "profound regret" at the Governor's veto. In a statement issued by the chancery, the Cardinal said:

"Today is a day of great sorrow and regret for us and for so many men and women of goodwill in our state. After so many hurdles and setbacks, this week our Legislature came so close to restoring the principle of human life to the law of the State of New York. It was encouraging to see the Legislature recognizing that a government's responsibility is to protect life, not to allow its destruction."

The White House said today there would be no comment on the veto.

In his veto message, the Governor alluded to the election-year pressure that was applied in obtaining the Legislature's approval—79-68 in the Assembly and 30-27 in the Senate—of the repeal of the 1970 law when he said:

"I fully respect the moral convictions of both sides in this painfully sensitive controversy. But the extremes of personal vilification and political coercion brought to bear on members of the Legislature raise serious doubts that the votes to repeal the reforms represented the will of a majority of the people of New York State."

When the abortion issue was debated for a total of 13 hours by both houses this week, reports circulated in the Capitol that some of those who voted for repeal did so as an election-year expediency and not because of personal abhorrence of the law. According to the reports, these legislators voted for repeal because they were confident of the Governor's veto.

The debate in the legislature covered the entire emotional range surrounding the issue of abortion—certainly one of the touchiest issues that has come before the lawmakers. The arguments ranged from unresolved questions about when human life actually begins to allegations that the Roman Catholic Church was trying to have its doctrines translated into state law.

In his veto message, the Governor said that "the very intensity of this debate has generated an emotional climate in which the truth about abortions and the present state abortion law have become distorted almost beyond recognition."

Reverting to the old state abortion law, the Governor said, would result in those who could afford abortions seeking them elsewhere "while the poor would again be seeking abortions at a grave risk to life in backroom abortion mills."

Mr. Rockefeller noted that the present law did not compel abortions but instead allowed persons who wanted them to obtain them under medically sound conditions.

"I do not believe it right for one group to impose its vision of morality on an entire society," the Governor said. Nor, he added, is it "just or practical for the state to attempt to dictate the innermost personal beliefs and conduct of its citizens."

Text of Abortion-Bill Veto

Special to The New York Times

ALBANY, May 13—Following is the text of Governor Rockefeller's message to the Legislature vetoing repeal of the state's liberalized abortion law:

The same strong reasons that led me to recommend abortion-law reform in my annual message . . . for 1968-69 and 1970 and to sign into law the reform that was ultimately adopted in 1970, now compel me to disapprove the bill just passed that would would repeal that reform.

The abortion-law reform of 1970 grew out of the recommendations of an outstanding select citizens committee, representative of all affected parties, that I appointed in 1968.

Under the distinguished leadership of retired Court of Appeals Judge Charles W. Froessel, the select committee found that the then-existing, 19th-century, near-total prohibition against abortion was fostering hundreds of thousands of illegal and dangerous abortions. It was discriminating against women of modest means who could not afford an abortion haven and the often frightened, unwed, confused young woman. It was promoting hypocrisy and, ultimately, human tragedy.

Connecticut Case Cited

I supported the majority recommendations of the Froessel committee throughout the public debate of this issue extending over three years, until the Legislature acted to reform the state's archaic abortion law. I can see no justification now for repealing this reform and thus condemning hundreds of thousands of women to the dark age once again.

There is, further, the recent Federal court decision invalidating the Connecticut abortion law, which is substantially the same as the pre-reform New York law. The law of that case, if upheld, would clearly invalidate the old New York law, as well, were the repeal of abortion reform allowed to stand. In such a circumstance, this state would be left with no law on the subject at all.

I fully respect the moral convictions of both sides in this painfully sensitive controversy. But the extremes of personal vilification and political coercion brought to bear on members of the Legislature raise serious doubts that the votes to repeal the reform has represented the will of a majority of the people of New York State.

Risk to Life Seen

The very intensity of this debate has generated an emotional climate in which the truth about abortions and about the present state abortion law have become distorted almost beyond recognition.

The truth is that this repeal of the 1970 reform would not end abortions. It would only end abortions under safe and supervised medical conditions.

The truth is that a safe abortion would remain the optional choice of the well-to-do woman, while the poor would again be seeking abortions at a grave risk to life in back-room abortion mills.

The truth is that, under the present law, no woman is compelled to undergo an abortion. Those whose personal and religious principles forbid abortion are in no way compelled against their convictions under the present law. Every woman has the right to make her own choice.

I do not believe it right for one group to impose its vision of morality on an entire society. Neither is it just or practical for the state to attempt to dictate the innermost personal beliefs and conduct of its citizens.

The bill is disapproved.

WOMEN URGE AMENDMENT.

Feminists Want Organic Law to Forbid Sex Discrimination.

At the first meeting of the Executive Committee of the Feminist Alliance in the home of Miss Henrietta Rodman, 315 East Seventeenth Street, yesterday afternoon, a letter was written to President Wilson asking that he use his influence to obtain an eighteenth amendment to the Constitution.

The amendment desired, according to Miss Rodman, is to the effect "that no civil or political right shall be denied to any person on account of sex." The letter was signed jointly by the members of the committee, and it was decided to appeal to political and suffrage organizations for support.

The committee also protested against the law by which American women forfeit their citizenship upon marrying aliens, and indorsed the Thompson Immigration bill now before the Senate.

April 13, 1914

EQUAL RIGHTS DRIVE STARTED ON STATES

National Party Forwards to Branches Measure for Adoption by All Legislatures.

SUPPLEMENTS FEDERAL BILL

Proposed Blanket Law Removes All Legal Discriminations Against Sex In State Acts.

Special to The New York Times.

WASHINGTON, Sept. 25.—The campaign to have all legal discriminations against women removed was carried into its second stage today, when a draft of blanket laws was sent from the headquarters of the National Woman's Party to all State branches except Wisconsin, where it had already been passed. It is proposed to have bills carrying out the proposals submitted to the State Legislatures without unnecessary delay.

The text of the blanket bill is as follows:

Section 1—Women shall have the same rights, privileges and immunities under the law as men, with respect to the exercise of suffrage; holding of office or any position under the Government, either State or local; eligibility to examination for any position affected by civil service regulations; freedom of contract; choice of domicile, residence and name; jury service; acquiring, controlling, holding and conveying property; ownership and control of labor and earnings;

care and custody of children, whether legitimate or illegitimate, and control of earnings and services of such children; acting as executors or administrators of estates of decedents; grounds for divorce; becoming parties litigant; immunities or penalties for sex offenses; quarantine, examination and treatment of diseases, and in all other respects.

Section 2—This article shall be construed as abrogating in every respect the common law disabilities of women.

Section 3—The courts, executive and administrative officers shall make necessary rules and provisions to carry out the intent and purposes of this statute.

Section 4—All acts and parts of acts in conflict with any of the provisions of this statute are hereby repealed.

This bill is supplemental to the proposed equal rights amendment to the Federal Constitution which Senator Curtis, the Republican whip, and Representative Fess, Chairman of the Republican Congressional Committee, have agreed to introduce in Congress on Oct. 1.

Maud Younger, National Legislative Chairman of the National Woman's Party, in a letter to the Senate Chairman, said that there were two phases of the question which had to be considered in drawing up the amendment and the bill. The first was that all the discriminations against women should be included, and the second that industrial legislation, such as the eight-hour law and the minimum wage, should not in any way be touched.

"At first," wrote Miss Younger, "it was thought that perhaps a clause specifically exempting industrial legislation would be necessary, but we are informed by our legal advisers that this is unnecessary. As our measures now stand, it seems that they neither approve nor disapprove such legislation—they do not touch it. The consensus of opinion among the lawyers whom we have consulted is that the Supreme Court could at present, if it wished, throw out the industrial legislation for women as unconstitutional under the Fifth and Fourteenth Amendments to the Constitution, and that it can also do so if our proposed amendment is passed, but that our amendment and bill will not make it any more likely that this legislation will be thrown out."

September 26, 1921

WOMEN WILL FIGHT FOR 'EQUAL RIGHTS

National Party Gathers in Detroit Convention to Speed Campaign for Amendment

MISS ALICE PAUL PRESENT

Militant Founder Comes From Abroad for First Activity Here in Many Years

By KATHLEEN McLAUGHLIN
Special to THE NEW YORK TIMES.

DETROIT, Oct. 6.—Currents of public opinion which during the last two years have swept numerical and strategic strength to the National Woman's Party may be also, its members feel, that "flood tide of fortune" on which the equal rights amendment may be forced through Congress. This sentiment dominated the group tonight on the eve of the opening of the biennial convention, unanimously conceded to be the most important to date in the fourteen-year history of the legislation.

No greater impetus could have been given the event than the attendance of Miss Alice Paul, the Quaker girl who was the founder of the Woman's Party but whose militant tactics in the days of the White House pickets accounted for the most dramatic chapter in the history of the American woman's struggle for suffrage. Miss Paul, who recently returned from an extended stay abroad, will be taking part in a large assembly in this country for the first time in several years.

If further assurance were needed that the senior members of the Woman's Party would be prominent in the rally, it could be found in the list of speakers scheduled. Hardly second to Miss Paul as an inspiration to her colleagues through the years is Mrs. Emma Guffey Miller of Pennsylvania, sister of Senator Guffey, who will address a "democracy for women" mass meeting Sunday night.

Others include Mrs. Helen Robbins Bitterman of Ohio, Mrs. Burnita Shelton Matthews, Mrs. Rebekah Greathouse, Mrs. Harvey Wiley and Miss Anita Pollitzer, all of Washington, and Mrs. Florence Bayard Hilles of Delaware, immediate past national chairman.

Campaign for Amendment

Mrs. Stephen H. Pell of New York, present national chairman, will preside at all the business sessions, at which the plans will be laid for an intensive campaign for adoption of the amendment when Congress reconvenes. The measure, reading merely, "Men and women shall have equal rights in the United States and in all places subject

'EQUAL RIGHTS' BY AMENDMENT?

to its jurisdiction," seeks to put women on a civic and legal basis identical with that of men.

For fourteen years its champions have labored throughout the forty-eight States to convince other women that only by such a blanket measure can the remaining discriminations in the law affecting women be abolished. Various large feminine organizations oppose the amendment on the ground that it would cancel more laws enacted for the protection of women than its benefits might effect.

Emergence of the amendment on the floor of the Senate last Spring was acclaimed by its sponsors with the greatest enthusiasm, even though its voting status was dubious because of the pressure of business, and it was sent back to committee on motion of Senator Borah. It had languished and died in committee in too many sessions not to have the committee vote constitute a yardstick of progress.

Since the last biennial, also, the major acceleration experienced by the Woman's Party in a number of years has developed, in the affiliation with it of the National Federation of Business and Professional Women, which has gone on record as favoring the amendment. The unit represents 65,000 women employers and employes of the country.

Candidates Among Guests

Representative Virginia E. Jenckes of Indiana will be the principal speaker tomorrow at the opening session, on "Women in Public Service." Women nominees for Congressional posts will also be in the group of invited guests, it was announced.

Miss Vida Milholland, a sister of Mrs. Inez Milholland Boissevian, ardent suffragette whose death followed her collapse on the platform in California during the campaign for the vote, will be a soloist on the program of the impending convention. She will sing at a luncheon Saturday which will feature a reunion of the women who picketed the White House and President Wilson, and who went to jail for their militant activities.

Mrs. Emma A. Fox, for several years parliamentarian for the General Federation of Women's Clubs and the National Woman's Party, will be honored at a dinner Saturday night, for her successful efforts in enrolling the Michigan State Federation of Women's Clubs among the list of State federations endorsing the equal rights amendment.

Pearl Buck Favors A Constitutional Guarantee Now

By PEARL S. BUCK
Nobel Prize Novelist

THE fact that there are honest and intelligent working women against the Equal Rights Amendment has made me consider and reconsider my own position in regard to a change which would take away the protective legislation which many women have given their lives to build up for other women. I fully appreciate the value of this legislation. Women do need special protection, not because they are individuals of a certain sort but because they are the mothers of children. It is obviously to the interest of the nation that strong, healthy children be born, and provision should and must be made that women can do their work and bear healthy children too.

But this could be done in the same way that any protective legislation is brought about. Men, as well as women, suffer certain liabilities occasionally as to health and physical handicaps, and yet no one thinks of laying upon all men the handicap of sex inequality because there is need for special protective legislation. Moreover, many women are not mothers and they suffer from the inequality without profiting from the special legislation, and even the mothers do not spend their entire time bearing children. The actual time given to bearing children is relatively little in any woman's life. Even if she stays with the children for a certain number of years, she has many other years in which to function as an individual.

Pearl Buck.

I feel, therefore, after the most careful study of all sides of the question, that no amount of special benefit to women is good enough to offset the basic damage done to human equality. Special benefit for women is a manifestation of that old-fashioned "chivalry" which has kept women so long upon a pedestal of inferiority to men. The nation must recognize the value of women not as dear and weaker possessions but as hu-

man creatures in their own right and with a function to perform in all parts of our national life. To announce this recognition the Equal Rights Amendment is necessary. Only thus can the fact be established once and for all that in our democracy there is no difference in value, so far as the State is concerned, between the rights and responsibilities of men and those of women. Upon this equality whatever legislation is necessary for men or women can then be built.

Nor do I believe for one moment that the effort put into previous legislation will be wholly lost. Some of it ought to be lost—those laws which have made it possible for women to do less work merely because they are women have been accompanied by the evil of lower wages for women because they had less responsibility. But the legislation which recognized the special function of women as mothers and potential mothers can and will be kept, for it is based upon physical facts of importance to the whole people.

The time has come, I believe, for our American democracy to declare itself on this matter of the equality of men and women in the State. Our enemies, both in Germany and Japan, have openly declared the opposite. For us to say that we believe in full equality of the sexes would at this moment carry special power both for the war and the peace.

Opposition Holds Such Action Would Prove Illusory

By ANNA LORD STRAUSS
President, New York City League of Women Voters

OF course I am in favor of women having full human rights. Every woman with a liberal outlook is, and so are the men, but I do not believe that the so-called Equal Rights Amendment is the way to obtain these rights.

Let us look at the record and see why we have not had equal opportunity. There are two major reasons. The first and most important is social custom. Throughout the ages the history of women shows that they have had to take second place. Not only in the past but at the present time there is strong prejudice against having women hold certain positions, practice in certain professions, be the top-ranking person when most of the subordinates are men.

There is no law which denies them these opportunities which are rightly theirs. There can be no law which will assure them these rights. They simply are not given the chance because of a point of view which has had a long history. The human race is slow to change its ways.

The second major reason is that there are laws which restrict women's rights. These are not Federal laws, they are State laws—and there are comparatively few of them left in the country as a whole. These laws, then, are a concern of the States and it is up to the citizens in those States to see that the laws are so changed as to give equal opportunity. An amendment to the Federal Constitution would be illusory. Leading legal authorities agree that it would create chaos in the legal structure of the country—that the courts

Anna L. Strauss. everywhere would be jammed with litigation for an indefinite period.

Take, for instance, New Jersey. The age of consent to marriage is 12 for girls and 14 for boys. The so-called Equal Rights Amendment will not resolve that difficulty—if a discrimination it is—for there will have to be a State law passed to determine which age is to be adopted both for girls and boys. Or take New York in which the age of consent is 18 for both sexes, while marriage is absolutely prohibited for girls under 14 and boys under 16.

It has heretofore been assumed that these distinctions in the law recognized what we considered to be established biological factors. For it is generally agreed that a mother is best qualified to take care of children in the home. But under this amendment she might jeopardize her present legal right to support from her husband for services in the home. There are endless examples that come to the mind of the confusion and wrong which would be done by such a sweeping amendment.

The proposed amendment would invalidate State legislation regulating hours of work and setting minimum wages for women workers. These laws have been passed because of the insistence of women in industry that there is need for such legislation. Many important groups have been concerned with women's place in the industrial field and have felt the necessity for legal protection. Adjustments are being made in the administration of these laws so that they do not interfere with the employment of women in war industries. But the protection that they afford will be needed during the post-war reconstruction.

A study of the amendment shows its inappropriateness as a part of the Constitution. No standard of equality is stated in the amendment. Does it mean that each State could determine equality within its own boundaries? The amendment authorizes Congress to enforce equality by appropriate legislation. Does this mean that Congress shall act in fields now reserved to the States — marriage and divorce laws, support laws, property laws and so forth? If so, the amendment would constitute one of the most extensive changes in the relation of States to the Federal Government in the history of the country.

Those in favor of the so-called Equal Rights Amendment have been trading on the phrase "equal rights." All of us would like to find a short and easy way to accomplish an end. But we have found from hard experience that the superficial manner of treating a basic subject leads one into many unforeseen difficulties. Yet a small group of women persist in calling for an overall sweeping amendment, instead of being willing to go into the States and tackle the specific laws which they wish changed.

Proponents of this amendment have also called it the Lucretia Mott amendment. I feel sure that she would never have subscribed to such an amendment. She was entirely too clear-sighted and practical a person ever to have believed that a social or biological revolution could be brought about by an amendment to the Federal Constitution.

March 28, 1943

WOMEN'S RIGHTS: Sex was kept out of the U. S. Constitution until 1920. But it reared its head that year with the passage of the Nineteenth Amendment, guaranteeing women the right to vote. And ever since it has been argued, in feminist circles, that women's other civil rights were inadequately protected in the Constitution. The question has been complex because in many states women are guaranteed special privileges—for example, in New York, the right to support after a legal separation. Many women were reluctant to get equal rights if it meant the loss of special privileges. Last week it appeared that they might get both.

On Thursday the Senate approved, 73—11, a proposed amendment to the Constitution that will give women equal rights without prejudice to special privileges. The proposed amendment now goes to the House, which pigeonholed a similar measure in 1950, and is not expected to act on the present proposal until next year. To become effective the measure must win a two-thirds vote in the House and then approval by three-fourths of the states.

July 19, 1953

PRESIDENT NAMES PANEL ON WOMEN

By ALVIN SHUSTER
Special to The New york Times.

WASHINGTON, Dec. 14—President Kennedy established today a commission headed by Mrs. Franklin D. Roosevelt to advance the cause of women's rights.

The President said the group, known as the President's Commission on the Status of Women, would make studies of "all barriers to the full partnership of women in our democracy."

He said he expected the commission to report by Oct. 1, 1963, on what remained to be done to "demolish prejudices and outmoded customs."

The emphasis in the President's statement was on setting up Federal employment practices as a showcase of the value of giving women equal job opportunities. And he set an example. There are fifteen women to eleven men on the commission.

Employment Practices

Specifically, he directed the Civil Service Commission to review all Federal personnel policies and practices affecting the employment of women. The object, he said, will be to assure that "selection of any career position is hereafter made solely on the basis of individual merit and fitness, without regard to sex."

Among other things, the new commission will also look into Federal employment policies and practices, as well as those of Federal contractors.

It also will study the effects of Federal insurance programs and tax laws on women's income, and will appraise Federal and state labor laws dealing with hours and wages.

The group will also presumably go into the advisability of the Administration's throwing its full support behind the oft-proposed constitutional amendment for "equal rights" for women. First proposed in 1920 and introduced at every session of Congress since then, the amendment has never succeeded in winning the approval of both Houses.

It is intended to eliminate "discrimination" against women in areas of employment and property rights and reads in part: "Equality of rights under the law shall not be denied or abridged by the United States or any state on account of sex."

December 15, 1961

JOBS-ISSUE BLOCKS ATTEMPT IN HOUSE TO VOTE ON RIGHTS

Southern Motions to Amend Bill Force a Delay, With New Debate Tomorrow

---

REPUBLICANS ARE ANGRY

But Halleck Fails to Prevent an Adjournment — Final Action Due Tuesday

---

By E. W. KENWORTHY
Special to The New York Times

WASHINGTON, Feb. 8—The House failed to complete action on the civil rights bill tonight after bogging down in a morass of amendments to the section outlawing discrimination by employers and labor unions.

At 10:12 P.M. the House adjourned until 10 A.M. Monday, when it will resume debate on one of the most controversial sections in the omnibus bill.

The chances for a final vote Monday on the whole bill are probably slim. However, a final vote must be taken by Tuesday.

On the question of adjournment, the Northern bipartisan coalition broke ranks for the first time.

G.O.P. Wants to Stay

The Republicans wanted to stay all night, if necessary, so that they could get away for the traditional Lincoln's Birthday speech-making.

They were resentful when Representative Emanuel Celler, Democrat of Brooklyn, who is floor manager for the bill, put the motion to adjourn.

As the Northern Democrats stood up in support of Mr. Celler, ironic cries of "Coalition! Coalition!" arose from the Republican ranks.

The Republican leader, Charles A. Halleck of Indiana, was so angry that he demanded a roll-call on adjournment, a most unusual request. The motion to adjourn carried, 220 to 175.

Fate Never in Doubt

However, with the Southerners showing no signs of running out of amendments, it was doubtful that action on the fair-employment section and the three remaining sections could have been completed by dawn.

It was a tumultuous day. The final fate of the section was never in doubt, as was demonstrated tonight when a motion to kill it entirely was easily defeated, 150 to 90.

Nevertheless, the civil rights supporters were forced to accede to some unexpected amendments, including one to include sex among the prohibited reasons for refusing employment, along with race, color, religion and national origin. Another amendment would allow an employer to refuse to hire "an atheist."

The Southerners were in no mood to hurry the proceedings to accommodate the Northern coalition, and they felt no obligation to do so. An agreement made by Representative Howard W. Smith, Democrat of Virginia, when his Rules Committee released the bill for action, was that a final vote would be taken by Tuesday.

And so the Southerners proceeded to offer amendments. Mr. Smith led off with the proposal prohibiting discrimination as to sex.

This amendment, Mr. Smith said, "will help an important minority."

"This bill is so imperfect, what harm will this little amendment do?" he asked.

Several times this week, similar amendments to other sections were defeated. But now every Congresswoman but one suddenly rose to its defense.

Asks 'Crumb of Equality'

Representative Katharine St. George, Republican of Tuxedo Park, said to the male members:

"We outlast you. We outlive you. We nag you to death. So why should we want special privileges? We want this crumb of equality. The little word 'sex' won't correct the bill."

Representative Martha W. Griffiths, Democrat of Michigan, said that, without the protection of this amendment, "white women would be at the bottom of the list in hiring" after white men and Negro men and women.

"It would be incredible to me that white men would be willing to place white women at such a disadvantage," she said.

Representative Catherine May, Republican of Washington, said, "I hope we won't overlook the

white native-born American woman of Christian religion."

Opposes Amendment

The only woman member to speak against the amendment was Edith Green, Democrat of Oregon, who has been fighting for years to get women equal pay for equal work.

She said she might be called "an Uncle Tom, or maybe an Aunt Jane," for what she was going to say but she asserted that the amendment might jeopardize the whole bill.

It was useless for the bill's managers to protest, and on the teller vote the amendment passed, 168 to 133.

When the vote was announced, a slight woman in the gallery jumped up and cried out:

"We made it! we made it! God bless America!"

Whereupon a guard promptly demonstrated that, despite the new amendment, some women were less equal than others. He threw her out.

The Smith amendment consumed two hours. Then Representative Graham B. Purcell Jr., Democrat of Texas, proposed that it be lawful for a church-affiliated school to insist on hiring individuals of its own denomination. After 75 minutes, the House agreed to this by a voice vote.

Representative John Dowdy, Democrat of Texas, then proposed that age as well as sex be added to the discrimination ban. Mr. Celler said that this would lead to endless confusion.

Mr. Smith, who is 81 years old, rose and said, "This is a right serious amendment for some of us."

He said that Mr. Celler, who is 76, was going strong after "the most grueling debate in my 32 years in the House."

Offers an Exhibit

"And yet he is opposing the amendment, and will put us out of business," Mr. Smith said. "I offer myself Exhibit B for this amendment."

The age amendment lost, 123 to 94.

Then Representative John M. Ashbrook, Republican of Ohio, proposed that an employer be allowed to refuse to hire an atheist without being guilty of discrimination.

There was a spate of oratory, most of it impassioned. Some members contended that atheism was not a religion and therefore could not claim the protection of the law. Others contended that the Constitution protected a citizen's right not to have any religion.

The House finally approved the amendment, 137 to 98.

Throughout the 11 hours of debate, there was never any doubt that ultimate approval would be given the section, which would create a Commission on Equal Employment Opportunity. Such an agency has long been called "F.E.P.C." for its prototype, the Fair Employment Practices Committee of World War II

Two things happened this morning to assure that the section would be included in the bill.

At a meeting with several Republican members of the Judiciary and Education and Labor Committees, Mr. Halleck agreed to support the F.E.P.C. title.

Mr. Halleck previously said that when he met late last October with President Kennedy and agreed to support the compromise coalition bill put together by the Judiciary Committee and the Department of Justice, he specifically excluded this section from the agreement.

Observers agreed that Mr. Halleck's decision to support the section would resolve the doubts of many Republicans, particularly those from the rural Middle Western and Mountain states.

The second thing that happened to assure passage was an agreement between the Judiciary Committee and some Republican members of the Education and Labor Committee on nine clarifying amendments to the coalition bill.

The Republicans sought these amendments to bring this section closer to the language of a fair-employment bill that was approved last fall by the Education and Labor Committee. When that bill failed to gain clearance from the Rules Committee, the Judiciary Committee attacked an F.E.P.C. section to the omnibus civil rights bill.

When President Kennedy sent his civil rights proposals to Congress last June, he said he favored a fair-employment agency. He did not, however, include it in his proposals for fear that its presence might jeopardize the whole bill.

By October, however, the Administration felt that the situation was more favorable and agreed to its insertion in the compromise bill.

Many Republicans look askance at the jobs proposal, and some Republicans in the Labor Committee believed their doubts could be eased by the nine amendments.

These were then offered as committee amendments. This meant they had the approval of Mr. Celler, the chairman of the Judiciary Committee, and of a majority of the committee.

The amendments also had the approval of William M. McCulloch of Ohio, the ranking Republican on the committee.

For Instance, Can She Pitch for Mets?

By JOHN HERBERS
Special to The New York Times

WASHINGTON, Aug. 19— A group of Government officials, labor leaders and personnel officers tackled today what experts on sex discrimination in employment call "the bunny problem."

The bunny problem is an extreme example of what might happen under the new Federal law banning discrimination in employment on the basis of race, color, sex or national origin—that is, a male applying for a job as a "bunny" in a Playboy club.

Other examples have been offered—the woman who applies for a job as attendant in a men's Turkish bath, the man who wants to clerk in a women's corset shop, the woman who wants employment aboard a tug that has sleeping quarters only for men. These all are lumped together under the bunny problem.

The Equal Employment Opportunity Commission, which must enforce Title VII of the Civil Rights Act of 1964, is expected to rule that, in cases such as these, sex is a bona fide occupational qualification under the law.

Section 703 of the law says it is not unlawful to hire only persons of a particular religion, sex or national origin when such hiring is "reasonably necessary to the normal operation of that particular business or enterprise."

But in a panel discussion on sex discrimination at the White House Conference on Equal Employment Opportunity, a staff member of the commission said that the bunny problem was not to be dismissed lightly. "The bunny question is interesting because everybody considers the answer to be obvious," said Richard K. Berg, deputy counsel. The obvious answer is no, the man could not get the job.

"But in terms of what bunnies do, it is something else— they serve drinks," Mr. Berg continued. He then raised the question of other businesses where pretty girls were hired to increase sales; for example, a hamburger stand.

"That is something the commission will have to decide," he said.

Another question raised was whether it would be unlawful for an executive to insist on hiring a secretary of a particular sex.

"Some men might find a female secretary disturbing," an unidentified male participant said.

"Could that be predetermined?" asked Miss Evelyn Harrison, deputy director of the Bureau of Programs and Standards of the Civil Service Commission.

Mrs. Mary D. Keyserling, director of the Women's Bureau of the Department of Labor, said that the law was not intended to work a hardship on anyone.

"He would not be compelled to take a dizzy blonde if that is upsetting to him," she said. But in the discussion that followed it was strongly implied that all women should not be ruled out for the man who preferred a male secretary.

A personnel officer for the Pennsylvania Railroad wanted to know if the company would be required to hire women as locomotive engineers.

"I don't know what to do when a woman applicant shows up," he said.

To this Mr. Berg replied, "The commission is going to put the burden on the employers. If they can't think of any reason not to do it [hire women for jobs traditionally held by men], then they better do it."

W. J. Trent, assistant personnel director of Time, Inc., New York City, asked what the commission intended to do about state laws that prohibited women from lifting more than a specified weight or working more than a certain number of hours. He asked whether refusal to hire women in jobs that required breaking these laws would be a violation of the Federal law.

Mrs. Keyserling said the commission could take one of two approaches.

First, it could rule that Title VII did not affect state laws except where those laws were used to maintain patterns of discrimination. Most organized groups have proposed this approach.

Secondly, it could rule individually on all complaints involving a conflict of state and Federal laws.

Discrimination Faced by Women Workers

To the Editor:

The ban on discrimination in employment on the basis of sex has not been treated by The Times in the seriousness it merits. The Times's stories ranged from the comic—"The Bunny Problem" in the Aug. 20 news article—to the tragic in its Aug. 21 editorial.

A little comedy in the news is a welcome change. And the tragic—"Everything has to be neuterized," or, "You can't even safely advertise for a wife" isn't frightening at all. But the subject also warrants a serious, factual treatment which The Times seems to be avoiding.

The White House Conference on Equal Employment Opportunity, held Aug. 19 and 20, involved many people seriously concerned with discrimination in employment, against Negroes primarily, but against women as well. While at this time in history discrimination based on race and color is the major problem, we need not blink at the discriminations that exist against the woman worker. Our struggles against the one injustice need not dilute our efforts to eliminate the other.

Man's Work World

Twenty-six million women are in the work force. One out of three workers is a woman. Women work for the same reasons men do—because they must work to support themselves and their dependents.

We need factual, unbiased

treatment of the story of discrimination against the woman worker in man's world of work.

Why are women generally in the lowest paid jobs? How many jobs are designated "men's jobs" merely because they are higher-paying rather than because women cannot perform them? How many jobs are "women's jobs" merely because they are menial, routine, monotonous and, of course, low-paying? Is bias against women in executive and administrative jobs based on fact or fancy? Are women excluded from certain jobs by force of tradition, whim, or misinformation rather than for real differences in the capacity to perform a job?

Occupational Qualifications

These matters were discussed at the conference. The Times saw only the funny bunny.

Actually the "bunny problem" is no problem at all. The law expressly recognizes that certain jobs may require a "bona fide occupational qualification" based on sex. The Times may rest assured: men will be men and women will be women, and the law does not even remotely suggest a "neuterization." Nor does it prohibit advertising for a wife—if that should be the way of romance.

So let us have our fun out of the sex angle—if we must. But let us also treat the plight of the woman worker with the seriousness it deserves from a great newspaper.

ESTHER PETERSON
Assistant Secretary of Labor
Washington, Aug. 26, 1965

On Being Female

AMERICAN WOMEN: The Report of the President's Commission on the Status of Women and Other Publications of the Commission. Edited by Margaret Mead and Frances B. Kaplan. 274 pp. New York: Charles Scribner's Sons. $6.95.

By EDWARD D. EDDY

THE Commission on the Status of Women, appointed by President Kennedy in 1961, has now issued its formal report, together with the reports of its various committees and a searching, even scorching, epilogue by one of the best of the female species, Margaret Mead.

The commission has dissolved so that, as a group, it will not have to carry on the endless discussion which its report will prompt. Is this, some will ask, the cry of the militant female, rising again in her wrath, setting down once more for all to ponder the demands of her disadvantaged self? The commission calls its report an "invitation to action."

Or is it merely the final gasp of the feminist movement, which will be "done in" by its own self-righteousness because it cannot withstand the inevitable snicker and snort? Marion K. Sanders, writing recently in Harper's Magazine, referred to the status of women as a problem which "has reached crisis proportions, comparable to air pollution and urban sprawl."

Apparently the commission feels that, despite the gains of this century and particularly of recent years, women continue to be a disadvantaged group. In Miss Mead's words, the commission concludes, in effect, that "any barrier whatsoever to full participation on the level of the privileged white, adult, American male . . . should be treated as a handicap so that it can be overcome." This is the implicit goal which the commission sets for American women. Its implications are both curious and disturbing.

THE major theme of the report is the necessity for freedom of choice among different life patterns. The commission holds that because women's lives are less likely than men's to follow continuous patterns, women should be able to move freely and equally from profession to parenthood to participation in public life. No barriers should exist if, when and as a woman wishes to change her status.

It must be this preoccupation with life-long equality for the female which has led the commission down an unfortunate, one-way street. It is both surprising and maybe even shocking to find a presidentially appointed group so completely misunderstanding the basic nature of its subject and so willing to capitulate to the demands of a materialistic society. Not a word is said about the power of women to shape ideas, to force the making of sound decisions, to act as conscience for the world. Instead the

Mr. Eddy comments frequently on women's education as president of Chatham College.

TOO many plans recommended to young women reaching maturity are only partially suited to the second half of the twentieth century. Women's ancient function of providing love and nurture stands. But for entry into modern life, today's children need a preparation far more diversified than that of the predecessors.—"American Women."

commission's report is a call for more more benefits, shorter hours, continuous education, Supreme Court seats and Social Security benefits for the widow "equal to the amount that her husband would have received at the same age had he lived."

There is even a recommendation of paid maternity leaves, but the commission should beware. If adopted, this will immediately place the white adult American male in the disadvantaged group.

Apparently the commission is concerned that many American women prefer to operate from within the structure of the home and family and that such a choice represents "a diminution of women's earlier drive for a chance to be persons in their own right, with work and interests of their own." Thus the call goes out for child-care day centers to relieve the mother, for prohibitions against compulsory night work, and for all sorts of protective legislation. One committee report notes, however, that "many women are still underprotected and some feel overprotected."

Miss Mead warns that while "the climate of opinion is turning against the idea that homemaking is the only form of feminine achievement . . . the pendulum must not swing too far, forcing out of the home women whose major creative life is grounded in motherhood and wifehood."

The commission's startling denial of the right of women to be female is nowhere better illustrated than in the section on education. It is a disappointing treatment, especially in scope, and suffers from an obvious lack of perception of the particular contribution which liberally educated women can make. The report concludes that "future American standards are likely to be more inwardly felt than those of the past, to be matters of taste rather than matters of emulation in the possession of material things." The emphasis, however, is completely on the need for vocational training and continuing education throughout life. Evidently liberal education is not considered important.

Even when the commission gets down to cases in its pursuit of the female fair share of materialism, it skirts the major problems. Why is it that both men and women prefer not to work for women? Certainly not just because the male lacks tolerance. Is there something inherently wrong with the woman who wants to lead several different kinds of life and, in doing so, doesn't mind giving up the

greater recognition which might come with concentration? What more do we need to know about women? And why no urgent commission call for research on what it recognizes as "the conflicting self-images, role, and practical realities" to which women are under pressure to conform, or "the complex motivations that determine their decisions?" Obviously American women are not contributing up to their potentiality, but it will take more than a Supreme Court decision on equality under law to create the right conditions.

In summary, this is an important book. It is also, regrettably, a badly organized, unevenly written and astoundingly naive treatment of a strategic subject. A picture does emerge but only from a hodge-podge of sweeping generalizations sandwiched between statistical detail.

The volume includes the reports of the various committees appointed by the parent commission, even though these reports frequently differ on major as well as minor points. One outstanding example is the committee recommendation regarding sex education and family planning, subjects of no small significance to women and to society. The commission report conveniently ignores anything so controversial.

American women can be thankful that Margaret Mead, who did not serve on the commission, was willing to add an epilogue. She has put her expert finger on the deficiencies. She is too polite to be cantankerous, but she knows when a grievous error has been made. She knows that the almighty dollar applied to the American female makes her neither pretty nor happy.

In a devastating, handsomely written interpretation of what the commission really meant to say. Miss Mead carries the commission's assumptions to their ridiculous extreme. If, as she points out, we adhere to the "American insistence that one's value as a person can be measured by money," then housewives ought to be paid for sweeping off the back porch on the grounds that this will give them dignity and college students provided with a salary because "they are learning to be the kind of persons needed by their society."

Miss Mead's tongue is in her cheek while the commission's tongue seems caught in its throat. In her epilogue, she provides a note of hope by managing to convey the idea that most women, like most men, are rather happy that there is a difference.

U.S. ACTS TO CURB SEX BIAS ON JOBS

Business Given Guidelines to Assure Equality

By NAN ROBERTSON
Special to The New York Times

WASHINGTON, Nov. 10

The Federal Government has officially served notice on employers that they will no longer be permitted to refuse to hire or promote women on the ground that their fellow workers or customers would not accept them.

The prohibition is only one of a set of precise guidelines offered to business to avoid lawsuits based on charges of sex discrimination under the Civil Rights Act of 1964.

The guidelines will be formally published in the Federal Register within 10 days.

Richard A. Graham of the Equal Employment Opportunity Commission said today that the Government had found that illegal discrimination against women — in hiring, job retention and promotions — was widespread. The commission is empowered to enforce the Fair Employment Practices section of the Civil Rights Act.

Prohibitions Specified

Mr. Graham disclosed new standards specifying what will be prohibited from now on. For one, it will be unlawful not to hire or promote women "because of the attitudes of fellow workers or clientele." It will also be unlawful to do the following:

¶Classify certain jobs exclusively for males or females unless sex is a bona fide occupational qualification.

¶Establish separate seniority lists based on sex.

¶Label jobs "light," or "heavy," when it is merely a subterfuge for the terms "female" or "male."

¶Forbid the hiring of married women if the ruling is not also applied to married men.

¶Place a help-wanted advertisement in a newspaper excluding applicants of one sex and limiting the job to applicants of the other sex.

Newspapers may place ads for "males" or "females" in separate columns for reader convenience provided there is a prominent disclaimer that notes Federal and state laws against sex discrimination.

Since the commission began operating July 2, 1965, it has received 2,300 complaints of discrimination under Title VII, the Fair Employment Practices Section, of the Civil Rights Act. Mr. Graham said that about 15 per cent of these cases alleged discrimination on the basis of sex.

False Assumptions Seen

The commission has found that such discrimination stems in part from a number of widespread and what it calls false assumptions — that men are less capable of assembling intricate equipment, for example; that women are not aggressive salesmen and that females are not qualified for managerial posts because of their "high turnover."

It has also found a striking similarity between sex and race discrimination in hiring and seniority.

Mr. Graham said "some common sense along with the legal approach will be required" in applying the law.

The commission will recognize a bona fide occupational qualification based on sex in these instances:

¶Where sex is vital in job performance, such as males to model men's clothes or females to perform the roles of women in a play.

¶Where it is significant "in terms of community standards of morality or propriety," such as a male to work in a men's washroom or a woman to work as a fitter in a brassiere and girdle shop.

¶Where sex is a bona fide factor in fulfilling provisions of other laws, which may require that only men masseurs may serve men or that women may work only certain hours.

However, Mr. Graham said, "customer or employer preference, or historical usage, tradition or custom" will not merit the grant of a bona fide occupational qualification without further justification.

Johnson Signs Order to Protect Women in U.S. Jobs From Bias

By MAX FRANKEL

WASHINGTON, Oct. 13 — President Johnson moved today to strengthen enforcement procedures to protect women against discrimination in the Federal Government and in the employ of its private contractors.

He signed an executive order extending the same review and appeal machinery that is already in force against discrimination because of race, creed, color or national origin.

Starting one month from today, the Civil Service Commission will be authorized to hear directly the complaints of Federal employes about discrimination based on sex. Starting a year from today, the Labor Department will be authorized to investigate complaints against such discrimination by all Federal contractors or subcontractors.

John W. Macy Jr., chairman of the Civil Service Commission, said at a White House briefing that about one-third of the complaints received about unfair employment practices and treatment on the job came from women. Most of these, he added, dealt with alleged discrimination in promotions rather than initial employment.

Title VII of the Civil Rights Act of 1964 proclaimed a policy of equal employment opportunities because of race, color, religion, sex or national origin. Two years ago, Mr. Johnson issued an executive order. No. 11246, to handle complaints by Government-supported employers but left matters affecting discrimination by sex to an already existing review machinery.

Since then, women's groups and the President's Citizens Advisory Group on the Status of Women were said to have expressed concern that the cases of women, would not be pursued with equal zeal unless all the enforcement procedures were identical.

Private contractors who are found guilty of tolerating a discernible pattern of discrimination are liable under these procedures to legal action to cancel their Government contracts.

To illustrate the problem facing women who seek administrative positions, Mr. Macy offered some statistics about the number of women in senior Government jobs. Despite "substantial improvement" over the last three or four years, he said, women still hold only 658 of the 23,000 jobs paying $18,000 a year, 74 of the 5,000 jobs paying $20,000; 41 of the 2,300 paying $22,000, and 36 of the 1,700 paying $25,000.

October 14, 1967

RULES ON SEX BIAS IN JOBS STRICTER

U.S. Lists Guides to Guard Women From Penalties by Federal Contractors

By ROBERT B. SEMPLE Jr.
Special to The New York Times

WASHINGTON, June 9—The Labor Department today issued detailed guidelines designed to eliminate discrimination against women in jobs paid for with Federal funds.

The guidelines go beyond an executive order signed by President Johnson on Oct. 13, 1967. That order provided a general ban on discrimination against women employed by contractors and subcontractors on Federal projects. But it did not identify the kinds of discrimination to be avoided.

The new guidelines, issued with some fanfare at a White House briefing, prohibit discriminatory techniques such as newspaper advertising labeled "male" and "female" unless sex is "a bona fide occupational qualification," penalties for women employes for taking time off to bear children and the denial of employment to women with young children "unless the same exclusionary policy exists for men."

In addition, the guidelines ban seniority based solely on sex and prohibit "discriminatorily restricting one sex to certain job classifications and departments."

Responsibility for enforcing the new prohibitions will rest with the Office of Federal Contract Compliance in the Labor Department. The guidelines are effective immediately and can be enforced by withholding contracts from contractors who fail to comply.

The gudelines were recommended by the President's Task Force on Women's Rights and Responsibilities. The group's 33-page report was released by the White House today, nearly six months after it was completed by a 13-member panel headed by Virginia R. Allan. Miss Allan is executive vice president of Cahalan Drug Stores, Inc., Wyandotte, Mich.

There was no immediate explanation of why the President chose to delay the report for so long. He has been under intense pressure from women members of Congress to release it.

The task force report contained a long series of recommendations, of which the President has publicly accepted only one—the new guidelines.

The task force said that "the United States, as it approaches its 200th anniversary, lags behind other enlightened and indeed some newly emerging countries in the role ascribed to women. It recommended the following:

¶Establishment of a permanent office of women's rights and responsibilities, whose director would be a special assistant reporting directly to the President.

¶A White House conference on women's rights and responsibilities in 1970, the 50th anniversary of the ratification of the suffrage amendment.

¶A special message to Congress calling for new legislation to strengthen Federal enforcement machinery, to liberalize the Social Security and income tax laws to benefit women employes and their husbands, and to provide increased assistance for the care of children of working mothers.

"American women are increasingly aware and restive over the denial of equal opportunity, equal responsibility, even equal protection of the law," the report said. "An abiding concern for home and children should not, in their view, cut them off from the freedom to choose the role in society to which their interest, education and training entitle them."

The new guidelines were hailed by Elizabeth Duncan Koontz, director of the Labor Department's Women's Bureau, as "a most appropriate milestone in women's progress."

Discrimination Is Found

WASHINGTON, June 9 (UPI) —A survey of some of the nation's most highly educated women and the men in their lives shows about 80 per cent of them believe that women suffer sex discrimination in the working world.

But the same survey shows that even educated men still tend to believe that a woman's rightful role is as wife and mother.

The survey was conducted nationwide by the American Association of University Women last winter.

The 56-question survey was mailed to association members and brought responses from 4,173 women and from 3,001 husbands and male colleagues.

Among the findings were:

¶A quarter of the women reported experiencing sex discrimination; the same proportion of men reported seeing discrimination against women.

¶Women in the South were least likely to agree that a woman's first responsibility was as wife and mother and most willing to give up femininity for job equality.

June 10, 1970

Equal Rights Amendment Passed by House, 354-23

By EILEEN SHANAHAN
Special to The New York Times

WASHINGTON, Oct. 12—The House of Representatives passed today, 354 to 23, a constitutional amendment prohibiting discrimination based on sex.

The amendment was passed in the form long favored by women's rights advocates.

The key vote was on the issue of including in the amendment provisions that would continue the legality of drafting men, but not women, into the armed forces and provisions asserting the validity of many existing laws that treat men and women differently.

Women's rights advocates said that these provisions nullified the intention of the Equal Rights Amendment, as it is known. They were stricken from the amendment by a vote of 265 to 87.

Today's vote marked the second time in two years that the House has passed the amendment in the form advocated by women's rights activists. Last year, there were only 15 votes against.

The amendment will now go to the Senate, which has never passed it in the version that feminists want, although it has passed amended versions three times.

The fate of the amendment in the Senate in the current Congress is uncertain. If the Senate does pass it, it must be ratified by 38 states to become effective. The Senate majority leader, Mike Mansfield of Montana, has placed the bill on the Senate calendar so it can legally be called up for a vote at any time. This was a device to keep the Senate Judiciary Committee, where there is strong apposition to the amendment, from burying it there.

Since Mr. Mansfield can bring up the bill at any time, the Judiciary Committee is expected to act on it.

But there appeared to be a strong probability that Senator Sam J. Ervin Jr. of North Carolina, the commitee's leading opponent of the amendment, would be able to attach provisions similar to those that feminists find unacceptable and that were defeated in the House today.

Whether these provisions could then be eliminated on the Senate floor was questionable. Women's rights groups expressed optimism that they would pick up more and more votes for their position as the 1972 elections drew closer.

The day's debate in the House was long and conducted before galleries that were two-thirds full of women of all ages --ranging from elderly veterans of the fight for the women's suffrage amendment, which was adopted in 1920, to college and high-school girls.

At one point in the debate, Representative Thomas G. Abernethy, Democrat of Mississippi, said that enactment of the amendment would mean that there was no way of compelling a man to support his family. And he said that his wife had instructed him to vote against the amendment "because she doesn't want to lose her home."

Mr. Abernethy was followed to the rostrum by Representative Bella S. Abzug, Democrat of Manhattan, who started her speech with the announcement, "I do not come here under instructions from my husband as to how to vote."

The galleries applauded and cheered—which is forbidden by the rules of the House.

Of the 11 women members of the House, nine, including Mrs. Abzug, voted for the amendment today. One absentee, Representative Edith Green, Democrat of Oregon, has supported it in the past. The lone opponent among the women members was Representative Leonor K. Sullivan, Democrat of Missouri.

The text of the amendment, H. J. Res. 208, is as follows:
Section 1. Equality of rights shall not be denied or abridged by the United States or by any state on account of sex.
Section 2. The Congress shall have the power to enforce, by appropriate legislation, the provisions of this article.

Section 3. This amendment shall take effect two years after the date of ratification.

Most of the debate focused on the question of whether women would have to be drafted, if men were, if the amendment were adopted.

The sponsor of the modification of the amendment that would have exempted women from compulsory military service Representative Charles E. Wiggins, Republican of California, said that the general counsel of the Department of Defense had told him it would be "impossible for the military to operate" if the amendment were adopted.

Not only would the services be forced to draft more women than they wanted, he said, but separate barracks and other separate facilities would not be permitted.

Representative John Conyers Jr., Democrat of Michigan, demanded to know why, if the military was concerned, it had not asked to testify at the hearings on the amendment. Mr. Wiggins said that he could not answer that question.

October 13, 1971

Equal Rights Amendment Is Approved by Congress

By EILEEN SHANAHAN
Special to The New York Times

WASHINGTON, March 22—The Senate passed the Equal Rights Amendment today, thus completing Congressional action on the amendment, which would prohibit discrimination based on sex by any law or action of any government— Federal, state or local.

The 49-year struggle of feminists to get the amendment through Congress ended at 4:38 P.M. when the 84-to-8 vote was announced.

Thirty-two minutes later, Hawaii became the first state to ratify the amendment when the state Senate and House of Representatives registered its approval at 12:10 P.M. Hawaiian standard time (5:10 P.M. Eastern standard time).

The Senate galleries, which were filled with women of all ages and more than a few men, mostly young, applauded, cheered and let out a few cowboy yells despite having been warned in advance by Senator William V. Roth Jr., Republican of Delaware, who was presiding, that such demonstrations were not permitted.

The next and final step before the amendment can go into effect is ratification by 37 more states, the three-quarters required by the Constitution.

The signature of the President is not required.

Confidence that ratification would be achieved swiftly was expressed by a number of supporters of the amendment.

Senator Birch Bayh, Democrat of Indiana, who led the Senate fight for the amendment, said he thought it would be ratified "with dispatch."

Present on the Senate floor when the amendment passed was Representative Martha W. Griffiths, Democrat of Michigan, who is generally given the largest single share of credit for enacting the amendment. Two years ago, she succeeded in a rarely tried parliamentary maneuver to bring the amendment to the House floor without the approval of the Judiciary Committee, which had

489

refused for decades even to hold hearings on the measure.

Also watching from the Senate floor when the amendment passed—a privilege that House members have—were Representatives Margaret M. Heckler, Republican of Massachuetts, and Bella S. Abzug, Democrat of Manhattan.

Mrs. Griffiths sat at the back-row desk usually occupied by Senator Edmund S. Muskie, Democrat of Maine, keeping her personal count of the roll-call.

Mr. Muskie returned from his campaigning in time for the roll-call, as did Senator Hubert H. Humphrey, Democrat of Minnesota. Both had missed what were generally considered to be key votes yesterday on changes in the amendment.

But two other Democratic Presidential candidates, although present yesterday, were absent today—Senators George McGovern of South Dakota and Henry M. Jackson of Washington.

Today's Senate debate centered, as it has from the outset, on what the consequences of the amendment would be.

Its principal opponent, Senator Sam J. Ervin Jr., Democrat of North Carolina, predicted many dire results. A series of seven amendments he offered were designed to thwart those results.

The Senate voted down all of Mr. Ervin's proposed changes. The largest number of votes that he mustered for any proposed change was 17.

The eight who voted against the Equal Rights Amendment included, in addition to Senator Ervin, only one other Democrat, John C. Stennis of Mississippi. The other opponents were Wallace F. Bennett of Utah, Norris Cotton of New Hampshire, Paul J. Fannin of Arizona, Barry Goldwater of Arizona and Clifford P. Hansen of Wyoming, all Republicans, and James L. Buckley of New York, Conservative-Republican.

How long it might take for the amendment to be ratified was unclear. Senator Bayh indicated he thought it would be two years. The amendment itself permits seven years to elapse before it dies, if unratified.

Common Cause, the organization headed by John W. Gardner that calls itself a public-interest lobby, announced

that it would get to work immediately in the 26 states where legislatures are in session now. Where legislatures are not in session, it will start organizing for ratification, Common Cause said.

It is agreed by all that considerable litigation would probably be required before all the effects of the amendment were known. The following, however, are some of the laws and practices that the amendment expected to invalidate:

¶Laws imposing greater restrictions on a woman's right, than on a man's, to buy or sell property or to conduct a business.

¶Laws setting different ages at which men and women attain legal majority or have the right to marry or become eligible for tax-supported retirement plans.

¶Differing admissions standards for boys and girls in tax-supported educational institutions and different facilities and curriculums—such as physical education programs and shop facilities — in public schools.

¶Laws establishing different jail sentences, by sex, for identical offenses.

¶Laws automatically giving preference to the mother in child-custody cases.

¶Laws granting alimony to women without reference to need and imposing the burden of child-support on the father, regardless of the relative economic situations of the two parents.

¶Regulations denying unemployment compensation payments to pregnant women who are still able and willing to work and laws that treat pregnancy differently from any other temporary physical disability.

¶Military rules setting higher entry standards for women volunteers than for men.

There is also general agreement that the amendment would require women to be drafted, if men were. The key vote in the Senate yesterday was over this issue, and Senator Ervin's amendment to prohibit the drafting of women was defeated, 73 to 18.

The main clause of the amendment is as follows: "Equality of rights under the law shall not be denied or abridged by the United States or by any state on account of sex."

The amendment is to take effect two years after ratification.

Women's Rights:

A Vote For Equal Status— And Equal Burdens

WASHINGTON — Everyone thought it was a shame that Mabel Vernon couldn't be there. A veteran of the fight for women's suffrage in the United States, one of the last survivors of the group of women who were arrested and jailed in 1917 for refusing to stop demonstrating for suffrage in front of the White House, Miss Vernon was sick last Thursday. She missed the Senate vote marking final Congressional approval of the Equal Rights Amendment.

The Amendment proposal now goes to the states. If approved by the necessary three-fourths, or 38, of the state legislatures, it will be the 27th Amendment to the Constitution. Its main clause: "Equality of rights under the law shall not be denied or abridged by the United States or by any state on account of sex."

Feminists had begun to seek adoption of such an amendment in 1923, just three years after women got the vote in the United States, though most people thought that the whole battle for women's equality had already been won. But then came the Great Depression, and World War II, and finally the postwar retreat into what Betty Friedan called "The Feminine Mystique" — the notion that women should feel 100 per cent fulfilled in their roles as wives and mothers.

Once the drive sparked by the new feminist movement resumed in earnest, it took less than three years to get the Equal Rights Amendment through Congress. One reason — but not the only one—was that the movement had advanced from "consciousness-raising" sessions to political activism. Well-organized women's groups in nearly every state threatened — in letters, telegrams, telephone calls and personal visits—to defeat members of Congress who voted against the amendment. A similar approach is already producing ratifications of the amendment by state legislatures, and feminists are beginning to hope that the ratification process might take less than two years. It cannot possibly be completed this year, because the

Go one better. Enlist for Ranger training.

Your future, your decision...choose ARMY

The Army may never be the same. Last week the Equal Rights Amendment passed Congress and was on its way to the state legislatures for approval. Will equal rights for women mean army service? "Advocates of the amendment say that women are ready to accept this obligation."

When Equality Isn't Equal	MEN	WOMEN
Overall Median Income	$7,529	$5,618
Income by Occupation		
Professional and technical workers	$9,868	$6,705
Clerical workers	7,006	5,570
Skilled blue collar workers	6,452	3,666
Service workers	5,778	3,272
Income by Education		
Less than 4 years of high school	$5,660	$3,132
High school diploma	7,362	5,500
1 to 3 years of college	8,310	5,608
4 years or more of college	10,726	6,852
		(1966 figures)

A recent study by two officials in the Census Bureau shows that women aged 30 to 44 who had worked every year since leaving school had much lower incomes than men who were the same age, had the same education and held the same type of jobs.

legislatures of fewer than the necessary 38 states meet in 1972.

But political power did not appear to be the only reason why the amendment went through Congress by such lopsided votes—354 to 24 in the House of Representatives last October and 84 to 8 in the Senate last week. There seemed to be a conviction on the part of many that the time had simply come to bring an end to sex discrimination that is sanctioned by law or by the practices of any government— Federal, state or local. That is what the amendment would do.

The list of such legal discriminations is long, though not all are to be found in all states and some exist in a mere handful. Laws and practices that the amendment would wipe out include higher entrance requirements for young women than for young men at state universities; differing curricula (home economics, shop, physical education) in the public schools; laws that limit the right of married women (but not men) to sell property or en-

gage in a business, without the consent of their spouses; differing rules for service on juries;

Opponents of the amendment expressed considerable fear that there would be other, undesirable, effects. They argued that separate rest rooms for males and females in public schools and other public places would be outlawed; that fathers would be absolved of all obligation to support their children and that laws that protect women from working long hours and lifting heavy weights would be wiped out.

Advocates of the equal rights amendment pooh-poohed the integrated rest room argument, saying that the established legal right to privacy would prevail—assuming anyone would ever sue to integrate rest rooms sexually. As for child support, that would be decided on an individual case basis, taking into account the needs and earning abilities of each parent. Finally, the advocates said, the "protective" laws don't protect women but just ban them from job and

overtime that they actually want. And such "protective" laws have almost all already been overturned under the 1964 Civil Rights Act anyway.

Both sides did agree that, under the amendment, women would have to be drafted if men were, but the advocates of the amendment said that women were ready to accept this obligation.

Even assuming prompt ratification of the amendment, there remained some questions as to how rapidly the status of women would actually improve. There are, for example, the feelings of many people who just don't feel women are capable of being engineers, crane operators, elective officials, business executives or judges and who are in a position to deny women the training and experience that would permit them to achieve these and many other positions.

An attempt to find out how much women are kept down by simple prejudice was undertaken recently by two Census Bureau officials, Larry E. Suter and Herman P. Miller. They studied 5,000 women aged 30 to 44 who had worked every year since leaving school, thus acquiring as much job experience as men in the same age group.

Their conclusion: "Women are unable to exchange education and occupational status into earnings at the same high rate as men even when they are full-time workers with considerable lifetime work experience. The inability of women to convert occupation status into income, to the same extent as men, suggested that much of the remaining unexplained difference in male-female earnings could be attributable to discrimination."

—EILEEN SHANAHAN

March 26, 1972

'West Side Story' Wins Oscar as Best Film

By MURRAY SCHUMACH
Special to The New York Times.

SANTA MONICA, Calif., April 9 — "West Side Story" overwhelmed all opposition tonight to become the best picture of 1961 and win nine other Oscars at the thirty-fourth annual presentation of the Academy of Motion Picture Arts and Sciences.

The Broadway musical that adapted "Romeo and Juliet" to New York juvenile warfare won, among its other honors, Oscars for its directors. Jerome Robbins and Robert Wise co-directed the movie, which was originally staged in New York by Mr. Robbins to music by Leonard Bernstein.

Partly obscured by the sweeping victory of "West Side Story" was the election of Sophia Loren as the best actress of the year for her performance in "Two Women." Her victory was the first time a major award in the world's most famous film competition was won by a foreign actress in a foreign-language film.

In the past, foreign stars have won Oscars in English-language movies and minor awards in the competition have been won by foreigners.

Among the important Oscars voted to "West Side Story" by secret ballot of 2,300 members of the Academy were awards to George Chakiris for best supporting performance by an actor and to Rita Moreno for best supporting performance by an actress.

Only "Judgment at Nuremberg" seemed to offer even token opposition as the theme songs from "West Side Story" echoed and re-echoed through the Civic Auditorium here each time another category was announced for the musical.

Abby Mann a Winner

For "Judgment at Nuremberg," Maximilian Schell received one of the coveted gold-plated statuettes for best performance by an actor. And Abby Mann received one for the script that he adapted from his original television drama about the trial of Nazis after World War II.

Ingmar Bergman's "Through a Glass Darkly," a Swedish drama recounting a woman's des____ on a ____ w____

United Press International Wirephoto

Rita Moreno and George Chakiris with awards they won as the best supporting actress and best supporting actor.

April 10, 1962

The Wrong Reasons

That attractive lady from Maine, Senator Margaret Chase Smith, has finally decided to enter the Republican Presidential primaries in New Hampshire and Illinois. One of the reasons that impelled her, she says, was to show that a woman could and should be a member of a national ticket. Some of those who heard her surmised that she would be happy to settle for second place on the ticket the Republicans will name in San Francisco next July.

Meanwhile the Erie County Democrats, under the leadership of that engaging politico Peter J. Crotty, have come out for the nomination of Attorney General Robert F. Kennedy for the Vice Presidency. Some of Mr. Kennedy's friends and allies do not think that this was doing Mr. Kennedy any favor. But to Mr. Crotty that is unimportant, compared to having a famous Catholic name on the ticket in his strongly Roman Catholic constituency.

Without any assessment of the qualifications of either the Senator or the Attorney General, we think they are being boomed for office now for the wrong reasons. The nominee for the Vice Presidency on both the Republican and the Democratic tickets should be selected solely because he is the best qualified person available to step into the Presidency, if fate should call him there. Considerations of religion or sex or race or family or place of residence should not enter into this choice. Ability to carry out the duties of the Presidency of the United States with distinction is the proper, and the only proper, criterion.

January 29, 1964

Woman Put in Charge Of All V. A. Personnel

WASHINGTON, Aug. 5 (AP)—The White House announced today the appointment of Miss Irene Parsons as assistant administrator for personnel of the Veterans Administration. This is the highest Government personnel job held by a woman.

In the $22,000-a-year post, Miss Parsons will be the top ranking woman in the Government's third largest agency.

Miss Parsons has been with the Veterans Administration since 1946.

Miss Parsons is a native of Wilkesboro, N. C., and a graduate of the University of North Carolina and George Washington University. She was a Coast Guard lieutenant during World War II.

Associated Press Wirephoto

Miss Irene Parsons at White House yesterday afternoon.

August 6, 1965

Working Wife Gets Approval of Men

By MARYLIN BENDER

THAT recently embattled American heroine—the housewife who longs for an identity beyond domesticity—is about to receive a pat of encouragement.

A psychologist and an educator who have been studying the role of women for more than a decade have turned their inquiry toward men. They report that men say they really like a woman who is active outside the home. Provided, of course, her activities don't interfere with her husband's comfort.

The psychologist, Dr. Anne Steinmann, and her colleague, Dr. David J. Fox, associate professor of education at City College, are reporting the results of their investigation tomorrow at a meeting of the Eastern Psychological Association at the Statler Hilton Hotel.

They asked 423 American men (white and Negro, college students, artists, professional and business men, the majority under 40) to reply to a series of questions that express value judgments about women's activities and satisfactions. They responded to the 34 statements as their ideal woman would.

When the Inventory of Feminine Values, as the questionnaire is called, was previously given to women they were asked to answer in three ways; in terms of how they felt, how their ideal woman would feel and how they thought men would want women to respond.

The researchers discovered a wide discrepancy between the active, self-assertive role women conceive for themselves and the passive, self-effacing women they think men want them to be.

The majority of the men surveyed said that "a woman should be active outside the family, have responsibility, use her talents, create, fulfill herself," Doctors Steinmann and Fox found. But when it came to specifics, they took a less liberal tack.

They drew back from the suggestion that at some point a wife's own work might be the most important aspect of her life.

April 15, 1966

1968: For Women, It Was a Year Marked by Numerous 'Firsts

By JUDY KLEMESRUD

THE year 1968 may well go down in history as the Year of the Woman.

In the last 12 months women have won new rights and offices and have been admitted to places where female faces had never been seen before. Many of these "firsts" were won by Negro women; in several cases they were the first Negro and the first woman to achieve distinction in a particular field.

In Mississippi, women won the right to serve as jurists for the first time. And in the Swiss cantons (states) of Basel and Berne, suffragettes finally won the right to vote.

The United States Equal Employment Opportunities Commission proved to be some women's best friend. It ruled that the airlines could not dismiss stewardesses when they reached their mid-30's or married. And it also ruled that newspapers could no longer segregate help-wanted ads by sex. As a result, that heading of a newspaper's classified department now reads something like: "Help Wanted — Male-Female."

Men were not the only ones wearing pants in 1968—nor were they the only ones using foul language. Four-letter and twelve-letter words became common additions to the vocabularies of women of the New Left and civil rights groups, many of whom regarded their usage as a natural outgrowth of the equality of the sexes.

All of a sudden, women were hot commodities at previously all-male institutions. Wesleyan University began admitting women in September, and others such as Yale and Princeton began wooing them to their Ivy-colored walls. Not to be outdone, several women's colleges, including Vassar and Bennington, announced plans to go "fully coeducational."

Even the Boy Scouts voted to take in girls. Beginning today, girls will be admitted to Exploring, the Scouts' character-building program for boys from 14 to 18.

A major breakthrough for women came when Muriel (Mickey) Siebert, 38, became the first woman to buy a seat on the 175-year-old New York Stock Exchange. It cost her $445,000, plus a $7,515 initiation fee.

"I had an incredible year, much better than I ever dreamed," Miss Siebert said yesterday in her office at 120 Broadway. "I grossed over $1,000,000 — and that was before volume discount!"

Member of the Big Board

Miss Siebert, who employs three men on her five-member staff, grossed about $500,-000 a year before she became a member of the Big Board. The bubbly blonde specializes in aviation and aerospace stocks, and her clients include nearly all of the nation's 25 largest mutual funds and several of the big New York City banks.

Another major "first" came when Mrs. Shirley Chisholm of Brooklyn became the first Negro woman member of Congress. The 42-year-old former school teacher won by a 2 to 1 margin in the 12th Congressional District in Brooklyn's Bedford-Stuyvesant section, where she was born and raised.

The 96-pound Mrs. Chisholm, the Democratic National Committeewoman from New York, defeated James L. Farmer, a former head of the Congress of Racial Equality and the Liberal-Republican candidate.

"I know freshmen are supposed to be seen and not heard," she said on the eve of her election. "But my voice will be heard. I have no intention of being quiet."

Horse-racing was another area where women made history. Two attractive equestriennes, Kathy Kusner and Penny Ann Early, became the first women to receive jockey licenses. Miss Kusner, 27, promptly broke her leg in a fall at the National Horse Show, and won't be able to attempt her track debut until 1969.

Miss Early ran into other problems. Jockeys boycotted her on her two attempts to become the first woman jockey to ride at Churchill Downs. As the year ended, she moved to California and was issued a license to ride at Santa Anita — but only as an exercise girl.

In the fashion world, Naomi Sims, a Negro model, became the first black woman to hit the cover of one of the big three of the women's magazine field — Ladies Home Journal, McCall's and Good Housekeeping. The willowy Miss Sims was on the cover of the November Journal, which also featured an interview with her.

Other Negro women who achieved "firsts" because of their race were Mrs. William (Kay) Dunham of Brooklyn, who became the first black Mrs. New York State; Federal Judge Constance Baker Motley, who became the first Negro trustee of New York University; and Mrs. Elizabeth D. Koontz, the first Negro to head the National Education Association.

In 1968, for the first time in the history of the civil rights movement, two women became major spokesmen for Negro organizations.

Spokesman for the Militants

Mrs. Coretta Scott King assumed the role for the Southern Christian Leadership Conference following the assassination of her husband, Dr. Martin Luther King Jr. And the attractive, bush-haired Kathleen Cleaver became a spokesman for the militant Black Panthers after her husband, Eldridge, disappeared on Nov. 24, the day he was supposed to turn him-

493

The Death and Life of Economies

By CHRISTOPHER LEHMANN-HAUPT

Jane Jacobs

THE ECONOMY OF CITIES. By Jane Jacobs. 268 pages. Random House. $5.95.

TO go straight to the heart of the radiant, harmonious and beautifully integrated theory that Jane Jacobs unfolds in "The Economy of Cities," let's take her favorite practical illustration from among hundreds in her book. In the early nineteen-twenties, Mrs. Ida Rosenthal, a custom seamstress who was making dresses in a small shop of her own in New York, grew dissatisfied with the way her product hung on her customers and began experimenting with underclothes. The result was the first brassiere and eventually the Maidenform Brassiere Company. (Prior to this, according to Mrs. Jacobs, "American women wore various under garments called corset covers, chemises and ferris waists.") This portentous event illustrates as well as any the cornerstone on which Mrs. Jacobs builds her theoretical edifice.

She translates the occurrence into a simple formula: $D+A \rightarrow nD$, in which D stands for a division of labor in an economic system (in this case dressmaking); A stands for new activities (such as manufacturing brassieres or body stockings); and nD stands for the resulting "indeterminate number of new divisions of labor." The equation is meant simply to illustrate how new work is added to old—how all economies grow.

Ideal City Envisioned

Mrs. Jacobs concludes that the only social setting in which her formula can work is the city. So she sets out to prove it by postulating the theoretical growth of an ideal city, accompanying every step with a dazzling variety of concrete illustrations from all over the world and all human history.

Stripped of illustration and violently oversimplified, her theory is that cities grow by converting imported goods and services into exports, which activity in turn produces additional imports. At a certain point the city reaches maturity and, if all goes well, it "continues to generate new exports and earn imports; replace imports with local production; generate new exports and earn imports; replace imports with local production, and so on.

"All these processes, taken together, compose two interlocking reciprocating systems; the first triggers off the second. If one process fails, the entire system fails and the city stagnates economically.

"Among the producers' goods and services that form in the course of these events are those that supply capital to new goods and services that are forming and growing, as well as to older goods and services. The root process is the adding of new work to older divisions of labor, to some of which still newer activities can be added." (We're back to Ida Rosenthal now.) "This underlying process, which I have symbolized as $D+A \rightarrow nD$, makes possible all others."

What this provides is a theoretical framework for the vision of city life that Mrs. Jacobs presented in her earlier book, "The Death and Life of Great American Cities." Except here the vestiges of apparent sentimental longing for a past age that clung to that book are gone and replaced by a tough-minded system of economic necessity.

New Work Generated

The ideal city must be diverse in economic and social activities that interact spontaneously, to generate new forms of work. If a single division of labor prevails over all others (as the steel industry in Pittsburgh and the automobile industry in Detroit have), if capital refuses to flow freely into unpredictable business activities (on the ground, for instance, that black businessmen may lack plans that appeal to white bankers), spontaneous generation ceases and the economy stagnates. No amount of artificial planning imposed from above will get it going again. (It is Mrs. Jacobs's conclusion that "from the symptoms to be observed, . . . the economy of the United States is in the process of stagnating.")

The major objection to all this is precisely that it is founded on the existence of cities. Everyone—you and I and the economists, anthropologists and archeologists—knows that urban technology grew out of rural agriculture. How is one to account for the development of agricultural economies with a theory based on the growth of cities?

Mrs. Jacobs's anticipation of and answer to that question is the most startling aspect of her whole argument and serves as her point of departure. Going back to the archeological evidence of a prehistoric city on the Anatolian Plain in Turkey, she advances the radical idea that not only did cities precede agriculture in human history, but that indeed "work that we usually consider . . . originated not in the countryside, but in the cities." And much of her ideal model of the modern city is evolved not from New York's West Village, where she has been such an activist, but from New Obsidian, her imaginary prehistoric city.

"The Economy of Cities" is an astonishing book. It blows cobwebs from the mind, and challenges assumptions one hadn't even realized one had made. It should prove of major importance.

The Ladies Home Journal

Model Naomi Sims, first Negro cover girl on a major women's publication.

self in for imprisonment on a charge of parole violation.

The Vietnam war produced several firsts for women, including the first combat decoration—an Air Force Bronze Star. It went to First Lieut. Jane A. Lombardi, 25, of Stockton, Calif., a nurse who helped evacuate 38 patients under fire during an attack on the air base at Danang.

The war also produced the first woman peace negotiator, Mrs. Nguyen Thi Binh, 42, who heads the National Liberation Front's delegation to the Paris talks. Communist source material describes her as "a dedicated fighter for freedom and democracy."

In education, Dr. Suzanne Keller, a sociologist, became the first woman to be granted professorial tenure in Princeton's 222-year-history. And Mrs. Maurice T. Moore, sister of the late Henry R. Luce, became the first woman named chairman of the board of trustees of the State University of New York.

In Washington, two major jobs in the Federal Government went to women in 1968. Mrs. Anthony Camps, 52, became the first woman to be vice chairman of the State Department's Policy Planning Council, an ivory-towered, brain-powered group of 12 persons—all men except Mrs. Camps—that since 1947 has helped plan the nation's long-range foreign policy.

And Mrs. Virginia Mae Brown, a 45-year-old West Virginia lawyer and mother, was named chairman of the Interstate Commerce Commission—the first woman ever to head an independent administrative agency of the Federal Government. "My friends call me 'Peaches,'" Mrs. Brown said, "but at the ICC they call me Commissioner Brown."

Court Rules Woman May Be a Baseball Umpire

By WILLIAM E. FARRELL
Special to The New York Times

ALBANY, Jan. 13—A Queens housewife, Mrs. Bernice Gera, won the approval of the state's highest court today to be an umpire in professional baseball.

The Court of Appeals, in a 5-to-2 decision, affirmed the judgments of the state's Human Rights Division and lower courts that Mrs. Gera, a 40-year-old resident of Jackson Heights, had been denied a position as a minor league umpire because of her sex.

"I'd like to start going into training now, and I hope I get a shot at the minor leagues this summer," Mrs. Gera said in a telephone interview. "I just want to be part of baseball."

Attempts to reach the minor league baseball associations that opposed Mrs. Gera's admission as an umpire to determine whether they planned to appeal today's decision to the United States Supreme Court were unsuccessful.

But Representative Mario Biaggi, a Bronx Democrat-Conservative, who has represented Mrs. Gera in court, said it was his understanding there probably would not be an appeal.

The litigation began in 1969 when, after graduating from an umpire school in Florida, Mrs. Gera was scheduled to make her professional debut in Auburn, N. Y., whose team is in

The New York Times
Mrs. Bernice Gera

the New York-Pennsylvania Professional Baseball League.

But Philip Piton, who was then president of the National Association of Professional Baseball Leagues, disapproved her contract and notified Mrs. Gera that she failed to meet umpire physical requirements of height of about 5 feet 10 inches, a maximum beginning age of 35 and an average weight of about 170 pounds.

Mrs. Gera is 5-2 and weighs 129.

She then instituted an action with the Human Rights Division, charging that she was being discriminated against because of her sex in violation of state law.

The minor league groups then took the case to court, contending that Mrs. Gera was not barred from employment because of her sex and that the physical standards espoused by the Office for Baseball Umpire Developments were reasonable.

In upholding the lower courts today, the Court of Appeals judges did not issue an opinion.

Mrs. Gera said tonight that she did not know whether her original contract was still valid, but she said she was determined to don an umpire's uniform.

"I used to put on hitting demonstrations for charities," she said, adding that her main goal was to be part of the game.

She said she did not belong to a women's liberation group but was a stanch adherent of work equality.

Last year, Mrs. Gera, with Representative Biaggi as her attorney, filed a $25-million law suit in Supreme Court in Manhattan against organized baseball, charging that her career as an umpire was "virtually destroyed."

Biaggi said the case was still pending and that he and Mrs. Gera now had to decide whether to pursue it.

The Congressman said the decision by the Court of Appeals "will open up umpiring to many other people."

The Human Rights Division said that Mrs. Gera's case was valid and ordered the minor league associations to "cease and desist from refusing to employ any individual because of her sex and to establish new physical standards which have a reasonable relation to the requirements of the duties of an umpire."

Umpire Liberated

Members of the National Organization for Women surrounded their only recruit from organized baseball, Mrs. Bernice Gera, yesterday as the the Queens housewife told why, after fighting six years in court to become the first woman umpire, she quit after one game. Mrs. Gera said her career as an umpire started and ended in a Class A New York-Penn League game Saturday night "because baseball fought me from the beginning and was going to fight me to the end." Mrs. Gera said, "I never was a member of a Women's Lib group before but I have joined the NOW organization to see this never happens to a woman again." In a release prepared by NOW, Mrs. Gera expressed a desire to get organized baseball "out of the hands of the sexist operators who control it." She said the struggle cost her "thousands of dollars although court costs were paid for by the Human Rights Commission." Mrs. Gera plans to write a book about her six years in court and seven innings on the diamond.

January 14, 1972

June 29, 1972

Women Managers and Marriage

Increased Freedom Posing Challenge To Family

By MARYLIN BENDER

If the presidents of two billion - dollar corporations were to marry each other, what would their family life style be? Obviously, different from the traditional work-obsessed husband and home-bound wife relationship.

The intriguing consequences for the family if women really do enter the managerial ranks of business in the next decade were explored by William J. Goode, Professor of Sociology at Columbia University and president of the American Sociological Association, at a recent conference sponsored by the Columbia Graduate School of Business at Arden House in Harriman, N. Y. His paper was entitled "Family Life and Women Managers."

Professor Goode might be called an honorary member of the women's liberation movement. A long-time student of family patterns and the socialization of women, he is an avowed supporter of women's rights. He has been quoted by major feminists such as Betty Friedan, Kate Millett and Cynthia Epstein.

In an interview based on his Arden House presentation, Professor Goode begins by repeating his pessimistic prediction that women will be the last group in our society to be freed because male managers will only grudgingly offer them opportunities for advancement.

•

Male managers rationalize not hiring women because they believe their duty is to children, home and husbands, Professor Goode suggests. He proposes that business adopt the same policy toward women that it has for men, namely, don't ask whether they will marry and have children but even hope they will neglect such outside distractions to give their best talents to the enterprise.

For the basis of discussion, he assumes that over the next two decades the utilization of women in higher managerial jobs will show a sharp increase. What then will be the consequences for the family?

QUESTION: Can we expect catastrophe or new harmony for the family if women move in numbers into the managerial levels of corporate society?

ANSWER: I might argue that females should experience no great shock or dislocation in running a corporation and a family simultaneously since management is inherently and organically a woman's job.

If our stereotypes of women are correct, they are trained in human relations, not test tubes and machinery; in insight; in the organization and maintenance of a social unit, the family; in command through persuasion and participation in taking care of subordinates so they will produce better.

However, analyzing the impact of being a manager on family life requires more than asserting the two tasks may be similar. In a different kind of social or economic position, people change and we have to ask how are they likely to change?

•

Q. What are the variables in the family life of women managers?

A. Women's independence for one. Women work in all societies and in most of them they do much of the dirty, drab and tedious work. But when they were put to work in factories at the earliest stages of industrialization, for the first time they were hired and promoted as individuals rather than as women attached to some man.

This variable is especially important with respect to entrepreneurship. Women who have been heads of companies in the past have typically got there because of family connection, very often as widows or heiresses.

Now we are proposing that women should be put in the topmost positions of large corporations, as men are, whether or not they have inherited large blocks of stock in the company itself or because they are married to someone who has a high political or corporate position. This will increase their independence substantially.

Q. It's often said that the successful manager needs a wife. What is the female manager to do?

A. If I may rephrase the question, consider what would their family life be if the presidents of General Motors and I.T.T. were married to one another.

Inevitably female managers will be married to other top-level managers, since people of the same class, education, race, ethnic group, religion and so on marry each other.

But high-level managers, professionals and research scientists are more likely than any other segment of the work force to work seven days a week and to take work home in the evening.

They not only spend long hours at their tasks but they also think about those tasks most of the time no matter where they are. On the other side, the amount of time that women spend in homemaker tasks has not diminished over the half-century. As Marx would have understood, the modern homemaker has a wide range of appliances to use, but she turns out more production in a given 10-to-14-hour day. But no machine will straighten a room after a cocktail party or socialize our children. As Alice Rossi pointed out, we are perhaps the first civilization to transform the socializing of children into a 24-hour job and it has been given to women.

Q. Are you suggesting that women who perform at the highest levels should have no families at all?

A. No. The social structure is changing, even if slowly. During the next two decades as a larger percentage of the top social stratum takes on different attitudes towards sex equality, they will behave differently. An erratically emerging set of changed attitudes will be encountered.

I make the prediction that women managers will in the future be perceived as much sexier and more womanly than now.

•

Professor Goode reviewed the negative stereotypes that attach to any minority that is discriminated against. He said women managers are supposed to be "tough, cold, bitchy and castrating women . . . frivolous but cunning . . ." Men are regarded as people, women are not. Furthermore, men are permitted several kinds of styles that give respect along with deprecation, such as "mad genius," "man about town." None of these is permitted to women, who are allowed a much narrower range within which to express their personalities, needs and motivations.

However, to the extent that corporations begin to utilize the imaginations and skills of womanpower, success will make women managers behave more humanely and less within the stereotype. He reiterates, "success is sexy" and that in the future this will apply to women as well as men.

•

Q. With what consequences?

A. It will be easier for women executives to be married. They will be worth more on the marriage market. They will not need as much as in the past to hold tight against emotional involvements and perhaps will not even have the need of finding a man whom they judge to be their superior. Since that number of men is statistically small, such women viewed their choice as being one between marriage and career. More women will be freer emotionally to commit themselves to a man.

Q. But hasn't the women's liberation movement had an impact on the kinds of marriage relationships viewed as tolerable?

A. It's possible that in the immediate future more men and women will live together without marriage for some time because they don't wish to enter the kinds of legal entanglements marriage now requires.

In the longer term future, there may be a movement toward more marriages based upon explicit contract . . . formal contractual relations that spell out what their obligations are to one another, how they shall operate a joint household and under what conditions and penalties they will be permitted to leave it.

•

Q. Isn't it inevitable that married women managers will have fewer children?

A. I fervently hope that

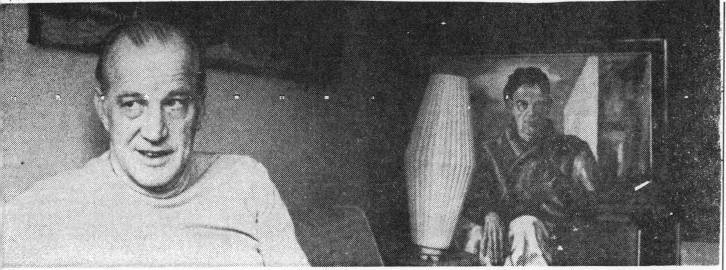

The New York Times/Tom Madden

William J. Goode, Professor of Sociology at Columbia, discusses women in business

the upper occupational strata will respond to the need for a reduction in population, but I would predict the increased percentage marrying in the future will balance off the possibly slight decline in fertility among those who do have families.

Q. You've been talking about the variable of women's independence. Are there others?

A. Time and energy budgets. Having housekeepers or husbands willing to help their wives are small contributions to the overriding burden women have of directing a household. I would characterize the nature of that job as containing hundreds of items that have relatively low importance but high urgency.

Women accomplish much less than men in their chosen areas of creativity, not because they have no free hours—homemaking is an intermittent task—but because there is no un-interruptible time. Also, they are socialized to respond to household urgencies. Men have been socialized simply not to respond to many household crises. Therefore it is much more difficult for a woman to get any creative work done at home than it is for a man.

It's not surprising that many young women now assert they simply will not marry at all. This is different from the choice between career and marriage 50 years ago. Today's young women like men and are willing to to live with them. They do not, however, wish to start

a household so that some man can achieve better.

●

Q. Aren't you being bearish about the future of marriage for creative, able women?

A. A goodly number of men will try to persuade women to settle down and take part in the joys of home life just as women once pleaded with the attractive bachelor to settle down to domesticity.

Furthermore, though there is somewhat more conflict in families where women are working, there is also likely to be much more satisfaction as well. The woman who enjoys her work is easier to live with.

Q. But returning to your variable of independence, why should creative women want to put up with the constraints of marriage?

A. The variable of independence is a negative element, I admit. People who enjoy more alternatives, whether in marriage and love, or in jobs, can afford to be more independent. The woman manager will be much less vulnerable to the economic threat of divorce. Her income is high, her social and friendship network is to a great extent her own. She possesses many advantages to offset in part the disadvantage of years.

●

Q. Doesn't increased independence build an increased element of instability into the woman executive then?

A. That's the challenge.

Through our imagination and in the face of the impossible time budgets and great independence of both partners, can we create any foundation for a stable and fulfilling relationship?

Q. And what effect on the children?

A. I foresee less effect on children than on the husband-and-wife relationship.

It will be psychologically more healthful for girls to be reared in an atmosphere where it is taken for granted they will use what talents they have. As for boys, our present system has created in males a high degree of anxiety about their own masculinity and this has created some viciously spiral problems in their sexual relations and for that matter, in the world of politics and business.

I believe children can thrive in an atmosphere of somewhat more neglect than they experience now, especially in the upper middle strata. Salutary neglect if husbands take a fair share of the burden of child-rearing. Women will not feel the same need to justify their intense concentration on the home if they have an outside job that is both fascinating and demanding. I believe that children would still obtain sufficient loving.

●

Q. Haven't some solutions been proposed such as communes and day care centers? Do they apply to the woman executive?

A. A commune does offer a partial solution though I

believe that all communes will have an extremely high rate of turnover and therefore will not furnish a viable solution for the problems I outlined.

A day care center program would also offer a partial solution for the child care problem. On the other hand, such centers are not predicated on any major change in society.

Q. What major change do you see affecting women managers?

A. Men and women might be not so compulsively work-driven. They might develop more flexible plans for their lives with respect to work. Husbands and wives might work only part-time for rather lengthy periods in their lives or might alternate at their jobs, men staying home for, say six months, and then turning the homemaking job over to their wives.

Suppose we had large-scale housing units—not true communes—in which there would be communal preparation of meals, services of various kinds, cleaning and the like.

If there were many top-level women managers, most of them married to men who also have high incomes, a number of such families could create small communities in which the range of services necessary to run households would be provided by an organization for that purpose. They could make their wishes known to the central organization, which is precisely what we do in the corporation itself.

December 26, 1971

It's Not All Fun and Glamour, Women Secret Service Agents Discover

By JUDY HARKISON

Special to The New York Times

WASHINGTON — The trouble with being a woman Secret Service agent is that while there are moments of fun and glamour, there are hours and hours of boredom and drudgery, the young women have told friends.

They can't speak for themselves because newspaper interviews are not permitted. Neither can they be photographed. "It would not be in the best interests of their job responsibilities," claims an equally anonymous voice in the Secret Service's public affairs section.

Five young women who can shoot .38-caliber revolvers have been working a year or so as security officers for the presidential staff and visiting foreign dignitaries—first in the White House with the Executive Protective Service, an arm of the United States Secret Service, and now with the Secret Service itself.

They have expressed disappointment that in the past much of their daily work was simply answering office telephones and that the adventures were few and far between. At least two have been heard to say that while they intend to remain through the election year, they would not make a career of it if their assignments didn't change.

Observers, surprised to see them trailing a foreign visitor, say they are on the ball and, although they don't look it, are tough.

One of them, by mistake, gave an example of her firmness when Prime Minister Golda Meir of Israel visited Washington and New York last month. Besides male Secret Service agents and Israeli security men, two of the women agents were assigned to guard Mrs. Meir.

When Secretary of State William P. Rogers stepped forth to greet the Prime Minister, one of the women agents, who went about her duties in a red rain slicker, didn't recognize him and quickly shoved him aside.

Mr. Rogers looked surprised but finally caught up with Mrs. Meir.

Observers said the officer was out of the big black limousine while it was still rolling. They thought at first she was an Israeli.

The Embassy of Israel said, no, she wasn't. "We have no women in our protective service," declared an Israeli spokesman. "Just because she was tough they thought she was Israeli, I said, 'That blonde chick belong to you.'"

Protection of Mrs. Meir not only meant slithering through crowds, but also standing long hours outside her room in the corridor of the Shoreham Hotel, while inside, the Prime Minister ate, napped, talked or read.

The Secret Service women were described as "efficient, enthusiastic and friendly" while they stood guard in the hallway. "I was impressed with them," remarked an Israeli official. "But that's a difficult job. I wonder how long their enthusiasm will last."

The women officers are Holly Hufschmidt of Milwaukee, Wis.; Sue Baker of Oak Ridge, Tenn.; Laurie Anderson of Jersey City, Kathryn Clark of Salt Lake City, and Phyllis Shantz of Rome, N. Y. They are all college graduates, single (a coincidence, said the Secret Service), in their twenties and all except Miss Clark were recruited from the District of Columbia's Metropolitan Police Department.

In late 1970 they became officers in the newly-formed Executive Protective Service, established for the security of the White House and foreign diplomatic missions. Last Dec. 15, they were sworn into the Secret Service as the first women agents in the organization's 106-year history.

Eugene T. Rossides, assistant secretary of the Department of the Treasury, said the women would be assigned to perform the same duties required of male special agents, which is protection as well as the investigation of cases involving counterfeiting and the forging and cashing of Government checks and bonds.

The women will soon enter the Treasury Law Enforcement Officers Training School. Subsequently, they will attend a Secret Service Training School for Special Agents.

Former colleagues of theirs at the District of Columbia police department say they are "a good cross section of policewomen—the girls are not at all alike."

Miss Shantz, who was graduated from the University of Maryland in 1969 with a degree in sociology and psychology, looks like a "swinger." With her very long black hair and stylish clothes, she is able to blend into different types of crowds and observe people, such as in a nightclub.

"Whenever they need someone to sit on a bar stool, she would be very useful," said Officer Mary Ellen Abrecht, D. C. policewoman coordinator. "She was also good at relating to the kids [she was assigned to the youth division] because she made a point of discussing things with them, and it always surprised them that she didn't talk like a cop."

Brown-haired Laurie Anderson was thought to be "very aggressive in the best police sense and could handle lots of difficult situations." Miss Anderson, a graduate in sociology from Beloit College in Wisconsin, worked as a student social worker while in school and spent a summer with the Headstart program in Plainfield. N. J.

For Holly Hufschmidt, a small woman with a blonde pixie haircut, one of her recent assignments was reported to be in Florida as one of the guards during West German Chancellor Willy Brandt's visit.

Last year, while she was stationed at the White House, one of her assignments was to go to school—the National Cathedral School for Girls. One of the students there was Kim Agnew, 16-year-old daughter of Vice President and Mrs. Agnew. Sue Baker also a blonde, spent two weeks at a girls' camp last summer with Caroline Kennedy.

Although the Secret Service announced that its women agents will perform the same work as the men, Officer Abrecht said she thinks this is questionable.

"My personal impression is that this whole thing is very token and they probably—and this is not based on fact but on fear—they probably will just use them for guard duty, the same thing they were doing for the White House," she said.

"Even though they were assigned to the Executive Protective Service they were doing a Secret Service job, protecting the President. The women were not getting the same assignments as the E.P.S. men, and they were not given much responsibility between projects.

"It's far from equality, what they have over there."

Corporate Tokenism for Women?

By MARYLIN BENDER

CHICAGO—Three corporate giants, recently and with fanfare, announced the appointments of women to the posts of assistant secretary.

In simultaneous moves, the General Motors Corporation, Pan American World Airways and the Dow Chemical Company promoted executive secretaries to jobs that might be described as low woman on the corporate totem pole.

"All they'll be doing is signing official documents and putting on the corporate seal," said a former executive secretary recently elevated to the post of equal opportunity coordinator of an oil company that has had female assistant secretaries for two decades without boasting about them. Is this just giving a title to women that looks good on paper?

Assistant secretaries are usually pegged one notch below officer, but Pan Am took pains to insist that its new assistant secretary was an officer.

None of these announcements mentioned that the United States Department of Labor's Revised Order 4 was to go into effect in early April and that it was exerting pressure on business to do something, at last, about bringing women into the corporate mainstream.

Prof. Eli Ginzberg, the manpower expert of the Columbia Graduate School of Business, has called Revised Order 4, which requires companies doing business with the Federal Government to take affirmative action to rectify sex discrimination, "the new reality."

"It will be years before we will be able to balance off the benefits and costs, but the employment picture will never be the same as it has been," Prof. Ginzberg predicted. "The pressure is on and it can go in only one direction—up."

●

Since James D. Hodgson, Secretary of Labor, signed Revised Order 4 in the first week of December, 1971, giving companies 120 days to comply with its directives, corporate managements and executive - search consultants have been thrashing about trying to decipher what consequences for them were buried in its turgid, bureaucratic prose.

Last week, the Urban Research Corporation held a two-day conference in Chicago in which 600 Government officials, corporate executives and feminists traded insults, intelligence and speculation about the new regulation.

Title VII of the Civil Rights Act of 1964 prohibited discrimination in employment on the basis of race, color, religion, national origin, or sex.

●

It set up the Equal Employment Opportunity Commission to investigate and try to conciliate complaints. But it has taken supplemental regulations to convince business that the Government meant what the law said.

Executive Order 11246 required affirmative action programs of Government contractors and subcontractors. It affected 260,000 companies, doing an $80-billion annual business with the Government.

Order 4, issued in January, 1970, provided guidelines for implementing such programs for minorities. Failure to comply meant cancellation of contract—a real threat, as evidenced by the well-publicized efforts of big business to hire, train and promote blacks.

Revised Order 4 added women to the list, covering an estimated one-third of the United States labor force. It demanded that Federal contractors with 50 or more employes and contracts of $50,000 or more set goals and timetables for correcting the underutilization of women "at all levels and segments of the work force."

It spelled out that women were likely to be underutilized as officials, managers, professionals, technicians, craftsmen and sales workers (except in certain retail occupations).

It asked companies to disclose their job classifications and who was filling them, as well as the availability and promotability of females in their organizations and the surrounding labor area.

They will also have to disseminate information about their willingness to hire, train and promote women in their consumer advertising and help-wanted advertising as well as through

William Negron

internal organization bulletins and programs.

Susan Davis, vice president of the Urban Research Corporation, said at the conference that business was "nowhere near implementation" of Revised Order 4. Some companies have taken the position: "What is the minimum we can get by on," she added.

●

She cited the General Electric Company, the Polaroid Corporation and Cummins Engine Company, Inc., as among "a handful of companies that have already set goals and timetables."

A quarter of those being hired for the assembly line at Cummins Engine are women and the company has set a 10-year goal of 25 per cent parity for women as supervisors, she pointed out.

Only a few companies, such as the International Business Machines Corporation and General Electric, have issued strong corporate policy statements of their commitment to equal opportunity for women, she said.

She congratulated the General Motors Corporation and the International Harvester Company for granting six weeks' sick leave for child bearing, which under the new guidelines is considered justification for a reasonable leave of absence.

●

She noted that the Boise Cascade Corporation had revised its personnel forms to omit questions about husbands and their rank and pay.

Blank spots in corporate consciousness were said to be the unwillingness to pay for management training for women, to admit that so-called women's jobs such as secretaries, nurses and assistants deserved higher pay and status, and to concede the tremendous need women have for part-time professional jobs.

During conference workshops on Revised Order 4 fears were expressed that sex - discrimination efforts might detract from minority programs and that additional proposed guidelines on religious and ethnic discrimination might dilute the women's cause.

Doubts about the efficiency and sincerity of the Government as enforcement agent were voiced by corporate equal employment coordinators, who complained of previous bureaucratic delay in reviewing affirmative action programs for minorities.

They were told that a new Order 14, soon to be issued, would simplify the maze of reports on minorities and women that corporations must now prepare for a variety of Government agencies.

Skeptics wondered whether the training in advancement of women could be accomplished without large allocations of corporate financial resources. They were told not to spend more money but to spend some of their existing funds on training women.

•

Several corporate managers of minority and women's programs complained of their top management's insincerity, and said their work was thwarted within their organizations.

"If they got a fink in your way, show him up to be a fink," a black male administrator shouted at a discouraged white female manager for a utility company.

"No one has the authority to tell a manager he will lose money out of his operating budget if he doesn't comply," another woman lamented.

Ray Graham, director of equal opportunity for Sears, Roebuck & Co., said his company was redesigning management evaluation programs to rate managers on their affirmative action performance.

Woman Wins Point

Alison Palmer, the Foreign Service officer who won a one-woman campaign after she had accused the State Department of sex discrimination, got her reward: she received a promotion.

Miss Palmer, who last August convinced a Civil Service Commission examiner that "solely because of her sex" her career had been adversely affected, will be-

Associated Press
Alison Palmer

come a Foreign Service Officer 3, on recommendation of the Board of the Foreign Service. That category makes her eligible to earn $23,300 to $28,000 a year. In her former rank, the salary ranges from $18,700 to $22,400.

Miss Palmer, who has been in the diplomatic service almost 11 years, has served in South Vietnam and in the Congo.

For More Women And More Minorities

Traditionally American colleges and universities have had relatively few women and minority-group members on their faculties and staffs. And those who were hired were more likely to be instructors —that is, in the lower echelons— than professors. This has led to charges of job discrimination by many of the institutions.

The issue has created a growing controversy because of confusing efforts by the Federal Government to increase the women and minority-group members on faculties of the 2,000 institutions that hold Federal contracts. Failure to act runs the risk of losing Federal contract funds, a serious matter for schools already having budgetary problems.

Columbia University had $13.8-million in Federal funds suspended until recently. Harvard, Cornell and the University of Michigan also have had funds held up for brief periods.

Columbia underscored the issue last week by releasing figures to support its claim that it wasn't doing badly compared with other comparable universities. For example, Columbia said that of 994 faculty members, 132 — or 13.3 per cent — are women. Some other figures: Harvard has 185 women in a total 2,093 for 8.8 per cent; Chicago has 86 in a total 1,103 for 7.8 per cent; University of California at Berkeley 235 in a total 2,137 for 11 per cent. Figures for minority-group members are comparably low.

As for claims that women and minority groups are relegated to the lower levels, American Council on Education figures show that 62.7 per cent of women staff members are in jobs paying $10,000 or less and 1.7 per cent make $20,000 or more (see chart).

The Government is acting under terms of a seven-year-old executive order 11246, originally signed by President Johnson, stipulating that every Federal contractor with 50 employes or more and a contract in excess of $50,000 is required to submit an "affirmative action plan" describing how it will change its hiring procedures to increase the number of women and minority-group members it employs. The Office of Civil Rights of the Department of Health, Education and

Welfare was given the responsibility for monitoring the colleges.

In an "affirmative action plan," the schools must set specific "goals and timetables" for hiring. But a basic difficulty is that nobody seems to have a clear definition of "goals and timetables."

J. Stanley Pottinger is the director of the Office of Civil Rights and he says he devotes about half of his time to affirmative action suits. Most of the pressure for such suits has come from women's groups.

"Nobody knows precisely what a plan should contain," Mr. Pottinger conceded in an interview in his Washington office. "In the commercial context, you can measure the number of people available for a particular position on the basis of information available by race, job, salary level, and geography. There is no similar mechanism for the university." The difference is that in industry and business the labor pool is considered to be confined to a certain area while the pool for higher education institutions can be on a national, or even international, level.

"Goals and timetables are fairly elusive things," and for the moment, the 32-year-old official continued, "there's no very effective way by which we can evaluate them." But the Civil Rights Office will soon issue a "70 page package with policy positions."

Mr. Pottinger's problem is compounded by the fact that his office has only 77 contract compliance officers — 58 men and 19 women. He says it is an "administrative nightmare" trying to monitor affirmative action plans at 2,000 institutions with so few people.

Prof. Sidney Hook, the outgoing president of University Centers for Rational Alternatives, and many other academicians believe that Mr. Pottinger's office is requiring universities to hire unqualified applicants to fulfill faculty hiring quotas. Mr. Hook asserts that some of the directives from the Civil Rights Office have been "in direct violation of the Civil Rights Act" of 1964. William Theodore deBary, vice president of Columbia, speaks of the "very subtle forms of influence that can develop when you are in a position of financial dependency on the Government."

Mr. Pottinger strongly denies that "goals and timetables" are "just a euphemism for quotas." A quota, he says, "means a level of employment is set in a given period of time and a failure to meet a quota would constitute a violation of the employer's commitment.

"A goal is a target of expected employment, also set by the employer, using his own best judgment

How Salaries of Men and Women Compare on College and University Faculties

Percentage of total members of each sex

Up to $10,000	27.9
	62.7
$10,000 to $14,000	38.1
	27.5
$14,000 to $20,000	24.6
	8.1
$20,000 and over	9.4
	1.7

Source: American Council on Education

of what he can recruit. A failure to meet that goal would not in itself constitute a violation. The standard to be used is good faith effort, not quotas."

But the lack of clear understanding of what constitutes a satisfactory plan has complicated the whole business. The impact can be seen in Columbia's interim plan, released late last month. Whenever an appointment is made which does not contribute to fulfillment of a previously stated goal, it becomes the responsibility of Vice President deBary's office to demonstrate to H.E.W. that a "good faith effort" was made to find a woman or minority-group member to fill the position.

"We cannot, in essence, hire, promote, or give a raise to anyone without clearing it over there," said Elie Abel, dean of the Columbia Graduate School of Journalism. "Are they really trying to tell us we cannot promote our own assistant professors without setting up a nationwide search?"

—CHARLES KAISER

April 2, 1972

First Woman Admiral
Alene Bertha Duerk

Special to The New York Times

WASHINGTON, April 27— The Navy's first woman admiral is a straightforward easy-going nurse more given to "reasoning" with people than hounding them. Capt. Alene Bertha Duerk, director of the Navy Nurse Corps, was driving alone through Ohio today, on the way to her mother's home in Holgate, when she first heard the radio reports of her nomination by the President. "I was surprised and thrilled," she remarked a few hours later, but true to her sense of orderliness she did not stop to telephone anyone and calmly continued her progress home.

Woman in the News

Captain Duerk, who enlisted as a Navy nurse 29 years ago at the height of World War II, has been a staff nurse, instructor, recruiter and, finally, administrator. She is an officer who has long believed in "organization of life and thoughts."

A member of the nominee's staff, Capt. Anna M. Byrnes, stressed that her boss was "very approachable — she doesn't stand on ceremony" and added, "She creates the atmosphere that makes it very easy to do your work." This remark, combined with the general feeling of jubilance emanating from the corps office today, seem to indicate that Captain Duerk had succeeded in communicating her personal philosophy to her associates.

Asserting that "you don't really gain anything" through strict discipline, the admiral-designate said, "I believe that the example that I set and the leadership I have should be so strong that people want to follow it, want to please. want to do."

Born in Defiance, Ohio, on March 29, 1920, Captain Duerk had decided in high school to pursue a nursing career and trained at the Toledo School of Nursing, graduating in 1941. She was commissioned as an ensign in 1943, serving for a period on the hospital ship Benevolence in the Pacific.

Released from the service in 1946, she remained in the Naval Reserve until called back to active duty during the Korean war. After serving at several naval hospitals, she was made a captain in 1967 and became director of the Nurse Corps, in May, 1970.

The corps, with 2,300 servicewomen, is the largest of the three branches of the Navy that are open to women —they also serve in the Waves and the Supply Corps. Captain Duerk will retain her duties as director and does not expect much change in her responsibilities, which include administration of nursing services in 39 Navy hospitals and a number of dispensaries.

Overtones of a reaction to the women's rights movement in the appointment were admitted by Vice Adm. George M. Davis, the Navy Surgeon General. Captain Duerk (rhymes with Dirk), having beat out "the competition of several qualified girls," will be "a visible representative of women," he said, adding his hopes that this will stimulate enlistments in the move toward an all-volunteer force.

"Pressures were indeed upon the Navy," Admiral Davis said. Since the Air Force and Army have recently appointed several women as general officers, he added, people were thinking, "Why haven't you given your girls a break in this regard?"

The nominee was more casual about the relationship between the women's movement and her own appointment. "Women have simply been moving into positions of responsibility," she said. "It's a natural thing."

But Captain Byrnes, who is responsible for recruiting Navy nurses, was more enthusiastic about the effect the action may have on attracting women into the service. "They can see that the sky's the limit now," she exclaimed.

April 28, 1972

Woman in High Post at F.B.I.

Barbara Lynn Herwig

By JUAN M. VASQUEZ

Special to The New York Times

WASHINGTON, May 11—Barbara Lynn Herwig recalls attending a recruiting session held by the Federal Bureau of Investigation when she was in law school. "After I was told they didn't accept women agents, well, I didn't expect to wind up here," she says. But today, the young lawyer was informed by L. Patrick Gray 3d that she would continue to be his special assistant as he moves into his new job as acting director of the bureau. The move means that, at the age of 27 years, she will become the first woman to play a major role in an agency that has been male-dominated since its birth half a century ago.

Woman in the News

"It may take a bit of getting used to," Miss Herwig said, "but I try to act like a professional, and I hope I will be accepted as one."

Then, in a tough tone followed by a quick laugh, she added, "I'd better be."

A colleague of Mr. Gray's staff commented: "If there are any die-hards in the F.B.I. who think this shouldn't happen, I can only say that there couldn't be a better person for the job."

Determination Is Cited

The qualities her friends cite are determination, perseverance and a quick mind, combined with a logical approach to problems and what one called "open-mindedness."

"She is really one of the few really bright, intellectual type conservatives I know," said one who knew her in college.

For Miss Herwig, who prefers the title Ms. but would like still better a "more pronounceable" title, the path from public school in California to F.B.I. headquarters

The New York Times
Logical and open minded

was as straight as an F.B.I. special agent

Miss Herwig, who was born Nov 1 1944, in Los Angeles, graduated from Stanford University in 1967 and obtained her law degree three years later from Boalt Hall Law School at the University of California, Berkeley.

In November, 1970, after an interview with a Justice Department recruiter who later went to the Supreme Court—Associate Justice William H. Rehnquist—she went to work for the Civil Division of the department in the appellate section here.

Backs Part of Movement

The following March, as she remembers, "I got a call and was asked if I'd like to be considered for the job of special assistant to Mr. Gray, and I said, 'Of course.'"

Of the acting F.B.I. director, she says, "He's a great man, you learn a lot from him." Mr. Gray calls her "an excellent appellate lawyer."

As to women's liberation, she said that she supported "that part of the movement that is for equal employment and equal pay, but I'm not in sympathy with that part of the movement that says men are bad, we should have a completely different society."

A law school friend recalled that Miss Herwig had been active in a women's movement at Berkeley that effectively campaigned against law firms with "sexist" leanings that recruited on the campus.

After graduation, the friend added, Miss Herwig "got to argue in court long before anybody else in our class that I can recall."

Miss Herwig conceded today that she had little knowledge of the internal workings of the Federal Bureau of Investigation. She did not know J. Edgar Hoover, although she "ran into him in the elevator a few times."

She said that she would like to help recruit women agents if Mr. Gray decided that the bureau should accept them. Her work for Mr. Gray has consisted of undertaking "special projects of any kind," she said, but she is not sure what her new responsibilities will entail.

Outside the office, as she described herself, she is a "book enthusiast" rather than a sports enthusiast. She lives alone in an apartment in the Southwest section of the city, not far from the Justice Department.

She has no pets. "I'd love to raise a tiger cub," she said, "a pet that would go well with the image of an ardent women's lib advocate." But in the next breath she confessed that among her favorite pastimes were sewing and cooking, at which she is said to be very adept.

Women Legislators Challenge Male Colleagues' Power

By EILEEN SHANAHAN

Special to The New York Times

POCONO MANOR, Pa., May 21—Women who serve in state legislatures believe that they are generally more industrious, more informed, more ethical, and more sexually pure and sober than their male colleagues but they still seldom reach leadership positions, according to views expressed at a meeting of women legislators here. They are beginning, however, to challenge their relatively powerless status inside the state houses.

In making their challenge, they may soon have their hand strengthened by a significant increase in their numbers. More women than ever before will apparently run this year for seats in state legislatures.

If any sizable number win, they will reverse a long down trend in the number of women legislators, which has reduced their numbers to fewer than 400 out of about 7,700 state legislators.

Problem Carrying the Ball

Views on the problems and potential of women legislators were exchanged here at a three-day meeting of 50 women legislators from both parties and 26 states. The 50 were chosen as outstanding women legislators by the sponsor of the meeting, the Center for the American Woman and Politics, which is a division of the Eagleton Institute of Politics. The institute is affiliated with Rutgers, the State University of New Jersey.

The participants in the conference reached a consensus on many issues, among them the following:

¶A woman legislator hurts her own standing with her male colleagues when she carries the ball on such "women's issues" as abortion, divorce law reform or ratification of the equal rights amendment. But most of the women nonetheless believe they must take the lead on such legislation, because the men will not.

¶The radical women's liberation organization make life harder for a woman legislator by

May 12, 1972

creating antagonism to any woman who asserts herself, even in a moderate way.

¶It is too early to assess the political impact of such relatively new women's groups as the National Organization for Women and the National Women's Political Caucus, neither of which tends to be closely tied to women who have actually won elections, except in a few states.

¶There is still a lot of bias against women running for office. If one has children and a husband, the voters tend to think she should stay home and take care of them. If she is single, an opponent is likely to campaign on his virtues as a "family man." Sometimes this backfires.

¶The one group that may be more pro-women than usual is young people. "The young are more accepting of anything different from what they've regarded as the Establishment," said Representative Grace T. Hamilton, Democrat of Georgia.

¶It is harder for a woman to raise money to run for office than it is for a man and, even if she raises enough to cover her campaign costs, serving in the legislature is likely to cost her money because of the low salaries and need to maintain two residences for part of the year.

The strongest theme of the conference turned out to be the extent to which women are said to be discriminated against once they get elected.

At the outset of the various discussion groups, most of the women said they were treated fairly, receiving good committee assignments by the second term, at the latest, for example. But as they exchanged experiences at this meeting, more and more said that they were the victims of serious discrimination.

Senator Clara Weisenborn, a Republican who has been in the Ohio Legislature for 18 years, said that women "are not privileged to know the mechanics that are going on in the inner circle because we are not committee chairmen."

She said the general lack of leadership positions for women was probably women's own fault "because we're not pushing." She added, "There isn't a single solitary door in this world that will open without pushing. I'm going back home and I'm going to turn the knob and push."

Successful efforts to give women greater positions of power were recounted by Nancy Brown Burkheimer of Maryland, president-elect of the National Order of Women

Legislators, and Representative Audrey Beck, of Mansfield, Conn.

In Maryland, women legislators achieved the co-chairmanship of a major committee and the chairmanship of a minor one when the women united in a woman's caucus and demanded such positions.

In Connecticut, the Democratic women presented a solid front and demanded that one of their number, Agnes Simons, be named assistant majority leader. After a six-month fight, they won.

What was seen as an equally serious problem with the lack of formal leadership posts was the nonparticipation by women legislators in night-time social activities with their male colleagues. It was agreed that serious legislative business is often transacted on these alleged social occasions.

'Select Circle' Stressed

Jess Unruh, the former Speaker of the California Assembly, who was one of the speakers at the conference, concurred in this evaluation.

"If you are not in the small, select social circle, you have no input," he said.

Almost all of those present agreed that because women legislators are seldom present for the evening events, for which they say lobbyists often pay, the women tend to vote more in the public interest and less for special interests.

The women legislators agreed that they tend to be much older than the men—the mid-fifties as against the mid-thirties — generally having raised their children at least to high school age before running for office.

Service in the legislature thus capped, for most women, a lifetime of service in community organization, they said. In addition, it was agreed, most have reasonably prosperous husbands who can support them.

For the male legislators, the situation was said to be different. They use the legislature as a stepping stone, the women agreed.

Representative Janet Merritt, Democrat of Georgia, summed up the point this way: "You have a group of young aggressive lawyers who go [to the legislature] not to serve the people but to build up their law practice. You have others, not good, who want to practice hanky-panky. The really good lawyers don't stay in politics or else they move on to higher office."

Companies Discuss Equal Opportunities for Women

By LEONARD SLOANE

About 300 representatives of companies that sell to the Federal Government wound up a two-day conference yesterday on equal opportunity for women in business.

The conference, sponsored by the Urban Research Corporation, included speeches and workshop sessions that delved into the practices and attitudes of corporations that must comply with Revised Order 4. This Federal order, which went into effect last April 2, provides for affirmative action programs of non-discrimination for large concerns that do business with Washington.

"You can view this as a compliance problem or as an opportunity to use a heretofore ignored talent pool," said John Naisbitt, president of Urban Research, which has presented three similar meetings over the last year. "This conference symbolizes that this is a subject matter we've got to deal with."

The keynote speaker at yesterday's session at the Americana Hotel was David J. Mahoney, chairman and president of Norton Simon, Inc. He discussed his company's views about what he called the "New American Revolution."

'Good for Business'

"The women's movement has been good for America and will be good for business," he said. Norton Simon is "committed to the active and aggressive development of new employment and promotion practices to move women into positions of greater responsibility."

Mr. Mahoney made it clear, however, that he was not proposing tokenism. "Company presidents should look for strong, capable women in their own organizations, give them some short-term development and then put them into top jobs at the corporate level," he asserted.

The Thursday keynote speaker, Aileen Hernandez, head of the national advisory board of the National Association for Women, said that corporations must reduce working hours and consider such new contract issues as parental leave and child care.

"Men eventually will embrace these changes," she said. "As the sole supporters of families, they are now disadvantaged and many are killed off yearly as the result of business tensions."

Another Thursday speaker, Eleanor Holmes Norton, chairman of the New York City Commission on Human Rights, said that "under our power to bring commission-initiated complaints against large corporations, we are securing hundreds of jobs for women." But she warned that "such clear progress must not blind us to widespread action now clearly under way to set us back."

The 29 workshops at the conference dealt with specific components of affirmative action. Co-sponsoring companies for the meeting were Atlantic Richfield, Bankers Trust, General Electric, International Business Machines, Norton Simon and Polaroid.

More Women Join Ranks of Nation's Police Forces

By DAVID BURNHAM

A small but growing number of policewomen are patroling the streets of American cities and responding to emergency calls in exactly the same way as male police officers.

One reason for the movement of women into what has traditionally been the male world of flashing lights and screaming sirens appears to be the belief that women tend to be less threatening than men and thus prompt less hostile reaction from the public.

Increasingly, too, women are being assigned to gritty, dangerous undercover details, primarily in drug investigations, as well as to the more routine duties, such as traffic control.

Generally, male police officers are nonplussed when they are assigned a woman partner on street duty, but they seem to get used to it fairly quickly.

At the same time, police officials say they are wary of putting married women, particularly those with children, in dangerous jobs, apparently under the belief that mothers should be exposed to danger less readily than fathers.

The women's rights movement and salary discrimination in other occupations seem to be important factors.

"Nine thousand dollars for a starting salary is better than what most women can earn at first, even with a master's degree," observed Marcella Daniels, a married college graduate who patrols the streets of Peoria, Ill.

With 40 women performing regular patrol work in Washington, more than a score in Miami, seven in Peoria, 15 undergoing training for such work in New York and other cities testing or exploring the concept, the use of women to patrol the streets appears to be an important new development in urban enforcement.

In Miami, where there are now 35 policewomen, including two sergeants, Chief Bernard L. Garmire finds that women have proved effective in all types of police work and says that "in certain situations they are more effective than men."

Chief Garmire cited a recent memo from C. E. Daniel, a black policeman who had been training a black female partner.

"I was a little reluctant about riding with a female partner," Patrolman Daniel said, "but

United Press International

Policewoman in Ann Arbor, Mich., frisking suspect before making arrest with partner

after a few hours I relaxed and realized that it had a great psychological effect on people in general. It was very beneficial in Liberty City [Miami's black area], especially in handling domestic disturbances. Women considered a policewoman as one of their own."

Less Violence Found

The extent of the growing trend toward a bigger role for women in police work and the merits of it are discussed in a report on "Women in Policing," to be published this week by the Police Foundation, a group established several years ago by the Ford Foundation to develop better approaches to police problems.

The report, written by the foundation's assistant director, Catherine Milton, says that the major reason for recommending a wider role for women is that it appears to reduce "the incidence of violence between police officers and citizens when women are assigned to patrol."

Mrs. Milton, previously on the staff of the International Association of Chiefs of Police, said that evidence from other fields and the experience of policewomen "suggest that women tend to defuse volatile situations and provoke less hostility than men."

Moreover, women undercover agents seem to have the same quieting effect on drug sellers and others they deal with.

The New York department utilizes several women — fewer than 10 — on its narcotics detail, primarily to buy from drug dealers.

One of them, a black woman whose name and age must remain confidential, regularly goes into the streets and into apartments where drugs are believed to be sold to make purchases. Normally, she will make more than one "buy" to establish that the suspect is in fact a dealer, not simply a one-time seller.

She holds the rating of a grade three detective and is paid $17,500 a year. "It's the easiest thing in the world to buy dope," she says. "The hardest thing is to stay alive."

Mrs. Milton, the author of the Police Foundation report, believes that a major reason for widening the opportunities for women in law enforcement is that the sex quotas maintained by many police departments and the separate promotion tests offered by some appeared to violate Federal and state laws outlawing discrimination against women.

She noted that the Law Enforcement Assistance Administration, the branch of the Justice Department that each year distributes millions of dollars in Federal grants, has already investigated and negotiated settlements of two complaints charging the departments in Wichita Falls, Tex., and Rochester with sex discrimination.

Despite the apparent benefits of using policewomen for

United Press International

Sister Mary Cornelia wearing pistol while on duty as a full-time dispatcher in Pontoon Beach, Ill.

a wider range of duties and the possible penalties of not doing so, Mrs. Milton found deep resistance to the concept in many police departments.

"Clearly," she wrote, "police departments are resisting a trend that is growing stronger. In effect, they are turning away female applicants by perpetuating arbitrary and discriminatory procedures which have evolved from the traditional assumption that policing is not a career for women, mostly because it is dangerous and may require 'unfeminine' behavior."

Chief Edward Davis of Los Angeles illustrated the deep feeling of some top police officials against the concept of using women on patrol during a recent recorded interview.

No Bandit-Wrestling

Asked whether he felt there was a place for women outside the normal clerical and other specialized jobs traditionally reserved for the country's 6,000 policewomen, he replied:

"Then are we going to let a 5-foot-2, 115-pound petit blonde girl go in there and wrestle with a couple of bank bandits? I personally don't think that's the role for women."

Mrs. Milton sees the situation differently. "By introducing women into jobs that have been held exclusively by men," she said in her report, "departments will be forced to rethink and re-evaluate traditional practices."

"For example, if a woman 5 feet 5 inches tall can perform the job of patrol, why can't a man who is the same height; if a woman needs better physical training, might not also a man; if a woman defuses a violent situation without having to make an arrest, shouldn't she or any man who does the same be given a high rating for effective law enforcement practice?"

Asked whether he felt the biological make-up of a woman might affect her performance, Chief Davis replied that "in the history of my wife and two daughters there were certain times during the month when they did not function as effectively as they did at other times of the month."

Another element blocking quick acceptance of women on patrol, according to Mrs. Milton, is the attitude of many policewomen themselves.

Discussing her research in New York, for example, Mrs. Milton said, "The most important obstacle to change is the resistance among the women themselves. Every woman interviewed agreed that the present situation is deplorable, but many find change acceptable in theory only."

This deep-seated feeling among many New York policewomen may be one reason that New York's first experiment is somewhat tentative.

Beginning June 23, according to Police Lieut. Victoria Renzulla, 15 volunteer policewomen now undergoing training will be assigned to work with the neighborhood police teams around the city. "Exactly how they will work will be within the discretion of the individual sergeant running each team," she explained.

The women training for neighborhood patrol work, now an experiment in New York, spend the mornings learning the art of self-defense: judo, jiu jitsui and aikido, firearms training, and baton (nightstick) work.

They spend the afternoons learning theory—laws and police and patrol techniques. They attend classes with visiting police and college teacher consultants for courses in human relations, community relations and awareness, the role of women as colleagues, citizens, victims and law-violators, and crisis intervention.

The women who have volunteered for the neighborhood patrol teams will not get any rise in pay. They now get from $12,500 to $14,500. One of them, Policewoman Ivy Forde, who has been doing clerical work in the first deputy commissioner's office and is the only black woman to volunteer for patrol, says she feels she has volunteered to be a pioneer.

Female Intelligence: Who Wants It?

There is plenty of it; the nation needs it—but our social scheme discourages it.

By MARYA MANNES

EVERY now and then there is a resounding call for a national resource—largely untapped and unmustered—referred to as the intelligence of women, or the female brain. Editorial writers, tired of outer space, say that if we are to win the race of survival and keep up with the Russians we must not squander this precious resource but rather press it into service.

Commenting on the number of women doctors, engineers, physicists and

A woman often suppresses her mental ability in favor of the primary need to be loved.

laboratory technicians in the Soviet Union compared to our paltry own, citing the desperate shortages in fields where the productive intellect is essential, they cry: "To the drawing-board, to the laboratories, to the computers!" And presidents of women's colleges beseech their students: "Use this brain you've got and we're training: society needs it!"

Gratifying though it may be to have the female intelligence not only publicly acknowledged but officially sought, these calls are met by a massive wave of indifference emanating from women even more than from men. We do not really believe either the acknowledgment or the demand for the kind of intelligence they speak of and claim they want, nor do we see any signs

MARYA MANNES, a regular contributor to The Reporter magazine, is the author of "More in Anger," a series of essays on American mores, and "Subverse: Rhymes for Our Time."

of a public attitude which would make its application either welcome or practical on a national scale.

The college presidents, the editorialists, the recruiters of resources are talking not of the intelligence which every woman needs to be a successful wife and mother or even a competent worker in office or factory or civic affairs. They are talking of the kind of free and independent intelligence which can analyze, innovate and create: the mind of the scientist and the artist, at liberty to roam in the world of abstractions and intangibles until, by will and effort, a concrete and tangible pattern is made clear.

Are women capable of this kind of intelligence? If they are not to the degree of genius—and the long history of man has produced no female Bachs or Shakespeares or Leonardos or Galileos—and although a Madame Curie is in lonely company, women have in every time given to the mainstream of the arts, letters and sciences. And when even a Jesuit priest-sociologist, Father Lucius F. Cervantes—whose recent book "And God Made Man and Woman" is a long and satisfied reiteration of the sacred differences between the two sexes—writes, "As far as has been ascertained there is no inherent intellectual capacity differential between men and women," then surely women are not by nature denied the ability to think creatively and abstractly.

IT is rather that this ability is unpopular with women because it is unpopular with men. Our prior need, in short, is to be loved. And if the possession of this kind of intelligence is a deterrent to love, then it is voluntarily restricted or denied by women themselves.

I have seen enough of this deterrence and this denial, since my youth, to believe it the common experience. And although it has not always been mine (I am fortunate in a happy marriage), I recognize only too well the signal of alarm in the eyes of men when a woman of intellect challenges their own.

It flashed even before I recognized it: boys at dances would forsake me soon for others, not—in Marty's language—because I was a "dog," but because I talked to them of sonnets or senses instead of about themselves. Used to a family where ideas were as much a part of the dinner table as food, I knew of no special kind of talk

geared to men rather than to women. Worse, I thought that to be interesting one had to say interesting things. This was possibly the greatest miscalculation since the Charge of the Light Brigade.

For most men, I duly discovered, prefer the woman whose interest lies not in her thoughts nor her speech nor her talents, but in her interest in them. Mind, they believe, interferes with this attention, and to some extent they are right. Right or wrong, the average American male is uneasy in the presence of markedly intelligent women; and the woman who wishes to change this unease into love must spend a good part of her life reining in her wits in the reluctant admission that they do her more harm than good.

Now there is a great paradox in all this. On the one hand, more girls go to college than ever before, and more colleges are equipped to develop their minds toward whatever intellectual goals they might aspire to. On the other hand, as President Thomas C. Mendenhall of Smith College recently —and sharply—deplored, there is a 60 per cent dropout of women students before graduation and most of this is due to their early marriage and almost immediate proliferation of the species.

In an open forum recently, I asked Millicent C. McIntosh, president of Barnard, and Dr. George N. Shuster of Hunter what they considered the purpose of higher education for women if they left the campus in droves for a career of total domesticity. Their answer, roughly, was this: "Our main aim is to turn out women who can apply a trained intelligence to the problems of daily living, and whose intellectual resources can enrich their lives and those of their children."

They agreed that only a small proportion of girls manifested a genuine drive toward intellectual excellence, or a sustained dedication necessary to the mastery of any art or science, and they deplored this. But the shared opinion seemed to be that a girl who went to college would not only be a more intelligent wife and mother than the girl who did not, but that in later life and increased freedom she could draw on greater reserves of mind and spirit.

And yet an English teacher at one of the Eastern universities said: "There is a terrible waste here. I've taught girls with as much, if not more, talent than many of the boys I've had in my classes: first-class writers and thinkers. And what do they do when they leave here? Work? Not on your life. They marry and have four children, and that's that."

THE argument, widely used, that a woman so trained can always return to her field when her children are grown and her time is her own, is specious, to say the least. In the sciences, if not in the arts, advances in theory and techniques are so rapid that a fifteen-year gap becomes unbreachable. Quite apart from that, the muscle of intellect degenerates with lack of use. The servantless young mother with small children has not the time, the place or the isolation necessary for any orderly process of thought or any sustained practice of the imagination.

Yet society—including most of the young women involved in this early and long domesticity—does not consider this condition even remotely tragic. On the contrary, there appears to be widespread approval of the return of women from the spurious and aggressive "independence" of their mothers to their prime function as the creators and guardians of the family.

Young girls themselves in countless numbers have chosen the security and closeness of a full household rather than the lonely road of individual fulfillment as creative identities. And although many young women work out of the home before and even after marriage, it is less for love of work than for love of a home in which a standard of living is more important than a standard of thinking.

Only a few seem to work because of an urgent need to be for once—if only part of every day—out of context and into their own skin, applying their intelligence singly toward matters not concerned with their personal lives.

Even this need, usually condoned for economic reasons ("She has to work to make ends meet") is criticized by those professionally concerned with allocating roles to the sexes, as an evasion of woman's prime responsibility and an indication either of maladjustment or of a false sense of values. And, although the country is full of educators charged with the development of the female intelligence, every social pressure is exerted on women from their childhood on toward one goal: marriage—the earlier the better—and babies, the more the better. And the girl who feels that she has something to give beyond her natural functions as a wife and mother is lonely, indeed—pitied even when she succeeds.

If television drama serials and mass magazine fiction are any indication of the national temper, there is only one "right" fulfillment for all women. The "career woman" may be admired for her success, but her absorption in her work—whether it be medicine, law, letters or art—is a tacit admission of her lack of fulfillment as a woman. And even if she marries and

Drawings by Susan Perl

NO RESPONSE—As long as the old view of woman's role remains unchanged, women will respond to the call to "use their brains" for the nation's good with massive indifference.

bears children, the assumption prevails that both her husband and her offspring will suffer from her preoccupation with the world outside.

Many housewives may secretly long for their independence, but they are secure in the knowledge that their own absorption in the home and the community is a guarantee against a continual conflict of loyalties and, indeed, against the natural hostility of men; a resentment, however covert, against the competition of the kind of female intelligence which, precisely because of its independence, is still called "masculine."

IF it is true that this kind of intelligence is undesirable to the majority of men, accustomed as they are to the "liberated" woman of today, what are the reasons?

I suspect that in the stormy sea of "equality," men are uncertain of the extent and nature of their dominance—if, indeed, they believe in it—and that they need a constant reassurance of their superiority in one field at least, that of the creative intellect.

They need not look far to see that it is they who formulate national policies, send rockets into space and govern the world of business, art and science. The challenge from women in these fields is still negligible, but it exists; a source of discomfort rather than satisfaction. And although many men are generous in their admiration of the few women who have achieved distinction in the laboratory or in letters or in scholarship, most men have no desire to be married to them. They take too much trouble.

And here we come, I think, to the root of the matter: a masculine laziness in the ways of love which inclines them to avoid rather than surmount this particular kind of challenge. It is far easier to choose the relaxed and compliant woman than one who makes demands on the intelligence. They may be intrigued by the brilliant woman, but they rarely want her for themselves.

For the qualities that form a creative intellect are hard to live with. The woman cursed with them can retain the love of men and the approval of society only if she is willing to modify and mute them as much as she can without reducing them to impotence. As one so cursed, however modestly, I herewith submit some hard-won suggestions:

I would counsel the woman of intellect to watch her wit. Though it need not be tinged with malice, it has of necessity an astringency which many people find disconcerting. In a bland society, the unsheathed dart can draw blood, if only from vanity. And after the tide of laughter at a woman's wit has ebbed, the wrack left in the public mind is a sort of malaise: "She has a sharp tongue" or "I wouldn't like to tangle with her."

CANDOR is a second danger. The woman who is honest with men is so at her own risk if this honesty requires either criticism or skepticism of their position. And if she has convictions opposed to those of the man she speaks with she will be wise to withhold them or speak them so softly that they sound like concurrence.

She must, above all, have no conviction that what she has to say is of importance, but train herself instead to listen quietly to men no more knowledgeable in a given subject than herself and, what is more, to defer to their judgment. This is not always easy, but a woman cannot afford the luxury of declarations, however pertinent, if she seeks—and what woman does not?—to attract.

A man who is intense or excited about his work can be highly attractive, but woe to the woman who is either. Most people cannot distinguish between the tiresome garrulity of a woman preoccupied with her affairs and the purely abstract passion of a woman concerned with the process of thought. A state of tension is inseparable from active intelligence, but it is socially unpermissible in women.

If such women are artists—and I use this to cover all forms of creative expression—and particularly if they have achieved any stature as such, they may have the attraction of rarity. There are even men who are mature enough and secure enough to cherish in them the capacity to create abstractly as well as biologically.

But they are rarer still, for the care and cultivation of an artist is a job that wives are

Modern courtship patterns hinder a thirst for culture.

trained for and few husbands want. The woman artist who has a husband and children must then, to quote Phyllis McGinley, have "three hands" —a mutation still infrequent but which the irradiation of women's minds may yet produce.

Is this irradiation really desirable? Are the full resources of the feminine intelligence really needed? And if they are to be mobilized for the national good, what is to be done about a climate of opinion satisfied with the overwhelming emphasis, on the part of the younger generation, on domesticity and large families? Do we need more babies or do we need more doctors and scientists and thinkers and innovators? Is it enough that we have a great pool of college graduates applying their intelligence to the problems of their homes and towns, or do we really

AND SO TO WED—Teachers say that marriage nullifies college training.

need more women able to come to grips with the major issues of our time?

If we do, changes will have to be made, many of which may well be unattainable at this time. But if the nation's leaders really want and need this kind of woman, the opinion molders of the mass media will have to start right now giving her an honorable place in society, and men will have to start giving her an honorable place in their hearts as well as in their professions.

For one thing, parents with daughters who show a genuine intellectual talent and aspiration in any field should not feel compelled to enter her in the infantile mating-marathon that pushes a girl toward marriage from the age of 12 on. It should be possible for such a girl to prefer an exciting book to a dull date without the censure of her family or her peers, and to continue her training through her twenties without courting celibacy.

Much has been said about the new sense of responsibility shown by the young in their early acceptance of marriage and parenthood. But time may show that the cocoon of a large-familied home is—like that of a large

corporation—the best protection from the loneliness of thought and a voluntary abdication of the burdens of personal freedom.

If a woman wishes to resume her chosen work after marriage and the bearing of children, there should be no stigma attached if she can afford to hire outside help for either home tasks or the care of the young. And we might begin to consider a pattern of community-supported nurseries which would permit the woman who cannot afford help to pursue her profession at least partially free from the continuous demands of child care.

A few months ago a delegation of Russian professional women visited this country, and one of them remarked in amazement at the lack of any such service. Our profusion of labor-saving gadgets did not, it seems, blind her eyes to the domestic entrapment of the young American woman.

As for college education, there should, I believe, be a division made between students merely marking time before marriage and girls seriously bent on a career or profession, confining the domestic-minded to a two-year course of liberal arts and reserving the four-year, degree-

granting course for the latter. After these have graduated, their entrance into the laboratories and offices of the country should be made on the same basis as that for equally qualified men—not, that is, as an interim occupation but as a chosen, sustained career.

And here, of course, is where the woman herself must be prepared to pay a fairly high price. If work is important to her she cannot allow herself the luxury of a large family or the kind of man who insists on one. Nor can she afford the close, and often cozy, community huddle in which women share their domestic preoccupations daily with one another. She must be prepared to fight for the freedom she wants at the risk of loneliness and the denial of a number of things dear to any woman.

As for men, they will have to stop thinking in terms of competition and think in terms of alliance instead: the alliance of companion intellects toward similar goals. If they can bring themselves to consider women primarily as human beings, they will be able to treat them intellectually as men and emotionally as women. If they do that, they will find the brilliant woman surprisingly docile and far from unfeminine.

Women often find themselves curbing a differing opinion.

If, however, men continue to subscribe to the prevailing belief that the American heroine must never be too intelligent for her own good and their own comfort, the cry for female brains will go largely unheeded—unless a national emergency makes it clear that we have for years been wasting one of the resources on which our strength depends and which other civilizations are using to their advantage.

A Huge Waste: Educated Womanpower

By MARY I. BUNTING

IN all the recent talk of America's affluent society, one prodigious national extravagance has been largely overlooked: the waste of highly talented, educated womanpower. The number of intellectually displaced women without productive outlets for their talents and education is growing yearly. Yet, to date, our efforts to stem the waste they epitomize have been meager, scattered and inadequate.

Women in America today are emancipated, educated and enfranchised. They are wonderfully long-lived and, to a large degree, they have become technologically only half employed in the home. Their academic success in our schools and colleges has been impressive and, contrary to the predictions of the last century, this has not interfered with their health or their fecundity.

Nevertheless, it must be admitted that their record of adult intellectual achievement has not fulfilled the promise of their student days. Perhaps there are innate limitations or perhaps, like plants kept under conditions that encourage vegetative growth but do not permit flowering, these women are the victims of cultural circumstances. The evidence is worth examining.

The factors involved are undoubtedly multiple and complex. Those most readily suspected may be most difficult to prove. Some may be so deeply embedded in our culture that we are scarcely aware of their existence, let alone their relevance.

In considering women and their potential contribution one must, I believe, begin with a restatement of the truism that is so often acknowledged but so seldom acted upon: the pattern of a woman's life, simply because she is a woman, differs radically from a man's. Most women marry, and during the early years of marriage and family are deeply absorbed in the varied, demanding and immensely satisfying responsibilities of a wife and mother.

THIS means, as a rule, at least a partial hiatus in any professional career. If that hiatus is allowed to continue too long, the intellectual interests and talent a woman discovered in herself before marriage are likely to become dulled and the education she acquired may become inadequate.

Thus, her ignorance is compounded. The degree she won ten years ago is not the equivalent of that achieved by today's young graduate. Therefore, if we wish to use the skills and proficiencies of able and educated women, we must plan to take into account these

MARY I. BUNTING is a noted biologist and teacher who became president of Radcliffe College last year. She has four children.

FAMILIAR STORY—The intellectual fires of bright young things in college often die down in marriage. Can they be made to blaze again?

basic facts about their lives and about the expansion of knowledge.

Few changes are so clearly necessary as those involving opportunities for higher education. At the present time educators seem rather like jockeys who have unaccountably lost interest in the outcome of the race some quarter-mile before the finish line. They seem little interested when the brilliant woman ceases to use her trained abilities, except as she becomes an embarrassing statistic in the academic "drop-out" rate.

Precious little attention has been given to designing educational opportunities to meet the needs of the married woman. Rather, we have assumed that if she marries early she is not interested in continuing her education. The possibility that the choice could be a question of timing rather than goals has not received serious attention. In so far as institutions of higher education have made it impossible for her to continue, they must at least share the responsibility for her "drop-out."

The rate of expansion of knowledge means that education must become a continuing part of adult living. Men today continue their studies well into adult life. Women can no longer expect to "finish" their educations before taking on home responsibilities.

EDUCATIONAL institutions, if they are concerned with the end product, must provide for, encourage and assist the able, part-time student—the married woman—by creating more flexible schedules. Too often they have been reluctant to consider the possibility of admitting part-time female students. In general, they shut the door or refuse financial aid or fail to open teaching or research opportunities to the married woman during that crucial period of her life when home responsibilities require a large part of her attention.

Actually, studying, in appropriate doses, mixes wonderfully well with homemaking. The time taken away from the family does not have to be excessive and offers precisely the contacts and the challenges most needed. The longer hours of study can be worked around the home schedules. Husband and, soon, children, will be doing their homework evenings. It is not so bad to open one's own briefcase and, in so doing,

perhaps one can be an even better homemaker. I well remember overhearing the voice of a 7-year-old guest who commented to my son: "It must be easy to do your homework when your mother and father are doing theirs."

Difficulties similar to those encountered in the academic world have faced women seeking to use their talents vocationally. The married woman who can work only part-time has few opportunities and the single girl is suspected of simply putting in time until she can marry.

EVEN the woman who is certified to teach finds that she cannot be employed on a part-time basis except as a substitute. Here again, the significance of the fact that a wealth of homemakers is available for employment if only jobs can be offered on a part-time basis seems to have escaped general attention.

In addition to difficulties of scheduling, the married woman encounters special financial problems. The working or the student mother is penalized by not being allowed to deduct the necessary expenses of child care from her taxable income. Many a woman eager to continue a professional career after marriage has been deterred by the realization that her household expenses might well outrun her prospective income. How many doctors, scientists and teachers have we lost because we have thrown up this block?

Why haven't we been more concerned with the higher education and later utilization of the married woman? What does this neglect signify? I think there is an answer which raises serious questions as to our fundamental values: We have not been greatly concerned because we have never really expected women to use their talents and education to make significant intellectual or social advances.

WE were willing to open the doors but we did not think it important that they enter the promised land. We urge the able boy to plan and work for the contribution he can make in the second half of his life, but we have not encouraged the girl to look beyond her early adult years. With the lack of expectation so prevalent, it is no wonder that most of the gifted children who fail to go on to college are girls.

When we see able high-school girls shunted off from academic courses into the easier vocational courses, even though this also means shunting them off from later opportunities, we can be sure the "hidden dissuaders" are at work. These are the subtle undercurrents in our society which shape our attitudes and often go unrecognized. They are the inherited influences, the cultural standards which produce, for example, the belief that a scientific career is somehow "unladylike," or that marriage should be enough of a career for any woman.

I recall a conversation with a girl who was the top student at Douglass College during the time I was there. She told me that if she had not won a full scholarship her parents would have refused to give her a liberal-arts education and would have insisted instead on her taking a nursing course or a degree from a teacher's college.

IT mattered not at all that she was uninterested in either nursing or teaching. These were practical courses; liberal arts would lead nowhere. Her parents were victims of the "hidden dissuaders," and so—almost—was she.

It may now be time to look at women's potentialities more objectively. Who knows what abilities might emerge if only the favorable cultural conditions could be achieved? Man has done little, if anything, to improve his genetic heritage over many thousands of years, and yet our evolving society has revealed all kinds of talents that would have seemed impossible in ancient times.

Perhaps women, because they are not the breadwinners, could be most useful as the trail-breakers, doing the unusual job that men cannot afford to gamble on. They may, in fact, be far more valuable working on the fringes, where there is always room, than competing with men in the intellectual market places. The unexplored is boundless.

This is the goal toward which the redesign of educa-tional and vocational opportunities for women should be directed. However, no reforms will work without a corresponding change in the popular attit   toward the educated woman. Unless her abilities and talents are recognized and valued by the community she will find it hard to sustain the enthusiasm needed for success in creative or professional work.

The Radcliffe Institute for Independent Study, founded last fall, is one effort to change the social climate for women. About twenty women, chosen as "Associate Scholars," will begin work on a part-time basis under its auspices next September. They will be Exhibit A in an experiment to test our faith in women's ability to contribute to scholarship and the creative arts.

THE program is tailored to fit the pattern of women's lives. Half-time postgraduate scholarships with stipends up to $3,000 are offered to women who wish to continue creative intellectual work along with homemaking or other responsibilities. These scholarships are awarded on the basis of the project prepared by the applicant and her qualifications for the task she has set herself. They may be renewed annually if the reviewing committee is convinced the Scholar is making satisfactory progress.

In general, a candidate must have a Ph.D. to qualify. However, a woman with equivalent experience — for example, the holder of an M. A. in Renaissance history who has taught at the college level and wishes to continue exploring a question she has long been interested in—would be acceptable. So would a person with background and achievement in the creative field.

A Scholar might be a woman who studied painting in college and exhibited professionally until she had children. Then she moved her brushes and easel, first from the nursery to a corner of her bedroom, and finally to the cellar. She wants to get back to painting. She wants to get back into the world of art and artists.

WE will give her time, a place to work, museums in which to study and teachers and critics to talk to about her ideas and experiments. Maybe at the end of her year she will be ready for a one-woman show. At least we can hope that she will have had enough concentrated re-immersion in art to be able to go on with it seriously.

The Scholar might have done promising graduate work in biology. Her two children are growing up fast. It seems harder and harder to concentrate on housework, P. T. A. meetings and cookie sales. She keeps speculating about the leads that were opening up during her last year in the laboratory. She has followed work in her field. She knows someone at Harvard whom she'd like to study with if she could only get back. If the department is interested, we will give her the opportunity, and we hope that as a result she will go on to make valuable contributions to biology.

Whatever their fields might be — whether writing, music, history, philosophy, anthropology or sociology — we expect the Scholars' accomplishments will be valuable in themselves. Once they have given new proof of their worth through their work at the Institute, they, and others like them, should be claimed for further work in academic institutions, businesses, science, the arts and the professions.

FOR each Scholar in the program the campus opens an opportunity to work in completely unrestricted fashion, drawing on the resources—physical and human—that we have. Scholars may use the libraries, the museums, the computers, the laboratories. The faculty of the college will be available to direct their study and offer criticism and consultation.

A scientist obviously cannot work without a laboratory. A historian would be helpless without a library. The artist, the poet, the playwright may not need or want any of the facilities we can provide. But in a more subtle way the college may be essential to her. It offers a place to work free from the unpredictable distractions of family life, the compulsion to pursue the daily routine at the expense of a half-finished conception or dream, and the guilt over children rebuffed, or questions unanswered.

The overwhelming response since plans for the Institute were announced last November indicates, I feel sure, the pressing need. Women trained in almost every area of educated skills are seeking only the chance to re-establish themselves as professionals. We shall have perhaps six or eight times as many qualified applicants as we have resources for.

Unfortunately, because of the home responsibilities of those for whom the program was designed, we can serve only people within easy traveling distance. Perhaps some of the colleges that have expressed interest in what we are doing will initiate similar plans soon for women in their areas.

Whether or not Radcliffe's plan succeeds in all its hopes, this will be an interesting cultural innovation. From it we shall learn all we can.

In urging a greater role for women in America's intellectual productivity, one cannot overlook the arguments against such a course. The viewers-with-alarm who attempt to correlate a high divorce rate, increased juvenile delinquency, even a deterioration in domestic cuisine, with the increase of working mothers have not, I suspect, pursued the arguments to their ultimate logic.

It could be argued, and more soundly, that many marriages break, many family relationships deteriorate for precisely the opposite reasons. The woman who, in her early thirties, sees her last child enter school and then faces blankly the next forty years left to her by the actuaries with no notion of how to realize herself as an individual, is likely to begin to blame the marriage for her plight. A dissatisfied woman is seldom either a good wife or a good mother.

THERE is, too, a certain measure of hypocrisy among the viewers-with-alarm. All too often, their criterion in judging harshly the mother with a job is not how much time she puts in with her children as compared with her bridge-playing neighbor, but rather whether she gets paid for whatever takes her away from home, and how much.

Once, the home was an economic unit demanding all the skill and perseverance and knowledge that a woman could muster. Today, however, with physical labor so greatly reduced, with her duties simplified, the mother who remains at home may be doing so primarily for the child. And in this world, with its new modes of communication, its new problems and interdependencies, it may not be at all propitious for a mother to remain entirely engaged in the relatively trivial tasks centered about Junior's creature comforts.

IF she is truly interested in the wealth she can contribute to her family, as well as to society, she must utilize the sum total of her trained talent. If she is interested in cultivating this wealth for her children, she must demonstrate through her own life the satisfaction that can be . so achieved. Motivation has always been imparted by example rather than by exhortation.

Each generation expects the next to be an improvement. We have today more women going to college and graduate school than ever before. But what improvement will that fact alone represent if we value their education too lightly to let them make full use of it.

If our national needs and purposes are to be fulfilled, it seems clear that all individuals should have the best of opportunities to employ all their talents. It is not so much for women as for our heritage and our aspirations that America must assess again, thoughtfully and purposefully, their places in our society.

May 7, 1961

COLLEGE ENTRANCE SUBJECT OF STUDY

House Unit Seeks Possible Bias Against Women

Coeducational colleges and universities that discriminate against women in their admissions policies should be deprived of Federal funds, Representative Edith Green declared yesterday.

The Oregon Democrat said she would propose such legislation if a study by her House subcommittee on education found that such practices did exist

Mrs. Green spoke at the annual meeting of the College Scholarship Service. She said that after passage of an unusual amount of education legislation, it was time for Congress "to stop, to look and to listen" before embarking on new educational programs.

Congress, she said, must give the colleges time to catch up on programs already passed — to staff and implement them. It should re-examine the role of government as a partner in education and consider such questions as the education of women, she added.

The meeting was attended by about 1,000 persons from the 661 colleges participating in the service.

Mrs. Green told a news conference later that coeducational institutions that receive Federal funds are no more justified in discriminating against women than against minority groups.

October 27, 1965

For Colleges, the Major Is Coeducation

By OLIVE EVANS

"Almost everyone I know is for it. Having just men is such an artificial environment, not like the way it'll be when we get out of here."

Thus a Wesleyan sophomore summed up his generation's attitude toward single-sex colleges and explained succinctly the galloping trend toward coeducation.

Yale, Wesleyan, Vassar and Bennington have made decisions—not for coordinate colleges like Radcliffe at Harvard or Pembroke at Brown —but for full coeducation. Williams, Trinity and Colgate are exchanging students with Vassar and Skidmore. Wellesley is "cross-registering" with M.I.T. Barnard and Columbia College are conducting a tentative courtship. Princeton has issued a 150-page report by a 10-member committee, recommending the admission of 1,000 women.

Coordinate Colleges Opened

Hamilton College (men) opened the coordinate Kirkland College (women) last September. Union College in Schenectady hopes to admit women in 1970. Sarah Lawrence and Bennington have begun to add men, and in the next two years Franklin and Marshall, Kenyon College, the University of the South and Georgetown University's now all-male College of Arts and Sciences plan to go coed. Connecticut College will take its first men in September.

Next month, Saint Xavier College, a 121-year-old Roman Catholic institution in Chicago, will admit its first men as students. And it will actively start seeking men for admission in the fall.

The effect has spilled over into college preparatory boarding schools. Prestigious Choate and exclusive Rosemary Hall have announced wedding plans; Horace Mann and The Hackley School plan to admit girls.

For Princeton, the decision will be an agonizing one, and alumni reaction will probably be the determining factor.

"CONFUSED—of course, I'm confused! I have a son at Vassar and a daughter at Yale!"

Outcries have already appeared among letters to the Princeton Alumni Weekly. A member of the 1927 class asserted: ". . . a basic requirement for admission . . . should certainly be a burning desire . . . to be a Princeton man. He should have decided that he wants to spend four years at Princeton, not Princeton with girls, or Princeton without clubs or any other Princeton. If he doesn't feel that way, he should go elsewhere. He will be happier and we will be better off without him."

At Yale, Dignity

Yale went coed amid a flurry of gentlemanly student activism. The chairman of the Student Advisory Board was refused permission to sit in on the meeting at Connecticut Hall where the president, Kingman Brewster Jr., recommended to the faculty that Yale admit 500 women in

1969 and thus proceed to coeducation "with style, dignity and decisiveness."

The Yale Daily News complained of the president's "fussiness" in wanting to describe carefully in admissions literature how women would be housed. "For 267 years," an editorial noted, "male students have been unhesitatingly entering Yale without this information."

Educational Advantages

It is the students, to a greater degree at some institutions than at others, who have pushed for coeducation. But they are supported on the whole by faculties.

Learning, it seems, gains through having both female and male attitudes on intellectual questions. Dating takes place in a more natural framework of day-to-day living, rather than during frantic weekends. The less attractive or less aggressive

511

boy or girl is seen as a whole person, rather than as a figure on the sidelines at mixers.

Faculty members generally prefer to teach coed classes, and young teachers find life at a coed college more stimulating socially.

Opposing views are few. One Vassar freshman was heard to remark, "Vassar will be a second-rate school. We'll have to refuse qualified women and take unqualified men."

Another anti-coed viewpoint contends that because women differ so much from men in their emotional make-up, they should be educated in a different style.

A more general fear, expressed even by those who favor coeducation, is that if coeducation means expansion, some schools may lose the smallness they treasure.

But the trend, as Alan Simpson, president of Vassar, pointed out, seems almost irreversible. Single-sex education, in the tradition of the English public school, has been a preference of the upper classes in this country. And state universities, heavily attended by the middle class, have a history of co-education.

More Attractive

Now even the most select colleges seek students from public high schools and recruit from among minority groups in poverty areas; for these students, the coed institution is more attractive.

The future of the women's college is very uncertain. Created to provide "separate but equal" education for women who were rebelling against Victorian mores, their feminist premise exists no longer.

Nightmares about expansion and higher costs, and cries of anguish at the toppling of tradition notwithstanding, coeducation fits the ideas, ideals and mood of today's young people—students and faculty alike. The "ayes" seem to have it.

New College Trend:
Women Studies

A new academic discipline is rising on the nation's campuses: women studies.

More than 60 colleges and universities around the country, apparently taking a hint from the black studies movement, are offering women studies courses this year. A year ago, only a handful of schools offered such courses.

The trend toward women studies, which has affected such schools as Yale, Cornell, Princeton, Wellesley and Northwestern, appears to have been generated not only by the women's liberation movement but also by pressures from students, teachers and alumnae who believe women are not getting fair academic treatment.

The trend has encountered some opposition, however, from faculty members who believe such fields as black studies and women studies are divisive and academically unsound.

Women as a Group

In general, women studies courses treat women as a group that has its own history, a unique role in society and special problems. The courses involve such matters as the contributions of women to science, history, literature and political science; discrimination against women, and the treatment of women in different societies.

At San Diego State College in California, 10 elective courses are offered. Fifty women and 20 men are enrolled in a course called "Contemporary Issues in the Liberation of Women," under the direction of Dr. Roberta Salper, 31 years old, a dedicated women's liberationist. The class examines such issues as abortion, divorce laws, contraception, sexual attitudes, child care and the role of minority group women.

At Princeton, where women were admitted last year, a similar course explores the impact of women on such social problems as drugs, racism, unemployment and pollution. Seventy-five per cent of the students in the course are men.

An idea of the purpose of such courses is provided by the San Diego State program's statement of purpose, which declares that the movement is "an attempt to repair the damage done to women by the omissions and distortions of traditional education and to illustrate at least one way of releasing the power and

The New York Times/William E. Sauro

Dr. Kay Boals, 26, at Princeton, where she conducts a course that looks into the impact of women on drugs, racism and other issues. Men form 75 per cent of class.

potential of more than half the population of this country."

"If it hadn't been for women's lib protests," said Dr. Salper from her West Coast office, "we wouldn't have this program at San Diego."

Stephanie Serementis, a neurobiology major at Cornell, believes there is discrimination against women students.

"I fight to be recognized in class," she said, "and if I'm a success, the teacher thinks I must be an exception to the female race."

At San Diego State, about 50 male professors recently attacked that school's program as "a radical innovation."

At Cornell, a questionnaire on the issue was distributed to the faculty last spring. Half of the 185 who responded supported the program and half opposed it.

An engineering professor, whose name was not disclosed by the university, commented on the questionnaire: "The idea is slightly absurd. Why don't you stop these attempts at fragmentalizing

The New York Times/Barton Silverman

At Douglass College of Rutgers University, New Brunswick, N. J., Mary McCarthy's novel "The Group," is discussed in a course called "Educated Women in Literature." Dr. Elaine Showalter, 29, leads study of portrayal of women.

higher education and devote yourself to real scholarship?"

A humanities teacher called the program a "disaster."

"Black studies is divisive enough," he said. "Female studies would inevitably be aimed toward political goals, which I am far from sharing."

Other authorities disagree.

"There are compelling reasons right now for an intellectual focus on women," said Dr. Jennie Farley, academic coordinator for female studies at Cornell.

"Take a problem like the population explosion," she said. "If we are to encourage women to have fewer children, we must give them some satisfactory alternatives to being only housewives and mothers."

Ella Kusnetz, a Cornell senior, said women studies were valuable to her as a student.

"I wish they had been offered when I was a freshman," she said. "I've never been as interested in academics. Female studies is a new reference, I have some identity now as a woman."

At Douglas College of Rutgers University, a women's school, a substitute for freshman English is "Educated Women in Literature," a course that concerns the portrayal of women in modern American literature. The class, led by Dr. Elaine Showalter, 29, recently discussed Mary McCarthy's description of women in "The Group," her novel about eight Vassar graduates.

"The direction the new courses will take is unclear," said Florence Howe, assistant professor of English at Goucher College, who is considered an authority on women studies by faculty members throughout the country.

"Nonetheless," she added, "the courses are multiplying rapidly."

Title Is Vague

Miss Howe is the director of the Modern Language Association's Commission on the Status of Women in the Profession, which is investigating the equality of women teachers. She has established a clearing house at Goucher for information on women studies.

The enrollment of men in the course at Princeton is at least partly a result of its vague title, "Political Modernization."

"Originally I thought the course was about underdeveloped nations," said Robert P. Thomas, a bearded sophomore from Washington. "It was a complete shock to find out what this was all about. Although I was a bit skeptical, I decided it would be a good time to find out what women's lib is all about."

"The majority of guys are all for women's lib as a result of taking the course," he said.

In a recent seminar involving nine students, eight of whom were men, the instructor, Dr. Kay Boals, 26, posed a question about Betty Friedan's "The Feminine Mystique."

Friedan Book Discussed

"Did you find Friedan's argument that there's no such thing as a happy housewife true?" she asked.

"Of course not," replied Mr. Thomas.

"But Friedan mentioned there were large numbers of suicides among the house-

wives she studied," argued a classmate.

"In the U.S. women either have to do their thing with grandchildren, or go out and get work," observed Mr. Thomas.

"But so many women over 40 can't get interesting jobs," said another student.

"Look, it's not just women who can't find interesting work," asserted Jonathan Winder. "I worked in a warehouse this summer where all these guys did was rip out slips from other forms. It may be chauvinistic to say, but I don't think women ever had it so good."

"The question isn't to decide who's oppressed but to end oppression of both men and women," said Dr. Boals. "However, that man ripping papers has it better than a woman caught in 'the mystique,' because her job is never finished."

The one woman student, Sherri Peltz, a junior, remained silent throughout the class.

In an interview later she explained: "I generally feel intimidated being the only girl and therefore find it difficult to say what I'm thinking."

January 7, 1971

513

SENATE OPPOSES COLLEGE SEX BIAS

Passes Ban on U.S. Aid to Schools Where Women Face Discrimination

By MARJORIE HUNTER
Special to The New York Times

WASHINGTON, Feb. 28—The Senate voted today to deny Federal funds to most public college and universities that discriminate against women.

While less sweeping than that sought by feminist groups, the Senate ban on sex discrimination in student admissions and faculty staffing is far stronger than one approved by the House last year.

The Senate provision, an amendment to the pending higher education bill, seeks to end sex discrimination in all public and private graduate schools and most public undergraduate colleges and universities. It was offered by Senator Birch Bayh, Democrat of Indiana, and was approved by voice vote.

Exemptions Proposed

It would not apply to military and maritime academies, military schools, private undergraduate institutions (such as Yale, Harvard or Vassar), or church institutions where the requirements would be "inconsistent with religious tenets."

Those traditionally one-sex colleges and universities that now are becoming coeducational would have seven years to complete the transition without facing the loss of Federal funds.

Furthermore, public institutions that have admitted only one sex since their founding would be exempt, pending further study. Government figures show that this would apply only to four institutions—Radford and Longwood Colleges in Virginia, Mississippi State College for Women and Texas University for Women. All of these admit women only.

The ban on sex discrimination would apply to student admissions, granting of scholarships and other forms of student aid, and the hiring, promotion and pay of faculty.

The amendment was attached to the pending $24-billion higher-education authorization bill after relatively little debate. Senate action on the full bill is expected Wednesday, opening the way for negotiations with the House on somewhat similar legislation.

As passed by the House last year, the bill would ban sex discrimination in all graduate schools receiving Federal funds. However, by a five-vote margin, the House struck from the bill a ban on such discrimination in student admissions in undergraduate colleges and universities.

The narrow margin involving undergraduate discrimination would seem to indicate a good chance that the House will agree to the Senate version.

In urging adoption of his amendment, Senator Bayh cited figures that, he said, clearly demonstrated "the persistent, pernicious discrimination which is serving to perpetuate second-class citizenship for American women."

He said that the average scholarship or loan was greater for men than for women ($760 for men, $518 for women) and that while women undergraduates received higher grades than men, few women were admitted to graduate schools.

Of students receiving medical, law or theology degrees in 1968-69, he said, 96 per cent were men. During the same period, he said, men received 87 per cent of other graduate degrees.

Mr. Bayh also cited figures showing that in 36 prominent law schools, only 35 of 1,625 faculty members are women, and that women receive substantially less than men holding the same faculty rank.

College Gives a New Meaning to Adult Education

By LINDA GREENHOUSE
Special to The New York Times

BRONXVILLE, N. Y., May 14 — Ten years ago, when Sarah Lawrence College opened its Center for Continuing Education, the idea of a special degree program for women who had dropped out of college years earlier was greeted in many academic circles with disdain.

"In the minds of many of our own faculty, adult education meant practicing your golf swing at the high school gym or brushing up on your French for a trip to Paris," said Melissa L. Richter, the center's director as well as the college's dean of graduate studies.

Ninety-nine graduates later, the center has changed the definition of adult education and provided a model for hundreds of similar programs at colleges around the country.

To mark the center's 10th anniversary this week, Sarah Lawrence is publishing the results of a survey that confirms, for the first time, what those involved with the program suspected all along: the women who return to school are more highly motivated, achieve better grades, drop out less frequently, and go on to graduate school twice as often as the college's ordinary 18-year-old to 21-year-old undergraduates.

In addition, the survey of 143 women who have passed through the program since 1962 showed that the chance to continue their interrupted educations had a profound effect on their own lives.

Two hundred twelve students who had enrolled in the program between September, 1962, and June, 1971, were surveyed, and 143 returned the questionnaires.

The center now has 112 students, including nine who will graduate in June. Most are women in their 30's who have young children at home. Typically, they left college, with no regrets, to marry and raise children, and only later developed career goals.

They take courses part-time, usually combining school with jobs and family responsibilities, and can take any number of years to get their degree. Most take about three years, although the recordholder so far is

Melissa L. Richter, the director of adult center.

Sally Levene, who first signed on as a special student in 1961, before the center was officially opened.

Eleven years and three leaves of absence later, (one for pregnancy, one to serve as a League of Women Voters president, and one to begin her present job as admissions counselor for the center), Mrs. Levene will become a Sarah Lawrence graduate next month. Despite her longevity as an undergraduate, her background is typical of students in the program.

She left Vassar College 21 years ago, at the end of her freshman year, to get married. As her family grew, she became deeply involved in community activities in New Rochelle and even took a few noncredit and correspondence courses.

By the time her third child was a year old — she has since had two more children —Mrs. Levene decided it was time to get a degree. Other nearby colleges discouraged adult students, often subjecting them to the same rigid social rules as regular undergraduates.

But at Sarah Lawrence, Esther Raushanbush, then dean and later president, was beginning to explore adult education, and Mrs. Levene was able to register for her first course.

A New Perspective

"The degree will add a new dimension to my life,"

514

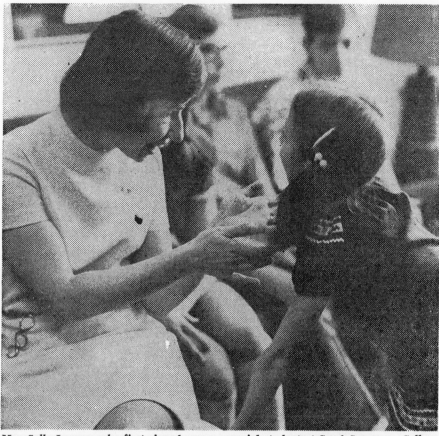

Mrs. Sally Levene, who first signed on as a special student at Sarah Lawrence College in 1961, with daughter. Mrs. Levene will graduate from the adult program next month.

she said the other day in the center's office, a red brick converted carriage house at the edge of the suburban Sarah Lawrence campus. "I think it's also given a new perspective on education to my youngsters, a respect for continuing their own education."

After 11 years, Mrs. Levene is not ready to leave Sarah Lawrence. She will stay on in the center's human genetics program, which leads to a master's degree and qualifies students to work as genetics counselors and associates to physicians in the genetics field.

Of the center's graduates who are not in graduate school, the greatest number are teaching. Others work in about two dozen widely varied fields.

Students take their first four courses at the center itself, choosing from a variety of courses taught in seminar style by Sarah Lawrence faculty members.

They begin at the center, Mrs. Richter said, because "they often have doubts and the need to gain confidence. Here, they don't have to apologize to anyone if their tools are a little rusty."

After that, they can matriculate as regular Sarah Lawrence undergraduates for as many courses as they need to meet their degree requirements.

All academic credits from other institutions are transferable, but a student needs at least 45 credits here before receiving a Sarah Lawrence degree.

Record a Good One

Once the rust is off, the adult students have little to be shy about. The 10-year survey shows that 16 per cent of them received A averages, compared with 7.5 per cent of a random sample of other Sarah Lawrence undergraduates. Sixty per cent went

on to graduate school, compared with 33 per cent of the younger Sarah Lawrence graduates and 32 per cent as a national average.

The dropout rate for the adult students was 22 per cent, compared with 36 per cent for the college as a whole and 52 per cent for the nation's undergraduates.

"We have discovered that there is no magic in ages 18 to 22 for students in higher education," Mrs. Raushenbush, now president emeritus, wrote in the introduction to the 10-year report. "Since that is so, we must actively design higher education to suit the middle years, as our present systems were designed for the young."

In addition to academics, the survey also asked students about the impact of the center on their lives. "The change has been so profound it is hard for me to recognize

my pre-Sarah Lawrence self," one woman answered.

Although 16 married women who entered the program were later separated or divorced, Mrs. Richter, a psychologist and biologist, said that for the most part the return to college had a positive effect on a student's family life. A large majority of the husbands, well educated and successful themselves, have actively supported their wives' educational ambitions, she said.

In the cases of marital break-up, Mrs. Richter said, "It's as if by finding themselves, they are able to be honest about a bad marriage for the first time."

The women often tell her, she said, that for the first time they no longer feel apologetic about their lack of education and "can start having real discussions with their husbands about something more than the dust under the table."

JOHNSON DISCERNS CRISIS IN FAMILIES

Tells Women's Parley That Ties Must Be Bolstered

By NAN ROBERTSON
Special to The New York Times

WASHINGTON, July 29 — President Johnson declared today that the family unit had collapsed among an alarming number of Americans, particularly Negroes.

He said that the nation must work to strengthen family ties, "in suburbia as well as in the slums."

"Our society and its success is built around a family unit," he told a White House meeting of 400 representatives of 44 state commissions on the status of women. Yet this fundamental unit is breaking down in all sections of society, the President said.

While stressing that he was "very proud" that more women had been brought into high Government positions in his Administration, Mr. Johnson said that "those women who stand insecurely and uncertainly on the lower rungs" of society must be quickly helped.

The President surprised the crowd with the statement that he had considered appointing a woman to the Supreme Court vacancy to which he named Abe Fortas yesterday. He implied he might yet name a woman to the Court.

"I looked yesterday at a number of women that I would hope could serve on the highest court of our land—where none have ever served," he said. "I didn't select one because, when I do, I want it to be absolutely without question the best person—male or female—available for the post."

At the same time, he painted a grim picture of other women who were "both breadwinners and mothers."

Many of them "face the uncertainties of the market place, the heartbreaking dilemmas of impoverished households, without training, often without motivation, very often without even the barest decencies of life, or even the emotional support of a husband," he said.

In recent days, the President has on many occasions turned the topic of Vietnam. Today he told his audience on the South Lawn about a "stack of letters" now on his desk from women, most of them wives and mothers of men in Vietnam, who supported his Vietnam policy.

A Southern mother of three sons wrote him to say she had lost one son in Vietnam, that another had been wounded in the Dominican Republic this spring and that the third was now in paratroop training in Texas, Mr. Johnson recounted. Nonetheless, he said she had told him how proud she was of him and Congress "for standing up and facing the enemy."

July 30, 1965

Who Marries Whom and Why

Marriage Is Not a Personal Matter

By JOHN FINLEY SCOTT
Assistant Professor of Sociology at the University of Washington

THE newest wrinkle in the old game of courtship is match-making by computer. It goes something like this: a young man lists in a "data bank" what he most desires in a prospective female companion and supplies information about his own characteristics. The computer compares the qualities and interests desired against those of a (presumably vast) inventory of candidates who have also put themselves on file. After some adjustment and compromise, our young man is presented with the name, address and telephone number of a "Miss Just-Right-and-very-nice-too." Since electronic match-making is not quite yet an exact science, he may also be informed of a few alternates (who are also very nice) in case something goes wrong and he doesn't quite hit it off with Miss Just-Right.

The fact that many "computerized introduction services" are pretty much fly-by-night operations does not mean that computer match-making is unworkable in principle. If marital felicity can be accurately defined, then it would seem that a compatible marriage partner would more likely be found among the thousands of candidates to which a computer could refer than among the handful that any one person could ever meet face to face.

But the problem is identifying "marital felicity"; what on earth *is* a successful marriage? Can any kind of successful matching be based on the verbal responses of the largely adolescent segment of the population that is on the verge of matrimony? Any programer will tell you that a computer is no better than the information put into it. In many respects, the verbal professions of persons facing marriage are the last things on which to base predictions about the future condition of the families thus formed. That a number of marriages—a minority, to be sure, but a substantial one—will terminate in divorce within three years will hardly be revealed through polling the expectations of brides-to-be.

Part of the problem with the sort of individualistic mate-selection that computer match-making proposes derives from the fact that marriage, though often regarded as an intensely personal affair, is one of the least individualistic of all social institutions. The family—which is, by the way, surprisingly invariant among societies in its basic features—has evolved not because it satisfies individual preferences but because it is socially useful. It combines the functions of reproduction, child care, sexual gratification and economic cooperation with an over-all efficiency that no alternative arrangement has so far been able to match. Since marriage is such a good thing from the society's point of view, it is convenient to make young people want to get married by teaching them that marriage satisfies their *own* needs, and to soft-pedal the demands of the larger society. This is why marriage (like the armed forces) is easier to enter than to leave. Young people are recruited to matrimony, but at the same time their hopes come to depend on frequently unrealistic aspirations and their ability to predict what lies ahead becomes limited.

Here lies the problem with any scheme of matchmaking that relies solely on the expressed preferences of the young people involved. This is hardly anything new: many parents, and most professional matchmakers —from Japanese villages to American suburbs—have known it for years. It would be interesting to see what kind of matches a computer would arrange if it interviewed parents as well as their eligible children.

516

FOR MEN

1. Which of the following activities most appeals to you?

(1) skindiving in Montego Bay
(2) touring the Rijksmuseum in Amsterdam
(3) watching a bullfight in Seville
(4) mountain climbing in Lausanne
(5) eating leberkase and drinking dark beer in a brauhaus in Munich

2. With which of the following cars can you most readily identify?

(1) Rolls Royce
(2) Mustang
(3) Cadillac
(4) Jaguar XKE
(5) Maxwell (vintage)
(6) Volkswagen

3. You are at a party where you don't know anyone. You would very likely:

(1) leave early
(2) find a comfortable chair in a corner
(3) join a conversation about sports
(4) introduce yourself to the women
(5) introduce yourself to the men

4. Which of the following fields are you most closely associated with or interested in?

(1) medicine and research
(2) law
(3) education
(4) social services
(5) advertising-public relations
(6) science and technology
(7) military service
(8) sales
(9) finance and industry

5. Your fiancee informs you that she has had relations with another man. You would probably:

(1) break the engagement
(2) marry her despite grave misgivings
(3) tell her it doesn't matter
(4) tell her of your own amorous adventures
(5) feel that her experience would make for a more successful marriage

6. Which of the following would probably give you the greatest personal satisfaction?

(1) working for the welfare of others
(2) traveling extensively
(3) being elected to public office
(4) earning a fortune
(5) raising a family

7. You've taken her out to dinner three or four times, but when you ask her to prepare the next meal herself, she informs you that she can't cook. You would most likely feel:

(1) angry
(2) dejected
(3) relieved
(4) indifferent
(5) hungry

FOR WOMEN

1. In which of the following situations would you feel most comfortable?

(1) exploring Vesuvius and the ruins of Pompeii
(2) sipping cappucino on the Via Veneto (Rome)
(3) boating off the island of Mykonos (Greece)
(4) conversing with peasants in Skoplje (Yugoslavia)
(5) visiting the Uffizi Galleries (Florence)

2. Of the following, which would you prefer?

(1) loving a man who did not love you
(2) being loved by a man you could not love
(3) neither loving nor being loved until the feeling was mutual, regardless of how long it took to come about

3. How well can you cook?

(1) expertly, exotic dishes and proper wines
(2) quite well, but nothing fancy
(3) hit or miss
(4) TV dinners and canned soup
(5) can-openers are for picture-hanging

4. Which of the following fields are you most closely associated with or interested in?

(1) nursing
(2) secretarial
(3) modeling or fashion
(4) sales or purchasing
(5) fine arts or design
(6) education
(7) business administration

5. Your date has spent his money on an electronic fish-finder, but you had wanted him to escort you to a concert. You would most likely:

(1) pay your own way
(2) lend him money
(3) find another date and let him go fishing
(4) treat him
(5) go fishing with him

6. You are with your friends when an argument develops about the evening's activity. You would:

(1) remain silent
(2) compromise
(3) go along with the majority
(4) insist upon your choice
(5) go off alone

7. Which of the following date ideas most appeals to you?

(1) dining and dancing
(2) horseback riding
(3) a picnic in the country
(4) watching TV
(5) attending a concert

8. How important is it that your match own and drive a car?

(1) very important
(2) moderately important
(3) he can borrow mine

Questions reprinted courtesy of Data-Date, Inc.

CHECK ONE—At left and right, excerpts from the sort of questionnaire a person in search of a date or mate might fill out for processing by computer.

We live in a society where unprecedented numbers of young people, aided by rapid social change, higher education, urbanization and widespread geographical and social mobility, negotiate marriages on their own, without the help of kith and kin. But the notion that the process as a whole is primarily an individual matter is a myth. When two people date who did not know each other beforehand, it is called a "blind date"—a name which stresses the fact that most dates are not blind. Wherever dating customs are studied closely — from church socials to Army barracks—intermediaries and "fixer-uppers" are found busily at work, pairing off the boys and girls in roughly the same way as the new computers. Considering the cost involved, it is economical for persons who date to rely on some outside help. For a young man, expected to take the initiative, dating is one of the most ruthless and unprotected forms of competition in which he can engage. He must put himself up for acceptance or rejection, and rejection can produce severe psychic wounds.

For a young woman, masculine attention in dating and courtship is the greatest social reward she will ever receive, and she therefore desires it to an extreme degree. But for her to accept dates indiscriminately is to run a variety of risks from boredom to sexual assault. The services of intermediaries, who present young men with invitations already accepted and young women with escorts already screened, are therefore greatly appreciated and widely practiced. But intermediaries bring their own interests into the transaction as well as those of the boy and girl whom they introduce. And since the dating career of any person is likely to make use of several intermediaries over time, dating and courtship thus become a thoroughly social process, affected by prevailing norms of mate selection even when the dating partners are not themselves committed to them. When young people today talk in all sincerity about their freedom to date anybody they please, they simply are not describing the entire process, of whose many controls they are often artfully kept unaware.

ONE very general answer can be given to the question of who marries whom: Most people marry someone pretty much like themselves. (If opposites do attract it has yet to show up in the statistics.) But scientific and garden-variety curiosity alike concentrate on the unexpected and unlikely combinations. It is rather like asking the question in a college classroom: "Which girls are going to get pregnant this semester?" Our curiosity runs so much to the irregular, the exotic and the immoral that we usually overlook the one obvious answer that covers almost all cases: "The ones who are married."

Unexpected marriages, like unexpected pregnancies, catch our attention when they deviate from social norms. The salient thing about marriage in this society—indeed, in any society with an organized system of kinship—is that it is regulated by the kinship-based groups which it affects. On the one hand, rules against incest drive young adults out of their own families; yet everywhere these young adults are expected to marry someone from a quite similar family. The anthropologist A. R. Radcliffe-Brown put the matter well when he referred to marriage as a "crisis."

Norms of mate selection—as sociologists rather coarsely phrase it—can be looked at as a classification of social groups in some of which marriage is to be preferred and in others is to be avoided. The practice of marriage within a group is called endogamy. All large groups formed by inheritance—what we call "ethnic groups"—will prefer endogamy to some degree. Since two parents who share the same ethnic traditions can pass them on more consistently than two whose backgrounds differ, endogamy makes a good deal of sense if one wishes to preserve traditions. And the more traditions are cherished, the stronger is the urge toward endogamy. American Jews, for example, voice great concern over the extent of Jewish exogamy—the opposite of endogamy—although, from a comparative point of view, it is amazingly small—probably less than 10 per cent of all marriages involving a Jew. But it seems that the only way for Jewish traditions to survive is through lifelong training of persons born into the group. (A Yiddish aphorism puts it: "A converted Jew is no Jew and no gentile.") Jewish control of endogamy is therefore remarkably strong, and the democracy and indulgence that seem characteristic of Jewish family life usually end abruptly when the prospect of intermarriage looms. Similar rules can be found among American Oriental population groups, the Mormons and, in weaker form, Roman Catholics (who more willingly accept converts).

One of the strictest rules of endogamy applies to "Negro-white" intermarriage. It is an essential part of the caste-like status of the black man and the innumerable rigid, two-class distinctions that derive from it. If, for a few generations, there had been practiced in America a degree of intermarriage amounting to 10 per cent of all marriages involving blacks, with the wife assuming the status of the husband and the children combining the genetic and social characteristics passed on by their parents, the contemporary racial situation would be profoundly different. "Black" and "white" would not be two discrete categories of color and (more im-

portant) of status, but a widely dispersed continuum, and the two-color caste system, with all its social consequences, would have crumbled in the face of the multiplicity of distinctions that in practice would have to be made. So patterns of marriage have historical consequences.

Predicting whether a certain proportion of marriages will be endogamous or exogamous actually depends on a few rather obvious variables. The relative numbers of the two sexes —the "sex ratio"—is one of the most obvious. It is historically important because men are more likely to migrate than women. This is largely why America, as a land of migrants, has been as much of a melting pot as it has. Many immigrant men who felt strongly about "marrying a nice (Jewish-Polish-Irish-Armenian, etc.) girl" found there wasn't enough of the kind they wanted to go around. Faced with the choices of marrying out or not marrying at all, many of them married out. The same thing goes on inside America today because men migrate to one place and women to another (there are usually more unmarried women than men in big cities, for example), so that rules for some sort of endogamous marriage get slighted in the competition for anyone to marry at all.

ANOTHER factor is the degree of parental control. This is important because it is the older generation that most respects the traditional rules of endogamy, while young people are easily swayed by personal attractions. Here residence is important. A young lady who lives at home and receives her suitors there cannot easily entertain young men of whom her parents strongly disapprove. Even when she is given much freedom, the elders can still influence her choice. Daughters can hardly fall in love with unsuitable men they never meet, and the chances of their not meeting them are greatly increased if the parents happen to have moved (for the children's sake, of course) to a class-homogeneous suburb. When a girl becomes infatuated with a boy beneath her station, parents can use the old stratagem of inviting him to a rather formal dinner, the better that his incorrigible unfitness for symbolically important occasions will be forced on the daughter's attention.

Today, however, parental control faces the peculiar threat of college education. When children live at home, parents can keep track daily of whom they are dating. But college often requires "dependent" and "irresponsible" children to live away from home. To be sure, a few young people have been going away to college for generations. But three trends combine to make college today a major threat to endogamy: (1) More persons of college age are in college (currently about 40 per cent); (2) An increasing proportion of students are

women; and (3) The average age at marriage has dropped (especially for women) to a point where it falls for many in the traditional undergraduate years.

College and matrimony thus combine to render the campus the most active marriage market of modern times. Even when children live at home while attending college (a growing trend as new campuses and junior colleges are built) the dating situation on the campus is hard for parents to control. Student bodies tend to be large and heterogeneous, and almost any of the many campus activities can be used for making contacts and thus beginning the process of dating and courtship. Not that parents have not fought back. College fraternities, and especially sororities, embody many ingenious arrangements whereby the courtship of young persons is kept in line with the desires of an older generation. Yet it is safe to predict that an increasing number of American marriages will be between persons who meet in college, and they are likely to meet under conditions largely indifferent to older rules of endogamy.

A third factor affecting the maintenance of endogamy is social mobility—the process by which members of a generation achieve a higher class position than that into which they were born. In America this movement is intimately related to higher education, for we widely believe that upward mobility is a good thing and that higher education contributes to it. But to the extent that young people start moving up before they are married, and that boys move up in different ways, or at different rates, than girls, then the traditional ways of pairing them off endogamously no longer work.

THE most basic difference here is that a man gains his status mainly through his job, whereas a woman's status is mainly conferred on her by her husband. We often speak as if occupational success were equally important for both sexes, but actually it is much less important for women. Women *can* gain a tolerable status through work, but a better one can usually be gained more easily through marriage. Where men move up most directly by competing for good jobs, women move up mainly by marrying men who move up. Marriage thus becomes the means of mobility for women. Insofar as she responds to the American dream of upward mobility, every unmarried American girl has a bit of the gold-digger in her.

Consider the situation of American Catholics. Catholic girls are expected to marry Catholic boys, but they also want to marry successful men. And it just so happens that, for most of the country, Protestant men on the average hold higher-ranked positions than do Catholic men. If the Catholic girl marries up, she is likely to marry out. And evidently this does occur, because more Catholic women marry outside their faith than do Catholic men. Among Jews, however, the situation is reversed. Men in this group are eminently successful and are "good catches" for girls of any faith who want to marry up. Evidently they do get caught, for many more Jewish boys marry gentiles than do Jewish girls.

The pressure for marrying up among women produces a kind of imbalance in marital bargaining, to the advantage of high-status men and low-status women and the disadvantage of low-status men and high-status women. A low-status man has little wealth or prestige to offer a wife. In addition, he must compete for a wife not only with others in his own station but with higher-ranked men as well.

A well-born woman, if she is to maintain through marriage the status conferred on her by her parents, must marry a man at least equally well-born —but for such men she faces a deadly competition from lower-status female rivals who also regard them as desirable husbands. As a result, low-status men are more likely to remain bachelors, and high-status women are more likely to remain spinsters. This is the "Brahmin problem," so named because it reached its most extreme form among the high castes of Hindu India (but it can be observed among Boston Brahmins as well).

IF a sociologist is so artlessly blunt as to ask young women whether they marry for money or for love, he will be lucky to escape with his questionnaire forms. Love, the girls indignantly tell us, conquers all. Lovable personal qualities eclipse Philistine wealth. But this is too simple by far.

On the one hand, there is a strong statistical tendency for women to marry up. If our hypothetical sociologist returns, suitably chastened, with a subtler set of questions on what makes men lovable, he will receive a list of characteristics of which many— urbane good manners, sensitivity, sophisticated good taste, interesting conversation, and so on—depend on expensive education and are thus associated with wealth. Money, in short, tends to be despised only in the abstract: in concrete form, enjoyed by the unmarried scions of a rich family, it is highly admired.

On the other hand, there probably never has been a society in which all lovable attributes were monopolized by one class. Love thus becomes a potentially random factor in marriage, one contrary to all rules of endogamy. In societies with stronger rules of endogamy than our own, love is not unknown, but it is strongly controlled and is regarded as irrelevant in the choice of marital partners.

The emotions of love are strong, but they are also ambiguous and volatile, and are therefore subject to deception and fraud. This places an emphasis on sincerity, but sincerity in love is very hard to assess. Young women are besieged with professions of love which they suspect are voiced simply to facilitate a quick seduction—and this is not what "love" means to most of them.

Especially where courtship tends to be individualistic, so that suitors cannot be effectively held to account for their promises, young women tend to measure the love of a young man not simply by what he says, but also by what he invests in the relationship. Often this is his money, but more often it is his time. Because any marriage market involves a wide age range of men competing for the smaller range of women in the years when they are young and pretty, the investment required in courtship gets bid up to a high level. Feminine nubility, thus rewarded, becomes a veritable institution in its own right. The extravagance of attention that young girls expect, however, paradoxically limits their chances for marrying well. Regardless of his income, the *time* of a successful man is always dear, while the adult male who is "still finding himself" is the one with the leisure to invest in courtship.

This applies also at the college level, where the pre-professional student who is going places occupationally has little time for dating and leaves most of the social life to the less ambitious campus playboys. This means that women who expect their suitors to spend a great deal of time in dating are likely to marry men of modest achievements in other areas.

NOW: How can all this be put in a matchmaking computer? It would be easy to specify the information that would be required, but awfully hard to find any way of digging it up. Getting it by simple interrogation—which is what the computers use now—would make the money-or-love question look like a masterpiece of diplomacy.

The problem, of course, is that the factors that do explain who is likely to marry whom are systematically obscured for the young people directly involved, the better to inspire them to get married in the first place. And if the parties involved *do* take a calculating attitude toward the bargaining and exchange that is part of any system of marriage, they are likely to practice fraud and deception, systematically misrepresenting their age, income, background and other assets and liabilities, just as in face-to-face contact they tell tall tales and white lies and wear elevator shoes and falsies.

The marriage practices of human society embody both ancient traditions and novel responses to changing times. The broad patterns of marriage—movement across class lines, the age at which it occurs, its impact on education and work-- can be pretty well predicted, and in fact are predicted by sociologists, demographers and insurance actuaries. But the narrow practical questions—"Will he marry her?" or "Will they be happy together?"— are likely to remain inexplicable, at least to the people involved. And the mystery is what gives these questions their abiding appeal. Successful computer matching—unlikely, anyway—would only spoil the fun.

For Divorced Wives, Alimony or Severance Pay?

WOMEN being divorced should not seek alimony from their husbands but rather "severance pay" for their domestic services, according to Clare Boothe Luce.

Women who want to avoid the "routine and menial tasks" of the housewife to pursue a career should not marry, advises the wife of the late publisher, Henry R. Luce.

Stand Again Domesticity

Or, "marry if you must," she writes in the April issue of McCall's magazine, out tomorrow, "but don't have children or make a home for your husband — unless he likes housework. Live with him in a hotel or small apartment, and eat your meals out."

Mrs. Luce wrote the April column before the death of Mr. Luce, who was her second husband.

When her first marriage to George Tuttle Brokaw ended after six years in 1929, she was awarded a reported settlement of $425,000. The only child of the marriage, a daughter, was killed in an automobile accident in 1944.

Mrs. Luce did not begin a career until after the dissolution of her first marriage, when she joined the staff of Vanity Fair in 1930.

She married Mr. Luce in 1935. During the 31-year marriage, which produced no children, she pursued a variety of careers that included playwrighting, newspaper reporting, politics and diplomatic service.

In her current column for McCall's, Mrs. Luce takes issue with the idea of realizing full equality between the sexes today—the rallying cry of the National Organization of Women.

Problems of Equality

Equal pay for equal work, yes, says Mrs. Luce, and she wishes NOW, the acronym of the organization, every success in its campaign to end job discrimination based on sex.

But the difficulty of full equality lies with "a fact that is plain to the most amateurish of sociologists," writes Mrs. Luce. "A vast amount of menial and routine work must be done daily or civilization would cease to function."

NOW may deplore the statistic that "fewer and fewer women are entering the professions in youth and persevering in them through maturity," she writes, but "the stark economic facts of domestic help alone explain why women are disappearing from the professions."

$10,000-a-Year Job

The work done "by one housewife cannot be bought for less than $10,000 a year," she contends. "Only talented married women, like Betty Friedan [president of NOW and author of "The Feminine Mystique"], who earn enough to command domestic services can continue in their chosen careers."

While wondering if Mrs. Friedan feels she is discriminating against her domestic help by not urging them to quit their menial jobs, Mrs. Luce agreeds with the author that divorced women should not receive alimony.

"In view of past services —often worth many thousands of dollars—rendered as domestics," Mrs. Luce says, "they should be given severance pay."

In an interview yesterday, Mrs. Friedan commented: "No man is ever asked to choose between his fulfillment in society and a home. Why should women who want a career remain celibate or give up the idea of having a home and children?

"Implicit in Mrs. Luce's thinking," Mrs. Friedan continued, "is the belief that patterns that now exist have to continue.

"Postpone marriage," Mrs. Friedan advised, "or childbearing until you have established yourself in your career and are able to pay for domestic help."

March 22, 1967

The Unmarried Marrieds On Campus

By ARNO KARLEN

THIS is the mythic creature of sex-revolution journalism, the collegiate beast with two backs. It's not at all like meeting the snark, the kraken, the Thirty-Sixth Hidden Saint. Ed and Louise are students who live together without ceremony and ring—according to many recent articles, the pinnacle of the new sexual freedom. They are attractive, likable, intelligent, articulate and earnest. When they talk about their life together, they are familiar, predictable and slightly boring. But that is the stuff myths are made of.

They met five years ago, when both were undergraduates of 21 in Cambridge, Mass. After a year of dating and then shacking up* on weekends, Ed spent a year abroad.

---
*Shacking up, as used here, means spending some nights and considerable daytime together, but without a permanent, joint living arrangement.

On his return they took an apartment, and they've lived in it through three years of graduate school. It is cozy, a bit shabby, full of records and books. They study together many evenings; texts lie on the kitchen table. They also go out together, see friends together, do things together. Like most college "unmarried marrieds" I know, they are relentlessly together.

They want to know why I'm here to talk to them and write about them. I explain that I've worked for several years on a book about sex behavior and sex attitudes that deals in part with college students. There have been many articles recently about mateships such as theirs. For instance, last year in Esquire . . .

Ed laughs. "I saw it. I know one of those couples. Both of them live here in Cambridge. But not together. The whole thing was a put-on."

"How many people do you know who really do live together?"

Ed says, "I know about a dozen couples who've done it. Most of them are married now because eventually the girl gets pregnant. Aside from them, almost everyone I know has at least spent weekends regularly with someone once. Of course, most of them are graduate students—undergrads aren't allowed to live outside dorms or can't afford to."

I ask why, after five years together, and three of domesticity, they haven't married. They answer in a light tone at first.

Louise: "But why should we?"

Ed: "Oh, I guess being married has advantages—income tax, not having to con some little old lady at the place we stay when we go skiing."

Louise: "If something came up like my having a child or our getting a joint grant, I guess we'd do it."

Ed: "Yes, there'd be penalties for the kid."

Louise: "If it lasts four years more, it'll be a common-law marriage. That's pretty ironic."

Ed: "The contract would create a mess if you had to get out of it. Besides, I can't see going to some

---
ARNO KARLEN is the author of a forthcoming book reporting research into sexual behavior and attitudes.

bureaucratic hack for it, let alone [with slow sarcasm] *a man of the cloth.*"

Me: "Is it just that you don't go to the trouble of observing a convention? Actually, it's less trouble spending a few dollars and a few minutes for a quick civil ceremony than years conning little old ladies and losing on income tax."

Ed: "Buffoons run our country. I don't want any participation in a country that elects a . . . a . . . well, you name them!"

Louise: "But it isn't political, our not being married. What marriage fulfills for people, our relationship fulfills for us. You know, someone did a test of American wives, and it turned out that they saw their husbands as breadwinners, fathers, companions and lovers, in that order. It ought to be reversed! And the women saw themselves as mothers first, then as housewives, and so on. Just keeping house and taking kids around the suburbs! I'd be terrible! When you marry you have to be ready not to go to a movie without first hiring a baby sitter. We want to go to California next year. How could we do it with kids?"

Me: "Maybe you could. If you're strong enough to live as you do, mightn't you be strong enough to be married without falling into the conventional patterns you hate? You seem to think that being a wife and mother has an irresistible negative force."

Louise: "No! That isn't so! I want kids very much, but I'd be happy to work four hours a day. I'd be a better mother, a better person to be around. You have to meet people outside your family. I'm afraid of the boredom I saw when I lived for nine years in the suburbs. I've actually met women who talk about their damned *appliances* all the time!"

Ed: "Louise, you're too angry. You're upset. He must have hit something."

Louise (pausing to think): "Yes. I guess so. I should think about that."

Me: "Do you have an agreement about sleeping with other people?"

Ed: "I made clear when I started living with her that a time would come when I'd want to sleep with other chicks. I can't imagine just making it with the same girl for 40 years. It's the same for her. The only real infidelity is living with someone you don't love."

Me: "Has either of you ever used that freedom?"

Louise: "Yes, when we were apart three years ago. But not since. We've had a running discussion about this; girls tend to be more upset about sex than men. Psychologically, it's **just not as simple with them. I know that when I first went**

to bed with guys I always thought there had to be involvement. Then I learned I could just sleep with a guy. I worked all that out before we lived together. Now it's settled. I just haven't met anyone who attracts me."

Me: "Not in three years?"

Louise: "There are 40 men where I spend my days, and there isn't one I'd want to sleep with. I guess we aren't on the lookout because we're happy together."

Ed: "I haven't met anyone I want more than Louise. But I was always reticent with women anyway. Now it just seems too far out of the way."

Me: "Do your parents know that you're living together?"

Ed: "Her parents know. They're very happy about it."

Louise: "Because they understand what we're into— that we really love each other. It's a stable thing."

Ed: "They're very liberal people. They've always let her do what she wants, and she's open with them. They're great. We spent vacations with them."

Louise: "My mother thinks it's fine. It's his mother who can't stand it."

Ed: "My mother's from a very conservative background. Trying to talk to her about us is like trying to talk to George Wallace about a black man."

Me: "Why do you think your friends have lived together?"

Louise: "Many of them think of marriage as a commitment, and that's why they don't want it."

ED and Louise are a small part of a small subculture of American college students. The majority of American undergraduates live at home or in supervised dormitories; with effort, some shack up for a night or a weekend. The unmarrieds are mostly older undergraduates and graduate students who live on their own away from home. Almost all of those I've met belong to the dissident youth subculture — intellectual, politically liberal-to-radical, from middle- and upper-middle-class backgrounds, anti-materialistic and anti-Establishment.

Within the dissident subculture the unmarrieds are taken for granted. Their friends casually say that what people do about sex — shacking up and living together — is their own thing. Nevertheless, a note of approval, even envy, often shows through the insouciant facade. Living together, for this subculture, represents true love and adulthood. More conventional students, unconnected with the life and values of the subculture, view the unmarrieds much as the media and its watchers do, through a filter of confused myths about hippies, sex and drugs. They, like most of the country, know it's going on somewhere—not here, but around the corner.

A number of the subculture's members shack up. But even within this minority only a tiny minority actually live together. We know that the so-called sexual revolution is really a leap in attitudes, expectations and verbal sophistication; in behavior it is a short hop. The most informed researchers say that sex activity among the rest of the population has risen slowly and steadily since about 1930, after the real revolution of the twenties. Since 1960 there has been a slight acceleration. Forty years ago, 15-20 per cent of college girls were non-virgins; today the figure is about 25 per cent. Among seniors it's 50 per cent, but the average marriage age for college girls has dropped to 22, and the majority of these girls still have all or most premarital intercourse with intended husbands. So, if we compare any category of sex behavior at a given age now with that of the middle fifties, there may be an increase of, say, five percentage points, at the outside.

But living conditions, due to affluence and more permissive regulations, are freer, so shacking up and living together *may* have increased a bit more than that rough figure of 5 per cent. Even if so, a much more significant change than numbers is taking place, and that is in the prevailing emotional atmosphere in these relationships.

Ed and Louise have much in common with the dissident

student world and the unmarrieds within it. First, their love life is more radical in theory than in fact. Ed says he has always been reticent with girls. Though Louise apparently talks casually about sex, she shows some signs of anxiety when doing so. They claim they've been faithful for three years, between ages 22 and 25. Judging by discussions with other individuals, I'd guess that it's probably true. In this age of foolproof birth control many of their enlightened, liberated friends have married because the girl had an "accident." (In the end, the unmarrieds do what the most conventional young people do—the girl gets pregnant to push the affair into a marriage.) Ed and Louise, too, talk as though a pregnancy could just "happen" to them.

And like many others in their world, especially other unmarrieds, they continually express the need for a cozy domestic nest. They are togetherness itself, and their lives seem to turn about The Relationship. Both verbally insist on financial independence, but exercise it little or not at all. The cry of independence, in fact, seems verbal protest against all evidence: "Just because I'm so dependent on you, don't think I'm dependent!" Further, the girl's family, more than the boy's, accepts or even encourages their living together. And when it comes to marriage and motherhood, the difficulties and unpleasantness are mentioned, not the rewards.

WHEN one listens to Jim and Edith, the pattern is repeated, and confirming details appear. Both are 21 and live together in Manhattan. He is a senior at N.Y.U.; she graduated last June from another school. Like Ed, he is tense, skittish, controlled, cerebral. Like Louise, she is more talkative and emotional. And, like Ed and Louise, they are reverential when they speak of The Relationship, but awkward when they talk about committed ties:

Jim: "Most of our friends live together—I'd say about eight couples. I mean, if you call living together one person sleeping overnight with the other fairly often. They don't move their things, just themselves. One keeps a separate apartment."

"Being a wife today is no more attractive
to many of the girls than a 9-to-5 job is to the boys."

Edith: "Whether you move into one place depends on how much you want to share a life. Often the guys don't want it; it's too close to being married. We don't know any couples who live the way we do. One couple did, but they got married."

Jim: "The N.Y.U. commuters are a different bunch, much more conservative. I know lots of people who shack up with girls; when college is over, they tend to get married. They don't see why they're making the distinction about marriage any more."

Edith: "They slide from dating into shacking up, and that slides into marriage."

Me: "But you slid into living together. Why not into marriage?"

Jim: "Ordinarily I'd be on my own, and I may be in the future. I feel young; I have no career I want to follow. I can't drag anyone around with me while I'm unsettled. Marriage is for people who know the structure they want in their lives."

Me: "Do you want children?"

Edith: "No."

Jim: "I can't drag her around, let alone a child."

Me: "Do your parents know that you're living together?"

Jim: "Mine know, and they're against it. They say, get married or live separately."

Edith: "My parents know, and I think my mother is glad that we're open about it."

Again, marriage and children are spoken of as "dragging someone around"—a psychologist would probably guess that this is a reflection of their own parents' basic feelings toward family and children. Jim is afraid of a permanent bond; Edith does not press for one, and typically she cites her mother's approval and doesn't mention her father, showing whose opinion matters.

As they tell it, the majority of their school is more conservative than they. But even within their intellectual, liberal student milieu, no others now live as they do, to their knowledge. Jim and Edith have agreed to be interviewed only on condition that no "personal matters"—sex—are discussed. When I ask at the end why they insisted on this prohibition, they seem even more tense than usual.

They resemble the other unmarrieds in not being freaky in clothing, manner or life style. In fact, they give an impression of being sensitive, edgy, unhappy and prematurely middle-aged. They are much more earnest about themselves than about anything outside themselves.

BY comparison, Gerald and Carolyn remind me more of students I knew who shacked up and lived together when I was an undergraduate in the middle fifties. Yes, students did it then—students I knew from Vassar and Swarthmore who snuck away to shack up on weekends, undergraduates at Antioch, the University of Chicago and Columbia who lived together in their early 20's. Some were like Jim and Edith, but the majority were not quite so owlishly pious about their love lives as the students to whom I've talked in the last few years.

Gerald would rather talk about his work or politics than about himself and Carolyn. He is a few years older than most seniors, active in radical politics, very hardworking, and with a clear vocational focus. Carolyn is an aggressive, intellectual girl several years younger. She has a sharp tongue and a combative spirit, and it is difficult not to smile when Gerald uses quiet, firm humor on her as an effective whip-and-chair. At their small liberal arts college, with its radical tradition and considerable freedom in living arrangements, they take living together pretty much for granted — though even here only a minority of students can or do have such an arrangement. They go places together but have separate activities as well. Their sprawling, disorganized apartment has no nestlike air.

This is Carolyn's first such arrangement. He has had several before, lasting from a few months to the better part of a year. Neither makes a cathedral of the relationship. It's part of their lives. If asked, they say simply that they love each other. They have no rationale for living together—it's what one does if in love but not ready for marriage. He has little conflict about it. She is combative and somewhat wary of the closeness; Gerald is working on that with affection, tenderness and exasperation.

Their attitude is the one I saw more often when I was a student: Edith and Jim's was common but not predominant. Like Gerald, many of the male students I knew in 1954 grew up in city neighborhoods and had parents without higher education. The country was less affluent, and some World War II and many Korean War vets were still in the schools; many students were in their middle 20's and had worked or been in the armed forces. They had been exposed to the adult world and tested as males and human beings to a greater degree than most students today. Like Gerald, many had a strong vocational commitment. They were less earnest about relationships, less theoretical about sex, more earnest about work.

Now many students come from affluent suburban families in which the father is a recessive figure. Psychiatrist Kenneth Keniston has described in his extraordinary book, "The Uncommitted," a personality frequently produced by such families, one basic to the dissident college culture today. The young men, says Keniston, are passive, unable to express anger and to commit themselves to people or work. They fail to identify with their fathers and with the world of work, assertion and competition in which the fathers are involved. Instead, they guardedly reach out for oceanic love in a relationship with a girl. Keniston did not study girls from this background, but those in the dissident subculture are often what one would expect — the emotive, controlling "mothers" their male counterparts grew up with and are still seeking. A psychiatrist at Gerald's college describes the situation this way:

"Among the students here I see a great many guys who are passive, unable to let themselves feel anger. But if you can't express anger, you can't really let other feelings go and get close to anyone. You turn off your feelings, don't even feel your anxiety. This sort of guy tends to pair up with a girl whose feelings are more accessible. But because her feelings are more turned on she feels anxiety more, so she sees her emotionality as something negative. The guy thinks he's getting a bubbly girl who'll bring him alive. The girl sees a strong male who will control her dangerous emotionality for her. When they get close they see each other more realistically. He sees that her emotion is used to control and manipulate. She sees that his strength is just constricted emotion, inability to feel.

"This isn't limited to the middle and upper-middle

classes. I've heard it described over and over by social workers in lower-class settings. It was the most common pairing I saw when I was a marriage counselor. But when I came to this college I thought at first that it was some kind of trick—the same type of couple coming into my office time after time as lovers."

Dr. Samuel Hadden, a distinguished psychiatrist in Philadelphia, says, "I've dealt with many of these kids—middle-class, intellectual, worked for McCarthy, and so on. Among such young people there seems to be a trend toward passive males and controlling girls. The male seems to be absolving himself of as much responsibility as he possibly can and the female, believing she makes herself more attractive, assumes more responsibility for herself and encourages him in his avoidance. It's related to a change in the family, and the devaluation of marriage. Being a man is a hell of a chore today, and many young men grow up very protected and a bit emasculated, with a somewhat feminine orientation. Being a wife is no more attractive to many of the girls than a 9-to-5 job is for the boys.

"If you want to see the roots of this, look to the parents. In many homes there is competition between husband and wife for the dominant role; many times daughters are reared with the idea that they mustn't be subordinate to any man. I had two sisters in here, two years apart, neither knowing the other had consulted me. They'd gone to a liberal-arts college; then their father insisted they spend a year at a business college. He said that then, if their marriages failed, they wouldn't be dependent on their husbands. They could walk out any time and support themselves. That's a hell of a way to get a woman to think positively about marriage. And sure enough, both girls were here divorced, having been prepared to terminate marriage as soon as difficulties developed."

Will is a tall, handsome young man of 25, sensitive and soft-spoken, when he speaks at all. He is trained in the visual arts and starting to work in his field. Georgina is a few years older, tall and slim and tomboyish. She is a nonstop talker, and at first she dominates the conversation. But eventually Will's tense reserve tends to control the entire room.

GEORGINA comes from a fractured family. She has outside work, but now spends most of her time working with Will. They have lived together for a year and a half, and they spend very little time apart. A great deal of the first hour is spent talking about the compromises of living with someone, and especially about conflicts in making daily decisions.

Georgina says, "Will and I were going together, and then we lived together after a few months. I mean, there were two apartments, but I stayed here most of the time. My mother came to visit, saw our places and said, 'His is grubby, but you could fix it up; it would be much cheaper if you moved in.' So I did. Until then I'd always needed the escape of my own apartment. The biggest hang-up in commitment is, if you have a fight, where do you run back to?

"Now our possessions are mixed up together—neither of us could sort out his own books any more. I've learned more about everything from this relationship. Until I lived with Will I slept with a lot of guys. I found sameness in the one-night things, though. This living with Will has been a real growth experience. I suspect that by the time I'm ready to have kids I'll really want them. We watched the birth of a baby on TV last night, and we were both in tears together.

"We make two concessions to the conventions. We have a second phone—it's a hot line for my outside work, because if they knew I lived with Will I might be in trouble. We have Mr. and Mrs. on the mail box, plus my 'maiden name.' This is a lower-middle-class neighborhood and the mailman refused to deliver mail to another couple like us near here."

I ask, "Why go to this bother instead of getting married?"

Will says, "Why should we? Why go out of our way?"

Georgina says, "I feel better for knowing we can split if it doesn't work."

They are monogamous in practice, but theoretically for sharing each other sexually with other people. Will says,

"It's selfish to deprive a loved one of an experience of pleasure and growth." I ask Georgina to imagine realistically her gut reaction on coming home and finding Will in bed with another girl. She is blank, cannot imagine it. Using the same words as Louise when asked that, she says, "I know he would never do anything that would hurt me." Will explains that he hopes he would react calmly if he discovered Georgina in such a situation.

They ask me what my reaction would be. I say, "My first impulse would be to throw him down the stairs and belt her in the mouth." Will shakes his head and says, "I feel a lot of pity for you."

Will and Georgina are no longer students, though Will was still a student when they met and began living together. But both still live in the same milieu as the students I interviewed, and this makes one wonder how much students should be singled out for their sexual behavior. If people leave home to live on their own at 18, we're hardly surprised at their having acquired some sexual experience after four or six years. We aren't even surprised if they grow up enough to go to bed only with people they'd want to breakfast with—that is, if they shack up. But when those who leave home for college mature sexually in this way, it's considered news, a revolution, a problem.

THERE are nonstudents whose lives follow the "student" pattern. There are Geralds among the college unmarrieds today, and there were Jim-Edith matches 15 years ago. I haven't done a systematic study of a rounded-out sample of student unmarrieds. But various studies and my own observations make me guess that there is a prevailing trend. I suggest it as a hypothesis that a social psychologist could check out:

Many, probably a large majority, of the unmarrieds live within the dissident student milieu to some degree. They are like their friends. In fact, they are almost "pure" examples of the type, and that is their special problem. The background from which so many come produces increasing numbers of people with a fear of commitment but a need for hothouse relationships—

and a conflict about sex roles coming largely from the diminution of the male parents in their families. They desperately need a sense of family, but lack basic trust in families. Most students who are torn between dependence and independence marry in their early 20's; they may resolve the conflict or carry it on in their marriage. But many of those who live together for a long time, as if married, act out the conflict dramatically. One hand pushes fearfully away from ties, the other clings to a mutually protective mateship.

We're used to male reluctance to take on marriage and family. Usually, in such circumstances, the girl's desire for them settles the matter one way or another. Among the unmarrieds the girls are as wary of marriage and parenthood as are the boys. Dr. Hadden mentioned a case in which the cue for this came from the girl's father. And, indeed, in some families one parent is "both mother and father" to the child emotionally, and this may be the father. But among most students I've talked to, fathers are hardly mentioned. The mother is the influential parent, and she supports the girl in staying uncommitted. In fact, one is reminded of the psychiatric truism that many children act out their parents' hidden fantasies. Mothers "trapped" in their marriages seem to be asking their daughters to stay free. Some unmarrieds don't fit this pattern, but many I've met in recent years fit it with provocative regularity. Ten and fifteen years ago it seemed to me that other patterns were at least as common.

I by no means suggest the unmarrieds run to the altar. I wish more students were shacked up or living together. The best preparation for a relationship is relationships; the best training for a good sex life is sex. We stunt the capacity for both in early life for many people, and they must catch up in their teens and 20's. I only regret that shifts in the family and in sex roles are not preparing people to enjoy the exploration more. Ventures in love and sexuality could be a joyful part of a joyful life. They needn't be life-engulfing and glum. I almost wish someone would take much of that unmarried vanguard by the hand and show it the joys of guiltless promiscuity. ■

A Day in the Life of One Husbandless Working Mother—It's No Picnic

CHARLOTTE, N.C. (AP)—"Shannon? Shannon? Come on, now, honey. It's time to get up."

Linda Stancil cooed softly to her 7-year-old daughter, and there was the soft pat-pat-pat sound of a mother's hand on a little girl's pajamas.

It was the start of another day for a husbandless working mother, one of hundreds of thousands of such women in America.

Mrs. Stancil, who tries to make the best of things for her daughter and her 6-year-old son, Bryan, looks a little older than her 28 years. Her face sometimes displays the effects of the daily pressure of working all day and being a mother and a father to the children at night.

She doesn't smile often and sometimes there are dark circles under her eyes.

Her weekdays start at 6 A.M. Sometimes, she says, she lies still after silencing the harsh buzzer of the alarm clock and longs to remain in the security of sleep where things are quiet and problems are forgotten.

But she gets up, gets herself ready for work and then rides herd on her two children to make certain that they get ready for school on time.

By the time she went to awaken the children on a typical morning, Bryan already was out of bed, standing sleepy-eyed in the doorway of his bedroom with his blond hair awry.

•

Mrs. Stancil walked into her daughter's bedroom, softly, as mothers do unconsciously, and flicked on the light.

Things move quickly around the Stancil house on weekday mornings.

The radio in Mrs. Stancil's bedroom could be heard clearly through the house. A disk jockey was warming up with practiced cheeriness. The Tijuana Brass came on strong.

"Bryan? How are you doing in there?" asked Mrs. Stancil as she passed by her son's room on the way to the kitchen. "Get dressed, now. Put your pajamas in your drawer and make your bed."

Was it yesterday that Mrs. Stancil was a child herself? Running, laughing, playing on her parents' farm in North Carolina.

"Momma, where's my belt?" Bryan asked from his bedroom. His voice had the same irritation as that of a grownup who has misplaced an item.

"I think it's hanging on the bathroom door," his mother replied from the kitchen as she poured hot water from a pan into a glass coffee pot.

"No, it isn't. That's my skinny one. I mean my black one."

Some of the hot water splashed onto one of Mrs. Stancil's hands and she grimaced.

"Mom-ma," Shannon called from her bedroom in a barely audible voice. Then came some mumbles.

"What, Shannon? What did you say?"

Mrs. Stancil rubbed ointment onto the injured hand.

"I said, why didn't you hem this dress up so I can wear it?" Shannon answered.

"I told you before that's a summer dress," her mother said.

It wasn't too many years ago that this 28-year-old mother was waiting in wild anticipation at her parents' home for her very first school day. Life was like a spring day then.

"Bryan, did you get that bed made yet? If you have, come on in here and get your breakfast." On her way to check on Bryan's progress, she glanced into her daughter's room and found her sitting listlessly on the edge of the bed, still undressed.

"What's going on here, Shannon?" Patting time was over. "Sit up here and get dressed. You're asking for it, young lady, and I mean it."

A momentary lull in the banter. The radio's song drifted into the bedroom.

Life is no picnic for Mrs. Stancil now. Dreams, perhaps of gaily papered walls in a new house and of love and warmth, had faded since her marriage at 17.

Her take-home pay of $70 a week and $120 a month for child support comes to about $400 income each month. Her Christmas present from her father was four new tires, and she was ecstatic. It was just what she needed.

"Momma! Shannon won't let me in the bathroom!"

"Well, you'll just have to wait until she's through."

"But she's not doing anything!"

"Yes I am!" came Shannon's angry retort from the bathroom.

Earlier, Mrs. Stancil had been asked about her budget.

"What budget?" she asked. It all goes for bills, so there's no need to make out a budget. When bread and milk run out a week before payday, she just has to "wait until the paycheck comes in to buy some more."

By 7:45 A.M., Mrs. Stancil managed to get the children into the car. She dropped them off at school, just a block away. It would be an hour before school started. Sometimes she lets them stay at home until classes begin.

Bills?

The monthly ones are $103 for rent, $33 for furniture, $15 for telephone, about $11 for electricity, about $25 for natural gas and about $20 for gasoline.

"Oh, yeah," she said. "And $2.10 for water."

Twelve dollars a week goes to a child-care center that keeps the children after they get out of school, and there are unfigured bills for groceries, doctor bills, medicine, clothes and car repairs.

Mrs. Stancil goes home for lunch. Her children eat at the school's cafeteria. At 5 P.M. she drives several blocks from work to the child-care center, which picks up the children after they get out of school.

Once at home, she must dive into preparing the evening meal, cleaning house, washing, ironing and other chores. She has little social life.

"Friends seemed to evaporate" when she and her husband separated four years ago. "You're no longer the single person you used to be, so you don't fit there. You're no longer the married person, so you don't fit there. You're just in a separate world."

The children were in and out of the house, the door banging shut each time. Minutes later they were feuding. Mrs. Stancil sent them both crying to their rooms.

She composed herself and smiled slightly.

Mrs. Stancil does date some. But her other-world position of being separated from her husband causes problems.

"I don't have very many friends who are men because you don't know what their interest is," she said. "Nine times out of 10 it isn't good. You know what they think about a woman who's separated."

It doesn't look as though life is going to get any easier for Mrs. Stancil. But, she said, "it was blind faith when I got married, and it's blind faith now that keeps me going. Blind faith that things will get better.

"They've got to."

Top Volunteer Mother
Arnette Thelma Giles

By NAN ROBERTSON
Special to The New York Times

WASHINGTON, Feb. 10 — When Arnette Thelma Peters Giles was growing up along the Gulf Coast in the early years of this century, her "childish dream" was to have "a huge house which would gather in all the unwanted children." "I knew all the heartaches and the disappointments," she said today. "I know what it is like to be unwanted, unloved and rejected." Mrs. Giles is 70 years old. In 51 years of marriage to the Rev. Charles Giles, a United Methodist preacher in Pearlington, Miss., she has reared 40 abandoned, poor children, many of them retarded, as well as five children of her own.

Woman in the News

Tonight, President Nixon gave her a $5,000 prize as the nation's outstanding volunteer of 1971 in ceremonies at the Kennedy Center for the Performing Arts.

"I never before in my life knew so much money all at once," Mrs. Giles said earlier.

Sharing the spotlight with Mrs. Giles last night was SERVE, an organization on Staten Island that was named as last year's outstanding group of elderly volunteers.

Workers from 60 to 96

SERVE is an acronym for Serve and Enrich Retirement by Volunteer Experience. Its 600 workers, who range in age from 60 to 96, assist at some 30 schools, social welfare agencies and health institutions in Staten Island, including the Willowbrook State School for the retarded.

Mr. and Mrs. Giles live in a nine-room frame house in the little country town on the Gulf of Mexico. Eleven children live with them.

The Gileses have adopted two. There are "some grandchildren," three sent "from the welfare" and a baby who was born of an unwed mother on the back seat of Mrs. Giles's car.

Mrs. Giles was abandoned first by her father, a lumber schooner sailor, and then by her mother when she was five years old and her brother was two and one-half. The children were shuffled about from relative to relative in Mississippi, Alabama and Louisiana.

"We never stayed in one place long," she said. "I'd gone to five elementary schools before I finished sixth grade."

She was married in 1920 at the age of 19 to Mr. Giles. Her fifth and last child was five years old when, in the depths of the Depression, she took in the 5-month-old infant of a dying neighbor.

That baby, Leonard Richmond Peters, now is a 37-year-old jazz musician in Los Angeles with a band of his own. He and the Gileses' other "children" are scattered across the land but still send

The New York Times

A gift for sharing

frequent letters and cards.

As a little boy, Leonard was originally labeled mentally retarded, but his foster parents saw his obvious musical ability and encouraged it.

Aid for Retarded

The couple helped develop even the children thought to be hopelessly retarded. A child given no chance to walk is now in the 11th grade; a present ward, deaf, dumb and weighing only 21 pounds when he came to the Gileses at the age of five, now can say "Mama" and "look."

Mrs. Giles calls the retarded ones "God's special children."

"The most they need is love and understanding," she said. "They're starved for love. If you show them any affection, you can get them to do almost anything."

When Hancock County opened its small school for the retarded, Mrs. Giles was asked to serve as a teacher's aide. With only nine grades of formal schooling behind her, she studied on her own and at night school, and three years ago, finally got her high school equivalency diploma. She is currently taking college courses in special education "to try to help the children more."

The National Volunteer Awards presented tonight were sponsored by the National Center for Voluntary Action, a private, nonprofit organization with headquarters in Washington. The winners were selected from 661 individuals and volunteer groups nominated by 31 states and Puerto Rico.

The judges on the final awards panel were Charles Evers, Mayor of Fayette, Miss.; Walter J. Hickel, former Secretary of the Interior and former Governor of Alaska; H. I. Romnes, board chairman of the American Telephone and Telegraph Company; Alvin Toffler, author of "Future Shock," and Mrs. Jacqueline G. Wexler, president of Hunter College of the City of New York.

When Smugness Collapsed

By FRANCES KAUFMAN

When I lived in Washington—with two babies and my husband, the young sister of a friend came to visit one night. She had just joined a liberation group at the university, and she had a list of complaints about the role of women in contemporary life.

"Why should I marry and have children," she asked, "and why should I marry someone who doesn't want to share the responsibilities of home and family with me? And why should a man's career and identity be more important than mine?"

The answer, I informed her smugly, was not to get so worked up about abstract concepts, and to choose wisely. Not all men, I informed her, make slaves of women; not all women had to have children; and, once women did have children, they had other choices beside full-time baby-sitting and drudgery.

First, motherhood has many satisfactions; second, if you play it wisely, you can always hire someone else to take care of the drudgery part; third, any man worthy of marriage to a woman like her had to understand her needs, and surely, would be more than happy to share the domestic responsibilities; and fourth, she could always choose to do what I was doing and have the best of all possible situations.

After all, I had a well-paying part-time job that allowed me to use my skills, and only took up twenty hours of the week, thereby leaving me with plenty of time for all the creative, pleasant things that life has to offer. Who'd want the obligations of supporting a family or working full time? Not I. I considered myself pretty free: my husband, a self-declared "feminist," was happy to see me working and satisfied, my children were young enough to be sleeping, eating, or otherwise occupied and distracted for the few hours I was away each day, and, because my salary afforded me the luxury of a full-time babysitter/housekeeper, I had plenty of time left to read books, listen to music, romp with the children, participate in the peace movement, even take an acting class or a long walk whenever I felt like it.

By the end of the evening, I had almost converted my young friend.

"Maybe," she thought, "there is hope."

Marguerite, wherever you are, I apologize. My "feminist" husband came home one night and announced that New York beckoned. He had been offered a better paying job with an expanding company that would afford *him* the chance to really grow professionally, and to provide *us* with a "better" way of life.

I objected—we already had a pretty comfortable way of life; all our material needs were satisfied, and we certainly didn't need more possessions; New York was a harder city to raise children in; I couldn't possibly live as close to my work as I did in Washington, where it took only fifteen minutes to travel to work; his entire raise in salary would only cover the higher cost of living in New York; and, besides, in a city crawling with writers and editors, who'd hire me? And who'd be willing to let me name my own hours and conditions of work?

When my objections failed to convince him, I kicked and screamed, held on by my fingernails while he tugged away at my confidence, and then, when all else failed, I flatly refused to leave. He, being a man first (a position far higher, I've discovered, on his list of priorities than that of feminist), and secure in the knowledge that his career and his happiness came first, assured me that he loved me, loved our children, needed all of us, but would somehow learn to manage without us if we chose not to join him in New York.

The battle was won. That kind of pressure I was in no way equipped to withstand. Wasn't I being selfish, trying to force my husband to give up what he wanted because I liked something better? Wasn't I creating grand issues where insignificant ones existed? And, worst, most devastating argument of them all, wasn't I trying to undermine his masculinity?

We moved. And my name went on the ever-growing list of the unemployed.

I have spent the last two years rationalizing all the problems away. I have joined committees that meet during the three hours the children are now in school. I have used up countless hours sewing clothes I don't need and probably will never wear (I'm an awful seamstress and nothing I make ever fits anyway); but it fills the time. I read endlessly, can even recite from memory the ingredients on the "King Vitamin" box. I take an occasional day off and haunt the museums, art galleries, movie theaters. I am, as they say, "up on things."

But, let me tell you, I'm lost. And I was probably lost, not at that crucial decision-making time two years ago, but long before I ever agreed to give up my career plans and teach school so that my new husband could finish his graduate work twelve years ago. I am definitely *not* one of the Pepsi generation, or the liberated generation; I belong, most certainly, to the last of the schlepp generation—two years too old for the pill, the Peace Corps, real liberation.

I don't know what the answers are. If I did, I wouldn't find myself wondering, in near-terror, what to do with myself on days when both my children are invited to friends' houses after school on the same day, and being furious that I have allowed myself to be lured into this trap; that I've let my life become so circumscribed that I have nothing to do some days. What I do know is that there will have to be major changes in the way we all live before anything changes.

Change will come only if they transcend the jargon of "concern" for cosmic problems as a substitute for sharing and loving and taking responsibility in their personal affairs. But if change is impossible, if we can't restructure things, then stop lying to us! It's a painful ruse. The women of my generation were not prepared for life. The realities of existence were not part of our training and education. We're not equipped to function in the lives we live.

February 7, 1972

The Frances Kaufman Letters

'I cannot sympathize'

To the Editor:

I too am a member of Frances Kaufman's "schlepp generation" (When Smugness Collapsed," Op-Ed, Feb. 7, 1972). I too was unprepared, both by education and family background, for the "realities of existence," for life as a "liberated woman." But I've learned a lot in twenty years.

If she's a writer, why isn't she freelancing articles or writing stories? Could she go to graduate school? At the very least she could take a volunteer job which would use her skills, and add to her credentials. Until Ms. Kaufman convinces me she's tried all possibilities, I cannot sympathize with her.
    MARY LOUISE WILLEY

'A self-pitying complaint'

To the Editor:

Oh, my God! Another one of those whining, self-pitying complaints from a middle-class, educated, talented woman about how society oppresses her! Did it ever occur to her that the man she married might just happen to be a selfish, self-centered, thoughtless human being as well as the product of a system she deplores? Perhaps not! To acknowledge that might be too much of an additional burden to an already-bruised ego.

JOEL POMERANTZ

'Stop shrieking'

To the Editor:

For one thing, she could stop shrieking, get off her pops, and get a job. Any job, if she's really "near terror" during the long afternoons. I cannot believe that in the whole great big city she cannot find the suitable means of enjoying life and feeling self-satisfaction.　EILEEN D. OBSER

'Everyone loses'

To the Editor:

It is not only the women of Frances Kaufman's generation who were unprepared for life. Everyone, men and women, are products of sexist society wherein only half the choices are open to each. The dichotomous conditioning process begins operating soon after birth—half the population is taught to dominate and be self-sufficient, the other half to nurture and submit. Everyone loses in the process and only with great effort do some people achieve a wholeness defined by humanity rather than by culturally defined sex role.

MARILYN SCHAPIRO

'Women's tyranny'

To the Editor:

Equality is equality. Ms. Kaufman was happy in Washington. Apparently Mr. Kaufman was not. Fair? Not by my equality standards. Because her husband sought a better position for himself, and she is having difficulty adjusting to a new situation, she should not snivel. To my mind, Ms. Kaufman is practicing women's tyranny, no liberation.　ALICE D'ANGELO

'Is a wife a slave?'

To the Editor:

Shame on Mrs. Frances Kaufman. She and all the would-be female liberationists overlook or ignore the specific freedom we wives have which is denied to our breadwinner husbands— the freedom of choice. Is a wife a slave because she has to run a household with all its concomitant duties?

DOROTHY H. HUGHES

A Married Couple's Response

To the Editor:

Bravo to Frances Kaufman for having the courage to speak out about her very personal discrimination, which has no doubt been duplicated in thousands of American homes. Why is it that men have been so imbued with their own sense of self-importance that even those who claim to be enlightened fail to consider their wives as they consider themselves?

Can a male human life be inherently more deserving of growth and fulfillment than that of a female? Should wives consistently surrender their own desires and goals for the sake of their husbands' careers or even for the supposed "greater good" of their marriages? The answer to both these questions must be no, a no founded on the integrity and value of all human life and based upon the proposition that we are indeed all created equal.

ARLENE SCHLISSEL

To the Editor.

The courage and perception shown by Ms. Kaufman are to be applauded.

There is a major paradox in a situation such as hers. Mr. Kaufman contended he had to move from Washington, D.C. to a new position in New York to further his career. The attendant challenge, prestige and remunerative aspects would be great fuel for his personal growth. Implicit in this attitude is the supposition that it will also be beneficial for the balance of the family.

Put another way, it means that he, she and the offspring run on the same fuel. Fortunately, our understanding of human behavior is such that we cannot blindly accept such a hypothesis as valid. Having her own sense of self, she needed her own fuel.

Two mature, considerate and equal individuals are required in the marital state—not an engine and a caboose.

THEODORE SCHLISSEL

'She is lost'

To the Editor:

Alas, poor Mrs. Kaufman, she is more lost than she realizes. She states emphatically she is not a member of the Pepsi generation, says she is not a member of the liberated generation and fears she is a member of the schlepp generation. She isn't.

She feels the women of her generation "weren't prepared for life." (Is anyone prepared for life?) Maybe it was being born in the Depression (or raised during it) or growing up during World War II—whatever the reasons —the schlepp generation did not expect life to be rosy and has coped with the realities amazingly well and is still plugging.

ELIZABETH B. MOYNIHAN

'Man and drudgery'

To the Editor:

Frances Kaufman and countless feminists along with her speak of the drudgery involved in being a housewife. Have these ladies thought about the drudgery in the jobs they take to liberate them? Also, but far more im-

portant, have they thought about the drudgery their husbands experience on their jobs?

NICKY SCHWARZ

'Lucky Mrs. Kaufman'

To the Editor:

I wonder how many men who aspire to write are in that situation the country over—working for small town papers or local magazines, trapped in the hinterlands by a wife, children, house with mortgage and a job that does afford a living, so that they don't dare give it up without the assurance of another one. Perhaps only persons who are or have been in that situation can realize how lucky Mrs. Kaufman is to have a breadwinner to pay the bills while she attacks the big market.　GLADYS DENNY SHULTZ

'I can sympathize'

To the Editor:

I can sympathize with Mrs. Kaufman but I am happy to say that she does not speak for me or for the many women like me who live happily in schleppdom.　NANCY JOLINE

To Julie and Abigail

By SHELLEY LIST

WESTPORT, Conn.—As you know, I'm 41. Divorced. Of course you know that. And I am fairly well "liberated" for the most part, having worked as a journalist for the last eight years—as soon as one of you left for nursery school and the other to first or second grade.

I always worked nearby in case one of you got sick, as happened often when the nurse would call the newspaper from school and talk about your temperature or fatigue and would I please come pick you up.

I always had help, one way or another, whether I could afford it or not, because I worked, and couldn't bear the thought of your coming home from school to an empty house. And because I hated housework; it was not something in which I excelled.

And for these five years of the divorce you have watched me become rather self-sufficient, independent. Men have been on the scene and we have all coped with the delight and despair and utter necessity of them.

I have been to a few consciousness-raising sessions, consisting mostly of suburban married women. And I would not change places with these women. Their marriages appear constricting to many of them, the constraints being very real, the monogamous state strangely confining. My own "libera-tion," self-imposed, has been out of desire and necessity. And at this point I am comfortable with it.

But what concerns me now, with your young womanhood approaching, and my "fulfilling" myself as a writer more and more is . . . priorities.

In other words, when you say to me, as one of you did recently after sharing an intimate confidence, your arm covering your eyes so I wouldn't see your pain, the tears escaping under your elbow down your cheeks, when you said to me, "Do you know this is the first time you have really talked to me in a long time, and I feel so much better just for that," I am taken aback.

And I think about your faces behind the shut door of my room when I confront the typewriter at night after being away at work all day. And I think about coming home from work at 7 or 8 o'clock sometimes, irritable and tired and ill-equipped to be an understanding mother.

And I think about Gloria Steinem and the beautiful sense she makes, and how right she is in demanding a re-evaluation of the relationship between the sexes, and the essential feeling of self-worth women must have as professionals and people, as well as females.

But I wonder what she would do at those moments when a daughter just needs her mother and whatever wise womanly self that mother can muster, and she is not there, but out fulfilling herself.

And when I pull your arm away from your eyes, and look at the moist brown, and kiss away the wetness, I wonder about liberation. I wonder about dedication to one's work. I read that politicians rue the traveling involved in campaigns because it takes them away from their families, and I wonder who is going to dry the eyes of the children of the women's caucus, and talk into the night about what it is just to be in this world, and especially what it is to be a woman.

I wonder about those feminists who decry having husbands or fathers for their babies. I respect their zeal and independence, but a baby becomes a person all too soon, and what a mother should give to that person as the maturer of the two is awesome.

So I am taken up short.

I am saying to you, I'm sorry when I throw you out of my room when I want to write. And I'm sorry that I miss those moments and let the days go by without sensing that we have not talked. And I'm saying I wonder if there is a way to be all things to all people, especially your children, and be "liberated" at the same time.

Shelley List is a newspaper editor and an author whose new novel is "Did You Love Daddy When I Was Born?"

March 17, 1972

The Question Is, What Is a Family, Anyway?

By ELIZABETH JANEWAY

Laments by Frances Kaufman and Shelley List—two women who struggle to cope alone with the social demands of the wife-mother role—call for some reality principles.

I want to suggest that we widen the context in which we look at these problems. The family, (as Talcott Parson says), is a subsystem of society, not a complete-in-itself operating unit. It can't, therefore, resolve dilemmas that surrounding circumstances create. It's too small. And today, it's smaller than ever. Sociologists still talk about "the nuclear family," but Mrs. List's family includes only one adult, not two. There are 20 million other people living in families with one, female head. Those are less-than-nuclear fam-ilies. Most families today can be described as less than nuclear—if you count how many working hours fathers and children are at home together, sharing each other's thoughts and company.

If a family runs into trouble, the reason may lie outside the family, in the surrounding circumstances. Trying to solve it inside the family won't work, and may make things worse because of the emotional strains that will result from effort and failure.

What is a family anyway? What is it supposed to do? Its economic functions have changed over the centuries, the emotional satisfaction provided there is always a personal thing, but the one task it's always undertaken has been the rearing of children. Believe me, working women know this just as well as mothers who can afford the choice to stay home.

Now, to raise the children well, a family has to be clued in to the operations of the community in which it exists. Adults have to understand the goals of a society (that doesn't mean they have to approve of them), and show the children how to operate within the guidelines these goals set. Processes of living ought to be understandable and open to exploration and participation.

Families have become isolated from the world of action. In his book on the alienated young, "The Uncommitted," Prof. Kenneth Keniston of Yale dubbed them "home havens," retreats from the rat race. No doubt that's a bitter and deserved comment on the rat race; but it raises a grave question. Can one really raise children successfully in a residential ghetto, cut off from the life of the world?

This is what women—mothers—are charged with doing. They have very little help. Cross-cultural studies show American women have less support today from family and community than mothers in other contemporary cultures and much less than did their mothers and grandmothers. And when they fail, they blame themselves. To bear a load of guilt on top of the task of doing alone one of society's major jobs is a shocking, a crippling burden which demands a conscious effort to set it right.

What the family needs is a re-creation, artificially, of the old community connections, the old extended family. Communal living is one way to do this and I expect it will spread in various forms. Another approach that can easily be undertaken and could have stunning effect is the establishment of childhood enrichment centers, or youth environments, or assemblies for educational opportunities. We call these places day-care centers now, and denigrate them in our own minds by doing so; for we appear to mean no more than places to dump children.

Giving them a new name won't ennoble them by itself, but adjusting our thinking and expectations to match the name can do so. I would like to see every plant, business, commercial establishment or gathering place above a minimum size establish such a center. Mothers (or fathers) could bring little children with them to the places where they work, could check on them during the day and be with them for meals. Older children could gather there after school. In so doing they would re-create something of the atmosphere of the old-fashioned big family which our attention to the population explosion has got to make less frequent. Retired men and women could come to talk and play with the children, and act as the grandparent generation, bringing a sense of the continuity of life to the everyday experience of growing up.

Government might well share the cost of these centers by granting a tax credit for establishing them, just as it does for other capital investment, and some government officials I've talked with agree. In fact, I would guess that industry, faced with government orders to cease discrimination against women, would find it profitable to have unworried mothers in the work force and to know that training given to young women would not be lost in the years when they might otherwise be dropouts.

Utopian? Nonsense. We're living with the alternative, and we know what it costs. Mothers of the World, Unite! What our children need from us isn't guilt, tears and frustration, but positive action to bring the community back home and open the home to the community.

Elizabeth Janeway is author of "Man's World, Women's Place."

Husband-and-Wife Team of Anthropologists Urge a New View of Marriage

By JOAN COOK

George O'Neill was a Columbia student and Nena, his wife-to-be, was a Barnard girl when they began to date. And when they were wed more than a quarter-century ago, the institution of marriage generally implied a set of customs and rules that were inviolate.

The husband was the breadwinner and undisputed head of the house. The wife was the unpaid housekeeper and governess for their children.

But times and the meaning of marriage have changed since the mid-forties, and observing these changes with a scientific eye from the perspective of a lasting marriage and parenthood (two sons, Brian, 21, and Michael, 25) were the O'Neills, both of whom are anthropologists.

History Repeats

The result of their observations and studies of male-female relationships inside wedlock is a provocative new book called "Open Marriage" (M. Evans and Company, Inc.; $6.95).

And in the strange way life has of repeating itself, Brian is currently a senior at Columbia, although there is a special Barnard girl, he's not talking.

"Just call me 'Son of Open Marriage,'" he said with a grin recently, when he dropped around to see his parents.

"Today, it's a whole different thing," his father acknowledged, returning the grin with interest. "Kids share dormitories, see each other under all kinds of conditions and, having put sex in perspective, are busy concentrating on building relationships. It's a much better way to go."

All of which fits into the O'Neill thesis that the only way to cope with the tensions of modern marriage is a new approach, one that is flexible enough to adjust to individual differences.

Mrs. O'Neill, who is working toward a Ph. D. in anthropology at Barnard, contrasted marriage contracts under the old, "closed" system with the new, "open" one they advocate.

The old contract, she said, demands: ownership of mate; denial of self; playing the couples game; rigid role behavior and absolute fidelity. On the other hand, she continued, the open contract offers independent living; individual freedom; flexible roles; mutual trust and expansion through openness.

"In the old contract, the man was dominant and out in the world, and the woman was domestic and stayed home with the children," she said. "Playing a passive role led to his growth and her stagnation. Under the open contract there is mutual growth that leads to synergy."

"Synergy," her husband interpolated, "is the combined, cooperative action of two people working in concert, where, as one person grows, he benefits and also gives the other partner an assist in her growth and vice versa."

Dr. O'Neill gave an example—the case of Jim, who loves fishing, and Mary who hates it. Jim loves Mary; Mary loves Jim.

"Under the closed marriage, Jim would either give up fishing or Mary would endure, but resent, going along or being stuck at home alone while he went off with friends," he explained.

"Under the open marriage, Jim would go fishing and Mary would go to an art exhibit or something she enjoyed, and both would come back to each other renewed and glad to be together," Mrs. O'Neill said.

One of the major misunderstandings in marriage today, the O'Neills said, is the issue of masculine and feminine roles.

"Some feminists would say that because women have done all the cooking in the past men should do all the cooking in the future, but substituting one tyranny for another isn't the answer," Mrs. O'Neill said.

"Whether the cooking chores are alternated or whether one cooks and the other cleans up, whatever the division is less important than its being based on the couple's priorities for the moment."

Do they practice what they preach?

Individual Priorities

"When George is deeply involved in something, I may do the cooking and the cleaning, but the next week he may be doing the whole thing," she said.

The foundation of an open marriage is communication, trust and respect, according to the O'Neills.

"That's not to say we never had a cross word," his wife said. "The book is not meant to be taken in one fell swoop, but more as a guideline to a more flexible way of life."

What about jealousy? Or the danger of infidelity? — Questions the couple are frequently asked.

Their theory is that the more two people do share voluntarily and the more freedom they permit each other to grow, the more they are going to want to be together rather than with someone else.

"The stronger the marriage grows, the less likely anyone from the outside can threaten it," Dr. O'Neill said.

Of course the possibility of infidelity exists, he said, but, in the case of a couple who are genuinely working toward an open marriage, it need not result in divorce.

"Of course both persons have to put something into it. We should make marriage harder and divorce easier. We look on divorce as a failure, but, if the sensible consensus is that this marriage is a failure, it should be terminated before the couple destroy each other," he said.

"Too many couples survive the seven-year itch to end up in the 17-year ditch when their children grow up and they find they have nothing in common," he added.

When, having married in good faith, one of the other balks at the idea of open marriage and resolutely refuses to grow, it is better to have it over and done with than drag along unhappily for years only to eventually end in divorce, Mrs. O'Neill asserted.

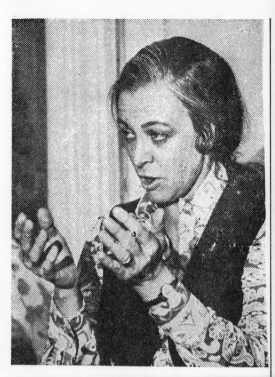

George O'Neill: "Too many couples survive the seven-year itch to end up in the 17-year ditch when their children grow up and they find they have nothing in common."

Nena O'Neill: "Some feminists would say that because women have done all the cooking in the past men should do all the cooking in the future, but substituting one tyranny for another isn't the answer."

February 3, 1972

A Day in the Life of Nonstop Housewife

By RALPH BLUMENTHAL

Sometime, somehow, the other day, between guest-teaching an elementary school art class, ministering to an ill daughter at home, making lunch and sending her son off to kindergarten, driving into Manhattan to check an exhibit of her paintings, taking her son to a birthday party, cooking dinner for the family and presiding over an evening meeting of the Queens community board, Mrs. Janet Langsam found time to take her other daughter shopping, pick up library books for the sick daughter and round up some support on the telephone for the proposed new Queens cultural center, of which she is an ad hoc board member.

"There are so many nice things to do in this world, why waste time sleeping?" she asked between nibbles on barbecued spareribs in a Chinese restaurant in Flushing after her meeting broke up at midnight.

Almost Tireless

Mrs. Langsam, whose name in German means "slow," is — as her husband, Edwin, puts it — "anything but."

Although there are other women chairing the 62 appointed community boards that advise their borough presidents on planning matters, probably none — male or female — is as tireless as the svelte, 36-year-old mother of three, who, one colleague commented, has "an inordinate ability to do the impossible."

At meetings of Queens Board 7, the last word is inexorably hers, although an accompanying smile usually eases the pain for the vanquished.

"I have a question! I have a question!" shouted an excitable citizen, interrupting her at a recent community budget hearing.

"Yes," she replied, fixing him with a stare of her green eyes, heavily framed with black eye-liner, "and *when* I recognize you, you'll ask one."

Time for Painting

Meanwhile, she finds time to paint — some of her huge acrylics are on exhibit at the New York University student center — and run an often frantic household in a plaster, red-roofed villa-style home in Whitestone, Queens.

"I just decided that having kids wasn't going to stop me from doing other things," Mrs. Langsam explained. "I wasn't going to let my life become one boring casserole after another."

Her husband (they were married 13 years ago when they met through a ski club and he turned out to be the boy next door in Far Rockaway, where she was born) agrees with his wife's attitude.

"No male chauvinist pig I," said Mr. Langsam, a producer of industrial films at the American Telephone and Telegraph Company. "From the beginning I was aware that my wife had many abilities and talents and I didn't want to see them obliterated under a pile of dirty dishes."

The Langsams catch up on life together on weekends, which they spend in an old schoolhouse they recently bought and converted in Chichester, N.Y., near Hunter in the Catskills. (The gymnasium, Mrs. Langsam found, was a perfect place to spread out her wall-size canvases.)

During the week, a typically frenetic schedule might resemble one she spent on a recent Monday.

The day began with an unscheduled distraction: an agitated hunt for her car keys. Then she drove off to Public School 79 in Whitestone to guest-teach, without pay, two hours of painting to the fifth-grade class of her daughter, Julie, who happened to be ill that day with a sore throat. Because Jonathan, who is 5, didn't start kindergarten until the afternoon, she took him along.

Shortly after 11 A.M., she rushed Jonathan home for lunch before his kindergarten class started. "He's got to have the fastest sandwich in the East," she said, maneuvering her blue Volvo through light traffic.

More Problems Solved

At home, more problems: Pajkos, the family's Hungarian sheepdog, had chewed on a letter that came from the bank. Besides handling that disaster and seeing to it that Jonathan ate his lunch and caught the school bus, she also made certain that Julie took her medicine. Then she handled a call from a newspaper inquiring about her exhibit. ("Well, they're large acrylic paintings, about 9 feet

Juggling Career, Husband and Child

By JUDITH WEINRAUB
Special to The New York Times

LONDON—Question: what kind of woman handles a full-time career commitment and successfully manages to fulfill her responsibilities to her husband and children?

Answer: she is likely to have been an only child from a higher than average social background; early in life she may have experienced family tension that dissuaded her from idealizing family life or placing full hopes for self-realization in it.

So say Robert and Rhona Rapoport, respectively an American social anthropologist and South African sociologist-psychoanalyst, who have studied working women, their jobs, their husbands and children for the past 5 years.

They have recently detailed some of their findings in "Dual Career Families," a series of case studies of the lives of five couples who manage to combine high-powered careers with family life. It was published in America last month (Penguin, $1.95).

"We wanted to get at the facts rather than living with stereotypes, so we took the hardest kind of situation possible," said Mrs. Rapoport recently at the Rapoport home in the Hampstead section of London.

"We looked for high fliers with an intact marriage, at least one child at home, and whose husbands were not in financial distress. There wasn't much offered."

"But the concept of the super-woman didn't hold up," added her husband. You don't have to be an Amazon."

What they did find in common in the families they studied was a flexibility about sex roles, a strong sense of organization and decision-making ability, and husbands who actively encouraged their wives' working.

"It's not only who the woman is, but also her job and her family setting that create the woman of a dual career family," Mrs. Rapoport explained. "You have to put the three together along with society's norms to see how the whole is facilitated."

Husband's Attitude

"There is no single most important factor, but the husband's attitude is crucial," admitted Mrs. Rapoport, who has studied and taught in America and England, as has her husband.

The Rapoports, a dual career family themselves (they have two children, Lorna, 13 and Alin, 9) admit their bias on the subject.

"At the heart of the project is an interest in helping women to realize their potential and enrich their lives," explained Mr. Rapoport. "But men and society can benefit as well."

"We differ from the radicals," he went on, "in that we feel this societal reorganization can be done in evolutionary ways."

"Even ten years ago, women stopped work at marriage. Now the woman who expects to work after a break for child care is the statistical norm."

Mrs. Rapoport, who never had to give up work totally when their children were young, explained that they felt the situation of the career-oriented woman had never been properly understood because it had never been studied in the context of the rest of her life.

Complex Lives

The results of their studies are not glowing success stories; they are detailed pictures of rather complex lives.

Although the most serious problem they found families encountered was finding the high-level child-care they demanded, other frequent areas of difficulty were overwork, a dependence on servants, a lack of free time and, inevitably, guilt.

"This idea of a dual career family is such a new one," said Mr. Rapoport. "There has always been so much guilt involved. You used to have to prove that you were not going to wreck your marriage or ruin your children. It wasn't felt that this life-style was a valid one."

On the plus side, however, the Rapoports found that many of the shibboleths about working mothers didn't seem valid. For example, having a working wife was not necessarily injurious to marital happiness or detrimental to children.

Said Mr. Rapoport: "Some

The New York Times/Larry Morris; Robert M. Klein
Mrs. Langsam puts son, Jonathan, on school bus

by 7 feet," she explained. "And I'm very talented and I'm a great painter and you can put that in your paper.")

That taken care of, she was off on her rounds again, pausing just long enough to tell Julie's baby-sitter: "If you're not going to finish your sandwich, give it to Pajkos."

After a trip to the N.Y.U. gallery at 566 La Guardia Place in Greenwich Village—during which she happened to run into her aunt from Far Rockaway—she headed home to get Jonathan and take him to a friend's birthday party, take her other daughter, Jackie, 10, shopping, make phone calls for the meeting that night and prepare a chicken dinner.

Shortly after 8 P.M. — Janet's always a little late, a friend explained—she showed

up at the meeting in a red turtle-neck and charcoal blazer and slacks and proceeded to handle the session with her usual aplomb.

When City Budget Director David Grossman told the meeting that Flushing had already been favored with more than its share of improvements, Mrs. Langsam had a tart answer.

"I hadn't noticed," she said.

Even after adjourning the meeting, there was still work to do. While walking to the exit, she briefed a reporter who had covered the session, paused to promise the custodian that she would try to get him a $20 fee for his late stay instead of the usual $15 and then drove around Flushing looking for a late-night restaurant to sit for one more interview.

January 15, 1972

of the women we interviewed said that they could stay at home if they wished but they wouldn't be fit to live with. There are so many strains in urban living today that you have to choose the strains that work best for you.

"People who criticize the dual career arrangement do so against a background of the illusion of a stress-free way, and there just isn't one."

"When we asked our daughter Lorna how she felt about her mother's work, she said it seemed quite natural," he said, adding "We've never known any other way."

To accommodate this particular life-style, which they say they feel more people will be choosing, the Rapoports suggest that certain changes will have to be made. Service occupations like cleaners should be upgraded to respectability, housework should be distributed more equitably between husband and wife, and a flexible balance of roles should be experimented with.

But, Mrs. Rapoport warned, "Don't think it will all get easier soon."

A Day in the Life of a Welfare Mother

The New York Times/Neal Boenz

Mrs. Bessie Johannes, a welfare mother, with her children. The curtains in front of crib are actually plastic carriers used on six-packs of soda cans.

At 8:30 in the morning, Bessie Johannes's day is just an hour old. Two babies lie in their cribs—one playing, one sleeping. Two older children are stepping from a bathtub. Each gets propped on a chair, dried and dusted with powder.

As they scramble to get dressed, Mrs. Johannes, a stocky woman in dungarees and sweater, pulls the bathtub plug and says with a wide grin, "I love bubble bath. It doesn't leave a ring."

At 25, Mrs. Johannes is a welfare mother. She lives in a four-room, five-flight walk-up in Harlem — 373 West 126th St. She gets no money from either her former husband—from whom she was divorced in 1969—or from her boyfriend, who fathered her two youngest children.

Every two weeks, she receives a check of $161.20, which she budgets to cover the $66.42 rent, food, gas, electricity, clothing and everything else. She cannot afford a phone. The bathtub —which twice a week becomes her laundry basin— sits within a wooden enclosure in her kitchen.

Alfredo, 6, and Nina, 5, return, breakfast on Instant H-O, and fuss with the two cats their mother got to ward off mice. Hustling the children off to the Grant Day Care nursery nearby is Bessie Johannes's first major task. It means running down to the ground floor to bring up a neighbor who will baby-sit while she takes them there.

For Mrs. Johannes, it is a good day when all her chores are done by noon: sweeping, washing, cooking, making beds. Today, they are. Five-month-old Denise has been fed and freshened.

"I thank God for Pampers," Mrs. Johannes says. "If I used diapers, I'd be bending over that bathtub 24 hours a day."

She starts a rice casserole for dinner, picks up 1½-year-old Virginia, plus yesterday's New York Post, and goes into her room, where an old

TV set ($35 at a thrift shop) hugs the edge of the bed. Switching on "Jeopardy," she simultaneously talks to her baby, pages through the paper, and outguesses the TV contestants.

Mrs. Johannes figures she is a little different from some welfare mothers. Her family came from Puerto Rico and were never on welfare. A graduate of Washington Irving High School, she went to work as a Teletype operator, married, and became pregnant immediately. But she continued to work until the birth of her third child, when she finally applied for welfare. "There is never enough money," she says. "But I make do. I manage better than most."

Place Is in the Home

Though she would like to work, she says a mother's place is in the home. "I say, if you plant a tree crooked, it grows up crooked. My children obey me. They say grace and go to church on Sunday. Welfare is no way of life for me. But I must wait till the children are older."

And there will be no more children for Mrs. Johannes. After the birth of Denise, she requested, and got, a tubaligation.

In the early afternoon, her landlord, Haskell Gray, comes by as he does every day. He deposits a small bag of Jamaican meat patties and promises that tomorrow he will fix the kitchen window, which, for several days, has been covered with cardboard.

"He's a sweet old man," Mrs. Johannes says after he leaves. "But with him it's always tomorrow, tomorrow."

"Look at that," she says, pointing to several dark, heavy wires which snake across the kitchen floor and out the back window. "I have DC current, and I'm hooked up to AC on the floor below. Now I always have to watch the children to make sure they don't chew it or spill anything on it, God forbid. I am in constant danger, but he won't get the current switched. And I can't afford the $95 to do it myself."

The rest of Bessie Johannes's day passes smoothly around the small kitchen table, where, in fact, most of her life is lived. It is here she reads her mystery books.

It is here she sits Virginia for lunch or crochets shawls for Nina. It is from here she observes her children at play —for she won't let them out on the streets by themselves. And it is from here, too, that she fashions whatever decorations hang in the house: the collage, made of nails, yellow string, and shoe polish color on wood; or the curtains made of plastic six-pack tops that separate two rooms.

Help From Sister

At 4 P.M., Mrs. Johannes's sister, Miriam Montalvo, arrives with Nina, Alfredo, and three children of her own. Mrs. Montalvo, who lives across the street in the Grant project, occasionally picks up the children, delivers phone messages and family gossip. They stand around the stove trading recipes.

After Mrs. Montalvo leaves, Mrs. Johannes starts frying chicken, and sends Alfredo down to the corner store to pick up four cartons of milk —the daily ration. Most of the food here is bought once a month—in bulk and on sale—from Finast or Shopwell on 125th Street. But today—with one week to go till her next check arrives — Mrs. Johannes has only 75 cents left. The milk will be bought on credit.

"And I keep this change," she says. "You never know if there's going to be an emergency, and I'll have to go somewhere by train."

When the children are fed and in bed, Mrs. Johannes makes her own dinner. Tonight, she is interrupted by her boyfriend, who brings kitty litter and looks in on the children. He chats for a while and leaves.

Mrs. Johannes drifts through the railroad flat toward the living room windows and points out the projects that loom over the tenements on her street.

"I want to live in a project," she says. "It's safer for the children, more rooms. But I won't get in. Some mothers have a much tougher time than me, and even they can't get in." She turns away.

"You should see my sister's place. Rugs on all the floors. French provincial furniture. Bookcases. The whole encyclopedia. But," she adds, "she's not on welfare."

GROUP QUESTIONS PARENTHOOD GOAL

Disputes View That Children Are Vital to a Marriage

Special to The New York Times

WASHINGTON, May 14— "The most common assumption among married people is that they should have children. The next most common assumption seems to be that children increase the happiness of a given marriage. There seems to be little evidence to support either of these assumptions."—Albert Ellis, the clinical psychologist.

The National Organization for Nonparents, a newly formed group of both parents and childless couples, is dedicated to dispelling this and other assumptions about parenthood and to showing the public what the group discerns as the realities of child rearing—that it is a tough, costly and full-time task requiring thoughtful planning.

The organization, based in Palo Alto, Calif., also wants to persuade the public that nonparenthood, far from being a tragic and empty state, can be life-enhancing, and it is working to eliminate the cultural bias and economic pressures that push people into parenthood.

The organization says that it has a membership of 500 and lists as directors doctors, psychologists, teachers, family planning experts and laymen.

Problems of Parenthood

At a news conference and dinner sponsored here by the organization as part of its national membership drive, members outlined the problems of parenthood.

"Parenthood is too often initiated by falling into a biopsychosocial trap," according to Dr. E. James Lieberman, a Washington member, who is a psychiatrist specializing in public health.

"Society, instead of permitting—much less encouraging—reflection, frustrates the considered judgment of many women about their own readiness for parenthood," Dr. Lieberman said. "Too often couples have children before they get a chance to adjust to each other."

Jim Bouton, the former baseball player, who is a member of the group, said that too many people had children for the wrong reasons.

"Too many couples don't look ahead," he aid. "Some view children as a $600 or $800 deduction at tax time, not thinking that the child, even if he is reasonably healthy, could cost them as much as $40,000 including college expenses."

Mr. Bouton, who said that he had a vasectomy after fathering two children and adopting a third, views population control as a necessity and a way out of poverty.

He offered a series of tax proposals that he said would relieve the overpopulation crisis and be more equitable to couples without children.

'Out of Wedlock'

By RAYMOND P. JENNINGS

BERKELEY, Calif.—We're grandparents again! Our first grandson (as yet unnamed), 9 pounds, 8 ounces, made his grand entrance on the stage of the last half of the twentieth century at 5:17 P.M., Sunday, July 11. I guess I could say all of the usual—and trite—things that are said at a time like this: a beautiful baby, a bundle of joy, the greatest child ever. He is all of that—and more.

But there is something more serious and important to be said. This child, born to our eldest daughter, is (to use the usual phrase) "born out of wedlock." After they learned the child had been conceived, his mother and father made the decision, thoughtfully and deliberately, not to marry. The father, a young man our daughter dated and liked very much while they were in the

Raymond P. Jennings is minister of the First Baptist Church, Berkeley. This article first appeared in his church bulletin.

Roland Topor

Army, has acknowledged his paternity, and the child will bear his name. But the two young people decided against marriage, feeling, among other things, that to get married just for the child's sake was not adequate grounds for a healthy marriage.

Our daughter squarely faced the various alternatives before her. One by one she put them aside; no abortion, no giving the baby up for adoption. She has determined to keep the child. We tried to be as supportive as possible and to affirm her determination, at first by long-distance telephone calls and again later when she came home.

During the past few weeks we have been going through the days of waiting with her—the days of expectation, her discomfort in pregnancy, the wondering if tonight would be the night. We have tried in some small way to make up for the absence of a father during these hours. We have shared in testing various names for sound and feeling—and Irene sat up all night in the fathers' room at the hospital. (Now she knows what that's like!)

We debate over how to handle the situation as it relates to friends and members of the church. This was not something one would be expected to announce publicly, and yet it was something that could not be hidden —nor did we wish to do so. We told some who are close to us; we resisted the fear of embarrassment. Now the child is here, and we make the announcement of his birth with all the joy and pride we could possibly have. This is our grandchild!

But more important, this is a human life with all the rights and dignity to which every human being is entitled. Of course we wish the circumstances might have been different—this is the kind of thing one thinks happens only to other families. But this time it happened in ours. And so, acknowledging the pain we feel, we also realize that there are really no "illegitimate" children; they have nothing to do with the circumstances of their birth (illegitimate parents, perhaps, but not illegitimate children). It is unfortunate—even tragic—that society attaches a stigma to a child for something for which he is not responsible. And so, while we know there will be special problems, this grandchild is going to be received in our family with all the love and joy and happiness with which we would greet any grandchild.

There is a sense in which this child seems symbolic of our times. There are increasing numbers of unwed mothers who are electing to keep their children. I suspect we will see more of this as the years go by. Surely the church and sincere Christians have an opportunity to demonstrate what love and acceptance mean—to show that, as Jesus made abundantly clear, persons are more important than any moral principles we might profess.

In all of this I am proud of the manner in which our daughter has assumed responsibility for her actions, of the love she has demonstratively evidenced for this child, even before its birth, and of the realistic and thoroughly human attitude she has nurtured within herself.

Apart from the additional reminder that I'm getting older, it's great to be a grandfather once more!

For These Women, Marriage Is Enough

By ENID NEMY
Special to The New York Times

CHICAGO—Mrs. John E. Swearingen rented a commercial vacuum cleaner the other day and gave her house-sized apartment a thorough cleaning. When she was finished with the oriental and tiger-skin and broadloom rugs, she began dusting. Her emerald ring glittered as the cloth whisked over French furniture, English furniture, a 12-panel Chinese screen, modern sculpture and scores of photographs taken with the world's beautiful and notable people.

By early evening, she had whipped the apartment into shape, had telephone conversation with two dozen people, attended a charity board meeting, taken a nap, made hors d'oeuvres and dressed to greet her husband.

"Everyone thinks my life is glamorous," said the svelte, blond wife of the chairman of the board of Standard Oil of Indiana, whose aggregate remuneration last year was $395,000.

"The general impression is that we have a houseful of servants, a chauffeur and live like a fairy-tale princess . . . that isn't quite the way it is," said Mrs. Gordon Metcalf, a soft-spoken, gray-haired woman who is married to the chairman of the board of Sears, Roebuck & Co.

Mrs. Metcalf lives in a modern three-bedroom apartment with an expansive view of Lake Michigan, does her own grocery shopping, a good deal of her own house work, and all the cooking, other than large-scale entertaining. Mr. Metcalf's listed remuneration last year was $385,000.

"My first responsibility is to make as comfortable as possible a home for my husband," said Mrs. Metcalf, who still remembers that her husband's salary was $27.50 a week when they were married 39 years ago and doesn't think that her life has changed too much in the intervening years.

•

"My wants are very simple," said the mother of three and grandmother of six. "But it's nice to know I can buy a new dress without thinking about it."

The wives of some of the nation's top executives don't, as some of them claim, live like the "average" person. Their household chores are made easier by the knowledge that they are done as a matter of choice, rather than necessity. They have few financial worries, they travel more extensively and more luxuriously than most, and they mingle with some of the industrialists, politicians and statesmen who shape the world.

But few of them, in this city at least, stay in bed until midmorning, spend the days at hairdressers or in the shops, or enjoy the services of staffs of well-trained servants. Their lives are adjuncts to those of their husbands and they walk the precarious line between

Mrs. Gordon Metcalf, wife of Sears Roebuck board chairman, says "My wants are very simple."

ever-ready availability and the retention of their own identities.

"As an executive wife, you don't pursue your own personal life as much as a career woman would," said Mrs. Graham J. Morgan, who before her marriage to the chairman of the board of U.S. Gypsum, taught school and worked in radio. "You gear yourself to your husband's life."

Mrs. Morgan, a handsome woman whose spacious apartment is furnished to complement paneled walls, parquet floors and inset columns of pink marble, gets up at 7 A.M. to breakfast with her husband before he starts his morning walk to the office.

"I've always felt that part of being a wife is being a companion," she said. "You have to grasp whatever moments you have together because executives lead such demanding lives."

The demanding lives, in many cases, mean rising by 6:30 A.M., arrival at the office by 8 A.M., and home for an early dinner with several hours of work following it, and bed by 10 or 11 P.M.

After 20 years of marriage, in which she has watched her husband rise from a junior executive to his present position (aggregate pay last year $240,000), Mrs. Morgan defines her responsibilities as providing a home with an atmosphere of "complete relaxation" and maintaining a totally flexible personal schedule.

"When I'm invited to go with my husband on a trip, nothing else is important and I really mean that," she said.

A whirlwind of energy, who keeps herself going with tea laced with honey in the comb, Bonnie Swearingen leads a completely business-oriented life.

"Anything else I do is sandwiched-in time," she said cheerfully. "Most of the corporation wives I know lead our lives in the shadow of our husbands but I don't think we lose our own identity."

A former stockbroker, who specialized in oil stocks and whose two ex-husbands were also in oil ("if they bottled oil, I'd use it as perfume") she approaches her new life as she did her career.

"I live on an uptick," she said. "I've just changed one hat for another. . . I took up stockbroking because I had a portfolio and I wanted to manage it myself. It's a sensible approach for any woman because the odds are with us that we are going to outlive our husbands. I don't have time to manage my portfolio any more but I'm very organized."

After her marriage three years ago, Mrs. Swearingen planned to decorate the sunswept apartment, almost framed by its water view, and return to her profession. Her husband raised no objections.

"But I found I couldn't . . . there just wasn't enough time in the day to operate," she said. "I don't miss it; there's too much else to do."

She is up at 6:45 A.M. daily to cook her husband's breakfast.

"When we were married, he insisted I get up with him so that I would be ready to go to bed early," she said. "I have to be a ray of sunshine because he gets a corporate look on his face at dawn."

The meal is almost always the same because her husband is, she said, a man of exact habit. One habit is coffee prepared 15 minutes in advance so it will be cold when served . . . "he doesn't want to waste a minute waiting for it to cool."

Once she rings for the elevator, hands her husband his attaché case, coat and hat, and kisses him good-by, she settles down to more tea and honey, reading the papers and tidying up ("my last maid was offered $200 a month more by someone else. . . I couldn't match that"). Then the telephone goes into action, with calls concerning anything from the Boys Club (as chairman of the ball last year, she raised $107,000) and the Illinois Children's Home to the Bonwit Teller advisory board.

•

In between the early-morning telephoning and the invariable late-afternoon nap, there are meetings, committee or business wives' luncheons, more meetings or fittings for charity fashion shows and the occasional shopping foray or expedition to the hairdresser.

If there are no evening engagements, dinner is early ("steaks, chops or hamburger . . . that's all I can make"); Mr.

Formerly a stockbroker, Mrs. John E. Swearingen (with husband) says she doesn't miss it.

Swearingen works in the library for a few hours and Mrs. Swearingen adjourns to the room known as the L.B.J. room, studded with pictures and trophies taken and shot at the Texas ranch.

The Swearingens travel constantly ("anything I do is subject to my husband's schedule and to immediate change") and despite her linguistic limitations ("I say Bon Jour You All"), Mrs. Swearingen said she enjoys meeting new people anywhere.

"I adore being around business men and women . . . they are much more intriguing to me than the jet set or artists . . but my husband never discusses business with me."

Mrs. Swearingen's wardrobe (50 evening gowns pressed and ready to wear) and jewelry collection ("it's my luxury") are both larger and more extravagant than most, generally attributed to the fact that she is younger than many wives in her position. But, withal, the Alabama-born extrovert considers herself economical.

"I experiment with fashion, I'm more adventurous than most corporate wives," she said. "My husband likes to see me neat, well groomed and never fussy and I think I've become more practical than I used to be."

What does her husband expect of her in areas other than fashion?

"He expects me to be what I am . . . useful, punctual, efficient, pleasant, alert and healthy. He has no patience with the opposites of any of these. He wants me to be feminine, to have a sense of humor without being witty and not to be too emphatic. I have learned quickly to compromise."

For Renée Crown, a Fine Arts graduate of Syracuse University and mother of seven children, her role as an executive's wife is a constant learning experience.

"It's a challenge," said Mrs. Crown, whose husband, Lester is president of Henry Crown Company, a concern that handles the family's investments, and of Material Services Corporation, a building services firm. "There is much more to it than material rewards. I'm doing things, seeing places and meeting people I never would have if I just led a quiet life with seven children."

●

Mrs. Crown runs her suburban Georgian home (seven bedrooms, two maids' rooms, indoor swimming pool, tennis court, sauna and three acres of grounds) with a live-in servant, a daily houseman and a semiweekly laundress. The five children at home, aged from 8 to 17, are assigned household chores as "responsibilities for living so well."

Although, like most wives, she is active in many charities, her life revolves around her husband and family. They have traveled together to Montreal for Expo, to Colorado for rapids shooting and are now planning an African safari.

"I don't think I sacrifice my children for any of my activities and my husband doesn't demand anything but I know pretty well what he wants and he knows it will be done. I want to do it . . . I want to please him. I chose my career. I've made my life and I have no regrets."

Marriage: Anachronism

By KATHRIN PERUTZ

Marriage is the hell of false expectations, where both partners, expecting to be loved, defined and supported, abdicate responsibility for themselves and accuse the other of taking away freedom.

Our modern legend has it that one man and one woman choose each other over all others and enter into love like an enclosed garden from which there is no retreat. Here they are their own place; each day they will feast on and with the beloved for they are blessed with happiness, their natural inheritance. Here legend ends, here Briar Rose is kissed by the king's son and whispers, "Is it you, Prince? I've waited so long." Her long sleep is over, and so is the fairy tale.

All husbands and wives know that moment: the sudden clarity when the honeymoon or partying have to stop, when the two who were brought together by God or judge resume their separate selves and wonder whatever made them do it.

The state of wedlock produces a kind of lockjaw which prevents the victim from talking about his plight. Not to have a "healthy relationship" is to admit invalidism, and most people would rather manipulate the symptoms than diagnose the malady. They babble about "meaning" and "communication" instead of finding something worth saying. A conspiracy is maintained against the unmarried, because marriage or the family is a perfect working mechanism of intake and output, a consuming function necessary for the economy of America. The image of marriage is held out like a national carrot, always in front of us, never seized, and we follow behind like beasts of burden.

For marriage as we insist on seeing it is an anachronism based on old roles, functions and imperatives. We say that marriage is "natural" and to that end develop anthropomorphic tautologies to show that animals "marry." But human behavior is purely human, and to call marriage as practiced today in America and Europe "natural" is to invoke sympathetic magic. Our marriage is neither a natural outcome of our standards and beliefs, nor is it an institution we can characterize as human because of its prevalence in history.

Only in Victorian times did marriage achieve its present sanctimony. Industrialization and the concept of modern democracy brought the idea of equals, the household lost eminence as the center of work and education, and romantic love was appropriated from the illicit to compensate husbands and wives whose relations to each other and their work were no longer obvious. Marriage, like other institutions, was to be the same for all classes, and so was both rigidified and sentimentalized.

We all suffer from it. A wife is still legally the property of, or at least answerable to, her husband. Social custom still requires that husbands are breadwinners. We marry for children despite overpopulation, and though our view of sex has radically altered in the last twenty years, marriage for sex remains as a quaint monument to a society that existed before birth control, penicillin and the discovery of female orgasm. In Victorian times, marriage provided containment. Now marriage is supposed to provide sexuality, and we expect sex to redeem us, though we are not closer to our bodies than we ever were.

When children are born, parents are terrified they can't do the job. Parents are the men and women who entered marriage as the most serious relationship of their lives, forgetting that they once were sons and daughters. They discarded their parents with the first whiff of adulthood, and now expect to have spontaneous love or interest in their children. So we maintain the untenable belief that our upbringing will not affect our bringing up. The American child is a creature of paradox, sentimentalized but not defined. He's given no true responsibility and is treated as though his existence were the symptom of a stage or phase, as though childhood had nothing to do with life or reality. A miniature adolescent, not adult, the American child has less security than any other, and is given rules but not values.

If we continue practicing this dangerous anachronism, we will lose not only ourselves and our mates, but also our children. Banalities about marriage suit us as well as the Emperor's new clothes. What we need is recognition that each person is himself, married or not; that the journey into oneself is more important than the ego trip; that we belong to each other only by willing it and by making a conscious commitment. We can't make promises to an impossible ideal, or take the name of someone else because we live with him, or vow to live forever with someone we have never lived with at all. The only true words of a wedding ceremony are: "I know you and I love you and I commit myself to you. I'll try to do you no harm." Children of such a union would have parents who know themselves, and they would have something to grow up to.

June 1, 1972

Wife-Husband Team to Head Bennington

The New York Times/Nancy Moran

Dr. Gail Thain Parker and husband, Thomas D., in Harvard's Winthrop House, where he is an administrator.

By IVER PETERSON

Bennington College in Vermont has chosen a 29-year-old Harvard professor, Gail Thain Parker, as its next president and her husband, Thomas, an administrator at Harvard, as vice president.

Dr. and Mr. Parker flew to Bennington yesterday from Cambridge after a special college committee of students, faculty and trustees had decided to recommend their appointments. The chairman of the Board of Trustees announced the appointments at the college's commencement ceremonies last night.

This is the first time that a major American college has chosen a wife and husband to take over its administration. A spokesman for the college said that the Parkers had been selected from among dozens of candidates after nearly a year of looking by a special search committee.

Bennington's presidency has been vacant since last September, when Dr. Edward J. Bloustein, 47, left to become president of Rutgers University.

Dr. Parker is an assistant professor of American history and literature at Harvard and one of the youngest tenured members of the faculty. She and Mr. Parker were undergraduate classmates there. They were married shortly before

537

they graduated in 1964, she summa cum laude—with highest honors — in American history and literature, and he magna cum laude — with high honors — in history.

She earned her Ph.D. in the history of American civilization — "The Dream of Success in America" was the title of her thesis — and has been teaching a course on "Women and Social Uplift" in American history and literature.

Dr. Parker was born in Chicago and raised in Evanston, Ill. Her father is assistant Dean of the University of Chicago Business School.

"It's an exciting opportunity," Dr. Parker said yesterday. She said that she and Mr. Parker would share the work at Bennington, although she would concentrate on academic issues and he on administration.

"It's really a job that will take an enormous amount of energy," Mr. Parker said, "and that's one of the advantages of having two people."

A spokesman for Bennington said that no special effort had been made to get a wife and husband team, and added, "They were married—they came together. It's not so much a case of dividing the job as sharing the job."

Mr. Parker, 30, earned a master's degree in education at Harvard and taught briefly in the Brookline, Mass. public school system while his wife worked on her Ph.D. He is now the senior tutor at Winthrop House, one of Harvard's undergraduate residences, where he counsels students, maintains academic discipline, and, he said yesterday, "helps students find their way through the academic bureaucracy."

At Bennington, he will serve as vice president of the college, a spokesman said.

He is from Oklahoma City, where his father is a businessman.

Dr. Bloustein, the former Bennington president, said in his offices at Rutgers yesterday that the selection of Dr. and Mr. Parker was in keeping with Bennington's reputation for innovative policies.

Dr. Parker was the senior resident of a woman's dormitory at Radcilffe for one year but has had little administrative experience beyond that.

Mr. Parker, however, has had wide experience in college admissions, financial aid to students and academic policy both at Winthrop House and in the Graduate School of Education. He will earn his Ph.D. in Education there next March, he said.

Dr. Parker will start at Bennington on Aug. 1 and Mr. Parker in September.

Problems Are Cited

Dr. Parker will face a number of immediate problems at Bennington that are common to many colleges and universities across the country.

The students—there are 440 women and 160 men—are demanding a greater voice in decisions affecting the curriculum and academic standards. And an expensive building program is under way on the college's 550-acre campus in southwestern Vermont.

A college official said that one of the factors that strengthened Dr. Parker's position in the search committee's view was her youth, and the presumption that this would make it easier for her to work with the students.

Dr. Parker is regarded at Harvard as a brilliant and serious scholar. She is also known to her friends for her quick and puckish wit.

She said that she was confident that her husband would not resent being outranked by her.

"After all," she said, "it isn't everyone who gets to sleep with the president."

Suggested Reading

Bird, Carolyn. *Born Female.* New York: D. McKay Co., 1968.

Breckinridge, S. P., "The Activities of Women Outside the Home," pp. 709–50 in *Recent Social Trends in the United States: Report of the President's Research Committee on Social Trends.* New York and London: McGraw-Hill Book Company, Inc., 1933.

Ditzion, Sidney. *Marriage, Morals and Sex in America—A History of Ideas.* New York: Octagon Books, 1953.

De Beauvoir, Simone. *The Second Sex.* New York: Random House, 1953.

Engels, Friedrich. *The Origins of Family, Private Property, and the State.* New York: International Publishers, 1969.

Firestone, Shulamith, ed. *Notes from the Second Year: Major Writings of the Radical Feminists.* New York: New York Radical Feminists, 1970.

Flexner, Eleanor. *Century of Struggle: The Woman's Rights Movement in the United States.* Cambridge, Harvard University Press, 1959.

Folsom, Joseph. *The Family and Democratic Society.* London: Rutledge and Kegan Paul, 1949.

Giedion, Siegfried. *Mechanization Takes Command.* Paper ed. New York: W. W. Norton & Company, Inc., 1969.

Ginzberg, Eli. *Life Styles of Educated Women.* New York: Columbia University Press, 1966.

Greer, Germaine. *The Female Eunuch.* London: MacGibbon and Kee Ltd., 1970.

Janeway, Elizabeth. *Man's World, Woman's Place: A Study in Social Mythology.* New York: William Morrow and Company, Inc., 1971.

Kamm, Josephine. *Rapiers and Battleaxes: The Woman's Movement and Its Aftermath.* London: G. Allen, 1966.

Kanowitz, Leo. *Women and the Law.* Albuquerque: University of New Mexico Press, 1969.

Komarovsky, Mirra. *Women in the Modern World: Their Education and Their Dilemmas.* Boston: Little, Brown, 1953.

Lasch, Christopher. *The New Radicalism in America, 1889–1963.* New York: Alfred A. Knopf, 1965.

Lifton, Robert J., ed. *The Woman in America.* New York: Beacon Press, 1965.

Lundberg, Ferdinand, and Marynia Farnham. *Modern Woman: The Lost Sex.* New York: Harper & Bros., 1947.

Maccoby, Eleanor. *The Development of Sex Differences.* California: Stanford University Press, 1966.

Mead, Margaret. *Male and Female.* Paper ed. New York: Dell Publishing Co., Inc., 1968.

Millett, Kate. *Sexual Politics.* New York: Doubleday and Company, Inc., 1969.

Myrdal, Alva, and Viola Klein. *Women's Two Roles—Home and Work.* London: Routledge & Paul 1956.

Newcomer, Mabel. *A Century of Higher Education for American Women.* New York, Harper & Bros., 1959

O'Neill, William. *Everyone Was Brave.* Chicago: Quadrangle Books, 1969.

Sanger, Margaret. *Woman and the New Race.* New York: Brentano's, 1920.

Showalter, Elaine, ed., *Women's Liberation and Literature.* New York: Harcourt Brace Jovanovich, Inc., 1971.

Sinclair, Andrew. *The Better Half.* New York: Harper & Row, 1965.

Index

Byline Index